VOLUME 2
1865 TO THE PRESENT
WITH READINGS

Rise of the American Nation

LIBERTY EDITION

LEWIS PAUL TODD   MERLE CURTI

EDITORIAL CONSULTANTS

PHYLLIS A. BAILEY — Coordinator of Social Studies, Baltimore County Public Schools, Towson, Maryland

MARV ELBERT — Social Studies Chairperson, Streamwood High School, Streamwood, Illinois

VIVIAN GLUCK — Assistant Principal, Supervision Social Studies, Stuyvesant High School, New York, New York

STANLEY HOLLIDAY — Supervisor of Social Studies, Indianapolis Public Schools, Indianapolis, Indiana

SARA KATZ — Teacher, East High School, Denver, Colorado

NORMA JEAN PETERS — Supervisor of Secondary Social Studies, Roanoke County Public Schools, Salem, Virginia

GARY SMUTS — Department Head of Social Studies, Cerritos High School, Cerritos, California

VERN WOLTHOFF — Teacher, Medford High School, Medford, Oregon

1865 TO THE PRESENT
WITH READINGS

Rise of the
American Nation

LIBERTY EDITION

LEWIS PAUL TODD   MERLE CURTI

 Harcourt Brace Jovanovich, Publishers

Orlando   New York   Chicago   San Diego   Atlanta   Dallas

LEWIS PAUL TODD has acquired national distinction as a teacher and writer on American history and related subjects. He taught American history for many years and was head of the Department of Social Studies at Bound Brook High School, Bound Brook, New Jersey. He also has taught American history, historical geography of the United States, American government, and related courses at Queens College, New York, at Western Connecticut State College, Danbury, Connecticut, and at New York University.

Dr. Todd is widely known among social studies teachers for his textbook writing and for his many articles and editorials in social studies journals. He has contributed to the Yearbooks and other publications of the National Council for the Social Studies (NCSS). For many years he was editor of *Social Education,* the official journal of the NCSS. Dr. Todd also has served as editorial writer for *Civic Leader.* In addition to his collaboration on *Rise of the American Nation,* he co-authored two series of social studies textbooks for elementary schools.

MERLE CURTI is Frederick Jackson Turner Professor of American History, Emeritus, at the University of Wisconsin (Madison) and has been Visiting Professor of History at the University of Tokyo. He has lectured at many American colleges and at Cambridge University. He also has served as honorary consultant in American cultural history, Library of Congress. Dr. Curti was formerly Professor of American History at Teachers College, Columbia University, where he and Dr. Todd began their collaboration on instructional materials for American history classrooms.

Professor Curti has been president of the American Historical Association, the highest honor a historian in the United States can receive. He also received the award of the American Council of Learned Societies for particularly distinguished scholarship. His long list of distinguished historical writings includes *Human Nature in American Thought: A History, The Social Ideas of American Educators, The Making of an American Community, The American Paradox: The Conflict of Thought and Action,* and *The Growth of American Thought,* for which he won the Pulitzer prize for history.

Requests for permission to make copies of any part of the work should be mailed to: Permissions, Harcourt Brace Jovanovich, Publishers, Orlando, Florida 32887

ACKNOWLEDGMENTS: For permission to reprint copyrighted material, grateful acknowledgment is made to Joan Daves Literary Agency for an excerpt from "I Have a Dream," an address by Martin Luther King, Jr., © 1963 by Martin Luther King, Jr., and to Harper & Row, Publishers, Inc. for an excerpt from *The Big Change* by Frederick Lewis Allen.

Printed in the United States of America
ISBN 0-15-376039-7

Contents

Readings

UNIT FIVE: **THE "GOLDEN TWENTIES" AND THE NEW DEAL (1920-1941)**

UNIT SIX: **FROM ISOLATION THROUGH WORLD WAR II (1920-1941)**

Text Maps

Charts

Special Features

Sources

Changing Ways with Technology

Historical Atlas
of the United States

Introduction

Beginnings to 1865

The roots of American culture

Not one of the men and women who settled in the Americas came to these lands empty-handed. To be sure, some arrived with little more than the clothing they wore. Others, even less fortunate, came as indentured servants who had sold their labor for a period of several years to pay for their passage across the ocean. Some, the tragic victims of slavery, arrived in chains to be sold to the highest bidder. Nevertheless, rich or poor, free or slave, every one of them brought along some part of the culture of their former homelands. Each person, regardless of his or her position in society, made a contribution to American culture.

What is culture?

Culture, simply defined, is the whole way of life of a people or a nation. It is the sum of all the things that distinguish one group of people or one nation from another.

Culture includes language, religion, laws, forms of government, methods of educating the young, means of communicating, ways of earning a living, games and recreation, habits and customs, and the organization of family and community life.

Culture is always changing. It develops and grows. It is the product of an endless interaction between human beings and their environment. Each greatly influences the other. The environment shapes in part the way a nation or a people lives. People, in turn, alter the environment. People who have an advanced science and technology are, of course, able to alter and control their environment far more effectively than men and women who must depend upon hand labor, simple tools, and traditional methods of working.

Europeans' advantages over the Indians

The culture that Europeans brought with them to the Americas gave them a decisive advantage over the Indians. As a result, European ways of living became firmly established in North America and in parts of Central and South America.

The **material culture** the Europeans brought with them included instruments of navigation, guns and gunpowder, iron and steel tools, plows, wheels, and a variety of domestic animals. Their **nonmaterial culture** included the alphabet, books and printing, the concept of the nation-state, and mathematics. These cultural developments, unknown to the Indians, gave the Europeans enormous advantages over the original inhabitants of the Americas. Because of their more advanced technology, the Europeans also had a great advantage in warfare. Equally important, they were conditioned by their culture to want to make use of America's natural resources and to reshape the environment to make it serve their own needs.

The European struggle for control

From the beginning, it was clear that the American continents were a rich prize for the nation that had the courage, enterprise, and ability to seize them. For more than 200 years the colonial nations of Europe took

The women who arrived at Jamestown in 1619 played a significant role in building the first European settlements in America.

part in a fierce struggle—diplomatic, religious, economic, and military— for control of one part or another of the Americas. The major powers in this conflict were Spain, France, and England. Portugal and the Netherlands also took part, and Sweden, too, was involved.

By 1763 the contest had for the most part been settled. Portugal remained in possession of Brazil. The Spanish flag flew over all the rest of South America; over nearly all of Central America; over a number of islands in the Caribbean Sea; over the city of New Orleans, east of the Mississippi River, and over the plains and mountains west of the Mississippi. France and the Netherlands retained only a few islands in the Atlantic Ocean and the Caribbean Sea. Great Britain controlled all of Canada and (with the exception of New Orleans) all of the area east of the Mississippi River. Thus by 1763 Great Britain had not only retained control over the 13 colonies it had planted along the Atlantic seaboard, but had also greatly expanded the area that it claimed in North America.

British culture in the colonies

All of the European nations shared a common background. All had inherited knowledge and skills from the past—from a past that reached far back into the beginnings of human history. The European ways of life had been shaped by contributions from primitive people, from the peoples of Egypt and Mesopotamia, from the Hebrews and Greeks and Romans, and from many peoples whom the Romans regarded as "barbarians." Europeans, like all peoples in all times, were part of the endless stream of history.

Each of the European nations reshaped this common heritage in its own way. Each developed its own variation of European civilization. Each carried its own way of life, its own culture, to the colonies overseas.

The British carried the English language, English law, and English political and economic and social institutions to the 13 colonies that were later to become the United States of America. The British also carried to their colonies a distinctive set of values and beliefs.

Especially important was the British emphasis on the rights of the individual. This emphasis helped to shape British law and British political institutions.

British law protected an individual against arbitrary arrest. It guaranteed each person a fair trial by a jury of that person's equals.

British law also included the right of an individual to be represented in government. The colonial assemblies were, in most ways, smaller versions of the Parliament that governed the people of England and Scotland.

There were, of course, many other traditions, practices, and beliefs that the British settlers carried overseas. They brought, for example, the institution of the established church, that is, an official church supported by public funds. They brought the class system—a system that designated individuals at birth as members of the aristocracy and various lower classes. Neither the established church nor the class system was peculiarly British. Both were part of the European way of life, and both were transferred to the colonies throughout the Americas.

However, the emphasis on the importance of the individual was a special feature of British culture. The men and women who settled the British colonies jealously guarded what they called "their rights as English subjects."

Greater importance of the individual

In North America many aspects of British culture that the early settlers brought to the colonies were changed. Climate, geography, and the influence of the Indians and of immigrants from other countries all helped to bring about changes.

From the beginning, the individual settler enjoyed increasing freedom in the colonies. For one thing, the English government did not itself establish any of the colonies along the Atlantic coast. Instead, it granted this right, in the form of charters, to private companies, to groups of persons, or even to individuals to build colonies overseas.

Moreover, the conditions of life in the colonies gave added importance to the individual. The colonists on the frontier had to clear the land, build their houses, and plant crops to provide their own food. Since the wilderness was vast, extending from the Atlantic Ocean to the Pacific Ocean, there were never enough men and women to do all the necessary work. Thus individual initiative and inventiveness were nourished and strengthened by the conditions of life in colonial America.

Breakdown of the class system

The growing importance of the individual greatly weakened the class system. It is true that in all the colonies except Rhode Island, Connec-

Indian tribes had well-developed cultures. The Eastern Woodland Indians, shown here, and other tribes helped the early European settlers to survive.

ticut, and Pennsylvania the governors and their associates continued to represent the aristocracy of the mother country. However, it was impossible to maintain the rigid class lines that separated the aristocracy and the lower classes in Great Britain. Poor settlers in the colonies could save their money and buy farms or could obtain free land on the frontier. With initiative and hard work they might prosper and become "independent." Even indentured servants, who were required to serve their masters for several years, could secure free or cheap land when their terms ended, and become farmers. African slaves were the only group unable to share these opportunities.

Nor was farming the only way for poor colonists to improve their lives. They could start their own businesses as skilled workers—bakers, shoemakers, tailors, gunsmiths, blacksmiths, silversmiths. They could build or buy fishing boats, start shipyards or sawmills, or become merchants. Also, more easily than in England, young men could attend one of the colonial colleges or become apprentices to gain enough training and education to enter the professions of medicine, law, and the ministry.

Social mobility, or the opportunity to improve one's position in society, was a distinctive feature of colonial life from the beginning. Many colonists took advantage of opportunities to achieve success. Benjamin Franklin, for example, started life as a poor boy and became one of the most distinguished men of his time, honored in Europe as well as in America.

Contributions of the Indians

The **environment** of the American colonies included far more than the climate and the land itself—the soil, forests, rivers and streams, rolling hills and sheltered valleys. It included the people—the Indians, the British settlers, the Africans, and the immigrants from many other lands.

One of the major contributions of the Indians was food. Long before the first Europeans arrived, the Indians had learned how to make use of a large variety of plants unknown in Europe. The list of these plants is long and impressive—corn, white and sweet potatoes, many varieties of beans, tomatoes, squash, pumpkins, blackberries, blueberries, cranberries, crab apples, chestnuts, peanuts, maple syrup.

The discovery of these foodstuffs created a revolution in Europe's eating habits. It provided both Europe and the Americas with food for their constantly growing population. The amazing truth is that more than half of all the agricultural goods produced in the world today have come from plants first discovered and cultivated by the Indians.

The Indians, moreover, helped to feed the first settlers, in Jamestown, in Plymouth, and in other new and struggling settlements. They also provided the colonists with seed and taught them how to plant, fertilize, and cultivate their crops. They taught the settlers hunting skills and forest lore.

Skillful Indian hunters provided furs for the colonies' important fur trade with Europe. The Indians also gave many new words and phrases to the English language.

Not least important, the presence of Indian tribes in the colonies forced the English settlers to join together and to organize for their own defense. In this respect, the Indians indirectly helped to strengthen the colonists' exercise of initiative, responsibility, and local government in the colonies.

Contributions of the Africans

Africans also contributed to the distinctive way of life that was developing in the American colonies. They were among the first newcomers other than the English to arrive in the British colonies. The earliest group landed in Virginia in 1619. For a number of years they worked as indentured servants, as did many of the early European settlers. By the middle 1600's, however, Africans were being transported to America as slaves. Even in slavery, the Africans adopted many American customs and contributed to the American way of life.

As workers—whether indentured servants, free individuals, or slaves—black Americans contributed their labor and their skill to the task of conquering the wilderness and transforming it into a productive land. As individuals—men and women from another continent and another way of life—they introduced new cultural traits into the colonies.

Like the Indians, black Americans by their very presence in the colonies forced the settlers to develop new social arrangements. Slavery compelled the colonists to create methods of controlling the labor and the lives of other human beings. It confronted all the colonists but particularly the slave owners with a moral problem that they were unable to solve except by the irrational declaration that Africans were inferior people.

Slavery and the moral issue it posed had far-reaching effects upon American society. As the years passed, it increasingly troubled the conscience of Americans. ("I tremble for my country when I reflect that God is just," Thomas Jefferson wrote.) It became an issue that deeply divided the nation and later contributed to a bloody war that nearly destroyed it. To this day practices adopted during the slavery era, as well as attitudes developed in the effort to justify the system, haunt American society. Traditions from the past continue to hamper efforts to eliminate discrimination and to provide the full equality to which black Americans are entitled under the law and as human beings. Thus, both directly and indirectly, people from Africa have had an incalculable influence upon American life.

Contributions of non-English immigrants

In the colonies, British culture was also greatly modified by settlers from many other lands. Swedes and Finns, who settled along the Delaware River, left their mark in many place names, such as Christiana and Hockessin, and in building what soon became known as the American log cabin. The Dutch in New Netherland had an even more lasting influence. They brought to the colonies a tradition of religious toleration and a belief in the value of elementary education. They brought interesting customs and architectural styles; and Dutch names of persons, places, and things soon became familiar — Roosevelt, Van Buren, Harlem, Brooklyn, cruller, boss, St. Nicholas.

By the late 1600's other immigrants from many countries were arriving in ever-growing numbers. The largest groups were those from Germany, Scotland, and Ireland. Many of these newcomers settled in the Quaker colony of Pennsylvania, but soon the stream of settlers flowed down the valleys into Virginia and the Carolinas.

All of the immigrants brought to America the language, clothing, customs, and ways of thinking and behaving of their mother countries. They tried to continue these everyday ways of life in their new homeland, but this proved to be impossible. As a result, they soon adapted the material aspects of their lives — houses, clothing, food, tools, weapons — to meet the needs of their new environment. More slowly, but just as surely, these groups of immigrants began to change and to modify the ideas and the ways of behaving that they had brought with them to the colonies.

Americans — a new people

From the earliest times America was regarded by Europeans as a "melting pot." Out of the mingling of peoples from many different lands, a "new people" and a new way of life were being fashioned.

"What," a French settler asked in the 1770's — "what then is the American, this new person?" Michel-Guillaume de Crèvecoeur answered his own question: "I could point out to you a family whose grandfather was English, whose wife was Dutch, whose son married a French woman, and whose present four sons now have four wives from four different nations. Americans are those who, leaving behind all their long-held prejudices and manners, acquire new ones from the new kind of life they have embraced, the new government they obey, and the new rank they hold. . . . Here individuals of all nations are melted into a new people, whose labors and posterity will one day cause great changes in the world."

Growth of religious toleration

The mingling of people of many different religious faiths encouraged the growth of toleration. Roger Williams in Rhode Island, Lord Baltimore in Maryland, and William Penn in Pennsylvania led the way by provid-

Colonial families often worked together to build homes and settlements. They also found time to enjoy themselves, as in this painting of a flax-making party.

ing religious freedom in their colonies. In other colonies as the years passed, Quakers, Baptists, Presbyterians, Catholics, and Jews secured freedom to worship in their own way. By the end of the colonial period the principle of an established church had been abandoned except in Connecticut and Massachusetts. When the new nation was being born, the First Amendment to the Constitution forbade Congress to make any law establishing or favoring a particular religion.

Growth of cooperation

Hand in hand with the growing emphasis on the rights of the individual was the growth of the spirit and practice of cooperation. From the beginning the shortage of labor compelled neighboring families to help each other. They gathered together to clear land, to build cabins, to harvest crops. They banded together for self-protection.

As the frontier moved westward, colonists cooperated in establishing new settlements, and in building roads, schools, and churches. The government was far away and often weak. Since the work had to be done, colonial men and women accomplished things by using their own initiative and joining together to do it. Visitors from foreign countries were amazed at the extent to which the colonists relied upon their own cooperative efforts.

Creating a distinctive American culture

During the colonial period there was, in the words of historian Frederick Jackson Turner, "a steady movement away from Europe, a steady growth of independence on American lines." Faced with the challenge of a new environment, the colonists became increasingly self-reliant.

Long before they broke with Great Britain the colonists had created a distinctively American way of life. They had moved toward the principle of religious freedom, had laid the foundations of free public education, and had strengthened the institution of representative government.

As late as 1776 most of the colonists insisted that they were loyal citizens of the British empire. Yet the fact was that during the colonial period they had been growing away from the mother country. They had begun to think of the colonies as *their* land, as a place apart from Great Britain.

In 1776 the colonists, recognizing their growing need for independence, declared their intention of separating from Great Britain. In 1789, following the victorious ending of the Revolutionary War and the ratification of the Constitution, the new nation was born. In 1789, however, the United States was a nation in name only.

A national language

Among the striking evidences of the new nation's spirit of independence were the efforts to mold a national "American" language distinct from English. "America," Noah Webster declared in 1783, "must be as independent in *literature* as is in *politics,* as famous for *arts* as for *arms.*" With this in mind, Webster labored at the tremendous task of preparing a dictionary — *An American Dictionary of the English Language* — in which the British spelling of many words was simplified. The dictionary, finally published in 1828, helped to establish a standardized American language.

Noah Webster also prepared a spelling book. First published in 1783, it was used in nearly every elementary school in America. By the time Webster died in 1843, more than 15 million copies had been sold. Before the book went out of use nearly 100 million copies had been sold. Like the dictionary, the spelling book helped to develop a uniform national language.

American history and geography

In addition to his work on the dictionary and the spelling book, Noah Webster edited a famous school reader, *An American Selection of Lessons in Reading and Speaking.* One of the major purposes of this textbook was to arouse Americans' feeling of national pride by focusing attention on the nation's heroes. In order to realize this purpose, Webster devoted more than half of his school reader to material from American history. He later wrote other books devoted entirely to American history.

Meanwhile, another scholar, Jedidiah Morse, was instructing American students about their country's geography. Morse, like Webster, stated that one of his purposes was to teach American history. His geographies were largely devoted to the story of American life.

American art

American artists also contributed to the growing spirit of **nationalism** — the people's feeling of pride and loyalty to the new nation. There were, for instance, the architects who designed the nation's capital. Although a French engineer, Major Pierre L'Enfant, planned the city of Washington, American architects played a large part in its design and construction. Benjamin Banneker, a free black from Maryland, helped to survey and lay out the final plan for the District of Columbia. Thomas Jefferson drew up plans for the Capitol Building, and although they were not used the architects did accept his proposal for the locations of the Capitol and the White House. Another American, William Thornton, and Benjamin Latrobe, an English citizen whose mother was born in Pennsylvania, designed the Capitol. As the city of Washington grew, it helped to give the American people a growing conviction that the new nation was solidly planted and destined to endure.

During this same period, artists like Charles Willson Peale, Gilbert Stuart, and John Trumbull began to devote much of their time to painting portraits of the nation's leaders. Their influence is shown by the fact that even today copies of their portraits of Washington, Jefferson, Franklin, and other leaders of the United States hang on the walls of public buildings all across America.

American literature

Literature as well as art helped to unite the American people. During the early 1800's a number of writers began to depict American heroes and themes. Some, such as Mason Locke Weems (better known as Parson Weems), who published a biography of George Washington, wrote in glowing terms about the founders of the nation.

Other writers, among them Washington Irving and James Fenimore Cooper, began to write about America itself. Irving turned chiefly to the Dutch society of the Hudson Valley, producing such works as "The Legend of Sleepy Hollow," "Rip Van Winkle," and the *Knickerbocker History of New York*. In his early novels Cooper wrote about the Indians and the frontier. *The Leather-Stocking Tales,* a series of novels, are only a few of the many books that he produced.

George Washington, portrait by Gilbert Stuart

America's culture-heroes

America's culture-heroes also helped to unite the American people. Every country has such figures—men and women, usually real but sometimes legendary—who represent the hopes and beliefs of the people and who serve as models of conduct in war and peace.

There were naval heroes like John Paul Jones and John Barry. The independence, courage, and skills of America's pioneers were represented by Daniel Boone and Davy Crockett. In later years, riverboat crews celebrated the deeds of Mike Fink, while lumber cutters told and retold the fabulous feats of the legendary Paul Bunyan and "Babe," his blue ox.

Black Americans, who contributed so much to the building of the nation but were denied their share in the American dream, had their own culture-heroes, among them Harriet Tubman. As a young woman, she escaped from slavery by fleeing to the North. Once free, she worked at any job she could get in order to earn the money she used to rescue more than 300 men, women, and children from slavery. As one of the leaders of the "underground railroad," she repeatedly risked her own life to free others.

Benjamin Franklin, another of the nation's leading culture-heroes, symbolized the "self-made" individual, that is, the person who achieves success solely through intelligence and hard work. Franklin strengthened the deeply rooted belief that every American, no matter what background he or she came from, no matter how deprived or poor, might rise to a position of wealth, fame, and influence.

Franklin also became a symbol of the American spirit of ingenuity and inventiveness. He demonstrated the value of learning by making a series of memorable inventions, among them the lightning rod, improved eyeglasses, and the Franklin stove.

America's leading culture-hero was George Washington. People looked up to him as "the father of our country." At the close of the Revolutionary War, he had helped to defeat a plot to make the new nation a monarchy by refusing to accept the title of king. Although he would have preferred to remain at Mount Vernon and run his plantation there, he could not refuse his nation's call to duty. He presided over the Constitutional Convention, and then served two terms as President of the new nation. Patriotism, self-sacrifice, and devotion to the common welfare made Washington a great hero to the American people. Indeed, Washington became a symbol of the nation itself.

America's value system

The aspirations and beliefs widely held by the people throughout the growing nation made up what is known as a **value system.** Most Americans, like their European ancestors and contemporaries, shared a common heritage of Judeo-Christian teachings. These included the belief that individuals were responsible to God for their conduct and would be rewarded or punished in a future life for their behavior on earth. Individuals had a duty to be kind and helpful to others, especially to those who were needy or suffering. Slavery and injustice thus were opposed to these beliefs, and this deeply troubled many Americans.

Americans believed in government based on law. They believed their nation was superior to any other on earth. They believed that theirs was a land of limitless opportunity in which all individuals could improve their position in life if they were hardworking, honest, and thrifty.

Closely related to faith in the United States as a land of opportunity was the conviction of most Americans that progress was inevitable. The future was certain to be better than the past. Education was important, not only because it was the means by which individuals could improve their position in life, but also because it was necessary for the progress of the nation as a whole. The system of free public schools that Americans developed reflected their belief in the importance of education.

Benjamin Franklin, portrait by Charles Willson Peale

The skilled hands of women workers were used to develop the important textile industry in New England.

Although Americans believed that thrift and planning were important in their personal lives, they did not have this same attitude toward the nation's natural resources. On this subject Americans gave little if any thought to the future. Most Americans assumed their nation's resources were inexhaustible. European visitors often were shocked by Americans' reckless misuse of their forests and soil.

Improvements in transportation and communication

Even with their widely shared beliefs, Americans could not have achieved unity as a nation without improvements in transportation and communication. The National Road, running from Maryland to central Illinois, was built between 1811 and 1853 with aid from the federal government. The Erie Canal, completed in 1825, connected the Great Lakes with the Atlantic Ocean. Soon a large system of roads and canals was established throughout much of the nation.

Steamboats on the rivers and, after 1830, a growing network of railroad tracks also helped to bind together the different parts of the nation. The telegraph strengthened these links of transportation and communication among Americans. All of these developments contributed to the growth of a national market and a national culture.

Labor-saving machines

The invention of labor-saving machines also contributed to the development of a national culture and a national market. Immigrants brought with them the tools, weapons, and skills of their homelands. In America, however, they modified and improved the European tools and machines to meet the needs of the new environment. For example, German gunsmiths who settled in Pennsylvania greatly improved the accuracy of rifles, which were so effective as weapons and in hunting for food and furs.

Faced with a vast continent to be conquered and a shortage of labor, Americans were forced to depend in large part upon what they could accomplish through their own efforts. The American environment required the colonists to develop individual initiative and inventiveness.

"Yankee ingenuity," as it came to be called, was one of the striking characteristics of the new nation. Shortly after the Revolutionary War, a young English mechanic named Samuel Slater built for his American employer the first power-driven textile mill in North America. Although Slater copied machinery he had worked on in England, he greatly improved it. At about the same time, Oliver Evans, an American inventor, built a grist mill that could be operated by one worker, who fed the grain in at one end and took out the ground flour at the other.

Another American, Eli Whitney, invented the cotton gin and, even more important, developed the principle of using interchangeable parts in the manufacture of new products. Other Americans made major contributions to the development of the steamboat, the steam railroad, steam-powered factories, labor-saving appliances for the home, and agricultural machinery. By the mid-1800's the United States was well on its way to becoming one of the world's leading industrial nations.

Divisions in the national culture

However, by the mid-1850's the United States was still far from being a completely unified nation. There were sharp divisions in the national culture. Americans were divided in matters of religion and on the issue of slavery.

Many Protestants who were descended from English-speaking colonial ancestors resented the ever-growing number of immigrants, especially those of the Roman Catholic faith. In the name of "Americanism," they demanded restrictions on immigration and were opposed to persons who were foreign-born serving in government jobs. Religious differences also led many Americans to persecute the Mormons, who belonged to the Church of Latter-day Saints. During the 1840's and 1850's, these religious differences became major political issues.

Even more serious were the differences rooted in sectionalism. The North, with its growing industries and factories and cities, was developing along very different lines from the West and especially the South.

By the early 1800's the South was developing what in certain respects was a national culture of its own. Climate, geography, and an agricultural economy based largely on the growth of cotton, tobacco, and rice gave the southern states a distinctive way of life. So, too, did the fact that relatively few European immigrants had settled in the South. The most critical difference between the North and the South concerned the issue of slavery.

As the forces of sectionalism grew stronger, they became increasingly serious. By 1861, when war broke out, the differences between the cultures of the North and South had become so great that the future of the nation itself was at stake.

The shaping of American democracy

Nothing is more crucial in any society than the power to make decisions. The person or persons who have this power are the real rulers of the society. The process by which decisions are made both reflects and determines the kind of society that develops in a nation. In an authoritarian society a single ruler or a small group of persons makes the major decisions. Through most of human history people have lived in such authoritarian societies. Because they were subjected to the will of their rulers, the people were known—and thought of themselves—as **subjects.** Their freedom and their rights as individuals were drastically limited.

The roots of American democracy

In a democratic society the power to make decisions is widely shared. The people in a democracy are considered citizens, not subjects. The extent to which citizens enjoy freedom of choice and are able and willing to participate effectively in the process of government is the true measure of democracy.

Democracy as we know it today did not exist in England or in colonial America. To be sure, the people of England enjoyed greater freedom than the subjects of any of the other major colonial nations. Although the right to vote was limited, those who could vote had the right to elect representatives to Parliament. In 1688, as a result of the "Bloodless Revolution," the principle that the politically active people, through their elected representatives, should possess the final governing authority was firmly established in English law.

The English men and women who settled in the American colonies brought with them the principle of representative government. Here, nourished in a new environment, it flourished. Steadily, through the years, individuals secured increasing freedom to make decisions—in the family, the local community, the state, and eventually at the national level.

Changing nature of the family

When the American colonies were founded, family life in Europe was highly authoritarian. By tradition and by law, the husband was, at least in theory, absolute ruler of the family. This pattern of family life was carried to the colonies, and it continued to exist all through the colonial period and well into the 1800's. The husband was expected to make all important decisions. The wife was subject to his authority, as were their children. Legally, he controlled any wages his children or his wife might earn, as well as any property they might inherit. His daughters—and sometimes his sons—could not marry without his consent. As late as the 1850's, a father might have the right to claim the wages of his sons until they were 21 years old.

There was a major exception to this pattern of family life. The owner of slaves completely controlled the lives of all members of a slave family. This weakening of the family in slavery was one of the system's most inhuman aspects.

Like all other aspects of European culture, however, the character of family life was modified in the American environment. The wife's influ-

In the colonies, all members of the family, young and old alike, helped to provide the family's food, clothing, and shelter.

ence increased as she worked side by side with her husband on the pioneer farm. In many cases she helped to defend their home and village during conflicts with the Indians. The influence of the sons also increased. Opportunities for them to become self-supporting and therefore independent were much greater in America than in Europe. They could leave home and get jobs in nearby towns, or find work on sailing ships, or move west and establish their own farms on the frontiers.

By the 1830's, 1840's, and 1850's, women were demanding—and beginning to win—changes in the laws to enable them to control their own wages and property. Some were even starting to demand the right to vote.

As a result of these and other changes, the authoritarian nature of the family began to break down. More and more, every member of the family began to share in the process of making decisions. This growth of democracy in family life meant increased personal freedom. It also helped to prepare Americans to take a more active part in the government of their communities, states, and nation.

Growing vitality of local government

Local communities, too, furnished fertile soil for the roots of democracy in America. The colonies were separated from England by a vast ocean. Even the fastest sailing ships needed about six weeks to cross. Also as the colonies grew, more and more of the villages were located far from the seats of the colonial governments. As a result, villagers and townspeople were required to take an active part in regulating their own affairs.

Citizens in the New England Colonies (Plymouth, Massachusetts Bay, Rhode Island, Connecticut, New Hampshire) had a greater part than any of the other colonists in making the decisions that affected their local communities. Of course, even in those colonies only white male settlers could take part in government. In New England, men who owned a certain amount of property and who were church members gathered at least once a year in town meetings. At these meetings they discussed local problems, elected town officials, and voted to levy taxes for support of schools and other community activities. Later, church membership as a requirement for voting was abandoned. Although ownership of property remained a requirement for voting, land was cheap. Thus a majority of townsmen had the right to take an active part in town meetings.

The situation in the Southern Colonies (Virginia, Maryland, the Carolinas, Georgia) was somewhat different. In contrast to the compact villages of New England, southern farms and plantations were widely scattered. The town meeting type of government was therefore not practical. Instead farmers and planters gathered on "Court Days" at crossroad settlements to hear—and sometimes to approve or protest—decisions that affected them. These decisions were made by justices of the peace and county lieutenants, who were appointed by the royal governors from among the prominent plantation owners.

The Middle Colonies (New York, New Jersey, Pennsylvania, Delaware) developed their own system of local government adapted from those practiced in New England and the Southern Colonies.

As the population moved westward, the settlers carried one or another of these types of local government to their new communities on the frontier. From the beginning, therefore, Americans acquired practice in self-government in their villages and towns. Long before the United States was created as a nation, most Americans had won a large measure of freedom in making decisions that affected their daily lives.

Growing power of the colonial assemblies

The distance between Great Britain and the American colonies also served to increase the amount of freedom enjoyed by the colonists. The colonies were simply too far away to be governed in every detail by the directors of the chartered companies, by the wealthy owners of the proprietary colonies, or by the king. Even if communications had been better, conditions in the colonies were so different from those in Great Britain that it would have been impossible—and foolish—for the British rulers to make all decisions affecting their colonies. Moreover, English colonists jealously guarded their "rights as English subjects"—including the right to take part in government through elected representatives.

As early as 1619, the London Company gave the colonists in Jamestown the right to take part in their own government. In July of that year 22 burgesses, or representatives, 2 from each of the settled districts along the James River, met in Jamestown. Each of the burgesses had been elected by the voters of his own district. The creation of the House of Burgesses, as the elected group was called, marked a significant step toward representative government in the British colonies.

Representative government in the Massachusetts Bay Colony developed in a different way. In 1629 a number of prominent Puritans in England secured a charter from the king and organized the Massachusetts Bay Company. Fortunately for the Puritans, the charter did not name the place where the directors of the company were to hold their yearly meeting. The directors, who were shrewd men, took advantage of this fact. They did so by voting to take the charter and move to North America, where they would be free to run the company as they pleased. In this way Massachusetts became, in effect, a self-governing colony, for many years almost independent of the English king and Parliament. At first only a few settlers were allowed any voice in the government. Soon, however, some of the newly settled towns demanded and secured the right to send representatives to Boston to meet with the governor and other officials and to help make the laws.

In the other colonies, as well as in Virginia and Massachusetts, elected representatives took part in the decision-making process. At first the governors of the royal colonies and the proprietary colonies could veto the actions of these assemblies, or groups of representatives. As the years went by, however, the colonial assemblies gained more and more influence. They had the power to vote taxes and to appropriate money for salaries and other expenses of government. Since they controlled all spending, they often refused to grant money unless the governing officials in the colony did as they wished. The colonial assemblies' experience in self-government proved invaluable to the colonists when the time came to create a new nation.

Written covenants and constitutions

During the colonial period Americans developed another extremely important check against the arbitrary use of power by appointed or elected officials. This was the written covenant, or agreement, voluntarily accepted by the people of the colony.

The earliest example of such an agreement was, of course, the Mayflower Compact. On November 11, 1620, shortly after the *Mayflower* had anchored off what is now Provincetown, the Pilgrim leaders gathered in the ship's cabin. There they wrote and signed an agreement to obey all laws that they themselves would adopt in the future.

Some years later, in 1639, settlers in the Connecticut Valley took an even more important step. Faced with the need to join together for certain common purposes, including self-defense, the settlers decided to adopt an official, written plan of government. The Fundamental Orders of Connecticut, as the document was called, was the first written constitution in America. In contrast to the Mayflower Compact, which was a general agreement in favor of majority rule, the Fundamental Orders set up a detailed plan of government.

The use of the written covenant, setting forth specific rules by which the people were to be governed, or to govern themselves, marked another significant step in the development of self-government in America. After the colonies declared their independence, each of the states as well as the national government adopted written constitutions.

Protest and rebellion

The right of people to protest and even to rebel against what they considered arbitrary use of power by the government also was strengthened during the colonial period. The victory of John Peter Zenger, who was brought to trial in 1735 for publishing articles criticizing the royal governor of New York, helped to establish the principle of freedom of speech as one of the foundations of democracy. This was only one example

17

Americans often moved unsettled areas seeking freedom and opportunity. Thus the Mormons crossed the plains to establish their church in Salt Lake City.

of the colonists' demanding the right to protest. Throughout the colonial period they did not hesitate to speak out when they believed it necessary to defend their interests.

When verbal or written protests failed, groups of colonists sometimes moved to unsettled areas where they were free to govern themselves in their own way. Roger Williams did just that when he fled from Massachusetts Bay Colony and founded what was to become Rhode Island. Through the years other groups followed his example, As late as 1847 the Mormons, fleeing persecution for their religious beliefs, crossed the plains of the west and built Salt Lake City, laying the foundations for the state of Utah. This method of securing the right to self-government was of course only possible in a country with an abundance of unsettled land.

As a last effort, some groups of colonists turned to direct action in their struggle against what they believed was oppressive authority. For example, in 1676 farmers in the less settled areas of Virginia, led by Nathaniel Bacon, rebelled against the government headed by Sir William Berkeley. Although the rebellion was put down, the government did make some concessions.

These and other attempts at rebellion when all other efforts failed provided precedents for the American Revolution itself. In the Declaration of Independence, Thomas Jefferson declared that when "a long train of abuses" threatens people with "absolute despotism, it is their right, it is their duty, to throw off such government, and to provide new guards for their future security."

The experiment with a league of states

As part of the British empire, the colonies had operated under the central authority of the British government. This authority was exercised by the king, by Parliament, and by agencies that the king and Parliament

18

created to manage the affairs of the colonies. The final power to make decisions remained in London.

Early in 1775, more than a year before the colonists declared their independence, the colonial governments began to crumble. British officials began to leave the colonies. The Tories, or those who remained loyal to the British king and Parliament, began to flee to Canada, the British West Indies, and Great Britain. By 1776 the Americans faced the problem of creating new state governments and a new central government.

The state constitutions that Americans wrote during the Revolutionary War reflected the people's deep-felt desire for a voice in their own government. All of the new governments were based upon written constitutions. These new constitutions also contained bills of rights guaranteeing to every citizen freedom from arbitrary government.

During the Revolutionary War, Americans also tackled the problem of building a central government. In their first efforts to govern themselves at the national level, the leaders of the 13 new states wrote the Articles of Confederation. However, this experiment with a league of more or less independent states was only partially successful.

There were two basic problems. First, there was the problem of dividing powers between the states and the central government. The Confederation was never able to provide a successful answer to this problem.

The signers of the Declaration of Independence proposed a revolutionary form of government—a democracy based on "the consent of the governed."

Second, the Confederation could not establish common, uniform laws for the states and the people of the states.

Even before 1787, a number of leader in America had become convinced that only a strengthened central government could remedy these weaknesses and secure order in the new nation.

Acting on this conviction, delegates from the various states met in Philadelphia in 1787. There they wrote the Constitution that, when ratified, became "the supreme law of the land," binding on both the states and the people of the states. (The Constitution appears on pages 722-55.)

Establishing the federal union

The Constitution of the United States created a federal union. It granted many important powers to the central government. Thus the central government now had the power and authority that it needed to deal with matters of common concern to all the states. By granting all other powers to the states, the Constitution guaranteed each state a large amount of independence in governing itself.

A federal system of government

This division of authority between the states and the central government, called **federalism,** provided a strong and effective system of government. Even so, disputes over where the final authority rested continued to arise. The issue reached the breaking point in 1861 when 11 southern states decided to withdraw from the Union and establish a Confederacy in which the ultimate power would be reserved to the states. Although the victory of the Union armies ended this greatest test of the federal system, the tug of war between the central government and the states continues to this day. Nevertheless, the principle of federalism has proven to be one of the nation's greatest sources of strength. This principle has worked as well with a federal union of 50 states as it did with the original 13.

James Madison, a leading member of the Constitutional Convention

Distributing power within the federal government

Those who wrote the Constitution believed in government under law, that is, government with written rules that must be applied equally to all citizens. They were aware that a misguided majority could be as great a danger to a government under law as a privileged ruling class or an all-powerful executive. Therefore, they were determined to protect the new nation from tyranny in any form.

Fear of tyranny by the central government was one of the major reasons for dividing power between the states and the federal government. This same fear prompted the founders of the nation to distribute the decision-making power *within* the federal government itself.

In an effort to prevent any one branch of the federal government from becoming too strong, the framers of the Constitution agreed that the executive, legislative, and judicial powers must be separated. To carry out this principle, they established three separate branches of the government, each having certain specified powers. To Congress, they gave the power to legislate, or make the laws (Article 1). To the Chief Executive, or President, they granted the power to execute, or carry out, the laws (Article 2). To the judiciary—the federal courts—they gave the power to interpret or rule on the meaning of the laws (Article 3).

Creating a system of checks and balances

Even these safeguards against tyranny did not satisfy the framers of the Constitution. As an additional protection, they wrote into the Constitution a system of **checks and balances.**

In order to prevent any one branch of the government from becoming too powerful, the Constitution provides checks on its power by the other two branches. For example, Congress has the power to enact laws, but the President has the power to veto them. However, Congress can by a two-thirds vote override the President's veto. The judiciary also has the power to check Congress. Ever since the famous decision of *Marbury v. Madison* in 1803, the Supreme Court has had the power to declare a law unconstitutional.

This is only a leading example of the carefully planned system of checks and balances written into the Constitution.

In practice, the exact powers of each branch of government have never been as clear as the framers of the Constitution intended. From time to time—and even today—there have been disagreements over which branch has the authority to take certain actions. In general, however, the system has worked remarkably well. It is a system that neatly balances effective government and freedom.

Identifying the source of final authority

In 1776 Thomas Jefferson outlined what was then a new and revolutionary theory of government. In the Declaration of Independence (see pages 720-21), Jefferson clearly and simply stated the basic principles of what today we call democracy: ". . . all men° are created equal," he wrote. ". . . they are endowed by their Creator with certain unalienable rights; . . . among these are life, liberty, and the pursuit of happiness." Governments exist in order to secure these rights, and the authority of all governments must be based on "the consent of the governed."

Those who wrote the Constitution made these ideals "the supreme law of the land." The Preamble makes this fact clear and beyond dispute. "We the people of the United States, in order to form a more

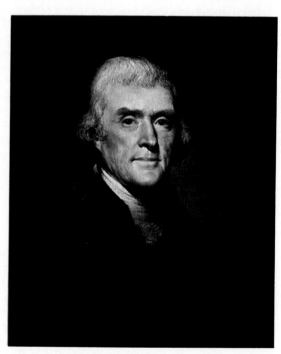

Thomas Jefferson, author of the Declaration of Independence and, later, President

°The term "men" used in the Declaration, the Constitution, and many other documents in American history really means "people" and refers to women and children as well as men.

perfect Union, establish justice, insure domestic tranquility, provide for the common defense, promote the general welfare, and secure the blessings of liberty to ourselves and our posterity, do ordain and establish this Constitution for the United States of America."

In addition to defining the purposes of the Constitution, the Preamble makes it clear that the government is established by consent of the governed. "We the people . . . ordain and establish" the government. This means that we, the people, have the final authority, the supreme power, in our nation.

Guaranteeing the rights of individuals

The separation of powers with checks and balances is just one way the Constitution protects each individual's rights. There are others.

Among the important guarantees of civil liberty in the Constitution as it was adopted in 1789 are prohibitions against ex post facto laws and bills of attainder. An **ex post facto law** – that is, a law passed "after the deed" – is one that sets forth a penalty for committing some action that was not illegal at the time it was committed. A **bill of attainder** is a law, or legislative measure, that punishes a person by fine, imprisonment, or confiscation of property without a trial in court.

The Constitution also guarantees that "The privilege of the writ of habeas corpus shall not be suspended, unless when in cases of rebellion or invasion the public safety may require it." The **writ of habeas corpus** is a legal document that requires that a person be released from prison unless that person has been formally charged with, or found guilty of committing, a crime.

The Constitution gives special protection to an individual accused of treason. The framers of the Constitution knew that the charge of treason often was used by all-powerful rulers to get rid of persons those rulers did not like. Moreover, the Constitution gives protection to innocent relatives of persons accused of treason. Only the persons guilty of treason can be punished. No penalty can be imposed upon their families or relatives.

These are only a few of the guarantees of personal rights that the founders wrote into the Constitution. They are important examples of the way in which the Constitution establishes a common standard of law for every American citizen, old and young, rich and poor alike.

The Bill of Rights

Despite the safeguards written into the Constitution, a number of states at first refused to ratify, or approve, it. They refused in part because they believed that it did not offer strong enough protection to the rights of individuals. They finally ratified it after they had been promised that a bill of rights would be added to the Constitution when Congress met.

In 1789–90 the first Congress of the United States drafted the first ten amendments to the Constitution. Among the guarantees of liberty in these ten amendments, known as the Bill of Rights, several are especially important. The First Amendment guarantees each American freedom of religion, speech, press, assembly, and petition. The Fourth Amendment upholds the principle of each citizen's right to privacy by prohibiting unlawful searches. The Fifth, Sixth, and Eighth Amendments protect accused persons from arbitrary arrest and from punishment by officials of the federal government.

The test of time

In their effort to protect the nation against tyranny by either a majority or a minority, the framers of the Constitution distributed the decision-making power throughout the government. Time has proven the wisdom of this provision. The Constitution has endured for nearly two centuries as the supreme law of the land. In general, it works as well today in a large industrialized nation of 50 states and 226 million people as it once did in a small agricultural nation of 13 states and 4 million people.

The compromise on representation

The Constitution was the product of a number of important compromises. If the delegates to the Constitutional Convention in 1787 had refused to compromise their differences, the writing of the Constitution would have been impossible.

One of the most serious conflicts of the Convention was the struggle between the large and small states over representation in Congress. The small states, fearful of being outvoted, insisted upon equal representation. The large states, unwilling to form the new federal union on this basis, insisted that the size of each state's population should determine the number of representatives it had in Congress. After a month of debate, the delegates agreed to accept a compromise. Each state, large or small, was to be represented by two Senators. Thus each state would have equal power in the Senate. In the House, however, each state's representation was to be based upon population.

The compromise on tariffs

Another source of conflict at the Constitutional Convention was the different economic interests of the North and South. Northern merchants wanted the central government to regulate commerce with foreign nations and among the states. Southern planters opposed this idea because they feared that the government would pass tariff laws and other legislation unfavorable to their interests. For example, if Congress imposed tariffs, or taxes, on exports, this would increase the cost of American tobacco to overseas buyers, and the planters' income might decline. Moreover, tariffs on imported goods might increase the price of the products the planters purchased.

The members of the Convention solved the problem by a compromise that gave Congress power "to regulate commerce with foreign nations, and among the several states," including the power to levy tariffs on *imports*. However, Congress was denied the power to levy tariffs on *exports*.

Compromises concerning slavery

The tragic contradiction between slavery and the noble principles outlined in the Declaration of Independence was not reconciled in the Constitution. In addition, two issues involving slavery caused bitter argument among the delegates.

One dispute arose over whether slaves should be included in counting population. Southerners wanted to count slaves in determining the number of representatives to be elected to the House of Representatives, but they did not want to count slaves for purposes of direct taxation. Northerners, on the other hand, thought that slaves should be counted for purposes of taxation, but not for representation. As a compromise, northerners and southerners agreed to count only three fifths of the total slave population for purposes of both representation and taxation.

There were also strong differences about regulating the slave trade. Southern planters were fearful that after Congress was given the power "to regulate commerce" and to tax imports, it would be able to prohibit the slave trade by law or by taxing the importation of slaves. As a compromise, the delegates agreed that until 1808 Congress should be denied the power to forbid the importation of any persons, such as slaves. Meanwhile no import tax could be levied in excess of $10 per person. By this compromise southerners won the right to import slaves for 20 more years and northerners secured the right to regulate the slave trade in the future.

The growth of the new nation

The new nation was created as a result of compromises. In the case of slavery, the compromises were unfortunate because they denied the principles of freedom upon which the nation was founded. Without them, however, it is doubtful that the Constitution could have been written.

Compromise as a solution to problems

As the years passed, the American people's ability to compromise made it possible for them to resolve serious conflicts or sometimes to put off the need to solve problems until some future time. In many other countries, the refusal or inability to reach compromise solutions often led to revolutions.

In the United States the use of compromise proved to be a substitute for revolution. By reconciling conflicting values and interests, the nation's leaders managed to resolve crises that might have destroyed the federal union.

Senator Henry Clay

The Missouri Compromise of 1820

The first serious clash between the North and the South developed early in 1819. Congress was about to admit Alabama as the eleventh slave state. With the entry of Alabama, power in the Senate would be equally divided. The North and the South each would have 22 Senators. This was the situation when the Territory of Missouri, in which slavery already existed, asked to be admitted. If Congress accepted Missouri as a slave state, the balance of power in the Senate would be upset, with the South having 24 votes to the North's 22.

At this point Representative James Tallmadge of New York presented an amendment to Missouri's application. Tallmadge proposed that no more slaves be allowed to enter Missouri. He also proposed to free all children born into slavery in Missouri after its admission as a state. This, however, was to be done gradually; the children of slaves were to become free only when they reached their twenty-fifth birthday.

Tallmadge's amendment touched off a bitter debate. At times the controversy became so heated that some political leaders talked boldly of "disunion" and "civil war." The issue had reached a deadlock when a group led by Senator Henry Clay of Kentucky proposed a compromise. At this time the people of Maine also applied to Congress to become a state. The admission of Maine would increase the number of free states in the Union. Clay therefore proposed that both Maine and Missouri be admitted together—one as a free state and the other without restrictions on slavery. As Clay pointed out, if this were done the balance of power between the North and the South in the Senate would not be changed. With Alabama, Missouri, and Maine in the Union, each section would have 24 votes.

Congress agreed to Clay's compromise proposal in 1820. As part of this compromise, however, slavery was prohibited in all other parts of the Louisiana Purchase north of latitude 36° 30′. Southern members of Congress accepted this ban because cotton could not be grown profitably on most farmland north of latitude 36° 30′.

In this way the crisis of 1819–20 had passed. Nevertheless, thoughtful people realized that a period of grave danger lay ahead of the young nation. John Quincy Adams wrote in his diary that the conflict over Missouri was "a mere preamble—a title page to a great, tragic volume."

The Compromise of 1833

Only a few years later Congress was faced with another very serious crisis. Once again, powerful groups in the North and the South clashed. This time the issue was the right of Congress to pass protective tariffs.

The issue arose in 1828 when the industrial interests of the North, joined by the agricultural interests of the West, succeeded in getting Congress to adopt a high protective tariff on imports. South Carolina and other southern states, led by Vice-President John C. Calhoun, bitterly opposed this so-called "Tariff of Abominations" on the grounds that it would force them to pay higher prices for goods manufactured in Europe.

The conflict smoldered for several years. Then, in 1832, Congress adopted a new tariff law. The Tariff Act of 1832 provided somewhat lower rates than the 1828 act. This new law was still a protective tariff, and therefore from the southern point of view it was no better than the old. South Carolina was convinced that the states that favored a protective tariff now controlled Congress. Therefore, it decided to take action.

In a convention called to act on the issue South Carolina adopted the Ordinance of Nullification.

Portrait by John Trumbull
Yale University Art Gallery

**Vice-President
John C. Calhoun**

25

The ordinance declared that the tariff acts of 1828 and 1832 were "null, void, and no law," and that they were not "binding upon this state, its officers, or citizens." It also contained a solemn warning that if the federal government tried to enforce the tariff law, South Carolina would leave, or secede from, the Union and become an independent nation.

President Andrew Jackson responded promptly. In "off-the-record" statements he warned that he was prepared to "hang every leader" who defied the authority of the federal government. For the public record, however, Jackson was more moderate, expressing his firm belief in the Union and his determination as President to enforce the law.

The crisis finally was resolved when both northerners and southerners agreed to another compromise proposed by Henry Clay. The Tariff Act of 1833 provided for a gradual reduction of tariff rates. At the same time, however, Congress passed the Force Bill, giving the President power to use federal forces, if necessary, to collect tariffs.

President Andrew Jackson

A new crisis develops

During the next 15 years Congress admitted six new states to the Union—three from the South, three from the North. In 1848 the uneasy balance still existed, with 15 slave states and 15 free states. During these same years the differences between the North and the South had been growing increasingly serious, with slavery the most bitter issue.

Then in 1849 California applied for admission to the Union. Southerners refused to consider the application because California's constitution prohibited slavery. If California entered as a free state, the balance between the sections would be upset in favor of the North.

Another issue before Congress was the controversy between the state of Texas and the newly acquired but still unorganized territory of New Mexico. Texas, where slavery was permitted, claimed that its boundary extended westward into an area that the federal government had recognized as belonging to New Mexico. Antislavery forces in Congress naturally tried to keep Texas' boundaries to the smallest possible limits. Southerners just as naturally were opposed to northern attempts to limit the area of Texas.

Arguments over other issues grew louder in both houses of Congress. Southerners sternly resisted a proposal to abolish slavery in the District of Columbia. They also resisted a northern proposal that New Mexico and Utah be organized into territories without any provision for slavery.

Many northerners were just as strongly opposed to a southern proposal to pass a new and more effective fugitive slave law. According to the original Fugitive Slave Law, adopted in 1793, state and local officials were responsible for capturing runaway slaves and returning them to their owners. In 1842, however, the Supreme Court had ruled that state law enforcement officers were not required to help federal officers to capture and return runaway slaves to their southern owners. The proposed new law now required state officials assist in capturing runaway slaves.

All of these issues were loaded with political dynamite. Any one of them could lead to a showdown between the North and South. In the opening months of 1850, many people felt that the United States was on the brink of disunion—perhaps on the brink of war.

The Compromise of 1850

Such was the situation when Henry Clay of Kentucky rose on the floor of the Senate to offer a compromise proposal. Clay, whose compromises had saved the Union from great danger in 1820 and again in 1833, was known and respected as "the Great Compromiser." Now, in 1850, ill and weary from years of devoted effort to hold the Union together, he pleaded once more for reason and moderation.

Clay's proposals included: (1) The admission of California as a free state. (2) The organization of the land acquired from Mexico (except California) into territories on the basis of "popular sovereignty," so that the settlers in each of the territories might decide for themselves whether or not they wanted slavery in their territory. (3) The payment of $10 million by the United States to Texas in return for Texas' abandoning all claim to New Mexico east of the Rio Grande. (4) The abolition of the slave trade—that is, of the buying and selling of slaves—but not of slavery itself in the District of Columbia. (5) The enactment of a more effective fugitive slave law, one that would compel state and local law enforcement officials to cooperate with federal officials in the capture and return of runaway slaves.

Clay's proposals provoked one of the most important and heated debates in American history, one that lasted more than six months. In the end, Congress adopted all of Clay's measures by substantial majorities. Compromise had once again saved the day.

The Compromise of 1850 lasted about four years. As it turned out, this period of relative calm proved to be merely the lull before the storm.

The Kansas-Nebraska Act

In 1854 Senator Stephen A. Douglas of Illinois sponsored and guided through Congress the Kansas-Nebraska Act. This act created two new organized territories in the West—Kansas and Nebraska. Both territories were north of the 36° 30′ line established by the Missouri Compromise and therefore closed to slavery. The Kansas-Nebraska Act now abolished this dividing line. The territories were now "perfectly free to form and regulate their domestic institutions in their own way. . . ."

The right of people in the territories to decide for themselves whether they wanted slavery or not was known as "popular sovereignty." Douglas had argued in favor of this procedure because he believed it was democratic. He had assumed that the people of Kansas would choose slavery and those of Nebraska would oppose it. He also had assumed that since the balance between the sections would be maintained, the measure would meet with approval in both the North and the South.

Douglas soon realized that his plan could not succeed. The Kansas-Nebraska Act immediately stirred up new arguments over the slavery question all across the nation. Throughout the North the issue of slavery again became the subject of heated discussion. The Fugitive Slave Law became increasingly difficult to enforce. "Anti-Nebraska" meetings in northern cities denounced Douglas for reopening the slavery dispute.

The issue of slavery divided the South and the North despite efforts at compromise. Here, newly purchased slaves are being sent to their owners.

"Bleeding Kansas"

Senator Charles Sumner of Massachusetts was one of many extreme antislavery people who believed that the Kansas-Nebraska Act would plunge the nation into serious trouble. "It puts freedom and slavery face to face and bids them grapple," he declared.

And grapple they did on the plains of the new Territory of Kansas. Northerners and southerners began to pour weapons and ammunition into the territory. Soon fighting broke out between the antislavery and the proslavery groups. At least 200 citizens lost their lives in the bitter strife. In the end it was necessary to send in federal troops to restore order.

Meanwhile, the settlers were trying to draw up a constitution and organize a territorial government. Hopelessly divided, they ended with *two* constitutions—one proslavery, one antislavery. Congress, also hopelessly divided over the issue, could reach no decision as to which constitution to recognize.

Fateful changes in the political parties

The Kansas-Nebraska Act and the struggle for control of Kansas widened the gap between the proslavery and antislavery groups within the two major political parties, the Whigs and the Democrats. Faced with this situation, antislavery forces in both parties decided to organize a new, purely sectional party. The Republican Party, as it was called, pledged itself to prevent the further expansion of slavery into the territories. Although its Presidential candidate failed to win the 1856 election, he did receive the electoral votes of 11 states, all in the North.

The growing split within the two major political parties into northern and southern wings and the formation of the purely sectional Republican Party were alarming developments. Other serious developments were to follow.

The Dred Scott decision

On March 6, 1857, the Supreme Court handed down the explosive Dred Scott decision. The Court ruled that the Missouri Compromise was unconstitutional because Congress had no power to exclude slavery from the territories. The Court based its ruling on the Fifth Amendment, which prohibited Congress from depriving any person of ". . . property, without due process of law." The Dred Scott decision was a clear victory for the proslavery South and a bitter blow for the antislavery forces in the North. It reinforced the belief of many northerners that southern slaveowners were determined to force their will on the entire nation.

John Brown's raid

Some two years later, in the fall of 1859, John Brown undertook to start a rebellion of slaves in Virginia. With money obtained from a number of New England and New York abolitionists, Brown armed a group of 18 men. On October 16 he seized the federal arsenal at Harpers Ferry in what is now West Virginia. He planned to seize the guns stored in the arsenal and give them to the slaves nearby. He would then lead the slaves in what he hoped would be a widespread rebellion.

It was a wild idea, certain to fail. Brown and his followers were captured. After being tried, Brown was hanged for "murder, criminal conspiracy, and treason against the Commonwealth of Virginia."

Many southerners believed that Brown's action represented northern opinion. They concluded therefore that slavery was no longer safe from direct attack. As a matter of fact, northern politicians and the majority of northerners were shocked at the news of the raid and quickly condemned it. However, extreme abolitionists regarded Brown as a heroic martyr. Ralph Waldo Emerson went so far as to declare that Brown was a "new saint" who would "make the gallows glorious like the cross."

Southern newspapers reported this small minority of abolitionist opinion as typical of northern thinking. To southerners John Brown's raid was convincing evidence that the North was determined to abolish slavery.

The breakup of the Union

By 1860 most of the ties binding the North and the South had been broken. The issue of slavery had split several churches—the Methodist, the Baptist, and one branch of the Presbyterian. Although many business ties still existed, the older political parties were divided and the new Republican Party was a purely sectional organization.

The final failure of compromise

The breakup of the Whig and Democratic parties into sectional groups and the election of the Republican candidate, Abraham Lincoln, to the Presidency did not make the breakup of the Union inevitable. There was still a genuine love of the Union in the South. However, the election of the Republicans strengthened southern extremists. They insisted that the Republicans, who now controlled the federal government, would not only confine slavery to the areas where it already existed, but would also try to abolish slavery altogether. Lincoln denied this.

In an effort to put such fears to rest, moderate leaders on both sides suggested a compromise that would guarantee slavery in the states where it was already established. Southern extremists demanded much more than this. They demanded guarantees of the right to extend slavery into the territories. Since the Republican Party was pledged to prevent the spread of slavery, the southern demands were completely unacceptable. So the last-minute efforts at compromise failed.

The steps toward war

South Carolina was the first state to leave the Union. Others soon followed its example, and early in 1861 delegates from six southern states met at Montgomery, Alabama, and drafted a constitution for the Confederate States of America. The Confederate Constitution resembled the Constitution of the United States. It created a federal government, but with some crucial differences. The Confederate Constitution stressed "the sovereign and independent character" of each state. It also guaranteed the right to own slaves.

The next, fateful step was now up to the government in Washington. Unless it was content to let the southern states depart in peace, armed conflict was only a matter of time. When President Lincoln sent reinforcements to Fort Sumter at Charleston, South Carolina, Confederate forces opened fire on the fort. Thus began, in the early morning of April 12, a terrible struggle that was to last for four long and bloody years.

Union advantages

The northern and western states — 24 in number before the war ended — held clear advantages over the 11 states in the Confederacy. The North had a population of some 22 million, the South only about 9 million, of whom 3½ million were slaves. The North was also greatly superior in manufacturing, in agriculture, in natural resources, in finance, and in transportation facilities. For example, when the war started, the North controlled 92 percent of the nation's industries and almost all of the known supplies of coal, iron, copper, and gold. The wealth of the Confederacy, by contrast, was largely in land and slaves. Moreover, at least during the early period of the conflict, the North was more united than it had ever been.

Confederate advantages

Considering the advantages enjoyed by the North, why did the Confederacy enter the conflict with confidence and why was it able to fight so effectively for four years? There are several answers to this question.

30

Cotton and other agricultural products formed the basis of the South's economy on the eve of the Civil War, as shown in this plantation scene.

First, the South needed only to fight a defensive war to protect its own territory until the North grew tired of the struggle—whereas the North had to invade and conquer the South, an area as large as Western Europe.

Second, southerners were fighting for the things all people cherish most—their homes, their independence, and the right to govern themselves in their own way. Northerners, by contrast, were fighting for something much more abstract, the idea of the preservation of the Union. After September 1862, however, when President Lincoln issued a preliminary Emancipation Proclamation,° northerners were also fighting to free the slaves.

Third, the armies of the Confederacy were led by able officers, men trained at West Point who knew the country they were defending. Probably the greatest military commander of the war was General Robert E. Lee, a Virginian, who resigned from the United States Army and supported his state when it joined the Confederacy.

Finally, the South hoped for support from other nations. Southerners believed that the textile mills of Great Britain and France were so dependent on southern cotton that those countries would come to the aid of the Confederacy.

Why the war broke out

None of this explains why efforts to compromise the differences between the two sections finally broke down and the Union was torn apart by armed conflict. There is no simple answer to this question.

At the heart of the matter, however, is the fact that during the first half of the 1800's the North and the South and the West had developed along different lines. The increasingly industrialized North with its growing factories and towns; the agricultural South with its increasing

°The final Emancipation Proclamation was issued on January 1, 1863.

31

dependence on its major crop, cotton; the new, growing West, with its restless pioneers moving toward ever-new frontiers—here were three radically different ways of life and different sets of values.

The rapid development of railroads linking the Northeast and the West during the 1850's and the growing dependence of each section on the other's food products and industrial output were among the important reasons why these two sections stood together when war came. Both also had a free labor system; both regarded slavery as evil and as a denial of the American dream of equality and freedom.

Thus the differences between the North and the South were not limited to slavery. The rural South and the rapidly developing industrial North held different views in regard to tariffs, federally financed public improvements, the control of money and banking, the disposal of public lands, and the issue of states' rights.

All of these factors helped to divide the nation and lead it down the road to armed conflict. For this reason, thoughtful historians do not attempt to give a short, simple explanation of why the North and the South went to war. Instead, they explain why northern extremists and southern extremists, a minority in each section, felt and acted as they did. Historians point out the great majority of the people in the North loved the Union and believed in it so strongly that they could not permit it to be destroyed. Historians also point out that many in the South who loved the Union and would have preferred to remain a part of it supported the Confederacy because they were determined to defend the principle of states' rights, to protect their homes, and to support the position taken by their relatives, neighbors, and friends.

A reunited nation faces the future

In 1865 the nation's terrible trial by fire and sword came to an end. The conflict had cost the American people billions of dollars. Far worse, large areas of the South lay in ruins, and hundreds of thousands of Americans had been killed or wounded. Not counting the wounded, the North had lost 359,000 people, the South about 258,000. Memories of these losses were to hang over the nation like a dark shadow for years to come.

The war had many far-reaching consequences. It ended the doctrine of secession. It strengthened the Union by increasing the power of the federal government at the expense of the states. It strengthened democracy by showing that a representative form of government could operate successfully in wartime. By freeing the slaves, it also gave the American people a new opportunity to demonstrate that they were committed without any exceptions to the principle that all individuals are equal under the law and are entitled to the "unalienable rights" of "life, liberty, and the pursuit of happiness."

Not least important, the victory of the North marked the triumph, not just of one section over another, but of city and factory over a rural, agricultural society. This victory insured the development of America as a powerful industrial nation.

In the spring of 1865, the people of the United States stood at the beginning of a new era. Great new opportunities were opening before them, but, of course, they could not know this at the time. They could look only into the immediate future. The big problem they faced, northerners and southerners alike, was "to bind up the nation's wounds" and to join hands as a reunited people.

Unit One

Rebuilding the Nation

1865-1900

Chapter 1
Restoring the South to the Union 1865-1900

1. President Lincoln strives for lenient reconstruction.
2. The nation struggles to restore order in the South.
3. The Radical Republicans enact a program of reconstruction.
4. White southerners regain control of their state governments.
5. The New South advances in agriculture, industry, and education.
6. Black southerners struggle for a place in the New South.

Chapter 2
Severe Trials for Democracy 1865-1897

1. Graft and corruption spread in the postwar years.
2. A start is made toward restoring honesty to government.
3. Efforts at political reform move forward.

Chapter 3
Conquering the Last Frontier 1865-1900

1. The Indians make their last stand on the Great Plains.
2. The government tries to "Americanize" the Indians.
3. Ranchers build a cattle kingdom on the plains.
4. Farmers plow the tough sod of the last frontier.
5. Miners discover new treasures in the western mountains.

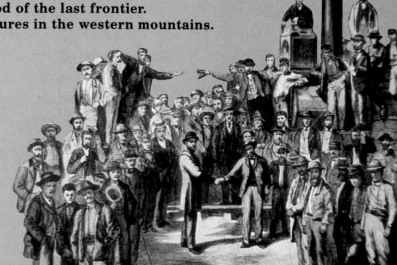

Chapter 1

Restoring the South to the Union

1865-1900

After the Civil War came to an end, bitterness between the North and the South continued for many years. In part this was the inevitable result of a terrible conflict in which most people on each side believed that their cause was right and just.

However, equally important as a cause of resentment was the decade of rebuilding the Union that followed the war. During this period bitter feelings arose over the stubborn political and constitutional problems involved in bringing the southern states back into the Union. There were also the grave economic problems of rebuilding devastated southern industries and reopening normal trade relations among the states. Finally, there was the continuing social problem of bringing black Americans into the mainstream of national life.

As you will read in this and the next chapter, these problems had to be dealt with at a time when both the North and the South faced a breakdown of public morality. Corruption then reached into every level of government—local, state, and national. This breakdown was due not only to the war, which had dislocated life in every section of the country. It was brought about also by the changes taking place in the United States during the latter half of the 1800's—the rapid development of industry, a flood of immigration, and the growth of cities.

THE CHAPTER IN OUTLINE

1. President Lincoln strives for lenient reconstruction.

2. The nation struggles to restore order in the South.

3. The Radical Republicans enact a program of reconstruction.

4. White southerners regain control of their state governments.

5. The New South advances in agriculture, industry, and education.

6. Black southerners struggle for a place in the New South.

1 President Lincoln strives for lenient reconstruction

On March 4, 1865, when the war was rapidly drawing to an end, President Lincoln stated the policy of reconstruction he intended to follow in regard to the South. The sullen roar of the cannons massed in front of Richmond would soon be stilled, but the moving language of Abraham Lincoln's Second Inaugural Address was destined to live on as part of the nation's heritage.

"With malice toward none," he said, "with charity for all, with firmness in the right, as God gives us to see the right, let us strive on to finish the work we are in, to bind up the nation's wounds, to care for him who shall have borne the battle, and for his widow, and his orphan—to do all which may achieve and cherish a just and lasting peace among ourselves and with all nations."

Lincoln's program. Lincoln's were not idle words. He had already begun to develop a program of reconstruction based upon "charity for all," and he fully intended to carry out that program.

As early as December 8, 1863, Lincoln outlined his program for restoring the South to the Union in his Proclamation of Amnesty° and Reconstruction. The practical, flexible program rested on Lincoln's theory that the Confederate states had never succeeded in leaving the Union. They had for a time left the family circle, but they were still part of the family. The immediate problem was to get them back into the circle quickly.

First, he offered full pardon to all southerners who would take an oath of allegiance to the Union and promise to accept federal laws and proclamations dealing with slavery. The only southerners who were excluded from Lincoln's offer were those who had resigned positions in the federal government to serve in the Confederacy, members of the Confederate government, high-ranking Confederate army and naval officers, and Confederates who had mistreated prisoners of war.

Second, Lincoln declared that a state could draw up a new constitution, elect new officials,

°**amnesty:** a broad pardon for offenses committed against a government.

and return to the Union on a basis of full equality with all other states when it met certain conditions. A minimum number of persons (at least 10 percent of those who had voted in the election of 1860) must take the oath of allegiance. Each person taking the oath must have been a qualified voter in the state before its secession from the Union.

In 1863 this program applied only to areas conquered by Union armies. Lincoln intended to apply it to all other Confederate areas as soon as they were in Union hands. Lincoln did not insist that this proposal was the only acceptable one. He agreed that Congress must give final approval to admitting members of Congress from the reconstructed states. More-

Lincoln pledged that "when I come to lay down the reins of power, [even if] I lost every other friend on earth, I shall at least have one friend left, and that friend shall be down inside me."

over, as time passed, Lincoln revealed flexibility in his own thinking. For example, in a letter written in 1864, he stated that the restoration of the southern states to the Union "must rest upon the principle of civil and political equality of both races; and it must be sealed by a general amnesty." In his last public address, delivered on April 11, 1865, only four days before his death, he declared that he favored giving the vote to those blacks who had fought for the Union and to those with some educational qualifications.

Opposition to Lincoln's program. Not all Republican leaders agreed with Lincoln's ideas on reconstruction. Many opposed the idea of pardoning former Confederates and allowing them to vote and hold office. These Republican leaders doubted the loyalty of former Confederates. They also doubted whether, if given political power, the former Confederates would permit blacks to enjoy legal and political rights.

The Republicans who were most opposed to Lincoln's reconstruction policy were called Radicals. The Radical Republicans were by no means a well-defined group. Different Radicals took different positions on political and economic issues and on methods of readmitting the former Confederate states. The two most outspoken Radicals were Senator Charles Sumner of Massachusetts and Representative Thaddeus Stevens of Pennsylvania.

Senator Sumner insisted on measures to guarantee the political and legal equality of black Americans and to educate them for the responsibilities of freedom. Representative Stevens wanted to punish the South for all the injustices and discriminations that black southerners had suffered under white rule. Stevens also wanted to do everything possible to make sure that in the future the freed slaves would be treated justly. Stevens also believed that political and legal rights for former slaves would be meaningless if the blacks did not have economic independence. He urged that the estates of "rebel traitors" be divided up and given to the freed slaves. Few Radical Republicans accepted so extreme a policy.

During the war and in the months following Confederate surrender, a majority of Republican leaders, more moderate in their views, lined up with Lincoln's reconstruction policies. However, many moderates agreed with the Radicals that Lincoln, in exercising his war powers, had encroached upon the constitutional powers of the legislative branch. They all felt that Congress, not the President, should lay down the rules for restoring the southern states to the Union.

Some Republicans frankly admitted that their thinking about reconstruction was influenced by practical politics. They believed that, when the war ended, white southerners would reject the wartime Republican Party and flock to the Democratic Party. Southern Democrats returning to Congress would probably support northern Democrats, thus making the Republicans a minority party. Such a combination might endanger measures supported by many Republicans—a high tariff, national banks, free land, and federal aid to railroads.

The Republicans could keep the Democrats from gaining majority power in state as well as federal governments in two ways. First, they could give voting rights to the former slaves. These new voters would support the Republicans at the polls in gratitude for emancipation. Second, they could keep former Confederate leaders from voting and holding public office.

Such political considerations played some part in shaping the attitudes of many Republicans toward reconstruction. Historians disagree as to how large a part. However, many Republican members of Congress approached the difficult problems of reconstruction with a genuine desire to help the freed slaves and to guarantee them fair treatment in American life.

The Wade-Davis Bill. Opposition to President Lincoln's plan for reconstruction found expression in the Wade-Davis Bill. Some Radical Republican members of Congress thought the bill was too mild. However, enough moderate Republicans supported it to allow the bill to be passed by a slender majority in early July 1864.

The Wade-Davis Bill provided for readmitting the southern states into the Union under harsher conditions than those favored by Lincoln. The bill was intended to give political power to southerners who had remained loyal to the Union. It was also intended to insure that the new constitutions of the southern states would recognize the freedom of black southerners. Finally, the bill was intended to insure that Confederate war debts were **repudiated,** or not paid.

President Lincoln refused to sign the Wade-Davis Bill. He felt that its rigid provisions

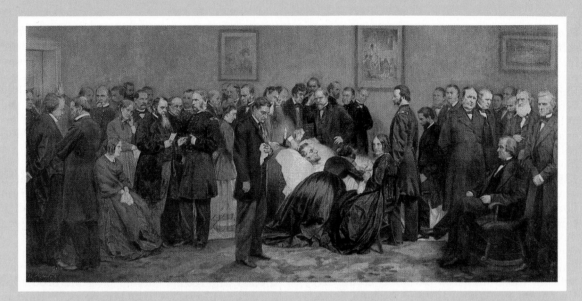

THE DEATH OF LINCOLN

It was Friday—Good Friday—April 14, 1865. The long war was finally over, and President and Mrs. Lincoln had arranged to go to the theater with friends. The play was a popular comedy called *Our American Cousin*.

At Ford's Theater the Lincoln party watched the performance from a special box that had been draped with flags. Shortly after ten o'clock, a former actor named John Wilkes Booth slipped quietly into the President's box. Resting his pistol on the back of Lincoln's chair, he shot the President in the head. Then Booth jumped to the stage, shouting "*Sic semper tyrannis!* [Thus always to tyrants!] The South is avenged!"

They carried Lincoln to a house across the street, for he was too badly wounded to be taken back to the White House. There he lay unconscious for hours. One eyewitness wrote that "the giant sufferer lay extended diagonally across the bed, which was not long enough for him." Physicians, cabinet officers, Mrs. Lincoln, their son Robert—all gathered in the small room.

What of Booth? He was a proslavery fanatic who apparently decided to kill Lincoln after the President's speech of April 11, in which he advocated limited suffrage for blacks. The assassin broke his left leg as he leaped to the stage but escaped on horseback. He ended up hiding in a Virginia barn, where he was found by Union soldiers. Whether Booth was shot or took his own life is unclear, but his end came on April 26.

Lincoln had lingered on through the night of April 14 and into the dark and gloomy morning of the next day. About seven o'clock he breathed his last. When told of Lincoln's death, Secretary of War Edwin Stanton said sadly, "Now he belongs to the ages."

would restrict him when the time came to rebuild the Union. He also believed that Congress did not have the constitutional authority to compel a state to abolish slavery. Abolition of slavery, he believed, would require an amendment to the Constitution.

Lincoln's assassination. Whether or not Lincoln could have won acceptance of his policy must remain unanswered. On April 14, 1865, he was assassinated in Washington, D.C., by John Wilkes Booth, an actor.

Sorrow and anger gripped the nation— South as well as North, black as well as white. White southerners had despised Lincoln during the war. Yet many had come to feel that he was a wise, compassionate leader who offered the best program of reconstruction. Flags flew at halfmast, bells tolled, and weeping crowds filed through the funeral train as it stopped in cities between Washington, D.C., and Lincoln's burial place in Springfield, Illinois. Meanwhile, Vice-President Andrew Johnson became President.

President Johnson. Andrew Johnson was a self-educated man. Without any formal schooling, he had spent his boyhood as a tailor's apprentice. Later his devoted wife had helped him to improve his meager writing ability. While still a young man, he was elected mayor of his community, a small mountain village in eastern Tennessee. This was the beginning of a political career in the Democratic Party that took him to the Senate of the United States in 1857. Although he owned a few slaves, Johnson disliked the large planters who were so influential in the South. He had resisted the secession of Tennessee in 1861.

Johnson's service for the Union during the war won him an appointment as military governor of Tennessee. He was responsible for controlling those areas of his state occupied by Union troops. When the Republicans, including Lincoln himself, feared that they might lose the Presidential election in 1864, Johnson, a Democrat, was placed on the "Union" ticket. The hope of the Republicans was that he would draw votes for Lincoln.

Andrew Johnson had many admirable qualities. He possessed a stubborn fighting spirit and the moral courage to act according to his convictions. Unfortunately, he was not a flexible man. Whereas Lincoln always tried to understand the positions of his political opponents, Johnson tended to insist upon the rightness of his own views. Johnson lacked sufficient patience, tact, and political skill to be the effective leader that the nation needed at this critical time in its history.

Johnson and reconstruction. One of Johnson's first decisions as President was to offer rewards for the arrest of Jefferson Davis and other former Confederate leaders. Most Radical Republicans were pleased with Johnson's action. The Radicals believed that he would help them carry out their harsher program of reconstruction.

President Johnson soon disappointed the Radicals. He adopted a more conciliatory attitude toward the South and claimed that he intended to follow Lincoln's program. For a time he seemed to be doing so. He officially recognized the reconstructed governments of Tennessee, Arkansas, Louisiana, and Virginia. Johnson also kept all of the members of Lincoln's cabinet.

In several ways, however, Johnson did not follow Lincoln's program, either in details or in general approach. Lincoln had kept an open mind about the best method of reconstructing the Union. Johnson refused to consider any plan but his own. His stubbornness antagonized the Radical Republicans, as did his policy of pardoning former Confederates. When the Radicals objected to his policies, Johnson answered their arguments with name-calling and personal abuse.

Johnson managed even to antagonize the moderate Republicans. Most moderates shared with the Radicals the belief that any program of reconstruction must provide civil and political equality for both races. Johnson opposed this viewpoint.

End of Presidential reconstruction. Nevertheless, the reconstruction program proceeded for a time along the lines laid down by Lincoln and modified by Johnson. Within a few months, all the former Confederate states except Texas had adopted new constitutions and organized new governments.

When Congress assembled on December 4, 1865, Senators and Representatives from the southern states, most of whom had been leaders in the Confederacy, were waiting outside the doors to take their seats in the national legislature. To many observers it looked as though the long and dreadful war was finally ended and the restored nation was about to start anew.

SECTION SURVEY

IDENTIFY: amnesty, reconstruction, Charles Sumner, Thaddeus Stevens, Wade-Davis Bill, John Wilkes Booth, Andrew Johnson.

1. (a) What did Lincoln mean when he said, "With malice toward none, with charity for all"? (b) What were the main terms of Lincoln's reconstruction plan? (c) Which terms show how he intended to put into practice the ideas expressed in his Second Inaugural Address?

2. (a) What were the main arguments against Lincoln's reconstruction plan? (b) Explain the reasoning of Lincoln's opponents.

3. (a) What were the provisions of the Wade-Davis Bill? Why did (b) Lincoln and (c) some Radical Republicans object to the bill?

4. To what extent was reconstruction policy (a) a struggle between the two major political parties and (b) a struggle between two branches of the federal government?

2 The nation struggles to restore order in the South

A new chapter in American history opened when Congress assembled on December 4, 1865, but it was not the chapter outlined by either Lincoln or Johnson. It proved, instead, to be one of the most troubled chapters in the nation's history.

Economic chaos in the South. The scene in the South at the end of the war was one of utter poverty. Crumbling chimneys rose from the ashes of once lovely mansions. Grass grew in the roads, bridges lay in ruins, and two thirds of the railroads were destroyed.

The devastation in the cities was especially grim. A visitor reported that Columbia, South Carolina, was "a wilderness of crumbling walls, naked chimneys, and trees killed by flames." Rubble covered the business section of Richmond, Virginia, one of the great southern manufacturing centers. The scene in Atlanta, Georgia, was one of devastation. City and countryside alike, wherever armies had fought, were largely in ruins.

Social chaos. The southern economy as well as southern property had been torn apart by the war. A citizen of Mississippi wrote in April 1865 that "our fields everywhere lie untilled. Naked chimneys and charred ruins all over the land mark the spots where happy homes . . . once stood. Their former inhabitants wander in poverty and exile, wherever chance or charity affords them shelter or food. Childless, old age widows, and helpless orphans beggared and hopeless, are everywhere." Conditions were not as bad as this everywhere, but they were bad enough.

The plight of some 3.5 million freed slaves was far worse. The former slaves were at last free, at least in name, but free to do what? Most of them had never been given an opportunity to learn how to read and write. None had owned land. Few knew what it was like to work for their own wages. Nor could most of their former owners pay them wages, for Confederate money was worthless and United States currency was scarcely to be found in the South. The land itself remained, but seeds and farm tools had almost disappeared.

After the war many schools were set up throughout the South to educate the newly freed slaves, young as well as old. One observer noted the eagerness of the new learners: "I have seen three generations sitting on the same bench, spelling the same lesson."

Disease, always the companion of hunger and lack of sanitation, swept across the South. It was especially serious in the cities and their outskirts, where uprooted people struggled to survive in makeshift shelters. Thousands died during the summer and winter of 1865–66. In some crowded urban areas, as much as one quarter to one third of the black population died of disease. The death rate among the white population was almost as grim.

Relief efforts for freed slaves. Even during the war, some abolitionists tried to aid the freed slaves who had fled into areas controlled by Union forces. When white planters abandoned their plantations on islands off the coast of South Carolina, black people there were left helpless and destitute. Idealistic men and women, white and black, helped the freed slaves to operate these plantations and to set up schools there. Outstanding among the volunteers was Laura Towne of Massachusetts. She looked after the health of former slaves, helped them with legal problems, and established the Penn School. This school later became a teacher-training institution with vocational as well as academic programs.

Elsewhere, relief societies financed by northern religious and charitable groups tried to fill the needs of freed slaves for food, shelter, jobs, and schooling. Josephine Griffing, an Ohio abolitionist and women's rights leader, set up one such program in Washington, D.C., that provided food, clothing, shelter, and job training for freed blacks. She also urged Congress to undertake a program to find places to live in the North and West for homeless black people and to help them become self-supporting citizens. She herself helped thousands find homes and jobs in many localities.

The Freedmen's Bureau. During the war, the United States Army provided food and clothing for impoverished southerners, black and white, in areas under its control. Once the war was over, it was clear that neither the army nor the voluntary relief societies could meet the pressing needs of southerners, especially the freed slaves. At the urging of Josephine Griffing and others, Congress in 1865 created the Freedmen's Bureau to look after "refugees, freedmen°, and abandoned lands." This was the first important example in the nation's history of federal support for needy and underprivileged people. The Freedmen's Bureau was headed by General Oliver Otis Howard of Maine. In 1867 General Howard also founded Howard University in Washington, D.C., which offered higher education to the freed slaves.

Northerners and southerners differed in their attitude toward the Freedmen's Bureau. Most northerners regarded it as an honest effort to help the South bring order out of chaos. Most white southerners, on the other hand, resented the bureau. They charged that many bureau agents encouraged the freed slaves to look upon their former owners as enemies and, by doing so, created racial friction.

White southerners also charged the bureau with raising false hopes among the freed slaves, thereby making readjustment increasingly difficult. One of these false hopes was the former slaves' belief that they would all receive farms. During the summer and fall of 1865, the rumor spread that every former slave would get "forty acres and a mule" as a Christmas gift from the federal government. This rumor was based on a statement in the

°**freedmen** was the term used in these years to refer to former slaves — women and children as well as men.

Freedmen's Bureau bill that abandoned land or land for which taxes had not been paid could be distributed among the former slaves. Many freed slaves accepted the rumor as truth. Overjoyed at the prospect of soon owning farms and understandably linking freedom with the right to choose where and how they worked, some freed slaves decided not to work for white southerners.

Restrictions on freed slaves. In this situation southern leaders began to take steps to restore life as they had known it. One step was the adoption of laws to regulate the conduct of the freed slaves.

Laws of this kind, known as "slave codes," had existed before the war. The new black codes, which varied from state to state, contained many of the same provisions as the old slave codes. As white southerners pointed out, however, they also included certain improvements in civil rights for the former slaves. Under the new codes, former slaves were permitted to own personal property, to sue and be sued in court, to act in court cases involving one or more black persons, and legally to marry members of their own race.

However, in general the codes denied blacks their basic civil rights. Mississippi, for example, using its old code, merely substituted the word "Negro" for "slave." Black southerners were forbidden to possess firearms unless licensed to do so. They were forbidden to assemble unless white southerners were present. Nor could blacks appear on the streets after sunset or travel without permits. Above all, the codes established white control over black labor. They prohibited black southerners from starting businesses. They provided for strict labor contracts, including severe apprenticeship regulations and stern punishments if contracts were broken. Some codes also restricted black southerners from renting or leasing farmland. The black codes indicated that white southerners had the intention of confining the freed slaves to a clearly defined, subordinate way of life.

Such was the situation in December 1865 when the newly elected Senators and Representatives from all the former Confederate states except Texas appeared in Washington to take their seats in Congress. The former Confederate states had taken some, but not all, of the steps required by both President Lincoln and President Johnson for readmission to the

Union. The new Senators and Representatives fully expected to take their seats in Congress and to share with northern members the task of rebuilding the Union.

Congress, however, refused to admit the southern Senators and Representatives. What motives prompted Congress to reject the South's newly elected representatives? Why did Congress refuse to accept Lincoln's and Johnson's programs for restoring the South to the Union?

Reasons behind rejection. From the time Lincoln's program began to take shape, Radical Republicans had argued that southern leaders could not be trusted. Now, in December 1865, the Radicals pointed to the black codes as evidence that white southerners were unwilling to recognize the complete freedom of black Americans.

The Radical Republicans also opposed the Lincoln and Johnson theory about the nature of the war. Both Lincoln and Johnson had argued that the conflict was a "rebellion of individuals." This being so, they believed that the President could use the pardoning power granted him by the Constitution to restore the South to the Union.

Senator Charles Sumner opposed Lincoln's theory with the "state suicide" argument. According to Sumner, the southern states, as complete political organizations, had committed "state suicide" when they seceded from the Union. Now, with the war over, they were like any other unorganized territory of the United States. This being the case, Congress alone had the constitutional right to establish the terms for admitting them to the Union.

Representative Thaddeus Stevens held an even more drastic point of view. According to Stevens, the former Confederate states did not exist even as territories. In Stevens's opinion they were "conquered provinces" and should be treated as such.

Historians cannot be sure of the motives that led Radical Republicans to take the positions they did. Some Radicals were influenced by economic and political considerations. However, a good many Radical and moderate Republicans had a sincere feeling of obligation to the freed slaves. They genuinely wanted to make sure that white southerners did not deprive black southerners of their freedom or take steps to reduce them to a permanently inferior way of life.

Many moderate Republicans shared Lincoln's attitude toward the South. If Johnson had been less insistent upon having his own way, if he had been willing to work with the moderate Republicans, they and the Democratic members of the House and Senate might have carried through a reconstruction program acceptable to white southern leaders. However, President Johnson would not change his views, and control of Congress passed into the hands of the Radicals.

SECTION SURVEY

IDENTIFY: Josephine Griffing, General Oliver Otis Howard, black codes, "rebellion of individuals" theory, "state suicide" theory, "conquered provinces" theory.

1. Describe the most pressing problems facing the South in 1865.
2. (a) Describe the work of the Freedmen's Bureau. (b) Contrast northern and southern opinions about the bureau.
3. (a) Name the main restrictions placed on black southerners by white southern leaders. (b) How did the new black codes differ from the old slave codes?
4. What reasons led Congress to reject the new southern members of Congress?
5. How did Andrew Johnson contribute to the problems of reconstruction?

3 The Radical Republicans enact a program of reconstruction

By refusing in December 1865 to seat the southern members of Congress, the Radical Republicans practically guaranteed their own control of both houses of Congress. Within a few months, they restored military rule in the South and sowed seeds of bitterness that were to live for many years.

The first steps. Congress immediately appointed a joint committee of six Senators and nine Representatives to study the entire question of reconstruction. While Congress waited for the committee's report, it passed a bill enlarging the powers of the Freedmen's Bureau. The new law gave the bureau power to prosecute in military courts, rather than in civil courts, any person accused of depriving freed slaves of their civil rights. President Johnson promptly vetoed the bill. He argued (1) that trial by military courts violated the Fifth Amendment of the Constitution and (2) that Congress had no power to pass *any* laws with 11 states unrepresented. Johnson's veto infuriated the Radical Republicans, who finally gathered enough votes to pass the bill over the President's veto.

In the meantime, Congress passed a civil rights bill. It was the first in a series of federal acts designed to give black Americans full citizenship and guarantee them complete equality of treatment. Johnson also vetoed this bill on the ground that it was an unconstitutional invasion of states' rights. Enough moderate Republicans joined the Radicals to pass the Civil Rights Act over Johnson's veto.

Johnson's vetoes cost him the support of moderate Republicans who, without any desire to punish white southerners, believed that Congress should protect the rights of former slaves. The vetoes also strengthened the influence of Thaddeus Stevens and the other Radical Republicans.

The Fourteenth Amendment. Congress feared that the Supreme Court might declare the Civil Rights Act unconstitutional. It decided to write the provisions of the act into the Constitution by amendment. This amendment, the Fourteenth, was the outcome of compromise between moderate and Radical Republicans. Some Radicals had hoped to outlaw all forms of racial segregation and discrimination. That objective does not seem to have been shared by the moderates, nor even by all Radicals who shaped the Amendment.

The Fourteenth Amendment (pages 748–49) made black Americans citizens of the United States and of the states in which they lived. It forbade states to deprive citizens of the rights of life, liberty, and property without due process of law or to deny any citizen "the equal protection of the laws." It went further and excluded former Confederate leaders from holding public office, state or federal. It provided for reduction of Congressional representation of states that deprived black Americans of their rights as citizens. The amendment also forbade southern states to repay Confederate war debts or to pay former slaveowners for the loss of their slaves.

Congressional elections of 1866. Tennessee ratified the Fourteenth Amendment in July 1866 and was immediately readmitted to the Union. On the advice of President Johnson, all of the other southern states rejected the amendment by overwhelming votes.

What would Congress do next? The answer depended in part on the Congressional elections in the fall of 1866. If the Democrats won control of Congress, they might return to Lincoln's and Johnson's programs or modify them. If the Republicans won, they might fight for further restrictions on the political role of the former Confederates and for stronger guarantees of the rights of blacks.

Several events helped to swing voters toward the Republicans. Violent race riots were especially influential in shaping public opinion. In Memphis, Tennessee, 46 blacks were killed and 12 black schools and 4 black churches were burned. In a riot at New Orleans, about 200 people, mostly black, were killed or wounded. Many northerners, shocked by such violence, began to feel that perhaps the Radical Republicans were right to demand further federal protection for the freed slaves.

In the late summer of 1866, President Johnson made a trip to Chicago, stopping along the way to make election speeches. When opponents heckled him, Johnson's answers often seemed to reflect a lack of understanding of the election issues, as well as bitter hatred of Radical Republicans. His language, often blunt and crude, antagonized many voters.

More important, however, as a reason for Republican strength was the memory of the war itself. During the terrible conflict, both sides had suffered immense casualties. Voters, fearful of losing the fruits of hard-won military victory, voted for Republican candidates.

In the election the Republicans increased their hold on both houses of Congress. With more than a two-thirds majority in both the Senate and the House, the Republicans, if they held together, could now override Johnson's Presidential vetoes.

Reconstructing the South. In March 1867 a combination of Radical and moderate Republicans passed, over Johnson's vetoes, a complete program for reconstruction. The new program contained five major provisions.

First, Congress divided the ten southern states that had rejected the Fourteenth Amendment into five military districts. Each

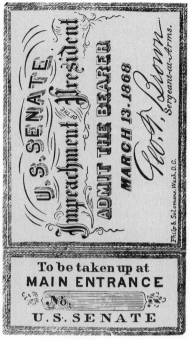

In February 1868 this House committee, led by an old, ill, and unforgiving Thaddeus Stevens (standing), drafted the articles of impeachment against President Johnson. Tickets for the trial that followed were in great demand.

district was under a military governor, with federal troops to maintain law and order while the states drafted new constitutions and organized new governments.

Second, Congress deprived most former Confederate leaders of the right to vote and hold office. The restrictions were the same as those that had already been written into the Fourteenth Amendment.

Third, Congress gave the freed slaves the right to vote and hold office.

Fourth, Congress authorized the states to write new constitutions that guaranteed freed slaves the right to vote.

Fifth, Congress required the states to ratify the Fourteenth Amendment.

The white southern governments that had been formed under the Presidential plan of reconstruction now had no choice but to accept the new program. One by one, the states held conventions and drafted new constitutions. They then organized their new governments and entered the Union under the terms that were laid down by Congress.

Johnson's impeachment and trial. By the summer of 1868, all but three southern states

had returned to the Union on the terms laid down by Congress. (Mississippi, Texas, and Virginia finally accepted the terms and were readmitted in 1870.) Meanwhile, the Radical Republicans determined to remove their hated enemy, President Johnson, from office.

Several things led the Radical Republicans to this decision. They certainly were affected by the emotional hatreds and tensions of the times. More important, the Radicals knew that the success of their reconstruction program depended heavily on its enforcement. They were convinced that Johnson would not enforce Congressional policy. He confirmed their suspicions when, by executive order, he restricted the power of military commanders in the South and removed commanders known to be sympathetic to Radical programs.

To find grounds for impeachment and to reduce the President's power, Congress in 1867 adopted the Tenure of Office° Act over Johnson's veto. Under this law the President could not dismiss important civil officers without the Senate's consent. Believing the law unconsti-

°tenure of office: the period during which an individual has the right to continue in office.

43

"Let Us Have Peace" was Ulysses S. Grant's campaign slogan in the 1868 Presidential election. This campaign poster mentions peace, but it plays up Grant's war record, which was the source of his great popularity.

tutional, Johnson decided to put it to a test. In February 1868 he demanded the resignation of Secretary of War Edwin M. Stanton. Stanton had consistently cooperated with Johnson's political enemies.

The House immediately adopted a resolution that "Andrew Johnson, President of the United States, be impeached of high crimes and misdemeanors in office." The Radicals also charged that Johnson "did attempt to bring into disgrace, ridicule, contempt, and reproach the Congress of the United States." The Radicals cited occasions when the President publicly made "with a loud voice certain intemperate, inflammatory, and scandalous harangues" against Congress "and did therein utter loud threats and bitter menaces."

Under the Constitution a President may be impeached on grounds of "treason, bribery, or other high crimes and misdemeanors" (pages 724, 725, and 738). Although the charges brought by the House against President Johnson were of doubtful legality, he was nevertheless impeached.

Johnson's trial before the Senate, presided over by Chief Justice Salmon P. Chase, lasted about two months. After prolonged debate it became clear that Johnson was not guilty of any offense for which he could legally be removed from office. Nevertheless, when the Senate vote was counted, it stood 35 to 19 against Johnson, just one vote short of the necessary two-thirds majority required for removal from office. Johnson continued to serve as President for almost a year, until his term expired, but his influence was at an end.

Decline of Radical power. It soon became apparent, however, that the Radical Republicans had overreached themselves. When they tried to remove the President from office, they lost the support of many moderate Republicans. Moreover, public opinion finally began to turn against them.

As the election of 1868 approached, the Republicans realized they were in trouble. In hopes of winning the election, they unanimously nominated Ulysses S. Grant for the Presidency. Grant had no political experience. He did not share the moral conviction of many Radical Republicans of the need to protect the freed slaves. Nevertheless, he was popular as a war hero.

The Democrats chose as their Presidential candidate Horatio Seymour, a wealthy New Yorker and former governor of his state. The Democratic platform denounced the Radical Republican program of reconstruction, declaring it unconstitutional. It also condemned the Radicals for their attempt to remove Johnson from office.

Economic issues were also important in the election of 1868. The platform of the Democratic Party, for example, favored a "cheap money" policy. During the war the federal government had issued $450 million in paper money known as "greenbacks." After the war, in 1866, the Republican Congress had provided for the gradual withdrawal of the greenbacks from circulation. By 1868 nearly $100 million had been withdrawn. In their 1868 platform the Democrats promised, if elected, to reverse this policy and reissue the paper money. The Democrats knew that this "cheap money" plank would antagonize wealthy bondholders.

44

Those bondholders fully expected that the money they had lent the government would be repaid in gold. The Democrats also knew that the proposal would appeal to many less well-to-do voters, particularly those who owed money. With more currency in circulation, debtors could more easily pay off their debts.

Republican candidate Ulysses S. Grant barely squeaked through to victory. Although he won by an electoral vote of 214 to 80, capturing 24 of the 36 states, his popular majority was only 309,000 out of almost 6 million votes.

The Radical Republicans studied the election returns with growing concern. They realized that many voters had turned against the Republicans because of their "hard money" policy. They also realized that the black vote had made possible their thin majority of the popular vote.

The Fifteenth Amendment. With this disturbing conclusion in mind, the Radicals drew up the Fifteenth Amendment and submitted it to the states for ratification. The Fifteenth Amendment was short and to the point: "The right of citizens of the United States to vote shall not be denied or abridged by the United States or any state on account of race, color, or previous condition of servitude."

The Fifteenth Amendment was ratified by the necessary three fourths of the states and became part of the Constitution in 1870. Mississippi, Texas, and Virginia—the last three southern states to return to the Union—were required to ratify the amendment as a condition for readmission.

Women, you recall, made many contributions to Union victory in the Civil War. Leaders of the women's rights movement expected, in return, that women would now receive the same legal protections and voting rights as blacks. Despite their protests, women were included in neither the Fourteenth nor the Fifteenth Amendments.

SECTION SURVEY

IDENTIFY: Civil Rights Act, due process of law, equal protection of the laws, Tenure of Office Act, Ulysses S. Grant, "cheap money."

1. (a) Explain how the new Freedmen's Bureau law and the Civil Rights Act aimed at protecting the freed slaves. (b) Why did Johnson veto both laws? (c) What were the results of Johnson's vetoes?

2. Describe the five major provisions of the Congressional plan for reconstruction.

3. (a) Why was Johnson impeached? (b) What were the consequences of his impeachment?

4. Source Study: (a) Read the Fourteenth Amendment on pages 748–49 and summarize the main ideas in each section. (b) Why did Congress propose the Fourteenth Amendment?

5. Source Study: Read the Fifteenth Amendment on page 749. (a) What does it provide? (b) Why was it passed? (c) What did the amendment do for the status of women?

4 White southerners regain control of their state governments

The Radical Republican program of reconstruction brought far-reaching changes to the South, but only for a relatively short time. For varying periods—as long as ten years in only three states—Radical Republicans and their allies controlled the former Confederate states.

Help from the North. In the ten years after the surrender of the Confederacy, the main concern of the federal government was the restoration of the Union. Providing aid to the war-ravaged South and to needy southerners took second place. The Freedmen's Bureau was severely limited by lack of funds and by opposition from most southerners and many northerners. Its work was supplemented, however, by teachers and missionaries, black as well as white. Most of the northern volunteers were moved by humanitarian and democratic ideals. Many won the confidence of the men, women, and children whom they had come to help. Others, equally well-meaning but unfamiliar with southern ways of life and perhaps less tactful, antagonized the people with whom they tried to work.

Carpetbaggers and scalawags. White southerners especially resented the arrival in the South of northerners whom they jeeringly called "carpetbaggers." This nickname implied, wrongly, that the newcomers were all fly-by-night adventurers who carried everything they owned in suitcases made of carpeting material, which were common at the time.

In all, 22 blacks from former Confederate states were elected to serve in Congress after the Civil War. Shown here are Senator Hiram Revels of Mississippi (far left) and six members of the House of Representatives.

The carpetbaggers came for many different reasons. Some sincerely wanted to help the freed slaves exercise their newly acquired rights. Some hoped to get themselves elected to political office. Some came to make their fortunes by acquiring farmland or by starting new businesses. However, some came for reasons of pure greed or fraud. Horace Greeley, the editor of the *New York Tribune,* wrote that such carpetbaggers were "stealing and plundering, many of them with both arms around the Negroes, and their hands in their rear pockets, seeing if they cannot pick a paltry dollar out of them."

Most white southerners and some northerners scorned the northern carpetbaggers who moved into the South. Especially strong scorn and abuse were directed toward those native-born southerners who had chosen to cooperate with the northern authorities.

Some of these native-born southerners had the best of motives. Having opposed slavery and secession, they had sympathized with the Union during the war. Now they believed that the best way to restore peace and prosperity to the South and to the nation was to forgive and forget. However, others were selfish and ambitious individuals who seized any opportunity to advance their own fortunes at the expense of their neighbors.

Whatever the motives of these native-born southerners, most were held in contempt by other white southerners. They were often referred to as "scalawags," which was a word used to describe scoundrels.

Reconstruction governments. Such were the individuals who largely controlled southern state governments during part of the Radical reconstruction period. Northerners held most of the important political offices, at least during the early years. They were able to get themselves elected partly because they persuaded the freed slaves to vote for them. Also, many white southerners were deprived of the right to vote and others refused to take part in political activities.

The enormous influence of northerners in southern politics can be seen by examining the election results in the seven southern states readmitted to the Union by 1868. As a result of the first postwar elections held in these states, 4 of the 7 governors, 10 of the 14 United States Senators, and 20 of the 35 United States Representatives were carpetbaggers. In general, southern scalawags and freed slaves had to be content with the less important state and federal offices.

Black southerners in public life. Blacks were elected to the southern reconstruction governments, and they played an important role in some of them. However, the black's role in these governments has often been exaggerated. Only one black American served briefly as a southern governor. In only one southern state — South Carolina — did black members for a time hold a majority in the state legislature. Only Mississippi sent black Senators, two of them, to Washington. One was Hiram Revels, a native of North Carolina who, after studying at Knox College in Illinois, had been a teacher and minister. The other was Blanche K. Bruce, who had escaped from slavery in Virginia and who had also been a teacher.

Many other blacks in reconstruction politics showed independence and political skill. Among them were Robert Brown Elliott of South Carolina, a brilliant lawyer and scholar, and P. B. S. Pinchback of Louisiana, son of a Mississippi planter and a black mother.

The blacks in public life during reconstruction did not demand revenge upon white southerners. In fact, most black leaders favored returning the right to vote to their former white masters. The records of those elected to the United States Congress compared well with the records of many of their white colleagues.

Reconstruction governments at work. The southern reconstruction legislatures started many needed and long overdue public improvements. The new legislatures, for example, strengthened public education and, for the first time, made it available to large numbers of black children.

The reconstruction governments also pushed forward other constructive programs. They spread the tax burden more equitably. They introduced overdue reforms in local government and the judicial system. They abolished imprisonment for debt. They extended the legal rights of women. They passed laws to protect homes and farms against illegal foreclosures — that is, against unjustified seizure by dishonest officials. Most of the southern state constitutions drafted during the period of reconstruction continued in effect for many years.

Such programs greatly increased the debts of the southern states. In addition, the reconstruction governments misspent huge amounts of money.

White southerners who had once dominated public life deplored large expenditures for needless luxuries authorized by legislators, white and black, in some reconstruction governments. They also denounced some reconstruction legislators for outright corruption.

Some of the new legislators were all too willing to enrich themselves while granting favorable railroad and corporation charters to business groups, often northern, who wanted to develop southern enterprises. However, southern Democrats who briefly controlled southern legislatures in the first years after the war had followed some of the same corrupt practices. As you will read, public morality in all sections of the United States sank to an extremely low level during the years following the Civil War.

Secret societies. Whatever the merits and demerits of the reconstruction governments may have been, most white southerners resented them. Since many former Confederate leaders were denied the vote and since others chose to boycott politics, some white southerners expressed their opposition by defying the law through intimidation and violence. By 1867 some white southerners were attacking carpetbaggers, scalawags, and politically active black southerners through a number of secret societies. The best known were the Knights of the White Camellia and the Ku Klux Klan.

These secret organizations tried to frighten black southerners and their white sympathizers into staying out of politics. Bands of hooded members clad in ghostly white costumes rode through the countryside at night, stopping now and then at a house to issue warnings. When warnings failed, cabins and churches were burned and some freed slaves were beaten or killed. White sympathizers and friends of blacks sometimes received the same treatment. Moderate white southerners, disgusted with the brutality and fearful of northern reaction, disapproved of these actions. However, for a time they were unable to prevent them.

Congress tried to end the lawlessness by passing a series of Military Enforcement Acts, sometimes called the Force Acts (1870–71). These acts gave the President power to use federal military forces to control the secret societies, to call upon the state militias when neces-

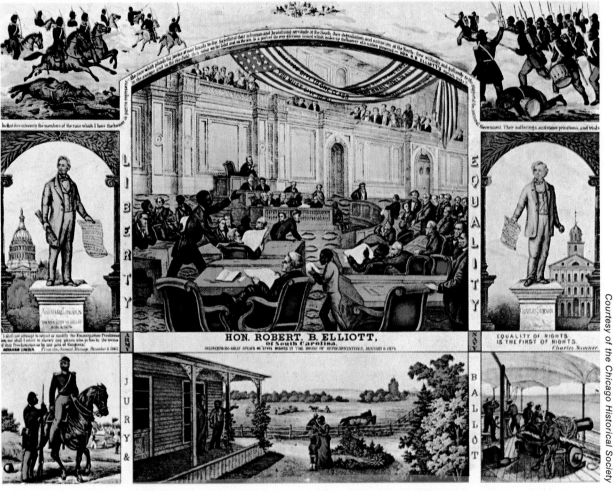

This magazine illustration features Representative Robert Brown Elliott speaking to Congress in 1874. The words at the top are his: "What you give to one class, you must give to all. What you deny to one class, you shall deny to all."

sary, and to suspend the writ of *habeas corpus.* They also provided for federal supervision of southern elections.

To many white southerners, the Force Acts seemed unduly harsh. Yet compared with the treatment of the losers in civil wars elsewhere, the former Confederates were not severely punished. There were never more than 25,000 federal troops in the occupied states after the war. No political leader was executed, few were imprisoned, and President Johnson made liberal use of his pardoning power. Jefferson Davis, for example, was released from prison within two years. Except for the loss of slaves, property was seldom seized by the federal government as punishment for what many northerners regarded as treason.

Further leniency prevailed in 1872, when Congress passed the Amnesty Act. This act restored political rights, including the right to vote, to about 160,000 former Confederates.

After 1872 only about 500 white southerners were still barred from political activity.

The Force Acts, the withdrawal of many southerners from the secret societies, and finally the Amnesty Act virtually ended the power of the Ku Klux Klan and other such groups at that time. Most white southerners began to vote again, and white southern leadership reemerged. The reconstruction governments in several states were thus replaced by governments representing traditional white southern rule.

The end of reconstruction. During the early 1870's, northerners began to lose interest in the problems of southern reconstruction. Radical Republican power and leadership was diminished by the death of Thaddeus Stevens in 1868 and of Charles Sumner in 1874.

At first many northerners had championed the cause of the freed slaves. Now they became disillusioned at reports, often exaggerated, of the political ineptness of black southerners. Some northerners seemed to ignore the fact that the former slaves had little, if any, education and no political experience. Other northerners grew weary of the problems of black southerners and less willing to press for an effective program to help them learn their new roles as citizens.

Many northerners began to say that perhaps the freed slaves *did* need the supervision of white southern leaders. Perhaps it would be better, they now said, to let southerners work out their own problems of government and race relations. Northerners justified their retreat by referring to the Constitution, which left many powers in the hands of the states. No doubt many northerners, sincere enough earlier in demanding equal rights for the freed slaves, were increasingly and uncomfortably aware that blacks were not treated as equal citizens in most northern states. Thus many northerners now found it easier to concentrate on strengthening national unity and to give less attention to the rights of black Americans. This attitude was shared by a growing number of northern businesses. It was clear that a disorganized, poverty-stricken South was not good for business on either side of the Mason-Dixon line.

In 1877 the last of the federal troops of occupation were withdrawn from the southern states, ending the reconstruction era. Reconstruction left many major problems unsolved and created new and equally urgent problems. This was true even though many forces in the North and the South continued working to reconcile the two sections.

SECTION SURVEY

IDENTIFY: Hiram Revels, Knights of the White Camellia, Ku Klux Klan, Force Acts, Amnesty Act.

1. (a) Define carpetbagger and scalawag. (b) For what reasons did the carpetbaggers go to the South?
2. How successful were the reconstruction governments?
3. (a) Why did some white southerners form secret societies during reconstruction? (b) How did the federal government react to them?
4. How did racial prejudice in the North influence the attitudes of some northerners toward reconstruction?

5 The New South advances in agriculture, industry, and education

During the 1880's many southerners began to speak of the "New South." Those who used this term urged southerners to abandon the one-crop system of agriculture. They should, instead, develop all the resources of a rich land —the minerals and the forests as well as the soil. Above all, those who shared these beliefs urged southerners to build up the region's manufacturing industries.

Breakup of plantations. One characteristic of the postwar South was the breakup of many, though by no means all, of the large plantations. This process started in 1865, immediately after the war ended. Planters, who had little if any cash to hire farm laborers, sold portions of their plantations to the more prosperous independent farmers. Between 1865 and 1880, the number of small farms more than doubled, while the size of the average southern farm decreased.

Some black southerners, who had emerged from slavery without education, without land, and almost without clothes, also benefited from the breakup of the large plantations. As the years passed, a small but growing number of former slaves acquired small farms.

Tenant farming and sharecropping. While some poor white southerners and a few black southerners became owners of small farms, many others became **tenant farmers**. Under this system, a planter usually rented portions of the plantation to several tenants, who supplied their own seed, mules, and provisions. The owner managed the scattered tenant holdings much as if these made up the old-time plantation. Thus some advantages of large-scale production were retained. Many tenants remained tenants all their lives. Others saved enough to buy land and become small landowners.

Less fortunate was the **sharecropper**. This farm worker furnished nothing but labor, getting a cabin, seed, tools, a mule, and a plot of land from the owner. In return for farming this land, the sharecropper received a percentage of the crop. Since sharecroppers did not get paid until harvesttime, they had to buy provisions

Savannah, Georgia, had been badly damaged during Union General William T. Sherman's "March to the Sea" in 1864. After the war Savannah was rebuilt. The city soon became an important cotton port on the Savannah River.

for their families on credit. To obtain credit, they had to give a lien, or mortgage, on the crops they expected to plant and harvest. The debts they could not pay at harvesttime were added to the bill to be paid a year later.

When the crops were harvested, almost all of the sharecroppers' share of the money usually went to pay their bills. Because they also had to pay interest on this debt, sharecroppers found it very difficult to get out of debt. As long as they were in debt, they were practically bound to the soil, since the law forbade them to leave the state until their bills were paid. Frequently the owner of the land also owned the store where the sharecroppers could buy their supplies on credit. Since the sharecroppers were seldom free from debt and almost never had any cash, they had to buy at the owner's store and go deeper into debt.

Many sharecroppers raised only cotton or tobacco since the landowner insisted on cultivating these crops exclusively. The owner argued that the sharecroppers did not know anything about other crops and that cotton and tobacco were the only dependable cash crops.

Although tenant farming and sharecropping existed in other parts of the country, these practices were especially widespread in the South. Indeed, tenant farming and sharecropping provided a workable solution to the frequently desperate economic situation of the postwar years. At the same time, they also made it difficult for the South to abandon its traditional one-crop system and to develop a diversified farming economy.

Agricultural progress. Despite the problems facing southern farmers, the South made considerable progress during the postwar years. Southerners, like farmers elsewhere in the nation, benefited from new developments in science and technology. During the 1870's and 1880's, improved machines for sowing, cultivating, fertilizing, and reaping were introduced. In 1872 both Alabama and Virginia established agricultural colleges. By 1900 all the other southern states had followed their example.

Cotton continued to be the most important single crop. Indeed, by 1871 the South was growing more cotton than it had in 1860. The older states increased their yield per acre by using commercial fertilizers and improved farming methods. Much of the total increase, however, came from the opening of new cotton lands in the Southwest. By 1900 Texas alone was planting and harvesting one third of all the nation's cotton.

Improved farming methods led to greatly increased production of tobacco, rice, sugar, corn, and other traditional crops. However, the most important change in southern agricultural life was the development of truck farming and fruit growing. Because of the growth of railroads and the invention of the refrigerator car, fresh vegetables and fruit could be shipped to northern cities. The long growing season in the South and an abundance of cheap labor also stimulated truck farming. As early as 1900, thousands of refrigerator cars were rolling northward with welcome cargoes of vegetables, watermelons, strawberries, oranges, apples, and peaches.

Industrial progress. An even more remarkable development in the New South was the growth of industry. In industry as in agriculture, the South responded to forces that were transforming economic life in other regions of the United States and, for that matter, in most of Europe.

Southern industrial development actually started before the outbreak of the Civil War. By 1860 about 10 percent of the manufactured wealth of the United States came from southern textile mills, ironworks, lumber projects, and sugar refineries. The war and reconstruction ruined many southern industries, and for nearly 20 years the South made little industrial progress.

By the late 1870's, more and more southerners felt that southern progress depended upon industrialization. The development of industry would enable the South to make better use of its rich natural resources.

Money to build factories, mines, steel mills, railroads, and other industries came in part from northern investors and in still larger part from the South itself. Profits from expanding agriculture were poured into new industrial ventures. In community after community, the people themselves gathered in mass assemblies to plan a factory, often a textile mill, and to raise the necessary capital. By 1900 more than 400 cotton textile mills had been built. Throughout the South farming villages were transformed into mill towns within a few short years. Poor whites provided most of the labor for the new factories. Black laborers were almost entirely excluded from the new industrial development.

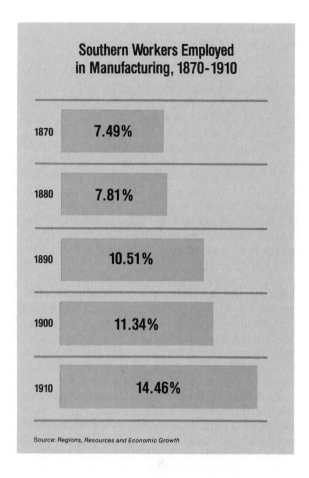

Southern Workers Employed in Manufacturing, 1870-1910

1870	7.49%
1880	7.81%
1890	10.51%
1900	11.34%
1910	14.46%

Source: *Regions, Resources and Economic Growth*

Many early mills were controlled by a single family or a small group of persons. They owned the houses in which the workers lived, the stores where they bought their goods, and the other town buildings. The men and women who worked in these mills depended on the owners for their jobs and had to spend their wages to rent company-owned dwellings and to buy supplies from company-owned stores. As a result, the labor organizations that were rapidly growing in the North during these years made little headway in the South.

The growth of southern industry also depended on improvements and extensions of southern railroads. The war left southern railroads in terrible condition, but old railroads were quickly rebuilt, and new lines constructed. By 1890 the southern railroad system was twice as large as in 1860.

Industrial development in the New South led to the growth of cities. Between 1870 and 1890 Durham, North Carolina, developed from a small village to a flourishing tobacco center.

51

Richmond, Virginia, and Nashville, Tennessee, became leading urban centers. The population of Atlanta, Georgia, increased from 37,000 to 65,000 between 1880 and 1890. Birmingham, Alabama, founded in 1871 on the site of a former cotton field, within a few years became a bustling iron and steel center, often called "the Pittsburgh of the South."

By 1900, southern manufactured products were worth four times as much as in 1860. With its growing industrial cities, its factories and mills and mines, and its developing transportation system, the South was beginning to be more and more like other regions of the United States. Nevertheless, the New South had a long way to go to catch up industrially with other sections of the country.

Educational developments. During the closing years of the 1800's, able and far-seeing leaders urged southerners to improve their educational system and thus make better use of their human resources. Southern education did improve, but every forward step was taken in the face of tremendous handicaps. Southern leaders had to deal with widespread poverty despite improving economic conditions. There was also a traditional reluctance to support public education with tax money. Maintaining separate schools for white and black children added to the cost of education.

Among the outstanding contributions to southern education were the gifts of northern philanthropists. Especially noteworthy were the gifts of George Peabody and John F. Slater, both northern millionaires. The Peabody Fund was created in 1867, the Slater Fund in 1882. Money from these funds helped to provide educational opportunities for white and black southerners alike in the postwar years.

The money from private sources, however, was only a fraction of what was needed. Most of the burden of rebuilding schools and opening up educational opportunities for whites as well as blacks had to be shouldered by the southern states. Slowly, as the economic situation improved, the South provided more opportunities.

The "Solid South." Most southerners belonged to the Democratic Party. There were southern Republicans, to be sure, but they were completely outnumbered in local, state, and national elections. For example, when the Presidential elections rolled around, the former Confederate states cast all their electoral votes for the Democratic candidates. Thus people began to refer to the southern states as the "Solid South."

The "Solid South" was born during reconstruction days, when Radical Republican governments controlled the southern states. In their determination to rid themselves of Republican rule, white southerners poured into the Democratic Party. After 1877, when the last federal troops were withdrawn from the South, most white southerners continued to support the Democratic Party.

SECTION SURVEY

IDENTIFY: New South, one-crop agriculture, "the Pittsburgh of the South," philanthropist, George Peabody, John Slater, "Solid South."

1. (a) Define tenant farming and sharecropping. (b) Explain why they were common in the postwar South. (c) Why was it hard for a tenant farmer or sharecropper to become a farm owner?

2. (a) Give three reasons for southern industrial development. (b) What were some results of industrial growth?

3. What handicaps hindered the development of education in the South?

4. Why did the South generally support the Democratic Party after the Civil War?

5. Graph Study: Look at the graph on page 51. What does the graph tell you about the growth of industry in the South after the Civil War?

6 Black southerners struggle for a place in the New South

Black southerners had hoped to share in the agricultural, industrial, and educational progress of the New South and in the nation's ideals of freedom and equality. They did not for several reasons. First, the federal government suspended its program for helping black southerners make the transition from slavery to freedom. Second and equally important, whites in both the North and the South continued to think of blacks not as equals but as inferiors. Third, white southerners feared that the white southern way of life would be threatened if blacks were not firmly "kept in their place."

Cartoonist Thomas Nast depicted a black man casting his vote in an election shortly after the Civil War. Who do you think the figures on the left represent?

Preventing blacks from voting. For more than ten years after white southern Democrats regained control of southern governments in 1877, many blacks continued to vote. A few even held public office.

Early in the 1890's, however, the new Populist Party threatened the power of both the Democratic and Republican parties (Chapter 2). In the South, Populist organizers had their greatest success among poor white people, but some also worked hard to win the support of black voters. Southern Democrats, alarmed by this development, attempted to prevent blacks from voting.

Beginning with Mississippi in 1890, the southern states adopted laws and framed new constitutions that in effect kept most blacks from voting on grounds other than "race, color, or previous condition of servitude." By the early 1900's, the guarantees of civil rights in the Fourteenth and Fifteenth Amendments had become largely ineffective in the South. In most areas, few blacks voted and fewer still held public office, even in minor positions.

A number of states adopted a **poll tax**—a fixed tax imposed on every voter—and also a **literacy test**—and examination to determine whether a person can read or write. Since many black southerners had little money and

little, if any, education, these laws kept large numbers from voting.

The poll tax and the literacy test also deprived many poor whites of the vote. To remedy this situation, several states, starting with Louisiana in 1898, added a "grandfather clause" to their constitutions. This clause declared that even if a man could not pay the poll tax or pass the literacy test, he could still vote if he had been eligible to do so on January 1, 1867, or if he were the son or the grandson of a man who had been eligible to vote on January 1, 1867. The grandfather clause was declared unconstitutional by the Supreme Court in 1915. While it was in force, it kept many black southerners from voting.

Segregating the races. Meanwhile, a pattern of segregation, or separation, of white and black southerners was taking shape.

Except in a few instances, the Radical Republicans had not tried to bring white and black children together in southern public schools. However, black and white southerners used the same transportation facilities and other public services. The Civil Rights Act of 1875 had declared that "all persons within the jurisdiction of the United States shall be entitled to the full and equal enjoyment of the ac-

Tuskegee Institute was the scene for many breakthroughs in agricultural research. George Washington Carver (center) joined the staff in 1896 and directed students in experiments that helped strengthen the South's economy.

commodations, advantages, facilities, and privileges of inns, public conveyances on land or water, theaters and other places of public amusement; subject only to the conditions and limitations established by law and applicable alike to citizens of every race and color, regardless of any previous condition of servitude."

Even after white southern rule was restored in 1877, southerners of both races often used the same transportation facilities and other public services. Then in 1883 the Supreme Court ruled against the Civil Rights Act of 1875 on the ground that the Fourteenth Amendment forbade only states, not individuals or corporations (such as railroads), from discriminating against black citizens. In spite of their decision, black and white southerners in many places continued to use the same public accommodations.

In 1881 Tennessee passed the first of the so-called "Jim Crow" laws. Under this law, white southerners and black southerners were required to ride in separate railway cars. Other states followed Tennessee's example. By the 1890's all southern states required such separation, not only in schools but in streetcars, railroads, and railroad stations. Within a few years, this pattern of segregation spread to parks, playgrounds, and other public facilities.

In 1896 the Supreme Court added legal support to segregation. In the case of *Plessy v. Ferguson,* the Court ruled that it was not a violation of the Fourteenth Amendment to provide "separate but equal" facilities for blacks. This 1896 ruling by the Supreme Court was a serious blow to the efforts of black Americans to improve their lives.

Black southerners' reactions. Confronted by segregation and denied their political and civil rights, some black southerners migrated to other nearby states, such as Oklahoma and Kansas, or moved to the growing northern cities. Most, however, stayed in the South and worked to develop their own black communities. Black southerners strengthened their own churches, lodges, and mutual aid societies, developed their own businesses, and, against handicaps, tried to secure an education. Their efforts began to produce results. In 1865 only about 5 percent of all black adults could read and write. By 1900 more than 50 percent possessed these basic skills.

Southern black leaders also protested the growing pattern of segregation and discrimination and the denial of civil rights guaranteed by the Fourteenth Amendment. On the lecture platform, in churches, in the press, and in conventions, they demanded their constitutional rights. In 1889 the former black abolitionist Frederick Douglass, now an old man, asked whether "American justice, American liberty, American civilization, American law, and American Christianity could be made to include and protect alike and forever all American citizens in the rights which have been guaranteed to them by the organic and fundamental laws of the land."

In Baltimore, E. J. Waring, a black lawyer, urged blacks to fight discrimination by lawsuits against officials and citizens guilty of violating their rights. In Memphis, Ida Wells Barnett, teacher and publisher, was dismissed from teaching for denouncing the inferior segregated schools for black children. She then launched a single-handed crusade against black lynchings—that is, the murder of black people by white mobs. Even after a mob broke into her newspaper office and threatened her life, she persisted in exposing the evils of "lynch law."

Booker T. Washington. The leading black voice from 1890 to 1915 was that of Booker T. Washington. The son of a slave mother and a white father, Washington received a vocational education at Hampton Institute in Virginia. He then founded and built Tuskegee Institute in Alabama. Washington was convinced that vocational education, not classical or liberal arts education, was necessary to provide black people with the skills they needed to earn a living. He felt that such education would prepare blacks for jobs in the skilled trades, small businesses, farming, and household work.

Washington also spoke out against lynching and illegal discrimination, especially in the years just before his death in 1915. Generally, Washington remained convinced that black southerners would make greater progress by avoiding protests and emphasizing vocational training and by owning farms, homes, and small businesses.

W. E. B. Du Bois. Booker T. Washington's views met a strong challenge from a younger black, W. E. B. Du Bois (doo·BOYCE). Born and reared in western Massachusetts, Du Bois studied in German universities and earned his Ph.D. at Harvard. At first he felt that if white Americans came to understand past black achievements and present black conditions, their attitudes toward black Americans would in time improve.

Gradually, however, Du Bois came to believe that only vigorous and continuous protests against inequalities and injustices, and effective appeals to black pride, could change existing conditions. In *The Souls of Black Folk,* a book of eloquent essays, Du Bois criticized

Booker T. Washington's emphasis on vocational training. He urged broader educational opportunities, including liberal arts education, for blacks. Du Bois urged blacks to demand their rights to have whatever kind of education they needed to achieve full equality and opportunity in American life. Along with a few likeminded black leaders, he organized a meeting in 1905 at Niagara Falls that demanded an end to all unequal treatment based on race and color.

The appeals and demands of the Niagara Movement aroused many Americans, white as well as black. One outcome was the formation of the National Association for the Advancement of Colored People (NAACP). The NAACP worked through the courts to end restrictions on voting and other civil injustices. In time it succeeded in winning Supreme Court decisions that declared unconstitutional the grandfather clause in southern state constitutions, jury trials conducted under mob pressure, and segregation by local law of housing for black people. The Urban League, likewise organized by both blacks and whites, fought for equal job opportunities for black workers and against discrimination in urban housing.

The work of the NAACP and the Urban League brought some progress for black citizens in the North and West. These national organizations were also represented in the southern states, but they made less progress there. Most black southerners continued to experience discrimination, segregation, and denial of equal rights.

SECTION SURVEY

IDENTIFY: segregation, "Jim Crow" laws, *Plessy v. Ferguson,* "separate but equal," Ida Wells Barnett, Booker T. Washington, W. E. B. Du Bois, NAACP, Urban League.

1. Why did black southerners not share in the progress of the New South?

2. Explain how each of the following affected the right of black southerners to vote: (a) poll tax, (b) literacy test, (c) "grandfather clause."

3. (a) How was a new pattern of segregation established in the South? (b) How did the Supreme Court contribute to the separation of the races?

4. Describe the disagreement between Booker T. Washington and W. E. B. Du Bois over what blacks should do to improve their situation.

Chapter Survey

Summary: Tracing the Main Ideas

In 1865, just before his tragic death, President Lincoln urged the victorious North to act "with malice toward none; with charity for all." This was the way, he felt, to build "a just and lasting peace."

President Johnson's efforts to apply Lincoln's policy by quickly restoring the Union were effectively blocked by the Radical Republicans, who controlled Congress. For various reasons, the Radical Republicans wished to decide how the former Confederate states should be reconstructed. The more extreme members of the Radical group wanted to transfer political power from the white leaders to the blacks.

Southern blacks, meanwhile, were faced with the challenge of developing new ways of life for themselves after more than two hundred years of slavery. They eagerly looked forward to the prospects of working at jobs of their choosing, of owning farms, of receiving formal education, and of taking part in the political process.

White southerners were disturbed at the prospect of living in a position of political, economic, and social equality with former slaves. They used every means at their command to defeat the northern program of reconstruction. Unable to enforce their will upon the South, northerners gradually lost interest. In 1877 the last federal troops were withdrawn from the former Confederate states.

During the 1880's and 1890's, the outline of a New South began to appear. With the slow but steady development of more varied agriculture, truck farmers began to ship growing quantities of fruit and vegetables to markets in the North. Southern mines began to supply increasing amounts of ore to southern furnaces. Textile mills and other factories began to transform quiet southern villages into growing towns.

In 1900 the South was still basically an agricultural region. Southerners were still struggling to recover from the economic disaster of the war. With the tragic exception of the blacks, who were desperately struggling to find a place for themselves in the New South, the southern states were making great strides forward. Like people in the northern and the western states, southerners were being swept along into the future by the growing forces of industry.

Inquiring into History

1. How did the Supreme Court decision in *Plessy v. Ferguson* reflect the spirit of the times?
2. Did the black codes and "Jim Crow" laws reestablish slavery in the South? Explain.
3. (a) What problems that caused the Civil War were solved by the war and reconstruction? (b) What new problems were created by the war and reconstruction?
4. If Lincoln had lived to carry out his plan of reconstruction, do you think he would have encountered the same difficulties that President Johnson did? Explain.
5. Why might the period of reconstruction be called the "tragic era"?

Relating Past to Present

1. Compare the federal government's attitude toward minorities during reconstruction and today.

2. Compare the relationship between the President and Congress during reconstruction with their relationship today.
3. During reconstruction only the South was prejudiced against black Americans. Today there is little difference among the various sections of the nation regarding racial prejudice. Do you agree or disagree with these statements? Use examples to explain your answer.

Developing Social Science Skills

1. Read *Freedom Road* by Howard Fast, a novel about reconstruction. (a) Write an essay discussing how reconstruction changed the lives of the people portrayed. (b) How is the novel's presentation similar to the account in your textbook? How is it different? (c) How do you account for these similarities and differences?
2. Construct a chart showing the differing ideas of Lincoln, Johnson, and the Radical Republicans on reconstruction.

Chapter 2

Severe Trials for Democracy

1865-1897

Change is often disturbing, and in no period of American history was change more disturbing than in the generation following the Civil War. You have read how white and black southerners struggled to adjust to the drastic changes that took place during the reconstruction period. Equally striking changes were occurring in the Northeast, the Middle West, and the West during these years.

The major cause of these changes was the rapid growth of industry after the war. New power-driven machinery was invented and installed in large factories. Giant corporations were organized. New methods of mass production were adopted. These exciting developments made many new products and services available to more and more Americans and helped to raise their standard of living.

There were dark shadows in this bright picture. As American industries grew, American cities also grew and became overcrowded. Other problems arose with the growth of the cities—problems of sanitation, disease, fire, and transportation.

In order to see this dramatic and disturbing period of American history clearly, it is necessary to look at it from several different points of view. In later chapters you will see how the growth of big business created complex problems, not only for many business people, large and small, but also for farmers, miners, and wage earners. In this chapter you will see how graft and corruption plagued American political life during the postwar years. This graft and corruption posed a major threat to the workings of the American political system. In this chapter you will also learn how repeated efforts were made to root out this dishonesty in government.

THE CHAPTER IN OUTLINE

1. Graft and corruption spread in the postwar years.
2. A start is made toward restoring honesty to government.
3. Efforts at political reform move forward.

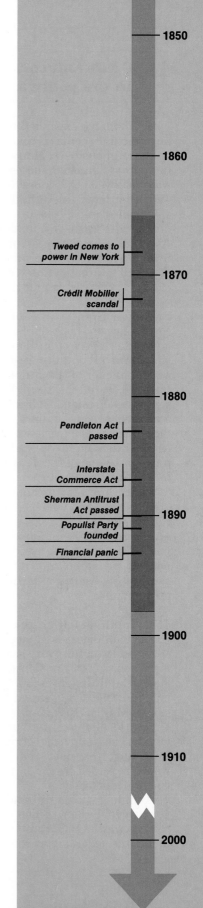

1850

1860

Tweed comes to
power in New York

1870

Crédit Mobilier
scandal

1880

Pendleton Act
passed

Interstate
Commerce Act

Sherman Antitrust
Act passed

1890

Populist Party
founded

Financial panic

1900

1910

2000

1 Graft and corruption spread in the postwar years

As industry expanded after the Civil War, huge fortunes could be and, in fact, were made by those in business. Many Americans seemed to approve financial success no matter how it was achieved. Operators of railroads, mines, and other businesses often did not hesitate to ask politicians for favors or to return such favors with cash payments or other rewards. As a result, graft and corruption infected every level of American government. It was Ulysses S. Grant's unhappy fate to occupy the White House at this disturbing time.

President Grant. In 1868, when he won the Presidency on the Republican ticket, Grant enjoyed the respect of millions of Americans. His well-earned reputation rested upon his success as commander of the Union armies during the latter years of the Civil War. Had he never served as President, Grant would have lived and died a popular hero. Unfortunately, his lack of political experience was a serious handicap. Grant's eight-year administration would prove to be one of the darker pages in the history of the Presidency.

Grant himself was honest and upright. His great weakness—which could have been a virtue if tempered by reason—was his total loyalty to friends. Being honest himself, he could not believe that his associates were any less honest. He stubbornly refused to admit that some of his friends used him to advance their own fortunes.

The Crédit Mobilier scandal. Even before Grant took office, the federal government was involved in an unsavory scandal. In 1861 California chartered the Central Pacific Railroad. A year later Congress chartered the Union Pacific Railroad. The Central Pacific was to build eastward from Sacramento, California, and the Union Pacific was to build westward from Omaha, in Nebraska Territory. When the two lines met, the East and West coasts at last would be joined by the nation's first transcontinental railroad.

Building such a railroad was extremely expensive and risky. Since the completed railroad would be important to national development, the federal government gave generous subsidies to the railroad companies. Among these subsidies were loans in the form of government bonds. The companies would receive $16,000 in bonds for every mile of track completed on the level plains, $32,000 for every mile through hilly country, and $48,000 for every mile in the mountains.

The small group of stockholders who controlled the Union Pacific Railroad looked greedily at these subsidies. They saw a chance to make enormous profits from the construction of the railroad itself. They organized a construction company called the Crédit Mobilier (kray·DEE moh·bee·LYAY). Their control of the Union Pacific enabled them to award construction contracts to their own construction company, the Crédit Mobilier. These contracts were paid for by other stockholders of the Union Pacific at several times what the job actually cost. As a result, much of the money invested by stockholders in the Union Pacific as well as a large share of the government subsidies flowed into the pockets of this small group of greedy men.

When Congressional committees finally investigated, they discovered that some members of Congress had owned stock in the Crédit Mobilier company. The company owners had given these members stock or had sold it to them at half price in an effort to bribe them and to block investigations.

The "salary grab" and tax scandals. In 1873, while the Crédit Mobilier scandal was occupying Congress, the Senators and Representatives voted themselves a 50 percent increase in salaries—from $5,000 to $7,500 per year. Moreover, each member of Congress would receive two years' back pay, or $5,000. The public was so outraged at this "salary grab" that Congress hastily repealed the act at the opening of its next session.

Public resentment had hardly died when another scandal made newspaper headlines. Secretary of the Treasury William A. Richardson signed a contract with a private citizen, John D. Sanborn. The contract gave Sanborn authority to collect overdue federal taxes, with the right to keep half of all he could collect. By various devious methods, Sanborn collected $427,000, keeping about half for himself.

When asked to explain the affair, Sanborn swore that he had kept only a small part of the "commission," having been forced to give $156,000 to his "assistants"! The "assistants" were politicians who had used their influence to swing the tax-collection contract to Sanborn. However, the contract was legal, and the "commission" was paid in full. A new law prevented the situation from recurring, however, and Richardson resigned.

The new Secretary of the Treasury, Benjamin H. Bristow, an honest official, discovered that taxes were not being collected on nearly 90 percent of the liquor distilled in the United States. Further investigation revealed that high public officials were guilty of blackmail and fraud.

According to the tax law, a distiller who failed to pay revenue taxes on distilled liquor had to pay a double tax if caught. Any informer who revealed to the government that a company had failed to pay its taxes received 10 percent of the tax penalty as a reward. Informers soon saw, however, that they could collect more by blackmailing the tax-evading company than by reporting the evasion. The Secretary of the Treasury discovered that a ring, or group, of whisky distillers and blackmailers had been defrauding the federal government of at least a million dollars a year.

Graft in the federal governments. Meanwhile, yet another scandal was unearthed. It was discovered that Secretary of War William W. Belknap had accepted $24,500 in bribes from a trader at Fort Sill in what is now Oklahoma. Belknap had decided to give the profitable trading rights with the Indians to a New York friend, but the trader who had the contract was making a huge profit from the Indians around Fort Sill. Therefore, the trader agreed to pay Belknap and his friend each $6,000 a year if he were allowed to keep his trading rights.

When evidence of this bribery was presented in 1876, the House of Representatives voted unanimously to impeach Belknap, who hastily resigned. Despite all the evidence, the Senate's impeachment trial failed to convict him. The Senators who voted "not guilty" claimed that because Belknap had resigned he was no longer subject to trial by the Senate.

There were still other evidences of graft in the federal government. The Secretary of the Navy "sold" business to builders and suppliers of ships. The Secretary of the Interior was involved with land speculators. President Grant himself had no part in these illegal activities. Nevertheless many people felt that Grant was at fault for allowing his friends to hide behind his good name.

Other scandals. Corruption was as bad, if not worse, in the state governments. In 1868 the Erie Railroad, which was controlled by Daniel Drew, James ("Jim") Fisk, Jr., and Jay Gould, wanted to sell $10 million worth of additional stock. Gould, to smooth the way, went to the New York State capital at Albany with a trunk full of money to bribe lawmakers to legalize the stock sale. Evidence suggested that the governor of New York sold his influence for $20,000 and that state senators got $15,000.

Perhaps worst of all was the corruption in municipal, or city, government. William M. Tweed, an uneducated chairmaker, rose in 15 years to be a multimillionaire "dictator" of New York City in the 1860's and 1870's. Working with Tammany Hall—as the city's Democratic **machine,** or political organization, was known—"Boss" Tweed largely controlled the city government.

Tweed gained control very simply. He or some of his followers met immigrant families when they landed, fed them, found them jobs and housing, and left them baskets of food at Thanksgiving and Christmas. After they secured the right to vote, the newcomers returned Tweed's "friendship" by voting for can-

According to one magazine, Thomas Nast's cartoons had more influence than cartoons "came near having in any [other] country." This one predicts "Boss" Tweed's escape from jail. Four years later Tweed did escape.

didates he favored. Moreover, when election outcomes seemed doubtful, the ballot boxes were stuffed with votes in favor of Tweed's candidates. That is, Tammany supporters voted several times, using different names and addresses each time.

How did Tweed use his power? He gave city jobs to many of his friends. He demanded kickbacks from people who wanted city jobs. He demanded bribes from companies that wanted to provide city services. A courthouse, started in 1868, was to cost $250,000. Three years later, still uncompleted, it had cost $8 million. In three years Tweed and his crooked ring stole an estimated $20 million from New York City. It is estimated that between 1868 and 1871 "Boss" Tweed's ring and his business friends cost the city close to $100 million.

Reasons for corruption. Why was public morality at such a low level in the years following the Civil War?

The war itself was partly responsible. In the crisis of wartime, the all-important consideration is to get things done quickly. Cost is secondary to what is considered national survival, and money flows freely into war industries. During the war years, with business booming, unscrupulous business interests and legislators had a rare opportunity to engage in dishonest practices. These practices were continued in the postwar years.

A related and equally significant explanation of the postwar graft was the rapid growth of large-scale industry, about which you will read in Chapter 4. In earlier times, when factories and businesses were small, their owners were well known in their own communities. If their practices were dishonest, they were likely to lose their neighbors' good will.

The new large corporations were impersonal. The people who controlled them were hardly known even by many of their own stockholders. Within the corporations, it was easier for dishonest individuals to get away with questionable practices.

SECTION SURVEY

IDENTIFY: Crédit Mobilier, "salary grab," graft, William Belknap, Tammany Hall, political machine, Tweed Ring.

1. Ulysses S. Grant's administration was a dark page in the history of the American Presidency.

What evidence in this section supports this conclusion?

2. Why did people blame Grant for the scandals that occurred during his administration?

3. Give examples of graft and corruption on the state and local levels during the postwar years.

4. Why was public corruption so widespread during the postwar years?

2 **A start is made toward restoring honesty to government**

Newspapers in the late 1860's and the early 1870's were filled with stories and cartoons attacking government graft among federal, state, and local officials. The most famous American cartoonist was Thomas Nast of New York, whose powerful cartoons in *Harper's Weekly* helped to reveal to the public the abuses of "Boss" Tweed and his associates.

These revelations of corruption stirred a widespread demand for reform. No reform movement aroused greater interest than the proposal to appoint persons to government jobs on the basis of merit. Under the spoils system, which Andrew Jackson had helped to extend, government jobs were given to political favorites. Under the proposed merit system, those who received the highest grades in competitive examinations would get the jobs. It would not matter whether they were Republicans or Democrats. All these public jobs in the federal, state, and local governments would be called **civil service** jobs.

Growth of the reform movement. In 1871, in response to the demand for reforms, Congress set up a Civil Service Commission to study the problem and to make recommendations. Although President Grant appointed able men to the commission, he gave it little support. In 1875 the chairman resigned in disgust and the commission was discontinued.

Meanwhile, in 1872, a group of reform-minded Republicans had started the Liberal Republican Party, nominating Horace Greeley, the editor of the *New York Tribune*, as their Presidential candidate to run against the regular Republican candidate, President Grant. The Democrats also nominated Greeley, hop-

AMERICA'S MASTER CARTOONIST

One Sunday in the summer of 1871, a bank officer visited a New York cartoonist named Thomas Nast. The visitor was authorized, he said, to offer Nast $100,000 for "art study abroad." Nast—who was just thirty-one and had a growing family—showed some interest, even greed. He pushed the amount to half a million. Suddenly he laughed and said, "Well, I don't think I'll do it. I made up my mind not long ago to put some of these fellows behind bars, *and I'm going to put them there!*"

"These fellows" were the Tweed Ring, and Nast was being offered a bribe to stop attacking them in his drawings. His best-known assault was to come a few months later. In "The Tammany Tiger Let Loose," a snarling beast in a Roman arena is about to devour the "Republic," pictured as a helpless young woman. In the stands sits Tweed as a bloated emperor. "What are you going to do about it?" asks a line under the drawing. New York citizens took such vigorous action that Tweed fled the country. But he could not escape Nast. Several years later, in Spain, he was identified by someone who recognized him from a Nast drawing. Tweed was returned to New York and sent to prison.

Nast did over 3,000 drawings in his twenty-five-year career. He helped modernize the political cartoon by simplifying and sharpening it. He not only popularized the Tammany tiger but also created Santa Claus as we know him, the Democratic donkey, and the Republican elephant. Lincoln called him "our best recruiting sergeant." Always a crusader, Nast summed up his goal in one sentence: "I try to hit the enemy between the eyes and knock him down!"

ing by this means to benefit from the split in the Republican Party.

The Liberal Republican platform included a pledge to fight corruption in public life and a specific plank, or section, urging civil service reform. Nevertheless, Grant was reelected President easily.

The defeat at the polls in 1872 was a disheartening blow to the reformers. Within a year, however, they began to gather strength. For one thing, new public scandals drove more Americans into the reform movement. Also, growing dissatisfaction with Grant's Republican administration enabled the Democrats to win control of the House of Representatives in the Congressional elections of 1874.

The election of 1876. The Democrats, heartened by the growing demand for reform, approached the 1876 elections confident of a victory. They chose as their Presidential candidate Governor Samuel J. Tilden of New York. Governor Tilden had won national attention by helping to break up the Tweed Ring in New York. The Democratic platform demanded civil service reform and an end to graft in public life.

The Republicans, who were running scared, nominated a man well known as a reformer, Governor Rutherford B. Hayes of Ohio. Hayes promised to work for civil service reform in the federal government. He also promised to end the troubled period of reconstruction.

Both Tilden and Hayes were wealthy. Both were closely associated with industrialists and business groups. Tilden's one big asset was the fact that he was running against a party that was identified with scandal.

The election gave Tilden 250,000 more popular votes than Hayes received. The first count of the electoral votes also gave Tilden an advantage over Hayes—184 to 165. Most newspapers at first reported Tilden had won.

However, the papers had jumped to the wrong conclusion. Tilden with his 184 electoral votes was one short of the necessary majority.

Ordinarily, when no Presidential candidate has a clear majority of the electoral vote, the House of Representatives chooses the President, but this was no ordinary election. Four states—South Carolina, Florida, Louisiana, and Oregon—had each sent in *two* different sets of returns. In all, 20 electoral votes from these four states were claimed by both the Republicans and the Democrats. Tilden needed only one of these disputed votes to win. Hayes, however, needed all 20.

The single disputed vote from Oregon was quickly settled in favor of Hayes. The 19 votes from the three southern states remained a problem. The Republicans claimed all three states for Hayes. The Democrats insisted that since these states were still under reconstruction governments, the will of the majority had not been expressed. For a time the controversy threatened to plunge the nation into violence.

Settling the dispute. Unfortunately, the Constitution provided no clear procedures for solving this situation. According to the Constitution, the votes had to be counted. But by whom? If the Republican-controlled Senate counted the votes, the Senators would throw out the Democratic returns and give the election to Hayes. If the Democratic-controlled House counted the votes, the Representatives would throw out the Republican returns and give the election to Tilden.

In order to break the deadlock, Congress created an Electoral Commission of 15 members. On it were five Senators, five Representatives, and five Supreme Court Justices. By previous arrangement the Senate chose three Republicans and two Democrats. The House chose two Republicans and three Democrats. Four Justices—two Republicans and two Democrats—were to name a fifth member of the commission—an independent voter without ties to either party.

It was generally understood that the independent member of the Electoral Commission would be Justice David Davis. At the last minute, however, Davis resigned from the Supreme Court because of his election to the Senate. His place on the Electoral Commission went to a Republican. It was not surprising, therefore, that when the disputed votes were counted, they went to the Republicans by a straight party vote of eight Republicans as opposed to the seven Democrats on the Electoral Commission.

Thus it was that Hayes, who had received a minority of the popular votes, entered the White House as President. The controversial election of 1876–77 did, however, represent a victory for compromise and for the process of orderly government.

Difficulties for Hayes. President Hayes had four difficult years in the White House. Throughout his administration the Democrats controlled the House and for two years, from 1879 to 1881, the Senate as well. Although the Democrats did not try to upset the decision of the Electoral Commission, they called Hayes "His Fraudulency" and "Old Eight to Seven" to remind him that they questioned his right to the Presidency.

Hayes also faced opposition from his own party. The election of 1876 split the Republicans into two groups—the Stalwarts and the Half-Breeds. The Stalwarts, sometimes called "Old Guard" Republicans, were against reform and reformers. They also opposed the President himself, whom they called "Granny Hayes." The Half-Breeds, led by James G. Blaine of Maine and John Sherman of Ohio, agreed with Hayes that at least some steps toward reform were needed.

To fulfill his promise of ending reconstruction, President Hayes named a former Confederate leader to his cabinet and withdrew the last federal occupation troops from the South. As the remaining reconstruction governments lost power, southern Democrats were free to manage state affairs in their own way. Southern Democrats elected to Congress from the "Solid South" now allied with northern Democrats to break the power of the Radical Republicans, who had controlled Congress during the period of reconstruction.

Hayes's battle for reform. In spite of strong opposition, Hayes was the first President to take serious steps to reform the civil service. He refused to follow the practice of many earlier Presidents of discharging thousands of officeholders and replacing them with political favorites. He also insisted that all persons recommended by members of Congress for jobs should be carefully investigated. He courageously removed a prominent Republican, Chester A. Arthur, from his job as Collector of Customs in New York because of Arthur's questionable political activities. One of his own cabinet members, Carl Schurz, a German-born

Republican, introduced the merit system into the Department of the Interior.

The election of 1880. Well before the nominating conventions for the 1880 elections, President Hayes announced that he would not run for reelection. The Stalwart wing of the Republican Party, fed up with talk of reform and eager to return to the "good old days," tried to win the nomination for former President Ulysses S. Grant. The Half-Breed wing of the party managed to block this attempt, and the Republican convention finally nominated a war veteran, General James A. Garfield of Ohio. To win the support of the Stalwarts, the convention nominated for Vice-President Chester A. Arthur, a leading Stalwart.

The Democrats also pinned their hopes for the Presidency on a war veteran, General Winfield S. Hancock of Pennsylvania.

During the campaign, neither the Democrats nor the Republicans faced up to basic problems of the new industrial age—labor legislation, regulation of railroads and other big business, the money issue, and an income tax. Thus it was a third party, the Greenback-Labor Party, as you will read, that squarely faced the controversial issues of the time.

Garfield won the election with an electoral vote of 214 to Hancock's 155. However, the popular vote was close—4,449,053 for the Republicans, 4,442,035 for the Democrats.

Civil service reform. On July 2, 1881, President Garfield was shot by a disappointed—and mentally unbalanced—government job seeker. Garfield died in September.

The President's tragic death shocked the nation into an awareness of the evils of the old spoils system. Chester A. Arthur, the new President, responded to the widespread demand for reform and supported the Pendleton Civil Service Act.

The Pendleton Act, which became law in 1883, set up a commission to give competitive examinations for those seeking government jobs. The first examinations were to include only about 12 percent of federal jobs, but the President was given authority to broaden the list. The Pendleton Act also forbade the party in power to ask for campaign contributions from federal officeholders. President Arthur appointed an able leader for the new commission and extended the list of jobs for which civil service examinations had to be taken.

Thus, after years of agitation, reformers at last managed to write into law the principle that federal jobs below the policy-making level should be filled by merit. A long step had been taken toward making government more honest and efficient.

The election of 1884. When the election year of 1884 rolled around, Chester A. Arthur made it clear that he wanted to run for the Presidency. However, his Republican Stalwart supporters had lost faith in him because of the reform activities he had supported. Instead of Arthur, the leader of the Half-Breed wing of the Republican Party, James G. Blaine, won the nomination.

Blaine was a handsome, colorful, and persuasive candidate, but during his long political career, he had made many enemies. These

In an attempt to save President Garfield after his assassination, his doctors used a device invented by Alexander Graham Bell. It found the exact location of the bullet near his spine, but blood poisoning set in and eventually killed Garfield.

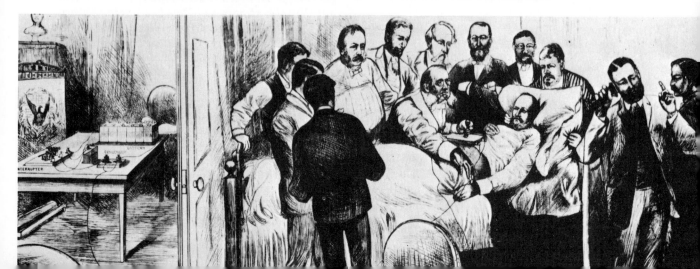

enemies now accused Blaine of having used his political influence to secure favors for big business — at a generous profit for himself. Unhappy with Blaine's nomination, a large group of Republicans, nicknamed "Mugwumps," bolted from the party and chose to support the Democratic candidate.

The Democrats made the most of Blaine's reputation as "a tool of the special interests." They chose a reformer as their Presidential nominee, Grover Cleveland, who had been governor of New York. Cleveland was known to be honest, courageous, independent — and stubborn when fighting for a principle.

In the campaign the big issues of the day were almost forgotten as the politicians heaped abuse upon the rival candidates. Each party raked over the personal life of the opposition candidate.

Throughout the campaign the two candidates, Blaine and Cleveland, ran neck and neck. Then, on the very eve of the election, at a reception given for Blaine by a group of Protestant clergy, a speaker called the Democrats the party of "Rum, Romanism, and Rebellion."

The speaker's use of the word "rum" was a deliberate attempt to smear the Democrats. His use of the word "rebellion" referred to the alliance between northern Democrats and the "Solid South" Democrats. Both references were bad enough, but the speaker's reference to "Romanism" — the Roman Catholic religion — was fatal. It was generally agreed that Blaine's failure to rebuke the speaker for this insult to Roman Catholic voters cost him the election. Grover Cleveland thus won the Presidency, squeaking through with 219 electoral votes to Blaine's 182.

The election of 1884 was the first Presidential victory for the Democrats in 28 years. It was one sign that memories of the Civil War were beginning to fade.

SECTION SURVEY

IDENTIFY: Thomas Nast, civil service, Horace Greeley, Samuel Tilden, Rutherford Hayes, James Blaine, James Garfield, Chester Arthur, "Mugwumps."

1. How is the spoils system different from the merit system of appointing people to government jobs?
2. In what ways was the election of 1876 one of the most unusual in American history?

3. What position did each of the following take concerning reform: (a) Liberal Republicans, (b) Stalwarts, (c) Half-Breeds?
4. (a) Explain the provisions of the Pendleton Act of 1883. (b) Why was it enacted?
5. What factors led to Cleveland's election in 1884?

3 Efforts at political reform move forward

When President Cleveland entered the White House in 1885, the movement for political reform entered a new phase.

Cleveland's firm stand. President Cleveland strongly believed that "a public office is a public trust." He took a firm stand on important issues, even though he knew that his action would antagonize influential members of his own party.

He supported civil service reform by doubling the number of federal jobs on the classified list. He took a step toward conserving the nation's natural resources by recovering vast areas of public land illegally held by railroads, lumber companies, and cattle interests. He signed a bill in 1887 creating a federal Division of Forestry.

One of his most courageous acts was his attempt to block "pension grabs" by veterans of the Union army. For many years the Pension Bureau had been very generous in handing out pensions. Now and then, however, requests for pensions were based on such flimsy grounds that even the bureau rejected them. Often, when this happened, the disappointed pension seeker asked his representative in Congress to get the pension for him by pushing a special bill through Congress. Cleveland vetoed more than 200 of these bills. He thus angered many ex-soldiers, who were united in the politically powerful veterans' organization the Grand Army of the Republic, known as the G.A.R.

Important laws. In addition to Cleveland's personal accomplishments, Congress adopted several important laws during the years from 1885 to 1889.

The Presidential Succession Act of 1886 provided that if both the President and the Vice-President died or were disabled, the cabinet officers would succeed to the Presidency in the order in which their offices had been created.

The Electoral Count Act of 1887 was designed to prevent another disputed election similar to the election of 1876. The act provided that if a state sent in more than one set of electoral returns, Congress had to accept the returns approved by the governor of the state.

In 1887 Congress tried to quiet the clamor of small business people and farmers against unfair business practices by the railroads. It passed the Interstate Commerce Act, about which you will read in Chapter 6. Congress refused, however, to accept President Cleveland's strong recommendation that tariff rates be lowered.

The election of 1888. President Cleveland's reform activities and especially his campaign for lower tariffs antagonized political leaders in his own party. Nevertheless, in 1888 the Democrats nominated him for a second term.

Although Cleveland won nearly 100,000 more popular votes than his opponent, Benjamin Harrison, he lost by an electoral count of 233 to 168. The Republicans won the Presidency and control of both houses of Congress.

Cleveland's policies reversed. Benjamin Harrison was a successful lawyer, a veteran of the Union army, and the grandson of former President William Henry Harrison. He was not, however, a strong President. In his opinion, his duty as Chief Executive was to follow the wishes of the Senators and Representatives, who in turn had the responsibility of carrying out the wishes of the people.

During President Harrison's administration, the Republicans reversed many of President Cleveland's policies. Instead of supporting the civil service system, they replaced Democratic officeholders (except those on the classified list) with Republicans. Congress passed an act that almost doubled the number of pensioners and their dependents. Congress also adopted the highest protective tariff the country had had up to that time, the McKinley Tariff of 1890.

The "Old Guard" Republicans did not have everything their way. In an effort to appeal to farmers, laborers, miners, small business people, and the American public in general, Congress passed two important laws in 1890. The Sherman Silver Purchase Act was in-

According to this cartoon, Uncle Sam had little reason to be pleased with Benjamin Harrison's Presidency. What failings does the cartoonist lay at Harrison's door?

tended to appeal to western mining interests. The act was also meant to increase the amount of money in circulation as a benefit to farmers, wage earners, and small business interests. The Sherman Antitrust Act was intended to protect the public from monopoly practices and other abuses of free enterprise that had arisen with the growth of industry. You will read about these two laws in the next unit.

Growing dissatisfaction. Neither the Sherman Silver Purchase Act nor the Sherman Antitrust Act stopped the growing dissatisfaction with President Harrison's Republican administration. Wage earners had no reason to hope their demands would be met by Republicans. Many farmers, abandoning hope of help from either party, began to join labor organizations in efforts to win control of the government and bring about reforms. Many Americans, struggling to make ends meet at a time of rising prices, blamed their troubles on the Republican-sponsored McKinley Tariff.

Two widely read books expressed the growing dissatisfaction with the concentration of wealth in the hands of a few. Henry George's *Progress and Poverty,* first published in 1879, contrasted the wealth of the privileged few with the poverty of many people. George blamed this inequality on the fact that a few persons had monopoly control over the nation's choicest land sites and other natural resources. George proposed a new system of taxing land. He thought that this system would abolish great fortunes and provide a good standard of living for everyone.

In 1894 the book *Wealth Against Commonwealth* by Henry Demarest Lloyd was published. The author concluded that the giant new corporations and business enterprises were running the new industrial economy for their own gain.

Lloyd's book expressed the deep discontent of millions of Americans. What concerned many Americans was that the new industrialism had created extremes of poverty and wealth. Expanding industries brought vast wealth to a few owners, while the majority of workers lived in poverty. For a solution to this problem, many Americans turned to government—whether controlled by Republicans or Democrats.

By 1892 the demand for government action could not be ignored. Owners of small businesses, wage earners in every section of the country, and especially the western farmers were calling for reform.

The election of 1892. Increasing discontent turned the election of 1892 into a spirited three-way contest. Both the Republicans and the Democrats realized that they had to do something about reform. They were prodded into action by the strength of a new party, the Populist Party, which had been created in 1891. The Populist Party, which you will read about later, was organized by farmers, but it also attracted wage earners and other discontented voters.

The Republicans were on the defensive. President Harrison and the Republican Party received widespread criticism. Nevertheless, the Republicans decided to stand on their record. The party nominated President Harrison for a second term.

The Democrats were eager to take advantage of the demands for reform from both workers and farmers. They nominated Grover Cleveland, who was already known as a champion of honest politics.

The Democrats won, with Cleveland gathering 277 electoral votes to Harrison's 145. The Democrats also won control of Congress, but

the new Populist Party—an out-and-out reform party—made a remarkable showing. Although the Populist candidate, James B. Weaver, collected only 22 electoral votes, his popular vote totaled more than 1 million. The Populist Party also elected three governors and numerous representatives to state legislatures and to Congress.

The Wilson-Gorman Tariff. From the beginning President Cleveland was in trouble. His election had stemmed in part from his promise to lower the McKinley Tariff. A tariff bill that he supported was introduced in the House in December 1893. By the time the bill had gone through the House and Senate, over 600 amendments had been tacked on to it raising tariff rates for particular products.

The Wilson-Gorman bill, as the amended bill was called, did provide overall lower average tariff rates than the McKinley Tariff. However, it was still a high protective tariff, and President Cleveland was furious. He refused to endorse it by signing it, preferring instead to leave it on his desk for ten days. After that time it automatically became law without his signature.

During the tariff debates in the Senate, powerful lobbies, or pressure groups, tried in every way possible to influence the votes of doubtful Senators. Producers of iron, steel, wool, glass, and hundreds of other products demanded tariff protection.

One of the most active lobbies was the American Sugar Refining Company, usually called "the sugar trust."° The original House bill had completely removed the tariff on raw and refined sugar. The sugar trust, determined to get the tariff restored, immediately went to work on the Senate. In the end, the trust won, and the tariff on sugar was restored.

The Wilson-Gorman Tariff cost the Democrats the support of millions of Americans who were convinced that the Democrats had broken their campaign promise to do away with a high protective tariff.

Decision against an income tax. The original tariff bill favored by President Cleveland would have sharply lowered the tariff rates. Expecting a loss in government revenue because of the lower rates, the House added a

°**trust:** a group of companies centrally controlled to regulate production, reduce production costs, and eliminate competition.

Panic hit the floor of the New York Stock Exchange as investors raced to sell their stocks in May 1893. Plunging stock prices set off a crippling depression that would last five years and cause hardship for millions across the nation.

clause to the tariff bill providing for a 2 percent tax on all incomes of more than $4,000.

The income tax clause provoked violent debate, but it finally became law. Opponents of the income tax immediately tested the new measure in the courts. In 1895 the Supreme Court declared it unconstitutional. The Supreme Court ruled against the income tax because it was a direct tax not apportioned among the states according to population, as required by the Constitution (page 724).

The Democratic administration could not be held responsible for the Supreme Court's negative decision on the income tax. Nevertheless, millions of Americans considered the Court's decision as merely one more example of how the government favored big business. Thus the Supreme Court's rejection of the income tax helped to fan the flame of protest sweeping the country.

Financial panic. On May 5, 1893, only two months after Cleveland took office, a financial panic began as the value of stocks on the New York Stock Exchange suddenly plunged. As the weeks passed, the situation rapidly became worse. Thousands of businesses failed. Facto-

ries closed their doors. Perhaps as many as 4 million workers were unemployed. The prices of farm produce dropped so low that farmers could not afford the cost of shipping it. By the end of the year, the American nation was in the grip of one of the worst depressions in its history.

SECTION SURVEY

IDENTIFY: "pension grabs," Benjamin Harrison, McKinley Tariff of 1890, Populist Party, Wilson-Gorman Tariff, lobbies, trust, panic of 1893.

1. What did Grover Cleveland mean when he said that "a public office is a public trust"?

2. Explain how each of the following laws helped to prevent a potential national problem: (a) Presidential Succession Act of 1886, (b) Electoral Count Act of 1887.

3. Summarize the main ideas in the writings of Henry Demarest Lloyd and Henry George.

4. How did the issue of tariffs play a part in politics during the 1880's and 1890's?

5. Cartoon Study: Look at the cartoon on page 65. What is the cartoonist's attitude toward Harrison? How does the cartoonist express this attitude?

Chapter Survey

Summary: Tracing the Main Ideas

Change, unrest, new ways of living, and new problems—these were characteristics of every section of the United States during the years from 1865 to 1900. Many of the new problems that Americans faced were the result of the Civil War, which for four long years had shaken the nation and disrupted long-established ways of living. To an even greater extent, however, the new problems were the result of the transformation of the United States from an agricultural nation into a great industrial power.

Industrialization, already under way before the war, roared ahead during the war years. Northern industry continued to expand after 1865 with ever-increasing speed. Industrialization was also transforming life in the South. As you will read in the next chapter, it contributed to the conquest of the last frontiers in the West.

The new ways of living brought serious problems as well as excitement and drama. Morality in public life sank to an all-time low as a "get-rich-quick" spirit and greed for power infected millions of Americans. Wealth and power became concentrated in the hands of a relatively few pioneers of the new industrial age. Through their control of the railroads, mines, factories, banks, and giant corporations, the new industrial and financial leaders exerted powerful influence over government at every level. The control exercised by this small group threatened the working of the democratic process.

There is, however, another side of the story. As Americans became increasingly aware of the threat to democracy, they began to take steps to correct the situation. In later chapters you will read how the American people undertook to solve the many problems that were confronting them.

Inquiring into History

1. Explain how the Pendleton Act made a significant contribution to the development of democracy in the United States.
2. During the late 1800's, many workers and farmers felt that the government favored big business and the well-to-do. (a) What events made them feel this way? (b) Do you think they were justified?
3. (a) Compare the views held by Grover Cleveland and Benjamin Harrison on the proper role of the President. (b) In what ways did their views affect their actions as President? Give specific examples to support your answer.
4. Historians have rated American Presidents by the following categories: great, near great, average, below average, and failure. Make a list of the Presidents elected between 1865 and 1896 and evaluate them according to these categories. What factors did you consider in making your judgments?

Relating Past to Present

1. (a) Name examples of graft and corruption in local, state, or federal government in recent years. (b) Compare the methods and motivations of these officials and of corrupt officials in the late 1800's.
2. Does the word "reform" seem to have a different meaning today from the one it had during the 1880's and 1890's? Explain.
3. (a) What groups of people made up the majority of the Republican Party and of the Democratic Party during the period from 1865 to 1897? (b) What major groups make up each party's majority today? Compare and comment.

Developing Social Science Skills

1. Study the cartoon on page 65. (a) Identify the characters shown in the cartoon. (b) What is the point of view of the cartoon? (c) How effective do you think the cartoon is?
2. Compare the Presidential Succession Act of 1967 (Amendment 25, see page 754) with the one enacted in 1886. Why do you think the act of 1967 was necessary?
3. Benjamin Harrison was elected President in 1888 although he received fewer popular votes than his opponent, Grover Cleveland, did. Consult an almanac or other reference books to find out if other candidates have won the Presidency despite receiving fewer popular votes than their opponents.

Chapter 3
Conquering the Last Frontier
1865–1900

Chief Joseph, leader of the Nez Percé Indians, surrendered to his conquerors sorrowfully, but with dignity. "I am tired of fighting," he said. "Our chiefs are killed. . . . It is cold and we have no blankets. The little children are freezing to death. . . . My heart is sick and sad. From where the sun now stands I will fight no more, forever." The year was 1877. The place was the plains of Montana, only a few miles from the Canadian border.

For years beyond memory, the Nez Percés had lived in the region where the present states of Oregon, Washington, and Idaho meet. For half a century, they had dwelt in peace with the whites.

By the mid-1860's, however, it had become clear that the peaceful days were ending. Land-hungry pioneers moving into the Pacific Northwest were looking with greedy eyes at the fertile valleys and hunting grounds of the Nez Percés. In 1877 the federal government ordered the Nez Percés to leave their homeland for a remote region. They started the move, but trouble broke out and a small band of Indians murdered 19 whites.

Certain that the United States Army would punish all of the Nez Percés, Chief Joseph decided to flee to safety and a new homeland in Canada. For two months the band of 200 warriors and 600 women and children outwitted and outfought much larger forces of pursuing troops. Finally, after traveling more than 1,300 miles (2,100 kilometers) through unbelievably rugged terrain, they were surrounded by United States troops and forced to surrender almost within sight of the border.

Thus, in 1877, Chief Joseph faced his conquerors on the last frontier of the West, the Great Plains. This vast area, stretching from the Canadian border to Texas, had belonged to the Indians from earliest times. Now it was being claimed by people from the North and South and from distant Europe. This is the story of the conquest of the Indians. It is also the story of the West itself and of new ways of life on the last frontier.

THE CHAPTER IN OUTLINE

1. The Indians make their last stand on the Great Plains.

2. The government tries to "Americanize" the Indians.

3. Ranchers build a cattle kingdom on the plains.

4. Farmers plow the tough sod of the last frontier.

5. Miners find new treasures in the western mountains.

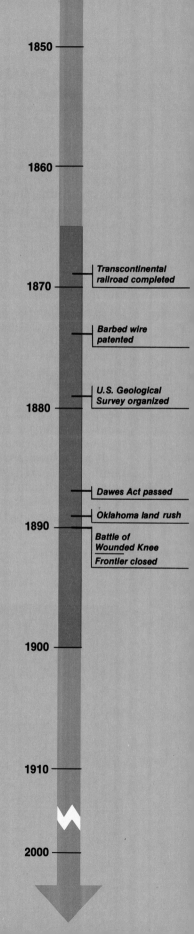

1850

1860

1870 — Transcontinental railroad completed

Barbed wire patented

U.S. Geological Survey organized

1880

Dawes Act passed

Oklahoma land rush

1890

Battle of Wounded Knee

Frontier closed

1900

1910

2000

1 The Indians make their last stand on the Great Plains

On their western edge, the prairies of the Middle West merge into the Great Plains. Although no sharp line separates the prairies from the plains, the 100th meridian is usually accepted as the dividing line. A traveler heading westward from the 100th meridian toward the Rocky Mountains will notice that the annual rainfall gradually decreases and the grass gets shorter.

The Great American Desert. It was along the line of the 100th meridian that the westward advance of the settlers halted for at least a generation during the early 1800's. The reluctance of the pioneers to settle on the Great Plains arose in part from misinformation. Earlier explorers, accustomed to wooded country with abundant rainfall, had established the idea that the Great Plains were arid and uninhabitable. Maps of the times called the plains the "Great American Desert."

For as long as the whites believed the plains to be barren desert, they were content to leave the region to the Indians. In fact, the federal government had moved many tribes to the plains from east of the Mississippi and prom-ised to keep white settlers out. "A country west of Missouri and Arkansas has been assigned to [the Indians], into which white settlements are not to be pushed," President Andrew Jackson had declared in 1835.

By the 1850's, however, the mistaken notion of the plains as desert was being dispelled. Traders and pioneers who crossed the plains on their way to California and the Pacific Northwest reported that much of the plains country was good for farming and cattle raising. White settlers gradually began to move onto the plains.

Bows and arrows against guns. The Plains Indians were determined to defend their hunting grounds and their way of life. They had learned what later white settlers would have to learn—how to adapt to the plains environment. Herds of wild horses, descendants of those of the Spanish conquistadors, now roamed the plains. The Indians had mastered these horses and had become expert riders. On horseback they could easily hunt the buffalo, or bison, which provided them with food, clothing, and shelter.

The Indians were powerful adversaries. They rode superbly. Before they secured rifles, they fought with spears and with short bows, from which they could drive their arrows with amazing rapidity and penetrating force. To protect themselves they used shields made of

Here artist George Catlin captures a moment in a Plains Indian buffalo hunt. The Indians who hunted with bows and arrows or with spears did not threaten to wipe out the buffalo population, but the white newcomers with rifles did.

buffalo hide. These they coated with glue made from horses' hooves and hardened over the fire to an almost iron-like consistency. A favorite Indian tactic was to gallop around the enemy, hiding behind their horses and shields and deliberately drawing enemy fire. When the enemy's ammunition was exhausted, the Indians darted in to strike with arrows and long spears.

Faced with these weapons and tactics, white intruders at first were at a disadvantage. Their long rifles could be reloaded and fired from the back of a galloping horse only with great difficulty.

The invention of the revolver in the late 1830's ended the Indians' temporary superiority in weapons. The revolver could be reloaded easily at full gallop. Several bullets could be fired in rapid succession without reloading. Armed with this new weapon, settlers in the 1850's could move out onto the plains with more confidence.

A new Indian policy. This new movement of white settlers brought about a change in government policy toward the Indians. In 1849 the Bureau of Indian Affairs became part of the Department of the Interior. The bureau had responsibility for carrying out the federal government's Indian policies. One early policy was **concentration.** This was the attempt to confine the Indian tribes to certain limited areas of the West. In these areas the tribes would be free to carry on their own affairs and continue their lives as hunters. It was hoped the policy would reduce warfare among the tribes and would clear routes for white settlers heading for California and Oregon.

More settlers on the plains. An individual traveling on foot across the Great Plains was in grave danger of dying from thirst, sunstroke, or cold. Thus the early pioneers who crossed the plains depended upon horses and oxen for transportation. A rider on horseback, however, could not transport goods in bulk. To fill this need, caravans of covered wagons set out upon the plains, forming circles around campfires at night for protection against Indian attack. As time passed, stagecoach lines offered a speedier form of transportation.

After the Civil War, the Great Plains attracted increasing numbers of land speculators, ranchers, miners, engineers, and farmers. These newcomers were determined to possess the land and its resources for themselves.

Government policy toward the Indians changed again, now calling for their resettlement on **reservations.** These were sharply defined tracts of land set aside by the government for the Indians. Most reservations were too small to support the hunting way of life. Therefore, the Indians were supposed to get food through government agents on the reservation. Also, the Indians were expected to take up farming, although reservations were usually located on the poorest land.

Railroads cross the plains. The railroads finally conquered the Great Plains for the white settlers. Construction of the first transcontinental railroad began in 1866. Chinese workers were imported to do most of the physical labor on the Central Pacific. Most of the workers on the Union Pacific, building from Omaha, in Nebraska Territory, were recent Irish immigrants. All work was done under the watchful eyes of scouts, who protected the railroad builders from hostile Indians. The Central Pacific and the Union Pacific met in 1869 at Promontory, in what is now Utah. This "wedding of the rails" was an occasion of jubilation. Silk-hatted gentlemen surrounded by grimy workers drove a golden spike to hold the last rails in place while the news was telegraphed to Americans everywhere.

The first transcontinental railroad contributed enormously to the nation's economic growth. It brought the Atlantic and the Pacific seaboards within a week's journey of each other and opened a speedy route to the rich resources of the West, a route followed by northerners and southerners alike.

The railroad also split the vast buffalo herds of the plains. The herds were split again and again as other rail lines were built across the grasslands. Finally the completion of the Northern Pacific Railway in 1883 sealed the fate of the last, northernmost buffalo herd (see map, page 78).

Destruction of the buffalo. The Plains Indians depended mainly on the buffalo for their living. Government agents and army officers, knowing this, sometimes encouraged the destruction of the great herds as a means of keeping the Indians on reservations. Parties of hunters debarked from trains with horses and equipment, killed the buffalo at will, and loaded the hides on trains bound for eastern markets. It has been estimated that between

White Bird, a Cheyenne who had fought against General Custer's troops as a boy, painted this picture of the Battle of Little Bighorn. News of Custer's defeat in the West by Sioux and Cheyenne Indians led by Crazy Horse and Gall reached the East just as the nation began celebrating its 100th birthday on July 4, 1876.

1871 and 1874, hunters killed nearly 3 million buffalo each year. By 1875, buffalo hides were selling from 65 cents to $1.15 apiece. The waste was frightful. Buffalo carcasses were abandoned, and for every hide taken, four were left on the plains.

The disappearance of the buffalo doomed the Plains Indians. The Indians saw the dwindling herds and the increasing number of white settlers. They saw the treaties, by which they agreed to give up land or to move to reservations, broken again and again by whites. They learned that the agents who ran the reservations were often corrupt. The Indians also came to resent the restrictions of the reservations and the attempts by the federal government to change their way of life.

Many Indians decided to resist the whites. They left the reservations and tried to resume their lives as hunters on the plains. This brought another change in government policy toward the Indians, one in which the United States Army played a key role. The army's mis-

sion was to keep the Indians on the reservations and to force the return of those who fled.

The Indian wars. Despite their advantages over the Plains Indians, white settlers and the army had to fight long and hard to drive them from their hunting grounds. Between 1865 and 1886, the United States conducted a costly and brutal campaign against the Plains Indians. In all the engagements of this campaign, former soldiers who had fought for the South or the North in the Civil War now fought together against the Indians.

In 1866 Congress decided to recruit four all-black regiments—the 24th and 25th Infantries and the 9th and 10th Cavalries—to fight in the Indian wars. One fifth of the army's soldiers on horseback in the western campaigns were enrolled in the 9th and 10th Cavalries.

During the 30-odd years of the Indian wars, the Indians fought back against white and black military forces in an effort to hold on to their lands and to keep their distinctive ways of life. As in earlier conflicts with settlers, the Indians were not always united in their struggle. Traditional tribal rivalries explain in part why the federal regiments were often able to enlist Indians as highly useful scouts.

Still, Indian resistance was remarkable. The smaller the area into which the Indians were driven, the more desperately they fought back. There was brutality on both sides, and army leaders fought not only with guns but also with broken promises. In 1877, the same year in which Chief Joseph made his heroic attempt to lead his people to freedom in Canada, President Hayes admitted, "Many, if not most, of our Indian wars have their origin in broken promises and acts of injustice on our part."

Custer's last stand. Just the year before, one broken promise had brought disaster. The Sioux had been promised as a permanent home the Black Hills in what are now South Dakota and Wyoming, which they considered sacred. However, after gold was discovered in the Black Hills, the 7th Cavalry, in 1876, was ordered to remove the Indians to a less desirable area. The removal operation was under the command of General George Custer, an experienced Indian fighter. Several years earlier, Custer had attacked a peaceful Indian village on the Washita River in Oklahoma. In the attack unarmed women and children as well as warriors were killed.

In June of 1876, General Custer attacked a large camp of Sioux and Cheyenne near the Little Bighorn River in Montana. The Sioux and Cheyenne warriors had two outstanding leaders. One was Sitting Bull, able, honest, and idealistic. The other was Crazy Horse, uncompromising, reckless, a military genius, and the most honored hero of the Sioux.

In fierce fighting along the Little Bighorn, Custer and his whole detachment of 264 troops were killed and some bodies mutilated. General Custer's last stand provoked long controversy, but none could deny that it was a major humiliation for the United States government. Still, the action at the Little Bighorn for a time marked the end of major fighting on the northern Great Plains. Troops pursued and harried the Sioux and Cheyenne until Crazy Horse and Sitting Bull were defeated and the Indians forced onto reservations.

Resistance ends in the Southwest. To the south and west, meanwhile, the Apaches continued their three centuries of almost uninterrupted war against the whites. First there had been the Spaniards, then the Mexicans, and finally the North Americans. From time to time, bands of Apaches and Comanches led by Cochise, Victorio, Geronimo, and others rode out of their reservations and spread terror along the Mexican–United States border. Finally, in 1886, Geronimo surrendered. With his surrender, organized resistance came to an end on the southern plains and in the rugged mountains of the Southwest.

The end of the fighting. It was on the northern plains, however, that the United States cavalry wrote the final bloody chapter in the long and tragic history of Indian-white warfare.

The events leading up to this final tragedy had their roots in 1889 with a religious revival that swept through the Indian tribes. The revival was celebrated in what the whites called the "Ghost Dance." It was based on the belief that an Indian Messiah was about to appear. With his arrival dead Indians would rise from their graves to join the living, the buffalo would again roam the plains, and the white intruders would vanish from the Indian lands like mist under the morning sun.

The Ghost Dance was not a call to war. It was, on the contrary, the celebration of a vision — the restoration of the old and treasured Indian way of life. As such, it awakened new hope in the hearts of a broken, despairing people. The Ghost Dance cult quickly gained followers, including many Sioux on the northern plains. White miners and settlers, alarmed at what they feared might be another outbreak of warfare, demanded that the army put an end to the activity.

At Wounded Knee in South Dakota in December 1890, a unit of the 7th Cavalry responded to this demand. The cavalry arrested a band of Sioux men, women, and children who were traveling to the Pine Ridge Reservation in search of food and protection. The troops surrounded the Indians and disarmed them. During the process a disturbance broke out, and someone fired a shot. Immediately, without warning, the troops opened fire with rifles and with Gatling guns, the earliest type of machine guns. They poured a deadly hail of lead into the band of unprotected Sioux, killing or mortally wounding 90 men and 200 women and children.

Many Americans expressed their horror at such brutality. Others rejoiced that at last General Custer had been "avenged." As for the Indians, the brutal massacre at Wounded Knee brought an end to all organized armed resistance in the United States.

SECTION SURVEY

IDENTIFY: Great American Desert, Bureau of Indian Affairs, concentration, reservations, transcontinental railroad, Chief Joseph, George Custer, Geronimo, Ghost Dance, Wounded Knee.

1. How did the following contribute to the defeat of the Indians: (a) the revolver, (b) the railroads, (c) the destruction of the buffalo?
2. Describe and explain the purpose behind each of these United States policies toward the Indians: (a) concentration, (b) reservations, (c) military force.
3. Compare the actions of Chief Joseph and Geronimo in response to United States policy toward the Indians.

2 The government tries to "Americanize" the Indians

The Indians, the first Americans, had once claimed all the North American continent as their own. By 1890 their conquerors had stripped them of most of their land and their freedom. They had also confined the Indians to reservations.

The reservations. On the reservations, far removed from their original tribal lands, the Indians confronted the problem of adapting their ways of life to unfamiliar climates and terrains. When they tried to escape, they were pursued, captured punished, and sent back to the reservation. To make matters worse, just when some of the Indians were beginning to adjust to their new environments, the government would move them to different reservations.

Legally, the reservation Indians were **wards** of the government, like minor children without parents. In return for the lands they had given up, they were supposed to receive certain supplies, such as blankets, seed corn, and basic food. These supplies were often poor in quality and quantity and slow in reaching the Indians. Some agents in charge of the reservations were honest, but many agents profited from corrupt deals with traders and with those who provided the supplies. The Indians were commonly treated with contempt or, at best, as children might be treated.

"Americanizing" the Indians. Even with the Indians confined to the reservations, there was still a serious "Indian problem" in the view of most white Americans. Most white Americans believed that it was necessary for the Indians to be "Americanized." This meant that the Indians had to be assimilated into the white

This photograph shows the Pine Ridge Indian Reservation in southwestern South Dakota. It was the final, government-run home of the Sioux, who had tried to stop the spread of settlement onto their lands but had been unable to do so.

These young men were part of an effort in 1900 to "Americanize" the Indians. They attended a school for Indians near Carson City, Nevada. Judging from the photograph, what means were used to "Americanize" them?

American way of life and forced to accept the culture of the dominant majority. To the Indians—reduced in numbers to between 200,000 and 300,000 at that time—this idea meant giving up many of their deeply held values and customs. These included the collective or tribal ownership and use of land; a belief that work was only a means of providing food and shelter, not an end in itself; marriage traditions, including having more than one wife; many religious beliefs; and even clothing styles and adornments. Indian men, for example, resented efforts to make them cut their long, braided hair. Nor did Indian men and boys accept the idea that they were supposed to plant and cultivate the soil; that had always been women's work.

The vast majority of white Americans neither understood nor appreciated the Indian cultures. They were unaware of the importance of these cultures to the Indians' sense of identity and self-respect.

Reform activities. Some Americans, however, were deeply troubled by the long history of the white settlers' injustice to the Indians.

Helen Hunt Jackson, in her book *A Century of Dishonor* (1881), provided documentary evidence of the government's broken promises. The reformers were also deeply disturbed by the corruption, inefficiency, and lack of leadership in the Bureau of Indian Affairs.

Sarah Winnemucca, daughter of a Nevada Paiute chief, played a unique role in urging reform. She was a scout, a guide, an interpreter at army posts, a teacher of Indian children, the widow of one army officer, and the wife of another. In lectures at Boston, San Francisco, and elsewhere, she spoke out against the injustices to her people. She denounced the corruption of agents of the Bureau of Indian Affairs and called for better distribution of lands to Indians. General Oliver Otis Howard, for whom she was a scout and interpreter, declared that she "should have a place beside the name of Pocahontas in the history of our country."

One reform group, the National Indian Defense Organization, argued that the deep-rooted cultures of the Indians could not be rapidly changed without grave consequences. Members of this group argued that the Indians should be allowed to retain their own traditions and customs. Most other reform organizations, however, believed that the Indians could and should be speedily "Americanized." They felt that the Indians must adopt Christianity, white American forms of education, and individual land ownership.

Reformers who urged individual land ownership for the Indians actually strengthened, without intending to, the more selfish interests of land speculators, miners, ranchers, and farmers who were already occupying the unsettled areas of the West. These groups, who wanted the more valuable parts of Indian reservations, supported the reformers' policy of individual Indian ownership. Since individuals could more easily be persuaded or bribed to sell their land, such a policy would open remaining reservation lands to white occupation.

Writing the policy into law. The federal government in the Dawes Act of 1887 made a general policy of what it had been trying to do in a piecemeal fashion. With the Dawes Act, Congress hoped to hasten the time when the Indians living on reservations would be successfully "Americanized."

The Dawes Act provided that each male head of an Indian family could, if he wished, claim 160 acres (64.8 hectares) of reservation land as his own. Bachelors, women, and children were to be entitled to lesser amounts. Legal ownership of the property was to be held in trust by the federal government for 25 years. During this period the Indians could neither sell their land nor use it as security for a mortgage. This restriction was intended to protect the Indians from unscrupulous land speculators. The Burke Act of 1906 modified this provision. It gave the Secretary of the Interior authority to reduce the 25-year trust period in those cases where the Secretary was persuaded that the Indians were capable of handling their own affairs.

The Dawes Act and the Burke Act also provided that Indians who accepted the land and abandoned their tribal way of life were to be given citizenship, including the right to vote. Meanwhile, Congress voted larger but still inadequate funds for the education of Indian children. Regular day schools or boarding schools far from their homes were set up. In these schools the children were taught, often by poorly trained and unsympathetic teachers, to look down on Indian ways of life as inferior and degraded.

Failure of the policy. The new laws persuaded and enabled some Indians to adopt the way of life of the white majority and to become American citizens. Even so, Indians who left the reservations to live in American towns and cities often met with discrimination in jobs and unfair treatment. Most Indians remained on the reservations, clinging as best they could to their tribal customs and living as wards of the federal government. The government policy of encouraging individual land ownership and individual farming among the Indians largely failed when land speculators found loopholes in the Dawes Act. Between 1887 and the 1920's, much of the reservation land was, in one way or another, taken from the Indians. The land that remained was generally eroded and inferior. Moreover, provisions for safeguarding the health of the Indians were neglected. Malnutrition and disease were widespread.

The late 1800's and early 1900's were in many ways the Indians' darkest period. Yet their vitality and spirit were not extinguished. Many continued to insist that they be treated as separate peoples with worthy ways of viewing human relationships, of understanding their environment, and of sensing their place in the universe.

SECTION SURVEY

IDENTIFY: ward of the government, "Americanization," Helen Hunt Jackson, Sarah Winnemucca, Dawes Act of 1887, Burke Act.

1. It has been said that much of United States policy toward Indians during the 1800's consisted of broken promises and acts of injustice. Give examples to support this view.

2. Describe the efforts by reformers to improve conditions for Indians during the late 1800's.

3. What arguments were made for and against "Americanizing" the Indians?

3 Ranchers build a cattle kingdom on the plains

Cattle raisers began to move out onto the Great Plains in the 1860's, long before the Indians were conquered. By the 1890's the cattle industry had become big business. Its prod-

This 1898 photograph shows how working cowboys actually looked and dressed. While the horse at right eats from its feedbag, the cowboys pause for a quick meal served from the tailgate of a chuck wagon.

ucts passed from the western ranges through the stockyards, slaughterhouses, and packing plants to become major items of domestic and world trade.

Rise of the Cattle Kingdom. Many of the animals for the cattle industry came from the ranches in southeastern Texas formerly operated by Spaniards and Mexicans. These ranches were occupied by the Texans, who also took over the huge herds of wild cattle, called longhorns, estimated in 1865 to number about 5 million head. The wild herds sprang from the cattle that were lost by the Spaniards and by the American wagon trains crossing the plains in earlier days.

It was no easy task for the first Texans to learn how to handle the cattle, wild or tame. A writer in the 1870's warned that "the wild cattle of Texas, . . . animals miscalled tame, are fifty times more dangerous. . . than the fiercest buffalo."

In learning how to handle cattle, the Texans owed a great deal to Mexican **vaqueros** (vah·KAY·rohs), or cowboys, and to Indians. Many slaves also learned the dangerous business of handling cattle. After emancipation freed slaves comprised perhaps one third of those working in cattle raising. With the aid of the horse, the saddle, the rope, and the revolver, white and black cowboys learned how to handle the longhorns on the open grasslands. Mexican Americans, who made up a large part of the cowboy population, continued to play an important role in cattle ranching. It became a profitable occupation and a distinctive way of life.

The long drive. People in the nation's growing cities needed enormous quantities of beef. The problem was to find a means of getting the steers to urban markets. The solution was transportation provided by the railroads, which in the 1860's began to push out upon the Great Plains.

As the steel rails moved westward, enormous herds of steers were driven from Texas north on long drives to towns that grew up along the railroads. By 1870, Kansas cattle towns like Abilene, Ellsworth, and Ellis, all on the Kansas Pacific Railroad, and Dodge City and Wichita on the Atchison, Topeka, and Santa Fe Railway had become roaring, riotous, lawless communities (see map, page 78).

During the early years of the long drives, nearly all the steers driven from Texas were

77

sold in the cattle towns at good prices. In time, however, the number of cattle began to exceed the demand. Texans who arrived in late fall were either unable to sell their steers or had to sell them at a loss.

The open range. At this point, enterprising cattle raisers began to winter their surplus steers on the open range, or unfenced grazing lands, near the cattle towns. After fattening them during the winter, they sold them at high prices in the towns before the new cattle drives from Texas arrived to glut the market.

This was not the first time that cattle had been pastured on the short grass of the Great Plains. Many wagon trains had wintered on

the plains, and the pioneers had discovered that their horses and cattle grew fat on the short and thin, but nutritious, grass. The open-range cattle industry did not develop, however, until the railroads provided access to markets and the Texans provided the cattle.

News that quick money could be made in the open-range cattle business soon reached the eastern seaboard and spread to Europe. The cattle rush that followed was similar to the gold rush that had populated California in 1849–50. Prices for land and steers soared as newcomers on the Great Plains staked out their claims.

People rushed to the cattle country to make their fortunes. They built dugouts, sod huts, or

WESTERN RAILROADS AND CATTLE TRAILS

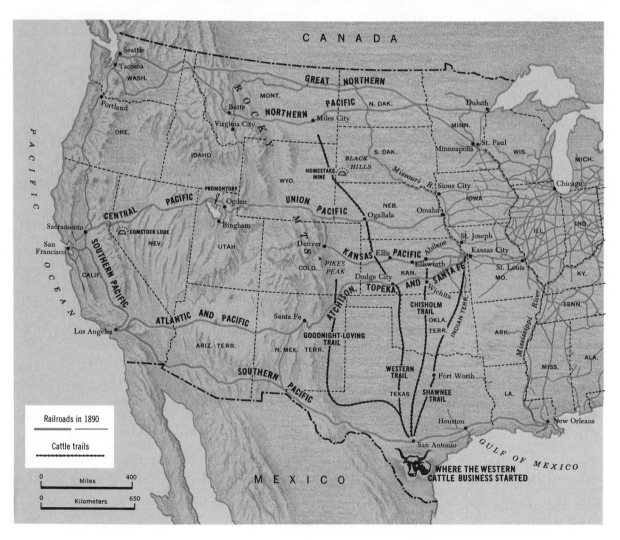

IT ALL STARTED IN MEXICO

What could be more American than a cowboy? From Paris to Peking, he is for millions *the* symbol of the United States. But the American cowboy—the whole cattle business, in fact—could never have existed without the Mexicans and the Spaniards before them.

First, of course, came the cattle themselves. In the days of the open range, the herds that roamed freely consisted of so-called Texas longhorns. These were descended from long-horned cattle first brought to America by Columbus in 1493.

Next was the horse. The type favored for ranging was descended from the mustang [Spanish *mestengo* (mes·TENG·goh), meaning "belonging to shepherds," and *mostrenco* (mohs·TRENG·coh), meaning "stray beast"]. The mustangs, like the longhorns, were the wild offspring of tame livestock introduced by Spanish settlers.

It was the Mexicans who first put men on horseback to roam the open range, round up wild cattle, and brand them to show ownership.

In fact, the first brand in America was probably the one used by Hernando Cortés. It was called Three Christian Crosses, and that is just what it looked like.

The Mexican cowboy was called a *vaquero* (vah·KAY·roh). In English this became the word "buckaroo," another term for a ranch hand. Almost everything the cowboy did or used on the job had a Spanish-Mexican origin.

When rounding up cattle, he used a rope called a lariat [Spanish *la reata* (LAH ray·AH·tah)] or lasso [Spanish *lazo* (LAH·soh)]. He protected his legs from thorny brush with chaps [Spanish *chaparreras* (chah·pah·RAY·rahs)]. If he got cattle into a *corral* [Spanish for "pen"], there was less danger of a stampede [Spanish *estampida* (ehs·tahm·PEE·dah)]. For fun he might ride bucking *broncos* [Spanish for "wild horses"] in a *rodeo* [Spanish for "cattle ring"]. But the cowboy had to be careful. If he celebrated too noisily, he might end up in the hoosegow [Spanish *juzgado* (hoos·GAH·doh)], or jail.

simple ranch houses and pastured their herds on the open grasslands. Some, though by no means all, did become wealthy.

Until the 1880's the cattle ranchers ruled the Great Plains. This was the period of the long drive, the open range, the roundup, and the picturesque roving cowboy.

End of the open range. The open-range cattle industry ended, however, almost as quickly as it had started. As the supply of steers rapidly increased, beef prices fell disastrously low. In 1885 a severe drought burned up the grasses on the overstocked range, and cattle starved by the thousands.

Even more disastrous for the cattle ranchers was the development of the sheep industry and farming. To be sure, Mexican Americans had been grazing sheep in New Mexico for a long time. However, the arrival in the 1880's of large numbers of sheepherders and farmers from the older areas of the United States doomed the open range. Sheep cropped the grass so close that little was left for the cattle. Farmers broke up the open range with their farms and barbed-wire faces (page 82). The cattle ranchers fought desperately to keep the range open, but it was a hopeless battle. By the late 1880's, the open, unfenced range was fast becoming a thing of the past.

By the 1890's the western cattle industry centered in the high plains running through eastern Montana, Wyoming, Colorado, the New Mexico Territory, and western Texas. Most ranchers by now owned their grazing land and fenced it in with barbed wire.

Ranches varied in size from about 2,000 to 100,000 acres (about 800 to 40,000 hectares). Western ranches had to be large since each steer required a grazing area of 15 to 75 acres (or about 6 to 30 hectares). The size of the area depended upon the amount of rainfall and the resulting growth of grass.

With the invention of better instruments for drilling into the ground and the improvement of windmills for pumping water, many cattle raisers watered their herds from wells scattered over their ranches. In years of abundant rainfall, cattle ranchers might prosper, since their herds could fatten on the natural grasses. In years of drought, they had to feed their cattle hay or cottonseed cake, a costly practice that could wipe out their profits.

Growth and specialization. The cattle industry tended to become more and more specialized. Many ranchers on the plains began to concentrate on breeding and raising cattle. The steers were then sold to farmers in the rich corn and pasture lands of the prairies. After being fattened for market, the cattle were shipped to nearby stockyards in Omaha, Kansas City, St. Joseph, Sioux City, St. Paul-Minneapolis, and Chicago (see map, page 78). There they were slaughtered and transported in refrigerator cars to eastern cities and sometimes from there to Europe.

Ranchers used the prairies, the semiarid plains, the high plateaus, and the mountain valleys of the West for cattle grazing lands. On these lands they produced a substantial portion of the nation's meat and wool. By the 1890's the western livestock industry had become an organized, specialized business, closely tied to the nation's economic life.

SECTION SURVEY

IDENTIFY: Cattle Kingdom, longhorns, vaqueros, long drive, open range, ranch.

1. What was the relationship between the railroads and the long drive?
2. (a) Why was the open range important to the cattle industry? (b) Why did it disappear?
3. Map Study: Look at the map on page 78. (a) Locate the original cattle-grazing area in Texas. (b) Locate three cattle trails and name them. (c) Why was Kansas City important to the cattle industry? (d) How can you tell that Chicago was an important trading center in 1890?

4 Farmers plow the tough sod of the last frontier

Farm families, single men, and some single women followed the cattle ranchers onto the prairies and plains. From 1870 to 1900, American pioneers settled more land than had all previous generations combined.

In the 263 years from the first tiny settlement at Jamestown in 1607 until 1870, white settlers claimed and occupied nearly 408 million acres (165 million hectares) of what had once been Indian land. This pace was almost leisurely compared to the speed with which later settlers conquered the prairies and the plains. In the 30 years between 1870 and 1900, pioneers settled an additional 430 million acres (174 million hectares). This was an area roughly equal to the combined areas of Norway, Sweden, Denmark, the Netherlands, Belgium, Germany, and France.

What was happening in America at this time to make possible the rapid settlement of the last frontier?

Free land. One attraction of the West was free land. In 1862 Congress enacted the Homestead Act, which granted 160 acres (64.8 hectares) to any individual who wished to settle a farm, or, as it was called, a "homestead."

Farmers as well as land speculators rushed to accept the offer. Thousands were ex-soldiers who sought new homes in the West. Thousands of others came from worn-out farms in the East, particularly from New England, in the hope of finding more fertile land. Still other

In 1888 these settlers in Custer County, Nebraska, used the side of a hill as the basis for their home. The house is part dugout and part sod walls and roof. Here the members of the family proudly pose in front of their home with their possessions — cow, horses, cart, and plow — for a traveling photographer.

thousands came from Europe. In many areas of the Middle West, more than half of the pioneer settlers were immigrants — Germans, Norwegians, Swedes, Danes, Czechs, Finns, and Russians.

Railroads and settlement. Without the railroad, however, the free land in the West, no matter how attractive, would have remained unpopulated. During the 1870's and the 1880's, four great transcontinental railroads crossed the prairies and the plains. These railroads along with their branch lines opened up the western country for settlement.

The rail lines into and through the wild western country were built only at enormous cost. Moreover, the investment was extremely risky. Investors did not know when, if ever, the new railroads would begin to make a profit and reward them for their risks. Thus the government, which was eager to have the railroads built, encouraged the pioneer railroad compa-

nies with cash subsidies and grants of land.

At the time the grants were made to the railroads, the land itself was almost worthless. Before the railroad companies could profit from their grants, they had to persuade people to move into the unsettled areas. Because the land was close to the railroads and therefore would be valuable, the railroad companies could hope to sell it, even though free land was available in more remote areas. More important was the fact that once the land was settled, the railroads would gain revenue from passengers and freight. In addition, any land that the railroads could not sell immediately would rise in value as settlers built farms, villages, and towns along the right of way.

With such things in mind, the railroads started extensive advertising campaigns. They sent literature and agents all over the United States and even into Europe. Life on the plains was pictured in glowing colors. As an added lure, prospective purchasers were sometimes

81

offered free railroad transportation to any land they might buy. The transatlantic steamship lines were always eager to obtain passengers and freight. They also began advertising campaigns in Europe.

The problems of houses and fences. Despite such efforts, settlers did not at first pour into the plains. For one thing, many still believed the old myth of the Great American Desert. An even more important factor slowing settlement was the scarcity of wood.

Pioneer families solved the problem of housing, as people have always done, by making use of whatever building material was available. On the plains this was sod. Cut out of the soil, bricklike chunks of sod formed the walls of shelters. With a few precious pieces of wood the settlers framed the roof, finishing it with a layer of sod to keep out wind and rain and snow.

Fencing presented an even more difficult problem. Pioneer families could not farm without fences to protect their crops, and on the plains there was no material for fences. The first pioneers tried everything, even mud

Changing Ways with TECHNOLOGY

DETAIL OF BARBED WIRE

BARBED-WIRE FENCE

On the Great Plains, fences were needed to hold range cattle and keep them off farmland. There were too few trees for stump fences or rail fences. However in 1874 farmers and herders began using barbed wire, which cattle learned to avoid. Fence posts were made from scrap lumber or from the few available trees.

walls, but without success. Ordinary wire strung between a few precious wooden posts was not effective. Cattle could get their heads through the smooth strands of wire and gradually work an opening in the fence.

The problem of fencing was finally solved by Joseph Glidden with his invention of barbed wire. Glidden took out his patent in 1874. Barbed-wire fences proved effective as a barrier to cattle, and within 10 years the open range was criss-crossed by a network of barbed-wire fences.

The problem of water. Scarcity of water, like scarcity of wood, was a problem that pioneer farm families had never had to face in the eastern part of the United States. Eastern farmers took their water from springs bubbling to the surface or from shallow wells. On the Great Plains, where the water was much deeper underground, machinery was needed to drill deeper wells. Once the well shafts had reached the water, the farmers then needed mechanical pumps to draw the water to the surface.

In a search for oil during the 1860's, petroleum companies developed new drilling machinery capable of penetrating farther beneath the surface than ever before. This machinery speedily found its way to the Great Plains. Farmers and ranchers used it to tap water supplies deep underground.

Meanwhile, other inventors were developing windmills capable of operating pumps to draw water to the surface. Daniel Halladay of Connecticut developed the self-governing windmill. This device automatically adjusted itself to wind pressure and thus operated at a uniform speed.

Windmills were first used on the Great Plains to provide water for steam locomotives crossing the plains and for herds of cattle. The windmill really came into its own when farmers began to settle on the semiarid lands. Factories producing windmills were soon doing a thriving business.

Other problems. Railroads, barbed wire, factory-made windmills—all products of the new industrial age—helped farmers conquer the Great Plains. So, too, did the development of dry farming. Dry farming involved deep plowing and careful cultivation to keep the surface of the soil pulverized and thus conserve as much precious moisture as possible.

The pioneer farm families had other prob-

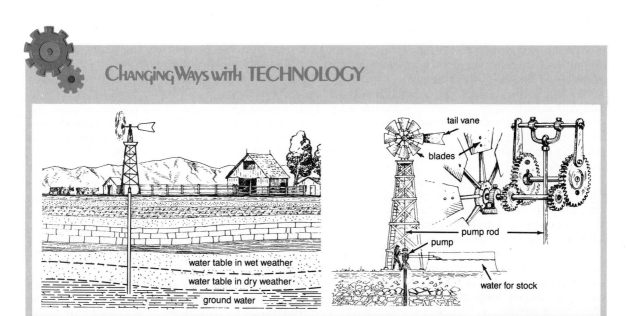

tail vane

blades

pump rod

pump

water for stock

water table in wet weather

water table in dry weather

ground water

WINDMILL FOR WATER

On the Great Plains, the table of ground water was so deep that human strength could not bring the water to the surface. The windmill solved this problem for settlers. The circular motion of the windmill blades was translated by a series of gears into the up-and-down motion of a rod. The rod powered a pump that brought water from the water table to the surface. Here the water flowed into tanks from which livestock could drink.

lems to solve, problems for which inventors, manufacturers, and agricultural experts had no ready answers. For one thing, the cattle ranchers resented the settlers who broke up the open range with their fences. Bitter fights raged in the early days between ranchers and farmers, and many unmarked graves soon dotted the plains. However, it was an unequal struggle, and by sheer force of numbers the farmers eventually won.

Nature also contributed to the settlers' difficulties. Until men and women learned how to deal with the plains environment, life was sometimes extremely harsh. The unrelieved round of daily labor impressed writers who tried to describe the life of the farmers on the Great Plains. O. E. Rölvaag (ROHL·vahg), author of *Giants in the Earth* and *Peder Victorious,* was one such writer. His novels provide a picture of empty plains and lives spent beneath a burning sun, of grasshopper plagues, of drought, of ruined crops, of bitter cold, and of blinding blizzards. Many pioneers gave up the difficult struggle and moved back east, but others remained.

Farm families in the 1880's and 1890's also encountered many new problems created by in-dustrialism. In the new industrial age, as you will read, farmers became increasingly concerned with freight and shipping charges, prices fixed in distant markets, the cost of farm machinery, interest rates on mortgages, and many other factors they could not control.

The Oklahoma Sooners. After the Civil War, many Plains Indians were moved to western portions of Indian Territory. This left a large area of unoccupied land in the central part of present-day Oklahoma. Several treaties had reserved these lands for the Five Civilized tribes—the Cherokees, Creeks, Chickasaws, Choctaws, and Seminoles. When white intruders moved onto this land, federal troops at first drove them off. In 1885, however, the government negotiated with the Creeks and Seminoles to open this part of Indian territory to white settlement.

In March 1889 President Benjamin Harrison issued a proclamation that set in motion a wild rush to the District of Oklahoma. The President announced that free homesteads of 160 acres (64.8 hectares) would be available "at and after the hour of twelve o'clock noon, on the twenty-second day of April." The army immediately set up patrols along the district boundaries to guard against premature entry and waited for the rush to begin.

It was a short wait. By April 22 almost 100,000 land-hungry pioneers—some in wagons, others on horseback—were packed solidly along the boundary line. Exactly at noon the officer in charge fired a shot, and the wild stampede began.

Even the swiftest riders discovered that they were not there soon enough. Many Sooners had evaded the patrols, slipped across the boundary, and staked out claims before the area was officially opened.

Within a few hours of the deadline, every inch of Oklahoma District was occupied. Thousands of disappointed landseekers started back along the roads they had eagerly traveled a short time earlier.

More land was soon available—again at the expense of the Indians. In 1889 land previously reserved for the Sauk, Fox, Potawatomi, Cheyenne, and Arapaho Indians were thrown open to white settlement. In the years that followed, the huge Cherokee Strip and reservations assigned to the Kickapoo, Iowa, Comanche, Apache, and Wichita Indians were also opened to settlement. All told, the Indians lost more than 11 million acres (nearly 4.5 million hectares) of land to white settlers.

The last frontier. The roll call of states entering the Union in the half-century after 1865 is an impressive one. Nebraska entered in 1867; Colorado in 1876; North Dakota, South Dakota, Montana, and Washington all in 1889; Idaho and Wyoming in 1890; Utah in 1896; Oklahoma in 1907; and New Mexico and Arizona in 1912.

In 1890 the Superintendent of the Census Bureau made a significant statement: "Up to and including 1880," he declared, "the country had a frontier of settlement, but at present the unsettled area has been so broken into by isolated bodies of settlement that there can hardly be said to be a frontier line."

SECTION SURVEY

IDENTIFY: sod houses, Joseph Glidden, Daniel Halladay, dry farming, Oklahoma Sooners, the last frontier.

1. How was western settlement speeded by (a) the Homestead Act and (b) the railroads?

2. How did the farmers on the plains solve the problems of housing and fencing?

3. Why was the windmill important to the Great Plains farmers?

4. Picture Study: Look at the picture on page 81. (a) What does it indicate about what life was like for farm families on the plains? (b) How did the natural environment affect farmers' lives?

---

5 Miners find new treasure in the western mountains

Developments of the new industrial age made it possible for the farmer to conquer the last western frontiers. The West, in turn, helped to speed the Industrial Revolution. From western farms came unending food supplies for the growing city populations. From western mines came an apparently limitless supply of gold and silver to provide capital to build industries. From other western mines came a steadily swelling volume of iron, copper, and other metals.

"Forty-Niners" and "Fifty-Niners." The discovery of gold in California drew fortune hunters by the tens of thousands to the Pacific coast in 1849–50. Some of the "Forty-Niners" made fortunes, but most were disappointed. Refusing to admit defeat, prospectors began to explore the valleys and slopes of the mountainous regions between the Pacific Ocean and the Great Plains. The development of mining communities again put pressure on the government to force Indians onto reservations.

In 1859, prospectors discovered gold near Pikes Peak in the unorganized territory of Colorado. More than 100,000 "Fifty-Niners" rushed to the scene to stake their claims. Caravans of covered wagons lumbered across the plains with the slogan "Pikes Peak or bust" lettered on the white canvas. Some prospectors shouldered packs and crossed the plains on foot. Others pulled handcarts behind them. Perhaps half of the fortune hunters returned the way they had come, with their slogan changed to "Busted, by gosh!" Nevertheless, enough remained to organize the Territory of Colorado in 1861.

Even more valuable than the Colorado deposits were the discoveries of silver in 1859 in

Taylor, Nevada, was one of many mining towns that boomed for a while, then faded away. Here it is in its heyday in 1881. Note the American flag flying at half-mast in honor of the recently assassinated President Garfield.

the western part of the Territory of Utah. Within a decade nearly $150 million worth of silver and gold had been extracted from the famous Comstock Lode in what is now Nevada (see map, page 78). By 1890 the total had reached $340 million. Enough of the early prospectors stayed after the stampede of 1859 to organize the Territory of Nevada, which became a state in 1864.

Gold in the Black Hills. In 1874, as you have read, prospectors found gold in the Black Hills of South Dakota (see map, page 78), and another gold rush followed. This area was Indian territory, the Sioux Reservation, which the federal government was supposed to preserve for the Indians. However, the government made only half-hearted efforts to keep prospectors out of the region. The lure of gold was too strong, and the government soon completely abandoned its efforts to protect the Indians. In 1877 the government opened the entire area to white settlers.

Early mining communities. During and after the Civil War, mining communities sprang up in many areas of the West. Life in these mining camps has been described vividly in *The Luck of Roaring Camp* by Bret Harte and in *Roughing It* by Mark Twain. These and other contemporary accounts present a picture of wild, lawless communities of tents, rough board shacks, and smoke-filled saloons strung along a muddy street.

Each mining camp passed through several stages of development. At first, people made their own laws, relying for safety upon fists or guns to protect themselves and their families. Then some citizens began to organize as private police forces, often called "vigilantes" (vij·ih·LAN·teez), in an effort to maintain order. Soon men and women built schools and churches—crude shacks, but important steps toward civilized living. With the schools and churches came organized local government. Then came the appeal to Congress for recognition as a United States territory. Eventually

The lack of women in mining camps did not mean that there could be no dances. "Ladies" at such a dance were often designated by their clothing or by a handkerchief on their sleeves.

the territory would adopt a constitution and be admitted to the Union as a state.

Today the mountain regions, the valleys, and the high plateaus of the West are dotted with abandoned mining communities—ghost towns. The gaping mine shafts and the sagging, windowless cabins stand as mute testimony to the fact that prospectors and miners once pioneered on this vast frontier.

Systematic exploration. The early discoveries of gold and silver acted like magnets, drawing adventuresome prospectors into the unexplored regions of the West. Before long, however, exploration was conducted on a more systematic basis, partly because of federal efforts. Between 1865 and 1879, the federal government sent many expeditions into the mountains, and in 1879 the United States Geological Survey was organized. Private industry also sent out carefully organized expeditions. The picturesque prospector with pack horse and hand tools continued to roam the mountains. Long before the end of the 1800's, however, an increasing number of the mineral deposits were discovered by expeditions equipped with the latest technological devices and knowledge of geology.

The development of the nation's industries brought a growing demand for metals of all kinds. Copper, needed when the electrical industry developed, was found in enormous quantities around Butte, Montana; Bingham, Utah; and in Nevada and Arizona. Lead and zinc were discovered in the same area. These and other metals have helped the United States to become the leading industrial nation in the world.

Mining as big business. Other developments brought about great changes in mining. New methods of extracting the metal from the ore were discovered. Colleges of mining engineering were opened, powerful machinery was invented, great corporations were organized, and armies of skilled technicians and engineers moved into the mining regions. New equipment and the growing knowledge of chemistry and metallurgy enabled companies to work low-grade ores with profit.

By the 1890's mining had become big business. Engineers, equipped with the latest tools of science and technology, were converting the West into a region of enormous value to the industrial development of the nation.

SECTION SURVEY

IDENTIFY: "Pikes Peak or bust," Comstock Lode, Bret Harte, Mark Twain, vigilantes, ghost towns, United States Geological Survey.

1. (a) Who were the "Forty-Niners"? (b) Who were the "Fifty-Niners"? (c) What impact did these people have on settlement of the West?

2. (a) Describe life in the early mining communities. (b) What stages of development did the communities go through?

3. How and why was the individual prospector replaced by organized mining expeditions?

4. What circumstances helped mining to become big business by the 1890's?

Chapter Survey

Summary: Tracing the Main Ideas

The conquest of the Plains Indians and the settlement of the land west of the Mississippi River took place, for the most part, during and immediately after the Civil War. Settlers poured into the prairies and plains in great numbers. By the 1890's they had settled so much of the West that the Superintendent of the Census Bureau announced that the frontier no longer existed.

This vast region, almost half of the total area of the present United States, had from time immemorial belonged to the original inhabitants, the Indians. The white government and the onrush of settlers drove the Indians from their lands and forced them to live on reservations. Efforts to "Americanize" the original Americans ended in failure.

The West that the whites had conquered was not one region, but many regions, each basically different from the others. The groups of settlers—cattle ranchers, farmers, and miners—learned to adapt themselves to their environment. They learned to make use of the most easily developed natural resources—the grasslands, the fertile soil, and the precious metals. As the years passed, they learned how to modify the environment and to seek out and develop other resources.

The conquest of the West was, in one sense, merely a prelude to an even larger chapter in American history—the transformation of the nation from a mainly agricultural country to one of the great industrial giants of the modern world. That industrial transformation is the subject of Unit Two and of later chapters in this book.

Inquiring into History

1. The United States tried to solve the "Indian problem" by eliminating the Indians. Do you agree or disagree with this statement? Give evidence to support your answer.
2. What actions did the federal government take to encourage the settlement and development of the West?
3. (a) Compare the problems that miners, cattle raisers, and farmers faced in settling the land west of the Mississippi River. (b) What solutions did each find for their problems? (c) How effective were these solutions?
4. The last frontier disappeared by 1890. (a) Explain how this occurred. (b) In your opinion, what is the significance of the frontier in American history?
5. (a) What effect did the Industrial Revolution in America have on the development of the American West? (b) What effect did the development of the American West have on the Industrial Revolution in America?

Relating Past to Present

1. (a) Is scarcity of water still a problem in the West? Give evidence to support your answer. (b) How do present methods of water conservation compare with those of the early West?

2. Compare American mining in the late 1800's to mining today in terms of (a) major minerals mined, (b) importance of these minerals to the economy, and (c) mining methods.
3. Do railroads today play the same role in the economy of the West that they did in the late 1800's? Why or why not?

Developing Social Science Skills

1. Study the map on pages 690–91. (a) Locate the Great Plains. (b) Name an important river that crosses the Great Plains. (c) With the help of the map and chart on page 694, determine from what other geographical areas new states entered the Union after the Civil War.
2. Prepare a bulletin board display about the cowboy's life. You might include such items as illustrations of equipment, lyrics from cowboy songs, and copies of paintings by Frederick Remington or Charles Russell.
3. Conduct research and prepare a report on one of the following: dry-farming methods; the role of women in the development of the West; the importance of blacks in western development; the life of Cochise, Black Elk, or Sarah Winnemucca.
4. Look at the pictures and read the captions on pages 82–3. How did the settlers of the Great Plains use technology to help them adapt to local conditions?

Unit Survey

For Further Inquiry

1. (a) Describe Reconstruction, as it was finally carried out under the Radical Republican Congress. (b) Do you think Reconstruction was successful? Explain.
2. Compare the situation of Southern blacks and western Indians from 1865 to 1900. Consider (a) economic status, (b) relations with the federal government, (c) treatment by whites.
3. Did the federal government become more powerful in the years after the Civil War? Give evidence to support your answer.
4. What evidence is there that industrialization was increasingly affecting the nation's development after the Civil War?
5. Trace the relationship between Congress and the President between 1865 and 1900.
6. Did the United States become more or less democratic during the years 1865–1900? Give reasons for your answer.

Projects and Activities

1. Imagine you are a journalist in the South just after the Civil War. Write a feature story describing the conditions that you observe in the cities and the countryside.
2. Write a skit about the impeachment of Andrew Johnson. Perhaps some of your classmates can join you in acting out the skit for the class.
3. On a blank map of the United States, illustrate the major events in U.S.–Indian relations from 1865 to 1900. Include such items as (a) battles, (b) signing of treaties, (c) establishment of reservations.
4. Conduct research and prepare an oral or written report on the roles of women on the "last frontier." Look into their political status, as well as their roles in daily life.
5. Select one event from the timeline here. (a) Form two hypotheses (educated guesses) about consequences that might have followed from the event. For example: 1874—grasshopper plague. (1) Many farmers soon went bankrupt. (2) The price of bread later went up. (b) Conduct research in order to test your hypotheses against additional information.

Exploring Your Region

1. Find out what life was like in your region at the time when it was part of the frontier. How do your findings compare with the account of the "last frontier" in your textbook?
2. (a) What were the main ways of making a living in your community in 1880? (b) What sort of economic relations did your community have with other areas of the country? (For example, did it send finished products to other areas? or buy food from other areas? or serve as a trading center for several areas?)

Suggested Reading

1. *Dr. George Washington Carver, Scientist,* Shirley Graham. Biography of the son of a slave whose determination enables him to become a distinguished scientist.
2. *Bury My Heart at Wounded Knee,* Dee Brown. A dramatic account of the "last frontier" from the Indian point of view.
3. *History of the Confident Years,* American Heritage. A highly illustrated history of the years from 1865 to 1900.
4. *Giants in the Earth,* Ole Edvart Rölvaag. Moving novel of the difficult life of pioneers in North Dakota.
5. *Duel in the Sun,* Nevin Busch. Excellent novel of the "wild west."

Unit Two

The Rise of Industrialism

1860's - 1890's

Chapter 4
Business Pioneers and the Growth of American Industry

1. Transportation and communications systems bind the nation together.
2. Expanding business creates more products for more people.
3. New forms of business organization appear as industry expands.
4. Business pioneers give new directions to American life.

Chapter 5
The Struggle of American Workers to Organize

1. Industrialism creates new problems for wage earners.
2. Immigration adds strength and variety to American society.
3. Wage earners organize to overcome their grievances.
4. Organized labor faces opposition as it seeks reforms.

Chapter 6
The Revolt of Farmers Against Big Business Practices

1. Farm life remains laborious, but simple.
2. Farmers face complex new problems in the industrial age.
3. Farm organizations join efforts to regulate the railroads.
4. Farm organizations put increasing pressure on government.
5. The farmers fail to win control of the national government.

Chapter 7
New Life Styles in the New Industrial Age

1. Cities grow and change under the impact of industrialism.
2. Education responds to the changing patterns of American life.
3. American writing reflects the new industrial age.
4. Architecture and other fine arts respond to a changing society.
5. New forms of recreation enrich American life.

Chapter 4

Business Pioneers and the Growth of American Industry

Changing Ways of American Life

1860's–1890's

In the 1870's a large majority of Americans lived in the country or in small rural villages and towns. This was the age of dirt roads, of carriages and wagons, and of covered bridges, their wooden sides plastered with circus posters and notices of county fairs. It was the age of oil lamps, woodstoves, the hand pump or the open well, and the Saturday-evening bath in a washtub in the center of the kitchen floor.

This was the age of sewing circles and spelling bees, the one-room schoolhouse, and the country store with its tubs of butter and pickles, its cracker barrel, and its clutter of groceries and clothing and household articles hanging from the ceiling and spilling over the shelves. Symbols of the age were the small family-owned factory and the blacksmith shop at the crossroads with its charcoal fire, its huge bellows, and its burly smith in grimy leather apron shaping and fitting a new set of shoes to a neighbor's horse.

But a new age was coming into being. Symbols of the new age were the rapidly growing cities, large factories with smoke pouring from their towering stacks, long lines of railroad cars rumbling across the countryside, and a growing number of farm machines standing outside barns or operating in the fields. In brief, life in the new industrial age was being transformed in many ways.

This, then, is the story of how America began to change from a rural, agricultural economy to an urban, industrial way of life.

THE CHAPTER IN OUTLINE

1. Transportation and communications systems bind the nation together.

2. Expanding business creates more products for more people.

3. New forms of business organization appear as industry expands.

4. Business pioneers give new directions to American life.

1 Transportation and communications systems bind the nation together

The heart of an industrial society is the city. It is here that most factories and workers are concentrated and that most raw materials are fashioned into finished products. It is also here that most goods and services are bought and sold.

If the city is the heart of an industrial society, the routes of transportation are the veins and arteries. Into the city flow the vital resources gathered from farm and mine and forest and sea. Out of the city flow the unending supplies of manufactured articles. These move day and night over a vast transportation network to every corner of the land and overseas to other lands.

Just as the human body cannot function without heart and veins and arteries, so an industrial economy cannot function without its urban manufacturing centers and an efficient system of transportation and communications.

The growth of cities. During the years between 1865 and 1900, the modern city with its busy railroad yards, its smoking factories, its wage earners, and its office workers took shape. During these years, scores of American cities grew from sprawling towns to huge urban centers. In 1870 about 75 percent of the people lived in the country or in communities of fewer than 2,500 inhabitants. By 1900 only about 60 percent of all Americans lived on farms or in small rural communities. The urban population had skyrocketed. In 1870 only about 10 million of the nation's total population of 40 million were urban dwellers. By 1900 more than 30 million of America's 76 million people lived in urban areas.

By 1899 the population of Chicago had passed the million mark. The city's position as a center of transportation was one reason for its remarkable growth. Every day steam-powered ships moved people and cargo between Chicago and other points along Lake Michigan, including Milwaukee.

Many revolutionary developments aided the growth of cities. Among them were the discovery of new sources of power, the application of hundreds of new inventions and new processes, and the enormous expansion of the nation's transportation and communications network.

The growth of railroads. Between 1870 and 1900, railway mileage in the United States increased from 53,000 miles (85,000 kilometers) to more than 190,000 miles (306,000 kilometers). During these same years, the railroads improved in speed, comfort, and safety. Double sets of tracks replaced single sets, allowing streams of traffic to flow in two directions at once. Iron rails, which had shattered beneath heavy loads, were replaced by steel rails. Bridges of iron and later of steel replaced wooden bridges. Coal, a more efficient fuel, replaced wood in the tenders of locomotives. In 1869 George Westinghouse patented the air brake, a system of power braking more efficient than the old hand brake. George M. Pullman's sleeping cars increased the comfort of passengers, and dining cars and parlor cars also appeared.

The success of the first transcontinental line (page 71) quickly led to the construction of several others. By 1893 a half-dozen major, or trunk, lines crossed the plains and mountains to the Far West. All over the United States feeder, or branch, lines linked the trunk lines with surrounding areas. Soon a network of steel rails served every part of the country.

Financing railroad construction. The construction of railroads, especially of lines reaching into the still unsettled West, was enormously expensive. To encourage the building of new lines, the government provided grants of land and loans of money.

The original land grants set aside large areas of land within which the railroad could claim a specified amount. Until the railroads exercised their claim, none of the land could be sold to the public. Some railroads ran into construction or other difficulties and did not exercise their choice for ten years or more. Others never exercised the right at all, and the government took title to the land. In round figures, the national government turned over 131 million acres (53 million hectares) of land to the railroads. At the time, this land was worth a total of approximately $123 million. The government also made loans of close to $65 million to the railroads.

In return, the land-grant railroads and their competitors carried government troops, military freight, and United States mail for less than the standard rates. In 1945 a Congressional committee reported that the railroads had already "contributed over $900 million in payment of the lands which were transferred to them under the Land Grant Act." In addition, the railroads repaid the original government loans along with an additional $103 million in interest.

Other transportation. While land transportation improved, traffic on the sea lanes and inland waterways also developed. After 1850, sailing ships on the oceans and on the Great Lakes were replaced by steam-driven, steel-hulled freighters and sleek passenger liners. These ocean-going vessels carried millions of emigrants from Europe to the rest of the world, mostly to the United States. They also carried raw materials and manufactured goods to and from the expanding world markets.

Meanwhile, in the growing urban areas, new methods of transportation enabled people to move quickly within the crowded cities. By the late 1800's, electric trolleys were rapidly replacing horse-drawn cars. Steam-driven and, later, electric-powered elevated trains rumbled along above crowded city streets. By the early 1900's, subway trains carried passengers below the streets of New York and Boston.

As steel-framed skyscrapers climbed higher into the air, elevators, powered first by steam and then by electricity, carried passengers and freight from story to story. Without the elevator skyscrapers could not have been used.

From telegraph to telephone. Equally important developments came in the field of communications. Until the 1870's the telegraph had been the most significant advance in communication since the invention of printing from movable type. From the 1870's on, however, major new inventions appeared one after the other.

The telegraph had been first successfully developed in the United States by Samuel F. B. Morse and in England by Charles Wheatstone during the late 1830's and the early 1840's—just as the new steam railroads began to appear. The telegraph moved across the country with the railroads. Indeed, without a telegraph

Before Christopher Sholes developed the typewriter, business correspondence had to be handcopied. As women learned how to operate the new machine, increasing numbers of them entered the nation's labor force.

system the nation's railroads could not have operated safely.

In 1866, about 25 years after Morse's invention, Cyrus W. Field succeeded in laying a transatlantic telegraph cable. During the next few years, additional underwater cables connected North America with other continents. Americans now had almost instantaneous communication with the rest of the world.

In 1876 Alexander Graham Bell, a teacher of the deaf in Boston, applied for a patent on a telephone he had invented. Bell's telephone quickly captured the public's imagination, and in 1885 the American Telephone and Telegraph Company was organized to put the new invention into widespread use.

Other inventions. The telegraph, the underwater cable, and the telephone were landmarks in the history of communications, but other important inventions and developments also reshaped American life. In the 1860's

Christopher Sholes of Wisconsin developed the typewriter, which later became an essential part of all business operations. An improved postal system, without which modern business could not function, was also developed.

New machines for making cheap paper from wood pulp and for printing newspapers, books, and magazines also contributed to more effective communication. There was also the camera, which later provided new forms of recreation as well as new techniques for industry and research.

By 1900, improvements in transportation and communications were binding all parts of the United States into a single complex economic unit. The National Banking Act of 1863 had established a sound, uniform currency for the entire country. Specialized business enterprises, both agricultural and industrial, sprang up in all parts of the land, each playing its part in the ever-expanding, interlocking economic system.

IDENTIFY: urban center, George M. Pullman, trunk lines, telegraph, Cyrus W. Field, Alexander Graham Bell.

1. Explain this statement: If the city is the heart of an industrial society, the routes of transportation are the veins and arteries.

2. (a) Why did the federal government help finance the building of the railroads? (b) What methods did it use? (c) How did the railroads repay the government for federal aid granted them?

3. Timeline Study: (a) Prepare a timeline of the major inventions mentioned on pages 92–3. Include at least one invention that depended for its development on an earlier invention.

2 Expanding business creates more products for more people

The industrialization of the United States was the result of many different developments in many different fields. These developments, taking place more or less at the same time, combined to transform the older ways of life. They included new sources of energy, new machines, new and bigger industries, and new methods of distributing and selling products and services.

New sources of energy. In the late 1700's, people learned how to convert the energy of wood and coal into steam and to use the steam as a source of power in tasks that had been done for centuries by human, animal, or water power. For more than a hundred years, the steam engine remained the most important "mechanical slave" ever developed up to that time. Then, in the late 1800's, two new sources of power—oil and electricity—were harnessed.

From earliest times people had known about the dark, thick substance that oozed from the earth in certain places and that is now called "petroleum," or "oil." In the early 1850's, kerosene, an efficient and inexpensive fuel for lamps, was first refined from petroleum. The growing demand for kerosene prompted Edwin L. Drake, a retired railroad conductor, to try to drill an oil well near Titusville, Pennsylvania, in 1859. While he was drilling, people thought he was crazy. When the oil began to flow, however, people quickly began sinking wells of their own.

Kerosene rapidly replaced whale oil as an efficient fuel for lamps. In every American city, peddlers carted kerosene through the streets, selling it from door to door. As the years passed, oil was also increasingly used as a lubricant for the nation's many new machines.

The development of the internal combustion engine, which burned gasoline or diesel fuel—both refined from oil—finally turned oil into one of the nation's major sources of power. In Chapter 9 you will read how oil as a source of power had a revolutionary affect on American life.

Power from electricity. Electricity, like oil, was known long before it was put to practical use. The work of two Italians, Galvani and Volta, led in the late 1700's and early 1800's to the invention of the storage battery. The storage battery supplied small amounts of electric current at low voltages and greatly aided those who were experimenting with the uses of electricity. The discoveries of the principles governing the electric motor and the dynamo had even greater effects. Although many persons contributed to these discoveries, a major share of the credit belongs to England's Michael Faraday and America's Joseph Henry.

Thousands of Americans first learned about the dynamo at the Centennial Exhibition at Philadelphia in 1876, where they saw one in operation converting mechanical energy into electrical energy. In 1882 Thomas Edison built in New York City the first large central power plant in the United States for generating electricity. Edison drove his dynamos with steam engines. Other steam-powered electric generating plants soon appeared in other cities. Another giant stride forward came in 1895 with the opening at Niagara Falls of the first large hydroelectric plant for producing electricity from water power. In spite of these developments, by 1900 only about 2 percent of America's manufacturing industries were powered by electricity.

Steel for new industries. Behind the story of new sources of power lies still another story—the discovery of new ways of producing steel. Steel, a mixture of iron, carbon, and other elements, was not a new material. People had made it for centuries and fashioned it into weapons, tools, and utensils. Until the mid-

1800's no one knew how to produce steel cheaply and in large quantities.

The United States had an abundance of the raw materials vital to the new industrial age — iron ore and coal. Immense deposits of iron ore lay near the western shores of Lake Superior. Nearly one half of the world's known coal deposits were waiting to be tapped.

In the 1850's Henry Bessemer in England and William Kelly in the United States independently discovered a new process for making large quantities of steel cheaply by burning out impurities in molten iron with a blast of air. During the next few years, even more effective processes were developed.

The annual production of steel in the United States soared. In 1870, for example, the United States produced only about 68,000 tons (about 62,000 metric tons) of steel. By 1918 production had increased to 44 million tons (40 million metric tons).

The growth of mass production. Much of the growing steel production at this time went into the construction of railroads, bridges, heavy machinery, factories, mills, and other industrial enterprises. American businesses were laying the foundations of an industrial system that eventually would make the United States the most productive country in the world. The system would also provide Americans with the highest national standard of living in history.

As businesses expanded and factories grew larger, their owners and managers developed more and more efficient methods of production. During the first half of the 1800's, Eli Whitney and others had developed interchangeable parts. This development in turn called for a **division of labor.** For instance, a shoemaker no longer made an entire shoe. Instead, in large shoe factories, one worker might run a machine that cut only heels. Another worker might run a machine that shaped soles. All the different parts were then brought together at a central location and assembled by other workers into a shoe. In this way, vast quantities of shoes could be made quickly and cheaply. This division of labor was soon adopted by most American industries. It made possible the **mass production** of products of every kind.

New ways of selling products. The small general store as well as the small family-owned factory became less important in

After 1859 the sound of an oil gusher was welcome to most Americans (though not to the young girl here). Such wells soon made the United States a major oil producer, adding greatly to its industrial growth.

America during the late 1800's. New types of stores arose to handle the ever-growing quantities of products from the nation's factories.

The **specialty store** concentrated upon a single line of goods — hardware, clothing, groceries, shoes, and so forth.

The **department store** combined many specialty stores under one roof. John C. Wanamaker opened one of the first department stores in the United States in Philadelphia in 1876. Marshall Field opened another in Chicago in 1881. Other department stores soon opened in other cities.

Chain stores—stores with branches in many cities—also began to appear. Pioneers in this field of selling were the Great Atlantic and Pacific Tea Company (A & P), founded in 1859, and the chain of stores started by Frank Woolworth in 1879. Chain stores, like department stores, bought goods in large quantities at low prices. They then passed on these low prices to their customers. Since women were commonly paid less than men, managers gladly hired women as clerks.

Large-scale professional advertising began to appear in the 1880's. Such advertising introduced new products, promoted mass purchasing, and helped create large national markets for the streams of new manufactured products that were now available.

Specialty stores, department stores, and chain stores were all part of the urban scene. In 1872, however, Aaron Montgomery Ward started in Chicago a mail-order business aimed at the rural market. A few years later, the Sears, Roebuck mail-order business was started. Montgomery Ward and Sears, Roebuck used the same business methods. Customers placed orders and paid for them by mail; their goods were shipped to them by mail or railway express. Catalogs from these two mail-order houses became prized possessions in rural households and in the bunkhouses and camps of cattle ranchers and sheepherders. They helped to bring the outside world to isolated farms and speeded the transformation of farm life.

SECTION SURVEY

IDENTIFY: Edwin L. Drake, Michael Faraday, Joseph Henry, Thomas Edison, Bessemer process, division of labor, mass production, Marshall Field, chain store.

1. In what ways did the revolution in power affect (a) workers and (b) manufacturers?

2. How did each of the following developments help transform the lives of average Americans in the late 1800's: (a) availability of kerosene, (b) cheap steel, (c) mass production?

3. What basic premise or idea did the following people have regarding the selling of goods: (a) Frank Woolworth, (b) John Wanamaker, (c) Montgomery Ward?

CHANGING WAYS WITH TECHNOLOGY

LANTERN

chimney

shade

flame regulator

reservoir and wick

TABLE LAMPS

KEROSENE LIGHTING

The wick was lit after it had absorbed kerosene from the reservoir. The glass chimney had to be cleaned frequently because soot from the flame accumulated inside.

3 New forms of business organization appear as industry expands

Most of America's factories and stores in the 1860's and 1870's were of the type known as **individual proprietorships**—small enterprises owned by individuals or families. The individual or the family members who owned a small factory knew all the workers, often by their first names. Most wage earners in the 1860's lived in small towns, worked in small factories, and often took part in community activities with their employers.

During the next 30 years, much of this small-town, personal relationship disappeared. It was crowded out by the huge industrial plant located in or on the outskirts of a large city and employing hundreds, even thousands, of wage earners, who were often strangers to one another and even more remote from the owners.

Partnerships. As businesses grew in size, the owners had to find ways of sharing expanding costs and responsibilities. The **partnership** as a form of business organization became more and more common.

A partnership of two or more persons offers greater capital and skill than a single person can usually provide, but partnerships do have one major weakness. Each partner is completely liable, or responsible, for anything that happens to the business.

Corporations. As industries grew another form of organization, the **corporation,** became more common. It gradually replaced individual proprietorship and partnerships as the leading form of business organization.

To start a corporation, three or more persons apply to a state legislature for a **charter,** or license, to start a specific business enterprise. This charter allows the interested persons to organize a corporation and sell shares of **stock,** or certificates of ownership, to raise the capital needed to carry on the enterprise. The **stockholders** or **shareholders** — those who invest money in the enterprise — may periodically receive **dividends,** that is, a share of the corporation's profits. Legally, a corporation is regarded as an individual — an "artificial person" entirely separate from its owners. It possesses certain rights, such as the right to make contracts, to buy and sell property, and to sue and be sued in court.

The corporation has important advantages over the individual proprietorship and the partnership. First, the corporation can draw upon very large supplies of capital because it can sell shares of stock to many people. Second, the charter gives the corporation perpetual life; that is, the corporation is not ended by the death or resignation of one or several of its owners. Third, stockholders can sell all or part of their stock whenever they choose. Finally,

Massachusetts had served as the cradle of the American Industrial Revolution. The state maintained its leading position in manufacturing during the late 1800's. The huge factory complex shown in this picture is the Assabet Manufacturing Company, located in Maynard, Massachusetts.

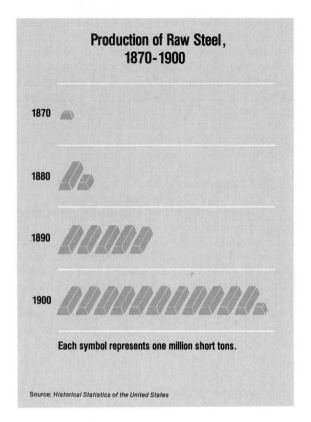

Production of Raw Steel, 1870-1900

1870

1880

1890

1900

Each symbol represents one million short tons.

Source: *Historical Statistics of the United States*

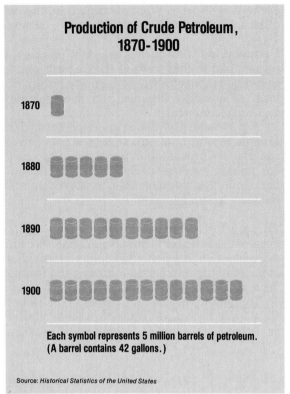

Production of Crude Petroleum, 1870-1900

1870

1880

1890

1900

Each symbol represents 5 million barrels of petroleum. (A barrel contains 42 gallons.)

Source: *Historical Statistics of the United States*

investors have only limited liability. That is, if the corporation fails, they lose only the money they have invested in its stocks; they cannot be made to pay any debts owed by the bankrupt corporation.

During the first half of the 1800's, only a few large American industries were organized as corporations, and these were usually owned by only a handful of persons. By the 1860's, however, business owners needed increasing amounts of capital to build, equip, and operate the new enterprises that were exploiting the vast resources of America's forests, soils, mines, and waters. Because corporations could gather large amounts of capital, they became very common after 1860.

Business consolidation. During the latter half of the 1800's, there was also a growing trend toward business combination, or consolidation. Corporations in the same type of business would frequently join together to create large combinations.

Economists have pointed out many advantages in these combinations. Several corporations, when banded together, could save some of the costs of production and distribution. They could eliminate competing salespeople and advertising. They could purchase larger quantities of raw materials at lower prices and make better use of byproducts. They could arrange better bargains with banks, transportation companies, and workers. In short, through consolidation, businesses could substitute cooperation for competition and thus reduce waste, costs, and risky losses.

These large enterprises sometimes presented dangers to important principles of freedom in the American economic system. Through consolidation a group of corporations might gain monopoly control over a particular field of business. Monopoly control could lead to restraint of trade. That is, it could reduce competition, which lies at the heart of a free enterprise economy.

For example, a business combination might have so much power that it could undercut prices until its competitors failed. Then the combination could raise prices to make up its losses. Or if a consolidated enterprise gained monopoly control of an entire business field, it could charge excessive prices for its products or services. In such cases, consumers lost the right to shop around for the best bargains. These and other economic practices stemming from monopoly created problems for everyone.

Corporation pools. One of the earliest ways in which corporations combined was by organizing **pools.** To form a pool, several corporations simply agreed to divide all their business opportunities among themselves. For example, several railroads serving the same city might agree on what percentage of local business each would handle. Or they might agree to charge uniform freight rates so that none would gain a price advantage. Or a group of manufacturing corporations might agree to divide the country into several market areas, each reserved for the sales force of one of the corporations in the pool and off limits to all the others.

Unlike the corporation, which operated under a legal charter, a pooling agreement had no legal standing. For that reason, courts refused to judge cases in which a member of a pool violated such an agreement with the other members. However, in 1887, pools were declared illegal in interstate commerce and practically disappeared.

Powerful trusts. Meanwhile, other business owners developed a second form of business consolidation, called the **trust.** Business owners who wanted to organize a trust first had to reach an agreement with the major stockholders in the several corporations involved. The promise of greater profits from a larger organization was often all that was needed to persuade stockholders to enter a trust.

Under the trust agreement, the promoters of the trust, called the "trustees," gained control of the stock in all the corporations and thus of the corporation themselves. In exchange, the trustees gave the stockholders of the corporations trust certificates on which dividends were paid out of the profits of the trust.

With control of the stock in their hands, the trustees could run several corporations as a single giant business enterprise. If the trustees could get control of enough corporations, they could secure monopoly control of an entire business. They could then control prices. They could, for example, lower prices temporarily in one area to drive a competitor out of business, while raising prices everywhere else.

During the 1870's and the 1880's, giant trusts swallowed up corporations in many of the nation's largest industries, including oil, steel, sugar refining, and whisky distilling. When a trust did get control of enough corporations to secure a monopoly and end competition, it often raised prices on the products it controlled. The consumers and smaller competing businesses complained bitterly as the trusts closed in on them.

Magazines and newspapers of the time were filled with articles, letters, and editorials pointing out the evils of the "all-powerful monopolies" and pleading with the government to step in and restore freedom of enterprise. However, local, state, and federal governments had passed no laws that said trusts and monopolies were illegal, although under the **common law,°** which courts might or might not enforce, "conspiracies in restraint of trade" were forbidden.

The Sherman Antitrust Act. Finally, in 1890, during the administration of President Benjamin Harrison, Congress passed the Sherman Antitrust Act. The public assumed that the act was intended to restore a larger measure of free competition by breaking up giant "trusts"—a term that had come to mean any monopoly or near-monopoly of an industry. This also seemed to be what Congress intended, for Section 1 of the act declared, "Every contract, combination in the form of trust or otherwise, or conspiracy, in restraint of trade or commerce among the several states or with foreign nations is hereby declared to be illegal." The act further stated that individuals and corporations found guilty of violating the law would be liable to legal penalties.

Actually, few Americans, including lawyers and members of Congress, understood what the new law did and did not prohibit. The act failed to define such words as "trust," "combination," "conspiracy," and "monopoly." Because of such loose wording, the Sherman Antitrust Act was difficult to enforce. The government lost seven out of the first eight cases that it brought against giant business combinations, or trusts.

In 1895 the Supreme Court handed down a decision in the case of *U.S. v. E. C. Knight Company* that made the antitrust law almost meaningless. The Court ruled that the company, which had control of 98 percent of the sugar-refining business, was not guilty of violating the antitrust law because its control of the

°**common law:** a system of law based upon custom, tradition, and precedents established by courts of law.

refining process alone did not involve restraint of interstate trade. A monopoly itself was not illegal, the Court stated. It became illegal only when it served to restrain interstate trade.

This and other decisions by the Supreme Court convinced businesses that they were free to consolidate. Thus the movement to form business consolidations actually speeded up in the years after the Sherman Antitrust Act was passed. Some historians see in this development evidence that the act was not really a reform measure. Such historians instead regard the act as an effort by big business to combat the growth of organized labor.

Despite its glaring weakness, the Sherman Antitrust Act was an attempt by the federal government to make rules for the conduct of big business. It established an important precedent for later and more effective laws.

Holding companies. After 1890 some of the nation's business leaders abandoned the trust for another form of business consolidation — the **holding company.** To form a holding company, it was necessary to get a charter from one of the states. The directors of the holding company then issued stock in the holding company itself. With the money raised by selling this stock, the directors bought controlling shares of stock in two or more corporations that were actually engaged in producing goods or services, such as manufacturing companies or transportation companies. The holding company did not itself produce either goods or services, but the company did control all the corporations whose stock it held.

After the 1890's the holding company became very popular. It was legal. It was responsible for its actions because, unlike the trust, it operated under a charter that could be revoked if the terms were violated.

Other ways to consolidate. Another form of consolidation was an **interlocking directorate.** In an interlocking directorate, some or all of the directors of one company served as directors of several other companies. Thus they could develop a uniform policy for the entire industry.

There were, of course, other ways to establish a uniform policy. Directors of different companies could simply meet and make secret agreements on prices and other matters.

Business leaders who tried to establish uniform policies for an entire industry — either through interlocking directorates or through secret understandings — were subject to prosecution under the Sherman Antitrust Act. However, it was difficult to prove that a monopoly existed. It was especially difficult when the monopoly had been created by means of interlocking directorates and secret agreements.

SECTION SURVEY

IDENTIFY: partnership, corporation, stock, dividends, business consolidation, monopoly.

1. What advantages does the corporation have over the partnership as a method of business organization?
2. (a) Summarize the provisions of the Sherman Antitrust Act of 1890. (b) Why was this law difficult to enforce?
3. How did the Supreme Court decisions in the late 1800's aid big business?
4. Chart Study: Make a chart entitled "Forms of Business Consolidation" with four columns headed Pools, Trusts, Holding Companies, and Interlocking Directorates. Below each heading (a) define this form of business consolidation, (b) give reasons for its creation, (c) name objections to it, and (d) name methods used to control its abuses.

4 Business pioneers give new directions to American life

Those who presided over the new world of throbbing machines, noisy factories, and crowded cities were the business leaders and the financiers. Their influence was reflected in local, state, and national politics.

Influence of business leaders. Between 1789 and 1860, thirteen Presidents had been elected — seven from the South, six from the North. Between 1860 and 1900, each of the seven Presidents elected was from the industrial regions of the Northeast or from the Middle West. On nearly all essential issues, moreover, the major differences between the Republicans and Democrats diminished during these years.

The business leaders of this period were not all of a single type. They varied greatly in personalities, abilities, and methods of doing business. They were pioneers, with the virtues as well as the shortcomings of pioneers. Some were rough, some were refined. All were eager to seize the unlimited opportunities of the new industrial world emerging around them. Some were fabulously successful. Others, the small business owners, never amassed fortunes or won great power. All of them—big-business leaders and small-business owners alike—shared the ideal of self-reliant individualism. This ideal was also shared by the few women who were permitted to take an active part in business. Among these women were Nettie Fowler McCormick in farm machinery, Lydia Pinkham in patent medicines, and Kate Gleason in machine tools.

Cornelius Vanderbilt. "Commodore" Cornelius Vanderbilt was born in 1794, when George Washington was President of the United States. By 1865 Vanderbilt, who had started life as a poor boy, had accumulated great wealth and owned a fleet of steamships worth $10 million. When he died in 1877 at age 82, he was worth $105 million.

Even in his seventies, "Commodore" Vanderbilt was an energetic man with a defiant bearing. He could hardly write, his spelling was impossible, and his temper earned him many enemies. He seemed to act on impulse, following his own hunches. He even consulted astrologers or fortunetellers about how to manage his business affairs.

What did Vanderbilt contribute to American life? For one thing, he consolidated the railroad companies that provided service between New York and Chicago. Before he took control of the different lines, passengers and freight had to be transferred 17 times between the two cities during a 50-hour trip. When he had completed the consolidation, one train made the entire trip in about 24 hours. He replaced iron rails and wooden bridges with steel rails and steel bridges. He built double tracks to make two-way traffic safe and speedy. He constructed new locomotives and terminals. Achievements such as these helped to make possible the rapid development of America's industrial economy.

Andrew Carnegie. Andrew Carnegie was another fabulous business leader during the early decades of industrialism. Born in 1835 in Scotland, Carnegie came to America at age 12 and

Cornelius Vanderbilt began work at age 16 by founding his own business. With money borrowed from his parents, he bought a boat and used it to ferry passengers and freight across New York Harbor.

Andrew Carnegie's philanthropy in his later years grew out of his personal philosophy, expressed in 1889: "The man who dies . . . rich dies disgraced."

MORE LUCK THAN PLUCK

"My brave boy, I owe you a debt I can never repay. But for your timely service I should now be plunged into an anguish which I cannot think of without a shudder."

Our hero was ready enough to speak on most occasions, but always felt awkward when he was praised.

"It wasn't any trouble," he said, modestly. "I can swim like a top."

"Our hero" was Ragged Dick, a New York City shoeshine boy. Saving the life of little Johnny Rockwell, who had carelessly fallen off a ferry boat, earned him not only the gratitude of the boy's father but also a job in Mr. Rockwell's business. From there, clearly, Ragged Dick would have smooth sailing on his way to fame and fortune.

Ragged Dick, published in 1868, was the eighth book written by Horatio Alger. It was the one that launched Alger on his own road to fame and fortune. The former Unitarian minister was to write over 100 novels. Almost all of them stuck to a very simple formula: poor boy works hard and makes good. The titles of Alger's books highlight this formula: *Fame and Fortune, Luck and Pluck, Strive and Succeed, Do and Dare.*

Few of Alger's thousands of readers read his books for their uplifting message. Few could have found much value in his wooden prose ("swim like a *top*"?). His world was a fantasy world. Although his heroes worked hard, they succeeded mainly through strokes of luck, which made for more interesting reading. Melodramatic events were common, as in Ragged Dick's act of heroism. What Alger did was write old-fashioned adventure stories in seemingly realistic settings. And Alger, like one of his characters, had his own stroke of luck. He combined these adventure stories with his formula at a time when the self-made millionaire had become a key figure in the American dream.

settled with his parents in Allegheny, now a part of Pittsburgh. At 14 he was working 12 hours a day as a bobbin boy in a cotton mill for $1.20 a week. He studied hard and at 16 was a telegraph clerk earning about $4.00 a week – a fair salary in those days. At 17 Carnegie became private secretary to the president of the Pennsylvania Railroad.

In 1850 Carnegie bought an oil well, and he made money in the new oil industry, but he soon turned to the steel industry. In it he spent the rest of his business life.

Carnegie frankly admitted that he knew nothing about steel manufacturing. His success lay in his ability as a seller and promoter. He knew how to gather around him people who were specialists. He was a relentless driver, never satisfied with himself or with others. One day he received a telegram from one of his plant superintendents: "We broke all records for making steel last week." Carnegie sent back another telegram: "Congratulations. Why not do it every week?"

Carnegie, however, also recognized the achievements of others. People he liked rose rapidly up the ladder to financial success. Charles M. Schwab, for instance, entered one of Carnegie's plants as a stake driver at a dollar a day. He became president of the Carnegie Steel Company at age 34. Schwab's share of profits in 1896 was $1.3 million. Similar stories are told of Carnegie's friendship for Henry Phipps, Henry C. Frick, and others.

By 1900 Andrew Carnegie, who began as a poor immigrant boy, was said to be the second richest man in the world. He owned all the types of property and equipment necessary for the mass production of steel, including deposits of iron ore, limestone, and coal; ships and railways to carry the raw material to smelters and mills; and huge steel plants from which the finished products poured forth.

Carnegie sold his steel property in 1901 for nearly $500 million. This tremendous financial deal was negotiated by J. P. Morgan, the most famous investment banker of the time. Out of the negotiations, in which 11 steel companies were merged, was born the mighty United States Steel Corporation, then the largest corporation in the world. Many economic historians have regarded this event as a critical point in the development of American capitalism. It marked a shift from **industrial capitalism,** in which corporations were controlled by their industrial owners, to **finance capitalism,** in which whole industries were dominated by bankers.

Carnegie retired in 1901. He spent much of the rest of his life giving away his money for education and other causes. "I started life as a poor man," he once said, "and I wish to end it that way." Before his death he had disposed of more than $350 million. Many public libraries stand today as monuments to Carnegie's generosity. Foundations created by his money still support causes such as education, world peace, and medical research.

John D. Rockefeller. Even richer than Carnegie was John D. Rockefeller, born in 1839, who during his lifetime accumulated the world's greatest fortune. One of five children, Rockefeller left high school after one year to work as a clerk for about $3 a week. In 1858, at age 19, he went into the wholesale food business. The Civil War brought large profits to the new company, and Rockefeller promptly invested his money in oil refineries. From this point on, oil became his major interest. He pioneered in developing the trust as a form of big business organization. Although he was ruthless in forcing his competitors to choose between joining him or going down to ruin, Rockefeller is given major credit for introducing order and efficiency into the highly chaotic and wasteful oil industry.

By 1900, Rockefeller's interests had broadened. He owned controlling stock in the gigantic Standard Oil Company, in railway lines, in steamship lines, in iron ore deposits in Colorado and in the Lake Superior region, in steel mills, and in many other enterprises. When the United States Steel Corporation was being organized by J. P. Morgan, Rockefeller sold to the newly formed corporation his iron ore deposits and Great Lakes steamers, receiving $80 million for the iron ore deposits alone.

Like Carnegie, Rockefeller later gave away many millions, and the foundations created with his money today continue to foster research and promote the welfare of the American people.

Pioneers of industrialism. These were only a few of the many pioneers of the new industrial society. Like other pioneers—cattle raisers, prospectors, frontier farmers, and wage earners—they helped to develop the resources of a new land. They were endowed with great energy and rare ability. They were gamblers, willing to take chances in the hope of gain. They were highly competitive people in a highly competitive society at a time when few laws had been passed to bring order into the mad rush of business enterprise. They were absorbed in the excitement of building a new industrial world, of creating huge fortunes, of securing power.

These business leaders have often been condemned as "robber barons" for their selfishness and ruthless business methods, for exploiting their workers and forcing their rivals out of business. At the same time, their critics have acknowledged that they also benefited the nation. They were responsible for building new industries, introducing efficient organization, and providing opportunities that enabled many people to invest their savings profitably in the new industries springing up all over the nation. However they are viewed today, these business leaders played an important part in an important period of the nation's development. They helped to give new directions to American life.

SECTION SURVEY

IDENTIFY: Nettie Fowler McCormick, J. P. Morgan, industrial capitalism, finance capitalism, Standard Oil Company.

1. (a) In what ways could Vanderbilt, Carnegie, and Rockefeller be considered "pioneers of industrial society"? (b) In what ways could they be considered "robber barons"?

2. What important contributions did the business pioneers of the late 1800's make to American economic life?

3. Find evidence to support the following statement: The most successful business leaders of the late 1800's generally believed in the ideal of self-reliant individualism.

Chapter Survey

Summary: Tracing the Main Ideas

During the years between 1865 and 1900, the United States grew rapidly. By the opening years of the 1900's, the United States had become the leading industrial nation in the world. Smoking factory chimneys, rumbling machinery, and long trains of freight cars pulling into and out of congested urban centers were symbols of the industrial world.

In the Northeast and Middle West and to a lesser extent elsewhere in the nation, industrialism was transforming the lives of the people. Raw materials from America's vast reservoir of natural resources poured into the mills and factories. Finished products in ever-growing quantities flowed from the factories into the marketplace and people's home's.

Mass production led to specialization. Financiers raised the capital to build the railroads and the factories. Manufacturers developed more efficient methods of producing goods. Merchants developed new methods of advertising and selling. Many workers—clerks, stenographers, managers, factory workers, and others—staffed the new industrial plants. New methods of business organization were developed and employed. Great corporations and combinations of corporations were increasingly replacing the individual or family-owned enterprises that had been the most common form of business organization.

Throughout America a new spirit of fierce competition drove people at a faster and faster pace. It was an exciting and a productive period in the nation's history, but some of the changes created problems for many people. Much of the nation's history since 1865 is concerned with the efforts of Americans to adjust their ways of life to the new forces of growing industrialism.

Inquiring into History

1. How were industrialization, improvements in transportation, and the growth of cities in America interrelated?
2. How did the abundance of natural resources and the development of advanced technology in America help contribute to its rapid growth as an industrial power?
3. (a) List the discoveries or inventions between 1865 and 1900 that you think did the most to encourage America's industrial growth. (b) How did each affect the growth of industry? (c) Were any of them interdependent?
4. (a) How do you suppose J. P. Morgan felt about the passage of the Sherman Antitrust Act? (b) What arguments might he have made to support his position?

Relating Past to Present

1. Read about one of the following inventions or innovations of the 1800's and trace its development to its present-day counterparts: telephone receiver/transmitter, typewriter, skyscraper, camera, dynamo.
2. Are today's objections to business monopolies the same as the ones raised during the period covered in this chapter? Explain.

3. Is it likely that a person today could rise "from rags to riches" as Vanderbilt or Carnegie did in their time?
4. (a) Should industries in the United States bear responsibility for what happens to the environment as a result of their activities? Why or why not? (b) How do the environmental efforts of government, business, and private groups today compare with those of the late 1800's?
5. Use reference books to find out the annual sales and total assets of the largest American corporations in 1900. (a) Are these corporations among the largest today? Why or why not? (b) Compare the 1900 figures with those of the largest corporations today, taking inflation into account. To what extent has big business gotten bigger in this century?

Developing Social Science Skills

1. Look at the graphs on page 98. What can you conclude from the information in the graphs about the rate of industrial growth in the United States after the Civil War?
2. Study the pictures in this chapter. (a) What evidence do they provide about industrialization? (b) Do any aspects of life under industrialization seem to be missing? (c) If so, how might you find out about these aspects of American life?

Chapter 5
The Struggle of American Workers to Organize

On April 14, 1865, when President Lincoln was shot in Ford's Theater in the nation's capital, the United States was still chiefly an agricultural country. By 1900 it had experienced a period of unprecedented industrial development and become the leading industrial and manufacturing nation in the world.

America's amazing industrial growth was possible because of a number of factors. Improvements in the transportation system allowed raw materials and finished products to reach their destination quickly and cheaply. The development of power-driven machines and the construction of giant factories and other industrial plants greatly expanded production. The organization of business into larger corporations and the cooperation of government added to the efficiency of industrialization. Finally, the machines in the new industrial plants were operated by rapidly growing numbers of workers.

The new industrial workers—women and children as well as men—came from America's farms and rural areas. They also came from Europe in the hundreds of thousands every year, a mighty flood of immigration.

Both the older Americans and the newcomers entered a new world when they moved into America's growing industrial communities. In the early days of power-driven machines and mass production, they were as much pioneers as those who had earlier pushed America's frontiers westward to the Pacific. Like pioneers in every age, wage earners in the late 1800's faced complex problems.

THE CHAPTER IN OUTLINE

1. Industrialism creates new problems for wage earners.

2. Immigration adds strength and variety to American society.

3. Wage earners organize to overcome their grievances.

4. Organized labor faces opposition as it seeks reforms.

Changing Ways of American Life

1860's–1890's

1 Industrialism creates new problems for wage earners

The industrial developments that transformed the United States between 1865 and 1900 created new problems as well as new opportunities for wage earners. Like all other Americans, wage earners had to adapt themselves to a rapidly changing industrial society.

New owner-worker relations. For one thing, large corporations hiring thousands of workers changed the old-time relations between owners and employees. In earlier days when factories were small, the owner knew the workers and sometimes took a personal interest in their welfare. In the huge factories, however, workers seldom saw the owners, most of whom were stockholders living in widely separated parts of the country.

Nor did many owners know at first hand what working conditions were like in their factories and mines. They bought shares of stock as an investment and hired managers to run the plants. As the factories grew larger, the workers, as individuals, became less important. If a worker objected to the way a factory was run, he or she could easily be replaced.

Workers in so-called "company towns" faced the greatest disadvantages. There were mining districts in Pennsylvania and West Virginia and textile-mill regions in the South where companies owned entire towns—all the houses, stores, and other buildings. The companies employed the teachers and the doctors. The local magistrates and the police owed their jobs to the company. In these towns workers did not dare to protest the rent they paid for their company-owned houses or the prices they paid in the company-owned store. Frequently, the workers received part of their wages not in cash but in credit at the company store.

Individual workers in the new industrial society could not hope to improve their working conditions. Nor could they reasonably hope to become an owner beyond, perhaps, buying a few shares of stock. To be sure, some workers

One byproduct of industrialism was the "company town." The one shown here is Butte, Montana, in 1890. It grew up around the Anaconda Copper Mining Company, which was then mining "the richest hill on earth."

did become supervisors and managers, and a few rose to positions of wealth and power. In general, though, as factories grew larger and more impersonal, it became harder for individual workers or groups of workers to bargain with employers over their wages and their working conditions.

Effects of mechanization. The use of power-driven machines in factories also created new problems for wage earners. Factory work became increasingly specialized and increasingly monotonous. Often machines were geared to high rates of output, and workers ended the day exhausted. Moreover, the new machinery often produced much more with fewer workers. Thus the installation of new machines could cause **technological unemployment** by throwing workers out of jobs. Sometimes new and different jobs were created because workers were needed to build and repair the machines. Also, the higher output of the machines increased the nationwide production of goods and thereby created new jobs of many kinds. However, displaced workers often found it difficult to learn new skills and get new jobs.

Machines were also physically dangerous. Until about 1910 little was done to safeguard workers from accidents. When an accident occurred, the worker was usually blamed. If disabled, he or she received no compensation to pay the costs of doctors and hospitalization. When a worker was killed, the worker's family was usually left without an income, for employers did not insure the lives of workers.

Industrial hazards were a major problem. Between 1900 and 1910, for example, 3 percent of all employed workers in the United States were killed or injured annually in industrial accidents. In 1911 a fire in the unsafe Triangle Building in New York City brought death to 146 women textile workers. In a strike just the year before, the women had protested against their unsafe working conditions.

Effects of the railroads. Before the nationwide network of railroads was built, American manufacturers usually sold their products only in nearby markets. With the railroad network, however, a manufacturer could hope to sell products anywhere in the country, provided the manufacturer's prices were as low as those elsewhere.

This creation of a competitive national market for goods also created a competitive na-

tional market for labor. For example, if cotton goods were being made cheaper in southern mills because of lower wages, then New England manufacturers of cotton goods were inclined to lower wages to compete with the lower-priced output of the southern mills.

Business cycles and the frontier. Like other citizens, workers were greatly influenced by what economists call the **business cycle.** This was the expansion of business and industry during periods of prosperity and their contraction during periods of depression. Workers lived in constant dread of being laid off or having their wages sharply reduced whenever business conditions took a downturn. Even when business was good, unemployment per-

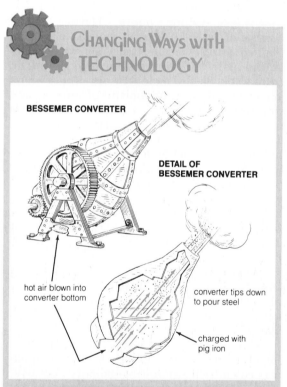

CHANGING WAYS WITH TECHNOLOGY

BESSEMER CONVERTER

DETAIL OF BESSEMER CONVERTER

hot air blown into converter bottom

converter tips down to pour steel

charged with pig iron

BESSEMER CONVERTER

Pig iron that was created in blast furnaces still contained impurities that had to be removed to produce steel. The Bessemer converter, developed in the 1850's, forced a blast of hot air through molten pig iron. Oxygen in the air combined with the impurities and they were burned out. A substance was added to remove excess oxygen and otherwise strengthen the mixture. The molten steel was then poured out and shaped.

sisted and brought misery to many industrial workers.

Between 1870 and 1900, hundreds of thousands of jobless persons searched for work. In 1889, a fairly typical year, about 19 percent of the workers in manufacturing and transportation were jobless.

As long as the frontier remained open, farmers on worn-out eastern land could choose between migration to the frontier or migration to the city. Many chose to continue farming and moved west. After about 1900, however, eastern farm families had fewer and fewer opportunities to find good, cheap western land. They turned in larger numbers to the cities for work, swelling the work force of the cities and driving down industrial wages.

Low wages and long hours. During the last quarter of the 1800's, many wage earners complained bitterly about their low wages. Unskilled male workers might earn no more than $10 a week. Skilled male workers—those whose jobs required a certain amount of training and education—might earn no more than $20 a week. In both skilled and unskilled jobs, the wage scale for women workers was even lower. In 1903, for example, a woman might receive $2.16 for a 62-hour workweek in a cap factory. Still, industrial expansion brought higher **real wages**° to workers as a whole. Nevertheless, large numbers of workers, like many farmers, believed that they were not receiving a fair share of the profits from the country's industrial growth.

Wages tended to be low for several reasons: the increasing power of employers over employees, the competitive national labor market, depressions, and the flood of immigrant workers into the labor market.

Wage earners also complained about their long working hours. After 1865 an 11-hour day was common in American industry. Yet even in the 1880's, many textile workers worked from 12 to 14 hours daily, and the 12-hour day was common in the steel industry.

It was indeed a new and rapidly changing world with which the American wage earner wrestled in the late 1800's. The problems of wage earners were complex, and the workers, the owners of the industries, and Americans in general lacked ready answers.

°**real wages:** wages measured in terms of actual purchasing power, or what the money will buy.

SECTION SURVEY

IDENTIFY: "company town," technological unemployment, Triangle Building fire, business cycle.

1. How did the move toward huge, corporation-owned factories change relations between owners and workers?
2. Discuss the problems faced by workers as a result of increasing mechanization.
3. How did each of the following affect workers: (a) railroads, (b) the business cycle, (c) the end of the frontier?
4. Picture Study: Look at the photograph on page 106. Do you find any evidence to show that industrialization could bring problems as well as benefits?

2 Immigration adds strength and variety to American society

Immigrants played an essential part in the industrial development of the United States between 1865 and 1900. Immigrants came seeking jobs and new opportunities. In trying to find places for themselves in their new homeland and in the industrial age, the immigrants were often greeted with suspicion.

The immigrants. Part of the difficulty was the overwhelming number of immigrants who poured into the country. From 1870 to 1899, more than 11 million women, men, and children entered the United States.

The changing character of immigration as well as the swelling tide alarmed many Americans. Until the early 1880's, most immigrants came from northwestern Europe—Great Britain, Ireland, Scandinavia, Germany, and the Netherlands. After 1890 an increasingly large number came from southern and eastern Europe—Russia (including Poland), Greece, Austria-Hungary, and Italy. The languages, customs, and ways of living of these immigrants were quite different from those of immigrants from northwestern Europe.

Effects of immigration on labor. The immigrants had an enormous influence on American life. Although some settled on farms, the great majority moved to the densely crowded slum areas of the cities. Here tenement owners

In 1869 Joseph Becker painted this picture of cheering Chinese "gandy dancers," or railroad workers. Gandy dancers took their name from the Gandy Manufacturing Company, which made tools used in railroad construction. Chinese immigrants supplied much of the labor that built the western railroads.

profited in higher rents from the competition for housing between native-born Americans and newcomers from Europe.

Most immediate of all, however, was the immigrants' effect upon established workers. Immigrants competed for jobs, thereby lowering wages. To be sure, immigrants helped to stimulate the economy by creating new demands for factory and farm products. Most wage earners, however, were more disturbed by the job competition of the immigrants than they were impressed with the stimulating effects of immigration.

Tensions on the Pacific Coast. Chinese workers on the Pacific Coast, particularly in California, were early victims of the rising distrust of all immigrants. By the terms of the Burlingame Treaty of 1868, Chinese people had the right to immigrate to the United States. For some years Chinese laborers had been welcome additions to the labor supply. They had been forced to accept the hardest and least desirable jobs for very low wages. They were the backbone of the construction gangs that built the western section of the first trans-continental railroad. By the 1870's nearly 75,000 Chinese workers had settled in California, where they made up about 20 percent of the labor force.

Then in 1873 a depression hit the country. As unemployment mounted, California workers worried that the Chinese would take their jobs at low wages. Fear and insecurity were intensified because the Chinese, for reasons not always of their own choosing, lived entirely to themselves. Thus they did not have an opportunity to learn and adapt to the ways of living accepted by most Californians.

Restricting Chinese immigration. Ill feeling was fanned into violence by crowds of unemployed California workers who gathered on street corners and sand lots. The "sand lotters" soon attacked the Chinese, killing some and burning the property of others.

In cooperation with distressed farmers, California workers were able to influence the writing of a new state constitution in 1879. California's new constitution discriminated against the Chinese by prohibiting them from owning property or working at certain jobs.

The opponents of Chinese immigration also succeeded in getting Congress to pass an exclusion bill in 1879. This bill prohibited all but a few Chinese from settling in the United States in any year. Because this bill violated the Burlingame Treaty of 1868, President Hayes vetoed it. Under pressure, however, the Chinese government agreed not to object if the United States regulated immigration. In 1882 Congress enacted a new Chinese Exclusion Act, which, with several extensions, continued in effect until World War II. The Chinese Exclusion Act forbade the immigration of Chinese laborers and denied American citizenship to Chinese born in China. Only students and a few other groups of Chinese could enter the United States.

Other restrictions. The Chinese Exclusion Act of 1882 was the first of a long series of restrictions on immigration, enacted mainly because of pressure from worker groups. The second was the repeal in 1885 of the Contract Labor Law.

The Contract Labor Law had been adopted by Congress in 1864, when booming wartime industries desperately needed workers. This law permitted American employers to recruit laborers in Europe. Under the law it was legal for employers to have workers abroad sign contracts agreeing to come to the United States to work for a specified employer for specified wages for a specified time. It was illegal for the workers to leave their jobs while the contract was in force. American workers objected to the law because (1) it came dangerously close to setting up a slave-labor system and (2) it subjected American workers to the unfair competition of cheap foreign labor.

After the repeal of the Contract Labor Law, American wage earners pressured Congress for other restrictive measures. One bill that kept coming up for 30 years would have forbidden entry to any immigrant who could not read and write. Congress actually did pass this law on several occasions, but each time the President then in office vetoed the bill. In 1917, however, Congress passed a "literacy test" bill over President Woodrow Wilson's veto, and the door to immigration was shut a little further.

The role of immigrants. Except for the Chinese Exclusion Act, the restrictions placed on immigration from 1865 to 1900 were relatively minor. Without the more than 11 million immigrants who poured into the United States between 1870 and 1900, profits to owners of industry would have been much smaller. As it was, employers could keep wages of immigrants lower than those of established Americans. Without immigrants America's industrial progress also would have been much slower. Immigrant muscles and brains helped to transform the United States from a predominantly agricultural country into a giant industrial power.

SECTION SURVEY

IDENTIFY: immigrants, slums, "sand lotters," "literacy test" bill.

1. How did the composition of the immigrant population change after 1880?
2. Discuss three ways in which immigration affected American workers.
3. Why did Congress pass the Chinese Exclusion Act of 1882?
4. (a) Explain the provisions of the Contract Labor Law of 1864. (b) Why was it repealed?
5. Give evidence to support this statement: Immigrant muscles and brains helped to transform the United States.

3 Wage earners organize to overcome their grievances

Faced with numerous problems brought on by the new industrial age, wage earners, like farmers, looked for solutions to their problems through organization.

The National Labor Union. Labor organizations were not new. During the war years 1861–65, however, as industry boomed and the cost of living soared, the labor movement gained new momentum.

In 1866 the National Labor Union was launched under the leadership of William Sylvis, an experienced and able organizer of iron molders. In 1868 the National Labor Union helped push through Congress a law setting an 8-hour workday for laborers and mechanics employed by or in behalf of the federal government. After unsuccessfully supporting a third-party movement in the election of 1872, this union faded away.

By 1890, when Thomas Anshutz painted this scene of steelworkers taking a lunch break, the United States had become the world's leading steel manufacturer.

The Knights of Labor. Far more important than the National Labor Union was the Knights of Labor, founded in 1869 in Philadelphia by Uriah S. Stephens, a tailor. The Knights of Labor tried to unite all American workers into one great union—foreign-born and native-born, blacks and whites, skilled and unskilled, women and men. Several women headed local units or "assemblies" and a few became national leaders. The Knights aimed "to secure to the toilers a proper share of the wealth that they create; more of the leisure that rightfully belongs to them." Among other things, they favored an 8-hour workday.

The Knights of Labor also tried to organize and run cooperative stores and manufacturing plants, as some farmers already had done. They hoped to save for themselves the profits that normally went to manufacturers and distributors and at the same time to produce lower-priced goods. However, most of their cooperative enterprises failed, largely because they did not have enough money to buy good machinery and to hire qualified managers.

In some of their efforts the Knights of Labor were more successful. They were influential, for example, in causing Congress to pass the Chinese Exclusion Act in 1882 and to repeal the Contract Labor Law in 1885.

The Knights of Labor officially frowned on strikes, preferring to settle disputes between management and laborers through industrial **arbitration.**° However, a successful railroad strike in 1885 did much to boost the group's membership. For the first time in American labor history, railroad operators met strike leaders on equal terms and agreed to labor's

°**arbitration:** the judging of a dispute between two sides by an impartial person whose decision they agree in advance to accept.

111

chief demands. When the railroad strike occurred, the Knights numbered about 500,000 members. By 1886 their membership had reached 700,000. This growth also owed much to the idealism and enthusiasm of Terence V. Powderly, who succeeded Uriah S. Stephens as leader of the Knights of Labor.

The Haymarket Affair. On May 4, 1886, while the Knights were at the peak of their power, a large group of workers gathered in Haymarket Square in Chicago. They were there to protest an attack on strikers on May 3 in which one striker had been killed and a number of others wounded.

The meeting was orderly and the crowd was just beginning to leave when nearly 200 police officers appeared. Suddenly, without warning, a bomb burst in the midst of the police. Seven people were killed and many others wounded.

No one ever identified the bomb thrower. Nevertheless, eight "radicals," who on earlier occasions had advocated violence, were arrested. Seven were sentenced to death, the eighth to 15 years in prison.

No evidence was ever produced to indicate that organized labor was responsible for the Haymarket Affair. Yet no other event during the 1880's did more to turn public opinion against organized labor.

Decline of the Knights of Labor. The Knights, as the leading labor organization, suffered most of all. The decline of the organization was almost as rapid as its rise. From 1886 to 1888, its membership dropped from the high of 700,000 to only 260,000, and by 1890 only about 100,000 members were enrolled.

There were several reasons for this decline in membership. For one thing, the Knights lost an important railroad strike in 1886. This strike angered the public because of violence accompanying it and because of shortages of food and coal resulting from it. In the second place, the Knights included too many opposing groups to develop real strength. Skilled workers especially disliked the Knights' policy of taking in unskilled workers, with whom they felt they had little in common.

Finally, Terence V. Powderly's aims came to be too general to satisfy numerous workers. Many wage earners were now convinced that a strong labor movement had to avoid political crusades and concentrate on improving conditions for specific groups of workers.

Other organizations rose to take the place of the Knights. Some, like the American Railway Union and the United Mine Workers, had specialized goals. The most important labor organization was the American Federation of Labor (A. F. of L.).

The A. F. of L. Started in 1881 under another name and reorganized in 1886, the A. F. of L. quickly replaced the Knights of Labor as the leading American labor organization.

Unlike the Knights of Labor, the A. F. of L. was a federation of separate national **craft unions.** Each craft union represented a group of skilled workers in a separate trade, or craft, such as carpentry, welding, or typography. The A. F. of L. sought to organize all skilled workers by their craft rather than by the industry in which they worked. However, the A. F. of L. did include a few **industrial unions** that tried to organize all workers, unskilled as well as skilled, in a single industry.

Each A. F. of L. union was free to bargain collectively for all its members, to call strikes, and to manage its own affairs. The A. F. of L. also differed from the Knights of Labor in keeping itself aloof from general reform movements and from independent or third-party political activities. The A. F. of L. was an economic organization of workers emphasizing craft unionism—"pure and simple unionism."

The A. F. of L. program called for an 8-hour workday and a 6-day workweek. It backed legislation protecting workers on dangerous jobs and compensating them and their families in case of injury or death. It also demanded higher wages and better working conditions. The A. F. of L. threw its weight in political contests to whichever party or candidate came closest to representing its aims.

The A. F. of L. accepted the capitalist free-enterprise system. Its leaders in general discouraged strikes and favored bargaining with management. The A. F. of L. did insist, however, on controlling the skilled labor market, on getting a larger share of the output of industry through higher wages and shorter hours, and on improving labor conditions.

With the exception of a single year, the president of the A. F. of L. from 1886 to 1924 was its principal founder, Samuel Gompers. Under Gompers's leadership the A. F. of L. grew rapidly. In 1890 it had only 100,000 members, but by 1900 membership had climbed to 500,000.

IDENTIFY: National Labor Union, Uriah Stephens, arbitration, strike, Terence Powderly, Haymarket Affair, Samuel Gompers.

1. Why did some American workers decide to organize unions during the mid-1800's?

2. Describe the (a) purpose, (b) successes, and (c) reasons for the decline of the Knights of Labor.

3. How did the American Federation of Labor differ from the Knights of Labor?

4. (a) What is the difference between a craft union and an industrial union? (b) Give examples of each today.

4 Organized labor faces opposition as it seeks reforms

When American workers began to organize during the late 1880's, they encountered many obstacles. The workers' attempts to form unions and to seek recognition of their unions' right to bargain for them met strong and widespread opposition.

Public opposition. During the late 1880's, Americans in general as well as the government usually supported employers in conflicts between employers and unions or between employers and workers striking for union recognition. This opposition to unions is not hard to understand. Most Americans had grown up in the older, rural America. Individual workers then had more control over their fates than they now had in the giant corporations. Most Americans also believed that employers had the right to hire and fire as they pleased.

Many Americans resented union demands for the **closed shop**. The businesses that had such agreements with a union could hire only union members. Employers resented this restriction on what they considered their right to hire anyone they pleased. Many workers also resented these closed-shop agreements, which forced them to join a union whether they wanted to or not.

Moreover, many Americans believed that most workers were quite content with their lot. The fact that as late as 1914 only about one worker out of ten belonged to a labor organiza-tion seemed to support this belief. Many Americans held that the best workers could still rise to become managers and even owners. Most Americans blamed the entire labor problem as well as industrial conflict itself on "power-hungry" labor leaders interested in their own personal advancement.

Immigrants and labor unions. Many union leaders were of foreign birth. In several labor organizations, especially in the textile and coal-mining industries, immigrant workers were a source of strength. Immigrant workers took leading parts in the strikes of New York garment workers as well as in the textile workers' strike in Lawrence, Massachusetts.

However, a great many immigrants opposed labor unions. Coming from rural backgrounds in Europe, most immigrants had no previous experience with labor organizations. Bewildered by their new environment, they often did not feel a need to join with native-born American workers in an effort to promote common interests.

Many immigrants had left Europe partly to be as free as possible from all sorts of restrictions. Thus they did not like labor unions, with their dues, their rules, and their insistence that no one work for less than a certain wage. Many immigrants felt that however bad working conditions in the United States might be, they were better than working conditions back in Europe.

Most immigrants, also, were unskilled workers. Thus the A. F. of L. made little or no effort to admit them to the craft unions. Finally, there was widespread prejudice among native-born American workers toward immigrant workers. This prejudice deepened when foreign-born workers were recruited by business managers to break strikes.

Women and unions. Many unions did not admit women to membership, but in a few craft unions women played important roles. Most notable was the International Ladies Garment Workers Union, in which Rose Schneiderman and Leona O'Reilly were leaders. The A. F. of L. expressed interest in organizing women but did not vigorously pursue this aim.

In 1903 the National Women's Trade Union League was founded, largely by middle-class women. It assisted women workers in several ways, especially by providing financial support during strikes. The league stressed voting rights for women as a means for advancing their economic equality and promoted minimum, or "living," wages for women.

Blacks and unions. Because of the racial prejudice of many white workers, blacks were excluded from most labor organizations. A notable exception was the Knights of Labor, which enrolled black workers without discrimination, at least until the organization's later years.

At first the leaders of the A. F. of L. favored including skilled black workers in their craft unions. They believed that if this were not done, black workers might undermine the purposes of the federation by accepting lower wages. When the machinists' union and others refused to admit blacks, Samuel Gompers, by then the dominant power in the A. F. of L., backed down. He insisted that union constitutions should not specifically exclude black members but admitted that in practice the unions might do so. The United Mine Workers and a few other A. F. of L. unions admitted black members on equal terms with white members. Most of the other unions insisted, however, that any black workers admitted to A. F. of L. membership had to be organized in separate unions.

Most northern blacks were unskilled workers. Thus after the decline of the Knights of Labor, the A. F. of L. policy of organizing only skilled workers in effect excluded black wage earners from northern labor organizations. In the South, where there were many skilled black workers, the labor market in the skilled trades was controlled by all-white A. F. of L. unions. As a result, many skilled southern black workers were forced to take jobs as unskilled laborers.

By 1902 in both the North and the South, 43 national labor unions had not a single black member, and 27 others had only a handful. Gompers argued that blacks had only themselves to blame for their exclusion because few were skilled workers and fewer still were willing to accept the self-discipline and cooperation necessary in trade unionism. Booker T. Washington, however, declared that the union movement itself was holding back the economic progress of black workers by refusing to admit them as apprentices and by making no effort to organize them.

The virtual exclusion of blacks from the American labor movement closed off to the great mass of black Americans an important opportunity to be included in the mainstream of American life. It also weakened the effectiveness of the labor movement itself.

Division in the ranks of labor. The mechanization of industrial plants also weakened the power of wage earners to unite. When factories were small, skilled workers could see that the work of unskilled workers, however minor, was an essential part of the production process. When factories grew large and workers became strangers, skilled workers came to look down on unskilled workers.

Thus the wage earners themselves divided into two groups: (1) a small number of skilled workers who gained more and more bargaining power with employers, and (2) a large number of unskilled, unorganized laborers whose voices and interests counted for very little.

Industry against the unions. With most Americans generally distrustful of unions, huge industrial enterprises did not find it difficult to influence public opinion and government in their own favor. They hired lawyers to fight their battles in the courts. They spent money on advertising and publicity to win public sympathy. They paid skillful lobbyists to get favorable laws passed or to defeat bills that employers did not like. Some corporations contributed to the political party they thought most likely to win an election, hoping to secure government favors.

To discourage workers from joining unions, employers also developed more direct methods. For example, employers' associations, made up of several manufacturers, compiled **black lists.** These were lists of workers considered as undesirable—sometimes because the workers were incompetent, sometimes because they were labor organizers, sometimes merely because they belonged to a union. A black list was circulated throughout an entire industry all over the country. Any person whose name appeared on a black list was barred from getting a job in that industry, at least under her or his own name.

Many employers also required workers applying for a job to sign a written agreement not to join a union. The workers called these agreements **yellow-dog contracts.** A worker who violated such a contract was fired.

Employers used still other methods to prevent workers from organizing. Sometimes pri-

The cartoonist who drew this picture in 1883 obviously saw the battle between management and labor as a very uneven one. What advantages does the cartoonist think that one side enjoyed over the other in the struggle?

vate detectives, posing as workers, joined unions and reported strike plans and names of union leaders to employers. Sometimes when strikes broke out, employers actually paid agents to commit acts of violence, which were then blamed on labor. At other times, the workers themselves resorted to violence. In either case, such violence gave employers a good excuse for calling in the local police, the state militia, or even federal troops to restore order and break the strike.

Sometimes employers fought strikes with another weapon—the **lockout.** They closed their plants, thus locking out the workers. Then they brought in **strikebreakers**— nonunion workers hired to do the work of those on strike—and the plant was reopened despite the angry strikers picketing outside its gates. At other times, owners simply locked their plants and waited until the hungry, impoverished strikers were willing to return to work on any terms.

Government support of industry. With public opinion on their side, employers counted on government aid in conflicts with workers. Despite some exceptions they generally got such aid.

In most serious labor disputes, governors sent the state militia to the scene, which was to the employers' advantage. Whenever they sent the militia, the governors argued that the troops were needed to protect property, prevent violence, and maintain order. Since the governors were sworn to uphold law and order, this seemed reasonable. On the other hand, the arrival of the state militia often made it impossible for the workers to continue to strike.

In the last quarter of the 1800's, the Presidents of the United States in general followed the example of the state governors in ordering troops to a scene of trouble. Thus during a series of railroad strikes in Pennsylvania and Maryland in 1877, when state troops could not restore order, President Hayes sent federal

Early in 1894 Coxey—together with a colorful Populist orator named Carl Browne—decided to make Congress aware of the problems of the down-and-out. "Browne," he exclaimed, "we will send a petition to Washington with boots on!"

Coxey had a sympathetic Congressman introduce bills based on his ideas. These provided for government sponsorship of vast road-building projects, which would furnish work for the unemployed. While the bills were in Congress, Coxey organized his march on Washington. Circulars proclaimed: "We want no thieves or anarchists to join us. We want patriots, not bummers." Only about a hundred men marched out of Massillon on that Easter Day, but additional recruits joined up as the group traveled eastward to Washington. By the time Coxey's "army" reached the nation's capital, at the end of April, it numbered about 500.

A big crowd lined Pennsylvania Avenue when Coxey's "army" trooped toward the Capitol on May 1. Coxey's daughter Mamie rode on horseback as the goddess of peace, dressed in white and carrying a tiny parasol. At the Capitol, however, hundreds of police kept the marchers back and prevented Coxey from speaking. Coxey and Browne were arrested—for walking on the grass. A few days later they were sentenced to twenty days in jail and fined $5 apiece.

Coxey's "army" seemed to be good for nothing but chuckles. But Coxey had the last laugh. In 1944, at the age of 90, he at last got to make his speech on the Capitol steps. By that time Congress had enacted the kinds of laws that Jacob Coxey had first called for fifty years earlier.

A PETITION WITH BOOTS ON

Jacob Coxey was a model citizen, a successful, hard-working quarry owner from Massillon, Ohio. But beneath his quiet exterior beat the heart of a reformer. The depression of 1893 had thrown thousands out of work, and Coxey thought the government should do something about it.

soldiers to keep the trains running. The strikes collapsed.

Federal troops also stepped in near Chicago in 1894 when a strike was called against the Pullman Palace Car Company by the American Railway Union led by Eugene V. Debs. The strike was supported by railway workers around Chicago and elsewhere, who refused to handle trains that included Pullman cars. When Governor Altgeld of Illinois refused to call out the state militia or ask for federal help, President Cleveland sent federal troops anyway. Cleveland declared that such action was justified in order to guarantee mail delivery, although mail trains were in fact running and

the mails were being delivered. Organized labor resented such use of federal troops.

The courts support industry. In the late 1800's, the courts generally sided with management. For example, during the Pullman strike the railroad owners asked a federal court in Chicago to issue an **injunction,** or court order, forbidding Debs and other labor leaders to continue the strike. The court issued the injunction. It claimed that the strikers had entered into "a conspiracy in restraint of trade" and were therefore violating the Sherman Antitrust Act of 1890, which declared such conspiracies illegal.

Debs defied the court order. He was promptly arrested and sentenced to six months in jail for refusing to obey the injunction. Labor denounced this conviction as "government by injunction," but the Supreme Court upheld the ruling. Debs was jailed, and the Pullman strike was broken.

After 1895, employers often secured injunctions to prevent or break up strikes. Labor leaders complained bitterly, but their only possible relief was (1) that the Supreme Court would reverse its decision in the Debs case, or (2) that Congress would modify the Sherman Antitrust Act so that it could not be used against labor unions.

Radical movements. After the Haymarket Affair of 1886, many Americans began to identify the labor movement with radicalism. However, most Americans in the 1880's and 1890's did not distinguish among the goals and methods of the three major radical movements —**anarchism, communism,** and **socialism.**

The anarchists believed that people could work and live happily together in voluntary associations if they could be freed from the restraints of government. They believed that their ideal society could be won only by the violent overthrow of the government and of capitalism—the economic system under which industry is owned and controlled by private individuals. Although the anarchists were few in number, their reputation for violence deeply alarmed the nation.

The best-known anarchist was Emma Goldman, an immigrant from Russia. Though feared and hated generally by the middle class and disliked by many workers, Goldman was appreciated in radical circles. She was a tough, fighting champion of working people, of free speech, and of complete freedom for women. Emma Goldman was also an uncompromising foe of militarism and the use of police force in what she regarded as the exploitation of ordinary people.

The followers of Karl Marx believed that wage earners would always be exploited under capitalism. They argued that capitalism had to be replaced by an economic system in which the workers could own and control the means of production.

In time, the followers of Marx developed into two separate groups. One group, known as Communists, insisted that the only way to build the new society of workers envisioned by Marx was by means of revolution and the violent seizure of power.

The other group, known as socialists, generally did not advocate revolution. The socialists believed that the workers, organized in unions committed to socialism and in a political party, could vote themselves into power and by democratic means could reconstruct the economic and social foundations of society. Socialist leaders included Daniel De Leon, Morris Hillquit, Kate Richards O'Hare, Eugene V. Debs, and Victor Berger.

The influence of the radical movements upon American labor organizations was never as strong as it became in some parts of Europe. Union members by and large continued to support Republicans, Democrats, or third-party candidates and policies according to the union members' personal judgment of issues and of their own best interests.

Influence of organized labor. In the face of strong opposition from management, government, and the middle class, organized labor made solid gains. For example, in 1896 there were 5,462 strikes. Of these, 3,913 achieved full or partial success for the workers. In 1903 there were 12,660 strikes that succeeded in whole or in part.

Despite setbacks, organized labor continued to fight for its aims and for public recognition and support. By the early 1900's, the lot of American workers was beginning to improve.

SECTION SURVEY

IDENTIFY: closed shop, National Women's Trade Union League, Pullman strike, anarchism, capitalism, Eugene V. Debs, Emma Goldman, communism, socialism.

1. Why did public opinion in the late 1800's usually support employers rather than workers?

2. Why did many immigrants oppose the labor movement?

3. (a) Why were black workers excluded from the labor movement? (b) What have been the long-term effects of this discrimination?

4. How were women workers treated by the labor movement?

5. How did employers use each of the following against organized labor: (a) publicity, (b) lobbyists, (c) political contributions, (d) black lists, (e) yellow-dog contracts, (f) lockouts, (g) strikebreakers?

117

Chapter Survey

Summary: Tracing the Main Ideas

The rapid development of large-scale industry between 1865 and 1900 created new problems for wage earners. They attempted to solve these problems by organizing labor unions. Through the labor movement, Samuel Gompers and other labor leaders outlined and pushed for a program of democracy that differed in many respects from the traditional ideas of democracy.

Democracy in the earlier days was largely based on the ability of the individual to help himself or herself. The growth of great corporations made it increasingly difficult for the individual worker to meet and solve his or her own problems. As a result, some workers organized unions through which they could act as a united group. They began to demand government protection in the form of laws providing maximum hours of work, minimum wages, and accident compensation.

By 1900, labor organizations were beginning to exert considerable influence upon government at both the state and the federal level. They were supporting those candidates in the major political parties who were most friendly to the progress of the workers. They were also insisting that it was their democratic right to organize, to bargain as a group, and to strike if necessary to protect their rights. Several bitter strikes had already occurred.

In their demands and in their actions, wage earners were reacting to the new industrial society that was transforming the United States. Like all other Americans, they were seeking to adjust to the industrial age.

Inquiring into History

1. In human terms, what did the United States lose in becoming an industrialized nation? What advantages did it gain?
2. The majority of immigrants coming to the United States during the late 1800's were between the ages of 14 and 45. Why do you think this was the case? How might this fact have been significant for the nation's economy?
3. In the period 1870–1900, what were the major grievances of working people against (a) employers, (b) state governments, and (c) the federal government?
4. In what ways were the radical movements and the labor movement connected during the late 1800's?
5. Give evidence to support the claim that both federal and state governments generally sided with industry and against labor in disputes during the late 1800's.

Relating Past to Present

1. How does the power that labor unions held during the period 1865–1900 compare to the power that they hold today? Use specific examples to support your answer.
2. Compare the demands that labor unions make today with the demands they made during the late 1800's.

3. In general, how did the courts treat labor unions in the late 1800's? Do the courts treat them differently today?
4. Using *Statistical Abstract of the United States* and *Historical Statistics of the United States,* compare the wage rates for and hours worked by American workers in the late 1800's and today. What does this information indicate about the standard of living of working Americans in the two periods?

Developing Social Science Skills

1. Study the graph of immigration on page 698. (a) During which decade did total immigration first reach 1 million? 2.5 million? (b) During which decade between 1860 and 1900 did the most immigrants come to the United States? About how many came? (c) Why do you suppose immigration might have dropped in the following decade?
2. Interview a member or leader of a labor union. Before beginning the interview, be sure to prepare your questions carefully. You might ask questions about union activities and goals, union accomplishments, and worker-employer relations.
3. Conduct research and prepare an oral report or bulletin board display on one of these people: Samuel Gompers, Eugene V. Debs, Emma Goldman, Rose Schneiderman, John Peter Altgeld, Daniel De Leon, George Pullman.

Chapter 6

The Revolt of Farmers Against Big Business Practices

1860's–1890's

After the Civil War, American farmers stood on the threshold of the industrial age. Yet neither the farmers nor the great majority of other Americans were aware of the sweeping developments that were about to transform life in America, in Western Europe, and eventually throughout the world.

By 1870 the symbols of the new industrial age were beginning to appear and to affect farmers' lives. Steel rails stretched across the prairies and through remote mountain valleys, opening up new farmland to settlement and bringing older farmland in closer touch with the cities. Farm machines had begun to appear on some of the nation's more prosperous farms, enabling the farmer to produce more goods with less labor. The rapidly growing industrial cities were opening up ever-larger markets for farm products. These and other related developments made the farmer an increasingly important part of the new industrial economy.

In the 1870's farm families had every reason to assume that better times lay ahead for the nation's rural population. Better times would eventually come, but not in the 1880's and 1890's. During this period American farmers instead were forced to confront a number of serious new problems.

THE CHAPTER IN OUTLINE

1. Farm life remains laborious, but simple.

2. Farmers face complex new problems in the industrial age.

3. Farm organizations join efforts to regulate the railroads.

4. Farm organizations put increasing pressure on government.

5. The farmers fail to win control of the national government.

1 Farm life remains laborious, but simple

Every ten years, as required in the Constitution, a federal census has been taken all across America. Occupations, income, and other information have been recorded and published by the government. The returns from the 1870 census showed that the nation's urban population was growing more rapidly than the rural population. In 1860 about 80 percent of all Americans lived in rural areas. By 1870 only about 75 percent lived on farms or in small towns and villages. Even so, the United States was still for the most part a farming country.

The 2.7 million farms that the census takers visited in 1870 varied greatly. Some were large, others small. Some farmers were prosperous; others just managed to earn a living. Regardless of their size or their degree of prosperity, the American farms of 1870 shared certain characteristics.

The day of hand tools. Manual labor and a few simple hand tools characterized work on most farms in 1870. It is easier, perhaps, to visualize life on the typical farm of 1870 by starting with things that the farm family did not yet have.

No farmers, for instance, had gasoline-driven machines or machines powered by electricity. Farmers pumped water by hand, lifted it in buckets from open wells, or, if they were fortunate, ran a pipe from a hilltop spring and allowed the water to flow to the barn and the farmhouse. There were no electric or gas stoves. Farm women usually cooked on iron, wood-burning stoves; only a few had the new kerosene stoves. There were no gas or electric lights; for lighting, farmers used smoky kero-

Winslow Homer's painting "Crack the Whip" captures an everyday scene of American rural life in the 1870's. Recess has released some of the students from their "little red schoolhouse," and they use their free time to play a game.

sene lamps and lanterns. There was no central heating; there were only stoves and, in the milder South, open fireplaces. In 1870 there was no free delivery of mail. Also there were no mail-order catalogs from which farm families could order their ready-made clothing, tools, or equipment.

On some of the nation's large and more prosperous farms, machines were becoming increasingly important. Steel plows were in general use. More horse-drawn corn planters, mowers, hayrakes, and reapers as well as steam-powered threshers were being manufactured in American factories and put to work in the fields.

In 1870 the average farmers depended almost entirely upon hand tools—axes, saws, spades, pitchforks, sickles, scythes, and rakes. For power they relied mainly on their muscles and on horses, mules, or oxen. There was nothing new in this situation. The lives of many American farmers in 1870 were not essentially different from the lives of American farmers in, say, 1770 or 1820.

The self-reliant farm family. Farming was not an easy way of life. The family rose at daybreak—or even earlier in winter—to milk the cows, bring in firewood, feed the pigs and chickens, and fill the water trough for the livestock. When night fell—and long after dark in winter—the family was still busy with its unending chores.

This hard life had its compensations. The family was its own boss. The land and the labor of the farmer, his wife, and their children provided most of their food, clothing, and shelter. A self-reliant farm family developed a spirit of independence that few wage earners could hope to enjoy.

Not all American farmers in 1870 shared this feeling of independence. Nearly one fourth of the families living on farms at this time did not own the land they worked. They either rented farms as tenants or operated them as sharecroppers. Sharecropping, as you have read, was especially common among black farmers in the South.

Social life. Except for farmers who lived close to a growing city or a large town, opportunities for social activities in 1870 were limited. Most farm families had only three centers of social activity—the nearest town, the church, and the school.

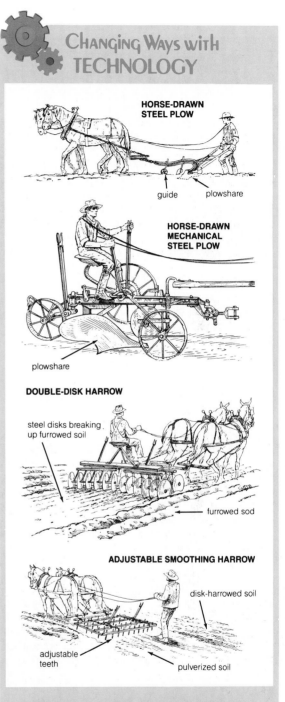

CHANGING WAYS WITH TECHNOLOGY

HORSE-DRAWN STEEL PLOW

guide plowshare

HORSE-DRAWN MECHANICAL STEEL PLOW

plowshare

DOUBLE-DISK HARROW

steel disks breaking up furrowed soil

furrowed sod

ADJUSTABLE SMOOTHING HARROW

disk-harrowed soil

adjustable teeth

pulverized soil

IMPROVED FARM IMPLEMENTS

The development of steel plowshares aided in turning over the tough sod of the prairie. Mechanical plows transferred much of the labor of plowing to a machine. The pulverizing of the soil, which was earlier done by hoes and rakes, was now performed by harrows. They were fast, thorough, and labor-saving.

THE COUNTRY STORE

Farmers and small-town Americans of the late 1800's could not have survived without the country store. In many communities it was the only place within walking or buggy distance where people could buy the necessities of life.

Food, of course, was basic, and much of it was sold in bulk. Ranged along the walls were barrels of flour and sugar, tubs of butter, baskets of eggs, huge blocks of cheese, bins of crackers, and slabs of bacon. Pickle vats, coffee grinders, and jars of spices gave off their distinctive smells.

For men there was chewing tobacco, cut to order. Women could buy family clothing from boots to bonnets or sew it, choosing from a big selection of fabrics, thread, and other supplies. Children were tempted by penny cards, arranged in rows in showcases or jumbled in jars.

The country store's wide range of household goods included crockery, cooking utensils, strong yellow laundry soap, stove polish, lamps, and the kerosene to fill them. Farmers could find seed, hay rakes, milking pails, and axes. Patent medicines promised to ease every ache and pain.

The country store (or general store, as it was often called) was more than a place to buy things. Often it housed the local post office. Above all, it was a sort of community center, where people met to talk and exchange news. In winter the locals gathered around the stove to discuss politics and swap stories all day long. "I am a storekeeper," wrote one merchant in an ad, "and am excessively annoyed by a set of troublesome animals, called Loungers, who are in the daily habit of calling at my store, and there sitting hour after hour." The owner may have felt better after letting off steam in print—but it is doubtful that he ever got rid of his "Loungers."

The Saturday drive to town in a wagon or buggy was a big weekly event. Even a 10-mile (16-kilometer) trip meant about four hours on the road. As for the "town," it might be nothing more than a country store at the crossroads, with a blacksmith shop on the opposite corner. On the other hand, it might be a sizable village or even a county seat with a courthouse, a railroad station, several stores, a bank, a doctor's office, a lawyer's office, and a cluster of houses.

These Saturday trips combined business with pleasure. While the farm women shopped and while the farmers arranged for the sale of their cash crops or settled accounts at the bank or the store, the children played with their friends. The shopping and the business gave families an opportunity to chat with neighbors, to catch up on the latest news, and perhaps to watch some horse trading in front of the blacksmith shop.

The Sunday trip to church was another bright spot in the week. The entire family, freshly scrubbed and dressed in their best clothes, drove to church in the wagon or buggy. There they worshiped, sang hymns, listened to the sermon, and afterward gathered in front of the church for leisurely talk before driving home once again.

The local school. On weekdays the children attended a one-room elementary school. To reach it, some of the boys and girls walked several miles along the country roads. School terms were short, for the children had to help with spring planting and fall harvesting. The teacher, usually a young woman, taught all grades. The emphasis in 1870, as in earlier times, was on "readin', 'ritin', and 'rithmetic." During the school term, the teacher often lived in the homes of the pupils, staying a month in one home, then a month in another, and so on throughout the term.

The school was also a community center. Graduation day was a big occasion, and now and then there were spelling bees and other events in which parents as well as their children could take part.

Loneliness of farm life. For most farm families, however, farming in 1870 was a hard, lonely way of life. It was especially hard and lonely on the prairies and plains.

Hamlin Garland, who spent his boyhood on farms in Wisconsin, Iowa, and the Dakotas, pictured in his writing the dreary loneliness in isolated farming communities. In his famous collection of tales, *Main-Traveled Roads,* Garland wrote:

"The main-traveled road in the West (as everywhere) is hot and dusty in summer, and desolate and drear with mud in fall and spring, and in winter the winds sweep the snow across it; but it does sometimes cross a rich meadow where the songs of the larks and bobolinks and blackbirds are tangled. . . .

"Mainly it is long and wearyful, and has a dull little town at one end and a home of toil at the other. Like the main-traveled road of life, it is traversed by many classes of people, but the poor and the weary predominate."

Immigrant farmers from Europe, who by 1870 were moving out onto the western prairies and plains, faced special difficulties. These immigrant pioneers had to adjust not only to a strange physical environment but also to a strange and bewildering social environment. Churches were different; schools were different; life in nearly every way was different from what they had known in the Old World. At first neither they nor their American-born neighbors understood each other's language and customs.

Hardest of all, perhaps, were the lives of black settlers who ventured onto the prairies and plains. One great exodus of about 15,000 blacks from the southern states arrived in Kansas in 1879, where they hoped to start new lives free from discrimination. These black newcomers—penniless, weary, and often ill from their long journey—took up homesteads in the unfamiliar lands. To buy a calf, a pig, a few chickens, or a plow, the men worked for wages on nearby farms, on railroads, or in mines. Despite these hardships, many of the black settlers managed to carve out homes for their families in Kansas. Smaller groups of blacks settled in other parts of the West. Most of them endured some form of discrimination from their white neighbors.

New problems. Most American farmers of the 1870's were not unhappy with their lot. They expected to work hard, and they expected to live more or less apart from their neighbors. The hardships that troubled them most were new ones growing out of the new industrial economy that was bringing changes to every part of American life.

SECTION SURVEY

1. In what ways was the life of farm families in 1870 quite similar to farm life in 1770 or 1820?

2. (a) List three adjectives that describe farm life in 1870. (b) Explain why you selected each adjective. (c) Do any of the adjectives seem to be negative? Are any of them positive? Explain.

3. Why was the Saturday drive to town such an important part of farm life?

4. (a) Compare the reasons for the movement of blacks to Kansas in 1879 to the reasons for the immigration of Europeans to America. (b) Compare the problems these blacks may have faced adjusting to their new homes to the problems the immigrants faced.

2 Farmers face complex new problems in the industrial age

For American farmers in general, the last 25 or 30 years of the 1800's brought new problems. Not all farm families were equally affected by these problems, but most of the nation's farmers found themselves in serious trouble. What were some of the new problems that farm families faced?

Overproduction and falling prices. The fundamental causes of agricultural discontent — overproduction and falling prices — were rarely understood by farmers.

From 1865 to about 1900, farmers produced more food than people could afford to buy. This increase of food in the American markets was the result of (1) the rapid opening of new farmland on the prairies and plains and (2) the development of new farm machinery and improved methods of farming.

Why did American farmers not sell their surplus products to other countries? They did, but competing agricultural countries such as Russia, Canada, Argentina, and Australia were also seeking customers and often had the same products that American farmers wanted to export. Thus there was an increased amount of certain kinds of food on the world market as well as in the United States.

In an open-market economy, whenever the supply of any commodity is greater than the demand for that commodity, prices fall. Starting in the 1930's, the federal government tried to support farm prices in the United States, but in the late 1800's, only a few farmers even suggested such a possibility. Thus farm prices kept falling.

Wheat, which had sold for $2.50 a bushel (35.2 liters) in 1868, dropped to about 78 cents a bushel in the late 1880's. Because of high transportation costs and other factors, however, the farmers actually often got only 30 cents a bushel. Corn fell to 15 cents a bushel and, being cheaper than coal, was often used for fuel. Cotton, which in the late 1860's had sold for 65 cents a pound (.45 kilogram),

This cartoon depicts the farmer of the late 1800's as a thin, tattered figure in contrast to the well-fed, well-dressed industrialists who were helped by tariffs passed by Congress and President McKinley (shown dressed as the waiter).

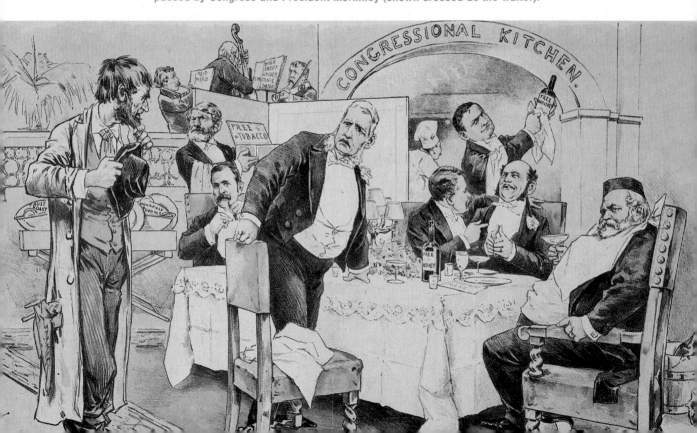

dropped to 5 cents a pound in 1895. Thus growers of these important staple crops were often farming at a loss.

High farm costs. To add to their difficulties, farm families had to pay high prices for their shoes, clothing, kerosene, furniture, farm machinery, household equipment, and other goods. In many instances, prices were high because cheaply made European goods had been kept out of American markets by the high tariffs put on imports to protect American manufacturers. In some instances, prices were high because they had been artificially raised by monopolies.

To make matters worse, farm families almost always owed money. Many had borrowed money in the form of mortgages to pay for their land, homes, and barns. They had added to this burden of debt by borrowing money to pay for fences, livestock, seed, and machinery. As prices for farm products fell, the farmers could not pay their debts. To head off disaster, they increased their mortgages by borrowing more money, thus adding to their debt.

The 1880's were often called "the decade of mortgages." Of the total number of farms in the country, 43 percent were mortgaged. In Kansas the number reached 60 percent. Of course, these mortgages often were necessary. By means of mortgages, families with little or no money could borrow the capital they needed to buy a farm, purchase farm machinery, or make improvements on existing farms. It was not so much mortgages themselves but rather the hard times and the high interest rates that troubled the farmers.

During the late 1800's, interest rates on western farm loans ran from 8 to 20 percent. These rates were higher than interest rates charged to industrial and commercial enterprises. Bankers and other money lenders justified the higher rates on farm loans on the ground that farming was a riskier business than industry or commerce. In addition to the high rates, money brokers charged a commission for arranging farm loans. In several farm states, loan brokers starting with nothing became millionaires within a few years.

The problem of money. The farmers blamed their troubles on the shortage of money, which was only part of the problem, but an important part. To understand the farmers' point of view, it is necessary to see how money affected their everyday lives.

The first thing to remember is that money is a **medium of exchange**—that is, something of value given in exchange for goods or services. Its value is determined by the goods or services it will buy. A flour miller might say, "One dollar will buy one bushel of wheat." A farmer might say, "One bushel of wheat will buy one dollar." The miller and the farmer are saying the same thing; both of them are stating the value of a dollar *and* the value of a bushel of wheat.

The second thing to remember is that there are two ways to change the value of a dollar *and* the value of a bushel of wheat. All other things being equal, if you *increase the amount of wheat*—for example, double it—then "one dollar will buy two bushels of wheat" or "two bushels of wheat will buy one dollar." If you *decrease the number of dollars in circulation*—say, by one half—you can accomplish the same result. For example, one half as many dollars will now buy just as much wheat. That is, "50 cents will buy one bushel of wheat" and "one dollar will buy two bushels of wheat," or again, "two bushels of wheat will buy one dollar." In practice, the problem of money value is not this simple, but the illustration may help to clarify the problem of western farmers.

Falling farm prices. Between 1870 and 1900, the price, or value, of farm products fell lower and lower. In other words, the value of money rose higher and higher. Consider a specific example. In 1868 Olaf Erickson sold 1,000 bushels (35,238 liters) of wheat at $2.50 a bushel. In 1868, then, his wheat brought him $2,500. Since his interest payments amounted to $250 that year, Olaf could pay this interest with the income from 100 bushels (3,524 liters) of wheat, or one tenth of his income. Each year from 1868 on, Olaf continued to grow and sell 1,000 bushels of wheat. But by 1890 wheat was bringing only 75 cents a bushel. Olaf's income in 1890, therefore, was only $750. Since his interest payments still amounted to $250, he now had to pay his debt with the income from 334 bushels (11,769 liters) of wheat, or one third of his total income.

As far as Olaf could tell, he had done nothing to cause this. Yet his income had dropped from $2,500 to $750 a year. Something was wrong. Olaf and his family were working as hard and raising as much wheat as ever.

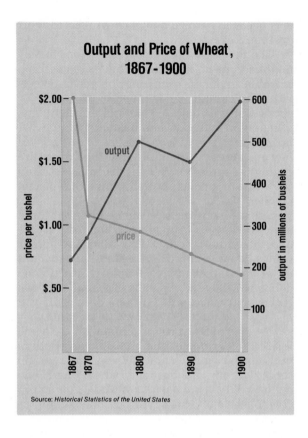

Output and Price of Wheat, 1867-1900

output

price

price per bushel

$2.00
$1.50
$1.00
$.50

output in millions of bushels

600
500
400
300
200
100

1867
1870
1880
1890
1900

Source: *Historical Statistics of the United States*

Clearly, Olaf reasoned, the *value of money* had changed. Money was harder to get; money was scarce or "tight." It had gone up in value. That was why, Olaf thought, the same amount of wheat brought him fewer dollars each year.

Olaf forgot that there were many more farmers in 1890, both in the United States and in other countries, than there had been in 1868. These farmers were producing far more wheat than they had produced in 1868.

Although Olaf did not understand the whole problem, he did have his finger upon one key to his difficulties. The supply of money in the United States was not expanding rapidly enough during the late 1800's to meet the needs of the new industrial economy. The answer, as Olaf saw it, was simple enough: Let the government increase the amount of money in circulation. This would "cheapen" the dollar and raise the price of farm products. Olaf could then pay his debts and buy the goods that his family needed.

The distributors. Farmers also blamed many of their difficulties on the distributors who bought from the farmers and sold to whole-salers and retailers. The services performed by these brokers, produce buyers, grain-elevator operators, and stockyard owners were important in the distribution of farm products. However, the farmers believed that the distributors were taking too large a share of the wealth produced on farms and ranches.

Many distributors no doubt did take advantage of the farmers. Farmers, having little cash and credit and needing money to pay their debts, had to sell their goods at harvest time even if prices were low. The distributors, backed by considerable capital, could afford to store what they bought from the farmers until prices went up. Of course, prices did not always go up, and distributors were sometimes ruined when prices fell.

The railroads. Farmers, especially on the prairies and plains, reserved their chief hatred, however, for the railroads. Like other Americans, including small business owners, farmers had at first welcomed the railroad with enthusiasm. They believed that it would open distant markets to them and increase the value of their farmland by bringing more farmers into the community. Farmers who could afford to do so often bought a few shares of railroad stock. The governments of small farming communities often invested money in railroad stocks and bonds in return for the railroad's promise to build a branch line to the community.

Unfortunately, events did not always turn out as the farmers expected. In the first place, the railroad stock that farmers owned represented only a small part of all the stock sold. Therefore the farmers had little voice in determining railroad policies.

In the second place, the farmers expected that competition among the railroads would keep freight rates low. In this hope they were also disappointed. For example, competing railroads bid against each other for long-haul shipments between two distant cities served by two or more lines, sometimes cutting their rates so low that they operated at actual losses. They made up these losses, however, by charging much higher rates for short-haul shipments to those communities that were served by only one railroad.

Farmers and other small shippers protested, of course, against this so-called "long-haul, short-haul abuse" on the part of the railroads. However, it was very difficult for them to do anything about the situation.

Many of the hardships that farmers faced in the late 1800's were new, strange, and complicated. Most farmers did not at first understand the complexities of overproduction, falling prices, "tight money," high interest rates, distributors, and high shipping costs. Like all other Americans, the farmers had to grope their way into the industrial age.

SECTION SURVEY

IDENTIFY: medium of exchange, "tight money," long-haul shipments, short-haul shipments.

1. What were the farmers' grievances against (a) the distributors and (b) the railroads?
2. How were the new problems that farmers faced in the late 1800's related to industrialization?
3. Graph Study: Look at the graph on page 126. How does it illustrate a major problem American farmers faced in the period following the Civil War?

3 Farm organizations join efforts to regulate the railroads

The farmers soon learned that only through cooperative action could they hope to share the advantages that were emerging from the new industrial economy.

The Grange. The first national farm organization, started in 1867, was called the Grange, or the Patrons of Husbandry. Its founder, Oliver Hudson Kelley, wanted to establish a national organization with a local chapter in every farm community. Farm families could meet in these chapters for recreation and to learn better ways of farming.

At first Kelley fought an uphill battle in organizing the Grange. By 1872, however, farm prices were falling rapidly, and the farmers, bewildered and disturbed, joined the Grange in growing numbers. By 1875 some 1.5 million farmers, most of them in the Middle West, were Grange members.

Farmers' cooperatives. Kelley had started the Grange primarily to combat social isolation and lack of educational opportunity. The farmers who joined in the 1870's, however, were more interested in solving economic problems and carrying out their slogans—"Cooperation" and "Down with monopoly."

Working together in the Grange and in other local farm organizations, many farmers set up cooperative associations, usually called **cooperatives.** Cooperatives owned and managed by the farmers themselves could bypass distributors. The cooperative could (1) sell the produce of a group of farmers directly to big-city markets and (2) buy farm machines, clothing, and household goods in large quantities at wholesale prices. Before long, farmers set up not only cooperative stores but also cooperative grain storage elevators, creameries, and even factories to manufacture their own farm machines and equipment.

Some of these early cooperative ventures were successful. However, most of them failed, partly because farmers often lacked business experience, partly because farmers did not have enough capital to compete successfully with established businesses. Despite failures the farmers did not give up, for they still had the possibility of political action.

Opposing unfair railroad practices. As early as 1870, farmers, the owners of small businesses, and lawyers persuaded the Illinois state legislature to investigate unfair practices by the railroads. In 1871 the Illinois legislature created a commission to fix maximum freight rates and made it illegal for a railroad to charge differential freight rates. The legislatures of Minnesota and Iowa passed similar laws, as did the legislature of Wisconsin, where the Grangers were the chief backers of railroad regulation.

The railroads opposed these laws and sometimes refused to obey them. In 1876 and 1877, the Supreme Court heard a series of cases known as the "Granger cases," of which the most far-reaching was *Munn v. Illinois.* The Court ruled that state legislatures had the right to regulate businesses that affected the public, including grain elevators and railroads.

Unfortunately for the farmers, the railroads either evaded the laws or exerted enough pressure on the legislators to get the laws repealed. The most serious blow for the farmers, however, came in 1886, when the Supreme Court qualified its decision in the "Granger cases." It now ruled that state legis-

This 1876 poster for the Grange, or the Patrons of Husbandry, reflects the central position that the farmers believed they held in the nation's work and life.

latures had no power to regulate traffic that moved across state boundaries. The Court held that only the federal government could regulate the interstate activities of railroads.

The Interstate Commerce Act. The 1886 Supreme Court decision led Congress to pass the Interstate Commerce Act of 1887 to correct a number of the railroads' practices.

Pooling arrangements by the railroads were one of the practices opposed by farmers, many business people, and the public. Several railroads operating in the same area and across state borders would join to form a pool. All members of the pool then agreed not to compete, but instead to charge certain agreed-upon rates. As a result, farmers and others using the railroads often had to pay exorbitant rates.

Another practice the public wanted corrected was the granting of special favors. In order to get business, competing railroads often gave large corporations especially low rates. Sometimes, instead of actually lowering the rates, the railroads agreed to grant **rebates,** that is, to refund part of the shipping charges.

Farmers, small businesses, and the public also complained, as you know, that railroads sometimes charged more for a short haul than for a long haul. It sometimes cost more to send goods a few miles than to send the same goods from, say, Chicago to New York.

SOURCES

MUNN v. ILLINOIS (1877)

Property does become clothed with a public interest when used in a manner to make it of public consequence, and affect the community at large. When, therefore, one devotes his property to a use in which the public has an interest, he, in effect, grants to the public an interest in that use, and must submit to be controlled by the public for the common good, to the extent of the interest he has thus created. He may withdraw his grant by discontinuing the use; but, so long as he maintains the use, he must submit to the control. . . .

Provisions of the act. The Interstate Commerce Act applied to all railroads passing through more than one state. The act made it illegal for such railroads to (1) make pooling arrangements, (2) give special favors in the form of lower rates or rebates, (3) charge more for a short haul than for a long haul over the same line, or (4) charge unjust or unreasonable rates. The act also required the railroads to print and display their rates and to give a minimum of ten days' public notice before they changed those rates.

Finally, the Interstate Commerce Act created an Interstate Commerce Commission (ICC) of five members appointed by the President and confirmed by the Senate. The commission had authority to (1) investigate complaints against the railroads, (2) summon witnesses, (3) examine a railroad's accounts and correspondence, and (4) require railroads to file annual reports about their operations and finances and to adopt a uniform system of accounting.

The commission, however, had no real authority to fix rates and to enforce its orders. If a railroad refused to accept the commission's proposals, the commission had to appeal to the courts for an order compelling the railroads to obey. In some instances, the courts refused to grant the commission's requests for such orders. In other instances, the courts reversed the commission's decision.

Despite its limitations, the Interstate Commerce Act was the first important attempt by the federal government to regulate transportation and to create a federal regulatory commission. Because the act set a precedent for more sweeping measures later adopted by Congress, it marked a turning point in the history of the relations between the federal government and business.

SECTION SURVEY

IDENTIFY: the Grange, Oliver Kelley, cooperatives, *Munn v. Illinois*, rebates.

1. (a) What were the goals of the Grange? (b) How successful was the Grange in achieving these goals?
2. (a) What were the provisions of the Interstate Commerce Act of 1887? (b) What were its limitations? (c) Why was the act significant?
3. What role did the Supreme Court play in the effort to regulate the railroads?

4 Farm organizations put increasing pressure on government

While struggling with railroad legislation, farmers also turned to a more serious problem —falling prices for farm produce. Ignoring the facts of overproduction and competition from farmers overseas, they blamed low farm prices solely on the scarcity of money.

Politics and paper money. The farmers' analysis of their problem was partly right, for during the late 1860's and the 1870's, money was becoming increasingly scarce. In 1865, for example, the amount of currency, or money of all kinds, in circulation in the United States averaged $31.18 per person. By 1878 the average had dropped to $17.08.

Faced with growing hardship, farmers demanded that the government increase the supply of currency in circulation. When neither the Republicans nor the Democrats promised to help them, farmers began to join the Greenback-Labor Party, commonly called the Greenback Party.

The Greenback Party took its name from the paper money known as "greenbacks," which had been issued by the government during the Civil War. After the war the government began to withdraw the greenbacks from circulation. Farmers and other "cheap money" advocates protested. They wanted *more,* not fewer, greenbacks in circulation.

The "cheap money" people did not get what they wanted. Instead, Congress adopted the Resumption Act in 1875. This act ordered the Secretary of the Treasury to redeem *in gold* all greenbacks presented to the Treasury on or after January 1, 1879. As a result of this compromise, by January 1, 1879, greenbacks were worth their full, or face, value in gold. Under these circumstances, owners of greenbacks did not bother to redeem them. Congress decided to allow 346 million greenbacks to remain in circulation as part of United States currency.

In 1875, dismayed by Congress's decision to redeem the greenbacks in gold, the "cheap money" advocates decided to take their case to the people at the polls. Although the newly organized Greenback Party did not win a significant number of votes in the 1876 election,

This is obviously the work of a cartoonist who had little respect for those who favored greenbacks. What devices does he use to make fun of these people? What kind of people does he show them to be?

began to fall. In 1874, for the first time in more than 30 years, 16 ounces of silver bullion were sold on the open market for *less than* one ounce of gold.

Faced with falling prices, silver producers remembered the government's offer to buy silver at the ratio of 16 to 1. They now tried to sell their silver bullion to the Treasury Department but discovered that in 1873 Congress had passed a law removing silver dollars from the list of standard coins. Furious at the loss of a profitable market for their bullion, silver producers denounced Congress for what they called the "Crime of '73."

The "Crime of '73" became a rallying cry for those who demanded that the government buy silver. This demand came mostly from westerners, but it was also supported by other Americans, including farmers, who wanted more currency in circulation.

The Bland-Allison Act. In 1877 Representative Richard P. Bland of Missouri introduced a bill calling for free and unlimited coinage of silver dollars at a ratio of 16 silver dollars to 1 gold dollar. When this bill reached the Senate, it was modified by Senator William B. Allison of Iowa to become the Bland-Allison bill.

The Bland-Allison bill authorized the Treasury Department to buy and to mint not less than $2 million and not more than $4 million worth of silver each month. President Hayes vetoed the bill, but Congress passed it over his veto in 1878. The new law was a partial victory for the silver interests, the Greenbackers, and other "cheap money" people.

Failure of the Greenbackers. The Greenback Party reached its greatest power in 1878, when it polled 1 million votes and elected members to Congress. This was a shock to the two major parties, but the triumph was short-lived. Two years later the Greenback Presidential candidate, General J. B. Weaver, received only 300,000 votes.

Although it failed to achieve its goal, the Greenback movement, like the Grange movement, taught the farmers several valuable lessons. The farmers learned from their experience with the Grange that they could, if united, gain influence in state legislatures. They learned from the Greenback movement that their influence might be felt even in Congress. Above all, they learned that the secret of power lay in organization.

the Greenbackers continued their battle for "cheap money."

The silver issue. Rutherford B. Hayes, who became President in 1877, successfully opposed the pressure of the Greenbackers to get more paper money into circulation. However, he was unable to block another move by the "cheap money" people to increase the volume of currency in the economy.

Back in 1834 the government had adopted a law providing for the coinage of both gold and silver, at a ratio of about 16 to 1. That is, the government offered to buy 16 ounces (453.6 grams) of silver for the same price it paid for one ounce (28.3 grams) of gold. At the time, silver was relatively scarce, and silver producers could sell 16 ounces of silver to private buyers for *more than* one ounce of gold. As a result, they did not take silver to the United States Mint to be coined into silver dollars.

In the 1870's, however, this situation changed. With the discovery of huge silver deposits in parts of Colorado and Nevada, the supply of silver increased tremendously. The value of silver **bullion,** or uncoined metal,

130

Farmers' alliances. Even before the Greenback Party began to break up, farmers were forming organizations called "alliances." During the early 1880's, the different state alliances in the North and Northwest set up a loose federation called the Northern, or Northwestern, Farmers' Alliance. The southern groups joined in a much more tightly knit organization known as the Southern Alliance.

Like the Grange, the alliances experimented with cooperative buying and selling organizations. They were prepared to take action to protect the farmers from the exploitation they were subjected to by manufacturers, railroads, and distributors.

Hard times in the late 1880's transformed the alliances into influential political organizations. By 1890, for example, the Southern Alliance had 3 million white members, while 1 million southern black farmers were enrolled in an affiliated Colored Alliance. A proposal to merge the Southern Alliance and the Northwestern Farmers' Alliance failed, however, because southerners insisted upon separate white and black lodges in the merged alliance. The Northern alliance leaders refused to accept this arrangement.

Desperate conditions. Starting in 1886, a 10-year series of droughts on the Great Plains turned farmland into arid desert. Driven to desperation, thousands of farmers finally gave up and moved back east. Others remained and continued to fight the land and those they held responsible for much of their trouble — the owners of railroads and factories, the directors of banks and insurance companies that held farm mortgages, and the distributors who bought and sold farm produce. The farmers also continued their pressure, along with other "cheap money" interests, to get the government to put more money into circulation.

Sherman Silver Purchase Act. In 1889 and 1890, six new states entered the Union — North Dakota, South Dakota, Montana, Washington, Idaho, and Wyoming. These states, all in the West, greatly increased the political strength of the farmers and the silver-mining interests in Congress. Members of Congress representing farming and silver-mining areas agreed to make a deal with the Republicans, who wanted to increase tariff rates. They agreed to vote for the McKinley Tariff Act if the high-tariff members voted for a "cheap money" bill.

As a result of this deal, the Sherman Silver Purchase Act became law in 1890. This act required the United States Treasury to purchase 4.5 million ounces (127.6 million grams) of silver each month at the market price and to pay for this silver with paper money that could be redeemed in gold or silver.

Silver miners hoped that the law would raise the price of silver, and farmers hoped that, by increasing the supply of money, it would raise the prices of farm produce. These expectations were not realized. The purchased silver was not coined, and the money in circulation did not greatly increase.

New farm leaders. Leaders of the Farmers' Alliances who supported the Sherman Silver Purchase Act and other legislation favorable to farmers became national figures. Among them was Ignatius Donnelly of Minnesota, a spellbinder on the platform and a pamphleteer with a biting literary style. In Kansas there was "Sockless Jerry" Simpson, who denounced the rich eastern monopolists. Kansas produced two other influential leaders — Mary Elizabeth Lease, a colorful and dynamic orator, and Annie Diggs, an editor and an effective behind-the-scenes political worker. One of the most effective of the speakers and writers was Sara Elizabeth Emery of Michigan. Her widely read book *Seven Financial Conspiracies,* which was published in 1888, called on farmers and workers to unite and break the "conspiratorial money power."

In the South a new group of political leaders representing the poorer farmers arose to challenge the leaders of the Democratic Party. Among them were Governor James Hogg of Texas, Tom Watson of Georgia, and "Pitchfork Ben" Tillman of South Carolina.

Thanks to such leaders, the voices of farmers would be heard more clearly in the nation. The needs and concerns of the farmers that these leaders addressed would become increasingly important in national politics.

SECTION SURVEY

IDENTIFY. Greenback Party, "cheap money," "Crime of '73," Farmers' Alliances, Sherman Silver Purchase Act of 1890, Sara Elizabeth Emery.

1. (a) What were the goals of the Greenback Party? (b) How successful was it in achieving these goals?

2. Explain how the Bland-Allison Act was a partial victory for "cheap money" advocates.

3. (a) What factors led to the passage of the Sherman Silver Purchase Act? (b) What were its provisions? (c) What did the act's supporters hope it would accomplish?

5 The farmers fail to win control of the national government

By 1890, American farmers were facing a major question: Should they form a third party? This was the question that farmers discussed in schoolhouses and Grange halls in the summer of that year. Many northern farmers favored a third party. Because of a split in southern Democratic ranks, most southern farmers opposed it.

The Populist Party. The Congressional elections in the fall of 1890 drew farm men and women into what seemed to be a fiery crusade. Speakers such as Mary Elizabeth Lease bluntly stated the farmers' grievances. In a powerful speech, she proclaimed, "Wall Street° owns the country. It is no longer a government of the people, by the people, and for the people, but a government of Wall Street, by Wall Street, and for Wall Street. The great common people of this country are slaves, and monopoly is the master. The West and South are bound and prostrate before the manufacturing East. . . . We want money, land, and transportation. . . . The people are at bay. Let the bloodhounds of money who have dogged us thus far beware."

Fired by this new militant spirit, Republican and Democratic farmers decided in 1891 to forget their political differences and form a third party. A meeting made up chiefly of Farmers' Alliance leaders from the West and Middle West launched the People's Party, or the Populist Party, at Cincinnati, Ohio, in 1891. In Omaha, Nebraska, the following year, the Populists drew up a platform and nominated James B. Weaver of Iowa for President of the United States.

°**Wall Street:** a street in New York City's financial district, the nation's principal financial center; often used as a symbol of large banking and business interests.

The Populist platform. On July 4, 1892, the Populists adopted their platform, demanding far-reaching reforms. In part, it stated, "We meet in the midst of a nation brought to the verge of moral, political, and material ruin. . . . The people are demoralized. . . . We have witnessed for more than a quarter of a century the struggles of the two great political parties for power and plunder, while grievous wrongs have been inflicted upon the suffering people. We charge that the controlling influences dominating both these parties have permitted the existing dreadful conditions to develop without serious effort to prevent or restrain them. Neither do they now promise us any substantial reform."

The Populist platform then listed the specific demands of the farmers: (1) an increase in the currency, to be secured by the "free and unlimited coinage of silver at a ratio of 16 to 1"; (2) government ownership of railroads, telegraphs, and telephones; (3) the return to the government of all land held by railroads and other corporations in excess of their needs; (4) a graduated income tax, requiring people with higher incomes to pay a proportionally higher tax; (5) a system of national warehouses where farm produce could be stored until market conditions improved, with the government providing loans on each deposit by a farmer; (6) democratic political reforms, including the direct election of United States Senators and the adoption of the secret ballot, the initiative, and the referendum.

The Populist Party had some support from industrial wage earners. Its platform demanded shorter working hours and restrictions on immigration, which many workers held responsible for unemployment and low wages.

The election of 1892. In the campaign of 1892, great crowds of farmers in the Middle West gathered at outdoor meetings and picnics to listen to eloquent Populist speakers. Weaver, the Populist Presidential candidate, traveled widely and spoke to enthusiastic audiences in the Middle West.

In the South, however, the story was different because of the racial situation. Conservative Democrats and Populists alike were willing to let black southerners vote—but only if it seemed certain that they could control the black vote. Populist leaders, however, urged poor farmers, white and black, to vote together against their "exploiters," the well-to-do planters and business people of the Democratic Party. This angered many white southerners, rich and poor alike, who feared that the Populist bid for black support might endanger white supremacy. Populist speakers in the South were greeted with howls and jeers.

The Populist bid for southern black votes was not very successful. The Populists did not attempt to build a strong or lasting alliance between poor white and black southerners. They did not work for federal supervision of elections, which would have guaranteed the right of black southerners to vote. Nor did the Populists support other efforts of southern blacks to overcome their grievances. Thus Populist candidates in the election of 1892 were generally defeated in the South.

President Benjamin Harrison, running for reelection on the Republican ticket, was defeated by the Democratic candidate, Grover Cleveland. The Democratic victory was a sweeping one, but the Populists made an impressive showing in the nation, despite their weakness in the South. They polled more than 1 million popular votes, won 22 electoral votes for their Presidential candidate, and gained seats in state legislatures and in Congress. Democrats and Republicans alike realized that the Populist movement was much more than the protest of a few discontented Americans.

Depression and discontent. For the two older political parties, however, the Populist movement was only the beginning of their difficulties. In 1893 the country sank into a serious economic depression. Farm prices plunged. Factories closed, and thousands of unemployed workers walked the streets trying to find jobs.

President Cleveland blamed the crisis on the Sherman Silver Purchase Act of 1890. He believed that it was not "tight money" that had led to the depression but rather uncertainty over the value of money. Cleveland insisted that the only way to end the depression was to accept gold as the single standard of value for the nation's currency. This was an oversimplified explanation, for the depression was worldwide, but there was some truth in the President's view.

Farmers and wage earners, on the other hand, blamed the depression on "tight money." They felt that the Sherman Silver Purchase Act had not gone far enough. They demanded that the government increase the amount of

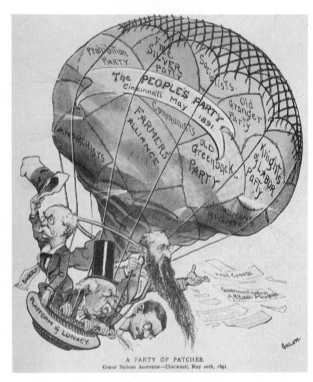

A PARTY OF PATCHES.
Grand Balloon Ascension—Cincinnati, May 20th, 1891.

Here the Populist Party is likened to a balloon made up of a crazy quilt of special-interest groups. Those riding about in the balloon are the groups' leaders.

currency in circulation by the "free and unlimited coinage of silver at a ratio of 16 to 1." They believed that the resulting increase in "cheap money" would end the depression.

Shrinking gold reserves. By 1893, however, the policy of **bimetallism** had become a matter of deep concern for the Treasury Department. This policy meant that two metals, gold and silver, furnished the security for all the nation's currency. The value of silver had fallen until the actual silver in a silver dollar was worth only 60 cents. Since silver as well as gold provided the backing, or security, for the nation's currency, more Americans began to grow uneasy about this situation. As a result, many people began to exchange their silver bank notes for gold coins rather than for silver coins. By March 1893 the gold reserves had shrunk to only a little more than $100 million.

The shrinkage in gold reserves created a serious government crisis. If the gold reserves completely disappeared, the government would not be able to keep its promise to exchange gold coins for paper money. It would, instead, have

133

In 1892 a Republican and a Democrat in Chicago bet on an election. The one whose candidate lost would have to pull a wagon through the streets of the city carrying the one whose candidate won. Joseph Kir painted the triumphant Democrat and the "workhorse" Republican in his picture "The Last Bet."

to pay with silver. Since by midsummer of 1893 the value of a silver dollar had fallen to 49 cents, prices would soar and the nation would head toward economic disaster.

Stopping the run on gold. President Cleveland called a special session of Congress to repeal the Sherman Silver Purchase Act. Representatives of silver mines, farmers, and "cheap money" people in general refused to consider repeal. By late fall, however, the administration finally had enough votes to push the repeal bill through Congress.

Repeal of the Sherman Silver Purchase Act stopped the flow of silver into the Treasury, but gold reserves continued to shrink. There were still many millions of silver bank notes in circulation, and the Treasury kept on redeeming them in gold. By 1895 the gold reserves had dropped to only $41 million. It seemed to be only a question of time before the United States would go off the gold standard—that is, would stop redeeming its paper currency with gold—and runaway inflation would start.

At this critical point, President Cleveland accepted the offer of a group of bankers headed by J. P. Morgan to lend gold to the government in return for government bonds as security. The arrangement worked. With leading bankers behind the government, confidence returned and the run on the gold reserves ended. Many Americans, those with "sound money" views, felt that President Cleveland and the bankers had acted wisely and had saved the nation from disaster. "Cheap money" Americans were furious and pointed out that the bankers had charged a generous commission for their services. They insisted that the President had made a deal with Wall Street.

Choosing candidates. By the time of the Presidential election of 1896, both major parties were split between the "sound money," gold-standard people and the "cheap money," silver people.

The Republicans chose as their Presidential candidate William McKinley of Ohio. Although McKinley tried to straddle the money issue, he came to be regarded as the leader of those people who favored the gold standard.

The Democratic convention opened with a bitter struggle between the "sound money" wing of the party and the "silver" wing. The "sound money" delegates were soon howled down, and "cheap money" delegates adopted a platform demanding "free and unlimited coinage of both gold and silver." The battle lines were drawn, with the Republicans on the "sound money" side and the majority of Democrats on the "cheap money" side. But the Democratic delegates had not yet selected a Presidential candidate.

William Jennings Bryan. The field was wide open when a handsome young lawyer stepped forward to address the convention. Only 36 years old, William Jennings Bryan of Nebraska had served in the House of Representatives for four years. This was his only political experience in the national capital. Nevertheless, his striking appearance and his compelling speech captured the attention of his audience.

"You come to us and tell us that the great cities are in favor of the gold standard," Bryan cried. "We reply that the great cities rest upon our broad and fertile prairies. Burn down your cities and leave our farms, and your cities will spring up again as if by magic; but destroy our farms and the grass will grow in the streets of every city in the country. . . .

"Having behind us the producing masses of this nation and the world, supported by the commercial interests, the laboring interests, and the toilers everywhere, we will answer their demand for a gold standard by saying to them, 'You shall not press down upon the brow of labor this crown of thorns, you shall not crucify mankind upon a cross of gold!'"

With the closing words of Bryan's "Cross of Gold" speech, wild tumult broke out at the convention. Here was the Democratic candidate!

The Democratic nomination of Bryan and the adoption of a platform demanding free and unlimited coinage of silver left the Populists in an awkward position. The Democrats had stolen their thunder. When they met in convention, the Populists decided to support Bryan as their Presidential candidate. To preserve their party identity, they nominated Tom Watson of Georgia for the Vice-Presidency rather than Arthur Sewall of Maine, who was the Democratic nominee.

Bryan's crusade. Bryan turned the election campaign into a crusade. In 14 exhausting weeks, during which he traveled vast distances by railroad, Bryan made 600 speeches to 5 million people in 27 states. Bryan's speeches succeeded in rousing his supporters to frenzies of enthusiasm.

The "sound money" people threw all their energy and resources into defeating Bryan. Under the leadership of Mark Hanna of Ohio, McKinley's campaign manager and a wealthy business leader, the Republicans raised at least $3.5 million to offset Bryan's $300,000 campaign fund. Some of this campaign fund was used to bring trainloads of people to McKinley's hometown to hear him read disarming speeches from his front porch. Nearly every influential newspaper in the country backed the Republicans. Many factories paid their workers on the Saturday before election with the warning that they would have no jobs if Bryan won the election.

McKinley's victory. Bryan lost with 176 electoral votes to McKinley's 271. The popular vote was much closer—7 million for the Republicans, 6.5 million for the Democrats. Although the country had decided in favor of the gold standard, the farmers and other "cheap money" advocates had come close to winning the Presidency and control of Congress.

Defeat in the 1896 election and the arrival of better times for the farmers ended the power of the Populist Party. As you will read, however, during the early 1900's, a new third party, the Progressive Party, as well as progressive Democrats and Republicans won many of the same reforms that the Populists had demanded.

SECTION SURVEY

IDENTIFY: Mary Elizabeth Lease, James Weaver, bimetallism, gold standard, William McKinley, William Jennings Bryan, "Cross of Gold" speech, Mark Hanna.

1. Explain how the Populist Party planks listed on page 132 would have helped farmers in 1892.
2. In the political struggle in the South, black southerners were caught in the middle. Comment.
3. How did the "tight money" and "cheap money" people each explain the cause of the depression of 1893?

Chapter Survey

Summary: Tracing the Main Ideas

Increasing industrialization created many new problems after 1870 for farmers as well as for all other Americans. Most farmers lost the individual freedom they had possessed when they produced a good part of what they needed on their own land. Overproduction brought falling prices and growing distress. Increasingly, farmers became dependent upon forces that they could not control. They depended upon the railroads that carried their goods to market and upon prices fixed in distant markets. They were also affected by tariffs that sometimes raised the cost of manufactured goods and by the supply of money made available by the federal government.

Faced with these new problems, farmers organized new political parties and increased their role in the old parties in an effort to influence state and federal governments. They hoped to secure laws that would regulate the railroads, the industries, and the other parts of the economic system and thus make life easier for farm people.

Industrialism brought benefits as well as problems. Power-driven machines made life immeasurably easier. Increased production enabled farmers to feed themselves and their fellow citizens far better than people had ever been fed before. Developments in transportation and communications broke down the isolation of farm life and brought farm families into touch with the life of the world beyond the borders of the farm.

It was as difficult for farmers as it was for all other Americans to adjust to the new industrial age. The problems were all too real. By the 1900's, however, farmers began to understand that Americans were becoming more and more interdependent. The farmers began to see that their best hope of realizing the bright promise of the new age was in learning to work together.

Inquiring into History

1. How did industrialization both benefit and hurt farmers during the late 1800's?
2. (a) Why did farmers favor "cheap money" (greenbacks) and free and unlimited coinage of silver? (b) To what extent were farmers successful in obtaining these things?
3. Explain why you would have felt as you did about "cheap money" vs. "sound money" if you had been (a) a debtor farmer, (b) a retired person living on a fixed income, or (c) a banker.
4. Give examples to support this statement: During the late 1800's, farmers learned that one way to gain power was through organization.

Relating Past to Present

1. How does the relationship between government and farmers today compare with their relationship during the late 1800's?
2. Find examples of recent third parties. How did their goals, methods, and results compare to those of the Populists?

Developing Social Science Skills

1. Choose an election discussed in this chapter. Design and prepare campaign posters—one for each major candidate in that election. Be prepared to explain why each poster would be effective in convincing people to vote for the candidate.
2. Imagine that you live on a farm in Kansas in 1880. Prepare a series of journal entries describing some typical activities, such as (a) a trip to town, (b) a day at school, (c) a meeting of the local chapter of the Grange.
3. Make a chart or graph presenting the following information: In 1820, one farm worker produced enough food to feed 4.5 people. In 1890 a farm worker produced enough for 6.5 people; in 1900, enough for 7 people; in 1950 for 16 people; in 1960 for 27 people; and in 1970 for 47 people. Then answer these questions: (a) Why do you think farm production per worker increased between 1820 and 1890? (b) Why can the farmers of the United States today feed the nation's large population even though there are fewer of them than there were in 1900?

Industry

The Corliss engine.

In 1876, to mark the nation's 100th birthday, Philadelphia held a huge Centennial Exposition. It housed thousands of exhibits from around the world and drew millions of visitors.

The big attraction was Machinery Hall, where America's new industrial processes were displayed. The wonder of the Hall was the giant 1,600-horsepower Corliss steam engine. The Corliss engine also stood as a symbol of the nation's growing industrial might. More than any other exhibit, it showed that America had taken its place among nations as an industrial giant.

Steelmaking was important to America's industrialization, but in the 1800's it was backbreaking and dangerous work.

The Industrial Revolution had far-reaching consequences and radically changed American life. It was the result of many events and trends that had their origins in Europe and colonial America.

Though originally a land of farmers, from its beginnings the nation was involved in commerce. The early colonists exported many of America's resources to Europe as well as some manufactured goods.

As industrialization increased, Americans made use of the nation's resources right in their own factories. Many people then left farms to become part of the growing urban work force. This industrialization was a slow process and progressed at different rates in different parts of the country.

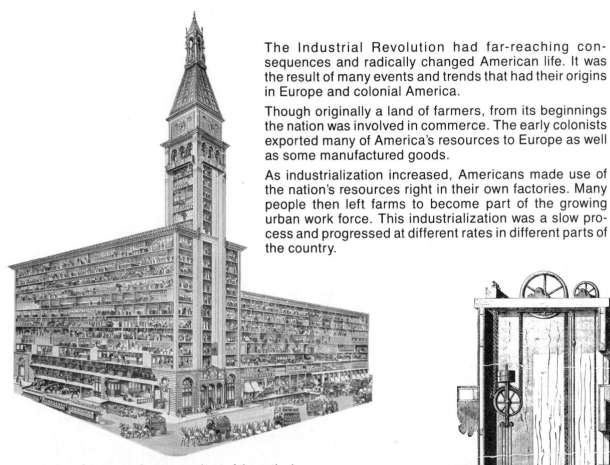

As new products poured out of the nation's factories, new means of selling them were required. The mail-order house of the late 1800's filled an important need.

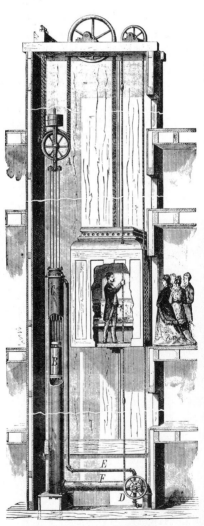

Steel beams were the stuff that made tall buildings possible; elevators, first common in the early 1800's, made them practical.

The Industrial Revolution in America started in New England's textile mills.

138

The ingenuity of American inventors such as Thomas Edison was a major factor in the nation's successful industrialization.

In time the new industrial technology moved into the countryside, as this portable steam engine and sawmill demonstrate.

Without its working people, America could never have become an industrialized nation. Many immigrants as well as women and children provided the human power industry needed.

The new technology is at work here. Computers run this steel mill.

"Think big but build small" was a lesson America learned from its space engineers. Soon microelectronics were adapted to many industries.

To some people the mid-1900's marked the beginning of a second industrial revolution. This new era was one of electronics and space-age technology. Computers, microcircuits, satellites, and synthetics were some of the tools of this new age.

The effects of industrialization in the 1800's were highly visible. Huge machines, towering smokestacks, and miles of highways and railroad tracks altered the American landscape. The effects of the new technology were less visible. One would have to look inside the home, the factory, and the laboratory to see how the new technology was changing life.

The Industrial Revolution helped to reshape the nation's landscape.

Chapter **7**

New Life Styles in the New Industrial Age

"We cannot all live in cities," Horace Greeley once remarked, "yet nearly all seem determined to do so." Greeley, the famous newspaper editor, was speaking of a change in the way Americans lived. From 1865 to 1900, people were moving away from the rural areas and into the great urban centers, a trend known as "urbanization."

What was the compelling attraction of the growing cities? The answer was "opportunity"—opportunity for adventure, opportunity to win fame and fortune. The city offered jobs in offices and factories, work in the building trades, employment for both skilled and unskilled workers, the chance to carve out a successful career in any of hundreds of enterprises. Many people, especially young people, were eager to share in the excitement of the new industrial age. They found the many attractions of urban life irresistible.

For a number of years, ways of life in the city and the countryside drew far apart, and terms like "city slicker" and "country hick" were often heard. As the years passed, however, the differences between life in rural and in urban areas became less marked.

THE CHAPTER IN OUTLINE

1. Cities grow and change under the impact of industrialism.

2. Education responds to the changing patterns of American life.

3. American writing reflects the new industrial age.

4. Architecture and other fine arts respond to a changing society.

5. New forms of recreation enrich American life.

Changing Ways of American Life

1860's–1890's

1 Cities grow and change under the impact of industrialism

The city had many faces. It was stores and banks and offices, museums and libraries and theaters, churches and schools. It was freight yards—and, in seaports, waterfronts—ringed by factories, warehouses, stockyards, and wholesale markets. It was drab tenement buildings crowded along narrow, dirty streets and alleys littered with rubbish. It was row after row of houses arranged, in newer cities, in a neat pattern of blocks or squares. It was pretentious mansions, the costly show places of the self-appointed leaders of "society." Mainly the city was people—rich people, people with modest incomes, poor people. All were affected by the new industrial way of life in the United States.

Concentration of wealth. In this new industrial age, wealth was concentrated in the hands of relatively few people. To be sure, some Americans had always been rich while others had been poor. However, the gap between the richest and the poorest had never been as great as it was in the late 1800's.

Many of the new millionaires built huge mansions filled with expensive and gaudy furnishings. They bought race horses, yachts, and summer estates. They traveled abroad. Sometimes they gave parties costing tens of thousands of dollars.

As time went on, however, the newly rich, and especially their college-educated children, smoothed off the rougher edges. Many business leaders accepted the responsibility for using their money to improve their communities. They gave money to build and support churches, colleges, art galleries, and libraries.

For example, during his lifetime Andrew Carnegie gave $60 million to help towns and cities establish free public libraries. Men of enormous wealth, such as Ezra Cornell, Leland Stanford, John D. Rockefeller, Sr., Jonas Clark, Matthew Vassar, and Cornelius Vanderbilt, founded or gave endowments to colleges and universities. J. P. Morgan, Henry C. Frick, Andrew W. Mellon, and dozens of others built up costly and valuable art collections, many of which were in time opened to the public. Others, including women, gave financial support to American symphony orchestras, social welfare, and the arts.

In 1892 Theodore Groll painted this busy scene of Indianapolis, Indiana, at dusk. He shows the hurly-burly and the general lack of organization that marked so many of the nation's fast-growing urban areas of the time.

The middle-income group. Lower down on the economic ladder were the professional people, the smaller business people, the clerks, the managers, and the more successful skilled workers. These people raised their standard of living and enjoyed "modern conveniences," such as gas and electric lighting, modern plumbing, and new household appliances. They went to the theater, used libraries, and bought magazines and books. Many of them sent their children not only through high school but also to college.

Women in religion and welfare. In activities such as religion and social welfare, several women achieved international reputations. Mary Baker Eddy founded Christian Science and contributed to its growth with her inspirational leadership and administrative ability. Other women were active in church missionary work abroad, establishing training schools, colleges, and hospitals in Turkey, Japan, India, and other countries. A number of Catholic women founded religious orders. The most famous was Mother Francis Xavier Cabrini. After emigrating from Italy in 1889, she established hospitals, orphanages, and schools in the Italian-American communities of New York, Chicago, and other cities. Mother Cabrini was the first American citizen to become a saint in the Roman Catholic Church.

The tireless and competent Clara Barton, after her contributions to nursing in the Civil War, established the American Red Cross. Despite opposition and indifference, she broadened its purposes to include not only aid to soldiers in wartime but also help to civilians in such disasters as floods, earthquakes, major fires, and epidemics.

Opportunities for women. New coeducational universities in the Middle West and the West and such women's colleges as Mount Holyoke, Wellesley, Vassar, and Smith in the East meant that more young women could obtain an education equal to that once enjoyed only by young men. Many people at first doubted that girls had the physical and mental ability to do college work, but the experiment proved successful. Women college graduates became increasingly active in civic affairs. Some became business executives, and others entered the professions. By 1900 there were 1,000 women lawyers, 3,000 women ministers, and 7,500 women doctors in the United States.

Maria Mitchell, an astronomer on the faculty of Vassar College, had discovered a comet that was named for her.

Non-college women who wanted careers or who were compelled by circumstances to work outside the home found new opportunities in business. The development of the typewriter meant more jobs as stenographers in offices, banks, and industrial plants. Tradition and prejudice, however, blocked opportunities to most of these women to advance into management positions.

A great many women of the white middle class joined the women's clubs that rapidly multiplied after the Civil War. These clubs at first concentrated mainly on discussions of literary and cultural topics. By 1900 they were also fighting for an end to political corruption,

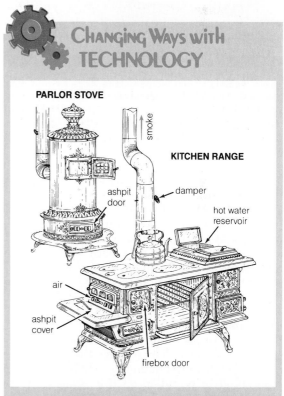

Changing Ways with TECHNOLOGY

PARLOR STOVE

KITCHEN RANGE

smoke

ashpit door

damper

hot water reservoir

air

ashpit cover

firebox door

HEATING AND COOKING

The parlor stove for heating and the kitchen range for cooking and heating were commonly used until the development of central heating, the gas range, and the electric range. Coal or wood was burned and ashes had to be removed frequently.

As a wealthy young woman, Jane Addams had complained, "I am filled with shame that with all my apparent leisure, I do nothing at all." But over the next 46 years, her efforts at Hull House aided thousands of the needy.

more conservative American Woman Suffrage Association. It worked for woman suffrage amendments to state constitutions. In 1890, after many years of rivalry, the two organizations merged as the National American Woman Suffrage Association.

Veterans of the women's rights movement were reinforced by younger leaders. Abigail Duniway of Oregon, a strong opponent of women's legal disabilities, became an effective speaker and lobbyist. Anna Howard Shaw, a graduate of Boston University in both theology and medicine, was a forceful speaker and untiring campaigner. Carrie Chapman Catt of Iowa, a pacifist as well as a women's-rights advocate, proved herself a brilliant orator and skilled administrator.

Despite the efforts of such leaders, progress toward women's suffrage was slow. The women suffragists were ridiculed and denounced by many women as well as men, by professional politicians, and by some religious groups. They also were opposed by the liquor industry, which feared that voting women might succeed in outlawing the manufacture and sale of alcoholic drinks.

Although by 1900 only a few western states had given women the right to vote, in the next 15 years the number grew. Meanwhile, in states that gave them limited suffrage, women took part increasingly in school-board elections and local politics.

for better health and recreational conditions, and for women's suffrage.

Black women also established clubs, which concentrated on social welfare. Active in this movement were Josephine Ruffin and Mary Church Terrell, who also were leaders in the founding of the National Federation of Afro-American Women and the National Association of Colored Women.

Toward women's suffrage. After the Civil War, you recall, women did not receive voting rights and other rights under the Fourteenth and Fifteenth Amendments. Differences over the stand to be taken on this issue split the women's rights movement. Elizabeth Cady Stanton and Susan B. Anthony refused to support the amendments. In 1869 they organized the National Woman Suffrage Association, which excluded men from membership. The Association adopted as its goal a women's suffrage amendment to the Constitution. Lucy Stone, her husband Henry Blackwell, Mary A. Livermore, and Julia Ward Howe launched the

Jane Addams. Jane Addams (1860–1935) was one of America's most influential women — a social reformer, humanitarian, and crusader for peace. Horrified by the suffering she saw in sprawling city slums, Addams decided to dedicate her life to helping the poor. In 1889 she opened Hull House in the slums of Chicago. She provided kindergartens for the children of working mothers, classes in child care, and recreational facilities for youth and adults. She also insisted on the collection of garbage from slum streets and fought incompetent and corrupt politicians and city officials.

For a time many business and political leaders opposed her as a dangerous meddler. Eventually, however, even her most bitter critics admitted that she was performing a great service. Social workers from all parts of the United States and from foreign countries visited Hull House. They then returned to their own communities to apply the new ideas that they had learned.

Jane Addams also helped secure child-labor laws and funds for public parks. In 1931 she received the Nobel Peace Prize for her active work in the cause of world peace. Her most enduring memorial was the growing recognition by people in all walks of life that they shared a responsibility for helping to reduce poverty.

The lower-income groups. On the lower rungs of the economic ladder in American life were the very poor people, including large numbers of immigrants and almost all Mexican Americans, Indians, and blacks. These lower-income groups enjoyed only a few of the advantages of the new urban culture. They could not afford to send their children to school beyond the elementary grades. In fact, children from poor families often had to take jobs in factories even before they finished elementary school. Nor could most of the poorer people afford to go to doctors or hospitals when they were sick.

Yet improvements in urban living affected at least a few of the poor. In the late 1880's, high-minded men and women founded social "settlement houses" similar to Chicago's Hull House in some of the worst slum areas of the major cities. These centers for recreation, education, and decent living gave hope to many immigrant youths and lightened the hardship of many elderly men and women. In addition, the Salvation Army, a religious group founded in England, provided food and shelter to many of the most poverty-stricken urban citizens. By 1900 some cities were building a few playgrounds in the poorest areas.

Opportunities to climb the economic ladder did exist, even for the poor. These opportunities far surpassed those in the Old World. They drew immigrants to the American cities in an ever-swelling volume. Finally, these opportunities encouraged many poorer people to struggle for an education and to rise above the environment into which they had been born.

SECTION SURVEY

IDENTIFY: Mary Baker Eddy, Mother Cabrini, Clara Barton, Maria Mitchell, women's clubs, Mary Church Terrell, National American Woman Suffrage Association, Jane Addams, settlement house, Salvation Army.

1. Explain what is meant by this statement: The city had many faces.

2. (a) What social-class divisions existed in the United States by 1890? (b) To what extent could a person move from one social class to another?

3. What is the relationship between the nation's industrialization and the women's rights movement?

4. Picture Study: Look at the painting on page 145. What evidence can you find in it of new inventions that were transforming American life?

2 Education responds to the changing patterns of American life

Like almost every other aspect of American life, education was transformed by the rising force of industrialism.

In 1870 about 7 million children were enrolled in American schools, most of them in the lower grades. Only 30 years later, in 1900, the number had more than doubled. During this same period, the number of high schools multiplied 10 times. This growth reflected not only the increasing throngs of children in America's cities but also the increasing wealth that could be taxed to support education.

From old ways to new. The character of the schools—including courses of study and methods of teaching—was also changing.

Pupils in the earlier rural classrooms were all too familiar with the sharp sting of the hickory stick, wielded by teachers on the theory "Spare the rod and spoil the child." Children learned reading, writing, and arithmetic and memorized a few more or less related facts about geography and history. The few students who went to high school or to a private academy spent much time learning Latin, Greek, and mathematics. Most educators believed that these subjects provided mental training and therefore fully equipped students for later life.

Some reformers began to demand a new program of education better suited to the industrial age. A few educational pioneers, such as Colonel Francis W. Parker of Chicago, stressed the idea that education is not just the memorization of facts but also the broadening of a child's experience. Education, Parker insisted, must prepare children to live in an ex-

Before 1860 women were admitted into only a few colleges. But by 1901, 128 women's colleges had been founded, other colleges had admitted women, and women made up one fourth of all undergraduates.

panding and complex world of science and industry.

John Dewey also stressed the idea that education is not something apart from the rest of life but an essential part of life itself. By the 1890's Dewey's experimental school in Chicago was attracting attention for its program of "learning by doing" and for its emphasis upon making children physically sound, intellectually competent, and socially well-adjusted. Ella Flagg Young, the head of the Chicago school system, worked closely with both Parker and Dewey. This able educator was the first woman to serve as head of a major school system in the nation.

Most schools, it is true, continued along more traditional lines. Nevertheless, Parker, Dewey, and other pioneers proved to have a great influence on the course of American education.

Influences of industrialism. The needs of the new industrial society were also reflected in the schools. By 1900, educational programs included the natural sciences and such "practical" and "useful" subjects as industrial designing, business arithmetic, bookkeeping, typing, stenography, shopwork, home economics, and manual arts. Superintendents and principals also became more businesslike in emphasizing efficiency and organization.

Colleges and universities. The colleges and universities also responded to the needs of the new age. New technical schools, such as the Columbia University School of Mines, the Massachusetts Institute of Technology, and the Case School of Applied Science, turned out more and more graduates prepared to take important jobs in railroad building, in mining, and in other engineering projects. The state universities and land-grant colleges emphasized practical training for a variety of fields.

Even the older colleges, which emphasized the classics, often added more scientific and "practical" subjects to their traditional courses of study. Under the influence of leaders like Charles W. Eliot of Harvard and Andrew D. White of Cornell, the colleges modified the old, rigid curriculum in which students studied mainly Latin, Greek, and mathematics.

Colleges and universities also enriched their educational programs by adding courses in the social sciences and modern languages as well as in the natural sciences. It was no longer possible for every student to take all the subjects in the curriculum. To meet individual needs, the elective system was introduced.

At the same time, marked progress was made in the professional studies of medicine and law. This was especially important, for people living in cities increasingly needed the services of good lawyers and doctors.

In these and many other ways, education responded to the changing patterns of everyday life after 1865.

SECTION SURVEY

IDENTIFY: Colonel Francis W. Parker, John Dewey, Ella Flagg Young, elective system.

1. What changes were made in the courses of study in public schools to meet the needs of the new industrial society?

2. Describe the ways in which colleges and universities responded to the needs of the new age.

3. Does education today reflect any of the ideas favored by Parker and Dewey? Explain.

3 American writing reflects the new industrial age

Newspapers, magazines, and novels also revealed the influence of the new urban industrial way of life. Most obvious was an enormous increase in circulation of printed material.

Newspapers and magazines. Between 1870 and 1900, the number of daily newspapers in the country increased from 600 to nearly 2,500. Their circulation multiplied six times—a jump far greater than the growth in population. This huge expansion reflected gains in the reading ability of many Americans and a growing interest in the events of the world beyond the local community.

Several mechanical inventions enabled publishers to print more newspapers, magazines, and books at lower costs. Most important of these inventions were the typewriter, improved printing presses, and the linotype, a fast and efficient typesetting machine.

Mass circulation was also stimulated by the rapidly developing art of advertising. Businesses were ready to advertise, but only in newspapers and magazines that reached large audiences. The desire to secure advertising stimulated publishers to print more and more "popular" articles written in a catchy style to attract the largest possible numbers of readers.

"Titans of the press." Three of the outstanding leaders of the new trend in journalism were Charles A. Dana, Joseph Pulitzer, and William Randolph Hearst.

Dana, publisher of the New York *Sun,* dug up sensational news and gave it prominent space on the front pages of his paper. Pulitzer, publisher of the New York *World,* followed much the same technique. His paper appealed to the general reader because of its human-interest stories and many articles on the scandalous activities of the rich and the tragedies of the poor. Stories by Elizabeth Seaman, who defied the prejudice against women reporters, were especially popular. Under the name Nelly Bly, she reported what she found when she worked in a factory, entered a mental institution by pretending to be insane, or got herself jailed. Pulitzer also developed the comic strip, the sports page, and a section with columnists, puzzles, and advice to readers.

Hearst, Pulitzer's chief rival, outdid Pulitzer at his own game. Hearst bought the New York *Journal* in 1895 and raised its circulation beyond that of any other paper. By denouncing the irresponsibility and selfishness of some of the well-to-do, Hearst appealed to the masses of people. His special success rested on his ability to hire gifted feature writers, able sports reporters, and popular comic artists. He also was able to get the most sensational news before anyone else and to play it up for all it was worth—frequently far more than it was worth.

Journalism as big business. Well before 1900 journalism adopted the methods of other big business enterprises. Leading publishers bought up small papers and organized great newspaper chains. Large chains could use the same feature articles, the same comic strips, and even the same editorials. This was especially true as the different parts of the nation and the world became increasingly interdependent and public interest reached out beyond the local community to national and world affairs. The newspaper chains also subscribed to great news-reporting services, or syndicates, such as the Associated Press (AP) and the United Press (UP), which collected news items from every corner of the earth. Even the newspapers that remained independent were influenced by the trend toward standardized practices in journalism.

By 1900 there also were numerous foreign-language newspapers for immigrants and about 150 newspapers for black Americans. Although these publications had limited resources, they served important functions. They gave their readers a sense of identity with other people of the same national origin or racial background. Most of these newspapers also were uncompromising in their opposition to discrimination.

Mass-circulation magazines. Like the newspapers, magazines adapted themselves to the changing times. Some of the older magazines, such as the *Atlantic Monthly, Harper's,* and *Scribner's,* continued to appeal to the better educated. Even before the Civil War, however, a new type of low-priced, popular magazine had appeared, which contained material aimed at mass circulation among "average" readers. The *Ladies' Home Journal,* established in 1883, was one of the most successful, providing reading material that interested millions of

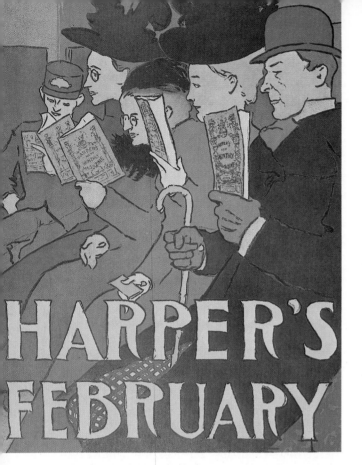

Started as a weekly in 1850, *Harper's* magazine remained popular into the 1900's. It published political cartoons, drawings of major events, and works of important writers, including Charles Dickens.

women. It further built up its circulation by setting its price at 10 cents. Under the editorship of a Dutch immigrant, Edward Bok, the *Ladies' Home Journal* sponsored many crusades to raise standards of living and improve community life.

Literature about urban life. American literature, too, reflected the growing influence of urban industrialism. The success stories for boys that Horatio Alger, Jr., and W. T. Adams (under the name of Oliver Optic) turned out by the dozens were extremely popular. These stories in a sense glorified an urban society in which a hard-working boy from humble beginnings could climb to the top by sheer pluck — and luck.

William Sydney Porter (O. Henry) struck a very different note with short stories that presented realistic pictures of American life, both urban and rural. Different again were the novels of Edith Wharton, which focused on the conflicts between the newly rich and older

well-to-do families of New York in the 1880's. Henry James's novels explored the tensions felt by the members of America's leisure class who chose to live in the sophisticated urban centers of Europe.

One of the best-known novels of the period was *The Gilded Age,* written by Samuel L. Clemens (Mark Twain) and Charles Dudley Warner. In a humorous but biting manner, the writers described the corrupt activities of politicians and land speculators in the nation's capital. Edward Bellamy's *Looking Backward: 2000-1887* contrasted an ugly urban America with an imaginary socialist America of the future. In Bellamy's future America, poverty and corruption have been eliminated and people live cooperatively in freedom and dignity. Among the ablest writers of his time was William Dean Howells. In *A Hazard of New Fortunes* and other realistic stories, he provided a faithful picture of middle-class life, chiefly in urban America.

Notable exceptions. There were, of course, many authors whose writing was not influenced by the changing ways of life. Emily Dickinson, for example, created short, thought-provoking poems that have since been recognized as gems of beauty and originality.

The growing reading public also enjoyed highly romantic and sentimental novels as well as colorful Wild West adventure stories that enterprising publishers put out in paper covers for only 10 cents. Many of these famous "dime novels" had the unfortunate side effect of reinforcing the stereotypes of Mexicans and Indians as villains.

Local-color writers. Some writers reacted against the more or less standardized ways of city life. They concentrated upon describing those regions of the United States that still largely followed the older, rural ways of living. One of these local-color writers, Edward Eggleston, touched a "folksy" note in describing life in rural Indiana in his book *The Hoosier Schoolmaster.*

The greatest of the local-color writers was Samuel L. Clemens (Mark Twain), the first important writer from west of the Atlantic seaboard states. His *Life on the Mississippi* dramatized the crude, vigorous, racy aspects of the American steamboat era. *The Adventures of Tom Sawyer* and *The Adventures of Huckleberry Finn* were landmarks in the representation of the adolescent American boy. At the same time, these books satirized the middle-class values and racial prejudices of a rural community in Missouri. Twain's *Roughing It* vividly portrayed the raw life of western mining camps.

The colorful and heroic verses of Joaquin (hwah·KEEN) Miller and the realistic stories of mining camps written by Bret Harte brought the Far West into the nation's literature. Helen Hunt Jackson also did much to increase the awareness of the Far West with her stories of Spanish missions and of Indian life in old California. Hamlin Garland, in *Main-Traveled Roads* and other books, wrote of the harsh conditions endured by many of the pioneers on the northern prairies.

The South, too, had its share of local-color writers. George Washington Cable, Kate Chopin, and Grace King presented life among the French-speaking Creoles of Louisiana. Thomas Nelson Page popularized a romantic image of master-slave relations on Virginia plantations before the Civil War. Joel Chandler Harris of Georgia won fame for his "Uncle Remus" tales, based on stories brought from Africa by slaves.

The writings of black authors also partly reflected the influence of the local-color school of writing. Local color distinguished *My Southern Home,* the last book of the pioneer black novelist William Wells Brown. Another important black writer, Paul L. Dunbar, was hailed as the first black American writer "to feel the Negro life esthetically and express it lyrically." Some of the novels and tales of Charles W. Chesnutt, a black writer of North Carolina, also reflected the local-color school of writing.

New England, like other regions, excited the imaginations of local-color authors, among them Mary E. Wilkins Freeman and Sarah Orne Jewett. These writers pictured the changes in rural life in New England as young people abandoned the rocky, unproductive family farms to seek their fortunes in the growing cities.

SECTION SURVEY

IDENTIFY: journalism, Elizabeth Seaman, Horatio Alger, Edith Wharton, Emily Dickinson, dime novels, local color, Mark Twain, William Wells Brown, Paul L. Dunbar, Sarah Orne Jewett.

1. What factors made possible the mass circulation of newspapers and magazines?

2. How did each of these people contribute to journalism: (a) Dana, (b) Pulitzer, (c) Hearst?

3. (a) Give evidence to show that newspaper publishing became big business. (b) How might this have affected the reading public?

4. Explain how some novels of the late 1800's reflected the growing influence of urban industrialism in American life.

4 Architecture and other fine arts respond to a changing society

Architecture and art, no less than journalism and literature, revealed the influence of urban life and the growth of industry in the years after 1865.

Decline and revival. For a number of years after the Civil War, American architecture reached what many have regarded as a low level. During the 1870's and 1880's, many successful business leaders and financiers poured fortunes into huge, gaudy mansions. These overdone showplaces as well as many equally tasteless public buildings and smaller houses were a far cry from the beautiful structures that Americans had designed and built along simple, classical lines during the late 1700's and the early 1800's.

Toward the end of the 1800's, however, a number of architects, notably Henry Hobson Richardson and Richard Morris Hunt, began to design more pleasing, practical houses and public buildings in a more dignified and restrained style.

The World's Columbian Exposition, or World's Fair, held in Chicago in 1893, helped to quicken public interest in good architecture. Many of the buildings that housed the exhibits were designed in the simple classical style. Thousands of visitors carried back to their home communities memories of beautiful structures with noble pillars and clean, direct lines that they had seen.

New trends in architecture. One structure at the Chicago World's Fair, the Transportation Building, heralded a new day in architecture. Its architect, Louis H. Sullivan, taught that "form follows function," meaning that the best-

The 21-story Flatiron Building, New York City's first skyscraper, was completed in 1903. It still stands as a landmark in the series of developments that helped make modern American cities possible.

designed building is one that has a style and uses materials perfectly suited to the purposes of the building. Gradually this idea was adopted by more and more architects, among them Frank Lloyd Wright. Wright started to practice his profession in Chicago in 1893 and became one of the world's foremost architects.

The availability of such new building materials as steel, concrete, and plate glass plus the necessities of urban life did much to stimulate a new type of business structure.

Skyscrapers. As city business districts became more crowded and as real-estate values soared, architects tried to solve the problem by building upward. How could they erect taller buildings? Ingenious architects constructed huge steel frames and filled the spaces with stone, brick, concrete, and glass. The Home Insurance Building, built in Chicago in 1884, set the example for these towering structures.

During the next few years, in both Chicago and New York, builders found ways to erect taller and taller skyscrapers.

The new towering buildings turned the narrow streets below into dark, gloomy canyons. To solve this problem, New York City adopted an ordinance requiring architects to set back the higher stories of all tall buildings so that more light would reach the streets. This ordinance accomplished its purpose. It also relieved the rectangular lines of the box-like skyscraper and accounted for the magically beautiful character of the New York skyline. Like many other activities of American life, architecture revealed more and more the influence of new times and new ways of living.

Painting and sculpture. The new industrial age had less influence on painters and sculptors than it did on architects. Between 1865 and 1900, the most important development in the fine arts was the increasing skill of American artists who had studied in European art centers. The improving standards in American art also rested in part on the ability and the willingness of wealthy Americans to collect masterpieces, to establish art schools, and to buy the works of American artists.

The themes that painters and sculptors chose often seemed to have little to do with the growing urban industrial society. Gifted sculptors created great statues of Lincoln and other national heroes. One outstanding creation was the Adams Monument in Rock Creek Cemetery in Washington, D.C., made by Augustus Saint-Gaudens (saint·GAW·dunz). This brooding, hooded figure, sometimes referred to as "The Peace of God," suggests the mystery of life and death.

A number of painters did equally outstanding work. George Inness captured on canvas the beauties of woodland scenes. Winslow Homer's brilliantly colored seascapes suggested the strength and primitive force of the sea. Mary Cassatt, influenced by the new French impressionist style and by Japanese art, painted portraits of women and children notable for lively charm and for exquisite tone and color.

The work of a number of artists, however, did reveal the influence of industrial and urban America. Thomas Eakins, for example, painted famous and wealthy Americans with such frank realism that they would not buy his works. Eakins, however, refused to change his style for the sake of immediate popularity and profit and continued to paint life as he saw it. In a painting designed to reveal the surgeon's scientific skill, *The Surgical Clinic of Professor Gross,* Eakins suggested very concretely the new scientific trend of the age.

SECTION SURVEY

IDENTIFY: architecture, Frank Lloyd Wright, Augustus Saint-Gaudens, Winslow Homer, Mary Cassatt, Thomas Eakins.

1. How did architecture in the late 1800's (a) meet the requirements of the urban industrial age and (b) take advantage of the new materials made available by the age?
2. What did Louis Sullivan mean by the statement that in architecture "form follows function"?
3. Describe the themes that inspired the noted American sculptors and painters of this period.

5 New forms of recreation enrich American life

Recreation, like all other aspects of everyday living, was transformed by the new urban industrial age. The well-to-do, having time and money, enjoyed such new and at first exclusive sports as tennis and golf. Gradually, however, the middle-income groups also began to enjoy such forms of recreation.

New types of recreation. For many thousands of American children and their parents in the late 1800's, one of the most memorable events of the year was the arrival of the circus. P. T. Barnum's tent circus, which he started in Brooklyn in 1871, was called "the greatest show on earth."

Equally awaited was the arrival of the Chautauqua (shuh·TAW·kwuh). The Chautauqua movement was an educational enterprise started in 1874 on the shores of Chautauqua Lake in upper New York State. Each year thousands of Americans from all over the United States traveled to Chautauqua Lake to enjoy a summer vacation and to benefit intellectually and spiritually from the lectures and sermons provided for them. Study groups using Chautauqua publications were organized in many towns and villages. As the years passed, the program at Chautauqua Lake became increasingly varied. Illustrated travel talks, stage presentations, and humorous acts were added to the more serious lectures and religious services. Other enterprising leaders also organized traveling tent programs similar to those earlier developed at Chautauqua Lake. By the early 1900's, the traveling Chautauquas were bringing a glimpse of the outside world into many rural communities.

The theater gained in popularity during the 1800's, particularly for middle-income groups. At its best the theater offered admirable plays performed by great actors, American and foreign-born. Some of the most appealing programs, however, were the melodramas that reminded city dwellers of their own rural background. Such plays as *Way Down East* and *The Old Homestead* attracted large audiences. There was also an equally popular series of melodramas on significant urban themes, such as *Bertha, the Sewing-Machine Girl.* Vaudeville shows, providing a variety of singing, dancing, and gymnastic acts, also attracted large audiences.

By 1900, amusement parks were attracting crowds of city people and making fortunes for their owners. In many cases trolley-car companies built amusement parks just outside the city, thereby reaping profits from the parks as well as from trolley fares.

Physical exercise and sports. During the last quarter of the 1800's, an increasing number of middle-class city dwellers became aware of the need for physical exercise, especially for youth. One answer was gymnasiums, which appeared in growing numbers in cities and towns as well as in schools and colleges.

In these years the bicycle changed from a clumsy, high-wheeled, dangerous contraption into something like the machine we know today. As a result, bicycling became a popular fad as well as a means of getting to and from work for many people.

These same years also saw the rapid development of three major spectator sports—baseball, football, and basketball.

Baseball in various forms had been played long before the first professional team, the Cincinnati Red Stockings, was formed in 1869. Seven years later, in 1876, the National League was organized. In 1900 the American League was formed. Well before 1900, urban

THE NATIONAL SPORT

King George III played a version of it as a boy. So did Washington's troops at Valley Forge. Even then the game, known as "rounders" or "base ball," was old. Some say it started in English villages in the 1500's, with players using milking stools as bases. (Baseball was *not* invented in 1839 by Abner Doubleday, though his claims were taken seriously at one time.)

Alexander Cartwright standardized rules and the diamond in 1845. The first recorded game played according to his rules took place the following year at Hoboken, New Jersey; the New Yorks defeated the Knickerbockers 23 to 1 in 4 innings. In those days the first team to get 21 aces (runs) won the game. Players still wore ordinary clothing, only the catcher used a glove, and umpires sometimes carried umbrellas to ward off sun and rain.

After the Civil War, baseball became truly the national sport. Then the rules became much like today's. The first professional teams appeared, and national leagues were formed.

Baseball as played in the early 1900's would be easily understood today, yet there were a good many differences. No blacks played in the major leagues. Players traveled by train, so schedules were less crowded and the season averaged around 140 games. There were no night games. A day game that went extra innings and had to be called on account of darkness was usually played out the next day.

Players wore bulky uniforms and, batting without protective helmets, were often "beaned" by pitched balls. Teams had fewer pitchers and they pitched more games. Even the ball was different, less lively than today's and likely to be used for an entire game. As a result, long balls and home runs were not common. But when bat and ball did connect, the crowd roared and baseball excitement filled the air.

dwellers in growing numbers were crowding into the ballparks to watch what would in time become one of America's favorite spectator sports.

Football, which evolved from the English game of rugby, also became increasingly popular. The first intercollegiate football contest, played between Rutgers and Princeton in 1869, had 25 players on each side. Within a few years, intercollegiate contests were being held in the West as well as in the East. Played mostly by college men, football in the early days was a rough-and-tumble game. It was so rough, in fact, that some people protested against its "brutality" and demanded its abolition. As the years passed, however, new rules of play were developed, and the game became better organized.

Basketball, which also became a typically American sport, was first played in 1892 by students at the Y.M.C.A. college in Springfield, Massachusetts. Its inventor, Dr. James Naismith, then an instructor in physical education, created the game to provide the same opportunities for recreation in the winter that baseball provided in the summer and football in the fall. Within just a few years, Naismith's game of basketball was being played all over the country.

The older rural forms of recreation—picnics, amateur baseball, horseshoe pitching—continued to enjoy popularity. Increasingly, however, the ways in which the people of the United States relaxed and amused themselves were being transformed in the new industrial age.

SECTION SURVEY

IDENTIFY: P. T. Barnum, Dr. James Naismith.

1. (a) What was the Chautauqua movement? (b) Why was it important to rural dwellers?

2. How did city dwellers satisfy their growing interest in physical fitness?

3. What three major spectator sports developed in the late 1800's?

Chapter Survey

Summary: Tracing the Main Ideas

Growing numbers of people poured into the great urban centers during the late 1800's. Each year the cities exerted a more and more powerful influence upon all aspects of American life, including education, journalism, literature, architecture, art, and recreation.

What had made the cities such a powerful influence?

In trying to answer this question we must remember that the cities were the centers of industry. Thus we find ourselves going back to the factories and mass production. And when we look at the factories, with their mass production, we find that they depended upon power-driven machines. And when we look at the power-driven machines—and the almost countless number of inventions and discoveries that made the new machines possible—we find ourselves face to face with science and technology—that is, with the application of science to industry. Or to put it in other terms, we come face to face with scientists, engineers, manufacturers, and business leaders. Without science and technology, there would have been no thriving factories and no large industrial cities.

The world of the late 1800's was changing with bewildering speed. New leaders were appearing, and new ways of living and working were transforming American society. The American people, rich and poor, city dwellers and country folk—had to adjust their lives to the new conditions.

The new age was full of promise for a richer and fuller life for all people everywhere, but before the promise could be realized, many problems still had to be solved. You will read about some of these problems and the ways in which the American people tried to solve them in the following chapters.

Inquiring into History

1. How did industrialization and urbanization affect (a) education, (b) architecture, (c) art, and (d) journalism?
2. How might American democracy have been affected by (a) the increase in educational opportunity and (b) the mass circulation of newspapers and magazines?
3. Explain how each of the following terms reflects the changing ways of American life during the late 1800's: (a) concentration of wealth, (b) settlement house, (c) elective system, (d) skyscrapers.
4. What might be the relationship between functionalism in architecture and an industrialized society?

Relating Past to Present

1. Does education today reflect the needs of our society? Explain.
2. Compare skyscrapers built in the late 1890's with those built recently in terms of (a) size, (b) cost, (c) structure and design, (d) materials used. What can you conclude from these differences?
3. Do you think that baseball and other sports have been affected by industrialization? Explain.
4. Do you think the federal government should be involved in the support of the arts? Why or why not?
5. Do newspapers today use any of the techniques practiced by Dana, Pulitzer, and Hearst? Why or why not?

Developing Social Science Skills

1. Examine the pictures on pages 146 and 150. How do they help to show the changes taking place during the late 1800's?
2. From primary and secondary sources, find out more about the women's rights movement between 1860 and 1900. (a) Who were the leaders? (b) What gains were made by women in these years? (c) What obstacles still existed? (d) What methods were most effective in promoting women's rights?
3. Read all or part of one of the novels discussed in Section 3. (a) Does the subject of the novel relate to industrialization or urban life? (b) Does the novel seem to express an opinion about the vast changes taking place in society at that time? Explain. (c) How does the novel's description of life in the late 1800's compare to the description presented in your textbook? How can you account for the similarities or differences?

Unit Survey

For Further Inquiry

1. After 1865 in what ways did the government encourage business and industry?
2. How important was each of these in bringing about industrialization in the United States: (a) individual business people, (b) discoveries and inventions, (c) abundant natural resources?
3. Why was city life so attractive to many people during the late 1800's?
4. What effects did large-scale immigration have on American society (a) during the late 1800's, (b) in the long run?
5. Compare the situation of farmers and industrial workers in the late 1800's in terms of (a) grievances, (b) methods of seeking improvement in their situation, (c) relationship with government.

Projects and Activities

1. (a) What is the theme of the timeline above? (b) Does that theme represent a significant aspect of life from the 1860's to the 1890's? Why or why not? (c) From the timeline choose one example of popular culture and one of high culture. Explain how you made your choices.
2. America has been described as a nation of immigrants. Look into your own family background to discover where your relatives or ancestors were born and why they came to the United States. You might also prepare a family tree.
3. Present a report on the problems and contributions of one of the immigrant groups in the United States.
4. Prepare a line or bar graph showing the growth of (a) coal production, (b) iron production, (c) oil production, or (d) railroad lines between 1860 and 1900. Beneath the graph, write a paragraph explaining what is shown on the graph and why it is important.
5. Imagine that you were preparing a museum exhibit on paintings of the industrial age. It will consist of five paintings of your choice. Select the paintings and write the catalogue for viewers of the exhibit. The catalogue should give facts about, as well as your comments on, each painting in the exhibit.

Exploring Your Region

1. Find out about the natural resources in your state—especially minerals or energy sources—that have contributed to the industrial growth of your region or the nation.
2. Prepare a bulletin board display about a city in your region that became important during the industrial age. The display can include pictures, charts, or short descriptions of the important historical facts in the development of the city.

Suggested Reading

1. *The Promised Land,* Mary Antin. Autobiography of a young Jewish immigrant and her struggle to rise above her difficult life in the Boston slums.
2. *Jane Addams: Pioneer for Social Justice,* Cornelia Meigs. Story of Jane Addams's career as a reformer and founder of Hull House.
3. *Altgeld's America: The Lincoln Ideal Versus Changing Realities,* Ray Ginger. A history of the vast changes taking place in the late 1800's as America was transformed from a rural to an urban, industrial nation.
4. *Everyday Life in the Age of Enterprise, 1865-1900,* Robert H. Walker. The story of popular culture and social life in the late 1800's.
5. *The Wind Blows Free,* Loula Grace Erdman. A novel of pioneers in the Texas Panhandle.
6. *The Age of Innocence,* Edith Wharton. A classic novel of high society in New York in the 1870's.

Unit Three

The Arrival of Reform

1897-1920

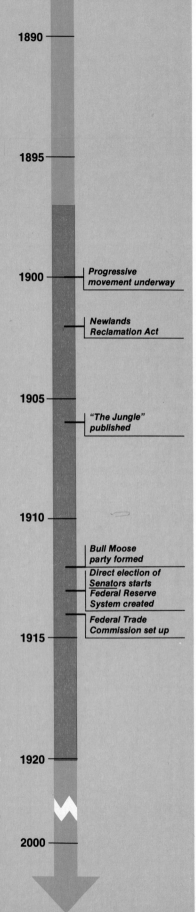

Chapter **8**

Reforms Under the "Square Deal" and the "New Freedom"

1897-1920

The election of William McKinley as President in 1896 marked the end of the Populist Party. Many Americans feared that it also marked the end of the reform movement. Within six years, however, a new reform movement, the progressive movement, would sweep the country. Three Presidents would contribute to this movement in different ways.

From 1901 to 1909, Teddy Roosevelt, colorful and dynamic, promised to give Americans a "Square Deal." On the whole, Roosevelt did much to fulfill this promise. From 1909 to 1913, William Howard Taft, a huge man, highly intelligent and thoroughly competent, advanced the reform movement. Taft, however, lacked Teddy's ability to capture the public's imagination. From 1913 to 1921, Woodrow Wilson, a scholar and idealist, promised Americans a "New Freedom" and took important steps toward this goal.

Each of these Presidents grappled with the same basic problem faced by earlier reformers—how to preserve and strengthen democracy in the industrial age.

THE CHAPTER IN OUTLINE

1. The progressives open the door to reforms in America.

2. The progressives promote more democratic forms of government.

3. Theodore Roosevelt promises Americans a "Square Deal."

4. Roosevelt acts to conserve America's natural resources.

5. The progressive movement gains and loses under Taft.

6. Wilson's "New Freedom" expands opportunities for Americans.

1 The progressives open the door to reforms in America

In 1897 McKinley and the conservative Republicans seemed to have a clear road before them. Having just defeated William Jennings Bryan in his bid for the White House, Republicans in Congress now passed the Dingley Tariff of 1897, which raised average tariff rates to a new high of 57 percent. In the meantime, the depression of 1893–96 gave way to prosperity. New corporations sprang up, and older corporations merged to form giant trusts and industrial concerns.

Surrounded by prosperity, many Americans in the late 1890's had forgotten the demands of the Populists and other reform groups. Yet by 1900 a new reform impulse known as the progressive movement was underway. This movement adopted and eventually achieved many of the goals of the Populists.

Aims of the progressives. The progressive movement cut across party lines. It included people from the Democratic Party as well as discontented Republicans. Leaders of the progressive movement had specific aims. (1) They wanted to restore control of the government to the rank and file of people. (2) They wanted to correct the abuses and injustices that had crept into American life in the age of urban industrialism. (3) They wanted to restore greater equality of economic opportunity by drawing up new rules for the conduct of business and the great private banks, or "money trust."

The progressives were optimists. They believed that these reforms would create a more prosperous and a more democratic country.

Robert M. La Follette. Robert M. "Fighting Bob" La Follette of Wisconsin was one of the outstanding leaders of the progressive movement. La Follette fought his way upward in local and state politics. He won victories over the Republican political machine that dominated Wisconsin. In doing so, he won a reputation for fearless honesty. An excellent speaker, he sought support from the farmers and working people and won the governorship of Wisconsin in 1900.

As governor, La Follette helped to break the power of the political machine that had been running the state. He persuaded legislators to levy heavier taxes on the railroads and on the newer **public utilities**—the gas, electric, and streetcar companies. He persuaded the legislators to create commissions to regulate these companies. He also started a movement for the conservation of Wisconsin's forests and water-power sites. Many of these sites had come under the control of big industrial corporations.

In the days before radio and television, campaigning for office meant that the candidates had to appear in person to spread their message. In his painting "Electioneering," artist E. I. Henry portrays one such appearance.

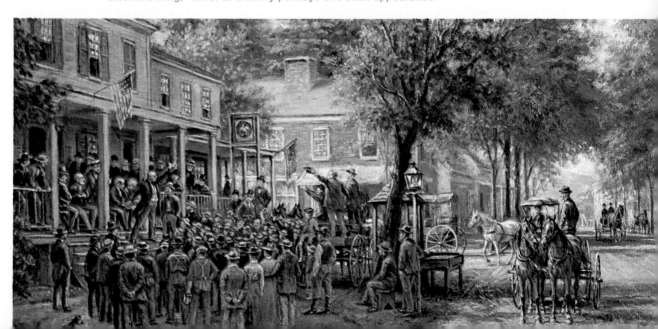

Under the leadership of Frances Willard, the Women's Christian Temperance Union had become a worldwide organization to be reckoned with by the mid-1880's. In addition to supporting the prohibition of alcohol, the W.C.T.U. called for a ban on all harmful drugs.

The La Follette administration promoted good government in Wisconsin by using university scholars to help legislators find needed facts and draft laws that the courts could not easily set aside. He also appointed scholars to serve on the new state regulatory commissions. The "Wisconsin Idea," as the movement started by La Follette was called, soon attracted nationwide attention.

Encouraged by La Follette's example, other public officials attacked corrupt government and powerful corporations. Joseph W. Folk became governor of Missouri in 1906 largely as a result of his success in prosecuting a ring of corrupt politicians in St. Louis. Charles Evans Hughes became governor of New York in 1907 chiefly because of his success in uncovering questionable business practices of certain insurance companies. Hiram Johnson became governor of California in 1910 after fighting the political bosses and powerful railroads that had great influence in the state.

Women reformers. Even though most women still lacked the vote, some of them took part in reforms whose purpose was to influence public opinion and government. The National Consumers League, in which Florence Kelley was a leader, brought unfavorable publicity to stores and companies that paid women less than men for equal work and that maintained unhealthful working conditions. The league urged the public to boycott consumer goods produced by child labor and by women who were unfairly treated. With the cooperation of the National Child Labor Committee, the league also secured legislation in the interests of women and children.

The Women's Christian Temperance Union (W.C.T.U.), founded in 1879, carried on a widespread campaign against the manufacture, sale, and consumption of alcoholic beverages. The W.C.T.U. stressed the physical, psychological, and social dangers of alcohol. It emphasized the threat posed by alcoholics to the well-being of their families. Frances Willard, president of the W.C.T.U. for 20 years, persuaded the organization to support women's suffrage as a means to achieve prohibition. The W.C.T.U. used education to achieve its goals. It did not approve of the tactics of Carrie Nation of Kansas, who invaded saloons with a hatchet to smash mirrors and bottles.

Many women also took part in the work of the Anti-Saloon League, which supported political candidates who pledged opposition to the liquor interests and opposed those who did not.

The muckrakers. The progressive movement also included many social workers, scholars, journalists, preachers, and novelists. Theodore Roosevelt applied the name **muckrakers** to the writers who exposed the evils and corruption in politics and the business world. Although Roosevelt used the term in an unfavorable sense, the writers accepted it with pride, and it came into popular use.

The muckracking movement is usually dated from an article, "Tweed Days in St. Louis," written by Lincoln Steffens and Claude H. Wetmore for the October 1902 issue of *McClure's Magazine.* The following month *McClure's* began to publish Ida M. Tarbell's critical *History of the Standard Oil Company.* Many other magazines also began publishing attacks on abuses in American life.

Muckraking novelists included Upton Sinclair, whose sensational novel *The Jungle* exposed unsanitary practices in the meat-packing industry. The book, incidentally, turned many of his readers into vegetarians. Frank Norris's novel *The Octopus* exposed the railroads' control over the political and economic life of the farmers. Jack London in *The War of the Classes, The Iron Heel,* and *Revolution* warned of a revolution that could wipe out private capitalism.

A few of the muckrakers called attention to the plight of American blacks. The most impressive work was *Following the Color Line* by Ray Stannard Baker, a series of magazine articles published as a book in 1908. This was a competent and honest report of segregation in the South and of racial discrimination in the North. As such, it put the problem of white-black relations in a nationwide context.

The root of the problem. The muckrakers brought to light many abuses in American life. Lincoln Steffens, however, pinpointed the basic problem in a series of articles later published as a book entitled *The Shame of the Cities.* Years later, in his *Autobiography,* Steffens summarized his conclusions. The basic problem facing Americans was not the development of industrialism or of business, large or small. The source of the evil was "privilege"—the demand for special privileges from government. This had to be controlled, according to Steffens, or abuses and corruption were sure to be the results.

SECTION SURVEY

IDENTIFY: Dingley Tariff of 1897, progressive movement, Robert La Follette, Charles Evans Hughes, Hiram Johnson, National Consumers League, Women's Christian Temperance Union, Lincoln Steffens, Ida Tarbell, *The Jungle, Following the Color Line.*

1. (a) In what ways did La Follette reform government in Wisconsin? (b) To what degree did his reforms reflect the goals of the progressive movement listed on page 157?

2. Describe the reform activities promoted by (a) Florence Kelley and (b) Frances Willard.

3. (a) Name three muckrakers and explain why they can be described as muckrakers. (b) What do their muckraking activities have in common?

4. What did Lincoln Steffens mean when he identified the basic problem and greatest evil in American life as "privilege"?

2 The progressives promote more democratic forms of government

Millions of Americans in the early 1900's shared the view that special privileges handed out by government were the source of corruption in public life. They also agreed that one way to combat the evils of special privileges was to restore the control of government to the people.

The Australian ballot. A major step toward more democratic government was the adoption of the **Australian ballot,** or secret vote. Until about 1890 each political party printed its own ballots in a distinctive color. Thus when a person cast a ballot—in open view of anybody who cared to watch—it was easy to determine how the person had voted. The secret ballot, developed in Australia and adopted in the United States, eliminated this open voting. Ballots listing the names of all candidates on a single sheet of paper were printed at public expense. The voters could then mark and cast their ballots in secrecy.

The initiative, referendum, and recall. In trying to secure a more democratic government, the progressives supported the use of the initiative, referendum, and recall. All of these reform measures had been advocated by the Populists in the 1890's.

The **initiative** enables voters in a state to initiate, or introduce, legislation at any time. Suppose, for instance, that a group of citizens wanted to increase the amount of state money spent for public schools. They would draw up a bill and attach to it a petition containing the signatures of a certain percentage of the voters in the state (usually from 5 to 15 percent, depending upon state law). When the petition was presented to the state legislature, the representatives were required by law to debate the bill openly.

The **referendum** was a companion to the initiative. By securing a specified number of signatures to a petition, voters could compel the legislature to place a bill before *all* the state's voters for approval or disapproval.

The **recall** enabled voters to remove an elected government official before the official's

These women and their offspring were just a few of the 15,000 supporters of women's suffrage who marched down New York's Fifth Avenue in May 1912. They were eight years from reaching their goal.

term expired. When a specified number of voters, usually 25 percent, presented a petition, a special election had to be held. In this election all of the voters would have the opportunity to vote for or against allowing the official to continue in office.

South Dakota, in 1898, was the first state to adopt the initiative and the referendum. Eventually 20 states adopted initiative and referendum procedures. A total of 12 states adopted the recall.

The direct primary. In trying to make government more responsive to the people's wishes, the progressives also advocated the **direct primary.**

Traditionally, all candidates for government office were nominated in political conventions. These were easily controlled by professional politicians. The direct primary remedied this situation by providing "a nominating election" well in advance of the regular election. Individuals who wanted to run for office would first get a specified number of signatures on a petition. Then they could have their names printed on the primary ballot of any one of the political parties. On the day of the primary election, the registered voters of each party then marked their ballots for the candidate of their choice. First adopted by Wisconsin in 1900, the direct primary soon spread to almost every state.

Women's suffrage. Although the progressives did little if anything to secure the vote for blacks, many promoted woman suffrage. By 1900 four states—Wyoming, Utah, Colorado, and Idaho—had granted full voting rights to women. Vigorous campaigns by woman suffragists between 1910 and 1914 led seven other states, all west of the Mississippi, to give women the right to vote.

Throughout the early 1900's, strong opposition existed even within progressive circles to a Constitutional amendment granting women the vote. Woodrow Wilson, the progressive Democrat who was elected President in 1912, opposed such an amendment on the ground that states alone had the power to fix suffrage requirements. In response, a group of militants led by the courageous and persistent Alice Paul, organized a demonstration against Wilson on his inauguration day that ended in a near riot. Other demonstrations bordered on violence when opposition to them mounted. Activist leaders were jailed and fined. Meantime the militants increased pressure on Congress.

Despite conservative disapproval of militant tactics, the vigorous participation of women in the war effort in World War I broke down much opposition. Finally, in 1920, with the ratification of the Nineteenth Amendment by the states, the right of women to vote throughout the United States was written into the Constitution.

Direct election of Senators. Another reform advocated by the progressives was the direct election of United States Senators. According to the Constitution, Senators were chosen by state legislatures. During the early 1900's, however, progressives in the House of Representatives urged the adoption of an amendment that would allow the people to vote directly for Senators. The Senate, which was often criticized as a "rich man's club" and which included many politicians who owed their jobs to political bosses and political machines, blocked this amendment.

In the end, however, the rising power of the progressives proved too much for the machine politicians. In 1913, in the Seventeenth Amendment, the right to choose Senators was given to the voters at large.

Reform of city government. While winning victories at the state and federal level, the progressives were also trying to reform corrupt city governments. Most municipal governments consisted of a mayor and a large city council, elected by the voters and given complete responsibility for running city affairs. Under this system a well-organized political machine, using corrupt election procedures, could easily win control of city governments.

Galveston, Texas, led the way to a new type of government in 1900 after a hurricane and tidal wave killed one sixth of the city's people and destroyed a third of its property. To meet the emergency, Galveston gave a commission of five persons extraordinary power to run the city. The **commission** form of government soon spread to other cities. By 1912 more than 200 American communities had adopted it. Supporters argued that it was simpler, more efficient, and less expensive than older types of city government.

In 1908 Staunton, Virginia, developed the **city manager** form of government. The city manager, an expert in municipal administration without political connections, is appointed by an elected city council or board of commissioners to run the city as efficiently as possible. City manager government soon spread to many cities.

The progressives were, indeed, a powerful force in American life in the early 1900's. In addition to bringing about these changes in government, they also sought to bring about changes in the relations between business and government.

SECTION SURVEY

IDENTIFY: Australian ballot, initiative, referendum, recall, direct primary, Seventeenth Amendment, city manager form of government.

1. How did the use of the Australian ballot help prevent abuses in elections?
2. How successful were women suffragists in reaching their goal during the progressive era?
3. How did the change in the method of electing Senators make the American political system more democratic?
4. It has been said that progressives sought to make America more democratic. Use specific examples to support or refute this statement.

3 Theodore Roosevelt promises Americans a "Square Deal"

President McKinley and the Republicans entered the elections of 1900 confident of victory. The Democrats, who had again nominated William Jennings Bryan, tried to make free silver a major campaign issue, but Americans in general, including most farmers, were enjoying prosperity. They returned President McKinley to the White House with an electoral vote of 292 to 155.

Six months after his second inauguration, on September 6, 1901, McKinley was shot by a half-crazed assassin. He died a few days later and, to the dismay of conservative Republicans, Vice-President Theodore Roosevelt became the nation's Chief Executive.

Roosevelt's background. Theodore Roosevelt was born in 1858 into a well-to-do New York family. He studied at Harvard, where he acquired a taste for history and politics. After graduation he served a two-year term, from 1882 to 1884, in the New York state legislature. For part of the next two years, he lived on a cattle ranch in Dakota Territory. Returning home in 1886, he unsuccessfully ran for mayor of New York City, then devoted the following three years to the study and writing of history.

During the next few years, Roosevelt served on the federal Civil Service Commission, as president of the New York City Police Commission, and as Assistant Secretary of the Navy.

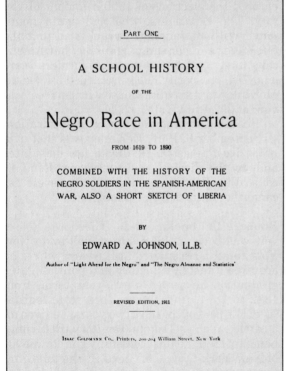

Edward A. Johnson, a black textbook author, is shown here with a page from his *School History of the Negro Race in America,* an important study in the growing literature on black Americans.

When war with Spain broke out in 1898, he resigned his Navy post to organize, with Leonard Wood, a volunteer cavalry regiment known as the "Rough Riders." After the war he became the Republican governor of New York. In that post his independent actions so alarmed the Republican political bosses that in 1900 they decided to get him out of active politics by "kicking him upstairs" into the Vice-Presidency.

This was the man who at age 42 became the youngest President the United States had ever had — and, as the conservative Republicans had correctly feared, one of the most independent.

Roosevelt was a good politician, ready to compromise when necessary. He did not start the progressive movement. Nor did he go as far as many progressives felt he could and should go, but he gave the progressive movement dramatic national leadership. His general popularity, his enthusiasm, his ability as a speaker, and his position enabled him to promote a number of reforms. One notable exception was government policy toward Indians, whose needs and rights were largely ignored.

Settling a coal strike. Less than a year after succeeding McKinley as President, Roosevelt took bold action in a struggle involving organized labor. In the spring of 1902, a strike broke out in Pennsylvania in the coal mines owned largely by railroad companies serving the region. The miners worked long hours, lived in company towns, and bought from company stores. Because of low wages, they found it hard to make ends meet. Organized as part of the United Mine Workers union, they had asked for a 9-hour day, a 20-percent wage increase, improved working conditions, and recognition of their right to bargain as a union. The mineowners refused to negotiate with the union, whereupon the miners went on strike.

By autumn the country faced a coalless winter with factories closed and homes without heat. The mineowners demanded that the President send federal troops into the area to break the strike. Roosevelt refused. Instead, he summoned representatives of the owners and of the union to meet at the White House.

At the meeting the mineowners refused to listen to a proposal for impartial arbitration. Furious at this lack of cooperation, Roosevelt let it be known that he might send the army to take over the mines in the name of the government. Faced with this prospect, the mineowners agreed to accept the decision of a board of arbitration.

After four months of study, the board gave the miners a 9-hour day and a 10-percent wage increase. However, the board did not grant the miners the right to negotiate as a union.

Although the miners won only part of their demands, the case was a landmark in the history of organized labor. For the first time, the federal government had stepped into a labor controversy to protect the interests of all concerned—wage earners, owners, and the public.

The Danbury Hatters' case. Organized labor was not pleased, however, with the outcome of another labor dispute. In 1902 the hatters' union started a nationwide effort to boycott, or to halt the purchase of, the hats produced by a manufacturer in Danbury, Connecticut. The hat company claimed that the boycott restrained trade and was therefore illegal under the Sherman Antitrust Act. After a long delay, the Supreme Court decided in favor of the hat manufacturer in 1908. As a result, the members of the hatters' union were held liable for three times the damages that the hat manufacturer had suffered.

Theodore Roosevelt was in no way responsible for the Supreme Court ruling. Nevertheless, organized labor, thoroughly alarmed at the outcome of the Danbury Hatters' case, held the government responsible for failing to draft laws that provided reasonable protection for labor unions.

Roosevelt and blacks. Some progressives fought the exploitation of black workers, established settlement houses for blacks, and organized national societies to protect the legal rights of black citizens. However, the progressives on the whole neglected the plight of black Americans. Many progressive leaders, to be sure, spoke out against racial injustice, but most of them believed that this problem could, at that time, be dealt with realistically only at state and local levels.

Theodore Roosevelt, too, did little to help the blacks. He did become involved in southern politics, where questions of segregation and black leadership were important issues. Thus, against the opposition of segregated southern Republican organizations, Roosevelt sometimes supported the claims of black politicians to federal office and to participation as delegates at Republican national conventions.

In such matters Roosevelt often used Booker T. Washington as his adviser. Once, after a conference with Washington, Roosevelt invited the black leader to lunch with him at the White House. When the episode became known, a storm of criticism swept the South. Roosevelt did not repeat the invitation.

In general, Roosevelt's neglect of blacks reflected the attitudes and prejudices of most white Americans, including most of the progressives, during these years.

Roosevelt as "trust buster." Under pressure from both reformers and business leaders, the federal government during Roosevelt's administration took steps toward regulating business practices in the interest of the public welfare. Before this time, as you recall, the federal government, with few exceptions, had not become greatly involved in business affairs.

Early in his first term, Roosevelt directed his Attorney General to bring suit under the Sherman Antitrust Act against the Northern Securities Company. This was a holding company that controlled the three leading

SOURCES

THEODORE ROOSEVELT'S "NEW NATIONALISM" SPEECH (1910)

Our country—this great republic—means nothing unless it means the triumph of a real democracy, the triumph of popular government, and, in the long run, of an economic system under which each man shall be guaranteed the opportunity to show the best that there is in him. . . .

I stand for the square deal. But when I say that I am for the square deal, I mean not merely that I stand for fair play under the present rules of the game, but that I stand for having those rules changed so as to work for a more substantial equality of opportunity and of reward for equally good service. . . .

Americans had long worried about the influence of trusts, as this 1880's cartoon, "Bosses of the Senate," shows. What symbols does the artist Joseph J. Keppler use to demonstrate how powerful these trusts had become?

railroads serving the country between Lake Michigan and the Pacific Northwest. "We do not wish to destroy corporations," Roosevelt announced, "but we do wish to make them subserve the public good." In 1904 the Supreme Court held that the Northern Securities Company did restrain trade and was illegal under the Sherman Antitrust Act.

Early in 1903, while the Northern Securities Company case was still pending in the courts, Congress passed the Expedition Act to speed up antitrust cases by giving them a priority over the other cases in federal courts. Another measure created the Department of Commerce and Labor, with a Secretary in the President's cabinet. The new department included a Bureau of Corporations authorized to investigate and report on corporate activities.

The election of 1904. Roosevelt's progressive ideas antagonized many Republican politi-

cal leaders. When election year 1904 rolled around, the Republican political leaders would have abandoned him in favor of a more conservative candidate had they dared. However, by this time Teddy Roosevelt enjoyed widespread popularity. No other Republican candidate had a chance of taking the nomination from him.

During the campaign, Roosevelt had announced that he was "unhampered by any pledge, promise, or understanding of any kind, save my promise, made openly to the American people, that so far as my power lies I shall see to it that every man has a square deal, no less and no more." This promise carried weight because Roosevelt had convinced voters that he meant what he said.

Roosevelt went on to win a resounding victory at the polls—336 electoral votes to 140 for his Democratic opponent, Judge Alton B. Parker of New York.

Renewed efforts at regulation. After 1904, encouraged by the Supreme Court decision in the Northern Securities Company case and by his reelection, Roosevelt started action against a number of other trusts. Altogether, 44 suits against trusts were started during his administration.

Even when the Supreme Court ordered a trust to dissolve, the business executives who had controlled the various corporations in the trust often continued to meet informally and share in the decisions of the separate corporations. By secret arrangements of this kind — often called "communities of interest" — the corporations continued to do informally what they had previously done as a trust. The advantages of large-scale operations for consumers and sometimes for the corporations were very great. Moreover, big business was so tied together that any attempt to break up a monopoly was like trying to unscramble the eggs in an omelet. The trend of the times was toward larger and larger business combinations. Neither Roosevelt nor anyone else could reverse this trend.

"Good" and "bad" combinations. Before leaving office in 1909, Roosevelt concluded that the problem of trusts was not simply one of size. What really mattered was whether a business combination, regardless of size, was "good" or "bad" for the public as a whole. He asked Congress to pass laws defining "good" and "bad" practices, but Congress refused.

In 1911, two years after Roosevelt left office, the Supreme Court adopted his point of view. The Court ruled that the Sherman Antitrust Act's prohibition of "all combinations in restraint of trade" should mean "all *unreasonable* combinations." The Supreme Court from then on decided whether a large business combination was "reasonable" or "unreasonable" by looking not merely at its size but also at its effect upon the public.

Important railroad legislation. The Roosevelt administration had more success in regulating railroads than in breaking up trusts. On the President's recommendations, Congress adopted two laws that put teeth into the Interstate Commerce Act of 1887 and strengthened the Interstate Commerce Commission.

The Elkins Act of 1903 made it illegal for a shipper to accept a rebate, just as the Interstate Commerce Act had made it illegal for

Cartoonist Clifford Berryman pokes fun at the idea of "good" and "bad" trusts. Bear-hunter "Teddy" has slain the "bad trusts." How does the cartoonist picture him dealing with the "good" ones?

railroads to give one. Many railroads approved of this act, for it freed them from giving special privileges to large shippers.

The Hepburn Act of 1906 gave the Interstate Commerce Commission authority (1) to regulate express and sleeping-car companies, oil pipelines, bridges, railroad terminals, and ferries doing business across state lines; (2) to fix "just and reasonable" rates, subject to approval by the federal courts; (3) to restrict the granting of free passes; and (4) to require that railroads use uniform methods of accounting.

Laws protecting public health. President Roosevelt also gave leadership to a movement to protect public health.

Government chemists had long known that the products of some distilleries, drug companies, and meat-packing plants were endangering public health. Patent medicines often contained harmful habit-forming drugs or ingredients that could not possibly relieve any ailments. Many canned foods were spoiled or were treated with poisonous preservatives. As Upton Sinclair had pointed out in his book *The Jungle,* meats in the packing houses were often from diseased animals.

Against the powerful opposition of the meat-packing interests, Roosevelt and the progressives in Congress secured passage in 1906 of the Meat Inspection Act. The act required government approval of all meat shipped from one state to another. Also under pressure from reform groups, including a women's letter-writing campaign, Congress passed the Pure Food and Drug Act of 1906. The act forbade the manufacture, sale, or transportation of impure food and patent medicines containing harmful ingredients. It also required patent-medicine containers to carry labels listing their exact contents. Five years later, in 1911, Congress supplemented this law by making it illegal to use false or misleading labels.

These acts helped to strengthen the developing theory that the federal government was responsible for protecting the public welfare.

SECTION SURVEY

IDENTIFY: Danbury Hatters' case, Northern Securities Company case, Department of Commerce and Labor, "Square Deal," Elkins Act of 1903, Hepburn Act of 1906, Pure Food and Drug Act of 1906.

1. (a) Why was organized labor pleased with Roosevelt's handling of the 1902 coal strike? (b) Was this a clear-cut victory for labor? Explain.
2. How did Roosevelt's attitude toward black Americans reflect the attitudes and prejudices of most white Americans of the time?
3. Roosevelt claimed to be a "trust buster." Do the facts support his claim? Why or why not?

4 Roosevelt acts to conserve America's natural resources

"The first work I took up when I became President," Roosevelt wrote in his *Autobiography,* "was the work of reclamation." This job of reclaiming and conserving the nation's natural resources proved to be one of his greatest contributions.

Wasted natural resources. Before Theodore Roosevelt became President, almost nothing had been done to safeguard the nation's resources. Indeed, Americans had always used their natural resources without regard for the future. Pioneer farmers had cut and burned their way westward, transforming forest land into farm land. The federal and state governments had carelessly encouraged waste, especially during the latter half of the 1800's. They handed over to private individuals and to corporations priceless natural resources — agricultural and grazing lands, forest regions, mineral deposits, oil fields, and water-power sites.

By 1900 only 200 million acres (81 million hectares) of the nation's original 800 million acres (324 million hectares) of virgin forest were still standing. Four fifths of this timber was privately owned. The executives who ran the nation's corporations cared no more about waste than the pioneer settlers had. Lumber companies destroyed forests without regard for wildlife, flood control, fire protection, replanting, or the preservation of young trees. Cattle raisers and sheepherders overgrazed semiarid lands, stripping them of their protective covering of grass. Often they helped turn these lands into dust bowls.

Coal companies worked only the richest and most accessible veins, leaving the bulk of the coal buried in abandoned mines. Oil companies allowed natural gas to escape unused into the air. The growing cities polluted rivers and streams with sewage and industrial wastes, destroying fish and creating a menace to public health. The American people were simply unused to thinking that their natural resources were exhaustible.

Early conservation efforts. By the late 1800's, a rapidly growing population was making heavier and heavier demands upon the nation's resources. The growing industries were devouring raw materials in ever larger quantities. A few thoughtful Americans realized that the nation's resources could not last forever.

As early as 1873, the American Association for the Advancement of Science had demanded some action to prevent the waste of natural resources. Because of these efforts and the efforts of other farsighted people, Congress in 1887 established the Forest Bureau in the Department of Agriculture. In 1891 Congress authorized the President to withdraw timberlands from public sale. Acting under this law, President Harrison set aside a national forest reserve of 17 million acres (7 million hectares), and Presidents Cleveland and McKinley more than doubled this area.

A small beginning toward the conservation of natural resources had been made. However, the public had not yet learned to think of the need for conservation as a serious national problem.

Roosevelt's leadership. President Roosevelt awakened public interest to the need for conservation, aroused Congress to action, and managed to get the federal and state governments to adopt new policies. In 1901 he warned Americans that "the forest and water problems are perhaps the most vital internal problems of the United States." In a special message to Congress, he reminded the legislators that "the mineral wealth of this country, the coal, iron, oil, gas, and the like, does not reproduce itself. . . . If we waste our resources today," he went on to say "our descendants will feel that exhaustion a generation or two before they otherwise would."

Roosevelt was never content with mere talk. During his administration he withdrew from public sale 150 million acres (60.7 million hectares) of forest land—an area much larger than France. He also withdrew millions of acres of coal and phosphate lands and potential water-power sites. In response to his urging, Congress created wildlife sanctuaries and national parks. In these activities, Roosevelt met opposition from private interests.

The Newlands Reclamation Act. One of the most important acts of his administration, however, received considerable support, especially from western members of Congress. Early in his Presidency, Roosevelt supported the Newlands Reclamation Act. This act provided that money from the sale of public lands in 16 western states and territories was to be used to build irrigation projects that would reclaim wasteland—that is, make it suitable for farming. Money from the sale of water to the farmers who settled on the reclaimed land was to go into a fund used to finance other irrigation projects.

Reclamation work started at once. Within four years 28 different irrigation projects were under way. By 1911 the Shoshone (shoh·SHOH·nee) Dam in Wyoming and the Roosevelt Dam in Arizona were in operation. Water from the enormous reservoir created by the Roosevelt Dam flowed through irrigation canals and ditches to transform 200,000 acres (80,940 hectares) of desert into rich farmland. As other projects were completed, additional thousands of acres of wasteland were brought under cultivation.

Paintings like Thomas Moran's "The Grand Canyon of the Yellowstone" helped acquaint Americans with the land's beauty and the need for national parks. Congress established Yellowstone National Park in 1872.

In 1903 Theodore Roosevelt (third from left) spent several days at Yosemite Park in California discussing conservation with the great naturalist John Muir (far right) and other concerned men of the day.

The White House Conference. In 1907 Roosevelt created the Inland Waterways Commission. After studying nearly every aspect of the conservation program, the commission urged the President to hold a national conference to publicize the need for conservation.

This meeting, the White House Conservation Conference of 1908, was a great success. One result was the appointment of a 50-member National Conservation Commission made up of nearly equal numbers of scientists, business executives, and political leaders. This commission went to work at once on a study of the country's mineral, water, forest, and soil resources. Another important outgrowth of the White House Conference was the appointment of state conservation agencies in 41 of the states by governors who were convinced of the need for them.

Thus Theodore Roosevelt helped to arouse public opinion to the need for conservation. Equally important, he established the foundations of a solid conservation program that would have far-reaching effects.

IDENTIFY: conservation, reclamation, natural resources.

1. What actions did Theodore Roosevelt take to arouse the nation to the need for conservation?
2. What was the significance of the Newlands Reclamation Act of 1902?
3. Why did some people oppose the idea of conserving natural resources?
4. In what ways did Roosevelt establish the foundations of a solid conservation program?

5 The progressive movement gains and loses under Taft

Despite a financial panic and depression in 1907, President Roosevelt's popularity with the public was at its peak in 1908. It was clear that the Republican nomination for another term was his for the asking, but Roosevelt stood by an earlier announcement that he would not run again.

The election of 1908. At the Republican convention in Chicago, Roosevelt supported his close friend and associate William Howard Taft of Ohio, who won the nomination on the first ballot. The Republican platform called for strengthening the Interstate Commerce Act of 1887 and the Sherman Antitrust Act of 1890, for conserving the nation's resources, developing an improved highway system, and revising the tariff.

The Democrats again chose William Jennings Bryan as their Presidential candidate. The Democratic platform condemned the Republican Party as the party of "privileges and private monopolies." It called for a lower tariff, new antitrust laws, a federal income tax, and restrictions on the use of court injunctions in labor disputes.

One unusual feature of the election campaign was the action taken by the American Federation of Labor. In 1908 the A. F. of L. abandoned its traditional policy of supporting friends of organized labor in both political parties and came out for Bryan and the entire Democratic ticket.

Despite the support of organized labor, the Democrats lost by a considerable margin, with Taft receiving 321 electoral votes to Bryan's

162. The Republicans also retained control of both houses of Congress.

Reforms under Taft. William Howard Taft, a Cincinnati lawyer and judge, had served the Roosevelt administration in the Philippines and in the War Department. Taft was a cautious man. His training as a lawyer and his temperament led him to stress the legalistic restrictions on his Presidential power. As one commentator put it, the change from Roosevelt to Taft was like changing from an automobile to a horse-drawn carriage. Despite his conservative nature, however, Taft recognized the force of the progressive movement and supported a number of important reforms.

Taft's administration chalked up an impressive list of accomplishments that progressives had favored. Taft's Attorney General started 90 antitrust suits against big corporations compared with 44 suits started under President Roosevelt. Following Taft's recommendation, Congress strengthened the Interstate Commerce Act by passing the Mann-Elkins Act of 1910. This new legislation placed telephone, telegraph, cable, and wireless companies under the jurisdiction of the Interstate Commerce Commission. Congress also created a new department with cabinet rank — the Department of Labor. In response to the growing attack upon the use of child labor, Congress established a Children's Bureau in the Department of Labor. It also established an 8-hour day for all workers on projects contracted for by the federal government.

The Taft administration also took steps to create a healthier political climate. President Taft himself added a considerable number of federal jobs to the civil service list. Congress adopted the Publicity Act requiring political parties to make public sources and sums of money spent in political campaigns.

Taft's administration was partly responsible for the adoption of a constitutional amendment to make possible a federal income tax. The Sixteenth Amendment, which had been proposed in 1909, was ratified in 1913.

Progressive opposition. In spite of these reforms, President Taft began to lose the support of the progressives in the Republican Party. As a result, he relied more and more on conservatives in the party.

The split between President Taft and the progressives appeared as early as April 1909, when Congress adopted the Payne-Aldrich Tariff. The progressives had worked for lower tariff rates, and at first Taft had supported their position. Then he switched to the high-tariff point of view and swung his influence behind the Payne-Aldrich measure. In the new act, some reductions were in fact made, but rates on many thousands of items were actually increased.

In the midst of the tariff battle, Taft was also violently attacked for his stand on conservation. Indeed, some of his most bitter critics charged that he had undermined Roosevelt's conservation program. Although this was an unfair charge, it is true that the conservation movement suffered a setback during the opening months of Taft's administration.

Taft's Secretary of the Interior, Richard A. Ballinger, was a cautious lawyer. Ballinger concluded that the President's authority to withdraw land from sale extended only to timber land. He therefore restored to public sale valuable water-power sites that President Roosevelt had previously withdrawn. Gifford Pinchot, head of the Forest Service under both Roosevelt and Taft, promptly protested. Taft sided with Pinchot, and the lands in question were returned to the forest reserve. However, Pinchot, an ardent conservationist, was convinced that Ballinger favored private interests and was opposed to the conservation program.

Pinchot's fears were strengthened when Ballinger allowed extensive coal lands and timberland in Alaska to pass into private hands. This action aroused a storm of controversy throughout the country. In the midst of the storm, Taft removed Pinchot from office.

Although Ballinger resigned in 1911 and the new Secretary of the Interior restored the Alaskan lands to the federal forest reserve, the damage had been done. Taft's stand on the Ballinger controversy cost the Republicans many votes in the Congressional elections of 1910. For the first time in 16 years, the Republicans lost control of the House of Representatives.

Actually, Taft did a great deal to advance the conservation program. With authorization from Congress, he withdrew almost 59 million acres (24 million hectares) of coal lands from public sale. He also signed the Appalachian Forest Reserve Act, which added large tracts of land in the southern Appalachians and in the White Mountains of New Hampshire to the federal reserves.

Roosevelt's spirited campaign captured the imaginations of cartoonists as far away as Germany. "I'm feeling like a bull moose," Roosevelt told a reporter, and thus was he depicted.

A victory for progressives. Early in 1910 the progressives of the Republican Party launched an attack upon the Speaker of the House. Since 1903 Speaker Joseph "Uncle Joe" Cannon of Illinois had been one of the most powerful officers in the government. As Speaker, he appointed all House committees and selected their leaders. He appointed himself head of the powerful Committee on Rules, which determined the order of business in the House. In this capacity, he could prevent any bill to which he objected from reaching the floor of the House for debate. Moreover, as presiding officer of the House he could determine who should speak during debate by recognizing or refusing to recognize anyone he pleased. As a result of these powers, "Uncle Joe" ruled the House with an iron hand.

The progressives charged that Cannon, a conservative, had used his great power to block progressive legislation. They planned to put an end to Cannon's control. In March 1910 Representative George W. Norris of Nebraska proposed an amendment to the House rules. He moved that in the future the Committee on Rules be elected by the members of the House and that the Speaker be excluded from membership on the Rules Committee.

Speaker Cannon, with solid support from the conservatives, fought desperately to maintain his power. After heated debate, about 40 progressive Republicans voted with the Democrats in favor of Norris's motion and stripped the Speaker of his traditional powers over the Committee on Rules. A year later the House deprived the Speaker of the power to appoint members of the remaining committees. The Speaker remained an extremely influential figure, but the Speaker's power was diminished.

Split in the Republican Party. By 1912 the Republican Party was split wide open, with the "old guard" on one side and the progressives on the other. Theodore Roosevelt, by now dissatisfied with Taft's leadership, decided to run again for the Presidency. To do so, Roosevelt had to brush aside the obvious candidate of the progressive forces, Robert M. La Follette of Wisconsin. Roosevelt also had to line up enough delegates to the nominating convention to insure his own nomination.

President Taft held the advantage that a President always has at a political convention. The Roosevelt supporters claimed that many of their delegates to the convention were refused seats by the Taft forces. Not surprisingly, the convention named Taft as its candidate. Angered by this, Roosevelt's supporters called another convention, which nominated him for the Presidency. Thus a new third party was launched—the Progressive Party, sometimes called the "Bull Moose" Party.°

The Bull-Moose Republicans with Teddy Roosevelt at their head adopted a platform calling for numerous reforms. The platform favored legislation in the interest of labor and advocated tariff reform. It endorsed the initiative, referendum, and recall, and it declared that it stood for government control over unfair business practices. In a spirited campaign, Roosevelt popularized his "New Nationalism" program. "New Nationalism," to Roosevelt, meant extending the powers of the federal government to make it an effective instrument in the battle for progressive measures and social reform.

°The party adopted as its emblem the powerful bull moose as a tribute to Roosevelt, who often used the term to describe a person's strength and vigor.

Wilson as the Democratic candidate. The Democrats were confident that the split in the Republican Party would insure their own victory. Their platform called for tariff reduction, banking reform, laws favoring workers and farmers, and the enforcement of stronger antitrust laws. As their candidate they chose Governor Woodrow Wilson of New Jersey.

Wilson, the son of a Presbyterian minister, had been president of Princeton University before he became governor of New Jersey in 1910. As governor, he fought the political machine bosses of his party, showing remarkable independence. He also took the lead in pushing through the legislature laws designed to reform the weak corporation laws of the state. As he showed more and more interest in other progressive measures, Wilson became the logical choice of the progressives in the Democratic Party.

An idealist and a man of convictions, Wilson was determined, courageous, and independent. He sensed the popular discontent in the country. His neatly turned phrases about establishing a "New Freedom" for ordinary Americans greatly appealed to those who were convinced that special privilege menaced the welfare of the nation.

The election of 1912. Still another party was involved in the election of 1912. The Social Democratic Party or Socialist Party had been organized in 1901. It had shown increasing strength in cities. In 1912, for example, 79 Socialist mayors were elected in 24 states. The Socialist Party candidate for President in 1912 was Eugene V. Debs.

The election proved to be a clear-cut victory for the progressives, a defeat for the conservatives. Wilson received 435 electoral votes and Roosevelt 88, whereas Taft received only 8.

Debs won no electoral votes but received almost a million popular votes.

Despite his overwhelming electoral vote, Wilson was a "minority" President. He received only 6 million popular votes out of a total of more than 15 million. Nevertheless, he could count upon widespread public support for his progressive "New Freedom" program.

SECTION SURVEY

IDENTIFY: Mann-Elkins Act of 1910, Publicity Act, Sixteenth Amendment, Gifford Pinchot, Joseph Cannon, "New Nationalism."

1. (a) Why did Taft's opponents consider him to be against conservation? (b) Do the facts support this charge against him? Explain.

2. (a) What were the reasons for the revolt against "Uncle Joe" Cannon? (b) What were the results?

3. Why did Roosevelt form the Bull Moose Party?

4. Chart Study: Make a chart comparing the parties, candidates, platforms, and results of the elections of 1908 and 1912.

6 Wilson's "New Freedom" expands opportunities for Americans

With his "New Freedom" program, President Wilson hoped to restore the equality of opportunity that many Americans enjoyed when the frontier was still open to settlers. He believed that this equality had been largely destroyed by the closing of the frontier, by great corporations, and by the often corrupt alliance of government and business.

SOURCES _____

WILSON'S "NEW FREEDOM" SPEECH (1912)

I take my stand absolutely, where every progressive ought to take his stand, on the proposition that private monopoly is indefensible and intolerable. And there I will fight my battle.

. . . I am for big business, and I am against trusts. Any man who can survive by his brains, any man who can put the others out of the business by making the thing cheaper to the consumer at the same time that he is increasing its intrinsic value and quality, I take off my hat to, and I say: "You are the man who can build up the United States, and I wish there were more of you." . . .

President Wilson at once recommended to Congress a positive program to promote the public welfare. Opposed by pressure groups and lobbies representing special business interests, Wilson used all his skills as a speaker to win popular support for his program.

Tariff reform. Like most Democrats, Wilson believed that high protective tariffs benefited the trusts by excluding from the country products that foreign manufacturers could make and market more cheaply. It was also true, of course, that tariffs protected jobs and helped workers maintain higher wages than foreign workers received.

To check the trend toward monopoly and reduce the cost of living, the Wilson administration pushed through Congress the Underwood Tariff Act of 1913. This act did not establish **free trade,°** but it reduced tariffs more than any tariff act had in the previous 50 years. It lowered duties on almost a thousand items, including cotton and woolen goods, iron, steel, coal, wood, agricultural tools, and many agricultural products. The average of all duties was reduced from 41 to 29 percent. The Underwood Tariff Act also included a section providing for an income tax. The new law provided for a graduated tax ranging from 1 to 6 percent on incomes over $3,000 per year.

The Underwood Tariff was passed against strong opposition, but it did answer the widespread cry for tariff reform. Moreover, its income tax provision laid down the principle that those with more income had to bear a heavier share of the expenses of government. This rule is sometimes called the "ability-to-pay" principle of taxation.

°**free trade:** the exchange of goods between countries unhampered by regulations or protective tariffs aimed to keep out foreign goods.

The Federal Reserve System. The second important achievement of Wilson's "New Freedom" program was in the field of money and banking. Almost everyone was dissatisfied with the existing banking system, but people disagreed on how to reform it.

In general, the more conservative business groups wanted greater private control over the existing banking system. They argued that this control would enable the stronger banks to help the less-favored banks in times of financial crisis.

On the other side were the Bryan Democrats and the progressive Republicans. They believed that the existing banking system was already dominated by the "money trust"—the great private investment banking firms like J. Pierpont Morgan and Company, which often controlled big business consolidations. The reformers wanted the government, not private bankers, to control the banking system. This control, they argued, would enable the government to regulate the amount of currency in circulation and thus help to stabilize prices.

The Federal Reserve Act of 1913 was a compromise between these two sides. It provided for the establishment of 12 Federal Reserve districts, each with a Federal Reserve Bank. The operations of these district banks were to be supervised and coordinated by a Federal Reserve Board in Washington, D.C. All national banks were to be members of a Federal Reserve Bank. All state banks that met certain requirements were invited to join.

The Federal Reserve Banks were strictly "bankers' banks." They provided services only for member banks, not for business concerns or private citizens. In times of crisis, when weak banks were on the point of failing, the Federal Reserve Banks could transfer money reserves and thus help prevent failure and the loss of people's savings.

SOURCES

WILSON ON AMERICAN IDEALS (1914)

My dream is that, as the years go on and the world knows more and more of America, it will also drink at these fountains of youth and renewal; that it also will turn to America for those moral inspirations which lie at the basis of all freedom; that the world will never fear America, unless it feels that it is engaged in some enterprise which is inconsistent with the rights of humanity; and that America will come into the full light of the day when all shall know that she puts human rights above all other rights and that her flag is the flag not only of America, but of humanity.

The Federal Reserve System also made it possible to put more money into circulation or to withdraw some from circulation according to the needs of the time. It thus provided a more elastic currency by controlling the amount of lending that member banks could do.

Antitrust laws strengthened. The third major achievement of Wilson's "New Freedom" program was its effort to strengthen the antitrust laws. The Clayton Antitrust Act of 1914 helped to put teeth in the older Sherman Antitrust Act.

The Clayton Act was aimed at business practices that until then had not been illegal. (1) It prohibited business organizations from selling at lower prices to certain favored purchasers *if* such price discrimination helped to create a monopoly. (2) It prohibited "tying contracts"—that is, contracts requiring a purchaser to agree not to buy or sell the products of a competitor. (3) It declared interlocking directorates illegal in companies with capital investments of $1 million or more. (4) It prohibited corporations from acquiring the stock of another company *if* the purchase tended to create a monopoly.

The Clayton Act also attempted to protect farmers and wage earners. The Sherman Antitrust Act of 1890 had been used on a number of occasions against labor unions. The Clayton Act, on the other hand, declared that labor unions and farm organizations had a legal right to exist. It said that they could not "be held or construed to be illegal combinations or conspiracies in restraint of trade, under the antitrust laws."

The Clayton Act also prohibited the granting of an injunction in a labor dispute *unless* the court decided that an injunction was necessary "to prevent irreparable injury to property." This act also declared that strikes, peaceful picketing, and boycotts were legal under federal jurisdiction.

Organized labor hailed the Clayton Act as a great victory. However, as you will read, the courts interpreted the act in such a way that the injunction continued to be used as a weapon against strikes.

The Federal Trade Commission. The Federal Trade Commission, created by Congress in 1914, was also part of President Wilson's "New Freedom" program. The commission was authorized to advise and regulate industries

Woodrow Wilson, shown here on a 1912 election campaign poster, believed that the duty of Progressivism was, "to cleanse, to reconsider, to restore . . . every process of our common life."

engaged in interstate and foreign trade. The commission was to be a bipartisan body of five members.

The commission was authorized to (1) require annual and special reports from corporations, (2) investigate the business activities of persons and most corporations, (3) publish reports on its findings, and (4) order corporations to stop unfair methods of competition. Among the unfair practices investigated by the commission were mislabeling, adulteration of products, and false claims to patents. If a corporation refused to obey an order to "cease and desist" from such practices, the commission could ask the courts to enforce its ruling. The law protected the corporation by providing that it could appeal to the courts if it considered the "cease-and-desist" order to be unfair.

The Federal Trade Commission was intended to prevent the growth of monopolies and to help bring about a better understanding between big business and the government.

Other "New Freedom" measures. The tariff, money and banking, regulation of trusts—these were the major problems tackled by Congress during Wilson's first administration. Much more reform legislation might have been adopted if the outbreak of World War I in

Europe in the summer of 1914 had not interfered. Even so, Congress found time to pass several other important measures.

In 1914 Congress adopted the Smith-Lever Act. Among other things, the act provided federal funds for rural education. The educational programs were to be carried on by the Department of Agriculture in cooperation with the land-grant colleges. Federal grants of money were to be matched by similar grants from the states receiving this aid. Three years later, in 1917, just before the United States entered World War I, Congress adopted the Smith-Hughes Act. This additional measure provided federal funds for vocational education in both rural and urban areas of the country.

The Federal Farm Loan Act of 1916 made it easier for farmers to borrow money. This act divided the country into 12 agricultural districts. It established a Farm Loan Bank for each district where farmers could get mortgages at rates lower than those available at regular banks.

Blacks and the "New Freedom." During the election campaign of 1912, Woodrow Wilson promised an officer of the National Association for the Advancement of Colored People (NAACP) that if elected he would promote the interests of black Americans in every way possible. Such was not the case, however. As President, Wilson seemed to agree with most white Americans that segregation was in the best interests of black as well as white Americans.

During Wilson's administration, white employees and black employees in government offices in Washington, D.C., were segregated. Many black office workers were dismissed in southern cities. A black journalist bitterly remarked that Wilson had given black Americans no part in the "New Freedom."

The election of 1916. By 1916 President Wilson had established himself as a vigorous leader. The delegates to the Democratic convention pointed with pride to his solid list of achievements and enthusiastically renominated him for a second term.

The Republicans chose Supreme Court Justice Charles Evans Hughes, former governor of New York, as their candidate. The Progressive Party nominated Theodore Roosevelt. However, Roosevelt was unwilling to split the Republican vote again, refused the nomination, and supported Hughes. The Progressive Party,

deprived of Roosevelt, decided not to nominate another candidate. As a result the Republicans, once more united, entered the campaign hopeful of victory.

The campaign of 1916 centered not only upon Wilson's record of domestic issues but also upon America's relation to the war that had broken out in Europe in 1914. Hughes toured the country, criticizing the Democrats for the Underwood Tariff and for their handling of foreign affairs. Wilson, on the other hand, contented himself with delivering speeches from the front porch of his summer home in New Jersey. Speakers for the Democratic Party adopted the slogan "He kept us out of war."

The election itself turned out to be one of the closest in American history. The final electoral vote was 277 for Wilson, 254 for Hughes. California proved to be the decisive state—the Democrats won in California by a margin of only 3,773 popular votes! Despite the closeness of the vote, Wilson had won against a united Republican Party, as had not been true in the election of 1912. Even more reassuring, he had collected nearly 600,000 more popular votes than Hughes.

Woodrow Wilson seemed to feel that his first term in office had accomplished his goals, though many progressives believed much remained to be done. In any event, it was not "New Freedom" measures that occupied the President during his second administration. Within a month of Wilson's second inauguration on March 4, 1917, the United States entered World War I.

SECTION SURVEY

IDENTIFY: "New Freedom," Underwood Tariff, free trade, elastic currency, "ability-to-pay" principle of taxation, Smith-Lever Act, Federal Farm Loan Act.

1. For what reason did Wilson start the "New Freedom" program?

2. (a) Describe the Federal Reserve System. (b) In what ways was it a compromise between the views of the conservatives and those of the progressives?

3. (a) How did the Clayton Antitrust Act of 1914 put teeth in the older Sherman Antitrust Act? (b) Why did organized labor praise the Clayton Act?

4. What was the function of the Federal Trade Commission?

Chapter Survey

Summary: Tracing the Main Ideas

The victory of the Republicans in the election of 1896 broke the strength of the Populist movement. With the triumph of the Republicans and with the return of prosperity, many people concluded that the reform movement had lost its force.

However, the reform movement was not dead. On the contrary, in the early 1900's it gained new life in the progressive movement. Guided by the progressives, including President Theodore Roosevelt, the relationship of government and business began to change. In earlier times, the government's role had been, in general, that of a referee who stood on the sidelines and stepped in only when it seemed that one of the players had disobeyed the rules. Now, in the twentieth century, the government was beginning to take a more active part, to accept more responsibility for regulating the activities of business in the interest of the public welfare. Both Republicans and Democrats were responsible for this changing view of the role of government in the new industrial age.

The reforms started under President Roosevelt were continued by President Taft and, to an even greater degree, during the Democratic administration of President Wilson. As you will read, the efforts were interrupted by the outbreak of World War I in 1914.

Inquiring into History

1. The basic issue with which Presidents Roosevelt, Taft, and Wilson had to deal was the role of government in the new industrial age. Explain.
2. Compare Roosevelt's "Square Deal" and Wilson's "New Freedom" in terms of (a) goals, (b) legislative accomplishments, and (c) long-range effects.
3. Present evidence to support or refute this statement: Despite his apparent weakness, President Taft was actually a more effective progressive President than Roosevelt.
4. To what extent did black Americans benefit from the progressive movement? Explain.
5. Did the ideals of progressivism agree with the ideals expressed in the Declaration of Independence and the preamble to the Constitution? Explain.
6. How might you have voted in the election of 1912 if you had been (a) a farmer, (b) a banker, (c) an Italian immigrant, and (d) a factory worker? Give reasons for your answers.

Relating Past to Present

1. Which critics in our society today might qualify for the title "muckraker"? Why?
2. (a) What are some of the reforms that are currently being proposed by the national government to help remedy problems of our society? (b) How do the problems and proposed solutions compare with those of the progressive era?

3. Pioneers, governments, corporations, and Americans in general have been responsible for the waste of America's natural resources and the pollution of its environment. Comment on this statement. Was it true in the early 1900's? Is it true today?

Developing Social Science Skills

1. Make a chart with these four headings: Social Reforms, Educational Reforms, Political Reforms, Economic Reforms. Fill in the chart by listing in the appropriate columns the reforms brought about during the progressive era (1895–1917). Then answer these questions: (a) Who benefited the most from each reform? (b) Did anyone get hurt by any of the reforms? (c) Which of these reforms do you consider the most important? Why?
2. Select a controversial issue of the progressive years and draw two political cartoons—one presenting each side of the issue. Give each cartoon a title that helps make clear the point of view presented in the cartoon.
3. Americans tend to elect Presidents who reflect the spirit of the times. Gather evidence to support or refute this hypothesis, using Theodore Roosevelt, William Howard Taft, or Woodrow Wilson as an example. Can you think of earlier Presidents who reflected the spirit of their times? Explain. Can this be said of any of our most recent presidents? Explain.

Chapter 9

"The Big Change" in American Ways of Life

1900–1920

As the United States approached the middle of the twentieth century, Frederick Lewis Allen wrote a book reviewing and interpreting 50 years of American history. He called this book *The Big Change* and gave it the subtitle *America Transforms Itself, 1900-1950.*

The transformation, as Allen saw it, was "in the character and quality of American life by reason of what might be called the democratization of our economic system, or the adjustment of capitalism to democratic ends." It was, he went on to say, "the way in which an incredible expansion of industrial and business activity, combined with a varied series of political, social, and economic forces, has altered the American standard of living and with it the average American's way of thinking and his status as a citizen."

During the years from 1900 to 1920, the United States was in full process of passing from a predominantly rural economy to a predominantly industrial economy. A growing number of Americans, including business owners and managers, became increasingly aware of the need to modify some of the attitudes and practices carried over from the early days of the Industrial Revolution. In 1920 there were still many large and difficult problems that remained unsolved. But "the big change" was already beginning to have an important influence on the direction of American life.

THE CHAPTER IN OUTLINE

1. New inventions and new ideas revolutionize American industry.
2. The lives of farmers improve in the early 1900's.
3. Conditions improve for industrial workers in the United States.

1 New inventions and new ideas revolutionize American industry

In 1900 America was still in the horse-and-buggy age, but that age would not last much longer. Great changes were already transforming the country, but even greater changes were to come.

Signs of change. In 1900, Americans still rode in horse-drawn streetcars. Hitching posts and watering troughs were common sights. Livery stables and blacksmith shops were centers of activity in every town. When night fell, the lamplighter turned on the gas lamps that still lighted the streets in most American cities and towns.

It is easier, perhaps, to picture the America of 1900 by listing the things that people did not have and did not know. There were no rock groups, no supermarkets, no income taxes. No one had heard of vitamins or antibiotics. Women could vote in only four states—Wyoming, Colorado, Utah, and Idaho. Motion pictures, radios, television, and airplanes did not exist. In those days automobiles were still curiosities, and people often called them "horseless carriages."

Yet, in 1900, Americans had already entered a new way of life. By 1900, railroad builders had laid down 192,566 miles (309,896 kilometers) of track. All the great trunk lines had been built across the continent. Day and night, long lines of freight cars rumbled across the country loaded with products of America's farmland, mines, mills, and factories. New railroad lines were still being built. By 1920 railroad mileage reached its high mark of 260,000 miles (418,500 kilometers) of track.

The horse-and-buggy age was fast drawing to an end when artist William Sonntag painted "The Bowery at Night," a picture of New York City. Soon automobiles would join elevated trains and trolleys in motorizing transportation.

Automobiles and highways. While this network of steel rails expanded, inventors in Europe and America were experimenting with a new source of power. This was the internal combustion engine, in which fuel, usually gasoline, was converted into a vapor and exploded within the engine walls. Among the American experimenters were Charles E. Duryea, George B. Selden, Elwood Haynes, Alexander Winton, and Henry Ford. These inventors and others developed the gasoline engine.

By 1900, "horseless carriages" were appearing on the roads. At first the automobile was an expensive toy for wealthy people. Mass production soon lowered costs, however, bringing the automobile within reach of people with modest incomes. Whereas in 1900 there were only 8,000 automobiles in the United States, by 1920 there were 8 million passenger cars and 1 million trucks.

Development of the automobile depended, of course, upon other inventions and developments. One was the discovery by Charles Goodyear of the process for vulcanizing, or hardening, rubber, for which he obtained his first patent in 1844. Other inventions led to improvements in refining petroleum into gasoline and in developing batteries, generators, and other electrical devices.

The development of the automobile also depended upon—and helped to stimulate—the construction of paved roads. In 1904 nearly all rural roads were little better than dirt lanes, although some were surfaced with gravel, clay, or crushed oyster shells. By 1924, however, 472,000 miles (760,000 kilometers) of rural highways had paved surfaces. By 1924, older roads were being widened, graded, and paved at the rate of about 40,000 miles (64,000 kilometers) a year, at an annual cost of approximately $1 billion.

The airplane. By 1900, Europeans and Americans, among them Samuel P. Langley, were experimenting with another new method of transportation—powered flight. Orville and Wilbur Wright, on December 17, 1903, became the first to put such a machine into the air. Their first flight went only about 120 feet (37 meters) and did not attract much attention. Within a few years, however, the first crude flying machines were being replaced by more effective planes, and air pioneers were making longer and longer flights. In 1919 a Navy seaplane crossed the Atlantic by way of the Azores. That

same year two Englishmen, John Alcock and A. W. Brown, flew nonstop from Newfoundland to Ireland.

Developments in communications. Equally revolutionary were developments in communications. People were barely getting used to the idea of the telephone when in 1895, an Italian inventor, Guglielmo (goo·LYEL·moh) Marconi, first demonstrated wireless telegraphy. Eight years later, from a station at Cape Cod, Massachusetts, he transmitted a message across the ocean to England and received a reply.

One of the most significant inventions in the field of communications was the three-element vacuum tube, invented by Lee De Forest in 1906. This invention made it possible to amplify even weak electrical impulses, or signals. Within a few years, wireless equipment had been installed on all large vessels. Wireless messages in the dots and dashes of Morse code were being sent over land and sea by powerful transmitters. Meanwhile, scientists and engineers were experimenting with transmitting the spoken word through the air. However, commercial radio broadcasting did not become a reality until the 1920's.

The motion picture. Several inventors, American, British, and French, contributed to the development of the motion picture. In 1895 two Americans, Thomas Armat and Woodville Latham, successfully used their projector in public showings.

In the early days, films ran only a few minutes. Then, in 1903, a pioneer "picture story" called *The Great Train Robbery* demonstrated the possibilities of the motion picture. Soon directors and producers were proving to ever larger audiences that the motion picture could do a great deal that was impossible on the stage. One early director, D. W. Griffith, won fame in 1914 for his film *The Birth of a Nation*. Night after night people crowded into the early movie theaters to watch such popular stars as Mary Pickford, Douglas Fairbanks, and Charlie Chaplin.

New methods of production. The new world that was coming into being in the early 1900's depended upon new power sources—oil and electricity. Between 1900 and 1920, oil production in the United States jumped from 63 million to about 443 million barrels a year. By 1914 nearly one third of the nation's factory machines were driven by electricity, and the use of electric power was rapidly increasing. High-voltage transmission lines carried the pulsing energy of dynamos—steam-driven or water-driven—to widely scattered cities. Smaller transmission lines carried electricity to towns and villages throughout the country and even to some isolated farms.

Productivity of America's factories was greatly increased not only by new sources of power but also by the **assembly line.** On an assembly line, workers stood at stations beside a slowly moving track, or conveyor belt. At each station, workers added a new part to the product on the track. Finally, a steady succession of finished products came off the end of the assembly line. Improved in the early 1900's by Henry Ford for use in the manufacture of automobiles, the assembly line soon became an essential part of America's developing industrial economy.

Increasing efficiency. The use of **efficiency engineering** also increased the productivity of factories. Frederick W. Taylor was a major contributor to this idea. Taylor wanted greater efficiency from machines and from the workers operating the machines. To get it, he developed "time-and-motion" studies of plant operation. Using a stop watch, Taylor timed the workers operating machines and counted the number of motions each worker made to complete a particular operation. Then he worked out ways to reduce the number of movements of the workers' hands and feet. Sometimes workers were trained to use their hands and feet more effectively. Sometimes the machine was redesigned and its controls placed in more convenient locations.

Taylor's methods made great economies possible in every stage of mass production. Each process in the mechanized industrial plant was simplified and speeded up along the assembly line. Each worker performed a highly specialized task, working with the least possible effort to produce the maximum output. However, some workers complained that such methods made them, more than ever, like parts in a great machine.

The "Ford idea." Henry Ford had made a major contribution to American industry in developing the assembly line. Even more important was his new and revolutionary theory of increasing employee wages.

THE PIERCE-ARROW CAR

Our idea is that the car should go "there and back" in the shortest possible time, with the least trouble to both owner and driver, with the greatest comfort to the owner in transit, at the least expense, weight of car and equipment considered, and without interruption of the trip by reason of or the fault of the car, and that it should do this not only now and then, but always. That is the service that the Pierce-Arrow Car is planned to perform.

The Pierce-Arrow Motor Car Company, Buffalo, N. Y.

The Pierce Arrow was for years the height of luxury in American cars. This advertisement refers to "both owner and driver," letting the reader know that this car demanded a chauffeur.

On January 5, 1914, Ford announced that he was nearly doubling the wages of the workers in his plants. Beginning immediately, he said, his 13,000 employees would receive a minimum wage of $5 for an 8-hour day. This announcement swept almost all other news off the front pages of America's newspapers. The New York *Herald* called it "an epoch in the world's industrial history."

Why was Ford's action considered so important? In taking this step, Ford had recognized an important fact about the American economic system. Rising wages gave American workers greater purchasing power to buy more and more of the products of America's expanding industry.

Ford was both warmly applauded and sharply criticized for his action. However, the criticism did not prevent the "Ford idea" from spreading to other industries. As the years passed, more people came to understand that mass production and mass purchasing power are interdependent. This understanding was an essential part of what Frederick Lewis Allen called "the big change" transforming America in the opening years of the twentieth century.

SECTION SURVEY

IDENTIFY: Charles Goodyear, Samuel Langley, Wright brothers, Guglielmo Marconi, *The Great Train Robbery,* assembly line, Frederick Taylor.

1. How did mass production of the automobile help to transform American life?
2. Why was the three-element vacuum tube an important invention?
3. (a) What is the purpose of efficiency engineering? (b) Give some examples of how it works. (c) What are its advantages? Its disadvantages?
4. (a) What was the "Ford idea"? (b) Why was it important to the American economy?

2 The lives of farmers improve in the early 1900's

By the early 1900's, the farmer had become an important part of the nation's industrial economy. To be sure, on thousands of small farms tucked away in mountain valleys and in other remote areas, farm families lived much as farmers had lived 100 years earlier. These more or less self-sufficient farms were exceptions. Most of the nation's farm produce was raised by farmers who, whether they liked it or not, had in many respects become owners of a business.

Growing demand for farm products. One factor that helped turn farms into businesses was the startling growth of America's city pop-

Even though tractors could outproduce horse-drawn machines, some farmers resisted buying them in the early 1900's. How does this advertisement for a tractor reflect that fact and how does it try to counteract it?

Have you placed a Sentimental Value on your Horses out of proportion to the work they are able to perform?

BAILOR MOTOR CULTIVATORS

ulation. Between 1900 and 1920, the urban population increased by about 24 million. Urban dwellers increased from about 40 percent of the total population to more than 50 percent. The swelling urban population was made up in part of farm youths leaving home to seek their fortunes in the cities. It was made up in much larger part of the more than 14 million immigrants who poured into the United States between 1900 and 1920. Regardless of the source, however, the growing urban population meant more mouths to feed and a growing demand for farm products. The commercial farmers struggled to meet this demand.

Commercial farms. Some farmers specialized in one, two, or three crops, or in raising dairy cattle or other livestock. Such **commercial farmers** needed money, or capital, to buy machinery and to hire labor. They had to keep careful accounts and to pay careful attention to market conditions. They were, in brief, one part of an abstract thing known as the "nation's economy." When the economy prospered, farmers likewise could hope to prosper. When the economy went into a depression, farmers were certain to suffer accordingly.

The rapidly growing demand for farm products enabled farmers to receive higher prices. Between 1900 and 1920, farm prices increased threefold. In the same period, the average value of farmland quadrupled. As prosperity spread, more and more farmers began to buy agricultural machinery.

Farmers had been using labor-saving machinery long before the turn of the century. Not until after 1900, however, did the shift from hand tools to power-driven machines begin to transform the farming industry. According to census records, in 1870 the total value of all farm implements and machinery in the United States amounted to $271 million. By 1900 the figure had risen to $750 million, by 1920 to $3.6 billion. One revealing measure of the machine age was the use of tractors. In 1910 there were only 1,000 tractors on American farms; by 1920 there were 246,000.

Gasoline and electricity revolutionized rural as well as urban life in the early 1900's. Power-driven machinery—pumps, plows, seeders, harvesters, milking machines, trucks, and tractors—eased the farmers' burden of labor, enabling them to produce far more products with much less toil. However, human sweat and muscle were still necessary on the commercial farms. The need for farm laborers to work on the commercial farms was met in part by an increase in immigration from Mexico and the Philippines, and, for a short time, from Japan.

Growth of scientific agriculture. Scientific knowledge as well as power-driven machinery helped to revolutionize farming. Chemists discovered new fertilizers and better methods of cultivation to stop soil exhaustion and replenish worn-out land. Biologists improved the life span and the productivity of livestock, plants, grains, and fruits. Bacteriologists discovered ways to check blights and diseases in both plants and animals. Scientists also developed new grains and fruits resistant to disease and better adapted to varying climatic conditions.

Federal aid to farmers. Much of the new research and experimentation was carried on by the Department of Agriculture and by the land-grant colleges that were created by the Morrill Act of 1862.

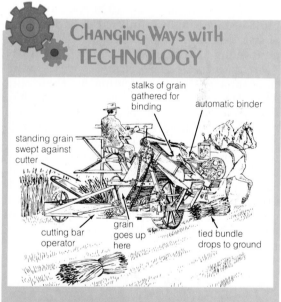

Changing Ways with TECHNOLOGY

stalks of grain gathered for binding

automatic binder

standing grain swept against cutter

cutting bar operator

grain goes up here

tied bundle drops to ground

REAPER-BINDER

The McCormick reaper developed in the 1830's cut the grain stalks and left them to be raked up by hand and tied in bundles. Many improvements led around 1880 to the reaper-binder above, which cut the grain stalks and tied them in bundles automatically.

In later years the federal government greatly expanded this program of aid to farmers. The Hatch Act of 1887, for example, provided money for agricultural experiment stations and farms in each state. The Smith-Lever Act of 1914 provided additional money for the employment of "county extension agents" who carried "practical information on subjects relating to agriculture and home economics" to the farmers of each county. The Smith-Hughes Act of 1917 provided money for the support of vocational education in public schools, including education in agriculture, industries, trade, home economics, and teacher training.

Changing ways of living. The new industrial age altered the everyday lives of farm families, too. By 1920 loneliness and social isolation were becoming memories to many of the nation's farmers. The slender threads of telephone wires were spinning a net of communications across the countryside. The automobile—notably Henry Ford's "Tin Lizzie"—was bringing the farm closer to the town and the city. Once a five-mile (eight-kilometer) drive to town had meant a one- or two-hour trip behind "Old Dobbin." By 1920 the same trip could be made in the family car in half an hour or less. This meant more trips to town, often for an evening at the movies.

With increased prosperity, farm families could provide better education for their children. The one-room school continued to dominate the rural educational scene, but more and more farm children came from miles around to enjoy the advantages of "consolidated schools," which served several towns or school districts. Many children were able to continue their education at the state university. For farm children, no less than for their parents, life "down on the farm" in the early 1900's was far more comfortable and interesting than it had ever been before.

SECTION SURVEY

IDENTIFY: self-sufficient farming, commercial farmers, "consolidated schools."

1. How did each of the following affect and change farm life in the years from 1900 to 1920: (a) urbanization, (b) mechanization, (c) scientific agriculture, (d) federal aid?

2. How did the social life of farm families change as a result of mechanization?

3. Why do you think it was necessary for farmers to receive federal aid during this period?

4. Picture Study: Study the advertisement on page 180. (a) What older product is the advertised product intended to replace? (b) What might be the advantages of this new product over the one it is replacing? (c) How does the ad try to persuade farmers to buy this product? (d) What other changes might the use of this new product bring to the lives of farmers?

3 Conditions improve for industrial workers in the United States

Conditions for the industrial worker as well as for the farmer improved considerably during the early 1900's. First, as you have read, wage earners benefited from the fast-increasing productivity of America's economic system. Second, through organization, wage earners were beginning to exert real influence on state legislatures and on Congress. Third, many Americans were beginning to realize that industrialization had raised serious problems that had to be solved if democracy itself was to survive. Fourth, through articles in popular magazines and in the daily newspapers, the general public was becoming increasingly aware of the wage earners' grievances.

Early social legislation. To improve the conditions of wage earners, legislators began to pass **social legislation,** as these laws were often referred to. These laws mainly were passed by the northern and western states. The South, with its newer industrial development, did little during this period to promote the welfare of workers through state laws.

In general, the first state laws improved working conditions and limited hours of work. As early as 1879, a Massachusetts law prohibited women and children from working more than 60 hours a week. Oregon enacted a similar law in 1903, and other states followed suit. Meanwhile, New York State passed a series of laws protecting workers as well as consumers.

The recognition that certain types of work involved special risk led Utah in 1896 to pass a law limiting the workday of miners to eight hours. In 1902 Maryland passed the first law to compensate workers for on-the-job accidents.

Working conditions like this in a Louisiana oyster-shucking plant were not uncommon in the early 1900's. Photos exposing the plight of child laborers did much to stir public sympathy and get protective laws passed.

This law was declared unconstitutional, but New York passed a successful compensation law in 1910, as did Wisconsin in 1911.

In 1912 Massachusetts set a precedent by passing the first minimum-wage law. The Massachusetts law established a minimum-wage rate—employers could not ask a wage earner to work below this rate.

Supreme Court objections. These early laws represented a new approach to the problems of wage earners in the emerging industrial society. Much of this early social legislation was declared unconstitutional by the Supreme Court. The Court ruled that limiting owners' control over their businesses deprived the owners of part of their property without the "due process of law" guaranteed in the Fifth and Fourteenth Amendments.

The Supreme Court also held that social legislation violated people's rights to enter into any contract they wished. According to the Court, when workers accepted employment and an employer agreed to pay them, a contract had been made even though the terms were not written down. Following this freedom-of-contract line of reasoning, the Supreme Court declared unconstitutional in 1905 a New York law that had fixed a maximum workday of 10 hours for bakers.

Changing Court attitudes. Many people argued that it was unrealistic to assume that the individual worker could actually bargain with a corporation that employed thousands of people. They insisted that in reality the Supreme Court was depriving all workers of freedom to bargain with their employers.

Supreme Court justices gradually changed their attitude toward social legislation. Like other citizens, they were influenced by the progressive temper of the times. The justices found other clauses in the Constitution that enabled states to limit people's right to do as they pleased with their property. The Court increasingly held that the Constitution had reserved to each state the power to enact laws necessary to protect the health and well-being of all of its citizens. On these grounds the Supreme Court upheld an Oregon law that provided a 10-hour day for women. This set a precedent for the Court's approval of other social legislation.

Federal labor laws. The states rather than the federal government enacted most of the early social legislation. However, the state laws were ignored, and certain states, especially in the South, lagged behind others. This situation prompted organized labor to seek relief through federal laws.

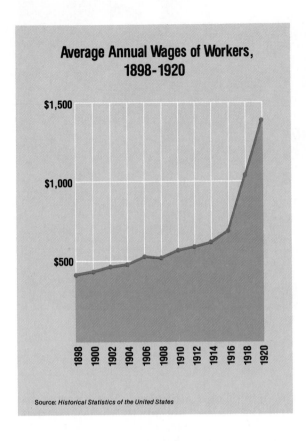

Average Annual Wages of Workers, 1898-1920

$1,500

$1,000

$500

1898 1900 1902 1904 1906 1908 1910 1912 1914 1916 1918 1920

Source: *Historical Statistics of the United States*

Except for its constitutional power "to promote the general welfare" and "to regulate interstate commerce," the federal government had little power to control labor relations. To be sure, the federal government did have the power to control working conditions for its own employees. In 1868, you recall, Congress established an 8-hour day for laborers and mechanics employed by or on behalf of the United States government. In 1892 all federal-government employees were given an 8-hour day.

Later, in 1906, acting under its power "to regulate interstate commerce," Congress passed an Employers' Liability Act. This act protected railroad workers from bearing all the costs of accidents that occurred on the job. Although this law was ruled unconstitutional, later legislation met the Court's objections.

In 1916, when the railroad workers' unions threatened to strike for an 8-hour day, Congress passed the Adamson Act. This act gave railroad workers the same pay for an 8-hour day that they had been getting for a 10-hour day.

During President Wilson's administration, Congress also granted labor's request that it be exempt from the charge of conspiring "to restrain trade." As you have read, the Clayton Antitrust Act of 1914 helped to modify some of the clauses in the Sherman Antitrust Act of 1890 to which labor had objected.

The IWW. Despite the progress in social legislation, many workers still felt the need to organize to win better working conditions. One union that appeared in the early 1900's was the Industrial Workers of the World (IWW). The IWW was set up as a radical union of skilled and unskilled workers. It demanded the overthrow of the capitalist system by general strikes, boycotts, and sabotage.

The IWW, or "Wobblies" as they were known, won some strikes in western mining and labor camps and in the textile mills of Lawrence, Massachusetts. It lost a textile strike in Paterson, New Jersey. Weakened in the years after by its reputation for violence and by federal prosecution, the IWW after 1918 ceased to be a challenge to more conservative trade unions.

Advances for organized labor. By the time World War I broke out in Europe in 1914, labor still had many grievances, and it was still far from its goals. Trade-union activities and political methods for achieving the goals had met only partial success. Nevertheless, organized labor could look back upon a number of reforms gained through 50 years of struggle. Perhaps most important, organized labor enjoyed a small but growing measure of public support.

SECTION SURVEY

IDENTIFY: social legislation, minimum wage, freedom of contract, Employers' Liability Act, IWW.

1. (a) Describe the various kinds of social legislation passed by the states to aid workers. (b) On what grounds did the Supreme Court declare this early social legislation unconstitutional?

2. (a) Why was it that for many years the federal government did not enact social legislation? (b) Why did it later begin to do so?

3. (a) Why did the IWW become less important after 1918? (b) What did its decline mean for the labor movement?

4. Graph Study: Look at the graph on this page. Does the evidence it gives indicate that conditions for workers were getting better or worse in the early 1900's? Explain.

Chapter Survey

Summary: Tracing the Main Ideas

During the years between 1900 and 1920, the United States completed the process of passing from a mainly agricultural economy to a mainly industrial economy. By 1920 the United States had become the most productive industrial nation on the face of the earth.

In 1900, Americans were still living in the horse-and-buggy age. It was, however, a dying age. Old ways were rapidly giving way to new. People living during the years between 1900 and 1920 saw the emergence of automobiles, airplanes, radios, motion pictures, assembly lines. These and many other developments greatly transformed the ways Americans were living.

The nation's rapidly increasing productivity and its steadily rising standard of living were only the most obvious signs of the new America. Less obvious, but equally important, were the changes that were beginning to take place in the thinking of great numbers of Americans.

More and more people were altering some of the attitudes and practices that they had carried over from the early days of the Industrial Revolution. More and more people were realizing that organized labor had an important role to play in the new industrial economy. Slowly but surely, Americans were taking the first halting steps toward what Frederick Lewis Allen called "the adjustment of capitalism to democratic ends."

In 1920 the American people still had a long, hard road to travel. Although they had no way of knowing it, the road along which they were moving would bring them by mid-century to the highest standard of living the world had ever seen.

Inquiring into History

1. Did industrialization strengthen the belief that America was the land of opportunity? Explain your answer.
2. In what ways did the revolution in communication help initiate reform movements and contribute to the growth of political democracy?
3. By having a national, rather than a local, transportation system, farmers had wider markets as well as more competition. How might this have affected their economic freedom?
4. In 1900 the United States was rapidly passing from a rural to an industrial economy. (a) What were some of the important changes taking place as a result of this revolution in American industry? (b) Why might it have been difficult for people to adjust to these changes?

Relating Past to Present

1. Compare the attitude of the federal government today toward social legislation with its attitude during the early 1900's. Give specific examples to support your answer.
2. (a) Which of the developments in transportation and communication that began in the early 1900's are still important in American life today? (b) How have they been improved or modified in more recent years? (c) Have any of them been completely replaced?
3. Are we still making what Frederick Lewis Allen called "the adjustment of capitalism to democratic ends"? Explain.

Developing Social Science Skills

1. Study the charts on pages 698 and 701. (a) What was the total population in 1900? In 1920? (b) Does immigration seem to have been an important cause of this population growth? Refer back to the chapter text. (c) Did most Americans live in urban or in rural areas in 1900? In 1920? (d) What factors may have accounted for the change?
2. The photograph on page 183 provides evidence about the life of some children during the early 1900's. Conduct research on other aspects of youth in America at that time, such as recreation, education, city life, country life, attitudes toward youth, and family life.
3. Study a Sears Roebuck or a Montgomery Ward catalog published around the turn of the century. What evidence do the ads provide about American life of the period? Name some things that have greatly changed since that time. Name some that have remained much the same.

Unit Survey

Tracing the Main Events: Technology and Change

1897	First subway is completed, in Boston.
1899	First motorized vacuum cleaner patented.
1901	First large oil strike, in Texas.
	Rockefeller Institute for Medical Research founded.
1902	Rayon patented.
1903	First transcontinental auto trip.
	Wright brothers make first airplane flight at Kitty Hawk.
1906	Mt. Wilson Observatory opened in California.
	First radio broadcast of voice and music.
1907	Electric washing machine developed.
1913	X-ray machine perfected.
	Woolworth Building in New York completed, tallest building in the world at the time.
1915	First transcontinental telephone call made.
1916	Thompson submachine gun invented.
1918	First successful helicopter flight.
1920	First national radio broadcast.

For Further Inquiry

1. (a) Make a list of characteristics that you think are necessary for a good President. (b) According to your list, which was the best President—Roosevelt, Taft, or Wilson? Support your answer with evidence.
2. Thomas Jefferson and Andrew Jackson both believed with Thoreau that "that government is best which governs least." Do you think this viewpoint became less practical by the 1900's? Explain your answer by referring to specific events.
3. (a) To what extent did the United States become more democratic during the Progressive era? (b) To what extent was it still undemocratic?
4. (a) Why was there a need for conservation of natural resources during the late 1800's and early 1900's? (b) What was done to make people aware of the problem? (c) Why might some people have opposed conservation?
5. How did industrialization affect (a) the make-up and location of America's population, (b) the daily lives of Americans, (c) differences among the regions of the nation?

Projects and Activities

1. Study the timeline here, which names some of the vast changes taking place in the United States during the early 1900's. (a) Which changes might especially affect the lives of women? (b) Which changes would have had an impact on the nation's health? (c) Which changes in these years would tend to make the nation seem smaller?
2. Interview an officer of a local bank to learn about the workings of the Federal Reserve System. Prepare a diagram or chart to illustrate how the system operates.
3. Read an article or book by a muckraker, such as Ida Tarbell's *History of the Standard Oil Company* or Lincoln Steffens *The Shame of the Cities:* (a) Write a paragraph summarizing the main point of the book or article. (b) What arguments does the author use to prove the main point? (c) Do you find the book or article persuasive? Why or why not?
4. Select an election discussed in Unit 3. Draw a map illustrating the results of the election. (You could use colors or other symbols to represent the states won by each candidate.)

Exploring Your Region

1. At your local library or newspaper office, locate copies of a local newspaper printed in 1900. Compare the prices of food and clothing in the advertisements with current prices. Then consult an almanac to find out the average family income in the United States in 1900 and the average family income today. Was it easier or more difficult to support a family in 1900?
2. Prepare a report on a national park located in your region. (a) Why was it founded? Under what circumstances? (b) How large is it? (c) What are its main features? If possible, include a map and pictures in your report.

Suggested Readings

1. *Up From Slavery,* Booker T. Washington. Autobiography of an ex-slave who became one of the foremost black leaders in America.
2. *The Age of Reform: From Bryan to F.D.R.,* Richard Hofstadter. A classic history of reform.
3. *How the Other Half Lives,* Jacob Riis. Written in 1890, this book is a famous exposé of slum conditions.
4. *The Jungle,* Upton Sinclair. The novel of conditions in the meat-packing industry that had a great impact on President Roosevelt.
5. *The Great American Novel,* Clyde B. Davis. A novel set in the Progressive era.

Unit Four

Becoming
a World Power
1898-1920

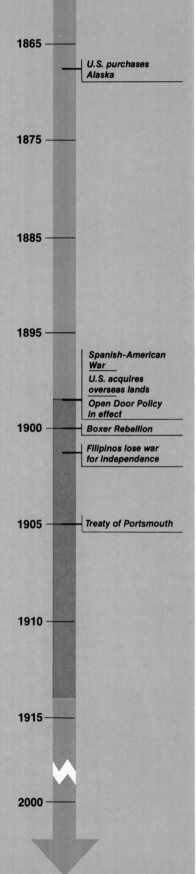

Chapter 10

American Expansion Overseas

1898–1914

From 1823 until the 1890's, Americans devoted most of their energy to the settlement and development of the continental United States. To be sure, Americans traveled to Europe and Europeans traveled to America. There was also vigorous trade between the two continents. However, it was the conquest of the West and, after 1865, the development of industry that occupied the American people.

By the 1890's, however, a revolution was taking place in American opinion. With the Middle West becoming a major industrial area, more Americans became interested in securing overseas markets where they could sell the surplus products of farms and factories. Some Americans even became interested in acquiring or controlling lands beyond the nation's continental boundaries.

In this chapter you will learn how Americans acquired a new interest in world affairs. You will learn, too, how they emerged from a brief war with Spain in 1898 in possession of the Philippine Islands and other islands in the Pacific Ocean. You will learn how this growing Pacific empire created new problems for the United States. You will also discover how it forced America's leaders to develop new policies for dealing with the nations of East Asia.

THE CHAPTER IN OUTLINE

1. American interest in expansion abroad increases.

2. The war with Spain turns the United States into a colonial power.

3. The United States takes over the Philippines, Hawaii, and Samoa.

4. The United States plays a larger role in East Asia.

1 American interest in expansion abroad increases

Great Britain, France, the Netherlands, Spain, Portugal—these were the old colonial powers. Back in the 1500's and 1600's, they had started their policies of **imperialism**—of establishing colonies and building empires for economic gain, prestige, and missionary purposes. Now, in the mid-1800's, these imperial powers owned and controlled a large portion of the world, but huge areas of it still remained unclaimed.

The new imperialism. During the latter half of the 1800's, there was a mad rush to gain ownership or control of the remaining uncolonized lands. Nations previously little interested in expansion joined the race—among them Belgium, Germany, Italy, Japan, and Russia. Within a few years, the rival colonial powers seized control over almost all of Africa and sliced off large portions of China and other areas in East Asia. By the early 1900's, most of the underdeveloped regions of the world had been divided among the rival colonial empires.

The Industrial Revolution was largely responsible for the mounting interest in colonies. Factories needed raw materials in ever-growing quantities. Manufacturers, to keep their factories operating, had to find new markets for their finished products. Improvements in transportation, especially in the steamship, enabled businesses to buy and sell in a truly worldwide market. As trade increased and profits accumulated, business executives and bankers looked overseas for opportunities to invest savings.

It is not surprising that Great Britain, the world's leading industrial power before 1900, built the largest empire. Right behind Great Britain were France, Belgium, the Netherlands, and Germany. Industrialization in each of these countries was in full swing by the late 1800's.

There were still other reasons for the growth of worldwide imperialism in the late 1800's and the early 1900's. One was the invention of new instruments of warfare, notably repeating rifles and machine guns. By 1900 these new weapons were becoming standard army equipment. With them small bands of professional soldiers could conquer and control people in underdeveloped regions who did not have similar weapons.

Another reason for the growth of imperialism was the attitude of people in the colonial powers. There were objectors in every country, but, in general, ordinary people were as eager for empire as were leaders of government and business. English factory workers, French shopkeepers, German farmers—these and other solid citizens of the colonial powers were all proud of their country's empire. With this support the governments of the colonial powers were able to spend the huge sums of money needed for armies to occupy the colonial territories and for navies to guard the sea lanes to and from the colonies.

A changing American attitude. Americans, with some exceptions, had never been interested in acquiring colonies. Indeed, Americans had cast off their own colonial status in the American Revolution. Thus American sympathies were with colonial peoples, not with the colonizing powers.

America's lack of interest in acquiring colonies is easy to understand. For 300 years the undeveloped American West was, in a sense, an American colony. Even as late as 1867, when Secretary of State Seward bought Alaska from Russia for just over $7 million, Americans referred to Alaska as "Seward's folly" and "Seward's icebox." It was not until 30 years later, in 1897, when gold was discovered in Alaska, that Americans began to realize what a great bargain they had made.

During the late 1800's, the United States became the world's leading exporter of agricultural products. By 1890, however, it was feeling the competition of such agricultural nations as Canada and Argentina. American growers and processors of grain, livestock, and cotton as well as the manufacturers of agricultural machinery were eager to sell their products abroad. It was not surprising, therefore, that America's agricultural interests in general supported government efforts to open up new markets overseas.

Although by 1890 the United States was rapidly becoming one of the world's leading industrial nations, there was a big difference between American and European businesses. European nations lacked sufficient raw materials and markets at home. They needed firm control of new sources of raw materials and new

During the Alaskan gold rush, every day hundreds of gold seekers landed in Alaska. The gold hunters lined up, with packs of supplies on their backs, to make the difficult climb through the pass leading to the gold fields.

markets. American businesses, operating in a young and only partly developed country, were not under the same pressure. The country as a whole, and especially the great American West, still offered large supplies of vital raw materials. There were almost limitless opportunities for the sale of manufactured goods and the investment of surplus money within the United States.

However, some American business leaders realized that this situation would not last forever. For this reason, by 1890 American business and agricultural interests were increasingly pleased to have the United States seek overseas for economic opportunities, if not for actual colonies.

American expansionists. Until 1898, at least, American interest in colonies was stimulated not so much by the leaders of big business as by preachers, scholars, politicians, and military leaders.

One advocate of American expansion was Josiah Strong, a Congregational minister and social reformer. His widely read book *Our Country*, written in 1885, argued that the American branch of the "Anglo-Saxon race"

was destined to extend its "civilizing" influence in Latin America, Asia, and Africa.

An even more influential book was written by Captain Alfred Mahan in 1890 under the title *The Influence of Sea Power upon History, 1660-1783.* Mahan's book attempted to show that the world's greatest nations had risen largely because of their sea power and that greatness depended upon sea power. Therefore, he argued, the United States had to strengthen its navy and also had to secure colonies overseas.

Mahan claimed that colonies were needed as naval bases and as refueling stations, or "coaling stations." He also pointed out that colonies would provide raw materials and markets. Colonies would thereby strengthen the industrial organization on which a modern sea power is forced to rely.

Strengthening the navy. Even before Mahan's book appeared, Congress had taken steps to strengthen the navy. These steps were needed. In 1880, for example, the United States had fewer than 100 "seagoing vessels." Many were "seagoing" in name only, with rusty boilers and rotted planking.

The situation began to change in 1882, however, when Congress authorized the construction of "two steam-cruising vessels of war." Three years later the Navy Department created the Naval War College at Newport, Rhode Island. About this time the Bethlehem Steel Corporation began to manufacture armor plate—tough steel sheets to protect the hulls and superstructures of warships. By 1895 the "White Squadron," sometimes called the "Great White Fleet," was under construction.

Ready for a new role. By 1895 some American business leaders were beginning to worry that their European competitors might gain control of the markets of underdeveloped areas. The nation's industrial system was rapidly becoming one of the most productive in the world. A new navy, small but modern and efficient, was ready for action. For these reasons and others, many Americans felt that the United States was destined to play a leading role in world affairs.

SECTION SURVEY

IDENTIFY: imperialism, Josiah Strong, Alfred Mahan.

1. How did the Industrial Revolution contribute to the mounting interest in acquiring colonies among the newly industrialized nations?
2. How did the transportation revolution encourage the search for colonies?
3. Why was the United States at first not interested in acquiring colonies?
4. Explain how each of the following affected American interest in colonies: (a) closing of the frontier, (b) industrial development, (c) growing power in world affairs.

2 The war with Spain turns the United States into a colonial power

The war with Spain, which lasted only a few weeks in the spring and summer of 1898, marked a turning point in American history. Before the war, the only lands the United States owned beyond its immediate boundaries were Alaska and the Midway Islands. The

United States had acquired the Midway Islands in the central Pacific in 1867. Within a few years after the war ended, however, the American flag flew over several islands in the Pacific. The United States was now deeply involved in East Asia, and American influence was strongly felt in the lands bordering the Caribbean Sea.

Trouble in Cuba. Cuba and Puerto Rico, both in the Caribbean, were the last remnants of Spain's once mighty empire in the New World. Spaniards had once called Cuba "the Ever Faithful Isle." In 1868, however, when a violent revolution broke out, the Cubans proved to be something less than faithful to their Spanish rulers. It took Spain ten years to crush this uprising. Spain did so only with a promise of long-awaited reforms, but discontent continued to smolder.

The trouble was that most Cubans worked at starvation wages for extremely wealthy landowners. To make matters worse, the Spanish government's policies, directed from Madrid, managed to anger the wealthier Cuban landowners as well as the landless workers.

Spanish misrule and an economic crisis finally plunged Cuba into another revolution. The United States was partly responsible for the economic crisis. In 1890, you recall, Congress adopted the McKinley Tariff Act. This act allowed Cuban sugar, the major crop of the island, to enter the United States free of duty. As a result, trade between the United States and Cuba prospered, reaching a total of more than $100 million a year. However, in 1894 the United States adopted the Wilson-Gorman Tariff Act. This act placed a 40-percent duty on all raw sugar imported into the United States. When the 1894 tariff went into effect, sugar piled up in Cuban warehouses, plantations closed, and thousands of Cubans lost their jobs.

Revolution in Cuba. Angered by the economic crisis and by Spain's failure to provide the long-promised reforms, the Cubans again revolted in 1895. Bands of revolutionists roamed through the countryside, killing, burning, and plundering.

The Spaniards, led by General Valeriano Weyler, nicknamed "The Butcher," responded savagely. General Weyler ordered all people living in territory controlled by the revolutionists into concentration camps run by the

Spaniards. Spanish soldiers then marched through the abandoned countryside, destroying buildings and putting to death all persons found in the area without permission. What the revolutionists had not destroyed during earlier raids, the Spaniards did. Large areas of Cuba were reduced to utter ruin. Starvation and disease plagued the land.

Growing American sympathy. Legally, the revolution in Cuba was no concern of the United States. Spain was a sovereign, independent nation, free to do as it pleased with its own colonies. This was freely admitted by the American government, which officially adopted a policy of neutrality.

However, the effects of the revolution were not confined to Cuba. The revolutionists themselves did everything possible to win American sympathy and support. They waged a vigorous propaganda campaign in America. José Martí, one of Hispanic America's greatest prose writers, aroused sympathy for Cuba by his persuasive articles. The revolutionists also bought quantities of American arms and ammunition, which they smuggled into Cuba.

The revolution also affected some American pocketbooks. Before the uprising began, Americans had invested more than $50 million in Cuban plantations, transportation projects, and businesses. These investments were in danger. Moreover, trade between Cuba and the United States was crippled by the revolution.

As months passed, more and more Americans expressed their sympathy for the revolutionists. They recalled their own struggle for freedom during the American Revolution.

American newspapers helped to inflame public opinion. Two New York papers— William Randolph Hearst's New York *Journal* and Joseph Pulitzer's New York *World*—were especially active in supporting the revolutionists. These publishers quickly discovered that sales skyrocketed when they printed sensational stories and pictures of the Spanish atrocities in Cuba.

Newspapers in other towns and cities quickly copied the financially successful methods of Hearst and Pulitzer. Before long, many Americans, feeding on the sensational stories and pictures, clamored for intervention. By 1898 even the more conservative newspapers, including weekly religious journals, insisted that the United States had the moral responsibility of restoring order in Cuba.

McKinley's attempts to avoid war. When President William McKinley was inaugurated on March 4, 1897, he strongly opposed war. The United States was just emerging from the depression that had started in 1893. The President, many of his advisers, and business leaders in general feared that war, or even the threat of war, would throw the country back into a depression. For nearly a year, the President held to an official policy of neutrality, but early in 1898 several events forced his hand.

On February 9, 1898, American newspapers headlined a letter written by the Spanish minister to the United States. In the letter, Dupuy De Lôme (LOH·may) described President McKinley as "weak and a bidder for the admiration of the crowd" and as a "would-be politician." The Spanish minister had written the letter to a friend in Havana. It was not meant for publication. Indeed, it had been stolen from the mails and sold to the press, but the harm was done. Unthinking Americans concluded that the uncomplimentary remark reflected the attitude of all Spaniards.

On February 16, Americans read even more startling news in their papers. The night before, the United States battleship *Maine,* which had been sent to Cuba in January to protect American lives and property, had sunk in Havana harbor with the loss of more than 250 American lives. Its captain stated that there had been an explosion of unknown origin and urged that "public opinion should be suspended until further report." In Havana flags flew at half-mast, theaters and places of business were closed, and expressions of sympathy were sent to Washington. All of this was brushed aside by the public. People jumped to the conclusion that the Spaniards had destroyed the ship. "Remember the *Maine!*" quickly became a national slogan.

Despite these incidents, President McKinley refused to declare war. Assistant Secretary of the Navy Theodore Roosevelt declared that the President "has no more backbone than a chocolate éclair." However, McKinley still hoped for a peaceable solution.

Spanish concessions. Late in March, with the President's approval, the Department of State sent an **ultimatum°** to Spain. In the ul-

°**ultimatum:** in diplomatic language, a final statement of terms whose rejection may lead to the breaking off of diplomatic relations or to war.

timatum the United States demanded that Spain (1) immediately cease all fighting and grant an armistice to the revolutionists, (2) negotiate with the Cubans for self-government or independence, and (3) abolish the concentration camps.

On April 9 the Spanish government accepted the ultimatum. The Spaniards hedged on the issue of independence, but the American minister in Madrid felt that with patience independence for Cuba could be achieved. In cabling the good news to President McKinley, he added, "I hope that nothing will now be done to humiliate Spain."

War declared. Despite the Spanish concession, on April 11, 1898, President McKinley asked Congress to intervene in Cuba. It seemed that the war spirit had proved too strong for the President to resist.

On April 19 Congress by large majorities voted to use the land and naval forces of the United States to secure full independence for Cuba. Congress also adopted the Teller Resolution. This resolution stated that the United States claimed no "sovereignty, jurisdiction, or control" over Cuba. The United States wanted only to **pacify,** or bring peace to, the beseiged Caribbean island. The resolution promised that once Cuba was free the United States would "leave the government and control of the island to its people."

Victory in the Pacific. Curiously enough, American fighting in the "war for Cuban liberty" started not in Cuba but in the Pacific. For weeks before Congress declared war, Theodore Roosevelt, the Assistant Secretary of the Navy, had been preparing for any developments. Roosevelt had sent orders to Commodore George Dewey, in command of a fleet anchored at Hong Kong, to prepare for action. When Dewey learned that war had been declared, he promptly headed for the Philippine Islands, the center of Spanish power in the Pacific.

On the night of April 30, 1898, Dewey's six ships slipped past the fortress of Corregidor and into the harbor of Manila, capital of the Philippines (see map, this page). At daybreak on May 1, the American warships opened fire. Their guns outranged those of the Spanish vessels, and by noon the one-sided battle was over. The Spaniards lost nearly 170 men and all their vessels. The Americans lost one man — who died of heatstroke.

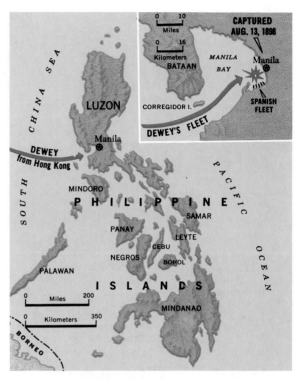

SPANISH-AMERICAN WAR: 1
(Philippine Islands)

Although Commodore Dewey controlled Manila harbor, he did not have a large enough force to land and seize the city. While he waited for a landing force to arrive from the United States, he sent arms and ammunition to a band of Filipinos led by Emilio Aguinaldo (ah·gwee·NAHL·doh). The Filipinos, eager to throw off Spanish rule and win their independence, prepared to attack Manila.

Two months passed. Then, early in August, American transports arrived with a strong landing party. The Spanish position was hopeless. Cut off by Dewey's warships, surrounded by Filipino revolutionists, and faced with an attack by an American army, Manila surrendered on August 13, 1898.

Victory in the Caribbean. Meanwhile, on April 29, Spain's Atlantic fleet under Admiral Cervera (sair·VAIR·ah) had sailed westward from the Cape Verde Islands for Cuba. The Spaniards slipped into the harbor at Santiago, Cuba, for refueling. Here they were bottled up by an American squadron commanded by Admiral William T. Sampson and Commodore W. S. Schley.

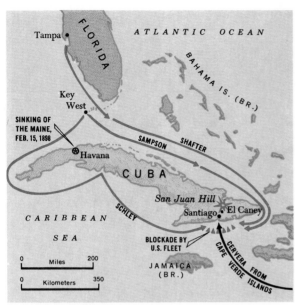

SPANISH-AMERICAN WAR: 2
(Cuba)

sonal direction of Clara Barton, provided such aid as it could.

On June 24 the two armies clashed. Slowly, fighting hard, the Americans under General William Shafter pushed the Spaniards back through the fortified village of El Caney and across San Juan Hill (see map, this page). By July 2, American forces had advanced to within a short distance of Santiago. It was this fact that led Admiral Cervera to make his desperate attempt to escape with the Spanish fleet. The destruction of the Spanish navy was the final blow. The Spanish commander at Santiago surrendered his forces on July 17, just 15 days after Cervera's defeat.

Black soldiers, who had not been allowed to mix with white troops on the ships carrying them to Cuba, fought well in several engagements. Frank Knox, later to be Secretary of the Navy, wrote home that he had never seen "braver men anywhere." He added, "Some of those who rushed up the hill will live in my memory forever."

Many Cuban patriots also fought and gave their lives for the freedom of their country. Among them was Cuba's great leader, José Martí, who was one of the first to die in the Battle of Dos Rios.

Meanwhile another American army, under General Nelson A. Miles, landed on the Spanish island of Puerto Rico, east of Cuba. The Americans encountered almost no opposition and by the end of July were in control of the island.

The rewards of victory. The United States entered the war claiming that it was fighting merely to free the oppressed Cubans. It ended the war with an empire on its hands.

American and Spanish commissioners met in Paris in October 1898 to negotiate a peace treaty. By the terms of the treaty, Spain surrendered all claim to Cuba. In addition, Spain ceded to the United States the following territories: Puerto Rico; the Pacific island of Guam; and the Philippines—in exchange for which the United States agreed to pay Spain $20 million. The United States also acquired Wake Island in the Pacific. American armed forces had landed on Wake on July 4, 1898. Congress later annexed Wake.

The Cuban and Puerto Rican people did not share fully in the fruits of victory. As you will read, their hopes and expectations of freedom and independence were only partly realized.

On Sunday morning, July 3, 1898, Cervera's fleet made a dash for the open sea, but the American ships were waiting. As the Spanish fleet raced out of the harbor and steamed along the coast, it was met by murderous fire (see map, this page). Within four hours the battle was over. Not a single Spanish vessel managed to escape.

Fighting in Cuba. In contrast to the United States Navy, which moved swiftly and efficiently, the War Department was quite unprepared. When the war began, the regular army numbered fewer than 30,000 officers and troops, including four regiments of black soldiers. It was scattered in small contingents all across the country.

More than 200,000 Americans immediately volunteered for war service, including four more units of black soldiers. The volunteers also included Theodore Roosevelt. Roosevelt resigned as Assistant Secretary of the Navy to lead a volunteer regiment of cavalry known as the "Rough Riders."

The first American troops to arrive in Cuba were improperly trained and equipped. The food was poor, and the army was without adequate hospital and sanitary facilities. Hundreds of American soldiers died needlessly from dysentery, typhoid, malaria, and yellow fever. The American Red Cross, under the per-

On July 2, 1898, the American Rough Riders, Roosevelt's volunteer regiment, captured this fort in Cuba, only to be trapped there later. This lithograph shows their rescue by black troops of the 24th and 25th United States Infantry Regiments.

Until 1898, except for the Midway Islands, the United States owned no overseas possessions. When the Senate ratified the peace treaty, however, the United States became a colonial power.

The expansionists—followers of Alfred Mahan, Theodore Roosevelt, and others—were delighted. Many other Americans were deeply troubled. Was it wise and proper, they asked, for the United States to join the European powers in the race for empire?

SECTION SURVEY

IDENTIFY: José Martí, William Randolph Hearst, Joseph Pulitzer, ultimatum, Teller Resolution, Commodore Dewey, Emilio Aguinaldo, Admiral Cervera, "Rough Riders."

1. (a) What were the causes of the Cuban revolt against Spain? (b) Why did this revolt affect the United States?
2. How did each of the following help bring about the war with Spain: (a) sensational press coverage, (b) the De Lôme letter, (c) destruction of the *Maine,* (d) American investments and trade with Cuba?
3. Where did the war over Cuban independence actually begin? Why?
4. The war with Spain marked a turning point in American history. Explain.

5. Map Study: Study the map on page 193. (a) What does the red arrow indicate? (b) What bodies of water are shown on the map? (c) On the large map, locate the area illustrated by the inset map. (d) When did Dewey capture Manila? Did he have any opposition? How can you tell from the map?

3 The United States takes over the Philippines, Hawaii, and Samoa

The Philippine Islands presented Americans with a difficult problem: Should the United States set the islands free, just as it intended to set Cuba free? Or should it force the Filipinos to accept American rule?

American dilemma. President McKinley wrestled with this problem. Finally he decided to establish American rule in the Philippine Islands. As he later explained, the United States could not return the Philippines to Spain, for "that would be cowardly and dishonorable." It could not give them to France, Germany, or Great Britain, for "that would be bad business and discreditable." It could not turn them over to the Filipinos, for they were "unfit for self-government." McKinley concluded, "There is nothing left for us to do but to take them all, and to educate the Filipinos, and uplift and civilize and Christianize them."

President McKinley's motives were better than his knowledge of the facts. His reference to "Christianizing" the Filipinos ignored the fact that many had long since been converted to Catholicism. A major exception was the Moros, a group of people who were Muslims.

Divided public opinion. Many Americans agreed with McKinley that it was America's duty to "educate" and "uplift and civilize and Christianize" the Filipinos. Others hoped to profit economically by following the path of world empire. Still others believed that America needed the islands as naval and military bases.

Opponents of imperialism viewed the decision with serious misgivings. They argued that in taking the Philippines the United States was violating its own Declaration of Independence and the principle that people had the right to live under a government of their own choice. "It will be only the old tale of a free people seduced by false ambitions and running headlong after riches and luxuries and military glory," warned Carl Schurz, a prominent Republican. A few opponents, including some blacks, argued that imperialism was based in part on the false assumption of white racial superiority. They argued that American expansion abroad could only work to the disadvantage of blacks seeking to improve their lives in the United States.

Conquest and early rule. The conquest of the Philippines turned out to be more difficult than the defeat of Spain. The Filipinos, led by Emilio Aguinaldo, fought as fiercely against American rule as they had against Spanish rule. For three years 70,000 American troops fought in the islands at a cost of $175 million and with a casualty list as high as that of the war with Spain. By 1902, however, the American forces were finally victorious.

Despite this unhappy beginning, the United States tried to live up to McKinley's promise "not to exploit, but to develop; to civilize, to educate, to train in the science of self-government." In the Philippine Government Act of 1902, Congress set up a government for the islands. The act provided for an appointed governor, a small elected assembly, and an appointed upper house. The United States Congress could veto all legislation. The plan did not go into effect until 1907. Meanwhile, William Howard Taft, the first governor, ruled wisely. He cooperated closely with the Filipinos and included many Filipinos in the new government.

Many Americans did not take the Filipino fight for independence seriously. What was the cartoonist's view? How are the Filipinos represented here? The United States? What is Uncle Sam holding? What does he intend to do?

Filipino dissatisfaction. Many Filipinos wanted full self-government—nothing less. Their dissatisfaction became apparent in 1907 when the elected lower house met for the first time. Three quarters of the representatives were pledged to work for independence. Their hopes rose in 1913 when Woodrow Wilson became President of the United States. Leading Democrats had opposed the conquest of the Philippines, and the Democratic Party had pledged itself to grant independence at the earliest possible date.

These hopes, however, were soon dashed. The Jones Act of 1916 did give the Filipinos the right to elect the members of both houses of the legislature. However, Congress did not grant independence but merely promised it "as soon as a stable government can be established."

Meanwhile conditions in the islands improved. Highways, railroads, and telegraph and telephone lines were built. Education reduced illiteracy from 85 percent in 1898 to 37 percent in 1921. Disease was greatly reduced and Filipino health steadily improved. Exports and imports swelled in volume as American tariffs on products from the Philippines were reduced and finally removed. Most important of all, the United States eventually kept its promise to set the islands free.

Early relations with Hawaii. Before 1865 about the only relations that the United States had with the Hawaiian Islands were through traders and missionaries. After 1865, American businesses began to develop the resources of Hawaii—chiefly sugar cane and pineapples. In 1875 Hawaii signed a treaty with the United States. In return for the right to sell sugar in the United States without payment of any duty, the Hawaiians promised not to sell or lease territory to any foreign power. In 1887, when this treaty was renewed, the United States leased Pearl Harbor as a naval base.

Native Hawaiians became increasingly alarmed as the wealth and power of the islands passed into foreign hands. Finally, led by Queen Liliuokalani (leh·LEE·woh·kah·LAH·nee), they announced their intentions to end foreign influence.

Revolution and annexation. The American businesses in Hawaii, aided by influential Hawaiians, met this challenge by starting a revolution on January 16, 1893. The American minister to Hawaii quickly intervened. Claim-

Queen Liliuokalani, the last monarch of Hawaii, wanted to reduce the influence of American business groups and missionaries over the affairs of the native Hawaiians but she lost her throne in attempting to do so.

ing that he was acting only to protect American lives and property, he requested the aid of marines conveniently at hand on a nearby warship. The Hawaiian soldiers, concluding that the marines had come to help the revolutionists, refused to fight. The new government, controlled by the foreign business interests and the missionaries, asked to be annexed to the United States. The American minister promptly raised the Stars and Stripes, and on February 1, 1893, marines began to patrol the islands.

When news of these events reached the United States, furious protests poured into Congress. Many Americans did not want island territory. They were indignant at the manner in which American marines had been used in Hawaii. They were also afraid that overseas expansion would lead to heavy military expenditures.

President Cleveland sent a commission to Hawaii to investigate. The commission ordered the American flag hauled down and heard evidence from both sides. The commission found that the revolution had been started largely by

American business groups, aided by the American minister and the marines, and that the Hawaiians had no desire to be annexed.

After studying the report, Cleveland concluded that Queen Liliuokalani should be returned to her throne. To do this would require the exercise of American force against the new government. By now Congress was fed up with the whole affair, and in 1894 it adopted a resolution refusing to interfere further in Hawaii.

Then came the war with Spain, which generated a new spirit in America. The question of Hawaii once again was brought up on the floor of Congress. This time, in 1898, by an overwhelming vote the islands were annexed to the United States and given territorial status.

American control of Samoa. As in Hawaii, American interests in the Samoan Islands were of long standing. In 1878 the United States secured from a Samoan chief the right to use the harbor of Pago Pago (PAHN·goh PAHN·goh) on the island of Tutuila (too·too·EE·lah) as a naval base. The Samoans granted similar privileges to Germany and Great Britain.

The three countries—Great Britain, Germany, and the United States—then scrambled to control the islands. At one point, in 1889, a naval clash among the three powers was narrowly avoided, largely because a typhoon blew the rival squadrons out to sea.

Finally, in 1899, the British withdrew and the islands were divided between Germany and the United States. Germany later lost control of its share of the islands when it was defeated in World War I. Tutuila, with its excellent harbor of Pago Pago, remained in the hands of the United States and became a major naval base in the Pacific.

SECTION SURVEY

IDENTIFY: William Howard Taft, Jones Act, Queen Liliuokalani.

1. Do you agree with the anti-imperialists who argued that the United States violated the Declaration of Independence when it took the Philippines? Why or why not?

2. How did the United States acquire Hawaii?

3. The scramble for the Samoan Islands demonstrated the rivalry among nations to acquire colonies. Explain.

4 The United States plays a larger role in East Asia

In 1900 United States territory in the Pacific included Hawaii, Midway, Guam, Wake, the Philippine Islands, and part of Samoa. With this new territory the American people assumed heavy responsibilities. These new responsibilities, plus events taking place in East Asia, led to a change in the United States' relations with China.

Early relations with China. America's interest in China began in the 1780's with profitable trade between the two countries. By the early 1800's, the China trade had become a flourishing business. Ships from Philadelphia, New York, and New England ports made the long, hazardous voyage around South America and up the West Coast to the Pacific Northwest. There they traded with the Indians, exchanging blankets, axes, guns, and other goods for furs. When they had a full cargo of furs, they sailed for China. There they traded the furs for tea, silk, porcelain, jade, and other valuable goods. Many merchants and shipowners in the United States as well as in Great Britain and other European countries made fortunes from the China trade.

As time passed, China's rulers grew disturbed at the influence of foreigners on their country. When China placed restrictions on British traders, however, Great Britain waged a successful war (1839–42) and forced the Chinese to open certain "treaty ports" to British trade.

Americans demanded and secured similar trading privileges. The American envoy to China, Caleb Cushing, negotiated a treaty that gave the United States all the trading privileges granted by China to other nations. In addition the treaty gave Americans the right of **extraterritoriality.** This meant that Americans in China who were charged with violations of Chinese laws had the right to be tried in American courts in China. Other foreign nations also secured similar privileges.

Crisis in China. These concessions from China encouraged foreign traders to settle there. As time passed, outsiders, including missionaries from the United States and other countries, exercised growing influence. Many

American troops move through rubble at the gate to the city of Tientsin after joining with other foreign troops to successfully put down the Boxer Rebellion and free the 300 hostages who had been trapped inside the foreign compound there.

of China's leaders strongly opposed this interference but were powerless to prevent it.

Among all the imperialistic powers interested in East Asia, the United States seemed least eager to grab Chinese territory. As a result, relations between the two countries remained friendly throughout the 1800's.

In the 1890's, however, a major crisis developed. Japan entered the race for colonies with an attack upon China in the Sino-Japanese War of 1894–95. In this war Japan won the large island of Formosa, territory on the Shantung Peninsula, and control of Korea (see map, page 344).

While China was helpless as a result of the Japanese attack, Germany, Russia, Great Britain, and France rushed in to seize their share of the booty. It appeared for the time that China would soon share the fate of Africa, which the European powers had already carved up and divided.

The Open Door Policy. The crisis in China posed a problem for the United States. Americans did not want Chinese territory. On the other hand, Americans did not intend to be squeezed out of the growing trade in Chinese markets by the other nations.

John Hay, who became Secretary of State in 1898, had a solution for the problem. He sent a note to all the powers concerned seeking two assurances. Hay asked (1) that they would keep open all "treaty ports" and (2) that they

would guarantee to all nations engaged in trade with China equal railroad, harbor, and tariff rates. In short, Hay asked for an Open Door Policy. Such a policy would insure American businesses the opportunity to compete on equal terms with other traders in China. Although the response to his note was not encouraging, Hay announced on March 20, 1900, that the Open Door Policy was in effect.

The Boxer Rebellion. Understandably, the Chinese resented the efforts by Japan, Russia, and western powers to control their country. On the rising tide of resentment, the Chinese launched a movement to drive all "foreign devils" from their country. The movement was led by a Chinese secret society that westerners called "the Boxers."°

In the spring of 1900, the Boxers suddenly attacked. They killed about 300 foreigners in north China. Then they surrounded the foreign area in Tientsin (TIN·TSIN) and the foreign legations in Peking, where men and women from many nations gathered for protection.

The foreign powers promptly rushed troops to relieve the besieged people. The force included 2,500 American troops from the Philippines as well as military units from Japan and several European nations. By August 14 the

°**the Boxers:** the Chinese name for this society literally meant "righteous harmonious band." Westerners wrongly translated the Chinese name to "righteous harmonious *fists*" and hence called the society "the Boxers."

199

A MEETING OF EAST AND WEST

"It is finally finished. The great agony is over! . . . The egg has hatched its chicken." What the American officer meant, he continued, was that "the Treaty between Japan and the United States was signed today." It was March 31, 1854, but the negotiations had begun several months earlier.

Commodore Matthew Perry had first anchored his small fleet in Yedo (Tokyo) Bay the previous July. The Japanese had never seen steamships before. One onlooker wrote admiringly of what he called a "fire wheel ship that runs as quick as a dragon in swimming." Perry delivered his proposals to government officials and promised to return the following year.

In February 1854, when the Americans steamed back, negotiations were stepped up, with formal processions, booming guns, and exchanges of gifts. For the emperor the Americans had brought a telescope, cases of firearms, clocks, and a barrel of whiskey. The Japanese presented their guests with fine silks, brocades, and lacquerware. There was entertainment, too: a minstrel show for the Japanese, a wrestling exhibition for the Americans. What made the biggest impression was a quarter-size steam locomotive—made to order in Philadelphia—with a tender and coach, set up to run on a 350-foot (160-meter) track. Japanese officials lined up eagerly for the privilege of riding atop the train as it scooted around in a circle.

However, it was not the gifts or the entertainment that "hatched" the treaty. Nor was it the magnificent banquet on board Perry's flagship, where one Japanese guest got so carried away that he threw his arms around the dignified commodore. It was Perry's ships and their bristling cannon. "We are without a navy and our coasts are undefended," said an official Japanese decree. Japan could do little but agree to increased trade—and plan to build its own "fire wheel ships."

force had relieved the foreigners in Tientsin and Peking, but not before 65 of the besieged had been killed.

The Boxer Rebellion provided an excellent excuse to seize additional Chinese territory, but John Hay took a firm stand in opposition. On July 3, even while the expeditionary force was fighting its way inland to Peking, he announced that the United States wanted to "preserve Chinese territorial and administrative entity . . . and safeguard for the world the principle of equal and impartial trade with all parts of the Chinese Empire."

Largely because of American influence, China did not lose any territory as a result of the Boxer Rebellion. China did, however, have to pay the foreign powers $333 million as compensation for loss, damage, and injury. The American share amounted to about $24 million. Half of this sum the United States government turned over to American citizens to compensate them for losses of personal property in China. The American government returned the rest of the money to China.

Grateful for this American action, the Chinese government used the money to send Chinese students to the United States. This fund enabled thousands of China's ablest youth to study in American colleges and universities. These students helped to build closer understanding between the two countries.

The Open Door Policy in China had other far-reaching results. It immediately involved the United States in the affairs of Russia and Japan, both of whom were expanding their influence in East Asia.

The opening of Japan. Before 1853 the Japanese had lived in almost complete isolation from the rest of the world. Japan's rulers forbade foreigners to enter Japan. Only the Dutch had won the right to carry on a limited amount of trade through one small Japanese port. In 1853, however, Japan's isolation was shattered when Commodore Matthew C. Perry arrived in Japanese waters with a squadron of American naval vessels. Perry demanded an audience with the Japanese rulers.

The presents that the Americans and Japanese exchanged during a conference in 1854 symbolized the difference between the two countries. The United States received gifts of silk, brocades, lacquerware, and other fine handmade articles. The Japanese received tokens of the new industrial world—a telegraph set, guns, and model railroad trains.

As a result of this conference and a later one, the United States and Japan signed the Treaty of Kanagawa. With this treaty both countries expressed a desire for peace, friendship, and developing trade. Japan also agreed to open two ports to United States trading vessels. Later, Japan opened other ports.

Japan's search for empire. Few events in modern history have had such far-reaching effects as the opening of Japanese ports. Two major developments followed at once. First, American and other traders started a lively commerce with Japan that grew to large proportions in the 1900's. Second, Japanese leaders were convinced that they should adopt the industrial techniques of the western nations.

By the late 1800's, Japan was a transformed country. However, the "new" Japan faced new problems. Knowledge of science, medicine, and sanitation had reduced the death rate, and the lower death rate meant a larger population. This created difficulties, for Japan was small, without enough farmland to feed its people adequately. The Japanese also needed raw materials for their new factories and markets for their products.

Faced with these problems, Japan started upon a program of imperialism similar to that being followed by other industrial nations. Japan needed colonies to secure food for its surplus population and to provide raw materials and markets for its growing industries. Thus Japan entered the race for empire and became one of the contestants in the struggle for control of East Asia.

As you have seen, Japan started its career as an imperial power with an attack upon China in the Sino-Japanese War of 1894–95. Ten years later Japan plunged into another war, this time with Russia.

The United States in the Pacific. Although the Russo-Japanese War of 1904–05 took place nearly half a world away from the United States, Americans were immediately concerned. Their new commitments in the Pacific had given Americans a direct interest in the affairs of East Asia. The war between Russia and Japan, fought on Chinese soil and in Pacific waters, threatened to interfere with American trading and missionary interests in China. It also threatened to weaken, if not destroy, the Open Door Policy.

Acting on his own authority, President Theodore Roosevelt warned Germany and France that if they aided Russia the United States would side with Japan. With Roosevelt acting as mediator, representatives from Russia and Japan met at Portsmouth, New Hampshire, during the summer of 1905. There they worked out terms for settling the conflict. In 1906 Roosevelt received the Nobel Peace Prize for his efforts.

The Treaty of Portsmouth transferred Russia's interest in Korea and Manchuria to Japan. It also gave Japan the southern half of Sakhalin Island (see map, page 344).

Roosevelt was delighted with the results of his efforts to end the Russo-Japanese War. The Treaty of Portsmouth left the Open Door Policy intact. It maintained for a time the balance of power in East Asia. None of the colonial powers, including Japan and Russia, had a dominant position in China. The doors of China remained open to American business and trade.

SECTION SURVEY

IDENTIFY: extraterritoriality, John Hay, Commodore Perry, Treaty of Portsmouth.

1. (a) Describe the circumstances that led to the Open Door Policy. (b) What were the provisions of this policy?

2. (a) What was the Boxer Rebellion? (b) How did it end? (c) What were its effects on United States–China relations?

3. (a) Why did Japan become imperialistic? (b) Why were Americans concerned about growing Japanese imperialism?

Chapter Survey

Summary: Tracing the Main Ideas

During the latter half of the 1800's, the major colonial powers of Europe engaged in a lively race for empire. The United States, however, was not especially interested in entering the race. To be sure, in 1867–68 Secretary of State Seward persuaded Congress to annex the Midway Islands and to purchase Alaska, but Congress did so reluctantly. Americans on the whole were indifferent.

Toward the end of the 1800's, American sentiment began to change. It was the Spanish-American War that finally started the United States down the road of colonialism.

The war with Spain in 1898 began in protest against Spanish policy in Cuba. It ended with a treaty in which Spain agreed to give up its claim to Cuba and in which the United States gained the Philippine Islands as well as Guam and Puerto Rico. In addition to the Philippines and Guam, the United States acquired other territories in the Pacific area. Hawaii was annexed in 1898 and a portion of Samoa was acquired in 1899. To protect its growing interests in the Pacific, the United States insisted upon an equal opportunity to share in the business and trade of East Asia. This Open Door Policy involved Americans in the troubled affairs of East Asia and committed the United States to a role of power politics in the Pacific.

America's interest in colonies was not confined to the Pacific area. As you will read in the next chapter, the Caribbean offered even larger and more inviting opportunities for the development of American interests.

Inquiring into History

1. Why did the foreign policy of the United States change from one of isolationism to one of expansionism?
2. What arguments did the expansionists use to defend their position?
3. Was there a contradiction in the United States' favoring the Open Door Policy for China and the policy of the Monroe Doctrine for the Western Hemisphere? Explain.
4. Some anti-imperialists argued that American imperialist policy worked to the disadvantage of black Americans at home. (a) How might this have been true? (b) Do you agree or disagree with their argument? Why? (c) What was the position of black Americans at home in the 1890's? (See pages 52–5.)
5. Why do you suppose the industrial nations were able to dominate the nonindustrialized areas of the world?
6. Recall American attitudes toward mercantilism before the American Revolution. What was our attitude toward our "mother country," Great Britain? Do you think you can generalize and say that most colonies feel this way about their mother country? Explain.

7. The consequences of moving into East Asia were to have a lasting effect on the nation's foreign affairs and domestic conditions. Explain.

Relating Past to Present

1. Is the United States involved overseas today for the same reasons it was involved during the period covered in this chapter? Explain.
2. Compare the role of the press today with that of the sensational press of the late 1890's.

Developing Social Science Skills

1. Examine the picture on page 199. (a) What details has the artist emphasized? (b) Do you think that the Japanese artist has painted American troops as they actually appeared? (c) What do you think influenced the artist to paint the picture in this particular way?
2. Study the world map on pages 712–13. (a) Indicate the territory held by the United States in 1900. (b) Locate the trade route often used by traders in the mid-1800's to get from the eastern United States to China. (c) What does the map suggest about the problems for the United States of governing territories such as the Philippines?

Chapter 11

American Expansion in the Caribbean

1898–1914

On December 10, 1898, the Spaniards signed the Treaty of Paris that formally brought the Spanish-American War to an end. For both the United States and Spain, the end of the war was a turning point.

By the terms of the treaty, Spain agreed (1) to leave Cuba, (2) to cede Puerto Rico and Guam to the United States, and (3) to cede the Philippine Islands to the United States in exchange for a payment of $20,000,000

The signing of the Treaty of Paris was a sad day for the Spanish nation. The Spaniards had reason for their sorrow. The war that they had fought and lost struck the final blow to the once mighty Spanish empire.

It was also a disappointing day for the Cubans who had hoped that peace would bring the freedom for which they had struggled and for those Puerto Ricans who had also hoped for freedom and independence.

For the American people, however, the war marked a crucial step forward on the path of empire and world power. After 1898, as you know, the United States rapidly became a major power in the Pacific and in East Asia. Between 1898 and 1914, as you will read in this chapter, it also gained power in the Caribbean and the rest of Latin America. This course of events turned the Caribbean Sea into what was sometimes called "an American lake."

THE CHAPTER IN OUTLINE

1. Americans begin to build an empire in the Caribbean.

2. The United States modifies and strengthens the Monroe Doctrine.

3. Conflict breaks out between the United States and Mexico.

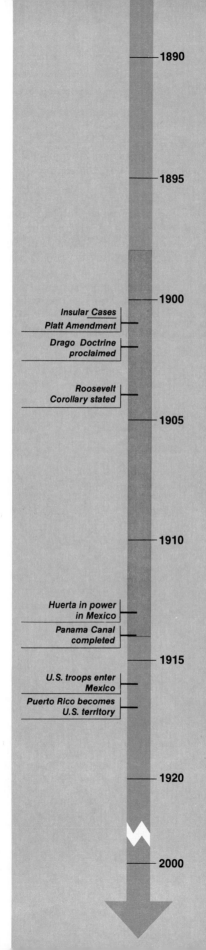

1890

1895

1900

Insular Cases
Platt Amendment
Drago Doctrine proclaimed

Roosevelt Corollary stated

1905

1910

Huerta in power in Mexico
Panama Canal completed

1915

U.S. troops enter Mexico
Puerto Rico becomes U.S. territory

1920

2000

1 Americans begin to build an empire in the Caribbean

Less than 20 years after the 1898 war with Spain, the American flag was flying not only over Puerto Rico but also over the Panama Canal Zone and the Virgin Islands. American advisers were helping to govern small countries in and around the Caribbean. In short, the United States had developed a revised foreign policy for the Western Hemisphere.

The new overseas possessions caused the American government to face several important questions: How would the United States respond to the desires of Cubans and Puerto Ricans for total independence? Were the people who lived in the newly acquired territories entitled to all the rights guaranteed by the Constitution to citizens of the United States? As the question was often stated, "Does the Constitution follow the flag?"

The Insular Cases. In the Insular Cases of 1901, the Supreme Court settled the issue of constitutional rights. It ruled that there were two kinds of possessions—incorporated and unincorporated. The incorporated possessions—Hawaii and Alaska—were destined for statehood. The citizens of these possessions were therefore entitled to all the constitutional rights guaranteed to United States citizens. The unincorporated possessions—Puerto Rico, the Philippines, Samoa, and others—were not destined for statehood. The people of these

In this 1904 cartoon President Theodore Roosevelt is depicted as a police officer. Do you think this view is a flattering or a critical one? Why?

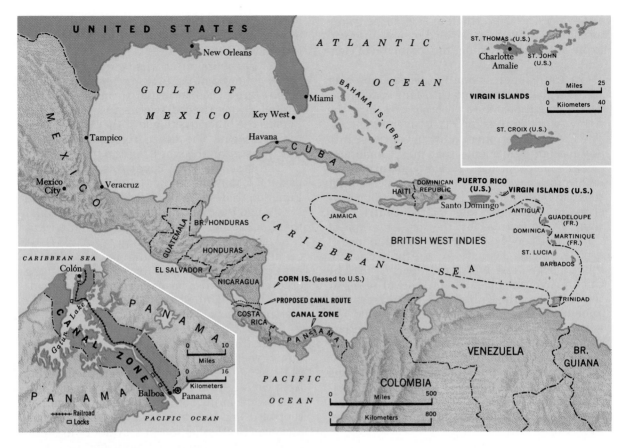

UNITED STATES EXPANSION IN THE CARIBBEAN, 1898–1917

areas were *not,* therefore, entitled to all constitutional guarantees. The people of the unincorporated possessions could not, however, be deprived of the fundamental rights of life, liberty, or property without the due process of law.

The Insular Cases and several similar Supreme Court decisions between 1901 and 1922 helped to develop an American colonial policy. However, it was Congress that passed the laws ruling America's growing colonial empire.

A government for Puerto Rico. In 1900, Congress passed the Foraker Act, which provided a new government for Puerto Rico. It would consist of a governor and an executive council appointed by the President of the United States and a lower house elected by the Puerto Ricans.

Discontented Puerto Ricans demanded a larger voice in their own government. In 1917, shortly after the Filipinos won a similar victory in the Jones Act of 1916, the United States adopted a second Jones Act. This act made Puerto Rico a United States territory and made the Puerto Ricans American citizens. In addition Puerto Ricans were also granted the right to elect members of both houses of their legislature.

In 1950 Congress gave Puerto Ricans the power to write their own constitution. In 1952, after the constitution had been ratified by popular vote, Puerto Rico became a self-governing commonwealth. It makes its own laws and controls its own finances. The United States, however, provides for the island's defense and includes Puerto Rico within its tariff system. It places no restrictions on immigration from Puerto Rico to the United States.

Strings on Cuban independence. Although Cuba was never considered an American colony, American influence over Cuban affairs remained strong after the war. The Teller Resolution, which Congress adopted in 1898, had pledged that the Cubans would be given their independence. Nevertheless, for three years after the war, Cuba was ruled by an American army of occupation under the command of General Leonard Wood.

In 1901 Congress finally turned Cuba over to the Cuban people, but with four conditions. These conditions were incorporated into the Army Act of 1901 as the Platt Amendment. (1) The Cuban government must never enter into any foreign agreements that might endanger Cuban independence. (2) The Cuban government must never incur debts that it could not repay in a reasonable time. (3) The Cuban government must give the United States "the right to intervene for the preservation of Cuban independence [and] the maintenance of a government adequate for the protection of life, property, and individual liberty." (4) The Cuban government must place naval bases at the disposal of the United States. Congress also announced that the United States would not withdraw its military forces until the Platt Amendment had been written into the new Cuban constitution.

This was not the "independence" Cubans had expected, yet they had to agree to American demands. Therefore, they accepted the Platt Amendment, and in 1902 the American forces were withdrawn.

An American protectorate. Actually, Cuba became a **protectorate** of the United States. That is, the United States, a strong nation, tried to supervise Cuba, a weaker nation, by keeping partial control over Cuban affairs. Cubans, who had fought for independence, resented this relationship.

Between 1906 and 1920, American troops landed in Cuba three times to maintain order and to protect American business and property. Moreover, American diplomatic pressure frequently forced the Cubans to accept policies favored by the United States. In 1934, as you will see, Congress abolished the Platt Amendment, thus ending America's role as "protector" of Cuba.

Growing interest in a canal. In 1898, when the Spanish-American War began, the U.S. battleship *Oregon* was in California waters. It immediately started to sail around South America in an effort to join the Atlantic fleet. Public imagination was stirred, and for six weeks daily reports of the ship's progress appeared in every newspaper. The *Oregon's*

lengthy voyage convinced many Americans that a canal between the Atlantic and the Pacific was needed.

In the years after the war, the United States followed along a path of empire. As the empire grew, people began to insist that the United States needed two navies—one in the Pacific, the other to safeguard the Atlantic and the Caribbean. The alternative to a two-ocean navy was a canal connecting the two oceans.

The best site for a canal was that narrow part of Colombia known as the Isthmus of Panama. Indeed, a French company in the 1880's had tried but had failed to build a canal there. Another possible canal route was through Nicaragua (see map, page 557). A canal in either place would enable a fleet to pass easily and quickly from one ocean to the other. It would also be of enormous commercial value to the United States as well as to the merchant fleets of the world.

The United States had considered building a canal through the Isthmus of Panama for many years. As early as 1850, the United States and Great Britain had agreed on terms for a canal in the Clayton-Bulwer Treaty. If a canal were built, both nations would together control it and guarantee that it be unfortified and open to all other nations, even in wartime.

By 1898, however, Americans had concluded that the canal was so vital to their national interests that the United States had to have exclusive control over it. In 1901 Great Britain agreed to give up all rights to share in the building and control of the canal. The United States was now free to build and operate the canal, but it was understood that the canal would be open to all nations, even in time of war.

Negotiations with Colombia. The next step was to secure a right of way either through Nicaragua or across the Isthmus of Panama. The United States decided in favor of the route across Panama, which was then a province of Colombia. Secretary of State John Hay immediately opened negotiations with the Colombian government, and a treaty was soon ready for ratification. In return for a 99-year lease to a 6-mile (10-kilometer) strip of land across Panama, the United States agreed to pay Colombia $10 million and a yearly rental of $250,000.

At this point Colombia's legislators adjourned without taking action, hoping to win

THE CONQUEST OF YELLOW FEVER

Walter Reed checked the time. It was 11:50 on the night of December 31, 1900. At his desk in an American army barracks in northern Cuba, he turned back to the letter he was writing his wife in the United States.

"Only ten minutes of the old century remain," he wrote. "The prayer that has been mine for twenty years, that I might be permitted in some way or at some time to do something to alleviate human suffering has been granted. A thousand Happy New Years!"

Reed was truly benefiting humankind, for he led a team that was conquering yellow fever. This tropical disease had killed countless victims over the centuries, but no one knew what caused it or how to prevent it.

In 1900 yellow fever broke out among American troops stationed in Havana. The United States government promptly sent a team of physicians headed by Reed to investigate. Its other members were James Carroll, Jesse W. Lazear, and Aristides Agramonte. Earlier investigators—including Dr. Carlos Finlay of Cuba—had already suggested that the disease was transmitted by a certain mosquito. The Reed commission decided that experimenting with human subjects was the only way to test this theory. Beginning in June 1900, Carroll, Lazear, and several other volunteers allowed themselves to be bitten by infected mosquitoes. Lazear died, but the others survived.

This courageous experiment proved at last what before had only been suspected. Armed with this knowledge, William C. Gorgas, chief surgeon of the American forces in Cuba, took steps to clean up mosquito-breeding areas in Cuba. Later he continued his work in Central America, making it possible for the United States to build the Panama Canal.

---

better terms. Many Americans, including President Theodore Roosevelt, were furious because Colombia's delay blocked the entire canal project.

Revolution in Panama. Fortunately for the United States, many leaders in the province of Panama also were angry at Colombia's delay. These leaders had dreamed of a canal that would place Panama at a crossroads of world commerce. Moreover, for years the people of Panama had resented control by Colombia. Columbia's delay was the last straw.

In Panama a group secretly organized a revolution. They were encouraged by representatives of the French company that had earlier tried to build a canal and now wanted to recover as much as possible of its investment.

One Panamanian leader secretly traveled to Washington and asked the American government for assistance. Although open aid was refused, the Panamanian left Washington convinced that the United States would not interfere once the revolution began.

According to rumors, the revolution was to begin on November 4, 1903. On November 2 an American gunboat, the *Nashville,* arrived at Colón (see inset map, page 205). Hardly had it landed when a Colombian ship arrived with Colombian soldiers. The Colombian generals commanding the expedition immediately proceeded to the city of Panama, leaving orders for the troops to follow. Shortly after they reached Panama, however, the Colombian generals were seized and jailed. The arrest of the Colombian generals was a signal for the outbreak of the revolution, and the city of Panama quickly fell under the control of the revolutionists.

Meanwhile, during a dispute that broke out in Colón, Colombian soldiers and naval officers threatened to kill every American in the city. At this point United States marines landed. Colombian authorities demanded to know what right the Americans had to interfere. The

The building of the Panama Canal was an enormous undertaking. In this photograph the 70-foot (21-meter) deep Miraflores Lower Locks stand near completion.

Americans said that in a treaty between the United States and Colombia signed in 1846 the United States had guaranteed free passage through the isthmus. The United States government also added that no Colombian troops would be permitted to land within 50 miles (80 kilometers) of Panama.

Right of way through Panama. Largely because of American aid, the revolution in Panama was a success. On November 4, 1903, the new government took control in Panama, and two days later the United States recognized Panama's independence. On November 13 the United States formally received the First Panamanian minister to Washington, Bunau-Varilla (boo·NOH vah·REE·yah). On November 18, only two weeks after the revolution broke out, Panama granted the United States the right of way across the isthmus for the canal.

In the Hay–Bunau-Varilla Treaty, Panama gave the United States a perpetual lease to a 10-mile (16-kilometer) strip of land between the Atlantic and the Pacific Oceans. In return for this land, the United States agreed to pay Panama $10 million outright and a yearly rental of $250,000.

Did the United States help to start the revolution in Panama? President Theodore Roosevelt once boasted, "I took Panama." At other times, he denied that the United States had in any way helped to carry out the revolution. One fact is certain—the revolution worked to the advantage of the United States—and Roosevelt made the most of the situation.

Colombia was furious, of course, and the affair added to the fear and distrust of the "Yankee" that was already strong in Latin America. In 1921 the United States tried to pacify Colombia by giving it $25 million as partial compensation for the loss of Panama.

Building the canal. Meanwhile, work on the canal progressed under the supervision of the United States Army Corps of Engineers. One of the first and most difficult tasks was to conquer malaria, yellow fever, and other tropical diseases. Until these diseases were brought under control, workers from the United States found it almost impossible to live in the Canal Zone.

Dr. Walter Reed and his colleagues working in Cuba discovered that yellow fever was transmitted by a certain mosquito, the *Stegomyia.* Using this and other medical discoveries, Dr. William C. Gorgas, the surgeon in charge of the American health program in Panama, was able to turn a deadly tropical jungle into a relatively healthful region.

By 1914 the canal was completed (see inset map, page 205) at the cost of approximately $400 million. Its completion was a major triumph of engineering and a personal triumph for the engineer in charge, Colonel George W. Goethals (GOH·thulz). The first traffic moved through the canal just as World War I broke out in Europe. Since then the canal has added immeasurably to the naval strength of the United States. Its value in peacetime for trade has been almost incalculable.

SECTION SURVEY

IDENTIFY: Insular Cases, protectorate, Hay–Bunau-Varilla Treaty, Walter Reed, George Goethals.

1. How did the Supreme Court answer the question, "Does the Constitution follow the flag"?
2. What provisions did Congress make for the government of Puerto Rico?
3. Why can it be said that the Platt Amendment made Cuba an American protectorate?
4. Why was the United States interested in a canal through Central America?
5. American policies in Latin America contributed to the growing distrust of the "Yankee" there. Explain.
6. Map Study: Refer to the map on page 205 to explain why the Caribbean Sea was once called "an American lake."

2 The United States modifies and strengthens the Monroe Doctrine

During the early 1900's, as you have read, the United States on a number of occasions intervened in the internal affairs of the smaller countries in the Caribbean area. How did the United States justify such interference?

Reasons for interference. Intervention was necessary, Americans argued, to maintain law and order in countries bordering on the United States. In the first place, the United States government had a duty to protect the lives and properties of its own citizens living in other countries. Second, the United States was determined as a matter of self-interest and self-defense to prevent European nations from intervening in the political affairs of the Western Hemisphere. There would be less chance for such intervention if law and order prevailed. Third, the United States was concerned about the defense of the canal it was then building across the Isthmus of Panama.

The Monroe Doctrine of 1823. Americans developed the argument of self-defense into a well-defined foreign policy. As you recall, the original Monroe Doctrine of 1823 warned the European powers (1) not to attempt any further colonization in the Americas and (2) not to interfere with independent nations in the Western Hemisphere.

When this warning was issued and for many years after, the United States did not have the naval strength to enforce it. However, as long as American and British interests did not clash in Latin America, the British Navy could be counted on to support Monroe's words. Moreover, the Latin American countries themselves made several efforts to cooperate in the organization of their own defense. In fact, Mexico, Argentina, and Chile did successfully resist European attempts to interfere.

The first test. The first major test of the Monroe Doctrine came during the 1860's, when Emperor Napoleon III of France tried to establish a French-dominated empire in Mexico. Napoleon III, together with Great Britain and Spain, sent an expedition to Mexico, supposedly to force Mexico to repay its debts. After Mexico repaid its debts, Great Britain and Spain withdrew, but Napoleon III refused to pull out his troops. Instead, aided by Mexicans who opposed the President, Benito Juárez (HWAH·res), the French troops installed Maximilian of Austria as emperor of Mexico. President Juárez fled to El Paso del Norte near the United States border.

The United States immediately protested that French occupation of Mexico was a clear violation of the Monroe Doctrine. However, the United States was fighting the Civil War and until 1865 was unable to take firm action. Then, with the war ended, the United States prepared to send an American army to the Mexican border — farther, if necessary.

The American army was not needed. Napoleon, faced with the danger of war in Europe and convinced that he could not hold Mexico, withdrew his forces. Juárez and his followers destroyed Maximilian's army and executed Maximilian in 1867.

Thus ended a difficult situation. However, the American government had shown its firm resolve to resist European interference in Latin America.

A second test. A second major test of the Monroe Doctrine came in 1895. The immediate issue was a boundary dispute between Venezuela and British Guiana (see map, page 205).

Great Britain had acquired British Guiana in 1814. Time and again Great Britain had pushed the western boundary of British Guiana onto territory claimed by Venezuela. Finally, in 1882, Venezuela had had enough. It demanded that Great Britain submit the controversy to **arbitration,** meaning that the British would have to agree in advance to accept the decision of a neutral party.

The British refused, and in 1895 Venezuela asked the United States to intervene. President Cleveland decided to act. In an extremely strong message, Secretary of State Richard Olney warned Great Britain that the United States would not tolerate any further interference with Venezuela and demanded an immediate settlement of the problem by arbitration.

Great Britain angrily rejected Olney's demands. In the first place, the British retorted, the Monroe Doctrine had not been violated. Second, the Monroe Doctrine was not a recognized part of international law. Third, the United States had no business interfering.

President Cleveland refused to accept this explanation. When the British refusal to arbitrate reached him, he appointed an American commission to investigate the controversy and reach a decision. This was a direct challenge to British imperial power.

Realizing that war between Great Britain and the United States was a real possibility, responsible leaders in both countries urged moderation. Partly because of their efforts and partly because of British difficulties in South Africa at the time, the British government suddenly reversed its position. It agreed to arbitrate the boundary dispute and even offered to help the American commission's investigation.

The Monroe Doctrine had been successfully upheld. On this occasion the United States could claim that it had used its foreign policy to protect a weak nation against a great power. Even more important, perhaps, was the fact that the British, desiring American friendship, now in effect recognized that the United States had special interests in the Caribbean area.

A third test. In 1902, seven years later, Venezuela found itself unable to repay debts owed to Great Britain, Germany, and Italy. After their demands for repayment produced no results, the three countries took joint action. They withdrew their diplomatic representatives, blockaded the Venezuelan coast, and seized several small gunboats.

At this point President Theodore Roosevelt warned the European powers that any attempt to seize territory in the Western Hemisphere would violate the Monroe Doctrine. Then he urged the countries involved to submit the dispute to arbitration. They did, and the matter was settled.

The Drago Doctrine. By the early 1900's, growing numbers of Americans were investing money in the Caribbean countries and other parts of Latin America. Latin-American leaders watched with concern the growth of American investments and the growing influence of the United States. In 1902 one of these leaders, Luis M. Drago, Argentine Minister of Foreign Affairs, expressed this concern in a policy for Latin America that came to be known as the Drago Doctrine.

Drago rejected the claim that any European nation had the right to use force to collect debts from a Latin-American nation. He argued that when individuals or nations lent money, they did so at their own risk.

Nearly all of Latin America's leaders as well as many United States citizens agreed with Drago. However, in 1904 President Roosevelt announced a policy that exempted the United States from the principle that foreign debts concerned only the debtor country and foreign investors.

The Roosevelt Corollary. The Dominican Republic was the reason for Roosevelt's announcement (see map, page 205). It owed long-overdue debts to several European countries as well as to American investors. When the European countries threatened to use armed force to collect the money, President Roosevelt at once intervened.

This cartoon refers to the Venezuelan crisis of 1902. "That's a live wire, gentlemen" says Uncle Sam. Whom is he warning? What is the live wire that he is pointing to? What does he imply would happen if they step on the live wire?

Roosevelt announced in 1904 that if it became necessary for any nation to interfere in the affairs of a Latin-American country, the United States had to carry out the task, not a European government.

The policy announced in 1904 came to be known as the Roosevelt Corollary to the Monroe Doctrine. With this policy the United States assumed the role of "international police officer" in the Western Hemisphere. On several occasions during the next two decades, the United States used the Roosevelt Corollary to justify its intervention in the affairs of several Latin-American nations.

There were, of course, two ways of looking at the Roosevelt Corollary. From the United States' point of view, the North Americans were protecting their weaker neighbors from European intervention. On the other hand, Latin Americans were well aware that the policy could be used against them and that it was basically an insult to their national pride.

Dominican Republic as protectorate. The United States first exercised its "international police power" by intervening in the affairs of the Dominican Republic. As part of an agreement with the Dominican government in 1905, President Roosevelt promised to guarantee the Republic's **territorial integrity.** That is, he promised to use American armed forces, if necessary, to prevent any European country from seizing Dominican territory. In exchange for this guarantee, the Dominican government agreed to allow an American agent to collect its customs duties. In addition it agreed to turn over 45 percent of the duties to the Dominican government and to use the rest of the money to pay foreign creditors.

Although customs duties doubled under American supervision and the financial position of the Dominican Republic improved, the Dominican people resented United States control. Finally, in 1916, during President Wilson's administration, the Dominican government announced it intended to end the protectorate.

The United States answered this challenge by landing marines and suspending the Dominican legislature. For eight years, until

The American flag flies high as the United States takes formal possession of the Virgin Islands from Denmark in 1917. For the next 14 years, this territory would be governed under the supervision of the U.S. Department of the Navy.

1924, the Dominican Republic was ruled by a Dominican military dictatorship under the American government. The United States withdrew its military forces in 1924 but did not end its role of "protector" until 1940.

Protectorate in Haiti. The same general methods used to secure control of the Dominican Republic were applied to Haiti (see map, page 205) in 1914. During Wilson's administration revolutions shook the debt-ridden Haitian republic, and the United States landed marines there.

The Haitians were then asked to ratify a treaty prepared by the United States Department of State. This treaty gave the United States the right to (1) supervise Haiti's finances, (2) intervene to maintain order, and (3) control the Haitian police force. After considerable American pressure, Haiti ratified the treaty, which went into effect early in 1916.

Neither the treaty nor the continued presence of American troops restored order completely. During the next four or five years, nearly 2,000 Haitians were killed in riots and other outbreaks of violence.

Nevertheless, some improvements did come to Haiti during the years of United States control. Some Americans, however, agreed with those Haitians who argued that better sanitation, health, and education and increased prosperity were not worth the loss of freedom.

Interference in Central America. Twice between 1900 and 1920, American military forces were used in Nicaragua and Honduras to gain a large measure of control over these republics. In addition, the United States had great influence over the governments of Colombia, Costa Rica, and Guatemala (see map, page 205). This influence was secured by a policy labeled **dollar diplomacy** by its critics.

Under the so-called dollar diplomacy, American bankers, sometimes by invitation of the Department of State, lent money to Caribbean governments. When the debtors failed to repay their debts or the interest on their loans, the United States government intervened to protect American investments. This intervention took various forms, including the landing of marines, the supervision of elections, and support to the political group that favored the United States.

The Virgin Islands. Back in 1868 Secretary of State Seward had tried to get Congress to buy three of the Virgin Islands (see map, page 205) from Denmark. Congress had refused; it refused again in 1902.

In 1917, however, with World War I raging in Europe, the United States feared that Germany might secure control of these strategic bases. It renewed the offer to buy the islands, and this time negotiations were completed. With the payment of $25 million to Denmark, the islands became outposts of America's Caribbean empire.

As the map on page 205 shows, the Virgin Islands lie at the eastern edge of the West Indies. United States naval bases on the islands, in Puerto Rico, and at Guantánamo Bay in Cuba help to guarantee American control over the Caribbean Sea and the approaches to the Panama Canal.

SECTION SURVEY

IDENTIFY: Napoleon III, Benito Juárez, arbitration, Richard Olney, Drago Doctrine, territorial integrity, dollar diplomacy.

1. (a) How did the United States justify its intervention in Latin-American affairs? (b) Do you agree that this intervention was justified? Why or why not?
2. (a) What were the provisions of the original Monroe Doctrine of 1823? (b) Describe two occasions on which the Monroe Doctrine was tested and upheld.
3. (a) In what way did the Roosevelt Corollary modify the original Monroe Doctrine? (b) Give examples of cases in which the Roosevelt Corollary was applied.
4. Cartoon Study: (a) What is the subject of the cartoon on page 211? (b) What attitude does the cartoonist seem to have toward this situation? How can you tell?

3 Conflict breaks out between the United States and Mexico

From the early 1800's and particularly after the Mexican-American War in 1848, the United States and Mexico had been uneasy, if not hostile, neighbors.

Unreconciled . differences. Relations between the two countries had been troubled by repeated acts of violence, some major, others minor. The Mexican people could not forget that through the Mexican-American War they had lost one third of their country to their powerful northern neighbor.

Moreover, in the years following the war, the borderlands between Mexico and the United States remained a source of tension. During the 1870's and 1880's, American troops often pursued bands of Indians across the border into Mexican territory. There were long-standing disputes involving the water rights to the Rio Grande and the Colorado River. Banditry, smuggling, and cattle rustling were common along the border. Underlying all of these conflicts was the deep-seated and mutually-shared prejudice of Anglo-Americans and Mexican Americans in the borderlands.

It was American investments south of the Rio Grande that eventually involved the United States in outright conflict with Mexico. By the time Woodrow Wilson became President in 1913, American citizens had invested nearly $1 billion in Mexican oil wells, mines, railroads, and ranches. Most of Mexico's trade was with the United States.

Dictatorship and revolution. Mexico was closely tied to the United States, and Mexico's President, Porfirio Diaz, was largely responsible for this. Diaz, although called "President," was actually a dictator. With the exception of three years from 1881 to 1884, he had ruled Mexico since 1877. During his long rule, he had brought peace and order to Mexico and had helped to develop the country's resources.

To develop Mexico's resources, Diaz had encouraged foreign investors to finance and operate mines, factories, and other industries by offering them special privileges. With this encouragement, foreign capital, much of it

This painting, "Impassioned Democracy," is part of a giant mural that decorates Mexico's Palacio Nacional. The mural was done by artist Diego Rivera in the 1930's as a visual record of Mexico's leading historical figures and issues.

from American investors, had poured into Mexico. Thus foreign investors and the privileged friends of dictator Diaz enjoyed most of the benefits of Mexico's developing economy.

In 1910 the Mexicans staged a successful revolution and restored constitutional government to their country. Diaz resigned and left for Europe. Francisco Madero then became President, but only for a short time. Early in 1913 Madero was assassinated by Victoriano Huerta (HWAIR·tah), who then seized control of the government.

Huerta had many enemies, including friends of the late President Madero. His enemies also included many Mexicans who demanded drastic social and economic reform. The struggle against Huerta, led by Venus-

tiano Carranza, plunged Mexico more deeply into bitter fighting and bloodshed.

Wilson's "watchful waiting." Many Americans were deeply troubled by this situation. Many were dismayed because Huerta had risen to power as the result of a cold-blooded murder. Others with investments in Mexico were disturbed by attacks on their property. President Wilson was urged to send military forces into Mexico to protect American investments and to restore law and order.

The President chose instead to follow a policy that he hoped would preserve the independence of the Mexican people. He outlined his policy in a speech shortly after his election. "The United States will never again seek one

214

additional foot of territory by conquest," he declared. "We have seen material interests threaten constitutional freedom in the United States," he went on to say. "Therefore we will now know how to sympathize with those in the rest of America who have to contend with such powers, not only within their borders but from outside their borders also." He then urged the Latin-American countries to settle the Mexican problem in their own way.

Although some European countries promptly recognized the Huerta government, Wilson refused to do so. He was convinced that the Mexicans themselves would soon get rid of Huerta. Meanwhile, the United States would follow a policy of "watchful waiting."

Wilson's refusal to intervene pleased most Latin Americans. However, many Americans criticized the President as they saw American lives and property destroyed in Mexico.

American intervention. As the months passed, even President Wilson began to lose patience. Hundreds of small revolutionary groups roamed Mexico, but they were not organized and Huerta remained in power. American citizens in Mexico were killed, and there were rumors that Huerta might try to confiscate, or seize, American property.

The final crisis came in April 1914, when a Mexican official arrested several American sailors near Tampico, Mexico, which was under martial law. The sailors were soon released, but Huerta refused to apologize for the incident. To make matters worse, a German ship arrived at Veracruz with machine guns and other military supplies for Huerta. President Wilson then ordered United States marines to occupy Veracruz. This action united Mexican public opinion against the United States.

The ABC mediation. At this critical stage, Argentina, Brazil, and Chile—sometimes called the "ABC powers"—invited President Wilson to send representatives to meet with Mexican leaders and those of other nations to try to reach a solution. Wilson accepted the invitation, and the conference was held at Niagara Falls, Canada. Among its other recommendations, the conference urged Huerta to retire. Huerta did retire, faced with the fact that his forces were being beaten by those of his rival, Carranza.

Carranza then established himself in power in Mexico, and American forces withdrew from Veracruz. In 1915 Carranza guaranteed that Mexico would respect foreign lives and property, and the United States recognized him as leader of the Mexican government.

American troops in Mexico. Carranza's reforms divided his followers, who began to quarrel among themselves. One of those who turned against Carranza was Francisco "Pancho" Villa (VEE·yah). Villa was angry at the United States for helping Carranza. Hoping to force American troops to intervene in Mexico, Villa and his followers in 1916 seized 18 Americans in northern Mexico and put them to death. Later, Villa crossed the border and raided Columbus, New Mexico, killing 17 Americans.

President Wilson announced he would send an expedition into Mexico to capture Villa "dead or alive." Carranza reluctantly agreed, and General John J. Pershing led some 5,000 troops across the border. The deeper Pershing pushed into Mexican territory, the more hostile the Mexicans became. For a time the threat of war hung over both countries. Finally, in January 1917, American troops withdrew from Mexico without having captured the elusive Villa.

Mexican immigration. One major result of the years of unrest in Mexico was the increased immigration of Mexicans into the United States. Many came as political exiles. Others came to escape from the uncertainties of life in a country torn by revolution. Still others came, as millions of immigrants from other countries had come, in search of a better life in a more prosperous country.

SECTION SURVEY

IDENTIFY: Porfirio Diaz, Victoriano Huerta, ABC powers, Venustiano Carranza, "Pancho" Villa, John Pershing.

1. Give examples to show how the economic interests of the United States and Mexico were closely interwoven.

2. What differences and events contributed to the growing hostilities with Mexico?

3. (a) Describe the circumstances that led to Wilson's policy of "watchful waiting." (b) Explain the policy. (c) Why did Wilson abandon "watchful waiting"?

4. How did the ABC powers help solve the conflict between the United States and Mexico?

Chapter Survey

Summary: Tracing the Main Ideas

The Spanish-American War of 1898 marked a turning point in America's position in the world. After the war the United States embarked upon a program of imperialism similar in many ways to that being followed by the powers of the Western world, as well as Japan.

The influence of the United States was particularly strong in the countries bordering the Caribbean Sea. The Panama Canal provided a connecting link between the various parts of America's rapidly growing empire. To protect that vital artery of trade, the United States took steps to bring other Caribbean countries under its influence. Each new step the United States government took, each new commitment it assumed, led to still further steps and still further commitments.

The United States had long before expressed its special interest in the Caribbean and the rest of Latin America by issuing the Monroe Doctrine. In 1904 the United States added the Roosevelt Corollary to the Monroe Doctrine.

The corollary stated that the United States could intervene in the domestic affairs of Latin American countries, including Mexico. The United States justified this intervention on the ground that it was acting as the friendly police officer for the Western Hemisphere. To Latin-Americans in general, however, the United States appeared instead more like a bully.

In the next chapter, you will see why and how the United States was drawn into World War I and how the nation emerged from that conflict as a great world power.

Inquiring into History

1. (a) How would you justify Theodore Roosevelt's policies in the Caribbean? (b) How would you criticize them?
2. It has been said that the Monroe Doctrine protected Latin America from Europe but not from the United States. Do you agree or disagree? Explain the reasons for your answer.
3. Theodore Roosevelt once boasted: "I took Panama." (a) What did he mean? (b) What does this say about the power of the Presidency? (c) What amends did the United States make to Colombia?
4. The Panama Canal created new commitments for the United States. Explain.
5. What is your opinion of dollar diplomacy? Explain.
6. President Roosevelt stated as his foreign policy, "Speak softly and carry a big stick, and you will go far." (a) What did Roosevelt mean by this statement? (b) Give examples to show that Roosevelt acted on this policy.

Relating Past to Present

1. Do you think Puerto Rico has benefited from its relationship with the United States? Explain.
2. In the 1970's Panama and the United States signed a treaty giving Panama greater influence and control over the Panama Canal. (a) What were the provisions of that treaty? (b) Do you think the United States should have agreed to such a treaty? Why or why not?

Developing Social Science Skills

1. Examine the cartoon on page 204. (a) Explain the subject of the cartoon. (b) What point of view is presented in the cartoon? (c) How effective is the cartoon in presenting its point of view? Explain.
2. Make a timeline for a bulletin-board display for the years 1898 to 1914. (The timeline on page 203 will help you get started.) Use pictures or drawings to show the major events in America's new role as a world power.

Chapter **12**

America's Involvement in World War I

1914–1920

On the morning of July 28, 1914, Americans opened their newspapers with shocked surprise. In screaming headlines the New York *Tribune* reported, "AUSTRIA DECLARES WAR, RUSHES VAST ARMY INTO SERBIA; RUSSIA MASSES 80,000 MEN ON BORDER." Other papers carried the same news.

In general, the reaction of the American public was one of both stunned disbelief and withdrawal. For many years and particularly during the early 1900's, governments and individuals had devoted much time and effort to develop international understanding and to promote peace. Now, in the summer of 1914, all of these efforts had suddenly gone up in flames. Well, if the Europeans chose to be so reckless, let them reap the consequences. The American people wanted no part of this European madness.

As the months passed, however, it became clear that the United States as a major power could not remain neutral. Step by step, the nation moved closer to involvement and in the spring of 1917 finally entered the war on the side of the Allies.

The conflict that started in 1914 was the world's first total war. Few people on the face of the earth remained unaffected. Before it ended four years later, 30 nations on six continents would be involved. More than 8 million fighting men would be killed and an equal number of civilians would lose their lives.

THE CHAPTER IN OUTLINE

1. Peace-keeping efforts fail and World War I breaks out.

2. The United States attempts to remain neutral.

3. The United States declares war and mobilizes its strength.

4. American troops and ideals help the Allies win the war.

5. The United States refuses to join the League of Nations.

1900

1905

1910

World War I begins

Lusitania sinks — 1915

U.S. enters World War I

Russian Revolution

Wilson issues Fourteen Points

Treaty of Versailles

U.S. rejects League of Nations

1920

1925

2000

1 Peace-keeping efforts fail and World War I breaks out

During the late 1800's and the early 1900's, the leading nations of the world had taken important steps toward international cooperation. By 1914 many Europeans and Americans were convinced that major wars would never again occur.

Growing interdependence. For nearly 100 years, a movement for international peace had been steadily gaining strength. During the early 1900's, antiwar societies in both Europe and America published pamphlets insisting that war was wasteful and failed to solve any problems—and that even the victors paid too high a price.

Industrial technology was rapidly breaking down the barriers of space and time and bringing the people of the earth closer together. Railway trains rumbled across national boundaries. Passenger ships and freighters steamed back and forth across the oceans. The telegraph, the telephone, and underwater cables linked people in all parts of the world.

The number, variety, and importance of activities that people of different nations could and did carry on together increased greatly. Many businesses now bought and sold in worldwide markets and built industries in different countries. Humanitarian associations, including the Red Cross, organized on an international basis. Professional groups—scientists, engineers, doctors, and scholars—formed international societies and pooled their knowledge for the benefit of all peoples.

Governments as well as individual citizens also engaged in a growing number of activities requiring international cooperation. By 1914 at least 30 international agencies of government were dealing with problems shared by many nations. Among them were transportation, communication, disease and sanitation, weights and measures, postal regulations, and maritime rules.

The Pan-American Union. Meanwhile the governments of the leading nations of the world had been making new efforts to prevent war. On several occasions during the late 1800's and the early 1900's, delegates from many different nations met to discuss the issues of war and peace. In 1889–90, delegates from the Latin-American countries and the

During the early 1900's members of the Women's Peace Party used fans to symbolize their hopes—that Americans would keep cool and not allow troubles elsewhere in the world to inflame them into going to war.

United States met in Washington, D.C., and organized the International Union of American Republics. The union aimed to abolish war and to substitute for it arbitration between the American republics.

In 1910 the name of the International Union of American Republics was changed to the Pan-American Union. Under that name it held periodic meetings to discuss common problems. (Later, in 1948, the members of the Pan-American Union created the Organization of American States, known as the O.A.S.)

In the early 1900's, United States expansion and interference in the Caribbean area angered many Latin Americans and thus weakened the influence of the Pan-American Union. Nevertheless, throughout the Americas the Pan-American Union was the symbol of hope for a new, more peaceful world.

The Hague Conference. Millions of people in both Europe and the Americas had also taken hope from two conferences held in Europe.

The First Hague Conference, called by the tsar of Russia, met at The Hague in the Netherlands in 1899. Twenty-six nations sent delegates. The delegates strongly urged nations to try to settle disputes through mediation or arbitration. In cases involving mediation, two or more nations engaged in a dispute would ask a disinterested third party or nation to recommend a solution. In cases involving arbitration, two or more nations engaged in a dispute would agree in advance to accept the decision of a neutral party. To encourage arbitration, the First Hague Conference organized the Permanent Court of Arbitration with headquarters at The Hague. The conference also tried to lessen the horrors of warfare by outlawing certain weapons and by drawing up rules for the conduct of war.

The Second Hague Conference, called by the tsar of Russia and President Theodore Roosevelt, met at The Hague in 1907. This time 44 nations sent delegates. The conference drafted additional rules for the conduct of war and adopted the Drago Doctrine. As you remember, this doctrine stated that no nation should use force to collect debts "unless the debtor country refused arbitration, or having accepted arbitration, failed to submit to the award."

The first two Hague Conferences encouraged those who were working to promote peace. A third conference was being planned when war broke out in Europe.

Other efforts to promote peace. Although President Roosevelt believed that some wars were necessary, he played a leading role in the peace movement. He was responsible for the 1905 peace conference at Portsmouth, New Hampshire. There Japan and Russia reached an agreement ending the Russo-Japanese War. President Roosevelt and his successor, President Taft, also played active parts in other international negotiations.

President Wilson, who took office in 1913, was an even stronger champion of international understanding. He supported his Secretary of State, William Jennings Bryan, who negotiated antiwar treaties with 21 nations in 1913 and 1914. These treaties declared that every dispute had to be submitted to a joint commission for investigation and recommendation. The nations signing the treaties promised not to go to war until the commissions had made their reports.

By 1914 such efforts had built what seemed to be a solid and enduring structure of peace. Why, then, did war break out?

The spark that led to war. In spite of the many efforts made to preserve peace in the early 1900's, the European nations during these years were standing on a powder keg. When a spark was struck to the powder, the hopes and plans for peace of peoples everywhere exploded.

The spark was struck in the Balkan Peninsula of Europe (see map, page 220) in the early summer of 1914. There Serbian nationalists had pledged to free all Slavs° living under the rule of the Austro-Hungarian empire. The Serbian nationalists assassinated the Archduke Franz Ferdinand, heir to the throne of Austria-Hungary, and his wife Sophie as they rode through the streets of Sarajevo (SAH·rah·yeh·voh), the capital of the province of Bosnia. Bosnia had only recently become part of the Austro-Hungarian empire.

The Serbian conspirators were caught and brought to trial, but Franz Joseph, emperor of Austria-Hungary, and his advisers decided to use this opportunity to destroy Serbia's power completely. Thus Austria-Hungary made certain harsh demands against Serbia, which Serbia refused to meet.

°**Slavs:** a people widely spread over central, eastern, and southeastern Europe whose languages come from the same basic root. The Slavs under Austro-Hungarian rule were called South Slavs.

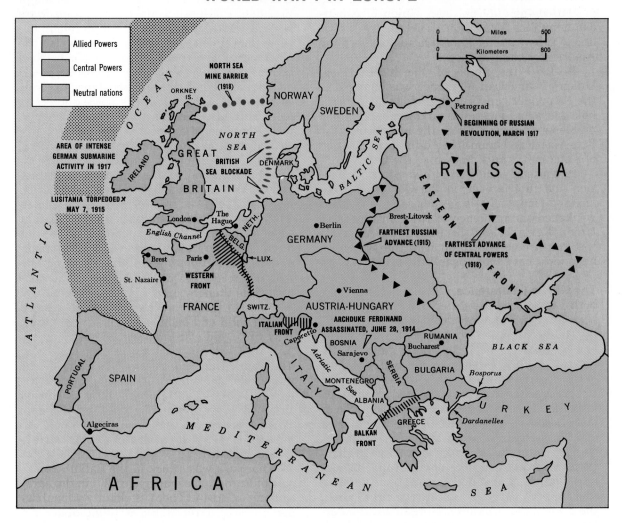

As tension grew, European diplomats struggled to solve the differences between Austria-Hungary and Serbia. The efforts failed and, with the support of Germany, its main ally, Austria-Hungary declared war on Serbia on July 28, 1914.

The movement of Austrian armies across the border into Serbia triggered a chain reaction. Within a week Austria-Hungary and Germany were at war with Russia, France, and Great Britain. Before the conflict ended, it had engulfed 30 nations on six continents. The nations siding with Austria-Hungary and Germany were known as the Central Powers. Those allying themselves with Russia, France, and Great Britain were referred to as the Allied Powers, or simply as the Allies.

Did the tragic incident at Sarajevo really start World War I? Yes and no. It was the immediate cause, the spark that touched off the explosion. However, there were deep, underlying causes that help to explain why the war came and spread so rapidly and widely.

Nationalism as a cause. An intense spirit of nationalism was one of the underlying sources of tension. The term **nationalism** often refers to the strong feeling people have for their own country. It may also refer to the desire of people ruled by others to throw off this foreign rule and create their own nation.

It was the desire to free certain Slavs from Austro-Hungarian rule that led the Serbian conspirators to assassinate the heir to the throne of Austria-Hungary. Austria-Hungary declared war on Serbia in order to crush this rising spirit of nationalism among the Slavic people. This spirit of nationalism was not confined to the Balkan Peninsula. In almost every country of Europe as well as in the colonies overseas, people ruled by other nations longed for independence.

Imperialism as a cause. Another source of tension was imperialism — the struggle for colonies. As you recall, during the late 1800's and the early 1900's the major powers of the world were engaged in a race for empire. By 1914, so far as colonies were concerned, the nations of Europe could be grouped into two classes: the "have" nations and the "have-not" nations.

Great Britain and France, each with huge colonial empires, were among the "have" powers. Although Russia owned no colonies, it possessed immense areas of underdeveloped land and thus was also a "have" nation.

Germany, on the other hand, was a "have-not" nation. It owned colonies in Africa and in the Pacific, but its colonial empire was relatively small, and Germany wanted additional territory. Italy was in a similar situation. One of the reasons that finally brought Italy into the war on the Allied side was a promise of colonies when the war ended.

International rivalries. Rivalry among nations was not, however, confined to the race for colonies. Austria-Hungary attacked Serbia partly to strengthen its hold on the Slavic peoples and partly to increase its influence in the Balkan Peninsula. Russia, on the other hand, came to Serbia's aid to prevent Austria-Hungary from increasing its influence.

France supported Russia not only because it was Russia's ally but also because it wanted to recover Alsace-Lorraine, a former French area that the Germans had conquered in 1871. Italy desired nearby territories within the Austro-Hungarian empire. Every Balkan country looked greedily at territory belonging to its neighbors. Russia longed for ice-free harbors in the Baltic Sea and for an outlet through the Dardanelles and the Bosporus into the Mediterranean Sea. Germany, the major Baltic Sea power, and Turkey, which controlled the Dardanelles, feared and distrusted Russia.

Systems of alliance. The mounting tensions with their accompanying plots and intrigues led to an armaments race, or race for military power. Long before 1914 the relative sizes of their navies and armies occupied a major part of the attention of all of the governments in Europe.

Besides building up their military forces, European nations tried to gain security with the **balance-of-power system.** This meant that every nation tried to increase its own strength by securing as many allies as possible. Thus Germany, Austria-Hungary, and Italy joined in what became known as the Triple Alliance. To maintain a balance of power, Great Britain, France, and Russia joined in what became known as the Triple Entente (ahn·TAHNT). Both of these rival alliances had been completed by 1907.

Austria's declaration of war on Serbia set the whole system of alliances into motion. Of all the nations, only Italy failed to live up to its treaty obligations, which pledged Italy to support Austria-Hungary and Germany. Waiting to see which side would promise the most, Italy did not enter the war until 1915, and then it fought on the Allied side.

Peace or war? During the early 1900's, as you may recall, strong forces pulled peoples and nations in two directions at the same time. With one hand, governments tried to strengthen the bonds between nations and build a solid structure of peace. With the other hand, governments plotted and schemed against one another and desperately planned for war or for the protection of their national interests in case war broke out.

SECTION SURVEY

IDENTIFY: interdependence, mediation, Slavs, Central Powers, Allied Powers, nationalism, imperialism, balance-of-power system, Triple Alliance, Triple Entente.

1. What was the purpose of the Pan-American Union?

2. Why did the first two Hague Conferences greatly encourage those who were working to promote peace among nations?

3. Why is the incident at Sarajevo considered the spark that set off World War I?

4. How did the following factors help cause World War I and encourage its rapid spread: (a) nationalism, (b) imperialism, (c) international rivalries, (d) the balance-of-power system?

2 The United States attempts to remain neutral

America's first reaction to the outbreak of war in Europe, as you have read, was one of shocked surprise and withdrawal. The war seemed unreal, a nightmare that surely would not last long.

American neutrality.   Nevertheless, the war was all too real, and President Wilson urged the American people to be "neutral in fact as well as in name" and "impartial in thought as well as in action." From the beginning, however, Americans were torn between the desire to avoid war and their sympathy for one side or the other.

Millions of recently naturalized Americans had friends and relatives in Europe. Men and women of German origin—or of Austrian or Turkish origin—wanted the Central Powers to

In 1914 heavy bombing nearly leveled the city of Reims in northeastern France. The bombing also destroyed the interior of the historic Reims Cathedral, including its irreplaceable stained glass windows.

win. Most Americans, however, were sympathetic to the Allied Powers. The ties of language, similar democratic governments, and deep-rooted traditions bound Americans to Great Britain. The ties with France were also strong. After all, the French back in 1778 had come to the aid of Americans fighting for their independence. As World War I went on, this sympathy for the Allies led thousands of young Americans to enlist in the British, Canadian, and French armed forces. A special unit of volunteer American fliers, called the Lafayette Escadrille, was created as part of the new French flying force.

Although in 1914 American sympathies were divided, most Americans supported the President's policy of neutrality and prayed for an early end to the war.

The German plan of attack.   The Central Powers, under the leadership of the German High Command, had every intention of ending the war quickly. They wanted to conquer France before the Russians could fully mobilize. With France at their mercy, they could then turn against Russia.

Long before the war the French, fearful of German attack, had built strong fortifications along the entire Franco-German frontier. However, the French had not fortified the border between France and Belgium. The French counted on an international agreement, which the Germans had signed, that in the event of war Belgium would be respected as a neutral nation.

The German Chancellor, however, declared that the international agreement respecting Belgium's neutrality was merely "a scrap of paper." The German High Command launched an attack against neutral Belgium and Luxembourg, intending to reach the borders of France in six days. As shown on the map on page 223, seven powerful German armies were to strike in a great wheeling action at northern France.

Failure of the plan.   The German plan failed, largely because Belgium resisted. Because of gallant resistance by the small Belgian army, the Germans took 18 days to cross Belgium, not the six called for in the German timetable. This delay gave General Joffre, commander of the French armies, time to rush troops to the Belgian border. In addition it gave the British time to transport an army of about 90,000 to northern France.

The French and the British arrived too late to save Belgium. Nor were they able to stop the Germans at the Belgian frontier. Crushed by the superior might of the Germans, the French and British retreated to the Marne River, where General Joffre hastily prepared his main defense.

Fighting against seemingly hopeless odds, the French and British stopped the Germans early in September 1914 at the Marne River in the First Battle of the Marne. The Germans then fell back to the Aisne (AYN) River, where they dug a line of trenches and checked an Allied counteroffensive.

The First Battle of the Marne was one of the decisive battles of the war. If the Germans had won, they might have crushed all remaining French and British resistance in a few weeks.

Stalemate on the Western Front. By 1915 the war in Western Europe had reached a stalemate. Both sides were dug in along a 600-mile (965-kilometer) line reaching from the Swiss border to the English Channel. During the next three years, both the Germans and the Allies, with only a thin strip of land called "no man's land" separating their trenches, fought desperately along the Western Front. Neither side was able to break through the enemy line or to end the trench warfare. Thousands died in this bloody struggle, but until the spring of 1918 neither side made a significant gain.

There were other fronts—and on all of them troops were fighting and dying. The Central Powers and Russia were locked in combat along the entire Eastern Front. Turkish troops defended a precarious line that reached southward through Palestine as far as Medina, in Arabia, against the British and French and their allies. The fighting forces of Austria-Hungary and Italy faced each other in the area of their common boundary north of the Adriatic Sea (see map, page 220).

The British blockade. The prospect of a long war was bad news indeed for Americans who hoped to remain neutral. It meant, among other things, that warfare on the high seas would grow fiercer as Great Britain and Germany tried to prevent supplies from the United States and other neutral countries from reaching the other side.

The British fleet controlled the seas, at least during the opening months of the war. It blockaded the German coast (see map, page

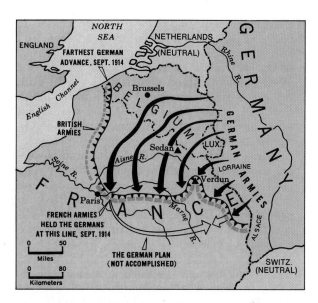

WESTERN FRONT: 1914–1917

220) and laid explosive mines in the North Sea. To the angry astonishment of Americans, the British navy also blockaded neutral countries, such as Norway, Sweden, Denmark, and the Netherlands, through which American goods flowed into Germany. American anger increased when the British began to examine American mail bound for Europe and ordered all neutral ships to stop at British ports, where their cargoes were searched. The United States protested that Great Britain's actions were illegal. Such actions violated the rights of neutrals to travel the high seas, provided they were not carrying war materials.

Submarine warfare. American anger at Great Britain subsided, however, in the face of German submarine warfare. According to international law, naval vessels of countries at war had the right to stop and search a neutral ship for weapons, munitions, and other materials useful in war, known as **contraband**. The naval vessel had the right to seize a neutral ship carrying contraband and take it into port as a prize of war. If it were impossible to take the neutral vessel into port, the warship was required to take its passengers and crew to a safe place before sinking the prize.

Submarines were not armed to defend themselves against enemy warships while on the surface. Thus they could not take seized vessels into port. Nor could submarines take the passengers and crew of a large vessel on board. Least of all could they surface and search neutral ships, for the moment they rose to the surface they were "sitting ducks" for even one well-aimed shot from a naval gun. Submarines were designed to lurk in the ocean depths, to strike suddenly without warning at an enemy ship, and to slip away quickly before a counterattack.

The German surface fleet, although powerful, was still no match for the British navy. The Germans, therefore, had concentrated on building submarines, called U-boats. Early in the war, the Germans notified President Wilson that they intended to turn their subma-

Notices like this one appeared in American newspapers, warning citizens of the dangers of sailing on British ships. Many Americans resented the threat that submarine warfare posed to freedom of travel.

NOTICE!

TRAVELLERS intending to embark on the Atlantic voyage are reminded that a state of war exists between Germany and her allies and Great Britain and her allies; that the zone of war includes the waters adjacent to the British Isles; that, in accordance with formal notice given by the Imperial German Government, vessels flying the flag of Great Britain, or of any of her allies, are liable to destruction in those waters and that travellers sailing in the war zone on ships of Great Britain or her allies do so at their own risk.

IMPERIAL GERMAN EMBASSY
WASHINGTON, D. C., APRIL 22, 1915.

rines loose in the Atlantic. President Wilson promptly replied that the United States would hold Germany responsible for any acts that endangered American property and lives on the high seas.

The *Lusitania*. The Germans were convinced that their submarine blockade would ruin Great Britain. They therefore ignored President Wilson's warning and ordered their U-boats to patrol the Atlantic shipping lanes. On March 28, 1915, a British steamer was torpedoed and sunk near Ireland, carrying to their deaths more than 100 persons, including an American.

This and other incidents led to the sinking of the British liner *Lusitania* off the southern coast of Ireland on May 7, 1915, with the loss of 1,198 lives, including 128 Americans. Since the *Lusitania* was carrying war materials bound for England, the Germans believed that their action was justified.

In three strongly worded messages to the German government in Berlin, the American State Department protested against the sinking of the *Lusitania*. The messages warned that any repetition of such action would have serious consequences. American anger at the *Lusitania* affair was still at the boiling point when on August 9, 1915, another U-boat sank the *Arabic,* a British liner, with the loss of two American lives.

Alarmed at the American reaction, Germany on September 1 gave a written promise that in the future "liners will not be sunk by our submarines without warning . . . provided that the liners do not try to escape or offer resistance." Americans had to be content with this promise.

The sinking of the *Lusitania* marked a turning point in American feeling about the war. Increasing numbers of Americans began to realize that the conflict in Europe was not far off but close at hand. They began to understand that neutrality might become impossible. Nevertheless, in 1915 most still hoped that the United States could avoid war.

More sinkings, more promises. In March 1916 the Germans broke their promise and attacked a French passenger vessel, the *Sussex*. Lives were lost and several Americans were injured. President Wilson threatened to break off diplomatic relations with Germany unless it agreed to abandon submarine warfare.

In what became known as the "*Sussex* pledge," Germany renewed its earlier promise not to sink liners without warning and without providing for the safety of the passengers. However, the Germans added an important reservation. They would keep the promise on condition that the United States would persuade the Allies to modify the food blockade of Germany, which, according to Berlin, was inflicting hunger and even starvation on the German people. The United States replied that the British blockade had nothing to do with German violation of American neutral rights on the high seas.

A rising war spirit. American opinion was divided over Wilson's efforts to enforce neutrality. Some people, including former President Theodore Roosevelt, felt that the United States was not firm enough. Others believed that the American government was unwisely going too far in its threatening demands on Berlin. Secretary of State Bryan, for example, resigned during the *Lusitania* crisis. In Bryan's opinion, the United States should forbid American citizens to travel on British and French ships. Bryan also believed that Congress should stop Americans from selling war materials to nations at war.

President Wilson refused to follow the advice of those who shared Bryan's views. Instead, Wilson supported a program for strengthening the army and navy. The National Defense Act, passed in June 1916, increased America's regular army from 106,000 to 175,000 soldiers and provided for officers' training camps. A three-year naval program was started in 1916. In 1916 the government also created the Council of National Defense and the United States Shipping Board. These agencies planned the mobilization of the country's resources in case of war and began a huge shipbuilding program.

The war preparations did not mean that either Wilson or the public had abandoned all hope of remaining neutral. Indeed, many Americans voted for the reelection of Wilson in November 1916 on the ground that "he kept us out of war."

Six months later, under the leadership of President Wilson and Congress, the American people entered the conflict, millions of them with considerable enthusiasm. What happened to lead the administration to abandon neutrality and take this step?

SECTION SURVEY

IDENTIFY: trench warfare, contraband, U-boats, *Lusitania,* "*Sussex* pledge."

1. President Wilson stated that the United States had to be "neutral in fact as well as in name" and "impartial in thought as well as in action." Why did many Americans find it difficult to maintain such impartiality?

2. America's neutral rights were violated by both Great Britain and Germany. Explain.

3. Map Study: Study the maps on pages 220 and 223. (a) Locate the area in the first map that is shown enlarged in the second map. (b) Which map would be more useful in gaining an overall impression of the war? In gaining information on military strategies? In naming the countries on each side? Explain your answers.

3   **The United States declares war and mobilizes its strength**

During the winter of 1916–17, all American hope of remaining neutral finally vanished. The German leaders themselves were largely responsible for this development.

Diplomatic relations broken. On February 1, 1917, Germany decided to renew unrestricted submarine warfare, thus going back on the "*Sussex* pledge." A German proposal to permit only one American passenger ship to sail to England each week added insult to injury.

The German High Command made this decision fully aware that it would almost certainly bring the United States into the war. The High Command took the calculated risk that submarines could destroy Great Britain's power and will to fight before the United States could provide effective help.

Wilson met the new challenge promptly. On February 3 he broke off diplomatic relations with the German government.

Moving toward war. On February 24, British naval intelligence agents revealed a German message they had intercepted and decoded. The message had been sent from Germany by Foreign Secretary Arthur Zimmerman to the German minister in Mexico. It contained instructions about what to do in case war broke out between Germany and the United States. In this event, the German minister was to offer Mexico an alliance with Germany. With German support Mexico was to attack the United States and "reconquer the lost territory in New Mexico, Texas, and Arizona." When Wilson released the Zimmermann note to the Associated Press on March 1, Americans were shocked and angry.

On March 12 President Wilson, through the State Department, announced that all American merchant vessels sailing through war zones would be armed for defense against German submarines. The public received this announcement with mixed reactions but in general approved.

Still other and deeper forces moved American sympathies toward the Allies and toward war with Germany. For one thing, American ties with Great Britain and France were traditionally closer than those with Germany. Not least important, American shipments of munitions to the Allied Powers had risen from $6 million in 1914 to nearly $500 million in 1916. By April 1917, American bankers had loaned about $2 billion to the Allies. Naturally, these American investors wanted an Allied victory. However, historians have found no evidence to show that economic interests consciously influenced Wilson's conduct in the critical weeks before the United States entered the war.

The President's "War Message." As the weeks passed, President Wilson reluctantly concluded that America's entrance into the war was inevitable. Supported by his entire cabinet, the President called for a special session of Congress. On April 2, 1917, a solemn and hushed group of Senators, Representatives, and distinguished guests gathered to hear President Wilson present his impassioned "War Message."

The President condemned Germany's submarine warfare as "the wanton and wholesale destruction of the lives of noncombatants, men, women, and children, engaged in pursuits which have always, even in the darkest periods of modern history, been deemed innocent and legitimate. Property can be paid for; the lives of peaceful and innocent people cannot be. . . . The challenge is to all mankind," the President declared. "The wrongs against which we now array ourselves are no common wrongs; they cut to the very roots of human life."

Wilson was too great an idealist to rest his case upon the evils of unrestricted submarine warfare alone. He also summoned the American people to rise in a crusade for a better world: "We are glad to fight thus for the ultimate peace of the world and for the liberation of its peoples, the German peoples included: for the rights of nations great and small and the privilege of men everywhere to choose their way of life and of obedience. The world must be made safe for democracy. Its peace must be planted upon the tested foundations of political liberty. We have no selfish ends to serve. We desire no conquest, no dominion. We seek no indemnities for ourselves."

Congress promptly declared war. The Senate approved a war declaration on April 4, the House on April 6, 1917. America's entry into the conflict had an immediate effect upon other neutral countries. Between April 1917 and July 1918, a number of Latin-American states declared war. Most of the other American countries, although unwilling to enter the war, severed diplomatic relations with Germany.

Raising an army. As soon as war was declared, the United States began to mobilize its work force, its industries, and its natural resources. On May 18 Congress adopted the Selective Service Act, which required the registration of all men between the ages of 21 and 30. The act was amended on August 31, 1918, to include all men between 18 and 45. During the war more than 24 million Americans were registered by their local draft boards, and 2.8 million of this group were drafted into the army. Before the war ended, more than 4.7 million Americans served in the armed forces.

About 371,000 black Americans served in World War I, but, as in earlier wars, they often met prejudice and discrimination. They were restricted to separate units, recreation centers, and living accommodations. Most of the 200,000 black troops sent to Europe served in noncombatant battalions, though many of them requested combat duty. All of the 10,000 blacks who served in the navy were assigned to noncombat duties.

As the war progressed, the bravery and courage of black units under fire were plain to see. The first Allied unit to drive through to the River Rhine was the 369th, a black regiment attached to the Ninety-third Division. For outstanding courage in battle, Henry Johnson and Needham Roberts of the 369th became the first black Americans to be awarded the *Croix de Guerre,* or Cross of War, a coveted French military honor.

Financing the war. To finance the war, Congress decided to raise approximately two thirds by borrowing, the remaining one third by taxing current income. The government borrowed money by selling war bonds. Through four Liberty Loan Drives and a Victory Loan Drive, the government borrowed more than $21 billion. The government also boosted income-tax rates and levied excise taxes on railroad tickets, telegraph and telephone messages, alcoholic beverages, tobacco, and certain amusements.

Mobilizing industry. Materials were as important as workers and money. The big problem was to stimulate production and prevent waste. To achieve this goal, Congress gave President Wilson sweeping wartime powers.

The President was authorized to set prices on many commodities, including such essentials as food and fuels. He was also authorized to regulate, or even to take possession of, factories, mines, meat-packing houses, food-processing plants, and all transportation and communication facilities. The President exercised these vast powers through a number of wartime agencies, or boards.

The War Industries Board, established in 1917, became the virtual dictator of manufacturing. It developed new industries needed in the war effort. It regulated business to eliminate waste and nonessential goods. Before the war's end, the War Industries Board was engaged in regulating the production of some 30,000 commodities.

Other federal agencies also took an active part in planning the war program. The War Finance Corporation loaned public funds to businesses needing aid in manufacturing war materials. The Emergency Fleet Corporation built ships faster than German submarines could destroy them. The Railroad Administration took over the operation of the railroads, reorganized the lines, and controlled rates and wages. The Fuel Administration stimulated a larger output of coal and oil and encouraged economies in their use.

Mobilizing labor. The successful mobilization of industry depended, of course, upon the full cooperation of labor. In an effort to deal

When the United States entered the war, the Army Air Service had only 130 pilots and only 53 serviceable planes. Dramatic posters like the one shown above helped to attract recruits and build up the service.

with labor disputes, President Wilson in April 1918 appointed the National War Labor Board. This board was authorized to arbitrate disputes between workers and employers. In June, Wilson appointed the War Labor Policies Board. This board could establish general policies affecting wages, hours, and working conditions. These measures and the cooperation of organized labor reduced labor disputes to a minimum during the war years.

As war-related industries expanded and more and more men entered the armed forces, women helped ease the labor shortages. They worked in shops, factories, the construction industry, and in steel mills. Some became conductors on trolley cars and engineers on trains.

Conserving food. The problem of food was equally critical. Late in 1917 Congress adopted and submitted to the states an amendment to

SERVICE

FALL IN!

NATIONAL LEAGUE foR WOMANS SERVICE

Colleges, schools, the press, churches, fraternal lodges, women's and civic groups all cooperated with the government's campaign "to sell the war to the American people." The poster shown here illustrates some of the roles occupied by women during World War I.

the Constitution prohibiting the manufacture, sale, or transportation of alcoholic liquors. The amendment was passed, in part, to help conserve grain, which is used in making alcohol. This Eighteenth Amendment was ratified by the necessary three fourths of the states in 1919 and went into effect on January 16, 1920.

The government also made other moves to guarantee food for the American people and their allies. Herbert Hoover, who had successfully managed food relief in war-stricken Belgium, was placed in charge of the Food Administration. Hoover brought about a vast expansion of agriculture and reduced the hoarding and waste of food. He encouraged people to plant "victory gardens" and urged them to observe "wheatless" and "meatless" days. The sale of sugar and other commodities was limited. All this took place without rationing. In-

stead the Food Administration, with the crucial help of women's groups, used persuasion to get people to cooperate.

Public opinion and dissent. The government also undertook to gain the cooperation of all Americans in the war effort. The Committee on Public Information circulated millions of leaflets describing in glowing language America's official war aims and denouncing the German government. Colleges, schools, the press, churches, fraternal lodges, women's organizations, and civic groups all cooperated with the government's campaign "to sell the war to the American people." In all sorts of public gatherings, well-known people gave brief speeches publicizing the nation's war aims and philosophy.

From the beginning most Americans enthusiastically supported the war. There were, however, some dissenters, who, in greater or lesser measure, were not in sympathy with the government's war effort.

To deal with those people, Congress in June 1917 adopted the Espionage Act. This act was aimed at treasonable and disloyal activities. In May 1918 Congress strengthened the Espionage Act by an amendment, often called the Sedition Act. This act provided penalties of up to $10,000 in fines and 20 years' imprisonment, or both, for anyone found guilty of interfering with the sale of war bonds, attempting to curtail production, or using "disloyal, profane, scurrilous, or abusive language" about the American form of government or about any of its agencies.

Under these laws, the Department of Justice arrested at least 1,597 persons. Of these, 41 received prison sentences of from 10 to 20 years. In addition, newspapers and periodicals found guilty of criticizing the government's conduct of the war were deprived of their mailing privileges.

Many loyal Americans, themselves thoroughly in sympathy with the war effort, objected to the Espionage Act and Sedition Act. They held that the constitutional rights of citizens should not be interfered with, even in wartime.

For the most part, however, Americans did not need arguments or laws to secure their loyalty. Americans entered the war on a great wave of enthusiasm. They were convinced, as Wilson had put it, that this was indeed a crusade "to make the world safe for democracy."

IDENTIFY: Zimmermann note, unrestricted submarine warfare, Selective Service Act, Henry Johnson, Espionage Act.

1. In his "War Message," President Wilson asked Congress to declare war on Germany. (a) What reasons did he give? (b) Why did he view the war as a crusade?

2. How did the United States mobilize (a) workers, (b) industries, (c) natural resources, and (d) public opinion?

3. In the crusade "to make the world safe for democracy," black members of the American armed forces often faced discrimination. Comment on this contradiction.

4. Picture Study: Examine the poster on page 228. (a) What roles does it show for women? (b) Were any of these roles new for women? (c) What effects do you think World War I may have had on the movement for women's rights?

4 American troops and ideals help the Allies win the war

America's declaration of war came none too soon. In the spring of 1917, the Allies were facing a grim situation, and by the end of the year their position was desperate.

The military situation in 1917. By early 1917 the Allies, who had suffered enormous losses, were war-weary and discouraged. In March they were further disturbed by news that the tsar of Russia had been deposed and a new revolutionary government established. America's entry into the conflict in April was one of the few bright spots in a year during which Allied fortunes sank lower and lower.

In the fall Germany threw a number of crack divisions into the Austrian campaign, and on October 24 the Austrians and Germans crashed through the Italian lines at Caporetto (see map, page 220). French and British troops, rushed from the Western Front, helped to stop the rout and saved Italy from collapse.

Most serious of all, however, was the news from Russia. On November 7 the Bolsheviks, a party of radical Communists, seized power. A month later the Bolsheviks signed an armistice with Germany. Almost three months later, in March 1918, they concluded the peace treaty of Brest-Litovsk (BREST lih·TOFSK). Meanwhile Rumania, unable to stand alone against the Central Powers in eastern Europe, in 1918 signed a peace treaty at Bucharest.

Thus, by the end of 1917, the Germans were free to concentrate most of their forces on the Western Front. General Ludendorff, commander of the German armies, prepared for an offensive intended to end the war before American troops could play an important role.

American naval forces. Meanwhile the United States Navy, which had been rapidly building its strength since 1916, went into action. Before the war ended, the United States had established 45 naval bases, which were located as far north as Murmansk, in Russia, and as far south as Greece.

In cooperation with the British Navy, American naval forces patrolled the North Sea and effectively bottled up the German fleet. They also laid most of a 230-mile (370-kilometer) barrier of mines that stretched across the North Sea from Norway to the Orkney Islands (see map, page 220). This barrier greatly increased the hazards for German submarines seeking to reach the open waters of the Atlantic Ocean or to return to their bases in Germany.

Meanwhile other naval vessels helped to convoy merchant ships and troop transports through the submarine-infested waters of the Atlantic Ocean. The convoy system was so effective that 2 million American soldiers or more were transported across the Atlantic with the loss of only a few hundred lives. It was a remarkable tribute to naval efficiency and a severe blow to the Germans.

The A.E.F. in France. While the United States Navy was busy on the high seas, American land forces were being organized. President Wilson appointed General John J. Pershing as Commander of the American Expeditionary Forces (the A.E.F.). Pershing had served in Cuba, in the Philippines, and as commander of the expedition sent into Mexico to capture Pancho Villa.

Pershing landed in France early in June 1917. By the end of June, the first regiments of the First Division arrived. On July 4 several thousand "Yanks" marched through Paris amid the heartfelt cheers of the French people.

American troops arrived in ever-swelling numbers. By the fall of 1918, more than 2 million had landed in France. To supply and maintain this huge army, the Americans built huge docks and railroads as well as networks of telephone and telegraph lines in Europe. They landed 17,000 freight cars and more than 40,000 trucks. The Americans also built training camps, hospitals, storage houses, and ammunition dumps.

Germany's last bid for victory. On March 21, 1918, the Western Front exploded into violent action once more. The Germans, reinforced by seasoned troops released from the Russian front, launched a powerful campaign, or "peace offensive," to end the war. At the end of two weeks, the Germans had gained a large area of land and inflicted 160,000 casualties. By the end of May, they were at the River Marne, only 37 miles (59 kilometers) from Paris.

Pershing's original plans had called for a period of training behind the lines before his troops went into action. He had also insisted that American troops fight as a separate army under their own top command. However, in the spring of 1918, he consented to putting every available soldier into the lines immediately. French, British, and American troops fought together under a unified Allied command directed by the French military leader Marshal Foch (FOSH).

Under the command of General John J. Pershing, the American Expeditionary Force distinguished itself during the allied victory drive. Here, in July 1918, American troops perform bravely at the front near Méry, to the east of Paris.

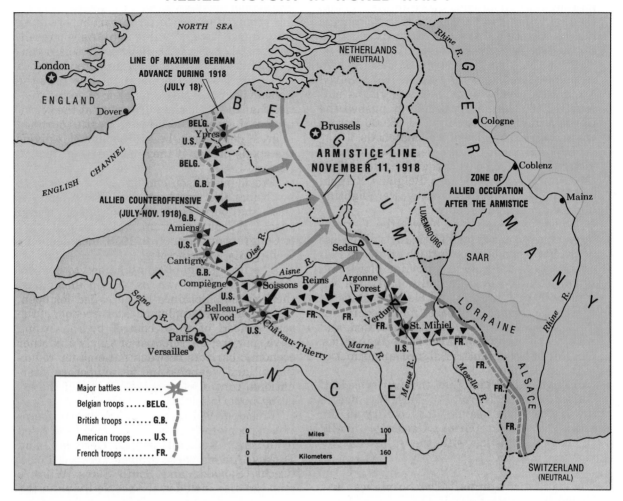

Stopping the German advance. Fighting desperately, French, British, Belgian, and American troops finally stopped the Germans. On May 28 the First Division of the United States Army took Cantigny (kahn·teen·YEE). Three days later the Third Division, in a last ditch defense of Paris, only 40 miles (64 kilometers) away, helped the French hold the Germans at Château-Thierry (shah·TOH teh·REE). At Belleau (BEL·loh) Wood the Second Division, strengthened by the 4th Marine Brigade, held back the Germans in six days of fighting (see map, this page).

Then, on July 15, the Germans threw everything they could into one final, ferocious assault around Reims (REEMZ). In this action, the beginning of the Second Battle of the Marne, the Allied lines held. On July 18 Marshal Foch ordered a counterattack spearheaded by the First and Second American Divisions and the First French Morocco Division. The Germans began to fall back. The tide at last had turned.

The Allied victory drive. The Allies now took the initiative. In July Foch launched a terrific offensive along the entire length of the line. The Germans were driven back.

The Americans fought as a separate army under General Pershing's command. The American troops, 500,000 strong and supported by French troops and British planes, launched a powerful attack on the area around St. Mihiel (SAN mee·YEL) in September 1918. After three days of savage fighting, this key section of the southern front was safely under American control.

231

Then, against heavy artillery and machine-gun fire, the Americans drove toward Sedan, the highly fortified position that the Germans had held since 1914. For 47 days the United States troops pushed toward their objective. The fighting in this tremendous Meuse-Argonne (MYOOZ ahr·GUN) offensive involved 1.2 million combatants. The Americans suffered 120,000 casualties, but they pushed the German line back and captured 28,000 prisoners and large supplies of war materials.

Important though they were, the American victories were only part of the offensive against the crumbling German lines. Belgians, British, and French, confident of victory, were fighting fiercely against the enemy.

Under such hammer blows, the German morale began to sag, and Germany's allies lost heart. In September the Turkish armies in Palestine and Arabia suffered crushing blows, and Bulgaria surrendered unconditionally. On November 3 the crews of the German ships at Kiel, a German naval base, mutinied rather than go to sea. Army units also mutinied, and riots broke out in a number of German cities. On November 3 Austria signed an armistice with the Italians.

Convinced at last that the war was lost, Kaiser Wilhelm II, ruler of Germany, fled to the Netherlands, leaving the country in the hands of revolutionists. Germany finally signed an armistice with the Allies on November 11, 1918.

The armistice terms. The armistice was signed in a railroad car in the forest of Compiègne (kon·PYEN·yuh) in France on the eleventh hour of the eleventh day of the eleventh month of 1918. The Germans signed grimly, for the terms were severe.

The Germans agreed to evacuate France, Belgium, Luxembourg, and Alsace-Lorraine without delay. They agreed to surrender to the Allies an enormous amount of war materials, including most of Germany's naval vessels, and to return prisoners, money, and all valuables which they had taken from the occupied countries. They agreed to renounce the Treaty of Brest-Litovsk with Russia and the Treaty of Bucharest with Rumania.

In addition, the Allies reserved the right to occupy all German territory west of the Rhine as well as a strip of territory about 18 miles (29 kilometers) wide along the east bank of the Rhine (see map, page 231).

Wilson's Fourteen Points. An American expression of idealism as well as American fighting strength played a large part in breaking the Central Powers' will to fight. As you recall, in November 1917 the Bolsheviks seized control of Russia and shortly thereafter signed a peace treaty with Germany. At this time the Bolsheviks published a number of secret treaties that the Allies had drawn up at the beginning of the war. These secret treaties outlined in great detail how the Allies planned to divide the spoils of war if they defeated the Central Powers.

President Wilson chose this opportunity to lay before the world what he firmly believed was "the only possible program for world peace." Wilson's program, which he presented to Congress on January 8, 1918, included fourteen points, or principles.

The first group of points aimed to end the causes of modern war, as Wilson understood these causes. Specifically, he called for open, instead of secret, diplomacy; for freedom of the seas instead of their control by the strong naval powers; for removal of tariffs and other economic barriers between nations; for reduction of land weapons; and for temporary international control of colonies in place of the existing imperialism.

President Wilson also called for the liberation of peoples whose lands had long been ruled by Russia, Austria-Hungary, Germany, and Turkey. Among these peoples were the Poles, Czechs, Slovaks, and South Slavs. Wilson's proposal also included the people living in the German-held region of Alsace-Lorraine. These and other groups were to have the right of self-determination. That is, they were to decide for themselves the country in which they wished to live.

The Fourteenth Point was the heart of President Wilson's program. In it Wilson urged the creation of a "general association of nations" to give "mutual guarantees of political independence and territorial integrity to great and small states alike."

Influence of Wilson's program. The Fourteen Points and statements explaining them were printed during the war in the languages of the peoples of central Europe. They were dropped by plane into the heart of enemy country. All this publicity encouraged the Slavic peoples within Germany and Austria-Hungary to boycott the war efforts of their rulers and to speed up their own liberation. Even the German people read the Fourteen Points and found in them hope for a just and lasting peace rather than a continued regime of absolute rule and militarism.

As defeat pressed closer upon them, the German and Austrian peoples saw in the Fourteen Points an escape from the harsh penalties that the Allies would otherwise impose upon them. Thus when the great German military offensives failed in the summer of 1918, and when President Wilson made it clear that he would not negotiate with any German authority that was not representative of the people, the people of Germany and Austria-Hungary took steps to overthrow their rulers.

SECTION SURVEY

IDENTIFY: Bolsheviks, convoy, General Pershing, Marshal Foch, armistice, Fourteen Points, self-determination.

1. What contributions did the United States Navy make to winning the war?

2. Who considered the armistice terms of 1918 severe? Why?

3. (a) How did Wilson's Fourteen Points help win the war? (b) Why was the Fourteenth Point the heart of Wilson's program?

4. Map Study: Examine the map on page 231. (a) What do the black triangles represent? The red solid line? The red arrows? (b) Name and locate three major battles. (c) What is the approximate distance from the capital of France to the capital of Belgium?

5 The United States refuses to join the League of Nations

On November 11, 1918, almost everyone in America took the day off from work. Factories, offices, stores, and schools closed their doors. Americans, old and young, poured into the streets of every city and town and village across the land to celebrate the armistice that ended World War I. In a joyful statement to the press, President Wilson announced, "Everything for which America fought has been accomplished." So it seemed to him, and so it

seemed to Americans in general on November 11, 1918.

Three weeks later, on December 4, 1918, the army transport *George Washington* steamed out of New York harbor for Europe. Its most distinguished passenger was President Woodrow Wilson, bound for the peace conference at Paris.

Wilson hoped to persuade the other representatives at the conference to adopt the Fourteen Points that he had earlier outlined as "the only possible program for world peace."

The "Big Four." The peace conference, which opened on January 18, 1919, had much of the tension of a melodrama. The stage, however, was the world. The principal characters were the chief officials of the four leading powers — Great Britain, France, Italy, and the United States. The outcome of the drama would affect millions of people.

Wilson arrived at the conference after a triumphal journey through Great Britain, Italy, and France. Masses of people had turned out to greet the man who symbolized their hope for a better world. Encouraged by this reception, Wilson felt that he could use his great popularity to bring about a just peace based on his Fourteen Points. However, the three other leading delegates at Paris, supported by powerful interests in their homelands, had very different aims.

David Lloyd George, the British Prime Minister, had just won a general election by using such slogans as "Hang the Kaiser" and "Make Germany Pay." He had no intention of becoming unpopular with the British voters by showing generosity toward the Germans. He had no wish to give up England's naval supremacy and accept Wilson's idea of "freedom of the seas."

The "Tiger" of French politics, Premier Georges Clemenceau (ZHORZH klay·mahn·SOH), believed that the only way to defend France was to crush Germany. Italy's Vittorio Orlando wanted to acquire territory that had been secretly promised to Italy when it joined the Allies in 1915.

Secret treaties. The united opposition of Lloyd George, Clemenceau, and Orlando was not the only problem President Wilson faced. There was also the problem of secret treaties. In 1917 the Russian Bolsheviks published secret treaties that the Allies had made before

EUROPE BEFORE WORLD WAR I

EUROPE AFTER WORLD WAR I

the United States entered the war. The new Communist rulers of Russia hoped to discredit the Allies by exposing these treaties as "imperialist diplomacy."

Under these treaties the Allies agreed to divide the spoils of victory. Great Britain was to take over Germany's colonies, except for certain territories in the Pacific Ocean that were to go to Japan. (Japan had declared war on Germany in 1914.) France, Russia, Serbia, and Italy were to enlarge their national boundaries at the expense of Germany and Austria-Hungary. Finally, Germany was to make huge payments, called **reparations,** to the Allies to compensate for damages resulting from the war. These secret treaties contradicted several of Wilson's Fourteen Points, such as open diplomacy, national self-determination, and the end of colonialism.

Wilson's dilemma. Faced with these secret treaties and with the opposition of Lloyd George, Clemenceau, and Orlando, Wilson could either compromise or walk out of the Paris Peace Conference. Indeed, at one point he almost did walk out, but he realized that such a step might be regarded as a confession of failure. He was also afraid that communism might

spread from Russia into central Europe if a peace treaty were delayed and conditions remained unstable. His strongest reason for staying, however, was his faith in a League of Nations. Such a League, he was convinced, would in time remedy any injustices that the peace treaty might contain.

The Treaty of Versailles. The final peace treaty, called the Treaty of Versailles, was completed and signed late in June 1919. The treaty showed the results of bargaining between Wilson on one side and Lloyd George, Clemenceau, and Orlando on the other.

The Treaty of Versailles and related treaties made important changes in the map of the world. Germany's colonies were given to the Allied victors, but under a **mandate system.** This system required the new owners to account for their colonial administration to the League of Nations.

Certain border areas of pre-war Germany were lopped off. One important area, Alsace-Lorraine, was returned to France. Other areas were included in a new country, Czechoslovakia, and in a recreated Poland. To satisfy the nationalist desires of various peoples in eastern Europe, several other independent states were created. These included Finland, Estonia, Latvia, Lithuania, and Yugoslavia. Certain border changes were made for Italy, Greece, Rumania, and Belgium (see maps, page 234).

Under the Treaty of Versailles, the German government had to accept full responsibility for starting the war and had to agree to remain disarmed. Germany also agreed to pay large reparations for war damage.

Wilson realized that vengeance and greed were weak foundations for a lasting peace, and he successfully opposed some of the more unreasonable Allied demands. Moreover, he had the great personal satisfaction of seeing the Covenant of the League of Nations written into the Treaty of Versailles.

The League of Nations. The League of Nations, with headquarters at Geneva, Switzerland, provided international machinery to make war less likely. The machinery consisted of (1) a permanent Secretariat, or administrative and secretarial staff; (2) an Assembly, in which each member nation had one vote; and (3) a Council, the all-important executive body. The Council had five permanent members—the five great powers of France, Great Britain, Italy, Japan, and the United States. Other nations were also represented by means of rotating membership. Germany and the Soviet Union (Russia) were excluded from League membership. Closely related to the League were the Permanent Court of International Justice and other agencies. They dealt with such issues as reducing armaments and improving conditions of health and labor throughout the world.

The League Covenant did not outlaw war. However, each League member agreed, before going to war, to make every effort to solve its difficulties in a friendly way and even then to wait during a "cooling off" period before striking a blow. If any member failed to do this, the other members might then decide, through the Council, to apply economic sanctions. This meant that they would refuse to trade with the offender. Moreover, the Council might go further and recommend the use of force against the aggressor nation. To forestall efforts to change the new map of the world by force, each League member was to guarantee the territorial integrity and political independence of every other member.

Weaknesses of the League. The League of Nations had several serious weaknesses. For

Representatives from 27 Allied Powers met in the mirrored Palace of Versailles, just outside Paris, to draw up the 1919 peace treaty. Woodrow Wilson, Georges Clemenceau, and David Lloyd George appear in the center of this painting.

one thing, taking action against an aggressor was almost impossible for several reasons. First, the term "aggressor" was not clearly defined. Second, the Council could only recommend that nations take action, but could not force them to act. Third, any Council member could block the wishes of the other members, because all important Council decisions had to be unanimous.

Another basic weakness of the League was its guarantee of existing political boundaries. When the map of Europe was redrawn, some peoples found that they were now part of a different nation—one that they did not want to belong to. These peoples had no way to secure further changes in their national boundaries.

A third weakness was the League's failure to provide adequate machinery for recommending solutions to economic problems that might lead to war. Trade rivalries, tariff barriers, and imperialism still existed, yet the League could not do much more than study such problems. Another weakness was exclusion of the Soviet Union and Germany from membership. Finally, the League was unable to tackle the problem of reducing armaments.

Despite its shortcomings, the League of Nations was a promising beginning in the difficult task of creating a new world order, dedicated to international peace and justice. In the 1930's about 60 nations belonged to the League. The League was bringing an important new ingredient into international affairs —the organized moral judgment of a majority of the nations of the world.

The Senate rejects the League. Early in July 1919, President Wilson returned from Paris to ask the Senate to approve the Treaty of Versailles and thus bring the United States into the League. The Senate shattered his hopes by rejecting the treaty. Senator Henry Cabot Lodge of Massachusetts, head of the Committee on Foreign Relations, and other Republican Senators opposed the League.

Many Americans thought that the Treaty of Versailles was unjust. They were unwilling to have the United States join a League that pledged its members to carry out the provisions of the treaty. Many Americans pointed with alarm to the article of the Covenant that pledged each member to guarantee the existing political boundaries of the other members. Americans argued that such a pledge might involve the United States in war.

Despite the opposition to the League of Nations, the Senate might have voted for it if Wilson had been willing to accept amendments proposed by Senator Lodge and his supporters. These amendments were designed to safeguard American interests and to prevent the United States from being drawn into European wars. Wilson believed, however, that these amendments would so weaken the League that it would become ineffective. He refused to compromise.

To win public support, Wilson traveled across the country making speeches in defense of the League. Finally, exhausted by the long strain, in the fall of 1919 he collapsed and for seven months lived in seclusion. His one remaining hope was that the public would support his cause by electing a Democratic President in the 1920 election. As you will read, the Republican landslide of that year and the election of President Harding seemed to indicate that Americans wanted to forget the League and world problems in general. They ignored Wilson when he warned, "Arrangements of the present peace cannot stand a generation unless they are guaranteed by the united forces of the civilized world."

The rise of Japanese, Italian, and German expansionism in the 1930's proved the accuracy of Woodrow Wilson's prophecy. For by that time, as you will read, the League of Nations had become too weak to prevent the outbreak of another world war.

SECTION SURVEY

IDENTIFY: "Big Four," reparations, Treaty of Versailles, mandate system, economic sanctions, Henry Cabot Lodge.

1. Compare the views of Wilson, Lloyd George, Clemenceau, and Orlando concerning the treaty of peace.

2. (a) Describe the structure of the League of Nations. (b) What machinery did the League set up for the prevention of war?

3. Describe some of the major weaknesses of the League.

4. (a) List two arguments presented by people who opposed the League. (b) What evidence is there that Americans generally agreed with these arguments?

5. Map Study: Using the maps on page 234, identify four ways in which the Treaty of Versailles changed the map of the world.

Chapter Survey

Summary: Tracing the Main Ideas

The outbreak of World War I in the summer of 1914 came as a blow to millions of Americans and other peoples throughout the world. During the opening years of the 1900's, great strides had been made toward international cooperation. Suddenly, in 1914, all hopes for peace were shattered under the blows of fierce national rivalries.

Despite America's desire to remain neutral, it became increasingly clear that the United States as a major power would not remain apart in a conflict involving the other great powers. Step by step the United States moved toward war and, in 1917, entered the conflict.

The war had far-reaching consequences for the American people. As "total" war it involved directly and deeply every man, woman, and child in the country and every part of life. It created a vast government bureaucracy to manage and control agriculture, labor, transportation, and the naval and military effort. Education, religion, and recreation were mobilized for the task of winning the war. The government directed and to a large extent controlled public opinion. Constitutional guarantees of freedom of speech and of the press were sometimes ruthlessly disregarded by the government in the name of "national security" and "Americanism."

In the United States and in other countries, war-weary people hailed the armistice of November 11, 1918, as a turning point in history. Hundreds of millions of people looked to the United States for leadership in the effort "to make the world safe for democracy." President Wilson reminded Americans that they had a major responsibility in the building of a lasting structure of peace. His advice went unheeded, however, and the United States turned its back on the League of Nations. During the 1920's and 1930's, the United States and the rest of the world disregarded the lessons of World War I. This neglect would lead, in 20 years, to the even more terrible bloodbath of World War II.

Inquiring into History

1. Why did the United States enter World War I?
2. What part did American troops play in the victory of the Allies?
3. The end of World War I brought with it a spirit of high idealism and hope to people throughout the world. Explain.
4. (a) How were the factors that led to World War I —nationalism, imperialism, international rivalries, and the balance-of-power system— related? (b) Did the Treaty of Versailles diminish any of these factors as a future cause of war? Explain.
5. (a) How was the League of Nations supposed to protect world peace? (b) Why did the United States not join the League?

Relating Past to Present

1. (a) Why are civil liberties often restricted during a period of crisis? (b) Have there been any recent instances of such restrictions?

2. Do other nations still look to the United States for leadership in the difficult task of building a peaceful world? Explain.

Developing Social Science Skills

1. Read excerpts from *Good-Bye to All That* by Robert Graves or *All Quiet on the Western Front* by Erich Maria Remarque, describing the fighting in World War I. (a) What does the author's attitude toward war seem to be? (b) How does the excerpt compare with your ideas about war? (c) What effects does fighting a war seem to have on individuals?
2. One method used by the government to encourage support of the war was the displaying of patriotic posters, such as the one shown on page 227. Create one or more posters that would have aroused Americans to serve their nation during the war either in the armed services or on the home front.
3. Create a cartoon depicting Wilson's failure to sell the League of Nations to the American people.

Unit Survey

For Further Inquiry

1. In acquiring overseas possessions, the United States was carrying on its tradition of "manifest destiny." Do you agree or disagree? Why?

2. How did Theodore Roosevelt interpret the power of the President in the area of foreign policy? Give evidence to support your answer.

3. How might you have felt about the control of Puerto Rico by the United States if you had been (a) an American farmer, (b) a citizen of Nicaragua, (c) a British merchant?

4. (a) Describe Wilson's 14 Points. (b) What was the reaction of Europe's leaders to them? (c) What factors might account for their reactions?

5. (a) Describe the United States' relations with Asia in the years 1898 to 1920. (b) Do they seem to be consistent with United States foreign policy in other parts of the world? Explain.

Activities and Projects

1. Study the timeline above. (a) Give two examples of "cause-and-effect" relationships shown on the timeline. Explain your examples. (b) Choose two other events on the timeline and add an event either before or after each one that will create a "cause-and-effect" relationship.

2. Read *All Quiet on the Western Front,* the well-known novel of the First World War. (a) What seems to be the author's attitude toward war? How can you tell? (b) How reliable is this novel as a source of information about World War I? Explain. (c) In what way is a novel a valuable source of information about an event or period in history?

3. Select one event in United States relationships with Latin America from 1898 to 1920. Write an account of the event as it might appear in a Latin American textbook for high school students.

4. Conduct research on one of these topics: (a) the role of blacks during World War I, (b) the role of women during World War I, (c) songs of World War I, (d) George Creel and the Committee of Public Information, (e) military technology of World War I.

5. Draw a map showing battles and other events of World War I that will illustrate why the war could be called a *world* war.

Exploring Your Region

1. Contact the local chapter of the Veterans of Foreign Wars or other veterans organization. Arrange to interview one or more veterans of World War I. Be sure to prepare your questions in advance. Perhaps the veteran would agree to let you tape the interview for presentation to your class.

2. Investigate the specific provisions of the Underwood-Simmons Tariff and find out about the economy of your region around 1913. How might the tariff have affected your region?

Suggested Reading

1. *Trail Blazer: Negro Nurse in the Red Cross,* Jean Pitrone. Story of a determined woman who became the first black nurse in the American Red Cross.

2. *The Making of a World Power,* Paul Angle, ed. Using many primary sources, this book tells the exciting story of the development of the United States into a world power.

3. *The Guns of August,* Barbara Tuchman. An award-winning history of the early days of World War I that reads like a novel.

4. *One of Ours,* Willa Cather. A novel of a young Nebraska man and how his life was transformed by World War I.

5. *They Came to Cordura,* Glencon Swarthout. A novel of the American expedition against Pancho Villa.

Unit Five

The "Golden Twenties" and the New Deal

1920 - 1941

Chapter 13

A Decade of Prosperity Ends in a Crash

1920-1932

The signing of the armistice on November 11, 1918, brought an end to World War I. It also marked the high point in Wilson's Presidential career. Democracy had triumphed. To many Americans, Wilson's vision of an orderly and peaceful world seemed about to become a reality.

The President's triumph was to be short-lived. During the next two years, he bore the heavy burden of frustration, shattered dreams, and broken health. Even before the armistice, in the Congressional elections on November 5, 1918, American voters revealed their dissatisfaction with Wilson's leadership by returning Republican majorities to both the House and the Senate. Two years later, in the elections of 1920, the voters of the country turned their backs completely on Wilson and the Democratic Party. They selected instead a Republican President, Warren G. Harding, to lead the nation.

During the 1920's three Republican Presidents—Harding, Calvin Coolidge, and Herbert Hoover—presided over a country that, on the whole, enjoyed a period of unparalleled prosperity. To be sure, there were hard times for many. Farmers suffered from higher operating costs and lower prices for their goods. Minorities still did not receive equal opportunities. Nevertheless, the nation's growing wealth was widely shared. By 1928, real wages were one third higher than they had been in 1914. Two out of three households owned automobiles.

But this era of the "Golden Twenties" ended with a stunning economic collapse. It was followed by the most shattering depression in American history.

THE CHAPTER IN OUTLINE

1. The Democrats lose popularity and face growing unrest.

2. Republicans assume responsibility for governing the country.

3. The Great Depression shatters the prosperity of the 1920's.

The Democrats lose popularity and face growing unrest

Before America's entry into the war, President Wilson had concentrated on his program of domestic reform. As you have read, his first administration, from 1913 to 1917, reduced tariffs, strengthened the antitrust laws, and established the Federal Reserve System. In these and other ways, Wilson tried to restore competition in American business and to protect consumers.

Even before the war, however, Wilson felt that the "New Freedom" program had largely achieved its goals. After the war he became deeply involved in organizing world peace. As a result, he had little time left for domestic affairs. Such problems included a postwar business slump, a decline in farm prices, and widespread unemployment.

Losing support at home. The American people, however, were tired of international issues. They were more interested in domestic affairs than in a peace treaty or a League of Nations. The Congressional elections of 1918, held just before the armistice, showed this. President Wilson appealed to the voters for a Democratic Congress. Instead, the voters elected a Republican majority in both the House and Senate.

When Wilson returned from the Versailles Conference in the summer of 1919, he found many Senators critical of the Covenant, or constitution, of the League of Nations. However, the President refused to compromise on the covenant's basic points and instead tried to win the public to his point of view.

Late in the summer of 1919, after three weeks of a grueling nationwide speaking tour, Wilson suffered a stroke. It left him partially paralyzed, and he remained an invalid until his death in 1924.

The postwar depression. Wilson's illness came at a time when the country was suffering from a severe postwar depression. With the signing of the armistice, the government began to cancel its wartime contracts. Wartime industries suddenly faced the problem of converting to peacetime production. New machinery had to be installed and new customers found. During the conversion, factories closed down or operated with greatly reduced labor forces.

Farmers also suffered during the transition from war to peace. As European farmland returned to normal production, the American farmers' wartime markets in Europe disappeared. Farm prices, which had soared during the war, dropped as competition increased. Wheat, for example, which had sold for as high as $2.26 a bushel (35.2 liters), dropped to less than $1 a bushel in 1922. Almost half a million American farmers, unable to pay their debts, lost their farms during this troubled period.

Wage earners also suffered. Many who had worked in government wartime agencies lost their jobs when the war ended. Hundreds of thousands of wage earners were thrown out of work when factories closed down or cut back operations. And the nation's war heroes were not spared. Many of the 4.5 million returning veterans could not find work.

As the depression deepened, as wages fell, and as more people lost their jobs, discontent swelled. To make things worse, the high cost of living rose even higher. In 1919 it climbed 77 percent above prewar levels. In 1920 it rose an additional 28 percent. Under such conditions, many workers resorted to strikes. During 1919 more than 4 million workers were at one time or another out on strike. Three strikes were especially serious.

The Boston police strike. On September 9 the Boston police force went on strike for higher wages and improved conditions, leaving the city without police protection. When rioting and looting broke out, the state guard was called in. The police force, realizing that the strike was lost, announced that they would return to their posts.

At this point, however, the Boston police commissioner refused to allow them to return to their jobs. He announced that he intended to hire a new police force. Governor Calvin Coolidge supported the commissioner. "There is no right," Coolidge flatly stated, "to strike against the public safety by anybody, anywhere, any time." Coolidge's statement was widely applauded. It brought him to public attention and helped him win the Republican Vice-Presidential nomination in 1920.

The coal strike. Less than two months after this police strike, on November 1, 1919, the United Mine Workers (U.M.W.) went out on strike. Led by their colorful and combative president John L. Lewis, they demanded higher wages and a shorter workweek. On November 9 United States Attorney General A. Mitchell Palmer secured an injunction ordering the officers of the U.M.W. to stop all activities tending to encourage the strikers.

However, the coal miners refused to return to work. Finally, on President Wilson's suggestion, the problem was submitted to a board of arbitration. The board gave the miners a 27-percent wage increase, but refused to consider a reduction in the weekly hours of work.

The steel strike. Discontent in the steel industry led to a strike involving more than 300,000 workers. The steelworkers had long been dissatisfied with their working conditions. In some plants they worked as long as 12 hours a day, 7 days a week. Moreover, they had not been able to form a union to bargain for them. During the summer of 1919, however, an A. F. of L. committee launched a vigorous organizing campaign in the steel towns. The strike started on September 22, 1919, after management refused to recognize the committee's right to speak for all steelworkers.

As the weeks passed, violence erupted around some of the steel mills. At Gary, Indiana, martial law was declared, and federal troops moved in to keep order. Finally, with public opinion running against the steelworkers, the strikers returned to their jobs in January 1920. Three years later, however, the steel companies agreed to the steelworkers' demand for an 8-hour day.

Labor's declining strength. The postwar depression did not last long. By early 1920 American export trade was soaring as orders for goods poured in from the war-devastated countries. The value of American exports rose to three times the 1913 level.

As economic conditions improved and jobs became more plentiful, many workers lost interest in unions. Membership in the A. F. of L., which had reached a peak of more than 4 million early in 1920, began to decline.

There were, of course, other reasons for the decline of the labor movement. The failure of the steel strike and of other strikes during 1919 discouraged workers. The use of the injunction, as in the strike of the United Mine Workers, was another discouraging factor. Also, Supreme Court decisions broadened the base for use of the injunction, restricted labor organizing activities, and ruled that legislation intended to improve working conditions was unconstitutional. Industrial management, moreover, launched a widely publicized campaign against the "union shop." In it labor unions were identified with socialism and communism. A "Red scare" that swept the country in 1919–20 caused many Americans, including many workers, to turn against organized labor.

Artist Ben Shahn was one who felt that Sacco and Vanzetti, two anarchists, were unjustly convicted of murder in 1921 because of their beliefs. His painting shows Sacco and Vanzetti after the execution with the judge and two of the trial's key witnesses.

The "Red scare." During the postwar years, federal and state governments conducted a vigorous drive against anarchists, Communists, and socialists. The Espionage Act, passed in wartime to punish treasonable or disloyal activities, remained in effect after the war. Under this law revolutionists and suspected revolutionists were arrested and fined. Some who were aliens were deported to the countries from which they had come.

One important reason for the postwar concern with radicals was the Russian Bolshevik Revolution of 1917. This event frightened many Americans who feared that radicals in the United States might try to follow the Bolshevik example. Rumors of revolutionary plots circulated widely from 1917 through 1920.

There was more than rumor to arouse alarm, even though radical leaders disapproved of acts of irresponsible violence. During the spring and summer of 1919, more than 30 bombs were discovered by postal authorities in packages addressed to prominent citizens. In New York City on September 16, 1920, a bomb exploded in crowded Wall Street at noontime, killing 38 persons and injuring hundreds.

Meanwhile, in the fall of 1919, Attorney General Palmer instructed agents in the Department of Justice to arrest radicals throughout the country. Among those arrested were several hundred aliens who were deported.

Many Americans, both Democrats and Republicans, criticized this drive against radicals, pointing out that many of the raids were conducted without search warrants. They argued that Attorney General Palmer's actions sometimes ignored the constitutional rights of free citizens.

The critics also directed their fire against state governments. During this postwar period, about one third of the states had passed laws to punish advocates of revolutionary change. By 1920 many Americans who had no sympathy with radicals were growing alarmed at the widespread violation of civil liberties. Leaders from both major political parties agreed with President Wilson that Americans could not solve their problems by trying to suppress unpopular political views.

SECTION SURVEY

IDENTIFY: John L. Lewis, Bolshevik Revolution.

1. (a) Describe the causes and nature of the depression that followed World War I. (b) How was the depression related to the many strikes that occurred in 1919?

2. During the Boston police strike, Governor Coolidge made this statement: "There is no right to strike against the public safety by anybody, anywhere, any time." (a) What did he mean? (b) Do you agree with his viewpoint? Why or why not?

3. Why did labor unions decline in the early 1920's?

4. (a) What conditions produced the "Red scare"? (b) Explain the arguments for and against the drive against radicals.

2 Republicans assume responsibility for governing the country

In the Presidential election of 1920, the country's unsettled condition gave the Republican candidate, Senator Warren G. Harding of Ohio, a clear advantage over his Democratic opponent, Governor James M. Cox of Ohio. Many voters blamed the administration in office for the troubled times, including the race riots and other minority problems. The Republicans' plea for a return to "normalcy" had great appeal. Many Americans were tired of Europe and its wars and tired of Wilson's attempts to "make the world safe for democracy." Business people were worried about the 1919 depression. Workers and farmers suffered from unemployment and falling prices.

The election of 1920. Warren G. Harding, the Republican candidate, was a genial Ohio newspaper owner who had climbed to the top of the political ladder in his own state. He had served as a United States Senator. Handsome and distinguished, with a warm, easygoing manner—much too easygoing, as it turned out—he had many friends in every walk of life.

Harding won the election with approximately 16 million votes to Cox's 9 million. The electoral vote was even more sweeping, giving Harding 404 to Cox's 127. Eugene V. Debs, the Socialist candidate, who was in prison for violating the Espionage Act, received nearly 1 million votes.

Farm relief and financial reform. Harding did not take over an easy job when he entered the White House. Late in 1920 a second postwar depression had hit the country. Farmers,

FLYING THE MAIL

Somebody plastered a postage stamp on actor Douglas Fairbanks's forehead before settling him on top of several bags of mail in the small plane. It was October 1918, and his flight from Washington, D.C., to New York was part of a publicity campaign to sell war bonds. After the flight Fairbanks scribbled his thanks to the pilot: "Handled with care—arrived right side up. Great trip."

Regular airmail service was just five months old. At this time the single route was between the nation's capital and its largest city. In 1921 a transcontinental route was tested, with a first flight that took over 33 hours. Gradually other routes were added until an airmail network crisscrossed the country.

Flying the mail in the 1920's was a serious business. Pilots rarely had companions, let alone famous ones. During the first few years, planes carrying mail flew only by day. In 1924, around-the-clock flights were started, with flashing beacons spaced every 25 miles (40 kilometers) to guide planes through the darkness. Even so, night flying was hazardous, for storms obscured beacons and landing fields were poorly lit.

The pilots who flew the mail in those early days needed nerves of iron. One of the best of them, Charles Lindbergh, had to abandon his plane and parachute to safety on four separate occasions in 1926. In a newspaper article of the time, the writer may have over-emphasized the romance, but certainly not the danger, of flying the mail:

Adventure rides with the United States mails today just as it did many years ago, when it went astride a wiry pony. Death lurks nearby just as it did when robbers and . . . Indians infested the lonely roads of the frontier. The means of transporting the mails have changed, but not the chances.

wage earners, business leaders, and the public in general were clamoring for government action and for President Harding's promised return to "normalcy."

Responding to widespread demands for help, Congress adopted the Emergency Tariff on May 27, 1921. This measure raised rates on some farm products but failed to raise farm prices generally. Congress also adopted the Budget and Accounting Act. This law was designed to reduce excessive spending and waste in government and to provide a more efficient method of handling government expenditures. It also created a Bureau of the Budget in the Treasury Department, with a director appointed by the President.

Up to this time, Congress had made annual appropriations on a piecemeal basis. No great concern was given to balancing the budget. Under the new system, all government agencies and departments had to submit annual requests for funds to the Director of the Budget. The director then drew up a detailed budget. Estimated income and expenditures for the coming **fiscal year**° were listed on this budget. The President submitted the budget to Congress. Congress could then raise or lower the estimates, if it so desired.

°**fiscal year:** the 12-month period considered as a year for general accounting and budgeting purposes. The fiscal year of the United States government begins on July 1.

Charles G. Dawes, the first Director of the Budget, was an extremely capable administrator. Under his leadership and that of the Secretary of the Treasury, Andrew W. Mellon, the government used surplus revenues to reduce the national debt. At the end of World War I, the debt totaled more than $25 billion. During the 1920's it was cut by about one third.

Some critics held that Mellon's financial measures reduced the taxes of the wealthy and placed too heavy a burden on the average wage earner, while checking a needed expansion of social services for the poor. However, most Americans approved of economy in government spending and of the reduction of the national debt.

War veterans. Congress also tackled the problem of the war veterans. Many war veterans as well as many other Americans felt that the government should provide "adjusted compensation" for veterans. These people pointed out that during the war members of the armed forces had risked their lives for low pay while workers at home earned high wartime wages in more or less safe jobs.

In 1921 Congress created the Veterans' Bureau. Harding then appointed Charles R. Forbes as its first director. The Veterans' Bureau handled veterans' claims for compensation and hospitalization, provided medical care for sick veterans, and administered the veterans' insurance program.

The Veterans' Bureau was only a partial answer to the demands of veterans. The American Legion, the Veterans of Foreign Wars, and other veterans' organizations continued to press for adjusted compensation. Congress responded in 1922 with a bonus bill. Harding vetoed the bill because it did not include any provision for raising the money to be spent.

The Fordney-McCumber Tariff. In 1922 Harding signed the Fordney-McCumber Act into law. The new tariff wiped out the reductions made in the Underwood Tariff of 1913 and set considerably higher rates on hundreds of manufactured products. It also continued the limited protection for farmers provided by the Emergency Tariff of 1921.

The Fordney-McCumber Tariff also authorized the President, under certain circumstances, to raise or lower any tariff rate by as much as 50 percent. As it turned out, most of the adjustments made were upward.

Public scandals. Despite some solid accomplishments, the Harding administration left a long, sorry record of corruption. Harding was not himself involved in the corruption. His mistake was in appointing certain undeserving men to office. His cabinet did contain such able and respected men as Charles Evans Hughes, the Secretary of State; Andrew W. Mellon, who headed the Treasury Department; and Herbert Hoover, the Secretary of Commerce. However, Harding's administration also contained dishonest politicians who disgraced his administration.

Self-seeking politicians known as the "Ohio Gang" placed one of their members, Harry M. Daugherty, in the cabinet as Attorney General. Daugherty used his position to protect persons who violated the Prohibition amendment. Another Harding official, Thomas W. Miller, defrauded the government in the sale of alien properties—that is, foreign-owned properties that were seized by the American government during World War I. Charles R. Forbes, the head of the Veterans' Bureau, could not satisfactorily account for $200 million spent by his organization.

The most famous scandal took its name from the naval oil reserve lands at Teapot

This cartoon shows the Senate washing out the "dirty linen" of the Harding administration. Several of President Harding's prominent political appointees were involved in the political scandals.

"The chief business of the American people is business," President Calvin Coolidge stated in 1925. Coolidge firmly believed that government should leave business to itself, without additional legal controls.

Dome in Wyoming. Secretary of the Interior Albert B. Fall persuaded the Secretary of the Navy, Edwin C. Denby, to transfer the Teapot Dome reserve and another oil reserve at Elk Hills, California, to Fall's jurisdiction. In return for bribes, Fall leased the oil reserves to private oil speculators.

Some hint of this corruption reached Harding early in 1923. However, the scandals did not become public until later, when Fall, Forbes, and Miller were prosecuted and imprisoned. Meanwhile, Harding's health broke under the strain, and he died in the summer of 1923 of a heart attack.

On Harding's death, Calvin Coolidge, the Vice-President, became President. Coolidge, a man of unquestioned honesty, helped to restore public confidence in the Republican Party.

The election of 1924. In the decade following their defeat in 1920, the Democrats gener-

ally failed to work out a clear-cut program to challenge the Republicans. They turned away from the spirit of reform that had marked Wilson's first administration. More and more the Democrats accepted the same conservative principles followed by the Republicans. As the years passed, it became difficult to distinguish between the two parties.

Only once during the 1920's did the Republican program face any serious opposition. Curiously enough, the opposition came in part from within Republican ranks.

The revolt broke out in 1924 when the Republicans nominated the staunchly conservative Calvin Coolidge for the Presidency. Coolidge believed that government should encourage, but not regulate, business. He also disapproved of special legislation to help workers or farmers.

Resisting these conservative policies, a group of progressive Republicans broke away and formed a new Progressive Party. They nominated Senator Robert M. La Follette of Wisconsin as their standard bearer. The Progressive Party received the backing of farmers, organized labor, and the socialists. The party called for federal credit and other assistance for farmers, and social legislation and additional laws to protect the rights of labor. In addition it advocated government ownership of railroads and water-power resources.

La Follette received almost 5 million votes, the largest number any third party had ever mustered. La Follette died shortly after the campaign, however, and the Progressive Party lost its strength and faded into insignificance.

The Democrats in 1924 nominated John W. Davis, a conservative corporation lawyer. During his campaign Davis concentrated on the scandals of the Harding era. The Republicans met this challenge by claiming credit for the prevailing prosperity, and this claim proved effective. Despite the Progressive revolt, which split the Republicans into two factions, Coolidge won the election by a landslide. He piled up 382 electoral votes to 136 for Davis and just 13 for La Follette.

Thrift in government. In a period of extravagance and "big money," Coolidge became a symbol of the thrifty, old-fashioned, simple country American. He emphasized thrift in government.

In 1924 Congress passed a bonus bill that provided adjusted compensation for all veterans except those with ranks above captain. The payments were not to be given in cash but in the form of a paid-up 20-year life insurance policy. Veterans who held the policy for 20 years would receive full compensation. In the name of economy, Coolidge vetoed the bonus bill, but Congress passed this bill over his veto.

Coolidge also vetoed a bill to stabilize farm prices by allowing the government to buy up farm surpluses and sell them abroad.

In other matters, too, Congress and the President disagreed, but the President remained popular. "Keep Cool with Coolidge" was a slogan of the day. He probably could have been re-elected in 1928, but a year before the election he announced that he did not choose to run.

The election of 1928. The Republicans then nominated Herbert C. Hoover of California. Hoover was a successful mining engineer with a notable record as administrator of food relief in Europe during and after the war and as Secretary of Commerce after 1921.

The Democrats nominated New York's governor Alfred E. Smith. Smith advocated a federal farm-relief program and also urged stricter regulation of public utilities. These planks in the Democratic platform had strong appeal for many Americans. However, Smith had political handicaps that cost him support within his own party. He was opposed to Prohibition, he was a Roman Catholic, and he had ties with the Tammany political machine in New York City. All these things made him unpopular with large groups of voters, especially in the South and West.

Hoover received 444 electoral votes to Smith's 87. Smith lost his own state of New York. In addition he lost several traditionally Democratic states in the South that for the first time since the Civil War gave their votes to a Republican.

Herbert C. Hoover. President Hoover expressed his political beliefs in the phrase "rugged individualism." His general point of view was very close to Harding's idea of "normalcy" and to Coolidge's belief that government should encourage business but not give special assistance to individuals. Hoover, however, displayed greater imagination than his Republican predecessors. He believed that experts in fields other than government could make important contributions to government.

He also believed that the government should take some part in planning for the social and economic development of the nation.

When Hoover took office, he looked forward to a long period of increasing prosperity. He believed that Americans now expected more than the necessities of life. "The slogan of progress," he declared, "is changing from the full dinner pail to the full garage." For about six months, booming business and heavy consumer buying seemed to bear out Hoover's optimistic prediction.

SECTION SURVEY

IDENTIFY: return to "normalcy," "Ohio Gang," Teapot Dome scandal, Robert La Follette, Alfred E. Smith, "rugged individualism."

1. How did Coolidge's election to the Presidency in 1924 reflect the temper of the times?
2. Despite some solid accomplishments, the Harding administration left a long, sorry record of corruption. Explain.
3. Compare the elections of 1924 and 1928 in terms of (a) parties, (b) candidates, (c) issues, and (d) results.
4. Cartoon Study: Look closely at the cartoon on page 245. (a) What do the elephant and donkey represent? (b) In a sentence or two, explain the meaning of the cartoon.

3 **The Great Depression shatters the prosperity of the 1920's**

Flourishing business conditions and a rising standard of living contributed to the political success of the Republican Party during the 1920's. Between 1922 and 1929, jobs were plentiful. Americans on the whole were better fed, clothed, and housed than ever before.

"Easy money." During the prosperity of the so-called "Golden Twenties," many Americans made and spent money with ease. Millions of workers received relatively high wages and many businesses earned large profits. An ever-growing number of stockholders received substantial dividends.

As Americans bought more and more consumer goods, the retail trade recorded ever-increasing sales. Some of the business profits supported expansion and new product research. Some paid for workers' recreational facilities, some for company programs providing insurance and pensions for employees. Large sums flowed into medical research, education, and the welfare of the poor.

As surplus income piled higher and higher, more and more Americans were tempted to invest their savings or their profits in the stock market, hoping for big returns.

Not all Americans shared in the prosperity of the "Golden Twenties." This was notably true of Indians, Spanish-speaking Americans, and most blacks. Many workers lost their jobs when new machines were installed in factories. Some, such as blacksmiths and harness makers, whose skills were no longer needed, found it difficult to adapt to the monotonous work on assembly lines. Furthermore, some industries —such as coal, textiles, and leather—never fully recovered from the postwar slump of the early 1920's.

Falling farm income. Finally, many farmers did not share in the general prosperity. One of their problems was a shrinking market for farm products. After 1918, as you recall, American farmers lost many of their wartime European markets. Moreover, during the 1920's Congress passed laws that almost ended immigration into the United States. As a result of these laws, American farmers lost a traditional source of new customers. Although the markets were shrinking, farm production—aided by new machines and techniques—rose by more than 20 percent between 1919 and 1929.

With fewer people able or willing to buy food and with more food available, farm prices dropped. While the farm prices were falling, the prices of industrial goods that the farmers needed rose higher and higher. Many farmers found it increasingly hard to meet their mortgage payments or the payments on their farm machines. Thus during the industrial prosperity of the 1920's, many farmers sank deeper and deeper into debt, and many lost their farms. The situation of sharecroppers and tenants, white and black alike, was even worse than that of the small farmers.

Effort to aid farmers. By the end of the 1920's, the nation's farm economy had deteriorated to the point that the government could no longer afford to ignore it. President Hoover gave his support to the Agricultural Marketing Act, which was adopted in the summer of 1929. This act created a Federal Farm Board with power to lend up to $500 million to cooperative farm groups to help them store crops during years when a surplus of farm products brought falling prices. The theory was that the farmers could sell their stored products later when prices went back up. Unfortunately, surpluses continued year after year and prices continued to fall. In the end the Farm Board used up its financial resources without bolstering farm income.

Prosperity ends in the crash. In spite of the failing agricultural economy, few Americans other than the farmers and those at the bottom of the economic ladder were concerned about the nation's economic health. Most Americans believed, with Herbert Hoover, that "we in America are nearer to the final triumph over poverty than ever before in the history of any land." Given this widely shared belief, the depression that started late in 1929 came as a stunning blow to most Americans.

SOURCES

HERBERT HOOVER'S "RUGGED INDIVIDUALISM" SPEECH (1928)

During one hundred and fifty years we have built up a form of self-government and a social system which is peculiarly our own. It differs essentially from all others in the world. It is the American system. It is just as definite and positive a political and social system as has ever been developed on earth. It is founded upon a particular conception of self-government in which decentralized local responsibility is the very base. Further than this, it is founded upon the conception that only through ordered liberty, freedom, and equal opportunity to the individual will his initiative and enterprise spur on the march of progress. And in our insistence upon equality of opportunity has our system advanced beyond all the world. . . .

Newspapers across the country chronicled the stock market crash of 1929. The superimposed picture shows the sad crowds that clustered around the Stock Exchange, vainly hoping to salvage some of their investments.

For years the prices of stocks had been moving upward. After Hoover's election in November 1928, moreover, a frenzy of speculation gripped the country. Convinced that they were entering "four more years of prosperity," investors bought feverishly. Despite repeated warnings that stock prices were too high, Americans, rich and middle class alike, invested in stocks, often on credit. During most of 1929, stock prices soared to ever higher levels.

The stock market crash. Then the bubble burst. On October 24, 1929, a panic of selling hit the New York Stock Exchange as frantic orders to sell stock came pouring in. The causes of this panic were chiefly overproduction and overspeculation. More goods had been produced than could be profitably sold. A great many stocks were either worthless or wildly inflated. That is, either the businesses behind such stocks existed on paper only, or the actual value of the stocks was far less than their market value.

Overproduction and overspeculation had caught up with the American people. The inflated prices of stocks tumbled downward. On October 29, prices sank to a shattering new low when over 16 million shares of stock were dumped on the market. By mid-November the average value of leading stocks had been cut in half, and stockholders had lost $30 billion. With this crash of the stock market, the Great Depression started.

At first business and government leaders tried to reassure the American people. "Business is fundamentally sound," announced Secretary of the Treasury Mellon. Such words, no matter how reassuring, could not stem the tide of economic disaster sweeping the country.

The Great Depression. Before 1929 ended, banks all over the nation were closing their doors. Businesses everywhere cut back production, and many concerns, finding themselves without customers, were forced out of business. Factories and mines were shut down. Empty railroad cars piled up on the sidings. By 1930 between 6 and 7 million Americans were un-

249

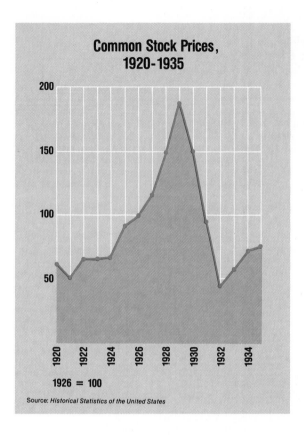

Common Stock Prices, 1920-1935

200

150

100

50

1920 1922 1924 1926 1928 1930 1932 1934

1926 = 100

Source: *Historical Statistics of the United States*

employed. The result was a chain reaction. Unemployment meant fewer customers; a decrease in customers caused further cutbacks in production; these cutbacks, in turn, resulted in more unemployment. By 1932 nearly 12 million Americans were out of work.

The depression struck at all classes. Many well-to-do Americans helplessly watched their fortunes, invested in stocks or businesses, disappear. The industrial workers and the farmers suffered most. Most wage earners had no savings to tide them over a period of unemployment. In every city thousands of unfortunate men and women stood in lines to get free meals of bread and soup. Families forced out of their homes moved to makeshift huts that they built on unused land at the edges of the city. Such huts were often made of scrap lumber, packing boxes, and corrugated iron.

For the farmers the depression came as a final blow. Between 1929 and 1932, farm prices fell lower and lower, and more and more farmers lost their farms to their creditors. In some midwestern states, desperate farmers used force to prevent sheriffs from foreclosing mortgages on their farms.

Many thousands of jobless people from cities and farms wandered over the land seeking jobs at any wages, hitchhiking or riding in freight trains and sleeping on park benches. Never had America known such widespread suffering.

Causes of the depression. There is no simple way to explain the Great Depression. President Hoover insisted that the major cause was the worldwide economic disorder that followed World War I. Many economists agreed. They pointed to the vast destruction of property during the war and the worldwide dislocation of trade during and after the war.

Other economists argued that America's high tariff policies helped to stifle world trade and hurt American business. High tariffs, they claimed, prevented other countries from selling their goods in the United States. This in turn prevented them from securing the dollars that they needed to buy American products.

Still other economists blamed the depression on the excessive borrowing of money—for stocks, for comforts purchased on the installment plan, or for the expansion of businesses. These critics also claimed that the federal government failed to control bank loans and to protect the public against the sale of stocks that had no value.

Some economists have argued that depressions are an inevitable part of the American economic system. According to this view, business expands during periods of prosperity in order to obtain the largest possible profits. When factories produce more goods than consumers can buy, the factories have to cut down on production, at least until their surpluses are consumed. For this reason, these economists have argued, prosperity and depression are inevitable parts of the business cycle.

Finally, some economists have traced the Great Depression to uneven distribution of income. These economists have argued that if farmers had received better prices for their products and if workers had received higher wages, the American people would have been able to buy a larger proportion of the surplus goods. Had this happened, these economists claim, the factories would have kept busy and the depression could have been avoided.

Hoover and the depression. The depression confronted the Hoover administration with two emergencies. First, there was the widespread misery of people without jobs or farms, without money to buy enough food or clothing, and increasingly without hope. Some Americans urged the federal government to extend direct relief to those in need. Hoover, however, believed that direct aid was a responsibility of local communities. Direct federal relief, he said, would create a vast, inefficient bureaucracy and undermine the self-respect of the persons receiving it. Unfortunately, local communities did not have the resources to cope with the ever-rising tide of human misery.

To the second emergency, the collapse of business and agriculture, Hoover responded more actively. He instructed the Farm Board to buy up agricultural surpluses in an effort to raise falling farm prices. With the support of Congress, he started several public works programs, among them Boulder Dam (later called Hoover Dam) on the Colorado River. These projects were intended to stimulate business and provide employment for jobless workers.

Also at Hoover's urging, Congress created the Reconstruction Finance Corporation (RFC) in February 1932. The RFC could lend large sums of money to banks, life insurance companies, railroads, farm mortgage associations, and other enterprises. Hoover hoped that federal loans would strengthen these key businesses and thus provide jobs for millions of workers. Although the RFC advanced nearly $2 billion in loans to American business before the end of the Hoover administration, the depression grew worse.

In response to a recommendation by Hoover, Congress also passed the Home Loan Bank Act in July 1932. This act created a series of special banks designed to provide financial assistance to savings banks, building and loan associations, and insurance companies—all of which lent money on mortgages. By providing financial aid to such institutions, Hoover hoped to reduce foreclosures on homes and farms as well as to stimulate the construction of residential buildings.

In adopting these measures, the President and Congress were accepting, for the first time, the idea that the government had to assume certain responsibilities when the nation's economy suffered a serious setback. Unfortunately, the measures adopted did not stop the downward trend.

The election campaign of 1932. In the summer of 1932, the Republicans renominated

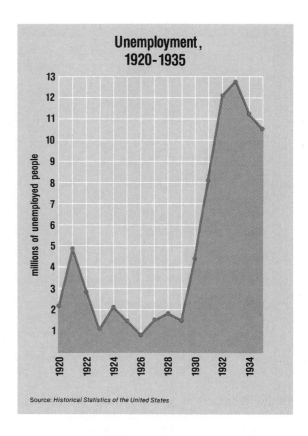

Herbert Hoover for President. As their candidate the Democrats chose Franklin Delano Roosevelt of New York.

Roosevelt had extensive political experience. He had served as a state senator in New York and as Assistant Secretary of the Navy. In 1920 he had been the Democratic nominee for Vice-President. In 1921 Roosevelt had been stricken with polio. Paralyzed from the waist down, he fought back to regain partial use of his legs. Roosevelt then regained the attention of the nation while serving as governor of New York.

There was really only one important issue in the campaign—the depression. Hoover continued to blame the depression on international conditions. He declared that his policies were beginning to bring recovery and that Roosevelt's would destroy the American system.

Both of these claims were rejected by Roosevelt. He maintained that Republican policies, not international conditions, were to blame for the depression. He argued that the federal government should help provide direct relief to the needy and direct aid to farmers. He called for a

Auto license tags like this one aimed to show the stand that the 1932 Democratic candidates, Franklin Delano Roosevelt and John Nance Garner, took favoring repeal of the Eighteenth Amendment that banned the sale of alcohol.

broad program of public works. He also demanded that safeguards be set up to prevent wild speculation and fraudulent issues of stock. To accomplish this he proposed laws to protect the bank depositor, the purchaser of stocks, and the homeowner. Referring to the unemployed workers, the desperate farmers, and others, Roosevelt stated that these "forgotten" Americans "at the bottom of the economic pyramid" had to have a "new deal."

Roosevelt's victory. Roosevelt and his running mate, John Nance Garner of Texas, won a sweeping victory in 1932, with Roosevelt winning 23 million popular votes to Hoover's 16 million. Roosevelt carried 42 states and piled up 472 electoral votes to Hoover's 59.

Moreover, the Democrats secured decisive majorities in both houses of Congress. These Democratic victories meant that Roosevelt's programs would have strong support in Congress.

A majority of voters throughout the 1920's had given the Republicans credit for the prosperity of those years. Now a great many Americans seemed to be saying that the Republicans would have to take the blame for the depression. Many of those who voted for the Democrats were really voting against Hoover rather than for Roosevelt. Many more saw in Roose-

velt the kind of dynamic personality that they believed was needed to lead the country out of its troubles.

Roosevelt had promised the American people a "new deal." During the four months between Election Day and Inauguration Day—March 4, 1933—workers, farmers, and even many business leaders waited hopefully to see how the new President would carry out his campaign pledge.

SECTION SURVEY

IDENTIFY: stock market crash, depression, RFC, Home Loan Bank Act, Franklin D. Roosevelt.

1. How do economists explain the major causes of the Great Depression?

2. (a) What measures did Hoover take to combat the depression? (b) How did these measures reflect his philosophy of government and the role it should take in economic affairs?

3. According to the 1920 census, more Americans were living in cities than on farms. How does this fact relate to the hardships experienced by the "little people" with the coming of the depression?

4. Graph Study: Look at the graphs on pages 250 and 251. How do they illustrate the events that are described in this section?

252

Chapter Survey

Summary: Tracing the Main Ideas

The joyous celebrations of victory that followed the signing of the armistice on November 11, 1918, soon came to an end. In 1919 and 1920, the United States was troubled by two short but severe postwar depressions, plus serious labor unrest and feverish concern over what was termed a "radical" threat to the country. During this period America's minorities suffered from renewed prejudice and discrimination.

By 1921, however, Americans were beginning to enjoy a decade of unparalleled prosperity. During the "Golden Twenties," as the decade was called, business activity reached an all-time high and relatively few Americans were unemployed.

Here and there warning voices called attention to the difficulties faced by large numbers of farmers and to other weaknesses of the economic system. For the most part, however, Americans were willing to believe that prosperity had come to stay.

Then, toward the end of 1929, the great industrial machine that the United States had built up began to grind to a halt. At first people refused to believe that the situation was serious. However, as the months passed, increasing numbers of businesses failed. Millions of Americans lost their jobs, farms, homes, and their life's savings. It became clear that the nation was confronted with a crisis of major proportions.

What was wrong?

Americans did not agree on all the answers to this very important question. They did agree that something had to be done to save the country from complete economic collapse.

In such an atmosphere, the election campaign of 1932 was fought. With the victory of Franklin Delano Roosevelt and the Democratic Party, Congress began a series of experiments that together came to be referred to as the "New Deal."

Inquiring into History

1. Why were Americans more interested in domestic affairs than in international relations in the year 1920?
2. Was the "Red scare" the first experience of this kind in American history? Explain.
3. During the Boston police strike, Governor Coolidge made the following statement: "There is no right to strike against the public safety by anybody, anywhere, any time." What did he mean? Do you agree or disagree with this viewpoint? Why?
4. The Fordney-McCumber Tariff of 1922 established high tariff rates. (a) How did this tariff affect foreign countries? (b) How did it affect American industries? (c) How did it affect American farmers?
5. When the cost of living goes up, how does it affect (a) buying power and (b) people living on fixed incomes?
6. Speaking in the 1920's, Herbert Hoover said, "We in America are nearer to the final triumph over poverty than ever before in the history of any land." (a) What facts supported his opinion? (b) Why were some Americans critical of his view?
7. Why was the Republican Party so successful in electing its candidates during the 1920's?

Relating Past to Present

1. Is it fair to blame or praise a President or a political party for (a) a war, (b) a depression, or (c) prosperity? Explain.
2. Compare the position of farmers in the 1920's with that of farmers today. Consider such factors as (a) the number of farmers, (b) the percentage of farmers in the population, (c) farm income, and (d) government farm programs.

Developing Social Science Skills

1. Find out more about the Sacco-Vanzetti trial which finally led to the execution of the two anarchists. (a) Where did they live? (b) What were their backgrounds? (c) Their beliefs? (d) Why did some people think they were innocent? (e) What do you think?
2. Interview one or more people who lived during the 1920's and 1930's to learn their impressions of each decade. Be sure to prepare your questions in advance of the interview. You might ask the following questions: (a) In what ways did your life change after the depression began? (b) Where did you live? (c) How did you spend each day? (d) What did you think should be done to end the depression?

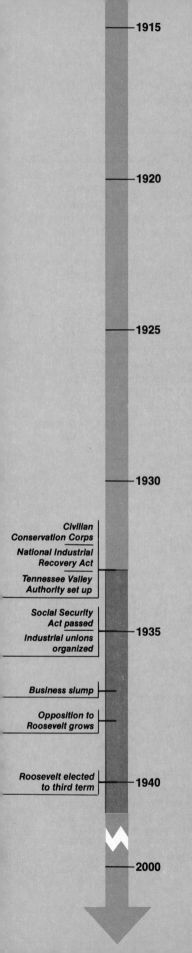

Chapter 14

The Great Depression and the New Deal

1933–1941

President Franklin Delano Roosevelt took office on March 4, 1933, at the height of the Great Depression. He began his administration with a ringing call to the American people to face the future with courage and faith. "The only thing we have to fear is fear itself," he confidently stated. His calm words helped to lift the nation from its despair and to rally the people behind the new administration.

The President outlined his New Deal program in a crisp, dramatic Inaugural Address. He then presented his proposals, with recommendations for immediate action, to a special session of Congress. He had called for this session himself upon taking office.

The New Deal had three general aims—relief, recovery, and reform. Because the American people were clamoring for action, the three aims were often mixed together as objectives of a single act of Congress. Sometimes measures adopted to realize one of the aims interfered with other measures designed to achieve the other aims.

The New Deal was interrupted by America's entry into World War II. But for eight years, from 1933 to 1941, a seemingly endless series of New Deal measures poured out of Washington. Each measure was meant in some way to contribute to the restoration of the nation's social, economic, and political health.

THE CHAPTER IN OUTLINE

1. New Deal measures provide relief and speed recovery.

2. Recovery measures stimulate agriculture and industry.

3. The New Deal carries out reform measures.

4. Opposition increases toward New Deal policies and programs.

5. New Deal reforms continue despite growing criticism.

6. The New Deal's great experiment comes to an end.

1 New Deal measures provide relief and speed recovery

By 1933 the American people had endured two full years of the depression. Each year, each month, each week, the situation had become increasingly desperate.

"I am afraid," Charles M. Schwab, chairman of the Bethlehem Steel Corporation said. "Every man is afraid."

These were true words. Rich and poor alike, Americans lived in growing fear. Despair was widespread throughout the nation. "We are at the end of our rope," retiring President Hoover declared on his last day in office. "There is nothing more we can do."

Restoring confidence. Fortunately, the incoming President, Franklin D. Roosevelt, did not share this fear. In his Inaugural Address, he challenged Americans to rise above their fear. Speaking in a strong, calm, confident voice, he promised "action, and action now."

Roosevelt's confidence was contagious. He had been in the White House only two months when Will Rogers, one of America's most popular humorists, expressed the feeling generally held throughout the nation. "The whole country is with him, just so he does something," Rogers declared. "If he burned down the Capitol, we would cheer and say, 'Well, we at least got a fire started anyhow.'"

President Roosevelt did indeed "get a fire started." On March 5, 1933, his first full day in the White House, he rolled his wheelchair into the Oval Office and began the "New Deal" for "the forgotten man." One of his first acts was to call a special session of Congress. During the next hundred days, he sent fifteen messages to the Congress, which responded by adopting fifteen major relief and recovery measures.

Restoring the banking system. On March 4, when Roosevelt took office, the nation's economic system was paralyzed. For months people had been selling stocks and rushing to the banks to withdraw their money before the banks failed. Throughout the country people were hiding their money in mattresses, under carpets, and in other places they considered safe. As a result of this run on the banks, many banks failed. Others closed their doors in an effort to avoid failure. With so many banks closed, the everyday business life of the nation ground to a halt. People could not pay their

In 1933, throngs of depositors like these in Ohio gathered to learn the fate of their savings. Many banks had failed. Others closed to avoid failure. Eventually the government stepped in and took action to protect the depositors.

FRANKLIN D. ROOSEVELT'S
FIRST INAUGURAL ADDRESS
(1933)

So, first of all, let me assert my firm belief that the only thing we have to fear is fear itself —nameless, unreasoning, unjustified terror which paralyzes needed efforts to convert retreat into advance. . . .

Our greatest primary task is to put people to work. This is no unsolvable problem if we face it wisely and courageously.

It can be accomplished in part by direct recruiting by the government itself, treating the task as we would treat the emergency of a war, but at the same time, through this employment, accomplishing greatly needed projects to stimulate and reorganize the use of our natural resources.

Hand in hand with this, we must frankly recognize the overbalance of population in our industrial centers and, by engaging on a national scale in a redistribution, endeavor to provide a better use of the land for those best fitted for the land. . . .

In the field of world policy I would dedicate this nation to the policy of the good neighbor— the neighbor who resolutely respects himself and, because he does so, respects the rights of others—the neighbor who respects his obligations and respects the sanctity of his agreements in and with a world of neighbors. . . .

---

bills by checks. There was not enough currency in circulation to meet the everyday needs of even a depressed economy.

On March 5 President Roosevelt issued a proclamation closing every bank in the nation for an indefinite period. The newly convened Congress then rushed through emergency banking laws forbidding any bank to reopen until it could prove its ability to carry on business without endangering its customers' deposits. Most banks were able to satisfy the financial authorities in the Treasury Department and quickly reopened.

In order to make sure people would never again lose their bank savings, Congress in June created the Federal Deposit Insurance Corporation (FDIC). The FDIC insured individual bank deposits up to $2,500. (The amount insured by the FDIC has been increased through the years to the present figure of $100,000.)

Cheaper dollars. Congress also authorized the Secretary of the Treasury to call in all gold coins and gold certificates then in circulation. With this action Congress abandoned the gold standard, which in the past had meant that all paper currency was redeemable in gold. In so doing Congress devalued the dollar. The administration hoped that cheaper dollars would help the farmers by forcing agricultural prices upward. In this respect, however, the measure was a disappointment.

Pump priming. In its efforts to revive the nation's economy, the New Deal followed a procedure called "pump priming." When the pump in a well does not draw water, it is sometimes necessary to prime the pump by pouring a little water down the well shaft. This water seals the crack around a washer in the shaft and thus helps to create a vacuum into which the well water rises so that it can be pumped up.

Roosevelt's administration planned to pump money into the nation's economy through federal loans and spending. The hope was that such action would stimulate the flow of more money.

One of the major pump-priming agencies was the Reconstruction Finance Corporation. The RFC had been started in Hoover's administration (see page 251). Under Roosevelt it continued to pour huge sums into the nation's economy. It did this in the form of loans totaling $11 billion to railroads, banks, insurance firms, and industrial enterprises. Much of this money was quickly repaid.

Direct relief for the unemployed. In addition to emergency measures to reopen the banks and to get more money into circulation, the New Deal provided direct relief to jobless, hungry Americans.

By 1933 nearly 14 million men and women were out of work. In response, the Roosevelt administration immediately launched what seemed at the time to be a colossal program of direct relief. In two years federal agencies distributed $3 billion to the states. Local authorities were allowed to use the money as they chose—to provide direct relief or jobs. At one time nearly 8 million families were on direct relief. However, few Americans liked this

CRITIC WITH A LASSO

He would amble out on stage wearing cowboy gear, a loose cowlick of hair falling over his forehead. He might do a few simple rope tricks with the lariat he always carried. But the important part of any appearance by Will Rogers was the talk—his dry, humorous comments on current events. He spoke sense so appealingly— not only on the stage but also on the radio and in a weekly newspaper column—that he once received 22 votes for President at a Democratic convention.

Will Rogers, born in Oklahoma in 1879 (he was part Cherokee), tackled almost any subject in the news. About taxation he said, "Income tax has made more liars out of the American people than golf has." On automobiles: "Ah, for the good old days, when you lived until you died and not until you were just run over." On men and women: "You know, women always could endure more than men. Not only physically, but mentally—did you ever get a peek at some of the husbands?"

It was politics that brought out the best, and sharpest, in the homespun humorist. "This President business," he wrote, "is a pretty thankless job. Washington, or Lincoln either, didn't get a statue until everybody was sure they was dead." Congress came in for a big share of ridicule: "All I can say about the United States Senate is that it opens with a prayer and closes with an investigation." And again: "America has the best politicians money can buy."

Few people ever took offense at Rogers's gibes. There was no malice behind them. He is probably best remembered for something he said about himself: "I joked about every prominent man of my time, but I never met a man I didn't like."

kind of help. What the unemployed wanted were jobs, and plans were made to replace direct relief with programs to provide work.

Work relief. The federal government attacked this problem in several ways. For instance, during 1933–34 it paid nearly $1 billion in wages to men and women on relief lists who were given jobs on "make-work" projects. Many of these projects—raking leaves and picking up litter in parks—had relatively little value. Critics of the New Deal called this kind of work "boondoggling."

President Roosevelt and other New Dealers knew that federal charity and "make-work" projects were at best necessary evils. What Americans needed and what the New Dealers wanted to provide was socially useful work. To this end, a new agency, the Works Progress Administration (WPA) was created in 1935, with Harry L. Hopkins as its head. The WPA cooperated with state and local governments, which shared in both the cost and the administration of the work relief program.

The WPA helped people in many different ways. By 1936 more than 6,000 schoolhouses had been constructed or repaired; new sewage plants had been built in 5,000 communities; about 128,000 miles (206,000 kilometers) of secondary roads had been constructed or improved. Many other public improvements had been made as well. Unemployed actors, musicians, and writers enriched American life by providing plays, concerts, guidebooks, and other forms of recreation. At the peak of its activity, in March 1936, nearly 4 million Americans were working for the WPA.

Work for youth. Perhaps the greatest tragedy of the depression was its effect upon millions of young Americans. Many were forced to leave school or college because they lacked food and clothing or were homeless. Those who graduated during the depression years faced unemployment. Thousands of jobless young Americans roamed across the nation in search of work.

Two agencies were created to bring immediate work relief to the nation's youths. In 1933 the Civilian Conservation Corps (CCC) was organized. At times as many as 500,000 young men between 18 and 25 were enrolled in the CCC. Nearly all of them were unmarried; most came from poverty-stricken families. These youths lived in work camps scattered across the land in which they received food, clothing, and shelter. They were also paid wages, which they were expected to share with their families. In the CCC they had opportunities for recreation and education.

The young Americans in the CCC did socially useful work. They built fire trails in the forests, cleared swamps, planted trees, built small dams for flood control, cleared land for public parks, and in other ways helped to conserve the nation's natural resources.

A second New Deal work relief measure aided young people who were still in school. The National Youth Administration (NYA), created in 1935, distributed federal money to needy students willing to work. These students were paid regular wages for performing useful tasks in and around their school. During its first year, the NYA gave jobs to more than 400,000 students.

The New Deal youth programs saved hundreds of thousands of youths from idleness, helped them to maintain their self-respect, and enabled many to get an education. It also kept many young Americans out of the overcrowded job market in business and industry.

Evaluating the relief program. The New Deal relief projects aroused much criticism. It is true that many mistakes were made; there was bad management; there was waste.

Some New Dealers admitted the truth of these criticisms. They explained, however, that there had been no successful past examples to follow in the gigantic tasks they had undertaken. They also pointed out that they had been handicapped by lack of trained personnel to carry out some of their programs.

Despite admitted weaknesses in the work relief program, New Dealers claimed that it had justified itself. Work provided by the federal government, they insisted, had saved millions of Americans from hunger and allowed them to retain some measure of self-respect.

SECTION SURVEY

IDENTIFY: New Deal, pump priming, direct relief, work relief, WPA, CCC, NYA.

1. What immediate problems faced Roosevelt when he took office in 1933?

2. How did the New Deal respect the rights of states in distributing funds for relief purposes?

3. Why can it be said that the greatest tragedy of the depression was its effect on millions of young people?

4. (a) What criticisms were leveled against the New Deal relief program? (b) How did the New Dealers answer these criticisms? (c) In your opinion were the New Deal measures well conceived? Explain.

2 Recovery measures stimulate agriculture and industry

The New Deal measures to provide direct relief and work relief were intended to meet the urgent needs of millions of suffering Americans. At the same time, the New Deal administration launched a recovery program designed to restore the nation's economic health.

Saving the farmers' homes. When Roosevelt became President, two out of every five American farms were mortgaged. Moreover, farmers all over the country faced mounting debts — back taxes, interest payments, and payments on the principal of their loans. Unable to pay their debts, many farmers lost their farms to banks, insurance companies, and private mortgage holders. Some farm families then rented as tenants the land they had once owned. Others were left homeless and jobless.

To relieve this situation, the federal government made available a huge sum of money that farmers could borrow at low interest rates. Some farmers borrowed to buy seed, fertilizer, and equipment necessary to continue operations. Others borrowed to buy back their farms or to pay their taxes.

Still others borrowed money from the government to refinance loans that they could not afford to repay at the time. Under the new government program, a farmer could borrow $5,000 from the Federal Land Banks to pay off the debt to a mortgage holder. The new loan

Poor farming methods and recurring drought turned much of the Middle West into a "Dust Bowl" during the 1930's. The Farm Security Administration (FSA) sent photographers to record the plight of farmers in the stricken area.

from the government could run as long as 50 years, with interest at 2 1/4 percent.

This liberal system of federal credit enabled hundreds of thousands of farm families to protect their land and homes. The farm credit programs were administered by the Farm Credit Administration (FCA), created in 1933.

Higher income for farmers. The New Dealers also tried to increase the farmers' income. The basic plan for farm recovery was simple. The first step was to raise the prices of farm products.

The government set out to increase farm prices by using the principle of supply and demand. Consider the example of a grocery store that has bought more oranges than it can sell. The surplus oranges are about to rot. What does the store do? It reduces the price of the oranges. Next time, of course, the store will order fewer oranges, hoping that by reducing the supply it can sell all the oranges at a good price. This is essentially the policy that the New Deal applied to farm goods in the Agricultural Adjustment Act of 1933.

Limiting farm production. The government reduced the supply of farm products by several methods. Under the Agricultural Adjustment Administration (AAA), farmers were urged to sign agreements not to use one quarter to one half of their land. The government then paid farmers a certain sum of money for each acre that they took out of production. The money for these subsidies, or benefit payments, came from taxes on the food processors—the meat packers, canners, flour millers, and others who prepared or processed farm products.

Under this program large amounts of farmland were taken out of production. In 1933 a million cotton planters plowed under cotton. They did not plant about 10 million acres (405,000 hectares) that they ordinarily would have planted. As a result the 1933 cotton crop was reduced by about 4 million bales and the price of cotton almost doubled. Meanwhile the cotton planters received almost $200 million in federal subsidies. Producers of wheat, corn, hogs, rice, tobacco, dairy products, cattle, rye, barley, peanuts, flax, grain, sorghum, and sugar signed similar agreements to limit their production.

Evaluating the farm program. New Dealers were pleased with their agricultural recovery program. They pointed out that the prices of

259

farm products had risen and farmers were earning more money. They also pointed out that farmers were now spending more money and thus helping to get industry rolling again. These favorable results, the New Dealers said, were the outcome of sound federal planning.

However, there was also severe criticism of the New Deal farm program. Critics pointed out that the money for subsidies came from taxes on the food processors. These taxes were passed along to consumers in the form of higher prices. Thus money was being taken from consumers and given to the farmers. While farmers were getting more money, city dwellers were experiencing a decline in purchasing power.

Also, the owners of large farms benefited far more from the program than did the owners of small farms. Poorer farmers felt that the benefit payments that finally filtered down to them were inadequate for their needs.

Many critics felt that the program resulted in red tape, confusion, and inefficiency. They believed that it concentrated too much power in too many government agencies.

Finally, millions of Americans condemned a program that deliberately decreased food supplies when hunger was widespread.

The AAA declared unconstitutional. The Supreme Court brought the Agricultural Adjustment Act of 1933 to an end. In a 1936 decision in the case of *United States v. Butler,* the Court stated that Congress had no constitutional right to regulate agricultural production. The Court ruled that this power belonged to the states and that the federal government had no authority to interfere.

Construction of public works. New Deal programs also attempted to revive the building industry. The New Dealers recognized that the building industry is one of the keys to a nation's economic health. The industry uses large quantities of materials from many sources. As a result, when construction work is going on, workers are busy in forests, mines, and factories throughout the country.

The building program of the New Deal started in June 1933. At that time, the Public Works Administration (PWA) began to contract with private firms for the construction of public works, such as bridges, government buildings, power plants, conservation projects, and dams. The federal government also en-

couraged states and municipalities to carry on their own building programs, offering them loans and gifts.

By the summer of 1936, public works projects included about 70 municipal power plants, several hundred schools and hospitals, nearly 1,500 waterworks, and many federal, state, county, and municipal buildings.

Repair and building of homes. The New Dealers also sought to revive the building industry by stimulating the construction of homes. Like so many New Deal measures, this program was double-barreled; it had as a second goal the relief of homeowners.

When President Roosevelt took office, an average of 1,000 American homes were being foreclosed and sold at public auction every day. In June 1933 Congress tried to end this situation by creating the Home Owner's Loan Corporation (HOLC). With money borrowed at low interest rates from this government agency, many homeowners could pay off their old mortgages. At the same time, they arranged with the HOLC to pay off their new mortgages over a long period with much smaller monthly payments. Between 1933 and 1936, the homes of more than 1 million American families were thus saved.

To provide further aid to the owners of homes and businesses and the building industry, the Federal Housing Administration (FHA) was established in 1934. The FHA encouraged banks to lend money to individuals for repairing and building homes and business properties. It did this by insuring the banks against losses on such loans. Yet so desperate was the financial position of most Americans that relatively few people were able to take advantage of the FHA loans.

A federal housing program to provide homes for the very poor was no more successful. Although the PWA lent and gave money to some 27 cities for clearing slums and building low-cost apartment houses, the results were disappointing. For one thing, rents for the finished apartments were usually more than poor families could afford.

Aid to transportation. No less important than the building industry to a nation's economic life is its transportation system. The depression hit the railroads a stunning blow. Between 1929 and 1933, almost one third of all the railroad companies in the United States went bankrupt. Others were saved from complete collapse only by loans from the RFC.

To recover lost business, some western railroads lowered their passenger rates from 3.2 cents to 2 cents per mile. The experiment proved so successful that the Interstate Commerce Commission ordered all lines to adopt the same rate. Government loans also enabled the railroads to install modern equipment, such as diesel engines and streamlined trains.

All of these measures helped the railroads. However, at the same time, the government also spent huge sums of money to improve the nation's highways and waterways, thereby giving a boost to the railroads' competitors.

The NIRA. All these New Deal recovery measures were more or less indirect methods of reviving the nation's industrial machine. With the National Industrial Recovery Act (NIRA), the New Deal tackled the problem head on.

The NIRA went into effect in June 1933 as a two-year emergency measure. It was intended to aid industry, consumers, and labor. Under the act employers would cooperate in stabilizing prices, finding employment for jobless workers, and raising wages. Cooperation was to replace competition as one of the major driving forces of American industry. Antitrust legislation, such as the Sherman and Clayton antitrust acts, was disregarded.

The NIRA provided that each industry should, with the aid of the National Recovery Administration (NRA), adopt a "code of fair practices." Once these codes had been approved by the President, they became binding upon the entire industry.

Some 95 percent of American industries adopted fair-practices codes within a few months. In general, the codes limited production and provided for the common control of prices and sales practices. Most codes also outlawed child labor and required that adults not work more than 40 hours a week and that wages not be less than $12 to $15 a week.

Perhaps the most important—and certainly the most controversial—provisions in the NIRA were contained in the famous Section 7a. This section guaranteed workers the right to bargain collectively with their employers.

Criticisms of the NIRA. Critics of the NIRA were many and outspoken. Owners of small businesses charged that the NRA codes of fair practices had mostly been made by and for large corporations. They insisted that the minimum-wage provisions in the codes favored the highly mechanized factories that could afford to pay higher wages. Other critics charged that it was difficult to enforce the codes. Also, the courts usually refused to enforce the fair-practices provisions of the codes. Finally, while the NRA was supposed to aid recovery by increasing the purchasing power of consumers, many manufacturers defeated this purpose by raising prices to cover increases in wages.

The main objection to the NIRA for many businesses was that it stimulated unionization and collective bargaining. Moreover, certain provisions in Section 7a of the act were not clear. For instance, did company unions, under the influence of managers and owners, have the right to engage in collective bargaining? Labor said that company unions could not honestly represent the workers and should be outlawed. Management disagreed.

The National Labor Board. To settle the confused points of the law, Congress established an agency that later became the National Labor Relations Board (NLRB). The board could conduct elections in plants and determine which labor organization had the right to bargain for all the workers in that particular plant. It also served as a board of arbitration to settle labor disputes.

The board was unpopular with business managers and owners. They claimed that it usually settled disputes in favor of labor. As a result, business began to oppose the entire NRA program. When management refused to grant union demands, a wave of strikes broke out. Despite these problems the National Labor Board, before the summer of 1935, settled more than four fifths of the 3,755 disputes referred to it and avoided nearly 500 strikes.

The NIRA declared unconstitutional. In May 1935, in the case of *Schechter v. United States,* the Supreme Court declared the NIRA unconstitutional. The Court held that in giving the federal government the right to regulate interstate commerce, the Constitution did not give the government the power to regulate every aspect of business.

The Wagner Act. One important idea in the NIRA was quickly reborn. In 1935 Congress passed the famous National Labor Relations Act. This measure was often called the Wagner

Act after one of its sponsors, Senator Robert F. Wagner of New York.

The Wagner Act, like the equally well-known Section 7a of the NIRA, guaranteed to labor the right to organize, to bargain collectively with employers for better wages and working conditions, and to engage in "concerted activities . . . for other mutual aid." The Wagner Act condemned as unfair to labor such practices as discriminating against or discharging a worker for belonging to a union. It also declared that the majority of the workers in any plant or industry could select representatives to bargain with management.

Under the Wagner Act, the organization of labor proceeded rapidly. While the Wagner Act was in a sense a reform measure, it was also intended to promote industrial recovery. It aimed to do this by guaranteeing to organized labor a better chance of raising workers' wages and thus increasing their purchasing power. No single measure of the New Deal aroused more controversy than the Wagner Act.

SECTION SURVEY

IDENTIFY: AAA, subsidy, bureaucratic, *United States v. Butler,* HOLC, Section 7a, NLRB, *Schechter v. United States,* Wagner Act.

1. (a) Explain the basic New Deal plan to aid farmers. (b) What were the major arguments for and against the New Deal farm recovery program?
2. Why did the Supreme Court declare the Agricultural Adjustment Act of 1933 unconstitutional?
3. What steps were taken during the New Deal to help the transportation industry?
4. (a) What was the aim of the NIRA? (b) How was the aim to be carried out?
5. Why did the Supreme Court declare the NIRA unconstitutional?

3 The New Deal carries out reform measures

Although relief and recovery measures were urgently needed in the early 1930's, only fundamental reforms could protect the nation against another depression. Such reforms became increasingly important goals of the New Deal in 1935 and thereafter.

Protection for investors. New Deal reforms strengthened banks in several ways. For example, the power of the Federal Reserve System was increased by placing commercial and savings banks under its supervision. The Federal Reserve Board was given additional power to regulate credit as a check upon reckless speculation.

Another series of laws was designed to protect the public against worthless stocks. Any bank, brokerage house, or salesperson that failed to give full and honest information about the true value of stocks and bonds offered for sale was subject to a severe penalty. In 1934 the Securities and Exchange Commission (SEC) was created to administer these laws and to regulate the stock exchanges.

Social security for the people. One key reform measure of the New Deal, the Social Security Act of 1935, tackled the problem of individual security. The act had three major goals.

First, it provided unemployment insurance for individuals who lost their jobs. The money to be used for this purpose was raised by a payroll tax on businesses employing more than eight workers.

A second goal of the Social Security Act was to provide old-age pensions ranging from $10 to $85 a month for persons over 65. The money for this purpose was raised by a payroll tax on employers and a social security tax on the wages of employees.

A third goal of the Social Security Act was to help the handicapped—the blind, the aged, the disabled—as well as dependent children. Federal pensions up to $20 a month were available for needy persons over 65, provided that the states paid an equal amount. Federal funds were also available for those states that sought to protect the welfare of the handicapped.

President Roosevelt called the Social Security Act "a cornerstone in a structure which is being built." It was admittedly only a beginning, for it did not include all workers. Nevertheless, by 1937 nearly 21 million workers were entitled to unemployment benefits, and 36 million retired workers to old-age pensions.

Electricity for homes. Another reform movement sought to bring electricity to more Americans. Despite widespread development of electric power up to the 1930's, only one third of America's homes had electricity. In rural areas only 15 out of every 100 houses were wired.

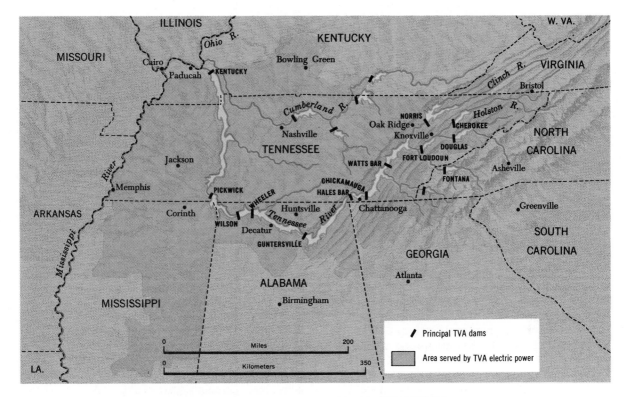

TENNESSEE VALLEY AUTHORITY

To solve this problem, the President in 1935 created the Rural Electrification Administration (REA). The REA had the responsibility of developing a program for generating and distributing electricity to isolated rural areas.

Regulating utility companies. In 1935 also, Congress passed the Public Utility Holding Company Act, also called the Wheeler-Rayburn Act. This measure gave the Federal Power Commission authority to regulate the interstate production, transmission, and sale of electricity. It gave the Federal Trade Commission similar authority over gas. It gave the Securities and Exchange Commission authority to regulate the financial practices of public utility holding companies.

By regulating the financial operations of the public utility holding companies, the New Deal hoped to end a trend toward monopoly in public utilities. The measure was designed to prevent any holding company from controlling more than a "single integrated public utility system" operating in a single area of the country. Under the law utility companies were forbidden to engage in any business other than the production and distribution of gas or electric power. They were also forbidden to issue new stocks and bonds without the approval of the Securities and Exchange Commission.

Finally, in a "death-sentence" clause, the Public Utility Holding Company Act gave the public utility holding companies five years to readjust their financial affairs. At the end of five years, any company that could not prove that it was actually distributing gas or electricity in a given area would be dissolved.

The TVA. With the creation of the Tennessee Valley Authority (TVA), Congress in 1933 launched the United States upon an experiment that had no parallel in American history. The scene of this monumental experiment included parts of seven states in the region drained by the Tennessee River and its tributaries (see map, this page).

The TVA moved into this region with a plan for the unified development of all its resources. The plan was to improve economic and social conditions for the benefit of the people who

263

lived in the valley. It would also benefit all Americans by setting a standard of cost for producing and distributing electric power.

Over the next ten years, the TVA constructed 21 large dams on the Tennessee River and its major tributaries and thousands of smaller dams on creeks and brooks. Power plants were erected to convert the "white coal" of the river into vast quantities of electricity. Whereas in 1935 only 1 in every 100 homes in Mississippi had electricity, by 1945 about 20 homes out of 100 were wired. The per capita consumption of electric power in the TVA region was 50 percent higher than the average per capita consumption for the entire United States. Moreover, rates for electric power had been cut by about one third.

The TVA dams were also planned as part of a program to control floods, to prevent soil erosion, and to restore the fertility of the land. Under the TVA fertilizer plants were opened, river and road transportation improved, and public parks, schools, and hospitals were con-structed. Vast changes have come to the region because of TVA programs.

Criticisms of the TVA. There is another side to the TVA story. Privately owned power companies, representing a $12 billion industry, bit-terly fought the TVA. They declared that the TVA was an unnecessary intervention by the federal government into the affairs of private industry. They insisted that the lower TVA rates for electric power were not the result of more efficient production. If the TVA paid taxes as all private industries did, critics in-sisted, the power agency would have to charge much more for its electricity.

Advocates of the TVA believed that its rates should be used as a standard to govern the rates charged by private power producers. The private power companies insisted that the TVA was an unfair standard, and the less ex-pensive electricity it generated was a gift from the taxpayers of the entire nation to the people of one region.

This 1933 painting shows the earliest of the TVA projects—the construction of the Norris Dam near Knoxville. The dam was named for Senator George W. Norris of Nebraska, who was an early and outspoken supporter of the TVA.

1. What were the three main purposes of the Social Security Act of 1935?

2. (a) What was the purpose of the Tennessee Valley Authority? (b) Although the TVA was located in a single region, how might it be seen as a benefit to the whole nation?

3. (a) What arguments have been used against the TVA? (b) Do you think these are valid arguments? Explain.

4 Opposition increases toward New Deal policies and programs

By 1936 the United States had made considerable progress in its battle against the depression. National income had risen sharply since 1932, having jumped from a low of less than $47 billion to almost $70 billion. Industrial production was double that of 1932.

However, the depression was far from conquered. In 1936 as many as 3.5 million people were still working on relief projects. Nine million men and women were still unemployed. Many factories and mines were still closed or were working at far less than full capacity.

Such was the situation when in 1936 the voters entered another Presidential election year. Should Roosevelt be reelected? Should the New Deal be continued? These were the big questions facing the voters.

Roosevelt's supporters. In June 1936 the Democrats enthusiastically renominated Roosevelt for a second term. Their platform strongly endorsed the New Deal.

Lined up behind the President were not only most Democrats but also countless rank-and-file Republicans. Most of the progressive Republican leaders who had supported him in 1932 continued to do so. Labor was overwhelmingly for the President, as were many farmers who remembered the New Deal benefits they had recently received. Many of those who had received federal relief money also supported Roosevelt. And finally, black voters in the North almost solidly rejected their traditional Republican ties and supported the party that, in some measure, had responded to their needs and grievances.

Roosevelt's critics. The President and the New Deal also had many critics, including a number of influential Democrats. Roosevelt's Republican critics included most big business leaders, many small business people who had suffered under the NRA, bankers, private power companies, newspapers, and many professional people. Some critics objected to Eleanor Roosevelt's efforts on behalf of black Americans.

Opponents of President Roosevelt sometimes claimed that he was undermining the Constitution. They pointed out that the Supreme Court had declared unconstitutional seven out of nine important New Deal measures. They insisted that the American way of life—individualism, free enterprise, and private property—was being abandoned for socialism and government control. Roosevelt's critics denied that the New Deal had restored prosperity. They pointed to the nation's continued unemployment. They stressed the fact that the administration had piled up a huge national debt of over $33 billion and had failed to balance the budget.

Republican promises. The Republicans in 1936 nominated friendly, thrifty Alfred M. Landon, Governor of Kansas, for President. Landon was a liberal Republican. Although he was in the oil business, he had the support of many farmers who trusted his judgment. Moreover, in a period when most states and the federal government had piled up huge debts, Governor Landon had balanced the Kansas budget.

The Republican platform promised to continue most New Deal measures, which, they claimed, they could carry out more effectively and economically than the Democrats. The Republicans also promised to balance the budget and to restore to the states certain powers that the federal government had seized to carry out the New Deal program. Thus the Republicans adopted what had traditionally been the Democratic states' rights position.

Roosevelt's victory. The election campaign was filled with angry charges and countercharges. More than 45 million Americans voted, reflecting keen popular interest. Roosevelt swept the country with an electoral

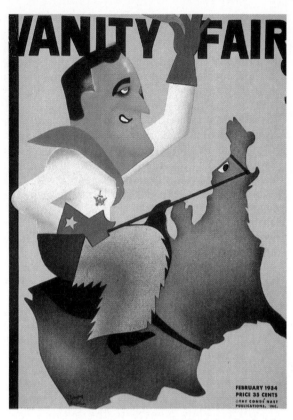

This 1934 cover of the magazine *Vanity Fair* reflected the thinking of those Americans who believed that Roosevelt had assumed too much power in the first year of his Presidency. Many of them were worried that Roosevelt would soon ride the nation into the ground.

vote of 523 to 8. Roosevelt's popular vote was also impressive—27,476,673 to Landon's 16,679,583. Moreover, the Democrats won or kept control of all but six governorships and maintained their leadership of both houses of Congress. Not since the reelection of President Monroe in 1820 had a Presidential candidate won such strong backing.

Roosevelt and the Supreme Court. Early in his second term, Roosevelt opened an attack on the Supreme Court. Roosevelt was upset because the Court had set aside as unconstitutional seven important New Deal laws. He was also disturbed because the Court had declared unconstitutional a New York State measure providing minimum wages for women and children. Moreover, the federal courts had used the injunction to block federal agencies from carrying out New Deal measures.

Roosevelt declared that all too often certain Supreme Court justices thought in terms of the "horse-and-buggy" era. "A dead hand was being laid upon this whole program of prog-

ress," the President later declared. It was, he said, the hand of the Supreme Court.

President Roosevelt asked Congress for power to appoint an extra justice to the Supreme Court for each existing justice who did not retire upon reaching age 70. At the time, six of the nine justices were 70 or older. Roosevelt's proposal, therefore, would have enabled him to appoint six new justices more favorable to the New Deal.

Changes in the Supreme Court. Although the President fought vigorously for his "reform" proposal, he lost. Members of Congress in his own party refused to support him, and public opinion ran against him. In general, people did not want to tamper with the delicate balance of legislative, executive, and judicial powers written into the Constitution.

Although Roosevelt lost the battle for Court "reform," he gained most of the things he wanted. The Court began to approve important New Deal measures. The National Labor Relations Act and the Social Security Act were tested and found constitutional. Moreover, the Court approved an act passed by the state of Washington establishing minimum pay for women and children. This act was almost identical to the New York State law that the Court had earlier declared unconstitutional.

Had the Court suddenly realized that it might be well to approve certain popular legislation to prevent a drastic reform of the Court itself? Many Americans believed this to be true. In any case, Roosevelt was able to replace, because of death or retirement, all but two of the original justices with members who appeared to be more sympathetic to New Deal legislation.

Business slump in 1937–38. Early in 1937, while the issue of the Supreme Court was being argued across the land, the nation's industrial machinery once again slowed down. By the autumn of 1937, factories were closing and unemployment was rising.

The Democrats spoke of what was taking place as a **recession,** that is, a business slump less severe than a depression. The Republicans, on the other hand, called it the "Roosevelt depression." Roosevelt's opponents blamed the Democrats and the New Deal for the present business slump in just the same way that the Democrats in 1931 had blamed the Republicans for the Great Depression.

Politics aside, there was fairly widespread agreement on the major cause of the slump. Instead of balancing the budget as he had promised to do back in 1932, Roosevelt had piled up the largest national debt in history. The Republicans had made the most of this fact in the 1936 election campaign. However, many Democrats and friends of the New Deal had also become increasingly uneasy about the mounting debt.

Mindful of the growing criticism, by 1936 Roosevelt had begun to cut spending for relief and public works. Unfortunately, private industry was not yet strong enough to give jobs to the men and women who were dropped from relief projects because of the cutbacks. Once again, therefore, the nation's economic system started on a downward spiral.

New pump priming. Fortunately, measures adopted to fight the Great Depression acted as brakes against the 1937–38 recession. More than 2 million wage earners in 25 states, protected by the Social Security Act, began to collect unemployment insurance. The new banking laws protected the savings of depositors. Many government agencies were ready to lend money to business and to construct public works, thus creating new jobs.

Roosevelt and Congress began once again to prime the economic pump by increasing government lending and spending. The Reconstruction Finance Corporation again came to the rescue of businesses in trouble. The WPA doubled the number of workers on its payroll from 1.5 million to 3 million.

By the end of 1938, the nation's economic machinery was once again picking up speed. The Democrats were quick to claim another victory for the New Deal. The Republicans, on the other hand, insisted again that recovery had come in spite of the New Deal. Many Americans, Democrats and Republicans alike, continued to express alarm at the ever-growing national debt.

SECTION SURVEY

IDENTIFY: Alfred M. Landon, recession.

1. (a) On what major issues did the election of 1936 focus? (b) What positions did each party take on these issues?
2. (a) Why did Roosevelt try to reform the Supreme Court? (b) Why did his plan fail? (c) What position would you have taken on the issue? Give arguments to support your opinion.
3. How did the measures adopted to fight the Great Depression act as brakes against the recession of 1937–38?

5 New Deal reforms continue despite growing criticism

During the 1936 election campaign, President Roosevelt had promised that, if reelected, he would continue the New Deal. Neither the business recession of 1937–38 nor the mounting criticism of his policies prevented Roosevelt from continuing his program.

The A. F. of L. and the CIO. As you may remember, the Wagner Act of 1935 guaranteed to workers the right of collective bargaining and forbade employers to discriminate against organized labor. Under the protection of this law, the American Federation of Labor began to organize unskilled workers in the mass production industries—steel, automobiles, aluminum, aircraft, utilities. However, the A. F. of L. did not move rapidly enough to please many labor leaders.

Growing impatience with the A. F. of L. led John L. Lewis, powerful head of the United Mine Workers, and a group of like-minded labor leaders to organize in 1935 the Committee for Industrial Organization (CIO). The CIO immediately launched a drive to organize workers in the automobile, steel, rubber, oil, radio, and other industries into industrial unions. The new industrial unions included all workers, skilled and unskilled, in an industry. The United Automobile Workers (UAW), for example, represented all workers in automotive plants. In earlier times workers in the automobile industry had negotiated contracts through many separate unions—electrical, welding, metalworking, and the like. Now they negotiated as a single powerful organization. The CIO also encouraged the inclusion of black workers in the new industrial unions.

Disturbed by the growing influence of the CIO, the leaders of the A. F. of L. ordered it to disband. When CIO leaders refused to obey this order, the A. F. of L. expelled them. However, the CIO continued to operate, and in May 1938

Here, auto workers in a General Motors factory stage a sit-down strike in 1936. It was through this 44 day sit-down strike at Flint, Michigan, that the GM workers won the right to be represented by the United Auto Workers.

it reorganized as a separate body, the Congress of Industrial Organizations (still called CIO), with John L. Lewis as its first president. By 1940 the CIO could boast of having 3.6 million members, roughly equal to the membership of the older A. F. of L.

The sit-down strike. Meanwhile, forceful organizing campaigns by both the A. F. of L. and the CIO resulted in a wave of strikes.

In November 1936 several hundred workers in the General Motors plant at Flint, Michigan, staged a **sit-down strike**. Instead of leaving the plant and organizing picket lines, the striking workers simply sat down at their machines and refused to work. They then announced that they would not leave until management granted their demands.

The sit-down strike, which made it impossible for management to bring in strikebreakers, proved extremely effective. Within a few months, this relatively new labor weapon spread to many other plants, involving more than half a million workers. All of the leading automobile manufacturers except Ford now

recognized the United Automobile Workers, the powerful new CIO union, as the bargaining agent for the automobile industry. The United States Steel Corporation, long a foe of labor unions, finally accepted the CIO steelworkers' union as the bargaining agent of the steelworkers. The CIO also organized the workers in many other industries.

In 1939 the Supreme Court ruled that sit-down strikes were illegal. Nevertheless the CIO — as well as the A. F. of L. — continued to forge ahead. In general, the Wagner Act of 1935, with its guarantee of collective bargaining, had given organized labor its great opportunity for growth.

Jurisdictional strikes. Much of the labor unrest of the late 1930's sprang from bitter rivalry between the A. F. of L. and the CIO. Disputes arose over which had **jurisdiction,** or the right, to enroll a particular group of workers. Sometimes these disputes led to jurisdictional strikes. In such cases management found it hard to know which side to recognize or to bargain with, and the government stepped in to settle the issue. The great wave of strikes that reached its peak in 1937 and 1938 diminished in the following years as both labor and management reluctantly came to accept government intervention.

Fair Labor Standards Act. The New Deal labor program did not merely encourage and support organized workers. It also aimed at reforming labor conditions in the United States. To this end, President Roosevelt in 1937 proposed the Fair Labor Standards Act, sometimes called the Wages and Hours Law. This law provided a minimum wage scale and a maximum workweek for many workers.

Strong opposition quickly developed to the Fair Labor Standards Act. Many employers claimed that it encouraged unneeded and unwise government interference and control over industry. However, the law went into effect in October 1938.

The Fair Labor Standards Act provided that a legal maximum workweek of 44 hours in 1938 be decreased to 40 hours by 1940, with time-and-a-half pay for overtime. It also provided that minimum wages of 25 cents an hour in 1938 be increased to 40 cents an hour by 1945. It prohibited the employment of children under 16 in industries producing goods for interstate commerce. The Department of Labor was responsible for enforcing the act.

Although the Fair Labor Standards Act affected only workers employed in interstate industries, by 1940 about 13 million men and women were benefiting from the law. Roosevelt hailed the new law as being, after the Social Security Act, "the most farsighted program for the benefit of workers ever adopted in this or in any other country."

Important though the Fair Labor Standards Act was, it did not insure freedom from racial discrimination in employment. In 1941 A. Philip Randolph, a powerful and militant black labor leader, threatened to march on the national capital with 10,000 blacks to demand equal employment opportunities. Responding to this pressure, Roosevelt established the Fair Employment Practices Committee (FEPC). The FEPC worked to counteract racial discrimination in industries that had contracts with the federal government.

Helping the farmers. Other far-reaching New Deal measures were meant to improve the economic position of the nation's farmers. In 1936, when the Supreme Court ruled against the Agricultural Adjustment Act of 1933, Congress passed another law.

The Soil Conservation and Domestic Allotment Act of 1936 set up a soil conservation program. Farmers who took part in the program leased part of their lands to the government. Under the supervision of state farm agencies, the farmers worked to restore the fertility of the leased land by practicing conservation measures, by using fertilizers, and by sowing soil-restoring plants, such as clover. In return, the farmers received a certain sum of money for every acre they withdrew from production.

By this means the government hoped to develop nationwide knowledge of sound conservation practices. Equally important, by limiting production the government hoped to raise the prices of farm products.

The Bankhead-Jones Act. With the Bankhead-Jones Farm Tenant Act of 1937, the New Deal undertook to help tenant farmers, sharecroppers, and migratory farm workers, who moved from place to place in search of jobs. The new law created the Farm Security Administration (FSA) to lend money at low interest to tenant farmers, sharecroppers, and farm laborers wishing to buy farms. Those who received the loans had 40 years to repay.

Agricultural Adjustment Act of 1938. The heart of the New Deal agricultural reform program was the second Agricultural Adjustment Act, passed in 1938. This act contained a number of important provisions:

(1) It provided payments to farmers in proportion to the number of acres that they withdrew from production and planted in soil-conserving crops.

(2) The government was authorized to decide the amount of various staple crops that could be marketed each year. With the approval of two thirds of the producers of these commodities in each locality, the government then assigned a certain allotment to each farmer. Farmers who exceeded this allotment had to pay a fine when they sold such crops during a time of surplus.

(3) When harvests were large, the surpluses were stored by the government for later use in lean years. However, farmers did not lose their income from the surplus crops. The government gave them commodity loans on all stored crops.

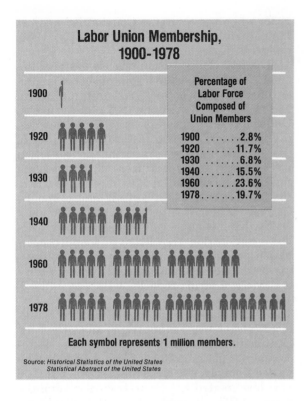

Labor Union Membership, 1900-1978

	Percentage of Labor Force Composed of Union Members
1900	2.8%
1920	11.7%
1930	6.8%
1940	15.5%
1960	23.6%
1978	19.7%

Each symbol represents 1 million members.

Source: *Historical Statistics of the United States*
Statistical Abstract of the United States

The amount of these loans was fixed at slightly below **parity**. Parity was a figure based on average prices of each of the commodities for the base period from August 1909 to July 1914, a relatively prosperous period for farmers. When the market price of a commodity rose to the parity level, farmers were to sell their stored crops and repay the loans. If the market price remained below parity, the farmers kept the money and the government kept their crops. By this method the government hoped to keep the price of agricultural products at a steady level and benefit both farmers and consumers.

(4) The act also authorized the government to insure wheat crops against drought, flood, hail, and plant diseases.

Evaluating the farm program. In 1932, in the depths of the Great Depression, farm income had sunk to less than $5 billion. By 1938 it had risen to more than $8 billion. By 1940 it totaled more than $9 billion.

Critics reminded the country that the increased income came from higher prices paid by consumers and from subsidies paid by the government—with taxpayers' money. These critics charged that money had been "taken from Peter to pay Paul."

Critics, including many farmers, also resented increasing government controls over farm production. They feared that subsidies would destroy farmers' independence. Moreover, critics charged that the government's price support program was causing America's agricultural products to lose out in the highly competitive foreign markets.

Such criticisms ended, at least temporarily, in 1941 when the United States was plunged into World War II. Then, as New Deal supporters were quick to point out, the country owed much to the farm legislation of the 1930's. This legislation had improved the economic condition of many Americans, had increased the fertility of millions of acres of land, and had enabled the United States to feed a large portion of the war-devastated world.

Housing for low-income groups. During his second term, Roosevelt also continued his efforts to ease the housing problem. The National Housing Act of 1937, usually called the Wagner-Steagall Act, had two aims: (1) to stimulate business by government spending for the construction of houses and (2) to "remedy the unsafe and unsatisfactory housing conditions and the acute shortage of decent, safe, and sanitary dwellings for families of low income in rural and urban communities."

The National Housing Act created the United States Housing Authority (USHA), which began an ambitious program of housing construction. By 1941 the USHA had lent $750 million for the construction of more than 160,000 housing units.

Other New Deal reforms. In 1938 Congress passed the Food, Drug, and Cosmetic Act, which replaced the earlier Pure Food and Drug Act of 1906. The 1938 act required adequate testing of new drugs before they were offered for sale. It also required manufacturers to list the exact ingredients of their products on their labels. In addition, the Wheeler-Lea Act, also passed in 1938, prohibited manufacturers from making false or misleading claims about their products in their advertising.

In 1939 Congress tackled the problem of improper political practices. The Hatch Act placed restrictions upon federal officeholders below the policy-making level in the executive branch of the government. Such officeholders were prohibited (1) from taking an active part in political campaigns, (2) from soliciting or accepting political contributions from workers on relief, and (3) from using their official positions to try to influence Presidential or Congressional elections. In 1940 the Hatch Act was amended to include state and local government employees whose pay came completely or partially from federal funds. The 1940 amendment also limited the amount of money a political party could spend in any one year. A maximum of $3 million was established. The amount any individual could contribute was $5,000 a year. This legislation was not effective because both parties soon found ways legally to avoid these limits.

SECTION SURVEY

IDENTIFY: John L. Lewis, CIO, industrial union, sit-down strike, jurisdictional strike, minimum wage, A. Philip Randolph, FEPC, parity, Hatch Act.

1. (a) Why was the CIO organized? (b) How did it differ from the A. F. of L.?

2. (a) How did the Fair Labor Standards Act benefit workers in the United States? (b) Why did some people oppose it?

3. What measures were taken from 1936 to 1938 to help improve the economic conditions of farmers?

4. Graph Study: Look at the graph on page 270. According to the graph, during what period did labor unions achieve their greatest growth?

6 The New Deal's great experiment comes to an end

By the middle of his second term, President Roosevelt's influence was beginning to decline. In 1937, as you have read, he had suffered a major defeat when he failed to push through Congress his bill for reorganizing the Supreme Court. In the Congressional elections of 1938, he suffered an even more serious defeat.

Congressional elections of 1938. As the elections approached, Roosevelt decided to liberalize the Democratic Party. Singling out those conservative Democrats who had voted

against his reform program, he urged voters to defeat them at the polls.

Roosevelt's effort to liberalize the Democratic Party failed. With only one exception, all the members of Congress whom Roosevelt had opposed were reelected. Moreover, the voters chose a great many new Democratic members who were foes of the New Deal. Adding to Roosevelt's dismay, the Republicans won additional seats in Congress. Nevertheless, the Democrats continued to hold a sizable majority in both the House and the Senate.

New Deal activities suspended. President Roosevelt, a shrewd politician, was quick to see the meaning of the 1938 elections. Realizing that public opinion was turning against him, he began to suspend earlier New Deal activities. By 1939 Congress was cutting appropriations for many New Deal agencies.

As a result of the threatening world situation, the PWA and the WPA shifted their attention from public works to projects involving national defense, such as the building of airports and military highways. Other New Deal agencies, such as the Civilian Conservation Corps and the National Youth Administration, ended operations when Congress cut off further appropriations. Although the TVA weathered attacks both in and out of Congress, the President's recommendation for similar projects in six other areas of the country received little support.

The driving impulse of the New Deal had spent itself. Those who maintained that the reform objectives of the New Deal were still far from being realized faced stiffer opposition and growing public indifference.

Opposition to New Deal finances. Much of the opposition to the New Deal came from people who believed that Roosevelt's financial policies were undermining the nation's economic system. In general, three different methods were used for financing New Deal relief, recovery, and reform programs.

One method was inflation. Although Congress authorized President Roosevelt to print paper money, he never did so. He did, however, take the nation off the gold standard. This cheapened the value of the dollar.

A second method was **deficit spending.** This meant that the government spent more than it received in taxes, leaving the budget unbalanced, or showing a deficit. In the 1930's the

As opposition to President Roosevelt's policies grew, he frequently took to the radio airwaves to defend them. The highly persuasive "fireside chats" often won support for his programs and reassured the nation.

national debt increased from about $16 billion to more than $40 billion. Men and women in both parties, but business leaders in particular, lost confidence in an administration that piled up a larger and larger national debt.

The third method by which the New Deal had financed the operation of new programs was by raising taxes. Despite strong opposition, Congress passed the Revenue Act of 1935, often called the Wealth Tax Act. With this measure Congress increased the income tax for individuals and large corporations and levied taxes on gifts and estates. In spite of these measures, the new revenue did not balance the budget, and the national debt continued to grow.

In the Revenue Act of 1936, Congress laid a steeply graduated tax on those corporate profits that were not distributed to stockholders. Business bitterly complained that the new tax would discourage business expansion and prevent the accumulation of surpluses for use in depression years.

In 1938, however, as a result of growing opposition to the New Deal, Congress began to reverse the taxation policy of earlier years. The Revenue Act of 1938 sharply reduced corporation taxes. In 1939 Congress abolished the tax on undistributed profits. At the same time, it raised the corporation income tax to a maximum of 19 percent. In addition, for the first time in history, Congress required employees of cities and states to pay taxes to the federal government.

A third term. Despite the fact that his influence was weakening, and despite the fact that the two-term tradition for Presidents was widely accepted as part of the unwritten Constitution, Roosevelt decided to run for a third term. The President did not at first announce his decision to the public, although he hinted that the critical world situation might compel him to be a candidate. However, behind the scenes he arranged matters so that it would have been almost impossible for any Democrat to run against Roosevelt without obtaining his consent.

The Democratic convention chose Roosevelt on the first ballot at Chicago in July 1940. It also, without general enthusiasm, accepted Henry A. Wallace of Iowa as his running mate. Wallace, a former Republican, had been Roosevelt's Secretary of Agriculture.

The Democratic platform promised to extend social security, to stress the low-cost housing program, and to advance government ownership of public utilities. The platform also promised to keep the United States out of the war that had broken out in Europe and to send no American armies abroad unless the nation were attacked.

Wendell Willkie. The Republicans chose as their candidate Wendell L. Willkie of New York, a powerful Wall Street lawyer with Democratic leanings and a long progressive record. Willkie favored many of the principles of the New Deal. On the other hand, he felt that the New Deal was extravagant. He also believed it had been administered in such a way as to endanger individualism, free enterprise, and democracy. Warmhearted and engaging, Willkie developed a strong following and became a formidable candidate.

The Republican platform condemned the New Deal for its "shifting, contradictory, and overlapping administrations and policies." It promised to revise the tax system to stimulate private enterprise and to promote prosperity. It also promised to keep the major New Deal reforms but to administer the laws governing these reforms with greater efficiency and less waste. The Republicans also demanded a constitutional amendment that would limit Presidents to a maximum of two terms in office. Like the Democrats, the Republicans promised to keep America out of war unless the nation were attacked.

The campaign of 1940. The threat of a second World War hung over the election campaign of 1940. Indeed, in the fall of 1940, while the American people were preparing to vote in the Presidential election, Great Britain was fighting desperately for survival.

Both Roosevelt and Willkie advocated a strong program of national defense. Both urged all aid to Great Britain short of war. In general, there was no important difference in their attitudes toward the terrible conflict that was raging abroad.

On domestic issues, however, they differed sharply. Willkie attacked Roosevelt for irresponsibility and Roosevelt attacked Willkie for "unwitting falsifications of fact." Willkie traveled thousands of miles through 34 states in a whirlwind campaign. Roosevelt limited himself to a few speeches.

Roosevelt won a sweeping victory in an election in which more Americans voted than in any previous contest in American history. But the returns clearly showed that the President had lost some of his earlier popularity. Roosevelt's 60 percent popular majority in the election of 1936 was reduced to just under 55 percent. In round numbers this meant that 27 million Americans voted for Roosevelt, and 22 million for Willkie. The popular vote was therefore much closer than indicated by the electoral vote of 449 for Roosevelt and 82 for Willkie. Although the Democrats retained control of Congress, the Republicans increased their strength in both Congress and the state legislatures.

During Roosevelt's third term, the New Deal domestic programs received less attention as foreign problems and war itself absorbed American energies. Thus a great period of reform in American history came to an end.

In August 1940, Wendell Willkie returned in triumph to his hometown of Elwood, Indiana, on his way to accept the Presidential nomination of the Republican Party. The wealthy New York lawyer was personable and charming and a strong candidate.

Whether this suspension of reform activities was the result of war or whether the reform impulse had spent itself remains unanswered.

SECTION SURVEY

IDENTIFY: deficit spending, national debt, Henry Wallace, Wendell Willkie.

1. (a) Describe the three methods used by New Dealers to raise money. (b) Why were these methods criticized?

2. Present evidence to support the view that Roosevelt's influence was decreasing by 1940.

3. In what ways did Roosevelt and Willkie disagree on domestic issues?

4. Do you think the fact that Roosevelt was running for a third term as President had any influence on the way people voted? Explain.

Chapter Survey

Summary: Tracing the Main Ideas

When Franklin D. Roosevelt became President of the United States in 1933, the nation was in the depths of the worst depression it had ever experienced. President Roosevelt, a person of great energy and overwhelming enthusiasm, inspired the people with his own confidence and faith in the future.

Surrounding himself with men and women who for the most part shared his views about the nation's problems, Roosevelt immediately opened a three-pronged attack upon the depression. In a series of relief measures, Congress, led by the administration, provided food, clothing, and shelter for the millions of unemployed and needy Americans. In a second series of recovery measures, Congress attempted to revive the nation's agriculture and industry and place the economy on a solid foundation. In a third series of reform measures, Congress developed a program designed to protect future generations from such a catastrophe.

By 1936 the New Deal program faced a large and growing body of opposition, some from within the Democratic Party itself. Many critics felt that the government was interfering too much with the free enterprise system and, in so doing, was threatening individualism and democracy.

By the end of 1938, the opposition had become so strong that President Roosevelt decided to postpone other far-reaching reforms that he had been considering. Indeed, during 1939, 1940, and 1941, the administration suspended the activities of several of the agencies created by the New Deal.

Another reason for the President's decision to postpone the reform program was his growing concern over the outbreak of war in East Asia and in Europe.

Inquiring into History

1. (a) Why was the New Deal controversial? (b) What were the major arguments in favor of the New Deal? (c) What were the major arguments against it?
2. Summarize the various ways in which the New Deal tried to help (a) the consumer, (b) low-income families on farms and in cities, (c) young people, (d) the aged, and (e) workers.
3. (a) Why did Roosevelt say that certain members of the Supreme Court thought in terms of the "horse-and-buggy" era? (b) How did he propose to remedy this situation? (c) How would his proposal have affected the balance of powers among the branches of the federal government?

Relating Past to Present

1. Which federal programs begun during the New Deal are still in operation today?
2. (a) How has history proved right the criticisms leveled against the New Deal? (b) How has history proved right the praise given to the New Deal?
3. Using the New Deal as a basis for comparison, how do you think the United States would react to such a severe economic crisis today?

Developing Social Science Skills

1. Read Herbert Hoover's "rugged individualism" speech of 1928 and Franklin D. Roosevelt's First Inaugural Address of 1933. (a) What is each President's view of the role of the federal government? (b) Based on these views, can you explain why each attempted to handle the depression in the way he did?
2. Draw a political cartoon that might have appeared in a newspaper during the Presidential election campaign of 1932, 1936, or 1940. Be sure that the cartoon clearly presents a point of view about a key issue or candidate of the campaign.
3. Read the novel *The Grapes of Wrath* by John Steinbeck or other novels set during the depression. (a) What problems brought on by the Great Depression did the characters face? (b) How did they try to solve these problems? (c) How does your impression of the Great Depression gained from the novel compare with that gained from your textbook? (d) How do you account for these similarities or differences?
4. Study the map on page 263. (a) Name five of the major dams in the TVA region. (b) Which states were included in the TVA region? (c) Why might the president of a privately owned power company in Alabama have opposed the TVA?
5. Write a caption story for the photograph on page 259. Make sure you describe the events that led to this view of devastating loss.

An American Album
Then and Now

Sports

Joe Louis, 12 years world heavyweight boxing champion.

Helen Wills Moody, 7 times U. S. women's singles tennis champion.

Babe Ruth, 11 years home run king of the American League.

Bobby Jones, 5 times U. S. amateur golf champion.

Jesse Owens, 4 Olympic gold medals in 1936.

The 1920's and 1930's were filled with great highs and lows, but one thing remained constant—America's love of sports and sports heroes. Sporting events offered people a chance to escape from their problems and lifted their spirits.

Of Babe Ruth, a fellow baseball player once said, "There was nobody like him...He was a god." Certainly the great slugger was no god, but to many Americans he and the other greats pictured here seemed almost superhuman.

The Puritans did not approve of sports, but that did little to keep America from becoming a nation of sports fans.

On these pages are just a few of the activities that have appealed to Americans from colonial days to the present. Individual tests of strength, courage, and endurance, simple team games, and highly organized ones have all been part of America's love of sports.

Lawn tennis was first played in America in 1874.

On the frontier, turkey shoots were popular and skills sharp.

Horse racing was the nation's first organized sport.

Long before the first settlers arrived, American Indians were playing lacrosse.

Football had its start on the nation's college campuses in the late 1800's.

In the late 1800's, ice skating was a social as well as a recreational activity.

Baseball began as a game called rounders in the early 1800's.

The heart pounds. The knees wobble. Sweat pours down the face. But the runner "never felt better." The runner has just finished 345th out of the 3,000 who entered this marathon.

This runner is not a star of the sports world, but simply one of millions of Americans trying to keep fit. Medical evidence has shown the links between exercise and good health. Americans have responded by lacing up running shoes, swinging tennis rackets, and pressing barbells. Spectator sports have long been big business in America. Today participant sports are, too.

For some, running was not only a way to keep fit, but a way to experience nature.

Thousands trained long hours in order to participate in the New York City marathon.

Chapter 15

From the "Jazz Age" Through the Great Depression

Writers and historians have pinned many different labels on the decade of the 1920's. Among these labels are the "Golden Twenties," the "Roaring Twenties," the "Age of Disillusionment," the "Decade of Wonderful Nonsense," the "Jazz Age," and the "Ballyhoo Years."

These labels suggest the character of the 1920's. These years were marked by widespread prosperity, by a sharp increase in the productivity of American industry, by disillusionment with the outcome of World War I, by an emphasis on the material aspects of life, and by the desire to get rich quick and to have a good time.

The decade of the 1930's was a very different story. The labels for the 1920's become a mockery when applied to the grim years of the Great Depression. The 1930's opened with the collapse of the nation's economy. Many banks failed and people throughout the nation lost the savings of a lifetime. Millions of Americans lost their jobs. Millions were homeless and hungry. Despair was widespread in the nation.

By the mid-1930's, however, hope was beginning to replace despair. Inspired by President Franklin D. Roosevelt and the New Deal, Americans in growing numbers faced the future with renewed faith and confidence.

Even so, progress was limited, and millions of men and women were still looking for work. Moreover, as the 1930's drew to a close, growing problems in Europe and Asia cast longer and darker shadows across the land.

1920's–1930's

THE CHAPTER IN OUTLINE

1. Machines continue to transform countryside, town, and city.

2. Industrialization speeds up changes in American society.

3. The depression drastically alters people's lives.

4. America's minorities struggle against hard times and discrimination.

5. Literature and the arts reflect changing ways and times.

1 Machines continue to transform countryside, town, and city

By 1920 the power-driven machine had become one of the dominant symbols of America. There were machines in factories, on farms, and in the home—and still the number and variety of machines kept multiplying. These machines helped transform America from a mainly rural to a mainly urban nation.

They also affected the daily lives of all Americans both in the city and on the farm.

Energy and efficiency. American industry in the 1920's could draw on vast reserves of energy to power its machines. There were enormous deposits of coal, huge underground pockets of oil and natural gas, water-power sites, and the know-how to generate large amounts of electrical power.

Use of the "new" sources of power, oil and electricity, soared during the 1920's. Between 1920 and 1930, petroleum production doubled. In the same years, production of electricity

In his 1928 painting "Boomtown," Thomas Hart Benton presented a view of America's spreading industrialization. Cars and the oil production on which they depend explain the boom experienced in this Western town.

went from 50 billion kilowatt-hours annually to 114 billion.

Manufacturers and engineers tackled the problem of using this abundance of energy most efficiently. Older machines were improved, and new machines were developed for factory, farm, and home. However, it was the organization of machines on a conveyor-belt assembly line that provided one of the striking characteristics of the American economy during the 1920's.

As you have read, mass production was an essential element of American industry long before the 1920's. Manufacturers had been using standardized interchangeable parts ever since Eli Whitney and European inventors had developed them more than a century earlier. The conveyor belt greatly increased the efficiency of the manufacturing process. First used on a large scale in automobile production by Henry Ford in 1914, the assembly line was soon adopted by other industries.

Efforts to increase efficiency were applied to workers as well as to machines. During the 1920's "time-and-motion" studies of machines and their operators were generally undertaken before a new machine or process was installed in an industrial plant.

Business executives also applied this efficiency engineering, or scientific management, to business planning and bookkeeping. This new approach to industrial efficiency was called "cost accounting." Cost accountants found out the cost of every item of machinery, materials, and labor that went into the total cost of producing or selling a product. They were then in a position to show business concerns how to cut costs and at the same time gain greater production at lower prices.

Bigger and bigger industries. Mass production could be carried on only by large, highly organized industrial concerns. During the "Golden Twenties," there was plenty of surplus capital to finance industrial development. As a result, older industries grew by leaps and bounds, while new industries climbed into the ranks of the giants.

Most of the growth of industry was the result of mergers—that is, the combining of two or more independent companies into one larger company. Between 1919 and 1929, for example, more than 1,000 mergers took place in manufacturing and mining. By 1930 only 200 corporations owned nearly half of the country's corporate wealth and one fifth of the total national wealth.

The attitude of government also encouraged the growth of large-scale industry. In the 1920's the government did not make any great effort to enforce the Sherman and the Clayton Antitrust Acts. Business and government were more interested in industrial efficiency than in industrial competition.

Advertising and marketing. Marketing techniques also became more effective during the 1920's. Advertising firms studied public psychology to discover how to appeal to consumers most effectively. Advertising firms also encouraged Americans to abandon the deeply rooted American ideal of thrift. In an age of abundance, they said, continued prosperity depended upon spending, not saving.

Mail-order houses, department stores, and chain stores continued to grow in number and size. The companies that had pioneered new methods of marketing during the late 1800's—Montgomery Ward, the Great Atlantic and Pacific Tea Company, F. W. Woolworth, Marshall Field, and Sears, Roebuck—were still among the leaders in their fields. These companies and many new ones were getting a big portion of the nation's retail business.

Two new developments that would contribute to a future revolution in the packaging of goods emerged in the 1920's. In 1923 Clarence Birdseye developed a method of quick-freezing for preserving perishable foods. In the same year, the Du Pont company bought the American patent rights to cellophane, a transparent wrapping material. By the late 1920's, frozen foods were being sold in stores, and cellophane was attracting attention.

The "automobile revolution." Even more important to the story of America's economic expansion in the 1920's was the development of the automobile. In 1920 about 8 million passenger cars and about 1 million trucks were registered in the United States. By 1930 about 23 million cars—an average of one car for every six citizens—and 3.5 million trucks were traveling the nation's roads.

This "automobile revolution" had far-reaching consequences. By 1930, cars, trucks, and buses had almost completely replaced horse-drawn vehicles. Even railroads and trolley cars were beginning to suffer from the competition of the gasoline-driven vehicles.

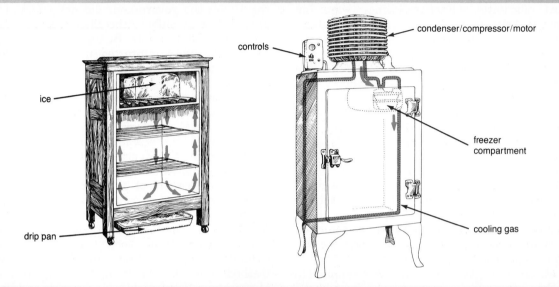

controls

condenser/compressor/motor

ice

freezer compartment

cooling gas

drip pan

ICEBOX AND ELECTRIC REFRIGERATOR

In an icebox warm air rises. At the top it melts some ice, which absorbs the air's heat. The chilled air falls and more rises to be cooled. As the air circulates, it refrigerates the contents of the icebox. The melting ice drips into a pan and is replaced periodically.

In an electric refrigerator, a refrigerant, such as ammonia, is changed back and forth from a liquid to a gas by a compressor. When depressurized, the liquid refrigerant evaporates and absorbs heat. The gas then flows to a condenser where it is repressurized and reliquefied.

By the end of the 1920's, the automobile industry had become the nation's biggest business, with an annual product valued at $3.5 billion in 1929. This new industrial giant used huge quantities of steel, glass, rubber, and other materials in manufacturing automobiles. It also created a rising demand for materials to build paved roads, garages, and service stations. It is estimated that 5 million persons, or one of every nine American workers, were employed in the automobile industry or a related business by 1930.

New industries. Many other new industries emerged during the 1920's. The increasing availability of electricity stimulated production of many labor-saving devicies for the homemaker. Among them were refrigerators, vacuum cleaners, toasters, electric fans, and electric stoves.

The chemical industry became one of America's most rapidly growing enterprises in the 1920's. By 1929 several American chemical companies were larger than any European competitors. In 1930 Du Pont, the giant among chemical companies, was producing 1,100 different products in 80 different factories in the United States. Among the products pouring out of the chemical plants were rayon, synthetic resins, and a growing variety of plastics.

Despite all the benefits, there was a negative side to the nation's rapid industrialization. Chemicals, gasoline, and other technical innovations began to pollute America's rivers and lakes—and even the air. In the cities, traffic and air pollution became problems. In the 1920's, however, few Americans paid much attention to these disadvantages. Most were content to enjoy the advantages of the machine age's quickening tempo.

Workers' gains and losses. The nation's growing industrialization greatly affected the lives of wage earners. The ever more rapid development of power-driven machines continued to free workers from backbreaking toil. Increases in productivity brought generally higher wages and an improved standard of living for the workers.

Wage earners at times benefited from the "time-and-motion" studies. Such studies could discover ways of lessening fatigue and eliminating accidents on the job. These studies showed that workers were happier and produced more when employers showed an interest in them. Applying this lesson, some employers introduced profit sharing and retirement plans and provided cafeterias, game rooms, and ballparks for employees.

Although employers as a whole showed increasing interest in working conditions, they opposed labor unions even more vigorously than before the war. A growing number of corporations in the 1920's started company unions. These were unions organized by the employers or their representatives rather than by the workers. Company unions as well as the higher standard of living contributed to the decline in strength of organized labor during the 1920's.

Urbanization. The growing industrialization also affected where Americans lived. It encouraged the movement of people from the countryside to cities and industrial centers. This is the process known as **urbanization.**

According to the 1920 census, the population of the United States was almost 106 million. For the first time in American history, those living in cities and towns outnumbered farm and country dwellers. The urban population then totaled 54 million, the rural population 51 million. By 1930 almost 69 million people lived in urban areas; the rural population, on the other hand, had reached only about 54 million. Moreover, a large percentage of the rural population lived in small towns and villages, not on farms.

Towns and cities were undergoing spectacular growth. Between 1920 and 1930, the rapidly growing population pushed 25 of America's older cities above the 100,000 figure. By 1930 as many as 93 cities had populations of 100,000 or more. Some of these urban areas more than doubled their population during this decade.

Changes in urban life. The very appearance of urban centers began to change. Huge new apartment houses appeared on what had been vacant lots or the sites of one-family houses. New skyscrapers pierced the skyline as builders tried to provide office space for the cities' growing industries. On the darker side, crowded housing conditions spurred the growth of slums in many cities.

Streets built in earlier times for horse-drawn vehicles and for a more leisurely way of life became increasingly crowded and noisy as automobiles and trucks multiplied. During the 1920's a new method of transportation, the bus, began to compete with the older electric trolleys. Although not a single bus was registered in the United States in 1920, about 40,500 were registered by 1930.

Perhaps most spectacular of all was the development of suburban areas. Streetcar lines and paved roads pushed out from the cities into the surrounding countryside. Farms in outlying areas were divided into building lots, and row after row of houses appeared in developments with such fanciful names as "Sunset Acres," "Grand View," and "American Venice."

Changes on the farms. By the 1920's developments in technology were breaking down the isolation and loneliness of farm life. Paved roads were reaching deeper into the countryside. Telephone and electric wires stretched along roads and across fields to farmhouses. Radio sets, a product of the 1920's, brought music, news, and entertainment into remote areas. Henry Ford's "Tin Lizzies" were parked beside barns and houses.

Machines also helped to ease farmers' burdens. Where electricity was available, it was used for lighting, for pumping water, and for refrigeration. Milking machines could now be found on many dairy farms. Trucks, tractors, and power-driven farm implements were being used by growing numbers of farmers. At the same time, more efficient farming methods and better plants and breeds of livestock were increasing farm productivity.

Farm problems. Increased productivity also created problems. A surplus of farm products drove farm prices downward. To be sure, not all farmers were hit equally hard by rising surpluses and falling prices. Dairy and truck farmers profited from the shift in American eating habits away from cereals toward more milk, butter, vegetables, and fruit. The citrus-fruit industries of California, Texas, and Florida experienced spectacular development. Tobacco growers also enjoyed a seller's market as cigarette smoking became more popular. The large, mechanized farms continued to prosper, mainly because they could afford the best equipment and could market their products most economically.

While the large, mechanized farms prospered, many of the small, family-owned farms were hard-hit. Handicapped by lack of money to buy expensive equipment, the farmers found it increasingly difficult to make a living.

These economic problems, coupled with the lure of the cities, led to a drop in farm population. Between 1920 and 1930, the number of people actually living on farms decreased from 31.6 million to 30.4 million. Young people in growing numbers were leaving farms to seek new opportunities in the booming cities.

SECTION SURVEY

IDENTIFY: assembly line, mass production, cost accounting, merger, Clarence Birdseye, cellophane, company union, urbanization.

1. Would it be correct to say that the machine and the word "efficiency" characterized America in the 1920's? Explain your answer.
2. (a) What was the "automobile revolution"? (b) In what ways did the automobile change life in the cities? In the country?
3. How were the lives of workers affected by (a) power-driven machines, (b) "time-and-motion" studies, and (c) company unions?
4. Graph Study: Reread this section, making note of all the population statistics given. Then make a line or bar graph showing the urban population, rural population, and total population from 1920 to 1930.

2 Industrialization speeds up changes in American society

The urbanization and industrialization of the 1920's altered the structure of American society. They led to changes in how people lived, learned, and amused themselves.

Growth of school enrollment. After World War I, it became increasingly clear that Americans needed a far more extensive education than that which had once been considered adequate. This fact, linked with the growth in urban population and improvements in transportation, led to an increased enrollment in the nation's schools.

In 1900 total high school enrollment had been under 700,000. By 1920, it had risen to about 2.5 million. The enrollment soared to 4.8 million by 1930 and continued to increase even during the heart of the depression.

The colleges showed similar gains. By the end of the 1930's, nearly 1.5 million students, or one out of every six or seven of college age, were enrolled in colleges and universities.

Minority groups made significant, though limited, gains in education. For example, a growing number of blacks in the North and South received a high school education, and more attended colleges and universities. By 1930 about 15,000 black Americans held academic degrees. Yet many blacks as well as Indians and Spanish-speaking Americans found that even an adequate elementary education was impossible to obtain. Because of prejudice and neglect, the doors of opportunity all too often remained closed to them.

Changes in the schools. To meet the needs of the enormously increased student body, American states and communities had to spend huge sums for new school buildings, textbooks, equipment, and teachers' salaries. The wealth created by the growing industrialization provided taxes that paid for these changes.

Some of the larger cities began to build high schools for as many as 5,000 to 10,000 students. In rural areas cars and buses permitted students from widely scattered areas to attend centrally located consolidated schools.

America's schools had to make other changes as well. Industrial society, with its emphasis upon highly specialized skills, called for men and women trained in mathematics, engineering, science, and the skilled trades. To meet the new needs, educators enlarged the curriculum to include more work in vocational training, home economics, commercial courses, health, physical education, foreign languages, and civic education. Special trade schools, technical schools, and commercial schools were built throughout the country in an effort to keep up with the machine age.

By the 1930's great strides were also being made in adult education. Radio stations began to give reports and commentaries on the news of the day. By 1936 at least 350 forums provided the chance to hear discussions of public issues. At the same time, vocational training for adults was also becoming more common.

Toward more effective education. During these years students of education were reaching new conclusions about how people actually learn and about the process of education. Educators, following the lead of psychologists William James and G. Stanley Hall, were proving that a child's mind can be molded — within limits. Other scholars, among them John Dewey, continued to teach that life itself is an education. They felt that the way to produce effective citizens is to give boys and girls actual experience in democratic living. Still other scholars, led by psychologists such as Edward L. Thorndike, worked out tests useful in measuring intelligence and evaluating the educational process.

New opportunities for women. During the 1920's the role of women underwent changes as striking as those in education. These changes brought new freedom and opportunity to women in American society.

An important step toward this new freedom was the adoption of the Nineteenth Amendment in 1920. This amendment gave women the right to vote in national elections. This right was a landmark in the struggle to win equality with men. The new League of Women Voters and other groups encouraged women to take an active part in political life.

Industrialization brought other changes in women's roles. The rapidly multiplying machines in mills, plants, and factories created new jobs on assembly lines for women. This was especially true in the textile and tobacco factories springing up in the South. Moreover, women were finding increasing opportunities to work as sales clerks, office workers, stenographers, and secretaries.

Equally important, the burden of housework was eased by new labor-saving devices — washing machines, irons, new types of stoves, vacuum cleaners, and refrigerators. Ready-made clothing and inexpensive sewing machines also relieved women of much of their labor. Packaged foods and canned goods helped to lighten the task of preparing family meals.

Middle-class women now had more time to read, to attend art exhibits, to hear lectures. Others now had time to work for civic improvements, to take part in political affairs, and to influence public opinion through such organizations as the League of Women Voters. Still others took active parts in parent-teacher associations. Never before had so many women found time and opportunity to develop interests outside the home.

The "new woman." The changing status and roles of women brought various expressions of a new sense of freedom. The "new woman," often a career woman, was more or less independent economically. She openly challenged what Charlotte Perkins Gilman, a leader of the new feminism, called "this manmade world." The new woman rejected the traditional female roles and refused to believe in the superior competence of men. She also denounced the different standards that were imposed on women in economic, sexual, and social relationships.

This defiance of conventional conduct among women was, in part, symbolized by the flappers. These young women, wearing above-the-knee dresses, bobbed hair, and lipstick, shocked older Americans as well as many people their own age. They took advantage of the freedom and mobility of the automobile, discussed sex openly and frankly, and smoked cigarettes. Flappers also defied the national Prohibition law by drinking in illegal bars called "speakeasies."

To some militant feminists, such indications of social freedom and equality did not go far enough. The Woman's Party challenged remaining legal discriminations against women. It demanded full equality in politics, business, the professions, sports, and the arts. In particular, the Woman's Party set as its goal an equal rights amendment to the Constitution of the United States that would outlaw all discrimination based on sex.

Influence of the automobile. Other changes in American society were a result of the nation's increasing prosperity.

By the 1920's the automobile was no longer the exclusive possession of the well-to-do. When working-class families were interviewed in a typical midwestern city in 1923, nearly half of them owned cars. The automobile was a major source of American recreation, as entire

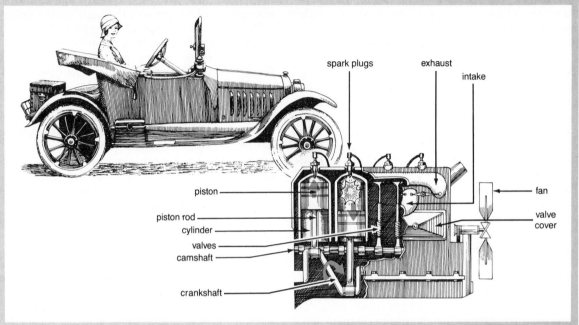

spark plugs   exhaust   intake   fan   valve cover

piston
piston rod
cylinder
valves
camshaft
crankshaft

INTERNAL COMBUSTION ENGINE

The internal combustion engine of an automobile changes up-and-down motion into rotary motion to turn the wheels. The intake valve admits a mixture of fuel and air into each cylinder, where a piston moves up and down. The piston rises and compresses the mixture and a spark plug ignites it. This ignition pushes the piston down and causes it to turn a crankshaft, which brings rotary motion to the wheels. The crankshaft also returns the piston to the top of the cylinder. Now an exhaust valve opens, and the piston pushes out the waste products of the ignition. After the piston falls again, it is ready to repeat the cycle. The ignitions in the cylinders are staggered by the timing of the spark plugs and by the design of the crankshaft so that the power that is generated can be spread out most evenly.

families piled into the car for an evening's ride or a weekend trip.

Although the automobile made travel comfortable and private, it also created new problems. Traffic accidents and deaths kept rising. Young people asserted their independence by driving off in the family car, free from parental supervision. Many Americans believed that the automobile was disrupting the family and destroying the nation's moral code.

The automobile also increased the difficulties of law enforcement by providing a convenient means of escape. It played a major role in the breakdown of Prohibition by providing a means for transporting illegal liquor.

Prohibition problems.   In January 1919 the Eighteenth Amendment was ratified (see pages 227–28). This amendment gave the federal government power to prohibit "the manufacture, sale, or transportation of intoxicating liquors."

In October 1919 Congress passed the Prohibition Enforcement Act, usually called the Volstead Act, over President Wilson's veto. This act defined as "intoxicating liquor" any beverage containing more than one half of one percent of alcohol, thereby making even beer and wine illegal.

The Prohibition experiment created serious problems in American life. Long coastlines in the east and west and unguarded frontiers to the north and south made it impossible to stop the flow of illegal liquor into the country.

Bootlegging became big business controlled by criminal elements in the large cities. The gangster Al Capone, who ruled Chicago's underworld, commanded a small army of gangsters equipped with revolvers, sawed-off shotguns, and submachine guns. Gang wars and other violence became common in many American cities during the "Roaring Twenties." Moreover, the gangs branched out to seize control of gambling establishments and dance halls. By the end of the decade, they had begun to develop the so-called "rackets." The racketeers collected "protection" money from businesses, threatening violence if their victims failed to pay.

The people themselves were partly to blame for this widespread violation of the law. Many Americans who were otherwise law-abiding refused to take Prohibition seriously. Finally, in 1933, the Prohibition era ended with the adoption of the Twenty-first Amendment, which repealed the Eighteenth Amendment. It returned the power to control the sale of intoxicating drinks to the states themselves.

Radio. Meanwhile another new development—radio—was helping to transform the lives of millions of Americans, both young and old alike.

KDKA, the first commercial broadcasting station, began to operate in Pittsburgh on November 2, 1920. Radio immediately became a craze. By 1929, sales of radio sets and parts amounted to almost $400 million. More than 600 broadcasting stations had been licensed, and one third of all American homes owned radio receivers.

Radio brought an enormous variety of information and entertainment directly to American families in their homes. The most popular programs featured "crooners," jazz musicians, comedians, sports announcers, and newscasters. However, many Americans felt that radio was not fulfilling its great promise as an instrument of education and culture. They criticized the dominant role of advertisers, who paid the broadcasting companies and entertainers and often determined what programs would be presented.

Despite the trivial content of many programs, however, radio served the nation in a variety of ways. By providing common experi-

Thousands of law officers like this one in Philadelphia tried to stop the flow of illegal liquor and beer during Prohibition in the 1920's. But as fast as government officials destroyed a supply of liquor, more was produced to replace it.

ences for all Americans, it increased the feeling of national unity. Radio also helped to overcome the isolation of rural life. It encouraged popular interest in current events, including sports, and offered useful information on health, home economics, and farming techniques. It made serious music available to more Americans than ever before. Finally, radio provided greater safety for airplanes and ships.

Sports. During the 1920's public interest in sports grew markedly. Baseball remained the most popular professional game, with between 9 and 10 million people attending major league games annually. Babe Ruth, who replaced Ty Cobb as the idol of fans, in 1927 astounded the baseball world with a record 60 home runs.

College football drew some 30 million spectators in the same year. Red Grange, a halfback for the University of Illinois, became a national hero. Jim Thorpe, with a Sauk, Fox, Potawatomi, and Irish heritage, also became a national hero. After playing football at Carlisle, an Indian college in Pennsylvania, he won medals in several events at the Olympic Games in Stockholm, Sweden, in 1912. Later, as an outstanding player in big league baseball and professional football, Thorpe was acclaimed as "the outstanding athlete of the half century." In boxing, fans in 1927 spent over $2.6 million to see the famous Dempsey-Tunney match. Amateur as well as professional interest also increased in such sports as golf, tennis, swimming, skating, and bowling.

Feats and fads. Americans in the 1920's were unusually responsive to new fads and fashions and dramatic public events. This period has been called the "Jazz Age" with some justice, for the rhythmic music of jazz was perhaps the most consistently popular of the new fashions. Other fads shifted rapidly from year to year: from the Chinese-originated game of mah-jongg, to crossword puzzles, to dances like the Charleston, to eccentric activities like flagpole sitting.

Some of the nation's enthusiasm was directed to individual accomplishments. The first glorified hero of the time was Charles A. Lindbergh, who in May 1927 made the first nonstop flight from New York to Paris in his plane *The Spirit of St. Louis.* Another fearless voyager was Commander (later Admiral) Richard E. Byrd. Byrd made the first flights to both the North and the South Pole. Other Americans who followed the example of Lindbergh and Byrd proved that the postwar period was an age of daring and feats as well as fads.

SECTION SURVEY

IDENTIFY: John Dewey, Edward Thorndike, Nineteenth Amendment, Charlotte Perkins Gilman, flappers, Woman's Party, Babe Ruth, Red Grange, Jim Thorpe, Charles A. Lindbergh, Richard E. Byrd.

1. (a) Why did school enrollment increase during the 1920's? (b) How did school curriculums change?
2. (a) How did women's lives begin to change during the 1920's? (b) What was the "new woman"?
3. What problems arose as a result of Prohibition?

3 **The depression drastically alters people's lives**

It can't be true! That was the initial reaction of Americans everywhere to the collapse of the nation's economy.

Unhappily, it was true. In a few short months during the winter of 1929–30, the prosperity and promise of the "Golden Twenties" had been replaced by unemployment, poverty, despair, and desperation.

What was it like? By 1932 industrial output had been reduced to half the 1929 figure. Wages had been cut by 60 percent, and one fourth of the nation's work force was jobless. The best estimates place the number of unemployed at 13 to 15 million.

A white-collar worker opened his pay envelope. It contained a pink slip informing him that his services were no longer needed. He had worked for the same company, one of the nation's largest corporations, for 40 years. He was 56 years old. He joined the millions of other jobless men and women.

No one really knew the number of people looking for work, and those seeking work were the breadwinners. Some 30 million others depended on them for food, clothing, and shelter.

These were the statistics. They translated into hunger, into the sad eyes of starving chil-

Much art in the 1930's depicted the plight of the down-and-out. In his painting titled "How Long Since You Wrote to Mother?" Raphael Soyer captured the loneliness of hungry men who came to missions for bread and coffee.

dren, into long lines of haggard men and women waiting for handouts of thin soup and dry bread provided by private and public charities. The men and women in the bread lines came from all walks of life and all social classes. There were former middle-income people and people from poor backgrounds. There were wage earners, business executives, and professional people. Hunger played no favorites.

Hunger was everywhere. "We saw a crowd of some 50 men fighting over a barrel of garbage which had been set outside the back door of a restaurant," one observer reported. This was not an isolated incident. Across the country men and women followed garbage trucks to the city dumps. Four hospitals in New York City reported 95 deaths from starvation in 1931. How many went unreported was never known.

Death came from self-inflicted causes as well. The Metropolitan Life Insurance Company reported that 20,000 Americans committed suicide in 1931.

Uprooted people. More than a million men and some women, many of them teen-agers, roamed the country looking for work. They rode the freight trains, thumbed rides on the roads, and did odd jobs where they could find them. They begged or stole food and slept wherever they could find shelter, on park benches or in shantytowns.

Every city had its shantytowns. Homeless people built them on vacant lots or on the city dumps out of packing boxes and scrap metal. "Hoovervilles" they were sometimes called, mocking the Hoover administration's failure to provide direct relief. There were also "Hoover blankets"—old newspaper used for warmth on park benches.

Many city people moved into the country hoping to find shelter and to raise their own food. Many farmers moved into the cities hoping to find work. People who had lost their homes or could no longer afford to pay rent moved in with relatives or friends. It was common to find several families crowded together in four or five rooms.

Rebellion on the farm. By 1932, farmers in some areas of the country were burning their corn to keep warm. Others armed with clubs, pitchforks, and shotguns confronted sheriffs who were trying to deliver foreclosure notices.

Other farmers, also armed, formed roadblocks and forced trucks loaded with milk to dump it on the road. With milk selling at 10 cents a quart in the stores, dairy farmers could not afford to operate. "They say blockading the highway's illegal," an Iowa farmer said. "Seems to me there was a Tea Party in Boston that was illegal, too."

The "Bonus Army." Farmers were not the only demonstrators. The "Bonus Army," 17,000 strong, arrived in Washington, D.C., in June 1932. They were veterans of World War I and they called themselves the "Bonus Expeditionary Force." Many arrived with their families. They traveled in freight cars, trucks, and wagons and on foot. They were in Washington to plead for a war bonus owed them. The money was not due until 1945, but they wanted it in advance.

They were allowed to live in empty government buildings and to camp on a swampy area across the Potomac River. The army provided them with tents, cots, field kitchens, and food. When the Senate refused to grant the bonus payment, most of them gave up and returned home with money provided by the government.

Some 2,000 of the veterans, many of whom had no place to go, decided to stay. They were ordered to leave. In a clash with the police, several veterans and police officers were killed. Army troops then moved in with machine guns, tanks, and tear gas. The troops drove the veterans from the buildings and broke up their encampment across the river, burning the shacks as they did so.

Slowing population growth. By the mid-1930's the New Deal had relieved much of the worst suffering and had restored a measure of hope. Nevertheless, grinding poverty continued to crush the dreams of millions of men, women, and children across the country. "I see one third of the nation ill-housed, ill-clad, ill-nourished," President Roosevelt said in 1937.

The Statue of Liberty still stood in New York harbor to welcome the poor, the homeless, the oppressed from other countries. However, the United States was no longer the "land of promise." Immigration had almost ceased. During the 1930's more people left America than entered it.

The number of marriages and the number of births also slowed. Many young people could not afford to marry and start families. In the decade of the 1930's, the population increased only about half as much as it had during the prosperous years of the 1920's.

More subdued living. Many of the rich and the well-to-do continued to live much as they had during the 1920's. For most Americans, however, even those who managed to hold onto their jobs, everyday life was much more subdued than it had been during the years of the "Golden Twenties."

Fewer people bought houses, household appliances, and new clothes. The sale of newspapers and magazines declined. At the same time, however, people read more, borrowing books from the public libraries.

People also tried to make things last. They kept their automobiles longer. This was possible, in part, because the number of service stations and repair shops doubled during the depression years.

Recreational activities reflected the slower pace of everyday life in the depression years. Not surprisingly, free recreation received the most attention. Hobbies, such as stamp collecting, became increasingly popular. So, too, did games that could be played at home, including cards, particularly bridge.

The radio. Radio, already popular in the 1920's, was the most common and the most influential form of entertainment in the 1930's. E. B. White, one of the keenest observers of the American scene, commented on the impact of the radio on rural folk. When they speak of "The Radio," White wrote, they have in mind "a pervading and somewhat godlike presence which has come into their lives and homes."

The growing popularity and influence of the radio, not only in rural areas but throughout the nation, was understandable. It provided something for just about everyone—news; music, including symphonies and operas; quiz programs and comedians; soap operas; church services; and adventure stories. All of these entered American homes through the mere turning of a dial.

President Roosevelt understood how effective radio could be in reaching people and broadcast a series of "Fireside Chats." These brought the people close to their government and added comfort and hope to the lives of millions. The "Fireside Chats" also helped Roosevelt gain and hold his popularity and win four successive Presidential elections!

1. How did some farmers react to the depression?
2. (a) What was the "Bonus Army"? (b) Was its stay in Washington, D.C., successful? Explain.
3. What effects did the depression have on population growth in the United States? Why?
4. Picture Study: Study the pictures in this section. Based on them, write a description of life during the depression.

4 America's minorities struggle against hard times and discrimination

The 1920's and 1930's were difficult times for America's minorities. They did not share equally in the growing prosperity of the "Golden Twenties." Later, when the depression of the 1930's hit, the minorities bore the heaviest burden.

Black migration to the North. Before World War I, many black families had moved from the South to the growing northern industrial centers. There they had hoped to escape poverty and discrimination and to find jobs, housing, and better education for their children.

World War I, with its heavy demand for industrial workers, had increased this migration. During the war about half a million southern blacks had found jobs in such places as the coal mines of West Virginia and Illinois, the steel mills of Pittsburgh, and the automobile factories of Detroit.

The movement into urban areas continued after the war. Between 1910 and 1930, the black population of the northern states rose from a little over 1 million to nearly 2.5 million. In the same years, the number of black wage earners in American industries nearly doubled, rising from about 600,000 to nearly 1 million.

Black families did not find in the North all the opportunities they sought. Blacks got the hardest jobs and the lowest pay. Northern white wage earners sometimes staged protest strikes against the hiring of blacks. Housing shortages, brought on by wartime building restrictions, also led to tensions when blacks tried to move into white neighborhoods in search of places to live.

Disappointed hopes. World War I, the war "to make the world safe for democracy," had naturally aroused the hopes of black Americans. Black soldiers returning from Europe, where they had been treated as equals, looked forward to new and greater freedom at home. They were angry and disappointed to find conditions in America little changed.

They were especially discouraged to find a new Ku Klux Klan operating in the North as well as in the South. The new Klan harassed Jews, Catholics, foreign-born citizens, and anyone else it chose to call "dangerous" and "un-American." However, blacks were the special object of Klan violence.

There were other reasons for black bitterness as well. In 1919–20 the nation's economy went into a postwar depression. This heightened the competition for jobs between blacks and whites and led to increased racial tension.

The riots of 1919. The rising tensions burst out in violence during the summer of 1919. Riots in more than 20 cities, northern and southern, brought death and injury to hundreds of men and women and destroyed thousands of tenements in city slum areas.

The riots generally began when blacks fought back against some especially discriminatory act. Frightened whites, convinced that black Americans were trying to threaten them and gain control, responded with more violence. Police forces, ill-equipped to deal with riots, usually sided with whites, causing blacks to take even more desperate actions.

The riots solved no problems. Nor did they spur local or national officials to try to remedy even the more obvious causes of the trouble. As a result, black Americans were now more ready to follow leaders who insisted that blacks had a lawful right to defend themselves when the law itself failed to do so.

Black pride. In the 1920's many blacks felt a growing sense of racial identity and pride along with an increasing interest in their African backgrounds. These feelings were strongly expressed by Marcus Garvey, a black immigrant from Jamaica in the West Indies.

Garvey became convinced that blacks could never win true freedom and equality in the

Black migration from the rural South to the urban North began during the first World War. The movement continued through the 1920's and the 1930's. Here black artist Jacob Lawrence depicts this trend in "The Migration of the Negro."

United States. He popularized among black city slum dwellers a form of black nationalism that emphasized a "back-to-Africa" movement. He eloquently described the achievements of black Africans and urged his listeners to return "home," where they might enjoy opportunities they could never find in white-dominated America.

None of Marcus Garvey's half-million black followers ever moved to Africa as he suggested. Nonetheless, Garvey's program did help to awaken in many blacks a new sense of racial pride.

Most black leaders of the 1920's opposed Garvey's movement as unrealistic and escapist. They insisted that blacks, having long been Americans, could and had to win the rights and opportunities that other Americans enjoyed. However, these leaders also encouraged American blacks to become interested in the achievements and hopes of black people in Africa and other parts of the world. Racial solidarity, they urged, should replace the narrow outlook that separated black Americans from blacks in other lands and that divided black Americans into different economic and social groups.

The "new Negro." Growing black pride was also stimulated by new achievements in arts and literature. One work that encouraged the rise of younger black leaders was *The New Negro* by Alain Locke, a professor at Howard University. This important book both reflected and encouraged the changes taking place in black communities.

The new black leaders insisted that the "new Negro" had to be proud of the black heritage. They insisted that black Americans stop being defensive and apologetic to white Americans. The "new Negro" had to realize that self-assertiveness, not accommodation, was the only effective way to gain full equality.

As part of this assertion of identity, many blacks came to believe that it was necessary to develop a separate black economy within the American economy. Businesses owned and operated by blacks would serve the black communities. The profits from these businesses would flow to blacks and further stimulate financial independence.

By 1929, blacks ran some 25,700 stores. Many factories, banks, and insurance companies were owned and operated by blacks as well.

Gains in civil rights.

The growing sense of pride and self-assertiveness led blacks in both the North and the South to make headway in their struggle for equal justice under the law. Black leaders denounced lynching, white terrorism, and discrimination in housing and in the courts. In these areas the efforts of the NAACP to bring lawsuits designed to bring about the enforcement of equal rights for blacks began to show important progress.

The major political parties did little to further the struggles of blacks in the 1920's. The Republican Party was trying to build strong political organizations in the South. As a result, the Republican administrations hesitated to meet the demands of southern blacks for federal protection of their voting rights or for a fair share of federally appointed jobs. Nevertheless, Oscar de Priest of Chicago ran as a Republican and in 1928 became the first black elected to Congress in 28 years.

The Democratic Party held power in the South and continued efforts to exclude black voters. In spite of this, Democrats in northern cities began to seek black support, and blacks slowly began to join the Democratic Party.

Blacks and the depression.

For blacks the coming of the depression was a catastrophe. Many businesses and banks owned by blacks went bankrupt. Black workers lived with the bleak knowledge that they were "the first fired and the last hired." During the worst years of the depression, an estimated two thirds of the blacks in American industry lost their jobs.

The New Deal provided black Americans with relief and employment in the Works Progress Administration, the Civilian Conservation Corps, and the National Youth Administration. By 1936, one sixth of those on relief were blacks. One black newspaper writer explained the meaning of one New Deal program to blacks: "The really important thing about the WPA is that it is a guarantee of a living wage." Blacks also had a share of new low-cost housing, and black farmers and sharecroppers received benefits from New Deal agricultural agencies. However, blacks suffered some degree of discrimination in almost all New Deal programs. A smaller percentage of blacks were employed in the work programs, and the housing and agricultural programs were particularly unfair to blacks.

Nevertheless, blacks did receive more aid under the New Deal than they had under Hoover's administration. In addition, at the urging of Eleanor Roosevelt, the President's wife, blacks were appointed to important federal positions. Among them were Mary McLeod Bethune, Ralph Bunche, and Robert C. Weaver. These and other leaders made up an informal group of advisers often called the "black cabinet."

Such New Deal actions revolutionized the voting habits of black Americans. By 1936, black voters were shifting to the Democratic Party. By the end of the decade, the Democrats had firmly secured the black vote.

The depression and the new opportunities provided by the New Deal increased the determination of blacks to win their legal and constitutional rights. In many northern cities, black leaders organized "don't-buy-where-you-can't-work" campaigns. In the rural areas, tenant farmers, black and white, often joined together against wealthy landlords. The National Negro Congress united black and interracial organizations from all across the nation in the struggle for black rights.

Despite these advances and the progress stimulated by New Deal programs, much remained to be done. For the vast majority of blacks, the elimination of prejudice and full acceptance into the mainstream of American life remained an unfulfilled dream.

Indian policy.

Other racial and ethnic problems in the nation were becoming critical in the 1920's. The policy of "Americanizing" the Indians under the Dawes Act (page 76) had failed. Individual farm ownership was contrary to Indian traditions. Many tribes had never engaged in farming. Indians who did try to learn modern methods of farming often had to struggle with worn-out, nonfertile land. As for education, the government-sponsored boarding schools and day schools deprived Indian children of their tribal identity but gave them no identity that they could find meaningful.

In 1924 the Indian population as a whole received United States citizenship, partly in recognition of the young Indian men who had fought in World War I. Citizenship did not lessen the harsh fact that Indian poverty was greater than that of any other group in the United States. The discovery of oil on some Indian lands brought unexpected wealth to a few Indians, but for most life was grim. Still, earlier predictions that the Indians were a vanishing race proved incorrect. The Indian population increased from about 243,000 in 1863 to about 350,000 in 1924.

Indians and the New Deal. In 1928 a report by the Institute for Government Research described the destructive conditions on Indian reservations. The report and other criticisms led Congress in 1934 to pass the Howard-Wheeler Act, or the Indian Reorganization Act.

The new law halted the breaking up of reservations by granting lands to individual Indians. It tried to restore to tribal ownership parts of reservations that had not yet become individual homesteads. The act also emphasized local control. It permitted tribes to choose whether or not they wished to practice local self-government. It allowed them to strengthen community life by reestablishing traditional beliefs, customs, and crafts. Under the act, Indians were allowed to engage in any business of their choice, to make contracts, and to sue or be sued in court.

The Howard-Wheeler Act also tried to teach Indians to use their land more effectively. Soil-conservation practices and improved methods of raising and marketing crops and livestock were taught. The new educational program included adults and children and made the school a center of community life.

Many problems remained in spite of the change in policy. Some tribes that had been more or less successfully "Americanized" disliked the new policy. They believed it would keep them inferior in American society. Efforts to improve unused Indian lands met with little success. Thus although the new policy brought greater freedom and recognition to the Indians, its aim of raising Indian standards of living was not realized.

Mexican Americans. As you may recall, many former citizens of Mexico became citizens of the United States at the close of the Mexican War in 1848. In the 1890's increasing numbers of Mexicans migrated into the United States looking for jobs. The need for labor during World War I and the desire of many Mexicans to escape the troubled economic and political conditions in Mexico increased the flow across the border. During the 1920's about half a million new Mexican immigrants arrived.

Most of these immigrants were poor families from rural areas. They were forced to work for low wages as migrant laborers in agriculture, in mining, and in railroad construction throughout the Southwest and, increasingly, the Middle West. They entered the United States speaking a different language and practicing different customs. For the most part poor and ill-educated, they met with prejudice and discrimination in jobs, housing, and schools.

Established labor groups resented them because they lowered wage scales by accepting, out of necessity, almost any rate of pay. White resentment also grew because these new immigrants could cross and recross the border as economic conditions in Mexico improved or worsened.

Despite these burdens, Mexican Americans took an increasingly active part in the organized labor movement. They shared each other's problems and developed a sense of cooperation through *mutalistas,* or self-aid societies. Particularly in New Mexico, they made their influence felt politically.

The United States and Mexico jointly developed a program to deal with immigration from Mexico. The Expatriation Program, as it was called, was designed to persuade Mexican immigrants to return to their own country. From the Mexican point of view, the purpose of the program was to revitalize the Mexican economy by making use of the skills the Mexicans had learned while in the United States. Some 500,000 men and women did return to Mexico. Only too often, however, they were disappointed with their decision. Conditions in their native land were bleak and they were ready, whatever the obstacles, to try once again to improve their lives in the United States.

The depression added to the burdens of the Mexican Americans. Jobs in agriculture and on railroads became scarce. Increasingly, the Mexican Americans moved from rural areas into the cities, where there was at least some hope, however slim, of finding work. At least in the cities, if jobs were not available, New Deal relief programs were.

SECTION SURVEY

IDENTIFY: Marcus Garvey, *The New Negro,* Oscar de Priest, "black cabinet," National Negro Congress, Indian Reorganization Act, *mutalistas,* Expatriation Program.

1. What factors helped cause the race riots of 1919?
2. (a) What does the term "new Negro" mean? (b) How did growing black pride affect business? How did it affect politics?

3. Why did blacks increasingly vote for candidates from the Democratic Party?
4. (a) What was American policy toward Indians during the 1920's? (b) How successful was it?
5. What was the situation of Mexican Americans during the 1920's and 1930's?

5 Literature and the arts reflect changing ways and times

During the 1920's and 1930's, writers and artists struggled to deal with new issues raised by changes in American society. At times, the struggle was with changing standards and values brought on by prosperity during the 1920's and depression during the 1930's. At other times, the struggle was to find new forms of expression that seemed appropriate to the machine age in America.

Concern for a vanishing past. Although American literature in many ways reflected the changing ways of life, one group of writers revealed their concern for a rapidly vanishing past. Edith Wharton and Ellen Glasgow contrasted the order and stability of bygone New York and Virginia with the restless materialism of the newly rich in a new age. In her writings Willa Cather recaptured the vitality and heroism of pioneer life in Nebraska and compared it to the empty lives of those whose major goal was material success.

Reactions to life in the 1920's. Many writers, however, focused directly on the conflicts and confusions of the emerging industrial world. T. S. Eliot in his poem *The Waste Land* (1922) pictured society in the machine age as grim, barren, standardized, cheap, and vulgar.

Several writers revealed the tragedy of equating success with money and the things money could buy. Theodore Dreiser's *An American Tragedy* (1925) unraveled the sordid story of a youth who deliberately let his girlfriend drown in order to pursue what in the end proved to be a futile goal. F. Scott Fitzgerald in his first novel, *This Side of Paradise* (1920), vividly pictured the confusion of the college "jazz set," bored with the futility of fast living and hard drinking. Later, in *The Great Gatsby*

(1925), Fitzgerald portrayed the emptiness of life devoted primarily to a frenzied struggle to make money. Sinclair Lewis wrote a number of books highlighting the deadening conformity and hypocrisy of middle-class life in America, among them *Main Street* (1920), *Babbitt* (1922), and *Elmer Gantry* (1927). In 1930 he received the Nobel Prize in literature, the first American writer to be so honored.

Literature of the 1930's. Several writers reacted forcefully to the crushing impact of the depression. The most gripping picture of those years was John Steinbeck's novel *The Grapes of Wrath* (1939). The story follows the sad fortunes of a poor but self-respecting Oklahoma family. Driven from their home in the dust bowl, they sought survival in California. Unhappily, life in California proved lonely and harsh. Sad though the story is, it ends on a glimmer of hope for the homeless, downtrodden wanderers.

Sinclair Lewis viewed the depression from a different angle. In a sobering novel, *It Can't Happen Here* (1935), Lewis contended that American society in the 1930's was ripe soil from which a dictatorship might arise.

Ernest Hemingway was another writer who came to grips with basic issues confronting America and the world. In *A Farewell to Arms* (1929), he stripped the romance and glamor from World War I. In *For Whom the Bell Tolls* (1939), he presented a graphic picture of the violence and brutality of the Spanish Civil War and in so doing provided a preview of World War II.

The Harlem Renaissance. Black writers and artists, inspired by the image of the "new Negro," produced important works that led to a cultural renaissance or rebirth. Their works aroused the interest of many white Americans while strengthening the growing pride of black Americans. This cultural rebirth of the 1920's centered in New York City's black community of Harlem. It has been called the "Harlem Renaissance," but its rich expressions were not confined to Harlem.

These new cultural contributions were marked by originality, freshness of style, and vigor. Jazz music, with its exciting and spontaneous rhythms, and the blues, reflecting the joy, laughter, sadness, and pain of black Americans, found outstanding composers and performers in the 1920's and 1930's. Among these

Edward Hopper, 1887-1967. "Early Sunday Morning." Oil on canvas. 19330. 35 × 60. Collection of Whitney Museum of American Art, New York.

One of the great painters who captured the look of America in the 1920's and 1930's was Edward Hopper. There is a quality of starkness and loneliness that can be found in many of his scenes such as this one, "Early Sunday Morning."

were W. C. Handy, Jelly Roll Morton, Louis Armstrong, and Duke Ellington. Black spirituals became part of the repertory of Marian Anderson, who in the 1920's was just beginning her career as one of the world's greatest singers of classical as well as folk music. Also during the 1920's, Paul Robeson began his brilliant career as an actor, concert singer, and civil rights activist.

The literature of the Harlem Renaissance reflected the racial pride of the "new Negro." Langston Hughes, Claude McKay, and Countee Cullen wrote verse marked by haunting bitterness and defiance but also by joy and hope. This many-sided emotional richness among black writers was exemplified by Jean Toomer's *Cane.* This work portrayed black environments in the rural South, in Washington, D. C., and in New York City. It starkly revealed its characters' intense emotions while also portraying their beauty and dignity.

Among the black writers of the 1930's, Richard Wright was a towering figure. In the four short novels that make up *Uncle Tom's Children* (1938), he explored Southern racial problems. His most famous novel, *Native Son,* is a harsh picture of life in the slums of Chicago. His autobiography, *Black Boy,* is a powerful portrayal of his family's experiences during his childhood years.

Journalism. Newspapers and magazines also reflected the influence of the machine age. By the 1920's journalism had become big business. *Reader's Digest,* started in 1922 by Dewitt Wallace, won nationwide circulation with its collection of condensed articles from other journals. *Time,* the brainchild of Henry R. Luce, was widely read for its concise reporting of current events. The enormous success of *Time* led to the founding of competitors, chief among them *Newsweek,* started in 1933 during the depth of the depression. Luce, who had made a fortune out of *Time,* bought the humorous magazine *Life* in 1936. He transformed it into the first American publication devoted to photojournalism, in which articles are developed largely through the use of photographs. It, too, soon attracted competitors, the most successful of which was *Look.*

Meanwhile, many of the individually owned newspapers were being bought by large newspaper chains. Chain newspapers ran the same syndicated columns and editorials, the same comics, sports news, and advertisements. They subscribed to the same news services—the Associated Press, the United Press, and the International News Service. Like the magazines, the newspapers reflected the problems of industrial America.

Painting and design. In painting and design, Americans were more and more influenced by such European artists as Cézanne, Manet, Monet, Degas, Matisse, and Picasso. Some modernists boldly experimented with geometric designs that often resembled machines in their emphasis on hard angles, masses, and abstract form. Many American artists continued to paint the more conventional themes, but they painted them in new ways. Others tried to reveal the meaning of the machine age in their paintings of factories, warehouses, slums, railroads, and other scenes of urban life.

New art forms. The machine age also opened up entirely new forms of art. In the hands of artists, the camera captured the spirit and meaning of the new age. New methods of art reproduction enabled people to own inexpensive yet excellent copies of the world's outstanding works of art. When these reproduction techniques were adopted by the mass-circulation magazines, millions of Americans were able to see the work of the world's greatest photographers, illustrators, and artists.

Aided by commercial artists and industrial designers, manufacturers began to produce telephones, furniture, fabrics, clothing, typewriters, glassware, refrigerators, stoves, automobiles, and many other articles that showed that machines and machine products might be beautiful in design and structure.

The movies. Motion pictures, the movies, were one new product of the machine age. They were a fascinating combination of new technology, big business, and art.

The movies rapidly became an important part of American life. In the 1920's huge and lavish motion picture palaces were built in large cities throughout the country. By the end of the decade, the motion picture industry had become the fourth largest one in the nation. Even during the hard times of the de-

pression, movies remained popular. In 1938, movie audiences numbered more than 80 million a week. In that same year, more than 500 American movies were produced.

The movies both reflected and shaped American society. Traditional values—the home, hard work, thrift—were usually upheld in movie stories. However, the movies often popularized less traditional values. The world of the "jazz set" and the flappers, when portrayed on the screen, looked glamorous. People began to copy the styles and manners of the movies.

Artistically, movies made great advances. Storytelling in the silent films of the 1920's was much more polished and sophisticated than in most prewar films. Directors also explored more demanding themes. Erich von Stroheim's *Greed* described with great power how greed for money warped the character and finally destroyed the lives of a working-class couple. Robert Flaherty's *Nanook of the North,* a documentary, captured the grandeur of nature and the difficulty of life in the Arctic. Great comics like Charlie Chaplin and Buster Keaton left audiences rocking with laughter—and furthered the art of silent-movie making.

In 1927 Warner Brothers released the first successful "talkie," *The Jazz Singer.* For a time, as moviemakers adapted to using sound, motion pictures became more stiff and stagy. Soon, however, sound techniques were mastered, and movies became more exciting and popular than ever.

In the 1930's Fred Astaire and Ginger Rogers sang and danced through a series of films that took people's minds off the problems of the depression. Directors like Howard Hawks, in *His Girl Friday,* and Frank Capra, in *Meet John Doe* and *Mr. Smith Goes to Washington,* studied manners and morals in contemporary society. John Ford, in *Stagecoach, Young Mr. Lincoln,* and *The Grapes of Wrath,* produced works that questioned and celebrated American history.

Architecture. Inspired by such outstanding architects as Louis Sullivan and Frank Lloyd Wright, other architects began to promote the idea that a building ought to use the materials and follow the forms most suitable to the purposes for which it was to be used.

For many people the skyscraper became a symbol of the influence of the machine upon architecture. Built of steel, glass, and concrete, it towered into the sky in order to use as little

INVASION FROM MARS

At eight o'clock on the evening of October 30, 1938, millions of radio listeners throughout the country heard the following announcement: "The Columbia Broadcasting System and its affiliated stations present Orson Welles and the Mercury Theater of the Air in *The War of the Worlds* by H. G. Wells."

There was a brief pause, followed by a weather report. Then an announcer declared that the program would be continued from a New York hotel. A jazz band came on the air. Suddenly the music stopped. An announcer, his voice tense and anxious, broke in to declare that a professor had just observed a series of explosions on Mars. Other announcements followed in rapid order. A meteor had landed near Princeton, New Jersey. Fifteen hundred people had been killed. No, it wasn't a meteor. It was a spaceship from Mars. Martian creatures were emerging from the ship. The creatures were armed with powerful death rays. They had come to wage war against the people living on earth.

An untold number of listeners were seized with panic. Some fell to their knees and began to pray. Others gathered their families, rushed from their homes, and fled on foot or by car into the night.

Yet it was only a radio play. CBS stated this fact clearly four different times during the hour-long program. Numerous explanations were advanced for the outburst of mass hysteria. But one thing was clear—the extraordinary power of broadcasting.

expensive ground space as possible. Upper stories were set back to prevent the streets from being darkened. In the emphasis upon clear-cut vertical lines and the massing of windows, the skyscraper was an excellent example of how purpose and materials dictated design.

Music and dancing. Music, too, showed the influence of the industrial age. Many people believed that jazz expressed the rhythms and the accelerated speed and energy of the machine. Music also became increasingly available through the radio, the phonograph, and musical instruments manufactured at lower and lower costs. Moreover, wealth created by the new industrial age supported symphony orchestras and opera companies.

Social dancing was transformed by jazz, while the dance as an art form was revolutionized by Isadora Duncan, Ruth St. Denis, Katherine Dunham, Ted Shawn, and Martha Graham. These dancers emphasized free and expressive movements in contrast to the traditional, formal patterns of the ballet.

SECTION SURVEY

IDENTIFY: Edith Wharton, Ellen Glasgow, Willa Cather, *The Waste Land, An American Tragedy,* F. Scott Fitzgerald, Sinclair Lewis, *The Grapes of Wrath,* Ernest Hemingway, Harlem Renaissance, *Cane,* Richard Wright, chain newspapers, Charlie Chaplin, *The Jazz Singer,* Frank Lloyd Wright, Isadora Duncan.

1. How did some writers show their disillusionment with the America of the 1920's?
2. How did the movies both reflect and shape American society?
3. How did the skyscraper symbolize the influence upon architecture of (a) land values and (b) industrialization?

Chapter Survey

Summary: Tracing the Main Ideas

During the 1920's the process of industrialization rapidly gathered momentum. Machines replaced or lightened human labor on the farm, in the factory, and in America's homes. The developing technology created a higher standard of living. At the same time, it began to give new directions to people's goals and to transform their daily lives.

Many critics of American life claimed that modern technology was standardizing life. These critics were disturbed that the machine, which had given people such immense power, was being used largely to make money and to provide more or less meaningless recreation.

Other students of American society defended the new technology. They pointed to the obvious fact that it relieved people of backbreaking toil and that it made possible more leisure, more consumer goods, more comforts, and more time for education and for pleasure. All of these advantages, they argued, provided a greater measure of freedom for the individual American.

As the 1920's drew to a close, however, the arguments over the advantages and disadvantages of modern technology were suddenly buried beneath the crushing impact of the Great Depression. For three desperate years, life for many Americans, and especially for the minorities, became a grim struggle for survival. The New Deal, born with the inauguration of President Franklin D. Roosevelt in March 1933, brought new hope to suffering Americans. In the following years, it brought growing relief from the heaviest burdens of unemployment and poverty.

The decades of the 1920's and the 1930's—the one characterized by widespread prosperity, the other by poverty and unemployment—left distinctive marks upon the American scene. Every aspect of life—including education, literature, and the arts—was influenced by the changing ways and times.

Inquiring into History

1. How did industrialization affect the lives of people (a) on farms and (b) in cities? Does industrialization always mean progress? Explain.
2. (a) How did the radio, movies, and newspaper chains contribute to conformity? (b) How did they contribute to individualism?
3. What are the relationships between industrialization and the role of women?
4. During the 1920's many black Americans left the South to go North. Did the northern cities turn out to be an escape to freedom? Explain.
5. (a) In what ways were the situations of blacks, Indians, and Mexicans similar during the 1920's and 1930's? (b) How were they different?

Relating Past to Present

1. Do you think television today has more, the same, or less effect on society than radio did in the 1920's? Explain.
2. Was poverty in the Great Depression different from poverty that exists today? If so, how?

3. What similarities can you cite between the woman's movement of the 1920's and the woman's movement of today? Explain.
4. During the depression, people were making special efforts to make their dollars stretch and such things as automobiles last. Do you think people have reasons to be doing the same sorts of things today? Explain.

Developing Social Science Skills

1. Read some of the poetry written by a poet of the Harlem Renaissance, such as Countee Cullen, Claude McKay, or Langston Hughes. (a) What do the poems tell you about the lives and concerns of black Americans in the 1920's? (b) What are the poet's attitudes about American society and values?
2. Assume that you lived during the Great Depression and your family left its home to seek jobs and a better life in another part of the country. Write a letter to a friend describing your experiences on the road and in your new home.

Unit Survey

For Further Inquiry

1. Explain how each of the following demonstrates a rejection of Progressivism and the ideals of the New Freedom: (a) President Harding's campaign slogan of "a return to normalcy," (b) President Coolidge's statement, "The business of America is business." (c) President Hoover's belief in "the American system of rugged individualism."
2. (a) Make a list of five words or phrases that describe American life during the 1920's. (b) Explain each of your choices.
3. (a) Why did the Great Depression happen? (b) Could such an economic collapse ever happen again? Why or why not?
4. Do you think the New Deal changed the basic character of the federal government? Why or why not?
5. Would either Hamilton or Jefferson have approved of the New Deal? Give evidence to support your answer.
6. (a) How did the depression affect the lives of America's minorities? (b) Why did it affect them that way?

Projects and Activities

1. Study the timeline here. (a) According to the timeline, was the situation of workers improving? How can you tell? (b) How were conditions for farmers? For Indians and blacks? (c) Does the information on the timeline seem to conform to the information in Unit 5? Which is more useful as a source of information about economic trends during the 1920's and 1930? Why?
2. Research the history of the Ku Klux Klan. How did the various stages of its history reflect the times?
3. Prepare a bulletin board display entitled, "Heroes of the Golden Twenties." Include in the display pictures, short biographies, or newspaper headlines to feature people such as Charles Lindbergh, Babe Ruth, Gertrude Ederle, and Bill Tilden.
4. Prepare a series of political cartoons on the New Deal. Be sure to keep the cartoons simple and to make clear the point of view expressed in each one.
5. Make a bar or line graph on one aspect of the 1920's and 1930's, such as (a) government spending, (b) average family income, (c) cost of living, (d) number of bank failures.

Exploring Your Region

1. In your community, try to locate buildings, roads, or bridges that were built during the New Deal. Find out the circumstances under which they were built. Prepare a map of your community that indicates their location.
2. Make a list of items in your home or school that were not yet invented or in use during the 1920's and 1930's. Describe what daily life would have been like without those items.

Suggested Readings

1. *Winged Legend: The Story of Amelia Earhart,* John Burke. Biography of America's outstanding woman aviator, whose plane disappeared over the Pacific in 1937.
2. *Black Boy,* Richard Wright. The story of the early life of a major American writer.
3. *The Great Depression,* David Shannon. Eyewitness accounts of life during the depression, including discussion of farming, relief, and education.
4. *Only Yesterday,* Frederick Lewis Allen. A popular history that documents the fads and fashions of the 1920's.
5. *Babbitt,* Sinclair Lewis. A satirical novel of middle-class life in the 1920's.

Unit Six

From Isolation Through World War II

1920-1945

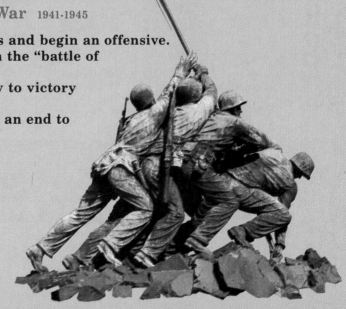

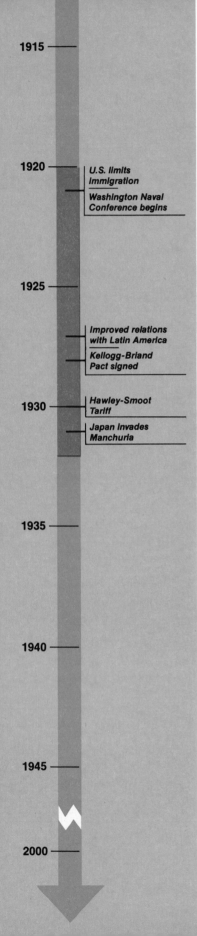

1915

1920 — U.S. limits
immigration

Washington Naval
Conference begins

1925

Improved relations
with Latin America

Kellogg-Briand
Pact signed

1930 — Hawley-Smoot
Tariff

Japan invades
Manchuria

1935

1940

1945

2000

Chapter 16

The United States Moves Toward Isolation

1920-1932

During the 1920's and 1930's, Americans had faced rapidly changing conditions at home. The economy had moved from a postwar depression to a boom to almost complete collapse in the Great Depression.

Relations with foreign nations went through equally complex changes during these years. The end of World War I in 1918 had released emotions long held in check. Millions of people on every continent mourned for loved ones killed in the war. Mixed with the sorrow, however, was wild joy that the war to end all wars was over. Millions of people offered prayers of thanksgiving and prayers for the fulfillment of President Wilson's vision of a world rebuilt on a foundation of lasting peace.

Wilson realized, as millions of Americans did not, that it is easier to win a victory on a battlefield than it is to build a lasting peace. He warned Americans that great problems remained to be solved and he challenged them to take up the responsibility of world leadership.

Unhappily, Wilson's plea went unheeded, and the idealism that marked the end of the war soon faded. Americans were tired of wartime restrictions and eager to return to the everyday business of living. Also, as the European Allies with whom the United States had fought began to quarrel over the spoils of war, Americans became increasingly disillusioned.

President Wilson struggled to keep his vision before the American people. However, during the 1920's, the American people rejected his policies, both domestic and foreign. They refused to join the League of Nations, and, in the following years, they turned their backs on Europe and on the chance to take on the challenge of world leadership.

THE CHAPTER IN OUTLINE

1. America closes its doors to Europe's people and goods.

2. The United States moves toward the Good Neighbor Policy.

3. Americans cooperate with other nations in efforts to prevent war.

1 America closes its doors to Europe's people and goods

After World War I, the United States in some ways drew back from involvement in world affairs. America refused, for example, to join the League of Nations in part to avoid becoming entangled again in Europe's troubles and quarrels.

The United States also tried, with considerable success, to keep out the people and products of Europe and Asia. The immigration and tariff laws passed during this period were the most restrictive in American history.

Closing the doors. During the 1920's the United States reversed one of its oldest traditions by almost completely halting immigration. Earlier, it is true, laws and international agreements had excluded the Chinese, the Japanese, and most other Asians. Despite these exceptions, few Americans had questioned the historic role of the United States as a place of refuge and of opportunity for immigrants. Indeed, during the decade before World War I,

more Europeans settled in the United States than in any previous decade.

Why did a nation of immigrants and descendants of immigrants suddenly close its doors? One reason was the anti-European feeling that swept over America after the war. However, certain Americans had reasons of their own.

Organized labor, for example, argued that new immigrants were willing to work for lower wages than American workers and thus pulled down the standard of living. Industrialists had formerly favored immigration as a source of cheap, unskilled labor. By 1920, with the railroads built and basic industries such as steel well developed, they no longer needed masses of unskilled workers. Finally, many established Americans felt that the newer immigrants, mainly from eastern and southern Europe, did not easily become "Americanized."

The immigration laws. Congress passed three laws in the 1920's that progressively restricted immigration from Europe. The Emergency Quota Act of 1921 introduced a **quota system.** This limited the number of Europeans and others who could be admitted to 3 percent of the total number of persons of their nationality

Ill-will toward the growing numbers of immigrants coming to the United States began long before the 1920's, as this 1891 cartoon shows. What is the cartoonist's opinion of the immigrants of the time? What evidence can you find of it?

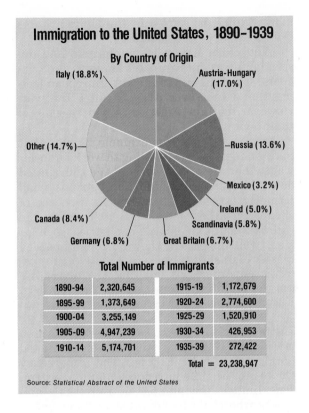

Immigration to the United States, 1890-1939

By Country of Origin

Italy (18.8%)
Austria-Hungary (17.0%)
Other (14.7%)
Russia (13.6%)
Mexico (3.2%)
Ireland (5.0%)
Canada (8.4%)
Scandinavia (5.8%)
Germany (6.8%)
Great Britain (6.7%)

Total Number of Immigrants

1890-94	2,320,645	1915-19	1,172,679
1895-99	1,373,649	1920-24	2,774,600
1900-04	3,255,149	1925-29	1,520,910
1905-09	4,947,239	1930-34	426,953
1910-14	5,174,701	1935-39	272,422
		Total =	23,238,947

Source: *Statistical Abstract of the United States*

residing in the United States in the year 1910. The act also set a total yearly limit of about 350,000 immigrants.

In 1924 an even more restrictive law reduced the yearly quota from 3 to 2 percent. It also changed the base year from 1910 to 1890. This change discriminated against Italians, Austrians, Russians, and other eastern and southern Europeans who had immigrated to America mainly after 1890.

Finally, the National Origins Act of 1929 shifted the base year of immigration to 1920. However, it counterbalanced this more liberal provision by reducing the yearly limit on immigrants to 150,000.

The new immigration policies aroused a great deal of bitterness, especially among eastern and southern Europeans. The Japanese were also aroused because the immigration act of 1924 ended the Gentlemen's Agreement of 1907. Japan had faithfully observed the agreement and resented the policies which closed the doors to Japanese immigrants.

The war of tariffs. While closing its doors to immigrants, the United States also raised tariff barriers to keep out foreign products. In fact,

the ink was hardly dry on the peace treaties before the nations of the world were engaged in another war—a trade war fought with tariffs. As you have read, the Fordney-McCumber Tariff of 1922 increased import duties on hundreds of items.

In 1930 Congress passed the Hawley-Smoot Tariff Act, providing for the highest tariff in American history. President Hoover felt that some of the rates were too high. He also pondered a petition signed by 1,000 leading economists who argued that such high tariffs would raise prices, create hardships for American consumers, and seriously interfere with world trade. Nevertheless, believing that protective tariffs encouraged business prosperity, Hoover signed the bill.

America's high-tariff policy proved a cruel blow to many countries in Latin America and in Europe. When America's high tariffs deprived these countries of their best markets in the United States, their economic strength declined. Factories closed, people were thrown out of work, and the surplus of farm products mounted steadily.

Some countries struck back by raising their own tariff barriers against American goods. Thus the high tariffs that Congress hoped would aid American industry in the end deprived many American businesses and farms of the foreign markets they badly needed.

War debts and high tariffs. America's high-tariff policy created still another problem. How could European countries pay their war debts to the United States if they could not sell their goods in this country?

The war had changed America's relation to Europe from debtor to creditor. Before the war American business leaders had borrowed money from Europeans to finance new industries. During the period before the United States entered the war in 1917, however, Europeans began to sell their American stocks and bonds to buy war goods. As the war progressed, the American government also loaned huge sums to the warring countries. As a result, by 1918 nearly all the European countries owed money to the United States. The total amounted to about $10 billion.

The American government reduced the interest rates on the loans. It also arranged for the debtor nations to repay the money over a long period of time. Despite the generous terms, the bankrupt European countries emerged from the war not knowing how they could repay their debts.

President Wilson reminded Congress of one possible solution to Europe's problems. He declared that if the United States wished Europe to repay its debts, Americans had to buy European products. However, this became impossible when the United States adopted a high-tariff policy.

War debts and reparations. The only other solution open to the European Allies was to collect war damages, or **reparations,** from Germany. They could then use this money to repay their war debts to the United States. In 1921 a Reparations Commission fixed the total of German reparations at $33 billion. Germany, however, was in the midst of a severe economic crisis and completely unable to pay such a huge sum. In an effort to secure the money, Germany borrowed from bankers in the United States and Europe.

There was a limit to the amount that the German government could borrow, and, as the years passed, the reparations had to be reduced. In spite of this relief, however, Germany's economic situation grew steadily worse. By 1930 the Germans could make no further payments.

A legacy of bitterness. Faced with this situation, the debtor countries notified the United States that they could no longer meet their payments on the war debts. They argued that they had contributed far more to victory in blood and sacrifice than had America. It would be only fair of the United States, they said, to cancel all war debts.

The American government refused to admit such a claim. It insisted that the war debts to the United States and German reparation payments to the Allies were two entirely separate matters. Americans pointed out that some of the loans—perhaps as much as a third of the total—had, in fact, been made after the armistice. Americans also reminded the European countries that they were not too poor to spend large sums for armaments.

In 1931 the debtors, with the exception of Finland, refused to make even a token payment. President Hoover then declared a year's halt, or **moratorium,** on the payment of war debts and reparations. However, Germany did not make any more payments, and the whole question was left unsolved.

In the end, most of the war debts and most of Germany's reparations remained unpaid. Nevertheless, America's unsuccessful attempt to collect the war debts increased Europe's resentment against the United States. Also, the European victors' unsuccessful attempt to collect reparations from Germany created a feeling of bitterness among the German people. This bitterness, as you will see, contributed to the rise of Adolf Hitler in the early 1930's.

SECTION SURVEY

IDENTIFY: quota system, Hawley-Smoot Tariff, reparations, moratorium.

1. List four reasons why various Americans favored restricting immigration after World War I.
2. (a) What reasons did the European Allies give for stopping payments on their war debts? (b) How did Americans answer these arguments?
3. In what ways did America's high-tariff policies backfire?
4. Graph Study: Look at the graph on page 304. According to the graph, from what countries did the largest percentage of immigrants come?

2 The United States moves toward the Good Neighbor Policy

During the early 1900's, you may recall, Presidents Theodore Roosevelt, William Howard Taft, and Woodrow Wilson had all intervened in Latin-American affairs. They had claimed that intervention was necessary (1) to safeguard the Panama Canal, (2) to prevent European countries from extending their influence in the Caribbean, and (3) to protect American citizens and property.

This Caribbean policy was continued by Presidents Harding and Coolidge. Critics of the policy—and there were many on both sides of the border—referred to it as "dollar diplomacy." Many Latin Americans called it "Yankee imperialism."

Investments and intervention. The prosperity of the "Golden Twenties" provided many Americans with money to invest. The underdeveloped countries of Latin America offered

President Coolidge (center) came to Cuba in 1928 to open the seventh Pan-American Conference there. He hoped his trip would show that the United States wanted to work together with Latin America.

many inviting opportunities for investment. American dollars financed the building of factories, railroads, mines, and ranches in the lands to the south. Whereas in 1913 United States investments in Latin America totaled $1.3 billion, by 1928 these investments totaled more than $5 billion.

American interest in Latin America grew in proportion to the amount of American money invested there. President Coolidge frankly declared that the United States government would protect the property and lives of American citizens wherever they went.

During these years many Latin-American countries were undergoing social and economic revolutions. Frequently two groups in a country struggled to gain control. Each group claimed that it alone represented the people and was the legal government. When this happened, the United States tended to recognize the group most friendly to American interests.

In some instances, the United States played an active role in the struggle for power. On oc-casion it forbade the sale of arms to the group it disliked and armed the group it supported. Worst of all from the Latin-American point of view, the United States sometimes sent armed forces to protect American lives and property.

Relations with Nicaragua. American policy toward Nicaragua offers an example of the kind of intervention that Latin Americans fiercely resented. The United States was particularly interested in Nicaragua because of large American investments there. Moreover, Nicaragua was close to the vital Panama Canal. Finally, there was the prospect that a new canal might eventually be built through Nicaragua itself. President Taft had sent marines into the country during an internal conflict to protect American investments and the nearby Panama Canal. President Coolidge withdrew the marines in 1925 but sent them back in 1926 when new disturbances broke out.

This policy was unpopular throughout Latin America. It was also unpopular with many Americans who claimed that the United States was really making war. President Coolidge denied this and spoke of the American occupation as a police duty. However, criticism was so strong that the administration took measures to solve the problem by more peaceful means.

In 1927 President Coolidge withdrew most of the marines, leaving only enough to protect American property if violence again broke out. This relieved some of the tension, but the Nicaraguans demanded the withdrawal of *all* marines and the end of American interference. In 1933 President Hoover finally withdrew all United States troops.

Relations with Mexico. Relations with Mexico also reflected the determination of the United States to protect American interests south of the Rio Grande. During Wilson's administration a sweeping social revolution in Mexico had raised new problems in the uneasy relations between the two countries. American lives and property suffered in the upheaval. Far more threatening to Americans who had invested in Mexican property was a new policy established in the Mexican constitution of 1917.

Article 27 of the Mexican constitution declared that "only Mexicans . . . have the right to acquire ownership [of, or] . . . to develop, mines, waters, or mineral fuels in the Republic of Mexico. The nation may grant the same right to foreigners, provided that they agree to be considered Mexicans in respect of such property, and accordingly not to involve the protection of their government in respect of the same." This article also canceled concessions made to foreigners by earlier governments. Foreign investors were quick to protest.

During 1917 and 1918, the United States was too involved in the European war to take any action in regard to Mexico. Moreover, not all of the provisions of the constitution were at once applied. However, after the armistice in 1918, oil investors and other American owners of property in Mexico clamored for intervention. These business interests were joined by many American Catholics who were disturbed by anti-Catholic provisions in the Mexican constitution and the anticlerical policies of the Mexican government. The situation grew worse when the Mexicans supported the anti-American faction in Nicaragua. By 1927, American-Mexican relations were close to the breaking point.

In 1927 the United States began slowly to modify its policy. President Coolidge took the first step by sending Dwight W. Morrow, a successful banker, as ambassador to Mexico. Instead of threatening Mexico with United States power, Morrow tried to understand the Mexican point of view. His sincerity, intelligence, and charm quickly won him many friends in Mexico. The skillful work of Morrow and other American "ambassadors of good will" repaired much of the damage done in the past. The Mexicans agreed to recognize American titles to subsoil minerals, such as petroleum, that had been in effect before the constitution of 1917.

New relations with Latin America. The Morrow mission marked a turning point in American relations with Mexico and with other Latin-American countries. From 1927 on, both Coolidge and his successor, Herbert Hoover, worked hard to develop friendlier relations with the Caribbean republics and with the South American nations. Coolidge went to Havana, Cuba, in 1928 and personally opened a Pan-American Conference. Hoover toured South America in the months before his inauguration.

Latin Americans were pleased by the friendly attention of an American President and a President-elect. They were also pleased

when the United States stopped using the 1904 Roosevelt Corollary to the Monroe Doctrine. The Corollary stated that the United States had the right to act as police officer of the Western Hemisphere.

In 1930 the State Department declared that the Monroe Doctrine would no longer be used to justify United States intervention in Latin-American domestic affairs.

Thus by the early 1930's, relations with Latin America had been considerably improved. The governments of these nations now encouraged American investments and gave those investments greater protection than in the past.

SECTION SURVEY

IDENTIFY: "Yankee imperialism," police duty, Dwight W. Morrow.

1. Why did United States Caribbean policy during the early 1900's arouse resentment in Latin America and criticism in the United States?

2. Why did many Latin Americans resent United States policy toward Nicaragua?

3. What were the reasons for American hostility toward Mexico from 1917 to 1927?

4. What steps did the United States take from 1927 to 1930 to improve its relations with Latin America?

3 Americans cooperate with other nations in efforts to prevent war

While the United States was improving relations with Latin America, it also took steps to move toward international cooperation.

America and the League of Nations. As time passed, American experts in international law, public health, and finance became important advisers in activities of the League of Nations. During Harding's administration the United States began to send observers to Switzerland to take unofficial parts in League committee work dealing with epidemics, slavery, and the narcotics trade. By 1924, American delegates were attending League conferences.

The League of Nations held its first informal meeting in Geneva, Switzerland, in 1920. No official American delegates attended the League's meetings at the start, though some Americans later served the League as advisers.

Both Harding and Coolidge recommended that the United States join the Permanent Court of International Justice, popularly known as the World Court, created in 1920 to arbitrate international disputes. However, the Senate, guarding its right to make treaties and influenced by Americans who feared "entangling alliances," agreed to join only on its own terms. The nations already belonging to the World Court refused to accept the Senate's terms, and the matter was dropped.

The armaments race. The government was more successful in its efforts to stop the naval armaments race in which it was engaged with Great Britain and Japan. Relations with Japan were particularly strained after World War I. Americans resented the Japanese occupation of the Shantung Peninsula in China. This occupation, begun in 1914, violated America's Open Door Policy, which was designed to keep China's territory intact and to prevent any single power from dominating China. Americans were concerned because Japan was allied with Great Britain.

As a result of the tension created by this situation, each of the three powers was rapidly building up its naval strength. Many people in all three countries feared that the naval armaments race might lead to war.

The Washington Conference. Against this disturbing background, nine powers with interests in Asia met in the American capital during 1921 and 1922. Secretary of State Charles Evans Hughes opened the Washington Naval Conference by boldly proposing a 10-year naval holiday during which no new warships were to be built. He suggested that the United States, Great Britain, and Japan each scrap enough of its own warships to bring the naval strength of the three great sea powers into a ratio of 5:5:3. These limitations applied only to capital ships, that is, to battleships and heavy cruisers. According to this plan, Great Britain and the United States would be equal in naval strength while Japan would have three fifths as much tonnage as each of the other two countries. France and Italy were to have fleets of equal size, with a ratio of 1.75 to the other powers.

At first, Japan refused to accept the plan. Finally, eager to make economies at home, the Japanese accepted the proposal on the condition that Great Britain and the United States would not further fortify any Pacific colonies, except Hawaii. These agreements were included in what came to be called the Five-Power Treaty.

Other agreements. The Five-Power Treaty was only one of the agreements reached at the conference. Among others were the Four-Power Pact and the Nine-Power Treaty.

In the Four-Power Pact, Japan, Great Britain, France, and the United States agreed to respect one another's rights in the Pacific. The four nations also agreed to consult with one another in the event of any act of aggression in the Pacific area.

In the Nine-Power Treaty, the nations represented at the Washington Conference guaranteed the territorial integrity of China. They promised to uphold the Open Door Policy by promoting trade and relations "between China and the other powers upon the basis of equality of opportunity."

Events in Asia following the Washington Conference seemed to justify the belief that a major step toward peace had been taken. Japan withdrew, at least partially, from the Shantung Peninsula. Japan also withdrew troops that had occupied parts of Siberia during the Russian Revolution. At a London Naval Conference in 1930, Japan agreed to extend the naval holiday. This agreement marked the high point of Japanese cooperation with the Western powers.

The attempt to outlaw war. The United States also tried to prevent war by what has been called a policy of "wishful thinking." In 1928 Secretary of State Frank B. Kellogg joined with the French foreign minister, Aristide Briand (ah·rees·TEED bree·AHN), in asking all nations to sign a pledge outlawing war "as an instrument of foreign policy." The signers were also to agree to settle all disputes by peaceful methods.

Eventually 62 nations accepted the document. However, the Kellogg-Briand Pact, or the Pact of Paris as it was called, proved to be little more than a statement of good intentions. In signing, each nation added its own reservations. Not one was willing to outlaw war waged in self-defense. Since nearly every nation going to war justifies its actions by pleading self-defense, this reservation destroyed the pact's effectiveness.

Finally, the document said nothing about enforcement. Those who signed it were not even bound to consult with one another in case some government acted aggressively.

The crumbling peace structure. The opening act in the tragedy that later engulfed the entire world began in 1931. Without warning, the Japanese army rolled across the frontiers of Manchuria (see map, page 321). China, large but helpless, could do little to defend its great northern province. Within a few months, the Japanese had torn the province away from the Chinese. A Japanese program to sweep

"foreign" influence out of the Far East and to build an Asia for Asians had begun.

Japan's aggression violated the Covenant of the League of Nations. It was an outright challenge to the Open Door Policy of the United States. Japan was bluntly reminded of these facts by Secretary of State Henry L. Stimson. In a formal note issued in 1932, Stimson protested Japan's flagrant violation of the Nine-Power Treaty and of the Kellogg-Briand Pact, both of which Japan had signed. President Hoover and Congress, however, were unwilling to use force or even economic sanctions to enforce the Stimson declaration.

Meanwhile, the League of Nations met to consider what action, if any, should be taken. President Hoover sent an American representative to this meeting. The League sent a commission to Manchuria to investigate, but beyond a statement of its agreement with Stimson's declaration, the League failed to act. Confident that the nations of the world would not act together to preserve peace, Japan withdrew from the League of Nations. It then made preparations to invade and conquer China and Southeast Asia.

The structure of peace had begun to crumble. As you will see, Fascist Italy and, after 1933, the rising Nazi regime in Germany realized that they too could safely embark upon programs of aggression. The peace structure was not firm enough to stand a heavy blow. The world powers, which by collective action might have reinforced the crumbling structure of world peace, were unwilling and unable to act together.

SECTION SURVEY

IDENTIFY: World Court, armaments race, Charles Evans Hughes, naval holiday, Frank B. Kellogg, Henry L. Stimson.

1. What conditions led to the Washington Naval Conference of 1921–22?

2. (a) What were the major provisions of the Five-Power Treaty? (b) What was the reason for the Four-Power Pact?

3. Why was the Nine-Power Treaty significant for (a) China, (b) the United States, and (c) Japan?

4. Why was the Kellogg-Briand Pact of 1928 little more than a statement of good intentions?

5. (a) How did the United States react to the Japanese invasion of Manchuria? (b) What was the reaction of the League of Nations? Why?

Chapter Survey

Summary: Tracing the Main Ideas

During the 1920's the American people as a whole rejected President Wilson's call to assume world leadership. To be sure, during the immediate postwar years, the United States did help Europe by supplying food, clothing, medical supplies, and huge loans of money. During the 1920's the United States worked closely with the League of Nations in efforts to reduce international friction and took steps to establish better relations with Latin America.

Nevertheless, the United States' refusal to join the League of Nations, its harsher immigration policies, and its higher tariff barriers did not win friends for America.

By 1932 the faith and good will that had been so widespread throughout the world in 1918 were rapidly evaporating. In place of the prosperity of the 1920's, the world was faced with a deepening economic depression. In place of faith and good will, the world was confronted by intense international rivalry and a growing feeling of suspicion and distrust. Japan had already begun its program of aggression, the Italians were threatening their neighbors, and the Nazi movement was gathering strength in Germany. The structure of peace was breaking into fragments.

Inquiring into History

1. During the years after World War I, the United States shut its doors to many immigrants and placed high tariffs on foreign goods. How are these two actions related?
2. What efforts toward world peace did the United States make during the 1920's?
3. What actions taken by nations during the 1920's caused resentments that might later flare into war?
4. The Kellogg-Briand Pact did not survive the challenges posed by the Japanese invasion of Manchuria. Why?
5. How would you characterize American attitudes toward (a) Europe, (b) Latin America, and (c) Asia during the 1920's? How do you account for those attitudes?

Relating Past to Present

1. Does the United States follow one or several policies in dealing with the nations of the world today? Explain.
2. How do United States relations with Latin American nations today compare with those of the 1920's?
3. In the period just studied, world peace was crumbling in part because the world powers could not act collectively to counteract aggression. Can you think of any events in recent years that might have destroyed world peace if left unchecked? How was peace maintained?

Developing Social Science Skills

1. Using the graph on immigration on page 698, (a) compare immigration to the United States from 1901–10 with immigration from 1921–30. (b) How do you explain this radical change? (c) What effect did it have on the makeup of our population? (d) What other effects may it have had on the nation? (Consider the contributions that immigrants have made to the United States throughout its history.)
2. Conduct research and prepare a report on United States relations with one Latin American country from around 1900 to 1930. Try to find material that gives the points of view of *both* nations.
3. Examine the cartoon on page 303. (a) Where does the scene take place? How can you tell? (b) Who are the hoards of people beneath the platform? (c) How would you describe them? (d) What evils does the cartoonist hold these people responsible for? How do you know? (e) How does Uncle Sam feel about these people? How can you tell?
4. Create a cartoon that exhibits a point of view opposite to the one put forth in the cartoon on page 303.

Chapter 17

Moving from Isolationism into War

1932–1941

In 1933, when Franklin Delano Roosevelt became President for the first time, it was clear that few Presidents had entered office under more unfavorable circumstances.

The Great Depression, the worst depression the country had ever experienced, was becoming worse week by week, not only in the United States but throughout the world.

Equally disturbing was the growth of warlike dictatorships in Asia and Europe. Americans were deeply troubled because the Japanese war machine had already rolled across the borders of Manchuria and, as you have read, seized that province from the defenseless Chinese.

However, there was no way for President-elect Roosevelt or anyone else to foresee that in 1933 Hitler would win control of Germany. No one could foresee that by 1936 a powerful German army would move into the Rhineland, violating the Versailles Treaty. Nor could anyone then know that by 1940 Hitler's Nazis, Mussolini's Fascists, and the Japanese warlords would have plunged the world into the most devastating conflict in its entire history.

During the 1930's the United States took an increasingly active interest in foreign affairs. It recognized the Soviet Union. It made provisions to grant independence to the Filipinos. It expanded the Good Neighbor Policy. Although the United States tried to remain neutral in a war-torn world, by the end of 1941 the American people found themselves playing a leading role in the struggle against the dictatorships.

THE CHAPTER IN OUTLINE

1. The United States broadens its relations with other countries.
2. Americans try to follow a policy of isolationism.
3. The nation finds isolationism difficult to maintain.
4. The United States becomes involved in World War II.

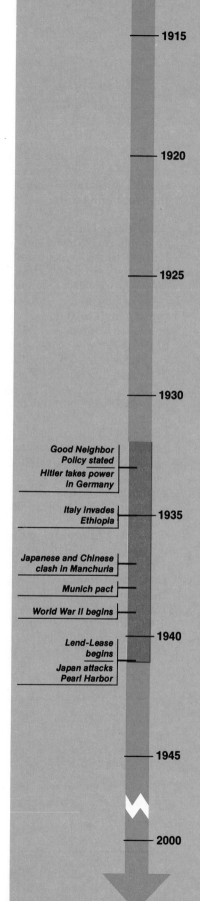

1915
1920
1925
1930

Good Neighbor Policy stated
Hitler takes power in Germany
Italy invades Ethiopia
1935
Japanese and Chinese clash in Manchuria
Munich pact
World War II begins
1940
Lend-Lease begins
Japan attacks Pearl Harbor

1945
2000

1 The United States broadens its relations with other countries

American foreign policy in the 1930's was influenced by two basic considerations: (1) the Great Depression at home and abroad and (2) the rise of dictatorships in Europe and Asia.

The Soviet Union. In 1933, during the first year of the New Deal administration, the United States recognized the Soviet Union. Those favoring this move argued that it was only realistic to recognize a regime that had been in power for 16 years. They pointed out that an increased flow of trade between the two countries would be helpful to the United States. Finally, they insisted that the two countries shared a concern about the threat of Japanese aggression.

In reply to these arguments, the opponents of recognition pointed out that the Communists made no secret of their goal of world conquest. This objection was met when the Soviet Union promised to stop all propaganda activities in the United States. As it turned out, this promise was not kept. Moreover, recognition of the Soviet Union did not greatly increase trade between the two countries.

Toward Philippine independence. In the Jones Act of 1916, as you may recall, the United States promised to give the Filipinos their independence. During the 1920's this action was postponed on the ground that the Filipinos were not yet ready for independence. In 1933, however, late in Hoover's administration, Congress passed an independence act for the Philippines over the President's veto.

The Philippine legislature rejected this measure. Many Filipinos feared that one of the act's provisions, giving the United States the right to keep military and naval bases, would enable Americans to continue their control in the Philippines anyway. Other Filipinos argued that once they were free, the United States would then raise its tariff barriers against Philippine products.

Trying to overcome these fears, Congress in 1934 passed the Tydings-McDuffie Act. This measure was more acceptable to the Filipinos. It provided for the establishment of a Philippine Commonwealth and outlined a gradual 10-year tariff increase on Philippine goods imported into the United States. This would give the Filipinos an opportunity to adjust to an independent economy.

Ten years after the establishment of a commonwealth—on July 4, 1946, as it turned out—the Philippines were to become entirely independent. The United States would retain its naval bases in the area, however.

The Good Neighbor Policy. During the 1930's the United States also redoubled earlier efforts to improve relations with Latin America. The policy started by Coolidge and Hoover was expanded by Roosevelt.

Self-interest as well as a genuine desire for friendship motivated the Good Neighbor Policy. During the 1920's many Americans began to realize that the United States could not afford to continue antagonizing its Latin-American neighbors. When the Great Depression came, this realization hardened into firm conviction. The United States needed Latin-American trade. The rise of dictatorships in both Europe and Asia further strengthened the conviction among Americans that the United States had to establish friendlier relations with Latin America.

SOURCES

PROCLAMATION OF PHILIPPINE INDEPENDENCE (1946)

Whereas it has been the repeated declaration of the . . . government of the United States of America that full independence would be granted the Philippines as soon as the people of the Philippines were prepared to assume this obligation; and

Whereas the people of the Philippines have clearly demonstrated their capacity for self-government; . . .

Now, therefore, I, Harry S. Truman, . . . do hereby recognize the independence of the Philippines as a separate and self-governing nation. . . .

In 1933 President Roosevelt declared, "In the field of foreign policy, I would dedicate this nation to the policy of the good neighbor—the neighbor who resolutely respects himself and, because he does so, respects the rights of others." Later that year, in a conference held in Montevideo, Uruguay, the United States joined the other American countries in a pledge not to interfere in the affairs of their neighbors. "No state," the pledge declared, "has the right to intervene in the internal or external affairs of another state."

The Montevideo Pact marked a turning point in United States relations with Latin America. As President Roosevelt put it, "The definite policy of the United States from now on is one opposed to armed intervention."

The policy in action. Nor were these mere words. In 1934 the United States canceled the Platt Amendment, under which it had claimed the right to intervene in Cuban affairs. That same year the remainder of American troops were finally withdrawn from Haiti. In 1936 the United States gave up its right to intervene in Panama's affairs. Also the United States gradually ended its control over the customhouses of the Dominican Republic—a control exercised since 1905.

The Good Neighbor Policy was put to a severe test in 1938. In that year President Lázaro Cárdenas (LAH·sah·roh KAHR·day·nahs) of Mexico confiscated the properties of all foreign oil companies. Foreign investors, including Americans, protested and demanded action from their governments. President Roosevelt refused to intervene on behalf of American investors. Instead, he urged the American oil companies to negotiate directly with Mexico. As a result of these negotiations, the Mexican government agreed to pay a small part of what the American companies had claimed.

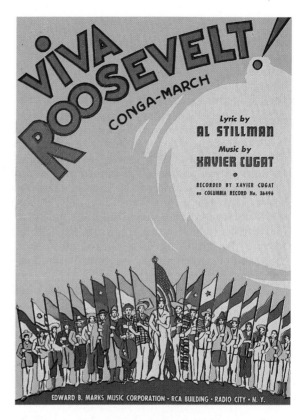

President Franklin Roosevelt's Good Neighbor Policy inspired this song, set to a Latin-American beat. The writers wanted to promote a spirit of friendliness throughout the nations of the Americas.

International trade agreements. The United States also tried to promote an international revival of trade. The Roosevelt administration offered to negotiate with any country special trade agreements that would provide for lowering tariffs.

In the Trade Agreements Act of 1934, Congress authorized the President to raise or lower existing tariffs by as much as 50 percent without Senate approval. As a result, the Roo-

SOURCES

ABROGATION OF THE PLATT AMENDMENT (1934)

Article I. The Treaty of Relations which was concluded between the two contracting parties on May 22, 1903, shall cease to be in force, and is abrogated, from the date on which the present treaty goes into effect.

Article II. All the acts effected in Cuba by the United States of America during its military occupation of the island, up to May 20, 1902, the date on which the Republic of Cuba was established, have been ratified and held as valid; and all rights legally acquired by virtue of those acts shall be maintained and protected. . . .

sevelt administration could bargain, or reciprocate, with other countries at its discretion. A nation that lowered its tariffs on United States goods would, in turn, receive more favorable tariffs on the goods that it sent to the United States. By 1940 Secretary of State Cordell Hull had signed 22 such reciprocal trade agreements.

Equally important was the provision of the Trade Agreements Act known as the "most-favored nation" clause. This clause offered any country the opportunity to be treated as well as the nation seemingly "most favored" in any tariff agreement. This act therefore helped to end tariff discriminations against the United States. The Trade Agreements Act also stimulated American business by improving trade relations with other nations.

New tariff agreements worked out with Canada and Great Britain under the Trade Agreements Act were especially important. They led to a great increase of trade between these countries and the United States. They also provided an economic foundation for the political cooperation that became so important in World War II.

SECTION SURVEY

IDENTIFY: dictatorship, Good Neighbor Policy, Montevideo Pact, Lázaro Cárdenas, reciprocal trade agreements, Cordell Hull, "most-favored nation" clause.

1. What were the arguments for and against recognition of the Soviet Union in 1933?

2. (a) What conditions led to the passage of the Tydings-McDuffie Act? (b) What was the major provision of the act?

3. (a) What were the conditions that prompted the Good Neighbor Policy? (b) Give examples of the United States following this policy.

2 Americans try to follow a policy of isolationism

In the early 1930's, the threat of war loomed larger and larger. In Asia and Europe, the militaristic leaders of Japan, Italy, and Germany started building up their armies and weapons arsenals. Their leaders seemed determined to prepare for aggression.

The rise of dictatorships. As the years passed, the Roosevelt administration had to deal with a growing number of totalitarian° rulers. In 1922 Benito Mussolini seized power in Italy as the leader of **Fascism.** Fascism was a system of government concentrating all political, economic, and cultural power in the state. It was dedicated to aggressive expansionism. Mussolini, a swaggering, domineering ruler, dreamed of controlling the Mediterranean and the Middle East.

The Japanese warlords who seized control of Japan in the late 1920's also had dreams of expansion and military glory. Their seizure of Manchuria in 1931 was only one step in a program designed to win complete control of East Asia and the Pacific.

Adolf Hitler, the Austrian-born, Jew-hating fanatic who climbed to power in Germany in 1933, was a ruthless dictator who also longed for conquest. Josef Stalin, who in the 1920's succeeded N. Lenin as the leader of the Soviet Union openly intended to spread communism throughout the entire world.

There were other dictators, including General Francisco Franco, who came to power in Spain in 1939 after a bloody civil war. However, the dictatorships of Japan, Italy, and Germany proved to be the most aggressive.

Hitler, Mussolini, and the Japanese warlords expressed their contempt for democracy. It was, in Mussolini's words, "a rotting corpse" that had to be replaced by "efficient" government and a "superior" way of life.

All of the dictatorships scorned the democratic rights of free speech and a free press. In totalitarian systems individuals existed to serve the state and had no rights except those that the state chose to give them.

All of the dictatorships glorified force. Compelling the people to work for "bullets rather than butter," they converted their industries to war production. Their major efforts were devoted to building powerful military machines.

Mounting tension. By the mid-1930's the dictators were ready to move. In 1935 Mussolini's blackshirted Fascists attacked the African nation of Ethiopia (see map, pages 320–31). They used bombers and poison gas against a practically defenseless people.

°totalitarian: This term refers to a dictatorship that exercises total control over a nation and suppresses individual freedom.

In 1934 and 1935, the Japanese broke the pledges made at the Washington Naval Conferences of 1921–22 and in later treaties. They began a rapid build-up of their navy.

Then in March 1936, German troops moved into the Rhineland (see map, page 318), clearly violating the Treaty of Versailles. In July civil war broke out in Spain. In October Germany and Italy signed a military alliance and began to call themselves the **Axis°** Powers. In November 1936 Germany, Italy, and Japan joined in an Anti-Comintern† Pact, thus hiding their aggressive designs under the pretense of resisting communism.

On July 7, 1937, Japanese and Chinese troops clashed on the Chinese-Manchurian border. This border incident developed into a full-scale war. In time, historians referred to it as the start of World War II in East Asia.

Roots of isolationism. Despite the growing threat to peace, most Americans remained determined not to become involved in war. They believed that the United States could and should isolate itself from other people's wars. Why did Americans feel this way?

In the first place, most Americans were disillusioned about the results of World War I. The war had not brought peace, disarmament, and democracy across the earth. Instead, it had been followed by constant quarreling among the European powers, by tariff wars, and by failures to reduce armaments.

Most important, the League of Nations had not become an effective instrument for peace. American isolationists refused to believe that the League might have been more successful had the United States joined. They argued that the League's weakness was the best possible evidence that the United States had been wise *not* to join. This widespread disillusionment became increasingly intense when the League failed to check the aggressions of Italy, Germany, and Japan in 1935–37.

American disillusionment about the war grew more intense in 1934 when the Senate started to investigate war profits. Figures re-

"Worker," this German election poster of 1932 urges, "Elect the Front-line Soldier, Hitler!" The Nazis won a majority of seats in the German Parliament and Hitler became the nation's supreme ruler.

leased by the Senate suggested that many American bankers and munitions makers had reaped rich profits from World War I. Many people concluded that America's loans to the Allies were largely responsible for drawing the nation into war. This conclusion has since been rejected by most historians. In the 1930's, however, it fed the spirit of disillusionment.

Disillusionment about World War I was not the only basis for American isolationism. Most Americans believed that the Atlantic and Pacific oceans would protect the United States from attack even if the dictators succeeded in crushing all opposition in Europe and Asia. Many also argued that the improved relations with Latin America gave the nation another safeguard against attack.

°**Axis:** a name made up by Mussolini, who said that the line from Rome to Berlin formed the "axis" on which the world would turn thereafter. Eventually Japan was included among the Axis Powers. The nations who fought the Axis Powers were known as the Allies.

†**Comintern:** an international organization, dominated by the Russian Communist Party, whose aim was to spread communism throughout the world.

Most Americans disapproved of acts of aggression by the Axis Powers. Even so, many were firm isolationists and joined groups that supported a policy of neutrality for the United States, as this poster shows.

The isolationists were strengthened by two other groups. Many Americans believed that the government's first responsibility was to combat the depression. Many others, deeply convinced pacifists, believed that all wars were unjustifiable and that the United States had to avoid being drawn into another conflict. Pacifism was strong, especially among young people, in both the United States and Great Britain during the 1930's.

Isolationism in practice. In 1934, American isolationists won a victory when Congress passed the Johnson Debt Default Act. This act forbade the American government and private citizens to lend money to any country that had **defaulted,** or failed to repay, its war debts.

The Johnson Debt Default Act underscored Americans' annoyance at the failure of all European nations except Finland to repay their war debts. Americans were especially annoyed because some of the defaulting nations were pouring money into weapons. Americans did not intend to provide them any more money for weapons or to risk becoming involved in another war because of entangling investments.

Between 1935 and 1937, the isolationists won other victories in a series of neutrality acts passed by Congress. These acts, which reflected widespread public sentiment against war, were prompted by Mussolini's attack upon Ethiopia, by the civil war in Spain, and by the aggressive actions of Germany and Japan.

In general, the neutrality laws did three things. (1) They prohibited the shipment of munitions to **belligerents,** or warring nations. (2) They authorized the President to list commodities other than munitions that could be sold to belligerents only on a "cash-and-carry" basis. (3) They made it unlawful for Americans to travel on the vessels of belligerent nations.

The neutrality laws were intended to keep Americans out of war and to prevent the involvement of American citizens in such disasters as the sinking of the *Lusitania* in 1915. With these laws the United States abandoned its long-established doctrine of freedom of the seas and withdrew the traditional rights of citizens to travel where and how they wished.

Dissatisfaction with neutrality. Isolationism by no means represented the thinking of all Americans. Many Americans were dismayed by totalitarian governments and their abandonment of individual rights that earlier generations had fought so hard to establish.

Still other Americans regretted that the neutrality laws made it difficult for the United States to help the victims of aggression. In their view, if the United States allowed aggressors to crush weaker neighbors, the United States might one day find itself surrounded by powerful enemies.

Finally, many citizens argued that the United States had a moral duty to aid the victims of unprovoked aggression. This attitude cut across party lines. There were internationalists as well as isolationists in both the Democratic and Republican parties.

Changes in policy. Between 1933 and 1937, President Roosevelt did not take a firm stand on America's responsibility in a troubled world. At times he sided with the isolationists, at other times with the internationalists.

By 1937, however, Roosevelt had become more deeply impressed with the seriousness of the world situation. He felt that the United States should take a positive stand against aggression. In a speech on October 5, 1937, the President said, "If we are to have a world in which we can breathe freely and live in amity without fear—the peace-loving nations must make a concerted effort to uphold laws and principles on which alone peace can rest secure. . . .

"When an epidemic of physical disease starts to spread, the community approves and joins in a quarantine of the patients in order to protect the health of the community against the spread of the disease."

Continuing isolationism. In the "quarantine" speech, Roosevelt expressed views that most Americans were not yet ready to accept. Proof of this came with the *Panay* incident. On December 12, 1937, Japanese planes bombed and strafed a United States gunboat, the *Panay,* and three American oil tankers on the Yangtze River in China (see map, pages 344–45). Several Americans were killed and many were wounded in the incident.

Secretary of State Hull immediately sent a sharp note to the Japanese government. He demanded full apologies, compensation, and a promise that no such incident would recur. The Japanese agreed to all of Hull's demands.

During this incident, the American public revealed how strongly it favored keeping out of war. A public opinion poll taken at the time showed that 54 percent of all Americans felt that the United States should completely withdraw from China.

By the end of 1937, the tide of aggression was rising rapidly in Asia as well as in Europe. Many Americans, including President Roosevelt, were becoming increasingly alarmed. Nevertheless, most Americans clung strongly to the belief that the United States could remain isolated.

SECTION SURVEY

IDENTIFY: totalitarianism, Benito Mussolini, Adolf Hitler, Josef Stalin, Francisco Franco, Axis Powers, isolationism, pacifists, belligerents, "quarantine" speech, *Panay* incident.

1. What were the philosophies of the totalitarian dictators in terms of (a) the role of the individual and the role of government and (b) the role of their nation in the world.
2. What were the roots of the widespread isolationism of the 1920's and early 1930's?
3. (a) What were the neutrality acts of 1935–37? (b) Why were they passed? (c) Why opposed?
4. What were the major events from 1935 to 1937 that threatened peace?

3 The nation finds isolationism difficult to maintain

By 1938 the dictators were becoming more ruthless. During 1938 and 1939, headlines of new aggressions and new crises often crowded other news off the front pages of America's newspapers.

The spread of warfare. In 1938, Japanese forces were attacking along the length of the Chinese coast and pushing inland up the river valleys. Meanwhile, in Europe the Spanish Civil War was bringing misery to hundreds of thousands of other people.

Spain had become an international battleground. Hitler and Mussolini were helping Franco. This provided them the opportunity to test their latest military equipment and to give picked "volunteers" actual battle experience. Soviet "volunteers" were fighting against Franco and his Nazi and Fascist allies. Among Franco's foes in the "International Brigade" were volunteers from many other countries, including the United States.

The United States reacted to this threat to world peace by joining France and Great Britain in a program of nonintervention. With President Roosevelt's approval, Congress in January 1937 barred all shipments of war materials to either side in the civil war in Spain.

New aggressions—and Munich. Another crisis developed when, on March 11, 1938, Hitler's powerful army moved into Austria (see map, page 318). Two days later Hitler announced the union of Austria and Germany.

With Austria under his control, Hitler turned greedy eyes toward western Czechoslovakia. This area, known as the Sudetenland (soo·DAY·tuhn·land), contained a large proportion of German-speaking people. Hitler demanded that Czechoslovakia turn over the region to Germany. Czechoslovakia, with one of the best-trained armies in Europe and with the sympathy of other democratic nations overwhelmingly on its side, refused to bow to Hitler's demands.

Tension was at the breaking point when Hitler and Mussolini met with the prime ministers of Great Britain and France at Munich.

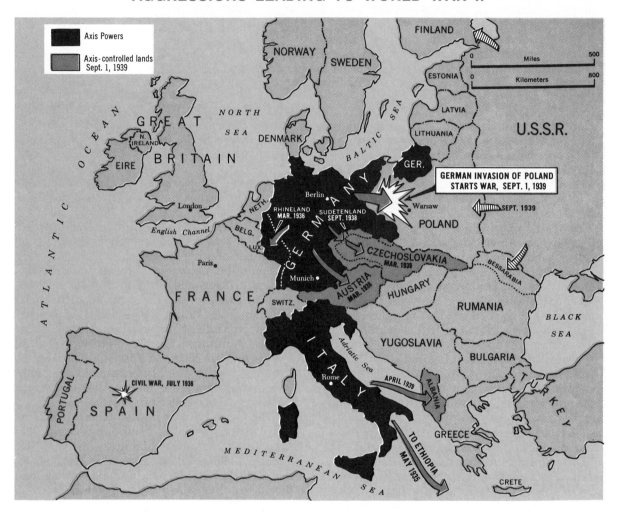

There on September 30, 1938, the four leaders signed a pact that gave Hitler almost all he demanded. The Czechs, forsaken by their friends, had no choice but to turn over most of the disputed region to Germany.

Neville Chamberlain, Prime Minister of Great Britain, returned to England blindly confident. He expressed the certainty that the Munich agreement had ended the threat of aggression in Europe. "I believe," he said, "it is peace for our time."

Other leaders did not share Chamberlain's confidence. They believed that his policy of appeasement would only lead Hitler to make further demands. Throughout Europe nation after nation tooled up to rearm themselves with greater speed.

Growing American concern. President Roosevelt viewed the events of 1938 with deepening concern. As early as January 28, in a special message to Congress, he coupled a promise to work for peace with a warning that it was time for the United States to build up its defenses. Congress increased appropriations for the armed forces and, in May, authorized more than $1 billion for a "two-ocean navy."

Roosevelt privately referred to the aggressions of Japan, Italy, and Germany as "armed banditry." Officially, however, the President sent personal notes to foreign rulers, including Hitler and Mussolini, urging them to settle their differences by negotiation and international cooperation. Since the United States was openly committed to a hands-off, isolationist policy, no one paid much attention to the President's words of caution.

Defending the Western Hemisphere. As the Czech crisis worsened, Roosevelt did make one commitment. In August 1938, in a speech to Canadians, he extended the protection of the Monroe Doctrine to Canada. He promised that "the people of the United States will not stand idly by if domination of Canadian soil is threatened by any other Empire."

Roosevelt's promise to Canada was only one of several steps the United States was taking to develop a defense policy for the nations of North and South America. Earlier, at the Buenos Aires Conference of 1936, the United States and the 20 other members of the Pan-American Union had agreed to regard a threat to any American country as a threat to the security of all. The 21 members also agreed to consult together if such a threat developed.

In December 1938, with the clouds of war rapidly gathering, the Pan-American Union met again in Lima, Peru. The delegates repeated their pledge to oppose foreign intervention in the Western Hemisphere.

Roosevelt's promise to Canada and the Declaration of Lima demonstrated that the Monroe Doctrine had become a multilateral, or many-sided, policy rather than a unilateral, or one-sided, policy. By 1938 it was clear, as Roosevelt said, that "national defense has now become a problem of continental defense."

New crises lead to World War II. On January 4, 1939, in his annual message to Congress, President Roosevelt warned that the world situation had become extremely grave. He urged greatly increased appropriations for the armed services. He also urged Congress to reconsider the neutrality legislation adopted during 1935–37.

The President's worst fears were soon confirmed. On March 15, 1939, Hitler's armies moved into the rest of Czechoslovakia. On April 7 Mussolini's troops invaded Albania (see map, page 318).

Awakening at long last to their common peril, Great Britain and France decided to stand firm. They announced that an attack upon Poland would mean war.

Great Britain and France also tried to get the Soviet Union to join with them in resisting, by force if necessary, any further aggression by either Hitler or Mussolini. It was with shock, therefore, that the domocratic nations learned on August 23, 1939, that the Soviet Union had just signed a nonagression pact with ots warring neighbor, Germany.

Seemingly freed by the Soviet pact from the danger of a two-front war, Hitler struck swiftly. On September 1, without warning, German bombers and powerful armored divisions crossed the border into Poland (see map page 318). On September 3, 1939, Great Britain and France declared war on Germany.

While Great Britain and France were busy mobilizing their armies, Soviet troops invaded Poland from the east. By the end of September, all organized Polish resistance had been crushed, and Germany and the Soviet Union divided Poland between them.

SOURCES

FRANKLIN D. ROOSEVELT'S "FOUR FREEDOMS" SPEECH (1941)

In the future days, which we seek to make secure, we look forward to a world founded upon four essential human freedoms.

The first is freedom of speech and expression—everywhere in the world.

The second is freedom of every person to worship God in his own way—everywhere in the world.

The third is freedom from want—which, translated into world terms, means economic understanding which will secure to every nation a healthy peacetime life for its inhabitants—everywhere in the world.

The fourth is freedom from fear—which, translated into world terms, means a worldwide reduction of armaments to such a point and in such a thorough fashion that no nation will be in a position to commit an act of physical aggression against any neighbor—anywhere in the world. . . .

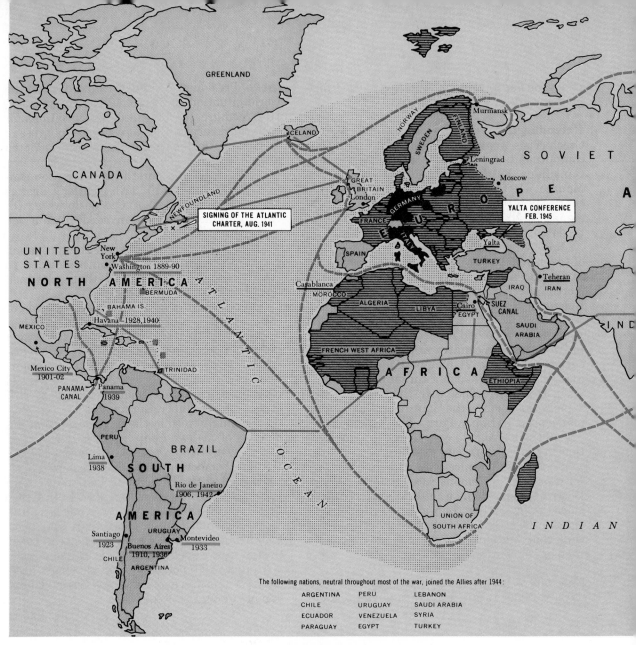

THE WORLD AT WAR: SEPTEMBER 1939 — AUGUST 1945

The following nations, neutral throughout most of the war, joined the Allies after 1944:

ARGENTINA	PERU	LEBANON
CHILE	URUGUAY	SAUDI ARABIA
ECUADOR	VENEZUELA	SYRIA
PARAGUAY	EGYPT	TURKEY

The Soviets then demanded and won the right to establish military and naval bases in Estonia, Latvia, and Lithuania, all independent republics at the time. (See map, page 318.) The Soviet Union also demanded the right to establish military bases on Finnish soil. Finland, too, was an independent republic. On November 30, after Finland refused to grant Soviet demands, the U.S.S.R. attacked its small neighbor. The Soviet government claimed that its actions were necessary to protect the Russian homeland from invasion.

Thus World War II started and began to spread across Europe.

SECTION SURVEY

IDENTIFY: Neville Chamberlain, Munich agreement, appeasement, Declaration of Lima, multilateral, unilateral, nonaggression pact.

1. How did the Spanish Civil War become an international event as well as an internal conflict?

2. (a) How did Neville Chamberlain view the Munich agreement? (b) Why did others have a different view?

3. (a) What actions did the United States take to prepare for the defense of North America? (b) How did these actions broaden the Monroe Doctrine?

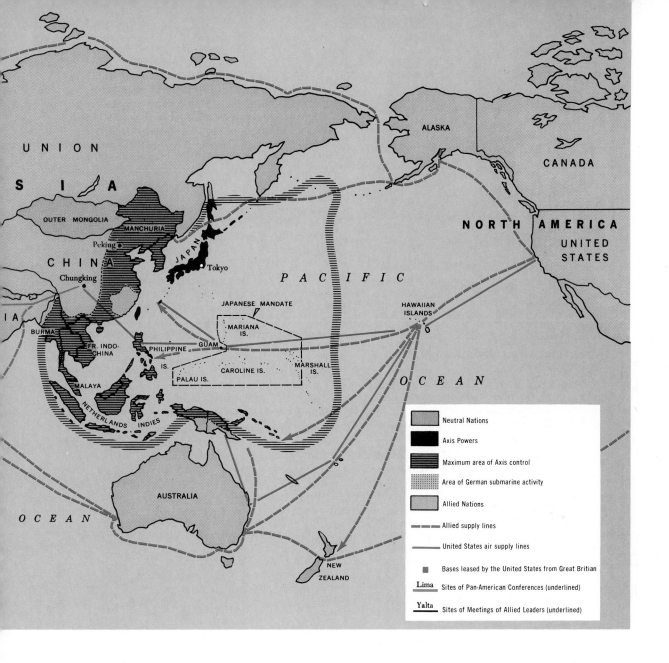

Neutral Nations

Axis Powers

Maximum area of Axis control

Area of German submarine activity

Allied Nations

Allied supply lines

United States air supply lines

■ Bases leased by the United States from Great Britian

Lima Sites of Pan-American Conferences (underlined)

Yalta Sites of Meetings of Allied Leaders (underlined)

4 The United States becomes involved in World War II

Although in 1939 Americans were overwhelmingly in favor of the Allies, they were determined to stay out of war. President Roosevelt voiced a widely shared feeling in a "fireside chat" over radio on September 3. He firmly announced, "As long as it remains in my power to prevent, there will be no blackout of peace in the United States."

Neutrality laws amended. On September 21, 1939, however, Roosevelt again urged Congress to amend the Neutrality Act of 1937. "I regret that Congress passed the Act. I regret equally that I signed the Act," he declared. Roosevelt pointed out that the existing embargo on the export of munitions actually favored Germany. If it were not for the embargo, Great Britain and France could use their control of the seas to secure from the United States the arms that they desperately needed. Adolf Hitler did not need military equipment, for he had been preparing Nazi Germany for war for many years.

THE WAR AGAINST THE JEWS

Our town is burning, brothers, burning. . . .
Don't look on with folded arms
While the fire spreads!

These lines from a Yiddish song describe the fate of thousands of Jewish communities in Europe after the Nazis rose to power in the 1930's. The fire in the song did spread, and millions died before it was put out.

From the beginning, Hitler based much of his Nazi message on anti-Semitism—the hatred of Jews—which had had a long history in Europe. Jews were blamed for every misfortune the Germans faced, especially their economic troubles after World War I. In 1933 the Nazis began a systematic program to settle the "Jewish problem" in Germany. Jews were deprived of their citizenship, forbidden to use public facilities, and gradually driven out of almost every type of work.

Thousands of Jews left Germany, some for other nations of Europe and some for the United States. (The best-known American immigrant was physicist Albert Einstein.) However, escape soon became almost impossible. One factor was the war itself. After it began in the fall of 1939, movement was extremely difficult. At the same time, Hitler's war against the Jews was extended to all the territories occupied by the Germans. Another factor was the reluctance of Allied nations to accept refugees. The United States held strictly to its immigration quotas and took in only about 100,000. England accepted 80,000, and Latin America only about half that number.

Some 8 million Jews were trapped in Europe —from Russia in the east to France in the west, from Norway in the north to Greece in the south. First they were isolated in ghettos or sent to concentration camps as forced laborers. In 1941 began what the Nazis called the "final solution"—extermination. (Actually, thousands of Jews had already died.) At special camps, such as Auschwitz and Treblinka in Poland, hundreds of thousands were mercilessly gassed and cremated.

Six million Jews died in what has come to be remembered as the Holocaust. (Another 6 million—gypsies, political prisoners, and prisoners of war—also perished in the camps.) Before they died, many of these victims of Nazi brutality sang this song:

Our brothers across the ocean
Cannot feel our bitter pain. . . .
Rivers of tears will flow,
When they will find some day
The biggest grave in the world
In Treblinka, in Treblinka.

After a six-week debate, Congress finally agreed on a compromise proposal. The new law abolished the arms embargo and allowed any country to buy weapons or munitions from the United States, provided that the goods were transported to that country on foreign ships. This new neutrality law, which went into effect on November 4, 1939, greatly helped the Allied nations resisting Hitler.

Declaration of Panama. While Congress debated the problem of neutrality, the delegates to the Pan-American Union issued a declaration. It warned all belligerent war vessels to stay out of a "safety zone" around the Americas roughly 300 to 1,000 miles (480 to 1,600 kilo-

meters) wide. Germany, Great Britain, and France challenged this declaration. They claimed that no nation or group of nations had the right to close any part of the high seas to their ships. The declaration was nevertheless an important indication of cooperation among the nations of the Western Hemisphere.

The fall of France. While Hitler carried on his **blitzkrieg**, or "lightning war," against Poland in 1939, the French mobilized. They prepared for an attack against the Maginot (mah·zhee·NOH) Line—the chain of forts along the eastern frontier. But Hitler did not attack. People joked about the "phony war," calling it a "sitzkrieg," or sitting war.

Great Britain and France declared war on Germany after Hitler invaded Poland in 1939. Here, German soldiers fire at snipers in the Polish capital of Warsaw. Scenes like this became common all across Europe in the next five years.

On April 9, 1940, the joking ceased as Hitler demonstrated the true meaning of "blitzkrieg." In the following weeks, his powerful armored divisions, supported by fighter planes and bombers, rapidly overran Denmark, Norway, the Netherlands, Belgium, Luxembourg, and northern France (see map, pages 332–33). On May 26 the British began a heroic evacuation of their troops from the beaches of Dunkirk, a seaport in northern France. Although the British were forced to leave much of their equipment, they succeeded in saving most of the troops. On June 10 Italy, sensing that France was doomed, declared war on France and Great Britain.

Hitler's blitzkrieg did not halt until June 22, 1940, when France signed an armistice with Germany. In London the French National Committee pledged continued resistance by the Free French under General Charles de Gaulle. The French nationalists began to rally parts of the French colonial empire against the Nazis. Meanwhile, Marshal Pétain (pay· TAN) became the leader of a German-controlled French government. Headquarters for the occupation government was at Vichy (vee·SHEE) in central France (see map, pages 332–33).

The Battle of Britain. With the fall of France, Great Britain stood alone and almost defenseless. On May 10, 1940, Winston Churchill replaced Neville Chamberlain as Prime Minister of Great Britain. With a rare gift for leadership, Churchill rallied the British people, strengthening their hopes and their will to fight. Churchill promised that the British would never surrender. If by chance Great Britain itself were to fall, he declared, "then our Empire beyond the seas, armed and guarded by the British fleet, would carry on the struggle until, in God's good time, the New World, with all its power and might, steps forth to the rescue and liberation of the Old."

By the end of June, with France under Nazi control, Churchill prepared his people for the coming Battle of Britain. "Hitler knows that he will have to break us in this island or lose the war," Churchill said. "If we can stand up to him, all Europe may be free and the life of the world may move forward into broad, sunlit uplands. But if we fail, then the whole world, including the United States, including all that we have known and cared for, will sink into the abyss of a new Dark Age. . . . Let us therefore brace ourselves to our duties, and so bear our-

"We shall defend our island, whatever the cost may be . . . ; we shall never surrender." This was Prime Minister Winston Churchill's pledge to the people of
Great Britain. Here, in 1940, Churchill gives his famous "V for victory" sign.

selves that, if the British Empire and its Commonwealth last for a thousand years, men will
still say, 'This was their finest hour.' "

The supreme test for the British came in
the late summer of 1940. In August Hitler
unleashed his fighters and bombers against
Great Britain. The Royal Navy fought back
furiously. The Royal Air Force, though almost
hopelessly outnumbered, flew day and night,
sometimes shooting down as many as 100 Nazi
bombers in a single 24-hour period. In October,
advised by his military chiefs that an attempt
to invade Great Britain would be suicidal,
Hitler postponed his invasion plan.

"Never in the field of human conflict,"
Churchill declared "was so much owed by so
many to so few." The proud leader was referring, of course, to the Royal Air Force.

American defense measures. During the
summer and fall of 1940, the United States was
strengthening its own defenses.

Many Americans feared the possibility of
subversive activities. To guard against such
activities, Congress passed the Alien Registration Act, commonly known as the Smith Act.
This law reinforced legislation controlling
aliens and made it illegal for any person in the
United States to advocate the overthrow of the
government by force or violence or to belong
to an organization that advocated the violent
overthrow of the government.

In July Secretary of State Hull and the
foreign ministers of the other American nations gathered in Havana, Cuba. They drew up
plans for preventing Germany from seizing the
Western Hemisphere colonies of the countries
it had conquered. The Act of Havana stated
that the moment any colony was in danger, the
American republics, acting singly or collectively, would take control of the colony. From
then until the end of the war, the colony would
be governed by a group of trustees from the
American republics.

Two weeks later President Roosevelt met with Prime Minister Mackenzie King of Canada. At this meeting the two leaders created a Permanent Joint Board of Defense to plan for the "defense of the north half of the Western Hemisphere."

In 1940 Congress furiously debated the pros and cons of the first peacetime draft in American history. The Burke-Wadsworth Act was finally passed and signed by President Roosevelt on September 16, 1940. The law required all men between 21 and 35 to register for the draft. It also made them liable for one year of military training.

Roosevelt's Lend-Lease proposal. By the end of 1940, American supplies were flowing to Great Britain and America's defense program was gathering momentum. Still, Roosevelt was worried that the British could not afford much longer to pay cash for needed war materials. In his annual message to Congress, Roosevelt declared, "Our country is going to be what our people have proclaimed it to be—the arsenal of democracy." Roosevelt proposed that the United States increase greatly its production of military equipment so that it could lend or lease to the British and to the other Allies any materials needed to carry on the fight.

Roosevelt's Lend-Lease proposal provoked a storm of controversy. Many people agreed with the President that the Lend-Lease proposal offered the best hope of avoiding full-fledged participation in the war. Others, including the isolationists, were sure that Lend-Lease would involve America in a shooting war.

Congress finally passed the Lend-Lease Act in March 1941. It appropriated an initial sum of $7 billion for ships, planes, tanks, and anything else that the Allies needed. When on June 22, 1941, Hitler's armies invaded the Soviet Union despite the German-Russian nonaggression pact, the United States made Lend-Lease materials available to the U.S.S.R.

The Battle of the Atlantic. The Lend-Lease arrangement inevitably drew the United States closer to war. By the spring of 1941, German and Italian submarines were turning the North Atlantic into a graveyard of ships. In April American naval vessels began to trail enemy submarines, radioing their location to British warships. In July American troops occupied Iceland (see map, pages 320–21) to prevent its occupation by Germany.

In September Roosevelt issued "shoot-on-sight" orders to American warships operating in the "safety zone" established back in 1939. American warships also began to accompany and protect, or **convoy**, merchant vessels as far as Iceland. In November Congress voted to allow American merchant vessels to enter combat areas. Roosevelt armed the merchant vessels and provided them with gun crews.

The Atlantic Charter. In 1941 the United States was moving rapidly toward undeclared war with Germany. That August, Roosevelt and Churchill met to discuss the larger issues involved in the conflict. At this meeting the two leaders drew up a broad statement of war aims that came to be called the Atlantic Charter.

Like Woodrow Wilson's Fourteen Points, the Atlantic Charter listed a number of common principles for building a lasting peace and a better world. In the Atlantic Charter, Roosevelt and Churchill pledged themselves to work for a world free of aggression, a world in which every nation, large or small, would have the right to adopt its own form of government. Once the aggressors were crushed, the Charter declared, all nations had to work together to free all people everywhere from the burden of fear and want.

Growing threat from Japan. While war raged in Europe, Japan was adding to its conquests in the Far East. In July 1941, Japanese troops occupied French Indochina (see map, pages 344–45). Thoroughly alarmed, President Roosevelt immediately froze all Japanese assets in the United States. He also placed an embargo on the shipment of gasoline, machine tools, scrap iron, and steel to Japan. Japan promptly retaliated by freezing all American assets in areas under its control. As a result, trade between the United States and Japan practically ended. Then in August the United States sent a Lend-Lease mission to China.

The Japanese were convinced that American resistance was stiffening. They began to make plans for an attack upon the United States. Even as its war leaders made the final preparations, however, the Japanese government sent a "peace" mission to Washington. On November 20, 1941, this mission demanded that the United States (1) unfreeze Japanese assets, (2) supply Japan with as much gasoline as it needed, and (3) cease all aid to China. The

The Japanese bombed the base at Pearl Harbor on the morning of December 7, 1941. The attack ended America's long period of isolationism and thrust the surprised nation headlong into the war that now spanned the entire globe.

United States refused to meet these demands but offered several counterproposals.

Pearl Harbor and war. On Sunday, December 7, 1941, the Japanese mission announced that further negotiations were useless. The Japanese said that the United States had failed "to display in the slightest degree a spirit of conciliation."

That morning, even before Japan's reply had been delivered to the American government, Japanese planes attacked without warning the United States fleet anchored in the huge American naval and air base at Pearl Harbor, in Hawaii (see map, pages 344–45). The Americans lost almost all of their planes and eight battleships and suffered the partial destruction of several other naval units. More than 2,000 soldiers, sailors, and civilians were killed, and almost 2,000 more were wounded. The same day the Japanese also attacked Wake, Midway, Guam, the Philippine Islands, and other American bases.

Shocked and angered, Americans almost unanimously supported President Roosevelt the next day when he asked Congress for a declaration of war against Japan. The Senate declared war unanimously, the House with only one dissenting vote. Great Britain and the governments-in-exile that had fled their countries when Hitler conquered them also immediately declared war against Japan. Three days later, on December 11, Germany and Italy declared that a state of war with the United States existed, whereupon Congress declared war upon those two countries.

SECTION SURVEY

IDENTIFY: Declaration of Panama, blitzkrieg, Charles de Gaulle, Marshal Pétain, Winston Churchill, Smith Act, Act of Havana, "arsenal of democracy," Lend-Lease, convoy, Atlantic Charter, Pearl Harbor.

1. How did the United States' arms embargo aid the aggressor nations?

2. What actions did the United States take to prepare for the possibility of war?

3. Trace the events that led to the Japanese attack on Pearl Harbor.

4. Map Study: Study the map on pages 320–21. (a) Locate the Axis Powers. (b) Where did Churchill and Roosevelt meet to sign the Atlantic Charter? (c) Trace the area protected by the Declaration of Panama.

Chapter Survey

Summary: Tracing the Main Ideas

During the 1930's the curtain began to rise upon one of the greatest tragedies of the modern world. The tragedy started with the Great Depression, which plunged millions of people all over the world into unemployment, confusion, and unrest. Then, in the middle 1930's, the armies of Japan, Italy, and Germany began to march across the troubled face of the earth, leaving death and destruction behind them. Before 1941 drew to a close, most of the nations of the world were involved in the most terrible conflict in human history.

The overwhelming majority of the American people were at first determined to remain out of the war. They supported Congress when it enacted neutrality legislation in 1935, 1936, and 1937. However, as the dictators crushed their weaker neighbors, Americans realized that the democratic way of life and the fate of free people everywhere were in danger. More and more, the Americans saw that by helping other nations to resist aggression, the United States would strengthen democracy and protect itself.

By 1939, when World War II broke out in Europe, the United States had begun to reverse its policy of isolationism. During the next two years, neutrality was abandoned as the United States became "the arsenal of democracy." American ships carried cargoes of war materials to Great Britain, the Soviet Union, and China. America's navy, air force, and army were strengthened with feverish speed. Then, on December 7, 1941, the Japanese struck at Pearl Harbor. The curtain had finally risen. The United States was at war.

Inquiring into History

1. How was the Great Depression related to the rise of dictatorships during the 1930's?
2. How were nationalism, imperialism, and belief in racial superiority related to the causes of World War II?
3. In 1938 the Latin-American nations became partners with the United States in enforcing the Monroe Doctrine. (a) Explain. (b) What steps led to this partnership?
4. Munich has become a symbol of the policy of appeasement. (a) What does this statement mean? (b) How did appeasement help lead to World War II?
5. (a) Why did many Americans believe in isolationism during the 1930's? (b) Why did that attitude start to change by the late 1930's?

Relating Past to Present

1. Do you think America's dealings with other nations today have been affected in any way by what was learned from the events leading to World War II? Explain.

2. Why might it be necessary to recognize a country's government, even if the United States does not approve of that government's policies?

Developing Social Science Skills

1. Draw a timeline for the years 1931 to 1939. (a) Below the line list the international events that led to World War II. (b) Above the line list United States actions or foreign policy decisions. (c) Find examples of actions on the top part of the timeline that led to actions on the bottom part.
2. Read the source on page 319. (a) What were the Four Freedoms? (b) Why might Roosevelt have given this speech? (c) To whom might he have been speaking? Explain.
3. (a) List the events that finally led to the outbreak of World War II. (b) On the map on page 318, locate the nations affected by these events. (c) Which nations were under Axis control by September 1, 1939? (d) Study the map on pages 320–21. What other European nations eventually came under Axis control? (e) Compare the map to a world atlas. What Mediterranean Islands were part of the Axis alliance? Can you say why?

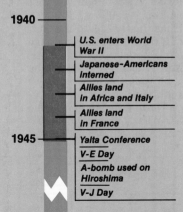

Chapter **18**

Americans in the Second World War

1941–1945

World War II had been under way a little more than two years when on December 7, 1941, Japan's savage blow at Pearl Harbor plunged America into the conflict.

America's enemies had the great advantage of what military leaders call "interior lines of supply and communication." Germany, Italy, and Japan were so situated geographically that the supply lines from their farms and factories to the fighting fronts were relatively short.

The United States and its allies, on the other hand, had to establish and protect supply lines that often stretched thousands of miles across sea and land to fighting forces in far-off areas of the earth.

America's enemies had an even greater advantage. They had been preparing for war for many years. During these years they had raised and trained huge armies and converted their factories to the production of war materials. They had built up vast supplies of rifles, machine guns, tanks, planes, and other instruments of modern warfare.

The United States, on the other hand, had not really begun to prepare for war until the summer of 1940. Even then preparations had been limited. Indeed, it was America's lack of preparation that led Hitler, Mussolini, and the Japanese war leaders to believe that they could win the war before the United States could mobilize its enormous resources.

Faced by such overwhelming odds, the American people grimly entered the conflict.

THE CHAPTER IN OUTLINE

1. The Allies overcome early disasters and begin an offensive.

2. Americans accept controls and win the "battle of production."

3. The Allies gradually fight their way to victory in Europe.

4. Allied victories in the Pacific bring an end to World War II.

1 The Allies overcome early disasters and begin an offensive

Throughout most of 1942, while Americans were desparately trying to convert to a wartime economy, the United States and its allies suffered a series of almost unrelieved disasters in every theater of the war.

Disaster in the Pacific. The scene at Pearl Harbor on the evening of December 7, 1941, was one of nearly total destruction. America's offensive power in the Pacific had been wiped out by the Japanese surprise attack.

The Japanese soon struck again in the Pacific. By the end of December, Japan had seized the American islands of Guam and Wake and captured the British colony of Hong Kong. They had also launched attacks upon Thailand, British Malaya, and the American-controlled Philippine and Midway islands (see map, pages 344–45).

The new year brought a mounting fury of destruction. Japanese conquests covered a widening area of the Pacific and Far East (see map, pages 344–45). On January 2, 1942, Japanese troops poured into Manila, capital of the Philippines. On January 11 the Japanese invaded Borneo and Celebes (SEL·eh·beez) in the Netherlands Indies. On February 15 the advancing tide of Japanese troops overran the British naval base at Singapore. Later in the month, in the Battle of the Java Sea, a Japanese naval force delivered a crushing blow to a fleet of American, British, Dutch, and Australian warships.

By the end of March, the Japanese had conquered most of the Netherlands Indies with its rich supplies of oil, tin, rubber, quinine, and other vital war materials. They had also seized Rangoon, Burma, and were driving British, Indian, and Chinese troops out of Burma.

In the Philippines, a small force of Americans and Filipinos under General Douglas MacArthur continued their heroic but hopeless resistance against the Japanese. In January 1942 Manila surrendered, and MacArthur's forces retired to the Bataan Peninsula. In March MacArthur himself was ordered to Australia to take command of the Allied forces in the South Pacific. Fighting against overwhelming odds, the hungry, sick, exhausted survivors on Bataan were captured on April 9. On May 6 the outnumbered and starving troops on the fortress of Corregidor guarding Manila Bay surrendered. The Japanese also cut the Burma Road, destroying the last land route to China (see map, pages 344–45).

Thus by the end of May 1942, less than six months after their attack on Pearl Harbor, the Japanese had overcome almost all opposition. They were poised to strike west at India, south at Australia, and east through Hawaii at the Pacific coast of the United States.

American gains in the Pacific. Despite some opposition at home, the United States accepted the British argument that the defeat of Hitler in Europe had to be the first Allied objective. However, the war in the Pacific proved to be more than a mere holding operation.

Japan suffered its first serious reverse early in May 1942. Carrier-based planes from a British-American naval force caught a Japanese fleet moving southward in the Coral Sea, off the northeastern coast of Australia. The planes sank or severely damaged more than 30 Japanese warships.

Japanese forces received another setback early in June 1942 when they launched a two-pronged seaborne attack on the Aleutian Islands and Hawaii. The ultimate Japanese objective was an invasion of the United States. American forces stopped the northern campaign, but only after Japanese troops had occupied the Aleutian islands of Attu and Kiska (see map, pages 344–45). American naval forces were able to block the southern campaign by defeating the Japanese in a major battle off the island of Midway.

Turning the tide in the Pacific. There are several reasons why the United States began to stem the Japanese tide. First, early in 1942 the United States and Great Britain had pooled their resources to create a unified Pacific command. Second, the American people were beginning to win the important "battle of production" at home. The products of the nation's farms and factories were pouring into Pacific supply depots and forward bases. Finally, time had been gained by the courageous resistance of Americans and Filipinos on Bataan and Corregidor.

On August 7, 1942, the United States undertook its first major offensive action when marines stormed ashore at Guadalcanal in the Solomon Islands (see map, pages 332–33). For four desperate months, American marines and army troops clung to a toehold around Guadalcanal's airport. They repelled savage attacks from the air, from the sea, and from the surrounding jungle.

In November the Japanese made a desperate effort to regain their former bases in the Solomons, which they needed to carry out their planned invasion of Australia. Admiral William F. Halsey intercepted the huge Japanese fleet and in a furious battle on November 12–15 completely routed the Japanese. The island of Guadalcanal was at last secure. The tide of battle in the Pacific had turned in the Allies' favor.

Disaster in Europe. The situation in the Atlantic and in Europe during most of 1942 was grave. German and Italian submarines in the Atlantic sank ships more rapidly than the United States and Great Britain could build new ones. Great Britain, now an isolated fortress in the Atlantic, could not hold out much longer unless reinforcements arrived and unless the devastating Nazi bombings were stopped.

On the continent of Europe, the tide of Axis conquest was rolling with terrifying speed. Yugoslavia fell to the Axis powers. The Greeks had been reduced to near starvation. The Soviet Union had lost its rich grainfields in the Ukraine region, and many Soviet industrial centers had been ruined. Part of the destruction was done by the Soviet people themselves. As they retreated before the Germans, they applied a "scorched-earth" policy to their land, destroying everything that they could not carry with them.

Despite Soviet resistance, the Nazi divisions rolled on in the summer offensive of 1942. The Germans overran the oil fields of the Caucasus and rumbled into the outskirts of Stalingrad on the Volga River (see map, pages 332–33). Beyond lay the Ural Mountains, where the Soviet people were feverishly building new industries to help in the war effort.

An American naval officer painted this picture of U. S. marines as they spearheaded the invasion of the Pacific island of Bougainville in 1943. By capturing this Japanese stronghold in the Solomons, the marines gave the Allies yet another stepping-stone on the path that would lead to Japan.

The Allies were able to turn the tables on the Axis forces in part because of the injection of U. S. manpower and materials into the war effort. Here, guarded by U. S. warships, a huge convoy moves toward an Allied battlefront.

In the Mediterranean the Axis forces were triumphant everywhere. German and Italian aircraft with bases in Italy, Greece, the Greek island of Crete, and North Africa all but forced British naval craft out of the Mediterranean. They thus denied the British the use of the Suez Canal route to the Indian Ocean. Great Britain was compelled to send its ships thousands of miles around Africa to reach Egypt, the Middle East, and India. By the autumn of 1942, the German *Afrika Korps* under General Erwin Rommel had advanced to the frontiers of Egypt. There the well-trained corps stood poised for a final thrust at the Suez Canal and the oil fields of the Middle East.

Allied victories. November 1942 marked a turning point of the war. In the Pacific, as you have read, the three-day naval battle of Guadalcanal started the Allies on their long drive toward Tokyo. In North Africa British General Bernard L. Montgomery caught Rommel by surprise late in October at El Alamein in Egypt and drove him back across the desert into Libya toward eventual defeat.

On November 8 a mighty invasion fleet led by General Dwight D. Eisenhower landed thousands of British, Canadian, and American troops on the northern coast of Africa (see map, pages 332–33. On November 19 the Soviet troops began to encircle the German forces at Stalingrad. Within several weeks the Soviet troops overwhelmed the Germans at Stalingrad and forced them to surrender.

"This is not the end," Winston Churchill said in November 1942. "It is not even the beginning of the end. But it is, perhaps, the end of the beginning." Subsequent events justified Churchill's reassuring words. Before 1942 was

over, the Allies held the initiative in Europe, as in the Pacific.

Wartime cooperation. How had the Allies been able to survive the earlier disasters? Why were they able in November 1942 to begin to seize the initiative? One answer is that the tremendous combination of America's human resources and war materials was beginning to have its effect. Another answer is that in their struggle the Allies were working as a team.

On January 1, 1942, the 26 Allied nations, calling themselves the **United Nations°**, issued a joint declaration. The countries (1) promised full cooperation in the war effort, (2) agreed not to make a separate peace, and (3) endorsed the war aims outlined in the Atlantic Charter by Churchill and Roosevelt (page 325).

Early in 1941, as you recall, even before the United States had entered the war, Congress laid the basis for cooperation among the Allies with the Lend-Lease program (page 325). After the attack on Pearl Harbor, the aid program went into high gear. The United States shipped immense quantities of war materials across the submarine-infested sea routes to its allies in the Pacific and to Great Britain, the U.S.S.R., and the British armies in Egypt and the Middle East. Before the war ended, Lend-Lease aid reached more than $50 billion. Of this total 69 percent went to Great Britain, about 25 percent to the U.S.S.R., and small quantities to other Allies.

Text continues on page 334.

°**United Nations:** The wartime Allies called themselves the United Nations. When in 1945 they formed a permanent organization, they continued to use this same name for that organization.

ICELAND

ATLANTIC

GREAT

NORTH
SEA

NORWAY

SWEDEN

FINLAND

Leningrad

ESTONIA

LATVIA

LITHUANIA

SOV

N.
IRELAND

EIRE

BRITAIN

DENMARK

BALTIC SEA

GER.

OCEAN

London

English
Channel

JUNE 6, 1944

Dunkirk

1942-45

1940-44

NETH.

Berlin

1945

GERMANY

Warsaw

POLAND

1945

1944

Kiev

UKR

NORMANDY

Paris

LUX.

BELG.

1945

1944

1945

CZECHOSLOVAKIA

FRANCE

Vichy

"VICHY FRANCE"

SWITZ.

Vienna

AUSTRIA

HUNGARY

1945

RUMANIA

1944

PORTUGAL

SPAIN

1944

ITALY

Rome

ADRIATIC SEA

YUGOSLAVIA

BULGARIA

1944

TU

SARDINIA

Anzio

Cassino
Naples

Salerno

ALBANIA

Strait of
Gibraltar

1942

Algiers

1943

1944

1943

GREECE

Casablanca

SP.
MOROCCO

Bizerte

Palermo

1942

1943

Tunis

SICILY

CRETE

MOROCCO (Fr.)

ALGERIA (Fr.)

TUNISIA (Fr.)

MALTA

MEDITERRANEAN

El Alamein

1943

1942

| 0 | Miles | 1000 |
| 0 | Kilometers | 1600 |

LIBYA

E G

WORLD WAR II IN EUROPE

Dark days for the Allies

1939

SEPT.–OCT. — German invasion and conquest of Poland.

1940

APR.–JUNE — German invasion of Denmark, Norway, Luxembourg, Belgium, Netherlands, France.

MAY — British evacuation from Dunkirk.

JUNE–JULY — Fall of France; establishment of Vichy government.

AUG.–OCT. — Battle of Britain (German air attacks).

OCT. — Axis aggressions in Balkans.

NOV.– FEB. 1941 — British offensive in Mediterranean and North Africa.

1941

FEB.–MAY — Battle of the Atlantic begins.

MAR.–APR. — Axis counteroffensive in North Africa.

APR.–JUNE — German invasion of Greece, Yugoslavia, Crete.

JUNE — German invasion of U.S.S.R. begins.

Allied gains: the tide turns

1942

MAY–AUG. — Allied air attacks on Germany begin.

OCT.–NOV. — Allied counteroffensive in North Africa begins.

NOV.– MAR. 1943 — Russian counteroffensives in U.S.S.R.; German surrender of Stalingrad.

1943

MAY — Allied victory in North Africa; end of African campaign.

JULY–AUG. — Allied invasion of Sicily.

JULY– JAN. 1944 — Russians drive Germans back in U.S.S.R. and enter Poland.

SEPT. — Allies begin Italian campaigns.

SEPT. 8 — Italy surrenders.

1944

JUNE 6 — Allied invasion along Normandy coast (Operation Overlord).

AUG. — Allied forces land in southern France.

AUG. 25 — Allies liberate Paris.

SEPT. — Allies liberate Belgium, Luxembourg.

SEPT. — Battle for Germany begins.

SEPT.–DEC. — Russians conquer Yugoslavia and Hungary.

DEC. — Battle of the Bulge (last German counteroffensive).

Allied victory in Germany

1945

FEB.–APR. — Allied invasion of Germany.

MAY 7 — Germany surrenders.

MAY 8 — V-E Day (end of war in Europe).

333

Lend-Lease was not a one-way arrangement. During the war the United States received in exchange goods and services valued at nearly $8 billion, most of which came from Great Britain. For example, when the American air forces began to arrive in England, the British provided bases, housing, and equipment. The Lend-Lease program was an outstanding example of Allied cooperation.

Cooperative planning. Joint planning of strategy was an even more decisive Allied effort. Shortly after the attack on Pearl Harbor, Prime Minister Churchill and a group of military, naval, and technical aides met in Washington, D.C., with General George C. Marshall, Chief of Staff of the Army, and the commanders of America's air, land, and sea forces. This meeting was the first of a series held by the Allied military leaders.

These conferences required a tremendous spirit of give-and-take. Final decisions were not always popular with all concerned. For example, the Soviets, hard-pressed in the summer of 1942, urged their Allies to relieve the pressure on the Soviet Union in Eastern Europe by opening a second front in Western Europe. Roosevelt and American military leaders finally agreed with Churchill that the Allies were not sufficiently prepared to do this. They decided instead to land troops in North Africa, where they could strike at southern Europe. Despite such differences among the Allies, the high degree of cooperation achieved was indispensable to the final victory.

SECTION SURVEY

IDENTIFY: Douglas MacArthur, William Halsey, "scorched-earth" policy, *Afrika Korps,* Erwin Rommel, Bernard Montgomery, Dwight D. Eisenhower, United Nations.

1. November 1942 marked a turning point of the war. Why?
2. How did the Lend-Lease program help both the United States and its allies?
3. (a) Why was Allied cooperation so important in winning the war? (b) In what specific ways did the Allies cooperate?
4. Map Study: Study the map on pages 332–33. (a) Locate the Axis countries. (b) In November 1942, which countries were under Axis control? (c) How does the map illustrate the fact that 1941 to mid-1942 were dark days for the Allies?

2 Americans accept controls and win the "battle of production"

The Allied victories were won on the farms and in the factories of the Allied nations as well as on the fighting fronts. By the end of 1942, the United States in particular had made itself "the arsenal of democracy."

Hitler's errors. When Hitler declared war upon the United States, he had already made two grave mistakes. First, he had failed to conquer Great Britain. He might have done this if he had launched an invasion immediately after the British armies lost most of their equipment at Dunkirk. Second, his surprise attack upon the U.S.S.R. in June 1941 and his failure to take Moscow led to the disaster of his troops at Stalingrad.

On December 11, 1941, Hitler made a third major mistake by declaring war upon the United States. He failed to realize how swiftly the American people could convert their peacetime industries to war production.

America's soaring production. One of the amazing demonstrations of America's productivity took place on the nation's farms. Despite the fact that 2 million agricultural workers served in the armed forces, farmers managed to raise record-breaking crops. They raised enough food to supply the American people as well as their Allies.

The output of America's mines and factories was equally impressive. For example, between July 1940 and July 1945, United States manufacturing plants produced 296,601 military planes, including about 97,000 bombers; 86,388 tanks; 88,077 scout cars and carriers; 16,438 armored cars; 2.4 million trucks; 991,299 light vehicles, such as jeeps; 123,707 tractors; 17.4 million rifles and side arms; 2.7 million machine guns; 315,000 pieces of artillery; and 41.4 billion rounds of ammunition.

In addition, America's shipbuilders created the greatest navy and merchant marine the world had ever seen. By 1943 five ocean-going vessels were being launched every 24 hours.

All in all, production during the war years was 75 percent greater than in peacetime. According to Donald M. Nelson, first chief of the

WOMEN IN THE COCKPIT

One afternoon at an Air Force base in Florida, a fighter pilot awaited his new plane, due to be ferried in from the factory. There was a heavy overcast.

Then we heard it. The apron sort of filled up with guys who wouldn't admit they were worried, of course. But they did want to see what was coming in through this stuff. Sure enough, a *Thunderbolt* broke out at about 500 feet, made a smooth turn to the end of the runway and rolled to as pretty a stop . . . as I ever saw. . . . I ran up to the wing and out stepped the teeny-weeniest little girl I ever saw in my life. . . . She had kind of a tired grin. "Your plane, captain?"

The "girl" (in the 1940's women were commonly called "girls" until they were elderly) was a member of the Women's Airforce Service Pilots, or WASP. She and others like her were constantly proving to astonished men that airplane controls responded as well to a woman's touch as to a man's.

The WASP, organized in 1942 by racing flier Jacqueline Cochran, trained about a thousand women. Their purpose was to free men for combat duty. A major WASP task was ferrying planes from factories to military bases. Its pilots also made weather flights and towed targets for aerial gunnery training.

In spite of their qualifications and excellent safety record, women in the WASP fought an uphill battle. They were never paid as much as men doing the same work and were never incorporated into the Air Force. By the end of 1944, when the shortage of male trainees had ended, the WASP was disbanded. Its members had made an important wartime contribution, however. They had also proved decisively, in the words of one woman flier, that "all a good airplane needs to fly it is a good pilot."

War Production Board, created in January 1942, "American industry turned out more goods for war than we ever produced for our peacetime needs—yet had enough power left over to keep civilian standards of living astonishingly high."

Financing the war. Where did the money come from to finance the war? A little more than one third came from taxes, which were raised to the highest level in American history. The government borrowed the remainder, chiefly by selling huge issues of bonds. Because of this borrowing, the national debt shot upward from about $49 billion in 1941 to nearly $259 billion by the spring of 1945.

The dollar cost of the war was staggering. By 1945, military expenditures totaled $400 billion. This was twice the sum that the federal government had spent for all of its activities, including all wars, between 1789 and 1940!

Government agencies. In its efforts to organize the war effort and to mobilize the nation's resources, the federal government created a complex network of agencies.

At the top there was a policy-making board called the Office of War Mobilization (OWM). Its job was to unify the activities of the many war agencies.

Just below the OWM was the War Production Board (WPB). This board affected the daily lives of nearly every man, woman, and child in the United States. The WPB controlled the allocations of raw materials to industrial plants. It searched the country for scrap iron and the nation's kitchens for fats, tin, and aluminum. It directed the conversion of factories from peacetime to wartime production and stimulated the construction of new plants.

In addition, the WPB restricted the production of all consumer goods that required materials necessary to the war effort. It rationed

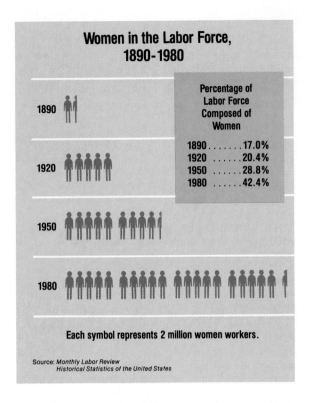

Women in the Labor Force, 1890-1980

	Percentage of Labor Force Composed of Women
1890	17.0%
1920	20.4%
1950	28.8%
1980	42.4%

Each symbol represents 2 million women workers.

Source: *Monthly Labor Review*
Historical Statistics of the United States

gasoline to conserve oil and rubber. It even controlled clothing styles to save wool, cotton, rayon, and other vital materials.

To prevent transportation shortages and bottlenecks, the federal government also created the War Shipping Administration and the Office of Defense Transportation. These agencies supervised the railroads, express services, and shipping. The result was that supplies and troops moved efficiently over land and sea.

Mobilizing human resources. The Office of War Information bolstered the morale of the armed forces and of civilians by publicizing the achievements of war production. It also gained support for Allied war aims by broadcasting them in dozens of languages to people all over the world.

The War Manpower Commission (WMC) discouraged men and women from working in nonessential occupations. By 1945 it had channeled nearly 30 million wage earners into the war production effort, including 12 million black American workers and 50,000 Indian workers. By 1943 the labor force included 2 million women working in war plants, replac-

ing men who had left to serve in the nation's armed services.

The WMC also operated the Selective Service System. By the end of the war, the Selective Service had drafted nearly 10 million out of the more than 15 million Americans who served in the armed forces. Included were more than 350,000 Mexican Americans and 1 million black Americans, among them both volunteers and draftees. Despite black protests, official military policy required blacks to serve in segregated units, as in previous wars. In 1944–45, however, some white and black troops in Europe were integrated to meet an emergency situation.

Also included in the armed forces were about 25,000 Indian volunteers. Among tribes with warrior traditions, the rate of enlistment was high. In general, the Indian volunteers enjoyed the respect of their white and black fellow soldiers. Indian soldiers who returned to the reservations after the war took back with them new ideas to their families and their tribal communities.

For the first time the American armed forces, which had previously used women only as nurses, accepted women in uniform to replace men in noncombatant jobs. More than 250,000 women entered the army (as Wacs), the Coast Guard (as Spars), the Navy (as Waves), and the Marine Corps. As full-fledged military personnel, women worked as machinists, storekeepers, office workers, radio operators, and drivers of jeeps and trucks. The performance of women in the armed forces and in the nation's war plants did much to break down prejudices about what women could and could not do.

Government price control. One of the ways in which the government most closely regulated the lives of civilians was through price controls. In World War I, the shortage of consumer goods and the increased purchasing power of industrial and agricultural workers had driven prices skyward. This brought on inflation and caused suffering, especially among the poor.

The government was determined to prevent inflation in World War II. As a first step, the government raised income taxes. This drained off dollars that would otherwise have been spent on goods in the stores. As a second step, the government encouraged Americans to buy war bonds, arguing that such purchases were both a patriotic duty and a sound investment. However, these measures alone could not prevent inflation.

In 1942, following the example of European governments, Congress created the Office of Price Administration (OPA). The OPA established ceilings, or top limits, on prices and set up a **rationing** system. The OPA issued ration books containing coupons that purchasers had to use in addition to money to buy gasoline, fuel, shoes, coffee, sugar, fats and oils, meat, butter, and canned goods. The OPA also established rent controls.

Despite these efforts, the prices of consumer goods rose, especially food prices. By 1944 the cost of living had risen 30 percent above 1941 prewar levels. Some Americans violated the price control and rationing system by paying exorbitant prices to obtain more than their share of rationed products. Most Americans, however, accepted price controls and rationing as wartime necessities.

Control of wages and profits. Shortly after the attack on Pearl Harbor, the leaders of organized labor promised President Roosevelt that American workers would not strike during the war. At the same time, they insisted that the government had to ensure that workers would be fairly treated. By the spring of 1942, however, the cost of living had risen, and workers were becoming restless.

In July 1942 the National War Labor Board (NWLB) tried to work out a compromise. It granted a 15-percent wage increase to meet the rises in living costs. Several months later Congress and President Roosevelt authorized the NWLB to freeze the wages and salaries of all workers at the newly established levels.

For a time there was relatively little trouble. However, as prices continued to rise, labor again became restless, and here and there strikes broke out. In such instances the government usually stepped in and for the most part settled the disputes quickly.

The government also tried to regulate profits—mainly by means of taxation. Personal income taxes were greatly increased for people in the higher income brackets. The most drastic means of controlling profits was the excess profits tax, levied in 1940. This tax obliged corporations to pay to the government as much as 90 percent of all excess profits. Americans did not like government controls. Nevertheless, they accepted them with the understanding that they would be removed when the emergency was over.

The Japanese Americans. The upheaval in everyday life resulting from these controls and from the whole vast war effort revealed the extraordinary willingness of the American people to make sacrifices for the national emergency. Despite discomforts and sacrifices,

Hastily built tarpaper barracks were the new homes for Japanese Americans in 1942 when they were forced to leave their former homes and relocate in detention camps. This camp was set up in the desert near Manzanar, California.

the people maintained a remarkably high level of morale.

Americans also suffered deep anxieties and fears. However, these fears did not lead to the widespread repressions of minority groups that occurred in World War I. The tragic exception to this overall tolerance was the forced relocation of some 100,000 Americans of Japanese birth or parentage.

After the Japanese attack on Pearl Harbor, many Americans were genuinely fearful of a Japanese attack on the United States. This fear was soon turned against the **Nisei**—native-born Americans whose ancestors came from Japan. As a result, most Japanese Americans—the great majority of whom lived in California—were forced to leave their homes and were taken to detention camps in other states, where they were imprisoned until the end of the war. Most of the Nisei lost their homes and businesses. Yet there had never been any real proof that these Japanese Americans had been disloyal. Indeed, nearly all of the Nisei remained loyal, patriotic American citizens despite their harsh, unfair treatment. Many of those allowed to serve in the armed forces distinguished themselves for bravery.

After the war Americans regretted their unjustified actions against the Nisei. In 1945 the Nisei were permitted to leave the detention camps and settle wherever they wished. In 1948 Congress passed an act to help the Nisei recover a part of their losses.

Minorities in wartime. American minorities contributed not only to the fighting but to efforts on the home front as well. In 1941 President Roosevelt directed that a Fair Employment Practices Committee be set up to end discriminatory hiring policies in defense industries. As a result, the doors of the defense industries opened to minority workers.

Less was accomplished, however, in promoting equal housing opportunities in the overcrowded cities. Discrimination on the part of white Americans led to outbursts of violence and even riots in several cities. In Detroit in 1943, for example, federal troops restored order after 25 blacks and 9 whites died in a riot.

In 1942 the United States and Mexico signed a treaty. Under its terms thousands of Mexicans known as **braceros** entered the United States on a temporary basis as farm workers. Their efforts helped keep vital food production high during the war.

Prejudice and discrimination against Mexican Americans in jobs, housing, and recreation facilities also aroused bitter resentment. This resentment, reaching a boiling point in Los Angeles in 1943, erupted in a riot between servicemen and Mexican Americans.

Aware of their contributions to the war effort, blacks and other minorities became increasingly restless. As they listened to patriotic speeches about freedom for all, they became more determined to make these ideals meaningful for themselves.

SECTION SURVEY

IDENTIFY: OWM, WPB, WMC, Selective Service System, price controls, rationing, Nisei.

1. (a) Why did the federal government establish controls and regulations over many aspects of American life during the war? (b) What were some of these controls? (c) How did they affect individuals?

2. How did the following contribute to the war effort: (a) unions, (b) women, (c) minorities.

3. Graph Study: Examine the graph on page 336. (a) About how many women were in the labor force in 1920? in 1950? (b) What percentage of the labor force were women in 1920? in 1950? (c) What may have contributed to the changes?

3 **The Allies gradually fight their way to victory in Europe**

In the summer of 1942, as the tide of war was turning in favor of the Allies, President Roosevelt and Prime Minister Churchill decided to strike at what Churchill called the "soft underbelly" of the Axis.

Victory in North Africa. The opening blow, as you recall, fell late in October 1942, when the British broke through Rommel's lines at El Alamein and began to drive the Germans back into Libya. Meanwhile, on November 8, a force of 500 troop transports and 350 warships under General Eisenhower's command landed thousands of Allied troops in French Morocco and Algeria. The African offensive was the greatest combination of land, sea, and air forces brought together up to that time.

The loss of French areas in North Africa was a serious blow to the Germans. Although they continued to fight with great skill, their efforts were hopeless. Allied planes and ships cut their supply lines from Italy. General Montgomery's British Eighth Army drove steadily westward, while American forces moved eastward. Outnumbered and caught between the jaws of two enemy forces in Tunisia (see map, pages 332–33), the Germans and Italians surrendered early in May 1943.

In the victory in North Africa, the Allies captured more than 250,000 Axis troops. Far more important, the Allied nations now had control of the Mediterranean, their warships protected by planes based at airfields along the North African coast. The Allies could ship supplies to India through the Suez Canal and to the Soviet Union by way of Iran.

Invasion of Italy. From their newly won North African bases, the Allies subjected Sicily and Italy to merciless bombing. Then, early in July 1943, British, Canadian, and American troops landed in Sicily. The Sicilians offered little resistance, and the crack German troops were greatly outnumbered by the invaders, who swiftly overran the island.

Americans and other Allied peoples were thrilled at the rapid conquest of Sicily and by other good news during the summer of 1943. Late in July the Italians ended Mussolini's dictatorial rule and organized a new government. Before dawn on September 3, the British Eighth Army landed on the southern coast of the Italian mainland. On September 8 the Italian government surrendered unconditionally, and the following day an Allied invasion force landed at Salerno.

Despite these great successes the campaign for Italy was one of the longest and most difficult of the war. German troops were rushed in to fill the gaps left by the Italians. Difficult mountain terrain and bad weather helped the Germans. On October 1 Naples fell to an American army under General Mark W. Clark, but for several months the Allies were unable to advance beyond Cassino (see map, page 332). In an effort to outflank the German lines, Allied troops landed on the Anzio beaches southeast of Rome on January 22, 1944, but the Nazis fought desperately and held them off. It was not until June 4, 1944, that the Allied armies entered Rome.

From Rome they moved north. Progress was slow, and every inch of soil was won at great cost by the Allies — Americans, British, Canadians, Indians, New Zealanders, South

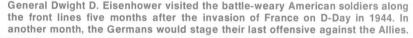

General Dwight D. Eisenhower visited the battle-weary American soldiers along the front lines five months after the invasion of France on D-Day in 1944. In another month, the Germans would stage their last offensive against the Allies.

Africans, French, Moroccans, Algerians, Senegalese, Poles, Greeks, Arabs, Brazilians, and a Jewish brigade from Palestine.

Importance of the Italian campaign. The victories of 1943–44 in Italy were immensely important. Through them the Allies strengthened their control of the Mediterranean. The loss of Italy deprived Germany of desperately needed troops. Moreover, from Italian bases Allied fliers were able to bomb southern Germany and the German-held Balkans, including the rich oil fields in Rumania.

Finally, in their efforts to check the Allies in North Africa and Italy, the Germans had been forced to withdraw troops from the Soviet front. This had helped the Soviet Union to regain great stretches of valuable farmland in the Ukraine. Despite the Italian campaign, however, the Nazis continued to concentrate most of their military forces against the Soviet Union, and the Soviets continued to call for a second front in Western Europe.

Victory in the Atlantic. The victories in Italy were possible only because the Allies had won control of the Atlantic Ocean. During the early months of the war, German submarines waged a mighty battle against ships carrying supplies to Europe. The Allies suffered staggering losses of ships, vital war materials, and lives.

Gradually, however, the Allies gained the upper hand. Radar and other devices for detecting planes and submarines were developed. New warships, including small aircraft carriers, were built by American and British shipyards. In 1942 the Axis sank 585 Allied and neutral vessels in the Atlantic. In 1943 the Axis sank only 110 ships. By the end of 1943, the Battle of the Atlantic was won.

Over the sea lanes, great convoys carried urgently needed military supplies to the Mediterranean war fronts and to Great Britain, which by 1943 had been converted into a vast base for the invasion of Western Europe.

Victory in the air. While the Allied navies were winning the Battle of the Atlantic, Allied planes began their offensive against Germany and German-occupied Europe. By early 1943 the Anglo-American air assault had become a major factor in the struggle. During the last year of the war, fleets of as many as 2,000 heavy bombers were dropping tons of bombs on a single target area.

The constant blows against German transportation centers, industrial plants, and military installations weakened German morale. The Allied air raids brought relief to Great Britain, which had suffered tremendous damage from German air attacks. They also helped Soviet armies who were seeking to drive the Nazis from Soviet soil.

Liberation of Western Europe. The terrific air assault on Germany was part of a larger strategy – the invasion and conquest of Germany. By June 1944 General Eisenhower, who had been named Supreme Commander of the Allied invasion armies in Western Europe, was satisfied that it was time to launch the attack.

Operation Overlord, as the invasion was called, began before dawn on the morning of June 6, 1944 (D-Day). More than 11,000 planes roared into the air. Some dropped airborne troops at key points a few miles inland from the German-occupied French coast. Others bombed roads, bridges, railway junctions, and German troop concentrations. Still others formed a mighty umbrella under which a huge invasion fleet of nearly 4,000 troop transports, landing craft, and warships moved across the English Channel to the Normandy beaches (see map, pages 332–33).

The Germans had worked for years to make these beaches unconquerable. Heavy artillery and machine guns were located in reinforced concrete pillboxes. Barbed wire and tank traps lined the shores. Other tangles of barbed wire were strung on steel and concrete piles and sunk just below the water's surface for hundreds of feet offshore.

Despite the years of preparation, the Germans were powerless to stop the invasion. The Nazis resisted fiercely, but they were outplanned, outnumbered, and outfought. Allied tank forces ripped through the German defenses and fanned out behind the lines. Aided by the French resistance, or underground movement, they quickly overran the countryside. On August 25, 1944, Paris fell. By this time the Allies had landed more than 2 million troops and millions of tons of munitions and supplies.

Meanwhile, early in August, the United States Seventh Army landed on the southern coast of France. It pushed rapidly up the Rhone Valley to join the Allied troops pouring in from Normandy. Within six months after D-Day, France had been liberated and the Allies had swept into the outer defenses of Germany's

Even in time of war there is a place for humor. Here, in caricature, an Iranian artist shows the Allied leaders hunting down Mussolini, Hitler, and Hirohito. Can you find President Roosevelt? Whom is he spearing?

famous Siegfried Line (see map, page 342). Here the attack at last ground to a halt. The Allied armies paused while new ports were opened, supplies were brought up, and military units were regrouped.

The election of 1944. The preparations for the final drive into Germany did not interfere with the regular November elections in the United States. The Republican candidate for the Presidency was Thomas E. Dewey, governor of New York. He had attracted national attention when, as a district attorney, he had successfully prosecuted racketeers in New York. The Republicans considered Dewey a strong candidate. However, the war was going well, and the Democrats argued that it would be unwise to replace experienced leaders. The argument proved convincing. Roosevelt, running for a fourth term, won with an electoral vote of 432 to Dewey's 99. The new Vice-President was Harry S. Truman of Missouri.

Germany's last counterattack. While the Allies were regrouping and the Americans were electing a President, the Germans were preparing a counterattack. On December 16 some 24 German divisions struck at a weakly held point in the Allied lines. German armored forces broke through, creating a dangerous bulge in the Allied lines. Christmas 1944 found the Allies fighting desperately in the Battle of the Bulge (see map, page 342), trying to prevent the Germans from plunging onward to the sea. Reinforcements were rushed up. The German divisions were shattered and thrown back behind the Siegfried Line.

Their defeat cost the Germans dearly in troops and equipment. Even more important, as General Eisenhower pointed out, was "the widespread disillusionment within the German army and Germany itself."

Invasion of Germany. By February 1945, Allied preparations had been completed for the invasion of Germany. The air forces continued to blast industrial areas, military bases, and transportation lines. Then, in March, the Allies crossed the Rhine, encircled Nazi troop concentrations, and plunged toward the heart of Germany (see map 342).

Meanwhile, the Soviets had been driving the Germans out of the Ukraine. They had conquered Nazi-held Rumania and Hungary and were closing in upon the Nazis from the south and east. Churchill had grown concerned over the Soviet Union's postwar intentions. He was alarmed at the deep penetration of the Soviet armies into Europe and argued that the Allies should race the Soviets to Berlin and Prague. This vital political problem might have been decided by the leaders of the Allied governments including, of course, President Roosevelt. Instead, the civilian leaders left the

ALLIED VICTORY IN EUROPE

decision to General Eisenhower. He, as Supreme Commander, concluded that his first objective should be the immediate and total destruction of the German armies. It would be "militarily unsound," he declared, to depart from this objective for political considerations. As a result of this decision, American forces under Eisenhower's command advanced only as far as the Elbe River (see map, this page). There on April 25 they joined the Soviet forces at Torgau.

Victory in Germany. Events that ended the war in Europe then followed in rapid order. On May 1 Hitler reportedly took his own life in the burning ruins of Berlin. On May 2 the Soviet troops hammered their way into the last Nazi strongholds of the city, and nearly 1 million German soldiers in Italy and Austria surrendered. Germany was in chaos. Within a week the Nazi forces in the Netherlands, Denmark, and Germany stopped fighting. Early on the morning of May 8, the German High Command surrendered unconditionally. Thus May 8, 1945 (V-E Day), marked the formal end of the war in Europe.

In Churchill's words, the victory over Ger-

many was "the signal for the greatest outburst of joy in the history of mankind." As for himself, he wrote, his joy was tempered by "an aching heart and a mind oppressed by forebodings." He was weighed down by the awful tragedy of the war and concerned over the postwar intentions of the U.S.S.R.

Revelations of Nazi horrors. The first outbursts of joy at the end of the war in Europe were soon dulled by shocking news coming out of Germany. During the war the few refugees that managed to escape Nazi control had brought reports of terrible persecution and massacres of Jews. When the Allied armies entered and occupied the conquered country, the full extent of Nazi horrors came to light.

The world now heard in detail the bloodcurdling crimes the Nazis had committed in their concentration camps. In one of the most terrible displays of brutality in human history, the Nazis had created these camps, or "death factories," to destroy their "political enemies" and to exterminate the entire Jewish population (see page 322).

The horrified world labeled this program of extermination the **Holocaust.** In it nearly 12 million men, women, and children, about half of them Jews, had been slaughtered after suffering indescribable anxieties, agonies, indignities, and tortures.

Roosevelt's death. President Roosevelt did not live to see the end of the war or to share in the world's horror over the Nazi atrocities. Worn out by his vast responsibilities, he died suddenly on April 12, 1945, in the "Little White House" at Warm Springs, Georgia. People all over the world were stunned at the news of his death. For three days American radio stations canceled programs to devote time to his memory. Vice-President Harry S. Truman, who now became President, declared, "His fellow countrymen will sorely miss his fortitude and faith and courage in the time to come. The peoples of the earth who love the ways of freedom and hope will mourn for him."

SECTION SURVEY

IDENTIFY: Operation Overlord, D-Day, Siegfried Line, Battle of the Bulge, V-E Day, concentration camps, Holocaust.

1. Why was the Allies' Italian campaign important?

2. (a) Why was it vital for the Allies to win the Battle of the Atlantic? (b) Why were they able to defeat the Germans in this battle?
3. Describe the events of 1945 that led to the fall of Germany and to the end of the war in Europe.

4 Allied victories in the Pacific bring an end to World War II

President Roosevelt's death in April 1945 came only a month before the Allied victory in Europe and only four months before the defeat of the Japanese ended World War II.

By 1943, you recall, the United States and its Allies were taking the offensive in the Pacific. The overall strategy, directed by Admiral Chester W. Nimitz, had three parts. (1) Air, land, and naval forces would strike westward at the Japanese-held islands in the Central Pacific. (2) A fleet under Admiral Halsey would drive the Japanese from the Solomon Islands. (3) General MacArthur would advance with troops along the New Guinea coast and on to the Philippine Islands. The ultimate objective was Japan.

Early victories. During 1943, American, Australian, and New Zealand troops pushed forward through the steaming jungles and across the vast stretches of the Central and South Pacific. The struggle was grim, for the Japanese clung to every foot of land. Few prisoners were taken.

Driving the Japanese from their threatening position before Port Moresby, which defended Australia, American and Australian troops fought their way up the New Guinea coast. Before the end of 1943, much of New Guinea had been recovered. American and New Zealand forces also won victories in the Solomon Islands.

Meanwhile, in the Central Pacific, Admiral Nimitz's powerful fleet moved into the Gilbert Islands, and American marines seized Tarawa and Makin (see map, page 344). Far to the north, Japan's troops were dislodged from the Aleutian strongholds of Attu and Kiska. The threat to Alaska was now ended.

Despite these successes, won at extreme cost in lives after ferocious fighting, the major Japanese positions remained untouched.

Island hopping. By 1944 a growing volume of troops and supplies was arriving in the Pacific. Powerful new warships and aircraft carriers, grouped into swift task forces, swept through the outer screen of protecting islands blasting Japanese installations and shipping routes. Carrier planes were raining explosives on the Japanese-held islands prior to invasion.

Suddenly, on January 31, 1944, the Allies struck again, this time against the Marshall Islands (see map, page 344). Three days later they seized Kwajalein (KWOJ·ah·lin), one of the keys to Japanese control of the Marshalls. Kwajalein was the first Japanese possession occupied by the Allies. Three weeks later Eniwetok (en·ih·WEE·tok) was stormed successfully. From these two bases, strong fleets of B-24 bombers began to blast Truk, a major stronghold in the Carolines and key to Japanese control of the Southwest and Central Pacific. Meanwhile General MacArthur, continuing his advance up the New Guinea coast, seized Hollandia. By July all of New Guinea was in his hands, with only bypassed pockets of Japanese troops left to surrender or to starve.

A month earlier, in June 1944, task-force raids and swift strikes by carrier-based planes pinned down Japanese air and naval forces and hammered the defenses of Saipan and Guam in the Mariana Islands (see map, page 344). Then under cover of intense air and naval bombardment, landing craft swept in upon the beaches. From fleets near the Philippines, the Japanese sent out swarms of planes, only to lose more than 400 in a few hours. The following day hundreds of American planes roared from the decks of carriers to strike a severe blow at the retreating Japanese fleet.

Though shocked and saddened by the appalling loss of life, the American people were thrilled at the victories on Guam and Saipan. They had long dreaded the thought of a slow, bloody, island-by-island advance to Japan. Now Americans realized that the nation's tremendous sea and air power enabled it to seize key positions in the Pacific, leaving Japanese forces isolated and helpless on numerous islands far behind the line of battle.

Victory in the Philippines. Probably the most gratifying news from the Pacific in 1944 was the reconquest of the Philippines. In October vast naval forces moved up from the New Guinea–Solomons theater of war and in from

Text continues on page 346.

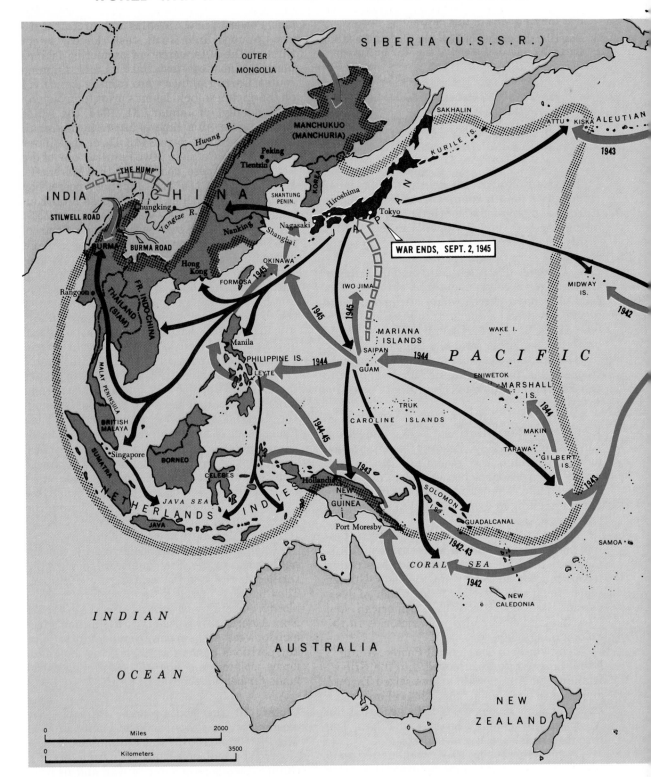

WORLD WAR II AND ALLIED VICTORY IN THE PACIFIC

SIBERIA (U.S.S.R.)

OUTER MONGOLIA

MANCHUKUO (MANCHURIA)

SAKHALIN

KURILE IS.

ATTU KISKA ALEUTIAN

1943

Hwang R.

Peking

Tientsin

KOREA

SHANTUNG PENIN.

Hiroshima

Tokyo

"THE HUMP"

INDIA CHINA

STILWELL ROAD

Chungking

Yangtze R.

Nanking

Nagasaki

Shanghai

WAR ENDS, SEPT. 2, 1945

MIDWAY IS.

1942

BURMA BURMA ROAD

Hong Kong

OKINAWA

1945

IWO JIMA

WAKE I.

Rangoon

FORMOSA

1945

1945

MARIANA ISLANDS

P A C I F I C

THAILAND (SIAM)

FR. INDO-CHINA

SAIPAN

1944

1944

Manila

PHILIPPINE IS.

1944

GUAM

ENIWETOK

MARSHALL IS.

LEYTE

1944

MALAY PENINSULA

TRUK

CAROLINE ISLANDS

MAKIN

1944

BRITISH MALAYA

1944-45

TARAWA

GILBERT IS.

SUMATRA

Singapore

BORNEO

1943

CELEBES

Hollandia

NEW GUINEA

SOLOMON IS.

1943

N E T H E R L A N D S

JAVA SEA

I N D I E S

JAVA

Port Moresby

GUADALCANAL

1942-43

SAMOA

C O R A L   S E A

1942

NEW CALEDONIA

INDIAN

OCEAN

AUSTRALIA

NEW ZEALAND

| 0 | Miles | 2000 |
| 0 | Kilometers | 3500 |

344

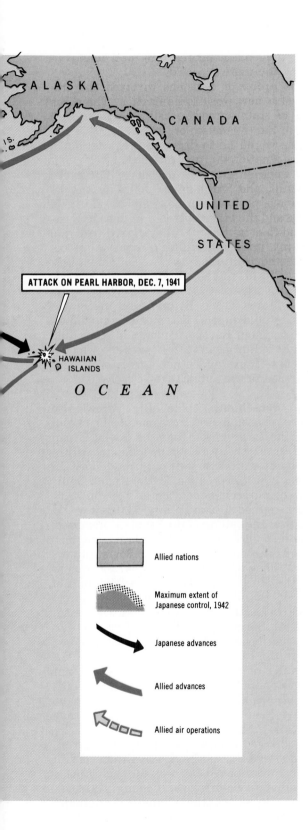

WORLD WAR II IN THE PACIFIC

Dark days for the Allies

1941

JULY	Japanese invasion of French Indo-China.
DEC. 7	Japanese attack Pearl Harbor.
DEC. 8–11	United States declares war against the Axis.
DEC.	Japanese invasion of Thailand and Br. Malaya; capture of Wake, Guam, Hong Kong; invasion of Philippines, Midway.

1942

JAN.	Fall of Manila.
JAN.–MAY	Japanese occupy Netherlands Indies and Burma.
FEB.	Singapore surrenders to Japanese.
FEB.–MAR.	Battle of the Java Sea.
APR.–MAY	Fall of Bataan and Corregidor.
MAY	Battle of the Coral Sea.
JUNE	Battle of Midway.
JUNE	Japanese occupy Attu and Kiska in Aleutians.

Allied gains: the tide turns

AUG.	U.S. marines land on Guadalcanal.
NOV.	Allied victory in naval battle of Guadalcanal.

1943

JAN.–SEPT.	Allied gains in New Guinea.
MAR.–AUG.	Allies force Japanese from Aleutians.
JUNE–DEC.	Allied offensive in South Pacific: Solomon Is.
NOV.–FEB. 1944	Allied offensive in Central Pacific: Gilbert Is., Marshall Is., Kwajalein, Eniwetok.

1944

APR.–JULY	Allies seize Hollandia and regain New Guinea.
JUNE–AUG.	Allies capture Saipan and Guam in Mariana Is.
OCT.	Allied campaign to reconquer Philippines begins.

1945

FEB.	Allies liberate Manila; end of Philippines campaign.
FEB.–MAR.	U.S. marines conquer Iwo Jima.
APR.–JUNE	U.S. marines conquer Okinawa.
MAY–AUG.	Allied air offensive against Japanese home islands.

Allied victory in the Pacific

AUG. 6	Atomic bomb dropped on Hiroshima.
AUG. 9	Atomic bomb dropped on Nagasaki.
AUG. 10	Japan surrenders.
AUG. 14	V-J Day (end of war in Pacific).
SEPT. 2	Japan signs formal surrender on U.S.S. *Missouri*.

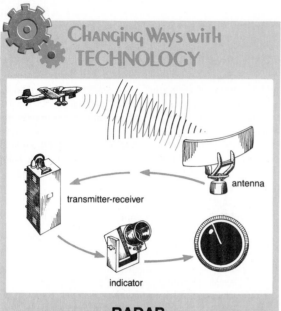

antenna

transmitter-receiver

indicator

RADAR

A radar transmitter sends out radio waves through an antenna. The radio waves bounce off objects and are received once again by the antenna. A receiver converts the detected radiation into spots of light on a cathode ray tube, which can be used to determine the location and speed of the object. Radar was first used on a large scale in World War II to locate airplanes and ships.

Saipan and Guam. The converging forces poured upon the beaches of Leyte (LAY·teh) in the central Philippines (see map, page 344) and eventually captured the island. Meanwhile, in the Battle of Leyte Gulf, American naval forces shattered Japan's remaining sea power.

Overcoming bitter land resistance, the conquering troops then spread over the Philippines. Early in February 1945, Manila fell to the Americans. "I shall return," MacArthur had promised when, following orders, he had left Corregidor in 1942. "I'm a little late, but we finally came," he said in Manila in 1945 as the American and Filipino flags were raised above the city.

The Yalta Conference. Long before the Allied victories in 1945, leaders of the great powers had met at a series of conferences to develop a common strategy and to form plans for a lasting peace. Early in February 1945, President Roosevelt, Prime Minister Churchill, and

Premier Stalin met at Yalta in the southern part of the Soviet Union (see map, page 320). There they made far-reaching decisions concerning the postwar world.

One group of decisions involved the creation of a new world organization. The three heads of state agreed to call a conference to meet in San Francisco on April 25, 1945. The purpose would be to draw up a charter for a new international organization.

In another group of decisions, Roosevelt, Churchill, and Stalin made plans for the occupation of postwar Germany and the future of Poland and the other liberated nations in Eastern and Central Europe. They agreed to divide Germany into four military zones to be occupied and controlled by the United States, Great Britain, the Soviet Union, and France. They also agreed that the "Big Three" — the United States, Great Britain, and the Soviet Union — would support free elections in Poland and throughout Europe. This would guarantee the right of Europeans to choose their own governments. These and other agreements were announced to the public.

Secret agreements. The "Big Three" also reached several secret agreements. In one of these, Stalin promised that the Soviet Union would enter the war against Japan within three months after the war in Europe ended. In exchange for this promise, Roosevelt and Churchill, upon recommendation of top military leaders, agreed to two points. (1) They would recognize the Mongolian People's Republic, which had once been part of China but now claimed its independence under Soviet protection. (2) They would allow the Soviet Union to have the Kurile Islands, the southern half of Sakhalin Island, an occupation zone in Korea, and certain rights in Manchuria (see map, page 344). Several of these territories and privileges had been held by Russia before it lost them in the Russo-Japanese War of 1904–05.

Details of the Yalta Conference did not become public until long after Roosevelt's death. Down through the years, critics have severely condemned Roosevelt for what they called his "surrender" to Soviet demands. The critics charged that as a result of his "surrender," Roosevelt gave the Soviet Union control of Manchuria, paved the way for the Chinese Communists' victory over Chiang Kai-shek (CHAHNG KI·SHEK), the Chinese Nationalist leader, and opened the door to Communist aggression in Korea. They also held him responsible for the Soviet occupation of East Berlin and East Germany and the creation of Communist governments in Eastern Europe. These governments were created without the free elections that Stalin had promised.

Roosevelt's defenders have replied to these charges by reminding the critics of the military situation at the time of the Yalta Conference. Soviet armies had already conquered most of Eastern Europe, including Poland. American troops, on the other hand, had not yet crossed the Rhine and were still fighting the Japanese in the Philippines. Moreover, Allied military leaders had warned that the invasion of Japan, scheduled for the spring of 1946, might cost the United States as many as 1 million troops.

Also, Roosevelt's defenders insisted, Stalin had given Churchill and Roosevelt reason to believe that the Soviet Union would cooperate in building a new world organization designed to establish the foundations of a lasting peace. As Churchill himself later wrote, "Our hopeful assumptions were soon to be falsified. Still, they were the only ones possible at the time."

The road to victory. On February 19, 1945, a week after the Yalta Conference ended, United States marines landed on the beaches of Iwo Jima (EE·woh JEE·mah). Nearly 20,000 American marines were killed or wounded in the successful effort to gain control of this barren volcanic island, only 750 miles (1,200 kilometers) from Tokyo (see map, page 344). Among the marines who helped raise a flag of victory over Iwo Jima was Ira Hayes, an Indian. Hayes later received the Congressional Medal of Honor as an outstanding hero of World War II.

A few weeks later, the largest landing force in Pacific history invaded Okinawa (oh·kih·NAH·wah), a Japanese island some 300 miles (480 kilometers) from the Japanese homeland. Despite bitter Japanese resistance, Okinawa fell in June 1945.

Japan's air and sea power were broken, but Japan still had many well-trained and well-equipped divisions of soldiers. It still controlled large areas of China, although badly needed American supplies were being flown across the eastern Himalayas and transported by trucks over the newly opened Stilwell Road (see map, page 344) to embattled Chinese troops. These supplies were only a fraction of what China needed, and Chinese troops were in no position to undertake a major offensive. Moreover, the

inner defenses on the Japanese homeland were strong. On the other hand, Japan was blockaded, and, after the war in Europe ended in the spring of 1945, the full weight of the Allies was available for the final struggle in the Pacific.

Day by day the American task forces grew bolder. They drove the remaining Japanese ships from the seas and shelled shore installations on the Japanese mainland. Day by day huge fleets of bombers, now within easier striking distance of Japan, dropped fire bombs and high explosives in devastating raids on the Japanese home islands. By the early summer of 1945, the blockade and the relentless bombings were destroying Japan's power to resist.

The end of World War II. With Roosevelt's death in April 1945, the responsibility for making decisions to bring about the defeat of Japan fell upon his successor, President Truman. In July Truman met with Stalin and Clement Attlee, the new British Prime Minister, at Potsdam, Germany. At this meeting the three

This statue of the raising of the flag at Iwo Jima can be seen in Washington, D. C. It commemorates the heroism of American marines in the Pacific.

This scene of destruction is Hiroshima, Japan, after it was hit by an atomic bomb dropped by an American bomber. Nearly 100,000 of the city's people were killed by the bomb which actually fell a mile from this site.

Allied leaders discussed plans for the control and occupation of Germany. They also issued an ultimatum to Japan, calling for its unconditional surrender. Japan rejected the ultimatum on July 29.

On August 6, 1945, at 8:15 A.M., a single American bomber flew high over the Japanese city of Hiroshima. No alarm was sounded. Then suddenly the city disintegrated in a single searing atomic blast. Nearly 100,000 of the 245,000 men, women, and children in Hiroshima were killed instantly or died soon after. A new force had been added to warfare, a force that would enormously complicate the postwar world.

In authorizing the atomic bombing of Hiroshima, President Truman knew that he had made an extremely grave decision. He had given the order only after days of conferring with his key military and political advisers. His decision was made to force Japan to surrender immediately and thus to save the lives of hundreds of thousands of American troops. Despite the devastation of Hiroshima, the Japanese failed to surrender.

On August 8 the Soviet Union declared war on Japan. On August 9 the United States drop-

ped a second atomic bomb. This one destroyed the city of Nagasaki. On August 10 the Japanese government finally asked for peace.

On August 14, 1945 (V-J Day), President Truman announced by radio that Japan had accepted the Allied peace terms. The formal surrender was signed on September 2, 1945. World War II had come to an end.

SECTION SURVEY

IDENTIFY: Chester Nimitz, Ira Hayes, Harry S. Truman, Potsdam Ultimatum, Hiroshima.

1. What was the Allied strategy for winning the war in the Pacific?
2. (a) Summarize the agreements reached at the Yalta Conference of 1945. (b) Explain the arguments made by some Americans for and against these agreements.
3. (a) Why did the Japanese finally surrender? (b) Was the dropping of the atomic bomb necessary to end the war? Explain.
4. Map Study: Examine the map on pages 344–45. (a) Trace the area of maximum Japanese control during the war. (b) With the help of the map, explain the island-hopping strategy.

Chapter Survey

Summary: Tracing the Main Ideas

The cost of World War II in human lives, money, and property was enormous. In the United States alone, the federal government spent more money than it had during the entire period from 1789 to 1940, including the cost of all earlier wars. Billions of dollars of property went up in smoke and flames. Parts of many of the world's major cities were reduced to rubble.

The loss of human life was staggering. According to General Marshall's final report, 201,367 Americans had been killed by the end of June 1945. About 600,000 had been wounded, and 57,000 were missing. Other nations lost much more heavily. It has been estimated that more than 3,000,000 Germans, more than 3,000,000 Russians, more than 1,500,000 Japanese, and more than 375,000 British troops were killed in battle. Civilian deaths resulting from bombs, starvation, disease, and concentration camps ran into countless millions. The exact number can never be known, for vast numbers of people simply disappeared. Many more millions of people were uprooted and left homeless as death and destruction raged across the face of the earth.

These were only some of the immediate and terrible effects of the most devastating war the world had ever seen.

Inquiring into History

1. What were the most important reasons for the Allied victory in Europe?
2. What role did science and technology play in winning the war?
3. What role did air power play in both the European and Pacific theaters of the war?
4. United States action against the Nisei was justified because the constitutional rights of all citizens are suspended in wartime. Do you agree or disagree? Why?
5. At certain times in a country's history, the power of a single personality becomes an extremely important force. Apply this idea to (a) Churchill in Great Britain, (b) Hitler in Germany, or (c) Roosevelt in the United States.

Relating Past to Present

1. Despite their deeply rooted belief in individualism and free enterprise, Americans accepted many new governmental controls during World War II. (a) Why? (b) Are there any circumstances under which Americans might accept such controls today?
2. The atomic bomb was used to end World War II. Are nuclear weapons an important part of America's defenses today?

3. If a war involving as many nations as World War II were fought today, what do you think its outcome would be?

Developing Social Science Skills

1. Use primary and secondary sources to find out more of the role of women during World War II. (a) Why did women enter the work force? (b) For the most part, what kinds of jobs did they work at? (c) What happened to these jobs at the end of the war? (d) What effects do you think the war had on the role of women in American society? Explain.
2. Study the maps on pages 332–33 and 342. (a) Trace the area on the map on pages 332–33 that corresponds to the area on the map on page 342. (b) Which map provides more information? (c) How do the purposes of the two maps differ? (d) How did the area of Axis control change from 1942 to 1945?
3. Use the *Reader's Guide to Periodical Literature* to locate articles written during the war years and post-war years about the Holocaust. (a) How much did the American people know about the Holocaust before the war's end? Explain. (b) What did the American people learn about the Holocaust after the war? How did they react?

Unit Survey

For Further Inquiry

1. In what ways did the "peace" ending World War I lead to World War II?
2. (a) What is isolationism? (b) Why was the United States basically isolationist after World War I? (c) In what ways was the United States *not* isolationist in that period?
3. During the 1930's, some nations resorted to dictatorship governments in order to resolve problems caused by the worldwide depression. (a) How might a dictatorship be able to solve such problems? (b) Why do you think the United States did not become a dictatorship during this period?
4. World War II was as much a battle of the scientists and engineers as a battle of the footsoldiers. Explain.
5. Review America's attempts to remain neutral before the War of 1812, World War I, and World War II. (a) What were the similarities and differences? (b) Why did each of these attempts fail?

Projects and Activities

1. Study the timeline here. (a) Which items concern an achievement or contribution of a minority person or group? (b) Which items concern Americans' reactions to minorities? (c) Which items concern government actions toward minorities? (d) Based on the timeline, write a short paragraph describing the status of minorities in America from around 1920 to 1945.
2. Examine the map on pages 344-45. (a) By what routes did the Allies try to attack Japanese areas from bases in India? (b) Locate examples of the "island-hopping" strategy. (c) Trace the boundaries of maximum Japanese control in 1942. Calculate the area (in square miles or square kilometers) of maximum Japanese control.
3. Investigate the Supreme Court cases, such as *Korematsu v. U.S.*, that arose from the internment of Japanese-Americans. (a) What were the major questions raised by the cases? (b) How did the Court resolve the questions?
4. Make a tape recording (from records or your own performing) of songs that were popular during World War II. You might include both patriotic and "pop" songs.

Exploring Your Region

1. Interview relatives or acquaintances who lived in your area during World War II. Ask them to comment on aspects of the war effort that directly affected their lives. You might ask them about such subjects as food and gas rationing, civil defense activities, changes in local factory output or employment.
2. Take a tour of local World War II memorials. Find out about ways in which the war dead are honored during the year.

Suggested Readings

1. *Pacific War Diary, 1942-1945,* James J. Fahey. The secret diary of an American sailor who fought in the Pacific during World War II.
2. *Diary of a Young Girl,* Anne Frank. A vivid account of a young Jewish girl and her family as they hide from the Nazis.
3. *Negro Medal of Honor Men,* Irvin H. Lee. Story of the heroic deeds of black soldiers in America's wars.
4. *No Time for Glory, Stories of World War II,* Phyllis Fenner, ed. Ten exciting short stories of World War II.
5. *Von Ryan's Express,* David Westheimer. An action-packed novel of British and American prisoners of war who make a daring escape in the last days of World War II.

Unit Seven

Reshaping the Postwar World

1945-1960

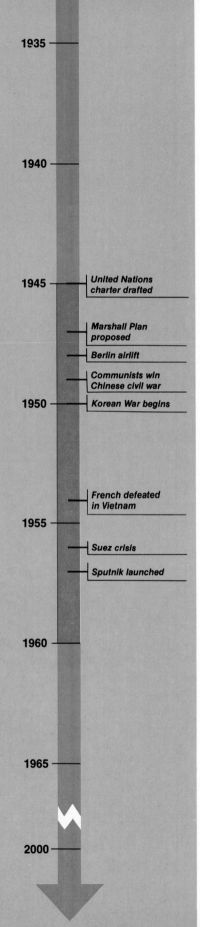

Chapter **19**

Assuming the Responsibilities of World Leadership

1945–1960

The end of World War II in 1945 brought rejoicing in all the victorious countries. But the joy and gaiety were restrained. The dominant feeling was one of immense relief.

The mood of the American people was summed up by the reporter who wrote that "everybody talked of the 'end of the war,' not of 'victory.' "

It was all so different from the aftermath of World War I. In 1918, Americans had been content to let the world take care of itself. In 1945 they felt they knew better.

Senator Arthur H. Vandenberg of Michigan, who in the 1930's had been one of the leading isolationists in Congress, spoke for millions of Americans when he was in London in 1944 during a German rocket attack. "How can there be immunity or isolation," he asked, "when man can devise weapons like that?"

Later, in the Senate, Senator Vandenberg renounced his isolationism. He came out in favor of American cooperation in building a new world order. "I want a new dignity and a new authority for international law," he announced. "I think American self-interest requires it."

In 1945 the American people were rapidly becoming aware that, like it or not, the United States was destined to play a new role in the world. However, not even the most farsighted among them realized the heavy burden of responsibility they would carry in the troubled years ahead.

THE CHAPTER IN OUTLINE

1. The United States helps to organize the United Nations.
2. The United States and the U.S.S.R. engage in a "cold war."
3. Growing nationalism and Communist aggression lead to a "hot war" in Asia.
4. The United States continues to meet the challenges of communism.

352

1 The United States helps to organize the United Nations

Even before World War II ended, many world leaders were considering ways to build an enduring peace. American officials were among the leaders in this effort.

During the war the Allies—or United Nations, as they called themselves—promised to join together to defeat Italy, Germany, and Japan (page 331). Allied leaders—among them Roosevelt, Churchill, and Stalin—agreed to convert the wartime alliance into a permanent organization for peace.

Many Americans pledged to support such an international organization of nations. Democrats and Republicans alike agreed to back a program of international cooperation.

Planning the United Nations. Delegates from the United States, Great Britain, the U.S.S.R., and China met in 1944 at Dumbarton Oaks, an estate in Washington, D.C. There they began planning for a postwar United Nations organization. On most of the questions concerning procedure, the delegates quickly reached agreement. Some problems, however, were more difficult to solve.

What, for instance, should they do about the U.S.S.R.'s demand that it be represented in the United Nations not by one delegation but by 16—one for each of the 16 Soviet republics? What should they do about the Security Council, the body that was charged with keeping peace in the world?

At Yalta in February 1945 (page 346), Roosevelt, Churchill, and Stalin reached agreement on several issues that had deadlocked the Dumbarton Oaks Conference. They agreed that two of the Soviet Union's 16 republics would be admitted to the United Nations as though they were independent nations. The leaders also worked out a compromise on voting procedure in the Security Council. Finally, they agreed to call a conference in San Francisco on April 25, 1945, to draw up the official Charter of the United Nations.

Delegates from 50 nations, representing three fourths of the peoples of the earth, took part in the San Francisco Conference. Despite their differences, the delegates all worked for one objective—to form a world peace organization. In just eight weeks, the Dumbarton Oaks and the Yalta proposals were reshaped into the

The United Nations' General Assembly serves as a forum for discussion of world problems and is often referred to as the "town meeting of the world." Membership in the Assembly consists of all members of the United Nations.

United Nations Charter. On October 24 — now celebrated as United Nations Day — the United Nations (UN) came into official existence.

Purposes and organization. The purposes of the UN are clearly stated in the Preamble to the Charter. "We the peoples of the United Nations, determined to save succeeding generations from the scourge of war, . . . to promote social progress and better standards of life in larger freedom, . . . have resolved to combine our efforts to accomplish these aims."

In general, the UN seeks to maintain peace, to provide security, to promote justice, to increase the general welfare, and to establish human rights. Six major organs and many related agencies were created to carry out the work of the UN.

(1) The Security Council was to be the police authority of the world, charged with preventing war. It was to consist of 11 members.° Five of these, the so-called "Big Five" powers — the United States, China, France, the Soviet Union, and Great Britain — were to hold permanent seats. The six nonpermanent members were to be elected for two-year terms. The Security Council was to have at its command an international military force to check aggression. On matters of peace and security, any one of the five permanent members could prevent action by its negative vote, or veto.

(2) The General Assembly was to be the "town meeting" of the world, in which all UN members were to be equally represented. It was to make recommendations for the peaceful settlement of disputes. It was to elect all the nonpermanent members of the Security Council and members of other agencies.

(3) The Economic and Social Council, composed of 18 members (now 57), was to study world economic, social, cultural, and health problems. It was to make recommendations on these problems to the General Assembly or to individual member countries.

(4) The International Court of Justice, modeled after the World Court, was to decide legal questions referred to it by disputing nations. It was to give advisory opinions when asked to do so, but it could not enforce its decisions.

(5) The Secretariat was to handle the administrative work of the UN.

°It later was increased to 15 members — five permanent members plus ten nonpermanent members.

(6) The Trusteeship Council was to look after the welfare of peoples living in colonial areas of the world.

Early years of the UN. Early critics of the UN insisted that it was doomed to fail because the member nations had not given up any of their national sovereignty. Other people, however, shared the opinion expressed by President Truman in 1945. "This charter," he stated, "points down the only road to enduring peace. There is no other."

As crises broke out in many parts of the world, Truman's statement took on new meaning. By 1948 the world situation had become so tense that Trygve Lie (TRIG·vuh LEE), the first Secretary-General of the UN, issued a warning. "The trouble," he declared, "lies in the intense conflict over the settlement of the last war . . . between the two most powerful single nations in the world today — the United States and the Soviet Union."

SECTION SURVEY

IDENTIFY: Dumbarton Oaks Conference, San Francisco Conference, "Big Five," Trygve Lie.

1. (a) What problems were left unsolved at the Dumbarton Oaks Conference? (b) How were these issues resolved later at Yalta?
2. What are the purposes of the United Nations?
3. What are the major functions of the Security Council and the General Assembly?

2 The United States and the U.S.S.R. engage in a "cold war"

At the end of World War II, millions of people throughout the world suffered from lack of food, clothing, shelter, and medical care. The United States responded generously to this desperate worldwide need for help.

America's new role. The United States played an active role in creating three important UN agencies: (1) the United Nations Relief and Rehabilitation Administration (UNRRA), (2) the International Bank for Reconstruction and Development, and (3) the International Monetary Fund. These agencies supplied food, clothing, shelter, and medical care to millions of people in war-damaged nations and provided money to rebuild ruined industries. A large part of the money for these activities came from the United States.

After the war ended, American dollars and supplies flowed directly to the war-devastated areas. Major contributions came from private American organizations—churches, schools, fraternal societies, and civic groups. An even larger contribution came from the United States government in the form of supplies, equipment, loans, and the assistance of specialists and experts.

Expanding Soviet influence. America's new role of world leadership brought it into conflict with the Soviet Union, which also emerged from the war as a major power. The postwar policies of the Soviet Union in some ways continued the expansionist policies of tsarist Russia. However, the U.S.S.R. now regarded itself as the leader of a Communist revolution destined to replace the "capitalist" and "imperialist" world—a world in which the United States was the principal power.

Even before World War II ended, the Soviets had begun to move aggressively against their weaker neighbors. In 1940 Latvia, Lithuania, and Estonia—countries to which the Russians had some historical claims—were incorporated into the Soviet Union. As a result of World War II, the U.S.S.R. also acquired large parts of Poland and Rumania. Through Communist governments that they helped to set up, the Soviets by 1948 had gained control of the "free" governments of Poland, Rumania, Hungary, Czechoslovakia, and the eastern part of Germany. Moreover, Soviet influence reached beyond Eastern Europe into the Mediterranean area. Moscow-trained Communists were especially active in Greece and Italy.

The U.S.S.R. was deeply entrenched in East Asia, as well as in Europe. As a result of the Yalta agreements and because of its last-minute entry into the war against Japan, the Soviet Union gained control of large areas that had been Chinese and Japanese territory.

Mounting tensions. The Communist leaders defended their actions on grounds of self-defense. They pointed out that in 1918–19 during the Bolshevik Revolution, the Allies, including American troops, had occupied north-ern Russia and Russian Siberia. Believing that war between communism and capitalism was inevitable, they feared that the United States would lead the capitalist nations in a new attack against the U.S.S.R. They reminded the world that the Nazi invasion of their country had cost them 21 million lives and the destruction of hundreds of their towns and cities. In view of these facts, the Soviets insisted on maintaining powerful military forces and on controlling bordering areas from which new attacks might be launched.

The United States objected bitterly to the Soviet Union's domination of its weaker neighbors. The United States, which had demobilized most of its own troops, resented the Soviet policy of maintaining huge military forces. Moreover, Americans loathed the ruthless methods used by the Soviet Union to crush all opposition. Most Americans regarded the Soviet Union as the world's newest aggressor.

As friction increased, the Soviet press and radio, rigidly controlled by the government, became increasingly anti-American. The Soviet government refused to join the United Nations Educational, Scientific, and Cultural Organization (UNESCO), which had been established to promote understanding among the peoples of the world. It permitted only a very few Americans to visit the U.S.S.R. or its satellite nations—those nations dominated by the U.S.S.R.

Deadlock over atomic energy. Inability to reach agreement on international control of the atomic bomb greatly added to the mounting tension between the United States and the U.S.S.R. Early in 1946, acting on American initiative, the UN created an International Atomic Energy Commission. At the Commission's first meeting, the United States representative, Bernard M. Baruch (buh·ROOK), presented America's proposal for international control.

Baruch proposed that complete control of atomic energy be turned over to an international agency responsible to the UN. This agency would have full authority to enter any country to inspect atomic energy installations. The United States—at that time the only nation that had atomic bombs—was ready, Baruch announced, to give up its secrets to the new world authority. However, he warned, the United States would not reveal any secrets until the UN provided for "immediate, swift, and sure punishment for those who violate the agreements that are reached by the nations." Baruch insisted that each of the "Big Five" on the Security Council give up its right to the veto on all matters involving atomic energy.

When the United States proposal reached the Security Council, the Soviet Union killed it by a veto. The Soviet Union then offered its own proposal. It opposed any system of international inspection and control. Instead, it insisted that the United States destroy its atomic bombs, that the UN declare atomic warfare illegal, and that all nations promise not to manufacture atomic bombs. However, the Soviet Union flatly refused to give up its veto right in the Security Council. This meant that if any nation, including the U.S.S.R., violated its promise not to make atomic bombs, the Soviet Union or any other permanent Security Council member could block all UN action by a single veto.

The Truman Doctrine. Wary of Communist aggression, the United States formulated a policy of containment. This policy aimed to contain, or restrict, Soviet expansion and to check the spread of communism. The new policy was first applied to Greece and Turkey.

In 1947, Greek Communists supported by the Soviets were about to seize control of the conservative Greek government. At the same time, the Soviet Union was trying to force Turkey to give up control of the Dardanelles, the strait between European and Asiatic Turkey. Soviet control of Greece and the Dardanelles would enable the U.S.S.R. to dominate the northeastern Mediterranean and the Suez Canal.

This situation prompted President Truman in 1947 to announce the Truman Doctrine. This doctrine stated that the United States had to "help free people to maintain their free institutions and their national integrity." He then asked Congress for authority to help the Greeks and Turks strengthen their armed forces to check the spread of communism. Congress responded with an initial appropriation of $400 million. In 1948 the United States also established and later increased its naval forces in the eastern Mediterranean.

The Marshall Plan. Aid to Greece and Turkey, however, was not enough to prevent the spread of communism. All of war-torn Europe was in economic difficulty. Throughout Europe Communists were winning converts among hungry, disillusioned people.

Early in June 1947, Secretary of State George C. Marshall suggested a solution to Europe's economic problems. The "Marshall Plan," as this program came to be called, proposed to help European countries to get their farms, factories, and transportation systems operating efficiently again. The United States would provide money, plus supplies and ma-

World War II left many European cities in utter ruin. With their economies, like their cities, in desperate need of restoration, many European nations looked to the United States for help. The Marshall Plan was part of America's response.

chinery, to any nation that would take part in the program. The Soviet Union and its satellites were included in the offer.

The Marshall Plan provoked heated Congressional debate. Those who favored the proposal insisted that the best way to block communism and strengthen America's own economic system was to restore Europe's economic health. Opponents of the program declared that the United States could not afford to "carry Europe on its back." In the spring of 1948, however, Congress approved the Marshall Plan, officially known as the European Recovery Program.

The Soviet Union and its satellites denounced the plan as "Yankee imperialism." Nevertheless, the Marshall Plan was an outstanding success. Slowly but steadily Europe began to recover from the war.

The Berlin airlift. Meanwhile tension had mounted in Germany. In 1945 the great powers had agreed to a joint occupation of Germany. Great Britain, France, and the United States occupied western and southern Germany, and the Soviet Union occupied eastern Germany. Berlin, within the Soviet-controlled zone, was also divided into four sections, each controlled by one of the four powers.

On June 24, 1948, the Soviets suddenly blocked all roads, canals, and railways connecting Berlin and the Western Zone of Germany. By this move they apparently hoped to force the three Western powers out of Berlin.

The British-American answer to the Soviet challenge was the Berlin airlift. Starting in the summer of 1948 and continuing for more than a year, British and American planes transported over 2 million tons of food and supplies to Berlin. This crisis in relations between the East and the West was finally resolved in 1949 with the aid of the UN.

NATO. The Soviet blockade of Berlin and communist efforts to wreck the Marshall Plan aroused growing alarm in Western Europe. In April 1949 nine Western European nations° joined the United States, Canada, and Iceland in an alliance known as the North Atlantic Treaty Organization (NATO).

In the Atlantic Pact—the treaty proposing the NATO alliance—each member nation

°Great Britain, France, Belgium, the Netherlands, Luxembourg, Italy, Denmark, Norway, and Porgugal. West Germany, Turkey, and Greece joined later.

SOURCES

THE MARSHALL PLAN (1947)

It is logical that the United States should do whatever it is able to do to assist in the return of normal economic health in the world, without which there can be no political stability and no assured peace.

Our policy is directed not against any country or doctrine but against hunger, poverty, desperation, and chaos. Its purpose should be the revival of a working economy in the world so as to permit the emergence of political and social conditions in which free institutions can exist. . . .

Any government that is willing to assist in the task of recovery will find full cooperation, I am sure, on the part of the United States government. Any government which maneuvers to block the recovery of other countries cannot expect help from us. Furthermore, governments, political parties, or groups which seek to perpetuate human misery in order to profit therefrom, politically or otherwise, will encounter the opposition of the United States. . . .

agreed that "an armed attack against one or more of them in Europe or North America shall be considered an attack against them all." They also agreed to resist such an attack with armed force, if necessary.

Since the Atlantic Pact was a treaty, it had to be approved by the United States Senate. Senate debate focused on whether or not the Atlantic Pact would compel the United States to go to war to assist a member nation without an act of Congress. This, you may remember, was the main issue that had kept the United States out of the League of Nations in 1919. However, in July 1949 the Senate did ratify the agreement. Eventually General Eisenhower was named Supreme Commander of the NATO forces.

Thus by the end of 1949 an American policy of containment had taken shape, at least in regard to Europe. NATO strengthened the military defenses of Western Europe. The Marshall Plan strengthened the economy of Western Europe, thus reducing the discontent that so often helped the spread of communism.

Meanwhile, however, trouble was brewing in the Middle East and in Asia.

IDENTIFY: UNESCO, satellite nations, Bernard Baruch, containment, George Marshall.

1. (a) Why did the Soviet Union try to expand its influence during the postwar period? (b) How did the Soviets justify their actions?

2. (a) Compare the Soviet and the American plans for control of atomic energy. (b) Why did efforts at control end in deadlock?

3. How did each of the following help to contain communism: (a) the Truman Doctrine, (b) the Marshall Plan, (c) the Berlin airlift, (d) NATO?

3 Growing nationalism and Communist aggression lead to a "hot war" in Asia

Postwar troubles were not confined to Europe. During President Truman's administration, growing tensions threatened peace in the Middle East and Asia.

Middle East tensions. Iran soon became a trouble spot. During World War II, both American and Soviet troops were stationed in Iran. After the war the United States pulled out its troops. However, the Soviets were eager to control the oil-rich land adjoining their border to the south and did not remove their troops. Tension mounted. Finally, after the UN intervened in 1946, the Soviets withdrew their military forces from Iran.

Meanwhile trouble broke out in Palestine, at the eastern end of the Mediterranean Sea. Since World War I, Great Britain had ruled Palestine under a mandate from the League of Nations. On May 14, 1948, Great Britain voluntarily gave up this mandate. The Jews in Palestine then proclaimed the independence of the new state of Israel.

This action angered Arabs and plunged Israel into war with the neighboring Arab countries of Egypt, Transjordan (later renamed Jordan), Lebanon, Syria, Iraq, and Saudi Arabia. The UN at once took steps to end the fighting. Finally a UN mission under the leadership of a black American, Dr. Ralph J. Bunche, managed to get both sides to agree to an armistice. As a result of his peace making efforts, Dr. Bunche received the Nobel Peace Prize.

Communist victory in China. While an uneasy peace was being restored in the Middle East, Chinese Communists were rapidly winning control of China. The struggle for control of China had begun long before World War II.

In 1927, four years before the Japanese moved into Manchuria, Chiang Kai-shek, leader of the Chinese Nationalist forces, opened war on the Chinese Communists. For a time China was torn by civil conflict. But after Japan attacked China, both of the opposing Chinese factions fought against the Japanese. During World War II, the United States encouraged such cooperation. Chinese troops heroically resisted the invading armies of Japan. In 1945, in recognition of these valiant efforts, China was admitted to the United Nations as one of the "Big Five."

With the end of World War II, the struggle between Chiang's Nationalist forces and the Chinese Communists once again erupted. The Soviet Union gave limited support to the Chinese Communists, led by Mao Tse-tung (MAU TSAY·TOONG). The United States at first provided military assistance to Chiang's Nationalists, but the Nationalists were weakened by internal conflicts and corruption. As the outlook for Nationalist victory grew dim, the United States withdrew its support. By 1949 the Communists had conquered most of China. Chiang and the Nationalist government, together with a small army, retreated to the island of Formosa, or Taiwan.

The United States continued to recognize the Nationalists as the legal government of China. Also, the Nationalists continued to represent China in the UN Security Council.°

The division of Korea. Meanwhile trouble was brewing in Korea. Between 1910 and 1945, the Koreans had been ruled by Japan. During the closing days of World War II, however, Soviet and American troops swept the Japanese out of Korea. After the war General Douglas MacArthur was appointed Supreme Commander of the Allied Powers and placed in charge of the occupation forces in Japan.† His responsibilities also included the southern portion of Korea.

°The People's Republic of China replaced Nationalist China in the Security Council in 1972.

†During the occupation period, relations between Japan and the Western powers were restored to a friendly basis. In 1951 Japan received independence in a treaty signed at San Francisco.

At the end of the war, a line drawn across the Korean peninsula at the 38th parallel (see map, page 360) separated American occupation forces in the south from Soviet occupation forces in the north. Americans and most other concerned peoples considered this a temporary arrangement.

Despite UN efforts to unite the country, Korea remained divided, and Soviet and American troops were not withdrawn. Then in 1948 North Korea and South Korea set up separate governments, each claiming authority to rule the entire country. The North Korean government, controlled by Communists and supported by the Soviets, called itself the "People's Republic of Korea." The South Korean government, of which Syngman Rhee (SING·man REE) had been chosen president in an election sponsored by the UN, called itself the "Republic of Korea." The United States and 30 UN members (but not the Soviet Union) recognized the Republic of Korea as the country's lawful government.

Finally the United States and the Soviet Union withdrew their troops. Each left behind a Korean army it had helped to train. These two Korean armies now faced each other across the 38th parallel.

The Korean challenge. On June 25, 1950, the North Korean army suddenly launched a full-scale invasion of South Korea. In an emergency session, the UN Security Council adopted a resolution ordering an immediate cease-fire. Had the Soviet delegate been present, he would undoubtedly have vetoed this action. However, the Soviet government was boycotting the Security Council because of its refusal to admit Communist China to the United Nations.

Meanwhile President Truman was busy conferring with the heads of the State and Defense departments. On June 27, 1950, the President pledged American aid to South Korea. That same evening the Security Council adopted a second resolution. It termed North Korea an "aggressor" and called on UN members to furnish all possible assistance to the South Koreans.

War in Korea. The UN itself had no troops to throw into action. Soviet vetoes in the Security Council had blocked every effort to create a UN military force. Although 19 UN members finally contributed assistance, the major burden

Ralph Bunche (right) took the job of peacemaker in Palestine with the knowledge that a predecessor had been assassinated for his efforts. Bunche received the Nobel Peace Prize for his work.

of defending South Korea against the North fell upon the United States.

In response to the UN's call, President Truman ordered the United States Seventh Fleet into action. It was charged with preventing any attack upon Formosa and blockading the Korean coast. Truman also ordered United States air and ground forces into Korea.

For a time it looked as though the North Koreans would overrun all of Korea. The South Koreans were hopelessly outnumbered. Neither they nor the first American troops rushed to the scene could stand up against the heavily armored, Soviet-made tanks of the North Korean army. By early August the South Korean and UN troops under General MacArthur were desperately defending a small area around Pusan in southeast Korea (see map, page 360).

Then the tide suddenly turned. On September 15, 1950, MacArthur staged a seaborne attack against Inchon and then swept eastward, recapturing Seoul (SOHL), the capital of South Korea. At the same time, a strongly reinforced UN army, now well equipped and powerfully supported from the air, attacked from southeastern Korea. The North Korean

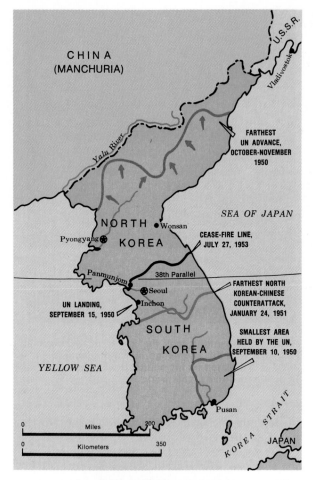

THE KOREAN WAR

Map labels:
CHINA (MANCHURIA)
U.S.S.R.
Vladivostok
Yalu River
FARTHEST UN ADVANCE, OCTOBER-NOVEMBER 1950
SEA OF JAPAN
NORTH KOREA
Wonsan
Pyongyang
CEASE-FIRE LINE, JULY 27, 1953
Panmunjom
38th Parallel
FARTHEST NORTH KOREAN-CHINESE COUNTERATTACK, JANUARY 24, 1951
Seoul
Inchon
UN LANDING, SEPTEMBER 15, 1950
SOUTH KOREA
SMALLEST AREA HELD BY THE UN, SEPTEMBER 10, 1950
YELLOW SEA
Pusan
KOREA STRAIT
JAPAN
Miles 0 200
Kilometers 0 350

forces, caught in a huge trap, began to break up. Thousands surrendered. The rest fled northward across the 38th parallel. Mac-Arthur's troops followed in hot pursuit. By November the UN forces were at the Yalu River, the boundary between North Korea and Communist China.

Then suddenly the tide turned again. Late in November hundreds of thousands of Chinese Communist "volunteers" swarmed across the Yalu River to reinforce the North Korean troops. The UN troops, their lines extended, were outnumbered in many cases by hundreds to one. Finally, after weeks of desperate fighting, MacArthur's forces managed to set up their defense line near the 38th parallel.

The Great Debate. The entry of Chinese Communist troops completely changed the na-

ture of the war. President Truman faced new, serious questions. Should he heed MacArthur's request and allow him to blockade the China coast and bomb the Chinese mainland? Should he also help Chiang Kai-shek's Nationalist forces to launch an invasion of China?

MacArthur's proposal provoked heated debate. His supporters argued that quick, decisive action would bring a speedy end to the Korean conflict. Those who disagreed argued that an attack upon Communist China might cause the U.S.S.R. to support its Communist ally openly. This would certainly start another world war.

MacArthur's opponents also pointed to another danger. If the United States committed its military forces to a major war in Asia, the Soviet Union would be free to do as it pleased in Europe.

Stalemate in Korea. By January 1951 President Truman had reached his decision. He ordered General MacArthur to establish the strongest possible defense line near the 38th parallel. However, he forbade blockading the China coast, bombing China, and using Chiang's troops to invade China. The war in Korea was to remain strictly a "police action" to protect South Korea. In 1951, therefore, the Korean War reached a stalemate.

MacArthur refused to accept Truman's decision as final and tried to appeal to Congress over the President's authority. In April 1951 President Truman removed MacArthur from his post. "I could do nothing else and still be President," Truman explained. General Matthew B. Ridgway replaced MacArthur as Commander of the UN forces.

American policy and Point Four. During 1951 and 1952, the United States continued the rapid buildup of its land, sea, and air forces. This military buildup was only part of America's response to the challenge of communism around the world. With economic aid and technical assistance, the United States helped less fortunate areas of the world to raise their standards of living. The Marshall Plan was intended primarily for Europe. A new plan, the Point Four program, was intended to help developing areas anywhere in the world. The Point Four program consisted of bringing many scattered activities for providing scientific and industrial aid into a carefully planned, coordinated program.

"In war there is no substitute for victory," said General Douglas MacArthur (seated next to driver), commander of UN forces in Korea. Here, seeking victory, he inspects troop positions along the front lines early in the war.

The Point Four program got off to a slow start. The Korean War, however, convinced even the most hesitant Americans that the world was facing a grave crisis. By 1952 most Americans believed that United States policy should include provisions for foreign aid and the strengthening of military defenses throughout the non-Communist world.

SECTION SURVEY

IDENTIFY: Ralph Bunche, Chiang Kai-shek, Mao Tse-tung, Taiwan, Douglas MacArthur, 38th parallel, Syngman Rhee, "police action," Point Four program.

1. Describe the postwar events that created tension in the Middle East.
2. (a) How did China come to have two governments by 1949? (b) What was the American position concerning China?
3. (a) What were the causes of the Korean conflict? (b) What issues provoked the Great Debate during that conflict?
4. Map Study: Examine the map on page 360. (a) Locate the line of farthest North Korean advance. (b) Describe the events of the war from September to November 1950. (c) What geographic advantage did China have when it sought to aid North Korea that the United States did not have?

4 The United States continues to meet the challenges of communism

Dwight D. Eisenhower was elected President in November 1952. When he took office, he and his Secretary of State, John Foster Dulles, continued the bipartisan foreign policy that had been followed since America's entry into World War II.

Ending the Korean War. During the 1952 election campaign, Eisenhower had promised to do everything within his power to end the Korean War. In December 1952 he visited the battle area for talks with political and military leaders. Peace talks were being carried on at this time in Panmunjom (PAN·MUHN·JUM) in Korea (see map, page 360). Finally, on July 27, 1953, North Korea and the UN signed an armistice agreement. This agreement recognized the division of Korea into two countries — North Korea and the Republic of South Korea.

In a formal treaty, the United States promised to defend South Korea against any future attack. The United States also undertook to

French troops look out glumly from their trenches at Dienbienphu, Vietnam, in May 1954. The French were unable to hold this key fortress and eventually faced defeat by Vietminh forces led by Ho Chi Minh after years of war.

help the South Koreans improve their economic and social conditions.

The Korean War had lasted three years and cost 33,629 American lives (and an estimated 1.5 million Communist casualties). The war had been unpopular at home. It did not change the dictatorship that ruled South Korea. It did, however, increase the prestige of the United Nations. It also showed that the prompt use of force could, at least in some cases, check Communist aggression.

Developments in Indochina. Only a few months after the Korean armistice, world peace was threatened by another crisis in East Asia. Ever since the end of World War II, Indochina, a French colony, had been torn by armed conflict. A group of revolutionary nationalists, the Vietminh (VYET·MEEN), who were mainly Communists, had been fighting to win control of the entire country from the French and their anti-Communist Vietnamese allies. When it became clear that Communist China was actively aiding the Vietminh, the United States during President Truman's administration began to send military equipment and economic help to the Vietnamese and French armies.

Early in 1954 the Vietminh, supported by the Chinese, launched a powerful drive against the French and their Vietnamese supporters. In May 1954 the key French fortress of Dienbienphu (dyen·byen·FOO) (see map, page 431) fell to the Vietminh.

In July 1954 a conference was held in Geneva, Switzerland, to discuss the fate of Indochina. Although the United States had helped finance the French cost of the war, it preferred to play the role of observer at Geneva. The delegates from France, Indochina, Communist China, the Soviet Union, and Great Britain recognized the independence of Cambodia, Laos, and Vietnam. The area of Vietnam to the north of the 17th parallel became the Communist state of Vietminh, later North Vietnam; the portion of Vietnam to the south of that line became South Vietnam (see map, page 431).

Changes in American foreign policy. Under President Eisenhower and Secretary of State Dulles, American foreign policy underwent several changes. Dulles announced a firmer American policy toward the Communist world. Instead of containment, Dulles spoke of a "rollback" of the Soviets in Eastern Europe.

Dulles also developed a policy that some people called **brinksmanship.** Dulles believed that the Communists only understood force. Therefore, he felt that in order to maintain peace the United States had to be ready to go to the brink of war. "The ability to get to the verge of war without getting into war is the necessary art," Dulles claimed.

Such a policy was increasingly frightening in the mid-1950's. By that time, both the Soviet Union and the United States had developed hydrogen bombs. These weapons were vastly more powerful than the atomic bombs dropped at the end of World War II.

Soon the United States and the Soviet Union were engaged in an arms race. Each side built up a stockpile of nuclear weapons. The reason for stockpiling was to threaten the other side. Each side was demonstrating its willingness to destroy the other if attacked. This policy was known as **massive retaliation.**

The United States also continued its efforts to strengthen Western Europe. In October 1954 the United States and its European allies agreed to give the Federal Republic of Germany (West Germany) full sovereign powers. They also agreed to admit West Germany to NATO and to allow it to build an army of 500,000 troops to serve under the NATO command. The United States, Great Britain, and France also agreed to regard an attack upon West Germany as an attack upon themselves.

Changes in Communist policy. In February 1956 startling news came out of the So-viet Union. Communist Party leader Nikita Khrushchev publicly attacked his predecessor, Josef Stalin, calling him a cruel tyrant. Stalin had died in 1953.

What was behind this attack? Was Khrushchev about to adopt a friendlier attitude toward the "free world"? Was he about to loosen the U.S.S.R.'s tight grip on its satellites in Eastern Europe? Would he be willing to end the arms race? Hope began to stir, and in the satellite countries people began to demand greater freedom from Soviet control.

In October 1956 the leaders of the Communist Party in Poland elected the Polish nationalist Wladyslaw Gomulka (VLAH·dee·slaf goh·MUL·kah) as first secretary of the party. Although a long-time Communist, Gomulka promised the Poles freedom of speech, press, and religion. Encouraged by Gomulka's stand, Poles staged anti-Soviet demonstrations in the streets. On several occasions they exchanged shots with Soviet troops.

The Polish revolt attracted worldwide attention. What would Khrushchev do? Instead of crushing the revolt, Khruschev surprised the world and granted concessions. He withdrew some Soviet troops from Poland and granted some freedom to the Poles.

Revolt in Hungary. Inspired by the example of the Poles, the Hungarians also rebelled against the Soviets. On October 23, 1956, Hungarian students and workers rioted in the streets of Budapest, demanding greater freedom.

Hungarian freedom fighters rebelled against the Soviets in October 1956. At first they appeared victorious and pushed the Soviets out of Budapest. However, Soviet troops later returned to ruthlessly crush all Hungarian resistance.

The next morning Soviet tanks, guns, and armored cars, supported by jet planes, moved into Budapest. Violent fighting broke out as units of the Hungarian army joined the "freedom fighters." After four days of fighting, the U.S.S.R. agreed to pull its troops out.

Even while the Hungarians were celebrating, Soviet forces began a massive attack upon Budapest. "All Budapest is under fire," the Budapest radio reported. "The Russian gangsters betrayed us."

Within a few days, the Hungarian fight for freedom came to a tragic end. With all organized resistance ruthlessly crushed, a new Hungarian government, a puppet of the U.S.S.R., began to round up the rebels and imprison them or deport them to the Soviet Union. Refugees by the thousands fled across the frontier into Austria.

Egypt and the Suez Canal. In the same week that the Hungarians rebelled, another crisis developed, this time over the Suez Canal in Egypt. For a few tense days, the world hovered on the brink of another war.

The Suez Canal, connecting the Mediterranean and the Red seas, ran entirely through Egyptian territory. Owned and operated by an international company, the canal was open on equal terms to ships of all nations. By arrangement with Egypt, British troops were stationed at the Canal Zone to safeguard it and protect British interests.

After World War II, the Egyptians became increasingly dissatisfied with British military occupation of the Canal Zone. Finally, in June 1956 the last British troops withdrew.

In the meantime, in 1954, Colonel Gamal Abdel Nasser led a successful revolution and became President of the Republic of Egypt. Nasser was determined to modernize the country and extend Egyptian influence throughout the Middle East. One of Nasser's major plans involved building a large irrigation dam and electric generating plant at Aswan on the Nile River. Furious when the Soviets, Americans, and British failed to finance the project, Nasser announced that Egypt was going to seize the canal and operate it.° The Western powers tried in vain to persuade Nasser to agree to international control by the 18 nations that regularly used the canal. Great

°In 1959 the Soviet Union agreed to provide money and engineers to build the dam. Construction began in 1960 and was completed in 1969.

Britain and France in particular saw Nasser's nationalization of the Suez Canal as a threat to the free flow of oil from the Middle East to Western Europe.

The Suez crisis. On October 29, 1956, the Israeli army moved rapidly westward through the Sinai Peninsula toward the Suez Canal. The Israeli government announced that its troops had invaded Egyptian territory to forestall a planned attack upon Israel by Egypt.

On October 30 the British and French issued a 12-hour ultimatum. They demanded that Egypt and Israel cease fighting and allow French and British troops temporarily to occupy key points in the Canal Zone. When Egypt refused, the British and French bombed Egyptian airfields and moved troops into the northern part of the Canal Zone.

In response the Soviet Union denounced Israel, France, and Great Britain as aggressors. It threatened to intervene with force if the three nations did not immediately withdraw.

The United States now found itself in an embarrassing position. Great Britain and France, its allies in NATO, had ignored both Washington and the UN. They had created a situation that could easily lead to a general war. Moreover, the United States was unwilling to permit the Soviet Union to claim that it was the only champion of Egypt and other small nations against "Western imperialism." Reluctantly the United States voted in favor of a UN General Assembly resolution calling for an immediate cease-fire and the withdrawal of British, French, and Israeli troops. Great Britain, France, and Israel accepted these terms.

The Eisenhower Doctrine. One result of the Suez crisis was that the United States adopted what came to be known as the Eisenhower Doctrine. In January 1957 President Eisenhower asked Congress to authorize him to use military force if this were requested by any Middle Eastern nation to check Communist aggression. He also asked Congress to set aside $200 million to help those Middle Eastern countries that desired such aid from the United States. Congress granted both requests. The United States thus indicated its intention of checking Communist influence in the Middle East.

The Eisenhower Doctrine was soon tested. Early in 1958 Egypt and Syria, linked in a temporary union, urged the other Arab nations to join them in opposing Western influence.

During the next few months, the Arab world was torn by intrigue. Rebellion broke out against the pro-Western government in Lebanon. In Iraq army officers killed the pro-Western leaders and seized control of the government. The leaders of Lebanon and Jordan, now convinced that their pro-Western governments would soon be overthrown, too, appealed to the United States and Great Britain for help. President Eisenhower immediately sent American marines to Lebanon. At the same time, Great Britain flew paratroopers into Jordan.

For several weeks American and British forces remained ready for any emergency. Late in September, after the Secretary-General of the UN reported that the situation was improving, Great Britain and the United States withdrew their troops.

The race into space. The crisis in the Middle East was not the major development of 1957–58. The most startling news, which broke on October 4, 1957, was compressed into a single word: *Sputnik*. The Russians had succeeded in orbiting an artificial satellite around the earth.

The American public, long convinced that no nation was superior to the United States in science and technology, was shocked. Recognizing the Soviet feat, President Eisenhower assured the American people that the United States had its own rocket and missile program. On January 31, 1958, the United States launched a small satellite, Explorer I, into orbit, and the space race was under way.

Rockets powerful enough to carry satellites into space could also be used to launch atomic and hydrogen bombs. By 1960 both the Soviet Union and the United States were building stockpiles of intercontinental ballistic missiles (ICBM's). Each of the missiles was equipped with a nuclear warhead. Push-button war that could destroy millions of lives in an instant had become a dreadful possibility.

Tension over Berlin. Meanwhile, in November 1958, the Soviet Premier issued an ultimatum on Berlin. Khrushchev gave the Western powers six months to agree to withdraw from Berlin and make it a free, demilitarized city. If the Western powers did not agree, the Soviet Union would turn over to Communist East Germany complete control of all lines of communication to West Berlin. If the Western powers then tried to gain access to West Berlin without the permission of the East German government, the Soviet Union would help the East Germans to meet force with force. The United States, Great Britain, and France replied by repeating firmly that they would remain in West Berlin.

During 1959, however, the situation began to improve. The Soviet Union met with the Western leaders in a "Big Four" foreign ministers' conference. Although the conference failed to reach any important agreements, it did open the door to further negotiations.

Premier Khrushchev himself seemed to be opening the door a bit wider when, in September, he visited the United States. At the end of his visit, he and Eisenhower issued a joint declaration, stating that the most serious issue facing the world was disarmament. They also agreed that the problem of Berlin and "all outstanding international questions should be settled, not by the application of force, but by peaceful means through negotiation."

SOURCES

DWIGHT D. EISENHOWER'S DISARMAMENT PROPOSALS (1955)

I should address myself for a moment principally to the delegates from the Soviet Union, because our two great countries admittedly possess new and terrible weapons in quantities which do give rise in other parts of the world, or reciprocally, to the fear and danger of surprise attack.

I propose, therefore, that we take a practical step, that we begin an arrangement very quickly; as between ourselves — immediately. These steps would include:

To give each other a complete blueprint of our military establishments . . .

Next, to provide within our countries facilities for aerial photography to the other country. . . .

FROM FICTION TO FACT

In Jules Verne's science fiction classic, *Twenty Thousand Leagues Under the Sea,* Captain Nemo performed an incredible feat. Submerging his electric-powered submarine, the *Nautilus,* under the Antarctic Ocean, he crossed the South Pole. It was a fascinating adventure story for readers of 1869, and later— but, of course, it was fiction.

At least it was fiction until 1958. In that year an American submarine actually made the first transpolar voyage, through the Arctic at the North Pole. This modern-day *Nautilus* (named after Verne's creation) was also the first nuclear-powered submarine. Since it was not dependent on oxygen, it could stay submerged much longer than previous underwater craft.

Preparations for the pioneering voyage of the *Nautilus* were highly secret. (The wife of its commanding officer, William Anderson, thought he was in Panama.) On August 1 the submarine, with 116 crewmen and scientific observers aboard, submerged off Point Barrow, Alaska. It carried ten special sonar instruments for ice detection, as well as a closed-circuit television system. The ship traveled through a series of underwater valleys, skirting vast blocks of ice that looked "like clouds going by extremely rapidly."

On Sunday, August 3, the *Nautilus* reported that its position was "latitude 90, longitude indeterminate"—in other words, the North Pole. The depth of the sea floor was 13,410 feet (4,087 meters), almost 2,000 feet (656 meters) lower than previous estimates.

The *Nautilus* continued its voyage, resurfacing on August 5 near the island of Spitsbergen. Commander Anderson was immediately flown to Washington, D.C., to receive the Legion of Merit from President Eisenhower. When questioned by reporters, he admitted that he could have made the crossing "in a much more relaxed fashion." But, he grinned, "we were in a hurry."

Encouraged by Khrushchev's apparent willingness to negotiate, the Western powers agreed to meet with the Soviet Premier at a summit conference.

Summit conference abandoned. The summit conference was never held. Early in May 1960, shortly before the conference was scheduled to open in Paris, Premier Khrushchev charged the United States with "aggression." He announced that on May 1 the Soviets had detected and shot down a United States plane flying over Soviet territory.

American officials at first insisted that the U-2, as the plane was called, was engaged in weather research and had strayed off its course. Later the United States admitted that the U-2 had been engaged in aerial reconnaissance over the U.S.S.R.

Premier Khrushchev was furious. He refused to take part in the summit conference unless Eisenhower agreed to stop all such future flights over his country, apologize for past acts of "aggression," and punish those responsible for the flights.

Hoping that the meeting could still be held, President Eisenhower announced that the U-2 flights had been stopped and would not be resumed. He refused, however, to apologize. Khrushchev, refusing to accept anything less than an apology, left for home. Plans for the conference had to be abandoned.

During the remaining months of his second term, President Eisenhower continued to seek ways of reducing world tensions. His efforts were fruitless. Khrushchev refused to budge.

SECTION SURVEY

IDENTIFY: Dwight David Eisenhower, John Foster Dulles, brinksmanship, arms race, Nikita Khrushchev, Gamal Abdel Nasser, nationalization, Aswan Dam, Sputnik, ICBM.

1. How did each of the following reveal the continuing challenge of communism: (a) developments in Indochina, (b) revolt in Hungary, (c) tension over Berlin?
2. (a) What were the causes and results of the Suez crisis in 1956? (b) Explain the position taken by the United States.
3. (a) What was the Eisenhower Doctrine? (b) How was it tested by events in the Middle East?
4. Why was the summit conference scheduled for May 1960 not held?

Chapter Survey

Summary: Tracing the Main Ideas

World War II transformed America's relations with the rest of the world. Any hopes that the United States could return to a position of isolationism vanished in the smoke and flames of the conflict. As the richest and most powerful nation on earth, the United States had to accept the responsibilities of world leadership. During the postwar years, these responsibilities proved far heavier than anyone could have foreseen as the war ended in 1945.

The immediate problem was the worldwide challenge of communism. During the Truman administration, the United States developed a foreign policy that sought to contain the Soviet Union and to check the spread of communism. The United States offered military aid to friendly as well as to uncommitted nations. It also formed collective defense arrangements, notably the North Atlantic Treaty Organization, with other nations. By such means the United States tried to build a shield of military might around the non-Communist world.

The United States also sought in a number of ways to remove the threat of war and to strengthen the foundations of peace. Under Democratic and Republican Presidents alike, the United States continued to support the United Nations, to work for disarmament, and to help less fortunate countries achieve a richer and more rewarding way of life. The United States developed the Marshall Plan and other programs of economic and technical assistance. Through such programs the United States brought new hope, first to the war-ravaged countries of Europe, later to the emerging nations of the underdeveloped world.

During the 1950's both Democratic and Republican administrations followed these two basic policies—one seeking to maintain the military defenses of the non-Communist world, the other to strengthen its economic foundations. America's leaders continued to insist that through firm resolve and through cooperation with allies, the United States would in time help people everywhere to realize the age-old dream of peace and freedom.

Inquiring into History

1. (a) In what ways is the United Nations a world government? (b) In what ways is it not?
2. In 1948 a world leader said, "The trouble lies in the intense conflict . . . between the two most powerful single nations in the world today—the United States and the Soviet Union." Give evidence to support this statement.
3. Was the Korean War a victory for the United States and the United Nations? Why or why not?
4. (a) How successful was the Marshall Plan? (b) What was its basic philosophy? Explain.
5. How effective were the actions taken by the United States during the years 1945–60 in meeting the challenge of communism?
6. The Eisenhower Doctrine was really an extension of the containment policy first developed during the Truman administration. Discuss.

Relating Past to Present

1. What do you think would be gained if the United Nations were given additional powers in order to protect world peace? What might be lost?

2. (a) How do the major areas of concern in foreign policy in the 1950's compare with those of today? (b) How does present United States policy toward these areas compare with policy in the 1950's?

Developing Social Science Skills

1. Study the primary source reading on page 357. (a) According to this document, what was the purpose of the Marshall Plan? (b) Which countries could expect to benefit from the plan? (c) What other kinds of primary sources might you investigate to learn more about the Marshall Plan? (d) What would be the advantages to a researcher of each of those sources?
2. Make a map of the world that (a) indicates the areas of influence of the United States and the Soviet Union in 1960 or that (b) illustrates the events in one world area where tension arose between the two powers during the 1950's. Be sure to include a legend on your map.
3. The U-2 incident raised important questions about the rights of one nation to spy on another. Is there evidence that such activities are going on today? Explain. How do you feel about the issue?

Chapter 20

Returning to Peace and Prosperity

1945–1960

International problems after World War II, as you have seen, were complex. Problems at home were equally involved. The nation had faced a decade of depression and almost five years of bitter warfare. Now Americans were eager to return to the business of daily life.

The problems of leading the nation through this period fell to Harry S. Truman, who had become President upon Roosevelt's death in April 1945. The new leader was almost 61 years old, gray-haired, plain, and folksy, with a winning grin and a liking for people. Born and raised on a Missouri farm, Truman had served overseas in World War I. After a successful career in local politics, he had been elected to the United States Senate. In the Senate he had supported New Deal programs and had attracted attention as head of a committee that investigated the national defense program. In 1945, after having served only a few months as Vice-President, he was suddenly elevated to the highest office in the land.

This was the new President who would have to handle the problems and challenges of the postwar period. The task he faced was enormous. Truman expressed it simply when he learned that he had become President: "I felt like the moon, the stars, and all the planets had fallen on me." Both Truman and his successor, Dwight D. Eisenhower, would struggle to deal with the huge burden of guiding the nation toward peace and prosperity.

THE CHAPTER IN OUTLINE

1. President Truman promotes a Fair Deal program.

2. President Eisenhower encourages Modern Republicanism.

3. The nation admits two states and prospers during Eisenhower's Presidency.

1 President Truman promotes a Fair Deal program

After World War II ended, the American people were concerned with two major efforts at home. (1) They wanted to transform the economy from wartime production to prosperous peacetime purposes. (2) Most Americans also wanted to resume and extend the social programs of the New Deal, many of which had been suspended during World War II.

Return of the armed forces. After Japan surrendered in August 1945, Americans were eager to return to peacetime conditions. They wanted their sons and daughters, brothers and sisters, husbands and friends, home again. Most of the men and women in the armed forces were just as eager to return to their homes in the states.

The nation's military leaders, involved in the postwar occupation of defeated enemy nations, reluctantly gave in to public pressure. Within two years after the war ended, the army, the navy, and the air force had sharply reduced their strength.

After World War II, the government did far more to help veterans return to civilian life than had ever been done before. Government help came through the Servicemen's Readjustment Act of 1944. This "GI Bill of Rights," as it was called, provided for (1) government loans to help veterans set up businesses or farms, (2) government loans to buy homes, (3) pensions and hospital care, and (4) educational opportunities. Under the GI Bill, hundreds of thousands of veterans received money for tuition, books, and part of their living expenses while they attended school or college.

The Employment Act of 1946. The federal government also, for the first time, assumed responsibility for maintaining a high level of employment. Although the Employment Act of 1946 did not guarantee "full employment," it did commit the federal government to maintain a strong economy and high employment through federal spending. The act's effectiveness was marred by the decision of Congress, against Truman's wishes, to abolish the Fair Employment Practices Committee. During the war this committee had helped to enlarge job and other opportunities for blacks and other minorities.

On their way home after serving in World War II, these soldiers look forward to starting their lives anew. Many of these returning veterans would use the G.I. Bill to help them go to college, buy homes, and begin businesses of their own.

Other postwar legislation. In August 1946 President Truman signed the Atomic Energy Act. This act established a government monopoly over the production of all fissionable materials. It placed the control of nuclear research and production in a newly created Atomic Energy Commission (AEC).

The National Security Act of 1947 centralized the responsibility for military research and planning. It created a new executive department, the Department of Defense, headed by a civilian Secretary of Defense. The act provided the new Secretary with three assistants, the Secretaries of the Army, Navy, and Air Force. The act also created the Central Intelligence Agency (CIA) to gather intelligence data abroad.

In 1947 Congress also proposed the Twenty-second Amendment (page 752), which became part of the Constitution in 1951. This amendment limited a President's length of service to two terms. The Twenty-second Amendment reflected the widely shared opinion that executive power might get out of hand if a President were not limited to eight years in office.

Postwar inflation. Some Americans had feared a postwar recession in the economy as industry shifted from wartime to peacetime production. However, there was no serious unemployment as veterans returned to civilian life. Most Americans—with important exceptions—had jobs and enjoyed a high degree of prosperity.

Prosperity did bring its own problems, including inflation. For more than a year after the war ended, President Truman kept wartime price controls (page 336). However, demands for ending these controls grew stronger. When Republicans, who opposed controls, gained a majority in Congress in 1946, Truman ended all controls on prices and wages, though not on rents.

Prices at once started to rise. High wartime wages, saved during the war years when most consumer goods had been scarce, had created an enormous reserve of purchasing power. With money to spend and an ever-increasing demand for goods of all kinds, American consumers created a seller's market for American business.

President Truman retained rent controls because of a severe housing shortage that would have caused rents to skyrocket. Few houses had been built during the Great Depression and almost none during the war, even though the population was increasing. Truman tried to provide government subsidies for new housing but failed. By 1947, however, the housing industry was moving into high gear. The housing situation, while still serious, began to improve.

Labor unrest. Rising prices led to demands for higher wages. In many cases industry met the demands—but raised prices to cover the increased costs of production. The rise in prices, in turn, spurred labor to demand even higher wages. Thus inflation continued its upward spiral, with workers blaming industry, industry blaming workers, and consumers caught in the middle.

Labor unrest led to strikes. In 1946 almost 4.6 million workers went out on strike at one time or another. Two of the most serious strikes involved the railroads and the coal-mining industry. President Truman, who was generally sympathetic to organized labor, ended the railroad strike by threatening to draft the strikers into the army. The federal government also ended the coal miners' strike by seizing the mines and issuing an injunction ordering the miners to return to work.

The Taft-Hartley Act. The postwar labor unrest and strikes led to public demand for stronger federal controls over organized labor. When the Republicans won control of Congress in 1946, they felt that their victory in part reflected a rising demand for new labor legislation. In June 1947 Congress passed the Labor-Management Relations Act, better known as the Taft-Hartley Act. President Truman vetoed the act, which he called "a clear threat to the successful working of our democratic society." Nevertheless, Congress passed the Taft-Hartley Act over his veto.

In general, the new law aimed to reduce the power that organized labor had won during the New Deal. The Taft-Hartley Act restricted the contributions of unions to political campaigns. It permitted management to seek injunctions to end strikes and to sue union officials for violations of contracts or for engaging in certain strikes. The law forbade closed-shop agreements requiring workers to belong to a union before they could be hired. It also gave the President power to require an 80-day cooling-off period when a strike threatened to affect the national health and safety. The law also required employers and union leaders to sign non-Communist oaths of allegiance.

Another provision of the Taft-Hartley Act allowed states to ban union-shop agreements within their borders. Such union-shop agreements require workers to join a union within a specified period after they are hired. By 1950, twelve states had passed legislation, known as **right-to-work laws,** barring such agreements.

The Taft-Hartley Act proved highly controversial. Supporters argued that it merely corrected the unfair advantages granted to labor in the Wagner Act of 1935 (page 261). Organized labor, on the other hand, protested that the new law deprived workers of many benefits won over a long period.

Gains for organized labor. During the postwar years, however, organized labor did make notable gains. Workers in general won substantial wage increases.

One labor agreement set an important precedent. In 1948, General Motors and the United Automobile Workers (UAW) signed a contract with an escalator clause. This clause tied wage increases to the cost of living. Other unions soon adopted similar contracts. Some union contracts linked pay increases to formulas based on increases in the cost of living as well as rising productivity. Union contracts often included welfare provisions, among them provisions for retirement pensions and health insurance.

The election of 1948. By 1948 the nation was enjoying a high level of prosperity. Under such favorable conditions, the Democrats met to choose their Presidential candidate.

The Democratic convention nominated President Truman on the first ballot. Largely at Truman's insistence and that of Mayor Hubert H. Humphrey of Minneapolis, the delegates included a strong civil rights plank, or section, in their platform. This plank urged Congress to guarantee the right of every adult (1) to vote and take part in politics, (2) to have an equal opportunity to work at any job for which he or she was qualitifed, (3) to receive personal security, and (4) to enjoy equal treatment in the armed services. The Democratic platform also favored repeal of the Taft-Hartley Act, federal support of housing, education and farm income, and broader social security benefits.

The Democratic platform split the party. Southern delegates vigorously opposed the civil rights plank. A number of southern Democrats formed a separate States' Rights Party and nominated Governor J. Strom Thurmond of South Carolina for President.

Former Vice-President Henry A. Wallace also left the Democrats to head a new third

In the 1948 campaign, Harry S. Truman promised, "there will be a Democrat in the White House—and you're looking at him." Few believed him, including this newspaper, which headlined his defeat before the returns were in.

party. Wallace's Progressive Party attacked Truman's foreign policy for being too anti-Communist. The Party warned that Truman's policies might lead to war with the Soviet Union. The Progressive Party also sought the support of labor and liberals by promising to renew and extend many New Deal measures.

With the Democrats divided, public opinion polls and most newspapers predicted that the Republican candidate, Governor Thomas Dewey of New York, would win. But President Truman launched a shrewd election campaign. He asked a special session of the Republican-controlled Congress to live up to its 1946 campaign promises and do something to halt rising prices and solve the housing crisis. When Congress adjourned without acting on these measures, Truman toured the country and denounced the legislators for failing to meet their responsibilities.

The election result was an astonishing victory for President Truman. He polled 49.4 percent of the popular vote to Dewey's 45 percent. Truman won 303 electoral votes, Dewey 189, and Thurmond 39. Wallace won no electoral votes at all. The Democrats also regained control of Congress and won many important state and city elections.

The Fair Deal. Heartened by his victory, President Truman decided to launch a broad program of reform. He urged Congress to adopt a Fair Deal program and extend some of the New Deal reforms. Many observers doubted that the President could win support for his program from the various groups in his own party. Time after time during Truman's second term, many southern and some northern Democrats did join the Republicans to block Fair Deal measures.

President Truman did, however, have some success with the Fair Deal program. Between 1949 and 1952, Congress did the following: (1) It extended social security benefits to include 10 million more persons. (2) The minimum wage for workers in interstate industries was raised from 40 to 75 cents an hour. (3) Congress authorized the federal government to clear slums and to build 810,000 low-income housing units over a six-year period. (4) Rent controls were continued to 1951. (5) A new Agricultural Act established farm price supports at 90 percent of parity through 1950 and thereafter on a sliding scale of 75 to 90 percent. (6) More federal employees were brought under civil ser-vice. (7) The work of the Reclamation Bureau in flood control, hydroelectric plants, and irrigation projects was expanded.

On the other hand, President Truman failed to persuade Congress to repeal the Taft-Hartley Act, to broaden support for education, to enact health insurance, and to secure all of the civil rights proposals he favored.

Concern over internal security. In 1947 President Truman asked the Federal Bureau of Investigation (FBI) and the Civil Service Commission to investigate the loyalty of all federal employees. By the end of 1951, more than 3 million employees had been investigated and cleared, 2,000 had resigned, and 212 had been fired as "security risks."

Meanwhile, in 1948 the FBI and the Department of Justice began an intensive investigation of Communist activity in the United States. Before the year ended, 11 Communist leaders had been indicted, tried, and sentenced to prison.

Finally, Congress passed the Internal Security Act of 1950. This law required all Communist organizations in the United States to file their membership lists as well as statements of their financial operations with the Attorney General's office.

In its deepening concern over internal security, Congress was reacting not only to the possibility of Communist subversion at home but also to the increasingly serious international situation. Both of these issues weakened the efforts to promote the Fair Deal program. Both also played major roles in the Presidential election of 1952.

SECTION SURVEY

IDENTIFY: GI Bill, Twenty-second Amendment, right-to-work laws, Hubert H. Humphrey, Strom Thurmond, Henry Wallace, Internal Security Act of 1950.

1. (a) Why was the Taft-Hartley Act passed? (b) What were its provisions?

2. (a) What were the provisions of the civil rights plank of 1948? (b) Why did these provisions cause controversy?

3. Describe some important achievements of Truman's Fair Deal program.

4. Chart Study: Make a chart comparing the parties, candidates, issues, and results of the election of 1948.

2 President Eisenhower encourages Modern Republicanism

In the 1952 Presidential campaign, the Republicans adopted the slogan "It's time for a change." However, they did not agree among themselves as to the nature of the change they wanted. Like the Democrats, they split into a conservative wing and a liberal wing.

The election of 1952. Confident of a Republican victory, each wing of the Republican Party fought vigorously to control the nominating convention. The conservatives failed to gain the nomination for their candidate, Senator Robert A. Taft of Ohio. The liberals won, nominating General Dwight D. Eisenhower for the Presidency and Richard M. Nixon of California for the Vice-Presidency.

In 1952 President Truman chose not to run for reelection. Consequently the Democrats then entered their 1952 nominating convention as a divided party. In general, conserva- tive Democrats had little liking for the New Deal and the Fair Deal. Moreover, southern Democrats differed sharply with many of their colleagues on the issue of civil rights. Faced with this party split, the Democrats finally chose Governor Adlai E. Stevenson of Illinois for their Presidential candidate and Senator John Sparkman of Alabama as their Vice-Presidential nominee.

Both parties waged hard-fought campaigns. The Republicans charged the Democrats with "political corruption" and promised to "clean up the mess in Washington." The Republicans condemned their opponents for steadily enlarging the powers of the federal government over the states. Further, Eisenhower charged the Truman administration with "bungling" in the Korean War.

Stevenson was an effective campaigner. He defended the Fair Deal and the foreign policies of the Truman administration. He insisted that there was no easy road to the "peace, prosperity, and progress" that the Republicans were promising the voters.

On November 4, 1952, voters in record numbers cast their ballots. Eisenhower won 57 percent of the popular vote and an overwhelm-

"I like Ike!" people chanted wherever Dwight D. Eisenhower appeared. When Eisenhower returned from service in Europe, he was one of the most popular persons in America—a fact that led to his landslide election as President.

TRIUMPH OVER A CRIPPLER

In 1921 Franklin D. Roosevelt—then a promising politician of 39—was vacationing at his family's summer home. Suddenly he was hit by a high fever, the onset of polio. When he recovered, his legs were paralyzed; never again could he walk without braces and canes. Roosevelt's election later to the Presidency was a vivid reminder for other polio sufferers that their lives might still be fulfilling. Still, the question remained: What could be done to control the spread of the disease?

Almost every year throughout the 1900's brought a worse epidemic. Most of the victims were children. (For this reason polio was often called infantile paralysis.) In the worst year of all, 1952, almost 58,000 Americans were struck. Of these over 20,000 were paralyzed and more than 3,000 died.

Medical experts knew that polio was caused by a virus. Yet much experimentation was needed before an effective vaccine could be produced. Beginning in 1939, a team of researchers led by a young doctor named Jonas Salk searched for such a vaccine. In 1953, having inoculated some 7,500 children (as well as himself and his family) with good results, Salk announced his findings publicly.

The following year over 1.8 million children took part in a testing program remarkable for its scope. Results were announced at Ann Arbor, Michigan, on April 12, 1955—a day chosen by chance but marking the tenth anniversary of the death of Franklin D. Roosevelt. Over 500 guests heard a report of the trials: the vaccine was 60 to 90 percent effective. Then Salk was introduced, and the room exploded with television lights, flashbulbs, and shouts of "It's here!" and "It's safe!"

Never again would polio attack with its earlier force. Soon doctors were also administering an oral vaccine pioneered by Dr. Albert Sabin. By the mid-1960's there were scarcely a hundred cases of polio in the entire United States.

ing majority of 442 to 89 in the electoral count. To the dismay of the Democrats, he carried even the traditionally Democratic states of Virginia, Tennessee, Florida, and Texas. Nevertheless, the Republicans won control of Congress by only bare majorities in both houses.

Eisenhower's background. Dwight D. Eisenhower, the newly elected President, had been born in Texas in 1890 and raised in Kansas. An average student and a good athlete, he entered West Point in 1911. After graduation he served in the army at posts in Texas, Kansas, France, and the Philippines.

As World War II drew nearer, Eisenhower's abilities as a planner and organizer attracted attention. He advanced rapidly in rank and was finally named Supreme Commander of the Allied Forces in Europe.

By the end of the war, Eisenhower was one of the country's most popular heroes. Both the Democrats and the Republicans urged him to accept nomination for the Presidency in 1948, although his political preferences were not known. Despite the pressure, Eisenhower at that time refused to get involved in politics. He left the Army to become President of Columbia University in 1948. In 1950, he returned to military service as the military commander of the NATO forces. Eisenhower held this position until he decided to run for the Republican nomination in 1952.

Eisenhower's administration. Eisenhower's style of Presidential leadership was a sharp change from the styles of Roosevelt and Truman. They had been active, vigorous leaders who had pressed Congress to pass their programs. Eisenhower believed that a President should not do too much leading. Instead, he felt that Congress should shape its own programs and that the President should carry them out. In carrying out these programs, Eisenhower expected his Cabinet members and his various appointees to handle the daily business of government. Only the most difficult problems were to be referred to him.

Economy in government and a balanced budget were "the first order of business" in Eisenhower's administration. Appropriations for defense and foreign aid were reduced significantly in spite of arguments from some Democrats that the administration was weakening national security. In 1956, for the first time in eight years, the government ended its fiscal year with a surplus.

Despite concern for a balanced budget, the Eisenhower administration did not attempt to repeal the basic social and economic legislation of the New Deal–Fair Deal era. President Eisenhower was personally in sympathy with much of this legislation. He supported a moderate extension of some of the New Deal- Fair Deal programs. This middle-of-the-road policy in domestic affairs—together with support for the United Nations, military aid for American allies, and economic and military help for underdeveloped countries—came to be called "Modern Republicanism."

Social legislation.   Early in April 1953, President Eisenhower signed a joint resolution of Congress, transforming the Federal Security Agency into the Department of Health, Education, and Welfare (HEW). Oveta Culp Hobby, who had commanded the Women's Army Corps, became HEW's first Secretary. In January 1954, in his State of the Union message, Eisenhower urged Congress to expand the social security program and consider ways of providing additional federal aid for housing, education, and health.

Congress responded by extending social security to an additional 10.5 million persons and by increasing benefits. By 1955 about 90 percent of the nation's workers were covered by social security.

Congress also set aside additional money for the construction of hospitals and for medical research. In 1955 it authorized $500 million for slum clearance and urban redevelopment.

However, Congress refused to appropriate money to build schools and raise teachers' salaries. Many members of both political parties feared that federal support of education might lead to federal control. In 1958, however, after the Russians had successfully launched several earth satellites, Congress adopted legislation providing loans for able students, chiefly for students of science.

The farm problem.   While dealing successfully with a number of domestic problems, the Eisenhower administration grappled with others for which there appeared to be no ready solutions. One such problem was the state of the nation's farms.

During the Eisenhower years, surplus crops from the nation's farms continued to be a problem. In an effort to discourage farmers from overproducing, Congress in 1954 replaced its fixed price support system with a flexible one.

Between 1952 and 1956, farm income dropped 26 percent. There were a number of reasons for this situation, including the loss of foreign markets and growing competition from farmers in other countries. Basically, however, the problem was an old one—overproduction in relation to the nation's needs. Since the early 1930's, farm productivity had almost doubled, largely because of advances in technology.

From 1942 to 1954, the government tried to guarantee farmers a fixed price support of 90 percent of parity. When prices dropped below this 90-percent level, the government bought surplus crops at the fixed price. Under this policy, grain elevators, warehouses, and storage facilities were overflowing. Storage charges alone were costing the government nearly a million dollars a day. Surpluses continued to pile up, and prices continued to fall.

In an effort to prevent these huge surpluses, Secretary of Agriculture Ezra Taft Benson persuaded the Eisenhower administration to end fixed price supports. In their place Congress adopted a flexible scale of price supports. This new policy aimed at discouraging farmers from growing crops that were flooding the market.

In 1956 the government made a major change in the farm program. The "soil bank program," as it was called, was designed to encourage the use of more land for providing forage, for growing trees, and for creating reservoirs. Farmers were to be paid for withdrawing land from commercial cultivation. By the end of 1958, the soil bank had paid $1.6 billion to farmers for withdrawing land previously used for growing crops.

Encouraging private business. The Eisenhower administration generally tried to reduce government interference with the states and with private business. For many years there had been controversy over the ownership of oil fields lying off the coasts of Florida, Louisiana, Texas, and California. Who owned these oil fields, the federal government or the states? With the approval of the Eisenhower administration, Congress settled this offshore oil controversy with the Submerged Lands Act of 1953, which gave the states control of the underwater oil deposits.

The Tennessee Valley Authority also became an issue in 1954 when the Atomic Energy Commission required additional electricity. Opposing a TVA proposal to build steam plants

Senator Joseph McCarthy (center) aired charges of communism against the U.S. Army during the 1954 Senate hearings. As millions of Americans watched the proceedings broadcast live on television, McCarthy's popularity plummeted.

to generate electricity for the AEC, the administration awarded the contract to a group of private utility companies. However, the contract aroused such a storm of controversy that it was canceled.

The Eisenhower administration made other efforts to encourage private enterprise. (1) Shortly after taking office, the President abandoned the wage and price controls imposed during the Korean War. (2) Former President Hoover agreed to head a new commission to recommend ways of securing greater efficiency in government and removing government competition with private business. (3) In 1954 Congress amended the Atomic Energy Act, giving private industry a larger opportunity to develop atomic energy for peaceful uses. (4) The federal government reduced or completely ended its participation in business activities. Among the activities curtailed were the manufacture of synthetic rubber, the operation of railroads, ships, and hotels, and the production of motion pictures.

Internal security. President Eisenhower faced the continuing problem of internal security during his administration. As you have read in Chapter 19, concern over the spread of communism became widespread after World War II. Revelations that American atomic secrets had been passed on to the Soviet Union, the victory of the Communists in China, and the outbreak of the war in Korea increased this concern.

During the Truman administration, Senator Joseph McCarthy of Wisconsin began to charge high government officials of sympathy with communism. In 1951 he even attacked General George C. Marshall, accusing him of conspiracy against the government. By the time Eisenhower became President, McCarthy, as head of a Senate subcommittee, was investigating the State Department and other government agencies. In his relentless hunt for Communists, he was joined by large numbers of private citizens. Actors, writers, educators, and other individuals and organizations were investigated and accused of communism or sympathy toward it.

Many Americans praised McCarthy for his patriotic zeal. Others criticized him for recklessness and disregard of constitutional rights. By the end of 1953, a national poll indicated that Americans who supported his activities outnumbered his critics by almost two to one.

The Senator was at the peak of his power and influence when he began to look for spies and Communists in the Army. The Army counterattacked with the revelation that McCarthy had attempted to use his influence to get the Army to give preferential treatment to one of the young men on his staff. McCarthy, claiming that the Army was trying to blackmail him in an effort to stop his investigation, demanded a public hearing.

The hearing, begun in April 1954 in full view of television cameras, continued into June. Huge numbers of Americans, sometimes numbering 20 million, watched the event daily on their television screens. Before it was over, Senator McCarthy was a discredited man. He had destroyed himself by his sarcasm, his endless interruptions, and his reckless and unsupported accusations. By the end of the year, the Senate had effectively finished McCarthy's career by voting to censure him. The vote was 67 to 21.

SECTION SURVEY

IDENTIFY: Adlai Stevenson, Oveta Culp Hobby, soil bank, Joseph McCarthy, censure.

1. What did Eisenhower think was the proper role of the President?

2. What was meant by Modern Republicanism?

3. In what ways did the Eisenhower administration encourage private enterprise?

4. (a) What problem faced farmers during the 1950's? (b) What attempts were made to solve this problem?

---

3 The nation admits two states and prospers during Eisenhower's Presidency

Toward the end of his first term, Eisenhower's popularity as President seemed undiminished. However, this popularity did not carry over to the Republican Party as a whole. In the 1954 Congressional elections, the Republicans had lost control of Congress. As the months passed, it became increasingly clear that Republican chances for victory in the 1956 elections depended upon Eisenhower's willingness to run for a second term.

The election of 1956. In September 1955 the nation was shocked to learn that President Eisenhower had suffered a heart attack. Even after his recovery was certain, the public wondered whether he would run for reelection. Eisenhower himself answered that question in February 1956 with the declaration that he was willing to be a candidate.

Both of the major parties held nominating conventions in August. The Republicans enthusiastically renominated Eisenhower and Nixon. The Democrats renominated Adlai Stevenson and chose as his running mate Senator Estes Kefauver of Tennessee.

In the campaign the Republicans reminded voters that the country was enjoying the highest standard of living in American history. The Democrats blamed the Republicans for the continuing high cost of living and for falling farm prices. They also charged that the Republicans had failed to develop an effective foreign policy.

In his bid for the Democratic nomination, Adlai Stevenson got a royal welcome. He was a popular candidate. However, he was unsuccessful in his attempt to unseat the even more popular Eisenhower from the Presidency.

Eisenhower's popularity returned him to the White House with a popular vote of more than 35 million to Stevenson's nearly 26 million and an electoral vote of 457 to 73. Nevertheless, the voters returned a Democratic majority to Congress, increasing the lead that the Democratic Party had won in 1954.

In the 1958 Congressional elections, the Democrats won by a landslide, piling up large majorities in both houses. Thus, for his last six years in office, Eisenhower had to work with a Congress controlled by the Democrats.

The Labor Act of 1959. During Eisenhower's second term, there were problems with organized labor. In 1957–58 a Congressional committee headed by Senator John L. McClellan revealed corrupt leadership in certain unions, notably in the powerful Teamsters Union. Several labor officials were brought into court and given jail sentences. The leaders of the AFL-CIO insisted that the corrupt practices were confined to only a small segment of organized labor. They took steps, however, to put their own house in order.

In the meantime, Congress adopted the Labor-Management Reporting and Disclosure Act of 1959. This law contained a number of important and far-reaching provisions: (1) It prohibited Communists or persons convicted of felonies within the five previous years from serving as officials or employees of labor unions. (2) It prohibited **secondary boycotts°** and the picketing of parties other than those directly involved in the strike. (3) It required labor unions to file with the Secretary of Labor annual reports giving complete information about their financial activities and other matters. (4) It required employers to report any loans or payments made to unions as well as any payments made to labor relations consultants. (5) It required national labor organizations to hold elections at least every five years. (6) It provided a bill of rights guaranteeing members of labor unions the right to attend meetings, nominate candidates for office, and vote in elections using secret ballots.

The new labor legislation went into effect in September of that year. In the meantime, President Eisenhower and Congress had been facing another difficult problem of labor-management relations.

°**secondary boycott:** the support of a boycott by other unions and other parties not directly involved in the dispute.

One of the outstanding events of the Eisenhower years was the opening of the St. Lawrence Seaway which made it possible for oceangoing ships to sail from the Atlantic to American and Canadian ports along the Great Lakes.

The steel strike of 1959. In 1959 the contract between the steel industry and the United Steel Workers of America came up for renegotiation. The workers asked for a wage increase and other benefits. They claimed that the steel industry could afford to meet these requests without raising the price of steel. The industry refused to discuss a wage increase unless the union would agree to changes in work rules.

In July the union called a strike involving 500,000 steelworkers and plants that produced 85 percent of the nation's steel. Negotiations dragged on for week after week. Finally, President Eisenhower, using powers granted him in the Taft-Hartley Act, asked for an 80-day anti-strike injunction. The injunction went into effect in November, and the workers returned to their jobs.

The injunction did not, of course, settle any of the issues. It was not until January 1960 that the union and the industry reached an agreement providing for step-by-step wage increases over a period of 30 months. In the dispute over work rules, the union maintained the right to place its own workers.

Gains for organized labor. During Eisenhower's administration organized labor won several notable advances. Congress raised the hourly minimum wage under the Fair Labor Standards Act from 75 cents to $1. In June 1955 the Ford Motor Company and the General Motors Corporation signed contracts that moved the United Automobile Workers toward a guaranteed annual wage. The new contracts provided, among other things, for the companies to pay unemployment benefits to the workers.

During the 1950's a growing number of unions set up welfare funds to aid unemployed, disabled, and retired workers. Some of the unions used surplus capital to buy stocks, bonds, and real estate.

In 1955 the A. F. of L. and the CIO voted to combine. The new organization, called the AFL-CIO, with George Meany as president and Walter Reuther as vice-president, had 15 million members.

Alaska and Hawaii. In 1959, during President Eisenhower's second term, Alaska and Hawaii were admitted as the 49th and 50th

379

states of the Union. They were the first states that did not share a common border with any of the other states. Alaska, now the largest state in the Union, adjoins northwestern Canada, far to the north of the state of Washington. Hawaii, a group of islands in the Pacific Ocean, is located about 2,400 miles (3,860 kilometers) west of California.

Alaska, as you have read, was purchased from Russia in 1867 by Secretary of State William Seward at a time when several nations were competing for its fur trade. So little was known then of its riches that for years Americans called Alaska "Seward's Folly." In the 1900's, however, Alaska became an important American source of timber and fish and of gold and other minerals. Later, in the early 1970's, a massive pipeline was built to transport enormous supplies of crude oil from the far north to the southern shore of Alaska for shipment in tankers.

Alaska's population today exceeds 300,000. About one fifth are native Americans — Eskimos of the north, Aleuts of the southwest and the Aleutian Islands, and various Indian tribes, mainly from along the southeastern coast of the state. Adult members of these minority groups became American citizens when Alaska became a state.

The first known inhabitants of the Hawaiian Islands were Polynesians. They were expert seafarers who probably sailed there in ocean-going canoes from other Pacific islands hundreds of years ago. Beginning in the late 1700's, European and American ships stopped in the islands for fresh water and food. American missionaries arrived in the 1820's. In the late 1800's, American planters, as you may recall, developed prosperous sugar and pineapple plantations and gained control of the islands. The United States annexed the islands in 1898, and Hawaii became a territory.

Many immigrants from Japan and other parts of East Asia came to the Hawaiian Islands to work on the plantations. They remained to become farmers, factory and service workers, and business people. Out of a population of more than 800,000, about 60 percent are of Japanese, Chinese, Filipino, Korean, or Polynesian ancestry or of mixed ethnic descent.

In 1959 the citizens of Anchorage, Alaska, celebrated their new statehood. Some of them added a 49th star to the American flag, which would soon be redesigned. Alaska adopted as its state motto "North to the Future."

Riding through the streets of Waikiki in an open car seemed a good way for Hawaiians to celebrate admission to statehood in their tropical climate in 1959. The headline of the newspaper proclaims the happy long-awaited event.

Continuing prosperity. By 1960, Americans still faced stubborn domestic and international problems. Nevertheless, they continued to enjoy a rising standard of living. To be sure, during the 1950's economic progress had been slowed down twice by recessions—the first in 1953–54, the second in 1957–58. The 1957–58 recession was the more severe of the two. Unemployment climbed to more than 5.5 million, the stock market slumped, and many Americans feared the country was entering another depression. However, by 1959 unemployed workers were returning to their jobs. The stock market had reached record high levels, business was booming, and a spirit of optimism prevailed throughout the land.

In 1950 the **gross national product°** (GNP) had been 264.7 billion dollars. By 1960 it had risen to about 510 billion dollars. Never before in the nation's history had so many Americans

°**gross national product (GNP):** the total money value of all goods and services produced in the nation.

enjoyed such prosperity. The enjoyment of "Eisenhower prosperity" was tempered, however, by the continuing need to struggle with communism and the growing tensions throughout the world.

SECTION SURVEY

IDENTIFY: AFL-CIO, George Meany, Walter Reuther, GNP.

1. (a) Why was the Labor-Management Reporting and Disclosure Act of 1959 passed? (b) What were its provisions?

2. (a) Why was Alaska called "Seward's Folly" during the 1800's? (b) Why would it be unlikely to be called a "folly" today?

3. Map Study: Turn to the map on pages 696–97 and answer these questions: (a) If it is 1:00 A.M. in Denver, Colorado, what time is it in Fairbanks, Alaska? (b) What is the capital of Hawaii? (c) How far is it from Ketchikan, Alaska, to Barrow, Alaska?

381

Chapter Survey

Summary: Tracing the Main Ideas

In 1945 the immediate problem facing the nation was that of converting from a wartime to a peacetime economy. During the postwar years, Americans met this problem squarely, made the necessary adjustments, and entered the 1950's on a wave of unprecedented prosperity. Harry S. Truman, a devoted follower of President Roosevelt, had some success in continuing the New Deal reforms with his Fair Deal program. Nevertheless, the Republican party made political gains.

With the election of Dwight D. Eisenhower in 1952, twenty years of government by the Democrats came to an end. President Eisenhower promised to reform the federal government by reducing spending, taxes, and regulations. He also wanted to transfer many federal programs to the state and local governments. The Republicans discovered that this was easier said than done. In 1960, when the Eisenhower administration drew to a close, the size of the federal bureaucracy remained about the same as it had been in 1952.

For a few years in the early 1950's, the search for Communists in government and in private life had seriously crippled the everyday life of the nation. Even so, the majority of Americans enjoyed eight years of relative calm and prosperity during the Eisenhower administration. There were, however, serious domestic problems calling for solutions. As you will see in the next chapter, important steps were made toward these solutions. Also, multiplying troubles in Africa, the Middle East, and Asia demanded attention.

Inquiring into History

1. Describe America's demobilization and conversion to peacetime after World War II. What problems did the nation face? What steps did it take to solve them?
2. From 1954 to 1960, the government operated with a Republican President and a Congress controlled by Democrats. (a) What does this tell you about the state of national politics at this time? (b) Why might this split in control of the Congress make it difficult for the Federal government to get things done?
3. Describe the tension between internal security and constitutional rights that arose during the 1950's.
4. Compare the Presidencies of Truman and Eisenhower in terms of (a) their attitudes toward the job, (b) the support they received from the American people, and (c) their accomplishments while they held office.

Relating Past to Present

1. In what ways have the states of Alaska and Hawaii contributed to the well-being of the nation as a whole?

2. (a) How does the situation of farmers today compare to their situation during the 1950's? (b) How does the government's relationship to farmers today compare to that of the 1950's?
3. President Eisenhower wanted to reduce the size of the Federal bureaucracy, but he failed to do so. Have any Presidents in recent years expressed the same wish? Have they succeeded or failed?

Developing Social Science Skills

1. Draw a political cartoon that might have appeared in a newspaper during the Truman or Eisenhower administration. Make sure that the cartoon presents a point of view about an event or person of the time.
2. Interview someone who was an adult during the 1950's. Ask him or her to share impressions of the political events of those years. (a) How does the information gathered from the interview compare to the information in your textbook? (b) What are the advantages of such an interview for learning about the events of an era? What might be the disadvantages of an interview as a source of information? (c) What other sources of information might be used for learning about the political events of a historical period?

Communications

The few bits of metal, wire, and wood hardly looked impressive yet they revolutionized communication and altered American life forever.

Until the mid-1800's, long-distance communication had depended on transportation. Letters, news, and messages of all types had to be carried to distant places by horse, boat, or train. Then in 1844 that unimpressive-looking device, Samuel Morse's telegraph, changed all that. The telegraph allowed messages to be sent in an instant over wires to distant points.

Today news is beamed around the world. Invisible signals are relayed across continents or bounced off satellites that orbit the earth. A television news bulletin that is broadcast from Illinois might be seen instantly in Australia.

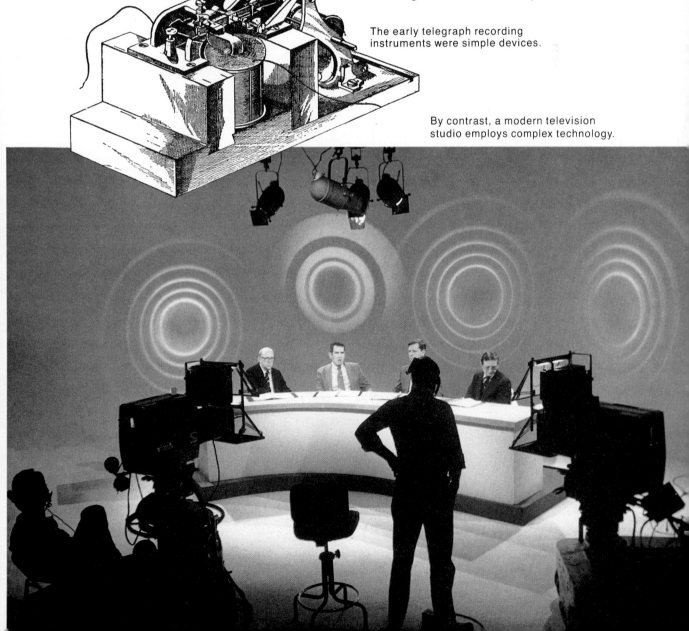

The early telegraph recording instruments were simple devices.

By contrast, a modern television studio employs complex technology.

Early humans communicated by word of mouth, gestures, and simple signals. In time people developed ways of communicating with pictures, for example, the Indian painting shown here. After centuries this led to written language. Movable type and the printing press made possible the wider distribution of the written word in books and newspapers.

Beginning in the mid-1800's, advances in communication came more quickly. The first transatlantic cable for the telegraph was laid in 1858. Less than 20 years later, Alexander Graham Bell invented the telephone. The wireless telegraph appeared 20 years after that. One by one new devices for communications were invented, binding Americans together and linking them with people across the seas.

Advertising was an important means of communication in the early days of the nation as it is today.

Before humans developed a written language, many important events were recorded in pictures.

NEWS! NEWS!!

AARON OLIVER, *Post-Rider*, WISHES to inform the Public, that he has extended his Route; and that he now rides thro' the towns of *Troy, Pittstown, Hoosick, Mapletown*, part of *Bennington* and *Shaftsbury, Peters*

The printing press, first used in the 1400's, made newspapers possible.

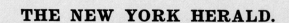

THE NEW YORK HERALD.

For its brief life, 1860 to 1861, the pony express was the fastest means of transcontinental communication.

In the 1920's listening to the radio required the use of earphones.

Photography, developed in the mid-1800's, was an important communications development.

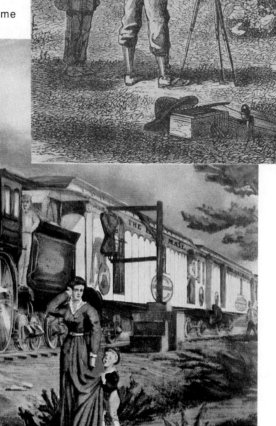

From its beginnings, the railroad became an important means of carrying mail.

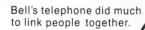

Bell's telephone did much to link people together.

Americans live today in a world where instant communication is a way of life. Telephones keep us in touch with our friends. Television and radio give us up-to-the-minute news. Home computers provide the latest stock-market prices and weather reports.

With 1,800 daily newspapers, 16,500 magazines, 7,500 radio stations, 900 television stations, and thousands of computers, the United States has the largest communications system in the world. New technological developments will put increasing amounts of information at our fingertips, changing the ways we live, work, and play.

The importance of the printed word in communications is demonstrated by the collection of newspapers and magazines at this newsstand.

Modern communications systems allow signals to be relayed instantly by satellite to stations all around the globe.

Microcircuits and computers have opened up new possibilities for the development of communications systems.

Chapter 21

Entering an Age of Rapid Growth and Change

Change and *growth* are the words that best describe American society in the years following World War II. To be sure, change has been a central feature of American life from the day the first European settlers landed on the shores of the New World. Through the course of the three and a half centuries that followed, Americans had lived with change as they conquered the continent. They had lived with change as they built it into one of the world's most prosperous nations.

But the new and startling fact in the postwar years was the *increasingly rapid rate* of change that Americans were experiencing. Never before in human history had so much change been compressed into such a brief span of time. One observer, writing in the early 1960's, declared that the changes in these years were "so wide-sweeping that they are taking us from one epoch of human history into another."

During the 1940's, however, not even the most far-sighted observers could foresee the amazing developments that would, in the years immediately ahead, profoundly alter older ways of living in the United States and throughout the world. In 1945 the opportunities and challenges of the new age had not yet been fully revealed.

By 1960 Americans had profited from the opportunities and had accepted the challenges of this new age. The United States was the richest, most productive nation in the world. This wealth was not shared equally among the citizens of the nation. Minorities still bore the burdens of poverty and prejudice. But they had taken major steps toward achieving full equality.

THE CHAPTER IN OUTLINE

1. Science and technology make revolutionary advances.

2. The nation builds an economy of abundance.

3. Most Americans enjoy the advantages of a booming economy.

4. Poverty in a land of abundance haunts the nation's minorities.

Changing Ways of American Life

1945–1960

1 Science and technology make revolutionary advances

Before World War II, major advances had been made in science in both Europe and America. Breakthroughs had been made by scientists working by themselves or with a few colleagues in the laboratories of prominent universities or private industry. During and after the war, however, scientific research and development became increasingly a carefully organized team effort.

The successful completion of the Manhattan Project, which led to the development of an atomic bomb in 1945, was not the end of atomic testing. Bigger, more powerful weapons were designed and built. This atomic device was exploded in the Nevada desert in 1951.

Organizing human intelligence. The distinguished scholar Alfred North Whitehead observed that when human beings began to organize research, they invented "the art of inventing." This "invention," he concluded, was one of humanity's greatest achievements. The first dramatic demonstration of what scientists and engineers could accomplish by such large-scale cooperation had occurred during World War II.

Late in 1939 the federal government committed its first funds for the exploration of atomic energy. This exploration soon became an all-out, top-secret effort to develop an atomic bomb for the United States. Thousands of the nation's leading scientists, engineers, and construction workers devoted their time and talents to what came to be called the Manhattan Project.

Never before had so much money ($2 billion), so much intelligence, and so much effort been channeled into a single undertaking. The atomic bombs that leveled Hiroshima and Nagasaki in August 1945 provided evidence, terrible though it was in this case, of the effectiveness of organized research. This effectiveness was to be demonstrated again during the 1960's with another massive project. This was the Apollo program—the successful effort conducted over nearly 10 years to land American astronauts on the moon.

The growth of organized research. The successes of wartime efforts like the Manhattan Project and the development of radar prompted government and private industry in the postwar years to devote more and more money to scientific research and development. In 1930 only $166 million was spent for this purpose. By 1960 the total had risen to more than $12 billion, approximately two thirds of which came from the federal government. However, most of the work itself was carried on in the laboratories of private industry, universities, and independent research institutes.

As a result of organized scientific activity, knowledge began to accumulate at a staggering rate. People began to speak of the "knowledge explosion." The amount of information available to the human race, it was estimated, was doubling every 10 years. Even more significant, each advance opened up new horizons for science and made possible further progress in technology. As you will see, new industries were created and thousands of new products became available. Most important, scientists made fantastic progress in understanding the basic forces of nature.

Each fresh discovery also created new problems. With the invention of the art of inventing, changes were occurring so rapidly that the world could never be the same again.

International scientific research. As the years passed, international scientific research came to be carried on by teams of scientists from many countries. For example, during the period from July 1, 1957, to December 31, 1958 —known as the International Geophysical Year—scientists of 66 nations worked together. They conducted worldwide studies of gravity, geomagnetism, meteorology, oceanography, solar activity, cosmic rays, and other fundamental subjects.

In 1959 the United States and 11 other nations, including the Soviet Union, signed a treaty governing the use of Antarctica. They agreed not to exercise any territorial claim over the vast, ice-covered continent. They also set the continent aside as a scientific preserve open to the scientists of all nations.

Looking ahead, in 1967 a similar treaty relating to outer space was signed by 62 countries. The treaty (1) prohibits the orbiting of nuclear weapons and (2) prohibits any nation from claiming sovereignty over the moon or any planet. President Johnson called the treaty "the first firm step toward keeping outer space free forever from the implements of war."

The computer revolution. The electronic computer was one of the most significant postwar products of the technological revolution. The first modern computers were developed shortly after World War II. By 1960 there were about 5,000 computers in use in the United States. Nevertheless, what was to become a computerized society was still in its infancy. Eventually, thousands of computers would be installed in laboratories, business offices, government agencies, hospitals, schools, banks, scores of other organizations, and increasingly in private homes.

In a fraction of a second, computers can perform calculations that even the most efficient individual could not complete in a lifetime. Computers available by the 1960's could perform in one second 357,000 additions or subtractions or 178,000 multiplications or 102,000 divisions. They were being used in laboratories to provide instant analysis of complex tech-

LOOK   JOHN DEMPSEY

"Merfson, I'm afraid I have some rather unpleasant news for you."

Automation was a topic of great interest and concern to many Americans in the 1950's. It was a source of hope to some, a source of worry to others. In this drawing, cartoonist John Dempsey presents a lighter view of one of the problems produced by automation.

nical problems that could not be studied in any other way. They were being used in businesses and banks for accounting, bookkeeping, and billing. They were being used by governments to check income tax returns and to record data on births, marriages, public health, car registrations, and criminal records. They were being used in industry to forecast economic trends and control assembly lines in automated factories.

In brief, machines were doing much of certain kinds of mental work once performed by men and women. In fact, any data that could be measured or counted could be handled more efficiently by computers than by human beings.

Business and industry automate. Other equipment performed still other operations far more swiftly and efficiently than individuals could hope to do. For example, the Bell Telephone Company reported that if it had not installed automatic switchboards, by 1962 a work force equal to the total of all the women in the nation between the ages of 18 and 30 would have been required to handle the 90 billion telephone calls made in the United States in that year alone.

389

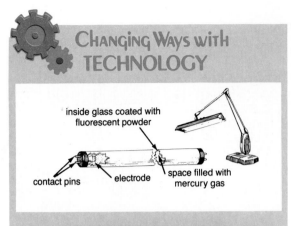

Changing Ways with TECHNOLOGY

inside glass coated with
fluorescent powder

contact pins   electrode   space filled with
mercury gas

FLUORESCENT LAMPS

Fluorescent lamps were introduced at the New York World's Fair of 1939–40. They use about one fifth of the electricity of an incandescent light bulb to produce the same amount of light. When an electric current is applied to the electrodes, an arc is created between them. The arc causes mercury gas in the tube to give off invisible, ultraviolet light. A coating on the inside of the glass absorbs the ultraviolet light and gives off visible light.

The automated machines used in many industries performed a whole series of operations. Some adjusted themselves to correct their own errors. Automated factories could turn raw materials into finished products with only a handful of technicians on the job to plan and control the process.

Americans watched the rapid increase in automation with mixed feelings. Some hailed it as a triumph of human ingenuity that would lead the nation to higher and ever higher standards of living. Others shared the deep concern of Walter Reuther, president of the United Automobile Workers, who was worried about jobs. He toured a plant in which automatic machines had reduced the number of workers from 800 to 15. Reuther agreed that the plant was indeed efficient. "But," he pointedly asked, "are these machines going to buy cars?"

The leaders of organized labor were not opposed to automation as such. Instead they criticized "irresponsibly introduced" automatic machines that could "result in unprecedented unemployment." They made it clear that they expected wage earners to receive a fair share of the prosperity that would come from increasingly efficient production.

SECTION SURVEY

IDENTIFY: Manhattan Project, "knowledge explosion," International Geophysical Year, automation.

1. Why can it be said that the organizing of research is one of humanity's greatest achievements? Do you agree? Why or why not?
2. In what ways have the United States and other nations cooperated in scientific research since World War II?
3. How have automation and computers affected business? Give some examples.
4. Cartoon Study: Examine the cartoon on page 389. (a) What is the unpleasant news for Merfson? (b) How can you tell? (c) What is the attitude of the cartoonist?

2 The nation builds an economy of abundance

The most obvious impact of the revolution in science and technology was upon the nation's economy. After World War II ended, the United States entered a period of unprecedented prosperity. This prosperity was built on what economists called "an economy of abundance." This term applied to an economic system that was capable of producing more goods and services than Americans as a whole could consume.

Growing productivity. In the 1950's a group of distinguished economists stated that "America today has the strongest, most productive economic system in human history. . . . The United States, with little more than 6 percent of the world's population and less than 7 percent of the land area, now produces and consumes well over one third of the world's goods and services and turns out nearly one half of the world's factory-produced goods."

During the 75 years preceding World War II, the United States had doubled its output of goods about once every 24 years. After World War II, the rate of growth climbed sharply. If it continued, the United States would double its production every 18 years.

The roots of prosperity. There were many reasons for America's remarkable economic growth. Among them were an abundance of natural resources, an excellent transportation system, and great numbers of skilled workers. Growth was spurred, too, by steadily improving labor-management relations, highly organized and efficiently managed industries, efficient methods of distribution, and an economic system that rewarded both individual effort and teamwork. The role of advertising in stimulating the desire of consumers for more goods and services also played a part in economic growth.

Above all, advances in science and technology sent the economy spiraling upward. Power-driven machinery and increasingly complex equipment were now common in nearly every field of human activity. They were found on farms and in mines, in factories and laboratories, in offices and homes. Out of America's industrial plants using new machines and new processes poured an endless variety of products in ever-increasing quantities.

American farm production was also setting new records. Advances in agricultural science and technology, in farm management, and in marketing helped make Americans on the whole among the best-fed people in the world. Each year the nation's farms produced huge amounts of food to feed Americans and to export to other nations.

New and expanding industries. New industries joined older ones in providing products, services, and opportunities for more and more Americans.

The aircraft industry, still in its infancy in the 1920's, grew in the years following World War II to a multibillion-dollar enterprise. Commercial airlines directly employed thousands of men and women. Many other thousands of workers were employed in the plants producing aircraft for the airlines and for private individuals, business firms, and the armed services.

The electronics industry had been small in the early 1920's. It boomed during World War II with the production of radio transmitters, radar, and other military equipment. During the postwar years, it grew still more rapidly with the production of television sets, computers, automation controls, radios, phonographs, and countless complex items for homes and businesses. In the late 1950's, the electronics industry received another big boost. It joined with the aircraft industry and hundreds of other enterprises in an entirely new undertaking—the space program.

Another completely new industry, atomic energy, also expanded greatly during the postwar years. Although military uses continued to dominate, peaceful applications of atomic energy were growing more numerous. For example, the first commercial nuclear-powered plant for generating electricity began operations near Pittsburgh in 1957. By 1960 three more plants were operating, and several others were nearing completion. Moreover, radioisotopes produced by nuclear reactors were being used for research in many fields, including

America's space program was, literally, getting off the ground in 1958 when this U.S. Army Jupiter-C Explorer II rocket was launched. Though it was a sign of things to come, few people then could have predicted the sweeping extent of today's space achievements.

medicine, where they were also used in the treatment of patients. By 1960 the United States and the world had crossed the threshold of the nuclear age. As you will read, the new age presented problems as well as promise.

While new industries grew, older industries modernized their plants and expanded their operations by mergers and by continuing to develop new products. Among the postwar industrial giants were the steel, automotive, petroleum, chemical, pharmaceutical, and business-machine industries. The giant of industrial giants was the American Telephone and Telegraph Company, which was the largest corporation in the world.

The revolution in transportation. The nation's advance into an economy of abundance would not have been possible without revolutionary developments in transportation.

In 1945, commercial airlines were still operating out of small airports. They carried only about 3 million passengers annually, most of them in two-engine, propeller-driven planes that could hold only 20 to 40 passengers. By the 1960's they operated out of huge, sometimes overcrowded airports. They used jet aircraft and carried more than 60 million passengers annually as well as ever-growing amounts of freight.

Speed as well as size and versatility became a major factor in aircraft design during the postwar years. By the late 1950's, jet aircraft had been designed for use on commercial air routes that could fly at 600 miles (965 kilometers) an hour, close to the speed of sound.

During the postwar years, traffic problems on the nation's streets and highways became an engineer's nightmare. Between 1945 and 1960, the number of automobiles, buses, and trucks more than doubled, from 31 million to nearly 74 million. The Federal Aid Highway Act, adopted by Congress in 1956, provided for the construction of 42,500 new miles (68,400 kilometers) of superhighways. Almost as soon as the act was passed, traffic experts began to talk of the need for an even more ambitious highway construction program.

As the number of cars on American roads quadrupled, the federal government started a $75-billion interstate highway program to accommodate them. Cloverleaf designs like this soon appeared across the landscape.

The railroads, once the main carriers of the nation's passengers and freight, did not share in the transportation boom. Although they still carried more than half the nation's freight, the railroads met stiff competition from the trucking industry. Moreover, they lost most of their passenger business to private automobiles, buses, and planes.

Some daily trains carrying workers to and from their city jobs were still crowded, but with few exceptions even the commuter railroads operated at a loss. Rising taxes and increasing operating costs added to the gloomy picture. Railroad managers argued that if commuter services were to continue in full force, federal, state, and local governments would have to subsidize train service. During the 1950's their pleas for help fell for the most part on deaf ears. By 1960 many railroads were in bankruptcy or nearing it.

However, the railroads were one of relatively few victims of the economic revolution that was transforming the nation. The American economy as a whole had never been more prosperous.

SECTION SURVEY

IDENTIFY: economy of abundance, Federal Aid Highway Act.

1. What were the causes of America's dramatic economic growth after World War II?
2. What new industries developed rapidly after World War II?
3. What was the connection between the transportation revolution and (a) the airline industry, (b) the trucking industry, and (c) the railroads?

3 Most Americans enjoy the advantages of a booming economy

The rapidly rising standard of living in the late 1940's and the 1950's sprang from phenomenal advances in almost every field of science and technology. There were, however, other contributing factors. For one thing, during the depression and the war—a period of more than 15 years—millions of Americans had not been able to buy the things they wanted and, in many cases, badly needed. Equally important, there was a postwar population explosion, called by some the "baby boom." It created millions of new citizens who required food, clothing, housing, education, and entertainment.

The population explosion. During the war and the prosperous postwar years, young people married earlier and had larger families. The resulting growth in population was spectacular. Where during the depression years of the 1930's the population increased by only 9 million, during the 1940's it rose by 19 million. In the 1950's it exploded with an increase of 28 million. In that single ten-year period, the increase was about equal to the total population of the country on the eve of the Civil War.

The nation's growing prosperity also attracted immigrants. Between 1951 and 1960, more than 2.5 million men and women arrived to swell the nation's population.

America's population was not only growing. It was also moving in a great human tide across the face of the land. Two major migrations of people—one into the central cities, the other out of them—were producing dramatic changes in American life.

Changes in the central cities. The migration into the central cities consisted for the most part of impoverished men, women, and children from the rural areas. Many of these came from the South and from Appalachia, the area around the Appalachian Mountains in the eastern United States. Growing numbers also poured into the cities from Puerto Rico and Mexico and increasingly as the years passed from other Spanish-speaking countries.

The hearts of the cities—the business and financial centers—were being completely rebuilt. Urban renewal programs were started during Truman's administration and continued under President Eisenhower. Under such programs older sections of cities were torn down. Old, decaying structures were replaced by new housing and buildings. In city after city, blocks of gleaming new office buildings and apartment houses towered as visible symbols of the nation's wealth and vitality.

At times, however, urban renewal programs destroyed good, low-cost housing. Such programs could disrupt established neighborhoods and force low-income families into poorer housing. At times the wealth and vital-

During the 1950's, a great building boom enabled millions of Americans to become homeowners for the first time. Giant residential developments like this one in California spread across former farmlands, turning them into suburbs.

ity of the business centers of cities stood in grim contrast to the decay in many surrounding residential areas. As you will see in Chapter 24, even while the nation as a whole was enjoying the economic boom of the postwar years, the central cities and the millions of newcomers to the cities faced increasingly critical problems.

The expanding suburbs. In the meantime, many young married couples were moving out of the cities to seek better living conditions for raising families. This movement strengthened the trend toward more widespread ownership of homes. By 1960 more than 60 percent of all American homes were occupied by people who owned them. One of America's oldest dreams was being realized.

All over the nation, families who could afford to do so were moving out of the older cities into the suburbs. The countryside around the cities was being leveled by bulldozers at a rate, according to one estimate, of some 3,000 acres (1,200 hectares) every day. Huge suburban housing developments were springing up almost overnight. Department stores and banks

were opening branches in the new suburban shopping centers. Many industries were also following the people out of the central cities. The new suburban communities had to create new schools, police departments, fire departments, water and sewage systems, churches, libraries, hospitals, parks, and scores of other public services almost from scratch. These expanding metropolitan areas were being tied together by the ever growing network of highways and superhighways.

Rural America was rapidly being replaced by a new and very different way of life. By 1960 almost 85 percent of the total increase in population was taking place around urban centers. These changes were creating new problems.

As the suburbs spread in an unplanned sprawl, the housing developments, shopping centers, highways, and roads ate up irreplaceable farmland at an alarming rate. The lack of planning contributed to the deterioration of the environment and of the quality of life itself.

The building boom. The changes in American life were also creating new opportunities. The movement into the suburbs stimulated a building boom. New jobs were available for millions of workers in housing, lumbering, and related industries. During the war years, almost no new houses had been built. After the war the pent-up demand for much-needed housing suddenly exploded.

Between 1950 and 1960, nearly a million new houses and apartments went up each year. In several of these years, the number even passed the million mark. The housing boom was accompanied by a similar boom in the construction of schools, hospitals, offices, factories, and government buildings. The need for highways to connect the suburbs with the central cities further stimulated the building boom.

More goods for more people. With jobs available and money to spend, Americans went on a buying spree. During the 1950's they bought nearly 50 million new automobiles. By 1960 about three fourths of all American families owned at least one car, and one out of every seven was a two-car family.

The sales of household appliances and other products also soared as the nation's young families furnished their new homes and older families began to enjoy the fruits of prosperity. Washing machines, dishwashers, toasters, vacuum cleaners, refrigerators, freezers, radios, and—newest of all—television sets poured from the factories into America's homes.

Television, invented and developed before World War II, appeared on the market in the late 1940's. By 1950 some 3 million Americans owned sets. By 1960 the number had risen to 50 million. More homes had television sets than had running water or indoor toilets.

A changing labor force. The labor force that produced these goods and services was different from that of only a generation earlier. It contained a much larger proportion of women. In 1940 one out of every four employed workers had been a woman. By 1960 the proportion had risen to one out of three.

The rapid rise in the number of women workers was the result of several developments. In the first place, the demand for workers during World War II broke down prejudices and gave women a chance to show that they could do as well as men in many different jobs. Even more significant, the rapidly expanding economy in the postwar years created thousands of new jobs. Many of these new jobs called for brainpower and manual dexterity

rather than sheer muscle. Moreover, the growing use of labor-saving appliances freed women from many of the burdens of housework.

Another striking change in the labor force was the growth in the number of white-collar workers — teachers, lawyers, doctors, computer operators, clerks, office workers, and so on. In 1956, for the first time, men and women in white-collar occupations, including the rapidly growing service industries, outnumbered blue-collar workers. By 1960 almost one in every seven Americans worked for the local, state, or federal government.

Leisure time. Shorter workweeks and paid vacations gave most Americans more leisure time than they had even dreamed of a generation before. Between 1940 and 1960, the average workweek dropped from 44 to 40 hours. In some of the skilled trades it was down to 35 hours. During this same period, the average paid vacation increased from one to two weeks.

With more free time and more money, Americans piled into their cars for vacations in the mountains, in the country, or at the seashore. Motels, fast-food chains, and service stations multiplied along the highways. Golf courses were crowded. Sailboats and power launches appeared in growing numbers on lakes and small harbors along all of the nation's coastline.

At home the major source of entertainment was the television set. In the average home, according to one estimate, the TV was turned on at least five hours every day. More than any other single development, television began to weaken regional differences and to shape a uniform culture for the entire country.

Television did not, however, devour all of America's newly-acquired leisure time. The sale of books, magazines, records, and tapes soared into the millions during the years following the war.

Need for better education. The changes transforming American life in the postwar years placed a heavy burden on the nation's educational system. The growth of population was in itself a problem. Between 1950 and the early 1960's, the number of students enrolled in America's schools and colleges increased from about 31 million to more than 50 million. This flood of students severely taxed the already overcrowded classrooms. And even larger numbers were certain to follow in the immediate future.

The number of students was not the only problem facing the schools. When the Soviet Union launched Sputnik in 1957, American confidence was shaken. Was the Soviet success due to a better educational system?

Critics in increasing numbers began to question the quality of American education. They charged that school standards were far too low. Schools, they said, were failing to prepare students for life in the rapidly changing postwar world. Such critics called for more demanding courses in mathematics, the sciences, English, and foreign languages.

In response to such criticism, Congress passed the National Defense Education Act in 1958. The act granted federal money to schools and colleges for teaching science and foreign languages. It also provided funds for loans to college students.

An uncommitted generation. Another issue troubled many older Americans. This was the indifference of young people as a whole to many of the traditional values of American life. The young men and women coming of age in the late 1940's and the 1950's were sometimes labeled as "the uncommitted generation." Their goals in life appeared to be a good job, a house in the suburbs, and a retirement program that would provide them with security in their old age. They were, it seemed, unconcerned about politics and reluctant to be bothered about the larger issues confronting the nation and the world.

This tendency to conform, to avoid controversy, was not confined to youth. It was widely shared among all age groups, women and men alike. During the 1950's America seemed on the verge of becoming a homogenized society. One historian referred to the decade of the 1950's as "the years of repose."

Books of the period. A number of the more serious books mirrored the attitudes and the problems of the times. Two of the best-selling books dealing with the war years were James Jones's *From Here to Eternity* and Norman Mailer's *The Naked and the Dead.* Among the

As television technology grew more sophisticated, a new teaching tool entered the classroom— educational television. Broadcast by the new network NET (National Educational Television), these televised classes had mixed success.

novels reflecting the deadening effect of conformity were Sloan Wilson's *The Man in the Gray Flannel Suit* and W. H. Whyte, Jr.'s, *The Organization Man.* J. D. Salinger's widely read *The Catcher in the Rye* vividly captured the life of an adolescent boy coming of age in the postwar years. Ralph Ellison's novel *Invisible Man* dealt with the attempt by a black to find his place in a hostile white society.

One of the most influential books of the 1950's was *The Affluent Society* by the Harvard economist, John Kenneth Galbraith. Galbraith reminded privileged Americans that in their pursuit of personal wealth they were neglecting the nation's poor, permitting the cities to decay, and causing the environment to deteriorate alarmingly.

SECTION SURVEY

IDENTIFY: "baby boom," urban renewal, suburb, National Defense Education Act of 1958, John Kenneth Galbraith.

1. During the 1950's America's population was moving in a great human tide across the face of the land. Explain this statement in terms of (a) the growth of central cities and (b) the growth of suburbs.

2. How were the following related to one another: (a) increased leasure time, (b) the two-car family, (c) the rising popularity of television?

3. Why were more women entering the labor force in the 1950's?

4. Graph Study: In 1930 the population of the United States was about 120 million. Make a chart or graph reflecting population growth in the years that followed: 1930's—increase of 9 million people; 1940's—increase of 19 million; 1950's—increase of 28 million. Why was the increase so great during the 1950's?

4 Poverty in a land of abundance haunts the nation's minorities

Millions of Americans did not share in the prosperity of the postwar years. The poor came from all races and all national backgrounds. They lived in rural areas and in the cities. However, it was the nation's minorities—particularly Indians, Hispanic Americans, and blacks—that bore the heaviest burdens of poverty. In their struggle to overcome prejudice and discrimination, America's minorities battled for freedom, justice, and dignity as well as for a share of the nation's material goods.

The first Americans. In this struggle no minority in the country faced more obstacles than the American Indians. In addition to discrimination, severe unemployment, and widespread poverty, the Indians have had to cope with numerous federal regulations and controls. Their problems have been compounded by shifting federal policies and programs.

The efforts to overcome these handicaps have been carried on by Indians from all walks of life—doctors, lawyers, scientists, writers, teachers, singers, athletes, and others. Theirs has been a long, difficult, and at times disheartening struggle.

Failure of the Reorganization Act. As you have read (pages 293–94), Congress had reversed a long-standing policy when it adopted the Indian Reorganization Act in 1934. This act was intended to encourage Indians to practice self-government and to strengthen tribal customs and tribal life. The promises of the act were seldom fulfilled. Some tribes that had already managed fairly well in adapting to the white culture rejected the new policy. They claimed that it would keep them in an inferior status in relation to the white majority.

Also, many of the 25,000 young Indians who had served in the armed forces during World War II were reluctant to return to tribal ways of life. These Indian veterans felt that the country for which they had fought and for which many had died owed them the full rights and opportunities of American citizenship. They believed that the complete recognition of these rights was more important than preserving tribal ways of life.

The termination policy. During the 1950's the federal government once again adopted a new Indian policy. In this policy it reversed much of the 1934 program and established entirely new goals. One of the new goals was known as "termination."

The termination program was intended to end all federal ties with the Indians. Responsibility was to be transferred to those states with large Indian populations. Acting under this policy, the government terminated federal ser-

Puerto Ricans were often at the bottom of the economic ladder, but many nevertheless had a fierce pride in their cultural heritage. This pride is evident here in their annual parade up Fifth Avenue in New York City.

vices for a number of tribes, including the Menominees of Wisconsin and the Klamaths of Oregon. The policy was a disaster for the Indians because states were unwilling or unable to provide needed services.

The second goal of the new Indian policy was to assimilate the Indians into the majority culture. This called for relocating as many Indians as possible in cities. The Bureau of Indian Affairs attracted thousands of Indians to cities with promises of job training and job placement. In many cases these promises were not kept. Some Indians managed to overcome great odds and achieve success. Many others, facing discrimination and without the support of tribal life, lived in loneliness and poverty in the cities, which remained for them a strange environment. Some, embittered by the experience, returned to the reservations. For most Indians, relocation, like termination, proved to be a failure.

Immigration from Mexico. People from Mexico also faced hardships during the postwar years. As you have read (page 338), the *bracero* program encouraged the entry of Mexican farm workers during World War II. The

policy of importing contract labor was continued after the war. From the Mexican point of view, it provided work for otherwise unemployed workers. It also provided relief through the money sent home by the *braceros* to impoverished Mexican families. However, opposition to the program was building up on both sides of the border. The Catholic Church opposed it on the ground that it broke up families. The Mexican government began to object because the Mexican economy was expanding and labor was needed in Mexico itself. The program also met growing opposition from organized labor in the United States. The newly-formed farm labor unions pointed out that it was competitively unfair to American workers.

Before the program was abandoned in 1962, more than 4.5 million Mexican workers had been imported as contract laborers into the United States. This number does not include the unknown number of illegal migrants, or undocumented immigrants.

Spanish-speaking immigrants. The *braceros* who came as farm laborers were required to return to Mexico after their contracts ended. During the 1950's, however, more than 360,000 Mexican immigrants entered the United States to become American citizens. They were joined by another 450,000 Spanish-speaking immigrants from countries in Central and South America and the West Indies. These newcomers came from all walks of life. A large percentage were highly educated professionals and white-collar workers.

Puerto Ricans. By the 1950's Puerto Ricans made up one of the largest Spanish-speaking groups in the United States. Unlike other immigrants, who had to be naturalized to become American citizens, Puerto Ricans were American citizens at birth. As you recall, Puerto Rico became an unincorporated territory of the United States in 1898 and then, after 1932, a commonwealth. Since 1898, Puerto Ricans have been legally entitled to the rights and privileges of American citizenship.

Even before the depression of the 1930's brought severe hardships to their island, many Puerto Ricans had migrated to New York City in search of jobs. During and after the depression, they came in ever-increasing numbers. Between 1945 and 1960, migration to the United States varied between 30,000 and 45,000 annually.

Puerto Ricans who moved to New York City, Newark, Chicago, and other northern cities faced many problems. Most came from rural villages. They lacked the skills necessary to compete for jobs in a highly complex urban environment. Many had only a limited knowledge of the English language, which handicapped them both in the labor market and in the schools. Perhaps most serious, they were victims of prejudice and discrimination.

Because of these handicaps, most of the newcomers were able to get only unskilled jobs that paid the lowest wages. Puerto Rican families were crowded into such tenement districts as Spanish Harlem in New York City.

In some ways the experience of Puerto Ricans in the United States resembled that of earlier immigrants. As you will see (pages 454–55), many gradually moved up the economic ladder and found places in small businesses, semi-skilled trades, the professions, and the arts. In the 1950's, however, progress of this kind remained beyond the grasp of most Puerto Ricans.

A major victory for black Americans. Black Americans returning from World War II, like other minority veterans, often faced bitter disappointments. In spite of their war service, they continued to be treated in many ways as second-class citizens. To be sure, by the 1940's blacks had won substantial successes in every field of activity — science, medicine, the professions, business, music and art, entertainment, and sports. At best, however, only a very small minority of American blacks had achieved such success. For most blacks, the doors of opportunity remained closed or at best only slightly open.

During the years after the war, the movement to end discrimination in government, business, education, and sports speeded up. President Truman urged Congress to adopt legislation strengthening civil rights laws and their enforcement. When Congress failed to act, Truman used his executive powers to order an end to segregation in the armed forces and in the government.

The Supreme Court rules. The most important development, however, was the Supreme Court decision of 1954 during Eisenhower's administration. In *Brown v. Board of Education of Topeka,* the Court reversed the 58-year-old *Plessy v. Ferguson* ruling (see page 54) that

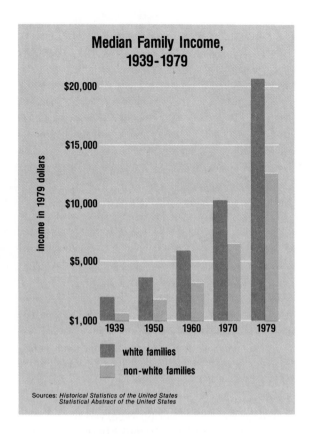

Median Family Income, 1939-1979

income in 1979 dollars

$20,000

$15,000

$10,000

$5,000

$1,000   1939   1950   1960   1970   1979

white families

non-white families

Sources: *Historical Statistics of the United States*
Statistical Abstract of the United States

"separate but equal" facilities were constitutional. The Court unanimously ruled that state or local laws requiring black citizens to send their children to separate schools violated the Fourteenth Amendment.

Several months after the 1954 decision, the Supreme Court required local school authorities to work out plans for gradually ending segregation in public school systems. The Supreme Court also instructed federal district courts to require local school authorities to "make a prompt and reasonable start toward full compliance" and to move "with all deliberate speed in carrying out the law."

Direct action. Encouraged by the Supreme Court ruling, civil rights supporters redoubled their efforts to break down discrimination. Dissatisfied with the slow response in a number of states to the Supreme Court's rulings, blacks turned to direct action.

Early in December 1955 Rosa Parks, a 40-year-old seamstress in Montgomery, Alabama, took a courageous step. Her action led to a nationwide protest movement. On her way home from work, Rosa Parks boarded a bus and took

A little over a year after Rosa Parks was arrested, she again boarded a bus in Montgomery, Alabama. This time, though, she was no longer expected to sit at the back. The successful boycott had enabled her to sit anywhere she chose.

a seat in the front section reserved for whites. The driver ordered her to move to the back. She refused and was arrested.

The next day, led by a 26-year-old minister, Martin Luther King, Jr., 50,000 blacks joined in a boycott of Montgomery's bus system. It was a peaceful protest, and it worked. When the bus system began to drift toward bankruptcy, King and other black leaders were arrested. Finally, almost a year after Rosa Parks's initial action, the Supreme Court declared that the Alabama segregation law was unconstitutional.

Inspired by the victory in Alabama, Martin Luther King called a conference of southern black leaders. Early in 1957 these leaders organized the Southern Christian Leadership Conference (SCLC). The organization announced to the nation that it intended to attack discrimination everywhere in the country by nonviolent means.

Congress finally acts. Efforts by both whites and blacks to avoid violence were only partially successful. Attempts to integrate schools as the Supreme Court had directed in 1954 led to violence in a number of communities. In 1957 President Eisenhower sent federal troops to Little Rock, Arkansas, to maintain order when several black students tried to enter the all-white high school.

Responding to the growing unrest and violence, Congress in 1957 adopted a Civil Rights Act designed to secure voting rights for black citizens. This was the first civil rights act since Reconstruction.

During the 1960's and the 1970's, the struggle by blacks and other minorities for freedom and justice became increasingly intense. You will read about this struggle and the government's response in Chapter 24.

SECTION SURVEY

IDENTIFY: termination, relocation, undocumented immigrants, Rosa Parks, Montgomery bus boycott, SCLC.

1. (a) Why did the Indian Reorganization Act fail? (b) What new Indian policy was set up in the 1950's? (c) How successful was the new policy?

2. (a) Identify several groups of Spanish-speaking Americans. (b) How are their backgrounds different from one another? (c) How has their treatment in the United States been similar?

3. Why is each important to the black civil rights movement: (a) *Brown* v. *Board of Education of Topeka,* (b) Eisenhower's action in Little Rock, Arkansas, in 1957, (c) Civil Rights Act of 1957?

Chapter Survey

Summary: Tracing the Main Ideas

During the years following World War II, the United States entered a period of rapid growth and spectacular change. Revolutionary developments in science and technology brought the nation to a position of unprecedented wealth and power.

Who in 1945 could have predicted the amazing developments that took place during the 1950's? Between 1945 and the early 1960's, an almost limitless variety of new products and services became available to a growing number of Americans. Young married couples could buy a new home for a down payment of only a few hundred dollars and have 30 years in which to pay the balance. Millions of cars rolled off the assembly lines. Labor-saving equipment for homes and farms poured out of the nation's factories in an unending stream. Medical science produced thousands of new medical products, including the priceless gift of anti-polio vaccine. Never before in history had so many people enjoyed so much prosperity.

There was, unhappily, a major flaw in the emerging economy of abundance. Millions of people shared only slightly, if at all, in the nation's new prosperity. Poverty in a land of abundance continued to haunt large numbers among the nation's minorities.

Inquiring Into History

1. (a) Why were the young people of the 1950's called the "uncommitted generation"? (b) Do you think it is appropriate to label the people of an era in this way? Why or why not?
2. Why has it become more and more important since World War II for American citizens to be educated?
3. What was the effect of the transformation of the United States from a rural to an industrial society on (a) workers, (b) black Americans, (c) Indians, and (d) young people?
4. (a) Explain why "change" and "growth" are good words to use in describing American society in the years after World War II. (b) What other words would be appropriate to describe those years? Explain.

Relating Past to Present

1. List some of the ways in which computers affect your daily life. Do you consider your contact with computer technology to be positive or negative? Explain.
2. What are some problems and some advantages of living in today's urban society? What were some problems and advantages of living in the rural society of the 1800's?

3. If the young people of the 1950's were called the "uncommitted generation," what might be a good term for the present generation? Explain.
4. Rosa Parks began her protest in Alabama alone. Can you think of more recent examples of people who on their own have taken courageous social action?

Developing Social Science Skills

1. Gather examples of pictures and drawings of American Indians from magazines and newspapers, package labels, book jackets, and other sources. (a) Do you consider the images presented of Indians to be positive or negative? (b) How might such images affect other people's attitudes toward Indians? (c) What sorts of images might Indians hope to see presented by the media?
2. Play a record of popular songs from the 1950's. (a) What is the subject of each song? (b) What do the songs tell you about the lives and concerns of young Americans in the 1950's? (c) How do the popular songs of the 1950's compare with those of today?
3. Visit your local library or historical society. Obtain maps of your community from 1950 and today. How has the map of the community changed over the years? Can any changes be traced to events discussed in this chapter?

Unit Survey

For Further Inquiry

1. Give evidence to support or refute this statement: After World War II, America's foreign policy goals were to maintain the military defenses of the non-Communist world and to strengthen its economic foundations.
2. (a) What was the Cold War? (b) In what ways was it a domestic as well as a foreign war?
3. Compare the administrations of Truman and Eisenhower in terms of (a) goals, (b) domestic achievements, (c) foreign achievements, (d) weaknesses.
4. Looking back, who might consider the 1950's the "good old days" or "happy days"? Who might not consider them to have been so good and happy? Explain.
5. Compare the situation of blacks, Hispanic Americans, and Indians during the 1950's.

Activities and Projects

1. Study the timeline above, on science and technology from 1945 to 1960. (a) Which events directly improved the quality of life for Americans? Explain. (b) Do advances in science and technology always improve people's lives? Give examples from the timeline to support your answer.
2. Prepare a map of the world in 1960 that focuses on a theme of your choice, such as Communist and non-Communist countries, members of the United Nations, "hot spots" of the world, or colonial and colonized countries. Be sure to give the map a title and to include a legend.
3. Imagine that you were a newspaper reporter for TASS, the official Soviet news agency. Write an article on one confrontation between the United States and the U.S.S.R. or on the general topic of the Cold War.
4. Watch a movie of the 1950's, such as "The Wild One" or "Rebel Without a Cause." Write a short report discussing how or if the movie reflects the spirit of the 1950's.
5. Prepare a pictorial timeline showing advances in transportation from 1900 to 1960. If possible, also include short quotations showing how people reacted to each innovation when it was introduced.

Exploring Your Region

1. Find out about one or more Indian tribes living in your region. In particular, try to discover how the tribe was affected by policies of the federal government, such as reorganization and termination.
2. Interview your principal or a teacher in your school who taught there during the 1950's. Try to find out how school curriculum and procedures were affected by such world events as the launching of Sputnik and the McCarthy hearings.

Suggested Reading

1. *Plain Speaking: An Oral Biography of Harry S. Truman,* Merle Miller. A candid look at Truman, the man and the President; written in lively style with many anecdotes.
2. *The Other America: Poverty in the United States,* Michael Harrington. The influential book that alerted affluent Americans to the plight of the poor.
3. *Realities of American Foreign Policy,* George Kennan. A noted diplomat explores the nature and goals of American foreign policy in the years after World War II.
4. *Seven Days in May,* Fletcher Knebel. A suspense-filled novel of intrigue at the highest levels of government.
5. *The Bridges at Toko-ri,* James Michener. An exciting Korean War novel.

Unit Eight

Into a New Era

1960-1980's

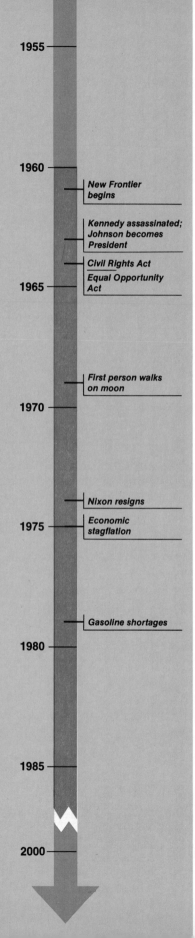

1955

1960

New Frontier
begins

Kennedy assassinated;
Johnson becomes
President

Civil Rights Act

Equal Opportunity
Act

1965

First person walks
on moon

1970

Nixon resigns

Economic
stagflation

1975

Gasoline shortages

1980

1985

2000

Chapter 22

Developments on the Domestic Front

1960-1980's

"Things are in the saddle, and ride mankind."

The words are those of Ralph Waldo Emerson, a keen observer of the human scene, who lived in Massachusetts more than a century ago. His observation could be accurately applied to the United States and the rest of the world during the years from 1960 through the 1980's.

During those years six different Presidents occupied the White House. They watched over the fortunes of the United States during one of the most turbulent periods in the nation's history. In these same years, the nation celebrated one of its proudest achievements when the first Americans landed on the moon. In these same years, many of the nation's cities, troubled by poverty and decay, exploded in riots. In this period the American economy at first prospered but later slumped sharply.

To what extent did these Presidents lead the nation and shape the course of events? To what extent were they themselves shaped and driven by forces beyond their control? Did they make policies, or were the policies forced upon them by events over which they had little if any control?

Such questions resist easy answers. Nevertheless, the questions themselves, even without answers, may help to illuminate the lives and the fates of the Presidents—Kennedy, Johnson, Nixon, Ford, Carter, and Reagan—who served the nation during those troubled years.

THE CHAPTER IN OUTLINE

1. Kennedy calls the nation to a "New Frontier."

2. Johnson urges Americans to build the "Great Society."

3. Nixon promises "to bring America together."

4. The Watergate scandals force Nixon to resign.

5. President Ford completes Nixon's second term.

6. Presidents Carter and Reagan face critical domestic problems.

1 Kennedy calls the nation to a "New Frontier"

The nation's unresolved problems at home and abroad were brought strongly to the attention of American voters in the Presidential campaign and election of 1960.

The election of 1960. Both the Republicans and Democrats nominated young, energetic candidates for the Presidency. The Republican nominee, Richard M. Nixon of California, had served in both houses of Congress. Since 1953 he had been Vice-President under Eisenhower. The Democratic nominee, John F. Kennedy of Massachusetts, had also served in both houses of Congress.

During the election campaign, the Presidential candidates faced each other in a series of television debates. Key issues were the nation's defenses and the economy, which had been in a recession since 1958. Kennedy called for a "supreme national effort" to reverse what

he called the downward trend of the nation's fortunes at home and abroad. He promised, if elected, "to get America moving again" by leading the nation to a "New Frontier."

Nixon insisted that the United States was stronger in relation to the Communist world than ever. He charged Kennedy with favoring "wild experimentation." Nixon promised, if elected, to build a more secure nation on the foundations of Eisenhower's policies.

Voters turned out in record numbers in the November election. Out of about 68 million votes cast, Kennedy squeezed through by a slim margin of 118,000 votes. In the electoral college, however, Kennedy won 303 electoral votes to Nixon's 219. Lyndon B. Johnson of Texas, who had been Democratic leader in the Senate since 1954, was elected Vice-President.

At 43 Kennedy was the first Roman Catholic and the youngest man ever elected President. He was acutely aware of the problems he faced. Barely half of the voters had shown a willingness to follow the new administration toward a New Frontier. Moreover, conservative Democrats in Congress, mostly from the

At his inauguration as President, John F. Kennedy stirred the nation when he said, "Let the word go forth from this time and place, to friend and foe alike, that the torch has been passed to a new generation of Americans. . . ."

South, had in the past voted with conservative Republicans to defeat measures similar to those Kennedy now wanted.

Economic problems. Once in office, Kennedy prepared to attack the related problems of unemployment and sluggish economic growth. The immediate problem was unemployment. In January 1961 more than 5 million Americans—nearly 8 percent of the total labor force —were unemployed. The unemployment rate among black Americans was double the rate for the nation as a whole.

The problem of unemployment had its roots in the nation's rapidly changing economic life. Some economists stressed that the American economy was not growing as rapidly as it should. Industries were not modernizing or building new factories as rapidly as many of them had done in the past.

Coupled with slow economic growth was the problem of automation, or the use of machines to do the work formerly done by men and women. Also, the increasingly complex American economy called for new skills on the part of workers. As a result, there were far fewer opportunities for the untrained and the poorly educated.

Encouraging employment and housing. In line with Kennedy's proposals, Congress took steps to increase spending power and retrain workers. Minimum wages were raised to $1.25 an hour, and 4 million more workers were included under wage-hour protection. The Area Redevelopment Act of 1961 authorized the federal government to make loans and grants to stimulate business and retrain workers in depressed areas. Congress also set aside $900 million for building public works in areas where more than 6 percent of the labor force was unemployed. In 1962, it passed the Manpower Development and Training Act providing for a three-year worker retraining program. Yet even with these and other measures, unemployment remained a major problem.

The Housing Act of 1961 tried to strengthen the nation's economic and social fabric. This act provided long-term loans at low interest rates to stimulate the construction of moderate-income housing. It included funds to provide hospitals and housing for the elderly. The largest authorization was for urban renewal, including the planning and improvement of mass transportation facilities. Congress also voted nearly $1.5 billion to aid in the construction of buildings for medical and dental schools and to assist colleges in building classrooms, libraries, and laboratories.

The Trade Expansion Act. In 1962 Congress took a major step to stimulate America's foreign trade. This step was prompted in part by the creation of the Common Market, a large trading area composed of six European nations. To improve trade among themselves, the Common Market nations gradually lowered the tariffs that had limited trade. By 1962 the Common Market nations were enjoying increasing prosperity. Recognizing that the Common Market could greatly affect the United States, Congress passed the Trade Expansion Act of 1962.

This act allowed the President, over a five-year period, to cut tariff rates 50 percent below the 1962 level or raise them 50 percent above the 1934 level. The President could also remove *all* tariffs on products for which the

SOURCES

We dare not forget today that we are the heirs of that first revolution. Let the word go forth from this time and place, to friend and foe alike, that the torch has been passed to a new generation of Americans—born in this century, tempered by war, disciplined by a hard and bitter peace, proud of our ancient heritage—and unwilling to witness or permit the slow undoing of those human rights to which this nation has always been committed, and to which we are committed today at home and around the world.

Let every nation know, whether it wishes us well or ill, that we shall pay any price, bear any burden, meet any hardship, support any friend, oppose any foe to assure the survival and the success of liberty. . . .

United States and the Common Market countries together accounted for 80 percent of all world trade.

The act contained an "escape clause" that allowed the President to retain or reimpose tariffs to protect industries hurt by tariff reduction. Endangered industries and workers in them could also receive loans and other government aid.

Congress passed several measures designed to aid the nation's farmers. These acts at best had limited success. By the end of 1963, the nation's farmers continued to struggle with surplus products and declining incomes.

The space program. In April 1961 the Soviet Union, which had launched the first satellite, made another advance into space. It sent the first astronaut, Yuri Gagarin, into orbit around the earth.

A month later Alan Shepard became the first American to make a rocket flight. Nevertheless Shepard did not orbit the earth as the Soviet had. Not until February 1962 was an American, Lieutenant Colonel John Glenn, launched into orbit.

President Kennedy, meanwhile, had become concerned that the United States might lose the race into space to the Soviets. He committed the United States to a program to make the United States first in space exploration. The United States, he declared, would land a man on the moon by 1970.

The space program also proved to be a source of new jobs for American workers. Soon some 9,000 firms were participating in the research and development of space-related products. By 1964 more than 30,000 scientists and specialists were working for the National Aeronautics and Space Administration (NASA), the agency in charge of the program. Estimates of the total number of Americans engaged in some phase of the space program ranged from 3 to 5 million. Moreover, by 1964 the program had created some 3,200 different products, many of which found their way into daily use.

The space program and the other parts of Kennedy's economic program seemed to be successful. By late 1961 the economy had begun to pull out of the recession. It then entered a time of growth that would last until 1970.

Changes in suffrage. During the Kennedy administration, several major changes took place in voting rights. The Twenty-third Amendment to the Constitution, adopted in 1961 (see page 753), enabled residents of the District of Columbia to vote in Presidential elections. The Twenty-fourth Amendment, adopted in 1964 (see page 753), forbade the poll tax as a requirement for voting in federal elections. Poll taxes had been used in many areas to prevent poor blacks from voting.

Other citizens fought for fairer representation in national, state, and local legislatures. Election districts in many states had remained unchanged for many years. However, the population in these states had generally shifted from rural to urban and suburban areas. This meant that rural districts were often overrepresented in the legislatures.

Between 1962 and 1964, the Supreme Court handed down several decisions relating to representation. The most far-reaching was the Court's "one person, one vote" ruling. According to this decision, election districts for state legislatures as well as for the House of Representatives must be as nearly equal in population as practicable. The Supreme Court thus set in motion a political revolution intended to make each citizen's vote have approximately equal value. This was meant to provide genuine representative government at both state and federal levels.

Unfinished business. During his time in office, Kennedy took important steps to insure equal justice for blacks (see Chapter 24). In June 1963, for example, Kennedy sent a civil rights bill to Congress. Despite his support, the chances of the bill's passage were uncertain. Kennedy also had plans for mass transit, medical care, and aid-to-education programs. By late 1963 he had not been able to get any of these programs through Congress.

Kennedy was reluctant to put too much pressure on Congress to pass these bills. The next year, 1964, was an election year. Kennedy, who had won so narrowly in 1960, knew he would need broad political support if he wished to be reelected.

One area of the nation where Kennedy's political support seemed weakest was the South. To build up enthusiasm for himself and his programs, Kennedy planned a trip to Texas in November 1963.

At 12:30 in the afternoon on Friday, November 22, 1963, while riding in a motorcade through Dallas, Texas, President Kennedy was killed by an assassin. Vice-President Johnson, who also was in the motorcade, immediately drove under close guard to the Presidential plane. There, in the cabin of the plane at 2:38 P.M., Lyndon B. Johnson was sworn in as the thirty-sixth President of the United States.

The tragic weekend. Americans reacted to the tragic news with shocked disbelief, then with deeply felt anger and grief. For three days, while the body of John F. Kennedy lay in state in the Capitol, radio and television stations suspended regular programming. All but the most essential businesses closed their doors. Messages of sorrow and sympathy poured in from all over the world. The leaders of many nations flew to Washington to pay their respects to the late President.

In the meantime, within an hour and a half of the fatal shooting, the Dallas police had seized a suspect, Lee Harvey Oswald. Oswald was placed under heavy guard in a Dallas jail. Two days later, while being moved from one jail to another, he was shot and killed in full view of millions of Americans who were watching the event on television. His murderer, Jack Ruby, pushed through a group of police officers to shoot Oswald at close range.

Americans were deeply troubled by this new act of brutality. With Oswald gone, grave questions remained unanswered. Was Lee Harvey Oswald truly the assassin? If so, had he acted alone? Or was he part of a conspiracy to assassinate President Kennedy? Was Jack Ruby part of that conspiracy, and did he kill Oswald to keep him from talking?

The Warren Commission. To answer these questions and to put an end to wild rumors and speculation, President Johnson appointed a commission to investigate the case. The commission was headed by Earl Warren, Chief Justice of the Supreme Court.

In September 1964 the Warren Commission released its report. After carefully examining the available evidence and the testimony of 532 witnesses, the commission unanimously concluded that (1) Lee Harvey Oswald had assassinated President Kennedy, (2) he had acted alone, (3) Jack Ruby also had acted alone, and (4) there was no evidence of a conspiracy.

The report did not, however, end the questions and speculations. Critics continued to question the procedures used by the commission as well as its conclusions. In 1979, a committee of the House of Representatives conducted its own investigation of the assassination. It heard from witnesses whom the Warren Commission had not called. It found experts who used new methods to study tapes made at the time of the shooting. Using these methods the committee found evidence that more than one gun had been fired at Kennedy. However, the committee could not say who had fired the other gun or guns, or who else might have been involved in a conspiracy.

SECTION SURVEY

IDENTIFY: New Frontier, automation, Common Market, John Glenn, NASA, Lee Harvey Oswald, Warren Commission.

1. What were the parties, candidates, issues, and results of the election of 1960?
2. (a) What actions did the Kennedy administration take in the areas of unemployment, housing, and foreign trade? (b) How effective were these actions?
3. Why did Kennedy believe it was important for the United States to land a man on the moon by 1970?
4. What was the significance for democratic government of the (a) Twenty-third Amendment, (b) Twenty-fourth Amendment, and (c) "one person, one vote" ruling?

2 Johnson urges Americans to build the "Great Society"

Five days after the assassination of President Kennedy, Lyndon B. Johnson, in his first Presidential address to Congress, dedicated himself to the "ideas and the ideals" that John F. Kennedy had "so nobly represented." President Johnson gave top priority to three items —a civil rights law, a tax cut, and an "unconditional war on poverty." Speaking quietly but firmly, he declared, "All this and more can and must be done." Thus the new President invited Americans to build what he would later call the "Great Society."

Johnson had served long years in both the House and the Senate. He knew the lawmakers well and how they thought and worked. Most important, he understood how to get legislation through Congress.

An impressive record.   Congress responded to President Johnson's leadership. Before adjourning in October 1964, Congress chalked up one of the most impressive legislative records in the nation's history. Most far-reaching was the Civil Rights Act of 1964 (see Chapter 24), but there were other important measures.

The Revenue Act of 1964 cut personal and corporate income taxes by $11.5 billion. By leaving more money in the hands of consumers and businesses, the new law greatly stimulated the economy.

The Economic Opportunity Act of 1964 marked an important attempt to "break the cycle of poverty." It created an Office of Economic Opportunity (OEO) and authorized $1 billion to begin the war against poverty. The new agency was to work with state and local governments to increase employment and expand training programs, especially for the nation's needy young people.

Congress also passed several other measures. For example, it authorized $375 million to help cities improve urban and commuter transit facilities. It also established a system to preserve federally owned wilderness areas. However, several measures strongly supported by President Johnson were still being considered when Congress adjourned to begin the 1964 election campaign.

The election of 1964.   The Republicans nominated Barry M. Goldwater, a conservative Senator from Arizona, for the Presidency and Representative William E. Miller of New York as his running mate. The Democrats nominated Lyndon B. Johnson and his choice for Vice-President, Senator Hubert H. Humphrey of Minnesota.

From the start of the race, both parties were divided. Goldwater was a firm conservative. He favored a sharply limited role for the federal government. Many moderate Republicans refused to support him. The Republicans also lost the support of most black voters. Goldwater was one of only six Republican Senators who had voted against the Civil Rights Act of 1964.

The Democrats, too, lost many loyal voters. Many white southern Democrats felt that President Johnson, a Texan, had betrayed them by leading the battle for the Civil Rights Act. They supported Goldwater because of his vote against the act and his support of states' rights.

In November nearly 70 million voters turned out. They elected President Johnson by an overwhelming electoral vote of 486 to 52. The popular vote was 42 million to 26 million. The Democrats also won substantial victories in state and local elections and in Congress.

Toward the "Great Society."   Encouraged by his sweeping victory, President Johnson challenged Americans to join him in building the "Great Society." He argued that Americans, now more prosperous than ever, could help build a new world, not just a new nation. Americans had three major tasks: "To keep our economy growing. To open for all Americans the opportunities now enjoyed by most Americans. To improve the quality of life for all."

By the time Congress adjourned in the fall of 1965, it had adopted laws dealing with all of the President's major recommendations. In one of the most far-reaching laws, the legislators provided a comprehensive program of aid to education (see Chapter 25). Congress also established Medicare, a national program of health insurance for persons over 65. Medicare provided basic health coverage, with social security paying the larger part of the costs of hospital treatment or home nursing care, the patient paying the rest. Medicare also included

After July 1, 1965, millions of the nation's senior citizens became eligible for Medicare. This program helped them to pay for the ever-increasing cost of their hospital, doctor, and other medical bills.

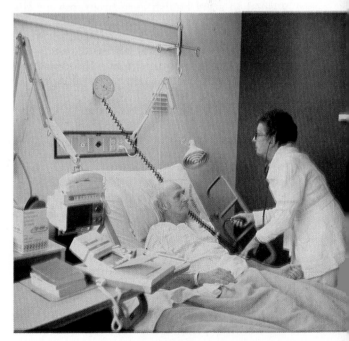

Shanks in The Buffalo Evening News

"Hope I know where we're goin'."

More than any President in modern history, Lyndon Johnson had control of Congress. To what does the cartoonist compare Johnson's persuasiveness? How is Congress portrayed? Is this a flattering view?

voluntary supplementary coverage, enabling individuals covered by social security to buy low-cost health insurance to cover doctors' bills and other health services. The Medicare bill also provided for federal grants to states that wished to start health care programs for the needy. Such care was known as Medicaid.

Responding to President Johnson's urging, Congress reduced federal excise taxes on automobiles, television sets, and other consumer items. The cut in excise taxes was designed to encourage Americans to buy more goods. This in turn would stimulate production and reduce unemployment.

In still other efforts to raise the standard of living of impoverished Americans, the legislators adopted several measures. Congress increased to $1.5 billion the funds for the Office of Economic Opportunity's anti-poverty program. Congress also voted $1 billion to help develop the depressed economy of the 11-state Appalachian region. In addition, Congress authorized $7.5 billion to improve the nation's housing. Much of this money was intended to help those who lived in low-income areas.

Loss of momentum. As it turned out, 1965 marked the peak of Johnson's program and

his popularity. Continued racial unrest in the nation damaged Democratic programs. Also, more people began to question increasing federal spending and government involvement in their daily lives. Most important, by 1966 the war in Vietnam, as you will read in Chapter 23, was absorbing more and more of the nation's resources and the administration's time and energy. As the war intensified, the President became the target of increasing criticism from Congress, from newspapers, and even from the pulpits of churches. Antiwar demonstrations disrupted the President's speeches at public ceremonies. Gradually, Johnson became more cut off from the American people. He was less able to get Congress to carry out his programs.

McCarthy's challenge. Eugene J. McCarthy, Democratic Senator from Minnesota, first revealed the extent of the dissatisfaction with Johnson. In November 1967 Senator McCarthy declared that he intended to campaign for the Presidency against Johnson. His purpose was to give voters a chance to show that they opposed the administration's Vietnam policy.

In the nation's first 1968 Presidential primary, held in New Hampshire in March, McCarthy made a surprisingly strong showing. In part his success was due to the thousands of young volunteers from all over the country who poured into the state to work for him. They campaigned hard for McCarthy because he inspired them with hopeful idealism.

Political developments. The New Hampshire primary triggered a series of political developments. A few days after the primary, Senator Robert F. Kennedy of New York announced that he, too, would seek the Democratic nomination for President. Senator Kennedy, a brother of the late President Kennedy, was an outspoken critic of President Johnson's Vietnam policy.

A second political development, one that stunned the nation, was President Johnson's declaration in March that he would not run for reelection. As Johnson later explained, he hoped that removing himself from the Presidential race would end the growing division among the American people over his conduct of the Vietnam War. Even some of Johnson's political enemies praised his decision.

President Johnson's withdrawal opened the door to the candidacy of Vice-President Hubert

Humphrey. He soon joined Senators McCarthy and Kennedy in the heated race for the Democratic nomination.

Two assassinations. Early in April 1968, the nation mourned the death of the great civil rights leader Martin Luther King, Jr. (see Chapter 24). In June the nation again grieved, this time for Senator Robert F. Kennedy, killed by an assassin's bullet just after he had won a close victory over Senator McCarthy in the California primary.

The assassinations of President John F. Kennedy, Martin Luther King, Jr., and Robert F. Kennedy led many people at home and abroad to wonder if violence was an ingrained part of American society. What, people asked, was happening to the nation? There was no easy answer, but President Johnson did appoint a commission to study the question of violence. Also, Congress, over strong opposition, passed a gun-control law, although critics called the new law a "halfway measure."

The end of a dream. Back in 1963 President Johnson had dedicated himself to building a Great Society—free from poverty, discrimination, and injustice. During his first two years in office, he made substantial progress toward that goal. Then, as the Vietnam War began to absorb the administration's attention, domestic programs suffered. Thus, Lyndon Johnson's dream of a Great Society became marred by the war abroad and by continuing unrest and violence at home.

SECTION SURVEY

IDENTIFY: Great Society, war on poverty, Barry Goldwater, Medicare, Medicaid, Eugene McCarthy, Robert Kennedy.

1. President Johnson believed that two goals of the United States were "to open for all Americans the opportunities now enjoyed by most Americans" and "to improve the quality of life for all." What legislation did he promote to achieve each of these goals?
2. With reference to the election of 1964, discuss (a) the candidates and parties and (b) the results for the parties and the nation.
3. In 1967 Eugene McCarthy triggered a series of political developments. What were they?
4. What did President Johnson hope to accomplish by refusing to run for reelection in 1968?

3 Nixon promises "to bring America together"

It was a restless, disturbed nation that in August 1968 watched the Presidential nominating conventions on television.

Choosing candidates. The Republicans, meeting first, gathered at Miami Beach. Richard M. Nixon, who represented the middle ground as well as the "establishment" of the Republican Party, was nominated on the first ballot. He chose Spiro T. Agnew, Governor of Maryland, as his running mate.

The Democratic convention, held later in Chicago, proved to be one of the most tumultuous in the nation's history. To Americans watching on television, the convention hall was a disorderly arena. There McCarthy and Kennedy supporters contended against "establishment" Democrats represented by Hubert H. Humphrey.

The bitter fight in the convention hall was reflected in the city's streets. Thousands of young people had gathered in Chicago to demonstrate against the Vietnam War and for candidates favoring peace. Claiming that the demonstrations had gotten out of hand, the Chicago police moved in. The violent confrontations that followed, resulting in numerous injuries, were also witnessed by millions of television viewers.

In the convention hall, the "establishment" won. Humphrey was picked on the first ballot and chose Senator Edmund S. Muskie of Maine as his Vice-Presidential candidate.

The campaign of 1968. The three main issues of the campaign were violence and disorder, Vietnam, and racial strife. Public opinion polls showed that seven out of every ten Americans were convinced that "law and order had broken down in the country." Two out of every three felt that the war in Vietnam was being badly managed. The overwhelming majority of white citizens believed that the civil rights struggle was going "too fast." An equally large majority of black citizens were convinced that the movement was "not going fast enough."

During the campaign neither Nixon nor Humphrey aroused great enthusiasm among voters. The emergence of a third-party can-

Here, during the 1968 Democratic convention in Chicago, National Guardsmen surround the hotel where party leaders were meeting. The troops had been ordered to keep demonstrators away from the hotel.

didate, George C. Wallace of Alabama, founder of the American Independent Party, further complicated matters.

George C. Wallace. From the beginning, third-party candidate Wallace hammered at the issue of law and order. Wallace also expressed opposition to existing welfare programs, forced busing of school children, and the federal enforcement of integration. He pledged, if elected, to repeal open housing legislation, to give the police greater power to deal with demonstrations and civil disorders, and to restore to the states and local communities control over welfare programs and the schools. As to Vietnam, he promised to end the war by negotiation, if possible, but to achieve a military victory if negotiations failed.

Richard M. Nixon. Nixon stressed the nation's need for new leadership. He declared that the Democrats had brought the United States close to disaster and that it was "time for a change." Like Wallace, he promised to restore law and order but added the word "justice" to his pledge.

Nixon insisted that the Democratic programs of massive federal spending to combat poverty had failed. He promised to review the entire welfare program and to turn over to private businesses the primary responsibility for retraining unemployed workers and rebuilding the cities.

Nixon also promised the nation that he would "bring an honorable end to the war" in Vietnam. He did not say how he would end the war, explaining that he did not wish to upset the delicate peace talks then going on in Paris.

Nixon was more specific, however, in his ideas about military policy and national defense. He favored a buildup of nuclear capability to insure that the United States held superiority over all potential enemies. His recommendations included the development of an anti-ballistic missile system (ABM).

Hubert H. Humphrey. During most of the campaign, Humphrey found himself in difficulty. His party was badly divided. Millions of people associated the violence in Chicago with the Democrats.

Humphrey was convinced that force, no matter how strongly applied, would not end the unrest and violence afflicting the nation. "We can only cut crime," he declared, "by getting at its causes: slums, unemployment, run-down schools and houses. This is where crime begins and that is where it must end." He cautioned that the attack against crime "must not jeopardize hard-won liberties of our citizens."

To meet the crippling problems of poverty and of urban decay, Humphrey called for "a Marshall Plan for the cities based upon self-help, local initiative, coordinated planning, and private capital."

Vietnam caused Humphrey the most trouble. At the start of his campaign, he lost much support by defending the unpopular administration policy. However, at the end of September he called for a halt to the bombing of North Vietnam, and his chances began to improve. They improved still further when, less than a week before the election, President Johnson announced that he had ordered a halt to all bombing north of the DMZ (Demilitarized Zone) that divided Vietnam, offering hope for an earlier end to the war.

The election results. The 1968 Presidential election was indeed a close one. Out of more than 71 million popular votes cast, Nixon's margin of victory over Humphrey was only 260,000 votes. The electoral vote of 302 for Nixon, 191 for Humphrey, and 45 for Wallace did not, however, reflect this closeness. The Democrats kept control of Congress.

Keenly aware of his narrow victory, President-elect Nixon pledged that his "great objective" would be to unite the country. Convinced that the "silent majority" of the American people stood midway between extreme conservatism and extreme liberalism, Nixon sought to hold to a "center" line.

To the moon. President Nixon was inaugurated on January 20, 1969. Just six months later, on July 20, 1969, American astronauts landed on the moon. The promise that President Kennedy had made back in 1961 to land a man on the moon before the end of the decade had been kept.

The costs were high. Three astronauts had died in a sudden flash fire. About $24 billion had been spent on the moon shot. Some critics argued that such money could have been better spent on solving problems at home.

Nevertheless, Americans stayed near television sets or radios for news when Neil Armstrong, Michael Collins, and Edwin E. Aldrin, Jr., lifted off in Apollo 11 for the moon. Millions of Americans watched in fascination four days later when the lunar lander named *Eagle* settled down on the moon's surface. Many felt a great pride when Armstrong stepped out of the spacecraft and onto the moon saying, "That's one small step for a man, one giant leap for mankind."

Difficulties with Congress. The Nixon adminstration, handicapped by a Democratic majority in Congress, had more trouble implementing its policies. In an effort to commit the Supreme Court to his own view of a strict interpretation of the Constitution, the President filled the vacancy created by Earl Warren's retirement by appointing Warren E. Burger as Chief Justice. However, Nixon was unable to secure Senate approval for two other nominees to fill a Supreme Court vacancy. Finally, the Senate approved Nixon's choice of Harry Blackmun, a respected moderate judge.

Differences between the administration and Congress also led to other compromises and stalemates. The President insisted on cutting down federal spending, contending that such spending was excessive and that many pro-

President Richard Nixon tried to get many programs passed into law, but Congress, with its Democratic majority, often foiled his efforts. According to this cartoon, what were some of the programs?

grams were unwise and poorly administered. But critics in Congress insisted that cuts in spending for social welfare, education, and other domestic programs were not justified. They also objected to the administration's reluctance to make substantial cuts in the military budget.

Difficulties at home. Nixon had inherited the Vietnam War from President Johnson. He also inherited the anger of antiwar protesters. Huge demonstrations were held in Washington, New York, and other cities calling for an end to the war. Nixon had announced that he had a plan to end the war, but for many of the demonstrators he was not moving fast enough.

Then in May 1970, the nation learned that President Nixon had ordered the invasion of Cambodia. Antiwar activists were outraged by this action. A wave of new protests swept across the nation.

At Kent State University, the protest turned violent. The National Guard was called out. On May 4, trying to break up a gathering of students, the Guard opened fire. Four students were killed.

413

A STEP, A GIANT LEAP

Down a ladder swung a heavy-booted foot. Over 500 million people, watching on television, saw it step out onto a powdery surface. Then they heard the voice of astronaut Neil Armstrong as he surveyed the gray and cratered landscape before him: "That's one small step for a man, one giant leap for mankind." It was Sunday, July 20, 1969, and the first humans had reached the moon.

The official name of this flight, Apollo 11, indicated that it was one of a series. The earliest Apollo missions had taken place in 1967, but the Apollo program had begun in 1961. At that time President Kennedy had committed the nation to a moon landing within ten years.

Early Apollo trials had tested the equipment in unmanned flight. Later ones carried fliers into earth and then lunar orbits. Apollo 7 (October 1968) was the first to broadcast live TV coverage from the cockpit. On Apollo 8 (December 1968), astronauts traveled faster than any humans up to that time. On Christmas Eve they read from the book of Genesis as they orbited the moon.

Apollo 11's Armstrong and Edwin Aldrin had landed on the moon in a small module called *Eagle.* It had separated from the command spacecraft, *Columbia,* which remained in orbit —commanded by Michael Collins—while the moon exploration took place. In two busy hours, the men installed scientific instruments, collected 50 pounds (22.7 kilograms) of moon rocks, and snapped hundreds of photographs. They also set up a metal flag and left a plaque, which read as follows:

HERE MEN FROM THE PLANET EARTH
FIRST SET FOOT UPON THE MOON
JULY 1969 A.D.
WE CAME IN PEACE FOR ALL MANKIND

Then *Eagle* lifted off, leaving behind footprints that might well last forever on the moon's airless surface.

The nation was shocked and sobered. Nixon's campaign promise to "bring America together" now seemed to ring hollow. The war in Vietnam still appeared to be tearing America apart.

Inflation and the energy crisis. Among the other serious problems facing President Nixon when he took office was inflation. The rising rate of inflation was partly a result of vast spending for the Vietnam War. It was also a result of basic problems in the American economy and society, and partly a result of international events. As you will read, Nixon's attempts to handle inflation met with mixed success.

The skyrocketing cost of oil was a major contributor to inflation in the United States and throughout the world. The major oil-exporting nations had in 1960 formed the Organization of Petroleum Exporting Countries (OPEC). OPEC wanted to get higher prices for its oil from importing countries. Then, in the fall of 1973, the Arab oil-producing nations sharply increased the price of oil, and in the midst of a new Arab-Israeli war, the Arab nations cut off all shipments to the United States and other industrial nations that had been supporting Israel. A few months later, the Arabs lifted their embargo, but OPEC kept oil prices high.

High oil prices and the embargo caused critical problems for Western Europe and Japan, which depended almost entirely on Arab oil. The United States, which depended upon Arab oil for only about 6 percent of its total requirements, also faced a serious situation.

For several years there had been a growing scarcity of energy in the United States. The 6-percent cutoff of oil coupled with soaring prices brought a serious "energy crisis" during the winter of 1973–74. The cost of gasoline, heating oil, and electricity rose drastically. In some parts of the country, shortages caused real hardships. As a result, Nixon announced a program to make the United States independent of all foreign countries for its energy requirements by the early 1980's.

Other important developments. In March 1971 Congress adopted the Twenty-sixth Amendment (page 755) lowering the voting age to 18 in both federal and state elections. When the amendment was ratified by the required 38 states three months later, the Census Bureau estimated that 25 million additional young people were now eligible to vote in the next Presidential election.

Shortly before the end of President Nixon's first term, he signed a $30.2 billion revenue-sharing bill. This act channeled federal revenue to states and local communities for various public programs. Nixon regarded this "new federalism" as an essential part of his program for decentralizing the power of the national government.

SECTION SURVEY

IDENTIFY: Spiro Agnew, George Wallace, Neil Armstrong, Warren Burger, inflation, wage and price controls, "energy crisis," Twenty-sixth Amendment, revenue sharing.

1. (a) What were the basic issues of the 1968 Presidential election? (b) What position did each candidate take on these issues?

2. (a) How did the Nixon administration try to control inflation? (b) How effective were its efforts?

3. (a) What was the "new federalism"? (b) What actions did Nixon take to promote the "new federalism"?

4. Cartoon Study: Examine the political cartoon on page 413. Then write a short paragraph explaining its meaning.

4 **The Watergate scandals force Nixon to resign**

Nixon's second term in office began with the triumph of a sweeping reelection victory. It ended less than two years later with a disgraced administration and with the President's resignation.

The election of 1972. At their 1972 convention, the Republicans again nominated Richard M. Nixon and Spiro T. Agnew. The Demo-crats nominated Senator George M. McGovern of South Dakota, a liberal, as their Presidential candidate. Governor George C. Wallace of Alabama, an early contender for the Democratic nomination, had been wounded by a would-be assassin and did not take an active part in the 1972 campaign.

The Democratic convention included among its delegates an unusually large number of black Americans, young people, other minorities, and women. Older party regulars believed that the newcomers were moving the Democrats too far to the left, beyond the majority views of the nation. They bitterly opposed McGovern's nomination.

From the start McGovern was in trouble. He chose Senator Thomas Eagleton of Missouri as his running mate. Then it was revealed that Eagleton had at one time been hospitalized for emotional illness. McGovern first announced his continued support of Eagleton. Then he changed his mind and asked Eagleton to step down. The Democratic National Committee then chose Sargent Shriver, former head of the Peace Corps, to replace Eagleton.

The incident called McGovern's judgment into question and cost him votes. In addition, many traditional Democratic voters opposed him, and others were lukewarm toward his candidacy. Nevertheless, McGovern campaigned tirelessly. He hit hard at inflation, corruption, what he called the Nixon administration's "indifference" to civil rights, and above all against United States participation in the Vietnam War.

Nixon was confident of victory. He could count on most of the 12 million to 15 million votes that might have gone to Governor Wallace if he had run. Moreover, Nixon's achievements in foreign affairs were widely praised by Democrats and Republicans alike. He had sharply reduced America's military role in South Vietnam and had improved relations with both Communist China and the Soviet Union. President Nixon also encouraged his supporters to spend heavily on whatever steps they thought were necessary to insure his reelection.

Nixon won one of the greatest victories in American history, winning about 47 million votes to McGovern's 29 million. The electoral vote was 521 to 17. Nixon's victory was largely personal, and Republicans failed to make significant gains in the House and Senate, which were controlled by the Democrats.

Nixon's social policies. President Nixon saw his landslide victory as a mandate, or command by the voters, to carry out his foreign policies and his domestic policies. These domestic policies called for a reduced role for the federal government.

Nixon believed that the expansion of federally funded social programs had worsened the conditions they were supposed to correct. He opposed large federal spending for job training for the handicapped, special education for the disadvantaged, and the use of school buses to speed up racial integration. He called for a halt to federal support for low-cost housing and urban renewal on grounds that neither had succeeded. He criticized publicly financed day care support for children of working mothers. He urged tighter controls over expenditures for Medicare and Medicaid, declaring his preference for private health insurance plans.

In January 1973 Nixon called for cutbacks or terminations in more than 100 federal programs in the next budget. To get his program through, he relied partly upon his Republican followers in Congress but also upon continuing support from conservative Democrats, chiefly from southern states.

Executive power. Although Nixon in general favored a reduced role for the federal government, his powers as President had grown. Ever since the 1930's, foreign and domestic problems had encouraged, if not required, increased executive power. During this time Congress had allowed a growth in power under both Democratic and Republican Presidents.

However, in Nixon's second term, critics began to worry about his use of executive power. At times Nixon seemed to believe that he as President was, or should be, above criticism or restraint. He had turned over much of the authority of Cabinet officers, where appointment required Senate approval, to his personally appointed White House staff. Nixon also held back vital information from Congress and the public. Members of the administration, especially Vice-President Agnew, attacked newspaper and television reporting as irresponsible and unfair. These events and others fed a growing uneasiness that Nixon's use of the Presidency threatened the constitutional balance of powers.

The Watergate affair. The threat to the balance of powers became clearer as a series of scandals emerged during Nixon's second term. The disastrous Watergate affair, as the scandals were called, began in June 1972 with an attempted burglary of the Democratic National Committee offices in Washington's Watergate Apartments complex. Five men were caught in the building. At first they gave false names, but they were soon correctly identified. The trail then led to the organization for which they had been working, the Committee to Reelect the President.

The White House tried to dismiss the episode as a "third-rate burglary," but news reporters refused to believe this. As the months passed, news reports began to unravel a tangled web of criminal activities that appeared to reach into the highest offices in the land. As a result, by 1973 both the legislative and the judicial branches of government had become actively involved in the Watergate investigations. A special Senate committee, chaired by Senator Sam Ervin of North Carolina, held televised hearings during the spring and summer of 1973. The Attorney General appointed a Special Prosecutor, who organized a staff and began to sift the evidence. A grand jury sitting in a federal district court headed by Judge John Sirica began to gather evidence and prepare indictments.

The resignation of Agnew. Meanwhile, the Justice Department had been investigating the financial affairs of Vice-President Agnew. By the fall of 1973, government investigators were prepared to indict Agnew for crimes, including bribery and extortion, committed while he was Governor of Maryland and Vice-President of the United States.

For a time Agnew angrily proclaimed his innocence of the alleged wrongdoings. However, in the late fall he decided to throw himself on the mercy of the court and plea-bargain for a light sentence.

Agnew's part of the bargain included his immediate resignation as Vice-President and a *nolo contendere* ("no contest") plea to a single count of tax evasion ($29,500 of undeclared income in 1967). In return, the Court agreed not to sentence Agnew to jail for the tax evasion and not to prosecute him for other criminal activities he allegedly committed.

The extremely lenient sentence—a $10,000 fine and unsupervised probation for three years—was widely criticized. Nevertheless, Attorney General Elliot Richardson defended it on grounds that a long trial "would have been likely to inflict upon the nation serious and permanent scars."

In accordance with the Twenty-fifth Amendment to the Constitution, President Nixon nominated a new Vice-President. He chose Gerald Ford, the Republican leader of the House of Representatives. The Senate confirmed the nomination.

Mounting evidence. Meanwhile, the Watergate investigations continued. The grand jury charged that members of the administration, if not the President himself, had approved the Watergate burglary and had then attempted to cover up the administration's part in the affair. The grand jury also charged that members of the administration, if not the President himself, had approved of the illegal entry into the offices of a psychiatrist. This break-in was undertaken in an effort to secure damaging personal evidence against one of the psychiatrist's patients, Daniel Ellsberg. Ellsberg had earlier released classified material relating to the government's plans and actions during the Vietnam War.

Investigators also uncovered evidence of the illegal use by the administration of wiretapping and bugging. There was also a plan to set up a secret White House group known as the "plumbers" authorized to break federal laws in the name of "national security." Investigators also claimed that the White House had tried to involve the CIA and the FBI in some of its illegal activities. They further claimed that during the 1972 election campaign huge sums of money had been collected from corporations with the understanding that the administration would do special favors for such contributors. As the months passed, additional evidence of wrongdoing steadily accumulated. Numerous officials of the White House staff were indicted. Some pleaded guilty and went to jail. Others went to trial; most of them were convicted and sentenced.

The White House tapes. From the beginning President Nixon protested that he was innocent of any wrongdoing. However, White House lawyer John W. Dean, who had already confessed to his own participation in the scandals, challenged him. Although the growing volume of evidence seemed to support Dean, it was his word against the word of the President. The issue remained unresolved.

In July 1973, however, the Senate committee investigating Watergate suddenly learned that for the past two years Nixon had been secretly taping everything said in his offices and over most of his White House telephones. This evidence could prove or disprove the President's claim of innocence of the charge of obstructing justice.

The Senate Watergate Committee and the Special Prosecutor immediately issued subpoenas. They requested President Nixon to turn over those tapes that contained discussions relating to the Watergate affair and the alleged cover-up. Nixon refused to surrender them on grounds of "executive privilege" and "national security."

The courts then ruled that the President had to release those portions of the relevant tapes that did not relate to national security. After considerable delay Nixon released some, but not all, of the tapes. A growing conviction that he was withholding damaging evidence became even more widespread when it was discovered that important parts of certain tapes had been erased. Finally, in August 1974, the Supreme Court ordered Nixon to release the requested tapes.

The Supreme Court ruling was the final blow to the President's efforts to conceal his part in the illegal White House activities during his administration. The tapes Nixon reluctantly turned over to the Special Prosecutor revealed that his repeated claims of innocence had been false. From the beginning he had been involved in efforts to cover up the Watergate affair.

Nixon's resignation. The revelation of Nixon's betrayal of the public's trust came as the House of Representatives was preparing to vote on the issue of Presidential impeachment. After a three-month investigation, the House Judiciary Committee had approved three Articles of Impeachment.

The three articles that the Judiciary Committee sent to the House charged the President with violating his oath of office by (1) obstruction of justice, (2) abuse of power, and (3) willful disobedience of subpoenas issued by the House of Representatives.

Faced with probable impeachment by the House and conviction by the Senate, President Nixon chose to resign. He submitted his resignation on August 8, 1974. He denied any guilt, however, and admitted only to having made

Just about two years to the day after Nixon had accepted the renomination of his party, he announced his resignation from the Presidency. Standing by Nixon in this photograph are his daughter and son-in-law.

some "mistakes" and to having lost his "power base" in Congress.

Nixon was the first President in the nation's history to resign from office. His departure brought an end to a grave constitutional crisis that had threatened to weaken, if not destroy, the democratic process. At issue had been the preservation of the system of checks and balances, the principle of the separation of powers, and the rule of law itself.

SECTION SURVEY

IDENTIFY: George McGovern, Senate Watergate Committee, Judge John Sirica, Gerald Ford, Articles of Impeachment.

1. (a) Why did Nixon win the 1972 election by a landslide? (b) Why was it called a "personal" victory?
2. (a) What was the "Watergate affair"? (b) What role did Congress have in investigating the affair? (c) What part did news reporters play? (d) What role did the courts have?
3. What were the events that led to President Nixon's resignation?
4. Why did some people think that Nixon's administration posed a threat to the principle of the separation of powers?

5 President Ford completes Nixon's second term

On August 9 the Vice-President, Gerald Ford, was sworn in as the 38th President of the United States. Following the procedure set forth in the Twenty-fifth Amendment, he nominated Governor Nelson A. Rockefeller of New York for Vice-President and Congress confirmed the nomination. Thus, for the first time since the Constitution was adopted, both the President and the Vice-President held their high offices by appointment, rather than through election by the voters.

Gerald Ford. Gerald Ford was an unpretentious man gifted with the common touch. Before Nixon appointed him to the Vice-Presidency he had represented his home state of Michigan in Congress for a quarter of a century. As leader of the Republicans in the House, Ford had won the respect of his colleagues in both political parties. He was liked and trusted for his honesty and his open, unassuming manner. "I am a Ford, not a Lincoln," he declared upon becoming Vice-President. In 1974 when he was sworn in as the nation's Chief Executive, he won respect for his candid assessment of his position. "I am acutely aware," he said, "that you have not elected me as your President by your ballots."

The Nixon pardon. A month after he took office, Ford lost much of the early confidence he had won. At that time he granted Nixon an unconditional pardon for all the federal crimes he "committed or may have committed or taken part in" while serving as President. Nixon accepted the pardon, which legally was an admission of guilt.

Ford's critics charged that by granting the pardon he had prevented the American people from ever learning the full truth about the Nixon administration. The critics pointed to the double standard of justice that gave Nixon a full pardon while his fellow conspirators were punished for following their leader's wishes. Some of the critics questioned whether the pardon had not been agreed upon in advance in exchange for Nixon's resignation.

President Ford insisted that these charges were not true. He defended the pardon on the ground that a public trial would have only prolonged the bitterness and the division produced by Watergate. He had acted, he said, because he wanted to heal the nation's wounds.

Ford's amnesty program. A week after he broke the news of the Nixon pardon, Ford dropped another bombshell with the announcement of an amnesty for the Vietnam draft evaders and military deserters. This, too, became a highly controversial issue and further lessened the President's initial popularity.

During the Vietnam War, thousands of young men had crossed the border into Canada or had gone to European countries to escape the draft. A smaller but still substantial number already in the armed services had deserted and fled the country. Both groups felt that the war was morally wrong and that for this reason they could not, in conscience, support it.

Ford declared that he could not condone the draft evasion and desertion. However, he added, it is time to "heal the scars of divisiveness." He then offered a conditional pardon. Those who wanted it would have to reaffirm their allegiance to the United States and agree to spend up to two years of alternative service working for the public. This service might be in hospitals, rehabilitation centers, conservation efforts, or similar activities.

Only a handful of the more than 200,000 resisters and deserters accepted the President's offer. They compared the conditional pardon they were offered with the full pardon granted Nixon. In their view, President Ford measured mercy and justice by a double standard.

Presidential leadership. In spite of his long and close ties with Congress, Ford found himself in repeated conflicts with it during the two years of his administration. In the Congressional elections of 1974, held only three months after Ford became President, the Democrats in both houses were able to greatly increase their already large majorities. Ford, a moderate conservative Republican, could not accept many Democratic proposals for social welfare programs.

Since Republicans in Congress could not defeat the bills, Ford used his Presidential veto to kill them. During his term in office, he vetoed more bills than any President had ever vetoed in such a short time. In most cases, Congress was unable to pass the bills over Ford's veto.

In an effort to beat inflation, President Gerald Ford announced his WIN program—*Whip Inflation Now*. Ford's program urged Americans to counteract rising costs by voluntarily curbing wage and price demands.

Economic problems. President Ford's frequent use of the veto was the result in part of his attempt to combat the problem of inflation. He had inherited this problem from Nixon, just as Nixon had inherited it from the years of the Vietnam War.

Ford, like Nixon, was convinced that excessive government spending was a major cause of the worst inflation the country had experienced since 1947. In 1973 inflation was driving up the cost of living at an annual rate of 9 percent. During 1974 the rate soared above 12 percent. People living on fixed incomes, principally the nation's elderly, were hardest hit.

Ford attempted to reduce federal spending and slow down the economy, but these efforts led to a sharp business slump. To add to the confusion, Ford and Congress disagreed over the best way to handle the still soaring cost of oil and gasoline and the threatening shortage of energy.

The election of 1976. With the election of 1976 approaching, Ford announced that he intended to run for the office that he had been occupying by appointment. His critics, including members of his own party, faulted him for lack of vigorous leadership. His supporters, although not all were enthusiastic about his candidacy, pointed out that he had helped to restore confidence in the Presidency.

Ford won a narrow victory at the nominating convention over Ronald Reagan of California, who represented the conservative wing of the Republican Party. The convention balanced the ticket with the choice of a Reagan conservative, Robert Dole of Kansas, as the Vice-Presidential candidate.

The Democratic convention again had a large representation of young delegates, women, blacks, and liberals. It chose Jimmy Carter of Georgia on the first ballot with Senator Walter F. Mondale of Minnesota as his running mate.

Carter had been almost unknown on the national stage when he first began to run for the nomination. His spectacular campaign in the state primaries attracted wide attention and led to his nomination.

Carter had attended Annapolis. After a successful career as a naval officer, he had returned to his home state of Georgia. There he had built up the family peanut business and later served as governor of the state.

The key issues in the election campaign were inflation and unemployment. Although Carter and Ford met in televised debates, the first since the Kennedy-Nixon debates of 1960, neither candidate aroused much enthusiasm. As a result, right up to election day a large number of voters had not decided for whom to cast their ballots. Political pollsters said the election was "too close to call."

Jimmy Carter won, but by the narrowest of margins—297 electoral votes to Ford's 241. The Democrats once again swept the Congressional contests.

SECTION SURVEY

IDENTIFY: Nelson Rockefeller, amnesty, stagflation, Jimmy Carter.

1. (a) Why did President Ford pardon Richard Nixon? (b) Why did some people criticize the pardon?
2. (a) How did President Ford attempt to fight inflation? (b) What were the results?
3. (a) Describe the events that led up to the nominations of Gerald Ford and Jimmy Carter for President in 1976. (b) Why was the general election too close to call?

6 Presidents Carter and Reagan face critical domestic problems

On January 20, 1977, Jimmy Carter was sworn in as the 39th President of the United States. Following the inaugural ceremony, he and his wife, Rosalynn, walked down Pennsylvania Avenue to the White House.

During the campaign Carter had promised, if elected, to stay in close touch with the American people. The walk—rather than the usual ride in a large limousine surrounded by Secret Service men—was a symbol of his intention to keep the promise.

Beginning "an open administration." The next day, as one of his first Presidential acts, Carter granted an unconditional pardon to the draft evaders of the Vietnam War. The pardon, which President Ford had refused to grant, did not include deserters, whose cases were to be treated individually.

In his first report to the nation, President Carter pledged, among other things, that government regulations would be written in "plain English." He said he would hold "town hall meetings" to keep in touch with the people. He also planned "call-in" sessions on the radio and TV networks to answer questions. He held the first of these "call-in" sessions early in March, and for two hours took phone calls directly from the people. A few days later, he made a trip to New England where he attended an old-fashioned New England town meeting and answered questions directed to him from the audience.

Before long, however, President Carter discovered that his executive duties left him little time for direct communication with even a sampling of ordinary citizens. Problems both at home and abroad confined him closer and closer to the White House. Within a few months, critics were complaining that he was too heavily preoccupied with foreign affairs. They claimed that he was neglecting the increasingly serious domestic problems, particularly unemployment, inflation, and energy.

Combating unemployment. Through the fall and winter of 1976–77, the nation seemed to be slowly but steadily recovering from the recession of 1972–75. Unemployment remained high, however, especially among blacks and Hispanics in the cities. For the country as a whole it averaged about 7 percent. This meant that approximately 7 million men and women were out of work.

Shortly after Carter took office, he sent Congress a plan designed to stimulate the economy and provide jobs. The plan called for a $50 rebate on 1976 taxes for every American citizen. It also called for tax cuts to encourage business to increase capital investments, which in turn would open new employment opportunities. Congress adopted the plan but, with Carter's approval, eliminated the rebates.

The efforts to reduce unemployment met only limited success. In the fall of 1978, almost two years after Carter became President, more than 6 million Americans remained jobless. Congress tried again to remedy the situation with a tax cut. The bill called for $18.7 billion of tax relief, mainly for upper-middle-class and wealthy Americans. Senator Edward M. Kennedy, speaking for large numbers of critics, urged the President to veto the bill. He claimed that it "unfairly ignored the needs of the average taxpayer for tax relief." Despite the widespread protests, Carter signed the bill.

At the same time, Congress adopted and the President approved the Humphrey-Hawkins "full employment" bill. The bill set as a national goal the reducing of unemployment to 4 percent by 1983. It also set as a goal the reducing of inflation to 3 percent by 1983 and to zero by 1988. The law did not say how the President and Congress would achieve these goals. It did, however, state that any programs used to combat inflation must not be permitted to interfere with efforts to reduce unemployment.

Other economic issues. During 1977 and 1978, while the Carter administration was struggling to combat unemployment, the cost of living rose sharply. By the fall of 1978, it was growing at the rate of 10 percent a year. Carter then tried to fight inflation with a voluntary system of wage and price controls.

The President's anti-inflation program was received with mixed reactions. Business, in general, favored it. Organized labor protested that it was unfair. Why, labor asked, had the President failed to include guidelines for interest rates, dividends, and profits?

President Carter also tried to raise the shrunken value of the dollar in the interna-

Following his inauguration in January 1977, President Jimmy Carter broke tradition and walked back to the White House from the Capitol Building, a surprise to the cheering crowds thronging Pennsylvania Avenue.

tional markets. At the same time, he attempted to reduce the nation's unfavorable balance of trade. This imbalance was especially marked in regard to Japan. The Japanese were successfully competing in the American market with automobiles, electronic equipment, agricultural and industrial machinery, and other products. The value of Japanese imports into the United States now far outweighed American sales to Japan.

Finally, in a further effort to control inflation, the President proposed to reduce federal spending. His "lean budget" reduced expenditures for social services while increasing military spending by 3 percent. It was severely criticized by farmers, minorities, and liberals in general.

The anti-inflationary measures also had an undesirable side effect. They increased unemployment. By the summer of 1980, America was moving deeper and deeper into a recession. With the Presidential elections approaching in the fall, this was worrisome news indeed for Jimmy Carter.

The energy problem. The energy problem remained the most urgent of all the long-term domestic problems facing the nation. Energy costs also contributed greatly to the soaring rate of inflation.

Four months after he took office, Carter sent his energy program to Congress. It emphasized the need for conservation. Speaking over the television networks, the President warned of a possible "national catastrophe" unless Congress and the people as a whole united behind the conservation effort.

Carter's program was called a "carrot-and-stick" approach. It mixed incentives to conserve energy with penalties to discourage wasteful practices. It proposed to increase the cost of domestically produced oil and gas by gradually deregulating prices of these fuels. The plan called for Presidential authority to impose additional taxes on gasoline to discourage its use. It stressed the development of other sources of energy, especially coal, nuclear power, and solar energy.

Not until the fall of 1978 did Congress pass an energy bill. The bill was a much watered-down version of Carter's original proposal. It provided some new taxes and tax credits and did begin to deregulate fuel prices. Congress also set aside $54 billion for highway improvement and the development of mass transit systems.

In the meantime Congress had created the Department of Energy (DOE). The DOE was given the major responsibility for improving older energy systems and developing alternative energy sources.

An energy crisis. Events overseas contributed to energy problems in the United States. A revolution in Iran (see page 442) stopped oil shipments from that country. This disturbed the flow of oil to nations around the world.

Americans felt the impact by the spring of 1979. Gas shipments to filling stations were reduced or cut off. Many stations cut back their business hours or closed altogether. Lines of cars waiting for gas soon jammed city streets. Waits of an hour or more were common. Several states adopted systems to restrict the days on which gas could be bought. To add to the crisis, oil exporting nations soon raised their oil prices, which sent the cost of gas and oil products soaring.

By the summer of 1979, Americans had cut back somewhat on their use of gas. The gas shortage eased, but the danger of another crisis

Signs of the worsening energy situation in the late 1970's were the seemingly endless lines of cars stretching from gas stations along jammed city streets in some parts of the nation. People often waited an hour or more to get gas.

still existed. In July Carter set forth another energy plan, calling for a massive program to develop synthetic fuels. The long-range goal of the plan was to cut importation of oil in half.

Obstacles to Carter's success. By the summer of 1980, a public opinion poll revealed that only 21 percent of the American people approved of President Carter's performance in office. This was the lowest figure for a President since the 1930's, when the poll was first taken. It was even lower than the figure for President Nixon at the height of the Watergate affair. Why was Carter's rating so low?

Part of the answer lay in Carter's inexperience. When running for office he had stressed his independence from Washington's political establishment. This helped him in the campaign but hurt him in office. He often had trouble enlisting support for his programs, even among members of his own party.

Part of the problem was the programs themselves. They were hard to define. He proclaimed his first energy program as "the moral equivalent of war" but failed to press Congress to pass the bill. He seemed changeable, almost fickle at times. In 1979 he changed five of his Cabinet members, among them the Secretary of HEW, whom he had just praised for doing an excellent job.

Part of the trouble lay in the nature of the problems Carter faced. Energy, inflation, unemployment, foreign affairs—they were all complicated. They had no easy solutions, and at times it seemed that Carter offered no solutions at all.

Choosing candidates. The campaign for the Presidential nominations in 1980 was a long one. Critics, in fact, began to ask whether the United States needed a system as lengthy, costly, and complex to nominate candidates.

Ronald Reagan was again a leading contender for the Republican nomination. He held off challenges from a variety of opponents and easily won the nomination at Detroit. He picked George Bush, one of those former opponents, as his running mate.

Jimmy Carter wanted to run for reelection. Usually a President in office has little trouble in securing his party's nomination. By early 1980, however, Carter's popularity was low. Many Democrats feared that if Carter ran again it would mean defeat for the Democratic Party in November. Senator Edward Kennedy

of Massachusetts challenged Carter for the nomination. As the incumbent, Carter had the edge and in the end won renomination from his party. Walter Mondale again was the candidate for Vice-President.

Many people were unhappy with the choice between Carter and Reagan. Representative John Anderson of Illinois recognized this dissatisfaction. Originally, he had tried for the Republican nomination but had lost to Reagan. Now he decided to run as an independent candidate who would appeal to such people.

The election of 1980. The election campaign of 1980 was hard fought. Reagan warned of the nation's military weakness. He also stressed Carter's failure to solve the nation's economic problems. He reminded voters of the ever-rising rates of inflation and unemployment and spoke of the current recession as the "Carter depression." If elected, Reagan promised, he would cut spending in government, cut taxes, and stimulate business.

Carter tried to remind people of his foreign policy achievements. For the first time since Herbert Hoover was President, he claimed, no American soldier had died in battle. He spoke of improved relations with China and the Egyptian-Israeli peace treaty. Carter pointed out the number of times in the past when Reagan had favored military intervention. Carter reminded voters that in a nuclear age a President had to show restraint.

Once again political pollsters said the election was too close to call. Thus, for many, the morning after election day was a surprise. Reagan had won a sweeping victory with 42,797,153 popular votes compared with Carter's 34,434,100. The electoral vote was 489 to 49. Anderson received no electoral votes.

Analyzing the results. More surprising than the size of Reagan's victory was the outcome in Congressional races. The Republicans won control of the Senate for the first time since 1952. The Democrats kept control of the House, but Republicans made gains there as well.

Many people asked if the Republican victory represented a new movement in politics. Were Americans becoming more conservative? Were they tired of massive federal programs that raised their taxes and complicated their lives as Reagan charged? Or had they simply rejected Carter for failing to handle the large problems adequately?

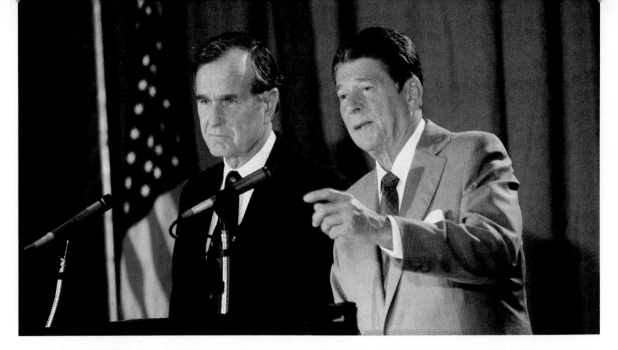

Ronald Reagan and George Bush proved to be a formidable team for the Republican Party. They won the 1980 election by a wide margin, foiling the bid by Democrats Jimmy Carter and Walter Mondale for reelection.

The Republicans take control. President Reagan entered office with widespread support from the public. His warm, winning, relaxed good nature and his reputation for managing personal differences added a nice touch to the "honeymoon" initially enjoyed by new administrations.

Reagan's popularity, high from the beginning, soared to new heights when, 70 days after he became President, he survived an assassination attempt. His courage and grace when he was shot, seriously wounded, and hospitalized won him the sympathy, good will, and respect of the American people.

Reagan's economic program. Reagan outlined his economic program during the election campaign. Once in office, he began immediately to try to win support for it and move it through Congress.

The first priority was victory over inflation. In order to win this victory, the government would have to balance the budget—that is, to reduce expenditures to match the amount of money available from taxes. The Republicans proposed to balance the federal budget by cutting government spending and by reducing taxes at the same time.

The Reagan program aroused a storm of controversy. Many critics charged that the proposed tax cuts favored the wealthy and corporations. They also claimed that spending cuts would damage programs that aided the needy, protected the environment, and supported public education. Critics also insisted that tax cuts could not be combined with the huge military spending Reagan was calling for. They warned that such a policy would only increase inflation.

In the face of such criticism, Reagan argued strongly for his economic program and won much public support. Plans for cuts in both taxes and federal spending were passed by Congress.

Yet even before his program took effect, Reagan called for additional spending cuts to balance the budget. For example, he proposed disbanding the Departments of Energy and of Education. How well the program would work, even with more cuts, remained to be seen.

SECTION SURVEY

IDENTIFY: Humphrey-Hawkins bill, fixed income, energy conservation, Department of Energy, Edward Kennedy, John Anderson.

1. What programs did President Carter support to (a) fight unemployment, (b) reduce inflation, and (c) solve the energy problem? How effective were his efforts in these areas?

2. What factors contributed to President Carter's unpopularity as President?

3. Describe the (a) candidates, (b) issues, and (c) results of the election of 1980.

424

Chapter Survey

Summary: Tracing the Main Ideas

John F. Kennedy's prediction in 1960 that the United States was entering one of the most critical periods in its history proved all too true. Between 1960 and 1980, the American people had to contend with the problems of unemployment, inflation, and the worldwide threat of a shortage of energy. As you will read later (see Chapter 24), the government and the American people also had to face the crisis confronting the nation's cities, a crisis closely related to the demands by the nation's minorities for freedom and justice.

The Presidents you have read about in this chapter also faced serious difficulties abroad. Warm relations with old allies cooled and old enemies became new friends. New nations began to play an increasingly important part in world affairs. The United States' foreign policies, of which you will read in Chapter 23, influenced and interacted with its domestic policies. Indeed, at times it was difficult to untangle the two.

Inquiring into History

1. Compare the goals and accomplishments of the New Frontier and the Great Society.
2. Make a list of the major legislation passed during the administrations of Presidents Kennedy, Johnson, Nixon, Ford, and Carter. (a) Which Presidents were most successful in getting legislation passed? Why? (b) Which Presidents were generally considered effective? How do their reputations compare with their legislative records?
3. It has been said that the United States has become more democratic in recent years. Do you agree or disagree? Give specific examples to support your answer.
4. List the key issues in the Presidential elections since 1960. (a) In which campaigns were the issues similar? (b) Why do you think these issues kept reappearing?

Relating Past to Present

1. In recent years television has become an important force in American politics. How does television affect elections during the campaigns and on election day?

2. Do you think Congress or the President should have the leading role in shaping government policies? Use examples from the Presidential administrations described in this chapter to support your opinion.
3. How did Reagan's plans for fighting inflation compare to Carter's plans? Carter was unsuccessful in his attempt to deal with the problem. Based on your knowledge of Reagan's administration, do you think he was more or less successful? Explain.

Developing Social Science Skills

1. Make line graphs to illustrate the ups and downs of inflation and unemployment since 1960. (Use a source such as *Statistical Abstract of the United States* to find the statistics.) Where the graph shows years of extreme highs or lows, explain why these extremes occurred.
2. Select one of the Presidential administrations discussed in this chapter. For display on the bulletin board, prepare an illustrated time line of the major events of the administration. Use pictures from magazines, newspaper clippings, political cartoons, or your own drawings to illustrate the time line.

1955	
	Chapter 23
1960	# Reexamining the Nation's Role in World Affairs
Cuban missile crisis	## 1960–1980's
Gulf of Tonkin Resolution	From the 1960's through the 1980's, Americans faced a complex, troubling domestic scene. First President Kennedy and later Presidents Johnson, Nixon, Ford, Carter, and Reagan all tried to cope with these domestic problems. Often, however, their attention was held by events overseas.
1965	
Arab-Israeli war	The United States had taken on the responsibilities of world leadership. Americans were now learning that such responsibility could be a heavy burden and could have serious effects on their lives at home. Worldwide problems—pollution of the environment, nuclear disarmament, feeding of the rapidly growing population—demanded attention. Trying to solve such problems required international cooperation, a sense of national purpose, and large sums of money.
1970	
Nixon visits China	
Détente with Soviet Union begins	America's growing involvement in Vietnam was of deepest concern because it affected all the other problems. This involvement in Southeast Asia would prove enormously costly in lives and resources. It would also deeply trouble large numbers of Americans and continue to haunt the nation long after the last Americans had left Vietnam.
Cease-fire in Vietnam War	
1975	In one sense, Vietnam was part of a larger issue confronting Americans: Had the United States assumed more responsibilities around the world than it could possibly meet, even with all its wealth and power?
Camp David accords signed	These were among the issues troubling Americans during the 1960's and 1970's and as the United States entered the third century of its history.
Iran seizes American hostages	
1980	
Hostages freed	### THE CHAPTER IN OUTLINE
	1. The United States assumes global responsibilities.
1985	2. The United States becomes deeply involved in Vietnam.
	3. World tensions are relaxed during the Nixon and Ford administrations.
	4. World tensions build up during the Carter and Reagan administrations.
2000	

1 The United States assumes global responsibilities

During the 1960's and 1970's, the dangers of nuclear war and Communist aggression continued to haunt Americans. At the same time, new global developments thrust increasingly heavy demands upon the American people and their leaders.

A changing world. One major development was the growing competition American business faced from Japan, the Soviet Union, and the Common Market countries of Western Europe. These nations, with modern, efficient industrial plants and equipment, had become serious competitors of the United States for world markets.

Another revolutionary development was the entry of a large number of new nations into the world community. By 1979 UN membership had grown to 151 nations. The new member nations represented more than 1 billion people. Most of these new nations had emerged from former colonies in the nonindustrial areas of Asia and Africa.

Shifting relationships. A third major development was the changing balance of world power. After World War II the Communist nations, led by the Soviet Union, had been aligned on one side, the United States and its allies on the other. During the 1960's this alignment began to crumble.

The newly independent nations of Asia and Africa were reluctant to tie themselves to either the Soviet Union or the United States. These nations, together with developing countries in Latin America, made up what came to be called the **Third World**. These Third World nations became increasingly important in world affairs.

Meanwhile the solid front of communism was breaking up as Communist China opposed the Soviet Union's leadership of world communism. By 1964 the leaders of the Soviet Union and Communist China were openly attacking each other's policies. By the late 1960's, the split between the two most powerful Communist countries was complete.

The solid front among anti-Communist nations was also becoming strained. President

In 1966 President Charles de Gaulle of France pulled his country out of the NATO alliance. What attitude does de Gaulle demonstrate in this cartoon? Do you think the cartoonist approves of de Gaulle's action?

Charles de Gaulle of France began to challenge America's leadership role. He hoped to establish France at the head of a group of nations with power and influence equal to that of the United States and the Soviet Union. In 1966 de Gaulle showed that the solid front had cracked by pulling France out of the NATO alliance.

By the 1960's all of the powerful nations—both Communist and non-Communist—were competing for the markets as well as the political support of the Third World nations. Thus many of the world crises facing the United States grew out of the problems of Africa, Latin America, and Asia.

Kennedy's foreign policy. In this rapidly changing world, President Kennedy and, later, President Johnson generally followed the basic foreign policy developed under Truman and Eisenhower. However, there were new steps in foreign policy during the early 1960's. The Trade Expansion Act of 1962 was passed to increase world trade as well as to meet the growing competition of the Common Market countries. Kennedy and Johnson also sponsored programs to strengthen international cultural relations by sending outstanding American musicians, theater groups, writers, and artists to visit friendly, neutral, and Communist countries.

The Peace Corps. The most imaginative new program was the Peace Corps. This was a government-supported organization of Americans who volunteered to live among the people of underdeveloped lands and to help them with day-to-day problems. In September 1961 the first American volunteers arrived in the African nation of Ghana to serve as teachers.

From the beginning the Peace Corps was a notable success. By 1970, Americans, mostly young men and women, were serving overseas in 59 different countries. The Peace Corps symbolized America's desire to provide humane assistance as well as economic and military leadership in the non-Communist world.

Trouble in Africa. President Kennedy had to deal with the problems of America's relations with the emerging African nations. The most serious crisis developed in the Congo (now the Republic of Zaïre).

The Congo, a former Belgian colony, became independent in June 1960. Many rival groups — among them pro-Communist and pro-Western groups — battled for control of the government. The problem grew worse when the mineral-rich Katanga province seceded from the newly formed nation.

In response to an appeal by the Congo government, the UN sent troops from African and Asian nations to police the troubled country.

The UN force prevented a full-scale civil war, but it was not at first able to end the bloodshed. A new crisis developed in 1961 when Patrice Lumumba, leader of the pro-Communist faction, was assassinated. Soviet Premier Khrushchev demanded withdrawal of all UN troops and threatened to intervene. President Kennedy warned that the United States would defend the UN operation.

With firm American backing, the UN continued its difficult peacemaking operation in the Congo. By 1965 the fighting ended and Katanga province rejoined the nation. By the late 1960's, most scars of the civil war seemed healed. The Congo (Zaïre) became one of the most prosperous African nations.

Cuba and the Bay of Pigs. President Kennedy faced a very serious problem in Cuba. Early in 1959, guerrilla forces led by Fidel Castro overthrew the government of Cuban dictator Fulgencio Batista (bah·TEES·tah). At first the United States welcomed Castro's rise to power. However, American sympathy rapidly faded when Castro began to act like a ruthless dictator. He put to death hundreds of political enemies, jailed thousands, and took control of foreign-owned property. In addition, he lashed out against "Yankees" and accepted a Soviet offer of military aid if the United States interfered in Cuba.

By the summer of 1960, the United States had placed an embargo on the purchase of Cuban sugar. It had also urged the Organization of American States (O.A.S.) to condemn Cuba's actions.

Kennedy had inherited a plan developed under Eisenhower to overthrow the Castro government. During 1960 a force of anti-Castro Cubans had been trained in Central America with the active support of the United States Central Intelligence Agency (CIA). The plan called for this force to invade Cuba. According to the plan, the Cuban underground would rise, join the invaders, and overthrow the Castro government. President Kennedy decided to allow the plan to be carried out.

On April 17, 1961, the invasion force landed on the beaches of the Bahía de Cochinos, or the Bay of Pigs. The invasion was a total failure. The Cuban underground never joined the battle. Most of the invading "Freedom Fighters" were killed or captured. In reply to a storm of criticism, President Kennedy admitted that the invasion attempt had been a mistake and assumed full responsibility for it.

The Alliance for Progress. To deal with the Communist presence in Cuba, Kennedy proposed a program called the Alliance for Progress. The United States and 19 Latin-American countries (all but Cuba) had joined the Alliance by 1961.

The Alliance members agreed to a 10-year program to improve social and economic conditions in Latin America. Finances for the program were to come from private and government sources in Latin America and the United States plus Japan, Western Europe, and international agencies such as the World Bank.

During the first four years, the United States contributed $4.5 billion to the program,

MISSILE ERECTOR

CABLE

MISSILE SHELTER TENT

TRACKED PRIME MOVERS

OXIDIZER TANK TRAILERS

FUEL TANK TRAILERS

Photographs like this, taken on October 23, 1962, by an American U-2 spy plane, supplied President Kennedy with evidence of a Soviet-constructed missile launch base in Cuba. Such evidence triggered the Cuban missile crisis.

the Latin-American countries $22 billion. Some progress was made, but the results were disappointing. Much of the money was used to help business interests and military forces in Latin America rather than the masses of poor people. Congress, increasingly impatient, began to reduce the budgets for the Alliance.

The missile crisis. Meanwhile, relations with Cuba worsened. The United States cut off all trade with Cuba. The O.A.S. did not go that far, but it did vote Cuba out of the organization in 1962. Castro announced his commitment to communism, and the Soviet Union stepped up shipments of military equipment to Cuba. This led to a frightening crisis in the fall of 1962.

In mid-October American intelligence sources reported that the Soviet Union was equipping Cuba with long-range jet bombers and offensive missiles that could deliver nuclear bombs to most of the eastern United States. On October 22 President Kennedy ordered the Navy to establish a blockade—or "quarantine"—against any further shipment of offensive weapons to Cuba. He also demanded that the Soviet Union immediately dismantle the Cuban missile bases and withdraw Soviet missiles and bombers from Cuba.

The world waited tensely for Khrushchev's reaction. Faced with the choice between nu-

clear war or meeting Kennedy's demands, Khrushchev backed down. During the next few weeks, the Soviets began to dismantle the missile bases and remove the missiles and bombers. Nonetheless, a Communist nation supported by the Soviet Union was now established only 90 miles (144 kilometers) from the United States.

The Dominican issue. Another Latin-American crisis arose in the spring of 1965. A revolution plunged the Dominican Republic into chaos. Calling the situation "grave," President Johnson ordered 400 marines into the Dominican capital, Santo Domingo. His aim was to protect the lives of Americans there. This was the first time since 1926 that the marines had been ordered into a Latin-American country. During the next two weeks, 22,000 additional American troops landed, and 10,000 more stood by in navy vessels offshore.

President Johnson justified his action on the grounds that it was necessary to prevent a possible Communist takeover and to enable the people to hold free elections. He made it clear that the American forces would be withdrawn as soon as the O.A.S. took responsibility for maintaining order.

Representatives of the O.A.S. accepted the responsibility. By midsummer a small force of

429

troops from four Latin-American nations had arrived in Santo Domingo. Some of the United States troops were then withdrawn. In late August both sides accepted a provisional president who governed until elections were held in June 1966.

Crisis in Berlin. In Europe, too, Kennedy faced a challenge from the Soviet Union. In 1961 Soviet Premier Khrushchev renewed his threat to end the Western nations' rights of free access to West Berlin. Kennedy warned in turn that the United States would not abandon West Berlin.

In August 1961 the East German government began to erect a wall along the line between East and West Berlin. The Berlin Wall cut off the escape of East Germans into West Germany. It became a grim symbol of the conflicts between the Communist and anti-Communist nations of Europe.

The nuclear test ban. In August 1961 Premier Khrushchev also announced that the Soviet Union intended to resume nuclear testing. This news shocked people everywhere, for in 1958 the nuclear powers—the United States, Great Britain, and the Soviet Union—had agreed to suspend all testing for three years. The three-year period had not yet expired. President Kennedy warned that if the Soviets carried out their plans, the United States would be forced in the interests of its own defense to resume nuclear testing.

Nevertheless, the Soviets began a series of nuclear tests in the fall of 1961. The following spring, after the Soviet Union had turned down repeated pleas for a fully effective test ban and a general arms reduction, the United States began its own tests.

The first breaks in the long deadlock came in 1963. In June Moscow and Washington agreed on a "hot line" to provide direct teletype communications between the two capitals to help prevent nuclear war by accident.

In July American, British, and Soviet representatives agreed to ban nuclear tests in the atmosphere, under water, and in space. Underground testing would continue. The United States Senate ratified the agreement, and it went into effect in October 1963.

Communist China. The United States met its most difficult problems in Asia. There Communist China continued to threaten trouble in much of Asia. In 1959 the Chinese Communists took over Tibet. In 1962, following a border dispute, they launched a large-scale attack on India. In response to appeals from the Indian government, the United States and Great Britain airlifted military supplies to the hard-pressed Indian troops. Then China announced a cease-fire and called for negotiations. India, shocked by what it considered unprovoked aggression, began to build up its defenses.

Conflict in Southeast Asia. In addition to China, the new countries of Southeast Asia—Laos, Cambodia, and North and South Vietnam became major crisis areas during the troubled 1960's.

The tiny kingdom of Laos was divided into three political factions—pro-Western, Communist, and neutral. In an effort to secure a strong pro-Western government, the United States poured millions of dollars into Laos. This effort failed. Finally, in 1962, after lengthy negotiations the Laotian factions agreed to a neutral government in Laos.

The United States also gave considerable military and economic aid to Cambodia in an effort to secure a pro-Western government. As in Laos, however, the policy failed. In 1963 Cambodia asked the United States to withdraw its military and technical personnel. You will read about increasing American involvement in Cambodia and in South Vietnam in the following section.

SECTION SURVEY

IDENTIFY: Third World, Trade Expansion Act of 1962, Peace Corps, Congo crisis, Premier Khrushchev, Fidel Castro, Bay of Pigs invasion, quarantine, Berlin Wall, "hot line."

1. (a) How did relationships among Communist nations change during the 1960's? (b) How did relationships among non-Communist nations change? (c) How did the rise of the Third World affect the foreign policy of both the United States and the Soviet Union?

2. The Cuban missile crisis brought the world to the brink of nuclear war in 1962. Explain.

3. Review United States relations with Latin America in (a) the Alliance for Progress and (b) the Dominican crisis.

4. (a) What was United States policy toward Asia in the early 1960's? (b) How successful was that policy?

2 The United States becomes deeply involved in Vietnam

The most serious problem that the United States faced between 1960 and 1980 was a war in South Vietnam. This war had a great impact on the image of America around the world. It also influenced the way Americans perceived their own country and its role in the world.

Background to war. As you have read (page 362), when France pulled out of Vietnam in the 1950's, an international agreement divided that country into two parts. Elections that would have reunited the country, scheduled for 1956, were never held. Instead Vietnam continued to exist as two nations. North Vietnam, with its capital at Hanoi, was under a Communist government headed by Ho Chi Minh. South Vietnam, with its capital at Saigon, was a republic whose president was Ngo Dinh Diem (NOH DIN DYEM). Diem's government had strong backing from the United States.

Although the promised elections were not held, many Vietnamese still wanted a united country. Vietnamese guerrillas, backed by North Vietnam, fought to overthrow Diem's regime and unite the countries. In 1960 the guerrillas took the name of the National Liberation Front (NLF). Their opponents referred to them as the Viet Cong (Vietnamese Communists).

American involvement. The United States was deeply concerned over events in South Vietnam. Not long before, Communists had taken over China and had barely been beaten back in Korea. Now a Communist movement was gaining strength in South Vietnam.

President Eisenhower warned of the danger of a "domino" effect in Southeast Asia. He meant that if the government of one nation there fell to the Communists, then the government of the neighboring nation would topple in turn. According to this view, all of Southeast Asia might end up in Communist hands if one nation fell. To prevent the fall of South Vietnam to the Communists, millions of dollars in military aid and 800 United States military advisers were sent to South Vietnam during Eisenhower's administration.

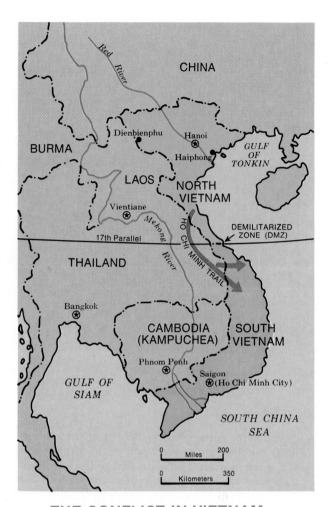

THE CONFLICT IN VIETNAM

Eisenhower's belief in a "domino effect" was shared by President Kennedy. Kennedy declared that United States foreign policy depended "in considerable measure upon a strong and free Vietnamese nation."

The formation of the NLF in 1960 was followed by increased guerrilla activity. In response, Kennedy increased the amount of military aid and the number of advisers to the threatened Diem regime.

The fall of Diem. However, Diem's administration was corrupt, and he became increasingly unpopular in South Vietnam. He harshly repressed Buddhists and political opponents. Also, his failure to control the NLF angered South Vietnamese military leaders. Kennedy pressured Diem to make reforms, but Diem failed to do so.

431

"Ike made a promise," President Lyndon Johnson often said, "and I have to keep it." Here, on a trip to South Vietnam, he visits some of the hundreds of thousands of American troops sent to that nation to try to keep the promise.

Finally, the United States government learned that South Vietnamese military leaders were planning to seize power from Diem. Kennedy made no effort to stop them or to inform Diem. In 1963, the military took over, and Diem was assassinated.

The new government fared no better than Diem's in the struggle against the NLF. The United States nevertheless remained committed to South Vietnam. After Kennedy's death, President Johnson stated, "I am not going to be the President who saw Vietnam go the way China went." He expanded American aid programs. By late 1964 there were 23,000 American advisers in South Vietnam.

The Gulf of Tonkin Resolution. On August 4, 1964, President Johnson appeared on television with shocking news. He announced that two American destroyers had been attacked by North Vietnamese torpedo boats in the Gulf of Tonkin (see map, page 431). The President stated that he had therefore ordered American planes to bomb North Vietnamese torpedo bases and oil refineries. He also asked Congress to grant him authority to take action against North Vietnam.

The President did not tell the nation that the American ships had been assisting South Vietnamese gunboats that were making raids on North Vietnam's coast. He also did not inform the nation that there was some doubt whether there had been any attack on the American ships at all.

Three days later Congress granted the President's request. It adopted what became known as the Gulf of Tonkin Resolution. This gave the President power "to take all necessary measures to repel any armed attack against the forces of the United States and to prevent further aggression."

The House voted unanimously for the measure. The Senate passed it by a vote of 88 to 2. Senator Wayne Morse of Oregon, who voted against it, warned that "we are in effect giving the President warmaking powers in the absence of a declaration of war. I believe that to be a historic mistake."

A turning point. As late as October 1964, President Johnson still stated that he did not intend to commit American troops to a war in Asia. "We are not," he declared, "about to send American boys nine or ten thousand miles away from home to do what Asian boys ought to be doing for themselves." Nevertheless, the Gulf of Tonkin Resolution changed the situation in South Vietnam and marked a turning point in United States participation there.

Viet Cong attacks in South Vietnam continued, and American responses grew stronger. In February 1965 President Johnson ordered American planes to bomb targets in North Vietnam. The bombing of North Vietnam would continue, with occasional pauses, until March 1968.

President Johnson ordered more United States ground forces to South Vietnam as well. In March 1965 the first marines landed there. By early 1966 there were 190,000 United States troops in South Vietnam. By mid-1966 the number was 265,000. By the end of 1967 it had risen to 500,000.

A widening war. As American aid increased, North Vietnam increased its support of the Viet Cong. Supplies flowed from North to South Vietnam over a network of routes that became known as the Ho Chi Minh Trail. As the war went on, troops from North Vietnam also moved south along the trail to join the Viet Cong in the fighting.

The United States tried in several ways to end the fighting. President Johnson halted bombing raids for brief periods. He also offered $1 billion in economic aid to Southeast Asia. Nevertheless, the North Vietnamese continued to insist that the United States had to get out of Vietnam before peace talks could begin. This the United States refused to do.

Differing strategies. Unlike the Communists, the Americans and the South Vietnamese relied heavily on air power in fighting the war. The Air Force poured bombs, napalm, rockets, and machine-gun fire on Viet Cong villages, hideouts, and supply routes in South Vietnam. In North Vietnam air raids were aimed at supply depots, industrial plants, and strategic roads and bridges. By the end of 1968, Americans had dropped more bombs on North Vietnam than they had used during all of World War II.

With support from the air, South Vietnamese and American ground forces carried out "search-and-destroy" missions against the Viet Cong. In areas they could not hold or defend, they moved the people to refugee centers and burned the villages.

The Viet Cong and the North Vietnamese, who lacked extensive air power, usually avoided large-scale fighting. Instead they used guerrilla tactics and terrorism. They planted bombs in a country marketplace or on a street in a busy city. They tortured or assassinated unfriendly village leaders. They practiced "hit-and-run" warfare, striking swiftly, then melting back into the jungle.

Effects of the war. The war had a shattering impact on all participants. In South Vietnam, a country about the size of the state of Washington, more than 1.6 million troops were fighting by 1968.° By that time American casualties totaled more than 27,000 killed and 92,000 seriously wounded.

Vietnamese civilians bore the heaviest burden of suffering. Though air strikes were aimed at military targets, civilians were often the victims. By the end of 1967, civilian casualties were totaling between 100,000 and 150,000 a year. By 1968 at least 2 million of the 16 million people of South Vietnam were displaced and had become refugees.

Elections in South Vietnam. The United States knew that the people of South Vietnam would have to have faith in their government if the war was to be won. For this to happen, the Vietnamese people would have to believe that their government was genuinely concerned about their welfare.

Unfortunately graft and corruption had continued under the rule of the military leaders who overthrew Diem. The United States urged these leaders to end corruption and move toward a more democratic form of government.

South Vietnam held elections in the fall of 1967. Defying the Viet Cong, who tried to sabotage the elections, an estimated 51 percent of those eligible voted. The South Vietnamese elected General Nguyen Van Thieu (nuh·WIN van TYOO) as President.

Some American observers saw the election as a positive step toward a stable, democratic South Vietnamese government. At the same time, American military leaders were issuing optimistic reports on the progress of the fight-

°By the end of 1968, troops in the war numbered as follows: on the allied side about 750,000 South Vietnamese, 540,000 Americans, 45,000 South Koreans, and 15,000 Australians, New Zealanders, Thais, and Filipinos. There were an estimated 300,000 Viet Cong and North Vietnamese regulars.

SOURCES

THE GULF OF TONKIN RESOLUTION (1964)

Whereas naval units of the Communist regime in Vietnam, in violation of the principles of the Charter of the United Nations and of international law, have deliberately and repeatedly attacked United States naval vessels lawfully present in international waters, and have thereby created a serious threat to international peace; and

Whereas these attacks are part of a deliberate and systematic campaign of aggression that the Communist regime in North Vietnam has been waging against its neighbors and the nations joined with them in the collective defense of their freedom; . . . Now therefore, be it

Resolved by the Senate and House of Representatives of the United States of America in Congress assembled, That the Congress approves and supports the determination of the President, as Commander in Chief, to take all necessary measures to repel any armed attack against the forces of the United States and to prevent further aggression.

---

ing. The war, they claimed, would be over soon. Victory was in sight.

The Tet offensive. In February 1968 came startling evidence that victory was not near. The Viet Cong and the North Vietnamese launched surprise attacks all across South Vietnam during Tet, the lunar New Year holidays. They seized partial control of or terrorized 26 of the provisional capitals of South Vietnam.

The South Vietnamese and Americans soon beat back this Tet offensive. Nevertheless, the cost of victory was high. Large sections of several cities were blasted into rubble. Thousands of soldiers and civilians were killed. Also, the Viet Cong gained firm control of large areas of the countryside.

Aftereffects of Tet. The Tet offensive dealt a staggering blow to predictions that the enemy was being defeated. It also demonstrated that the "other war"—the effort of the Saigon government to win the loyalty of the Vietnamese people—was still far from won.

At the end of March 1968, with the Tet offensive still a raw memory, President Johnson declared that the United States would limit its bombing to invasion routes and to the area immediately north of the Demilitarized Zone (DMZ). This was a supposedly neutral strip of land separating North and South Vietnam.

The Hanoi government responded to Johnson's steps with the long-awaited offer to begin peace talks. In May 1968 the United States and North Vietnam began these talks in Paris.

Criticism of the war. The Tet offensive contributed to the mounting criticism of the war in the United States. By the fall of 1968, the Vietnam conflict had become the second longest war in American history and the third largest in terms of lives lost and money spent. Only the Revolutionary War had lasted longer, and only World War I and World War II had cost more in money, resources, and lives.

Growing numbers of Americans were convinced that the Vietnam War was a grave mistake. They felt that the conflict was basically a civil war in which the United States should have no part. Moreover, they added, the United States was destroying South Vietnam in the process of "saving it" from communism. These critics urged an immediate end to the bombing and a rapid end to the war.

A constitutional question. Congress criticized the war as well. In March 1968 the Senate Foreign Relations Committee held a televised hearing on the conduct of the war.

At the heart of Congress's concern was an issue of constitutional powers. The Constitution makes the President the commander in chief of the nation's armed forces. It also gives him extensive powers over the conduct of foreign affairs. Nevertheless, the Constitution reserves to Congress the power to declare war. Now in Vietnam the United States was engaged in an undeclared war over which Congress had little control.

Most Americans agreed that at times the President had to make major decisions without waiting for Congress to act. Did this mean, however, that in matters of war and peace the role of Congress was no longer relevant? No one, it seemed, had a conclusive answer.

The costs of commitment. Members of Congress and many Americans were also concerned with the larger issue of American foreign policy in general. The American commitment to stop the spread of communism had become enormous. By 1969 the United States was providing some form of aid to 70 nations. It had formal commitments to defend 42 nations against any form of aggression, Communist or otherwise. To back up these commitments, the United States had 3.5 million men and women in the armed forces. Another 1.2 million civilian employees supported these troops. As of January 1968, total military expenses amounted to $87.6 billion a year, or a total expenditure of $439 for each American.

Critics pointed out that Congress voted only $24 billion for human needs—health, education, and welfare—in that same year. They claimed that the war and huge foreign commitments drained resources that could be spent on problems at home.

Critics also claimed that military expenses were contributing to inflation at home. This would raise prices and make it more difficult to sell American products abroad. Thus even the economy would be damaged.

President Johnson's decision. Such criticisms of the war continued to mount. Debate over the course of the war spilled out onto the streets. Huge demonstrations were held to protest the war. At times, prowar and antiwar demonstrators clashed. Many people feared that the country was being torn apart.

President Johnson was eligible to run for reelection in 1968. Nevertheless, growing criticism of the war and strengthening political opposition meant his victory would be doubtful. In March 1968, when he announced the bombing limits, he also announced that he would not seek reelection.

SECTION SURVEY

IDENTIFY: Ho Chi Minh, Ngo Dinh Diem, NLF, Viet Cong, "domino effect," Gulf of Tonkin Resolution, Ho Chi Minh Trail, "search-and-destroy" missions, General Thieu, DMZ.

1. Trace the steps of American involvement in South Vietnam starting in 1962.

2. (a) What was the Tet offensive? (b) What were some of its consequences?

3. What were some of the arguments presented by opponents of the Vietnam War?

4. Source Study: According to the Source on page 434, why was the United States justified in taking action in South Vietnam?

3 World tensions are relaxed during the Nixon and Ford administrations

The war in Vietnam remained the most serious problem confronting the nation when Richard M. Nixon became its next President in January 1969.

Nixon's plan for Vietnam. During the election campaign, Nixon had declared that if elected he would "bring an honorable end to the war." Nixon's plan called for the gradual withdrawal of American troops as soon as the South Vietnamese showed that they were able to defend themselves. The plan also replaced the "search-and-destroy" policy with a "protective-reaction" policy. Under this new policy, American troops would engage the enemy only when attacked or threatened by attack. Nixon hoped that the new tactics would both reduce American casualties and help quiet the fierce opposition to the war.

The invasion of Cambodia. The Nixon plan disappointed those Americans who wanted a quick end to the nation's military involvement in Vietnam. They were further disheartened in the spring of 1970 by Nixon's startling announcement that South Vietnamese and American troops were crossing the border into "neutral" Cambodia. The objective of the invasion, Nixon said, was to destroy North Vietnamese and Viet Cong supply centers and camps along the eastern border of Cambodia. As soon as these centers from which the Viet Cong had been launching their attacks against South Vietnam had been wiped out, the troops would be withdrawn. Nixon promised that all American forces would be out of Cambodia by the end of June.

President Nixon kept his promise. In the meantime, however, the American invasion of Cambodia had triggered widespread antiwar demonstrations in the United States. Further, it intensified a long-standing conflict between Communist and non-Communist forces in the Southeast Asian nation.

The cease-fire agreement. The "protective-reaction" policy and the withdrawal of some American ground troops from South Vietnam during Nixon's first term in office did reduce American casualities. However, there was no reduction in the fury of the air war. American air power destroyed large areas in South Vietnam that were controlled by the Viet Cong and the North Vietnamese. American planes also mined the harbors of North Vietnam and rained bombs upon North Vietnamese supply routes and ammunition centers in Laos and Cambodia.

Meanwhile the negotiations in Paris continued. Nixon's foreign policy adviser, Henry Kissinger, patiently tried to break the deadlock. Just before the Presidential election of 1972, Kissinger announced that "peace is at hand," but the welcomed announcement was premature. The United States continued military operations for two months, including massive bombing of Hanoi during December. Early in January 1973, a cease-fire agreement finally was reached.

There were three key terms in the agreement. (1) The continued presence of North Vietnamese military forces in South Vietnam was tacitly agreed to. (2) South Vietnam was assured that it was to have a government of its own choosing. (3) The United States guaranteed continued economic and military aid to South Vietnam. President Nixon then withdrew the remaining American troops from South Vietnam. As a result of continuing pressure, most American prisoners of war were later released by North Vietnam.

The costs of war. American participation in this longest and most unpopular war in the nation's history had been enormously costly. By the spring of 1973, when the last troops left Vietnam, direct expenditures totaled $137 billion. Some 45,729 Americans had been killed in action and more than 300,000 wounded. As for the people of Southeast Asia, estimates put South Vietnamese deaths at 160,903 and those of the Viet Cong and North Vietnamese at 922,295. In addition, more than 6 million refugees were uprooted and made homeless. Large areas of Vietnam, Laos, and Cambodia had been devastated.

The Vietnam War left feelings of anger and division in American society. The sharp disagreement over what to do about thousands of American draft resisters and deserters who had fled to Canada, Sweden, and elsewhere was but one example of this lingering bitterness (see Chapter 22).

Most Americans agreed that there had to be "no more Vietnams." One element that had contributed to involvement in Vietnam was the President's war-making power (see page 432). Once the war in Vietnam had started, Congress could at any time have ended America's involvement by cutting off funds for further military operations. However, Congress was reluctant to take this step while American troops were in the conflict.

After the war's end, Congress addressed the issue. In November 1973, Congress overrode Nixon's veto of its War Powers Resolution. The law provided that no President could send American troops into combat for a period longer than 60 days unless Congress approved. The law also provided that Congress could, by a concurrent resolution, order the immediate removal of troops from an area of combat.

Later events in Southeast Asia. The peace in Southeast Asia did not last long. Communist forces there took the offensive in 1973 and 1974. In Cambodia, during 1974 and 1975, Communist troops captured much of the country and surrounded the capital of Phnom Penh. In April 1975 the remaining Americans were evacuated by helicopters and the Communist armies took control of Cambodia.

Meanwhile in South Vietnam, resistance to the Communists also was crumbling. By March 1975, South Vietnamese troops were in retreat before the advancing North Vietnamese and Viet Cong. In a last desperate effort to prevent a complete collapse of South Vietnam, President Ford asked Congress to vote $722 million in emergency military aid. Congress, certain that the South Vietnamese cause was hopeless and fearing a renewal of America's involvement, refused to support him.

By the end of April, Saigon was surrounded. American helicopters and ships lying off the coast withdrew the remaining Americans as well as 100,000 South Vietnamese. The Vietnamese refugees, for the most part destitute, were temporarily housed on American military bases until they could be relocated in the United States. Thus, with the Communist takeover of South Vietnam, three decades of fighting in Vietnam came to an end.

Nixon's foreign policies. Apart from the unpopular Vietnam War, Nixon's foreign policies won widespread approval. His success in improving relations with Communist China and the Soviet Union was impressive.

Nixon, like other recent Presidents, insisted upon maintaining a military force strong enough to meet any challenge to the nation's interests and security. He demonstrated his opposition to communism by insisting upon the continued exclusion of Cuba from the O.A.S. This opposition was also apparent in his approval of the secret use of funds by the CIA to try to prevent a Socialist-Communist election victory in Chile. The CIA later made it difficult for the Marxist government elected by those parties to govern. Like earlier Presidents, Nixon largely ignored the denial of human rights in anti-Communist countries that received American military and economic assistance in exchange for military bases. These countries included Spain, Greece, South Korea, South Vietnam, and Iran.

Nixon's foreign policy stressed skillful, realistic, and flexible diplomacy that would recognize changing conditions in the world. Nixon's chief adviser on foreign policy was Henry Kissinger. Kissinger was a refugee from Nazi Germany who had become a professor of political science at Harvard University.

Without conferring much with the Department of State, Nixon and Kissinger planned the broad outlines of American foreign policy. Their "personal diplomacy" involved an unprecedented number of conferences with leaders in other countries. President Nixon himself traveled to Western Europe, the Soviet Union, China, Canada, Iceland, and the Middle East for talks with other heads of state. Shortly after his reelection in 1972, he appointed Kissinger Secretary of State.

A new policy toward China. In one of his most dramatic moves, Nixon visited the People's Republic of China in February 1972. With this visit, the door that had been shut and barred between the two countries for more than 20 years began to swing open. Each government promised not to seek dominance in the Asian Pacific region, to cooperate in preventing other powers from doing so, and to avoid international war. Both governments agreed to develop trade, improve cultural and scientific relations, and work to restore full diplomatic relations. As for the major obstacle to improved relations, President Nixon promised eventual withdrawal of United States military forces from Taiwan and Indochina. In what was regarded as proof of America's desire to cooperate, the Nixon administration used its influence to support China's ally, Pakistan, when war broke out between Pakistan and India over the independence of East Pakistan (renamed Bangladesh).

Détente with the Soviet Union. In May 1972, three months after Nixon had visited Peking, he met for talks with Soviet leaders in Moscow. Nixon and Communist Party Secretary Leonid Brezhnev (BRESH·nev) agreed to cooperate in efforts to improve trade and to tackle world problems involving space, health, and the environment.

Early in 1972 the world was surprised to learn that a secret arrangement had been made for President Nixon to visit China. Just months earlier, the idea of an American President strolling in Peking would have been unthinkable.

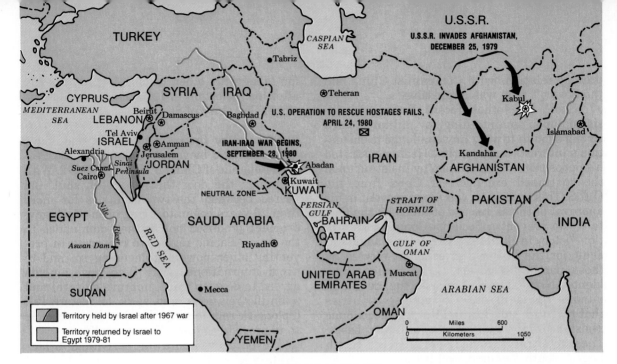

THE MIDDLE EAST

Nixon and Brezhnev also signed two documents intended to limit nuclear armaments. These documents were based upon earlier negotiations known as the Strategic Arms Limitation Talks (SALT). One of the documents, an executive agreement, froze offensive missiles at near existing levels for a five-year period. The other document, a treaty requiring Senate approval, limited each nation to two antiballistic missile sites in its territory. It also placed a limit on the size of American and Soviet land-based and submarine-based missile forces. The Senate ratified this treaty in August 1973. Throughout the world, people hoped that the United States and the Soviet Union were moving away from the confrontations of the Cold War. The two countries seemed to be entering a period of **détente**, or the gradual relaxation and reduction of tensions between them.

Arab-Israeli conflict.   One area of the globe that posed a threat to détente was the Middle East. As you have read, the Middle East had long been an area of international tension. After the Suez crisis, the bitter quarrel between Israel and the Arab nations continued.

Another crisis came in 1967 when Israelis believed that the Arab nations were massing large military forces to destroy Israel. In June 1967, powerful Israeli forces struck at Egypt, Jordan, and Syria, defeating them in a war

lasting only six days. After the war Israel kept large areas of land that had belonged to these three Arab states.

The Arab nations were bitter at their defeat and doubly determined to destroy Israel. They began sending trained guerrillas into Israel. The Israelis continued to strike back.

For many years the Soviet Union sent aid of various kinds, including military aid, to the Arab nations but not to Israel. The United States tried to help the Arab nations overcome their poverty, and it gave military aid to those nations resisting communism. It also gave military aid to Israel.

The Yom Kippur War.   Another Arab-Israeli war erupted in October 1973. The war provided a major test of détente and of Secretary Kissinger's skill as a diplomat. Egypt and Syria, seeking to recover territories lost in the 1967 war, suddenly launched an attack upon Israel. The Israelis at that time were observing Yom Kippur, a day holy to Jews. They were caught by surprise and suffered heavy casualties.

By the second week of the war, however, Israeli troops were driving back Syrian tanks in the north and had crossed the Suez Canal in the south. Soon Israeli forces were within 60 miles (96 kilometers) of Cairo.

In the meantime the United Nations had called for a cease-fire, but the fighting continued. The Egyptians, faced with almost certain defeat, called upon the Soviet Union for help. The Soviets, angered by American failure to get Israel to accept the cease-fire, now threatened to send their own troops to help end the fighting. President Nixon immediately ordered a "precautionary alert" for all American forces around the world. A major military confrontation between the Soviet Union and the United States now seemed possible.

Fortunately, the two great powers persuaded the Arabs and the Israelis to accept the cease-fire and to prepare for negotiations. Détente had survived its first critical trial.

However, many Israelis were bitter at being forced to end the fighting just as a final victory was within their grasp. Also, the Arabs were angered by American support of the Israelis. Several Arab nations cut off all shipments of oil to the United States and other countries that were friendly to Israel. Although the immediate crisis was over, the cease-fire had brought only an uneasy peace.

President Ford's foreign policy. On August 9, 1974, Gerald R. Ford replaced Nixon as President. One of his first acts was to ask Henry Kissinger to continue to serve as Secretary of State. This move indicated that Ford intended to follow the basic foreign policy developed during the Nixon administration.

Congress, in which Ford had served for a quarter of a century, was prepared to accept the President's leadership. However, early in 1975, when Ford urged Congress to provide $222 million in military aid to Cambodia, Congress refused. Congress made it clear that it was determined to close the door on further military adventures by the United States.

A few months later, however, Congress joined in the praise of Ford's action in the *Mayaguez* incident. In May, the *Mayaguez,* an unarmed American cargo ship, was seized by Cambodian Communists. Ford promptly sent air, sea, and ground forces to free the vessel and its crew of 39 men. In the action 15 American servicemen were killed, 50 wounded, and 3 missing. The President was sharply criticized for what many considered an unnecessary and ill-timed venture. Others applauded him for acting decisively.

Changes in détente. When Ford became President, he had taken over negotiations on a trade agreement between the United States and the Soviet Union. Senator Henry Jackson

of Washington was one of many critics of the proposed agreement. Jackson insisted that trade between the two nations should not be freer until the Soviet Union relaxed its restrictions on the emigration of its citizens, including political dissenters and Jews who wanted to move to Israel.

In the fall of 1974, the Soviet Union apparently accepted the "Jackson amendment." They agreed at that time to increase the number of exit visas for Jewish citizens. A few months later, however, the Soviets rejected the trade agreement. Moscow declared that it could not allow the United States to interfere with Soviet emigration policy.

The Soviet rejection was a setback for the policy of détente. As you will see, during the Carter administration this rift in the policy became noticeably wider.

SECTION SURVEY

4 World tensions build up during the Carter and Reagan administrations

The period of détente between the United States and the Soviet Union promoted by President Nixon and encouraged by President Ford did not last long after 1976. By 1980 tensions were approaching the breaking point.

President Carter's goals. Several months after his inauguration in January 1977, President Carter outlined the goals of his administration in a speech delivered at Notre Dame University. "We are now free," he declared, "of that inordinate fear of communism which once led us to embrace any dictator who joined in that fear. We fought fire with fire, never thinking that fire is better fought with water."

Carter then went on to express the hope that the great powers would resolve not to try to impose their social systems on other countries. During his administration, he said, he intended to work to improve America's relations with its allies, to advance human rights everywhere in the world, and to make genuine progress in arms control.

Carter's inexperience hindered his efforts to carry out this program. In addition, he at times had to resolve the conflicting views of the men and women he had chosen to advise him on foreign affairs. His Secretary of State, Cyrus R. Vance, was an experienced diplomat who preferred to handle problems through patient negotiations. Vance often clashed with the President's tough-minded National Security Adviser, Zbigniew Brzezinski (zuh·BIG·nee·ehv bruh·ZHIN·skee), a Columbia University professor of political science. Brzezinski was more inclined to take a hard line, particularly on issues involving the Soviet Union.

The Panama Canal treaties. The first major test of the President's program developed over the Panama Canal treaties. As soon as the treaties were ratified, Panama would begin to exercise almost total control over the operation of the canal itself. By the year 2000, Panama would gain complete control of the canal.

The treaties caused a storm of controversy in Congress and throughout the country. Critics argued that the United States was surrendering national property and endangering the nation's security. Supporters, including the President, insisted that the United States had never possessed sovereignty over the Canal Zone. They also pointed out that the terms of the treaties prevented any hostile country from ever securing control.

After an extended and often bitter debate, the Senate finally ratified the treaties by a close vote in the spring of 1978.

The issue of human rights. In August 1975 the leaders of 33 European nations plus the United States and Canada had gathered in Helsinki, Finland. There the leaders signed a statement outlining the basic goals of "peace, security, justice, and cooperation." High on the list of commitments was the pledge to support "human rights."

Carter, as President, also placed the issue of human rights high on the list of priorities for his administration. Nevertheless, Carter's commitment to freedom and justice for all people everywhere met with mixed reactions both at home and abroad.

Not surprisingly, strong opposition came from countries ruled by military dictatorships. Many leaders from such countries often ignored the rights of their subjects. At the same time, however, many diplomats both in the United States and among its allies felt that by insisting upon worldwide observance of human rights the President was interfering in the domestic affairs of other countries. These critics reminded Carter that the United States would resent any effort by other nations to interfere in America's domestic affairs. They argued that the President's emphasis upon this issue did not help to relax international tensions or to promote world peace.

Africa. African affairs were another source of trouble for Carter. The huge continent had vast natural resources, a population of nearly half a billion, and a growing number of newly independent states. As a result, it was the scene of competition between the United States and the Soviet Union. Both powers as well as the other industrial nations attempted to establish their influence and their social and political systems in the African nations.

In 1975, during President Ford's administration, Portugal had withdrawn from Angola, and this last remaining colony in Africa won its independence. Angola was then torn by a civil war. Cuban troops trained and equipped by the Soviets soon moved in to support the Communist-inspired leaders.

Henry Kissinger, then Ford's Secretary of State, warned that the United States could not remain indifferent to Soviet interference in Africa. Yet Americans were reluctant to become involved in another Vietnam-type military venture. Thus, there was little the United States could do. As it developed, the Soviet success in Angola led to similar Cuban-Soviet intervention in other African countries, notably Ethiopia.

During Carter's administration the United States tried to counteract Communist intervention in Africa. The United States encouraged the African states to deal with their own problems and to solve them in their own way. Andrew Young, a black civil rights activist who had supported Carter's election campaign, served the President as Ambassador to the United Nations. Ambassador Young was an outspoken critic of white imperialism in Africa. He sharply criticized the Union of South Africa's racial policies and practices. He also strongly supported black majority rule in Rhodesia (now Zimbabwe).

Young's interest in and concern for Africa and the developing countries made him an influential figure in the United Nations. His followers were dismayed, therefore, when in August 1979 he resigned his post as Ambassador. Young's unauthorized meeting with a representative of the Palestine Liberation Organization (PLO) embarrassed the administration and forced him to submit his resignation. President Carter accepted the resignation with "deep regret."

The Middle East. The troubled Middle East provided the President with a major foreign policy achievement. The renewal of war between Egypt and Israel was a danger when Carter became President. The first really hopeful development came at the end of 1977 when President Sadat of Egypt accepted Premier Begin's invitation to visit Israel. A few weeks later, Begin returned the visit and the door was opened to the first peace negotiations since the Arab-Israeli War of 1973. During the next nine months, Secretary of State Vance worked with the Egyptians and the Israelis in an effort to hammer out an agreement. These discussions ended in a stalemate.

At this point, President Carter invited Begin and Sadat to meet with him in Washington and they accepted. At the end of 13 days of secret discussions at Camp David, the President's mountain retreat in nearby Maryland, they reached a tentative framework for a peace settlement.

In April 1979, gathered on the White House lawn, the three men signed a formal peace treaty. The treaty ended 30 years of war between Egypt and Israel. After the signing, in an emotion-filled moment, the three embraced. Each of them quoted the prophet Isaiah: "And they shall beat their swords into plowshares and their spears into pruning hooks."

Working out the details of the treaty proved a harder task. What should be done with the

This was the happy moment for which the Camp David meetings on Middle East peace were aiming—the signing of a framework for peace by Carter (center), Begin (right), and Sadat (left) at the White House.

lands Israel had occupied during the wars? How should Palestinian demands for a homeland on the Israeli-controlled West Bank of the Jordan River and on the Gaza Strip be handled? Israel did, among other things, return the Sinai to Egypt. Nevertheless, little progress was made on the remaining problems. The possibility of renewed war in the Middle East remained a constant threat.

President Carter's personal efforts to solve the Arab-Israeli conflict did not meet with unqualified approval. The Arabs were furious at what they called Sadat's "betrayal." Also they criticized Carter for bringing Egypt and Israel together into even an uncertain relationship. But many American critics felt that the President had tilted his influence toward the Egyptian-Palestinian side in order to maintain the good will of the Arab oil-exporting nations, particularly Saudi Arabia.

Iran. For many years Iran, across the Persian Gulf from Saudi Arabia's rich oil fields, had been a key to United States defense arrangements in the Middle East. Back in 1953 the United States had helped overthrow what it considered a pro-Communist government in Iran. With American backing the Shah Mohammed Reza Pahlevi had been restored to his throne. During the 1970's the Shah received about $8 billion worth of American military equipment. The Shah harshly repressed political opponents. His secret police, some of whom had been trained by Americans, were accused of torturing and murdering such opponents.

Anger against the Shah flared up in a revolution in 1979, and the Shah fled the country. His government was overthrown by a militant religious leader, the Ayatollah Khomeini (AH·yah·tol·ah HOH·may·nee) and his followers. The new leaders blamed the United States for the sufferings the Iranian people had endured under the Shah. They bitterly resented President Carter's decision to admit the Shah into the United States for medical reasons at the very time the Iranian leaders were demanding his return for trial.

American hostages in Iran. In an attempt to force the United States to return the Shah to Iran, on November 4, 1979, a group of Iranian militants seized 53 American diplomatic and consular personnel. The militants held their captives as hostages in the American Embassy and in the Foreign Office in Teheran.

President Carter reacted by freezing some $8 billion of Iranian assets held by the United States and warned Iran of possible boycotts. He urged America's allies to add their pressure in defense of international law.

After almost six months, the Iranian leaders had either refused or were unable to secure the release of the hostages. President Carter then ordered a daring military rescue mission. The mission ended in disaster due to mechanical failures in the desert some 200 miles (320 kilometers) from Teheran. Eight American marines and airmen lost their lives and several others were seriously wounded in the flaming crash of a helicopter and a transport plane.

Reaction to the rescue mission. President Carter was both praised and blamed for undertaking such a desperate rescue mission. His supporters applauded him for acting decisively and, in so doing, for upholding national honor. His critics included many of America's allies and his own Secretary of State, Cyrus R. Vance. Vance strongly opposed the use of military force as a solution to the problem. On this matter, he disagreed with National Security Adviser Brzezinski. As a result, Vance offered his resignation and Carter accepted it.

The hostages remained in Iran, and it seemed that little progress was being made toward their release. American naval and air forces in the Indian Ocean and the Persian Gulf area continued the buildup in strength that had been started several months earlier.

The situation grew still more dangerous when a border dispute led to war between Iran and Iraq in September. Iran accused the United States of pushing Iraq to go to war to punish Iran for holding the hostages.

Finally, the Algerian government helped to negotiate an agreement between Iran and the United States. On January 21, 1981, just as Ronald Reagan took his oath as President, the hostages were freed. After 444 days of captivity, they returned to the United States as heroes.

The Carter Doctrine. Early in January 1980, the Soviets invaded Afghanistan, a Muslim country on the eastern border of Iran. They intended to replace the existing pro-Communist head of government with another leader whom the Soviets considered more receptive to Soviet influence. As the map shows (page 438), Soviet troops in Afghanistan were close to the Persian Gulf, the lifeline to vital oil supplies.

President Carter labeled the Soviet move a serious threat to world peace. He then warned the Soviet Union to withdraw from Afghanistan. When the Soviets showed no intention of withdrawing, the United States made several countermoves. Carter ordered a cut in sales of electronic equipment and grain to the Soviet Union. The United States withdrew from the 1980 summer Olympics in Moscow, and urged other countries to follow suit. Congress made it clear that a key arms limitation treaty between the Soviet Union and the United States would be postponed indefinitely. Its failure would mean that a new arms race costing both countries vast sums was almost certain.

Finally, the President announced what was called the "Carter Doctrine." He declared that any use of military force by the Soviet Union in the Persian Gulf would be met with a major military response by the United States. The United States thus seemed to be stating that its national interest included the defense not only of Japan and Western Europe, but also of the Middle East and the Persian Gulf.

Reagan's foreign policy takes shape. By the time President Reagan took office, détente was, at best, in a shaky condition. The world faced the possibility of returning to another dangerous period of Cold War.

After 444 long days of captivity, Americans held hostage in Iran were at last freed. Here, in February 1981 at a ceremony held at the White House, President Ronald Reagan welcomes them home to their grateful and happy nation.

Reagan soon made it clear that he would oppose Soviet expansion everywhere, even at the risk of confrontation. Reagan continued the buildup of America's military presence in the Persian Gulf and the Indian Ocean. He warned the Soviets that military intervention by them in Poland would have the gravest consequences. On the other hand, Reagan removed the embargo on agricultural exports to the Soviet Union that Carter had ordered.

Reagan's Secretary of State, Alexander Haig, pointed out that the lifting of the grain embargo did not mean a softening of the administration's position toward the Soviets. Haig warned that there could be no talk of arms limitation until the Soviets abandoned their aggressive meddling in other countries.

In the case of El Salvador, the administration moved from warnings to action. This tiny Central American country was torn by civil war. Guerrilla fighters, supported by some intellectuals and peasants, battled to dispossess the ruling classes and to redistribute the land and other resources. Some of the arms for the guerrillas came from the Soviet Union and Cuba. The Reagan administration countered by increasing its military aid to the government of El Salvador and by sending advisers to assist the troops. Critics feared that the United States was becoming involved in another war like that in Vietnam. Reagan denied this possibility and insisted that the United States could not allow Communist actions to go unchallenged.

Reagan's first budget was evidence of his determination to defend American interests with force if necessary. Military spending, already on the rise before Carter left office, jumped sharply upward. Proposed military expenditures over five years, according to Reagan's plan, would reach $1.3 trillion. The Reagan administration also urged its NATO allies and Japan to increase their military spending.

Under President Reagan's leadership, the United States seemed prepared to challenge Soviet expansion anywhere in the world. That was the message spelled out in the buildup of the nation's military strength. Thus the prospect for a renewal of détente seemed dim.

SECTION SURVEY

IDENTIFY: Cyrus Vance, Zbigniew Brzezinski, Angola civil war, Andrew Young, President Sadat, Premier Begin, Shah Mohammed Reza Pahlevi, Ayatollah Khomeini, Carter Doctrine.

1. What were President Carter's foreign policy goals?

2. (a) What were the terms of the Panama Canal treaties? (b) Why did they cause controversy?

3. (a) How did President Carter move Israel and Egypt closer to peace? (b) What problems remained?

4. Describe the events that led to the taking of American hostages in Iran in 1979.

5. (a) Why did President Carter consider the Soviet invasion of Afghanistan to be a serious threat to world peace? (b) How did he respond?

Chapter Survey

Summary: Tracing the Main Ideas

When John F. Kennedy became President in January 1961, the United States and the Soviet Union were locked in the Cold War. During the next two years, the situation rapidly worsened. The Soviet attempt to install long-range missiles in Cuba brought the two great powers to the brink of a nuclear war. Fortunately, reason prevailed, and the Soviet Union withdrew the offensive weapons.

Under President Johnson the United States became involved in what turned out to be the longest and most costly war in the nation's history. The Vietnam conflict was costly in lives, in money and resources, and in its divisive effect upon the American people.

During the Nixon-Ford years, the United States withdrew from Vietnam, reopened its ties with China, and began to establish improved relations with the Soviet Union. Détente with the Soviet Union offered visions of improved international relations and even a lasting peace.

During President Carter's term, however, the period of détente seemed to draw to a close.

There were a few heartening developments in America's foreign affairs during the Carter years. The highlight was the peace treaty between Egypt and Israel negotiated with Carter's personal help. However, by 1980 no decisions had been reached on the basic issues dividing the Arabs and the Israelis, and the treaty itself hung in the balance.

A more immediate threat to peace was the revolution in Iran and the Soviet invasion of Afghanistan. These events transformed the oil-rich Persian Gulf into a tinderbox. Détente appeared to be a thing of the past. With the buildup of both Soviet and American military forces in the Middle East, world tensions again approached the breaking point.

Inquiring into History

1. (a) What was the policy of détente worked out by Nixon and Kissinger? (b) What major changes among Communist nations made this new policy possible? (c) How did the Arab-Israeli War of 1973 test the policy of détente?
2. (a) Why did the United States commit itself to opposing Communist expansion in Southeast Asia? (b) Describe the actions taken by the Kennedy, Johnson, and Nixon administrations with regard to the conflict in Vietnam.
3. Describe the impact of the Vietnam War on (a) Vietnam and (b) the United States.
4. How did competition between the United States and the Soviet Union affect events in (a) Africa and (b) the Middle East during the 1960's and 1970's?

Relating Past to Present

1. (a) What are the goals of American foreign policy today? (b) Of the Presidents' foreign policies discussed in this chapter, which was most similar to today's policy? Which was most different?

2. (a) What are the trouble spots in the world today? (b) How are the events occurring there today influenced by the events that occurred during the 1960's and 1970's?

Developing Social Science Skills

1. Study the excerpt from the Gulf of Tonkin Resolution on page 434. (a) What power does it give to the President? (b) According to the document, what events led Congress to pass the Resolution? (c) How could this Resolution be used later to justify sending American troops to Vietnam?
2. Write one of the newspaper accounts described here: (a) a Palestinian account of the Camp David meeting among Sadat, Begin, and Carter, (b) a Panamanian account of the Panama Canal treaties, (c) a Congolese account of the Congo crisis in 1960–61.
3. Examine the map on page 438. (a) Parts of what three continents are shown? (b) Locate the Persian Gulf and Suez Canal. (c) Using the map, explain the Carter Doctrine and its importance. (d) Why can the Middle East be called the "crossroads of the world"?

Chapter 24

Reaching for Greater Freedom and Justice

Changing Ways of American Life

1960's–1980's

Give me your tired, your poor,
Your huddled masses yearning to breathe free.

These words, engraved on the pedestal of the Statue of Liberty, are those of Emma Lazarus. The words are hers, but the vision they reveal grew out of the thirteen original British colonies along the Atlantic seaboard.

From colonial days to the present, more than 50 million immigrants have come to America. They have come seeking larger opportunities than they could have hoped for in the lands of their birth. The great majority of those who came during the past century entered through New York harbor. Their first glimpse of the New World was the Statue of Liberty, the symbol of freedom and justice.

However, in recent years the ports of entry for the immigrants and the countries of their origin have changed dramatically. Many of the newcomers entered through Florida or crossed the border from Mexico or passed through the ports along the Pacific coast. Today men, women, and children from Asia, Mexico, Central and South America, and the West Indies far outnumber immigrants from Europe.

These were not the only ones "yearning to breathe free." The nation's minorities, including blacks and Indians, had long carried a burden of prejudice and discrimination. Now they were demanding that the vision of freedom and justice be fulfilled. They were demanding that the United States truly become a nation of equal opportunity for all.

Thus the nation entered a time of unprecedented upheaval. The land itself—the farms, the suburbs, the cities—was transformed. Even the values the American people lived by were tried and tested and sometimes reshaped.

THE CHAPTER IN OUTLINE

1. New patterns of population growth and distribution alter ways of life.
2. Black Americans demand equal rights and opportunities.
3. Hispanics share the struggle for freedom and justice.
4. Indians refuse to accept the role of "vanishing Americans."
5. Women redouble efforts to win equal rights and opportunities.

1 New patterns of population growth and distribution alter ways of life

During the years after 1960, America's population continued to grow and shift. The movement from rural to urban areas continued. This, in time, led to a severe crisis for American cities.

Growth of population. By 1980 there were 43 million more people living in the United States than there had been in 1960. The increase in that 20-year period alone—from 179 million in 1960 to more than 226 million in 1980—almost equaled the total population of the country a century earlier.

One reason for this growth was the remarkable advances made by medical science. Antibiotics and many other drugs created in the postwar years made important contributions. So, too, did new methods and improved instruments for diagnosis and treatment. As a result, doctors were able to reduce the nation's death rate, especially among children, and to prolong life.

In the years following World War II, the birth rate soared to an average level of 3.5 births per woman. By the 1970's, however, the birth rate was slowing down. In December 1972 the Census Bureau reported that it had dropped to about 2 births per woman. This is the level of Zero Population Growth (ZPG). This birth rate replaces the existing population but does not increase it.

The birth rate reached its lowest point in the nation's history in 1976. Although it rose slightly during the remaining years of the 1970's, it seemed having two children was the popular goal for many American families.

The redistribution of people. The growing mobility of Americans also had far-reaching effects, particularly after 1960. Americans were increasingly able and willing to move from place to place. In earlier times many people had lived their whole lives in the areas in which they were born. However, by the 1960's and 1970's, this pattern was changing. One out of every five Americans was moving to a new residence each year.

These population movements affected different sections of the country in different ways. The West and the South, particularly the Sunbelt areas, became the fastest-growing sections of the nation. In 1964 California passed New York to become the most populous state. During the 1970's about 40 percent of the nation's total population growth occurred in the Sunbelt states of Florida, Texas, and California.

Meanwhile, the states of the Northeast were losing population in relation to the rest of the country. By 1980 the high cost of home heating during the cold winters was convincing more and more people to move to the warmer Southern states.

Change in rural population. Another dramatic change in American life was the sharp decline in farm population. Between 1940 and 1980, the number of people living on farms dropped from more than 30 million to around 6 million. In some years more than 1 million men and women left the farms to seek better opportunities elsewhere.

Despite the shrinking farm population, America was producing more food and other farm products than ever before. By the 1970's

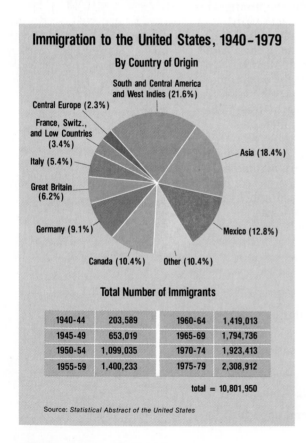

Immigration to the United States, 1940–1979

By Country of Origin

- South and Central America and West Indies (21.6%)
- Central Europe (2.3%)
- France, Switz., and Low Countries (3.4%)
- Italy (5.4%)
- Great Britain (6.2%)
- Germany (9.1%)
- Canada (10.4%)
- Other (10.4%)
- Mexico (12.8%)
- Asia (18.4%)

Total Number of Immigrants

1940-44	203,589	1960-64	1,419,013
1945-49	653,019	1965-69	1,794,736
1950-54	1,099,035	1970-74	1,923,413
1955-59	1,400,233	1975-79	2,308,912

total = 10,801,950

Source: *Statistical Abstract of the United States*

THE TALL SHIPS

"All you look at for three weeks is the water and your crewmates. When we see land, we shout and jump. I think I lost my girlfriend because I go to sea so often. Are there girls in New York?"

The 20-year-old naval cadet may not have found a romantic replacement in New York, but he undoubtedly received a warm welcome. He was one of the crew on the German training vessel *Gorch Fock,* one of the tall ships that sailed up the Hudson River on July 4, 1976. The stunning naval parade of which it was a part was the highlight of New York City's observance of the bicentennial of the United States.

The waters were full of ships that day. Along the shores were anchored 53 warships, representing 22 nations. Between their ranks cruised some 200 sailing vessels of Operation Sail (Opsail for short). Its stars were the 16 tall ships—square-riggers with a mast height of more than 127 feet (38.7 meters). There are only 20 of these left in active service, and they had come from all over the world: the *Amerigo Vespucci* from Italy, the *Nippon Maru* from Japan, the *Dar Pomoza* from Poland, the *Sagres II* from Portugal, and the *Kruzenshtern* from Russia. They were led up the Hudson by the United States square-rigger *Eagle* and escorted by spouting fireboats. Other notable ships in the waters that day were a Chinese junk, a replica of a Viking boat, and the English schooner *Sir Winston Churchill,* with an all-woman crew, as well as over 10,000 small private craft.

Some 6 million people watched the naval parade that day. The gesture of international good will lifted the spirits of all who saw it. But the day was more. It was a visible bridge between the present and the past. It reminded those who saw it that, for all the striking changes of the past 200 years, the United States as a nation still endured.

each farm worker was producing enough food for more than 50 people. American farms were producing more than enough food to feed Americans. Huge surpluses for hungry people overseas were also available. From the 1960's to the 1980's, farm products were a substantial part of the nation's total exports.

Efficient, large-scale corporation farms and spectacular developments in agricultural science and technology made such productivity possible. Better strains of plants, greater use of fertilizer, and improved breeds of livestock were just a few major developments. They combined to raise the average yield of some farm crops by as much as 50 percent. At the same time, worker productivity increased twice as fast on the farm as in industry.

Although the farm population was shrinking, the 1980 census revealed a surprising fact. For the first time since the 1820 census, rural areas and their small towns were growing faster than metropolitan areas. Between 1970 and 1980, nonmetropolitan areas grew by 15.4 percent. Metropolitan areas grew only by 9.1 percent.

Technological advances now allowed many businesses to move out of urban centers. Improved transportation and communication systems meant that rural areas were no longer as isolated as they once had been. Also the rural areas, at least for the time being, did not suffer from many of the problems that troubled the nation's older urban areas.

Urban areas. Many of those who left farms moved to urban areas. These urban areas included central cities and the suburbs around them. These cities and their suburbs were

No sign was needed here. The ruined building says it all. Buildings like this were on the increase as the middle class fled the cities, leaving them to the urban poor, minorities, and new immigrants.

closely related. Originally the cities were the work-places and the suburbs were the living areas. Gradually such a clear distinction faded. The real boundaries between the cities and the suburbs became harder to draw.

These city-suburbs combinations were given the name of Standard Metropolitan Statistical Areas (SMSA's). By 1980 there were over 280 SMSA's in the nation. Over 72 percent of the nation's population lived in such areas.

New immigrants. These SMSA's received a swelling tide of men and women from other lands. During the 1960's and 1970's, immigration increased sharply. Patterns of immigration also changed dramatically.

The Immigration and Nationality Act of 1965 abolished the old national origins acts of the 1920's (see page 304). It also changed the ethnic character of the nation's population. The new law provided for the annual admission of 120,000 immigrants from the Western Hemisphere and 170,000 from all other nations. No more than 20,000 could come from any single country. Preference was to be given to members of families of American citizens and to those men and women with specialized training and skills.

One result of the law was a sharp increase in the number of Asians and Hispanics entering the country. By the mid-1970's more than 300,000 were arriving each year. In 1977, for example, some 150,000 Asiatics and more than 200,000 Hispanics entered.

Most of the newcomers, although by no means all, were poor. Most settled in the cities. There they moved into the homes and apartments left by the white middle class who had moved to the suburbs or back to rural areas. As immigrants and minorities moved into the cities, increasing numbers of whites moved out. This "white flight" contributed greatly to the decay of the cities.

The urban crisis. In the 1960's and 1970's, conditions in America's cities became desperate. Urban renewal programs had helped rebuild the business and financial areas of many cities. However, the older residential areas had often become heavily overcrowded. Many had deteriorated into slums. Property owners, discouraged by the flight of the middle class to the suburbs, refused to spend money to repair their buildings. The core areas of the cities were so badly run down that they needed to be entirely rebuilt. This would take years and require the investment of billions of dollars.

Meanwhile, people living in the slums needed more and better services — health, education, sanitation, recreation, and police and fire protection. They also needed jobs and job-training programs. However, the cities did not have the finances to do the work that had to be done. The people most able to pay the taxes needed to support such programs were leaving. Those least able to pay and most in need were becoming more numerous. City after city faced the prospect of bankruptcy.

"Social dynamite." The urban crisis was in fact a national crisis. In 1961 James B. Conant of Harvard issued a report titled *Slums and Suburbs* that attracted nationwide attention. The report pointed out the alarming contrast between the poverty of life in the decaying cores of the cities and the growing wealth of the suburbs.

Nevertheless, during the next two decades, conditions grew steadily worse. "We are allowing social dynamite to accumulate in our large cities," Conant warned.

1. What were two major changes in the United States population between 1960 and 1980?
2. How was each of these areas affected by population movements between 1960 and 1980: (a) Southwest, (b) Northeast, (c) rural areas, (d) suburbs?
3. What factors contributed to the urban crisis of the 1960's and 1970's?
4. Graph Study: Study the graph on page 446. From what nation did most immigrants come in 1949? in 1979?

2 Black Americans demand equal rights and opportunities

The "social dynamite" that Conant had warned about exploded in city after city during the 1960's. Meanwhile, black Americans had grown frustrated with their slow progress toward full equality of opportunity. They became increasingly insistent upon "freedom now."

The civil rights movement. During the 1950's blacks at long last began to receive support from both the Supreme Court and Congress. As you have read (page 399), in 1954 the Supreme Court ruled that state and local laws requiring blacks to send their children to separate school systems violated the Fourteenth Amendment. Three years later Congress adopted the Civil Rights Act of 1957. This law, strengthened by a related act in 1960, authorized the Department of Justice to sue local officials who tried to prevent blacks from voting.

These developments were immensely encouraging. More immediately important, however, was action taken by the blacks themselves. Under leaders such as the Reverend Martin Luther King, Jr., they began to use nonviolent methods, such as boycotts and peaceful demonstrations, to win their rights.

The civil rights movement that got under way in the late 1950's and early 1960's was a heroic struggle led and sustained by blacks. However, it also drew the active support of whites—particularly ministers, rabbis, nuns, priests, lawyers, writers, and students. The mass media also helped to stir the conscience of white America by bringing the details of the struggle into millions of homes.

Direct action. The movement developed a number of tactics to speed the integration of all public facilities. In addition to the boycott, which had been effective in Montgomery, Alabama (see page 400), the sit-in became a useful device. In February 1960 four black students in Greensboro, North Carolina, refused to leave a "whites-only" lunch counter at a department store until they were served. Day after day they returned. Meanwhile demonstrations in their support were staged across the nation. In July the Greensboro lunch counter was finally integrated. Similar sit-ins spread rapidly over the South to press for the integration of movie theaters, libraries, parks, and other public gathering places.

"Freedom rides" and "freedom marches" by whites and blacks also dramatized the struggle for civil rights. In 1963 A. Philip Randolph, a veteran black trade union leader, organized a march on Washington. More than 250,000 men, women, and youths gathered in the nation's capital to support passage of a civil rights bill. The highlight of the event was Martin Luther King's speech "I have a dream."

Other demonstrations followed, including the 1965 march for voting rights by more than 3,000 blacks and whites from Selma to Montgomery, Alabama. Thousands of walkers, blacks and whites, were led by Martin Luther King and protected by the National Guard along the 54-mile (86-kilometer) route.

Achievements. Congress responded to the protest movement with the Civil Rights Act of 1964 and the Voting Rights Act of 1965. The 1964 measure outlawed racial discrimination in employment and in public accommodations. The 1965 act authorized federal supervision of registration in districts where fewer than half of those of voting age were registered.

By the mid-1960's race barriers had been largely broken down in hotels and restaurants, in buses and trains and airlines, and in other public places. Impressive gains had also been made in voter registration. In 1965, for example, only 6 percent of the black citizens of Mississippi were registered to vote. By 1967 more than 33 percent had been registered.

In March 1965, Reverend Martin Luther King, Jr. (center) led a march from Selma, Alabama, to the state capital at Montgomery to demand voting rights for blacks. Such marches effectively demonstrated to the American people the need for federal civil rights legislation.

The gains in school desegregation in the South were slower. By 1967 token desegregation was a fact throughout the South. Nevertheless, only 16 percent of black southern students attended integrated schools.

In the fall of 1969, the Supreme Court, in its toughest ruling to date, ordered an end to all racially segregated school systems "at once." By the early 1970's, many southern school districts were integrated, and the movement continued throughout the decade.

By the 1970's, in fact, school segregation was more widespread in northern cities than in the South. The courts then began to rule against this **de facto segregation°** in the northern schools. Often they ordered the busing of students from one school to another to achieve a desired balance of races. Opposition to such busing was often fierce. Demonstrations, at times violent, erupted over busing in Boston, Chicago, and other cities.

A shifting emphasis. In spite of the gains, by the mid-1960's many blacks were frustrated. Essential though civil rights were, they did not

°**de facto segregation:** segregation that exists not by law, but because of neighborhood residence patterns.

provide adequate housing either in rural areas or in overcrowded city slums. They did not provide the training or education that allowed disadvantaged people to build a better way of life. It was also becoming clear that integrated schools were not necessarily better schools in terms of the quality of education they provided.

By the mid-1960's the goals of the movement had shifted from civil rights to economic and social issues—jobs, housing, and discrimination by businesses and by organized labor in hiring practices. But as the war in Vietnam absorbed more and more of the nation's resources, black Americans felt that their problems were being neglected. Their goal of equal opportunity seemed as remote as ever.

Violence in the inner city. The depth of black frustration was starkly revealed in riots that broke out in the community of Watts in Los Angeles, California, in the summer of 1965. The National Guard was finally called in to restore order. In the riots 4,000 persons were arrested, hundreds were injured, 34 were killed, and the damage from burning and looting totaled $35 million.

This urban violence shocked the nation. It especially alarmed those Americans, black and white alike, who had believed that the civil rights movement was making progress and that race relations were improving. Any lingering optimism in that regard was swept away during the next two years when rioting broke out in cities across the nation. Among the hardest hit were Detroit, Cleveland, Newark, Baltimore, and the nation's capital, Washington, D.C.

Many Americans, black as well as white, blamed the violence on a group of new militant black leaders, but this was by no means the whole truth. The rate of unemployment among black workers the country over was double that of white workers. Among black teenagers in the inner cities the jobless rate was much higher. As the riots demonstrated, poverty from which there seems to be no escape is a fertile breeding ground for violence.

New leaders and "black power." One of the best known of the new black leaders was Elijah Muhammad, who headed the Black Muslims, the largest and economically most powerful black group. Another was Malcolm X, formerly a Muslim minister, who preached that the black and white races could exist only if they were completely separated from each other. Before his death, however, Malcolm X gave up his rigid racist position, referring to it as "sickness and madness." In 1965 he was assassinated by black radicals he had antagonized.

Among the other new leaders were Floyd McKissick and Stokely Carmichael, who had been active in militant civil rights organizations. Also included were the founders of the Black Panther Party—Huey P. Newton, Bobby Seale, and Eldridge Cleaver. The Black Panthers advocated immediate confrontation with "the white power structure" and the use of force, if necessary, to protect black Americans against aggressive "white racism."

Black extremists demanded "black power." In economics, black power seemed to mean the growth of independent black businesses. In education it meant local community control of largely black schools. In politics it meant the growth of political power either by the formation of a black political party or by control of politics in black neighborhoods through bloc voting. Socially it meant black self-reliance, self-respect, and racial pride.

Moderate black leaders shared many of the objectives of the black power movement, but they rejected its tactics. Among these leaders were Roy Wilkins of the NAACP and Dr. Martin Luther King, Jr., head of the Southern Christian Leadership Conference (SCLC). King, the most influential of the black leaders and a devoted advocate of nonviolence, denounced the appeal to black racism and the threatened use of force. Those who rejected integration and called for a separation of the races, he believed, did a cruel disservice to black people.

Signs of progress. By the mid-1960's the black power movement was making gains. Politically these gains were revealed in the election of black Americans to public office—for example, Edward W. Brooke of Massachusetts to the United States Senate; Carl B. Stokes and Richard Hatcher as mayors of Cleveland, Ohio, and Gary, Indiana, respectively; Julian Bond to the Georgia legislature. In addition, the Supreme Court also had its first black member, Justice Thurgood Marshall.

In the spring of 1968, Congress adopted a new civil rights act. The new act extended federal protection to civil rights workers and also included a guarantee of open housing. The open-housing provision barred discrimination in the sale or rental of all housing with the exception of owner-occupied homes sold directly by the owner.

The Kerner Commission. In the summer of 1967, President Johnson appointed a National Advisory Commission on Civil Disorders headed by Governor Kerner of Illinois to investigate inner city riots and violence. The Kerner Commission's report in 1968 was the most thorough federal study of the race problem.

The report acknowledged that gains had been made in civil rights laws and desegregation. However, it warned that little or nothing had been accomplished in those basic areas that mattered most to a majority of America's black people—housing, jobs, and economic security, educational opportunities, and living conditions in the inner cities. "Our nation," the Kerner Commission reported, "is moving toward two societies, one black, one white—separate and unequal."

SOURCES

MARTIN LUTHER KING, JR.'S "I HAVE A DREAM" SPEECH (1963)

I say to you today, my friends, that in spite of the difficulties and frustrations of the moment I still have a dream. It is a dream deeply rooted in the American dream.

I have a dream that one day this nation will rise up and live out the true meaning of its creed: "We hold these truths to be self-evident; that all men are created equal."

I have a dream that one day on the red hills of Georgia the sons of former slaves and the sons of former slaveowners will be able to sit down together at the table of brotherhood. . . .

I have a dream that my four little children will one day live in a nation where they will not be judged by the color of their skin but by the content of their character.

I have a dream today. . . .

The commission warned of continued disorder and the destruction of democratic values unless improvements were made at once in those basic areas. This could be done, it said, only by "commitment to national action—compassionate, massive, and sustained."

The death of Martin Luther King, Jr. The assassination of Martin Luther King, Jr., Nobel Peace Prize winner and most respected of black leaders, on April 4, 1968, fell with stunning force on all Americans, white and black alike. Dr. King was in Memphis, Tennessee, to lead a nonviolent demonstration when he was killed by an assassin's bullets. In the last speech he made before his death, Dr. King said, "It is no longer a question of violence or nonviolence. It is nonviolence or nonexistence."

Dr. King's death was a grim reminder of the importance of the Kerner Commission's warnings. While the nation mourned the loss of a leader who had devoted his life to a nonviolent solution of the race issue, riots broke out in various cities across the country. Chicago and Washington were the worst hit.

Political advances. The massive effort called for by the Kerner report did not develop. Yet neither its worst predictions nor the revolution threatened by radical black nationalists had taken place either.

In 1975 the Civil Rights Commission reported that many black citizens, as well as members of other minorities, were still prevented from voting by various unfair means. Even so, black citizens were making important political gains. By the end of the 1970's, 4,503 black Americans were serving in elected public offices. This number was only 10 percent of all such offices, but it was an improvement over earlier years. By 1980 there were 17 black members of the House of Representatives. There were black mayors in such cities as Los Angeles, Atlanta, Detroit, Gary, Newark, and Washington, D.C.

Andrew Young, a civil rights leader, served during part of Carter's administration as the outspoken United States Ambassador to the United Nations. Carter also appointed the first black woman to a Cabinet post. This was Patricia Harris, Secretary of Housing and Urban Development and, later, Secretary of Health, Education, and Welfare.

New black leaders were gaining greater political power. They were learning how to get out the black vote, an important factor in the election of President Carter in 1976. They were forming political alliances and making effective use of lobbying tactics.

An uncertain outlook. The Equal Rights Commission brought lawsuits against corporations and labor unions to end unfair employment practices. In a number of schools and businesses, **affirmative action** programs were begun. This meant that blacks and members of other minorities were at times given preference when applying to schools or for jobs. They were given preference even when their qualifications were no better than those of other applicants. The idea behind such programs was to make up for past discrimination, which had left blacks and minorities at a disadvantage. Nevertheless, many Americans objected. Such programs, they said, did not represent the ideal of "equal justice for all." They were instead, critics claimed, reverse discrimination.

The number of blacks attaining middle-income status also was growing, at least until the recession of the mid-1970's. Nevertheless, the rate of unemployment among black workers continued to be far greater than among whites. In the mid-1970's the median income for white families was $14,000, for black families only $9,000. Moreover, 30 percent of blacks lived below the poverty line, in stark contrast to 10 percent of whites.

In summary, black Americans had made gains on all fronts, but the longest and hardest road still lay ahead. Martin Luther King, Jr., had dreamed of a nation in which men and women and children of every race and creed would be united in peace and justice. Whether and when this dream would be realized remained an open question as the nation moved into its third century.

SECTION SURVEY

IDENTIFY: Martin Luther King, Jr., sit-in, A. Philip Randolph, de facto segregation, Elijah Muhammad, Malcolm X, Black Panther Party, black power, Thurgood Marshall, Andrew Young, affirmative action.

1. What were some actions taken by Congress and the Supreme Court since 1954 to guarantee the civil rights of all Americans?

2. What types of actions did civil rights groups take during the 1960's and 1970's in their effort to end

discrimination and increase opportunities for blacks?

3. In view of the many gains made by blacks by the mid-1960's, why were so many still frustrated?

4. What is the relationship (a) between poverty and violence and (b) between neighborhood housing patterns and school segregation?

5. (a) What is the purpose of affirmative action programs? (b) Why do some people oppose them?

3 Hispanics share the struggle for freedom and justice

The discrimination suffered by blacks was also experienced in varying degrees by other ethnic groups. The Hispanics, some 15 million according to one 1980 estimate, were second only to blacks in terms of numbers. There are some estimates that they will overtake the blacks and become the nation's largest minority during the 1980's.

The Hispanics. The Hispanics are people from a number of different Spanish-speaking countries and their offspring. They include large numbers of Mexicans, Puerto Ricans, Cubans, Filipinos, Dominicans, and recent immigrants from other South American countries and the West Indies. All of these people share a common Spanish-influenced heritage. In addition to the Spanish language and Spanish cultural traits, they often share the ties of the Roman Catholic religion.

Despite their common heritage, the Hispanics are a varied group. These immigrants represent a wide range of jobs, from farm workers to lawyers. In fact, more than 30 percent of the immigrants from South America have been highly educated professionals and white-collar workers. The most numerous of the Hispanics are the Mexican Americans. Among them are the descendants of Mexicans living in California, New Mexico, Arizona, and Texas when these lands belonged to Mexico. These people often call themselves Hispanos.

Migrant farm workers. Most of the recent Hispanic immigrants, including the undocumented or illegal migrants, came from poor rural areas to seek a better life in the United States. The great majority worked for the large commercial farms. Most were illiterate, at least in English, and insecure in their jobs. As migrant workers these men, women, and children labored for low pay in lettuce and asparagus fields, citrus groves, and apple orchards. They moved as the crops matured to Oregon, Washington, Nebraska, and the Great Lake states, living in substandard shacks or mobile trailers. They received little benefit from the social legislation that was intended to protect workers. "We were jailed, beaten, even killed," wrote the historian Dr. Julian Navo.

From the early 1900's on, some efforts had been made to organize the migrant workers. These early efforts met only limited success. In the 1960's, however, Cesar Chavez made headway in organizing the workers in the California vineyards and lettuce fields. Sympathetic priests, civic groups, and idealistic students aided in his efforts. In 1965 he launched a strike that led to a nationwide boycott of produce not bearing the label of the United Farm Workers. In 1970, the strikers finally won. Although the gulf between Mexican Americans and other farm workers was still wide, it had begun to narrow.

Mexican Americans have had success in winning political power, especially in the southwestern states. Henry Cisneros, who is pictured here, was elected mayor of San Antonio, the third largest city in Texas.

453

Mexican Americans in cities. In time, large Mexican-American communities or *barrios* grew up in such cities as El Paso, Los Angeles, Denver, Seattle, Minneapolis, and Chicago. The residents of the *barrios* met with prejudice and discrimination in employment, in courts of law, in relations with the police, and in schools where English was often an unknown language to them.

Despite obstacles, an increasing number of Mexican Americans went to high school and college, acquiring vocational and professional skills. Loyal to family and to their Mexican-American culture, the city dwellers contributed to the economic development of the country as well as to the arts. During the Vietnam War, the death rate for Mexican-American servicemen was higher than that for any other group. This was due largely to the fact that many fought in high-risk branches of the service, such as the Marines.

The Chicano movement. Inspired in part by the struggles of blacks for their rights, Mexican Americans in the 1960's took increasing pride in their Hispanic background. They, too, struggled to win their civil rights. They also fought to overcome the prejudice that many "Anglos," as they called other Americans, held against them.

Referring to themselves as "Chicanos," leaders of the movement used boycotts, sit-ins, demonstrations, political organizations, and the courts to secure their rights. In New Mexico, Reies López Tijerina formed an organization to regain land that, he claimed, Anglos had taken illegally. In Denver, the boxer, newspaper editor, and poet Rodolfo "Corky" Gonzales won recognition for his work in the Democratic Party. He organized demonstrations and became one of the leaders of the Chicano movement. In Los Angeles Vilma Martinez, like a growing number of Mexican-American women, took an active part in defending the rights of her people.

Many new militant organizations sprang up. One of them, *La Raza Unida,* sought to register Mexican Americans and to see that they voted. Youth organizations also demanded Mexican-American studies and the use of Spanish in high schools and colleges.

Mexican-American studies soon were recognized in many schools and colleges. Able Mexican-American historians, social scientists, and humanists were professors at leading universities. *El Grito del Norte* and other newspapers and periodicals were further evidence of the vitality of the Chicano movement.

The Puerto Ricans. Puerto Ricans made up the second largest Spanish-speaking group in the United States. As you recall, Puerto Rico has long had a special commonwealth relationship with the United States. The inhabitants of the island are legally American citizens. Many Puerto Ricans have left their homeland in search of jobs in the United States. By 1975 more than 5 million Puerto Ricans, including mainland-born descendants, were living in the United States.

The Puerto Ricans were concentrated in New York. There, by the mid-1970's, they made up 10 percent of the city's population. Large numbers also lived in Newark, Philadelphia, Cleveland, Chicago, Boston, and other cities. In these urban areas they faced problems of unemployment, poor housing, prejudice, and discrimination.

The lives of young Puerto Ricans were especially difficult. Making up 33 percent of New York's school population, they were handicapped because they did not speak English. The dropout rate was very high. Street gangs, friction with the police, and high unemployment added to their problems. Yet many realized that education was a road to a better life. Evidence of this was the fact that in 1975 more than 17,000 young Puerto Ricans were enrolled in colleges and universities.

Despite difficulties and discrimination, many Puerto Ricans moved up the economic ladder. Some found places in small businesses, in semi-skilled trades, and in offices. By the late 1970's, about 10 percent of employed Puerto Rican males held professional or technical jobs. More and more were able to leave the crowded slums for better living conditions in the cities or in the suburbs. In the field of the arts, entertainment, and sports, José Feliciano, Rita Moreno, and Roberto Clemente became well known.

Puerto Ricans realized that political methods could improve their position and as a result they set up political organizations. Other politicians soon became aware of their bloc-voting power. In 1970 Herman Badillo of New York City became the first Puerto Rican member of Congress.

Many Puerto Ricans, on the other hand, rejected the "establishment." They emphasized forceful demands and revolutionary tactics to win greater opportunity. Frustration and pride led some to support Puerto Rican independence. Nevertheless, in a number of elections Puerto Ricans have rejected both statehood and independence, preferring instead to remain a commonwealth.

The Cubans. In 1959, as you have read (page 428), Fidel Castro overthrew the government of the reactionary dictator, Fulgencio Batista. When it soon became clear that Castro wished to create a Communist state, refugees began to escape to the United States. Many crossed the 90-mile stretch of water in small fishing boats. From 1961 to 1970, more than 208,000 arrived. During the 1970's the number landing on these shores each year increased steadily. In 1977 alone more than 66,000 entered the United States. Most of them settled in the Miami area.

In an effort to relieve the strain on the city, county, and state, the federal government set up the Cuban Refugee Program. With an annual budget of $40 million, it provided welfare assistance, health services, and vocational training. The refugees, largely middle class, used their assets, skills, and initiative to set up businesses and other enterprises. As a result of their efforts, they soon became an important part of the Miami area's economy.

Efforts by the refugee program to promote settlement in other parts of the country were effective. By the mid-1970's half of the Cubans were living in New York, Chicago, Los Angeles, and other cities. In 1979 the Census Bureau estimated that the Cuban population in the United States had reached 700,000.

Then, in the spring of 1980, a flood of refugees began to pour into Florida. The "Freedom Flotilla," an improvised fleet of privately owned boats, ferried them from Cuba to southern Florida. It was a dangerous, haphazard operation. Some of the boats, estimated to number more than 2,000, were capable of carrying only five or ten people.

At first President Carter welcomed the refugees with "open heart and open arms," but he soon was forced to change his position. By the end of May, more than 60,000 refugees had entered and several thousand more were arriving each day. Increasing numbers of American citizens objected to the arrival of the Cubans. They claimed that the nation was in a recession and that unemployment was high. They feared that the newcomers would take already scarce jobs.

Each year, uncounted thousands of aliens pour into the United States, some legally and some illegally. These newcomers were among the more than 100,000 Cubans who sailed here from their homeland in 1980.

Opposition to the uncontrolled flood of people approached the stage of violence. Finally the Carter administration announced that the "Freedom Flotilla" would be shut down. By that time, more than 125,000 Cubans had entered the United States.

SECTION SURVEY

IDENTIFY: Hispanos, migrant farm workers, Cesar Chavez, *barrio,* "Anglos," Chicanos, Rodolfo "Corky" Gonzales, Vilma Martinez, Herman Badillo, "Freedom Flotilla."

1. (a) What cultural characteristics do most Hispanics share? (b) From what nations do they come?

2. (a) In general, how have Mexican Americans been treated by other Americans? (b) What actions have members of the Chicano movement taken? (c) How successful has the Chicano movement been?

3. Compare the situation of Puerto Ricans with that of Mexican Americans in terms of (a) problems and (b) attempts to solve the problems.

4. (a) Why have many Cubans come to the United States since 1959? (b) How has the Cuban Refugee Program tried to help them adjust to their new life?

4 Indians refuse to accept the role of "vanishing Americans"

From the day the Europeans first invaded their land, the American Indians were forced to battle for sheer survival. A century ago they made their last desperate stand against the United States Army on the Great Plains. By 1892 the wars were over and the Indians had been subdued. Events would demonstrate that they had not been defeated.

Years of frustration. For the next 75 years, government policies toward the Indians changed repeatedly. In some cases they even reversed themselves. Such policy shifts left the Indians confused and frustrated. They also helped to keep the Indians the poorest of the poor among the nation's minorities.

Yet the American Indians refused to fulfill some earlier predictions and vanish. Against great odds they not only survived but also increased in numbers. According to the Bureau of the Census, in 1970 there were about 800,000 Indians living in the United States. More than 350,000 of these are in urban centers, the rest in rural areas.

Growing awareness. In the 1950's the government had adopted a policy designed to "terminate" its responsibilities to the Indians and to relocate them in cities. The policy, as you have read, proved to be a disaster.

Following the example of the blacks, Indian activists in the 1960's began to form organizations to promote Indian interests. They fought to overcome the damage caused by such policies as termination.

One of the oldest of the organizations was the National Congress of American Indians (NCAI). Founded during World War II, the NCAI became increasingly active during the 1960's. Other organizations, among them the National Indian Youth Council and the Native American Movement, joined in the battle for Indian rights.

Books, several written by Indians, attracted public attention to the problems of the Native Americans. The books and the publicity they received helped to stir the consciences of growing numbers of American citizens.

The New Indians by Saul Steiner alerted readers to a new "uprising" led by Indian intellectuals who wanted to develop "red power." In 1969 Vine Deloria, Jr., a Standing Rock Sioux and a former director of NCAI, published one of the most influential books, *Custer Died for Your Sins.* In it Deloria outlined the tragic history of broken white promises, set forth the goals Indians were struggling to achieve, and provided a glimpse of what white Americans could learn from the First Americans. A year later Deloria continued his indictment of white America and his plea for understanding with another book, *We Talk, You Listen.* The following year Dee Brown's *Bury My Heart at Wounded Knee* appeared and became one of the most widely read of the recent books.

People began to pay attention to Indian problems. President Johnson was one of them. In 1968 he asked for, and Congress passed, a program of more than $500 million in aid to the Indians.

Violence. The growing awareness of Indian problems was quickened by militant Indian action. One group of Indians took over Alcatraz Island, a former Federal prison in California, to dramatize their demands.

The American Indian Movement (AIM) was launched by young urban Indian leaders in the late 1960's. In the fall of 1972, some 500 members of AIM banded together, calling themselves "The Trail of Broken Treaties." They marched on Washington, D.C., occupied the Bureau of Indian Affairs, and did some $2 million in damage. They finally received official promises that the government would pay attention to their complaints.

In February 1973, members of AIM seized the trading post and church at the Sioux Pine Reservation in Wounded Knee, South Dakota. This was the village where in 1890 United States cavalry units had brutally massacred more than 200 Indians. For 71 days heavily armed Indians and United States marshals grimly confronted each other over the barricades that separated them. In the end, after the government promised to consider their demands, the Indians surrendered.

The end of termination. Meanwhile the federal government had once again reversed itself. In 1970 President Nixon asked Congress to repeal the termination policy of 1953. He then announced a policy of "self-determination without termination." From now on, Nixon declared, the Indians would be encouraged to develop their own tribal life on their reservations. In supporting them the government would provide assistance for housing, vocational training, and economic development.

Although Indians welcomed the new policy, they could not forget the repeated reversals in the past. They continued to fear that termination would be renewed.

As it turned out, Congress failed to pass the necessary laws to make the proposed policy effective. Moreover, the tactics employed by AIM angered the Nixon administration. As a result the reform movement begun by the federal government was only partially carried out. However, the federal government did lay to rest the policy of termination.

Moving forward. Although AIM's violent tactics lost some support for the Indians, other Indian leaders continued to move toward their goal of running their own lives in their own way. These leaders increasingly relied on educational activities and on court action to gain their ends.

The Indians made gradual progress. By 1975, for the first time in history, Indian men and women made up a majority of the employees of the Bureau of Indian Affairs. At the same time, more and more schools and colleges had developed programs of Indian studies that informed students of the Indians' part in the nation's life.

The Indians won other victories as well. For example, the Indians of the Taos Pueblo in New Mexico recovered 48,000 acres (19,400 hectares) of land, including the sacred Blue Lake, that had been made part of a national park. Indians in Maine, who claimed that more than half of the state had been illegally taken from them, took their case to the courts. Congress awarded them $81.5 million and the right to purchase up to 300,000 acres (120,000 hectares) of land.

The Indian today. Today, as in the past, generalizations about the Native Americans must be made carefully. The Indians of the United States are now divided into more than 450 tribes or communities and speak more than 100 different languages. Although most continue to battle poverty, many have become well-to-do and some have become wealthy. Many are highly educated and highly skilled.

Here, in northern New Mexico, is the Blue Lake, for centuries held sacred by the Indians of the Taos Pueblo. The lake had been made part of a national park in the 1970's, but finally, the federal government returned Blue Lake to its traditional Indian owners.

There are Indian doctors, lawyers, scientists, and engineers. A large number have become completely "Americanized." However, many refuse to abandon traditional ways and continue to live apart from the mainstream of American culture.

For the most part, the First Americans remain intensely proud of their heritage. They believe that they have contributed richly to American life. They also believe that they have much more to contribute—if America will pause long enough to listen.

SECTION SURVEY

IDENTIFY: NCAI, Vine Deloria, Jr., AIM.

1. (a) What methods have Indians used to dramatize their needs and problems? (b) Which have been most effective? Explain.

2. (a) What was President Nixon's Indian policy? (b) How effective was it?

3. Describe the progress made by Indians in recent years.

457

Women redouble efforts to win equal rights and opportunities

American women make up nearly 53 percent of the population. They are the largest group struggling against discrimination. During the 1960's the struggle came to be known as women's liberation or the women's rights movement and gathered strength.

Reasons for early successes. In part the movement gained strength because of the growing number of American women who were now employed. By the mid-1970's women made up about 50 percent of the nation's labor force. Their average wages, however, were only 60 percent of those paid to men doing comparable work. Even more revealing, only a small percentage of women held higher-paying and more responsible positions. Among the directors of large corporations, for example, only 3 percent were women.

Another factor in the rise of the women's rights movement was the civil rights movement. Many women had been actively involved in the civil rights movement and had gained ability and confidence for their own struggle.

Their struggle was also aided by a clause in the Civil Rights Act of 1964. This clause outlawed discrimination based on sex in employment. Using this clause, women battled to secure equal treatment in business, education, and the other professions.

Growing numbers of women agreed with movement leaders that sex discrimination kept many women from realizing their full potential. According to public opinion polls, a majority of American women did not feel that taking care of a home and raising children were restrictive or frustrating roles. By the mid-1970's, however, a majority of American women did approve of equal opportunities for their sex in all areas of life.

Women's rights organizations. One of the first and most prominent groups within the women's rights movement was the National Organization for Women (NOW). NOW and other feminist groups shared a number of goals. They demanded equal treatment of women in educational programs, including faculty appointments in universities. They worked for publicly financed day-care centers for children. They attempted to get state laws forbidding abortion repealed. They strongly opposed the treatment of women as sex objects. Some of the groups also insisted that men should share in the tasks of homemaking and childrearing.

The ERA. Most of the women's rights organizations pressed for a Constitutional amendment to guarantee women equal rights. By 1978 the Equal Rights Amendment (ERA) that had been passed by Congress in 1972 had been ratified by 35 of the required 38 states. By 1980, however, no additional states had ratified the amendment.

Why had the ERA become stalled?

Many American women believed that the ERA would deprive them of more than it gave them. They feared it might make them subject to the military draft or end alimony payments to women or put an end to laws protecting women in the workplace. More deeply, many of these women believed that such an amendment would help to destroy the traditional bonds of the family.

These women organized their own countermovement. They put pressure on state legislatures and succeeded in preventing ratification in key states. By the early 1980's, passage of the ERA seemed doubtful.

New freedoms for women. Despite the stalling of the ERA, steps were being made toward meeting some goals of the women's rights movement. Legal suits were filed against businesses, colleges, and other institutions. Such suits charged the institutions with sex discrimination in hiring, pay, and promotion practices.

Women also entered careers in fields formerly dominated by men. Women enlisted in the armed forces in growing numbers. Women became police officers and ministers. They won new recognition in sports such as tennis and golf. As a result of such changes, there were fewer strict barriers between men and women in dress and social customs.

In 1973 the Supreme Court ruled that women had the right to have abortions before the sixth month of pregnancy. This controversial decision clashed with existing laws in most of the states. The states then began to change their laws to conform to the Court's ruling. At the same time, anti-abortion groups chal-

In the fall of 1981, Sandra Day O'Connor of Arizona was sworn in as a Justice of the United States Supreme Court. She is seen in this photograph with the other members of the Court. Chief Justice Warren Burger is the fourth from the left.

lenged the right of the Court to make such a decision. They demanded a Constitutional amendment banning abortions.

Political gains. In political affairs women were still underrepresented. However, change was in the air.

Several women in Congress became nationally known. Among them were Bella Abzug, Shirley Chisholm, Barbara Jordan, Elizabeth Holtzman, and Nancy Kassebaum. Of the 52 women who ran for Congress in the 1980 race, 19 were elected.

Women scored impressive gains in state and local politics as well. Approximately 500 women served in state legislatures. Many more took active roles in local party politics. In Connecticut, Ella Grasso served as an extremely popular governor until she resigned because of poor health in 1980. In San Jose, California, Janet Hayes became the first woman mayor of a large American city. Jane N. Byrne was later elected mayor of Chicago.

Other women in government included Carla Hills, Secretary of Housing and Urban Development under President Ford. President Carter appointed two women, Juanita Kreps and Patricia Harris, to his Cabinet. The most widely noted appointment, however, was that of Sandra O'Connor, who was named by President Reagan to a seat on the Supreme Court.

The balance sheet. By the 1980's, despite some growing resistance, the women's rights movement was advancing toward many of its goals. The effects of the movement seemed likely to be far-reaching. Even the women who defended traditional roles and actively opposed the movement did so using political methods and styles that seemed far from traditional.

SECTION SURVEY

IDENTIFY: NOW, Equal Rights Amendment, Shirley Chisholm, Nancy Kassebaum, Ella Grasso.

1. What are some of the goals of the women's rights movement?
2. Why did the women's rights movement gain strength by the mid-1970's?
3. Why did some people object to the women's rights movement?

459

Chapter Survey

Summary: Tracing the Main Ideas

More than two hundred years ago, the American nation was founded on the principle that "all men are created equal." By the 1980's the promise of 1776 remained only partially fulfilled.

Even so, during the years after World War II, and particularly during the past two decades, the movement toward freedom and justice for all Americans has made steady progress.

Despite progress, problems still remained. The cities, in which so many of the poor and the minorities were concentrated, continued to decay. Also, from the mid-1970's on, the nation's economic health was poor. Soaring prices and scarce jobs damaged the chances of many minority members to better their lives.

In spite of these obstacles, however, blacks, Hispanics, Indians, and the largest group of all, women, were demanding and winning a share of "the American dream." They had moved a great deal closer to full equality. A great distance remained to be traveled.

Inquiring into History

1. Describe the major changes that have occurred in the population of the United States in the years since 1960.
2. (a) How are the problems of Hispanics, blacks, and Indians similar? (b) How are they different? (c) Compare the recent progress made by each group.
3. Today women make up more than 50 percent of the population of the United States. Nevertheless, they are often considered a minority. Why do you think this is so?
4. Equal rights movements often suffer from conflicts between their moderates and militants. (a) What sorts of tactics might be favored by moderates? By militants? (b) How did such conflicts affect the black civil rights movement? (c) How did similar conflicts affect the movement for Indian rights?

Relating Past to Present

1. During the 1800's many Americans considered the United States to be a "melting pot" of many peoples. How would you describe the United States today? Explain.
2. Though there has been a steady decline in the farm population since 1940, many young people today look at farming as an enviable occupation. How do you explain this interest? Why do you suppose even the most interested find it difficult to take up farming?
3. What is the present federal policy toward (a) urban problems, (b) affirmative action, and (c) school desegregation? How does it compare with the policies discussed in this chapter?

Developing Social Science Skills

1. Examine the chart on page 699, showing the national background of immigrants. Design and draw a world map that illustrates the immigration of the people from these countries to the United States.
2. (a) Use the *Reader's Guide to Periodical Literature* to locate articles supporting and opposing the Equal Rights Amendment. Make a list of the most compelling arguments on both sides of the issue. (b) Based on your research, take a stand on the ERA and defend your position in a paper or a speech.
3. Create a cartoon comparing the equal rights movement to the civil rights movement.

Chapter 25

Into the Future

On January 21, 1981 Ronald Reagan was sworn in as the fortieth President of the United States. His Inaugural Address that day was solemn. In the years after World War II, the nation had reached a level of wealth, productivity, and power never before approached in history. By 1981, however, formidable problems had emerged. Inflation, unemployment, and a deepening recession seemed to defy solutions. Continued poverty in a land of abundance troubled many Americans. A growing loss of confidence in the government cast a darkening shadow over the democratic process. Schools and colleges, faced with rising costs and falling enrollments, began to rethink their purposes and their programs. Shortages and soaring prices convinced many Americans that they could not continue to depend upon oil as a major source of energy.

By 1981 it had become clear that Americans could no longer take for granted the prosperity so many of them had enjoyed for so many years. As never before in the nation's history, men and women in every walk of life faced the urgent need to reexamine the nation's goals as well as their own personal objectives.

In his Inaugural Address, Reagan recognized this need. He called for a "new beginning" and an "era of national renewal." He said, "The crisis we are facing . . . does require . . . our best effort, and our willingness to believe in our capacity, to perform great deeds; to believe that together with God's help we can and will resolve the problems which now confront us."

Changing Ways of American Life

1960's–1980's

THE CHAPTER IN OUTLINE

1. Americans begin to reexamine their goals.

2. The American economy remains a source of continuing concern.

3. The United States attempts to resolve its energy crisis.

4. Americans share a growing awareness of environmental issues.

1 Americans begin to reexamine their goals

Change is by definition an unsettling experience. As the dictionary reminds us, "to change" is "to alter, to become different." Increasingly during the years after World War II, change uprooted traditional values, beliefs, and behavior of Americans and people everywhere on the planet.

Change and its effects. It was not just change, as such, that was so unsettling. Throughout human history people have been compelled to adapt to changing ways and times. The disturbing difference in the second half of the twentieth century was the increasingly swift rate of change.

The rate of change was particularly rapid in the areas of science and technology. According to one estimate, 90 percent of all the scientists who have ever lived were alive and active in the 1970's. This intense scientific activity throughout the world brought new discoveries, new ideas, new processes, and new inventions in an ever-growing volume.

Nothing in the universe was too small to escape the attention of science; nothing was too immense or too remote in time or place. Scientists explored particles of the atom and stars so distant that their light has taken more than 10 billion years to reach earth. Every field of science was probed, and the answers to questions merely prompted scientists to raise still more questions.

Research produced a vast tidal wave of new developments. Many such developments had unexpected and unplanned effects on daily life. People everywhere were finding it more and more difficult to adapt their personal lives and their institutions—religious, educational, social, economic, political—to the demands of changing ways and times.

Space exploration. Many of the things accomplished by science would have been dismissed a generation ago as wild imaginings. The world was startled when in 1957 the Soviet Union launched the first artificial satellite, Sputnik. Yet by 1969 two American astronauts, Neil Armstrong and Edwin E. Aldrin, had landed on the moon. By 1981 American scientists were testing the *Columbia*, a reusable space shuttle, with the aim of starting regular manned flights.

Today hundreds of satellites orbit the earth. They serve numerous purposes. Some relay television, radio, and telephone messages across continents and the seas. Some survey military activities, search the earth for oil and other resources, and provide data on the weather. Others enable ships at sea to determine their exact location within a matter of seconds. Still other space craft have explored the solar system, reaching out as far as Jupiter and Saturn and sending scientific data and photographs back to earth.

Other scientific advances. The exploration of outer space was paralleled by equally dramatic discoveries on earth. Medical science made major advances in the cure and control of disease. New materials and techniques enabled medical researchers to produce such products as artificial skin and mechanical hearts. Insecticides, pesticides, herbicides, and thousands of drugs, many of them unknown in the natural world, were created and produced in chemical laboratories.

In biological laboratories scientists experimented with such basic life characteristics as the nature of cells. This experimentation involved splicing together genes from different organisms to form what is known as recombinant DNA. Researchers hoped that the new or different forms of life created in the process would have some practical value—either medical, scientific, or industrial.

Many scientists and nonscientists insisted that this type of experimentation was dangerous and should be abandoned. Others would permit it to continue only under the most rigid supervision. In June 1980, however, the Supreme Court ruled that scientists could patent such new forms of life. In this particular case, patent rights were issued to the "inventor" of a newly developed strain of bacteria that would eat crude oil.

Another major scientific breakthrough was the development in the 1960's of ways to generate, amplify, and control beams of pure, or "coherent," light. Lasers, as they are called, were used to perform surgical operations, including delicate operations on the eye. Far more powerful lasers were being developed by the military as anti-tank and anti-satellite weapons. Laser technology also made it possible to transmit telephone messages through glass fibers,

"We are really in the space business to stay," said Robert Crippen after he and John Young took the *Columbia* on its near-perfect first flight. He was voicing the hope that space shuttle flight would soon become a common occurrence.

rather than through copper wires. These were only a few of the rapidly developing uses of laser technology.

The emerging computerized world. The computer was the key to the new world that was emerging out of the amazing advances in science and technology. Scientists continued to refine and improve computer designs and functions. By 1980 a tiny silicon chip no larger than a small coin could outperform the earliest room-sized computers. The largest computers could perform up to 800 million calculations a second and store as many as four million words. All of the stored data was instantly retrievable and could be communicated at the speed of light to any designated location on the earth.

Advances in design allowed computers to be used in more and more areas. Computers guided robot welders on automobile assembly lines. In hospitals computers were linked to X-ray machines. These CAT scanners, as they were called, provided detailed cross-sectional views of vital organs. Small-sized computers were increasingly found in people's homes, aiding them with bank accounts and budgets or entertaining them with electronic games.

Computer scientists agreed that the computer was still in its infant stage of development. No one doubted that these "thinking machines" would continue to increase the efficiency of the human mind. Yet the spread of computers created new problems. Advances in computer technology meant the loss of jobs for some people. Also the spreading use of computers meant that more information about individuals was being collected in computer memories. The individual's right to privacy could be threatened if unauthorized people gained access to such information. How computers would be used in the future depended, finally, upon the values that men and women held and chose to guide their lives.

A revolution in values. A revolution in manners, morals, and values, as well as in science, also characterized the 1960's and 1970's. This

463

development was not confined to the United States. The experience was shared to a greater or lesser degree by all of the world's industrialized nations and even by some of the developing nations. Nor was this revolution limited to the young, although they often led the way.

The development got under way in the United States in the opening years of the 1960's. Inspired by the relatively young President Kennedy, young people increasingly committed themselves to causes. Some joined organizations like the Peace Corps. Others became active in the civil rights movement.

The high hopes that blossomed in these years withered after the assassination of President Kennedy and America's growing involvement in the war in Vietnam. Many young people became angry, resentful, and frustrated over Vietnam and over continuing poverty and discrimination in their own country. Some of these young people, unable or unwilling to find their place in society, rejected the beliefs and practices of the older generation. As a visible sign of their independence, they adopted dress, hair styles, and ways of living that set them apart from the "establishment." Some of them "dropped out" from the traditional world and joined communes. Others experimented with drugs. Still others turned to political activism and attempted to revamp or overthrow the established order by means of organized protest, political action, and, at times, violence.

During the 1970's the earlier, more violent aspects of the rebellion died down. For one thing, the large majority of America's youth did not drop out or fight against the "system." Instead, they continued their education and their search for ways to earn a living. Moreover, some changes had been made in the "system." For example, young people had been granted a more important role in society. The Voting Rights Act of 1970 and the Twenty-sixth Amendment in 1971 extended to 18-year-olds the right to vote.

In still other ways the "revolution" left its mark on American society. Older Americans were also affected by the changes it brought with it. Divorce rates climbed. Growing numbers of single-parent families took their place alongside the traditional family group—father, mother, and children. Some workers, unhappy with what they saw as the pressures and demands of the traditional business world, sought out less financially rewarding but more personally satisfying jobs. Subjects rarely if ever discussed in private social gatherings as recently as the 1960's were now frankly considered in books, family magazines, motion pictures, and television programs.

There were changes on the political scene as well. Although they had only recently won the right to vote, increasing numbers of young men and women failed to register and exercise that right. The majority of those who did indicate an interest in the political process listed themselves as independents. This movement away from the Democratic and the Republican parties was not limited to young people. It was a growing trend among all age groups. By 1980 there was widespread concern throughout the country that the nation's traditional two-party system was in trouble.

Demand for a return to "basics." By the late 1970's, however, signs of a strong reaction to the turmoil of the earlier years was apparent. Parents called for increased discipline and a "return to basics" in the schools. Other Americans felt that traditional goals and purposes were in danger of being lost. Groups such as the Moral Majority pressed for a return to what they insisted were the traditional values in all aspects of American life. Many observers felt that the strong Republican showing in the 1980 elections offered firm evidence that the nation had entered a more conservative time in its history.

New demands on education. Fast-moving developments created both problems and opportunities for the educational system. During the 1960's one of the more serious problems was overcrowding as the children born during the years of the postwar "baby boom" reached school and college age. Reversing traditional policy, Congress came to the aid of the hard-pressed educational system with federal financial assistance.

During the 1970's, however, even with this federal support, the nation's educational institutions suffered an increasingly serious financial crisis. Although enrollments had begun to decline, expenses skyrocketed, partly because of inflation.

Public schools faced additional problems. Although school enrollments on the whole declined, inner city schools often remained overcrowded. Racial tensions and lack of discipline in some public schools led many parents to enter their children in private schools instead.

These crises came at a time when the schools and colleges were confronted with the heaviest responsibility they had ever been expected to carry. Overriding all other issues was the basic question: What kind of education should American schools provide to prepare their students for life in a complex, rapidly changing world?

The evidence was overwhelming that poorly educated, poorly trained men and women had little hope of earning an adequate living in an increasingly complex society. Far more serious from society's point of view was the fact that inadequately educated citizens could not help to solve critical problems facing the nation and the world.

Strong efforts to improve the quality of education began in the late 1950's with improvements in the teaching of mathematics, physics, chemistry, biology, and other natural sciences. By the mid-1960's these efforts had broadened to include the humanities and the social sciences. Grants from the federal government and from private foundations helped to fund projects to improve both the curriculum and methods of learning. These projects were developed and tried out in research centers and in hundreds of schools.

Efforts were also made to improve the quality of education for disadvantaged students. The Head Start program sponsored by the federal government tried to provide pre-school children with rewarding learning experiences.

These and other developments, including the use of closed circuit television, computer terminals, and other kinds of technology in the classrooms, represented an effort to improve the quality of American education. In 1979 Congress undertook to strengthen this effort by creating a separate Department of Education.°

Foreign aid and defense. By 1980 the issue of assistance to the developing nations had become urgent. For one thing, the world's food supply and distribution of it had not kept pace with its exploding population. By 1980 this had passed the 4.5 billion mark. Moreover, many new nations had been created. The United Nations included 151 members, three fourths of them developing countries.

Compounding the problem was the fact that the gap between the rich, industrialized countries and the poor, developing nations was becoming steadily wider and deeper. By 1980 the problem of providing food and other necessities for hundreds of millions of men, women, and children in the poorer nations had reached crisis proportions.

It was plain that the rich, industrial nations would have to play an important part in solving the problems of poverty and hunger in the world. Self-interest, as well as America's cherished belief in human dignity and equality of opportunity, seemed to place a special responsibility on the United States. But by the late 1970's the United States was experiencing serious needs among its own people. How much foreign aid could it afford to give?

At the same time that Americans were deciding how much aid to give other nations, they were trying to determine how much to spend to protect themselves from other nations. In other words, how much of the nation's wealth should be spent on its defense?

During the war in Vietnam in the 1960's, defense spending had represented almost 45 percent of the federal budget. After that the percentage dropped steadily to a low of about 25 percent under President Carter.

President Reagan feared that such cutbacks in spending had given the Soviet Union the chance to gain military superiority. Soviet military spending, he asserted, had greatly increased while America's military budgets had been cut. The only way to counter the growing Soviet threat was with a massive buildup of American arms.

Thus Reagan proposed a program of military spending that would cost $1.3 trillion over a five-year period. Defense spending would climb to over 30 percent of the federal budget. Critics were quick to contrast the Reagan administration's 1980 budget recommendation of $151.5 billion for national defense with the $9.6 billion allocated for foreign aid. Critics also pointed out that most of the money budgeted in recent years for foreign aid was for military assistance, not for the relief of poverty and suffering in the developing countries.

Reexamining government's role. One of the major questions that Americans would have to answer concerned the role of the federal government in their lives.

As you have read, some founders of the nation were concerned that the federal government not have too much power. During the early

°The former Department of Health, Education, and Welfare (HEW) then became the Department of Health and Human Services.

1800's debates on how powers should be divided between federal and state governments were common. The Civil War seemed to settle the question, firmly establishing that the federal government had supreme authority.

Nevertheless, the federal government remained reluctant to assert authority in matters of daily life and business. For example, the first federal regulatory agency was not formed until 1887. Also, until the 1930's the federal government took no major role in trying to end the economic depressions into which the country plunged from time to time.

The Great Depression that started in 1929 led to a larger role for the federal government as state and local governments were powerless to relieve the widespread suffering. President Franklin Roosevelt's programs, such as Social Security, brought the federal government into daily life in an unprecedented way.

World War II and America's new role as world leader also encouraged the growth of the federal government. By the 1960's federal programs under Kennedy's New Frontier and Johnson's Great Society were enormous. Presidents Nixon and Ford promised to reduce the size and role of the federal government. In spite of their promises, public employment and federal spending increased.

More and more people began to question the role that the federal government was playing. Disenchantment with the federal government was heightened by the Watergate scandals and rising inflation and unemployment rates.

During the election campaign of 1980 Ronald Reagan asked for the chance to reduce federal involvement in some aspects of people's lives. In his Inaugural Address he cautioned, "In this present crisis, government is not the solution to our problem; government is the problem." In his first messages to Congress, President Reagan called for sharply reduced federal programs in social welfare, education, research, and support of the arts. His calls received much early popular and Congressional support.

Nevertheless, how much the federal government's role could be reduced remained in question. The extent to which the federal government was involved in daily life was not always apparent. For example by 1980, government payments to individuals made up 28 percent of total personal income in the nation. Cutting back on this involvement would mean sacrifice and hardship for many citizens.

SECTION SURVEY

IDENTIFY: lasers, Head Start program, Twenty-sixth Amendment, Moral Majority.

1. Describe some ways in which scientific research and technology have changed the daily lives of Americans.

2. (a) What problems did the educational system face during the 1960's and 1970's? (b) Describe some of the efforts to solve these problems.

3. What did President Reagan mean when he said, "In this present crisis, government is not the solution to our problem; government is the problem"?

2 The American economy remains a source of continuing concern

When President Reagan in his Inaugural Address said "in this crisis . . . government is the problem," the crisis he spoke of was an economic one and had been building throughout the 1970's. In the 1980 Presidential campaign, the economy was the key issue.

The problem of inflation. The most troubling issue was the most obvious one — inflation. Inflation can be simply described as a significant rise in the cost of materials for agricultural and industrial production, labor, consumer goods, services, and credit. It can also be thought of as an overabundance of money in relation to the goods and services that money can buy.

When such a situation exists, prices rise. In 1971 a gallon of gas cost about 37¢; by 1981 it cost about $1.27. In 1971 a rib roast sold for $1.18 a pound; by 1981 it was $3.69 a pound.

Inflation, which was an international problem, was only part of the economic trouble. On many fronts — productivity, growth, investment — America seemed to slip as world leader.

Many economists traced the serious problems with the economy back to the mid-1960's. At that time, inflation was less than 2 percent a year, and the economy seemed healthy. However, the United States was growing more deeply involved in the Vietnam War. The federal government spent heavily for this war without increasing taxes. Money was pumped into the economy and the federal debt rose.

Signs of a troubled economy are unemployment lines like these. During the 1960's unemployment only once dropped to 5 percent. During the 1970's it never dropped below 5.8 percent, reaching a high of 8.5 percent in 1975.

At the same time that President Johnson was waging the war in Vietnam, he declared a war on poverty in the United States. This war on poverty also pumped money into the economy and increased the national debt.

Attempts to curb inflation. President Johnson at last called for a tax increase to cut the growing deficit and cool down the economy. The tax increase did not take effect until 1969, when Richard Nixon took office.

By then inflation was increasing at the rate of 4.7 percent a year. Americans were demanding that the President take action to halt it.

At first, President Nixon tried two methods of controlling inflation. He cut federal spending for education, welfare, housing, urban renewal, and anti-pollution measures, reducing the budget by several billion dollars.

Nixon also encouraged the Federal Reserve Board and the nation's banks to increase interest rates sharply. The "tight money" policy, as it was called, was intended to make borrowing more expensive. This in turn would cut into the overabundance of money that allowed Americans to bid up the prices of goods and services.

Despite these measures, inflation continued at an alarming rate. Finally, in August 1971,

Nixon announced a new economic program. Its main feature was a 90-day freeze on wages, prices, and rents. A Cost of Living Council was set up to develop guidelines for wages, prices, and profits after the freeze ended. Although both business and labor were unhappy with parts of the program, the rate of inflation did slow a little.

Encouraged by this development, Nixon eased the controls in January 1973, claiming that inflation was moderating and the economy was beginning to slow down. With restraints removed, prices began to soar. Nixon again applied partial controls, which he removed in 1974. Once more inflation shot up, and this time the rate was increased by new OPEC (see page 414) demands for higher oil prices.

Inflation and stagflation. When President Ford took office, the annual rate of inflation was 12 percent. Ford, like Nixon, was convinced that excessive government spending was a major cause of inflation. Ford tried to reduce government spending and slow down the economy. By 1975 the rate of inflation had dropped to 7 percent.

Ford's efforts, though, had unfortunate results. They brought about a nationwide slump

467

in business, or recession, the worst since before World War II. During the winter of 1974–75, the nation's industrial output dropped, and millions of people lost their jobs. By the summer of 1975, more than 8 million men and women were unemployed.

A new word, **stagflation,** was used to describe the puzzling combination of a stagnant economy and a high rate of inflation. Traditional measures for aiding the economy were not effective with stagflation. Cuts in spending by the government to reduce inflation produced longer unemployment lines. Increased government spending and tax cuts did help to stimulate employment, but they also increased inflation.

The recession did, finally, slow inflation. When President Carter took office in 1977, the inflation rate was 4.8 percent. However, the rate of unemployment remained high, about 7 percent. Carter tried to reduce this unemployment by putting more money into the economy. Federal spending was increased and federal taxes were cut. Such policies led to another rise in the inflation rate, and by late 1978 it had risen to 10 percent.

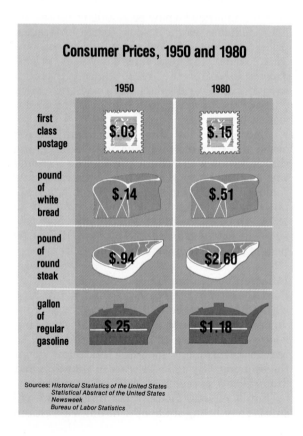

Consumer Prices, 1950 and 1980

	1950	1980
first class postage	$.03	$.15
pound of white bread	$.14	$.51
pound of round steak	$.94	$2.60
gallon of regular gasoline	$.25	$1.18

Sources: *Historical Statistics of the United States*
Statistical Abstract of the United States
Newsweek
Bureau of Labor Statistics

To combat inflation, Carter called for a program of voluntary wage and price controls. If workers accepted federal guidelines, they would limit wage increases to a maximum of 7 percent, including fringe benefits. Business, for its part, would voluntarily limit price increases to a maximum of 5 percent.

Stronger measures, higher inflation. Carter's voluntary controls did not halt the rising cost of living. The increase was speeded along by OPEC's sharp boosts in the price of oil. By the spring of 1980, the rate of inflation was more than 18 percent a year. The value of the dollar was shrinking. In 1980 it took nearly $5 to buy what $1 had bought in 1940.

The nation's economy was in serious trouble, and the Carter administration redoubled its efforts to find a cure. The Federal Reserve Board tightened credit. Leading commercial banks raised the prime rate of interest on money borrowed to over 20 percent. Carter now also tried to cut federal spending. The anti-inflationary measures had the undesirable side effect of increasing unemployment. America was moving into another recession.

By 1980 the inflation crisis had become serious indeed. In the early years of the inflationary boom, incomes had kept ahead of costs. For example, from 1967 to 1973 the average real income of Americans, adjusting for inflation, rose 17.5 percent. But from 1974 to 1978 it rose only 5.5 percent. Starting in 1979 real income actually declined.

One economist put it this way: "The two-earner family has about peaked, average real weekly earnings are falling, and now you are going to have to put teenagers to work just to keep income stable."

The impact of the economic problems can be expressed another way. In 1972 the United States had the highest standard of living in the world. By 1980, it had slipped to fifth place.

With less real income, Americans were less ready to make major purchases, especially when they faced high interest rates on borrowed money as well. Thus industries vital to the nation's economy, such as the automobile and the housing industries, suffered. Because the inflation rate was usually higher than the rate of interest banks paid on savings accounts, people were also less willing or able to save.

Inflation and business. Inflation ate away at the welfare of businesses as well as that of

468

At this American plant, automobiles move along a robot welding assembly line. Investment in such equipment was necessary to insure that the American automobile industry remained competitive with those of other nations.

individuals. You have seen that people's unwillingness to make large purchases cut into business sales. Additionally, a reduced rate of savings meant that there was less money available to invest in business.

Inflation also made business less willing to make necessary commitments in costly new equipment. Without such new equipment, the productivity of some of the nation's key industries declined.

The results were striking. In the 1960's the rate of the nation's economic growth averaged 4.1 percent a year. In the 1970's it was only 2.9 percent. Likewise, the output of goods and services per worker, which had been growing at 1.9 percent a year from 1968 to 1973, dropped to .7 percent a year from 1973 to 1979.

World competition. The economic picture looked gloomier still when America's economic performance was compared with that of rival industrial nations. Japan and West Germany, in particular, made amazing economic strides. They invested heavily in new and efficient technology and were able to seize a sizable share of markets in other countries and even in the United States.

In 1962, United States-made aircraft commanded over 70 percent of worldwide sales. By 1979, the figure had shrunk to 58 percent. In this country, the records of automobile sales showed how the United States was losing ground to foreign competition. In 1960, almost 96 percent of all cars sold in this country were American-made. Twenty years later only 79 percent were produced here.

Reagan's program. These, then, were some of the challenges that Ronald Reagan faced when he took office in 1981. Constructing a strong new economic program was his first order of business.

Reagan's first priority was victory over inflation. In order to win this victory, the government would have to balance the budget—that is, reduce expenditures to match the amount of money available from taxes.

The Reagan administration called for a two-pronged attack on the problem. One prong was a sharp reduction in federal spending except for defense. The idea was to reduce expenses by cutting back on some programs, dropping others, and eliminating wasteful practices.

The second prong was a tax cut. This called for across-the-board reductions in personal and corporate taxes. Reagan hoped that these reductions would encourage people and businesses to save and invest. It was assumed that this would lead to the modernization of old plants and the construction of new ones.

This investment would help to revitalize the economy. Revitalization would mean more goods and services, stabilized prices, and more jobs. With more workers on the job and more taxpayers, the government would be able to balance the budget.

That was the broad outline of President Reagan's plan. He and his staff then began to work with Senators and Representatives and soon got the program through Congress.

Reagan had stated, during his Inaugural Address, that he intended to "put America back to work." How well his plan would accomplish this goal remained to be seen.

SECTION SURVEY

IDENTIFY: inflation, Cost of Living Council, stagflation.

1. How can government actions affect the rate of inflation?
2. How did world competition affect the United States economy?
3. Describe President Reagan's program for improving the nation's economy.
4. Chart Study: Look at the chart on page 468. How much did the price of each item rise? What was the percentage of increase for each item?

3 The United States attempts to resolve its energy crisis

Energy topped the list of critical resources. Without it American productivity would be drastically reduced. Sources of energy provided essential power for American farming, lumbering, mining, manufacturing, transportation, communications, heating, cooking, lighting, air-conditioning, and countless other tasks. Americans and people in other industrial countries lived in a world dominated by machines dependent on energy resources.

Dependence upon fossil fuels. The fossil fuels—coal, oil (petroleum), and natural gas—made up 95 percent of the energy resources in the United States in 1980 and a slightly larger percentage for the world as a whole. The world's dependence upon fossil fuels was, however, relatively new.

It was with the Industrial Revolution, hardly more than 200 years ago, that the change came. Only then did people begin to make heavy use of the fuels that had been buried in the earth for millions of years.

During the past 50 years, the industrial nations consumed an alarmingly high percentage of all the fossil fuels that existed on the planet. The United States was the world's largest producer, importer, and consumer of energy resources, mainly oil. The energy required to power America's machines and to heat and cool homes and other buildings doubled between 1950 and 1970 and was expected to double again by the mid-1980's.

The end of an era. By the 1980's, however, it was becoming increasingly clear to the United States and the other industrialized countries that they could not continue much longer to depend upon oil as their principal source of energy. Known reserves of the most widely used fossil fuels—oil and gas—were dwindling steadily. The cost of discovering and developing new sources of these fuels was rising rapidly. In the United States by 1980 domestic deposits of oil supplied only about half of the nation's energy needs.

Twice in the 1970's, the American people were shocked into the awareness that their standard of living and even the security of the nation itself depended upon decisions made in and by other countries. For a nation accustomed to think of itself as a world leader, the discovery was immensely disturbing.

The first shock came in 1973. At that time foreign oil producers formed a cartel, or pool, designed to eliminate competition among themselves and to control the price of oil on the world market. Within a few months, OPEC had increased the price of oil from $4 to $11 a barrel. Even more disturbing, OPEC, which was angered by American support of Israel, temporarily halted all shipments of oil to the United States.

The second shock came in 1978–79 when Iran, which supplied 10 percent of the world's petroleum, was torn by revolution. All shipments of oil from the Iranian oil fields to the United States were cut off.

In the meantime, during the 1970's OPEC had been steadily raising prices. By 1980 the OPEC countries were demanding $28 to $40 a barrel, the price was still rising, and no top limit was in sight.

The era of cheap oil, and therefore of cheap energy, had come to an end. Alternative sources would have to be found. The nation's prosperity and independence in coming years depended upon the success of the search for these alternatives.

Natural gas and coal. For the short term, natural gas, which in 1980 was supplying about one third of United States energy, would continue to be available. However gas, like oil, was becoming increasingly expensive. It, too, was limited in amount. In time gas reserves, too, would be exhausted.

The expanded use of coal, which during the 1970's provided about 18 percent of the energy consumed in the United States, seemed at first glance to provide a more realistic alternative to oil. It was estimated that the world's coal reserves, of which 20 percent are in the United States, were large enough to meet the projected world energy demands for the next 200 to 300 years. Coal was also a potential source for so-called synthetic fuels. These were fuels that could be processed from coal. They included both liquid fuel and gas.

There were, however, serious questions as to the wisdom of depending upon coal as a major source of energy. In the past the mining of coal was enormously costly in terms of human life. Deep mining has been the world's most hazardous occupation. Miners lived with the everpresent danger of accidents and the possibility of suffering from black lung disease. Surface or strip mining was less costly in terms of human life and health. However, such mining could damage the environment.

Increased use of coal as a fuel also presented grave hazards to the environment. The effect of burning coal upon the world's climate was becoming a matter of increasing concern. "Acid rain" produced by chemicals released into the air by burning coal killed all the fish in many lakes and threatened both forests and farmlands.

Advances in technology helped to ease some of these problems. Nevertheless, much more research and planning are still needed.

Nuclear energy. Another energy option included a formidable challenge. This was the continuing development of nuclear power.

After World War II nuclear fission, the splitting of atoms, seemed to promise a safe, cheap, clean, and unlimited source of power. The failure of nuclear fission reactors to meet this early promise was not due entirely to technical problems, although these have been, and continue to be, very difficult and complex. The failure was due in part to the warnings of environmentalists and nuclear scientists, who insisted upon increasingly strict safety precautions. As nuclear knowledge has accumulated, a growing awareness has developed of the terrifying risks posed by this immensely complex technology.

These risks were clearly demonstrated in the spring of 1979 in what was generally acknowledged to be the nation's most serious nuclear accident. The accident occurred when the cooling system failed in a reactor at the

In March 1979 atomic energy experts raced to the Three Mile Island nuclear power plant. The plant's cooling system had malfunctioned, threatening a dangerous core meltdown. A disaster was averted, but clean-up costs were in the billions.

SOLAR-HEATED HOUSE

Solar collectors fitted with absorber plates are positioned on the roof to receive maximum sunlight. The plates heat air which is circulated through the collectors. The heated air is blown by a fan through ducts to the basement. There it heats storage rocks, which, in turn, heat a water system. Another fan circulates heat from the storage rocks throughout the house.

Three Mile Island power plant on the Susquehanna River near Harrisburg, Pennsylvania.

The core of the reactor, where radioactive materials produce the heat used to generate power, was damaged. For a time it seemed that a complete core "meltdown," which would release deadly radiation into the air, was possible. While scientists and engineers struggled to cool the reactor, plans were made to evacuate people within the surrounding area. Fortunately, the reactor was finally brought under control before a meltdown occurred.

The near-disaster heightened world-wide concern over the safety—and cost—of nuclear power. A year and a half after the accident, the power company reported that the cleanup work would cost an estimated $2.8 billion. The damaged reactor could not be back in operation before 1985, if then. Meanwhile, in other countries as well as in the United States, nuclear authorities began to develop stricter regula-

tions for the design, location, and operation of power plants.

The problem of nuclear accidents was only one of the questions that troubled many scientists. How, they asked, is it possible with our present limited knowledge to determine what impact such nuclear installations might have upon human beings and all other forms of life? How could an absolutely foolproof method be developed to seal, transport, and store the deadly wastes produced by nuclear reactors?

The nuclear outlook. Energy from nuclear fission clearly presented serious problems. Nevertheless, many scientists and engineers believed that generating plants using nuclear materials could be reasonably safe sources of energy. Painstaking efforts were carried on throughout the world to control the hazards of nuclear energy. By 1980 more than 20 nations were operating nuclear generating facilities.

472

The United States had 72 plants in operation in 26 different states, and 90 construction permits had been granted for additional plants.

Scientists were also probing a potentially safer source of nuclear energy than the present process of splitting the atom. In 1980 the House of Representatives voted overwhelmingly to commit $20 billion over the next 20 years in an all-out effort to harness nuclear fusion. This is the process that feeds the fires of the sun. Up to now, scientists have been able to use it only to provide the awesome destructive power of the hydrogen bomb. If fusion could be tamed and controlled, it would provide the world with a virtually unlimited source of energy. Moreover, unlike nuclear fission with its deadly waste products, the principal by-product of fusion is non-radioactive helium.

Energy alternatives. There were, of course, other energy alternatives. One was the increased use of power generated by falling water—hydroelectricity. There were, however, limits to the amount of energy that could be secured from this source. Also, construction of the necessary dams would mean the flooding of valuable timber areas and irreplaceable farmland.

Another energy option was the development of geothermal energy, or power generated from hot gases and steam in the depths of the earth. Several such plants were operating in Europe and the United States. Any substantial increase in the use of geothermal energy would depend on further research and development.

One other potential source of energy was the ebb and flow of the ocean tides. The La Rance Tidal Project, located near St. Malo, France, had been harnessing this tidal energy successfully since 1968. It was the largest such project in the world. However, other countries, including China and the Soviet Union, also operated tidal generating plants. In 1980 Canada, determined to harness the tides in the Bay of Fundy, started construction of what would be the world's largest tidal plant.

The most promising possible energy source was the sun—the original source of all energy, past, present, and future. Solar energy is inexhaustible. Scientists estimated that all of the United States' energy requirements for an entire year could be met by the amount of solar energy that falls on the surface of Lake Erie in a single day!

Efforts to harness solar energy were increasingly successful in recent years. For example, solar batteries were developed to supply electricity to spacecraft. They were at first used in situations where only small amounts of electricity were needed and the high cost was not a problem. Moreover, current research was rapidly reducing the cost of solar batteries, and the prospects for the future seemed highly promising.

In the meantime, researchers in many countries were developing practical solar energy devices to provide hot water, to heat homes, and to supply energy for other uses. In 1975 President Ford signed into law the Solar Heating and Cooling Act to encourage the development of such devices in the United States over the next five years. The Carter administration offered tax incentives to encourage the adoption of other energy conservation measures.

America's energy future. A group of distinguished scholars brought out one of the most comprehensive studies of America's energy future in 1979. The report, *Energy Future,* concluded that none of the present conventional sources of energy—oil, natural gas, coal, and nuclear—would be likely to supply significantly more energy in the future than they were supplying in 1979.

The report contended that America's future depended upon the development of "unconventional" sources of energy—solar and conservation. Conservation includes the increasingly efficient use of conventional sources of energy. The report found that conservation could supply as much as 40 percent of the nation's energy needs during the 1980's. Solar energy, given substantial government support, could by the year 2000 supply some 20 percent of America's energy requirements.

Changes in government policy. The federal government was criticized for failing to act decisively on the energy problem. In the late 1970's it finally began to move.

In 1977 Congress made a modest beginning with the creation of a new Cabinet-level Department of Energy (DOE). One of the major functions of the new department was to conduct research and help coordinate efforts to develop solar energy and other alternative energy sources.

In 1978 President Carter, acting in spite of

strong public opposition, announced that he was going to remove controls regulating the price of domestic oil. The price of American-produced oil and gasoline immediately began to rise to the levels charged by the OPEC countries. Consumers reacted to the higher prices by reducing their consumption of gasoline and oil. This is what the President had hoped would happen when he announced deregulation. At the same time, however, the profits of the oil companies began to climb to record highs.

The following year President Carter presented a comprehensive energy program to Congress and to the American people. He proposed limiting oil imports to the 1977 levels, providing more aid for mass transit systems, and developing energy conservation measures. The heart of his program was a plan for encouraging private industry to develop synthetic fuels and the use of solar energy. The President believed that the entire cost could be covered by a tax on what he termed the "excess" profits of oil companies.

The Reagan administration brought a different approach to the energy problem. President Reagan favored some of Carter's moves. For example, he speeded up deregulation of domestic oil prices. Reagan argued that higher prices for domestic oil would encourage oil companies to search for and develop America's resources. This would, he believed, help free the nation of dependence on foreign oil.

In other areas Reagan's policies differed from Carter's. During his election campaign Reagan spoke of eliminating the Department of Energy. Although he took no immediate steps to do so, he did play down the importance of that department. Also, Reagan was not deeply committed to synthetic fuels projects. He favored heavy cuts in federal support for such projects.

Thus, by the early 1980's, several important changes had taken place in the nation's views on energy. American citizens, stung by higher prices and shortages, did take steps to conserve. Use of gasoline, for example, fell sharply. Owners of homes and businesses added insulation to their buildings and turned down heat in winter and cut back on air-conditioning in summer. Energy companies also made serious efforts to find new fuel sources. How long it would take for the nation to achieve energy independence remained a question.

Windmills have long been features of the American landscape. Today scientists are studying the possibility of using windmills to generate electricity. This gigantic device was built as an experiment by NASA.

ERDA/NASA
100kW EXPERIMENTAL WIND TURBINE
TOWER HEIGHT   100 FEET
BLADES, TIP TO TIP   125 FEET
ELECTRICAL POWER 100kW from 18-40m
INSTALLED   SEPT. 4, 1975
ACHIEVED RATED   DEC. 18, 1975
POWER

SECTION SURVEY

IDENTIFY: fossil fuels, cartel, OPEC, strip mining, acid rain, hydroelectricity, geothermal energy, conservation.

1. Why was it necessary for Americans to find alternatives to oil as an energy source?
2. (a) Name some of the alternative energy sources being used in the United States today. (b) What are the advantages and disadvantages of each?
3. Compare and contrast the energy programs of Presidents Carter and Reagan.

4 Americans share a growing awareness of environmental issues

The energy crisis of the 1970's was part of a broader problem. Learning to manage energy resources was just a step toward learning to manage the overall environment.

Geothermal power stations, like this one in California, produce energy while doing little harm to the environment. The station draws on the natural heat of the earth in the form of hot water or hot gases and converts it into electricity.

The impacts on the environment. By the 1960's and 1970's it was becoming ever more clear that serious damage was being done to the most essential of all the natural resources —air, water, and the earth itself.

Clean air in many cities had been replaced by smog. Some 200 million tons of pollutants poured into the air each year from motor vehicles, industries, homes, and power plants. Human and industrial wastes pouring into the nation's rivers had turned many into virtual sewers. Growing shortages of fresh water in many areas of the country led to strict regulations and sometimes to rationing.

The earth, as well as the air and the water, was deteriorating. Fertile land was being bulldozed to build highways, shopping malls, and housing developments. Irreplaceable farmland was vanishing at an estimated rate of 10,000 acres (4,000 hectares) every day.

The problem of wastes. The wastes produced by our industrial society created problems for every form of life on the planet. Urban areas alone generated hundreds of thousands of tons of garbage and solid waste every day. Hazardous wastes from chemical plants, nuclear reactors, and other industries polluted the air and accumulated in thousands of dumps across the countryside.

Finding proper ways to dispose of all the wastes, both liquid and solid, was difficult. Much of it could be burned. However, burning introduced pollutants into the air, and some burning wastes released poisonous fumes.

Burial was another widely used method of disposal. Some wastes decomposed safely or remained harmless underground. Other buried wastes could become deadly threats to the environment. This fact was driven home to the nation in a number of incidents. One of the worst disasters came to light in Niagara Falls, New York, in 1978.

There homes had been constructed near a ditch known as Love Canal. The chemical company that owned the ditch dumped steel drums of chemical wastes into it. The company covered the wastes and turned the land over to the city for use as a school and playground.

In time the steel drums rusted and deadly chemicals leaked out. They bubbled to the surface in foul-smelling pools and oozed into the basements of nearby homes. Residents complained of strange skin rashes and breathing problems. A higher than normal percentage of them suffered cancer. Likewise, an abnormal number of children were born with birth defects.

Finally in 1978 President Carter declared a state of emergency in the area. The state government in the end agreed to evacuate about 800 families and to purchase their homes.

Managing resources. Many concerned citizens worried not just about pollutants added to the environment but also about resources removed from it. Oil shortages during the 1970's made clear that one day fuel might run out. Suddenly Americans began to realize that other vital resources might also be limited.

Much of the astonishing productivity of the United States has come from resources within its own borders. At the beginning of the 1900's, the United States produced about 15 percent more raw materials than it consumed. By 1940, however, American industry consumed more raw materials than the nation produced. Since then the gap has widened significantly.

During the past 25 years the United States has become increasingly dependent upon the rest of the world for a large part of the materials it needs to maintain its industrial productivity. Since 1954 the American people have used more minerals than the rest of the world has used since the beginning of human history! In the mid-1960's the United States contained only 6 percent of the world's population. Yet it was consuming more than 50 percent of the world's output of oil and nearly 90 percent of the total output of natural gas. It also consumed vast quantities of iron ore to produce half the world's supply of steel.

Some resources, such as lumber, are renewable. Others, such as metals, can be recycled. Still others, such as fossil fuels, can be used once—and then they are gone forever. Very few—solar energy is one—are inexhaustible.

The slow awakening. By the mid-1960's one historian reminded Americans that "less than a century divides the era when America was looked upon as a Garden of Eden or savage wilderness. Frankly, no people have ever so quickly subdued their natural environment." Usually Americans accomplished this with little concern for the laws of nature or for the consequences of violating these laws.

To be sure, as early as the 1890's the federal government had begun to reflect the concern of a few Americans about the need to conserve the nation's resources (see page 166). However, the early conservation movement, important though it was, had limited goals. The first conservationists were mainly concerned with regulating the use of particular resources— forests, wildlife, minerals, and the soil. A half century later, by the 1950's, more and more people were beginning to understand that the earth itself—including all its resources and all forms of life—was being endangered by the waste and misuse of resources.

Major credit for arousing public concern probably belonged as much to Rachel Carson as to any other single person. In her bestselling book *Silent Spring,* published in 1962, she warned that "along with the possibility of the extinction of mankind by nuclear war, the central problem of our age has . . . become the contamination of man's total environment." This warning received nation-wide attention and influenced the thinking of government officials and private citizens alike. During the next few years growing numbers of ecologists, biologists, and other scientists expressed alarm over the reckless misuse of the environment.

Government action. The Kennedy and Johnson administrations responded to these warnings with new programs to safeguard the environment. In addition, state and local governments stepped up their environmental efforts. In 1970, during Nixon's first term, Congress created the Environmental Protection Agency.

By the mid-1970's an impressive body of federal, state, and local laws had been enacted. Laws regulated the use of pesticides, insecticides, and other potentially dangerous sprays. Species of wildlife threatened with extinction had been protected. Automobile manufacturers had to provide pollution control devices on exhausts of cars, trucks, and buses. Clean-air standards had been established for factories, office buildings, and apartment houses. New waste disposal and sewage treatment plants were being built to prevent further pollution of the land and water and to clean up the rivers and lakes.

Efforts had also been made to restore the natural beauty of the countryside by regulating unsightly junkyards and dumps. Federal and state governments set aside more land to preserve as wilderness or parks for future generations. Considerable progress had been made

PEDAL POWER

The young Californian stood on the coast of southern England and gazed toward France across the English Channel. "It just seemed to go on and on," he recalled later. "I concluded that everybody here was right—we were crazy." Even so, Bryan Allen and his companions went ahead with their plans. Their goal was to fly across the Channel using only human muscle power—that is, Allen's pedaling. Their reward, if successful, would be a prize of £100,000 (about $220,000) offered by a British industrialist. There would also be the satisfaction of having achieved both an air record and an ecological breakthrough.

Allen, who had been training by bicycling for months, was now ready. So was the plane, the *Gossamer Albatross,* designed by Paul Mac-Cready. Built of the lightest carbon-filament tubing sheathed in translucent plastic, the fragile craft weighed just 75 pounds (34 kilograms). Inside the tiny cockpit was Allen's bicycle-like apparatus, its pedals connected to a propeller. He hoped to make the flight in a little under two hours.

Allen took off early on the morning of June 12, 1979. "What audacity," he thought, "to challenge the elements in such a machine." The flight was not an easy one. Air currents sometimes forced the *Gossamer Albatross* down to less than a foot above the choppy waves of the Channel. Allen's radio failed and his water supply also gave out. Head winds cut into his speed, while leg cramps caused him terrible pain.

Then the coast of France came into sight! Allen regained hope, running on reserves he never knew he had. After almost three hours in the air, the exhausted pilot landed among 300 welcomers. Engineer MacCready summed it up: "It's a specialized thing . . . but it certainly does alter one's perspective of what man is capable of, both in design and actual powering of things."

in the management and conservation of America's forests, soil, and water. Only a small beginning had been made in conserving and recycling natural resources.

Economy and environment. In spite of the complexity of environmental problems mentioned above, not all Americans felt that increased action by the federal government was necessary. As economic conditions in the nation worsened in the late 1970's, many people called for the government to ease environmental regulations.

These critics argued that meeting strict clean air and clean water requirements costs billions of dollars. Foreign businesses that did not have to meet these standards were able to produce goods more cheaply and thus gain a larger share of the world market. Also, critics charged, federal regulations were often unclear and contradictory. These critics wanted the cost of such regulations to be weighed against the benefits they produced. Only if the benefits exceeded the costs would the regulations be enforced.

Many Americans also believed that restrictions on the use of federal lands should be relaxed. They felt that since the nation's industries desperately needed mineral resources, it made good sense to search for them on federal lands.

President Reagan agreed with many of these points. He proposed cutting back and simplifying environmental regulations. He also encouraged the search for mineral resources on federal lands. One of the first acts of his Secretary of the Interior, James Watt, was to propose opening sections of the sea floor off California to oil exploration. Environmentalists argued that the risk of oil spills on these sites posed a grave threat to a particularly scenic area of the California coast.

A global matter. Whatever actions the United States took regarding the environment would have consequences far beyond its borders. The same was true for any actions taken by other nations.

Worldwide developments have brought increasing pressure upon the natural environ-

Wrangell, Alaska, is located in an area of great beauty and rich natural resources. The citizens of Wrangell, like other American citizens, will face important decisions in the years to come about how to manage those resources while maintaining the natural environment.

ment. First, world population has been doubling nearly every 35 years. Just to maintain people's standards of living at their present level would require, during the next generation, the production of twice as much food, clothing, shelter, and industrialized goods. The demand upon increasingly scarce raw materials, many of them irreplaceable, will be enormous. Yet such a great increase in production would do nothing to improve the living conditions of most of a projected world population of more than 6 billion men, women, and children by the year 2000.

A question of responsibility. The United States is one of the world's richest nations. It produces more than 25 percent of all the grain grown on the face of the earth. It also has the largest pool of scientists, engineers, and management experts of any industrial nation. With so much wealth and so much talent, the United States cannot avoid sharing the responsibilities of world leadership.

During the twentieth century Americans have been foremost in the movement into the scientific-technological world. Because they have often led the way, Americans have been among the first to meet the consequences of the reckless use of land and resources.

Urgent though the challenges are, the American people had reason to move into the

future with confidence. The same scientific genius and engineering talents that unknowingly created many of the as yet unsolved problems remain available to solve them.

In 1976 Americans had celebrated their nation's 200th birthday. They looked back with pride upon all those years of growth. For generation after generation, Americans had repeatedly demonstrated an amazing ability to adjust to changing ways and changing times. Americans in the 1980's were, for the most part, certain that in future years they would meet and overcome new problems and challenges. They recognized that, more than ever before, the power to shape the future lay in their hands.

SECTION SURVEY

IDENTIFY: smog, Love Canal, Rachel Carson, James Watt.

1. By the mid-1970's, what steps had the federal government taken to try to protect the environment?

2. In what ways is the United States dependent on other nations in order to maintain its industrial productivity?

3. Why have some people called for easing environmental regulations?

4. Is environmental pollution simply an American problem? Explain.

Chapter Survey

Summary: Tracing the Main Ideas

Through the centuries the nation has grown from a rural society of small villages and towns to an urban society of large cities and suburbs. The economy of the United States has developed from a simple one based on self-sufficient farming to an infinitely more complex one based on the technology of an industrial society. The nation has emerged from relative isolation to a role of world leadership.

As the nation moved into the third century of its existence, a new generation of Americans faced new problems, new challenges, and new opportunities. The federal government and its budgets had grown greatly since the 1930's, and many citizens were asking if such growth was necessary and helpful. The American economy, a marvel to people the world over, seemed to falter in the face of continuing problems with inflation and increasing international competition. The American land, with its beauty and its wealth of natural resources, needed thoughtful care and management to insure that its treasures would be passed on to future generations.

The American people have solved many immense problems during the course of their nation's history. They need only the will and the commitment to meet the new challenges of the future.

Inquiring Into History

1. How have computers changed Americans' way of life?
2. Describe the economic problems facing the United States when Ronald Reagan became President.
3. Can the United States try to solve its economic problems without regard for the economic situation in the rest of the world? Why or why not?
4. (a) What are some causes of the environmental problems that the United States faces today? (b) How are Americans trying to solve these problems?

Relating Past to Present

1. "Human history becomes more and more a race between education and catastrophe." How does this statement apply to the world today?

2. Pollution of the land and water and misuse of resources began with the first European settlements in America. Explain.

Developing Social Science Skills

1. Read the financial section of a daily newspaper for a week or more. (a) What factors do economists seem to consider in judging the state of the economy? (b) What connections seem to exist between the value of the dollar and the price of gold? between interest rates and stock market averages? (c) What actions for solving economic problems does the newspaper seem to favor?
2. Draw a series of political cartoons about issues discussed in Chapter 25. Be sure your cartoon clearly presents a point of view about the issue.
3. List the advantages and disadvantages of using each of the following as a major source of energy: oil, natural gas, coal, nuclear, solar. Then rank them according to your findings.

Unit Survey

For Further Inquiry

1. Why might conflicts arise between the two goals of protecting the environment and decreasing United States dependence on foreign oil?
2. Do you think that during the 1960's and 1970's the United States assumed more responsibility around the world than it could meet? Give evidence to support your answer.
3. (a) What is the Third World? (b) How did its emergence affect the relationships between the United States and the Soviet Union?
4. Consider the New Deal, the Fair Deal, the New Frontier, and the Great Society. (a) How were they similar? (b) How were they different?
5. Make a chart comparing blacks, Hispanics, Indians, and women in terms of (a) problems, (b) goals, (c) methods used to achieve goals, (d) degree of success.
6. Of the six Presidents since 1960, which do you think was the best? Be sure to explain the standards by which you made your judgment.

Projects and Activities

1. (a) Based on the timeline here, what evidence is there that United States foreign policy has stayed basically the same since 1960? (b) What evidence is there that American foreign policy has changed in significant ways since 1960? (c) Make a timeline of domestic events since 1960. Do there seem to be any connections between foreign and domestic affairs? Explain.
2. Study the map and charts on page 708 concerning America's world trade. (a) In which area of the world are America's major trading partners? (b) Does the United States import more than it exports? How can you tell? (c) Does the United States export more raw materials or manufactured goods?
3. Listen to a record of speeches by Dr. Martin Luther King, Jr. (a) Summarize briefly the main point of each speech. (b) Do you find the speeches persuasive? Why or why not?
4. Draw political cartoons that might have appeared during the administration of one of the Presidents discussed in Unit 8. Be sure to make clear the point of view of each cartoon.

Exploring Your Region

1. What is being done in your area about the energy crisis? (For example, is there increased availability of gasohol? More solar energy in use? More incentives to install insulation in houses?)
2. Prepare a map of all or part of your municipality, divided into its voting precincts. Indicate how each precinct voted in the Presidential election of 1980. Try to find out why the voting results were the way they were. (You might look into the number of voters registered in each party in each precinct or the ethnic or economic breakdown of the population in each precinct.)

Suggested Readings

1. *Promises to Keep,* Chester Bowles. Autobiography of a man who served in diplomatic and other posts under six American Presidents.
2. *The Mexican American People: The Nation's Second Largest Minority,* Leo Grebler, Joan W. Moore, and Ralph C. Guzmán, et al. Thorough study of Mexican Americans in the Southwest.
3. *Silent Spring,* Rachel Carson. An influential and moving warning about pesticides.
4. *Roots,* Alex Haley. Story of the author's search for his own past—from Africa in the 1700's to the American South today.
5. *When the Legends Die,* Hal Borland. A novel of Tom Black Bull, a young Indian man, who tries to "find himself" after leaving the reservation.

Readings

Unit One

Rebuilding the Nation

1865–1900

CHAPTER 1
RESTORING THE SOUTH TO THE UNION

LINCOLN'S RECONSTRUCTION POLICY

Many people have wondered if the reconstruction period might have been different if Lincoln had lived. They wonder if Lincoln, who was more flexible and tactful than Andrew Johnson, might have been better able to deal with the Radical Republicans who wanted to punish the South. Of course, it is not possible ever to know, but we do know that Lincoln wanted to follow a moderate policy in restoring the South to the Union.

In this speech, delivered on April 11, 1865, just four days before he was assassinated, Lincoln explained the reconstruction policy he favored. In it he explains why he believes Louisiana has met the conditions necessary to restore it to the Union.

What are Lincoln's main arguments for readmitting Louisiana to the Union? What is his viewpoint about giving blacks the right to vote? Do you think his ideas are effective? Explain.

Adapted from Arthur Brooks Lapsley, ed., The Writings of Abraham Lincoln. *New York: G. P. Putnam's Sons, 1906.*

Fellow citizens: We meet this evening not in sorrow, but in gladness of heart. The surrender of the principal Confederate army gives hope of a righteous and speedy peace.

Because of these recent successes, we must think more than ever about re-establishing national authority—about reconstruction. This task is filled with great difficulty. Unlike a war between independent nations, there is no authorized group for us to negotiate with. No one person has authority to surrender on behalf of any other person. We simply must begin with and help bring together the disorganized elements. And we, too—the loyal people—differ among ourselves about the methods and measures of reconstruction.

We all agree that the seceded states are out of their proper practical relationship with the Union. We also agree that the only object of the government, civil and military, in regard to those states, is to get them back into their proper practical relationship with the Union. I believe that it is not only possible, but in fact easier, to do this without deciding or even considering whether those states have ever been out of the Union. Finding them safely at home, it would be completely useless to worry about whether they had ever been gone.

The number of voters on which the Louisiana government rests would be more satisfactory to all if it totaled 50,000, or 30,000, or even 20,000, instead of 12,000, as it does. It is also unsatisfactory to some that the vote is not given to colored people. I would myself prefer that it were now given to the very intelligent, and those who serve our cause as soldiers.

Still, the question is not whether the Louisiana government, as it stands, is quite all that is desirable. The question is, Will it be wiser to take it as it is and help to improve it, or reject it? Can Louisiana be brought into proper practical relation with the Union sooner by keeping or by getting rid of its new state government? Some 12,000 voters in the state have sworn loyalty to the Union. They have held elections, organized a state government, and adopted a free-state constitution. This gives the benefit of public schools equally to black and white, and gives the legislature the power to grant the vote to the colored people. This legislature has already voted to ratify the Thirteenth Amendment, recently passed by Congress abolishing slavery throughout the nation. These 12,000 persons are thus fully committed to the Union and to maintaining freedom in the state. They are committed to the very things, and nearly all the things, the nation wants. They ask the nation's recognition and its assistance to make good this commitment.

Now if we reject them, we do our utmost to disorganize them. We, in fact, say to the white people: You are worthless or worse. We will neither help you nor be helped by you. To the black people we say: This cup of liberty which these, your old masters, held to your lips, we will take from you. We will leave you to gather the spilled and scattered contents in some way. If this course, discouraging and paralyzing to both white and black, helps in any way to bring Louisiana into a proper practical relationship with the Union, I have so far not been able to see it.

If, on the contrary, we recognize and support the new government of Louisiana, the opposite is true. We encourage the hearts of 12,000 to stick to their work and fight for it, and feed it, and grow it, and ripen it to a complete success. The colored people, too, in seeing all united for them, are inspired with energy and courage. Grant that they get the vote. Will they not gain it sooner by saving the steps already taken toward it? Granted that the new government of Louisiana is related to what it should be only as the egg is to the chicken, we shall have the chicken sooner by hatching the egg than by smashing it.

A NORTHERN TEACHER IN GEORGIA

By the end of the war large parts of the South were in ruins and many southerners suffered great hardships. Things were especially difficult for the freed slaves. Many suffered from disease and hunger, and many died. Few had job skills or were able to read or write. They lacked jobs and land and often even homes. Something had to be done to help the freed slaves adjust to a new way of life.

Even before the end of the Civil War, many northerners—especially New England abolitionists—had gone into Union-occupied areas of the Confederacy to help the former slaves. They established schools and helped the freed slaves to find homes and jobs. Among these were Sarah Chase, a Quaker from Worcester, Massachusetts, and her sister Lucy, who went to the South early in 1863. They helped to establish schools and taught in various parts of the South for the next seven years.

How would you describe Sarah Chase's attitude toward the people in Columbus, Georgia? Toward her pupils? What future does she see for families in the South who favored the Union?

Reprinted from Dear Ones at Home, *edited by Henry L. Swint,* © 1966. Reprinted by permission of Vanderbilt University Press, Nashville, Tennessee.

Columbus, Georgia
February 5, 1866
Dear Mrs. May [a member of the New England Freedman's Aid Society in Boston]:

When I last wrote we had just opened a school at Savannah: There were already several schools there and Colonel Sickles [the military governor of the Carolinas] was managing the affairs of the Freedmen's Bureau in a most admirable manner. So it did not seem right to stay in that charming city, though we could have found enough important work there to fill every moment. Wishing to work where there was the most need—there are so many places where nothing has been done for the freedmen, and where they are sorely persecuted—we came here. A schoolhouse built by the soldiers had just been destroyed by the citizens. The feeling is intensely bitter against anything northern. The affairs of the Bureau have been very much mismanaged in Columbus, and our government has been disgraced by the troops who were stationed here. Now the troops have been withdrawn, and the people are annoyed by the presence of the Bureau and "a few pious and enthusiastic northeastern schoolteachers." "Both must be cleared out of the place," says the daily press. We have never been treated rudely by any of the citizens, but we know that we are generally discussed, and that many plans are proposed for "getting rid" of us.

We have glorious schools, and I am so satisfied with the work here that nothing in the world could make me wish to be in another place, or doing anything else. In my own day school and night school, I have 140 pupils. They have made truly wonderful progress in the five weeks I have been teaching.

How much I wish you could see my school! A more earnest, fine-looking group of students could not be found. I find the people here more tidy and thrifty than in any other place I know, even though many are very poor and nothing has been given them from the North. They are always cheerful and hopeful, ever anxious to improve.

How I wish I were rich! For the first time in my life I say it, for I have so much need of money here. We are too far from the North to make it worthwhile to send any boxes here because it costs too much. But I ought to have money to buy a piece of cloth, or drugs or a splint for a broken limb, or a piece of bedding for some good old soul—someone who has "raised eight children for missus as if they were my own; and nursed master so well the doctor said I saved his life; and now I'm too old to work—I'm turned out to die like a dog." Though I receive money from home, the expense of living is very great. And no individual's funds are enough for everything that is needed.

There are a number of colored people in this place who are very well-off. They cheerfully do what they can, but in a population of about 8,000, they can do little. I shall organize mutual help societies in the Negro churches (Baptist and Methodist) as soon as possible. Large numbers of black people are working for their food alone, and the white people tell them that they are not free yet. Across the river, in Alabama, several Negroes have been shot *because* they were free!

Union! I can more easily believe in the lion and the lamb lying down together than in a union of the North and South. In all the counties around here, the Union families are being persecuted. People here say that those who favor the North cannot live in their communities. We now have with us a family who fled for their lives from their plantation 14 miles [22 kilometers] away. They have never owned slaves and have always been loyal. Consequently the neighbors have been killing their cattle and taking their farm tools and doing many things to make them leave their place. A few nights ago, a regular armed force from the county surrounded their house. They were going to kill the whole family but, finding that one of the sons was not there, they left to decide whether to put it off for another time. During that time a part of the family escaped to the woods.

Such things happen all the time. But it is not a good idea to write North about them. If they get in print, it gives encouragement to many communities who are ready to act in the same way. Now that the military courts are withdrawn, I see only two alternatives for southerners who favor the Union in many parts of the South—either enduring constant persecution, or moving to the North.

STEVENS PRESENTS A RADICAL VIEW

President Johnson and the Radical Republicans in Congress had very different ideas about reconstruction. Even so, for a time most of President Johnson's version of Lincoln's moderate reconstruction program was followed. Then in 1866, the Radical Republicans won control of Congress. With a majority large enough to override President Johnson's veto, Congress took control of reconstruction.

One of the leaders of the Radical Republicans was Thaddeus Stevens, who favored a harsh reconstruction program. This selection is a part of Stevens' speech of January 3, 1867, in favor of such a reconstruction program, which Congress passed over President Johnson's veto on March 2, 1867.

In Stevens' view, what was the legal position of the Confederacy during the Civil War? What was its position afterward? What reasons does he use

to prove that the President has no authority to reconstruct the nation? What do you think of his reasons?

Adapted from Congressional Globe, 39th Congress, 2nd Session Part I, January 3, 1867.

Since the surrender of the armies of the Confederate States of America, a little has been done toward establishing this government upon the true principles of liberty and justice. But it will be only a little if we stop here. We have broken the chains of four million slaves. We have allowed them to walk about— so long as they do not walk in paths which are walked on by white people. We have allowed them the privilege of attending church—if they can do so without offending the sight of their former masters. We have even given them that highest and most agreeable proof of liberty— the right to work.

But how have we added to their liberty of thought? In what way have we taught them about and granted them the privilege of self-government? We have forced upon them the privilege of fighting our battles, of dying in defense of freedom, and of bearing their equal share of taxes. But where have we given them the privilege of taking part in the formation of the laws for the government of their native land? By what laws have we made them able to defend themselves against oppression and injustice?

Do you call this liberty? Do you call this a free republic, where four million people are subjects but not citizens? Twenty years ago I spoke against this—the tyranny in my native land. Then, twenty million white people held four million black people in slavery. I say it is no nearer a true republic. Now, twenty-five million of a privileged class keep five million from taking part in the rights of government.

Nearly six years ago a bloody war started between different sections of the United States. Eleven states having a very large territory, and ten or twelve million people, aimed to break their connection with the Union. They wanted to form an independent empire, founded on the principle of human slavery and excluding every free state. They did not aim to reform the government of the country, but they claimed their independence of that government and of all obligations to its laws. The "Confederate States" had as perfect and absolute control over those eleven states as the United States had over the other twenty-five.

The two powers prepared to settle the question by arms. They each raised armies of more than half a million men. The war was regarded by other nations as a public war between independent enemies. The two sides regarded each other as such, and claimed to be governed by the laws of war in their treatment of each other. On the result of the war depended the fate of the warring parties.

The Union armies triumphed. The Confederate armies and government surrendered unconditionally. The law of nations then fixed their condition. They were subject to the controlling power of the conquerors. No former laws, no former treaties existed to bind opposing sides. They had all been melted and destroyed in the fierce fires of the terrible war.

In a monarchy, the king would have fixed the condition of the conquered provinces. He might have extended the laws of the empire over them, allowed them to keep some of their old institutions, or have enforced new laws.

In this country, sovereignty rests with the people, and is exercised through Congress. The legislative power is the only protector of that sovereignty. No other branch of the government, or other department, no other officer of the government, holds one single part of the sovereignty of the nation. No government official, from the President and Chief Justice down, can take any action which is not directed by the legislative power.

Since the President is only the servant of the people, who issue their commands to him through Congress, where does he obtain the constitutional power to create new states? Where does he get the power to remake old ones, to establish laws, to fix the qualification of voters, to declare that states have the right to command Congress to admit their Representatives?

To reconstruct the nation, to admit new states, to guarantee republican governments to old states—these are all legislative acts. The President claims the right to make use of them. Congress denies it and claims the right to belong to the legislative branch. This I take to be the great issue between the President and Congress.

The President wants to pardon the conquered rebels from all the expense and damages of the war. He insists that those of our people who had property burned or destroyed by rebel raiders shall not be paid back, but shall bear their own loss. He desires that the states created by him shall be accepted as valid states. At the same time he declares that the old rebel states are still in existence, and always have been, and have equal rights with the loyal states. He is determined to force a solid rebel delegation into Congress from the South.

In opposition to these things, a part of Congress seems to desire that the conquered side shall, according to the law of nations, pay at least a part of the expenses and damages of the war. The loyal people who were plundered and ruined by rebel raiders should be paid back in full. A majority of Congress desires that treason shall be made hateful, not by bloody executions, but by other adequate punishments.

There are several good reasons for the passage of this bill [the reconstruction program]. In the first place, it is just. I am now speaking of granting the vote to Negroes in the rebel states. Have not loyal blacks as good a right to choose rulers and make laws as rebel whites? In the second place, it is a necessity in order to protect the white people who are loyal to the Union in the seceded states. The white Union people are in a great minority in each of those states. With them the blacks would act together as a group. In most states they would form a majority, control the states and protect themselves.

Another good reason is, it would insure the power of the Republican Party. I believe that the safety of this great nation depends upon the continuing power of the Republican Party.

For these, among other reasons, I am for giving the vote to Negroes in every rebel state. If it is just, it should not be denied. If it is necessary, it should be adopted. If it is a punishment to traitors, they deserve it.

But it will be said, as it has been said, "This is Negro equality!" What is Negro equality about? It means, as understood by honest Republicans, just this much and no more: Every person, no matter what his or her race or color, every human being who has an immortal soul, has an equal right to justice, honesty, and fair play. The law should secure those rights for people. The same law which condemns or acquits Africans should condemn or acquit white people. The same law which gives a verdict in a white person's favor should give a verdict in a black person's favor using the same set of facts. Such is the law of God and such ought to be the law of humans.

JOHNSON IS FOUND NOT GUILTY

President Johnson's policies, his inflexible stand on reconstruction, and his vetoes of Congressional reconstruction bills made him a hated enemy to the Radical Republicans. They became determined to remove him from office, since they were convinced that Johnson would not enforce their reconstruction program. The House of Representatives impeached Johnson in February of 1868, and he was brought to trial in the Senate in March. During the Senate trial, it seemed clear that the President had not committed any offense for which he could legally be removed from office. Nevertheless, he was found not guilty by the margin of a single vote.

Although never a popular President, Andrew Johnson's dignified behavior during the House impeachment and the Senate trial won the respect of the American people. In this selection, the Senate trial is described by William H. Crook, a White House guard.

According to Crook, why was the trial so important? From this account, what do you think had more effect on the outcome of the trial—legal arguments or behind-the-scenes influence on the voting?

Adapted from pp. 125-134 of Through Five Administrations: Reminiscences of Colonel William H. Crook, *edited by Margarita Spalding Gerry. Copyright 1907, 1910 by Harper & Brothers. Reprinted by permission of Harper & Row, Publishers, Inc.*

On the 23rd of March, when the actual trial began, the President said good-by to three of his lawyers, who had come to the White House for a final discussion. I was near them as they stood together on the porch. Mr. Johnson's manner was calm and unconcerned. He shook hands with each of them in turn, and said:

"Gentleman, my case is in your hands. I feel sure that you will protect my interests." Then he returned to his office. I went off with the lawyers. At the President's request, I went with them to the Capitol every day.

When, from my seat in the gallery, I looked down on the Senate chamber, I almost had a moment of terror. It was not because of the gathering. It was rather in the thought that one could feel in the mind of every man and woman there: For the first time in the history of the United States, a President was on trial for more than his life—his place in the judgment of his country's people and history.

The trial lasted three weeks. The President, of course, never appeared. In that respect the proceedings lacked the spectacular interest they might have had. Every day the President had a meeting with his lawyers. Otherwise, he attended to the routine work of his position. He was absolutely calm through it all.

As the trial went on, the belief grew with me—I think it did with everyone—that the weight of evidence and constitutional principle lay with the defense. There were several clever lawyers on the prosecution side, but most of the proceedings showed personal feeling and prejudice rather than proof. Every appeal that could be made to the passions of the time was used. By comparison, the calm, ordered, masterly reasoning of the defense must have made everyone believe in the truth of its cause.

But the legal struggle, after all, was hardly the contest that counted. The debate was for the benefit of the country at large. While the legal experts argued, the enemies of the President were working in other ways. The Senate was thoroughly checked for votes. Personal appeals and influence were constant. Every personal motive, good or bad, was used. Long before the final vote, it was known how most of the men would probably vote. Toward the end, only one doubtful vote remained—that of Senator Ross of Kansas. It looked as if Kansas—which had been the fighting ground of rebel guerillas and northern abolitionists—was to have the determining vote.

Kansas was, from the beginning, abolitionist and Radical. It would have been supposed that Senator Ross would vote with the Radicals.

Then the Radical forces in the Senate and the House put pressure on the Senator from Kansas. Party discipline was used, and then ridicule. Either from uncertainty, or policy, or a desire to keep his associates in uncertainty, Ross refused to say how he would vote. In all probability he was honestly trying to decide for himself.

The last days before the vote was to be taken were breathless ones. The country was paralyzed. Business in Washington was almost at a standstill.

On May 16th the vote was taken. Everyone who by any possible means could get a ticket of admission to the Senate chamber arrived early that morning at the Capitol. The floor and galleries were crowded.

The journal was read. The House of Representatives was told that the Senate, "sitting for the trial of the President upon the articles of impeachment," was ready to receive the other house in the Senate chamber. The question of voting first upon the eleventh article was decided.

The clerk read the legal statement of those crimes of which, in the opinion of the House of Representatives, the President was guilty. At the end, the Chief Justice directed that the roll be called. The clerk called out:

"Mr. Anthony." Mr. Anthony rose.

"Mr. Anthony"—the Chief Justice looked at the Senator—"how say you? Is the respondent, Andrew Johnson, President of the United States, guilty or not guilty of a high misdemeanor as charged in this article?"

"Guilty," answered Mr. Anthony.

A sigh spread round the room. Yet Mr. Anthony's vote was not in doubt. A two-thirds vote of 36 to 18 was necessary to convict. Thirty-four of the Senators were pledged to vote against the President. Although there was some doubt, it was thought that Mr. Fowler of Tennessee would most likely vote for the President. Senator Ross was the only one whose vote was really in doubt. No one knew his position. When Fowler's name was reached, everyone leaned forward to hear his answer.

"Not guilty," said Senator Fowler.

The tension grew. There were many names called before that of Senator Ross was reached. When the clerk called it, and Ross stood up, the crowd held its breath.

"Not guilty," replied the Senator from Kansas.

The Radical Senators, who had been with Ross only a short time before, turned to him in a rage. All over the hall people began to stir. The rest of the roll call was listened to with lessened interest, although there was still the chance of a surprise. When it was over, and the result—35 to 19—was announced, there was a wild outburst, chiefly groans of anger and disappointment, for the friends of the President were in the minority,

I did not wait to hear the verdict read—it would be no surprise to me, as I had been keeping a list of the votes on a slip of paper—I ran downstairs at top speed. In the corridor of the Senate I came across a curious group. In it was Thaddeus Stevens, now completely disabled, whose two attendants were carrying him high on their shoulders. All around him, the crowd, unable to get into the courtroom, was calling out: "What was the verdict?" Thad Stevens' face was filled with rage and disappointment.

He waved his arms in the air and shouted in answer:

"The country is going to the devil!"

I ran all the way from the Capitol to the White House. I was young and strong in those days, and I made good time. When I burst into the library, where the President sat with three other men, they were quietly talking. There were no signs of excitement.

"Mr. President," I shouted, too excited and filled with delight to stop myself, "you are acquitted!"

Everyone stood up. I made my way to the President and took hold of his hand. The other men surrounded him, and began to shake his hand. The President responded to their congratulations calmly enough for a moment, and then I saw that tears were rolling down his face.

LAUNCHING THE "NEW SOUTH"

In 1886, a group of New York business leaders asked Henry W. Grady, the editor of the Atlanta newspaper the *Constitution,* to come to New York to speak before their group. In his speech, Grady spoke of the "New South" and described the many changes that had taken place during the years following the war. Afterward, the speech became well known, and the term the "New South" became famous. It convinced many people that the South had changed.

And indeed by the 1880's, the South had changed in many ways. Many large plantations were broken up and many small farms were started. Improved farming methods were used and crops other than cotton were grown. Industry began to develop, and with industry came the growth of cities.

Why do you think Grady spends so much time describing "the footsore Confederate soldier"? To what groups of people do you think this speech might appeal? What is his advice to northerners regarding blacks? Was this advice followed?

Adapted from Daniel J. Boorstin, ed., An American Primer, *Vol. I. Chicago: University of Chicago Press, 1966.*

Dear to me is the home of my childhood and the traditions of my people. I would not, if I could, dim the glory they won in peace and war. Nor would I by word or deed take anything from the splendor and grace of their civilization—never equaled before and perhaps never to be equaled again. There is a New South, not the result of protest against the old, but the result of new conditions, new adjustments, new ideas, and new hopes.

Dr. Talmadge [the previous speaker] has drawn for you the picture of your returning armies. He has told you how they came back to you, marching with proud and victorious step, reading their glory in a nation's eyes! Will you be patient while I tell you of another army that returned home at the close of the war. This army marched home in defeat and not in victory, in sorrow and not in splendor, but in glory that equaled yours, and to hearts just as loving. Let me picture for you the footsore Confederate soldier, as he turned his face southward from Appomattox in April 1865. Think of him as ragged, half-starved, heavy-hearted, weak from want and wounds. Having fought to the point of exhaustion, he surrenders his gun, shakes the hands of his comrades in silence, and—lifting his tear-stained, pale face for the last time to look at the graves that dot the old Virginia hills—pulls on his gray cap and begins the slow and painful journey home. What does he find when he reaches the home he left so prosperous and beautiful? He finds his house in ruins, his farm destroyed, his slaves free, his animals killed, his barns empty, his trade destroyed, his money worthless. His social system has been swept away. His people are without law or legal status. Crushed by defeat, his very traditions are gone. He has no money, credit, job, material, or training. Besides all this, he is faced with the problems of establishing a status for the freed slaves.

What does he do—this hero in gray with a heart of gold? Does he sit down in gloom and despair? Not for a day. The soldier stepped from the trenches into the fields. Horses that had charged Union guns now marched before the plow. Fields that ran red with human blood in April were green with the harvest in June. There was little bitterness in all this. Cheerfulness and frankness were widespread.

But in all this what have we accomplished? What is the sum of our work? We have found out that, in general, the free Negro counts more than he did as a slave. We have built schools and made them free for white and black. We have built towns and cities and put business above politics. We have challenged your spinners in Massachusetts and your ironmakers in Pennsylvania. We have established thrift in city and country. We have fallen in love with work. We have restored comfort to homes from which culture and elegance never left. Above all, we know that we have achieved in these times of peace a fuller independence for the South than that which our fathers sought to win in the political arena by their words or on the battlefield by their swords.

It is a great privilege to have had a part, however small, in this work. Never was a nobler duty given to human hands than the uplifting and rebuilding of the fallen and bleeding South, misguided perhaps, but beautiful in its suffering, and honest, brave, and generous always.

But what of the Negroes? Have we solved the problem they present, or progressed in honor and fairness toward the solution? Let the record speak. No section shows a more prosperous working population than the Negroes of the South. They share our schools, have the fullest protection of our laws and the friendship of our people. Self-interest, as well as honor, demands that they should have this. Our future, our very existence, depends upon our working out this problem in full and exact justice. We understand that when Lincoln signed the Emancipation Proclamation, your victory was assured. For he then committed you to the cause of human liberty, which weapons cannot overcome. Those of our leaders who pledged to make slavery the cornerstone of the Confederacy doomed us to defeat, committing us to a cause that reason could not defend or the sword maintain.

The relations of the southern people with the Negroes are close and friendly. We remember how for four years they guarded our defenseless women and children, whose husbands and fathers were fighting against their freedom. Whenever they struck a blow for their own liberty they fought in open battle. When at last they raised their hands so that the chains might be struck off, those hands were innocent of any wrong against their helpless charges, and worthy to be taken in loving grasp by every person who honors loyalty and devotion. Ruffians have mistreated them, rascals have misled them. But the South, with the North, protests against injustice to this simple and sincere people.

Law can bring the Negro only liberty and the vote. The rest must be left to conscience and common sense. It should be left to those among whom the Negroes' lot is cast, with whom they are closely connected. Their prosperity depends upon having intelligent sympathy and confidence. Faith has been kept with the Negroes in spite of statements to the opposite by those who claim to speak for us or by our enemies. Faith will be kept with them in the future.

But have we kept faith with you? In the fullest sense, yes. We fought hard enough to know that we were beaten. The chains that had held the South in narrow limitations fell forever when the chains of the Negro slave were broken. Under the old system the Negroes were slaves to the South and the South was a slave to the system.

The old South based everything on slavery and agriculture. The new South presents a perfect democracy. Its social system is less splendid on the surface but stronger at the center. It has a hundred farms for every plantation, fifty homes for every mansion, and industry that meets the complex needs of this complex age.

The new South loves its new work. Its soul is stirred with the breath of a new life. It is thrilled by the realization of growing power and prosperity. It understands that its emancipation came because in the wisdom of God its honest purpose was crossed and its brave armies were beaten.

This is said in no spirit of apology. The South has nothing for which to apologize. It believes that the late struggle between the states was war and not rebellion, and that its convictions were as honest as yours.

BOOKER T. WASHINGTON EMPHASIZES HARD WORK

By the 1880's, black southerners were segregated from white southerners in schools and public facilities. Also, black Americans were now denied their political and civil rights. Some black leaders spoke out against this discrimination and urged blacks to struggle for their rights; other leaders disagreed.

In a speech in 1895 at the Atlanta Exposition, Booker T. Washington suggested that black Americans should follow a moderate course. His speech became known as the Atlanta Compromise because it seemed to indicate that black Americans should accept segregation. In actuality, Washington believed that if blacks gained job skills and training they would become necessary to the South's economy, and thus would become respected and regain their civil rights.

What does Washington mean when he advises blacks to "cast down your bucket"? When he advises whites to do the same? How does he try to encourage his black listeners? How does he try to reassure his white listeners?

Adapted from Booker T. Washington, Up From Slavery: An Autobiography. *Garden City. N. Y.: Doubleday, Page and Company, 1900.*

One third of the population of the South is of the Negro race. No project seeking the material, civil, or moral welfare of this section can ignore this part of our population and reach the highest success. I bring to you the feeling of the masses of my race when I say that in no way have the value and manhood of the American Negro been more fittingly and generously recognized than by the managers of this magnificent Exposition. It is a recognition that will do more to strengthen the friendship of the two races than any happening since the dawn of our freedom.

Not only this, but the opportunity given here will awaken among us a new era of industrial progress. We were ignorant and inexperienced, and it is not strange that in the first years of our new life we began at the top instead of at the bottom. A seat in Congress or the state legislature was more sought than land or industrial skill. The political convention or election speeches had more attraction than starting a dairy farm or truck garden.

A ship lost at sea for many days suddenly sighted a friendly ship. From the mast of the unfortunate ship was seen a signal, "Water, water; we die of thirst!" The answer from the friendly ship came back at once, "Cast down your bucket where you are." A second time the signal, "Water, water; send us water!" ran up from the distressed ship. It was again answered, "Cast down your bucket where you are." And a third and fourth signal for water was answered, "Cast down your bucket where you are." The captain of the distressed ship, at last listening to the advice, cast down his bucket, and it came up full of fresh, sparkling water from the Amazon River. To those of my race who depend on bettering their condition in a foreign land or who don't realize the importance of developing friendly relations with southern whites, who are their next-door neighbors, I would say: "Cast down your bucket where you are." Cast it down in making friends of the people of all races by whom we are surrounded.

Cast it down in agriculture, in industry, in commerce, in domestic service, and in the professions. In this connection it is well to remember that whatever other signs the South may have, when it comes to business it is in the South that the Negro is given a chance in the commercial world. Our greatest danger is that in the great leap from slavery to freedom we may overlook the fact that most of us are to live by the productions of our hands and fail to keep in mind that we shall prosper as we learn to dignify and glorify common labor and put brains and skill into our occupations. We shall prosper if we learn to draw the line between the superficial and the substantial, the ornamental things of life and the useful things. No race can prosper till it learns that there is as much dignity in tilling a field as in writing a poem. It is at the bottom of life we must begin, not at the top. Nor should we permit our problems to overshadow our opportunities.

To those of the white race who look to the immigrants of foreign lands for the prosperity of the South, I would repeat what I say to my own race, "Cast down your bucket where you are." Cast it down among the eight million Negroes whose habits you know, whose loyalty and love you have tested. Cast down your bucket among these people who have, without strikes and labor wars, tilled your fields, cleared your forests, built your railroads and cities, and brought forth treasures from the earth. Casting down your bucket among my people, helping and encouraging them, you will find that they will buy your extra land, grow crops in the waste places in your fields, and run your factories. While doing this, you can be sure in the future, as in the past, that you and your families will be surrounded by the most patient, faithful, law-abiding, and unresentful people that the world has seen. We have proved our loyalty to you in the past, nursing your children, watching by the sickbeds of your mothers and fathers, and often following them with tear-filled eyes to their graves. So in the future, we shall stand by you with a loyalty that no foreigner can equal. We are ready to lay down our lives, if need be, in defense of yours. We shall join our industrial, commercial, civil, and religious life with yours in the way that shall make the interests of both races one. In all things that are purely social we can be as separate as the fingers, yet one as the hand in all things essential to mutual progress.

The wisest among my race understand that demonstrating on questions of social equality is foolish. Progress in enjoying all the privileges that will come to us must be the result of severe and constant struggle rather than of forcing. No race that has anything to contribute to the markets of the world is banished for long. It is important and right that all privileges of the law be ours. But it is much more important that we be prepared for making use of these privileges. The opportunity to earn a dollar in a factory just now is worth much more than the opportunity to spend a dollar in an opera house.

W. E. B. DU BOIS OFFERS HIS VIEWS

Booker T. Washington was the best known leader of black Americans in the late 1800's and early 1900's. However, there were other black leaders who disagreed with Washington's emphasis upon job training and vocational education for black Americans.

Among those who disagreed was W. E. B. Du Bois, a Harvard-educated black scholar. He felt that talented blacks should not be content with vocational education but should go to colleges and universities. He also came to believe that only strong protests against inequality and discrimination could bring about change. In 1903 Du Bois singled out Washington and his Atlanta speech for criticism, and he made his own suggestions for the advancement of black people.

Why, according to Du Bois, did Booker T. Washington win such wide popularity when he did? Do you think Washington asked blacks to give up the three things that Du Bois lists? What does Du Bois advise black people to do?

Adapted from W. E. B Du Bois, The Souls of Black Folk, *6th ed. New York: A. C. McClurg & Co., 1905.*

Easily the most striking thing in the history of the American Negro since 1876 is the importance of Mr. Booker T. Washington. It began at the time when war memories and ideals were rapidly passing. A time of astonishing commercial development was beginning. A sense of doubt and hesitation overtook the freedmen's sons — it was then that his leadership began. Mr. Washington appeared with a simple, definite program, at the moment when the nation was a little ashamed of having given so much sentiment to Negroes, and was concentrating its energies on dollars. His program involved industrial education, pleasing the South, and acceptance and silence as to civil and political rights.

It startled the nation to hear a Negro proposing such a program after many years of bitter complaint. It startled and won the applause of the South. It interested and won the admiration of the North. And after a confused murmur of protest, it silenced if it did not convert the Negroes themselves.

To gain the sympathy and cooperation of the white South was Mr. Washington's first task. At the time Tuskegee [the school started by Booker T. Washington] was founded, this seemed, for a black person, almost impossible. And yet ten years later it was done in the words spoken at Atlanta: "In all things purely social we can be as separate as the five fingers, and yet one as the hand in all things essential to mutual progress." This "Atlanta Compromise" is the most notable thing in Mr. Washington's career. The South judged it in different ways. The radicals saw it as a complete surrender of the demand for civil and political equality. The conservatives regarded it as a working basis for joint understanding. So both approved it. Today its author is certainly the most distinguished southerner since Jefferson Davis, and the one with the largest personal following.

Mr. Washington represents in Negro thought the old attitude of adjustment and giving in, but adjustment at such a time as to make his program unique. This is an age of unusual economic development, and Mr. Washington's program naturally has an economic basis. It becomes a gospel of work and money and almost completely forgets the higher aims of life. Moreover, this is an age when the more advanced races are coming in closer contact with the less developed races, and race feeling is therefore stronger. Mr. Washington's program, for all practical purposes, accepts the inferiority of the Negro race. Again, a reaction against wartime feelings has led to race prejudice against Negroes, and Mr. Washington withdraws many of the high demands of Negroes as American citizens. In other periods of prejudice all the Negro's tendency to self-assertion has been called forth. At this period a policy of giving in is advised. In the history of

491

nearly all other races and peoples, the policy suggested for such crises has been that self-respect is worth more than lands and houses. And that a people who on their own surrender such respect, or stop struggling for it, are not worth civilizing.

In answer to this, it has been claimed that the Negro can survive only through giving in. Mr. Washington asks that black people give up, at least for the present, three things—

First, political power,

Second, demand for civil rights,

Third, higher education of Negro youth. They should concentrate all their energies on industrial education, on gaining wealth, and on pleasing the South. This policy has been courageously and insistently encouraged for over fifteen years, and has been triumphant for perhaps ten years. What has been the result? In these years there have occurred:

1. The disfranchisement [taking away the vote] of the Negro.

2. The legal creation of a separate status of civil inferiority for the Negro.

3. The steady withdrawal of aid from institutions for the higher training of the Negro.

These movements are not, to be sure, direct results of Mr. Washington's teachings. But his propaganda has, without a shadow of doubt, helped speed them up. The question then arises: Is it possible, and probable, that nine million people can make effective progress along economic lines if their political rights are taken away, and they are made an inferior group and allowed only the smallest chance of developing their outstanding people? If history and reason give any distinct answer to these questions, it is *No.*

In failing to declare plainly and without doubt the demands of their people, even at the cost of opposing an honored leader, the thinking classes of American Negroes would be avoiding a heavy responsibility. They would be avoiding a responsibility to themselves, to the struggling masses, to the darker races of people whose future depends so largely on this American experiment, and especially to this nation. It is wrong to aid a national crime simply because it is unpopular not to do so. The growing spirit of kindliness and understanding between the North and South after the differences of a generation ago ought to make everyone happy, especially those whose mistreatment caused the war. But if that understanding is to be marked by the industrial slavery and civic death of those same black people, then those black people should oppose such a course by all civilized methods—even though it involves disagreement with Mr. Booker T. Washington.

CHAPTER 2
SEVERE TRIALS FOR DEMOCRACY

AN ENGLISH REFORMER ATTENDS A POLITICAL CONVENTION

In the 1870's, George Holyoake, a social reformer, came over from England to visit the United States. He was interested in visiting and studying the cooperatives formed by American farmers.

Holyoake was also very curious about American politics, and he admired "the republican equality and the republican freedom of America." He wrote: "The minds of the people, like keyless watches, wind themselves up and always keep going." Because of this interest in politics, he attended a Republican Party convention in 1879 at Saratoga, New York. This is his description of that meeting.

Do you think Holyoake is serious about his description of the convention's procedures? Can you think of some reasons why Americans at this time were willing to listen to such long speeches? What does Holyoake admire about the convention?

Adapted from pages 48-53 from Among the Americans by George Jacob Holyoake, used with the permission of Greenwood Press, the reprint publishers, a division of Congressional Information Service, Inc.

The object of the convention, called by the Republican leaders, was to choose a candidate for governor of New York and other state officers. My wish was to see not only what was done, but also how it was done and where it was done.

The convention was held in the Town Hall. It was not bad inside. There was more space than we reserve for speakers in England. But in the center of the stage was a small, ugly desk. The president hit its hollow top with a pitiful wooden hammer, setting off weak echoes within it. Nobody had thought that the grandest use of a public hall is a public meeting.

I had heard a good deal in England about American political organization. It did not appear in the physical arrangements of the meetings though it showed in the proceedings. The names of the candidates for the chief office were read over. The popular name was that of "Alonzo B. Cornell," the son of the founder of the Cornell University. Mr. Cornell received the nomination for governor of New York State. That day I heard his name said a thousand times. Each delegate was called upon to announce aloud the name of the candidate he was voting for. There was only one Cornell, yet nobody answered as we would do in England — "Cornell." Each said, "Alonzo B. Cornell," or "Jehosophat P. Squattles," or whatever was the name of the other candidate.

An hour was spent over that new governor's name, yet if "Alonzo B." had been eliminated the business would have been finished in a third of the time. (Mr. Cornell himself was a modest, pleasant gentleman, with a business-like method of speech.)

The character of every people, like that of every individual, is made up of contradictions. The Americans, as a rule, catch on to things quickly. Their conversation is clear, bright, and precise. Their understanding is direct. Yet these quick-witted listeners will tolerate speakers who are long-winded, indirect, and speak endlessly. They will sit and listen to them for long periods of time.

At the New York convention a "program of principles" called a "platform" — was read. No one could make sure what was meant, and a professor of memory could not remember half of what was written. All I remember was that the platform ended with some statements about things in general. Yet there were parts of it which showed intelligence — if only the writer had known when to stop.

I regretted not being able to go to Syracuse to see the Democratic convention. I was told the Democratic conventions were marked by great activity and disorder. The *New York Tribune* said that there would be many "large heads" at Syracuse. I wanted to see "large heads," as I had no idea what a political "large head" was. I was told that the Democrats are more boisterous in their meetings than Republicans. The Democrats seem to be like our Tories at home — indignant at any dissent at their meetings, but persistent in interrupting the meetings of others.

The Saratoga convention was characterized by great order and attention to whoever desired to speak. If anyone had a question, the answer was "The Chair takes a contrary view; the Chair decides against you." The chairman was an institution, or a court of authority. This I found to be a rule in America. The immediate attention given to anyone who wanted to speak was greater than in England. In England the theory of a public meeting is that anyone present may speak, but we never let them do it. If the chairman is willing the audience is not. At several public meetings that I attended in America the right of a person on the floor seemed equal to that of those on the platform. Citizens seemed to recognize the equality of each other. In England there is no public sense of equality. There is always somebody who is supposed to be better than anybody.

GROWING UP REPUBLICAN

In the years after the Civil War, loyalties to political parties became especially strong. The party that a person supported was often the result of tradition and family upbringing. For example, a person who was brought up in a family that supported the Democratic Party would almost never vote for a Republican candidate. And a person raised in a family that supported the Republican Party would not vote for a Democratic candidate.

In these years, there were few Americans who were "independents." Most people supported either the Republican or Democratic Party, or perhaps a smaller third party. And there was very little "ticket splitting," or voting for some of the candidates of both major parties, as there is today. In this selection, Sarah Smith Pratt tells what it was like to grow up in a Republican home in Indiana.

What attitudes does the writer have toward her father? Do you think that the author's attitudes toward political parties might have changed if the visiting Methodists had been Democrats instead of Republicans? Is party loyalty as strong in your family as it was among the Smiths?

Adapted from Sarah S. Pratt, The Old Crop in Indiana. *Indianapolis: The Pratt Poster Co., 1928.*

Although we lived in a Democratic stronghold, our family happened to be Republican. I realize now that the great shaping force of Republicanism in my youth was my father. He was a perfect example of the "waving-the-bloody-shirt" type — intolerant of everything he did not approve of. He was of that great group of good men who are upset by wrongdoing, but are never willing to hold office. He had great influence throughout the county we lived in because of his education, moral courage, and ability to speak well. He was listened to with respect by a large group of farmers. Nick Smith's [the author's father] opinions were quoted all over the county. He was the delight of the virtuous and the terror of the wrongdoer. He loved to criticize liquor-sellers and Democrats.

He had come from Baltimore and settled in Indiana about 1836, bringing a stock of farm tools, roofing material, vats, tanks, and hydraulic rams, all greatly needed in that new country.

I was surrounded with Republicanism from the very minute I was born. Editorials read aloud from the newspapers of that day, explained loudly to my mother and filled with criticisms of the "jackasses" and "natural-born fools" who headed the other party — these stamped themselves forever on the well-behaved children who sat and listened.

And yet my father's hunting friend and the companion of his long Sunday walks was Walter Beach, a strong, outspoken Democrat.

My first knowledge of the word "Democrat" came because of Dash, my dog. One night he was found near the kitchen door of the editor of the *Times.* The *Times* was the Democratic newspaper — the *Journal,* the Republican. This editor, because he was short and somewhat pompous, was called "Whistlebreeches."

"Whistlebreeches shot Dash last night. He's lying dead in their yard," my brother came and told us as we were at breakfast.

"Get the wheelbarrow, Lutie, and get him and bury him in the yard — that — that Democrat," my father said as he gulped down his coffee.

When I saw this editor go past our house on his way home at noon, despite my grief I was interested in the name I had heard my father call him: Democrat!

"What *is* a Democrat, Papa? I think it is such a pretty word."

"Democrat," exploded my father, "a Democrat is a man —" he said, too mad to know just what to say. "A man who — who —"

"Now, Nicholas, be careful before the children. Don't say anything mean. You know our minister is a Democrat and so is our doctor."

My father, feeling a little ashamed by this time, said nothing, but he had left a bad impression of the party started by Jefferson. I still think "Democrat" is a great word. It is perhaps the most important of human meanings and — in its perfection — the most unreachable.

An event which deepened my respect for the party in power [the Republican Party] occurred right after the war when a Methodist conference was to be held in Delphi. Brother Sims and Brother McIntosh asked our parents to entertain some of the visiting clergy. We were Episcopalians, but joyfully opened our doors to the visitors. Three of their most interesting men stayed at our house. Two of them were celebrities. The third was a professor from New Orleans. These good-humored men were soon well liked by the whole household. One of them was Elder John L. Smith, a noted man in his day. Another was John Hogarth Lozier — called Chaplain Lozier because of his work in the army, and admired by hundreds of soldiers. The third was a brown-eyed professor.

All the men were strong Republicans. My father, pleased beyond measure to find his own feelings backed up by three such men, showed them the greatest hospitality. There never were more cheerful or wittier talks than those that lasted these three days at our home.

Chaplain Lozier was a writer of verses, many of which had been set to music. Some of them described political events. He had a popular song set to the tune of "Wait for the Wagon." He would recite this line by line and we would all sing it:

In Uncle Sam's dominions in 1861
The fight between the Union and secession
   was begun
The South declared they'd have the rights
That Uncle Sam denied
Or in his Union wagon they would not longer
   ride.

Wait for the wagon, the old Union wagon,
Wait for the wagon and we'll all take a ride.

This visit served to deepen my belief that the Republican Party was even greater than I had thought it was. Of course, there were good Democrats—old Dr. Blanchard and Lawyer Sims and plenty of good people who were our neighbors. But to think that from the outside world had appeared Elder Smith wearing a long black coat and silk hat, carrying a gold-headed cane, and having elegant manners. He was a Republican. And there was Chaplain Lozier, who could make poems and have them printed and sung. He too was a Republican. And there was Professor Henry Jackson, who could write in French and teach in a young woman's school. And he too was a Republican. Altogether, the greatness of the Republican Party was increased in my mind by this visit of these loyal Methodists.

"WHY GREAT MEN ARE NOT CHOSEN PRESIDENTS"

Many historians believe that there have been very few great American Presidents—perhaps seven or eight at most. In his book *The American Commonwealth*, James Bryce, an English scholar, tried to explain why Americans have elected so many ordinary Presidents. This work has been called "the greatest book written about this country." Bryce visited the United States three times before he wrote his study. And he later served as the British ambassador to Washington. Although this selection may seem critical, Bryce actually had a favorable opinion of the American system of government.

What are the three main reasons Bryce gives for the lack of "great men" who have held the office of President? Do you think that American Presidents still have the characteristics Bryce describes?

Adapted by permission of G. P. Putnam's Sons from The American Commonwealth *by James Bryce. Copyright ©️ 1959 by G. P. Putnam's Sons.*

Europeans often ask, and Americans do not always explain, how it happens that this great office—to which any man can rise by his own merits—is not more frequently filled by great men. In America, which is a country where political life is unusually keen, it might be expected that the Presidency would always be won by a man of brilliant gifts. But since the heroes of the Revolution died out with Jefferson and Adams and Madison some sixty years ago, no person except General Grant has reached the office whose name would have been remembered if he had not been President. No President except Abraham Lincoln has shown rare or striking qualities in the office. Who now knows or cares to know anything about the personality of James K. Polk or Franklin Pierce? The only thing remarkable about them is that, being so ordinary, they should have climbed so high.

Several reasons may be suggested for this fact, which Americans are themselves the first to admit.

One is that the number of people with great abilities drawn into politics is smaller in America than in most European countries. In France and Italy, half-revolutionary conditions have made public life exciting and easy to enter. In Germany, a well-organized civil service develops the art of government with unusual success. In England, many persons of wealth and leisure seek to enter politics, while vital problems touch the interests of all classes and make people eager observers of the political scene. In America, many able men rush into a field which is comparatively small in Europe, the business of developing the material resources of the country.

Another reason is that the methods and habits of Congress, and indeed of political life generally, seem to give fewer opportunities for personal distinction. There are fewer ways in which a man may win the admiration of his countrymen by outstanding thought, speech, or ability in administration.

A third reason is that important men make more enemies than less well-known men do. They are therefore less admirable candidates. It is true that the important man has also made more friends, that his name is more widely known, and that he may be greeted with louder cheers. Other things being equal, the famous man is preferable. But other things never are equal. The famous man has probably attacked some leaders in his own party, has replaced others, has expressed his dislike of some group, has perhaps committed errors which can be turned into offenses. No man can be in public life for long and take part in great affairs without causing criticism. People constantly search out all the corners of a Presidential candidate's past life. Therefore, when the choice lies between a brilliant man and a safe man, the safe man is preferred. Party feeling, strong enough to support a man without positive merits, is not always strong enough to gain forgiveness for a man with positive faults.

A European finds that this needs to be explained. For in the free countries of Europe, brilliance or some striking achievement is what makes a leader triumphant. Why should it be different in America? Because in America party loyalty and party organization have been so perfect that anyone chosen as a candidate by the party will get the full party vote if his character is good and his "record," as they call it, is unstained. The safe candidate may not receive quite so many votes from the moderate people of the other side as the brilliant one would, but he will not lose nearly so many from his own party. Even those who admit he is only ordinary will vote for him when the moment for voting comes. Besides, most American voters do not object to ordinary candidates. They have a lower idea of the qualities necessary for a statesman than those who direct public opinion in Europe. They like their candidates to be sensible, vigorous, and, above all, what they call "magnetic." They do not value, because they see no need for, originality or profundity, a cultured background or great knowledge. Candidates are selected by small groups of persons who run the political party but are usually commonplace men.

It must also be remembered that the merits of a President are one thing and those of a candidate another thing. An important American is reported to have said to friends who wished him to be a candidate, "Gentlemen, let there be no mistake. I would make a good President but a very bad candidate." Now to a party it is more important that its choice should be a good candidate than that he should turn out to be a good President. It will be a misfortune to the party, as well as to the country, if the candidate elected proves to be a bad President. But it is a greater misfortune to the party if it is beaten, for it will then lose four years of national patronage.

After all—and this is a point much less obvious to Europeans than to Americans—a President need not be brilliant. Englishmen, imagining him as something like their Prime Minister, assume that he ought to be a great speaker, having also the power to propose a great policy or write a good law. They forget that the President does not sit in Congress. His main duties are to promptly and effectively carry out the laws and maintain public order, and choose the executive officials of the country. Firmness, common sense, and, most of all, honesty are the qualities which the country needs in its chief executive.

So far we have been considering personal merits. But in the selection of a candidate many other considerations have to be regarded. The chief of these is the amount of support which can be secured from different states or regions of the Union. State feeling and sectional feeling are powerful factors in a Presidential election. The Northwest, including the states from Ohio to Dakota, is now the most populous region of the Union, and therefore counts for most in an election. Thus a northwestern man makes the best candidate. A large state casts a greater vote in the election, and every state is of course more likely to be carried by one of its own citizens than by a stranger. Therefore a man from a large state is preferable as a candidate. The problem is further complicated by the fact that some states are already safe for one or the other party, while others are doubtful. Most of the Northwestern and New England states are certain to go Republican. All of the Southern states are (at present) certain to go Democratic. It is more important to please a doubtful state than one you have already. Thus a candidate from a doubtful state, such as New York or Indiana, is to be preferred.

KEEPING PUBLIC SERVANTS ON THEIR TOES

The years after the Civil War were years of graft and corruption at all levels of American government. As a result, many writers and journalists tried to make Americans aware of the dishonesty in their governments, in the hopes of ridding the nation of dishonest officials. These writers often used humor to show the faults of government officials. Thomas Nast's famous cartoons of Boss Tweed and the Tammany Ring were one example. Another was the books of David R. Locke, a favorite humorous writer of this period. Lincoln said of one of Locke's earlier books, "For the genius to write such things, I would gladly give up my office." In a later book, Locke wrote down the sayings of "a wise Persian man living in New Jersey." The purpose of this book was to poke fun at American government.

How does Locke make fun of legislators? Do you think he is serious about the remedy he suggests? Do you think this selection still applies to American politics today?

Adapted from David R. Locke, The Morals of Abou Ben Adhem, *Upper Saddle River, N.J.: Literature House/Gregg Press, 1969.*

Abou Ben Adhem was not in a good mood. He had put a large sum of money in a bank in New York. The bank had failed because of the strong desire of its cashier to view the sights of the Old World. As the cashier took with him over half a million dollars, the bank had to close. The directors were very sorry, but Abou's money was gone. He was not in a good mood.

At this point a man from Albany approached, bowing deeply three times. "Mighty Abou," said he, "I am a member of the New York legislature."

"Away, man! I want no favors. I have no need of votes. I have no money to spend. I have no desire to be severe, but, sir, whenever I see a member of a legislature, I think that Nature is wasteful. There is a great deal of lightning wasted. Away!"

"Mighty Abou, you mistake me. I am, it is true, a member of that legislature. But I am an honest man. If you will take the trouble to remember, you will remember that there are two or three such as I."

Abou looked at him with a long stare of painful astonishment, ending with a long whistle of disbelief.

"I am an honest member of the legislature of the state of New York," continued this man, "and I desire advice and enlightenment so that I may be of some use to my fellow citizens. Tell me, what can we do in the way of lawmaking that will get rid of all crime in the country? Is there no cure for it?"

Abou looked at him closely.

"I will trust you," he said. "I will believe that you are an honest man, despite the position you hold. And I will give you the information you desire.

"Sweet sir," continued Abou, "three hundred years ago there was a kingdom to the north of what is now Persia in which these things of which you complain did not happen very often. In that blessed land there was almost no crime—no accidents, no mistakes, no nothing. Life there was like a calmly flowing river. The people lived happily and died regretfully. I helped to organize that community. I was the author of the system that brought it about. I—"

"Three hundred years ago?" asked the stranger.

"Three hundred years ago,—did I not say so?"

"I beg your pardon; but, give me, oh give me, the system by which this most desirable state of things was achieved."

"I will. We had in Koamud, which was the name of the kingdom, no prisons, no reform schools, no civil-service examinations, no boards of any kind—nothing of the sort. If the government wanted a postmaster, for example, it did not go foolishly talking about qualifications or anything of that sort. It simply posted on the door of the post office a printed statement of what would be required of the postmaster. Then the first man who said he wanted the position was appointed."

"Were no bonds required of him?"

"No. He took the position, and undertook his duties."

"But suppose he stole money?"

"He was immediately caught and hanged."

"Hung for stealing?"

"Certainly, and for a mistake as well. If there was an error in his accounts by so much as a pound of twine, he was hung immediately."

"But suppose such irregularities were the result of bad business habits?"

"Then he was hung for being a bad businessman. What we wanted was honesty and ability. We treated everyone else the same way. Suppose a railroad train ran off the track. Suppose we discovered that a rail was out of order, or that the roadbed was not properly kept up. We hung the president, directors, and superintendent. If the accident was caused by any slip on the part of the conductor, he was hung.

"Once we hung all the officials of the Teheran and Ispahan Railroad, and from that time there were no accidents on that line. Their successors were very careful. The superintendent slept very little. The company hung up a small gallows in the cab of every locomotive to remind the engineer of his fate in the event of trouble.

"Then we carried the same rule into everything. The people put their money into the First National Bank of Picalilly. Very good. The bank failed one morning. The authorities took the president, cashier, and board of directors out and hung them all, because they had been guilty of letting the bank fail.

" 'I didn't steal a dollar of this money,' said the president.

" 'Makes no difference,' said the judge, 'where it was lost. You haven't got it.'

" 'But you won't hang a man who has not stolen, will you?' says the president.

" 'I will hang you for being an idiot. I shall hang you for risking money that was not yours to risk.'

"And up he went.

"In fact, they hung them more mercilessly for being fools than for any other crime. If a man said, 'I stole it,' they felt a sort of pity for him. If he said, 'I lost it,' they felt none at all, and hung him up in a minute."

"What was the effect of this vigorous hanging?"

"Splendid. Bank officials made no mistakes in their figures and none in their business. The officers of the government were rather careful about their accounts, for they were hung for mistakes as well as for stealing. The presidents and directors of railroads took care of their tracks, and a more watchful and careful set of men than the conductors, engineers, and switchmen you never saw.

"The effect was good in another way. This system reduced the population greatly, but it make a magnificent race of men and women. You see, the vicious and the careless were all hung, leaving only the industrious and clear-headed to live. Consequently, it was a splendid people. I am, perhaps, a fair example. There were no lunatics, idiots, triflers, or dishonest people left to spread mischief and danger."

"Is that government still in existence?"

"Alas! no. There sprang up a class of people who began to feel sorry for criminals. They got into the habit of visiting them just before they were hanged, and sending them flowers, and begging the governor to pardon them. They created sympathy for them, and finally some escaped. Then it was all over. The moment there was any doubt as to the certainty of punishment, people became almost as bad as they are here. Then I left the country.

"Go to Albany, my friend, and make but one penalty — hanging — for all crimes or mistakes, in public or private. True, it would cause a heavy expense on each county for a gallows. It would probably make New York one of the smallest cities, as far as population, in the country. In a week you probably couldn't get a quorum in the New York legislature. But the final effect would be splendid. The next generation would be fifty percent better than this, and the improvement would go on and on to the end of time. I have spoken. Leave me, for I am tired."

The stranger went away sorrowful.

"The idea is good," said he to himself, "but I dare not urge it. If hanging were the rule for crimes or mistakes, how long would my children have a father?"

CHAPTER 3
CONQUERING THE "LAST FRONTIER"

SITTING BULL SPEAKS OF THE WHITES

Many Indian leaders became well-known figures during the long period of conflict between the Indians and white settlers on the Great Plains. One of the most famous of these leaders was Sitting Bull, a chief of the Sioux. Although he became well known as a great warrior and war chief, he also was respected as a religious leader or "medicine man."

In the first selection, Sitting Bull speaks of the relationship between Indians and white people. In the second reading, he talks about Custer's "last stand." Although most people at the time thought that Sitting Bull was one of the chiefs who led the Sioux at Little Big Horn, he did not take part in that battle.

What wrongs does Sitting Bull accuse the whites of committing against the Indians? What crimes is he accused of by whites? How does he defend his own actions? What do you think of his arguments?

Adapted from Cry of the Thunderbird: The American Indian's Own Story, *edited by Charles Hamilton. New edition copyright 1972 by the University of Oklahoma Press. Reprinted by permission of the publisher.*

What treaty that the whites have kept has the red man broken? Not one. What treaty that the whites ever made with us red men have they kept? Not one. When I was a boy the Sioux owned the world. The sun rose and set in their lands. They sent ten thousand horsemen to battle. Where are the warriors today? Who killed them? Where are our lands? Who owns them?

What white man can say I ever stole his lands or a penny of his money? Yet they say I am a thief. What white woman taken as captive was ever insulted by me? Yet they say I am a bad Indian. What white man has ever seen me drunk? Who has ever come to me hungry and gone without food? Who has ever seen me beat my wives or abuse my children? What law have I broken? Is it wrong for me to love my own? Is it wicked in me because my skin is red? Because I am a Sioux? Because I was born where my fathers lived? Because I would die for my people and my country?

*　　*　　*　　*

The palefaces had things that we needed in order to hunt. We needed ammunition. Our interests were in peace. I never sold that much land. [Here Sitting Bull picked up with his thumb and forefinger a little dirt, lifted it, and let it fall and blow away.] I never made or sold a treaty with the United States. I came in to claim my rights and the rights of my people. I was driven by force from my land. I never made war on the United States government. I never stayed in the white man's country. I never committed any robberies in the white man's country. I never made the white man's heart bleed. The white man came onto my land and followed me. The white man made me fight for my hunting grounds. The white man made me kill him or he would kill my friends, my women, and my children.

We have all fought hard. We did not know Custer. There were not as many Indians as the white man says. There were not more than two thousand. I did not want to kill any more men. I did not like that kind of work. I only defended my camp. When we had killed enough, that was all that was necessary.

A PROPOSED SOLUTION TO THE "INDIAN PROBLEM"

The "Indian problem" had begun when the Europeans first settled in America. Conflict between the two groups centered largely on the concept of land ownership and differing ideas and ways of life. For the Indians, the problem was how to remain on the land where they had lived and hunted for centuries. For the white settlers, the problem was how to get the land and what to do with the Indians.

During the late 1860's, a long period of conflict began. As white settlers began to move beyond the Mississippi River, they came into conflict with the Indians who lived and hunted on the Great Plains. Thoughtful Americans wondered how the Indians could be removed from these lands without violating ideals of justice and humanity. General Nelson A. Miles, an Army officer with experience in Indian wars, offered his solution to the "Indian Problem" in an article that was published in 1879.

Does Miles think that the Indians are equals of the whites? Do you think he is fair in his summary of the relations between Indians and whites? What are the major features of the plan that Miles proposes? Did the government follow his advice and adopt his plan?

Adapted from Nelson A. Miles, "The Indian Problem," North American Review, *March 1879.*

Strange as it may seem, after nearly 400 years of conflict between the European and American races on this continent — a conflict in which war and peace have alternated almost as frequently as the seasons — we still must ask the question, What is to be done with the Indians?

The real issue is this: Shall we continue the uncertain and expensive policy that has hurt our name as a nation and a Christian people? Or shall we work out some practical and just system by which we can govern one quarter of a million of our people? Can we secure and maintain their loyalty, raising them from the darkness of barbarism to the light of civilization? Can we put an end to these endless and expensive Indian wars?

In considering the subject, it might be well to examine first the causes of the present situation. If we dismiss from our minds the prejudice we have against the Indian, we can understand more clearly the feelings of both races.

The Indians have the same motives that govern all other people. The lack of confidence and the bitter hatred now existing between the two races have been caused by the warfare that has lasted for centuries. And stories of bad faith, cruelty, and wrong have been handed down by tradition from father to son among both groups of people. It is unfair to suppose that one side has always acted rightly, and that the other is responsible for every wrong that has been committed. We might speak of the treachery of the red man, the violence of his crimes, the cruelties of his tortures, and the hideousness of many of his savage customs. We might try to estimate the number of his victims. Yet at the same time the other side of the picture might appear equally black with injustice.

One hundred years before the Pilgrims landed at Plymouth, the Spanish government issued a decree which allowed American Indians to be made slaves. Later they were sold into slavery in Massachusetts, Rhode Island, Pennsylvania, Virginia, the Carolinas, Georgia, and Louisiana, and hunted with dogs in Connecticut and Florida. They were, for all practical purposes, disfranchised by our original Constitution. By either war or treaty, nearly every tract of land which was desirable to them and valuable to the white settler was taken away. Step by step, they were driven back from the Atlantic to the Far West. Now there is scarcely a spot of ground upon which the Indians have any certainty of remaining permanently.

It may be well to remember that for the most part Europeans were treated kindly by the Indians when they first landed on American shores. When Europeans came to make permanent settlements, they were supplied with food, which enabled them to last through the long and cheerless winters. For a time during the early settlement of this country, peace and good will existed, only to be followed by warfare.

The available land that can be given to the Indians is being rapidly decreased. They cannot be moved farther west. Some political party or administration must take the responsibility of protecting their rights of person and property.

The advantage of placing the Indians under some government strong enough to control them and just enough to command their respect is clear. It is therefore suggested that a system which has proved to be practical should receive at least a fair trial. The government employs army officers who, by long and faithful service, have established reputations for integrity, character, and ability. These officers have commanded armies, reconstructed states, and controlled millions of dollars' worth of public property. During years of experience on the frontier, they have opened the way for civilization and Christianity. The services of these officials could prevent war and uplift the Indian race.

Allowing the civilized and semicivilized Indians to remain under the same supervision as at present, the President of the United States should have power to place the nomadic, or wandering, tribes under the control of the War Department. Officers of known character and experience, who would be interested in improving the Indians' condition, should be placed in charge of the different tribes. One difficulty in the past has been that they have been managed by officials too far away, who knew nothing of the people they were dealing with. The Indians, as far as possible, should be kept in sections of the country to which they have already adapted.

Every effort should be made to locate the Indians by families. The ties of relationship among them are much stronger than is generally supposed. By this means, the Indians will become independent of their tribal relations, and will not be found crowded together in large and unsightly camps, as are common now.

The officers in charge should have enough force to preserve order, patrol the reservations, recover stolen property, arrest the lawless, and keep the Indians upon their reservations and within the limits of their treaties. The officer in charge should have the power to control or prevent the sale of ammunition, as well as to stop the sale of liquor among the Indians. Many thousands of Indian ponies, useful only for war or hunting, should be sold and the money used to buy domestic animals.

The warriors may be made to care for their flocks and herds. The work of the Indians that is now wasted can be used for peaceful and useful pursuits. Yet the great work of reform must be mainly with the young people of the different tribes.

Several years ago I suggested that our unoccupied military posts be used as schools. As many Indian youths as can be gathered voluntarily should be placed at these schools, especially the sons of chiefs who will in a few years govern the different tribes. They should be taught the English language, habits of work, the benefits of civilization, and the power of the white race. After a few years, they would return to their people with some education, with more intelligence, and with their ideas of life entirely changed for the better. They would, in turn, be able to educate their own people. Their influence for good could not be estimated. The expense of educating them would be less than at present, and thousands would benefit. The Indians, as they become civilized and educated, as they acquire property and pay taxes toward the support of the government, should have the same rights of citizenship as all other men enjoy.

A race of savages cannot by any human means be civilized and Christianized within a few years of time. Neither will 250,000 people with their descendants be destroyed in the next 50 years. The white man and the Indian should be taught to live side by side, each respecting the rights of the other. Both should live under wholesome laws, enforced with authority and justice. Such a government would be most helpful to the Indians. It would also be satisfactory to three other groups: (a) people who have invested their capital and are developing the wealth that for ages has lain in the Western mountains; (b) people who have left the overcrowded centers of the East, and whose homes are now on the plains and valleys of the Far West; and (c) the soldiers who are called upon every year to withstand greater exposure and suffering than is required by the troops of any other nation on the globe.

RESISTING "AMERICANIZATION"

After many years of conflict on the Great Plains, the Indians were defeated and forced to live on reservations. Even so, many Americans still felt that the "Indian problem" had not been solved. They believed that the Indians had to be "Americanized."

As a result, the United States government tried to "Americanize" the Indians in various ways. Education was considered especially important in this effort. Consequently, many Indian children were sent to boarding schools many miles away from their homes. By 1898 some day schools had been built near the reservations. In this selection, Helen Sekaquaptewa, a Hopi Indian born in Arizona, tells of her experiences at a day school in the early 1900's.

Were Hopi parents opposed to education? Why do you think that hiding the children was a serious and rather desperate game?

Adapted by permission of the publisher from Me and Mine: The Life Story of Helen Sekaquaptewa, as told to Louise Udall. Tucson: University of Arizona Press, copyright 1969.

By the time I was old enough to go to school, a day school had been built near the village. Children up to the third grade could go to school by day and live at home. This was a favor to the Hopi parents. Still, many of them tried to prevent their children from attending the day school.

When we were five or six years old, we and our parents became involved with the school officials—assisted by the Navajo police officers—in a serious and rather desperate game of hide-and-seek. Every day the school principal sent out a truant officer, and many times he himself went with the officer. They went to Hopi homes to take the children to school.

When September came, there was no peace for us. Early in the morning, from our houses, we could see the principal and the officer start out from the school, walking up the trail to "get" the children. Parents tried every day in different ways to hide us from them, for once you were caught, you had lost the game. You were discovered and listed and you had to go to school and not hide any more.

Sometimes, after a very early breakfast, somebody's grandmother would take a lunch and go with a group of eight to twelve little girls and hide them in the cornfields away from the village. On another day another grandmother would go in the other direction over the hills among the cedar trees. We would play in a narrow valley, have our lunch, and come back home in the afternoon. Men would be out with little boys playing this game of hide-and-seek.

A place where one or two small children could be hidden away quickly was the rabbit blanket. A rabbit blanket is made by cutting dressed rabbit skins in two-inch strips and weaving them together with wool thread. When not in use, in warm weather, this blanket is hung by the four corners from a hook in the rafter beam. But once it was discovered, this hiding place was out. The school officer would feel the rabbit blanket first thing when he came into the room.

Most houses have a corn storage cupboard in a wall. A cloth covered the front, making a good place to keep the corn dry and clean. One day the officers were only two doors away from our home when my mother became aware of their presence. She grabbed her young son Henry and put him in the cupboard just in time to win the game—that day.

Our houses were two and three stories high. When a lower room became old and unsafe, it was used as a dumping place for ashes, peach stones, melon and squash seeds, and bits of discarded corn. Anything that could be eaten was preserved in the ashes, and the room was gradually filled. In time of famine these bits of food could be dug out and eaten. In my home such a room was about three-fourths filled. One September morning my brother and I were hidden there. We lay on our stomachs in the dark, facing a small opening. We saw the feet of the principal and police officers as they walked by, and heard their big voices as they looked about wondering where the children were. They didn't find us that day.

I don't remember for sure just how I came to be "caught." Maybe both my mother and I got a little tired of getting up early every morning and running off to hide all day. She probably thought to herself, "Oh, let them get her. I am tired of this. It is wearing me down." The hide-and-seek game continued through September. But when October came, the colder weather was on the school's side.

So one morning I was "caught." Even then, it was the rule among mothers not to let the child go voluntarily. As the police officer reached out to take me by the arm, my mother put her arm around me. Tradition required that it appear that I was forced into school.

I was taken from the village to the schoolhouse, along with several other children. First, each of us was given a bath by one of the Indian women who worked at the school. Then we were dressed in cotton underwear, cotton dresses, and long black stockings and heavy shoes supplied by the government. Each week we had a bath and a complete change of clothing. We were allowed to wear the clothes home each day, but my mother took off the clothes of the hated white man as soon as I got home, until it was time to go to school the next day.

Names were given to each child by the school. Mine was "Helen." Each child had a name card pinned on for as many days as it took the teacher to learn and remember the name she had given us. Our teacher was Miss Stanley. She began by teaching us the names of objects around the room. We read a little from big charts on the wall later on, but I don't remember ever using any books.

A feud developed over the years as the people were divided into sides for and against those who came from the outside. These two factions were known as the "Friendlies" (to the government) and the "Hostiles" (to the government). Later these groups were known as the "Progressives" and the "Traditionals."

Those who put their children into school voluntarily were given an ax, a hoe, a shovel, or a rake. (Stoves and wagons they had to work for.) "Hostile" parents scornfully rejected these tools even though they would have served them better than the tools they made of wood or stone. These gifts were looked upon only as a bait that would end in no good to the Indians. "Hostile" parents warned their children, when they were leaving for school, "Don't take the pencil in your hand. If you do, it means you agree to what they want you to do. Don't do it."

The attitude of the parents carried over to their children, as was shown on the school grounds. The children of the "Friendlies" made fun of us, calling us "Hostiles," and they would not let us join with them in their play. Going back up the trail after school was often a skirmish. The "Friendly" children often ran ahead up the trail and gathered rocks and threw them down at us when we came to the bottom of the steep rocky ledge. Sometimes we would try another way up to avoid being hit by rocks.

I liked school. It was pleasant and warm inside. I liked to wear the clothes they gave us at school; but when I learned that the kids were "hostile" to us, I didn't want to go to school. Everyone, even the principal and the teachers and employees, were more or less against us.

The Mennonites had a church in Old Oraibi, but our parents would not let us go even to their Sunday School. We wanted to go, and sometimes we went to Sunday School by a back path. They would give us a little ticket each time we came, and on Christmas they gave a big prize to the one who had the most tickets. We did not understand much of what they said, but it was nice to be there. I received a few tickets but gave them away. I did not dare accept a present.

A NORWEGIAN FARM WOMAN WRITES HOME

Pioneering farmers followed the miners and cattle raisers toward the "last frontier" as they settled and farmed the land on the Great Plains. Although plains farming was difficult, backbreaking work, thousands of families moved to the

Gro Svendsen and her husband, Ole, left Norway in 1862 to settle in Iowa. Her life on the Great Plains was far from easy, and she died in 1878 after giving birth to her tenth child. But in this selection, a letter written in 1873 to her parents, she tries to tell of the good things in her life on the plains.

What does Gro Svendsen's letter tell you about the lives of pioneer farmers on the Great Plains? What things in her life make her happy? What are her chief worries? How do you think you would have liked living on the plains in the 1870's?

Adapted from Frontier Mother: The Letters of Gro Svendsen, *translated and edited by Pauline Farseth and Theodore C. Blegen, published by The Norwegian-American Historical Association, 1950, pages 121-123. Reprinted by permission of the publisher.*

December 6, 1873

My beloved Parents:

I am writing you, my dear parents, in the hope that you are still living and in good health. I should have written you a long time ago. At least I should have thanked you, Father, for your last letter dated the first of March.

I must tell you first of all that we are all well. My health is not always of the best, but so far God has spared me from any long illness, and so I feel that I cannot complain. Rather I should thank God for His infinite goodness.

The children have always been in good health. They are growing strong and healthy. Little Bergit was small and frail for a long time, but this summer she has grown plump and fat. Steffen is very healthy looking, chubby and fat; his cheeks are pink and white like a rose. I wish his grandmother could see him. I am sending you pictures of Svend and Niels and Carl and Albert so now you can see what they look like. Ole was not at home when the pictures were taken, so he was left out. Niels is just as tall as Svend, but not so fat. Many who do not know them think they are twins.

My four oldest children have been attending Norwegian school this fall, but I must sadly confess that they are far behind in their studies. If they were at home in Norway, I know full well that they would have learned a great deal more. We so seldom have Norwegian school, and it is slow work to try to teach the boys at home.

When I wrote you last spring I told you that we were very much concerned about Ole's fa-ther, who had been kicked by a horse and was very ill. However, when Ole arrived there, his father had gotten well again.

Store-Ole was here a couple of weeks ago. He stayed a little over a week. His family is well. They like their new home very much and are more than happy over having moved there, in spite of the fact that their harvest will be poor this year because of the locusts that attacked their grain.

Here, also, the crops will be poor. This spring the locusts destroyed our fields, too. In many places there will be no harvest. We did get a little, enough for our own living, but none to sell. So it will be difficult to pay our many debts. We were forced to buy our land for $480. Since we had no money, we had to borrow. Then we had other bad luck. One of our horses had a sore leg this summer. At the time when there was most work to be done we couldn't use him, so we had to buy another horse that cost $150. The sick horse is well again, and now we have three draft horses and one colt. We still owe for the new horse. His name is Jack.

Times have been hard this fall—much harder than any since we came to this land. The future is uncertain. No one knows what tomorrow will bring.

We have been thinking of selling this land and moving up to Rock County [Minnesota] in order to be near Store-Ole. If the opportunity should come, we might move. If we did sell, we should have to get enough for our land so that we would have a few hundred dollars to start all over again in our new home. In the meantime we shall await whatever life may bring.

From what I have said you will see that we are not rich. But though we have no material wealth, we have nevertheless possessions of greater worth—a quiet and peaceful home with many children, all normal, gifted with health and intelligence, spirited, cheerful, and happy. We have other possessions, too. I could not name them all, but all these blessings seem to be of far greater value than money. I am more than satisfied and thankful to God for all His goodness toward His unworthy children.

This letter, which should reach you before Christmas, will be short. But I wanted you to know that we are all well.

A joyous Christmas and a blessed New Year to you, my dear parents, sisters, and brothers.

With love from
Ole and Gro

Unit Two

The Rise of Industrialism

1860's–1890's

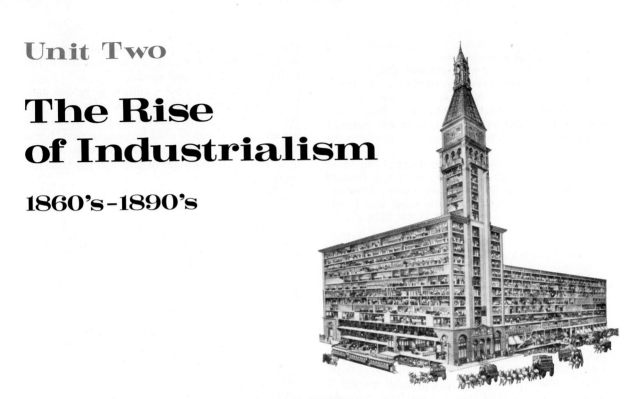

CHAPTER 4
BUSINESS PIONEERS AND THE GROWTH OF AMERICAN INDUSTRY

CARNEGIE MAKES A DEAL

In the years after 1870, as industry grew rapidly in the United States, several business leaders came to control entire industries and became enormously wealthy. One of them, Andrew Carnegie, was a Scottish immigrant who settled in the city of Pittsburgh. He studied and worked hard and eventually gained control of many steel mills. Carnegie's steel mills were Pittsburgh's most important industry.

In the following selection from Carnegie's autobiography, he describes what he thinks are the main reasons for business success. He also tells about an early business deal he took part in.

According to Carnegie, what policy is "the true secret of success"? Do you think that Carnegie is correct when he says that quality is the basis of business success? Why? What characteristics of a good business leader does Carnegie show here?

Adapted from Autobiography of Andrew Carnegie. © 1920 by Louise Whitfield Carnegie. *Copyright renewed 1948 by Margaret Carnegie Miller. Reprinted by permission of Houghton Mifflin Company.*

The Keystone Bridge Works have always been a source for satisfaction for me. Almost every company that had tried to build iron bridges in America had failed. Many of the bridges that they built had fallen. Some of the worst railway disasters in America were caused that way. But nothing has ever happened to a Keystone bridge, and some of them have stood where the winds were strong.

Luck had nothing to do with it. We used only the best material and enough of it, making our own iron and later our own steel. We inspected everything very carefully, and would build a safe structure or none at all. When asked to build a bridge which we knew was not strong enough or was poorly designed, we refused. We guaranteed any piece of work that had the stamp of the Keystone Bridge Works (and there are few states in the Union where they are not to be found).

This policy is the true secret of success. It will be uphill work for a few years until your work is proven, but after that it is smooth sailing. Instead of objecting to inspectors, all

504

manufacturing companies should welcome them. A high standard of excellence is easily maintained, and people are educated in the effort to reach excellence. I have never known a company that became successful unless it did good, honest work. Even in these days of the fiercest competition, when price is very important, at the root of great business success there still lies the much more important factor of quality. The effect of attention to quality upon everyone in the firm, from the president of the concern down to the lowest worker, cannot be overestimated.

The president of an important manufacturing work once boasted to me that their workers had chased away the first inspector who had appeared, and that they had never been troubled with another since. This was said as if it ought to be a matter of sincere congratulation, but I thought to myself: "This concern will never stand the strain of competition; it is sure to fail when hard times come." The result proved the correctness of my belief. The surest basis for a manufacturing concern is quality. After that, and a long way after, comes cost.

I gave a great deal of personal attention for some years to the affairs of the Keystone Bridge Works, and when important contracts were involved often went myself to meet the parties. On one such occasion in 1868, I visited Dubuque, Iowa, with our engineer, Walter Katte. We were competing for the contract to build the most important railway bridge that had been built up to that time, a bridge across the Mississippi.

That visit proved how success often depends upon small and unimportant things. We found we were not the lowest bidder. Our chief rival was a bridge-building company in Chicago to which the board of directors who were in charge of building the bridge had decided to give the contract. I stayed and talked with some of the directors. They knew nothing about the advantages and disadvantages of cast-iron and wrought-iron. We had always made the upper part of the bridge with wrought-iron, while our rivals' was made of cast-iron. I explained the result of a steamer striking against the one and against the other. In the case of wrought-iron, it would probably only bend. In the case of cast-iron, it would certainly break and down would come the bridge. One of the directors was able to back up my argument. The other night, he said, he had run his buggy in the dark into a cast-iron lamppost, which had broken to pieces.

"Ah, gentlemen," I said, "there is the point. A little more money and you could have had the indestructible wrought-iron and your bridge would stand against any steamboat. We never have built and we never will build a cheap bridge. Ours don't fall."

There was a pause. Then the president of the bridge company asked if I would excuse them for a few moments. I left the room. Soon they called me back and offered the contract, provided we built the bridge at the lower price, which was only a few thousand dollars less. I agreed to this. That cast-iron lamppost so conveniently smashed gave us one of our most profitable contracts. What is more, it obtained for us the reputation of having won the Dubuque bridge against all competitors.

The moral of that story lies on the surface. If you want a contract, be on the spot when it is given. A smashed lamppost or something equally unthought of may secure the prize if the bidder is there. And if possible stay until you can take the written contract home in your pocket.

LIFE BEHIND A TOY COUNTER

What was it like to work as a salesperson in a department store? In the late 1800's, a Canadian sociologist wanted to find out more about the lives and working conditions of sales clerks in large stores. As a result, she decided to take a job as a saleswoman. For several days during the Christmas season she worked in a New York department store. For one week's work she earned $2.00 in wages and $3.25 in commissions. However, 30 cents was taken from her salary because she arrived at work late three times. (Every time sales clerks were late, 10 cents was deducted from their weekly salary.)

What seems to be the store's attitude toward its employees? Toward the public? Do modern department stores operate differently? If so, in what ways?

Adapted from Annie M. MacLean, "Two Weeks in Department Stores," American Journal of Sociology, *Vol. IV, May 1899, in Neil Harris, ed.,* The Land of Contrasts. New York: George Braziller. 1970.

The hurried breakfast, the rush out into the street crowded with people carrying their lunches, and the streetcars packed with pale-faced sleepy-eyed men and women made the working world seem very real. Hurrying workers filled the center of the city. No one was stirring. I reached the store promptly at eight, the time of opening. The manager said he would give me two dollars a week plus 5 percent commission on sales. I was then given a number, and by "424" I was known during my stay there.

I was sent to the toy department, where I found sixty-seven other people who were to work with me. The place was filled with all kinds of toys, from a monkey beating a drum to a doll that said "mamma." Our business was first to dust and arrange the stock. Then we stood ready for customers. Our business was to see that no one escaped without buying something. The confusion can be readily imagined. As soon as the elevators emptied themselves on the floor, there was one mad rush of clerks with a quickly spoken, "What would you like, madam?" or, "Something in toys, sir?" The majority of answers were rude. Some people were amused, and a few were alarmed at the urgency of the clerks. One young boy, on being asked by half a dozen clerks at once, threw up his hands in horror, and said, "For God's sake, let me get out of here!" He ran down the stairs, not even waiting for the elevator. The cause of such wasteful activity on the part of so many employees was the 5 percent commission, which could add two or three dollars a week to one's salary.

One of the difficult things at first was trying to remember the prices, for they were frequently changed during the day, and the penalty for selling something at a lower price was that one was immediately fired. Selling above price, however, met with no disapproval. Every morning there were special sales. Sometimes articles that had sold for one dollar would be reduced to ninety-eight cents. Again, twenty-five-cent articles would be offered at a bargain for forty cents "today only." The manager's brief instructions each morning kept us aware of the bargains. The charms of the bargain counter disappear when one has been behind the scenes and learned something of its history. The humor of it seemed to impress the clerks, for often they would exchange knowing winks when some customer was being victimized.

Oh, that first morning! The hours seemed days. "Can I possibly stand up all day?" was my main thought, for I soon learned that anyone who was found sitting down would be harshly criticized. Later in the week, one of the girls who was exhausted sat for a moment on a little table that was for sale — there was not a seat of any kind in the rooms, and the only way one could get a moment's rest was to sit on the children's furniture that was for sale on one part of the floor. The manager came along and found the poor girl resting. He called out in rough tones: "Get up out of that, you lazy hussy; I don't pay you to sit around all day!" By night the men as well as the women were limping wearily across the floor. Many sales were made under positive physical agony.

How well I remember my first sale there! The people were slow to arrive that morning; in fact, they were slow every morning. We hardly ever had any business until eleven o'clock, and the greatest rush came about six. From twelve thirty to two was a busy time also. My first two customers were types that were common. First a woman with a businesslike expression came to me and demanded that I show her building blocks. They were shown, but proved unsatisfactory. The dolls' buggies, boys' sleds, laundry sets, and skates were examined in slow succession. I was asked about the prices and merits of everything. Then she looked at me and said: "I do not intend to buy today; I just wished to examine your goods." Still I had not a sale on my book and she had taken half an hour of my time.

The next customer was a man who wanted a boy's sled at a cost of one dollar and a half. Now, we had none at that price, but we had them at one dollar and thirty-five cents, and one dollar and sixty-five cents, either of which I thought would suit him. But I was mistaken. He gave me a look of utter scorn, and then criticized me for advertising things we did not have in stock. I meekly suggested that I was not responsible for the ads that appeared in the morning papers. But he was not at all pleased by this. I felt rather upset, but the comforting voice of a cashier said "Don't mind him, he's only a cheapskate."

Thus encouraged I started out on another sale. This time it was a small boy who wanted to buy, and the bright-faced little fellow did me good. He had eighty cents, he said, and he wanted presents for the baby, and Tom, and Freda, and Cousin Jack, and several others. I suggested one thing after another, till finally he had spent his money.

The boy was happy, and so was I. I looked

admiringly at the eighty cents set down on my sales sheet. It meant that I had earned four cents in commission. After that the sales came frequently. They were all small, of course, and amounted to only $14.98 for the day. But this was more than I sold any day after that. It has often been noticed that new clerks do better at first than they do later. With me, freshness and interest in the novelty helped to take away my tiredness, and thus invited sales.

My first day ended at six thirty. I went wearily to the coat-room and more wearily to my boarding place. When I arrived there, I could only throw myself upon my small white cot in the dormitory and wonder if it would be all right for a working girl to cry. Presently I was dreaming that blows from an iron hammer were falling upon me. In a little while it was morning, and another day had begun.

A TRUST IS BORN

In the 1870's and 1880's, the rapid growth of American industry was greatly spurred by the trend toward business consolidation, or combination. Companies used this form of business organization to gain control of a large part of the market in a certain industry—for example, oil. When the corporations in an industry joined together into one large trust, they gained many advantages. The large size of the trust enabled it to take advantage of the money-saving techniques of mass production and cheap marketing. The trust also could limit production, fix prices, and secure lower railroad rates. Trusts were so effective that they were able to drive out most competition and establish a monopoly or near-monopoly. The American tobacco trust, formed by James Buchanan Duke, is a good example of how such a giant business combination worked.

How were James Duke's business efforts aided by technology? By advertising and promotion? How did he gain the support of bankers?

Excerpt from The Potentates: Business and Businessmen in American History *by Ben B. Seligman Copyright © 1971 by the Estate of Ben B. Seligman. Reprinted with the permission of The Dial Press.*

It became evident that any business that might develop a wide market for its product would end up in a financier's hands. Entrepreneurs themselves might become financial tycoons, as was the case with James B. Duke. For if money could be made by supplying consumers with goods and services, much more could be made by controlling stocks and bonds. Duke and his tobacco empire are striking not so much for size or importance of product, but because they show the methods that were used in bringing together various branches of a new industry and the way in which a new technology—mechanized cigarette-making—could promote consolidation.

Tobacco had been an important plantation crop before the Civil War. After the war, John Ruffin Green sold tobacco under the trade name of "Bull Durham." (It was named after Durham, North Carolina, the town in which it was processed.) The picture of the bull became a well-known trademark that Blackwell and Carr, who took over after Green, fought to protect. They learned quickly that testimonials and advertising were essential in convincing the consumer to smoke their tobacco or buy their chewing plug. By 1884 the Blackwell and Carr factory had become the largest in the world. Soon many brands of tobacco were being produced in Durham. Those who processed the tobacco were determined to make the city the tobacco capital of the South.

However, the North Carolina town of Winston, near the sleepy village of Salem, soon began to rival Durham as a center for manufacturing tobacco products. One of the aggressive young salesmen in that area was R. J. Reynolds, who headed a family firm there. Lewis Ginter and John Allen had a thriving business in Richmond. Liggett and Myers was a growing firm in St. Louis. There was a great demand for tobacco all over the nation. Chewing and smoking brands were produced in ever-increasing quantities to satisfy it. Concerned with the protection of their trademarks, which clearly distinguished one brand from another, manufacturers passed out premiums and coupons. They gave rebates to dealers, and paid bribes to put their brands in certain stores.

It was not long, however, before Buck Duke would take over all the others. Born in 1856, James Buchanan Duke was named after the Democratic President elected in that year. Duke's father had been a small farmer before the Civil War. Afterward he returned to the land to grow and sell tobacco. His little tobacco curing factory grew steadily. By 1872 it was producing 125,000 pounds [577,000 kilograms] of tobacco a year. In 1874 the elder Duke and his two sons, James and Ben, moved the factory to Durham. The elder Duke took both boys in as partners to form W. Duke & Sons. To obtain more capital, several partners from outside the firm were brought in.

Cigarettes had been popular in Europe for many years, though in America they could not yet compete with plug and smoking tobacco. But Duke felt that he was hitting his head against the stone wall of Bull Durham. Blackwell and Carr had moved far ahead of their rivals in selling plug and smoking tobacco. Duke knew that he could not compete with them, and so he decided on cigarettes. But these had to be rolled by hand. Although Duke had some of the best workers in the business, their output was still too small for an expanding market. Then the Dukes obtained a cigarette machine, which could turn out 120,000 cigarettes a day. Realizing that cigarettes were popular in cities, Duke set up a branch in New York. He successfully competed with the better-known firm of Ginter and Allen. He gave premiums and matched Ginter ad for ad. A favorite selling method was to place a picture of a pretty girl in each package of cigarettes. He sent clever salespeople on the road to find business. People were hired to go from store to store asking only for Duke's product. Incoming immigrants were given free cigarettes at ports of entry. By 1890 W. Duke and Company had become first in the tobacco industry.

Meanwhile, Duke was watching developments in oil, steel, whisky, and sugar. All were being combined through trusts. Why not tobacco? But first one had to get into the good graces of financiers. Duke began to negotiate for small thirty-day or sixty-day loans with New York bankers, always paying them back promptly. Soon Duke had established a line of credit with the powers that counted.

Finally, Duke was able to convince four other large companies that they all ought to get together. In 1890 the American Tobacco Company was started, a combination of Duke, Ginter, and three others. This was 90 percent of the cigarette industry. Capitalization was set at $25,800,000, though the combined tangible assets were just slightly over $3,000,000. Eight years later another company was formed to handle plug tobacco. Dealers were forced to take other items through tie-in sales. If they wanted cigarettes, they had to also take the trust's tobacco plug.

American Tobacco continued to expand by all means available, some fair, many unfair. Almost absolute control over cigarette-making machinery was worked out. Dealers refusing to take the trust's products were blacklisted and subjected to ruinous price wars. Through all these operations, Buck Duke ruled with a iron hand. He fired his star salesman, Edward Small, when he refused to move his family to Cincinnati. By 1905 American Tobacco and its related Consolidated Tobacco Company, both headed by Duke, controlled three fourths of the smoking-tobacco, and over nine tenths of the snuff, in addition to having almost complete control of the cigarette market.

Four other firms were taken over in the early 1890's. Liggett and Myers was then taken over. In 1899 it was R. J. Reynolds' turn to join the trust.

Stocks and bonds were controlled to yield a profit to insiders. Operations were always carried out in secret. Duke used several techniques to dominate the market. One was price-cutting. Another was to form phony "independent" companies to make it look as though there were competition. Duke also offered premiums and rebates, created rival brands to confuse consumers, and took over more competitors. Once a market had been won, retail prices were kept at the same level, while the jobber was squeezed with higher wholesale prices.

Nor was the foreign market neglected. Duke tried to get his products into Japan, but the government there decided to set up its own monopoly. He bought a factory in England, but the Imperial Tobacco Company was formed so British manufacturers could protect English people against American cigarettes. After several years of conflict, the usual cartel agreement [a cartel is an international trust] was reached. The United States and Cuban markets were given to Duke, Great Britain was given to Imperial, and the rest of the world was shared through the British-American Tobacco Company. The entire industry, with the exception of cigar-making, was now controlled by the "Tobacco Trust."

ROCKEFELLER'S ACHIEVEMENTS

Probably no single business leader of the late 1800's received more praise or criticism than John D. Rockefeller. Born into a poor family, in time he came to control the nation's oil industry. In 1870 he organized the Standard Oil Company and located his oil refineries in Cleveland.

Like many other industrial leaders of the time, Rockefeller used unfair business methods. For example, at times he would cut prices until competing companies went bankrupt or sold out to him.

By 1882 the Standard Oil Trust had been formed. Just five years later, in 1887, Rockefeller controlled 95 percent of the oil refineries in the nation.

In this selection, historian Allan Nevins gives his analysis of Rockefeller and his methods. He describes Rockefeller's innovations, or the changes he introduced to American industry. According to Nevins, what important characteristic of the new industrial era did many people fail to see? What was Rockefeller's goal? With what historical figures does Nevins compare industrial leaders? What do you think of this comparison?

Adapted from Allan Nevins, John D. Rockefeller, *Vol. II. Copyright 1940 Charles Scribner's Sons; copyright renewed 1968 Allan Nevins. Reprinted with the permission of Charles Scribner's Sons.*

It is plain that the place Rockefeller holds in American industrial history is that of a great innovator. Early on, he saw the advantage of combination and order in an industry that was bloated, lawless, and chaotic. Following this vision, he formed a scheme of industrial organization which, magnificent in its harmony and strength, world-wide in its scope, possessed a striking novelty. He met great opposition. Producers, rival manufacturers, courts, legislatures, presidents, and public opinion fought him at every step. He and his partners marched from investigation to investigation, from lawsuit to lawsuit, under a growing load of criticism. But they moved forward. They believed that the opposition was mistaken and irrational. They felt that the full victory of competitive laissez-faire individualism would mean a step backward, confusion, and general loss.

The dominant ideal of pioneering America was one of complete independence and self-sufficiency. Long after the new industrial era was far advanced, people held on to the old faith in a self-balancing system of private ownership, small-unit enterprise, and free competition. They believed that this system would give every person a reward roughly equal to his or her work, integrity, and ability. They were slow to see that the industrial system was not self-balancing, that it grew less so decade by decade. They were slow to see that people were less and less independent, more and more interdependent. They were reluctant to admit that free competition was steadily becoming more restricted, and that its character was changing. It was no longer a competition of small business and individual firms. It was becoming a competition organized by great corporations.

Rockefeller was a realist. Partly by intuition, partly by hard thought, he understood the real nature of economic forces and the real motives behind American industry. He and the other leaders of the "heroic age" in American business development were the guiding forces of our industrial society. Many of the forces and elements in that society were unreasonable and wasteful. Rockefeller wished to bring about a more reasonable and efficient pattern. Behind this desire he placed a good mind, a skill in organization, and a dynamic personal force which were not surpassed, and possibly not equaled, by those of any other industrial captain in history.

Rockefeller's economic foresight, and the courage he showed in sticking to it, deserve praise. He knew that he was carrying through a great experiment, and he believed the experiment to be sound and wise. Any careful analysis of the work of the best leaders shows that money was not the central object, but a by-product. Greedy people exist, but they seldom obtain great fortunes, for greed tends to defeat itself in complex business operations. Those who built the really great economic structures were not thinking mainly of dollars, or they would have stopped after their first great business successes.

One great fact to be remembered when studying Rockefeller and other captains of industry is that American business has typically been a more optimistic, lighthearted undertaking than business in other lands. The best business people have been great adventurers. The giants of the "heroic age" of industry can be compared with the famous Elizabethan captains—with Drake, Hawkins, Cavendish, Frobisher, Cabot (some of whom were good business people, too). In business, Americans of the nineteenth century found the Great Game. They played it with enjoyment and enthusiasm, they enjoyed it even when it was dangerous, and they took its ups and downs calmly. Of all its leaders, none showed more boldness or swiftness than Rockefeller, and none more balance in accepting defeats and victories. Love of the game was one of the motives, particularly as his keen eye saw a pattern in the game that less intelligent people missed.

"IT IS ALL WRONG TO BE POOR"

During the years of the late 1800's, some Americans became very wealthy by amassing fortunes in business and in the stock market. Newspapers and magazines told of the fabulous fortunes that were being made and how the rich lived. Many Americans soon began to envy the lives of the very wealthy. The great American dream of becoming rich was shaped during these years.

Russell Conwell, a Union army officer turned preacher, said that there was no point in envying the rich. Instead he suggested that everyone should settle down and make money where he or she lived. He preached this message more than 6,000 times all over the United States in a famous speech called "Acres of Diamonds." The title of the speech came from its opening story, which told of a rich Arab who sold his lands to go in search of diamonds. The new owner of the Arab's land then found these same riches on the very property that the Arab had sold.

Why, according to Conwell, is it a person's duty to get rich? What do you think of Conwell's speech? Do you agree with his ideas?

Adapted from pp. 17–59 of Acres of Diamonds *by Russell H. Conwell. Copyright 1915, 1943 by Harper & Row, Publishers, Inc. printed by permission of Harper & Row, Publishers, Inc.*

Now then, I say that the opportunity to get rich, to obtain great wealth, is here in Philadelphia now, within the reach of almost every man and woman who hears me speak tonight. I mean just what I say. I have come here to tell you what in God's sight I believe to be the truth. If my years have been of any value in teaching me common sense, I know I am right. The men and women sitting here, who found it difficult perhaps to buy a ticket to this talk, have within their reach "acres of diamonds," opportunities to get wealthy. There never was a place on earth more suited to this purpose than the city of Philadelphia today. Never in the history of the world did a poor person without money have such an opportunity to get rich quickly and honestly as he or she has now in our city.

I say that you ought to get rich. It is your duty to get rich. How many of my religious brothers and sisters say to me, "Do you, a Christian minister, spend your time going up and down the country advising young people to get rich, to get money?" "Yes, of course I do." They say, "Isn't that awful! Why don't you preach the gospel instead of preaching about people making money?" "Because to make money honestly is to preach the gospel." That is the reason. The people who get rich may be the most honest people you find in the community.

"Oh," but says some young man here tonight, "I have been told all my life that if a person has money he is very dishonest and dishonorable and mean and contemptible." My friend, that is the reason you have none, because you have that idea of people. The foundation of your faith is altogether false. Let me say here clearly, and say it briefly—ninety-eight out of one hundred of the rich people of America are honest. That is why they are rich. That is why they are trusted with money. That is why they carry on great enterprises and find plenty of people to work with them. It is because they are honest.

Says another young man, "I hear sometimes of people who get millions of dollars dishonestly." Yes, of course, you hear this, and so do I. But such people are so rare a thing in fact that the newspapers talk about them all the time as a matter of news until you get the idea that all the other rich people get rich dishonestly.

My friends, drive me out into the suburbs of Philadelphia, and introduce me to the people who own their homes around this great city, those beautiful homes with gardens and flowers. I will introduce you to the very best people in character as well as in enterprise in our city. A man is not really a true man until he owns his own home. Those who own their homes are made more honorable and honest and pure, and true and economical and careful, by owning their homes.

Money is power, and you ought to be reasonably ambitious to have it. You ought to because you can do more good with it than you could without it. Money printed your Bible, money builds your churches, money sends your missionaries, and money pays your preachers. (You would not have many of them if you did not pay them.) The person who gets the largest salary can do the most good with the power that is given to him or her.

I say, then, you ought to have money. If you

can honestly obtain riches in Philadelphia, it is your Christian and godly duty to do so. It is an awful mistake of these religious people to think you must be awfully poor in order to be religious.

Some people say, "Don't you sympathize with the poor people?" Of course I do, or else I would not have been speaking all these years. I sympathize with the poor, and the number of poor who are to be sympathized with is very small. While we should sympathize with God's poor — that is, those who cannot help themselves — let us remember there is not a poor person in the United States who was not made poor by his or her own shortcomings, or by the shortcomings of someone else. It is all wrong to be poor, anyhow.

Greatness consists not in the holding of some office. It consists in doing great things with little means and in the accomplishment of great purposes from the private ranks of life. To be great at all one must be great here, now, in Philadelphia. He who can give to this city better streets and better sidewalks, better schools and more colleges, more happiness and more civilization, more of God, he will be great anywhere. Let every man or woman here, if you never hear me again, remember this. If you wish to be great at all, you must begin where you are and with what you are, in Philadelphia, now. He that can give to this city any blessing, he who can be a good citizen while he lives here, he that can make better homes, he that can be a blessing whether he works in the shop or sits behind the counter or keeps house — whatever be his life, he who would be great anywhere must first be great in his own Philadelphia.

CHAPTER 5
THE STRUGGLE OF AMERICAN WORKERS TO ORGANIZE

CHANGING CONDITIONS BEWILDER A WORKER

Walter Wyckoff wanted to find out how other people in the United States lived. Consequently, soon after he graduated from Princeton University, he decided to travel across the country.

Along the way, Wyckoff worked at many different jobs. One of his jobs was construction work for the World's Columbian Exposition in Chicago in 1892. In this selection he writes of the working conditions at the Exposition. These conditions were typical of the new industrial age. Individual workers had become unimportant, and relationships between boss and worker were impersonal.

Why is "Mr. Ford" confused by his new surroundings? By his new job? What is his attitude toward unions? Do you think that joining a union would have helped him?

Adapted from Walter A. Wyckoff, The Workers. *New York: Charles Scribner's Sons, 1899*

Our work was the general care of all the plank roads on the grounds. They had been put in fairly good condition, but they received hard use, and constant repairs were necessary. We were, therefore, to give our attention, up to five o'clock in the afternoon, to those sections of the road which most needed repairs. After five, when the work for the day was over, our duty was to go over all the roads and see that they were in good condition for the next morning.

Our job is not easy. The roads constantly need to be repaired. A good deal of hard work is necessary to keep them in order. It is mostly pick and shovel work, the hardest kind of work as far as my experience goes. The old trenches must be kept open and new ones dug, and sometimes the sides of long sections of the road must be buried under a layer of earth to prevent the bare planks from twisting out of shape in the sun.

Among the workers on the grounds, none has interested me more than an American carpenter with whom I sometimes spend an evening. The man is lonely and uncomfortable in his new surroundings. The conditions he faces as a worker are as disturbing to him as the unfamiliar surroundings of his daily life. He holds on to his individuality, but the new things which face him here make that difficult.

The man is a master carpenter from a village home in Ohio. But the certainty of steady work for many months at four dollars a day was tempting enough to cause him to leave his family behind and come here. He had arrived a few days ago and had found work right away.

Seeing the man, a tall, fine-looking, self-respecting American worker, and hearing him speak, and learning even this little of his history, you could see his past. You could almost see a comfortable wooden cottage, which he had built himself, with a garden plot about it and flower beds in front, standing on a well-shaded village street. He owns the cottage and the plot of land, and his children were born there. He is an officer of the village church and has been justice of the peace, and more than once he has served as school trustee. The idea of social inequality is new to him, and it makes him self-conscious. In his home village his family and the families of all his neighbors are all equals. The only exceptions are the minister, the doctor, the village lawyer, and the schoolmaster, because of their special education. His children study and play at school with the children of all his neighbors, and meet with them at church and elsewhere.

But here things are new and strange. He is no longer a man with a name to distinguish him, but has become a worker with a number on his jacket. He goes to work as just one in an army of ten thousand numbers. Home has changed to a barrack. There he, a number, sleeps in a numbered bunk, and eats as one of half a thousand men. His comfort and convenience are not considered, and his views have no bearing whatever on the course of things.

The superintendent of the building upon which he works, whose energy and skill he admires, shifts him about with dozens of other men, having no more regard for him as an individual than if he were a piece of wood. Once he spoke to his superintendent about some detail of the work and found him a most appreciative listener. Then he started to talk about a subject of general interest, only to find that by some mysterious change he was speaking to a stone wall.

And now something else faces him which he regards as another loss of his individuality. He is urged to agree to this loss, and it gives him some concern. He knows very little about labor unions, and now he is bombarded with appeals to join one.

Management does not discriminate between union and nonunion workers in employing people at the Exposition. But many of the union workers here are making the most of the present opportunity. They want to publicize their principles and bring desirable nonunion workers into their organization. My carpenter friend, whom I shall call Mr. Ford, has received much attention.

Two or three times he has asked me to go with him in the evening to meetings which are held near the fairgrounds, and hear speeches from delegates from the Central Labor Union. These we have not found very helpful. There has been a good deal of beer-drinking and much useless speech, which has grown heated at times. Now and then a plain, matter-of-fact worker has given us an interesting talk on the history of unionism and on the need of organization among workers as the only means of safeguarding their interests.

Mr. Ford, much confused, has listened to all this. We have talked it over together on the way back to our rooms, and sometimes late into the night. I have tried to explain to him, as well as I understand it, the idea for labor organization, and the necessity for it which has grown out of the great industrial change since the middle of the 1800's. But Mr. Ford, for all practical purposes, belongs to another period. The industrial change has hardly affected him. He served his apprenticeship, and then was a journeyman and then a master carpenter in due course. In his experience, work has always had its basis in a personal relation, as, for example, between himself as a contractor and the person whose job he undertook and from whom he received payment. A similar personal relation has always existed between himself and the people he has employed.

This new relation between a worker and an impersonal corporation which hires him is one that he does not readily understand. And this merging of one's individuality in an organization which attempts to regulate hours, wages, and employers is a thing he hates.

"Why," he said to me, "I give up my independence, and I'm no better than the worst carpenter in the group. We all get union wages alike. There's no reason for a man to do his best. He ain't a man any more, anyway. He's only a part of a machine. Why, such work as some I see done here, I'd be ashamed to do by moonlight, with my eyes shut. But it makes no difference in the union, you're all on the same level, as nearly as I can make out."

A DISILLUSIONED IMMIGRANT

During the late 1800's and the early 1900's, millions of immigrants from many countries came to America. This huge group of newcomers to the United States is often referred to as the "New Immigration." They consisted mainly of immigrants from nations in southern and eastern Europe. For the most part, the newcomers were unskilled workers who had no choice but to live crowded together in slum neighborhoods in the large cities of the East.

During the New Immigration, for the first time, large numbers of Jews from eastern Europe, especially Russia and Poland, came to America. One of these immigrants was Anzia Yezierska, a sixteen-year-old girl who arrived in New York in 1901. In this selection she tells of her dreams and expectations before her arrival and her reactions to what she found.

What expectations did Anzia Yezierska and her family have? What caused her first doubts about America? Do you think that her experiences in America were typical of most immigrants in the late 1800's and early 1900's? Why?

Adapted from Hungry Hearts *by Anzia Yezierska, copyrighted by Louise Levitas Henriksen. Reprinted by permission of the copyright holder.*

We traveled in steerage [the section of the ship where those who paid the cheapest fares were crowded together under the decks]—dirty bundles—foul odors—seasick people—but I saw and heard nothing of the stinking dirtiness and ugliness around me. I seemed to float in showers of sunshine. Sight after sight of the new world were in my imagination. From everyone's lips flowed the golden legend of the golden country:

"In America you can say what you feel—you can join your friends in the open streets without fear."

"In America there is a home for everyone. The land is your land. Not like in Russia where you feel yourself a stranger in the village where you were born and lived—the village in which your father and grandfather lie buried."

"Everyone is like everybody else in America."

"All people can do what they want with their lives in America."

"Plenty for all. Learning flows free like milk and honey."

"Learning flows free."

The word painted pictures in my mind. I saw before me free schools, free colleges, free libraries, where I could learn and learn and learn and keep on learning.

In our village there was a school, but only for Christian children. In the schools of America I'd lift up my head and laugh and dance—a child with other children. Like a bird in the air, from sky to sky, from star to star, I'd soar and soar.

"Land! Land!" came the joyous shout.

"America! We're in America!" cried my mother, almost crushing us in her happiness.

Everyone crowded and pushed on deck. They strained and stretched to get the first glimpse of the "golden country," lifting their children on their shoulders that they might see beyond them.

Men fell on their knees to pray. Women hugged their babies and wept. Children danced. Strangers hugged and kissed like old friends. Old men and women had in their eyes a look of young people in love.

Age-old visions sang themselves in me—songs of freedom of an oppressed people.

America! America!

*   *   *   *

Between buildings that rose up like mountains, we struggled with our bundles. Up Broadway, under the bridge, and through the crowded streets of the ghetto, we followed our friend, Gedalyeh Mindel.

I looked about the narrow streets of squeezed-in stores and houses, ragged clothes, dirty bedding hanging out of the windows, ashcans and garbage cans piled up on the sidewalks. A sadness pressed down my heart—the first doubt of America.

"Where are the green fields and open spaces in America?" cried my heart. "Where is the golden country of my dreams?"

A loneliness for the sweet-smelling silence of the woods that lay beyond our mud hut built up in my heart, a longing for the soft earth of our village streets. All around me was the hardness of brick and stone, the stinking smells of crowded poverty.

"Here's your house with separate rooms like in a palace." Gedalyeh Mindel opened the door of a dingy, airless apartment.

"Where's the sunshine in America?" my mother cried in dismay.

She went to the window and looked out at the wall of the next house. "Like in a grave so dark."

513

"It ain't so dark, it's only a little shady." Gedalyeh Mindel lighted the gas. "Look only." He pointed with pride to the dim gaslight. "No candles, no kerosene lamps in America, you turn on a screw and put to it a match and you got light like with sunshine."

Again the shadow fell over me, again the doubt of America!

In America there were rooms without sunlight, rooms to sleep in, to eat in, to cook in, but without sunshine. And Gedalyeh Mindel was happy. Could I be satisfied with just a place to sleep and eat in, and a door to shut people out—to take the place of sunlight? Or would I always need the sunlight to be happy?

And where was there a place in America for me to play? I looked out into the alley below and saw pale-faced children running in the street.

"Where is America?" cried my heart.

*   *   *   *

My eyes were shutting themselves with sleep —the dead-weight sleep of complete exhaustion.

"Heart of mine!" my mother's voice moaned above me. "Father is already gone an hour. You know how they'll squeeze from you a nickel for every minute you're late. Quick only!"

I grabbed my bread and herring and ran down the stairs and out into the street. I ate running, blindly pushing through the hurrying crowds of workers—my haste and fear choking each mouthful.

I felt a strangling in my throat as I neared the sweatshop [the factory where she worked]. All my nerves screwed together into iron hardness to withstand the day's torture.

For an instant I hesitated as I faced the window of the old building—dirt and decay cried out from every crumbling brick.

In the shop, raging around me the roar and the clatter, the clatter and the roar, the grind of the pounding machines. Half maddened, half deadened, I struggled to think, to feel, to remember—what am I—who am I—why was I here?

I struggled in vain—confused and lost in the noise.

"America—America—where was America?" it cried in my heart.

The factory whistle—the slowing-down of the machines—the noon hour had come.

I woke as from a nightmare—a tired waking to pain.

In my brain reason began to dawn. In my heart feelings began to pulse. The wound of my wasted life began to hurt and ache. My childhood ended by work—must my youth die too—unlived?

The odor of herring and garlic—the hungry eating of food—laughter and loud, vulgar jokes. Was it only I who was so unhappy? I looked at those around me. Were they happy or only not aware of their slavery? How could they laugh and joke? Why were they not torn with rebellion against this grind—the crushing, deadening movements of the body, where only hands live and hearts and brains must die?

A touch on my shoulder. I looked up. It was Yetta Solomon from the machine next to mine.

"Here's your tea."

I stared at her, half hearing.

"Ain't you going to eat nothing?"

"Yetta! I can't stand it!" The cry broke from me. "I didn't come to America to turn into a machine. I came to America to make from myself a person. Does America want only my hands—only the strength of my body—not my heart—not my feelings—my thoughts?"

AN ITALIAN BOY LOSES AN "I"

In 1896, when he was nine years old, Leonard Covello came to America with his mother and two younger brothers. (His father had made the trip earlier to earn money for their passage.) Like thousands of other "New Immigrants," they came from Italy. And like thousands of other immigrants, they found that becoming American brought both pleasure and pain.

Many years later, Covello wrote of his experiences as a newcomer. He stressed the culture conflict that developed between immigrant parents and their children. Covello wrote: "We soon got the idea that 'Italian' meant something inferior, and a barrier was erected between children of Italian origin and their parents. This was the accepted process of Americanization. We were becoming Americans by learning how to be ashamed of our parents."

What do you think of the education Leonard Covello received as a young immigrant? Why was his father so upset by the family's name change in school? Has anyone in your family ever changed his or her name? Why? What would you do if something like this happened to you?

Adapted from The Heart Is the Teacher *by Leonard Covello and Guido D'Agostino. Copyright © 1958 by Leonard Covello. Reprinted by permission of Lurton Blassingame, the authors' agent.*

Every day in school before receiving our bowl of soup we recited the Lord's Prayer. I had no idea what the words meant. I only knew that I was expected to bow my head. I looked around to see what was going on. Swift and simple, the teacher's blackboard pointer brought the idea home to me. I never looked around again after that.

I learned arithmetic and penmanship and spelling—every misspelled word had to be written ten times or more in my notebook. I do not know how many times I wrote "I must not talk." In this same way I learned how to read in English, learned geography and grammar, the states of the Union, all the capital cities and choice bits of poetry and sayings. Most learning was done in unison. That is, all the children recited to the teacher while they stood at attention. Repetition. Repetition until the things you learned beat in your brain even at night when you were falling asleep.

Silence! Silence! Silence! This was the characteristic feature at school. You never made an unnecessary noise or said an unnecessary word. Outside in the hall we lined up by size, girls in one line and boys in another, without a sound, to go to the assembly. Eyes front and at attention. Lord help you if you broke the rule of silence. I can still see a distant relative of mine, a girl named Miluzza, who could never stop talking. She stood in a corner behind Mrs. Cutter [the teacher] throughout an entire assembly with a spring-type clothespin fastened to her lower lip as punishment. Not at all frightened, instead defiant—Miluzza with that clothespin hanging from her lip. . . .

The piano struck up a march and from the hall we paraded into assembly—eyes straight ahead in military style. Mrs. Cutter was there on the platform, her eyes reaching every corner of the assembly hall. It was always the same. We stood at attention as the Bible was read and at attention as the flag was waved back and forth, and we sang the same song. I didn't know what the words meant, but I sang it loudly with all the rest, in my own way, "Three Cheers for de Red Whatzam Blu!"

One day I came home from school with a report card for my father to sign. I remember that my friend Vito Salvatore happened to be there, and Mary Accurso had stopped in for a moment to see my mother. With a tired look my father looked over the marks on the report card and was about to sign it. However, he paused with the pen in his hand.

"What is this?" he said. "Leonard Covello! What happened to the *i* in Coviello?"

My mother stopped sewing. Vito and I just looked at each other.

"Well?" my father insisted.

"Maybe the teacher just forgot to put it in," Mary suggested. "It can happen." She was going to high school now and spoke with an air of authority, and people always listened to her. This time, however, my father didn't even hear her.

"From Leonardo to Leonard I can follow," he said, "a perfectly natural process. In America anything can happen and does happen. But you don't change a family name. A name is a name. What happened to the *i*?"

"Mrs. Cutter took it out," I explained. "Every time she pronounced Coviello it came out Covello. So she took out the *i*. That way it's easier for everybody."

My father hit the table with his fist. "And what has this Mrs. Cutter got to do with my name?"

"What difference does it make?" I said. "It's more American. The *i* doesn't help anything." It was one of the very few times that I dared oppose my father. But even at that age I was beginning to feel that anything that made a name less foreign was an improvement.

Vito came to my rescue. "My name is Victor —Vic. That's what everybody calls me now."

"Vica. Sticka. Micka. You crazy in the head!" my father yelled at him.

For a moment my father sat there, bitter rebellion building in him. Then, with a shrug of giving up, he signed the report card and shoved it over to me. My mother now suddenly entered the argument. "How is it possible to do this to a name? Why did you sign the card? Narduccio, you will have to tell your teacher that a name cannot be changed just like that."

"Mamma, you don't understand."

"What is there to understand? A person's life and his honor is in his name. He never changes it. A name is not a shirt or a piece of underwear."

My father got up from the table, lighted the twisted stump of a cigar and moved out of the argument. "Honor!" he muttered to himself.

"You must explain this to your teacher," my mother insisted. "It was a mistake. She will know. She will not let it happen again. You will see."

"It was no mistake. It was done on purpose. The *i* is out, and Mrs. Cutter made it Covello. You don't understand!"

"Will you stop saying that!" my mother insisted. "I don't understand. I don't understand. What is there to understand? Now that you have become Americanized you understand everything and I understand nothing."

With her in this mood I dared not answer. Mary went over and put her hand on my mother's shoulder. I called to Vito and together we walked out of the apartment and downstairs into the street.

"She just doesn't understand," I kept saying.

"I'm gonna take the *e* off the end of my name and make it just Salvator," Vito said. "After all, we're not in Italy now."

Vito and I were standing unhappily under the gas light on the corner. Somehow or other the joy of childhood had left us. We were only boys, but a sadness that we could not explain pressed down upon us. Mary came and joined us. She had a book under her arm. She stood there for a moment, while her dark eyes looked at us questionably.

"But they don't understand!" I insisted.

Mary smiled. "Maybe some day, you will realize that *you* are the only one who does not understand."

FEAR OF THE IMMIGRANT

For the millions of immigrants who came to America in the late 1800's and early 1900's, their first sight of their new land was the Statue of Liberty. It stands on an island at the entrance to New York Harbor. And for most newcomers the statue with its uplifted torch was a wonderful and welcome sight.

However, not all Americans in these years welcomed the newcomers. Many Americans were worried by the "New Immigrants," whose ways of life and customs seemed so strange and foreign. Thomas Bailey Aldrich, a writer and editor of the *Atlantic Monthly* magazine, expressed the fears of many Americans in his poem "Unguarded Gates."

How does Aldrich picture the United States in the first stanza? Where do members of the "motley throng" come from? What two frightening things do they bring with them?

From "Unguarded Gates" in The Works of Thomas Bailey Aldrich, *Poems, Vol. II. Boston: The Jefferson Press.*

Wide open and unguarded stand our gates,
Named of the four winds, North, South, East, and West;
Portals [gates] that lead to an enchanted land
Of cities, forests, fields of living gold,
Vast prairies, lordly summits [mountains] touched with snow,
Majestic rivers sweeping proudly past . . .
A realm [land] wherein are fruits of every zone, . . .
A later Eden planted in the wilds. . . .
Here, it is written, Toil shall have its wage,
And Honor honor, and the humblest man
Stand level with the highest in the law.
Of such a land have men in dungeons dreamed. . . .

Wide open and unguarded stand our gates,
And through them presses a wild motley throng —
Men from the Volga and the Tartar steppes,
Featureless figures of the Hwang Ho,
Malayan, Scythian, Teuton, Celt, and Slav,
Flying the Old World's poverty and scorn;
These bringing with them unknown gods and rites,
Those, tiger passions, here to stretch their claws.
In street and alley what strange tongues are loud. . . .

O Liberty, white Goddess! is it well
To leave the gates unguarded? . . .
Lift the down-trodden, but with hand of steel
Stay those who to thy sacred portals come
To waste the gifts of freedom. Have a care
Lest from thy brow the clustered stars be torn
And trampled in the dust. . . .

THE NEED FOR UNIONS

In the late 1800's and early 1900's workers faced many problems that were the result of the new industrial age. In order to try to solve these problems, workers began to join together and to organize into unions. However, the right of workers to organize unions and to bargain collectively with employers became an important issue. At times, it seemed that most Americans and even state governments and the federal government were opposed to this effort. Union leaders often had great difficulty in persuading working people to join labor unions. In this selection John Mitchell, president of the United Mine Workers from 1898 to 1908, argues in favor of labor unions.

Why is it impossible for an individual worker to bargain effectively with an employer? What, according to Mitchell, is the basic principle of trade unionism? How do you think you would have felt about labor unions in these years?

Adapted from John Mitchell, Organized Labor: Its Problems, Purposes, and Ideals. *Philadelphia: American Book and Bible House, 1903.*

In its basic principle, trade unionism is plain and clear and simple. Trade unionism starts by recognizing that under normal conditions individual, unorganized workers cannot bargain advantageously with the employer for the sale of their labor. Since workers have no money saved, they must sell their labor immediately. Moreover, they have no knowledge of the market and no skill in bargaining. Finally, they have only their own labor to sell, while the employer uses hundreds or thousands of workers and can easily do without the services of any particular individual. Thus workers, if bargaining only for themselves, are at a great disadvantage.

Trade unionism recognizes the fact that under such conditions labor loses value. The labor which workers sell is, unlike other commodities, a thing which is of their very life and soul and being. In the individual contract between a rich employer and a poor worker, the laborer will get the worst of it. Workers are constantly weakened because of wages too low to buy nourishing food, hours too long for enough rest, working conditions that destroy moral, mental, and physical health, and dangers that may cause accidents and disease. The "individual bargain," or individual contract, between employers and workers means that the condition of the worst and lowest worker in the industry will be that which the best worker must accept.

From first to last, from beginning to end, always and everywhere, trade unionism is opposed to the individual contract. It is this principle, the absolute and complete end of contracts between employers and individual workers, upon which trade unionism is founded. There can be no lasting prosperity for the working classes, no real and lasting progress, until this principle is firmly and fully established.

Trade unions were founded to find a substitute for the individual bargain. A trade union, in its usual form, is an association of workers who have agreed among themselves not to bargain individually with their employer or employers, but to agree to the terms of a collective or joint contract between the employer and the union. The difference between the individual and the collective or joint bargain is simply this: In the individual contract one worker in a hundred refuses to accept work, and the employer keeps the service of ninety-nine. In the collective bargain the hundred employees act together and the employer keeps or fires all of them on the same terms. The ideal of trade unionism is to combine in one organization all the workers employed, or capable of being employed, at a given trade. And to demand and secure for each and all of the workers a definite minimum standard of wages, hours, and conditions of work.

To carry out a joint bargain, it is necessary to establish an accepted minimum of wages and conditions which will apply to all. This does not mean that the wages of all shall be the same, but only that equal pay shall be given for equal work. There cannot be more than one minimum wage in a given trade, in a given place, at a given time.

The recognition of the union is nothing more nor less than the recognition of the principle for which trade unionism stands—the right to bargain collectively and to insist upon minimum standards.

There are many employers who are willing to give up the principle of the individual bargain but do not accept the principle of the collective bargain. These employers state that they do not insist upon dealing with their employees as individuals, but that they must keep the right of dealing with "only their own employees." They say that they must not be forced to permit a worker who is not their own employee to interfere in their business.

The right to bargain collectively, however, or to take any other united action, necessarily involves the right to representation. Experience and reason both show that a person who is dependent on the good will of an employer is in no position to negotiate with him. If he insists on what he considers to be the rights of the workers represented by him he may be fired or at least lose his employer's favor. Not only should workers have the right of making collective contracts, but they should also have the right of being represented by whomever they wish. To deny the right of representation is tyranny.

HARDSHIPS OF RURAL LIFE

A world away from the rapidly growing, crowded cities of the East and Midwest, with their working-class slums and mansions of the rich, were the farms of the Great Plains. Eugene V. Smalley, a well-known journalist in the years after the Civil War, traveled through the Great Plains, where he visited many of the farms. He wrote about the lives of the farm families on the plains. In this selection, he emphasizes the isolation of farm life and suggests what could be done to make farm life more pleasant.

Why are American farmers so isolated? How does their condition compare with that of European farmers? What solution does Smalley suggest? What factors, which he could not take into account, eventually brought about changes in the situation?

Adapted from E. V. Smalley, "The Isolation of Life on Prairie Farms," Atlantic Monthly, *September 1893.*

In no civilized country have the farmers so poorly adapted their home life to the conditions of nature as have the people of our vast plains region. This is a strong statement, but I am led to this conclusion by ten years of observation. The European farmer lives in a village, where considerable social enjoyment is possible. The women talk together at the village well, and visit frequently at one another's homes. The children find playmates close to home. There is a school, and if the village is not a very small one, a church. The old men gather on summer evenings to smoke their pipes and talk of the crops. The young men play ball on the village green. In a word, something takes place to break the monotony or sameness of daily life. The houses, though small and with little furniture, have thick walls of brick or stone that keep out the summer's heat and the winter's cold.

Now contrast this life with the life of a poor settler in North or South Dakota or Nebraska. Every homesteader must live upon his claim

for five years to confirm his title to it. If the country were so thickly settled that every quarter-section of land, or 160 acres [64.7 hectares], had a family upon it, each family would still be half a mile [.8 kilometer] from any neighbor. But many settlers own 320 acres [129.5 hectares] and a few have 640 acres [259 hectares]. Then there are sections of land set aside for schools and other sections are not occupied at all. Thus the average space separating the farms is, in fact, always more than half a mile [.8 kilometer]. Many settlers must go a mile or two to reach a neighbor's house.

If there is any region in the world where the natural sociable instinct of people should be upheld, that region is our northwestern prairies. A short hot summer is followed by a long cold winter. The treeless plain stretches away to the horizon in every direction. In summer, it is covered with grain fields or grass and flowers, and is lovely in its color and vastness. But one mile of it is almost exactly like another. When the snow covers the ground it is bleak and depressing. There are no birds left after the wild geese and ducks have flown south. The silence of death rests on the vast landscape, except when it is swept by cruel winds.

In such a region, you would expect the houses to be strongly built, but they are not. The new settlers are too poor to build a house of brick or stone. Instead, they haul a few loads of lumber from the nearest railway station. Then they put up a frail little house of two, three, or four rooms that looks as though the prairie winds would blow it away. The barn is often made of sod walls with a straw roof. A barbed-wire fence surrounds the barnyard. There are usually no trees.

In this small, cramped home, the farm family sees nothing more cheerful than the distant houses of other settlers, just as ugly and lonely, and stacks of straw and unthreshed grain. In the summer there is a school for the children, one, two, or three miles away. But in winter the distances across the snow-covered plains are too great for them to travel. Each family must live mainly to itself. A drive to the nearest town is almost the only pleasure. There are few social events in the life of these prairie farmers to liven up the monotony of the long winter evenings.

Visits from neighbors are few, because of the long distances which separate the farmhouses. Another reason is the differences among the people. They have no common past to talk about. They were strangers to one another when they arrived in this new land, and their work and ways have not thrown them together much. Often the strangeness is increased by differences of national origin. There are Swedes, Norwegians, Germans, French Canadians, and perhaps even Finns and Icelanders. The Americans themselves come from many different states. It is hard to establish any social bond in such a mixed population.

An alarming amount of insanity occurs among farmers. In proportion to their numbers, the Scandinavian settlers send the most people to the insane asylums. The reason is easy to see. These people came from cheery little farm villages. Life in their homeland was hard and full of work, but it was not lonesome. Think for a moment how great the change must be from the white-walled, red-roofed village in Norway to an isolated cabin on a Dakota prairie. It is little wonder that so many Scandinavian farmers lose their mental balance.

There is only one solution for the dreariness of farm life on the prairies. The isolated farmhouse must be abandoned, and the people must draw together and live in villages. The peasants of the Russian steppes did this centuries ago, and so did those on the great plain of the Danube. In the older parts of our prairie states, titles to homestead claims are now nearly all confirmed, so farmers no longer have to live on the land they farm. They might go out with their teams to till their fields, and return at evening to village homes. It would be entirely possible to divide the land over again so that each settler would still have 160 acres [64.7 hectares], and no one would live more than a mile from the farthest limit of his farm. The homes of the families would surround a village green, where the schoolhouse would stand. There would probably be a store and a post office. An active social life would soon develop in such a community.

If the plains people were thus brought together into towns, some home industries might be established that would add to family incomes, or at least save expenses. The economic weakness of farming in the North is based on the idle period of the farmer and the work animals during the long winter. If it were possible to bring back to the farm some of the crafts that were carried on in the country thirty or forty years ago, there would be a great gain in comfort, intelligence, and happiness.

According to habit, American farmers feel they must live upon the land they till, and must have no near neighbors. This habit will be hard to break, but I believe it must in time give in to the advantages of living closer together. I have known instances, however, where efforts at more neighborly ways of living have been made on a small scale, and have failed. In the early settlement of Dakota, sometimes four families, each taking a quarter-section homestead, would build temporary houses at the quarter-sections' meeting line, in order to be near each other. But a few years later, when they were able to put up better buildings, they moved to the opposite sides of their claims. They did so, they said, because their chickens got mixed up with those of their neighbors. In these instances, I should add, the people were Americans. There is an individuality about the average American farmer, the result of generations of isolated living, that does not encourage living close to others.

I am aware that nothing changes so slowly as the customs of a people. It will take a long time to change the settled American habit of isolated farms. If it is ever changed, the new system will have to be introduced near the top of the rural social scale, and work down gradually to the masses. A group of farmers of superior intelligence and of above-average means must set an example and establish a model farm village. Such an experiment would be widely discussed by the newspapers. This extensive free advertising could hardly fail to interest other people in the idea.

The farmers of the West have thus far been engaged in a hard struggle to establish themselves on the soil, obtain the necessities of life, and pay off their mortgages. They are getting ahead year by year. In the older settled districts good houses are taking the place of the pioneer homes, and the towns show progress. Before long these prairie people will begin to try to solve the problems that come with a higher civilization. Then it will be found, I believe, that the first great step toward more comfortable living, intellectual development, and social enjoyment is the abandonment of the lonesome farmhouse and the establishment of the farm village.

A POPULIST ANALYZES FARMERS' PROBLEMS

During the hard times of the 1880's and 1890's farmers throughout the country gathered in Grange halls and other meeting places to discuss their problems and to demand relief. As this happened, the Grange, a national farm organization founded to provide community activity for farm families, began to work for the improvement of farm conditions. The Grange established cooperatives, and its members went into politics. Then in the early 1890's members of the Grange and other farmers formed their own political party—the Populist Party.

In 1890, William Peffer, a Kansas lawyer and journalist, was elected to the Senate on the Populist Party ticket. In this selection, he summarized the farmers' complaints against the manufacturers, the banks, and the railroads.

According to Peffer, how had the farmers' situation changed between the 1840's and the 1890's in terms of self-sufficiency, cash, and competition? Who or what was to blame? Why did the political power of farmers decline?

Adapted from William A. Peffer, The Farmer's Side: His Troubles and Their Remedy. *New York: D. Appleton and Co., 1891.*

A hundred years ago 90 percent of our population lived on farms. Transportation was so expensive that surplus wheat and corn could not be sold 50 miles [80 kilometers] away from a market town. Now great cities have grown up, the market has expanded, and distance is practically meaningless. From a small area along the Atlantic coast, we have spread across the continent. We travel by railroad from Boston to San Francisco in less than six days.

The American farmer of today is a completely different sort of person than he was 50 or 100 years ago. A great many men and women now living remember when farmers were largely manufacturers. That is, they made a great many tools and other things for their own use. Every farmer had tools with which he made wooden tools such as forks and rakes, handles for his hoes and plows, spokes for his wagon, and various other things.

Then the farmer produced flax and hemp and wool and cotton. These fibers were prepared on the farm. They were spun into yarn, woven into cloth, made into clothes, and worn at home. Upon every farm geese were kept. Their feathers were used in the home's beds and pillows, and the surplus was sold at the nearest market town.

When winter came, animals raised on the farm were butchered. Meat for family use during the next year was prepared and preserved in the smokehouse. The orchards supplied fruit for cider, for apple butter, and for preserves. Wheat was threshed, a little at a time, just enough to supply the needs of the family for money. Everything was saved and put to use.

One of the results of that sort of careful planning was that only a small amount of money was required to carry on the business of farming. A hundred dollars a year was probably as much as the largest farmers of that day needed to pay for workers, repairs of tools, and all other expenses, because so many things were paid for with farm crops.

Now we find that nearly everything has been changed. All over the West farmers thresh their wheat all at one time, get rid of it all at one time, and in a great many instances waste the straw. They sell their hogs, and buy bacon and pork. They sell their cattle, and buy fresh beef or canned beef or corned beef. They sell their fruit, and buy it back in cans. If they raise flax at all, they thresh it, sell the seed, and burn the straw. Instead of having clothing made on the farm or by a neighbor woman or country tailor a mile away, they either buy their clothing ready-made at the nearest town, or buy the cloth and have a city tailor make it.

Instead of making tools which they use on the farm, they go to town to purchase even a handle for an ax or a mallet. They purchase twine and rope and all sorts of material made of fibers. Indeed, they buy nearly everything now that they once produced, and these things all cost money.

Besides all this, there is something even stranger. In earlier times the American home was a free home. There was not one case in a thousand where a home was mortgaged to secure the payment of borrowed money. Only a small amount of money was then needed to carry on the business of farming, and there was always enough of it to supply the demand. Now when at least ten times as much is needed, there is little or none to be obtained. Nearly half the farms are mortgaged for as much as they were worth, and interest rates are very high.

As to the cause of such changes in the condition of farmers, it is the railroad builder, the banker, the moneychanger, and the manufacturer who have hurt the farmer. The manufacturers came with their factories. The wagonmaker's shop in the neighborhood has given way to the large company in the city where people by the thousand work and where a hundred or two hundred wagons are made in a week. The shoemaker's shop has given way to large companies in the cities where most of the work is done by machines. The old smokehouse has given way to the packing house. The farmer now is forced to go to town for nearly everything. Even a hand rake to clean up the yard must be bought at the city store.

And what is worse, if they need a little more money, they are forced to go to town to borrow it. But they do not find the money there. In place of it they find an agent who will "negotiate" a loan. The money is in the East, at a distance of a thousand, three thousand, or five thousand miles [1,600, 4,830, or 8,050 kilometers]. The farmers of the country today are maintaining an army of distributors, loan agents, bankers, and others, who are absolutely worthless for all good purposes in the community.

These things, however, involve only the mechanics of farming. The farmers' territory has been invaded by people who buy large tracts of land and operate these large farms like factories. This is "bonanza" farming. The aim of some of the great "bonanza farms" of Dakota is to use machinery so effectively that farming one full section, or 640 acres [259 hectares], represents one year's work for only one person. Railroad companies gave special rates to the bonanza farmers. And while this disastrous competition was going on, ranchers too took possession of vast areas of the public lands and raised cattle by the million at no expense beyond the cost of herding.

These are some of the causes of the hard times in the farming industry. It was impossible for the average farmers to hold their own with such odds against them.

While these problems were increasing, other forces were operating to add to farmers' difficulties. The people were rapidly taking on

debts, while prices of farm products fell very low. While one hundred dollars had the same value in 1889 as it did in 1869, lower farm prices made it worth more. It requires twice as many bushels of wheat or of corn or of oats, twice as many pounds of cotton or tobacco or wool, to pay off a debt in 1887 as it did to pay a debt of the same amount in 1867.

It is frequently said that the farmers themselves are to blame for all these problems. But that is not true. The farmer has been the victim of a gigantic scheme of plunder. Never before has such a vast combination of brains and money forced people into labor for the benefit of a few.

In the beginning of our history nearly all the people were farmers, and they made our laws. But as the national wealth increased, they came to supply the needs of those who own or control large fortunes. Farmers worked while others reaped the harvest. It is greed that robbed the farmers. High interest rates took all their money. And now, when their problems are becoming worse and disaster overtakes them, they appeal to those they have made rich only to learn how poor and helpless they are.

From this testimony readers need have no difficulty in determining for themselves "how we got here." Money [bankers and financiers] rules our financial policy. Money controls the business of the country. Money is robbing the people. These people of Wall Street hold the bonds of nearly every state, county, city, and township in the Union. Every railroad owes them more than it is worth. Every trust and combine made to rob the people had its beginnings in the example of Wall Street dealers. This dangerous power which money gives is taking away the liberties of the people. It now has control of nearly half their homes, and is reaching out its clutching hands for the rest. This is the power we have to deal with.

UNITED AGAINST A "COMMON ENEMY"

All farmers faced the problems of debt, overproduction, and low prices during the hard times of the 1880's and 1890's. But these years were especially difficult for black farmers in the South. Some leaders hoped that poor blacks and whites could work together to solve their problems. One man who hoped this was possible was T. Thomas

Fortune. Born a slave in Florida, Fortune attended Howard University after the Civil War. He later became the publisher of a newspaper, the New York *Age*.

According to Fortune, what was the chief mistake the North made after winning the Civil War? What reasons does he give for industrial slavery being oppressive? Do you think his hope for the future is realistic?

Adapted from Black and White: Land, Labor and Politics in the South *by Timothy Thomas Fortune. Reprinted by Arno Press, Inc., 1968.*

I know it is not fashionable for writers on economic questions to tell the truth. But the truth should be told. During the war the government confiscated the slave population of the South, but it left to the rebels a far more valuable kind of property. The slave, the perishable wealth, was taken by the government and then freed. But property in land, the wealth which does not perish, was left to the rebels.

The United States took the slave but left the thing which gave birth to *personal slavery* and is now fast giving birth to *industrial slavery*. The latter is more agonizing and much worse than that other slavery, which I once withstood. The old slaveholders had to feed, clothe, and house their property, and take care of it when disease or accident threatened its life. But industrial slavery requires no such care. The new slaveholder only wants to obtain the most labor for the least cost. He does not regard the worker as of any consequence when he can no longer produce. Having worked him to death, or ruined his health and robbed him of his labor, he turns him out upon the world to live upon the charity of people or to die of starvation. He knows that there is no profit in wasting time and money upon a disabled industrial slave. He makes wealth and death at one and the same time. He could not do this if our social system did not give him a monopoly of the soil from which a living must be obtained.

I think of the absolutely destitute condition of the colored people of the South at the close of the war. I remember the moral and intellectual harm slavery did them. Not only were they bankrupt, but they were absolutely cut off from the soil, with no right or title to it. Now they have already got a respectable slice of land. They have eagerly taken hold of the opportunities for educational development provided by good men and women. They have bought homes and supplied them with articles of convenience and comfort, often of luxury. I am surprised not at this progress, but that the race did not terrorize and rob society as society had for so long terrorized and robbed them. The thing is strange and marvelous, in the extreme. Instead of becoming outlaws, as the situation would seem to have indicated, the black men and women of the South went to work to better their own lives and the crippled condition of the country, which had been produced by the ravages of rebellion. Meanwhile, many white people of the South, the capitalists, the land-sharks, and the ruffians organized themselves into a band of outlaws. They deliberately murdered innocent men and women for political reasons, and robbed them of their honest labor because they were too lazy to work themselves.

But this highly abnormal, unnatural condition of things is fast passing away. White people, having asserted their superiority in matters of assassination and robbery, have settled down on a barrel of dynamite, as they did in the days of slavery. They will await the explosion with the same self-satisfaction true of them in other days.

The future struggle in the South will be, not between white people and black people, but between capital and labor, landlord and tenant. Already the armies are gathering on the field.

The same battle will be fought upon southern soil that is in preparation in other states where the conditions took longer to develop but are no more deep-rooted or harmful. The social problems in the South will be found to be the same as those in every other section of our country. Questions of "race," "condition," etc., will be properly adjusted as people become better off and forget the unhappy past.

The hour is coming when the working classes of our country, North, East, West, and South, will recognize that they have a *common cause*, a *common humanity*, and a *common enemy*. If they want to triumph over wrong, without distinction of race or previous condition, *they must unite!* When the battle begins, the rich, be they black or be they white, will be found upon the same side. And the poor, be they black or be they white, will be found on the same side.

Necessity knows no law and discriminates in favor of no person or race.

CHAPTER 7
NEW LIFE STYLES IN THE NEW INDUSTRIAL AGE

THE MAKING OF A NEW YORKER

From 1865 to 1900, more and more Americans left farms and small towns to live in the cities. In 1869 no American city had a population of 1 million, but by 1890 New York, Chicago, and Philadelphia each had more than 1 million people.

What caused so many thousands of people to leave their homes and try to start a new life in the city? This great movement of people had many causes. People were attracted to the cities by hopes of jobs and high wages; many also came to escape the dullness of farm life. Cities were interesting places with their bright lights, tall buildings, and bustling activity. The largest American city was New York City. Its crowded streets and activity fascinated many people, especially writers like William Sydney Porter, better known as O. Henry. In this selection, O. Henry writes about "the making of a New Yorker."

What do you think of O. Henry's description of various cities? To what kind of woman would you compare your town? What turns Raggles into a New Yorker? Do you think an incident like this could happen?

Adapted from "The Making of a New Yorker" from The Trimmed Lamp *by O. Henry, published by Doubleday & Co., Inc.*

Besides many other things, Raggles was a poet. He was called a tramp. But that was only a way of saying that he was a philosopher, an artist, a traveler, a naturalist, and a discoverer. But most of all he was a poet. In all his life he never wrote a line of poetry; he lived his poetry.

Raggles' specialty, had he used ink and paper, would have been sonnets to the cities. He studied cities. A city to Raggles was not only a pile of bricks and mortar, with a certain number of inhabitants. It was a thing with a characteristic and distinct soul, an individual life with its own special flavor and feeling. Two thousand miles [3,220 kilometers] to the north and south, east and west, Raggles wandered, studying cities. And when he found the heart of a city and listened to its secret confession, he went on to another.

Through the ancient poets [those of Greece and Rome] we have learned that cities are like women. So they were to poet Raggles. His mind carried a clear idea of the figure that symbolized and typified each one.

Chicago seemed to swoop down upon him with a breezy suggestion of plumes and perfume.

Pittsburgh impressed him as a royal and generous lady—homely, hearty, with a red face, washing the dishes in a silk dress and white slippers, and telling Raggles to sit before the roaring fireplace and drink champagne along with his pigs' feet and fried potatoes.

New Orleans had simply looked down upon him from a balcony. He could see her thoughtful, starry eyes and catch the movement of her fan, and that was all.

Boston appeared to the poetic Raggles in an unusual way. It seemed to him that he had drunk cold tea and that the city was a white, cold cloth that had been wrapped tightly around his head to spur him to some unknown but tremendous mental effort.

One day Raggles came to the heart of the great city of Manhattan. She was the greatest of all. He wanted to classify and label her and arrange her with the other cities.

Raggles landed from a ferryboat one morning and walked into the center of the town confident and at ease. Without money—as a poet should be—but with the excitement of an astronomer discovering a new star, Raggles wandered into the great city.

Late in the afternoon he came out of the roar and commotion with a look of terror on his face. He was defeated, puzzled, frightened. Other cities had been as easy to read and understand as a child's book. But here was one as cold, glittering, serene, and impossible as a four-carat diamond in a window to a young man in love looking at it and feeling his modest clerk's pay in his pocket.

The greetings of the other cities he had known—their homey kindliness, their rough charity, friendly curses, talkative curiosity, or indifference. This city of Manhattan gave him no clue. It was walled against him. Never an eye was turned upon him. No voice spoke to him.

On Broadway Raggles, the successful suitor of many cities, stood, shy, like any country youth. For the first time he experienced the sad humiliation of being ignored. And when he tried to understand this brilliant, swiftly changing, ice-cold city he failed completely. The houses were defensive walls. The people were bright but bloodless ghosts.

The thing that weighed heaviest on Raggles' soul was the spirit of absolute egotism that seemed to fill the people. Humanity was gone from them. They were like gods of stone, worshiping themselves. Frozen, cruel, cut to an identical pattern, they hurried on their ways like statues brought to life, while soul and feeling lay dead in the marble.

Gradually Raggles became aware of certain types. One was an elderly gentleman with a snow-white, short beard, pink, unwrinkled face and stony, sharp blue eyes. He seemed to personify the city's wealth and icy unconcern. Another type was a tall, beautiful woman, calm, dressed like the princesses of old, with eyes coldly blue. And another was a broad, swaggering, grim fellow, with large cheeks, a baby's skin, and the knuckles of a prize fighter. This type leaned against cigar signs and looked at the world with scorn.

Raggles got up his courage and begged for money. The people passed on without a wink of an eyelash to indicate that they were aware of him. And then he said to himself that this fair but pitiless city of Manhattan was without a soul, and that he was alone in a great wilderness.

Raggles started to cross the street. There was a blast, a roar, a hissing and a crash as something struck him and tossed him over and over six yards [5.5 meters] from where he had been.

Raggles opened his eyes. And then a hand soft as a falling petal touched his head. Bending over him was the woman dressed like a princess of old, with blue eyes, now soft with human sympathy. Under his head on the street were silks and furs. With Raggles' hat in his hand and with his face pinker than ever from an outburst against reckless driving, stood the elderly gentleman who personified the city's wealth. From a nearby cafe hurried the man with fat cheeks and baby skin, carrying a glass full of a red liquid.

"Drink dis, sport," he said, holding the glass to Raggles' lips.

Hundreds of people surrounded him in a moment, their faces wearing the deepest concern. Two policemen got into the circle and pressed back the crowd of people wanting to help. A newsboy slipped one of his papers beneath Raggles' elbow, where it lay on the muddy pavement. A brisk young man with a notebook was asking for names.

A bell clanged importantly, and an ambulance cleared an opening through the crowd. A cool surgeon asked, "How do you feel, old man?" The princess of silks and satins wiped a red drop or two from Raggles' head.

"Me?" said Raggles, with an angelic smile, "I feel fine."

He had found the heart of his new city.

In three days they let him leave his bed for the convalescent ward in the hospital. He had been there an hour when the attendants heard sounds of a fight. They found that Raggles had assaulted and hit another patient.

"What's all this about?" asked the head nurse.

"He was speaking badly about me town," said Raggles.

"What town?" asked the nurse.

"Noo York," said Raggles.

NEW YORK: ANOTHER VIEW

Although cities held great attractions for many Americans, the ugliness and the problems caused by rapid growth and by too many people could not be hidden. All large cities had slum areas, where people lived crowded together in dirty, foul-smelling dwellings. Many of these dwellings were airless and without plumbing.

In New York City thousands of people lived crowded together in such run-down tenements. Many of these tenement-dwellers died of disease and lack of proper food. These conditions in city slums alarmed many people. One of them, Jacob Riis, a newspaper reporter, wrote about slum neighborhoods in New York City and took pictures of the conditions there. This selection is from his most famous book, *How the Other Half Lives*, written in an effort to improve such conditions.

What are the worst features of tenements, as Riis describes them? What effect do they have on children who live in them? Do you think that slums have changed since 1890?

Adapted from Jacob Riis, How the Other Half Lives. *New York: Charles Scribner's Sons, 1890.*

There are tenements everywhere. Suppose we look into one on Cherry Street. Be a little careful, please! The hall is dark and you might fall over the children pitching pennies back there. Not that it would hurt them. Kicks and punches are their daily diet. They have little else. Here, where the hall turns into complete darkness, is a step, and another, and another. A flight of stairs. You can feel your way if you cannot see it. Stifling? Yes! What do you expect. All the fresh air that ever enters these stairs comes from the hall door that is forever slamming, and from the windows of dark bedrooms.

That was a woman filling her pail you just bumped against. The sinks are in the hallway, so that all the tenants may get to them—and all smell horrible in the summer. Hear the pump squeak! It is the lullaby of tenement-house babies. During the summer, when a thousand thirsty throats want a cooling drink in this block, the pump is worked in vain. But the saloon, whose open door you passed in the hall, is always there. The smell of it has followed you up.

Here is a door. Listen! That short hacking cough, that tiny, helpless cry—what do they mean? They mean that the soiled bow of white you saw on the door downstairs [when someone died, a bow was hung on the door—black for an adult, white for a child] will have another story to tell—oh, a sadly familiar story—before the day ends. The child is dying with measles. With half a chance it might have lived. But it had none. That dark bedroom killed it.

"It was took all of a sudden," says the mother, smoothing the little body with trembling hands. There is no unkindness in the rough voice of the man in overalls who sits by the window grimly smoking a clay pipe, while he watches his child die, bitter as his words sound: "Hush, Mary! If we cannot keep the baby, need we complain—such as we?"

"Such as we!" What if the words ring in your ears as you grope your way up the stairs and down from floor to floor, listening to the sounds behind the closed doors—some of quarreling, some of coarse songs, more of cursing. They are true. When the summer heat comes with its suffering, its meaning is more terrible than words can tell. Come over here. Step carefully over this baby—it is a baby, in spite of its rags and dirt—under these iron bridges called fire escapes. They are loaded down, despite the warnings of the firemen, with broken household goods, with washtubs and barrels, which no one could climb over to escape from a fire.

This gap between dingy brick walls is the yard. That strip of smoke-colored sky up there is the heaven of these people. Do you wonder that the name does not attract them to the churches? That baby's parents live in the back tenement here. This tenement is much like the one in front we just left, only fouler and darker. A hundred thousand people lived in back tenements in New York last year.

What sort of an answer, do you think, would these tenement-dwellers give to the question, "Is life worth living?"

HOW MUCH PROGRESS FOR WOMEN?

In 1876 Americans celebrated their centennial. One important feature of this celebration of the nation's first one hundred years was the Philadelphia Centennial Exposition. This huge exposition glorified human achievements and progress in many fields. However, there was at least one group of Americans who were not happy with the progress they had made. At this time, American women were still struggling to gain the right to vote and to be considered as social equals. In this selection Elizabeth Cady Stanton, a leader in the women's rights movement, tells about the Woman's Pavilion, or building, at the Exposition.

How did Elizabeth Cady Stanton describe the efforts of some American women to improve their lives? What was her attitude toward the Woman's Pavilion? If you were asked to set up a Woman's Pavilion today, what kind of exhibits would you want to display in it?

Adapted from Elizabeth Cady Stanton, Eighty Years and More. *New York: European Publishing Co., 1898.*

The Woman's Pavilion on the centennial grounds was an afterthought, as religious philosophers claim woman herself to have been. The women of the country, after having contributed nearly $100,000 to the centennial, found that no provision had been made for the separate exhibition of their work. The centennial board then decided to raise funds to build a separate building, to be known as the Woman's Pavilion. It covered an acre of ground, and was built at a cost of $30,000—a small sum in comparison with the money which had been raised by women and spent on the other buildings.

The Pavilion was no true exhibit of woman's abilities. Few women are, as yet, owners of the businesses which their work makes profitable. Cotton factories, in which thousands of women work, are owned by men. The shoe business, in some branches of which women are doing more than half the work, is under the ownership of men. Rich embroideries from India, rugs of downy softness from Turkey, the muslin fabric of India, Waltham watches (whose finest mechanical work is done by women), and ten thousand other industries found no place in the pavilion. Said United States Commissioner Meeker of Colorado, "Woman's work makes up three fourths of the exposition; it is scattered through every building. Take it away, and there would be no exposition."

But this pavilion did one good service for the woman by showing her capabilities as an engineer. The boiler, which provided the force for operating the pavilion, was under the care of a young Canadian girl, Miss Allison. She had loved machinery from childhood, and had spent much time in her father's large mills. When she was chosen to run the pavilion machinery, it caused much opposition. It was said that the committee would, some day, find the pavilion blown to bits; that a woman engineer would spend her time reading novels instead of watching the steam gauge; that the idea was impractical. But Miss Allison soon proved both her abilities and the falseness of these statements by taking her place in the engine room and managing its workings with perfect ease. She declared that the work was cleaner, more pleasant, and much less tiring than cooking over a kitchen stove. "Since I have had to earn my own living," she said, "I have never done work I like so well. Teaching school is much harder, and one is not paid so well." She was confident that she could manage the engines of an ocean steamer. There were thousands of small engines in use in various parts of the country, she said. There was no reason why women should not be employed to manage them, following the profession of engineer as a regular business.

But the Woman's Pavilion would have been truly historic if some displays had hung upon its walls. These displays might have included the yearly protest of Harriet K. Hunt against taxation without representation. Another might have been the legal papers served upon the Smith sisters for their refusal to pay taxes while unrepresented. Still another might have been papers issued by the city of Worcester for the forced sale of the house and lands of Abby Kelly Foster, the abolitionist, because she refused to pay taxes without representation. With these should have been exhibited framed copies of all the laws bearing unjustly upon women—those which rob her of her name, her earnings, her property, her children, her person. Another exhibit might have included the legal papers in the case of Susan B. Anthony, who was tried and fined for claiming her right to vote under the Fourteenth Amendment; and the decision of Mr. Justice Miller in the case of Myra Bradwell, denying national protection for woman's civil rights.

Woman's most fitting contributions to the Centennial Exposition would have been these protests, laws, and decisions, which show her political slavery. But all this was displayed in rooms outside the exposition grounds, where the National Woman's Suffrage Association raised its flag and made its protests.

To many thoughtful people it seemed unreasonable for women to complain of injustice in this free land, among such universal rejoicing. When the majority of women are seemingly happy, it is natural to suppose that the discontent of the minority is the result of unfortunate individual circumstances. But the history of the world shows that the great majority, in every generation, just accept the conditions into which they are born. Those who demand larger liberties are always a small minority, whose claims are made fun of and ignored. We would honor any Chinese woman who claimed the right to her own feet so that she could walk; the Hindu widow who refused to climb upon the funeral fire of her husband; and the Turkish woman who threw off her veil and left the harem.

Why not honor as well the intelligent minority of American women who protest against the false disabilities by which their freedom is limited and their development stopped? That only a few protest against the injustice of long-established laws and customs does not disprove the fact of the oppressions. The satisfaction of the many, if real, only proves their lack of concern. That a majority of the women of the United States accept, without protest, the disabilities which grow out of the fact that they cannot vote is simply an evidence of their ignorance and cowardice. The minority who demand a higher political standing clearly prove their greater intelligence and wisdom.

A CLOSE-UP OF MARK TWAIN

Two important writers of the late 1800's were Mark Twain and William Dean Howells. Twain described the new industrial age in his book *The Gilded Age*, but he was even more popular as a local-color writer who captured the frontier spirit and humor of the West. Howells was famous for his realistic writing. His best-known book, *Silas Lapham*, told about the lives of some newly rich Americans.

Howells and Twain were close friends. And when Twain died in 1910, Howells wrote a tribute to the man he called "the Lincoln of our literature." Although he called it *My Mark Twain*, he noted that he always called Twain by his real name, Samuel Clemens, because his pen name "seemed always somehow to mask him from my personal sense." In this selection, Howells speaks of visiting Twain at his home in Hartford, Connecticut.

What does Howells admire most about Twain's style? What was Twain's attitude toward writing in sequence? What do you think of his method of writing?

Adapted from My Mark Twain *by William Dean Howells. New York: Harper & Brothers.*

Clemens and his architect had planned a luxurious study over the library in his new house. But as his children grew older, it was given to them to use as a schoolroom. He then used the room above his stable. There we used to talk together until he discovered that he preferred to use the large billiard room at the top of his house as a place to write and meet friends. It was pretty cold up there in the early spring and late fall weather. But by lighting all the gas burners and building a fire, we could keep it well above freezing. Here he wrote many of his tales and sketches, and for all I know, some of his books.

We took special pleasure in looking out of the high windows at the pretty Hartford landscape, and down to the tops of the trees covering the hillside near his house. We agreed that there was a charm in trees seen from such a point of view. He had not been a country boy or, rather, a village boy, for nothing. Nothing that nature can offer the young was lost on him. We were natives of the same vast Mississippi Valley. Missouri and Ohio were close enough so that we had learned many of the same ways of talking. I had outgrown mine because I read more, but I gladly recognized the phrases which he used for their lasting juiciness.

His natural use of words formed the backbone of his style. I may have read more, but he was always reading some vital book. It might be some out-of-the-way book, but it had the root of the human matter in it. Perhaps it was a book of great trials, an autobiography, a history, or a narrative of travel—something that showed him life at first-hand. As I remember, he did not care much for fiction, and he had certain distinct dislikes. One was for my dear and honored favorite, Jane Austen. As for plays, he hated the theater, and said he would rather add a list of numbers than follow a plot on the stage. Generally, I think his pleasure in poetry was not great, and I do not believe he cared much for the usual accepted masterpieces of literature. He liked to find out good things and great things for himself. Sometimes he would discover these in a masterpiece new to him alone.

Of all the literary men I have known he was the most unliterary in his background and manner. I do not know whether he knew any Latin, but I think not. German he knew pretty well, and enough Italian to have fun with it. But he used English in all its various forms as if it were native to his own air, as if it had come up out of American, out of Missourian ground. His style was what we know, for good and for bad. But his manner, if I may separate the two, was as entirely his own as if no one had ever written before. He was not enslaved to the consecutiveness in writing which the rest of us are chained to. That is, he wrote as he thought, as all people think, without sequence, without an eye to what went before or should come after. If something occurred to him beyond or beside what he was saying, he put it down on his page, and made it as much at home there as its nature would allow. Then, when he was through with this idea, he would go back to his original thoughts, and keep on with what he had been talking about. He followed this manner in the construction of his sentences, and the arrangement of his chapters.

I helped him with a Library of Humor, which he once edited. When I had done my work according to tradition, with authors, times, and topics carefully studied in order, he tore it all apart, and threw in the pieces wherever he wanted to at the moment. He was right. We were not making a textbook, but a book for the pleasure rather than the instruction of the reader. He did not see why the principle on which he built his own tales and novels should not apply to it. On minor points he was, beyond any author I have known, without favorite phrases or pet words. He also was not against repeating words many times. If a certain word served him better than a substitute, he would use it on a page as many times as he chose.

SMALL-TOWN PLEASURES

During the new industrial age, American customs and ways of life were changing. The rapid growth of industry and cities caused great changes in the way Americans acted, thought, and lived. The old customs gave way to the new, in recreation just as they did in everything else. Organized sports took the place of the simpler games of frontier days. The circus and "Wild West" show were new and popular forms of entertainment.

In small towns, however, recreation continued to follow the more traditional ways. Here, people played games rather than watched them, and they attended picnics and fairs. In this selection, writer Albert Britt, born in 1874, talks about his boyhood on a farm in southern Illinois and the pastimes he enjoyed.

What were the main amusements of Albert Britt's youth? How did the way he played baseball differ from the way you play it? What pleasures did he have that you lack? Which ones do you enjoy that he lacked? Would you want to change places with him?

Taken from An America That Was *by Albert Britt. © by Albert Britt 1964. Used by permission of Crown Publishers, Inc.*

Sunday was a day of rest for older people, and the place to rest was a comfortable chair indoors. Only extreme heat could drive them outside to soft grass and the shade of convenient trees. After I had become a city person, I thought of a walk in the woods or through the fields as a form of recreation and my divorce from the farm was complete. Fields and woods were for work and not for idle walking by grown people.

Even mild games were thought to be beneath the dignity of adults, although croquet was permissible. Tennis was unknown to us, although it was creeping into the towns. There was one exception in the case of tennis. Bill Adcock, a prosperous farmer, liked what he heard about this game and came home from town one day with a full set of the necessary equipment, net, rackets, and balls. My brother-in-law Dan saw it and liked the game but not enough to spend money for the equipment. A long fishnet, which he tied himself, made a fair net. He could make his own rackets, which he did— wooden paddles of at least the right shape and size. Balls of course he could not make, so he had to buy them. The result was a game that was a mockery of lawn tennis, even as it was played in that early day. But Dan had an idea. Paddle tennis is with us today.

Of course, being good Americans, we played baseball, but no games on Sunday, although batting and fielding practice were allowed. Neighborhood baseball rose and fell as the number of active young men varied. There were two or three seasons when we Tylerville players thought rather well of ourselves because of a young farmer nearby who could manage to pitch a curve ball. Unfortunately, his control was uncertain and our dream of a township championship never got to first base.

Diamonds were set up wherever there was a large enough stretch of level pastureland to give the players at least a chance to field the ball, although I remember one diamond where a long hit into right field had a better than even chance of rolling down a slope into a creek at the bottom. There were bitter arguments over the scoring of such a hit. Some held the theory that a hit was a hit. Others maintained that such a performance was an act of God and not a home run. Umpires, when there were any, generally followed the rule of safety-first by balancing an outrageously wrong decision in favor of team A by an equally absurd error in behalf of team B at the first opportunity. There were few pitchers' battles, and scorers were kept busy. Thirty-two to twenty-five was thought of as a close game and was entirely satisfactory to those who were watching.

A small, coal-mining community ten or fifteen miles [16 or 24 kilometers] away in the next county went in strong for baseball and turned out a team that could give a busy afternoon to towns two or three times their size. Wherever they went, a crowd of rooters went with them, not only to cheer but also to bet. Those were good times for coal miners and pay was high by our standards. The rooters were well supplied with money. In the early stages of the game, the bettors walked up and down in front of the spectators showing their money and looking for customers. If there were local laws against public betting, they never applied inside the baseball field when the miners were playing.

When scores were close and hits were important, men who had bet money on the game pleadingly offered "A dollar for a hit!" and if a lucky batter got a hit he gathered in a small harvest of silver dollars from the dust at his feet. These miner-sportsmen were way over our heads and we watched them in silent awe and admiration.

Our money operations were limited to occasional collections to buy new balls. Players supplied their own bats and gloves, although most of us played barehanded. Charlie Glass was our most admired catcher because of his willingness to stand close behind the bat without mitt, mask, shinguard, or chest protector. It was not our courage but our lack of money that fixed the limit of our equipment. League balls cost a dollar or more, and a lost ball might throw us into bankruptcy. Unless it was lost, a ball stayed in play as long as the stitching held.

Picnics were favorite summer affairs, usually requiring an anniversary or some celebration for an excuse. Farmers were not likely to go on picnics for the mere joy of spending time with Nature. We were in close touch with Nature twelve months of the year and knew it for what it was, a cold-blooded creature who could deal blessing or blight with equal indifference. The Fourth of July was always a good time for a picnic, giving opportunity for a patriotic display and lots of good food at the same time. There were Sunday School picnics, Old Settlers' meetings, country school picnics, and sometimes political picnics.

A big social event was the county fair, which was usually held in early September. That was the week when rain was a catastrophe, however much it might be needed. The fair was a combination livestock show and exhibition of farm machinery and farm products, fruit, vegetables, grain, jams, jellies, preserves, pickles, rows of canned fruits from farm kitchens. Blue, red, and white ribbons, emblems of awards, were proudly displayed by the happy winners. There were side shows too —the fat, tattooed, or bearded lady, a snake charmer with a snake wound around her, the grisly bones found in a cellar somewhere that bore witness to a mysterious murder. In the afternoon there were running and trotting races.

One popular feature was the balloon lift. This always drew a crowd, from the building of the fire that heated the air to lift the big balloon to the moment when the daring pilot cut loose with his parachute and floated down, usually to land in the middle of a cornfield half a mile away.

For country people the fair was another and bigger picnic with fried chicken, lemon pie, and endless visiting. Farmers from all over the county met and gossiped around the pens of fat hogs or prize-winning cattle, and women made envious comments on the blue-ribbon peaches or the excellence of a patchwork quilt that the judges had ignored. There were exhibits of work done in country schools. One year our district walked off with some kind of ribbon. The reason for our achievement is forgotten, but it is certain that samples of my penmanship were not included in the exhibit.

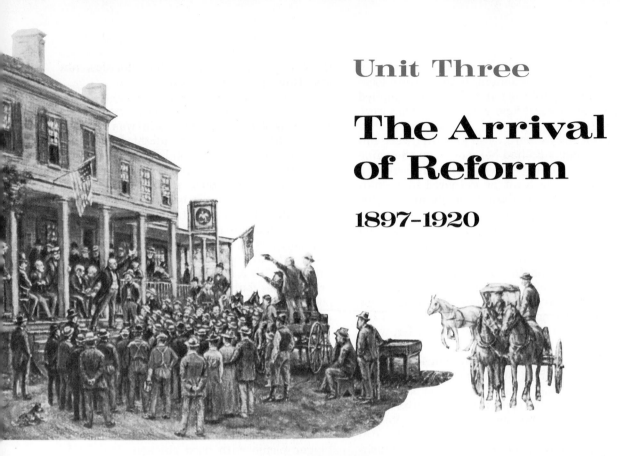

The Arrival of Reform

1897-1920

CHAPTER 8
REFORMS UNDER THE "SQUARE DEAL" AND THE "NEW FREEDOM"

HOW TAMMANY HALL OPERATES

By the end of the 1800's corrupt political machines controlled the governments of many large cities. Tammany Hall in New York City was one of the most powerful of these political machines. It stayed in power through graft, by securing the votes of immigrants through favors, and by running a "balanced ticket" so that a member of each major ethnic group held a top position in city government. An important politician in Tammany Hall for many years was George Washington Plunkitt.

In 1905 a young newspaper reporter, William L. Riordan, wrote a book about Plunkitt. He recorded Plunkitt's own words on how he became a powerful politician and a millionaire.

How does Plunkitt distinguish between honest and dishonest graft? Can you think of similar examples in politics today? What services does Plunkitt perform for poor families?

Adapted from William L Riordan, Plunkitt of Tammany Hall. *New York: McClure Phillips & Co., 1905.*

Everybody is talking these days about Tammany people growing rich on graft, but nobody thinks of drawing the distinction between honest graft and dishonest graft. There's all the difference in the world between the two. Yes, many of our people have grown rich in politics. I have myself. I've made a big fortune out of the game, and I'm getting richer every day. But I've not gone in for dishonest graft—blackmailing gamblers, saloon-keepers, and so on. And neither have any of the people who have made big fortunes in politics.

There's an honest graft, and I'm an example of how it works. I might sum up the whole thing by saying: "I seen my opportunities and I took 'em."

Just let me explain by examples. My party's in power in the city, and it's going to undertake a lot of public improvements. Well, I'm told ahead of time, say, that they're going to lay out a new park at a certain place.

I see my opportunity and I take it. I go to that place and I buy up all the land I can in the neighborhood. Then the board of this or that makes its plan public, and there is a rush to get my land, which nobody wanted before.

Ain't it perfectly honest to charge a good price and make a profit on my investment and foresight? Of course, it is. Well, that's honest graft.

Or supposing it's a new bridge they're going to build. I find out and I buy as much property as I can that has to be used for the road approaches to the bridge. I sell the property at my own price later on and drop some more money in the bank.

Wouldn't you? It's just like looking ahead in Wall Street or in the coffee or cotton market. It's honest graft and I'm looking for it every day in the year. I will tell you frankly that I've got a lot of it, too.

I'll tell you of another case. They were going to fix up a big park. I learned of it and went looking about for land in that neighborhood. I could get nothing at a bargan except a big piece of swamp, but I bought it right away and held on to it. What happened was just what I counted on. They couldn't make the park complete without Plunkitt's swamp, and so they had to pay a good price for it. Anything dishonest in that?

I don't own a dishonest dollar. If my worst enemy was given the job of writing an epitaph for my grave marker he couldn't do more than write:

"George W. Plunkitt. He Seen His Opportunities, and He Took 'Em."

What's important in holding your grip on your district is to go right down among the poor families and help them in the different ways they need help. I've got a regular system for doing this.

If there's a fire on Ninth, Tenth, or Eleventh Avenue, for example, any hour of the day or night, I'm usually there with some of my election district captains as soon as the fire engines arrive. If a family is burned out, I don't ask whether they are Republicans or Democrats. I don't refer them to the Charity Organization Society, which would investigate their case in a month or two and decide they were worthy of help about the time they are dead from starvation. I just get a place for them to live, buy clothes for them if their clothes were burned up, and fix them up till they get things running again. It's philanthropy, but it's politics, too—mighty good politics. Who can tell how many votes one of these fires brings me? The poor are the most grateful people in the world, and, let me tell you, they have more friends in their neighborhoods than the rich have in theirs.

If there's a family in my district that needs help, I know it before the charitable societies do. Me and my men are the first to help. I have a special group of people to look up such cases. The result is that the poor look up to George W. Plunkitt as a father, they come to him when they're in trouble, and they don't forget him on election day.

A MUCKRAKER ATTACKS CITY CORRUPTION

By 1900 many Americans felt that something had to be done to reform American government and American life. This reform movement was known as the Progressive movement. Some of the most important supporters of the Progressives were the writers and newspaper reporters who were making Americans aware of how widespread the corruption and abuses had become in the United States.

These crusading, reform-minded writers were disliked by some Americans, including Theodore Roosevelt. In a speech in 1906, he described them by referring to a character in the book *Pilgrim's Progress*—"the man with the muckrake." One writer, Lincoln Steffens, proudly adopted the term "muckraker" to refer to anyone who wanted to uncover, or rake up, corruption. Soon the term became very popular.

Steffens became famous because of his magazine articles on corruption in American cities. The following selections are from his book *The Shame of the Cities*.

Why, according to Steffens, do business leaders make bad politicians? Who does he think is to blame for corruption? What solution does he propose?

Adapted from Lincoln Steffens, The Shame of the Cities. *New York: McClure Phillips & Co., 1904.*

There is hardly a government office from United States Senator down to alderman in any part of the country to which some business leader has not been elected. Yet politics remains corrupt and government pretty bad. Business leaders have failed in politics as they have in good citizenship. Why?

Because politics is business. That's what's the matter with everything—art, literature, religion, journalism, law, medicine. They're all business, and all as you see them.

Make politics a sport, as they do in England, or a profession, as they do in Germany. Then we'll have—well, something else than we have now—if we want it, which is another question. But don't try to reform politics with the banker, the lawyer, and the merchant. For they are business people and there are two things that make it very difficult for them to achieve reform: One is that they are different from, but no better than, the politicians. The other is that politics is not "their line."

There are exceptions both ways. Many politicians have gone into business and done well. (Tammany ex-mayors, and nearly all the old bosses of Philadelphia, are important financiers in their cities.) Business managers have gone into politics and done well. (Mark Hanna, for example.) The politician is a businessman with a specialty. When a businessman in some other line learns the business of politics, he is a politician, and there is not much reform left in him. Consider the United States Senate, and believe me.

The commercial spirit is the spirit of profit, not patriotism; of credit, not honor; of individual gain, not national prosperity; of trade, not principle.

We cheat our government and we let our leaders rob it. We let them persuade and bribe our power away from us. True, they pass strict laws for us, but we let them pass bad laws too, giving away public property in exchange. Our good, and often impossible, laws we allow to be used for oppression and blackmail. And what can we say? We break our own laws and rob our own government—the woman at the tax office, the lyncher with his rope, and the captain of industry with his bribe and his rebate. The spirit of graft and of lawlessness is the American spirit.

The people are not innocent. This will not be news to many observers. It was to me. When I set out to describe the corrupt systems of certain typical cities, I meant to show simply how the people were deceived and betrayed. But in the very first study—St. Louis—the startling truth showed that corruption was not merely political. It was financial, commercial, and social. Its offshoots were so complex and far-reaching that one mind could hardly grasp them all.

The corruption of St. Louis came from the top. The best citizens—the merchants and big financiers—ruled the town, and they ruled it well. They set out to overtake Chicago. The commercial and industrial war between these two cities was a picturesque and dramatic spectacle such as is seen only in our country. Business leaders were not just merchants, and politicians were not just grafters. The two kinds of citizens got together and used the power of banks, railroads, factories, the prestige of the city, and the spirit of its citizens to gain business and population. And it was a close race. Chicago, having a head start, always led. But St. Louis had spirit, intelligence, and tremendous energy. It pressed Chicago hard. It excelled in a sense of civic beauty and good government. There are those who still think it might have won. But a change occurred. Public spirit became private spirit, and public enterprise became private greed.

Along about 1890, public franchises and privileges were sought, not only for legitimate profit and common convenience, but also for loot. Taking only slight but always selfish interest in the public councils, leading merchants and financiers misused politics. Other less important and even less honest men, catching the smell of corruption, rushed into the Municipal Assembly, drove out the remaining respectable leaders, and sold the city—its streets, its wharves, its markets, and all that it had—to the now greedy business people and bribers.

So gradually has this taken place that these same citizens hardly realize it. Go to St. Louis and you will find the habit of civic pride in them. They still boast. The visitor is told of the wealth of the residents, of the financial strength of the banks, and of the growing importance of the industries. Yet the visitor sees poorly paved streets full of garbage, and dirty or mud-filled alleys. He passes a broken-down firetrap of a building crowded with the sick, and learns that it is the city hospital.

In Pittsburgh graft falls into four classes: franchises, public contracts, vice, and public funds. There was, besides these, a lot of other loot—public supplies, public lighting, and the water supply. But I cannot go into these. Neither can I stop to discuss the details of the system by which public funds, earning no interest, were put in favored banks from which the city borrowed money at a high interest rate. All these things were managed well within the law. That was the great principle underlying the Pittsburgh plan.

The vice graft, for example, was not blackmail as it is in New York and most other cities. It is a legitimate business, conducted not by the police, but in an orderly fashion by syndicates. The leader of one of the parties at the last election said it was worth $250,000 a year. I saw a man who was laughed at for offering $17,500 for the slot-machine concession. He was told that it was leased for much more. "Speakeasies" [unlicensed drinking places] have to pay off so many people that even though they may earn $500 or more in 24 hours, their owners often just about make a living.

We Americans may have failed. We may be selfish and influenced by gain. Democracy with us may be impossible and corruption inevitable, but these articles, if they have proved nothing else, have shown that we can stand the truth. There is pride in the character of American citizenship. This pride may be a power in the land. So this record of shame and yet of self-respect, disgraceful confession, yet a declaration of honor, is dedicated, in all good faith, to the accused—to all the citizens of all the cities in the United States.

A MUCKRAKER ATTACKS BIG BUSINESS

The muckrakers told Americans of the many abuses in their society. Their books and articles made many Americans deeply concerned about the consequences of the great industrial growth and business consolidation then taking place. They brought many of the unfair business methods and practices of large industries to the attention of the public.

Probably the most famous of all muckraking reports about American industry was Ida Tarbell's *History of the Standard Oil Company.* **In this series of newspaper articles, which later became a book, she exposed the practices and policies of that giant monopoly.**

According to Ida Tarbell, how are the large profits of the Standard Oil trust being used? Why does she regard transportation as the key to Standard Oil's monopoly? What does she believe is the "ethical cost" of the oil industry monopoly? What solutions does she suggest?

Adapted from Ida M Tarbell, History of the Standard Oil Company. *New York: McClure Phillips & Co., 1904.*

The profits of the present Standard Oil Company are enormous. For five years the dividends have been averaging about $45 million a year. When we remember that probably one third of this great yearly profit goes into the hands of John D. Rockefeller, that probably 90 percent of it goes to the few people who make up the "Standard Oil family," the Standard Oil Company becomes a much more serious public matter than it was in 1872, when it began to take over the oil business.

For, consider what must be done with the greater part of this $45 million. It must be invested. The oil business does not need it. It has money for all of its ventures. The money must go into other industries. Naturally, these other interests will be connected to oil. One such interest will be gas, and we have the Standard Oil people steadily taking over the gas interests of the country. Another will be railroads, for all industries depend on transportation. Besides, railroads are one of the great consumers of oil products and must be kept in line as buyers. So we have the directors of the Standard Oil Company acting as directors on nearly all of the great railways of the country. They will go into steel, and we have Mr. Rockefeller's great holdings in the steel trust. They will go into banking, and we have the National City Bank and its connected institutions in New York City and Boston, as well as a long chain running throughout the country.

No one who has followed this history can expect that these holdings will be bought on a rising market. Buy cheap and sell high is a rule of business. When you control enough money and enough banks, you can always work it out so that a stock you want will be temporarily cheap. No value is destroyed for you—only for the original owner. This has been one of Mr. Rockefeller's most successful maneuvers in doing business. The result is that the Standard Oil Company is probably in the strongest financial position of any organization in the world. And every year its position grows stronger, for every year another $45 million is poured into taking over the property most essential to keeping and broadening its power.

In spite of the Interstate Commerce Commission, the crucial question is still that of transportation. Until the people of the United States have solved the question of free and equal transportation, there will always be a trust question. As long as it is possible for a company to own the carrier on which a great natural product depends for transportation, and to use this carrier to limit a competitor's supply or to cut it off entirely, it is foolish to talk about constitutional amendments limiting trusts. As long as the Standard Oil Company can control transportation, as it does today, it will remain master of the oil industry. The people of the United States will pay a high price for oil because of their indifference in regard to transportation. And they will see an increasing amount of natural resources and transportation systems owned by the Standard Oil monopoly.

If all we suffered was limited business opportunities for a few hundred men and women and a constantly rising price for refined oil, the case would be serious enough. But there is a more serious side to it. The ethical cost of all this is the main concern. We are a commercial people. We cannot boast of our arts, our crafts, our culture. Our pride is the wealth we produce. As a consequence. business success is holy. We justify practically any methods to achieve it.

Very often people who admit the facts, who see that Mr. Rockefeller has employed force and fraud to obtain his ends, justify him by declaring, "It's business." That is, "It's business" has come to be a legitimate excuse for hard dealing, sly tricks, special privileges. It is a common enough thing to hear people arguing that the ordinary laws of morality do not apply in business.

Now, if the Standard Oil Company were the only company in the country guilty of the practices which have given it monopolistic power, this story never would have been written. But it is simply the most outstanding example of what can be done by these practices. The methods it uses with such skill, constancy, and secrecy are used by all sorts of business people, from corner grocers up to bankers. If exposed, they are excused on the ground that this is business. If the point is pushed, frequently the defender of the practice falls back on the Christian doctrine of charity, and points out that we are only human and must allow for each other's weaknesses! If this excuse were carried to its logical conclusion, our business people would be weeping on each other's shoulders over human weakness, while they picked each other's pockets.

And what are we going to do about it? For it is *our* business. We, the people of the United States, and nobody else, must cure whatever is wrong in the industrial situation, typified by this account of the growth of the Standard Oil Company. It is clear that our first task is to obtain free and equal transportation privileges by railroad, pipeline, and waterway. It is not an easy matter. It is one which may require severe methods. But the whole system of rate discrimination has been nothing but violence. Those who have profited by it cannot complain if curing the evils they have caused brings hardship to them. At all events, until the transportation matter is settled, and settled right, the monopolistic trust will be with us, a barrier to our free efforts.

As for the ethical side, there is no cure but in an increasing scorn of unfair play—an increasing sense that a thing won by breaking the rules of the game is not worth winning. The business person who fights to obtain special privileges, to crowd competitors off the track by unfair methods, should be treated just the way we treat the doctor or lawyer who is "unprofessional" or the athlete who abuses the rules. Then we shall have gone a long way toward making business a fit profession for our young people.

PRESIDENT ROOSEVELT URGES BUSINESS REFORM

President Theodore Roosevelt was a skilled politician whose bold acts and personality captured the imagination of Americans. His efforts to regulate the trusts made many Americans think of him as the leader of the progressive movement. In fact, he was less a crusader than many other progressive reformers. He believed that reform had to come slowly and had to be carefully planned.

However, Roosevelt did make an enormous contribution to the progressive movement. His popularity and his support of many of the progressives' aims helped to publicize the movement and gained it widespread support. The following selection is from his first annual message to Congress in 1901.

How would you describe Roosevelt's attitude toward the "captains of industry"? Why does he recommend caution in dealing with them? What is the "widespread belief" among Americans about trusts? Does he agree with it? What does he think should be done?

Adapted from James D. Richardson (comp.), A Compilation of the Messages and Papers of the Presidents, *Vol. X. 1789-1902. Washington: Bureau of National Literature and Art, 1903*

The tremendous and highly complex industrial development which went on during the last half of the 1800's brings us face to face, at the beginning of the 1900's, with very serious social problems. Old laws and old customs were once quite enough to regulate the accumulation and distribution of wealth. They are no longer enough.

The growth of great industrial centers has meant a startling increase, not only in wealth itself, but in the number of very large individual and corporate fortunes. The creation of these great corporate fortunes has not been due to the tariff, nor to any other governmental action, but to natural causes in the business world, operating in other countries as they operate in our own.

The process has created much opposition, a great part of which is wholly without cause. It is not true that as the rich have grown richer the poor have grown poorer. On the contrary, never before has the average wage-earner, farmer, or small trader been so well-off as in this country at the present time. There have been abuses connected with the accumulation of wealth. Yet a fortune gained in legitimate business can be acquired only when the person doing so brings great benefits to others.

The captains of industry who have built the railway systems across this continent, who have developed our industry, have on the whole done great good to our people. Without them our development could never have taken place. Moreover, we should realize that it is important not to interfere any more than is necessary for the public good with the strong and forceful people upon whom the success of business operations rests.

Another reason for caution in dealing with corporations is to be found in international business. The richest concerns and those managed by the ablest people are naturally those that take the lead in the struggle for commercial supremacy among the nations of the world. America has only just begun to dominate the international business world. It is of the greatest importance that this position not be placed in danger.

Moreover, striking with ignorant violence at the interests of one set of people almost inevitably puts the interests of all in danger.

The basic rule in our national life is that, on the whole, and in the long run, we shall go up or down together. Disaster to great business concerns never limits its effects to the people at the top. It spreads throughout, and while it is bad for everybody, it is worst for those farthest down.

All this is true. And yet it is also true that there are real and serious evils. A practical effort must be made to correct them.

There is a widespread belief among the American people that the great corporations known as trusts are harmful to the general welfare. This belief does not spring from a spirit of envy or lack of pride in the great industrial achievements. It does not rest upon ignorance of the fact that a good deal of capital is needed to accomplish great things. It is based upon the sincere belief that combination and concentration should be, not forbidden, but supervised and within reasonable limits controlled. In my judgment this belief is right.

It is no limitation upon property rights or freedom of contract to require that when people receive from the government the privilege of doing business under corporate form, they should be truthful as to the value of the property in which capital is to be invested. Corporations engaged in interstate commerce should be regulated if they harm the public. Great corporations exist only because they are created and safeguarded by our institutions. It is therefore our right and our duty to see that they work in harmony with these institutions.

The first essential in determining how to deal with the great industrial combinations is knowledge of the facts. In the interest of the public, the government should have the right to inspect and examine the workings of the great corporations engaged in interstate business. Publicity is the only sure remedy we now have. What further remedies are needed in the way of governmental regulation, or taxation, can only be determined after publicity has been obtained.

The large corporations, commonly called trusts, though organized in one state, always do business in many states. There is a complete lack of uniformity in the state laws dealing with them.

Therefore, in the interest of all the people, the nation should take over the supervision and regulation of all corporations doing an interstate business. There would be no hardship in such supervision; banks are subject to it, and in their case it is now accepted as a simple matter of course.

When the Constitution was adopted at the end of the 1700's, no human wisdom could foretell the sweeping changes which were to take place by the beginning of the 1900's. At that time it was accepted as a matter of course that the states were the proper authorities to regulate the comparatively insignificant corporations of the day. The conditions are now wholly different. Wholly different action is called for.

THE GROWING INTEREST IN CONSERVATION

One of Theodore Roosevelt's most important achievements was the interest he helped create in the conservation of America's natural resources. In 1908 he held a White House conference on conservation. At this conference more than a thousand delegates listened to speeches expressing concern over how the nation's resources were being used and suggesting reforms. A few speakers such as George Kunz, a mineralogist, also stressed the need to protect America's natural beauty.

In his speech, from which this selection is taken, Kunz speaks of human beings as having passed through various stages of development—savagery, barbarism, and civilization. His remarks reflected the widely held theory of the time that all peoples had progressed through the same well-defined steps on their way to modern civilization.

How does Kunz link the appreciation of the beauty of nature and the development of civilization? Why does Kunz believe that some higher judicial power must weigh the merits of "conflicting interests"? Do you think that present-day Americans have followed Kunz's advice?

Adapted from George F. Kunz Proceedings of a Conference of Governors. *Washington: Government Printing Office 1909.*

The great forces of nature have created the mineral wealth stored beneath the earth. They have carved the hollows and valleys in which our lakes lie and our streams flow. They have lifted up our mountain ranges and have made the soil that feeds our forests and crops. These same forces have made the various features called scenery, which delights the eye, and stirs the imagination. And scenery in turn has affected our movements, our life, and our de-

velopment. Thus, for many reasons, human history has always been identified with the natural landscape.

In recommending to the conference the protection of American scenery, I deny that there is a conflict between the idea of preserving scenery and the idea of properly using our material resources. Every interest represented in this conference is looking forward to the same goal—the greatest happiness and good for the greatest number of people. That will be reached best by friendly cooperation, by mutual adjustments, and by reasonable concessions when necessary.

The purpose of our organization is to encourage the beautiful without preventing the development of forests, mines, railroads, or water power. But it must not be forgotten that there are many factors in reaching human happiness.

In the lowest status of savagery, when humans are nearest the beasts of the field, happiness depends almost exclusively upon satisfying bodily needs. But as we lift ourselves up through the stages of savagery, and through barbarism into civilization, a new element of happiness becomes important. In this rise, with its accompanying intellectual development, our thoughts constantly range farther and farther from the narrow limits of our own bodies for satisfaction. While meeting physical wants is the first necessity, other needs must also be met.

The wholesome pleasure which one obtains from being in nature is a characteristic of our civilization. We cannot get rid of it even if we wanted to. It makes us better, happier, more efficient citizens. It is a fact of human nature to be honestly recognized. It should not be put aside as empty sentimentalism any more than using the physical resources of the land would be held in contempt as too commercial.

Our goal should therefore be to see how closely we can get together so as to join our interests for the common good. It is at this point that we need some judicial power higher than the individual to weigh the merits of conflicting interests. There are occasions, for instance, when the value to the community of damming a given stream at a given place may not be truthfully expressed in dollars and cents. When we balance all considerations, we may find that the location of the dam farther upstream or farther downstream, or on some other stream, or even preventing it from being built, may contribute to the greatest good for the greatest number. Thus, the necessity for regulation by some branch of government representing all interests is apparent. It is proper that the law should regulate the destruction of trees, rocks, river banks, and other notable features of the landscape.

Nothing is more valuable in creating a love of beauty in the average person than the scenic beauty of forests, mountains, and rivers. For this reason, such objects of natural beauty should be carefully guarded against injury or destruction.

BLACK AMERICANS AND PROGRESSIVE REFORMS

Although the reforms of the progressive movement brought important benefits to most Americans, it did little to improve the lives of black Americans.

When Theodore Roosevelt became President, many black Americans expected that they would be included in the progressive reforms. They remembered his praise of black troops during the Spanish-American War. He stirred the hopes of black Americans by inviting Booker T. Washington to dinner at the White House and by condemning lynching. Yet during Roosevelt's Presidency, the earlier hopes of black Americans were not realized. Roosevelt and most progressive reformers ignored the need to improve conditions among blacks. In the following selection, a visiting English writer, H. G. Wells, tells of the plight of black Americans.

What is the basic question that Wells asks about black people? What kinds of answers does he receive? Why does he admire black Americans? What future does he see for them?

Adapted from H. G. Wells, The Future in America. *New York: Harper & Brothers, 1906.*

In regard to the colored population, just as in regard to the great and growing numbers of Jews, and the growing numbers of Roman Catholics, I have tried time after time to get some answer from Americans to the question that is to me the most obvious. "Your grandchildren and the grandchildren of these people will have to live in this country side by side. Do you think—do you believe it possible—that under the increasing pressure of population and competition, they will be living then in just the same relations that you and these people are living in now? If you do not, then what relations do you suggest should exist between them?"

It is not too much to say that I have never once had the beginning of an answer to this question. Usually one is told with great seriousness that the problem of color is one of the most difficult that we have to consider. The conversation then breaks up into long stories and unfavorable statements about black people.

Whatever America has to show in heroic living today, I doubt if it can show anything finer than the quality of will, the constant effort hundreds of black people are making today to live blamelessly, honorably, and patiently. They get for themselves what scraps of refinement, learning, and beauty they can. They keep their hold on a civilization they are begrudged and denied. They do it not for themselves only but for all their race. Each educated colored person is an ambassador to civilization. They know they have a handicap. Yet each one, I like to think, is aware of being a representative, fighting against injustice, insult, and the unspeakable meannesses of bigoted enemies. Every one of them who remains decent and honorable does a little to beat that opposition down.

But what patience the Negroes need! They cannot ever show contempt. They must regard as superior those whose daily conduct is clear evidence of moral inferiority. Negroes must go to and fro self-controlled, without all the equalities that the great flag of America proclaims —that flag for which black people fought and died. Negroes must take second place to the strangers who pour in to share the nation's wealth, strangers ignorant even of its language. That Negroes must do—and wait. The Welsh, the Irish, the Poles, the white South, and the Jews may have grievances and complain aloud. Negroes must keep still. The others may be hysterical, revengeful, threatening; their wrongs excuse them. For Negroes there is no excuse. And of all the races upon earth, which has suffered such wrongs as this Negro race? Those people who scorn them have sinned against them beyond all measure.

No, I can't help idealizing the dark submissive figure of the Negro in this spectacle of America. The Negro seems to me to sit waiting —and waiting with a marvelous and constant patience—for finer understanding and a nobler time.

THE BIRTH OF THE PROGRESSIVE PARTY

The summer of 1912 was an exciting time in American politics. After the Republicans nominated Taft for the Presidency, Roosevelt split with the party. He and a group of his supporters, together with a wide variety of reformers, joined together to form a third political party known as the Progressive (or "Bull Moose") Party. They held a convention in August at Chicago, where the delegates sang "Onward Christian Soldiers" and drafted a platform which they called "A Contract with the People." They nominated Roosevelt for President and Hiram Johnson of California for Vice-President. In this selection Jane Addams, who took part in the convention, describes it.

To Jane Addams, which was more important, having Roosevelt as party leader or having a reform platform? From what you have read, do you think her judgment was correct?

Adapted with permission of Macmillan Publishing Co., Inc. from The Second Twenty Years at Hull-House *by Jane Addams. Copyright 1930 by Macmillan Publishing Co., Inc., renewed 1958 by John A. Brittain.*

From various directions, people were drawing toward a new political party. It was at first as if one heard in the distance the grave and measured step of history. But the pace increased during the first half of 1912, and became absolutely breathless by midsummer. It was in August 1912 that the Progressive Party was organized.

Suddenly, as if by magic, the city of Chicago became filled with men and women from every state in the Union who were moved by the same needs and hopes. They showed each other common sympathies and memories. They urged methods for righting old wrongs and establishing new standards. For three days they defined their purposes and joined their wills.

Among the members of the platform committee for the new party were social workers, others closely identified with religion, and still others who were scholars. Sometimes when we came across members of the American Economic Association, or of the Civil Service Reform League, or similar groups, we feared that a few people were trying through the new party to obtain measures which, although worthy, had only limited support. To me, this was very alarming. But I gradually discovered that the situation was in reality the very opposite of this. The dean of a university law school acted as head of the resolution committee, and others who knew law supplied information. But these people, together with the so-called "practical" members of the committee, were not representing the opinion of any individual nor the philosophy of any group. They were trying, as conscientious American citizens, to meet the basic duty of adapting the laws to the changed conditions of national life.

Delegates had all experienced the frustration and disappointment of individual effort. They had come to this first national convention of the Progressive Party not only to urge reform legislation, but to test its usefulness through the consent of their fellow citizens, to throw their measures into the life of the nation itself. They believed that the program of social legislation placed before the country by the Progressive Party was of great importance to the average voter regardless of party.

In the hope that the political organization of the nation might never again get so far away from the life of the people, the platform recommended equal suffrage, direct primaries, and the initiative and referendum. We quoted to each other the saying of Walt Whitman, that it seemed to him unbearable that large groups of people should follow those who do not believe in people. We placed at the head of our precious new party two men of political wisdom who had shown an understanding not only of the social demands of the people but also of the people themselves. We realized that Colonel Roosevelt possessed a unique power. In spite of our belief in our leader, however, I was there — and I think the same was true of many others — because the platform expressed the social hopes so long ignored by the politicians.

Although we were all quite well aware that the convention was far from being united, it seemed to us at the moment as if it really were. Certainly, for the time being, all doctrines and group egotisms were dropped. Or rather, they were melted down by overwhelming good will and enthusiasm.

The Progressive convention has been described many times, perhaps never quite adequately. It was a curious moment of release from inhibitions. It did not seem in the least strange that quiet, reserved men and women should speak aloud of their religious and social beliefs, confident that they would be understood. Because we felt so at home in that huge Coliseum, there was a quick understanding of those hidden feelings which we were mysteriously moved to express.

During the three days of the Progressive convention, one could almost hear the breakdown of the well-worn slogans which had provided the old parties their election battle cries for half a century. The sound was not unlike the uproar which accompanies a great religious conference. The old-line politicians were as much surprised to find that politics had to do with the matters discussed at the Progressive convention as the social workers were delighted to discover that their long concern for human needs had come to be considered politics. Nevertheless, in spite of the careful platform building, the entire noisy convention was well described as the "barn raising of a new party."

WILSON'S "NEW FREEDOM"

President Woodrow Wilson was a progressive of a different sort from Theodore Roosevelt. While Roosevelt distinguished between good and bad trusts and declared that the government should not break up large corporations but regulate them, Wilson believed that all large trusts were bad. He felt that the trusts were too powerful to be controlled and that the antitrust laws should be used to break them up. Wilson used the phrase "a New Freedom" to describe his program of reform. He also wrote a book called *The New Freedom* in which he outlined his reform philosophy. The following selection is taken from that book.

According to Wilson, what special interests endanger the United States? How? Why does Wilson feel that the trusts must be broken up? What does the term "New Freedom" mean to Wilson?

From the book Woodrow Wilson, The New Freedom, *by William E. Leuchtenburg.* © *1961, by Prentice-Hall, Inc. Published by Prentice-Hall, Inc., Englewood Cliffs, New Jersey 07632.*

We have entered a very different age from any that came before us. We have entered an age in which we do not do business the way we used to do business. We do not carry on any of the operations of manufacture, sale, transportation, or communication as people used to carry them on. There is a sense in which the individual has been submerged. In most parts of our country people work not for themselves, not as partners in the old way in which they used to work, but generally as employees of great corporations. There was a time when corporations played a very small part in our business affairs. Now they play the chief part, and most workers are the servants of corporations.

You know what happens when you are the servant of a corporation. Your individuality is swallowed up in the individuality and purpose of a great organization.

American industry is not free, as once it was free. American enterprise is not free. The person with only a little capital is finding it harder to get into the field, more and more impossible to compete with big business. Why? Because the laws of the country do not prevent the strong from crushing the weak. That is the reason. And because the strong have crushed the weak, the strong dominate the industry and the economic life of this country. What this country needs above everything else is laws which will look after the people who are striving to succeed rather than the people who are already successful.

Don't fool yourselves for a moment as to the power of the great interests which now dominate our development. They are so powerful that it is almost questionable whether the government of the United States can dominate them or not. Go one step further, make their organized power permanent, and it may be too late to turn back. The roads divide at the point where we stand. They stretch out to regions far separated from one another. At the end of one is the old, tiresome scene of government tied up with special interests. At the other shines the free light of individual freedom, the light of unrestrained enterprise.

I believe in human liberty as I believe in the wine of life. There is no salvation for workers in the small favors of industrial masters. Guardians have no place in a land of free people. Prosperity guaranteed by trustees has no prospect of lasting. Monopoly means the wasting away of enterprise. If monopoly continues, it will always control government. I do not expect to see monopoly hold back itself.

The government of our country cannot be placed in the hands of any special class. The policy of a great nation cannot be tied up with any particular set of interests. I want to say again and again that my arguments do not involve the *character* of the people to whom I am opposed. I believe that the very wealthy who got their money by certain kinds of corporate enterprise have closed in their horizon, and that they do not see and do not understand the people. It is for that reason that I want to break up the little group that has determined what the government of the nation should do. We must save our government from the domination of special classes, not because these special classes are necessarily bad, but because no special class can understand the interests of a great community.

The meaning of liberty has deepened. But it has not stopped being a demand of the human spirit, a basic necessity for the life of the soul. And the day is at hand when it shall be realized on this consecrated soil—a New Freedom. It will be a liberty widened and deepened to match the broadened life of the modern American, returning to us the control of our government. It will throw open all gates of lawful enterprise, releasing energies and warming the generous impulses of our hearts. It will be a process of freedom and inspiration, full of a breath of life as sweet and wholesome as the airs that filled the sails of Columbus, giving the promise and boast of magnificent opportunity in which America dare not fail.

A SPANIARD REPORTS ON THE 1916 ELECTION

In the election of 1916, the Democrats nominated Woodrow Wilson for a second term and the Republicans chose Charles Evans Hughes, Chief Justice of the Supreme Court, as their candidate. Theodore Roosevelt was again chosen by the Progressive Party. During the campaign, Americans were especially concerned with foreign affairs. With World War I raging in Europe, Wilson's slogan—"He kept us out of war"—attracted many voters. Other issues, of course, were important in the campaign. A Spanish writer, Julio Camba, was in the United States at the time of the election and wrote this account of the campaign.

What, according to Camba, are the "two basic tendencies" in American life? How does the election match them against each other? Camba calls the American President a "kaiser" (German for "emperor"). Do you think the term is accurate?

Adapted from "Un Año en el otro mundo" by Julio Camba, from This Was America *by Oscar Handlin, published by Harvard University Press. © 1949 by the President and Fellows of Harvard College; renewed © 1977 by Oscar Handlin. Reprinted by permission of the publisher.*

The battle has already taken shape. The Republican and Progressive parties have met in Chicago to nominate candidates. Soon the Democratic Party will meet. Afterwards, in the month of November, will come the elections, first for the electoral college, then for the President. The names which are most often heard now are Wilson, who is now President, Roosevelt, and Hughes.

We must prepare to see one of the most picturesque spectacles in the world—that is, a Presidential election in the United States. To give you an idea of the sporting spirit with which the people regard such equal contestants, it is necessary to quote the following paragraph from the *Evening Post:* "It is a pity that two men as famous as Wilson and Hughes could not appear together on the same platform! That would be a sensational match, and spectators would pay a fabulous price for admission."

Hughes holds over Wilson the enormous advantage of the offensive. The ex-justice can attack all the Presidential acts of Wilson, who will have to make great efforts to defend them. In his turn, Hughes will have to show how he would have acted if he had been President. Hughes can depend on a greater number of personal sympathizers than Wilson, who seems to make enemies of his friends. Wilson, in turn, enjoys great intellectual prestige. He writes very well, speaks well, and is considered a most honorable and well-intentioned man.

The candidates are ready. The boxers have put on their gloves. The first round is about to begin.

There are two basic tendencies in the life of this country. One is an idealistic and humanitarian tendency with a great moral content, which reaches from William James, the philosopher, to Henry Ford, the manufacturer of automobiles. The other is a materialistic tendency without any content of idealism, a tendency of capitalism and imperialism. The two tendencies, as may be seen in this election, are now in a state of balance.

It is certain that Hughes and Roosevelt, as against Wilson, represent the second of those tendencies. Hughes stands for the Wall Street capitalists, who gained him the nomination. He speaks for the trusts. He represents the scorn of money for moral values. His friends have put signs all over New York which read: "We don't want professors meddling in our affairs," and "What's the use of democracy in business?" Hughes, in short, represents the materialism of a civilization in which quality counts for nothing. What counts are dollars, many dollars, business, bridges, telephones, cranes, skyscrapers, noise, speed.

If matters continue as they have until now,

and if Hughes does not win this time, he (or someone else who represents the same things) will win in four years. The second tendency is steadily winning out over the first. By the same degree that a people enriches itself with material possessions, it also loses some of its spiritual content. The 1800's are dying in the trenches of Europe. At the end of the war, France, Germany, England, and Italy will face in the United States a people whose ideals are those of the corporation—to do business. And *what is the use of democracy in business!* What help is democracy in making money?

This moral difference between that which Hughes represents and that which Wilson represents is, without doubt, much more important for the relations of North America with the rest of the world than the possible difference of opinion between those two men on the European war. One must, moreover, be aware of the position of the President of the United States to understand the importance of the election. The President of the United States is a kaiser [emperor]. He is elected, by a democratic process, a kaiser for four years; yet he is a kaiser who gets what he wishes.

WHAT DID THE PROGRESSIVES ACHIEVE?

The progressive movement came to an end when the United States entered World War I. It had started to slow down with the outbreak of war in Europe in 1914. With their attention now on foreign affairs, many Americans became less interested in reform. A great many Americans also felt that the progressive movement had achieved its aims and that further reform was not needed. Then, too, many Americans were tired of the endless talk about reforming the ills of society. What had the reform movement of the early 1900's accomplished, they wondered? Richard Hofstadter, a leading modern historian who has studied this period, gives his answer to this question. The following selection is from the introduction to his book *The Progressive Movement: 1900–1915.*

According to Hofstadter, what did Americans accomplish during the period from the end of the Civil War to 1900? What price did they pay for these achievements? How does he describe the chief characteristics of the movement?

From the book The Progressive Movement 1900–1915, *by Richard Hofstadter, editor,* © *1963, by Prentice-Hall, Inc. Published by Prentice-Hall, Inc., Englewood Cliffs, New Jersey 07632.*

For a long time historians have written of the period between 1900 and 1914 as the Progressive era, and of its variety of reform agitations as the Progressive movement. In using these terms, historians have followed the example of many of the period's leading figures. They liked the ring of the word "Progressive" as applied to themselves. The people of that age were proudly aware, even as they were fighting their battles, that there was something distinctive about the political and social life of their time which sharply marked it off from the era of materialism and corruption.

From the end of the Civil War to the close of the 1800's, the physical energies of the American people had been organized for a remarkable burst of material development. But their moral energies were relatively inactive. Certain moral aspects of the American character had become all but invisible. It was as though the controversy over slavery, the Civil War itself, and the difficulties and failures of Reconstruction had exhausted the moral and political capacities of the people. They abandoned crusades and reforms and jumped instead into the rewarding tasks of material achievements.

During this period Americans had filled up a vast area of land between the Mississippi River and California. They had crossed the country with a railroad network of more than a quarter of a million miles. Still more impressive was the growth of the urban and industrial part of the economy. Whole systems of industry and whole regions of industrial production were created. The urban population jumped from 9.9 million to 30.1 million. Thoughtful observers could see that the day was not very far off when the rural population would be outnumbered and the characteristic problems of the nation would be city problems.

By 1900 it became increasingly evident that all this material growth had been achieved at a terrible cost in human values and in the waste of natural resources. The land and the people had been robbed. Farmers had received small returns for their work. They had had little or no protection against exploitation by the railroads, against the high cost of credit, or against an unjust burden of taxation. At the same time the cities that grew with American industry were themselves industrial wastelands—centers of illegal activities and poverty, ugly, full of crowded slums, badly managed. Industry, after a period of great competition, was rapidly becoming concentrated. Big business choked free competition and concentrated political power in a few hands. Moreover, business, great and small, had lowered the character and quality of politics. Working with powerful bosses, business had won favors and privileges in return for its grants of money to corrupt political machines. Domination of the nation's affairs by political bosses and business organizations was now seen to be a threat to democracy itself.

What had happened, as a great many people saw it at the beginning of the Progressive era, was that in the extraordinary outburst of productive energy of the past few decades, the nation had not developed at the same time the means of meeting human needs or controlling or reforming the evils that come with any such rapid change. The Progressive movement, then, may be looked upon as an attempt to develop the moral will, the intellectual insight, and the political and administrative agencies to remedy the evils of a period of industrial growth. Since the Progressives did not believe in revolution, it was also an attempt to work out a strategy for orderly social change.

What were the main qualities of Progressivism? The name itself may be slightly misleading. Of course, the Progressives believed in progress. But so did a great many conservatives. The distinguishing thing about the Progressives was something else, which for lack of a better term might be called "activism." They argued that social evils will not remedy themselves, and that it is wrong to sit by without doing anything and wait for time to take care of them. As one writer put it, they did not believe that the future would take care of itself. They believed that the people of the country should be stimulated to work energetically to bring about social progress. Progressives believed in energy and governmental action.

If the people were sufficiently aroused, they would grab power away from city and state bosses and millionaire senators and take it back into their own hands. Having done so, they would use their regained power—through the city, state, or federal governments—to solve social and economic problems. Tenements would be gotten rid of. The labor of women and children would be forbidden. The Negro race would be supported in the struggle for its rights. High tariffs and monopoly prices would be regulated out of existence. Social legislation would protect the working classes from the terrible dangers of industry. Dangerous foods and falsely advertised drugs would be driven off the market. Unfair competition by the great corporations would be subject to constant government control. The concentration of business control in the hands of a few powerful banking interests would be broken up. Better credit would be provided for farmers and small business owners. The commercial exploitation of vice and drink would be reduced or eliminated.

The Progressive movement depended on the civic alertness and the aroused mood of a great part of the public. Such a mood cannot last forever. Perhaps what was most remarkable about the Progressives was their ability to maintain enthusiasm for reform as long as they did.

Despite the briefness of many of its achievements, the heritage of the Progressive movement cannot be considered small or unimportant. The Progressives developed for the first time on a large scale a type of realistic journalism and social criticism that has become a permanent quality of American thinking. They gave a new strength to a climate of opinion hostile to monopoly. They forced big business to operate carefully and even to exercise some self-restraint. The traditions of responsible government and forceful leadership of men like Theodore Roosevelt and Woodrow Wilson established unforgettable high points in American leadership. Finally, the reforms of the Progressive era established a basis for further reforms to be passed when the need for them was felt.

The men and women of the Progressive movement must be considered the pioneers of the welfare state. This was not because they sought to promote the growth of big government for its own sake. But they were determined to remedy the most pressing and dangerous social ills of industrial society. In the attempt they quickly learned that they could not achieve their aims without using the power of government. Moreover, they declared—and they were the first in our history to do so with real practical success—the idea that government cannot be seen only as a cold and negative policing agency. Instead it has a wide responsibility for the welfare of its citizens, and for the poor and powerless among them. For this, Progressivism must be understood as a major part in the history of the American conscience.

CHAPTER 9
"THE BIG CHANGE" IN AMERICAN WAYS OF LIFE

THE ALL-POWERFUL TELEPHONE

In the early 1900's, many great changes took place in the United States. These changes were the result of new inventions and new methods of industrial production. One of the important inventions of this period was the telephone. In 1911 Arnold Bennett, an English writer, visited the United States. He was both fascinated and terrified by the widespread use of the telephone and he wrote the following selection about this "evil" invention. In fact, he became so interested in this new device that he took a tour of the New York City phone company to learn more about how the telephone system worked.

How do you think Bennett really feels about the telephone? Why does he use this "comic-horror" style of writing? What are his feelings about the telephone operators? To whom does he compare them?

Adapted from Your United States *by Arnold Bennett. Reprinted by permission of Mrs. Dorothy Cheston Bennett.*

What strikes and frightens the backward European as much as anything in the United States is the efficiency and fearful common use of the telephone. I think of the big cities as great heaps pierced everywhere by elevator shafts full of movement. I think of them too as being threaded, under pavements and over roofs and between floors and ceilings and walls, by millions upon millions of live threads that unite all the privacies of people—and destroy them in making them public! I do not mean that Europe has failed to adopt the telephone, nor that in Europe there are no hotels with the dreadful curse of an active telephone in every room. But I do mean that the European telephone is a toy, and a somewhat clumsy one, compared with the serious American telephone. Many otherwise highly civilized Europeans are shy when speaking into a telephone, as they would be in speaking to a king or queen. Average middle-class Europeans still speak of their telephone, if they have one, in the same falsely casual tone as Americans tend to speak of their motor-car. It is nothing—but somehow it comes into the conversation!

"How odd!" you exclaim. And you are right. It is we Europeans who are wrong, through no particular fault of our own.

The American is ruthlessly logical about the telephone. The only occasion on which I was in really serious danger of being taken for a madman in the United States was when, in a Chicago hotel, I permanently removed the receiver from the telephone in my room. The whole hotel was horrified. Half of Chicago shuddered. In response to a request from the management, I put the receiver back. On the horrified face of the manager I could read the unspoken question: "Is it possible that you have been in this country a month without understanding that the United States is primarily a vast collection of telephone booths?" Yes, I gave in and admired! And I predict that on my next visit I shall find a telephone on every table of every restaurant that respects itself.

It is the efficiency of the telephone that makes it irresistible to a great people whose passion is to "get results"—the speed with which the communication is given, and the clear loudness of the telephone's voice in reply to yours. These things are completely unknown in Europe. If I were to live in the United States, I too should become a victim of the telephone habit, as it is practiced in its most advanced form in suburban communities. There a person takes to the telephone as people in more decadent lands take to drugs. You can see them in the morning at their bedroom window, pouring confidences into their telephone, thus combining the joy of an innocent vice with the healthy freshness of breeze and sunshine.

Now it was obvious that behind the apparently simple outer aspects of any telephone system there must be a complex and marvelous secret organization. In Europe my curiosity would probably never have been excited by the thought of that organization. At home one accepts everything as a matter of course. But in the United States, partly because the telephone is so much more wonderful and terrible there, and partly because in a foreign land one often has whims, I wanted to see the mysteries hidden at the other end of all the wires. Thus, one day, I paid a visit to a telephone exchange in New York. There I saw what nine hundred and ninety-nine out of every thousand of the most eager telephone users seldom think about and will never see.

My first impression was a murmuring sound, as of hundreds of scholars in a school learning their lessons, and a row of young women seated on stools before a long machine of holes and pegs and pieces of elastic cord—all looking extremely serious. One saw at once that none of these young women had a single moment to spare. They were all involved in the tremendous machine, were part of it, keeping up with it and in it, and not daring to take their eyes off it for a moment. What they were saying it was impossible to guess. If one placed oneself close to any particular young woman, she seemed to utter no sound, but simply and without stopping, pegged and unpegged holes at random among the thousands of holes before her. She apparently did this in obedience to the signaling of tiny lights that continually went on and off.

We who had entered were ignored. We might have been ghosts, invisible and silent. Even the supervisors did not turn to look at us as they moved restlessly behind the stools. And yet somehow I could hear the delicate shoulders of all the young women saying, without speaking: "Here come these tyrants again, who have invented this exercise which nearly but not quite cracks our brains for us! They know exactly how much they can get out of us, and they get it. They are cleverer and more powerful than we are, and we have to give in to their discipline. But—" And afar off I could hear: "What are you going to wear tonight?" "Will you dine with me tonight?" "I want two seats." "Very well, thanks, and how is Mrs. . . . ?" "When can I see you tomorrow?" "I'll take your offer for those bonds." . . . And I could see the inside of endless offices and living rooms. But of course I could hear and see nothing really except the low, serious voices and quick movements of those completely absorbed young women on stools exactly alike.

I understood why the telephone service was so efficient. I understood not only from the conduct of the long row of young women, but from everything else I had seen in the precise and evilly clever arrangement of the whole establishment.

FORD DESCRIBES THE FIRST ASSEMBLY LINE

American business and industry continued to expand rapidly during the early years of the 1900's. One of the most far-reaching developments in industry before America's entry into World War I was the introduction of the modern assembly line, pioneered by Henry Ford in the production of automobiles. In this selection, Ford describes how the idea for the assembly line came about.

Do you think that you, as a worker, would have shared Ford's enthusiasm for this new production method? What were some of its advantages? Some of its disadvantages?

Adapted from My Life and Work *by Henry Ford in collaboration with Samuel Crowther. Reprinted by permission of Seabury-Wilson Home, Inc.*

A Ford car contains about 5,000 parts, counting screws, nuts, and everything. Some parts are fairly large, and others are hardly larger than watch parts. In our first assembling, we simply started to put a car together at a certain spot on the floor. Workers brought to it the parts as they were needed in exactly the same way that one builds a house.

When we started to make parts, it was natural to create a single department of the factory to make each one. Usually one worker performed all of the operations necessary on a small part. But the rapid speedup of production made it necessary to work out some plans of production so that workers would not be falling over one another.

The first step forward in assembly came when we began taking the work to the workers instead of the workers to the work. We now have two general principles in all operations— that a worker should never have to take more than one step, if it can possibly be avoided, and that no worker need ever bend over.

The principles of assembly are these:

1. Place the tools and the workers in the sequence of the operation so that each part used in making the automobile will travel the least possible distance while in the process of finishing.

2. Use work slides or some other form of carrier so that when a worker completes his operation he drops the part always in the same place. That place should always be the most convenient to his hand. And if possible have gravity carry the part to the next worker for his operation.

3. Use moving assembling lines by which the parts to be assembled are delivered at convenient distances.

The result of the application of these principles is the reduction of the necessity for thought on the part of the workers and the reduction of their movements to a minimum. They do as nearly as possible only one thing with only one movement.

Along about April 1, 1913, we first tried the experiment of an assembly line on a small generator. We try everything in a small way at first. We will rip out anything once we discover a better way, but we have to know absolutely that the new way is going to be better than the old before we do anything drastic.

I believe that this was the first moving line ever installed. The idea came in a general way from the overhead cable that the Chicago packers use in cutting up beef. We had previously assembled the generator in the usual way. With one worker doing a complete job, he could turn out from thirty-five to forty pieces in a nine-hour day, or about twenty minutes for each assembly. What he did alone was then divided into twenty-nine operations. On an assembly line, that cut down the time for each assembly to thirteen minutes, ten seconds. Then we raised the height of the line eight inches [20 centimeters]—this was in 1914—and cut the time to seven minutes. Further experimenting with the speed cut the time down to five minutes.

In short, the result is this: with the aid of scientific study one worker is now able to do somewhat more than what four workers did only a few years ago. That line established the efficiency of the method and we now use it everywhere. The assembling of the motor, formerly done by one person, is now divided into eighty-four operations—those workers do the work that three times their number used to do.

WHY A MINIMUM WAGE?

Henry Ford also brought great changes in the field of labor relations. In 1914 the Ford Motor Company astonished the business world by voluntarily reducing the weekly hours of work and providing a minimum daily wage of $5 for each of its workers. The $5-a-day wage was nearly double what Ford and other automobile companies had been paying. In the following selection Ford explains the philosophy behind this policy.

According to Ford, what is the relationship between a business and its employees? What mistake can employers make in determining wages? On what basis should wages be determined? Why, in Ford's view, did his company establish its minimum wage?

Adapted from My Life and Work *by Henry Ford in collaboration with Samuel Crowther. Reprinted by permission of Seabury-Wilson Home, Inc.*

What good is industry if it is so unskillfully managed that it does not return a living to everyone concerned? No question is more important than that of wages—most of the people of the country live on wages. The scale of their living—the rate of their wages—determines the prosperity of the country.

It is not usual to speak of employees as partners, and yet what else are they? Whenever people find the management of a business too much for their own time or strength, they call in assistants to share the management with them. Why, then, if people find the production part of a business too much for their own hands, should they deny the title of "partner" to those who come in and help them produce? Every business that employs more than one person is a kind of partnership. The moment a person calls for assistance in business—even though the assistant be but a child—that moment the person has taken a partner.

No person is independent as long as he or she has to depend on another's help. It is a mutual relation. The boss is the partner of the worker; the worker is partner of the boss. It is useless for one group or the other to think that it is the one necessary unit. Both are necessary. They are partners. When they pull and push against each other, they simply hurt the organization in which they are partners and from which both draw support.

It ought to be the employer's ambition, as leader, to pay better wages than any similar line of business, and it ought to be the workers' ambition to make this possible. Of course, there are workers in all factories who seem to believe that if they do their best, it will be only for the employer's benefit—and not at all for their own. It is a pity that such a feeling should exist. But it does exist and perhaps it has some justification. If an employer encourages workers to do their best, and the workers learn after a while that their best does not bring any reward, then they naturally drop back into "getting by." But if they see the profit of hard work in their pay envelope—proof that harder work means higher pay—then they also begin to learn that they are a part of the business, and that its success depends on them and their success depends on it.

"What ought the employer to pay?" "What ought the employee to receive?" These are minor questions. The basic question is, "What can the business stand?" Certainly no business can stand to pay out more than it makes. When you pump water out of a well at a faster rate than the water flows in, the well goes dry.

Employers can gain nothing by looking over the employees and asking themselves, "How little can I get them to take?" Nor can employees gain much by glaring back and asking, "How much can I force them to give?" In time, both will have to turn to the business and ask, "How can this industry be made safe and profitable, so that it will be able to provide a sure and comfortable living for all of us?"

It ought to be clear that the high wage begins down in the factory. If it is not created there, it cannot get into pay envelopes. There will never be a system invented which will do away with the necessity of work. Nature has seen to that. Idle hands and minds were never intended for any one of us. Work is our sanity, our self-respect, our salvation. So far from being a curse, work is the greatest blessing. True social justice flows only out of honest work. The worker who contributes much should take away much. Therefore no element of charity is present in the paying of wages.

The kind of workers who give the business the best that is in them are the best kind of workers a business can have. And they cannot be expected to do this indefinitely without proper recognition of their contribution. People who come to the day's job feeling that no matter how much they may give, it will not give them enough of a return to keep them from being poor are not in shape to do a day's work. But if people feel that their day's work is not only supplying basic needs, but is also giving them a margin of comfort and making them able to give their families opportunities and pleasure, then their job looks good to them and they are free to give it their best.

I have learned through the years a good deal about wages. I believe in the first place that, all other considerations aside, our own sales depend in a measure upon the wages we pay. If we can distribute high wages, then that money is going to be spent. It will serve to make storekeepers and distributors and manufacturers and workers in other lines more prosperous. Their prosperity will show up in our sales.

We announced and put into operation in January 1914, a kind of profit-sharing plan. The minimum wage for any class of work and under certain conditions was $5 a day. At the same time we reduced the working day to eight hours—it had been nine—and the week to forty-eight hours. This was entirely a voluntary act. It was to our way of thinking an act of social justice, and in the last analysis we did it for our own satisfaction. There is a pleasure in feeling that you have made others happy—that you have lessened in some degree the burdens of other people—that you have provided something out of which may be had pleasure and saving. Good will is one of the few really important assets of life. Determined people can win almost anything they go after, but unless they gain good will, they have not profited much.

Unit Four

Becoming a World Power

1898-1920

CHAPTER 10
AMERICAN EXPANSION OVERSEAS

AMERICA'S "ANGLO-SAXON" MISSION

A great change took place in American foreign policy in the late 1800's. The nation's traditional isolationist policy was replaced by a policy of expansionism. During these years a number of writers developed arguments in favor of American expansion overseas as well as in the Western Hemisphere.

One of the most influential of these writers was Josiah Strong, a Congregational minister. His arguments in favor of American expansion were based, however, on two false beliefs. One was the concept of an Anglo-Saxon "race," which to Americans meant the people of Great Britain and their descendants. The other belief, called social Darwinism, applied the theories of scientist Charles Darwin—especially the theory of the "survival of the fittest"—to peoples and nations. Many Americans misused Darwin's theories to claim that the earth should belong to the energetic, the strong, and the fit—that is, to the American people.

How do Anglo-Saxons represent the two "great ideas" that Strong describes as the basis of civilization? Why does he predict that Americans will "Anglo-Saxonize" the human race?

Adapted from Josiah Strong, Our Country: Its Possible Future and Its Present Crisis. *New York: Baker & Taylor for the American Home Missionary Society, 1885.*

Every race which has deeply impressed itself on the human family has been the representative of some great idea—one or more—which has given direction to the nation's life and form to its civilization. The Anglo-Saxon is the representative of two great ideas, which are closely related. One of them is that of civil liberty. Nearly all of the civil liberty in the world is enjoyed by Anglo-Saxons: the English, the British colonists, and the people of the United States. Some peoples, such as the Swiss, are allowed by their neighbors to maintain it. Others, such as the French, have experimented with it. But, in modern times, the peoples whose love of liberty has won it, and whose genius for self-government has preserved it, have been Anglo-Saxons.

The other great idea represented by the Anglo-Saxon is that of a pure, spiritual Christianity.

It is not necessary to argue that the two great needs of human beings are, first, civil lib-

547

erty, and second, a pure, spiritual Christianity. These are the forces which, in the past, have contributed most to advancing the human race. They must continue to be, in the future, the most efficient aids to its progress. It follows, then, that Anglo-Saxons, as the great representative of these two ideas, have a special relationship to the world's future. They are divinely commissioned to be, in a sense, their brother's keeper.

Another important fact is the Anglo-Saxon's rapidly increasing strength in modern times. In 1700 this race numbered less than 6 million persons. In 1800, Anglo-Saxons (I use the term somewhat broadly to include all English-speaking peoples) had increased to about 20 million. In 1880 they numbered nearly 100 million, having increased almost five times over in 80 years.

In 100 years the United States has increased the size of its territory ten times. There can be no reasonable doubt that North America is to be the great home of the Anglo-Saxons, the principal seat of their power, the center of their life and influence. Our continent has room and resources and climate, it lies in the pathway of the nations, and it belongs to the zone of power. Already, among Anglo-Saxons, we lead in population and wealth.

Moreover, our social institutions are stimulating. In Europe the various classes of society are, like the layers of the earth, fixed and rigid. There can be no great change without a terrible upheaval, a social earthquake. Here, society is like the waters of the sea, constantly moving. All people are free to become whatever they can make of themselves. They are free to transform themselves from rail-splitters or tanners into the nation's President. Our aristocracy, unlike that of Europe, is open to all comers. Wealth, position, influence, are prizes offered for energy. Every farmer's child, every apprentice and clerk, every friendless and penniless immigrant, is free to enter the contest. Thus many causes combine to produce here the most forceful and tremendous energy in the world.

What is the significance of such facts? It seems to me that God, with great wisdom and skill, is training the Anglo-Saxon race for an hour sure to come in the world's future. Up until now in the history of the world there has always been unoccupied land westward. Into this the crowded countries of the East have poured their surplus populations. But there are no more new worlds. The unoccupied farmlands of the earth are limited, and will soon be taken.

The time is coming when the pressure of population on the means of subsistence will be felt here as it is now felt in Europe and Asia. Then the world will enter upon a new stage of its history — the final competition of races. The Anglo-Saxon is being trained for this. Long before our numbers reach a billion, the expansionist tendency inherited by this race, and strengthened in the United States, will assert itself. Then this race of unequaled energy, with all its numbers and the might of wealth behind it — the representative of liberty and Christianity — having developed aggressive traits to force its institutions upon all people will spread itself over the earth. If I predict correctly, this powerful race will move down upon Mexico, down upon Central and South America, out upon the islands of the sea, over upon Africa, and beyond. And can anyone doubt that the result of this competition of races will be the "survival of the fittest"?

Is there room for reasonable doubt? This race, unless weakened by alcohol and tobacco, is destined to drive out many weaker races, absorb others, and mold the remainder, until, in a very true and important sense, it has Anglo-Saxonized humankind.

AN AMERICAN SOLDIER LOOKS BACK

Americans entered the Spanish-American War in 1898 with great enthusiasm. But the Americans were almost as unprepared for war as the Spaniards. American soldiers were sent off to war without proper equipment. In a climate where temperatures often were above 100 degrees Fahrenheit (38° Celsius), American forces were issued heavy woolen uniforms. Their weapons were outdated Springfield rifles that were almost useless, and their food supplies often consisted of spoiled canned meat. Diseases such as malaria, typhoid, dysentery, and yellow fever were widespread.

Of the 5,400 men who died in the war, over 5,000 died from disease. Only 400 lost their lives in battle. Jacob Judson, an Illinois militia officer who received his training for combat near Tampa, Florida, wrote this account of the war more than fifty years later.

From Judson's account, what hardships could have been prevented? What is Judson's attitude toward his experiences? Do you think that his description is accurate? Explain.

Adapted from a letter of Jacob Judson, Illinois National Guard, April 15, 1956; now in the Manuscript Collection of the Chicago Historical Society. Reprinted by permission of the Chicago Historical Society.

We of the Spanish War who are still living can look back on our war experience, and can thank our Heavenly Father for being alive today. It's remarkable what our bodies can stand, when I think back on our Picnic Island days in Tampa, Florida—untrained men in a heavy rain, a fierce storm blowing our tents out into the sea, no protection, our clothing soaked to the skin. At sea they gave us canned corned beef that stunk so we had to throw it overboard. Then our landing at Sebony in Cuba, camping at the foot of a hill, with large land crabs crawling over us at night. After that our long march toward San Juan Hill through jungles and swamps, joining up with Rough Riders on Kettle Hill, heavy rains pouring down, no tents for cover, every man for himself, standing in trenches in a foot of water and mud, day and night. When off duty, we massaged our feet to get them back in shape. When the sun came out, our boys would help each other by wringing out wet clothes and blankets, quickly cutting down branches from trees, and constructing an overhead protection by laying on palm leaves. Abel Davis and I found a spot under a tree not far from Teddy Roosevelt's tent.

For lack of proper food men grew weak. Our food ration consisted of a slice of salt pork, hardtack, and some grains of coffee that we had to crack between stones or rocks. Then came the issue of wool-lined underwear in a tropical climate, and orders to burn the underwear we brought from home. After that, you would see the boys in the river streams, their backs covered with boils. Wool-lined underwear and salt pork do not go in a tropical climate.

Then came malaria. It was my duty in the mornings to take our sick boys to the division hospital. There were no doctors in attendance, just a hospital corps sergeant who issued pills out of one bottle for all sicknesses. Sick men lay on cots, their mouths, ears, and noses full of flies. I would go over to these poor boys and with my finger clear their mouths of flies—not so much as a piece of paper to cover their faces. Other boys lay day and night on the edge of the sinks; because of malaria they had no control of their bowels. Morning sick detail would come along and take away any that had died. Their bodies would be buried on a hillside. If heavy rains washed away the soil, a second burial was necessary.

I was one of the fortunate boys. It had been my privilege to train Abel Davis when he joined up with the First. We were very close pals. Abel Davis had a brother who was a doctor in Chicago. This doctor gave Abel a box containing medicines for malaria and other tropical sicknesses, so when I came down with malaria Abel took care of me. There were very few doctors; most of them were down with malaria themselves. Abel pulled me through. Then he came down with the malaria himself, and I used his medicines until he got better. If it was not for that box of medicines, I think both Abel's bones and mine would lie in Cuban hills today.

Colonel Teddy Roosevelt said "The Spanish War was but a drop in the bucket as compared with the war following." This statement was no doubt true. The next war had troops spread all over Europe. But the soldier [in World War I] had full modern equipment, proper clothes, healthy, nourishing food, and the very best medical care, none of which was given the Spanish War soldier.

When the war ended and we landed at Montauk, Long Island, our boys were thin, underweight, and yellow as lemons. It took us years to recover. So I say: Let us thank God for taking care of us all these years.

IN DEFENSE OF IMPERIALISM

The success of the United States in the Spanish-American War led some Americans to dream of a colonial empire. Leading the enthusiasm for overseas possessions was Albert J. Beveridge, a young lawyer from Indiana. In the following speech, delivered in 1898 during his campaign for the Senate, he made a strong appeal for action. After his election, he continued to favor and encourage a policy of expansionism.

What are Beveridge's arguments in favor of expansion? How does he support his case by appeals to his listeners' pride? To their feelings of competition? To their sense of duty?

Adapted from Modern Eloquence, *Vol. 10, by Albert J. Beveridge, edited by Ashley H. Thorndike. Reprinted by permission of Mrs. George W. Hibbitt and Mrs. Ashley Thorndike.*

It is a noble land that God has given us—a land that can feed and clothe the world; a land set like a guard between the two oceans of the globe. It is a mighty people that God has planted on this soil. It is a people descended from the most masterful blood of history and constantly strengthened by the strong working folk of all the earth. It is a people imperial by virtue of their power, by right of their institutions, by authority of their heaven-directed purposes.

It is a glorious history our God has given His chosen people. Its keynote was struck by the Liberty Bell, and is heroic with faith in our mission and our future. It is a history of leaders who expanded the boundaries of the republic into unexplored lands and savage wildernesses. It is a history of soldiers who carried the flag across blazing deserts and through hostile mountains. It is a history of a multiplying people who overran a continent in half a century. It is a history of prophets who saw the consequences of evils inherited from the past, and of martyrs who died to save us from them.

Therefore, in this campaign, the question is larger than a party question. It is an American question. It is a world question. Shall the American people continue their restless march toward the commercial supremacy of the world? Shall free institutions extend their blessed reign until the empire of our principles is established over the hearts of all humankind?

Have we no mission to perform, no duty to discharge to our fellow humans? Has the Almighty Father given us gifts and marked us with His favor, only to rot in our own selfishness? This happens to people and nations who are cowardly and self-absorbed—China, India, and Egypt.

Shall we be as the man who had one piece of gold and hid it, or as he who had ten pieces of gold and used them until they grew to riches? And shall we gather the reward for carrying out our high duty as the sovereign power of earth? Shall we occupy new markets for what our farmers raise, new markets for what our factories make, new markets for what our merchants sell? Shall we take advantage of new sources of supply for what we do not raise or make, so that what are luxuries today will be necessities tomorrow? Shall our commerce be encouraged until American trade is the imperial trade of the entire globe?

The opposition tells us that we ought not to govern a people without their consent. I answer: The rule of liberty, that all just government takes its authority from the consent of the governed, applies only to those who are capable of self-government. I answer: We govern the Indians without their consent, we govern our territories without their consent, we govern our children without their consent. I answer: How do you assume that our government would be without their consent? Would not the people of the Philippines prefer the just, humane, civilizing government of this republic to the savage, bloody rule of plundering from which we have rescued them?

Shall we turn these people back to the bloody hands from which we have taken them? Shall we abandon them to their fate, with the wolves of conquest all about them—with Germany, Russia, France, even Japan, hungering for them? Shall we save them from those nations, to give them a self-rule of tragedy? It would be like giving a razor to a baby and telling it to shave itself.

They ask us how we will govern these new possessions. I answer: Out of local conditions and necessity. If England can govern foreign lands, so can America. If Germany can govern foreign lands, so can America. If those nations can supervise protectorates, so can America. Why is it more difficult to govern Hawaii than New Mexico or California? Both had a foreign population. Both were more distant from the seat of government when they came under our control than Hawaii is today.

Will you say by your vote that American ability to govern has decayed, that a century's experience in self-rule has failed? Will you show by your vote that you do not believe in American vigor and power and practical sense? Or will you say that we are of the ruling race of the world—that ours is the blood of government, the heart of authority, the brain and genius of administration? Will you remember that we do only what our fathers did—we simply pitch the tents of liberty farther westward, farther southward. We only continue the march of the flag.

There are so many real things to be done—canals to be dug, railways to be laid, forests to be felled, cities to be built, fields to be tilled, priceless markets to be won, ships to be launched, peoples to be saved, civilization to be proclaimed, and the flag of liberty flung to the eager air of every sea.

We cannot escape our world duties. We must carry out the purpose of a fate that has driven us to be greater than our small intentions. We cannot retreat from any soil where Providence has placed our flag. It is up to us to save that soil for liberty and civilization. For liberty and civilization and God's promise fulfilled, the flag must from now on be the symbol to all humankind.

A CRITICISM OF IMPERIALISM

Not all Americans favored the United States' new policy of overseas expansion. Many well-known Americans spoke out against expansionism. After the Spanish-American War, Carl Schurz, a liberal reformer, became a leading opponent of American expansion. Schurz, who had originally come to the United States from Germany, had been a lawyer, an abolitionist, a Senator from Missouri, and Secretary of Interior in President Hayes' cabinet.

Schurz was especially opposed to the American annexation of the Philippines. The following are selections from a speech he gave on the subject in 1899. According to Schurz, how did earlier American territorial gains differ from those of the 1890's? How does Schurz regard the effort to "Americanize" foreign peoples? Do you think he is more concerned about the effects of expansion on people in the territories or their effects on Americans?

Adapted from Frederick Bancroft, ed., Speeches, Correspondence and Political Papers of Carl Schurz, *Vol. 6. New York: G. P. Putnam's Sons, 1913.*

According to the solemn proclamation of our government, the Spanish-American War was undertaken only for the liberation of Cuba, as a war of humanity and not of conquest. But our easy victories put conquest within our reach. When our troops took over foreign territory, a loud demand arose that, pledge or no pledge, the conquests should be kept, including even the Philippines on the other side of the globe.

Why not? was the cry. Has not the career of the Republic almost from its very beginning been one of territorial expansion? Has it not acquired Louisiana, Florida, Texas, the vast areas that came to us through the Mexican War, and Alaska? Has it not digested them well? Were not those acquisitions much larger than those now thought of? If the Republic could digest the old, why not the new? What is the difference?

Look with a clear eye, and you will soon discover differences that should warn you to look out. There are five of great importance.

1. All the former acquisitions were on this continent and, except for Alaska, on our borders.

2. They were located not in the tropical but in the temperate zone, where democratic institutions do well, and where our people could move in great numbers.

3. They were very thinly settled—in fact, without any population that would have been in the way of new settlements.

4. They could be organized as territories in the usual manner. It was expected that they would presently come into the Union as self-governing states with populations much like our own.

5. They did not require an increase in our army and navy, either to subject them to our rule or to protect them from foreign attack.

Compare now our old acquisitions on all these important points with the ones now under discussion.

They are not continental, not bordering our present land, but are overseas—the Philippines are many thousand miles distant from our coast. They are all located in the tropics, where people of the Northern races, such as Anglo-Saxons, have never moved in large numbers. They are more or less densely populated, parts of them as densely as Massachusetts. Their populations consist almost exclusively of races to whom the tropical climate is well suited—Spanish mixed with Negroes in the West Indies, and Malays, Tagals, Filipinos, Chinese, Japanese, Negritos, and various more or less barbarous tribes in the Philippines.

The question is asked whether we may hope to adapt those countries and populations to our system of government. At this, those who favor annexation answer cheerily that when they belong to us, we shall soon "Americanize" them. This seems to mean that Americans in sufficiently large numbers will move there to change the character of the people until they are more like us.

This is a false belief. If we go honestly about

it, we may indeed accomplish several helpful things in those countries. But one thing we cannot do. We cannot strip the tropical climate of those qualities which have kept people of the Northern races, to which we belong, from moving and settling there in large numbers. It is true that you will find in towns of tropical regions a few persons of Anglo-Saxon or of other Northern origin—merchants, railroad builders, speculators, professional people, and mechanics. But their number is small, and most of them expect to go home as soon as they make some money.

The scheme of Americanizing our "new possessions" in that way is therefore absolutely hopeless. The forces of nature are against it. Whatever we may do for their improvement, the people of the Spanish islands will outnumber us. The vast majority are completely alien to us, not only in origin and language, but in habits, traditions, ways of thinking, principles, ambitions—in short, in most things that are of the greatest importance in human and political cooperation.

What, then, shall we do with such peoples? Shall we organize those countries as territories with a view to their eventual admission as states? If they become states on an equal footing with the other states, they not only will govern themselves, but will take part in governing the whole Republic. They will share in governing us, by sending Senators and Representatives into our Congress to help make our laws, and by voting for President and Vice-President. The prospect of such consequences is so alarming that you may well pause before taking the step.

But this may be avoided, it is said, by governing the new possessions as mere dependencies, or subject provinces. This would be a most serious departure from the rule that governed our former acquisitions. It is useless to speak of the District of Columbia and Alaska as proof that we have done such things before and can do them again. Every honest person will at once admit the great difference between those cases and the permanent establishment of arbitrary government over large territories with millions of inhabitants. The question is not only whether we can do such things, but whether having the public good at heart, we *should* do them.

If we adopt such a system then we shall, for the first time since the abolition of slavery, again have two kinds of Americans. There will be Americans of the first class, who enjoy the privilege of taking part in the government in accordance with our Constitutional principles. And there will be Americans of the second class, who are to be ruled by the Americans of the first class.

This will be a difference no better—rather somewhat worse—than that which existed 125 years ago between English people of the first class and English people of the second class. The first were represented by King George and the British Parliament. The second group consisted of the American colonists. This difference led to the American Declaration of Independence—a document which, I regret to say, seems to have lost much of its charms among some of our citizens. Its basic principle was that "governments derive their just powers from the consent of the governed."

We are now told that we have never fully lived up to that principle. Therefore, we may now throw it aside altogether. But I say to you that, if we are true believers in democratic government, we should move in that direction and not away from it. If you tell me that we cannot govern the people of those new possessions in accordance with that principle, then I answer that this is a reason we should not attempt to govern them at all.

If we do, we shall change the government of the people, for the people, and by the people into a government of one part of the people, the strong, over another part, the weak. Abandoning such a basic principle may at first seem to involve only distant lands, but it can hardly fail to affect democratic government at home. And I warn the American people that a democracy cannot deny its faith in a vital principle—it cannot long play the role of king over subject populations without creating in itself ways of thinking and habits of action most dangerous to its own vitality.

THE WHITE MAN'S BURDENS, PRO AND CON

In 1899 Rudyard Kipling, a British writer, wrote a poem called "The White Man's Burden." The poem, written and published in the United States, immediately became a popular defense of expansionism and imperialism. Kipling wrote that the "white man's burden," or responsibility, was to take up the task of governing what Kipling described as childlike and untamed people. He argued that it was the duty of more advanced nations to bring civilization to the backward peoples of the earth.

The poem was imitated and made fun of by many Americans, especially those who were against expansion in the Philippines. The first stanza of Kipling's seven-stanza poem appears here. Following it are poems which are imitations of and answers to his poem.

What is Kipling's attitude toward conquered peoples? What is the point of the first poem that imitates the Kipling poem? Of the second? Of the last, four-line poem?

First poem from Rudyard Kipling, "The White Man's Burden," 1899.

Second, third, and fourth poems adapted from Little Brown Brother *by Leon Wolff, by permission of Barthold Fles, Literary Agent. Copyright 1960, 1961, by Leon Wolff.*

Take up the White Man's burden—
   Send forth the best ye breed—
Go bind your sons to exile
   To serve your captives' need;
To wait in heavy harness,
   On fluttered folk and wild—
Your new-caught, sullen peoples,
   Half-devil and half-child.

*   *   *   *

Pile on the brown man's burden
   To gratify your greed;
Go, clear away the Negroes
   Who progress would impede;
Be very stern, for truly
   'Tis useless to be mild
With new-caught sullen peoples,
   Half devil and half child.

Pile on the brown man's burden,
   And if ye rouse his hate,
Meet his old-fashioned reasons
   With Maxims [a Maxim gun was a kind of machine gun] up-to-date;
With shells and dum-dum bullets [bullets made to expand on impact and thus create a large wound],
   A hundred times make plain
The brown man's loss must ever
   Imply the white man's gain.

*   *   *   *

Take up the sword and rifle,
   Send forth your ships with speed,
To join the nations' scramble,
   And vie with them in greed;
Go find your goods a market;
   Beyond the western flood,
The heathen who withstand you
   Shall answer it in blood.

Take up the sword and rifle,
   Still keep your conscience whole—
So soon is found an unction [remedy]
   To soothe a guilty soul.
Go with it to your Maker,
   Find what excuse ye can—
Rob for the sake of justice,
   Kill for the love of man.

*   *   *   *

We've taken up the white man's burden
   Of ebony and brown;
Now will you tell us, Rudyard,
   How we may put it down?

FROM THE HAWAIIAN VIEWPOINT

By the late 1800's Americans owned most of the sugar plantations in Hawaii and had obtained a treaty that allowed Hawaiian sugar to enter the United States duty free. However, the McKinley Tariff Act of 1890 threatened the Hawaiian sugar planters by allowing all foreign sugar to enter the United States duty free and by giving a two-cent per pound subsidy to American sugar producers. Shortly afterward the planters asked that Hawaii be annexed by the United States, believing this was the only way to save their sugar industry.

Queen Liliuokalani, who was supported by the Hawaiian people, opposed annexation. And in 1893, because of her efforts against them, the planters and other Americans in Hawaii revolted against her rule and set up their own government. In this selection, the queen tells what happened in Hawaii during the years before the islands were annexed.

Why did the Hawaiians allow Americans to take over their government? For what actions does Queen Liliuokalani criticize the Americans?

Adapted from Hawaii's Story by Hawaii's Queen *by Liliuokalani, published by Charles E. Tuttle Co., Inc.*

It has been said that the Hawaiian people under the rule of the chiefs were harshly ruled.

Under the monarchy, it was held, their condition greatly improved, but the native government in any form finally became intolerable to the better informed part of the community. I shall not examine such statements in detail. But I do feel called upon to make a few remarks from my own—that is to say, the native Hawaiian—viewpoint.

I shall not claim that in the days of Captain Cook our people were civilized. I shall not claim anything more for their progress in civilization and Christian morality than missionary writers have. Perhaps I may safely claim even less, admitting the criticism of some intelligent visitors who were not missionaries. In other words, the habits and prejudices of New England Puritanism were not well adapted to a tropical people, and could not be thoroughly absorbed by them.

But they have accepted Christianity in substance. I know of no people who have developed a tenderer Christian conscience, or who have shown themselves more ready to obey its commands. And where else in the world's history have savage people, pagan for ages, with fixed customs and beliefs, made equal progress in civilization and Christianity in the same amount of time?

Does it say nothing for us that we have always recognized our Christian teachers as worthy of authority in our councils? That while four fifths of the population of our islands were killed by diseases introduced by foreigners, the ruling class held on to Christian morality, and gave its strong support and service to the work of saving and civilizing the masses? Has not this class loyally held on to the brotherly alliance made with the better group of foreign settlers, giving freely of its authority and its substance, its sons and daughters, to cement and prosper it?

Why should it be thought strange that education and knowledge of the world have made us able to see that as a race we have some special mental and physical requirements not shared by other races? That certain habits and ways of living are better for our health and happiness than others? And that a separate nationality and a particular form of government, as well as special laws, are, at least for the present, best for us? These things were ours until the pitiless and tireless "annexation policy" was effectively backed by the naval power of the United States.

Before this we had allowed foreigners to give us a constitution and control the offices of government. Not without protest, indeed, for this grabbing of power caused us much humiliation and distress. But we did not resist it by force. It had not entered our hearts to believe that these friends and allies from the United States would ever go so far as to overthrow our form of government, grab our nation by the throat, and turn it over to a foreign power.

Perhaps there is a kind of right, known as the "Right of Conquest," under which robbers may take whatever they are strong enough to grab from others. I will not pretend to decide how far civilization and Christian teachings have outlawed this right.

If we have been friendly to those who sought our ruin, it was because they were Americans, like those whom we believed to be our dearest friends and allies. If we did not resist their final outrage by force, it was because we could not do so without striking at the military might of the United States. The conspirators, having actually gained possession of the government, refused to give up their conquest. So it happens that the people of the islands have no voice in determining their future, but are in a condition like that of the American Indians.

It is not for me to consider this matter from the American point of view. The current question of annexation, however, involves a departure from the established policy of that country and a dangerous change in its foreign relations. I am able to say, with absolute authority, that the native people of Hawaii are entirely loyal to their own chiefs, and are deeply attached to their own customs and government. They either do not understand, or bitterly oppose, the scheme of annexation.

Perhaps I may say here a final word about the Americans who favor this annexation of Hawaii. I observe that it is pretty much a party matter, favored chiefly by Republican leaders and politicians. But is it really a matter of party interest? Is the American Republic to decline and become a colonizer and a land-grabber? And is this prospect acceptable to a people who depend upon self-government for their liberties? There is little question but that the United States could become a successful rival of the European nations in the race for conquest and could create a great military and naval power if such is its ambition. But is such an ambition praiseworthy? Is such a departure from established principles patriotic or wise?

CHAPTER 11
AMERICAN EXPANSION IN THE CARIBBEAN

A CANAL BUILDER AT WORK

Americans in the early 1900's were proud of their great achievement in building the Panama Canal. Much of the credit for this feat belonged to Colonel Goethals, who was appointed chief engineer by Theodore Roosevelt in 1907. Goethals had to deal with a labor force of 30,000 workers, overcome landslides that delayed the work, and solve enormous engineering problems. Offices, schools, houses, recreation centers, machine shops, and dining halls—all had to be built. Goethals spent time each day listening to workers' complaints, and he soon won the respect and dedication of the workers. In this selection Arthur Bullard, who traveled to Panama in 1909, tells about the building of the canal.

What do you think of Goethals' "Court of Justice"? Was it necessary for Goethals to be an "absolute autocrat" in these circumstances? Why? What is Bullard's opinion of Goethals?

Adapted from Arthur Bullard, Panama: The Canal, the Country and the People. *New York: The Macmillan Co., 1914.*

"Tell me something about Colonel Goethals." My friend was a keen observer who had already given me much information about life and work in the Canal Zone.

"You want to know about the old man?" he said after a moment's thought. "Well the most distinctive picture of him I have is this. I used to live at Culebra. One night I was sitting out on the porch, smoking. There were only a few lights here and there in the Administration Building. One by one they went out, all except that in the old man's office. It was almost ten o'clock when his light went out. It was the dry season. A full moon, as big as a dining-room table, was out—a gorgeous night. The old man came out and walked across the grass to his house. He didn't stop to look up at the moon; he just walked along, his head a little forward, still thinking. And he hadn't been in his own house ten minutes before all the lights were out there. He'd gone to bed. The only time the colonel isn't working is from 10 P.M. to 6 A.M., when he's asleep."

That seems to be the thing which impresses our men down here most of all about the boss. He is always on the job.

Just what is the job?

Strictly speaking, it is administrative, rather than constructive, engineering. The type of the canal was decided upon before the present commission was installed. They have had but few changes of importance to make: widening the channel in the Cut, increasing the size of the locks, and moving the Pacific locks inland, beyond the range of a hostile fleet. Their work has been the perfecting of details and the carrying out of what had been already determined.

Colonel George Washington Goethals, the Chief Engineer and Chairman of the Panama Canal Commission, is now at the head of this great national job of ours. A visitor to the Isthmus who has not included the colonel among the sights has missed more than half of what there is to see down here. You will not have to wait long before you are brought into the throne room, and are face to face with the most absolute autocrat in the world.

Many people have described Colonel Goethals as having a boyish face. But they must have seen him with his hat on, for his hair is white. If, as they say, his face looks 20 and his hair 60, I could not see it, for his eyes—which dominate—look 40. He is broad-shouldered and erect. Above everything, he looks alert and fit. Although he does not spare himself, he has not lost a day from malaria.

Of course, the first thing you do will be to hand him your perfectly useless letter from your representative in Congress. Useless, because even if you have no letter he will show you every courtesy he can without interfering with the job. And he will not interfere with the job even if you bring letters from all the members of Congress.

Like every man who accomplishes a great amount of work, he believes in routine.

Six mornings a week he is "out on the line." He took me along on one of these inspection trips. It was before seven when we reached Pedro Miguel, and we walked back through the Cut to Empire. It was four hours of bitter hard walking, for the colonel kept to no well-worn path. Whatever interested him he wished to see close up. The colonel said, "The only way to keep your health in this climate is to take a little exercise every morning." Doubtless it is true, but I had rather die quickly than keep alive at that rate.

He spends his afternoons on routine desk work, signing papers, approving reports, and so forth. It is part of his system that he discourages oral reports. Everything comes to him on paper. If he wants to talk with any of his subordinates, he generally does it during his morning trips—on the spot. Perhaps the phrase he uses most frequently is, "Write it down."

The afternoon office work is often interrupted by callers. The stream of tourists grows steadily, and the colonel realizes that it is we, the people of the United States, who are doing this canal job. Anyone who is sufficiently interested to come down and look it over is welcome.

The most remarkable part of Colonel Goethals' routine is his Sunday Court of Low, Middle, and High Justice. The colonel holds a session every Sunday morning. I had the good fortune to be admitted one Sunday morning to the audience chamber.

The first callers were a Negro couple from Jamaica. They had a difference of opinion as to the ownership of $35 which the wife had earned by washing. Colonel Goethals listened until the fact was established that she had earned it, then ordered the man to return it. He started to protest something about a husband's property rights under the English law. "All right," the colonel said, decisively. "Say the word, and I'll deport you. You can get all the English law you want in Jamaica." The husband decided to pay and stay.

Then came a Spanish worker who had been hurt in an accident. The colonel called in his chief clerk and told him to help the unfortunate man prepare his claim. "See that the papers are prepared correctly and have them pushed through."

A man came in who had just been thrown out of the service for brutality to the men under him. This action was the result of an investigation before a special committee. The man wanted his job back. The colonel read over the papers in the case, and when he spoke, his language was vigorous. "If you have any new evidence, I will instruct the committee to reopen your case. But as long as this report stands against you, you will get no mercy from this office. If the men had broken your head with a crowbar, I would have stood up for them. We don't need slave drivers on this job."

Then a committee from the Machinists' Union wanted an opinion on some new shop rules. A nurse wanted a longer vacation than the regulations allow. A man and his wife were dissatisfied with the house they had been given. A supervisor of steam shovels came in to ask advice about applying for another job under the Panama government. The end of the canal work is approaching and the farsighted men are beginning to look into the future. "Of course I can't advise you," the colonel said. "You know I would hate to see you go. But if you decide that it is wise, come in and see me. I may be able to give you some introductions which will help you." (And, as everyone knows that a letter of introduction from the chairman of the commission would look like an order to the Panama government, there is another man who will want to vote for Goethals for President in 1916!)

An American Negro introduced some humor. He was convinced that his services were of more value than his foreman felt they were. The colonel preferred to accept the foreman's judgment in the matter. The dissatisfied worker announced that he was the best blacksmith's helper on the Isthmus and that he planned to appeal this decision. The colonel's eyes twinkled. "To whom are you going to appeal?" he asked. For the fact is that the decisions made in these Sunday sessions will not be changed before the Day of Judgment.

The procession kept up till noon—pitiful, patience-trying foolishness, with occasional humor. "Once in a while," the colonel said, "something turns up which is really important for me to know. And, anyway, they feel better after they have seen me, even if I cannot help them. They feel that they got a fair chance to state their troubles. They are less likely to cause discontent. But it is a strain."

COLOMBIA PROTESTS AMERICA'S ACTIONS

The actions taken by the United States to obtain the right to build a canal across the Isthmus of Panama increased the Latin American nations' distrust of their neighbor to the north. Colombia, which was forced to give up the territory of Panama, felt especially threatened. However, that small nation realized that it could not resist the power of the United States. Consequently, leaders of Colombia's government, who were seeking payment for their former territory of Panama, appealed to world opinion for support.

The following selections are from a pamphlet written by Colombia's foreign minister, Francisco José Urrutía, to present his nation's case. A year after the canal was officially opened in July 1920, the United States paid $25 million to Colombia, which in turn recognized the independence of Panama.

What does Urrutía mean by "the crime committed in 1903"? What action does he threaten to take against the United States? Do you think this was a serious threat?

Adapted from Francisco José Urrutía, A Commentary on the Declaration of the Rights of Nations. *Washington, D.C.: 1916.*

Until 1903 the relations between Colombia and the United States were most friendly. Good will toward Colombia was always recognized by the United States, not only in negotiations about the Panama Canal but in all matters.

The statement that Colombia ever opposed the opening of the Panama Canal is absolutely untrue. On the contrary, the entire diplomatic history of Colombia, from the time of its freedom from Spain, shows how great was its desire to see the canal built. Out of regard for self preservation, it did try to bring this about without harming its own sovereignty.

With the canal now open, Colombia cannot ignore the fact that this great work is one of the chief factors in the future material development of the world. But as long as the agreement giving a lawful title to the United States is not carried out, Colombia will also maintain that the work, great as it is, stands as a monument to an even greater crime. It will insist that Colombia and Colombia alone is the lawful owner of the Isthmus of Panama. If the formal opening of the canal should take place before a final settlement is arrived at, Colombia will be forced once more to protest to the other nations of the world, against the violation of its sovereignty.

In the eyes of the people of Colombia and of all America, the Panama Canal stands for the victory of might over right, the triumph of force over law. It stands for this far more than it does for the splendid conquest of tropical nature by the science and energy of the people of the United States. The United States has the power to remove this feeling, to change this state of affairs, and to insure that the canal shall be what it would have been without the crime committed in 1903 — a great and powerful link uniting Colombia and the United States.

Reference has been made to the danger threatening the canal if it were attacked from Colombian territory, and of the necessity of preventing an alliance between Colombia and any other nation. If any such danger or any such necessity exist, the best guarantee of the safety of the canal lies in an agreement with Colombia. Fear that the Panama Canal might be attacked some day from Colombian territory may be avoided by the United States. This cannot be through a policy of force, but through a policy of friendship and justice. Such a policy calls for returning — by means of payment for past grievances — the ancient and traditional good will and friendship between Colombia and United States.

If the safeguarding of the Panama Canal enters into the scheme of the national defense of the United States, it is natural to suppose that that protection would be sought in an honest and loyal manner by encouraging the friendship of Colombia and by respecting its sovereignty. It can never be reached by returning to a policy already disapproved by both the American continents.

AN AMERICAN IN MEXICO, 1914

After a revolution broke out in Mexico in 1910, relations between Mexico and the United States became troubled. At first President Wilson, who was anxious not to intervene in Mexico, followed a policy of "watchful waiting." However, in 1914 several American sailors were arrested in Tampico. When the Mexican government refused to apologize by firing a 21-gun salute, Wilson sent American troops to take Veracruz.

The anxious days that followed are described in the following selection by Edith O'Shaughnessy, the wife of Nelson O'Shaughnessy, American charge d'affaires at the United States embassy in Mexico City. Although O'Shaughnessy had to support Wilson's actions, in later years he declared that Wilson's Mexican policy was "brutal, unwarranted, and stupid."

What does Edith O'Shaughnessy think of America's intervention in Mexico? What are her feelings toward President Huerta?

Adapted from A Diplomat's Wife in Mexico *by Edith O'Shaughnessy, published by Harper & Brothers, Inc.*

April 18th. 6:30 p.m.

It makes me sick with dread to think of the probable fate of Americans in the deserts and mountains of Mexico. Someone has made a mistake, somewhere, somehow, that we should come in to give the final blow to this distracted nation, which still holds on, and rightly, to the little sovereignty we have left it. The foreign powers think we are playing the most cold-blooded, most cruel game of grab in history.

10 p.m.

If we get through this, the next incident will mean war. I hope that the leaders in Washington will appreciate some of the difficulties Nelson has to meet, and act accordingly. How glad I am that I haven't sent my son or my jewels with various terror-stricken friends who have fled. War hasn't come yet. After everything is said and done, everything depends on the life of that wise and patient old Indian [Huerta], who —whatever his sins—is legally president of Mexico. Chase legality out of Latin America and where are you? After him will come anarchy, chaos, and finally intervention—the biggest police job ever undertaken in the Western Hemisphere, however one may feel like making little of it from a military standpoint.

April 19th. 2:30 a.m.

I can't sleep. National and personal problems keep running through my brain. Three railroad men came to the embassy this evening. They brought reports of a plan for the massacre of Americans in the street tonight. But, strange and wonderful thing, a heavy rain is falling. It is my only experience of a midnight rain in Mexico, except that which fell upon the mobs crying "Death to Diaz," nearly three years ago. As all Mexicans hate to get wet, rain is as effective as shellfire in clearing the streets, and I don't think there will be any trouble. Fate seems to keep an occasional unnatural shower on hand for Mexican crises.

Had this war been started by a great incident or for a great principle, I could stand it. But because the details of a salute could not be decided upon, we cause ourselves, and inflict on others, the horrors of war. It is no situation for amateurs. The longer I live the more respect I have for technical training. Every foreign office in Europe or any other continent keeps experts for just such cases. I may become an in-

terventionist, but *after* Huerta. He has proved himself greatly superior, in executive ability, to any leader Mexico has produced since Diaz, in spite of his lack of balance and his surprising childishness. He would have sold his soul to please the United States and gain recognition. [Wilson refused to recognize the Huerta government.] In that small, soft hand (doubtless bloody, too) were possibilities of bringing back prosperity.

April 20th

My heart is sick. Wednesday that great fleet arrives. What is it going to fight? It can't bombard Veracruz. The streets are full and the houses overflowing with fleeing people. It can't climb the mountains and protect the countless Americans living inland. Huerta's army is engaged in the north in a death struggle against enemies of the government, armed with our guns. Oh, the pity of it!

And this city, beautiful Mexico City, so wonderfully located in the very center of the Western Hemisphere, a great continent to the north and the south, halfway between immense oceans, and lifted nearly 8,000 feet [2400 meters] up to the heavens!

April 21st

We are at war. American and Mexican blood flowed in the streets of Veracruz today. The story that reaches us is that the captain of the German ship *Ypiranga* tried to land 17 million rounds of ammunition. Admiral Fletcher protested. The captain of the *Ypiranga* insisted on doing it. The admiral prevented him by force, and they say, took the town—thus putting us on a war basis. Whether this is a true version of what has happened I don't know. It has been many a year since American blood flowed in the streets of Veracruz. General Scott took it in 1847. The endless repetitions of history!

April 22nd

The newspapers are rather fierce this morning. One headline in the *Independiente* says that "the Mexican bullets will no longer spill brothers' blood, but will hit blond heads and white breasts swollen with vanity and cowardice." The newspapers add that the Americans landed "without a declaration of war, like criminals." It is impossible to expect the Mexicans to grasp the idea that the landing of our troops was a simple police measure. In the face of the facts, I am sure such distinctions will be overlooked. At 7:30 an officer appeared in the drawing-room, saying that President Huerta was outside. There was no time to ring for servants. I went to the door and waited while the fearless old Indian, in his gray sweater and soft hat, came quickly up the steps. It was his first and last visit to the embassy during our stay there.

I led him into the drawing-room, where we had a strange and moving conversation. I could not, for my country's sake, speak the endless regret that was in my heart for the official part we had been forced to play in the action carried out by us to his country's undoing. He greeted me calmly.

"Señora, how do you do? I fear you have had many annoyances."

Then he sat back, quietly in a big armchair, impersonal and mysterious. I answered as easily as I could that the times were difficult for everyone. I said that we were very grateful for what he had done for our personal safety and that of other Americans. I asked him if there was anything we could do for him. He gave me a long, piercing look, and after a pause, answered:

"Nothing, Señora. All that is done I must do myself. Here I must remain. The moment has not come for me to go. Nothing but death could remove me now."

I felt the tears come to my eyes, as I answered—"Death is not so terrible a thing."

He answered again, very quietly, "It is the natural law, to which we must all give in. We were born into the world according to the natural law, and must leave according to it—that is all."

He does not want us to leave by way of Guadalajara and Manzanillo. He is giving us his train tomorrow night to take us to Veracruz. There will be a full escort, including three officers of high rank.

I was dreadfully keyed up. I felt the tears come to my eyes. He seemed to think that it was fear that moved me, for he told me not to be anxious.

I said, "I am not weeping for myself, but for the tragedy of life."

And, indeed, since seeing him I have been in a sea of sadness, personal and impersonal—impersonal because of the crushing destiny that can overtake a strong man and a country, and personal, because this many-colored, vibrant Mexican experience of mine is drawing to a close. Nothing can ever be like it.

As we three [Huerta, Edith, and Nelson] stood there together he said, very quietly, his last word:

"I hold no ill will toward the American people, nor toward President Wilson." And, after a slight pause, he added, "He has not understood."

It was the first and last time I ever heard him speak the President's name. I gave him my hand as he stood with his other hand on Nelson's shoulder, and knew that this was indeed the end. I think he realized that my heart was warm and my sympathies rushing out to beautiful, agonizing Mexico. For, as he stood at the door, he suddenly turned and made me a deep bow. Then, taking Nelson's arm, he went out into the starry, perfumed evening, and I turned back into the house I was so soon to leave, with the sadness of life like a hot point, deep in my heart. So is history written. So do circumstances and a man's will seem to raise him up to great ends, and so does destiny crush him.

I am sad, very sad, tonight. Whatever else life may have in reserve for me, this last conversation with a strong man of another temperament than mine will remain on my heart—his calm, his philosophy on the eve of a war he knows can only end in disaster.

CHAPTER 12
AMERICA'S INVOLVEMENT IN WORLD WAR I

WILSON'S "WAR MESSAGE"

After World War I broke out in Europe in 1914, the United States managed to keep out of the war for nearly three years. During this period both sides—the Allies and the Central Powers—violated American neutrality. American ships bound for Europe were stopped by both Great Britain and Germany. However, in 1917 Germany sharply increased submarine warfare against the United States.

After months of growing tension over German submarine warfare and its violation of the rights of neutral shipping, President Wilson asked

Congress to declare war on Germany. On April 2, 1917, Wilson went before Congress and delivered his "War Message." It was passed by the Senate two days later, by a vote of 82 to 6, and by the House on April 6, by a vote of 375 to 50.

For what reasons does Wilson argue that the United States must enter the war? According to Wilson, what are America's war aims?

Adpated from A Compilation of the Messages and Papers of the Presidents, *Vol. XVII. New York: Bureau of National Literature, Inc., n.d.*

I have called the Congress into special session because there are serious, very serious, choices of policy to be made, and made immediately. It was neither right nor constitutional that I should take the responsibility of making them.

On February 3rd, 1917, I officially informed you of the announcement of the Imperial German Government that on and after February 1st, it would put aside all restraints of law or humanity and use its submarines to sink every ship that tried to approach the ports of Great Britain and Ireland, the western coast of Europe, or any of the ports controlled by the enemies of Germany within the Mediterranean.

The new policy has swept every restriction aside. Ships of every kind, whatever their flag, type, cargo, destination, or errand, have been ruthlessly fired on and sent to the bottom of the sea without warning and without thought of help or mercy for those on board. Even hospital ships and ships carrying relief to the stricken people of Belgium have been sunk with the same reckless lack of sympathy or of principle.

I was for a little while unable to believe that such things would, in fact, be done by any government that considered itself civilized. International law had its origin in the attempt to set up some laws which would be respected and observed upon the seas, where no nation had the right of control. That law has been built up by painful stage after stage, always with a clear view of what the heart and conscience of humanity demanded.

I am not now thinking of the loss of property involved, great and serious as that is, but only of the reckless and wholesale destruction of the lives of noncombatants, men, women, and children, engaged in activities which have always, even in the darkest period of modern history, been regarded as innocent and legitimate. Property can be paid for; the lives of peaceful, innocent people cannot be.

The present German submarine warfare against commerce is a warfare against humankind. It is a war against all nations. American ships have been sunk, American lives taken in ways that have stirred us very deeply. But the ships and people of other neutral, friendly nations have been sunk in the same way. There has been no discrimination. The challenge is to all people. Each nation must decide for itself how to meet it.

When I addressed Congress on February 26th, I thought that it would be enough to assert our neutral right with arms; our right to use the sea against unlawful interference; our right to keep our people safe against unlawful violence. But armed neutrality, it now appears, will not work. Because submarines are, in effect, outlaws when used as the German submarines have been used against merchant shipping, it is impossible to defend ships against their attacks. (The law of nations has assumed that merchant ships would defend themselves against cruisers or visible ships chasing them upon the open sea.) Under the present circumstances, we have to destroy the ships on sight.

The German government denies the right of neutrals to use arms at all within certain areas of the sea. The Germans say that the armed guards which we have placed on our merchant ships will be treated as outside the protection of law and dealt with as pirates would be. Armed neutrality is weak enough at best. In such circumstances it is likely only to produce what it was meant to prevent—it is practically certain to draw us into the war without either the rights or the effectiveness of belligerents.

There is one choice we cannot make, that we are incapable of making. We will not choose the path of submission and suffer the most sacred rights of our nation and our people to be ignored or violated. The wrongs against which we now array ourselves are no common wrongs; they cut to the very roots of human life.

With a strong sense of the solemn and even tragic character of the step I am taking and of the grave responsibilities it involves, but in unhesitating obedience to what I see as my constitutional duty, I advise that the Congress declare the recent course of the Imperial German Government to be, in fact, nothing less than war against the government and people of the United States. I advise that it formally accept the status of belligerent which has thus been thrust upon it. I advise that it take immediate steps not only to put the country in a more thorough state of defense, but also to use all its power and resources to defeat the German empire and end the war.

We are now about to accept battle with this natural foe of liberty and shall, if necessary, spend the whole force of the nation to end its power. We are glad, now that we see the facts with no veil of false pretense about them, to fight thus for the ultimate peace of the world and for the liberation of its peoples, the German peoples included; for the rights of nations great and small and the privilege of human beings everywhere to choose their way of life and obedience. The world must be made safe for democracy. Its peace must be planted upon the tested foundations of political liberty.

We have no selfish ends to serve. We desire no conquest, no dominion. We seek no payment for ourselves, no material compensation for the sacrifices we shall freely make. We are but one of the champions of the rights of humans. We shall be satisfied when those rights have been made as secure as the faith and the freedom of nations can make them.

Just because we fight without hatred and without selfish objectives, seeking nothing for ourselves but what we wish to share with all free peoples, we shall, I feel confident, conduct ourselves without passion and observe the principles of right and fair play we are fighting for.

It is a distressing and oppressive duty which I have performed in thus speaking to you. There may be many months of fiery trial and sacrifice ahead of us. It is a fearful thing to lead this great peaceful people into war, into the most terrible and disastrous of all wars, with civilization itself in the balance. But the right is more precious than peace. We shall fight for the things which we have always carried nearest our hearts — for democracy, for the right of those who submit to authority to have a voice in their own governments, for the rights and liberties of small nations, for such a universal domination of right as shall bring peace and safety to all nations and make the world itself at last free.

To such a task we can dedicate our lives and our fortunes, everything that we are and everything that we have. We can do this with the pride of those who know that the day has come when America is privileged to spend its blood and its might for the principles that gave it birth, happiness, and peace. God helping us, we cannot do otherwise.

WOMEN UNITE TO SUPPORT THE WAR

American women made a great contribution to the war effort. Many of them took over jobs in factories and industry. Many others did volunteer work for organizations such as the Red Cross. They spent many hours preparing bandages to be used in hospitals and first-aid stations. Mary Carolyn Davies, an American writer, described this experience in a poem she called "Fifth Avenue and Grand Street." In the poem, Fifth Avenue stands for wealth and fashion, while Grand Street, on New York's Lower East Side, was a low-income area where many immigrants lived.

What do you think the writer is trying to say in this poem? Why does it apply especially to women? Do you think she is right?

"Fifth Avenue and Grand Street" by Mary Carolyn Davies. Reprinted by permission of Miss Laura Benet.

I sat beside her, rolling bandages.
I peeped. "Fifth Avenue," her clothes were saying.
It's "Grand Street," I know well, my shirtwaist [a kind of dress] says,
And shoes, and hat, but then, she didn't hear,
Or she pretended not, for we were laying
Our coats aside, and as we were so near,
She saw my pin like hers. [Many women during the war wore a star-shaped pin to show that someone close to them was serving in the armed forces.]
And when girls are
Wearing a pin these days that has a star,
They smile out at each other. We did that,
And then she didn't seem to see my hat.

I sat beside her, handling gauze and lint,
And thought of Jim. She thought of someone too;
Under the smile there was a little glint
In her eyelashes, that was how I knew.

I wasn't crying—but I haven't any
Pride in it; we've a better chance than they
To take blows standing, for we've had so many.
We two sat, fingers busy, all that day.

I'd spoken first, if I'd known what to say.
But she did soon, and after, told of him.
The man she wore the star for, and the way
He'd gone at once. I bragged a bit of Jim;
Who wouldn't who had ever come to know
Him? When the girls all rose to go,
She stood there, shyly, with her gloves half
    on,
Said, "Come to see me, won't you?" and was
    gone.

I meant to call, too, I'd have liked it then
For we'd a lot in common, with our men
Across. But now that peace is here again
And our boys safe, I can't help wondering—
    Well,
Will she forget, and crawl back in her shell
And if I call, say "Show this person out"?
Or still be friendly as she was? I doubt
If Grand [Street] will sit beside Fifth Avenue
Again, and be politely spoken to.

We're sisters while the danger lasts, it's true;
But rich and poor's equality must cease
(For women especially), of course, in peace.

ACTION AT THE FRONT

During World War I, about 8 million soldiers
were killed and about 20 million were wounded in
the fighting. It was the first war in which tanks, di-
rigibles, and airplanes were used. And it was the
first war in which submarines and machine guns
were used on a large scale. The use of these
weapons, and of poison gas, for mass killing
greatly increased the horrors of the fighting. On
the western front, soldiers spent weeks in muddy,
rat-filled trenches facing steady artillery bom-
bardments and the threat of poison gas.

Eldon Canright, a private from Wisconsin,
spent 180 days in the trenches along the western
front. In this letter home, he tells his family what
the fighting there was like.

How would you describe Canright's attitude
toward the fighting? Does he seem to share the
war aims that Wilson outlined for the nation?

*Adapted from "Some War-Time Letters" by Eldon J.
Canright in the* Wisconsin Magazine of History, *V: 192-195
(1921-1922). Reprinted by permission of the State Historical
Society of Wisconsin.*

Somewhere in France
July 8, 1918

My Dear Folks:
I believe I have told you in another letter that
because of the fine record we have made since
we have been at the front, we have been chosen
as "shock troops." Well, we sure are being
shocked!

Try and picture the very worst thunder-
storm you have ever heard. Then multiply it by
about 10,000 and you will get some idea of the
battle that has been and still is raging along
this front and in which we are taking a very active part!

The battle started shortly after midnight a
few days ago and has been raging ever since! It
started with a very heavy bombardment all
along the front, and as the country here is very
flat, you can see for a long way. I can tell you
that it is some sight at night to see the blinding
flashes of the guns all along the line. Even far
off on the horizon you can see the pink glow
flare up and die down and flare up and die
down again—very much like a city burning in
the distance. The roar and crash of the guns
just seems to tear the air into pieces, and
explosions shake the ground. To add to the confusion you have the whine and shrieks of the
shells, some coming and some going! And signal rockets of all colors are constantly shooting
up into the air, and that is the way the army
"talks" at night. It's a wonderful sight! The
first night, a shell struck an ammunition supply and rockets went shooting in every direction. It lasted for several minutes and was very
thrilling!

Of course every so often the Germans send
over poison gas. We have to be constantly on
the alert for it and wear our gas clothes most of
the time, and carry our gas masks all the time!

We all have cotton in our ears. Still, the
noise of the guns has made some of us temporarily deaf. We have not taken off any of our
clothes or gone to bed since the battle started.
When it slows up a little we just lie down on
the ground, right by the guns, and get what little rest and sleep we can. Our meals are
brought to us, as we may not leave the position
long enough to go and get them!

The first day they shot down an observation
balloon right near us. A pilot attacked it and
hit it with his machine gun. The balloon came
down in flames, but the observer jumped out
and landed with a parachute! However, about a
minute later, even before the observer had hit

the ground, another airplane had rushed up after the plane that "got" the balloon. The second plane shot him down and he came tumbling out of the clouds with his plane in flames. That happened three days ago, and the burned and broken airplane is still lying there, and so are the two pilots. They are an awful sight. And when the wind is in the right direction (or rather wrong direction) we get a very disagreeable odor, and there are several dead horses, etc., lying out there, too. No one has had time to bury them yet!

During the daytime there are a great many airplanes flying overhead, constantly trying to "see" what the other side is doing. We have seen some very exciting air battles. It is nothing unusual to see anywhere from two to two dozen airplanes fighting and chasing each other in and out of the clouds as they try to get into position to fire—we can hear the "spitting" of their machine guns as they fire. Sometimes you can hear them fighting when they are above the clouds, too! And twice a very daring German pilot flew down over our position and turned his machine gun on us! We could hear the "whang and spit" of the bullets as they struck the ground within a few feet of us! He flew so low that we could see the black cross on the plane and see the pilot shooting at us! But they didn't stay long. They would just shoot down and fire and then away they'd go before we had a chance to shoot back at them.

You see, we are right out in the open with no trenches to protect us, and so we are an easy mark for anything like that! And the Germans have been sending over many shells, too! So the field around our position is all torn up with shell holes—some big ones, too. One of those big shells makes a noise like the rumble and roar of a freight train going about 1,000 miles [1609 kilometers] an hour! When we hear them coming we say, "Here comes another of the devil's fast freights!" And when they burst, a mountain of rocks and dirt shoots up in the air higher than the trees! They make a hole about eight feet [2.5 meters] deep and about fifteen feet [4.5 meters] in diameter. And shell fragments scatter for about 300 feet [91 meters]. A shell fragment makes an awful wound, too, as it just tears a great hole in you, while a bullet just drills a clean round hole! So you can imagine what would happen if one of those shells should make a "direct hit" on our position!

There is, or rather was, a little town over in a clump of trees near here—now there isn't even a wall or a piece of a house standing. There are just broken bricks and pieces of plaster scattered around.

Another thrilling sight is to see the ammunition caissons [wagons] bringing up ammunition. Each caisson is drawn by six horses hitched in teams of two, and a man rides the left horse of each team. They generally come up just before dark and you can see the long line of caissons stretching away down the road, and coming at a gallop. The horses are covered with sweat and lather when they get here! We unload the caissons in a hurry and then they start back again, at a gallop, as the Germans are apt to shell the road at any time—so they are running for their lives! In fact the other night the road was shelled when they were bringing up ammunition! The driver swung off the road and came through the fields, spurring the horses to even greater speed!

This kind of warfare means a great many killed and wounded. But I prefer it, as it is the only way to end the war—just kill off all the Germans!

I have given you details and described disagreeable things, but I just want you to know what war is and what it means for us and for everyone!

But I think it's great sport and certainly am glad I'm here and taking part in this—one of the greatest battles the world has ever known.

Love,
E.J. Canright,
Medical Department
149th Field Artillery
A.E.F.,
A.P.O. No. 715

CELEBRATING THE ARMISTICE— IN FRANCE

For Americans the end of the war came less than two years after they entered the conflict. For Europeans the agony of the war had lasted longer —for four long years. During this time, millions of people had died and millions of others had suffered great hardships.

Mildred Aldrich, an American news reporter and writer, spent the war years living in France. She had worked for several years as a reporter and editor in Boston, then had moved to France in 1898 and bought a small house in the country near the Marne River. The Battle of the Marne in 1914 was fought in the area near her house. In this selection, she tells of the end of the war and how she and her French neighbors reacted to the news of peace.

What does Mildred Aldrich think about the armistice terms? Would you say that her outlook is more French than American? More American than French? A mixture of both?

Adapted from Mildred Aldrich, When Johnny Comes Marching Home. *Boston: Small, Maynard and Company, 1919.*

Saturday morning [November 9] we read about the armistice in the newspapers. Stiff as the terms were, we knew that Germany could not hesitate, just as we knew that the French would not discuss. I had only to look at the two maps I had studied two days before to know that Germany was forced to accept even if the terms had been harder. Yet I could have cried to think it had come so soon. I knew that once Germany had, with Wilson's aid, been allowed to talk, the armistice was inevitable. Beaten to the point where its case was hopeless, and where the final surrender of its army was in sight, it could save itself from invasion only by accepting any terms proposed. As for the Allies, no matter how they felt, they could hardly go on with the fighting once Germany gave in. Much as one grieved that the surrender was made with Germany still the invader, the order to "cease firing" meant the saving of thousands of lives.

The expected news came early Monday morning. As we expected, the Germans had accepted the hard terms of the "unconditional surrender," and the order had been given to "cease firing" at eleven. We had known it would come, but the fact that the order had been given rather surprised us. To realize that it was over! How could one in a minute?

I was up early to wait for the papers. It was a perfectly white day. The whole world was covered with the first frost and wrapped in a deep white fog, as if the huge flag of truce were wound around it. I went out on the lawn and looked toward the north. The fog was so thick, I could not see as far as the hedge. Yet out there I knew the guns were still firing. Between them and me lay such devastation as even the imagination cannot exaggerate, and such suffering and pain as human understanding can but partly understand. Four years and four months—and how much is still before us? The future has its job laid out for it. Are ordinary humans capable of handling it?

Later, as I stood near the road, I heard footsteps running toward me on the frozen ground. Out of the fog came Marin, the town crier, with his drum on his back. He waved his drumsticks at me as he ran, and cried, "I am coming as fast as I can, Madame. We are ringing our bells at four—at the same time Clemenceau reads the terms in the Chamber of Deputies and Lloyd George reads them in London." As he reached the corner just above my gate he swung his drum round and beat it like mad.

It did not take two minutes for all our little village to gather about him. In a loud, clear voice he read the order of the day, which officially announced that the war had ended at eleven o'clock. The inhabitants of the town were authorized to hang out their flags, light up their windows, and join in a dignified celebration of the liberation of France. Then he slowly lifted his cap in his hand as he read the last phrase, which begged them not to forget to pray for the brave soldiers who had given their lives that this day might be, and not to forget that to many among us this day of rejoicing was also a day of mourning.

There was not a cheer.

Amelie told the whole story when she dropped on a bench at the kitchen door, and with dry eyes and tightened lips exclaimed, "Finally! It's over. We beat them!"

After all, that was the important thing. It was not what we hoped for, or what we wanted, but the killing was over. I don't see how the French, on whose bodies and souls the burden had fallen, can, even in their disappointment, have any other thought just now.

Less than an hour after Marin passed over the hill, the mayor and his associates arrived to present me formally with the thanks of the town for the part I had taken in sharing the hard days with them. I did so wish again for some magic means by which every one of the American women who had stretched out generous helping hands across the sea to this little place could have seen the scene, and heard me try to make a French speech. I stumbled a bit, but the French are good at understanding. As far as their faces went I might have been rivaling the best French speaker. I put the honors where they were due. But in spite of all I said, for the moment I was to them—America.

They all went out on the lawn before leaving to look off toward the battlefield. It was still covered with fog, although the mist had thinned. "There," said the mayor, making a sweeping gesture toward the north, "there after all it was decided, perhaps, right under our eyes. Without that victory, all the aid the States sent us later would have been in vain." Perhaps. At any rate that is still the opinion of everyone.

Then we all shook hands at the gate, and they hurried back to ring the church bells to salute the victory. I did not go with them, as they suggested. I was content to sit here on the spot where I had watched in those hot days of September 1914.

The mist was lifting slightly. All along the valley the bells rang for hours, cut at regular intervals by the booming of the guns at the forts.

I sat on the lawn alone, thinking that all over France—wherever the bells had not been destroyed—this same scene was being carried out. I was sure that in Paris, where Clemenceau was standing before the deputies, his reading of the terms of the armistice was being emphasized by guns saluting the victory and by cheers in the streets.

WILSON DEFENDS THE LEAGUE

At the end of World War I, President Wilson attended the Versailles Conference, where he helped to write the peace treaty. When he returned home in 1919, he asked Congress to ratify the treaty. However, there was a bitter debate in the United States over whether the Senate should ratify the Treaty of Versailles, and thus approve America's joining the League of Nations. Many Senators were opposed to the United States' joining the League. They feared that membership in the League would involve America too deeply in European politics—perhaps even lead the nation into another war.

President Wilson, however, believed strongly in the League. As a result he decided to appeal directly to the American people for support. On a cross-country speaking tour in the fall of 1919, he made thirty-seven speeches in twenty-nine cities. But the tour ended suddenly when Wilson suffered a stroke. The following selection is from a speech Wilson gave on September 4, at the beginning of his speaking tour.

Why, according to Wilson, is the League "unique in the history of humankind"? What arguments does he offer to urge the United States Congress to ratify the treaty?

Adapted from War and Peace: The Public Papers of Woodrow Wilson, *Vol. 1, Harper & Row, Publishers, 1927.*

After all the discussion of the Treaty of Versailles, perhaps you would like to know what is in it. I find it very difficult in reading some of the speeches that I have read to form any idea about that great document. It is a document unique in the history of the world for many reasons. I think I cannot do you or the peace of the world a better service than by pointing out to you what this treaty contains and what it seeks to do.

In the first place, my fellow Americans, it seeks to punish one of the greatest wrongs in history, the wrong which Germany sought to do to the world and to civilization. Germany attempted an intolerable thing, and it must be punished for the attempt. The terms of the treaty are severe, but they are not unjust.

I can state that the people associated with me at the Peace Conference in Paris had it in their hearts to do justice and not wrong. But they knew, perhaps with a greater sense of what had happened than we could possibly know, the many solemn agreements which Germany had disregarded, the long preparation it had made to defeat its neighbors, and the complete disregard it had shown for human rights. They had seen their lands destroyed by an enemy that devoted itself not only to the effort at victory, but to the effort at terror. There is a method of adjustment in that treaty by which the reparation shall not be pressed beyond the point which Germany can pay. But it will be pressed to the greatest point that Germany can pay—which is just, which is righteous. For, my fellow citizens, this treaty is not meant only to end this single war. It is meant as a notice to any government which in the future may attempt such a thing that humanity will unite to inflict the same punishment on it.

There is no national triumph sought in this treaty. There is no glory sought for any particular nation. The thought of the leaders collected around that peace table was of their people, of the sufferings that they had gone through, of the losses they had suffered. Let us never forget the purpose—the high purpose, the disinterested purpose—with which America lent its strength not for its own glory but for the defense of humanity.

As I said, this treaty was not intended only to end this war. It was intended to prevent any similar war. I wonder if some of the opponents of the League of Nations have forgotten the promises we made our people before we went to that peace table. We had taken men from every household, and we told mothers and fathers and sisters and wives and sweethearts that we were taking those men to fight a war which would end all wars. If we do not end wars, we are unfaithful to the loving hearts who suffered in this war.

That is what the League of Nations is for—to end this war justly, and then to serve notice on other governments which might consider trying to do the same things that Germany attempted. The League of Nations is the only thing that can prevent another dreadful catastrophe and fulfill our promises.

When people tell you, therefore, that the League of Nations is intended for some other purpose than this, answer: If we do not do this thing, we have neglected the central promise we made to our people. The rivalries of this world have not cooled. They have been made hotter than ever. The harness that is too unite nations is more necessary now than it ever was before. Unless there is this assurance of combined action before wrong is attempted, wrong will be attempted just as soon as the most ambitious nations can recover from the financial stress of this war.

Now, look at what else is in the treaty. It is unique in the history of humankind, because the heart of it is the protection of weak nations. There never was a congress of nations before that considered the rights of those who could not enforce their rights. There never was a congress of nations before that did not seek to bring about some balance of power by means of serving the strength and interest of the strongest powers concerned. This treaty says people have a right to live their own lives under the governments which they themselves choose to set up. That is the American principle, and I was glad to fight for it. If there is no League of Nations, the military point of view will win out in every instance, and peace will not last.

Some people have feared with regard to the League of Nations that we will be forced to do things we do not want to do. If the treaty were wrong, that might be so. But if the treaty is right, we will wish to preserve right. I think I know the feelings of our great people better than do some others I hear talk.

The heart of this treaty then, my fellow citizens, is not even that it punishes Germany. That is a temporary thing. It is that it corrects the age-old wrongs which characterized the history of Europe. There were some of us who wished that the treaty also would reach some other age-old wrongs. It was a big job. I do not say that we wished that it were bigger. There were other wrongs elsewhere than in Europe which, no doubt, ought to be righted, and some day will be righted, but which we could not include in the treaty because we could deal only with the countries that the war had affected.

Have you ever thought, my fellow citizens, about the real source of revolution? Revolutions do not spring up overnight. Revolutions come from the long suppression of the human spirit. Revolutions come because people know that they have rights and that they are disregarded. When we think of the future of the world in connection with this treaty, we must remember that one of the chief efforts of those who made it was to remove that anger from the heart of great peoples who had always been suppressed, who had always been the tools in the hands of governments not their own. The makers of the treaty knew that if these wrongs were not removed, there could be no peace in the world. This treaty is an attempt to right the history of Europe.

If I were to state what seems to me the central idea of this treaty, it would be this: Nations do not consist of their governments but of their people. That is a simple idea. It seems to us in America to go without saying. But, my fellow citizens, it was never the leading idea in any other international congress made up of the representatives of governments. They were always thinking of national policy, of national advantage, of the rivalries of trade, of the advantages of territorial conquest. There is nothing of those things in this treaty.

I have not come to debate the treaty. It speaks for itself, if you will let it. The arguments against it are directed against it with a great misunderstanding of it. Therefore, I am not going anywhere to debate the treaty. I am going to explain it. And I am going, as I do here today, to encourage you to assert the spirit of the American people in support of it. Do not let people pull it down. Do not let them misrepresent it. Do not let them lead this nation away from the high purposes with which this war was fought. When this treaty is accepted, soldiers will not have to cross the seas again. That is the reason I believe in it.

I say "when it is accepted," for it will be accepted. I have never had a moment's doubt of that. The only thing I have been impatient of has been the delay. Do you realize, my fellow citizens, that the whole world is waiting on America? The only country in the world that is trusted at this moment is the United States. The peoples of the world are waiting to see whether their trust is justified or not. That has been the reason for my impatience. I knew their trust was justified, but I resented the time that certain people wish to take in telling them so. We shall tell them so in a voice as true as any voice in history. In the years to come, people will be glad to remember that they had some part in the great struggle which brought about the fulfillment of the hopes of humankind.

SENATOR BORAH ATTACKS THE LEAGUE

The bitter debate over ratification of the Treaty of Versailles and joining the League of Nations lasted for many months. By the time the Senate voted in November 1919, forty-five amendments and three "reservations," or special clauses to protect American interests, had been added to the treaty. When the final vote was taken on November 19, the Senate rejected the treaty, and thus refused to have the United States join the League of Nations.

One of the leading foes of the treaty, Republican Senator William E. Borah of Idaho, delivered the following speech during the Senate debate over the treaty's approval. His speech clearly reflected the views of those Americans who opposed the treaty.

To what American tradition does Borah appeal? Why does he believe that the treaty represents a danger to the United States? How does he use American history to strengthen his case against the treaty?

Adapted from American Problems: A Selection of Speeches and Prophecies by William E. Borah, *Horace Green (ed.).* Reprinted by permission of Dodd, Mead & Company, Inc.

What is the result of this Treaty of Versailles? We are in the middle of all of the affairs of Europe. We have entangled ourselves with all European concerns. We have joined in alliance with all the European nations which have thus far joined the League, and all nations which may be admitted to the League. We are sitting there dabbling in their affairs and meddling in their concerns. In other words — and this comes to the question which is fundamental with me — we have surrendered, once and for all, the great policy of "no entangling alliances" upon which the strength of this Republic has been based for 150 years.

Will my friends who talk of reservations tell me where is the reservation in these articles which protects us against entangling alliances with Europe?

Will those who are differing over reservations tell me which one protects the doctrine laid down by our first President? That fundamental proposition is surrendered, and we are a part of European turmoils and conflicts from the time we enter this League.

You have put in here a reservation concerning the Monroe Doctrine. I think that, as far as language could protect the Monroe Doctrine, it has been protected. But as a practical matter, tell me honestly, as people familiar with the history of your country and of other countries, do you think that you can meddle in European affairs and keep Europe from meddling in your affairs?

There is another and even more pressing reason why I shall vote against this treaty. It endangers what I believe to be the underlying, the very first principles of this Republic. It is in conflict with the right of our people to govern themselves free from all restraint, legal or moral, by foreign powers. It challenges every principle of my political faith. If this faith were mine alone, you could accuse me of arrogance. But I am only being faithful to American ideals as they were created by those who built the Republic and as they have been extended throughout the years.

I will not, I cannot, give up my belief that America must, not alone for the happiness of its own people, but for the moral guidance and greater happiness of the world, be permitted to live its own life. Next to the tie which binds a person to his or her God is the tie which binds a person to his or her country. All schemes, all plans, however ambitious and fascinating they seem, which would compromise our country's freedom of action, I reject absolutely.

Senators, we should not close our eyes to the fact that democracy is something more than just a form of government by which society is restrained into free and orderly life. It is a moral and spiritual force as well. And these are things which live only in the air of liberty. The foundation upon which democracy rests is faith in the moral instincts of the people. Its ballot boxes, the vote, its laws and constitutions are but the outward sign of the deeper and more essential thing—a continuing trust in the moral purposes of the average man and woman.

When this is lost, your outward forms, however democratic in terms, are a mockery. You cannot mix the distinguishing virtues of a real republic with the destructive forces of the Old World and still preserve them. You cannot tie a government whose fundamental principle is that of liberty to a government whose first law is that of force and hope to preserve the former. These things are in constant conflict. One must in time destroy the other.

We may become one of the four dictators of the world, but we shall no longer be master of our own spirit. And what shall it profit us as a nation if we share with others the glory of world control but lose that fine sense of confidence in the people, the soul of democracy.

Look upon the scene as it is now presented. Behold the task we are to take on. Then think of the method by which we are to deal with this task. When this League is formed, four great powers representing the dominant people will rule half of the inhabitants of the globe as subject peoples—rule them by force, and we shall be a party to the rule of force. There is no other way by which you can keep people in subjection. You must either give them independence, recognize their rights as nations to live their own life and set up their own form of government. Or you must deny them these things by force. That is the scheme, the method proposed by the League.

We are told that this treaty means peace. Even so, I would not pay the price. Would you buy peace at the cost of any part of our independence? We could have had peace in 1776. The price was high, but we could have had it. James Otis, Sam Adams, John Hancock, and Joseph Warren were surrounded by those who encouraged peace and British rule. All through that long and trying struggle, there was a cry of peace—let us have peace.

We could have had peace in 1860. Lincoln was advised by people of great influence and wisdom to let our brothers—and, thank heaven, they are brothers—leave in peace. But the tender, loving Lincoln, bending under the fearful weight of almost certain civil war, an apostle of peace, refused to pay the price. A united country will praise his name forevermore—bless it because he refused peace at the price of national honor and national integrity. Peace upon any other basis than national independence, peace bought at the cost of any part of our national integrity, is fit only for slaves.

But your treaty does not mean peace—far, very far, from it. If we are to judge the future by the past, it means a war. Is there any guarantee of peace other than the guarantee which comes from the control of the war-making power by the people? Yet the people at no time and in no place have any voice in this scheme for world peace.

Can you hope for peace when love of country is disregarded in your scheme, when the spirit of nationality is rejected, even scoffed at? Your treaty in a dozen instances breaks the divine law of nationality. Peoples who speak the same language, kneel at the same ancestral tombs—moved by the same traditions and common hopes—are torn apart, broken in pieces, divided, and given to hostile nations. And this you call justice. No, your treaty means injustice. It means slavery. It means war. And to all this you ask this Republic to become a party. You ask it to abandon the principles under which it has grown to power and accept the principles of repression and force.

I turn from this scheme based upon force to another scheme, planned 143 years ago in old Independence Hall, in the city of Philadelphia, based upon liberty. I like it better. I have become so used to believing in it that it is difficult for me to reject it.

America will live its own life. The independence of this Republic will have its defenders. Thousands have suffered and died for it, and their sons and daughters will not be betrayed into the hands of foreigners. The noble face of our first President, so familiar to every boy and girl, looking out from the walls of the Capitol in stern reproach, will call those who come here for public service to a reckoning. The people of our beloved country will finally speak, and we will return to the policy which we now abandon. America, free in spite of all these things, will continue its mission in the cause of peace, of freedom, and of civilization.

Unit Five

The "Golden Twenties" and the New Deal

1920-1941

CHAPTER 13
A DECADE OF PROSPERITY ENDS IN A CRASH

BLACK AMERICA'S GREAT MIGRATION

For black Americans, the war years and the period following World War I were a time of tremendous change. During these years, black families in ever-increasing numbers moved from the South to the cities of the North. Nearly one million black Americans took part in this so-called "Great Migration."

Why did so many people leave the South? Crop failures caused by floods and the boll weevil (an insect that destroys cotton) led to great hardships, especially for farm workers. At the same time, northern factories needed workers to replace those who had left to serve in World War I. Thus the hope of greater opportunities, higher wages, and a better life caused more and more black Americans to move to the North. In this selection, Charles Johnson, a black sociologist, tells us about the Great Migration.

How does Johnson describe the migration? What are some of the things that caused it? In what ways did the new Negro culture in the North differ from that of the South?

Adapted from Charles S. Johnson, "The New Frontage on American Life," in Alain Locke, ed., The New Negro. *New York: Albert and Charles Boni, 1925.*

The cities of the North—stern, impersonal, and enticing—needed people with strong muscles. Europe, suddenly at war, had stopped supplying them, when thousands of blacks came from the South like a silent shadow. There were 500,000 people in the first three-year period. They had come first to the little towns of the South, then to the cities near the towns. Sooner or later, they boarded a special train bound for the North, to go to the cities which attracted them, to their bright lights and high wages, crowds, excitement, and struggle for life.

There was Chicago in the West, known far and wide for its great stockyards; Chicago, remembered for the fairyland wonders of the World's Fair; home of mills yelling for workers.

And there was Pittsburgh, gloomy and cheerless, and the nearby towns of Bethlehem, Duquesne, and Homestead. One railroad line

569

brought in 12,000 new laborers free. The railroads, the vast construction projects of the state, and the large mills wanted workers.

And there was New York City, with its Harlem—the Mecca of Negroes the country over. Old families, brownstone mansions, a step from Broadway. It had factories and docks, large clothing industries, and buildings to be "superintended." It was a land of opportunity for musicians, actors, and those who wanted to succeed, and the national headquarters of everything but the government.

And there was Cleveland, with a faint southern feeling but with iron mills; St. Louis, with great foundries, brick and pottery works; Detroit, the automobile center, with its high wages reflecting the daring economic policies of Henry Ford; Akron and its rubber; Philadelphia, with its comfortable old traditions; and the many little industrial towns where fabulous wages were paid.

Migrations, says one expert, are nearly always due to the influence of an idea. In the case of the Negroes, it was not just an idea, but an idea that was made possible. By tradition, Negroes are rural types. Their usual occupation is agriculture. Their mental and social habits have been adjusted to such an economy.

The South has few cities. The life of the section is based not on manufacturing but on the soil—and more than anything else, the fluffy white bolls of cotton. Cotton is King. When it lives and does well, there is comfort for the owners. When it fails, as is most often the case, a heavy heel twists on the neck of the black tenant farmer. The sharecropping system causing dishonesty and holding Negroes always in debt and almost in slavery; the fierce hatred of poor whites in frightened and desperate competition; the cruelty of the masters; the dullness of rural life; the hope for something better; distant flashes of a new country, calling—these were the soil in which the idea of migration took root and flowered. There was no slow, deliberate making of plans, or inspired leadership, or forces dark and mysterious. To each person in his or her setting came an impulse and an opportunity.

There was Jeremiah Taylor, of Bobo, Mississippi, old and worn out and resigned to his farm. One of his sons came in one morning with the report that folks were leaving "like Judgment day." He had seen a labor man who promised a free ticket to a railroad camp up North. Jeremiah went to town, half doubting,

and came back excited and decided. His son left, he followed. In four months his wife and two daughters packed their possessions, sold their chickens, and joined them.

Into George Horton's barber shop in Hattiesburg, Mississippi, came a white man from the North. Said he: "The colored folks owe a debt to the North because it freed them. The North owes a debt to the colored folks because after freeing them it took away their living. Now, this living is offered with interest and a new birth of liberty. Will the colored people live up to their side of the bargain?" The deciding argument was free transportation. Hattiesburg contributed forty men.

And there was Joshua Ward, who had prayed for these times and now saw God cursing the land and stirring up his people. He would ask for his anger no longer.

Rosena Shephard's neighbor's daughter went away. Silence for six weeks. Then she wrote that she was earning $2 a day packing sausages. "If that lazy, good-for-nothing gal can make $2 a day, I can make $4," and Mrs. Shephard left.

Clem Woods could not tolerate any fellow's getting ahead of him. He did not want to leave his job and couldn't explain why he wanted to go North. His boss proved to him that his chances were better at home. But every person who left added to his restlessness. One night a train passed through with two coaches of men from New Orleans. Said one of them: "Good-by, I'm bound for the promised land," and Clem got aboard.

Mrs. Selina Lennox was slow to do anything, but she was a friendly person. The emptiness of her street wore upon her. No more screaming, darting children, no more bustle of men going to work or coming home. The familiar greetings of women who were shopping, the smell of boiled food—all these were gone. Mobile Street, once noisy, was now very quiet, as if some disaster threatened. Now and then the Italian storekeeper, confused and sad, would walk to the middle of the street and look first up and then down and walk back into his store again. Mrs. Lennox left.

George Scott wanted more "free liberty" and accepted a railroad ticket from a stranger who always talked in whispers and seemed to have plenty of money.

Dr. Alexander H. Booth's practice declined. Some of his patients who had left and had owed him money for a long time paid up with an air of superiority that made him very angry. In their letters they said such things as "home ain't nothing like this" or "nobody who has any grit would stay." The doctor left.

Jim Casson in Grabor, Louisiana, had paid his poll taxes, his state and parish taxes. And yet there was no school for his children.

Miss Jamesie Towns taught fifty of the colored tenants' children for four months, out near Fort Valley, Georgia. Her salary was reduced from $16.80 to $14.40 a month.

* * * *

There is a new type of Negro—a city Negro. He is being shaped out of strangely different elements of the general background. This is a fact overlooked by students of human behavior. In ten years, Negroes have been actually transplanted from one culture to another.

Once there were personal and close relations, in which individuals were in contact most of their lives. Now there are group relations, in which the whole structure is broken, and people are in contact at only one or two points of their lives. The old controls are no longer expected to operate. The newcomers are forced to change their lives.

With Negroes in more industrial contact and competition with white workers of greater experience and numbers, bad feelings build up. The fierce economic fears of workers in competition are increased by racial differences. Beneath the disastrous East St. Louis conflict was a boiling anger toward southern Negroes coming in to "take white people's jobs."

Here lies one of the points of highest tension in race relations. White workers have not, except in a few instances, overcome hatred based on race enough to allow Negro workers the same privileges they themselves enjoy. While refusing Negroes admission to their unions, they grow furious over their dangerous borings from the outside. Where there is agitation and unrest, there is change. Old traditions are being shaken and rooted up by new ideas. In this the year of our Lord 1925, extending across the entire country, seventeen cities are in violent agitation over Negro residence areas. Once Negroes were silent. Now they are more apt to act with conviction. Claude McKay, the young Negro poet, caught the mood of the new Negro in this, and he turned it into fiery verse which Negro newspapers copied and recopied:

If we must die, let it not be like hogs,
Hunted and penned in an inglorious spot.

Less is heard of the two historic "schools of thought" clashing over the question of industrial training versus higher education for the Negro. Both are, sensibly, now taken for granted as quite necessary. The industrial schools are concerned with adjusting their courses to the new fields of industry in which Negro workers will play an increasing role. The universities must meet the demand for trained Negroes in business, the professions, and the arts. The level of education has been raised through the work of both types of schools.

Thus the new frontier of Negro life is spread out in a jagged, uneven, but progressive pattern. For a group historically kept back and not readily assimilated, contact with its surrounding culture causes uneven results. There is no fixed racial level of culture. There are as many differences in culture, education, and sophistication among Negroes as between the races. It is likely that the culture which has both nourished and abused Negro strivings will, in the end, be enriched by them.

STOCK MARKET FEVER

During the 1920's, more and more Americans invested their money in stocks. So many people were buying and selling stocks that the New York Stock Exchange had to close down several times during its regular Saturday trading sessions. This was the only way that the brokers' clerks could catch up each week with all the paper work required by the enormous volume of stocks being bought and sold. It seemed at times that everyone was speculating in the stock market.

In this selection, newspaper writer Franklin P. Adams makes fun of this frenzied stock buying in a poem called "American Bores Common."

Why is the author critical of the great increases in buying and selling stocks? Did he himself invest in the stock market? Why or why not?

"American Bores Common, Ex. Div.," from Christopher Columbus and Other Patriotic Verses by Franklin P. Adams. Copyright 1931 by Franklin P. Adams. Reprinted by permission of Viking Penguin, Inc.

In days of not so very old
Bores did I know a million fold.
They used to tell me this or that:

How cheap—or dear—they'd leased a flat;
They used to tell me of That Kid—
What little Elsie said or did;
They used to tell me of the trains
Between New York and Tiger Plains,
And of how fast they made the trip
From house to office—zippety zip!
Of girls they used to talk—and boast.
Of games, perhaps, they talked the most;
Of fights and baseball games they'd seen;
Of single strokes from tee to green;
Of backhand drives and passing shots;
Of hands that won stupendous pots.
They used to tell, with silly pride,
How yesterevening they were Fried.
They used to tell, the bores supreme,
Of this or that Uncanny Dream.
But nowadays the bores I find
Are of a single, standard kind:
For every person I may meet
At lunch, at clubs, upon the street,
Tells me, in endless wordy tales,
Of market purchases and sales;
Of how he bought a single share
Of California Prune and Pear;
Or how he sold at 33
A million shares of T. & T.
How McAvoy and Katzenstein [stock market
    brokers]
Told him to sell at 99;
Of thousands lost and millions made
In this or that egregious trade;
How bright he was to buy or sell
FP, GM, X, or GL.
In herds, in schools, in droves, in flocks
The men and women talk of stocks.
They talk in couples and in crowds,
And I, whose head is in the clouds,
Who hold that Mind is more than Matter,
Am bored by all this market patter.
How long can any land be sane
With all its mind on moneyed gain?
And whither, prithee, do we drift
Whose port is Gain instead of Thrift?
It makes me ill, and even sicker
To see so many watch the ticker.

To Mammon bends the national knee;
What fools these stock-mad mortals be!
Ill fares, as Goldsmith [a British writer of
    the 1700's] used to gab it,
The land where everyone's a Babbitt [a per-
    son who strives for money and success, ig-
    noring artistic and intellectual values].
But what a zob they made of me!

I sold a stock at 43
A month ago, and up to date
It's selling at 388.

Ill fares the land, as said before
Where everyone's a stock-mad bore.

WHAT CAUSED THE DEPRESSION?

The stock market crash of October 1929 was the beginning of the Great Depression that lasted through the 1930's. During this period of hard times, banks and businesses closed down and many millions of Americans were forced out of work.

What caused the depression? Economists have developed many conflicting theories about the direct and indirect causes of the depression. Some blame the lack of prosperity in American agriculture during the 1920's and the farmers' reduced buying power. Some blame the unequal distribution of income. Others blame overinvestment in the stock market. Still others feel that the huge government debts among nations put too much pressure on the world economy.

The following selection was written by John Kenneth Galbraith, a present-day economist. In it he gives his explanation of this crisis in America's economy.

What explanations of the depression does Galbraith disagree with? What evidence does he give to support his statement that the economy in 1929 was "basically unsound"?

Adapted from The Great Crash: 1929 *by John Kenneth Galbraith. Copyright 1954, © 1955, 1961 by John Kenneth Galbraith. Reprinted by permission of Houghton Mifflin Company.*

The collapse of the stock market in the autumn of 1929 was a natural result of the speculation that went before. The only question about that speculation was how long it would last. Sometime, sooner or later, confidence in increasing stock values would weaken. When this happened, some people would sell. There would be a rush to unload. This was the way past speculative orgies had ended. It was the way the end came in 1929. It is the way speculation will end in the future.

We do not know why a great speculative orgy occurred in 1928 and 1929. The long accepted explanation that credit was easy and so people were forced to borrow money to buy common stocks on margin is obviously nonsense. On many occasions before and since, credit has been easy, and there has been no speculation whatever. Furthermore, much of the 1928 and 1929 speculation occurred using money borrowed at interest rates which for years before, and in any period since, would have been considered exceptionally high. Money, by ordinary standards, was tight in the late 1920's.

Far more important than the rate of interest and the supply of credit is the mood. Speculation on a large scale requires a sense of confidence and optimism. People must also have faith in the good intentions of others, for it is through others that they will get rich. When people are cautious, questioning, or suspicious, they resist speculative enthusiasms.

Savings must also be plentiful. Speculation, however it may rely on borrowed funds, must be nourished in part by those who participate. If savings are growing rapidly, people will be willing to risk some of it against the prospect of a good return. . . .

A great many people have always felt that a depression was inevitable in the 1930's. There had been (at least) seven good years; now, by a law of compensation, there would have to be seven bad ones.

There is also the belief that economic life is governed by an inevitable rhythm. After a certain time, prosperity destroys itself and depression corrects itself. In 1929 prosperity, in accordance with the law of the business cycle, had run its course.

Neither of these beliefs can be seriously supported. The 1920's, by being comparatively prosperous, did not call for the 1930's to be depressed. In the past, good times have given way to less good times and less good or bad to good. But change is normal in a capitalist economy. No inevitable rhythm required the collapse of 1930–40.

Finally, the high production of the 1920's did not, as some have suggested, outrun the wants of the people. During these years people were indeed being supplied with an increasing volume of goods. But there is no evidence that they had no more desire for automobiles, clothing, travel, recreation, or even food. On the contrary, all later evidence showed (given the income to spend) a capacity for a large further increase in consumption.

What, then, were the causes of the depression?

There seems little question that in 1929 the economy was fundamentally unsound. This is a circumstance of first-rate importance. Many things were wrong, but five weaknesses seem to have had an especially close bearing on the disaster. They are:

1. *The bad distribution of income.* In 1929 the rich were clearly rich. It seems certain that the 5 percent of the population with the highest incomes in that year received approximately one third of all personal income. The proportion of personal income received in the form of interest, dividends, and rent—the income, broadly speaking, of the well-to-do—was about twice as great as in the years following World War II.

This highly unequal distribution of income meant that the economy was dependent on a high level of investment or a high level of luxury consumer spending or both. The rich cannot buy great quantities of bread. If they are to get rid of what they receive it must be on luxuries or through investment in new plants and new projects. Both luxury and investment spending are subject to wider changes than the bread and rent outlays of the $25-a-week worker. This high-bracket spending and investment was especially open, one may assume, to the crushing news from the stock market in October of 1929.

2. *The bad corporate structure.* . . . American business in the 1920's had opened its hospitable arms to an exceptional number of promoters, grafters, swindlers, imposters, and frauds. In the long history of such activities, there was a kind of flood tide of corporate theft.

3. *The bad banking structure.* The banking structure of the United States was weak. When one bank failed, the assets of others were frozen while depositors elsewhere had a warning to go and ask for their money. Thus one failure led to other failures, and these spread with a domino effect. Even in the best of times local misfortune or isolated mismanagement could start such a chain reaction. (In the first six months of 1929, 346 banks failed in various parts of the country; their deposits totaled nearly $115 million.) When income, employment, and values fell as the result of a depression, bank failures could quickly become an epidemic.

4. *The doubtful state of the foreign balance.* During World War I, the United States became a creditor nation, rather than a debtor nation. In the ten years following the war, the surplus

of exports over imports, which once had paid the interest and principal on loans from Europe, continued. The high tariffs, which restricted imports and helped to create this surplus of exports, remained.

Before the war, payments on interest and principal had in effect been deducted from the trade balance. Now that the United States was a creditor, they were added to this balance. During most of the 1920's, the difference was covered by cash—that is, gold payments to the United States—and by new private loans by the United States to other countries. But countries could not make up for their bad trade balance with increased payments of gold, at least not for long. This meant that they had to increase their exports to the United States, reduce their imports, or not pay their past loans. President Hoover and the Congress moved quickly to get rid of the first possibility—that the accounts would be balanced by larger imports—by sharply increasing the tariff. Accordingly, debts, including war debts, were not paid and there was a decline in American exports. The reduction was not great in relation to the total output of the American economy, but it contributed to the general suffering and was especially hard on farmers.

5. *The poor state of economic knowledge.* . . . It seems certain that the economists of the late 1920's and early 1930's were almost determined to be wrong. In the months and years following the stock market crash, they gave advice that was constantly on the side of measures that would make things worse. Asked how the government could best help economic recovery, the sound and responsible adviser suggested that the budget should be balanced. Both political parties agreed on this. . . .

A commitment to a balanced budget meant there could be no increase in government spending to expand purchasing power and relieve suffering. It meant there could be no further tax reduction. But taken in the strictest sense it meant much more. From 1930 on the budget was far out of balance. Balance, therefore, meant an increase in taxes, a reduction in spending, or both. The balanced budget was not the only restraint on government policy. There was also the fear of "going off" the gold standard and, most surprisingly, of risking inflation. . . .

It is in light of the above weaknesses of the economy that the role of the stock market crash in the great tragedy of the 1930's must be seen. The collapse in securities values affected first the wealthy and the well-to-do. In the world of 1929 this was an important group. Its members spent a large proportion of the consumer income. They controlled the greatest share of personal saving and investment. Anything that struck at the spending or investment by this group would of necessity have broad effects on spending and income in the economy at large. . . .

The stock market crash was also an exceptionally effective way of exploiting the weaknesses of the corporate structure. Many companies were forced by the crash to cut down on spending. Their later collapse destroyed both the ability to borrow and the willingness to lend for investment.

The crash was also effective in bringing to an end the foreign lending by which international accounts had been balanced. Now the accounts had, in the main, to be balanced by reduced exports. . . .

Finally, when the misfortune had struck, the attitudes of the time kept anything from being done about it. This, perhaps, was the worst feature of all. Some people were hungry in 1930 and 1931 and 1932. Others feared that they might go hungry. Everyone suffered from a sense of complete hopelessness. Nothing, it seemed, could be done. And given the ideas which controlled policy, nothing could be done.

If the economy had been basically sound in 1929, the effect of the great stock market crash might have been small. But business in 1929 was not sound. On the contrary, it was exceedingly fragile. It was open to the kind of blow it received from Wall Street. . . .

HOOVER'S "AMERICAN PLAN"

As the United States sank deeper and deeper into the worst depression in its history, Americans searched for workable solutions to their economic problems. The nation had never before faced such widespread poverty and so much suffering. But President Hoover believed the nation was suffering only from "frozen confidence" and that prosperity was "just around the corner." Because of this outlook, Hoover tried to use traditional methods to deal with the crisis. Although he realized that some government action was necessary, he was only willing to take limited measures, such as helping to provide some new jobs and making loans to businesses.

In the following speech of June 1931, Hoover outlined his views on how to deal with the depression. Does Hoover oppose or favor the idea of government planning? What argument does he use to support his position? Do you agree or disagree with his arguments? Explain.

Adapted from "Address to the Indiana Editorial Association," in State Papers and Other Public Writings of Herbert Hoover, *Vol. I, edited by William Starr Myers. Reprinted by permission of the Herbert Hoover Foundation.*

We have many citizens insisting that we produce an advance "plan" for the future development of the United States. They demand that we produce it right now. I presume the "plan" idea is an infection from the slogan of the "five-year-plan" through which Russia is struggling to save itself from ten years of starvation and misery.

I am able to propose an American plan to you. We plan to take care of a 20 million increase in population in the next twenty years. We plan to build for them 4 million new and better homes, thousands of new and still more beautiful city buildings, thousands of factories. We plan to increase the capacity of our railways, to add thousands of miles of highways and waterways, to install 25 million electrical horsepower, to grow 20 percent more farm products. We plan to provide new parks, schools, colleges, and churches for these 20 million people. We plan more leisure for men and women and better opportunities for its enjoyment.

We not only plan to provide for all the new generation. We shall, by scientific research and invention, lift the standard of living of the whole population. We plan to secure a greater distribution of wealth, a decrease in poverty, and a great reduction in crime. And this plan will be carried out if we just keep on giving the American people a chance. Its moving force is in the character and spirit of our people. They have already done a better job for 120 million people than any other nation in all history.

Some groups believe this plan can only be carried out by a fundamental, a revolutionary, change of method. Other groups believe that any system must be the outgrowth of our character and traditions. They believe that we have established certain ideals over 150 years, upon which we must build rather than destroy.

If we analyze the ideas which have been put forward for handling our great national plan, they fall into two main types. The first holds that the major purpose of a nation is to protect the people and to give them equality of opportunity. It holds that the basis of all happiness is in the development of the individual, and that we should steadily build up cooperation among the people themselves to this end.

The other idea is that we shall, directly or indirectly, regiment the population into a bureaucracy to serve the state. It holds that we should use force instead of cooperation in planning, and thereby direct every person as to what may or may not be done.

These ideas present themselves in practical questions which we have to answer. Shall we abandon the philosophy and beliefs of our people for 150 years by turning to a belief that is foreign to our people? Shall we establish a giveaway from the federal treasury? Shall we undertake federal ownership and operation of public utilities instead of regulating them? Shall we protect our people from the lower standards of living of foreign countries? Shall the government, except in temporary national emergencies, enter into competition with its citizens? Shall we regiment our people by extending the arm of bureaucracy into a great many affairs?

Our immediate task as a people is to defeat the forces of economic disruption and pessimism that have swept over us. The duty of government in these times is to use its agencies and influence to strengthen our economic institutions; to inspire cooperation in the community so as to keep up good will and keep our country free from disorder and conflict; to cooperate with the people so that the deserving shall not suffer; and to strengthen the foundations of a better and stronger national life. These have been the objectives of my administration in dealing with this, the greatest crisis the world has ever known. I shall stick with them.

CHAPTER 14
THE GREAT DEPRESSION AND THE NEW DEAL

ROOSEVELT ON GOVERNMENT AND THE ECONOMY

In 1932 the Democratic Party nominated Franklin D. Roosevelt as its candidate for President. Roosevelt had served as Assistant Secretary of the Navy under President Wilson and had become governor of New York in 1928. But he was not well known to many Americans when he began his Presidential election campaign. His campaign travels to all parts of the nation and his speeches promising to act immediately to end the depression won him victory in the 1932 election.

In his Inaugural Address, Roosevelt promised "a new deal for the American people," and he outlined his program for ending the depression. He believed that the Great Depression was a grave crisis that had to be fought with bold new governmental programs. In the following speech delivered in San Francisco on September 23, 1932, Roosevelt summarized his ideas about what the role of the federal government should be in ending the crisis.

According to Roosevelt, what are the two basic economic rights of all Americans? How can they be guaranteed by business? By government?

Adapted from The Public Papers and Addresses of Franklin D. Roosevelt, *Vol. I, published by Random House, Inc.*

I want to speak not of politics but of government. I want to speak not of parties but of universal principles. They are not political, except in that larger sense in which a great American once defined politics—that nothing in all of human life is unrelated to the science of politics.

A look at the situation today indicates only too clearly that equality of opportunity as we have known it no longer exists. Our industrial system is built. The problem just now is whether under existing conditions it is not overbuilt. Our last frontier has long since been reached. There is practically no more free land. More than half of our people do not live on farms, and they cannot make a living by cultivating their own property. There is no safety valve in the form of a Western frontier to which those thrown out of work by the Eastern economic machines can go for a new start. We are not able to invite immigrants from Europe to share our endless plenty. We are now providing a drab living for our own people.

Our system of constantly rising tariffs has at last reacted against us. It has closed our Canadian frontier on the north, our European markets on the east, many of our Latin-American markets to the south, and a sizable part of our Pacific markets on the west.

Just as freedom to farm has ended, so also opportunity in business has narrowed. It still is true that people can start small businesses, trusting their own shrewdness and ability to keep ahead of competitors. But area after area has been taken over altogether by the great corporations. Even in the fields which still have no large companies, the small operator starts under a handicap. The statistics of the past 30 years show that the independent business owner is running a losing race. Perhaps he is forced into bankruptcy. Perhaps he cannot get credit. Perhaps he is "squeezed out" by highly organized corporate competitors—as your corner grocery store owner can tell you.

Recently a careful study was made of the concentration of business in the United States. It showed that our economic life is dominated by some 600 corporations that control two thirds of American industry. The other third is shared by 10 million small businesses. More striking still, it appears that if the process of concentration goes on at the same rate, at the end of another century all American industry will be controlled by a dozen corporations, run by perhaps a hundred people.

Clearly, all this calls for us to think over our values. A builder of more industrial plants, a creator of more railroad systems, an organizer of more corporations, is as likely to be a danger as a help. The day of the great financial promoters to whom we granted anything if they would build or develop is over. Our task now is not discovery or exploitation of natural resources or producing more goods. It is the less dramatic task of managing resources and businesses already in existence. We need to get back foreign markets for our surplus production, and solve the problem of underconsumption. We must adjust production to consumption, distribute wealth and products more fairly, and adapt existing economic organizations to the service of the people. The day of enlightened management has come.

In older times the central [national] government was first a place of refuge, and then a threat. In the same way, in our present economic system the huge corporation is no longer a servant but a danger. I would draw the parallel one step farther. We did not think, when national government became a threat in the 1700's, that we should abandon the principle of national government. Nor today should we abandon the principle of corporations, just because their power can be abused. In other times we dealt with the problem of an overly ambitious central government by changing it gradually into a constitutional democratic government. So today we are changing and controlling our economic units.

As I see it, the task of government in its relation to business is to help in developing an economic declaration of rights, an economic constitutional order. Happily, the times indicate that to create such an order not only is the proper policy of government, but is the only line of safety for our economic structures as well. We know now that these economic units cannot exist unless prosperity is uniform. Purchasing power must be well distributed throughout every group in the nation. That is why even the most selfish corporations would be glad to see wages raised and unemployment ended, and the Western farmer restored to prosperity. That is why some enlightened industries themselves try to limit the freedom of action of each business group within the industry in the common interest of all.

I feel that we are coming to see that private economic power is a public trust. I believe that in order to keep that power any individual or group must fulfill that trust. The people who have reached the top of American business life know this best. Happily, many of them urge that we adopt this greater social contract.

The terms of that contract are as old as the Republic, and as new as the new economic order.

Every person has a right to life. This means the right to make a comfortable living, a right that may not be denied. We have no actual famine. Our industrial and agricultural systems can produce enough and still have capacity to spare.

Every person has a right to individual property. This means a right to be assured of the safety of one's savings. In all thought of property, this right is supreme. All other property rights must give way to it.

These two requirements must be satisfied chiefly by the individuals who control the great industrial and financial concerns which dominate our industrial life. They are not business leaders, but rather princes of property. I am not prepared to say that the system which produces them is wrong. But I do say that they must take the responsibility which goes with the power. Many enlightened business leaders know this.

The responsible heads of finance and industry, instead of acting alone, must work together to achieve the common good. They must, where necessary, sacrifice this or that personal advantage and seek a general advantage. It is here that government comes in. Whenever the dishonest competitor or the reckless promoter refuses to join in achieving a goal recognized as being for the public welfare, the government may properly be asked to apply restraint. Likewise, if the group should ever use its collective power against the public welfare, the government must be swift to protect the public interest.

The government should take over the function of economic regulation only as a last resort when private initiative has finally failed. As yet there has been no final failure, because there has been no attempt.

The final goal of the Declaration of Independence was liberty and the pursuit of happiness. We have learned a great deal about both in the past hundred years. We know that individual liberty and individual happiness mean nothing unless both are achieved without one man's meat being another man's poison. We know that liberty which robs others of basic rights cannot receive governmental protection.

All this is a long, slow task. Human endeavor is not simple. Government includes the art of making a policy, and using political techniques to secure as much of that policy as will receive general public support. We must build toward the time when a major depression cannot occur again. If this means sacrificing the easy profits of inflationary booms, then let them go, and good riddance.

Faith in America, faith in our tradition of personal responsibility, faith in our institutions, faith in ourselves, demand that we recognize the new terms of the old social contract.

577

We shall fulfill them. We must do so. Otherwise, a rising tide of misery, caused by our common failure, will swamp us all. But failure is not an American habit. In the strength of great hope we must all share our common responsibility.

WPA AND THE ARTS

Enormous problems faced President Roosevelt when he took office in March of 1933. Millions of Americans were unemployed, thousands stood in "bread lines" for food every day. As part of the New Deal, Roosevelt planned programs to provide direct relief for the unemployed. Several government agencies also were set up to provide work for jobless Americans.

One of these agencies was the Works Progress Administration (WPA). The WPA provided jobs not only for unemployed factory and office workers but also for artists, writers, musicians, and actors. Through the Arts Projects, the WPA decorated post offices and other government buildings with murals. It performed free concerts, staged plays and musicals, and wrote a set of guidebooks about America. In this selection, writer Robert Bendiner describes the WPA Arts Projects.

What were the four main types of Arts Projects? What were their major accomplishments? Does the federal government offer aid to America's museums, theaters, and other cultural centers today? Do you think that it should? Explain.

Adaptation of "WPA, Willing Parton of the Arts," (pp. 178-200) in Just Around the Corner, *by Robert Bendiner. Copyright © 1967 by Robert Bendiner. Reprinted by permission of Harper & Row, Publishers, Inc.*

In the history of the world, few depression governments have given housewives free piano lessons. Fewer still have put thousands of artists to work. And before the 1930's probably none had given stage people an annual wage, even a small one, to put on free puppet shows and classical plays. But the New Deal did all of these things. In addition, it paid $90 a month to unemployed reporters, unpublished writers, skilled researchers, and others to prepare some 250 books about America.

It has been pointed out over and over that the Arts Projects, as these operations of the Works Progress Administration were known, produced no Mozarts or Da Vincis. Neither did they produce lasting works of drama or fiction. What they did do was to help many talented people through the hard times. And they exposed to those talents millions of Americans who would otherwise never have known their charms. This introduction of struggling artists helped to destroy in four years certain American myths that had been around for a hundred years—that painting had to be European to have merit, and required weath to be appreciated; that all concerts except those by the town band were in the nature of good works to which dutiful women dragged long-suffering husbands; and that except for four or five cities the American people required no theater at all.

Statistics are no key to quality, but they *can* point to a highly stimulated interest in music, painting, and plays. By the end of the 1930's, nearly 70 art centers were flourishing in communities where many art teachers had never before seen a professional painting. Some 60,000 Americans had taken painting lessons from government-paid artists. Offices and lobbies in government buildings across the land boasted murals and new paintings. Audiences estimated at 100 million people had heard some 150,000 free concerts, most of them by three dozen newly created symphony orchestras. And a half-million Americans each month had enrolled in free music classes, 40,000 in New York City alone.

A visiting English critic was amazed. "Accidentally WPA has dug up an extraordinary amount of talent," said Ford Madox Ford. "Art in America is being given its chance, and there has been nothing like it since before the Reformation."

Certainly a Reformation was not what Harry Hopkins [head of the WPA] and his aides had in mind when they thought of the Arts Projects. What interested them was the hope of creating a whole new idea of government relief. In three years the country had come a long way from the Hoover view that direct aid to the victims of flood or earthquake was right and proper but not aid to the victims of human-made economics. For a time, welfare was the answer, then work of any kind for any purpose. Now the time had come for "maintaining the morale and skills" of the unemployed by paying them to perform the work they could do best until private business was ready to rehire them.

While the Public Works Administration went on with its building, the newly planned

Works Progress Administration would serve human beings. WPA funds would be spent on people, not things. What they were to do would be determined by what they *could* do, not by what the community might lack in the way of parking lots or sewage disposal plants.

Carrying the idea further, WPA proposed to help *all* the jobless artists who might come to it for help, rather than just the truly gifted, who would most likely be the least in need. For years government agencies had hired the best artists, or those it considered such, to do murals and sculpture for its buildings. Now the problem was to employ not just the best, but also those who were merely good — in practice even those who were mediocre and sometimes those who were not very good, who also had to eat.

Of all Americans engaged in the arts in the 1930's, the worst off by far were show people [entertainers]. Some 40,000 show people were extremely poor. So it was that, of all the good works of the WPA, the Federal Theater Project had the greatest opportunity, made the biggest splash, and left the most vivid memories.

One of the great charms of the Federal Theater was that it really covered the country. WPA shows were not just for New York, Chicago, and San Francisco. They were also for Tacoma (Washington), Reading (Pennsylvania), and Timberline Lodge (Oregon), not to mention Gary (Indiana), Peoria (Illinois), and Red Bank (New Jersey). They brought theater to towns in the United States that had not seen live actors for years. And they were received with great enthusiasm.

Three other WPA efforts in the arts left more visible reminders than the Federal Theater. About the Music Project I know little beyond the story of a violinist in a WPA orchestra in Florida. He apologized to the audience, on behalf of himself and the other musicians, for the quality of their concert. Their hands were still stiff, he explained, from their previous relief job, which was building a highway. The lasting work that the Music Project did was to search out and record the real folk music of America — the songs of the Southern mountaineers, the Indian-flavored songs of early Oklahoma, the Cajun songs of Louisiana, and the African-inspired songs of the Mississippi bayous.

On the Art Project, as the painters' and sculptors' unit was called, nobody pretended that the quota of genius was high. Considering the varied talents it had to work with, the Art Project sensibly made no attempt to have everyone paint. Of the 4,000 to 5,000 federally enrolled artists, far fewer than half were engaged in painting pictures or sculpturing or doing murals. Many taught free art classes. Some took photographs of old and decaying American houses. Others worked on posters and stage sets for the Federal Theater.

But the Art Project's real monument was the Index of American Design. For this magnificent work, still widely used, some 400 people reproduced in oil and watercolor the native art with which Americans, from early settlers to late Victorians, had decorated their homes, their possessions, and themselves. Here appeared in all their brightness the scarlet tulips that enlivened the coffeepots of the Pennsylvania Dutch, the embroidery of seventeenth-century Massachusetts, and the wonderful carved figureheads from New England ships. It was this great work, with its 7,000 skillful illustrations, that convinced many Americans that we had a native art after all.

It was charged that the fourth of the federal projects in the arts, the WPA Writers' Project, had little to do with writers. True, the memorable names connected with it can be counted on the fingers. What passed for a Writers' Project was essentially what writer Bernard DeVoto called it, "a project for research workers." Happily, good writers and skilled journalists, headed by Henry Alsberg, its first national director, turned out the most colorful series of guides a nation could ask for. A one-time newspaper reporter, Alsberg felt that Americans might want to know more about places, people, and things in the United States than they could get from filling-station maps. There had not been a guide to America since 1909.

Alsberg's feeling was right. It fitted in, moreover, with the concept that ran through all the Arts Projects — namely, that given the talent available and the controversy that creative work might involve, their best contribution would be to expose Americans for the first time to true, detailed, and vivid information about America. The result was that the guides — one for each of the 48 states, 30 for major cities, and 20 others for great travel arteries like *U.S. One* and *The Oregon Trail* — were remarkably rich.

It was, all in all, a magnificent experiment and one that went far to support sculptor Gutzon Borglum's letter when the WPA was still a developing idea of Harry Hopkins: "I want to suggest that you make your aid to the creative ones among us greater, more effective in scope. You are not after masterpieces, and you should not be discouraged if you have many failures. The real success will be in the interest, the human interest, which you will awaken, and what that does to the nation's mind. I believe that's the door through which you can coax the soul of America back to interest in life." It certainly coaxed it over to a somewhat *different* life.

HOW SOCIAL SECURITY WAS BORN

Today, Americans take for granted many of the economic and social benefits provided by the federal government. Many of these programs began during the New Deal. One of the most significant programs was social security.

The idea of old-age and unemployment insurance had first been suggested during the progressive era. But the depression brought new demands for such a program. After two years of planning with members of Congress, the Roosevelt administration set up a program of old-age and unemployment insurance. This program, spelled out in the Social Security Act, was passed by Congress in 1935. In this selection, Frances Perkins — Secretary of Labor in President Roosevelt's cabinet and the first woman to serve in the cabinet — outlines how the social security law came about.

How was the social security bill's passage through Congress affected by personal factors? By public opinion? Do you think social security is a good program? Why or why not?

Adapted from The Roosevelt I Knew *by Frances Perkins. Copyright 1946 by Frances Perkins. Copyright © renewed 1974 by Susanna W. Coggeshall. Reprinted by permission of Viking Penguin, Inc.*

Before his inauguration in 1933, Roosevelt had agreed that we should explore at once methods for setting up unemployment and old-age insurance in the United States. Therefore, early in 1933, the President encouraged Senator Robert F. Wagner and Representative David J. Lewis, who were both deeply interested in the subject, to go ahead with their bill on unemployment insurance. The bill, in a rough draft, was offered frankly for educational purposes. It was hoped that in the course of holding hearings the Congressional committees and the introducers of the bill would work out a satisfactory unemployment insurance law.

The President asked me to discuss the matter in as many groups as possible. I began in the cabinet. I made a point of bringing it up at least at every second meeting. In time, the other cabinet members became sincerely and honestly interested.

Hearings were held before Congress. Effective people were invited to testify before the Congressional committees. I myself made over a hundred speeches in different parts of the country that year. I always stressed social insurance as one of the methods for helping the unemployed in times of depression and for preventing depressions. We encouraged others to talk and write about the subject.

The Wagner-Lewis bill in Congress covered only unemployment insurance, but there was a great demand for old-age insurance also. It was easy to add this feature — and politically almost necessary. The President began telling people he was in favor of adding old-age insurance clauses to the Wagner-Lewis bill and putting it through as one program.

A great deal of educational work was done in 1933. But by June 1934 the Wagner-Lewis bill had not reached committee agreement. There had been differences of opinion in the testimony and recommendations to Congress. We began to see that there must be further study and a more complete plan before the bill could be presented to Congress for action.

The President had put the program on the must list. But the weather grew hot and Congress was very tired. Roosevelt decided that it might be better to tell Congress that he would be happy to agree to their adjourning if they understood that he would have a study made during the summer and would present a full program on economic security on January 1 when Congress met again. Congress gladly agreed.

Since members of the cabinet had developed great interest in the social security program, I suggested that it might be well to have the study made by a cabinet committee. The President readily agreed. He saw at once that a program developed by a committee of the cabinet would be under his control. It would not be likely to get off into the kind of political discussion and publicity that might cause doubt and delay.

The members of the cabinet Committee on Economic Security appointed by the President were the Secretary of Labor [Frances Perkins], chairman; Secretary of Agriculture Henry Wallace; Secretary of the Treasury Henry Morgenthau; and Attorney General H. S. Cummings. Harry Hopkins was added because of his vital experience as administrator of the relief program.

It was evident to us that any system of social insurance would not relieve all poverty. Nor would it relieve the sufferings of the presently old and needy. Nevertheless, it was also evident that this was exactly the right time to look ahead to future problems of unemployment and unprotected old age. It was never, I think, suggested by any reasonable person that relief should be abandoned in favor of unemployment and old-age insurance, but it was thought that there could be a blend of the two.

I took pains to make certain that Roosevelt understood and pledged himself to support the program as we worked it out. It must be made clear that this technique of using a cabinet committee to develop the program for him did not mean that he was evading the great issue. I had more than one special conference with him about the subjects we would have to consider in the cabinet committee.

I asked him if he thought it best for me to be chairman, since the public knew I favored the general idea. Perhaps it would be better, from the point of view of Congress and the public, if the Attorney General were chairman.

He was quick in his response. "No, no. You care about this thing. You believe in it. Therefore I know you will back it more than anyone else, and you will drive it through. You will see that something comes out, and we must not delay. I am convinced. We must have a program by next winter and it must be in operation before many more months have passed."

I indicated to him that there were sound arguments, advanced by many thinkers, that since we were in the midst of deflation [a decline in prices, caused by a decrease in the supply of money, or in spending] the collection of any money for reserves, no matter by what method, would be further deflationary.

"We can't help that," he answered. "We have to get it started or it never will start."

He was aware that 1936 was not too far away, that there might be a change of administration, and that this program, which in his own mind was *his* program, would never be ac-

complished, or at least not for many years, if it were not put through immediately.

By the time the study was fully started, the President's imaginative mind had begun to work on it. At cabinet meetings and when he talked privately with a group of us, he would say, "You should make it simple – very simple. So simple that everybody will understand it. And what's more, there is no reason why everybody in the United States should not be covered. I see no reason why all children, from the day they are born, shouldn't be members of the social security system. When they begin to grow up, they should know they will have old-age benefits direct from the insurance system to which they will belong all their life. If they are out of work, they get benefits. If they are sick or disabled, they get benefits.

"And there is no reason why only the industrial workers should get the benefit of this. Everybody ought to be in on it – the farmer and his wife and his family.

"I don't see why not," he would say, as I began to shake my head. "I don't see why not. Cradle to the grave – from the cradle to the grave they ought to be in a social insurance system."

It was not that I did not admire his bold idea of including every person. But I felt that it was impractical to try to develop and manage so broad a system before we had some experience and machinery for the first and most pressing steps.

Moreover, I felt sure that the political climate was not right for such a universal approach. I may have been wrong. Having the administrative responsibility, I was more alarmed than he about how we were going to achieve it. The question of financing was most important. Roosevelt, because he was looking at the broad picture, could skip over that difficult problem.

It is difficult now to understand fully the doubts and confusions in which we were planning this great new undertaking in 1934. The problems of constitutional law seemed almost impossible to overcome. I drew courage from a bit of advice I got accidentally from Supreme Court Justice Harlan Stone. I had said to him, at a social occasion a few months earlier, that I had great hope of developing a social insurance system for the country, but I was deeply uncertain of the method. I said laughingly, "Your Court tells us what the Constitution permits."

Stone had whispered, "The taxing power of

the federal government, my dear. The taxing power is sufficient for everything you want and need."

This was a windfall. I told the President but bound him to secrecy as to the source of my sudden superior legal knowledge. I insisted in the cabinet committee that the taxing power was the method for building up the fund and determining its expenditure for unemployment and old-age benefits to be paid in the future.

The bill with the cabinet committee's recommendations was prepared the first week in January 1935. We took it to the President to see how it should be introduced in Congress. We thought it would be wise to have it referred to a special committee on social security, if possible a joint committee of the Senate and House. Since the measure rested primarily upon the constitutional taxing power of the federal government, it would have gone ordinarily to the Ways and Means Committee.

The news got around that a special committee was being recommended. Representative Robert L. Doughton of North Carolina, chairman of the Ways and Means Committee, went to see the President. He was angry that anyone had thought of bypassing him, though he had never made a speech in the House that had indicated he had any interest in social security. It was a surprise to find out that he cared.

As a result the President said to me, "No, no, it will never do. We will have to put it through the Ways and Means Committee. It is the only thing to do. You will hurt Bob Doughton's feelings if you don't."

The Ways and Means Committee had a number of able members. They put their minds to this new problem not only of finances but of social and economic policy for the whole United States.

The House committee and other members of Congress began to hear from the voters in favor of the social security bill. It was soon clear that it was going to be moved along. In August 1935 Republicans as well as Democrats voted for the bill. There were only a very few who had the courage to vote against it.

I remember that when I appeared before the Senate Committee old Senator Thomas Gore raised a sarcastic objection. "Isn't this socialism?" he asked me.

My answer was, "Oh, no."

Then, smiling, leaning forward and talking to me as though I were a child, he said, "Isn't this a teeny-weeny bit of socialism?"

When the law was signed by the President [on August 14, 1935], we had a little ceremony in his office and he gave out the usual pens. I had brought in not only Congressman Doughton, but also Senator Wagner and Congressman Lewis, and one or two other members of Congress, and had provided the pens for them. As he was signing the copies of the bills with pens that would be given to its sponsors, the President looked up at me. "Frances, where is your pen?" he asked.

"I haven't got one," I replied.

"All right," he said to his secretary, "give me a first-class pen for Frances." And he insisted I was responsible for the bill and thanked me personally in very appreciative terms.

THE NEW DEAL IN HISTORY

For decades now, Americans have been thinking, talking, and writing about the New Deal. During the 1930's — the years of the New Deal — people's feelings were especially strong. Some Americans in those years thought that the New Deal was a radical threat to the American way of life. Others believed that the New Deal programs were moderate reforms necessary to help the nation recover from the depression.

Like other Americans, historians, too, have held strong opinions about the New Deal. In 1945 historian Henry Steele Commager reviewed the record of the New Deal and summed it up in a magazine article. In the following selection, based on that article, Commager explains his reasons for forming a favorable conclusion about Roosevelt and the New Deal.

What did Commager believe were the major achievements of the New Deal? Why do you think Commager concluded in 1945 that the New Deal "is here to stay"? Can you name some of the New Deal laws, programs, or reforms that still exist today?

Adapted from "Twelve Years of Roosevelt" by Henry Steele Commager, in The American Mercury, April 1945, pp. 391–401. Reprinted by permission of The American Mercury Patrons, Inc.

Now that the bitter quarrels over New Deal policies have been drowned out by the war [World War II], it is possible to evaluate those policies in some historical perspective. Those policies have been decisively voted for four times by large popular majorities. They have been turned into reality so fully that controversy about them is almost irrelevant. It should be possible to fix, with some degree of accuracy, the place occupied by Roosevelt in American history.

We can see now that the "Roosevelt revolution" was no revolution. Rather it was the high point of 50 years of historical development. Roosevelt himself, though clearly a leader, was an instrument of the people's will rather than a creator of, or a dictator to, that will. Indeed, the issue of the expansion of government control for democratic purposes began in the 1890's. A longer perspective will see the 50 years from the 1890's to the present as a historical unit. The roots of the New Deal go deep down into our past. It is not understandable except in terms of that past.

What was really only a new deal of the old cards looked, to startled and troubled Americans at the time, like a revolution for two reasons. It was carried through with breathless rapidity. And, in spirit at least, it contrasted sharply with what came immediately before it. But if the comparison had been made, not with the Coolidge-Hoover era, but with the Wilson, the Theodore Roosevelt, even the Bryan era, the contrasts would have been less striking than the similarities.

Actually, the precedents for the major part of the New Deal legislation were to be found in these earlier periods. Regulation of railroads and of business dated back to the Interstate Commerce Act of 1887 and the Sherman Act of 1890. The farm relief program of the Populists and of Wilson anticipated much that the Roosevelt administration passed into law. The beginnings of conservation can be traced to the Carey Act of 1894 and the Reclamation Act of 1902.

Power regulation began with the Water Power Act of 1920. Supervision over securities exchanges began with laws of the Harding and Coolidge administrations. Regulation of money is as old as the Union. The fight which Bryan and Wilson waged against the "money power" and Wall Street was more bitter than anything that came during the New Deal. Labor legislation had its beginnings in such states as Massachusetts and New York over 50 years ago. Much of the program of social security was worked out in Wisconsin and other states early in the 1900's.

There is nothing remarkable about this. Nor does it lessen in any way the significance of President Roosevelt's achievements and contributions. It is to the credit of Roosevelt that he worked within the framework of American history and tradition.

What, then, are the major achievements, the lasting contributions, of the first three Roosevelt administrations? First, perhaps, comes the restoration of self-confidence, the reassertion of faith in democracy. Those who lived through the electric spring of 1933 will remember the change from depression and discouragement to excitement and hope. Those able to compare the last decade with previous decades will agree that interest in public affairs has rarely been as widespread, as alert, or as responsive.

All this may seem indefinite. If we look to more definite things, what does the record show? Of primary importance has been the physical rebuilding of the country. It became clear, during the 1920's and 1930's, that the natural resources of the country—its soil, forests, water power—were being destroyed at a dangerous rate. The development of the Dust Bowl, and the migration of farmers to the Promised Land of California, the tragic floods on the Mississippi and the Ohio, dramatized to the American people the urgency of this problem.

Roosevelt tackled it with energy and boldness. The Civilian Conservation Corps enlisted almost 3 million young men. They planted 17 million acres in new forests, built over 6 million small dams to stop soil erosion, and fought forest fires and plant and animal diseases. To check erosion, the government organized a cooperative program which obtained the help of over one fourth of the farmers of the country. More important than all this was the TVA, a gigantic laboratory for regional rebuilding.

Equally important has been the New Deal achievement in human rehabilitation. Roosevelt came into office at a time when unemployment had reached perhaps 14 million, and when private solutions had failed. It was perhaps inevitable that he should sponsor a broad program of government aid. More important than relief was the acceptance of the principle that the government was responsible for the welfare and security of its people.

That this principle was bitterly opposed now seems hard to believe. Its establishment must stand as one of the main achievements of the New Deal. Beginning with emergency legislation for relief, the Roosevelt program in the end included the whole field of social security — unemployment assistance, old-age pensions, aid to women and children, and public health. It involved programs of rural rehabilitation, the establishment of maximum hours and minimum wages, the prohibition of child labor, and reform in housing.

In the political field the achievements of the New Deal were equally notable. First we must note the steady trend toward the strengthening of government and the expansion of government activities — whether for good or bad only the future can tell. As yet no better method of dealing with the problems of a modern economy and society has shown itself. It can be said that though government today has, quantitatively, far greater responsibilities than it had a generation ago, it has, qualitatively, no greater power. For our constitutional system remains as it always was. All power still resides in the people and their representatives in Congress. They can at any moment take from their government any power.

We seem to have overcome our traditional distrust of the government and realized that a strong state could be used to benefit and advance the nation. That is by no means a New Deal achievement. But it is a development which has gained much from the experience of the American people during the Roosevelt administrations.

It has meant, of course, a marked federal centralization. Along with this has come a great increase in the power of the President. The charge that Roosevelt has been a dictator can be dismissed, along with charges that Jefferson, Jackson, Lincoln, Theodore Roosevelt, and Wilson were dictators. American politics simply doesn't run to dictators. But Roosevelt has been a "strong" executive — as every great democratic President has been a strong executive. There is little doubt that Roosevelt accepted this situation cheerfully.

The New Deal, as far as can be foreseen, is here to stay. There seems no chance of a reversal of any of the major developments in politics in the last twelve years. This was recognized by the Republicans in 1940 and again in 1944. Both platforms endorsed all the essentials of the New Deal.

And what, finally, of Roosevelt himself? It may seem too early to fix his position in our history. Yet that position is reasonably clear. He takes his place in the great tradition of American liberalism, along with Jefferson, Jackson, Lincoln, Theodore Roosevelt, and Wilson. Coming to office at a time when the very foundations of the republic seemed threatened, he restored confidence and proved that democracy could act as effectively in crisis as could totalitarian governments.

A liberal, he put government clearly at the service of the people. A conservative, he pushed through reforms designed to strengthen the natural and human resources of the nation, restore agriculture and business to their former prosperity, and save capitalism. He saw that problems of government were primarily political, not economic. He saw that politics should control the economy, not the other way around.

"The only sure defense of continuing liberty," Roosevelt said, "is a government strong enough to protect the interests of the people, and a people strong enough and well enough informed to maintain its sovereign control over its government." The Roosevelt administration proved once more that it was possible for such a government to exist and such a people to flourish, and restored to the United States its position as "the hope of the human race."

A CRITIC LOOKS AT THE NEW DEAL

The verdict of history about the New Deal has not been all favorable. Some critics of the New Deal charge that it expanded the authority of the federal government by taking away powers of state governments. They point out that the New Deal programs greatly increased the national debt. Critics also argue that the Roosevelt administration helped labor unions to become much too powerful.

John T. Flynn was one of these critics who believed that Roosevelt's New Deal policies were disastrous for the nation. Flynn was particularly worried about the growth of the government bureaucracy and its increasing power. In this selection from his book *The Roosevelt Myth,* written in 1948, Flynn also bitterly attacks Roosevelt himself as well as his policies.

According to Flynn, what were some myths about Roosevelt? What changes did Roosevelt make in the American economic and political systems? What do you think of Flynn's criticism of Roosevelt? Why do you think Roosevelt provoked such strong feelings?

Adapted from The Roosevelt Myth *by John T. Flynn, published by The Devin-Adair Company, Inc., Old Greenwich, CT. Copyright © 1948, 1956 by John T. Flynn. Reprinted by permission of the publisher.*

Many good people in America still cherish the false idea that Roosevelt performed some amazing achievement for this country. They believe he took our economic system when it was completely broken down and restored it to vitality. They think he took over our political system when it was weakest and restored it to its full strength. He put himself on the side of the underprivileged masses. He transferred power from the great corporation executives to the simple working people of America. He controlled the adventurers of Wall Street, and gave security to the humble men and women of the country.

But not one of these claims is true. He did not restore our economic system to vitality. He changed it. The system he so stupidly moved us into is more like the bureaucracy of Germany before World War I than our own traditional order.

Before his regime we lived in a system which depended for its expansion upon private investment in private enterprise. Today [1948] we live in a system which depends for its expansion and vitality upon the government. This is a prewar European importation. And it was imported at the moment when it had fallen apart in Europe. In this system the government takes by taxes or by borrowings the savings of all the citizens and invests them in non-wealth-producing undertakings in order to create work.

Behold the picture of the American economy today. In America today every fourth person depends for a livelihood upon employment either directly by the government or indirectly in some industry supported by government funds. There is a public debt of $250 billion, compared to a pre-Roosevelt debt of $19 billion, and a government budget of $40 billion instead of $4 billion before Roosevelt. Inflation has doubled prices and reduced the lower-paid employed workers to a state of poverty as bad as that of the unemployed in the depression. More people are on various kinds of government relief than when we had 11 million unemployed. Bureaucrats are in every field of life. And the President is calling for more power, more price-fixing, more regulation, and more billions. Does this look like the traditional American scene?

No, Roosevelt did not restore our economic system. He did not construct a new one. He substituted an old one which lives upon permanent crises and an armament economy. And he did not by a process of orderly design and building, but by a series of mistakes. He moved one step at a time, in flight from one problem to another. Now we have a state-supported economic system that will continue a little at a time to destroy the private system until it disappears altogether.

Roosevelt did not restore our political system to its full strength. One may like the shape into which he battered it, but it cannot be called a repair job. He changed our political system with two weapons—blank-check congressional appropriations and blank-check congressional legislation. In 1933 Congress gave up much of its power when it put billions into his hands. It gave him a blanket appropriation to be spent at his own will. And it passed general laws leaving it to him, through great government bureaus that he set up, to fill in the details of legislation.

These two mistakes gave Roosevelt a power which he used ruthlessly. He used it to break down the power of Congress and concentrate it in the hands of the executive. The result of these two betrayals—the smashing of our economic system and the twisting of our political system—can only be the planned economic state. This, in the form of either communism or fascism, dominates the entire continent of Europe today. The capitalist system cannot live under these conditions. Free representative government cannot survive a planned economy. Such an economy can be managed only by a dictatorial government. The only result of our present system—unless we reverse the drift—will be the gradual disappearance of the system of free enterprise under a free representative government.

There are people who honestly defend this change. They at least are honest. They believe in a planned economy. They believe in a highly centralized government operated by a powerful executive. They do not say Roosevelt saved our system. They say he has given us a new one. That is logical. But no one can praise Roosevelt for doing this and then insist that he restored our traditional political and economic systems to their former vitality.

Roosevelt's star was sinking sadly in 1938 when he had 11 million unemployed and when Hitler made his first war moves in Europe. The cities were filling with jobless workers. Taxes were rising. The debt was soaring. The war rescued him and he seized upon it like a drowning man. By leading his country into the fringes of the war at first and then deep into its center all over the world he was able to do the only things that could save him—spend billions to spread the hot flames of war hysteria and put every man and woman into the war mills. Under the pressure of patriotism, he could silence criticism and work up the illusion of the war leader.

On the moral side, I have barely touched that subject. It will all still be told. But go back through the years, read the speeches and platforms and judgments Roosevelt made, and consider them in the light of what he did. Look up the promises of thrift in public office, of balanced budgets and lower taxes, of honesty in government, and of security for all. Read the speeches he made promising never, never again to send our sons to fight in foreign wars. He broke every promise. He betrayed all who trusted him.

The figure of Roosevelt exhibited before the eyes of our people is false. There was no such being as that noble, selfless, hard-headed, wise, and farseeing combination of philosopher, philanthropist, and warrior. It has been created out of pure propaganda. A small collection of dangerous people in this country are using it to advance their own evil purposes.

CHAPTER 15
FROM THE "JAZZ AGE" THROUGH THE GREAT DEPRESSION

A REVOLUTION IN MANNERS AND MORALS

In many ways, the society we live in today took shape after World War I. Cities and suburbs began to look the way they do now. Things we take for granted, such as automobiles and canned foods, first came into wide use in the 1920's. And along with these material changes came changes in the way people lived, acted, and thought. One writer, Frederick Lewis Allen, described these changes in people's lives as a revolution in manners and morals. In the following selection from a well-known book he wrote about the 1920's, Allen tells about the revolution that took place during those years in the lives of American women.

What were some of the major changes in women's actions and attitudes? Do you think Allen is right in calling the changes in women's lives during the 1920's "revolutionary"? What are some changes in society in recent years that have affected women's lives? Do you consider these changes "revolutionary"?

Adapted from pp. 94-109 in Only Yesterday by Frederick Lewis Allen. Copyright 1931 by Frederick Lewis Allen; copyright renewed 1959 by Agnes Rogers Allen. Reprinted by permission of Harper & Row, Publishers, Inc.

A revolution in manners and morals was beginning to affect men and women of every age in every part of the country. A number of forces were working together to make this revolution inevitable.

First of all was the state of mind brought about by the war and its conclusion. A whole generation had been affected by the eat-drink-and-be-merry-for-tomorrow-we-die spirit which accompanied the departure of the soldiers to the training camps and fighting front. It was impossible for this generation to return unchanged when the war was over. They found themselves expected to settle down into the dull routine of American life as if nothing had happened. They couldn't do it, and they said so.

The revolution was speeded up by the growing independence of the American woman. She won the vote in 1920. She seemed, it is true, to be very little interested in it once she had it. She voted mostly as the men about her did. Few of the younger women had even a slight interest in politics. To them it was a low and useless business, without flavor and without hope. Nevertheless, winning the vote had its effect. It greatly strengthened woman's position as man's equal.

Even more marked was the effect of women's growing independence from housekeeping. Smaller houses were being built, and they were easier to take care of. Families were moving into apartments, and these required even less of the housekeeper's time and energy. Women were learning how to make lighter work of the preparation of meals. Much of what had once been housework was now either moving out of the home entirely or being made easier by machinery. Women were slowly becoming freed from routine to "live their own lives."

And what were these "own lives" of theirs to be like? Well, for one thing, they could take jobs. Up to this time girls of the middle classes who had wanted to "do something" had been largely restricted to school-teaching, social-service work, nursing, stenography, and clerical work in business firms. But now they poured out of the schools and colleges into all kinds of new occupations. They crowded the offices of publishers and advertisers. They sold antiques and real estate, opened little shops, and invaded the department stores. Married women who had children and could not seek jobs cheered themselves with the thought that homemaking and child-rearing were really "professions," after all. No topic was so furiously discussed at luncheon tables from one end of the country to the other as the question whether the married woman should take a job, and whether the mother had a right to. And as for the unmarried woman, she no longer had to explain why she worked in a shop or an office. It was not working that now had to be defended.

With the job—or at least the sense that the job was a possibility—came a feeling of economic independence. With the feeling of economic independence came a weakening of husbandly and parental authority. Unmarried women were leaving the shelter of the family home and getting apartments of their own. Yet even the job did not provide the American woman with that complete satisfaction which the management of a mechanized home no longer provided. She still had energies and emotions to burn; she was ready for the revolution.

Like all revolutions, this one was helped by foreign propaganda. It came, however, not from Moscow, but from Vienna. Sigmund Freud had published his first book on psycho-analysis at the end of the 1800's. But it was not until the war that Freudian ideas began to circulate widely among the American public.

The principal forces which stimulated the revolution in manners and morals were all 100 percent American. They were prohibition, automobiles, confession and other popular magazines, and the movies.

When the Eighteenth Amendment was ratified, prohibition seemed to have an almost united country behind it. Evasion of the law began immediately, however. Strong and sincere opposition to it quickly gathered force. The results were the bootlegger, the speakeasy, and a spirit of deliberate revolt which in many communities made drinking "the thing to do." From these facts in turn flowed further results: the cocktail party, and the general transformation of drinking from a men's pastime to one shared by both men and women together. Meanwhile a new sort of freedom was being made possible by the enormous increase in the use of the automobile. The automobile offered an easy way of escaping temporarily from the supervision of parents and chaperons, or from the influence of neighborhood opinion.

Finally, as the revolution began, its influence led to confession magazines and sensational motion pictures. These in turn had their effect on a vast number of readers and moviegoers who had never heard and never would hear of Freud.

The most obvious sign of what was taking place was the great change in women's dress and appearance. Skirts became shorter and shorter, until they finally reached the knee. With the short skirt went an extraordinary change in the weight and material and amount of women's clothing. The boyishly slender figure became the aim of every woman. The flesh-colored stocking became as standard as the short skirt. Petticoats almost disappeared from the American scene. In fact, the tendency of women to do away with one layer of clothing after another became so great that in 1928 the *Journal of Commerce* estimated that in the previous 15 years the amount of material required for a woman's complete outfit (except for her stockings) had declined from 19¼ yards to 7 yards [17.6 meters to 6.4 meters].

Not satisfied with the freedom of short and skimpy clothes, women sought, too, the freedom of short hair. During the early years of the decade, the bobbed head became increasingly frequent among young girls, chiefly on the ground of convenience. In the late 1920's bobbed hair became almost universal among girls in their twenties, very common among women in their thirties and forties, and by no

587

means rare among women of sixty. Women universally adopted the small cloche hat which fitted tightly on the bobbed head.

The manufacturers of cosmetics and the owners of beauty shops made enormous profits. The popularity of rouge and lipstick spread swiftly to even the smallest village. Women who in 1920 would have thought the use of makeup immoral were soon applying it regularly and making no effort to hide the fact. Beauty shops had sprung up on every street to give "facials," to make war against the wrinkles and sagging chins of age, to pluck and trim and color the eyebrows, and otherwise to heighten and restore the bloom of youth.

These changes in fashion—the short skirt, the boyish figure, the straight, long-waisted dresses, the use of makeup—were signs of a real change in the American feminine ideal (as well, perhaps, as in men's idea of what was the feminine ideal). Women were determined to have freedom—freedom to work and to play without the restrictions that had bound them before to lives of comparative inactivity. But what they sought was not the freedom from men which had put the suffragists of earlier years into hard straw hats and mannish suits and low-heeled shoes. The women of the 1920's wanted to be able to attract men even on the golf links and in the office. Nor was the post-war feminine ideal one of maturity or wisdom or grace. On the contrary: the search for slenderness, and the boyish figure, the popularity of short skirts—all were signs that, consciously or unconsciously, the women of this decade worshiped youth. They wanted to be—or thought men wanted them to be—men's casual and light-hearted companions. Youth was their pattern.

TRYING TO BE A CAREER WOMAN

Though women in the 1920's had many new freedoms, they did not always find their new freedom an easy experience. Should a married woman work? What was a suitable career for a woman? These were questions women faced.

Elisabeth Stern, a writer, was trained as a social worker. After her marriage—to her supervisor—she stayed home to raise a family. However, during the flu epidemic of World War I, her husband became ill and she supported the family by working in a department store. After her husband recovered, she continued to work but as his assistant. In this selection she tells of a new job opportunity and the many problems it presented.

Why did Elisabeth Stern hesitate to take the new job? Do you think the board's questions to her were fair? In what ways have conditions for working women changed since the 1920's? What problems do women face today?

Adapted from I Am a Woman—and a Jew *by Elisabeth G. Stern. Reprinted by Arno Press, Inc., 1969.*

One day in late winter, a long, important-looking envelope came to the office with the name of a well-known woman in the corner. "For you, Mrs. Morton" [Elisabeth Stern's married name], said the typist.

The letter told me they were planning to open a "health center" in the industrial neighborhood where the Hungarians lived. What they thought of was a place where clinics would be held and free medical treatment given, and where, during the summer, clubs, classes, and community activities would be developed. In time, they would open a camp for children. The president of a large business had signed the letter as chairman of the committee.

They knew, he said, that I had done this sort of work. They wanted me to talk the matter over with them. There were a number of candidates for the position, but they had written to three they particularly wished to have as "first choice." The salary was almost as much as my husband was making.

This was not "just writing." It was not "assisting my husband."

This was a real job for me to do myself, one requiring training, certain special abilities, and experience.

Had I been gathering that experience in the years when I was simply meeting each problem of our life as it came along? I thought over my teaching, my work in the department store, my work with my husband. Curious. I had been an "executive"—why, for years.

Here was an opportunity that any man could be satisfied to have, and at a salary equal to a man's. We had friends teaching in the university who were earning $2,500 a year as heads of their departments. We knew a minister whose parish paid him $1,800 a year, and he was an old man with four degrees.

My husband, whose work this was, who was my chief, received only $700 a year more than this letter offered me.

Could a woman—I—be worth this much? The war had created new conditions, of course. Before, when a woman asked for work, she understood she must expect at least $1,000 a year less than a man, even as an "executive" in a business or profession. I had women friends teaching in colleges and doing social work, who held positions exactly equal with men, and who cheerfully accepted salaries less than half those of the men.

But every woman I knew who had outstanding work, a "big job," was an unmarried woman, or a widow. Married women, at the head of a work as important as a *man's*—and well-paid—were still practically unknown.

What would our friends and neighbors say if I went away every day to the office—to another office than my husband's? When I had worked at the store my husband was ill. He had been home, and the children had been under his care part of the time. What would people say if I left my children—to do work that was not my husband's, but my own entirely?

If I took this new job, I would be away from nine to five daily, six days a week. My work would be more exacting than my husband's. I would have to leave my children completely in the care of strangers.

The community felt itself very broadminded when it said, "Oh, she's not an old maid, she's an unmarried woman with a lot of brains who hasn't found a man big enough for her to marry." But the married woman who went to work had to prove that her husband was a man big enough for her to have married. She could not be "bigger" than he. She could not really be as "big."

All these things went through my mind. It will seem strange to women today, but I was afraid to take the work offered me.

Days passed, almost a week, and I could not make a decision. One laughs at these things later. I smile, too, to think now of my fear and hesitation. But I smile as one does at something done by a younger sister.

One morning I turned to my husband and told him of the new offer, of the letter that had been lying under my pillow for almost a week now.

"Do you want me to do this?" I asked.

He sat thoughtful, silent, a while. "I do not know," he said finally. "It means a great responsibility. It means a real opportunity. It's a really excellent salary." His grave eyes came to mine, worried then. "It is so big a salary that I am troubled by it. It will mean that you must give yourself completely to your work. You'll have to work so hard! I've hoped that after—that store work—you'd never do anything except what you felt you might drop when you wished. I want you to feel that you are free to do anything you like. Do you want to give up writing?"

I think, if he had not said that, I should never have answered the letter. But I understood what he wished to tell me. He wanted me to have a sheltered life, with the responsibility of earning our income on him and the pleasure of economic freedom for me—the fun of writing whenever I wanted to stop working, instead of the serious job of the daily task, the concrete thing, with monthly salary and hourly duties.

"I'd like to do—this," I said.

I met my board one Thursday morning, five people who met in the office of the chairman. Two were women. Of the men one was young and enthusiastic and impractical, and the other was an older man with quiet voice and movement. They had heard of me, knew my work and my husband. They spoke well of my husband.

We discussed the plans they had in mind, and the work done in the past. We decided what activities it might be practical for us to begin with.

Then there was a pause.

"Mrs. Morton," came the voice of the chairman, "this work we are planning will take all your time and all your energy. We know you are a married woman, and we believe, at least I do," and he smiled in a very kind, fatherly way, "that married women are going to become more and more important in all kinds of work in the future, in professions and business equally. We're employing numbers of women in our bank every day. But I want to ask you two questions now. The first is this: you have children, have you not?" I nodded. He went on, slowly, "We did not know you had a family when we first began to consider you. That I will tell you frankly, Mrs. Morton. How will that fit in with your work? Will your husband agree to your giving all your time to this work?"

The other four waited, with him, for me to answer. I understood that these two questions had been discussed before I came in. They had been objections raised by someone.

I thought of the children. Had I neglected them? I wanted to smile, openly, at the question. What work would I do which I could promise to put first, before them? The fact that I was their mother answered that question. I could only work harder, give myself doubly. Nothing would ever come that could stand before them in my thought.

"I held a professional job even when my little daughter was a baby," I answered, letting that speak for me.

The larger of the two women shook her head. "But that's it, Mr. Blank," she said. "Let us be frank, Mrs. Morton. I've heard a great deal about you from Mr. Blank. I think this is your work. But I'm an old-fashioned woman," she admitted. "I do not feel quite easy about seeing young wives and mothers leave their homes. I was a schoolteacher myself, and I gave up my work as soon as I married. However, I am willing to keep up with the times," and she smiled to Mr. Blank. "I feel we ought to be intelligent. It is not clear to me, though," she confessed, "that your children do not suffer by having their mother away on other interests. I can understand that writing would not interfere so with your home. Please do not think I am being too personal, but we have to be in this matter. Can you give your children the proper care if you come to us—and are you doing social work because you want to, or just as a stop-gap?"

It was shrewd of her. She was more acute about me than was I myself.

But at the time I did not think of her shrewdness. I thought only how unfair her questions were. I thought that if I were an unmarried woman, I would never have been asked if my dependents were cared for. I would not have been asked to assure them that I would not neglect the work I was paid to do for some other interest. It was because I was a married woman, a mother, that I was in this undignified position and questioned in this way.

"I do not think," I said, "I wish to speak about my children and the care I give them. It seems to me that if a woman is capable of arranging for the lives of several hundred people, she is equally able to arrange the lives of those dearest to her. I do not wish to discuss how I plan to do so. That seems to be my personal business."

The large lady grew red. She did not answer. The chairman sat back, too. I had been "independent" to the board. I had not been polite and respectful. In other words, I had destroyed my opportunity.

I said good-by, and said good-by to $2,800 a year as I went out.

The house was empty and still when I came in, for my husband was away, the children were at school. I had to get rid of some of the disappointment that I felt. I set to work, scrubbed and washed and swept. I tore through that house with broom and mop. This is what "they" thought I ought to do!

My husband listened to the account of the meeting quietly. "You were right," he said finally. "You could never have started the job under such conditions. Your board would have said that you were giving only part of your attention to the work, that you were thinking of your children and your home. It would have been an impossible situation."

It was true, and I knew it. But still, disappointment ate at me. I had thrown it all away. A man would never have done it. He would have known how to speak, how to smooth things out. Only women were emotional and hasty.

"A man wouldn't have had to meet such a situation," my husband said. "Do you think he would be asked, even if he were a widower, how he planned to take care of his children?"

I looked at him. "Did you want me to have that job?" I asked, for the second time. "Did you really want me to have it?"

He did not answer immediately. "I don't know," he said slowly. "I don't really care what you do, just so it makes you happy. I would prefer you not to have burdens to weigh you down, like, I suppose, a man carries. That's not because I don't believe you can carry them. It is just that I prefer to do that for us."

"Do you think of me," I asked then, "just as a—well, a little girl? Don't you think—well, that I am as mature as you, as capable?"

At that he laughed, his rare, deep laugh. "I know that is disturbing you," he answered. "You want to be thought 'just as good as a man'—in anything. You feel unhappy because you are afraid I do not regard you so. I suppose you are just as mature as a man, as capable. But," and here he smiled at me again, "it is not because you are capable and a good executive that I love you, my darling."

He did not say quite what I wanted him to say. He did not say I was as capable as a man. But I was satisfied.

"There'll be other opportunities," he said. "Meanwhile, let's get back to my work."

A BLACK WRITER ON THE HARLEM RENAISSANCE

During the 1920's, there was a cultural renaissance, or rebirth, in black culture that came to be known as the "Harlem renaissance." An extremely talented group of writers and poets began to speak out against injustices in America and to write of the joys, sorrows, and hopes of black Americans.

Black pride was aroused by these writers and by America's growing interest in black music, art, and entertainment, especially in the Harlem area of Manhattan in New York City. Jazz music became the rage, and many black entertainers became extremely popular and famous, as did many nightclubs in Harlem. In this selection, Langston Hughes, one of the leading black writers of that time, writes about the Harlem renaissance.

How was the work of black writers and black entertainers of the period affected by white audiences? What is Hughes' attitude toward black intellectuals? Toward the ordinary people of Harlem?

Selection adapted from "When the Negro Was in Vogue" from The Big Sea *by Langston Hughes. Copyright 1940 by Langston Hughes. Copyright renewed © 1978 by Arna Bontemps and George Houston Bass. Reprinted by permission of Hill and Wang, a division of Farrar, Straus & Giroux, Inc.*

The 1920's were the years of Manhattan's black Renaissance. It began with the musical revue *Shuffle Along.* It reached its peak just before the crash of 1929, the crash that sent Negroes, white folks, and all rolling down the hill.

Shuffle Along was a honey of a show. Swift, bright, funny, carefree, and gay, with a dozen danceable, singable tunes. Everybody was in the audience—including me. People came back to see it many times. It was always packed.

To see *Shuffle Along* was the main reason I wanted to go to Columbia. When I saw it, I was thrilled and delighted. From then on I was in the gallery of the Cort Theatre every time I got a chance. *Shuffle Along* gave just the proper push—a pre-Charleston kick—to that Negro vogue of the 1920's that spread to books, African sculpture, music, and dancing.

The 1920's brought the rise of Roland Hayes, who packed Carnegie Hall; the rise of Paul Robeson in New York and London; the booming voice of Bessie Smith on thousands of records; and the rise of that grand comedienne of song, Ethel Waters. The 1920's brought Louis Armstrong and Josephine Baker.

White people began to come to Harlem in large numbers. For several years they packed the expensive Cotton Club on Lenox Avenue. But I was never there, because the Cotton Club was a Jim Crow club for gangsters and rich whites. They did not want Negro customers, unless you were someone famous like Bojangles [a dancer]. So Harlem Negroes did not like the Cotton Club and never appreciated its Jim Crow policy in the very heart of their dark community. Nor did ordinary Negroes like the growing numbers of whites in Harlem after sundown, filling the little cabarets and bars. Formerly only colored people laughed and sang there. Now strangers were given the best ringside tables to sit and stare at the Negro customers—like amusing animals in a zoo.

The Negroes said: "We can't go downtown and sit and stare at you in your clubs. You won't even let us in your clubs." But they didn't say it out loud—for Negroes are practically never rude to white people. So thousands of whites came to Harlem night after night, thinking the Negroes loved to have them there. They firmly believed that all the people who lived in Harlem left their houses at sundown to sing and dance in nightclubs, because most of the whites saw nothing but the nightclubs, not the houses.

Some of the small clubs had people like Gladys Bentley, who was something worth discovering in those days, before she got famous. For two or three amazing years, Miss Bentley sat and played a big piano all night long, without stopping. She slid from one song to another, with a powerful and continous underbeat of jungle rhythm. Miss Bentley was an amazing exhibition of musical energy—a large, dark, masculine woman, whose feet pounded the floor while her fingers pounded the keyboard—a perfect piece of African sculpture, made alive by her own rhythm.

But when the place where she played became too well known, she began to sing with an accompanist, became a star, moved to a larger place, then downtown, then to Hollywood. The old magic of the woman and the piano and the night and the rhythm are gone. But everything goes, one way or another. The 1920's are gone and lots of fine things in Harlem night life have disappeared like snow in the sun—since it became completely commercial, planned for the downtown tourist trade, and therefor dull.

The dancers at the Savoy even began to

practice acrobatic routines. They did absurd things for the entertainment of the whites that probably never would have entered their heads to attempt just for their own amusement.

Some critics say that that is what happened to certain Negro writers, too. They stopped writing to amuse themselves and began to write to amuse and entertain white people. In so doing they distorted their material and left out their American brothers of a lighter complexion. Maybe it's true, since Negroes have writer-racketeers like any other race. But I have known almost all of them, and most of the good ones have tried to write honestly and express their world as they saw it.

All of us know that the happy, sparkling life of the so-called Negro Renaissance of the 1920's was not so happy and sparkling beneath the surface. But it was a period when, at almost every Harlem uppercrust dance or party, one would be introduced to various distinguished white celebrities who were there as guests. It was a period when preachers opened up shouting churches as sideshows for white tourists. It was a period when every season there was at least one hit play on Broadway acted by a Negro cast. And when books by Negro authors were being published with much greater frequency and given much more publicity than ever before or since. It was a period when white writers wrote about Negroes more successfully (commercially speaking) than Negroes did about themselves. It was the period when Ethel Barrymore appeared in blackface in *Scarlet Sister Mary!* It was the period when the Negro was in vogue.

I was there. I had a swell time while it lasted. But I thought it wouldn't last long. For how could a large and enthusiastic number of people be crazy about Negroes forever? But some people in Harlem thought the race problem had at last been solved. They were sure the New Negro would lead a new life from then on in green pastures of tolerance created by Countee Cullen, Ethel Waters, Claude McKay, Duke Ellington, Bojangles, and Alain Locke.

I don't know what made any Negroes think that—except that they were mostly intellectuals doing the thinking. The ordinary Negroes hadn't heard of the Negro Renaissance. And if they had, it hadn't raised their wages any. As for all those white folks in the speakeasies and night clubs of Harlem—well, maybe a colored man could find *some* place to have a drink that tourists hadn't yet discovered.

AN AGE OF HERO-WORSHIP

Throughout the history of the United States, certain men and women have become heroes to the American people. In earlier times these heroes were often famous generals or politicians. Americans also seemed to greatly admire men and women known for outstanding individual achievements. In this selection, writer Bruce Bliven suggests that in the 1920's such hero-worship seemed more intense and involved more people. One of the most popular heroes of the period was Charles Lindbergh, but many other Americans also became objects of national hero-worship.

Why, according to Bliven, did Americans worship heroes so much in the 1920's? Do you agree with his reasons? Why do you think none of the "heroes" Bliven mentions was a woman? Who are some people that you especially admire today? Why do you feel this way about them?

Adaptation of "Worshiping the American Hero" by Bruce Bliven from America as Americans See It *edited by Fred J. Ringel. Copyright 1932, by Harcourt Brace Jovanovich, Inc.; copyright 1960, by Fred J. Ringel. Reprinted by permission of the publishers.*

For some years past, the most persecuted man in the world has undoubtedly been Charles A. Lindbergh, the American flyer. For a long time, he never dared to appear in public without a police guard, lest his clothes be torn from his back and his life put in danger by frenzied hero-worshipers.

He was driven nearly to desperation by the crowds which gathered at every landing field where his airplane was expected. These crowds, in their eagerness to be near him, refused to leave a clear space in which he could land. When he toured the United States to increase interest in flying, he was driven through the streets of each city in an automobile. Several of his friends had to catch as best they could the heavy packages of candy and the wreaths of flowers which lovesick women tossed at him from the crowd.

Hero-worship is not a new phenomenon in American life. But like many other things nowadays, it is speeded up and achieved on a larger scale. Thirty years ago, after the Spanish-American War of 1898, Admiral Dewey was the subject of equal worship. It ended overnight, however, when he hurt the country's feelings by making a technical transfer to his wife of a house which had been presented to him by the people. Another hero of the same war, Richmond Person Hobson, became the target of masses of strange young women who insisted, one after another, on kissing him in public.

As we have it today, however, hero-worship is a product of our times, especially of the movies and the radio. For twenty-five years movies were silent. A deep psychological need grew among most people to see in person, and to hear the voices of, those whom they had so often followed as gray shadows on a silver screen. The popular movie star dared not appear in public without a disguise, and counted his or her fan mail by hundreds of thousands of letters each year. Then came the radio and it reversed the process. Millions wanted to see the owner of the voice to whose tones, musical or otherwise, they responded night after night. There are several persons, quite unknown a few years ago, who now receive a fee as high as $1,000 a performance just to stand upon a stage.

Americans' love of sport, and their admiration of athletics, of course, accounts for much of the present hero-worship. The typical American attitude toward athletics is still one of spectatorship rather than participation. The outstanding figures in sports—"Babe" Ruth in baseball, Bobby Jones in golf, W. T. Tilden in tennis, Red Grange or Albie Booth in football— are the objects of the greatest public interest. They can, and some of them do, earn large sums of money by endorsing certain advertised products, by writing for the press, and by appearing in vaudeville theaters. For that matter, anyone who has become somewhat known, by whatever means, can take advantage of it to some extent. The woman who shoots her husband or boyfriend writes her life story from her prison cell for some sensational newspaper. The winner of an endurance contest, who has rocked in a rocking chair, or ridden a bicycle, or sat in a tree, longer than anyone else, is an outstanding hit in a theater, though often completely forgotten soon afterward.

What we have seen in recent years is the creation of a vast new machinery for making everyone aware of any new person or idea. Of this machinery the movies and the radio are but a part, although an important one. Let anyone say or do anything interesting, and within a week everyone in America has heard his voice on the radio, seen his photograph and read his interviews in the newspapers, seen and heard him in the movies. This fact has a double result. It not only creates heroes by

magic, but it guarantees that people will tire of them with equal speed. Just as a popular song now runs its course and dies in half the time it did a few years ago, there is no one so completely forgotten as the person in the spotlight last year.

The movie is the deadliest of all enemies of these soon-forgotten celebrities. They are now required to make a speech before the camera, and rarely do they come through this ordeal well. They have trouble talking, they perspire, make mistakes in grammar, or what is worse, read a speech which was obviously prepared for them by someone else. It seems probable that when television comes along, only the very sturdiest of our heroes will be able to last.

Are Americans more interested in hero-worship than the people of other countries? Or is it just that the hero-making machinery exists here in more complete form than elsewhere? Certainly hero-worship is not unknown in Europe. American movie stars are mobbed more mercilessly in London than they are in New York. Lindbergh was never in greater danger from the bear-like affection of the mob than at Le Bourget airport in Paris. The making of mob-idols is neither uniquely an American phenomenon nor one of the present age alone. In explanation of America's attitude there are several things to be said, though I can hardly do more than suggest them here.

1. The Americans are only very partially believers in the theory of democracy. While their politics are republican, their business life —which is to them far more important—is conducted on strictly autocratic lines. In this country, as elsewhere, the mob desires ruthless leaders whose strength and success make up for their own weakness and failure.

2. A common error is to suppose that the American temperament is like the English, or that of other North European peoples. It is not. In its intensity, violence of thought and action, and changeability, it is much more Latin than Nordic.

3. It must be remembered, moreover, that America is not so much a nation as a parliament of nations. It has become a commonplace to point out that New York City alone has more Irish than Dublin, more Italians than Naples, more Jews than Jerusalem. Not only in New York but throughout America, these groups with their various racial backgrounds and cultural heritages are vaguely conscious of their differences from one another. They do

what they can to find a common meeting ground. It is not too fanciful to say that when they all worship the same hero at the same moment, they feel a sense of kinship to each other which they can acquire in no other way.

4. Most important of all, however, is a feeling at which I have already hinted. Americans, like other Western peoples, feel an uneasy, increasing sense of insecurity in the modern world, where they seem more and more to be the puppets of great economic forces which are beyond anyone's power to control. In this predicament they turn with relief to anyone who, in any field, appears to stand out beyond everyone else. They feel that the world needs giants —as perhaps it does. When they find them, they pretend that they are even taller than in fact they are.

A TEENAGER ON THE SOUP LINE IN THE DEPRESSION

Many Americans today sometimes wonder what life was like during the Great Depression. They have seen movies and read stories about people standing in soup lines or bread lines, about people going hungry, about jobless people hitchhiking around the nation looking for work. But do these movies and stories give a true picture of the times? What was life really like during the 1930's?

In the late 1960's, writer Studs Terkel decided to find out about American life during the Great Depression by interviewing people who remember those times and asking them how the depression had affected them. He spent months interviewing people and used their conversations in his book *Hard Times*. In this selection, Peggy Terry tells about her experiences as a teenager from Oklahoma during the depression.

Have you ever heard persons who lived during that time talk about the depression? How did the depression affect them? Do they mention the "feeling of together" that Peggy Terry speaks of? How does she compare poor people today with those she knew as a young girl?

Adapted from Hard Times: An Oral History of the Great Depression *by Studs Terkel. Copyright © 1970 by Studs Terkel. Reprinted by permission of Pantheon Books, a division of Random House, Inc.*

I first noticed the difference when we'd come home from school in the evening. My mother'd send us to the soup line. And we were never allowed to curse. If you happened to be one of the first ones in line, you didn't get anything but water that was on top. So we'd ask the guy that was putting the soup into the buckets— everybody had to bring their own bucket to get the soup—he'd dip the greasy watery stuff off the top. So we'd ask him to please dip down to get some meat and potatoes from the bottom of the kettle. But he wouldn't do it. So we learned to curse.

Then we'd go across the street. One place had bread, large loaves of bread. Down the road just a little way was a big shed, and they gave milk. My sister and me would take two buckets each. And that's what we lived off for the longest time.

I can remember one time, the only thing in the house to eat was mustard. My sister and I put so much mustard on biscuits that we got sick. And we can't stand mustard till today.

There was only one family around that ate good. Mr. Burr worked at the ice plant. Whenever Mrs. Burr could, she'd feed the kids. But she couldn't feed 'em *all*. They had a big tree that had fruit on it. She'd let us pick those. Sometimes we'd pick and eat 'em until we were sick.

Her two daughters got to go to Norman to college. When they'd talk about all the good things they had at the college, she'd kind of hush 'em up because there was always poor kids that didn't have anything to eat. I remember she always felt bad because people in the neighborhood were hungry. But there was a feeling of together. . . .

When they had food to give to people, you'd get a notice and you'd go down. So Daddy went down that day and he took my sister and me. They were giving away potatoes and things like that. But they had a truck of oranges parked in the alley. Somebody asked them who the oranges were for, and they wouldn't tell 'em. So they said, well, we're gonna take those oranges. And they did. My dad was one of the ones that got up on the truck. They called the police, and the police chased us all away. But we got the oranges.

It's different today. People are made to feel ashamed now if they don't have anything. Back then, I'm not sure how the rich felt. I think the rich looked down on the poor as much as they do now. But among the people that I knew, we all had an understanding that it wasn't our fault. It was something that had happened to the system. Most people blamed Hoover, and they cursed him—it was all his fault. I'm not saying he's blameless, but I'm not saying either it was all his fault. Our system doesn't run by just one person, and it doesn't fall by just one person, either.

Did I feel a sense of shame? I remember it was fun. It was fun going to the soup line. 'Cause we all went down the road, and we laughed and we played. The only thing we felt is that we were hungry and we were going to get food. Nobody made us feel ashamed. There just wasn't any of that.

Today you're made to feel that it's your own fault. If you're poor, it's only because you're lazy and you're ignorant, and you don't try to help yourself. You're made to feel that if you get a check from Welfare that the bank at Fort Knox is gonna go broke.

Then I got married. My husband and me just started traveling around, for about three years. It was a very nice time, because when you're poor and you stay in one spot, trouble just seems to catch up with you. But when you're moving from town to town, you don't stay there long enough for trouble to catch up with you. It's really a good life, if you're poor and you can manage to move around.

I was pregnant when we first started hitch-hiking, and people were really very nice to us. Sometimes they would feed us. I remember one time we slept in a haystack, and the lady of the house came out and found us and she said, "This is really very bad for you because you're going to have a baby. You need a lot of milk." So she took us up to the house.

She had a lot of rugs hanging on the clothesline because she was doing her house cleaning. We told her we'd beat the rugs for her giving us the food. She said, no, she didn't expect that. She just wanted to feed us. We said, no, we couldn't take it unless we worked for it. And she let us beat her rugs. I think she had a million rugs, and we cleaned them. Then we went in and she had a beautiful table, full of all kinds of food and milk. When we left, she filled a gallon bucket full of milk and we took it with us.

You don't find that now. I think maybe if you did that now, you'd get arrested. Somebody'd call the police. The atmosphere since the end of the Second War—it seems like the minute the war ended, the propaganda started. In making people hate each other.

FLEEING THE DUST BOWL

American farmers in the plains states were hit by a terrible drought during the 1930's. This lack of rain caused large areas of the Great Plains to dry up and turn into what came to be called "the Dust Bowl." The situation in Oklahoma and other states of the Great Plains was so serious that thousands of farm families were forced to leave their farms. Many of them headed west to California to look for jobs as migrant farm workers.

These poor and desperate Americans were models for the characters in a famous novel written by John Steinbeck, *The Grapes of Wrath*. Woody Guthrie, a song writer, also told of the lives of these people in some of his folk songs. The following selection includes Guthrie's memory of what it was like to wander across America in the 1930's, as well as two of his songs about the Dust Bowl.

What is Guthrie's point in the song "Do Re Me"? To whom is he speaking in "Pastures of Plenty"? How have the lives of migrant workers changed since the 1930's?

I got a few little jobs—helping a water-well driller, hoeing figs, irrigating strawberries in the sandy land, laying roofs, hustling sign jobs with a painter.

I followed the oil towns and found myself as far west as Hobbs, New Mexico. I'd learned how to play a guitar, a few of the easy chords, and was making saloons like a preacher changing from street corner to street corner.

I hit Pampa in the Panhandle of Texas, and stuck there a while. Then the dust storms begun blowing blacker and meaner, and the rain was getting less, and the dust more and more. I made up a little song that went:

'37 was a dusty year
And I says, Woman, I'm leavin' here.

And on one dark and dusty day, I pulled out down the road that led to California.

The further west you walk, the browner, hotter, stiller and emptier the country gets.

I met the hard-rock miners, old prospectors,

desert rats, and whole swarms of hitchhikers, migratory workers—squatted with their little piles of belongings in the shade of the big sign boards, out across the flat, hard-crust, gravelly desert. Kids chasing around in the blistering sun. Ladies cooking scrappy meals in sooty buckets, scouring the plates clean with sand. All waiting for some kind of a chance to get across the California line.

*   *   *   *

Do Re Me

Lots of folks back east, they say,
Is leavin' home every day,
Beatin' a hot old dusty way to th' California
    line.
'Crost th' desert sands they roll
Gettin' outta that old dust bowl,

They think they're a-goin' to a sugar bowl
But here's what they find:

> Oh, the police at the port of entry say,
> "You're number Fourteen Thousand for to-
> day! Oh!

"If you ain't got th' do re me, folks,
If you ain't got th' do re me,
Why, ya better go back t' beautiful Texas,
Oklahoma, Kansas, Georgia, Tennessee;
    California is a garden of Eden,
    A paradise to live in or see;
    But, believe it or not,
    You won't find it so hot
    If you ain't got th' do re me!"

If you wanta buy a home or farm,
That cain't do nobody harm,
Or take your vacation by the mountains or sea,
Don't swap your old cow for a car,
Ya better stay right where you are;
Ya better take this little tip from me.

Cause I look thru the want ads every day
But the headlines in the papers always say:

Chorus: "If you ain't got. . . ."

Yes, guess I'm what you'd call a migrant worker. Guess you had to think up some kind of name for me. I travel, yes, if that's what you mean in your red-tape and your scary offices, but you can just call me any old word you want to. You just set and call me off a whole book full of names, but let me be out on my job while you're doing the calling. Thataway, we can save time and money and get more work turned out.

I ain't nothing much but a guy walking along. You can't hardly pick me out in a big crowd, I look so much like everybody else. Streets. Parks. Big places. I travel . . . yes, I travel. Ain't you glad I travel and work? If I was to stop, you'd have to up and leave your job and start traveling, because there's . . . a lot of traveling that's got to be done.

*   *   *   *

Pastures of Plenty

It's a mighty hard row that my poor hands has
    hoed;
My poor feet has traveled a hot, dusty road;
Out of your dust bowl and westward we rolled;
And your deserts was hot and your mountains
    was cold.

I worked in your orchards of peaches and
    prunes;
Slept on the ground in the light of your moon;
On the edge of your city you'll see us and then
We come with the dust and we go with the
    wind.

California, Arizona, I make all your crops,
Then, it's north up to Oregon to gather your
    hops,
Dig the beets from your ground, cut the grapes
    from your vine,
To set on your table your light sparkling wine.

Green pastures of plenty from dry desert
    ground
From that Grand Coulee dam where the water
    runs down;
Ever' state in this union us migrants has been;
We'll work in this fight and we'll fight till we
    win.

Well, it's always we rambled, that river and I,
All along your green valley I will work till I
    die;
My land I'll defend with my life if it be,
'Cause my pastures of plenty must always be
    free.

WINNING A SIT-DOWN STRIKE

By the middle of 1934, after some improvement in the economy, American business and industry again began to slow down. As a result, some Americans began to criticize many of Roosevelt's policies, and their opposition increased during Roosevelt's second term. However, organized labor, especially the members of the newly formed CIO union, continued to support President Roosevelt. They believed that the New Deal's labor policy had brought great benefits and greater economic freedom to working people.

In this selection, Bob Stinson, an auto worker, tells of the first sit-down strike in the General Motors plant at Flint, Michigan, in 1936. When interviewed by writer Studs Terkel many years later, Stinson clearly recalled the day he and the other workers won their strike.

What was the situation in Flint just before the strike? Why did the strikers make special efforts to take care of company property? Are unions a more powerful force in the United States today than they were in 1936? Explain.

Condensed from Hard Times: An Oral History of the Great Depression *by Studs Terkel. Copyright © 1970 by Studs Terkel. Reprinted by permission of Pantheon Books, a division of Random House, Inc.*

Everybody has to have something they're really sold on. Some people go to church. If I'd had anything I'm really sold on, it's the UAW [United Automobile Workers].

I started working at Fisher Body in 1917 and retired in '62, with 45 years service. Until 1933, no unions, no rules: you were at the mercy of your foreman. I could go to work at seven o'clock in the morning, and at seven fifteen the boss'd come around and say: come back at three o'clock. If he preferred somebody else over you, that person would be called back earlier, though you were there longer.

I left the plant so many nights hostile. If I were a fella big and strong, I think I'd a picked a fight with the first fella I met on the corner. It was lousy. You might call yourself a man if you was on the street, but as soon as you went through the door and punched your card, you was nothing more or less than a robot. Do this, go there, do that. You'd do it.

We got involved in a strike in Detroit, and we lost the strike. Went back on our knees. That's the way you learn things. I got laid off in the fall of '31. I wasn't told I was blackballed, but I was told there was no more jobs at Fisher Body for me. So I came to Flint and was hired right off the bat.

We had a Black Legion in this town made up of stool pigeons and bigotty kind of people. They got themselves in good with the management by puttin' the finger on a union organizer. Once in a while, a guy'd come in with a black eye. You'd say, "What happened?" He'd say, "I was walking along the street and a guy come from behind and knocked me down."

The Black Legion later developed into the Flint Alliance. It was supposed to be made up of good solid citizens, who were terrorized by outside agitators, who had come in here to take over the plant. They would get schoolkids to sign these cards, [and] housewives. Every shoe salesman downtown would sign these cards. Businessmen would have everyone in the family sign these cards. They contended they had the overwhelming majority of the people of Flint.

Most people in town was hopin' the thing'd get solved. They had relatives and friends that they knew working in the plant; [it] was no bed of roses. They did accept some of this outside agitator stuff that got in the paper. I think anybody who reads this stuff day after day accepts a little bit of it. The great majority of the people was neutral.

There was fear. You kept your mouth shut when you was in strange company. Every time you put a union button on, you were told to leave the plant. You were fired so fast, it made your head spin.

The Flint sit-down happened Christmas Eve, 1936. I was in Detroit. When I came back, the second shift [the men who worked from 4:30 P.M. to 12:30 A.M.] had pulled the plant [struck]. It took about five minutes to shut the line down. The foreman was pretty well astonished.

The boys pulled the switches and asked all the women who was in Cut-and-Sew to go home. They informed the supervisors they could stay, if they stayed in their office. They told the plant police they could do their job as long as they didn't interfere with the workers.

We had guys patrol the plant, see that nobody got involved in anything they shouldn't. If anybody got careless with company property —such as sitting on an automobile cushion without putting burlap over it—he was talked to. You couldn't paint a sign on the wall or anything like that. You used bare springs for a bed. 'Cause if you slept on a finished cushion, it was no longer a new cushion.

Governor [Frank] Murphy said he hoped he would never have to use National Guard against people. But if there was damage to property, he would do so. We invited him to the plant and see how well we were taking care of the place.

They'd assign roles to you. When some of the guys at headquarters wanted to tell some of the guys in the plant what was cookin', I carried the message. I was a scavenger, too.

The merchants cooperated. There'd be apples, bushels of potatoes, crates of oranges that was beginnin' to spoil.

The soup kitchen was outside the plant. The women handled all the cooking, outside of one chef who came from New York. He had anywhere from ten to twenty women washing dishes and peeling potatoes in the strike kitchen. Mostly stews, pretty good meals. They were put in containers and hoisted up through the window. The boys in there had their own plates and cups and saucers.

Most of the men had their wives and friends come down, and they'd stand inside the window and they'd talk. Find out how the family was. If the union supplied them with enough coal.

We had a ladies' auxiliary. They'd visit the homes of the guys that was in the plant. They would find out if there was any shortage of coal or food. Then they'd maneuver around amongst themselves until they found some place to get a ton of coal.

Some of 'em would have foremen come to their homes: "Sorry, your husband was a very good operator. But if he don't get out of the plant and away from the union, he'll never again have a job at General Motors." If this woman was the least bit scared, she'd come down and cry on her husband's shoulder. He'd more than likely get a little disturbed, get a hold of his strike captain. Sometimes you just had to let 'em go. Because if you kept them in there, they'd worry so much over it, that'd start ruinin' the morale of the rest of the guys.

Morale was very high at the time. It started out kinda ugly because the guys were afraid they put their foot in it and all they was gonna do is lose their jobs. But as time went on, they begin to realize they could win this darn thing, 'cause we had a lot of outside people comin' in showin' their sympathy.

Nationally known people contributed to our strike fund. Mrs. Roosevelt for one. We even had a member of Parliament come from England and address us.

Lotta things worked for the union we hadn't even anticipated. Company tried to shut off the heat. It was a bluff. Nobody moved for half an hour, so they turned it back on again. They didn't want the pipes to get cold. If the heat was allowed to drop, then the pipes will separate—they were all jointed together—and then you got a problem.

Some of the time you were scared, because there was all kinds of rumors going around. We had a sheriff—he came in one night and read the boys the riot act. He told 'em they had to leave. He stood there, looked at 'em a few minutes. A couple of guys began to curse 'im, and he turned around and left.

The men sat in there for forty-four days. Governor Murphy was trying to get both sides to meet on some common ground. I think he lost many a good night's sleep. We wouldn't use force. Mr. Knudsen was head of General Motors and, of course, there was John L. Lewis [founder of the CIO]. They'd reach a temporary agreement and invariably the Flint Alliance or GM headquarters in Detroit would throw a monkey wrench in it. So every morning, Murphy got up with an unsolved prolem.

John L. [Lewis] was as close to a Shakespearean actor as any I've ever listened to. He had more command of language. He made a speech that if they shoot the boys out at the plant, they'd have to shoot him first.

Finally, we got the word: THE THING IS SETTLED. My, you had to send about three people, one right after the other, down to some of those plants because the guys didn't believe it. Finally, when they did get it, they marched out of the plants with the flag flyin' and all that stuff.

When Mr. Knudsen put his name to a piece of paper and says that General Motors recognizes the UAW-CIO—until that moment, we were non-people, we didn't even exist. That was the big one.

THE GOLDEN AGE OF RADIO

Although Americans underwent many hardships during the Great Depression of the 1930's, not all was gloom and misery. The entertainment industry did a thriving business. Hollywood, for example, turned out such all-time movie favorites

as "Gone With the Wind" and "The Wizard of Oz." Over 60 percent of all Americans went to the movies every week. (It was possible to see a double feature for as little as ten cents.)

Even cheaper was radio. The 1930's were the heyday of this medium, and many different types of shows were broadcast live from stations all over the country. Whole families gathered around the radio to relax, much as they watch television today.

Joseph Julian, the author of this account, began his radio career as a bit actor and sound-effects man in 1932, in the depths of the depression. Here he talks about some of his experiences in the mid-1930's.

How did radio as Julian describes it differ from radio today? Can you see any advantages of radio as compared to television? Explain.

Edited from This Was Radio: A Personal Memoir *by Joseph Julian. Reprinted by permission of Viking Penguin Inc.*

Gradually, I began getting more auditions —and winning a few now and then. I picked up isolated jobs on shows like *Flash Gordon; Inner Sanctum; Joyce Jordan, Girl Interne;* and *Renfrew of the Mounted.*

Waiting in the studio for a *Renfrew* rehearsal to start, I got into a conversation with a tall, distinguished-looking gentleman named Brad Barker. In the middle of a discussion, he suddenly excused himself, walked over to a large cardboard cylinder mounted on a metal frame, put his mouth to one end, and emitted the blood-curdling howl of a timber wolf. This was the opening signature of *Renfrew of the Mounted,* a weekly series of half-hour stories of manhunts and battles between the good guys and bad guys in the Canadian wilderness.

Barker (what's in a name?) was one of a small group of specialists who made a good living doing animal sounds, baby noises, and screams—which were always in demand.

The animal imitators could come up with just about anything asked of them, from the chirp of a canary (any age) to the roar of a rhinoceros.

Donald Bain, one of the best, could meow and bark and spit, as both characters of a cat and dog fight. Some actors once played a dirty trick on him. They accompanied him to the Automat, where he regularly had lunch, then one telephoned from the outside and had him paged. Pretending to be the director of a radio show, he told Bain he needed someone in a hurry who could do a good cat and dog fight,

and that he had been recommended. Would he be willing to do a short audition over the phone? Whereupon Bain furiously snarled and meowed and spat and barked into the receiver, while everyone in the restaurant roared at the antics of this seemingly crazy little man.

The baby criers were usually women, who carried a small pillow around with them, into which they gurgled, whined and bawled. Sometimes they would also lisp the words of a young child.

The screamers? You might think anyone can scream? Not so. 'Tis an art. There are all kinds of screams: some that are short and eerie, others that are long and shrill. And screams you might hear in a Gothic tale, of the victim before the kill. Some screamers were better than others, but they all saved the throats of the actors for whom they doubled, enabling them to continue the performance without hoarseness.

The most powerful casting director at that time was Frances von Bernhardi, who worked for Frank and Anne Hummert, an incredibly successful husband-and-wife team that dominated the field of radio drama. Former journalists, they pioneered the format of the daily series and filled them with the same low common denominator—sentimentality.

The Hummerts themselves usually dreamed up a show's original concept, building it around a folksy or easily identifiable character. They employed a large stable of writers. One group worked exclusively at developing story lines and plots. When approved by the Hummerts, the scripts were passed along to the dialogue writers. There were many do's and don't's. For instance, all characters had to be constantly identified by name:

JOHN: Why, hello, Henry!
HENRY: Hello, John.
JOHN: Haven't seen you in a long time, Henry.
HENRY: Yes, that's true, John.
JOHN: How about joining me for a drink, Henry?
HENRY: Why, I'd like to, John.

Unnatural? Yes, but they felt it was essential to know who was talking to whom at all times. They must have thought their listeners were pretty stupid not to be able to tell from the dialogue itself.

Plot lines were often altered by a performer's real-life situation. Some contracts provided they be written out of the show for a few weeks in order to rehearse a Broadway play. The writers would then invent a reason for the character's disappearance. Perhaps he would be sent on a journey abroad, or to a rest home, or, perhaps, to jail. The same when an actor took sick. And, if he suddenly quit or was fired, there were always easy ways of killing him off—a heart attack, an auto accident, a murder.

Long pauses could never be indicated in a script. "Dead air" was forbidden. The theory was that during even a five-second silence, a hundred thousand listeners might be just tuning in. Hearing nothing, they'd turn to another station, losing all those customers for the sponsor's product.

To snag new listeners, and for those who may have missed a chapter, each episode of a serial had to be preceded by a short summary of the plot:

> ANNOUNCER: Yesterday, we left Alice in her living room, along with John Hennesy, her sister Gwendolyn's husband. John had just confided that he had always been in love with Alice, and had made a terrible mistake in marrying Gwendolyn. Gwendolyn, who had left the house moments before, suddenly remembered she had forgotten some books she wanted to return to the library. As she reentered the living room, John had just put his arms around Alice's waist. Gwendolyn froze as she heard John say:
> JOHN: Darling, I love you more than anything in this world!

This would be followed by a music sting (*sharp chord*), the organ music would fade, and the announcer would come in with the first commercial. Generally there was an opening, middle, and closing commercial—a terrible price that listeners didn't seem to mind paying for their addiction to "soaps."

* * * *

By the late thirties network programming had pretty well standardized its form. Its main categories—drama, comedy, and music—were served up in quarter-, half-, and one-hour slices of time.

Most of the dramas were, of course, the daytime "soaps"—so called because they were listened to mostly by women while doing their washing and cleaning, who were thus presumably vulnerable to sales pitches by the soap company sponsors.

In the evenings dramas were always on the menu, but the emphasis was on comedy and music.

Most of the important comedians sprang full-blown from vaudeville—especially those whose specialty was essentially non-visual, such as the joke tellers. But these comics paid a price for their new popularity. In vaudeville, a comedy routine lasted for years; in radio, it was consumed in a night. The strain of building a new show every week took its toll, and there were many breakdowns and retirements and comebacks among the nation's top funny men.

There was also a kind of humor special to radio. Mock insults and feuds between two leading comedians would boost each other's ratings, and sometimes could be kept running for months, such as the one between Jack Benny and Fred Allen, in which Allen kept finding new ways to describe Benny's stinginess. One evening a sketch had Benny being held up by a thief who snarled, "Money or your life!" The long, long period of dead air that followed became hilarious, and was topped by Benny finally saying petulantly, "I'm thinking it over." This just couldn't be as funny in any other medium. And there was Allen's classic retort to an insult by Benny: "If I had my writers here you wouldn't talk to me like that and get away with it!"

Speaking of comedy, probably the most unique comedy performance in radio history occurred in 1937 when, during a newspaper strike, the mayor of New York City, Fiorello H. La Guardia, took to the air to read funny papers to the children. The kids "didn' wanna know from nothin" about wages and working conditions—they missed their funnies! La Guardia, mayor of *all* the people, understood what that deprivation meant. Every evening, for as long as the strike lasted, he would act out all the parts in his high squeaky voice and slight lisp, gesturing dramatically as he described the pictures and read the ballooned dialogue of the comic strips that regularly appeared in the New York papers. It was something to hear—and behold.

Unit Six

From Isolation Through World War II

1920-1941

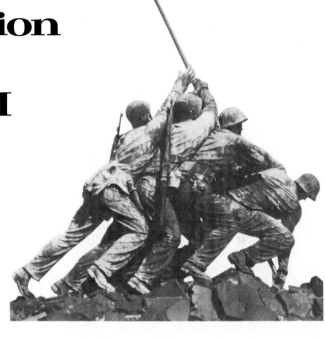

CHAPTER 16
THE UNITED STATES MOVES TOWARD ISOLATION

HOPE FOR A RICH FUTURE

In the 1920's, Congress passed several laws to limit immigration into the United States. These laws reflected a widespread feeling of prejudice and intolerance toward the large groups of immigrants who came from southern and eastern Europe in the late 1800's and early 1900's.

Not all Americans felt this way about the newcomers. Many Americans believed that the vitality and strength of the United States were based on the great diversity of its people, cultures, and ideas. They did not view their nation as a "melting pot," where people's differences were "melted down" and everyone was "Americanized." Horace Kallen, a scholar and writer, held this view, suggesting that the ideal nation was one in which each group maintained its identity and contributed its special talents to society.

What two alternatives does Kallen believe Americans face? Which one does Kallen favor? Would you say that American society today has become either of Kallen's alternatives?

Adapted from Culture and Democracy in the United States, *by Horace M. Kallen. Copyright 1924 by Boni & Liveright, Inc., copyright renewed 1952 by Horace M. Kallen. Reprinted by permission of the Liveright Publishing Corporation.*

Today the descendants of the colonists appear to be making a new Declaration of Independence. Again, as in 1776, Americans of British background fear that certain possessions of theirs, which may be lumped under the word "Americanism," are in danger. The danger comes, once more, from a force across the ocean. But this time the force is regarded not as superior, but as inferior. The relationships of 1776 are thus reversed. To save the unalienable rights of the colonists of 1776, it was necessary to declare all people equal. To save the unalienable rights of their descendants in the 1900's, it becomes necessary to declare all people unequal. In 1776 all people were as good as their betters. In 1920 people are permanently worse than their betters.

In 1776 most white people in the colonies *were* actually rather free and rather equal with respect to each other. I speak not so much of the absence of great differences in wealth, as of the fact that the white colonists were similar to each other. They had ethnic and cultural unity and the same background and ideals. Their 150-year-old tradition as Americans blended with their older traditions as Britons. They did not, until the quarrel with the mother country began, regard themselves as anything but English subjects, sharing England's dangers and England's glories.

In time, the nation created by the Declaration of Independence gained all the continental area known as the United States. The French in Louisiana and the Germans in Pennsylvania remained at home. But the descendants of the British colonists traveled across the continent, founding new settlements. If the population of these settlements had continued to grow in the same proportion as it did between 1810 and 1820, Americans of British background would have totaled over 100 million today. The inhabitants of the country today do number over 100 million. But they are not the children of the colonists and pioneers. They are later immigrants and the children of later immigrants, and they are not only British but of all the other European backgrounds.

First came the Irish. They were ethnically different from the British and Catholic in religion. They came seeking food and freedom. Their area of settlement is chiefly the East.

Behind the Irish came large numbers of Germans, quite different in speech and customs. They were culturally and economically far better off than the Irish. They settled inland, over a stretch of territory extending from western New York to the Mississippi.

Beyond the Germans, in Minnesota and the Dakotas, are the Scandinavians. Beyond these, in the mountain and mining regions, are central and eastern and southern Europeans—Slavs of various stocks, Magyars, Finns, Italians. Across the Rockies, a group of Americans of British background balances the small group on the Atlantic seacoast. They are flanked on the south by Latins—Spaniards, Mexicans, Italians—and scattered groups of Asiatics—and on the north by Scandinavians. The distribution of the population along the two coasts is similar. On the Atlantic shore French-Canadians, Irish, Italians, Slavs, and Jews alternate with the British-American population and each other.

Of all these immigrant peoples, most were of peasant stock. They were unable to read or write, surviving on a minimum of food and a maximum of work. The fearful Americans think that their coming to the United States was determined not by any spiritual reason, but because of the steamship agencies and economic need or greed. This opinion ignores four significant exceptions and one notable one. The significant exceptions are the Poles, the Finns, the Bohemians, the Slovaks. Political and religious and cultural persecution plays a large role in their movement here. The notable exception is the Jews. The Jews, more than any other people, come with the attitude of the earliest settlers. For they come because of persecution and disaster and are in search of economic opportunity, liberty of conscience, and civil rights.

All immigrants and their children undergo "Americanization" if they remain in one place in the country long enough—say six or seven years. In general, "Americanization" seems to mean the adoption of the American kind of English speech, American clothes and manners, and the American attitude in politics. "Americanization" means, in short, the disappearance of the outward differences upon which so much race prejudice is based. It appears to mean the blending together, by "the miracle of assimilation," of Jews, Slavs, Poles, French, Germans, Hindus, Scandinavians, and so on. They all are to become similar in background, tradition, outlook, and spirit to the descendants of the British colonists—the "Anglo-Saxon" stock.

Broadly speaking, these elements of Americanism are somewhat outward, the effect of environment. Along with them go American individualism, the American tendency to look on the bright side of things, and the other "pioneer" virtues. They are purely reactions to the country's natural wealth. As such they are common to all societies where the relation between population and resources is similar.

America is at the parting of the ways. Two genuine social alternatives face Americans, either of which they may achieve if they wish. What do Americans want to make of the United States—a unison, singing the old British theme "America," the America of New England? Or a harmony, in which that theme shall be dominant perhaps, but one among many, and not the only one?

In the United States, the whole social situation is favorable to the idea of unison — everything is favorable except the basic law of America itself and the spirit of American institutions. To achieve unison would require violating them. Fundamentally it would require completely nationalizing education, doing away with every form of parochial and private school, ending instruction in all languages except English, and concentrating on the teaching of history and literature based on the English tradition.

Achieving the other alternative, a harmony, also requires united public action. But this action would not go completely against the ideals of America's fundamental law or the spirit of American institutions. It would seek simply to eliminate the waste and the stupidity in the society's organization, by way of freeing and strengthening those strong forces now at work. Taking the existing ethnic and cultural groups, it would seek to provide conditions under which each group might attain cultural perfection that is *proper to its kind*. All of the various nationalities which make up the American nation must first of all be taught this fact. Perhaps is used to be, to patriotic minds, the outstanding idea of "Americanism" — that democracy means self-realization through self-control and self-discipline.

What is essential in the life of humankind is its inborn positive quality — its inner inheritance. People may change their clothes, their politics, their religions, their philosophies, to a greater or lesser degree. They cannot change their grandparents. Jews or Poles or Anglo-Saxons, in order to stop being Jews or Poles or Anglo-Saxons, would have to cease to be. They inherit their selfhood and the kind of happiness they pursue. This is what, in fact, democracy in operation assumes. There are human capacities which it is the function of the nation to liberate and protect.

As intelligence and wisdom gain over "politics" and special interests, the outlines of a possible great and truly democratic nation can be seen. Its form would be a federal republic. It would be a democracy of nationalities, cooperating voluntarily through common institutions. Thus "American civilization" may come to mean the perfection of the cooperative harmonies of "European civilization" — an orches-

tration of humankind. As in an orchestra, every type of instrument has its specific tone and its proper theme and melody in the whole symphony. So in society, each ethnic group is like a natural instrument. The harmony and discords of them all make the symphony of civilization.

TWO BRITISH VIEWS OF AMERICAN ISOLATION

Right after World War I, the European nations believed that the United States would join the League of Nations and use its influence and power to help keep the peace in Europe. These hopes ended with the Senate's rejection of the Treaty of Versailles. How did Europe react to America's refusal to join the League? For the most part, Europeans were quite critical of it.

Some Europeans, however, tried to analyze more thoughtfully the reasons behind America's return to its traditional policy of isolation. Among them were two British writers, J. A. Spender and Collinson Owen. The first selection is taken from a book by Spender; the second is from a book by Owen.

What does Spender think is the main reason for American isolationism? In Owen's analysis, what incorrect belief does he think helps to explain American actions since the war? In your opinion, do these two articles agree or disagree about the causes of American isolationism?

Adapted from Through English Eyes *by J. A. Spender. Reprinted by permission of the Estate of the late J. A. Spender.*

Adapted from The American Illusion *by Collinson Owen, published by Ernest Benn Limited. Reprinted by permission of the publisher.*

The first thing, it seems to me, is for Europeans to realize that the United States is not a European power. The habit of treating it as if it acted from the same motives, sympathies, and dislikes as European nations has been the source of much misunderstanding. Most Americans still think they are lucky not to be in Europe and not to be forced to mix themselves in its very tangled affairs. To these — the vast majority of Americans — participation in the war to meet the German challenge was a break, but not a change, in their traditional policy. They regard it as common sense to keep out of Europe if they can.

But this is not the only opinion in America.

A large minority of important and politically knowledgeable people have a generous desire to do what they think is their duty to the world. And the whole business community wants to trade with Europe, lend it money, and get back from it what it owes. This "common sense," this idealism, and this commercial ambition are all factors in American policy. We have to consider their interaction in attempting to judge any particular part of its policy.

At the present moment America is seeking a compromise which it hopes will give it the best of all possibilities. It will trade in Europe, maintain its claims on Europe, and shout "Hands off Europe." This annoys and confuses the Europeans. It involves America in such apparent contradictions as starting an enormous program of naval construction at the same time it is proposing a plan for all nations to give up war. There is, nevertheless, a search for the right and wise policy going on all the time, and to treat it with distrust would be a great mistake. It is better to consider what has happened and why it has happened.

The British people should not hastily condemn American policy. The American state of mind corresponds almost exactly to that of the British until quite recently. For a large part of my life—roughly from the year 1880 to the year 1904—it was the aim of both British political parties to stay clear of "continental entanglements." We said to ourselves that the sea made us safe and that we should be able to sit quietly on our island. Why, we asked, should we meddle in quarrels which did not concern us when we had the whole British Empire demanding our extra energy and capital?

It was not argument but events which drove us out of our "splendid isolation." Very reluctantly we came to the conclusion that we must either help to control events on the continent or be controlled by them. Whether we chose rightly or wrongly history must decide. But by the beginning of the 1900's we had discovered that nonintervention was not, as we had supposed, an easy and simple solution, but the most difficult and complicated of all foreign policies. As much as Great Britain might have wished to turn its back on its neighbors, they could not or would not turn their backs on it. Every year these points of contact and friction seemed to increase.

I am not suggesting that American policy will follow the same or a parallel course. Their 3,000 miles [4,830 kilometers] of ocean seem to make it even more obvious common sense for Americans to stand apart than our 21 miles [34 kilometers] of English Channel made it for us. The possibilities of meeting between the United States and other nations are fewer than those between the British Empire and other nations. An attack on the United States from Europe would be far more difficult than an attack on the British Isles from the continent. But Americans too discovered in 1917 that it was impossible for them to remain outside a great European struggle. At the end of it, their President said that there would be no neutrals in another war. Thus he proposed a League of Nations to keep the peace. Europeans accepted it and America rejected it. Europe is thus left with an American institution which America refused to accept—an American orphan left on Europe's doorstep. The United States still believes, in spite of its experiences of 1917, that nonintervention is a possible policy. At all events the United States is determined that it alone will decide whether, when, and how it will intervene.

The real cause of all this misunderstanding of America is the Great War. Before then all the European nations were aware of the United States, but not obsessed by it. Many of the workers and farmers of these countries may have dreamed of America as the great land of opportunity. But most accepted America much as America thought of itself: a very great country, but a country still in the making. It was a country which had made remarkable progress considering the short time it had been a nation. But it was a country which still had a very long way to go before it could be regarded as a nation as European nations thought of the term. It was not even a real naval or military power, in days when to be a great naval or military power was one of the proofs of civilization.

But the war changed all that. While all Europe was locked in its four years' struggle, America stole up on us like a bill collector in the night. The war changed us, and seemed to change America. But the fact is that, riches apart, America was exactly the same country after the war that it was before it. Essentially it still remained the same partly developed community. In many ways frontier conditions still ruled, side by side with great material prosperity.

*　　*　　*　　*

Perhaps the most startling discovery one can make in the United States is the fact that many Americans have come to the conclusion that they really won the war.

When this rumor first began, some two or three years after the war was over, no sensible person in Europe paid any real attention to it. No doubt that attitude was then correct. But things have changed very much since then. There are many individuals in the United States who are much too fair and sane to believe in any such fantastic idea. But the people as a whole, aided by the superpatriots, part of the press, the politicians, the movies, and that curious belief that everything American is necessarily best, have now convinced themselves that it was what America did that really mattered. The years 1914–17 are forgotten. Everyone's memory is concentrated on 1918.

This false idea shared by a very large part of a vast nation is not just something to be made fun of. It has its direct effect on international politics. The more firmly America believes this idea, the more likely it is to feel strengthened in its official attitude toward Europe as a continent of warring barbarians, full of old-fashioned treaties and secret diplomacy.

It is a difficult subject to discuss even with some of the best and most open-minded Americans. Although they know that such a claim is absurd, on the whole they would like to feel that America's participation was the really deciding factor.

If the war was really a fight to maintain what we call civilization, against the scientific, military barbarism of the Germany of 1914, then in upholding civilization, the Allies by the middle of 1917 were almost bled to death. The war by that time had become a blood tax on those nations which believed in upholding this civilization. America believed in this ideal, as it assured us both before and after its participation. The blood tax it was called upon to pay in saving it was very, very small. That is the only point of view that needs to be presented in any discussion of whether or not America won the war.

But it would be useless to present such a view to most Americans. They have become convinced of their comforting false idea. And they believe that the soldiers who crossed the Atlantic to Europe were noble crusaders such as the world had never seen before. It is the habit, of course, of every nation to praise the courage of its own soldiers in war. But though this is a tendency common to all nations, the United States—so far as the last war is concerned—easily goes beyond any other in praising its soldiers. If ever there was a sort of inferiority complex about America's late entrance in the war, it has long since been forgotten, and has been replaced by a mass-produced self-satisfaction and pride concerning the events of 1914–18.

It is a self-satisfaction which has a very definite business as well as patriotic value. So long as America feels like this, there can be no uneasiness of mind concerning Europe's war debts. "Those Europeans" may be feeling the pinch a bit, but they're always getting into wars anyhow, and don't know how to finish them when they begin. America had to do that for them, spending a lot of its own best blood and its own good money in the process. Too much talk about generosity to France and the rest of them becomes tiresome after that.

LOBBYING FOR DISARMAMENT

After World War I, the major military powers of the world held a series of conferences aimed at limiting the naval armaments race. At the Washington Naval Conference of 1921, the United States, Great Britain, and Japan agreed to a ten-year "naval holiday." During this time they would build no new warships.

In 1930, as this period was drawing to a close, these same nations, plus France and Italy, met in London to renegotiate. Now Great Britain and France went further, urging the abolition of battleships and submarines. The Americans objected, arguing instead for parity (that is, equality). This would allow the United States to build *more* warships, since it had had fewer than the British to begin with.

Earlier, President Herbert Hoover had pledged to reduce American naval strength. What was happening now? To many, it seemed that the United States was opposing real disarmament. One critical group was the Women's International League for Peace and Freedom. It sent the President a strongly worded letter of complaint. The next day Dorothy Detzer, executive director of the league (referred to here as the W.I.L.), was asked to visit the President.

What does the league want the American delegation to do? How does Hoover respond to the league's proposal? How does Detzer explain Hoover's reluctance to "offer a program of real naval disarmament"?

Adapted from Appointment on the Hill *by Dorothy Detzer. Copyright 1948 by Dorothy Detzer. Reprinted by permission of Holt, Rinehart and Winston, Publishers.*

The President spoke about the contents of the letter. He said he knew that the public was disturbed by "rumors" from London that the naval conference was deadlocked, and that the U.S. delegation was in great part responsible for this situation. He recognized, too, the sincerity of the W.I.L. in pressing for more affirmative action. But he felt sure, he said, that we would not be so vocal and persistent if we knew all the facts.

In our letter, he reminded me, we had pointed out that private citizens were not always in a position to know the facts. He knew our interest, respected our energy. Therefore, he had decided to take me into his confidence. If I understood the real situation, he hoped the situation itself would persuade me to divert the present flood of W.I.L. criticism into equally vigorous public support for the government's undertaking at London.

At this point, Mr. Hoover took from his pocket a key and unlocked a deep drawer in the desk. From the drawer, he drew out a bulky package of dispatches. "These," he said, placing the package on his desk, "are the decoded cables sent to me by the U.S. delegation in London. I want you to read them. For I am sure when you have done so, you will agree with me that your letter was based on a misunderstanding."

I picked up the first cable and began to read. The President picked up a pencil and began to "doodle." It took me almost an hour to read through the thick pile of confidential dispatches. In that hour, there unfolded before me the whole inside story of that naval conference.

When I laid down the last decoded cable, dated only that day, the President looked up from the paper he was covering with elaborate patterns of intricate circular designs.

"Well," said the President gently as he smiled across the desk at me, "don't you agree now that your letter was based on a misunderstanding?"

I hesitated. I liked this shy, gray President. There was something strangely appealing about his very shyness. He did not seem like the controversial storm center of editorials and cartoons, or even the formal official who received White House delegations. He was just a man in a blue serge suit with very kind, tired eyes. My immediate instinct was a protective one. Who was I to add even a fraction to the heavy burden he carried? Yet I knew integrity demanded my first loyalty.

"No, Mr. President," I said after the momentary pause. "To me, those dispatches only confirm the rightness of our letter."

"What do you mean?" he asked, swinging his chair about in a motion of impatience. "Can't you see all the complications—all the difficulties?"

"Yes, I think I do," I answered. "They are even worse than I had imagined."

"Then why do you say those dispatches confirm the rightness of your letter?"

"Because," I answered, "these dispatches have convinced me that the U.S. delegation is allowing the difficulties to block the achievement of your announced policies."

Mr. Hoover made another gesture of impatience.

"Why do you say that?" he asked.

"Mr. President, I didn't have to read these dispatches to know that the U.S. delegation in London is concentrating all its effort on the principle of parity, and not on reduction," I answered. "That certainly is no secret; the press reports that fact every day. Yet you stated publicly, before the conference convened, that our country was prepared to reduce its naval strength in proportion to any other nation, and that it only remained for the other nations to say how low they would go—they couldn't go too low for us. But our delegation, instead of supporting the proposals now before the conference for the abolition of battleships and submarines, blocks those proposals by its demands for parity. And won't parity mean a new super battleship for us as well as an extension of our cruiser program? That, it seems to me, contradicts your pledge that the United States would go as low as any other nation. Therefore, if the conference fails, why won't the fault lie with the United States, Mr. President?"

"But since reading those dispatches," said the President, "you certainly must see that there are other factors which must be considered in this situation also; and because of those factors, you should realize that if the conference fails the responsibility will not rest on the United States."

"Mr. President," I said, "I am sorry, but I can't understand what you mean. The factors you refer to certainly complicate the problems. I can't, of course, know all that is involved by just reading those dispatches. But in spite of such limited knowledge, what I *do* know convinces me that the United States will be responsible for the outcome of the conference. And as we suggested in our letter, it would seem that that responsibility is yours, Mr. President."

Mr. Hoover looked as though I had struck him. He swung his chair around in a half circle so that his back was partly toward me. He gazed silently out of the window across Executive Avenue. Opposite, the White House grounds lay lovely and serene in the gathering spring twilight. Inside the room, there was only a prolonged silence, and the pallid dusk of early evening. What should I do? Should I leave? But one didn't just leave a President; one had to be dismissed. I must wait; his was the next move. Yet after what seemed to be an endless time, I half rose in my chair.

"Mr. President," I asked quietly, "do you want me to leave?"

The President turned slowly in his chair. "No, sit down," he said wearily. "I want to ask you a question." There was a long pause. Then looking up he said, "What would you do now if you were the President of the United States?"

This time, I felt as if the President had struck me.

"Mr. President," I said, trying to make my tone as light as possible, "I don't suppose a President of the United States will ever ask me that question again. And perhaps you will think that only arrogance or ignorance would lead me to answer it. I hope it is neither; for I want to answer it.

"Go on," he said. "I want to hear what you would do."

"Mr. President," I began, "you don't know it, but in one sense we have shared a tremendous experience. Only you were the chief of the American Relief Administration in Europe [after World War I], and I was only an ordinary relief worker with the Friends' Mission. But however different our status in that work, we both know what war means to all the little people. If I were President of the United States, I would never forget for one moment all those little people. Remembering them, I would discard all ideas of 'parity' and 'limitation' and 'reduction,' and I would offer at London a program so daring and inspiring that the world would rise up and call me blessed. You can do that; you have the power. You would be opposed and attacked, of course, by the vested interests in war, but those are the ones who are never shot at or starved." I paused. "Why can't you do that?"

"I can't," said the President, swinging his chair around toward the window again. "I can't. Besides, you forget this is not a disarmament conference. This is a conference on limitation."

"I haven't forgotten that, Mr. President," I said. "But certainly you can 'limit' things down to nothing. And what other nation has such an opportunity as the United States now? We have two big oceans on either side of us, friendly neighbors to the north and south. Who threatens us? We are powerful, and rich, and safe. We could go farther than any other nation. If you would offer a program of real naval disarmament, supplemented perhaps with a positive economic program, think what that would mean for peace. Why can't you do something like that before it is too late?"

"I can't," he said. "I can't."

"Well, if you can't do all of that," I pursued, "why can't you accept the proposals for the abolition of battleships and submarines? If the other nations are making those proposals just as a bluff, why don't you call their bluff? But if they are honest, what a good start that would be. If the United States doesn't respond now, it may be forever too late."

The President was silent for a long moment; then he raised his hands in a gesture of futility, and dropped them on the desk. "I can't," he fairly whispered. "I can't."

I looked at the weary profile silhouetted against the window. In it was sadness, and worry, and frustration. "He's trapped," I said to myself, "trapped. He holds the most powerful position in the most powerful nation in the world, and yet for some reason the President of the United States is not a free agent."

I looked at my watch; it was six o'clock. I had been there two hours. I rose to my feet. "It is six o'clock, Mr. President. Don't you want me to go?" Mr. Hoover's eyes never moved from the window. It was a moment before he jerked slightly, as though aware that someone had just spoken.

"What did you say?" he asked.

"Perhaps you would like me to go," I said.

"Oh, yes—yes," he answered. "Yes, of course."

"Thank you very much for letting me talk to you," I said, feeling a little at a loss to know how to end such an interview.

I got my coat off the rack and went out into the lovely April evening. I would go to the office now and type a memorandum while the events of the last two hours were still fresh in my mind. Tomorrow I would take it to the bank and place it in my safety deposit box. This was a memorandum which could not be dictated to a secretary nor put in the office files. For I was burdened with a secret: the naval conference would fail.

CHAPTER 17
MOVING FROM ISOLATIONISM INTO WAR

A "BUG'S-EYE" VIEW OF EUROPE

Don Marquis, a newspaper writer, became famous as the creator of an imaginary insect named Archy. Archy, a cockroach, was a shrewd observer of people and events, and he did not hesitate to express his opinions on any subject. He had very strong viewpoints, especially about American society.

Each night, Archy used Marquis' office typewriter to write down his ideas about what was happening in the world. Archy supposedly operated the typewriter keys by jumping on them head first. Because he was unable to move the shift key on the typewriter, he was not able to use capital letters or punctuation. In this selection, you will read Archy's view of "post war europe."

To what "mutual animosities," or hatreds, do you think Archy is referring? According to Archy, when will wars cease permanently? Do you think that using a make-believe character to express opinions is effective? Explain.

"the league" by Don Marquis. Copyright 1935 by Doubleday & Co., Inc. From the Book The Lives and Times of Archy and Mehitabel. *Reprinted by permission of Doubleday & Co., Inc.*

the league

if the league of nations
can survive the mutual animosities
of the powers which belong to it
it is safe from the activities
of the countries which stayed outside of it
it furnishes a wonderful mechanism
with which to do what the powers
want to do if they only knew
what they wanted to do
incidentally i wonder why europe of today
is always referred to by highbrow writers
as post war europe

they seem to think that the war
which started in nineteen fourteen
is over with whereas there have been
merely a few brief truces
that war is merely worrying through
its first half century
and will only cease permanently
when a generation comes along
which has forgotten all the old feuds

archy the cockroach

THE MENACE OF HITLER

Many Americans were deeply concerned about events in Europe in the late 1930's. They were disturbed by the rise of dictators in some European nations and the aggressive ambitions of these dictators. With each new act of aggression by Germany, Italy, and Japan, some Americans feared that war was certain.

One person who was especially concerned about these events was Dorothy Thompson, a famous journalist whose newspaper and magazine writings were well known to Americans. During these years, it was said that she was "the equivalent of a troop of tanks in the prewar skirmishing with Adolf Hitler." The following selection was written on February 18, 1938, shortly after Austrian chancellor Kurt von Schuschnigg had met with Hitler and agreed to admit Nazi members into the Austrian cabinet. Still not satisfied with this agreement, Hitler sent an army into Austria a few weeks later. Austria then came under the total control of Germany.

Why, as Dorothy Thompson sees it, does Germany want Austria? What two alternatives does she predict for the future? Was her prediction correct?

Write it down. On Saturday, February 12, 1938, Germany won the world war, and dictated, at Hitler's mountain retreat, a peace treaty to make the Treaty of Versailles look like one of the great humane documents of the ages.

Write it down. On Saturday, February 12, 1938, Nazism started on the march across all of Europe east of the Rhine.

Write it down that the world revolution began in earnest—and perhaps the world war.

Write it down that the democratic world broke its promises and gave in, not in the face of strength, but of terrible weakness, armed only with ruthlessness and daring.

What happened?

On February 4, Hitler ousted his chief of staff and fourteen other generals. Why? Because the army leadership refused to move against an unarmed, friendly country—their German-speaking neighbor, Austria. Why did they refuse? Because of squeamishness? Hardly. Because they thought that Britain and France would interfere? Perhaps. Or because they themselves feared the ultimate catastrophe the future would bring as a result of this move? I think this is the best guess.

A week later, Hitler, with his reorganized army, made his move. How did he make it? He called in the chancellor of Austria, Doctor von Schuschnigg, and gave him an ultimatum. Sixty-six million people against six million people. German troops were ready at Austria's borders. Hitler's generals stood behind him as he interviewed the Austrian chancellor. Hitler taunted his victim. "You know as well as I know that France and Britain will not move a hand to save you." Hitler will doubtless hail this meeting as a friendly reconciliation between two German-speaking peoples and the strengthening of peace in eastern Europe.

What does the chancellor of Austria really think about Nazism?

He expressed himself hardly more than a month ago, on January 5, in the *Morning Telegraph* of London.

This is what he said:

"There is no question of ever accepting Nazi representatives in the Austrian cabinet. An enormous distance separates Austria from Nazism. We do not like arbitrary power, we want law to rule our freedom. We hate terror. Austria has always been a humanitarian state. As a people, we are tolerant by nature. Any change now in our *status quo* could only be for the worse."

Why does Germany want Austria? For raw materials? It has none of any importance. To add to German prosperity? Austria is a poor country with serious problems. But strategically it is the key to the whole of central Europe. Czechoslovakia is now surrounded. The wheat fields of Hungary and the oil fields of Rumania are now open. Not one of them will be able to withstand the pressure of German domination.

It is horror walking. Not that "Germany" joins with Austria. We are not talking of "Germany." We see a new Crusade, under a pagan symbol, worshiping "blood" and "soil," preaching the holiness of the sword and glorifying conquest. It hates the Slavs, whom it thinks to be its historic "mission" to rule. It subjects all of life to a militarized state. It persecutes men and women of Jewish blood. Now it moves into the historic stronghold of Catholic Christianity, into an area of mixed races and mixed nationalities, which for a thousand years the Austro-Hungarian Empire could rule only with tolerance. Adolf Hitler's first hatred was not communism, but Austria-Hungary. Read *Mein Kampf* [Hitler's book]. And he hated it for what? For its tolerance? He wanted 80 million Germans to rule with an iron hand an empire of 80 million "inferiors"—Czechs, Slovaks, Magyars, Jews, Serbs, Poles, and Croats.

Today, all of Europe east of the Rhine is cut off completely from the western world. The swastika banner, we are told, is the crusader's flag against Bolshevism [Communism]! Madness! Only the signs on the flags divide them [Germany and the Soviet Union].

And it never needed to have happened. One strong voice of one strong power could have stopped it.

Tomorrow, one of two things can happen. Despotism can stop where it is, through the lack of real leadership and creative brains. For the law of despotisms is that they kill off the good, and the brave, and the wise. Perhaps all of Europe east of the Rhine will become, eventually, a no-man's land of poverty, militarism, and despair. But nonetheless a plague spot.

More likely the other law of despotism's nature—the law of constant aggressiveness—will cause it to move farther and onward, made bolder and stronger by each success.

To the point where civilization will take a last stand. For take a stand it will. Of that there is not the slightest doubt.

Too bad that it did not take it this week.

LONDON DURING THE BLITZ

After Hilter's invasion of Poland in September 1939, Great Britain and France went to war against Germany. By June 1940 Hitler's blitzkrieg warfare had been so successful that only Great Britain was left to fight Nazi Germany. Then Hitler decided to try to bomb Great Britain into surrender.

All during these long months of war, foreign correspondents, or reporters stationed abroad, kept the American people informed about the war. One of these correspondents was Edward R. Murrow. He was in England during the Battle of Britain, and his radio reports of the nightly Nazi air raids made him famous. Night after night he told Americans of the courage of the British people, the daring of the Royal Air Force pilots, and the horrors they faced. The following are selections from Murrow's broadcasts during the Battle of Britain.

In what ways does Murrow describe the air raids? Why do you think his reporting job was so difficult? What opinions do you think Americans formed from these broadcasts?

From In Search of Light: The Broadcasts of Edward R. Murrow 1938–1961 *edited by Edward Bliss, Jr. Copyright 1941 by Edward R. Murrow. Adapted by permission of Alfred A. Knopf, Inc.*

September 10, 1940

This is London. And the raid which started about seven hours ago is still in progress. Larry LeSueur [a fellow correspondent] and I have spent the last three hours driving about the streets of London and visiting air-raid shelters. We found that like everything else in this world the kind of protection you get from the bombs on London tonight depends on how much money you have. On the other hand, the most expensive dwelling places here do not necessarily provide the best shelters, but certainly they are the most comfortable.

We looked in on a renowned hotel tonight and found many old dowagers [women] and retired colonels settling back on the overstuffed settees [couches] in the lobby. It wasn't the sort of protection I'd seek from a direct hit from a half-ton bomb, but if you were a retired colonel and his lady, you might feel that the risk was worth it because you would at least be bombed with the right sort of people.

Only a couple of blocks away we pushed aside the canvas curtain of a trench cut out of a lawn of a London park. Inside were half a hundred people, some of them stretched out on the hard wooden benches. The rest huddled over in their overcoats and blankets. Dimmed electric lights glowed on the whitewashed walls, and the cannonade of anti-aircraft and reverberation of the big stuff the Germans were dropping rattled the boards underfoot at intervals. One woman was saying sleepily that it was funny how often you read about people being killed inside a shelter. Nobody seemed to listen. Then over to the famous cellar of a world-famous hotel, two floors underground. On upholstered chairs and lounges there was a cosmopolitan crowd. But there wasn't any sparkling conversation. They sat, some of them with their mouths open. One of them snored. King Zog [the former king of Albania] was over in a far corner on a chair, the porter told me.

The number of planes tonight seems to be about the same as last night. Searchlight activity has been constant, but there has been little gunfire in the center of London. The bombs have been coming down at about the same rate as last night. It is impossible to get any estimate of the damage. Darkness prevents observation of details. The streets have been deserted, save for a few clanging fire engines during the last four or five hours. The planes have been high again tonight, so high that the searchlights can't reach them.

Once tonight an anti-aircraft battery opened fire just as I drove past. It lifted me from the seat and a hot wind swept over the car. It was impossible to see. When I drove on, the streets of London reminded me of a ghost town in Nevada — not a soul to be seen. A week ago there would have been people standing on the corner shouting for taxis. Tonight there were no people and no taxis. Earlier today there were trucks delivering mattresses to many office buildings. People are now sleeping on those mattresses, or at least they are trying to sleep.

And so London is waiting for dawn. We ought to get the all clear in about another two hours. Then those big German bombers that have been lumbering and mumbling overhead all night will have to go home.

610

September 13, 1940

This is London at 3:30 in the morning. This has been what might be called a "routine night" — air-raid alarm at about nine o'clock and intermittent bombing ever since. I had the impression that more high explosives and fewer incendiaries [fire bombs] have been used tonight. Only two small fires can be seen. Again the Germans have been sending their bombers in singly or in pairs. The anti-aircraft barrage has been fierce but sometimes there have been periods of twenty minutes when London has been silent. Then the big red buses would start up and move on till the guns started working again. That silence is almost hard to bear. One becomes accustomed to rattling windows and the distant sound of bombs, and then there comes a silence that can be felt. You know the sound will return. You wait, and then it starts again. That waiting is bad. It gives you a chance to imagine things.

The scale of this air war is so great that reporting it is not easy. Often we spend hours traveling about this sprawling city, viewing damage, talking with people and occasionally listening to the bombs come down, and then more hours wondering what you'd like to hear about. We've told you about the bombs, the fires, the smashed houses and the courage of the people. We've read you the communiques and tried to give you an honest estimate of the wounds inflicted upon this, the best bombing target in the world. But the business of living and working in this city is very personal — the little incidents, the things the mind retains, are in themselves unimportant, but they somehow weld together to form the hard core of memories that will remain when the last all clear has sounded. That's why I want to talk for just three or four minutes about the things we haven't talked about before; for many of these impressions it is necessary to reach back through only one long week. There was a rainbow bending over the battered and smoking East End of London just when the all clear sounded one afternoon. One night I stood in front of a smashed grocery store and heard a dripping inside. It was the only sound in all London. Two cans of peaches had been drilled clean through by flying glass, and the juice was dripping down onto the floor.

Today I went to buy a hat — my favorite shop had gone, blown to bits. The windows of my shoe store were blown out. I decided to have a haircut; the windows of the babershop were gone, but the Italian barber was still doing business. Someday, he said, we smile again, but the food doesn't taste so good since being bombed. I went to another shop to buy flashlight batteries. I bought three. The clerk said, "You needn't buy so many. We'll have enough for the whole winter." But I said, "What if you aren't here?" There were buildings down in that street, and he replied, "Of course we'll be here. We've been in business here for a hundred and fifty years."

September 18, 1940

There are no words to describe the thing that is happening. Today I talked with eight American correspondents in London. Six of them had been forced to move. All had stories of bombs, and all agreed that they were unable to convey through print or the spoken word an accurate impression of what's happening in London these days and nights.

I may tell you that Bond Street has been bombed, that a shop selling handkerchiefs at $40 the dozen has been wrecked, that these words [of the broadcast] were written on a table of good English oak which sheltered me three times as bombs tore down in the vicinity. But you can have little understanding of the life in London these days — the courage of the people, the flash and roar of the guns rolling down streets where much of the history of the English-speaking world has been made, the stench of air-raid shelters in the poor districts. These things must be experienced to be understood.

September 22, 1940

I'm standing again tonight on a rooftop looking out over London, feeling rather large and lonesome. In the course of the last fifteen or twenty minutes there's been considerable action up there, but at the moment there's an ominous silence hanging over London. But at the same time a silence that has a great deal of dignity. Just straightaway in front of me the searchlights are working. I can see one or two bursts of anti-aircraft fire far in the distance. Just on the roof across the way I can see a man wearing a tin hat, a pair of powerful night glasses to his eyes, scanning the sky. Again, looking in the opposite direction, there is a building with two windows gone. Out of one window there waves something that looks like a white bed sheet, a window curtain swinging free in this night breeze. It looks as though it were being shaken by a ghost. There are a great many ghosts around these buildings in London. The searchlights, miles in front of me, are still scratching that sky. There's a three-quarter moon riding high.

Down below in the streets I can see just that red and green wink of the traffic lights, one lone taxicab moving slowly down the street. Not a sound to be heard. As I look out across the miles and miles of rooftops and chimney pots, some of those dirty-gray buildings look almost snow-white in this moonlight here tonight. And the rooftop spotter across the way swings around, looks over in the direction of the searchlights, drops his glasses and just stands there. There are hundreds and hundreds of men like that standing on rooftops in London tonight watching for fire bombs, waiting to see what comes out of this steel-blue sky. The searchlights now reach up very, very faintly on three sides of me. There is a flash of a gun in the distance but too far away to be heard.

AMERICA, "THE ARSENAL OF DEMOCRACY"

When World War II broke out in Europe in 1939, the United States faced the problem of what role, if any, it would take in the conflict. During the following year, as Hitler's armies defeated one country after another, the debate over what course of action America should take became increasingly heated.

At first, most Americans wanted to remain out of the war. But by 1940, with Great Britain the only nation left in the struggle against Nazi Germany, many Americans became deeply concerned. Some Americans began to question whether neutrality was a wise policy for the nation. Then, near the end of 1940, President Roosevelt dramatically declared that he favored aiding Great Britain with weapons and military supplies. In a historic "fireside chat," broadcast to the American people over radio on December 29, 1940, President Roosevelt argued that the United States could not remain neutral.

Why does Roosevelt believe America is in great danger? What will happen if Great Britain is defeated? What actions does Roosevelt urge America to take?

Adapted from "Fireside Chat," December 29, 1940, by Franklin D. Roosevelt, from the National Archives and Record Service, Franklin D. Roosevelt Library.

This is not a fireside chat on war. It is a talk on national security. The whole purpose of your President is to keep you now, and your children later, and your grandchildren much later, out of a last-ditch war for the preservation of American independence and all of the things that American independence means.

Never before since Jamestown and Plymouth has our American civilization been in such danger as now.

For, on September 27, 1940—by an agreement signed in Berlin—Germany, Italy, and Japan [the Axis powers] joined together. They threatened that if the United States interfered with their expansion program—a program aimed at world control—they would unite against us.

The United States has no right or reason to encourage talk of peace until there is a clear intention on the part of the aggressor nations to give up all thought of dominating or conquering the world.

Some of our people like to believe that wars in Europe and in Asia are of no concern to us. But it is a matter of most vital concern to us that European and Asiatic war makers should not gain control of the oceans which lead to this hemisphere.

Does anyone seriously believe that we need to fear attack while a free Britain remains our most powerful naval neighbor in the Atlantic? Does anyone seriously believe, on the other hand, that we could rest easy if the Axis powers were our neighbors there?

If Great Britain goes down, the Axis powers will control the continents of Europe, Asia, Africa, and Australia, and the oceans as well. They will be able to throw enormous military and naval resources against this hemisphere. It is no exaggeration to say that all of us in the Americas would be living at the point of a gun—a gun loaded with explosive bullets, economic as well as military.

We would enter upon a new and terrible period in which the whole world, our hemisphere included, would be run by threats of brute force. To survive in such a world, we would have to convert ourselves permanently into a militaristic power with a war economy.

Some of us like to believe that even if Great Britain falls, we are still safe because of the Atlantic and the Pacific oceans. But the width of these oceans is not what it was in the days of clipper ships. At one point between Africa and

Brazil, the distance is less than from Washington to Denver, Colorado—five hours for the latest type of bomber. And at the north of the Pacific Ocean, America and Asia almost touch each other.

Frankly and definitely there is danger ahead—danger against which we must prepare. But we well know that we cannot escape danger, or the fear of it, by crawling into bed and pulling the covers over our heads.

There are those who say that the Axis powers would never have any desire to attack the Western Hemisphere. This is the same dangerous form of wishful thinking which has destroyed the powers of resistance of so many conquered peoples. The plain facts are that the Nazis have said, time and again, that all other races are their inferiors and therefore subject to their orders. And most important of all, the vast resources and wealth of this hemisphere make up the most tempting loot in all the world.

The experience of the past two years has proven beyond doubt that no nation can appease [make concessions to] the Nazis. No one can tame a tiger into a kitten by stroking it. There can be no appeasement with ruthlessness. There can be no reasoning with a bomb. We know now that a nation can have peace with the Nazis only at the price of total surrender.

The American appeasers ignore the warning to be found in the fate of Austria, Czechoslovakia, Poland, Norway, Belgium, the Netherlands, Denmark, and France. They tell you that the Axis powers are going to win anyway. They argue that the United States might just as well use its influence to achieve a dictated peace and get the best out of it that we can.

They call it a "negotiated peace." Nonsense! Is it a negotiated peace if a gang of outlaws surrounds your community and, on threat of death, makes you pay tribute to save your own lives?

The British people are conducting an active war against an unholy alliance. Our own future security is greatly dependent on the outcome of that fight. Our ability to keep out of war is going to be affected by that outcome.

I make this direct statement to the American people. There is far less chance of the United States getting into war if we do all we can now to support the nations defending themselves against attack by the Axis than if we go along with their defeat, then wait our turn to be attacked.

If we are to be completely honest with ourselves, we must admit there is risk in any course we may take. But I believe that most of our people agree that the course I suggest involves the least risk now and the greatest hope for world peace in the future.

The people of Europe who are defending themselves do not ask us to do their fighting. They ask us for the implements of war—the planes, the tanks, the guns, the freighters which will enable them to fight for their liberty and our security. We must get these weapons to them in sufficient volume and quickly enough so that we and our children will be saved the agony and suffering of war which others have had to endure.

There is no demand for sending an American military force outside our own borders. There is no intention by any member of your government to send such a force.

Our national policy is not directed toward war. Its only purpose is to keep war away from our country and our people.

Democracy's fight against world conquest is being greatly aided, and must be aided still more, by the rearmament of the United States and by sending every ounce of munitions and supplies that we can possibly spare to help the defenders who are in the front lines. It is no more unneutral for us to do that than it is for Sweden, Russia, and other nations to send steel and ore and oil into Germany every day.

This is not a matter of feelings or of controversial personal opinion. It is a matter of realistic military policy, based on the advice of our military experts. These experts and the members of Congress and the Administration have one single purpose—the defense of the United States.

I want to make it clear that it is the purpose of the nation to build now with all possible speed every machine and factory that we need to manufacture our defense material. We have the people—the skill—the wealth—and above all, the will.

We must be the great arsenal of democracy. For us this is an emergency as serious as war itself. We must apply ourselves to our task with the same determination, the same sense of urgency, the same spirit of patriotism and sacrifice as we would show if we were at war.

A FAMOUS FLYER URGES
NEUTRALITY

In March 1941 Congress passed the Lend-Lease Act, which permitted the United States to send unlimited weapons and military equipment to Great Britain. But even after passage of this law, Americans continued to debate the nation's role in the European war. On one side were the interventionists, who wanted the United States to enter the war on the side of the Allies. On the other side were the isolationists, who thought Americans should keep completely out of Europe's affairs.

One of the best-known isolationists was the famous American flyer Charles A. Lindbergh. He became a leading member of America First, a nationwide organization that favored arming for defense but argued that the United States could not save the Allies. Lindbergh made the following speech at an America First meeting in New York City on April 23, 1941.

Why does Lindbergh oppose America's entry into the war? What does he urge Americans to do? Why does he think his position is wise?

Adapted from "We Cannot Win This War for England" by Charles A. Lindbergh, in Vital Speeches of the Day, *1941. Reprinted by permission of Vital Speeches of the Day.*

I know I will be severely criticized by the interventionists in America when I say we should not enter a war unless we have a reasonable chance of winning. That, they will claim, is far too materialistic a view. But I do not believe that our American ideals and our way of life will gain through an unsuccessful war. And I know that the United States is not prepared to wage war in Europe successfully at this time.

I have said it before, and I will say again, that I believe it will be a tragedy for the entire world if the British empire collapses. That is one of the main reasons why I opposed this war before it was declared, and why I have constantly favored a negotiated peace. I did not feel that England and France had a reasonable chance of winning. France has now been defeated. Despite the propaganda and confusion of recent months, it is now obvious that England is losing the war. I believe this is realized even by the British government. But they have one last desperate plan remaining. They hope that they may be able to persuade us to send troops to Europe and to share with England

militarily, as well as financially, the fiasco of this war.

I do not blame England for this hope, or for asking for our assistance. But we now know that it declared a war under circumstances which led to the defeat of every nation that sided with it, from Poland to Greece. We know that in the desperation of war England promised to all these nations armed assistance that it could not send. We know that it misinformed them as it has misinformed us about its military preparations, its military strength, and the progress of the war.

In time of war, truth is always replaced by propaganda. I do not believe we should be too quick to criticize the actions of a warring nation. But we do have a right to think of the welfare of America first, just as the people in England thought first of their own country when they encouraged the smaller nations of Europe to fight against hopeless odds. When England asks us to enter the war, it is considering its own future, and that of its empire. In making our reply, I believe we should consider the future of the United States and that of the Western Hemisphere.

It is not only our right, it is our duty as American citizens to look at this war objectively and to weigh our chances for success if we should enter it. I have attempted to do this, especially from the standpoint of air power. I have been forced to the conclusion that we cannot win this war for England, no matter how much aid we send.

I ask you to look at the map of Europe today and see if you can suggest any way in which we could win this war if we entered it. Suppose we had a large army in America, trained and equipped. Where would we send it to fight? The campaigns of the war show only too clearly how difficult it is to force a landing, or to maintain an army, on a hostile coast.

Suppose we took our navy from the Pacific, and used it to convoy [to provide naval protection to] British shipping. That would not win the war for England. It would, at best, permit it to exist under the constant bombing of the Germans. Suppose we had an air force that we could send to Europe. Where could it operate? Some of our squadrons might be based in the British Isles. But it is physically impossible to base enough aircraft in the British Isles alone to equal in strength the aircraft that can be based on the continent of Europe.

I have asked these questions on the assumption that we had an army and an air force large enough and well enough equipped to send to Europe, and that we would dare remove our navy from the Pacific. But the fact is that none of these assumptions are correct. Our army is still untrained and inadequately equipped for foreign war. Our air force lacks modern fighting planes because most of them have already been sent to Europe. We have only a one-ocean navy.

When these facts are stated, the interventionists shout that we are defeatists, that we are undermining the principles of democracy, and that we are giving comfort to Germany by talking about our military weakness. But everything I mention here has been published in our newspapers, and in the reports of congressional hearings in Washington. Our military position is well known to the governments of Europe and Asia. Why, then, should it not be brought to the attention of our own people?

I say it is the interventionists in America, as it was in England and in France, who give comfort to the enemy. I say it is they who are undermining the principles of democracy when they demand that we take a course to which more than 80 percent of our citizens are opposed. [According to public opinion polls, by December 1941 only 20 percent of the American people were in favor of declaring war on Germany.] I charge them with being the real defeatists, for their policy has led to the defeat of every country that followed their advice since this war began. There is no better way to give comfort to an enemy than to divide the people of a nation over the issue of foreign war. There is no shorter road to defeat than by entering a war with inadequate preparation. Every nation that has adopted the interventionist policy of depending on someone else for its own defense has met with defeat and failure.

There is a policy open to this nation that will lead to success—a policy that leaves us free to follow our own way of life and to develop our own civilization. It is not a new and untried idea. It was favored by Washington. It was incorporated in the Monroe Doctrine. Under its guidance the United States has become the greatest nation in the world.

It is based upon the belief that the security of a nation lies in the strength and character of its own people. It recommends the mainte-nance of armed forces sufficient to defend this hemisphere from attack by any foreign powers. It demands faith in an independent American destiny. It is a policy not of isolation, but of independence; not of defeat, but of courage. It is a policy that led this nation to success during the most difficult years of our history, and it is a policy that will lead us to success again.

We have weakened ourselves for many months by dabbling in Europe's wars. While we should have been concentrating on American defense, we have been forced to argue over foreign quarrels. We must turn our eyes and our faith back to our own country before it is too late. And when we do this, a different outlook opens before us. Practically every difficulty we would face in invading Europe becomes an asset to us in defending America. Our enemy, and not we, would then have the problem of transporting millions of troops across the ocean and landing them on a hostile shore. They, and not we, would have to provide the convoys to transport guns and trucks and munitions and fuel across 3,000 miles [4,800 kilometers] of water. Our battleships and submarines would then be fighting close to their home bases. We would then do the bombing from the air and the torpedoing at sea. And if any part of an enemy convoy should ever pass our navy and our air force, they would still be faced with the guns of our coast artillery and behind them the divisions of our army.

The United States is better situated from a military standpoint than any other nation in the world. Even in our present condition of unpreparedness, no foreign power is in a position to invade us today. If we concentrate on our own defenses and build the strength that this nation should maintain, no foreign army will ever attempt to land on American shores.

War is not inevitable for this country. Such a claim is defeatism in the true sense. No one can make us fight abroad unless we ourselves are willing to do so. No one will attempt to fight us here if we arm ourselves as a great nation should be armed. Over 100 million people in this nation are opposed to entering the war. If the principles of democracy mean anything at all, that is reason enough for us to say out. If we are forced into a war against the wishes of an overwhelming majority of our people, we will have proved democracy such a failure at home that there will be little use fighting for it abroad.

AN EDITORIAL ON THE DANGER OF NEUTRALITY

Charles Lindbergh, America's flyer-hero and a leader of the isolationist America First Committee, attracted nationwide attention with the speech he made on April 23, 1941, urging that the United States should stay out of the war in Europe. A week later, on April 30, *The New York Times,* one of the nation's most influential newspapers, published a strong editorial challenging Lindbergh's point of view. The *Times* editorial, which follows, argued forcefully that the United States had no choice but to aid England in its fight against Nazi Germany.

What reasons does the *New York Times* give to explain why the United States must aid England against Germany? What does the paper claim will happen if England is defeated? Do you think the arguments in the editorial are effective or not? Why?

Condensed from "Editorial Challenging Lindbergh's Views on Entry into World War II" in The New York Times, *April 30, 1941. © 1941 by The New York Times Company. Reprinted by permission.*

Those who tell us now that the sea is still our certain bulwark [defense], and that the tremendous forces sweeping the Old World threaten no danger to the New, give the lie to their own words in the precautions they would have us take.

They favor an enormous strengthening of our defenses. Why? Against what danger would they have us arm if none exists? To what purpose would they have us spend these almost incredible billions upon billions for ships and planes, for tanks and guns, if there is no immediate threat to the security of the United States? Why are we training the youth of the country to bear arms? Under pressure of what fear are we racing against time to double and quadruple our industrial production?

No man in his senses will say that we are arming against Canada or our Latin-American neighbors to the south, against Britain or the captive states of Europe. We are arming solely for one reason. We are arming against Hitler's Germany—a great predatory [warlike] power in alliance with Japan.

It has been said that if Hitler cannot cross the English Channel he cannot cross 3,000 miles [4,800 kilometers] of sea. But there is only one reason why he has not crossed the English Channel. That is because 45 million determined Britons, in a heroic resistance, have converted their island into an armed base, from which proceeds a steady stream of sea and air power. As Secretary [of State Cordell] Hull has said: "It is not the water that bars the way. It is the resolute determination of British arms. Were the control of the seas by Britain lost, the Atlantic would no longer be an obstacle—rather, it would become a broad highway for a conqueror moving westward."

That conqueror does not need to attempt at once an invasion of the continental United States in order to place this country in deadly danger. We shall be in deadly danger the moment British sea power fails; the moment we are compelled to divide our one-ocean Navy between two oceans simultaneously.

The combined Axis fleets outmatch our own: they are superior in numbers to our fleet in every category of vessel, from warships and aircraft carriers to destroyers and submarines. The combined Axis air strength will be much greater than our own if Hitler strikes in time—and when has he failed to strike in time? The master of Europe will have at his command the resources of 20 conquered nations to furnish his materials, the oil of the Middle East to stoke [run] his engines, the slave labor of a continent to turn out his production.

Grant Hitler the gigantic prestige of a victory over Britain, and who can doubt that the first result, on our side of the ocean, would be the prompt appearance of imitation Nazi regimes in a half-dozen Latin-American nations, forced to be on the winning side, begging favors, clamoring for admission to the Axis? What shall we do then? Make war upon these neighbors, send armies to fight in the jungles of Central or South America; run the risk of outraging native sentiment and turning the whole continent against us? Or shall we sit tight while the area of Nazi influence draws ever closer to the Panama Canal, and a spreading checkerboard of Nazi airfields provides ports of call for German planes that may choose to bomb our cities?

But even if Hitler gave us time, what kind of "time" would we have at our disposal?

There are moral and spiritual dangers for this country as well as physical dangers in a Hitler victory. There are dangers to the mind and heart as well as to the body and the land.

Victorious in Europe, dominating Africa and Asia through his Axis partners, Hitler could not afford to permit the United States to live an untroubled and successful life, even if he wished to. We are the arch enemy of all he stands for: the very citadel [stronghold] of that democracy which he hates and scorns. As long as liberty and freedom prevailed in the United States, there would be constant risk for Hitler that our ideas and our example might infect the conquered countries which he was bending to his will. In his own interest he would be forced to harry [harass] us at every turn.

Who can doubt that our lives would be poisoned every day by challenges and insults from Nazi politicians; that Nazi agents would stir up anti-American feeling in every country they controlled; that Nazi spies would overrun us here; that Hitler would produce a contin-ual series of lightning diplomatic strokes—alliances and "nonaggression pacts" to break our will; in short, that a continuous war of nerves, if nothing worse, would be waged against us?

And who can doubt that, in response, we should have to turn our own nation into an armed camp, with all our traditional values of culture, education, social reform, democracy, and liberty subordinated to the single, all-embracing aim of self-preservation? In this case we should indeed experience "regimenta-tion." Every item of foreign trade, every trans-action in domestic commerce, every present prerogative [right] of labor, every civil liberty we cherish, would necessarily be regulated in the interest of defense.

CHAPTER 18
AMERICANS IN THE SECOND WORLD WAR

AN ARMY NURSE IN THE PHILIPPINES

After the Japanese attack on Pearl Harbor in December 1941, the United States entered World War II. The early months of the war were a disaster for the United States. The Japanese armed forces moved steadily through Southeast Asia, conquering nation after nation and invading island chains in the Pacific Ocean. American and Filipino troops under General Douglas MacArthur struggled to defend the Philippine Islands. But early in January 1942 Manila, capital of the Philippines, was forced to surrender. American forces then retreated to the Bataan Peninsula and the island of Corregidor. There they fought heroically, until Bataan was conquered on April 9 and Corregidor finally fell on May 6.

Thousands of American soldiers, including many sick and wounded, were trapped in the Philippines. In this selection, an army nurse at Bataan and Corregidor describes the last weeks.

What were the conditions at Hospital Number 1 on Bataan? What was the mood of the patients? Of those working in the hospital?

Adapted from "An Army Nurse at Bataan and Corregidor" as told to Annalee Jacoby; from History in the Writing *by Gordon Carroll. Copyright 1945 by Time Inc. Reprinted by permission of Time Inc.*

Conditions at Hospital Number 1 were not too good during the last few weeks we spent there. Patients were flooding in. We increased from 400 to 1,500 cases in two weeks' time. Most of them had serious wounds, but nine out of ten patients had malaria or dysentery be-sides.

We were out of quinine [a drug used in treating malaria]. There were hundreds of gas gangrene cases, and our supply of vaccine had run out months before. There were no more sulfa drugs. There weren't nearly enough cots, so triple-decker beds were built from bamboo, with a ladder at one end so we could climb up to take care of the patients. They had no blankets or mattresses.

There was almost no food except carabao [water buffalo]. We had all thought we couldn't eat carabao, but we did. Then came mule, which seemed worse, but we ate that too. Most of the nurses were wearing government-issue heavy-laced men's shoes. [From the term "gov-ernment issue" came the name for American soldiers in World War II—GI's.] We had to keep our feet taped up to walk in them. Our uniforms had been gone for a long time, so we mostly wore size 32 air corps coveralls. We carried steel helmets and gas masks even in the wards, but we didn't expect to use them.

We went about our work feeling perfectly safe because of the Red Cross markings on the roof. When bombers came overhead on April 4, we hardly noticed them. Then suddenly incendiary [fire] bombs dropped. They hit the receiving wards, mess hall, doctors' and officers' quarters, and the steps of the nurses' dormitory, setting fire to all the buildings but luckily not hitting the wards. Several people walking outside were killed. The patients were terrified, of course, but behaved well. The Japanese prisoners were perhaps the most frightened of all. Everything was a blur of taking care of patients, putting out fires, straightening overturned equipment.

We remained frightened until two hours later when someone heard the Japanese radio in Manila announce that the bombings had been an accident and wouldn't happen again. After that, we wouldn't even leave the hospital for a short drive. We felt safe there and nowhere else.

The morning of April 7 we were all on duty when a wave of bombers came over. The first bomb hit near the Filipino mess hall and knocked us down before we even knew planes were overhead. An ammunition truck was passing the hospital entrance. It got a direct hit. The boys on guard at the gate were shell-shocked, smothered in the dirt thrown up by the explosion.

Hospital patients picked us up and we began caring for patients hurt by shrapnel [bomb fragments]. Everything was terror and confusion. Patients, even amputation cases, were falling and rolling out of the triple-decker beds. Suddenly a chaplain, Father Cummings, came into the ward, threw up his hands for silence and said: "All right, boys, everything's all right. Just stay quietly in bed, or lie still on the floor. Let us pray." The screams stopped instantly. He began the prayer just as a second wave of planes came over.

The first bomb hit near the officers' quarters, the next struck the patients' mess hall just a few yards away. The shock waves bounced us three feet off the cement floor and threw us down again. Beds were tumbling down. Flashes of heat and smoke burned our eyes. But through it all we could hear Father Cummings' voice reciting the Lord's Prayer. He never stopped, never even fell to the ground, and the patients never moved. Father Cummings' clear voice went through to the end. Then he turned quietly and said: "All right, you take over. Put a tourniquet on my arm, will you?" And we saw for the first time that he'd been badly hit by shrapnel.

The next few hours were a nightmare, except for the way everyone behaved. We were afraid to move, but realized we had to get to work. One Filipino with both legs amputated— he'd never gotten out of bed before by himself— rolled onto the ground and said: "Miss, are you all right, are you all right?" The ward boys all told us, "You go on outside—don't stay here any longer. We'll take care of everything." We tried to care first for the patients most seriously hurt. A great many all over the hospital were bleeding badly. We went to where the bomb had hit the ward and began pulling patients from the crater. I saw Rosemary Hogan, head ward nurse, and thought for a moment her face had been torn off. She wiped herself with a sheet, smiled and said: "It's nothing, don't bother about me. Just a nose bleed." But she had three shrapnel wounds.

It would be hard to believe the bravery after that bombing if you hadn't seen it. A soldier had risked his life by going directly to the traction wards where patients were tied to beds by wires. He thought it was better to hurt the men temporarily than to leave them tied helpless above ground where they'd surely be hit by shrapnel, so he cut all tractions and told the patients: "Get under the bed, Joe."

We began immediately to move patients to another hospital. We were so afraid the Japanese would be back again the next day that even the most serious cases were moved, because giving them any chance was better than none. There were only 100 patients left the next morning. We worked all that day making up beds to admit new patients. It never occurred to anyone that we wouldn't go on as usual. Suddenly, after dark, we were told we were leaving in 15 minutes—that we should pack only what we could carry. Then we heard that the Japanese had broken through and the Battle of Bataan was over. The doctors all decided to stay with the patients, even doctors who had been told to go to Corregidor.

We left the hospital at 9 that night—got to Corregidor at 3 in the morning. The trip usually took a little over an hour. As we drove down to the docks, the roads were jammed. Soldiers were tired, aimless, frightened. Cars were overturned. There were bodies in the road. Clouds of dust made it hard to breathe. At midnight on the docks we heard that the Japanese had burned our hospital to the ground.

Bombers were overhead, but we were too tired to care. We waited on the docks while the navy tunnel and ammunition dump at Marivales were blown up. Blasting explosions, blue flares, red flares, shrapnel, tracers, gasoline exploding—it was like a hundred Fourths of July all at once, but we were too frightened to be impressed. As we crossed the water with Corregidor's big guns firing over our heads and shells from somewhere landing close by, the boat suddenly shook and the whole ocean seemed to rock. We thought a big shell had hit the water in front of us. It wasn't until we landed that we learned that an earthquake had hit just as Bataan fell.

Corregidor seemed like heaven that night. They fed us and we slept, two to an army cot. We went to work the following morning. Months before, patients on Corregidor had filled a few side tunnels only. Now they were in doubledecker beds all along the halls and in the main tunnel. There was constant bombing and shelling—sometimes shock waves from a bomb outside would knock people down at the opposite end of the tunnel. Emperor Hirohito's birthday, April 29, was a specially bad day. The bombing began at 7:30 in the morning and never stopped. Shelling was heavy; soldiers counted over 100 explosions per minute. Dive bombers were going after the gun on the hill directly above our heads and the shock waves inside were terrific.

The worst night on Corregidor was when a bomb hit outside the tunnel entrance. A crowd had gone outside for a cigarette and many were sleeping on the ground at the foot of the cliff. When the first shell hit nearby, they all ran for the tunnel, but the iron gate was shut and it opened outward. As more shells landed, they smashed men against the gate and twisted off arms and legs. All the nurses got up and went back to work—the operating room was overflowing until 5:30 in the morning. There were many amputations.

At 6 o'clock one evening, after the usual bombing and shelling, 21 of us were told we were leaving Corregidor by plane. We don't know how we were selected. Everyone wanted to leave, of course, but morale was splendid. Everyone realized the end was getting close, but none gave up hope.

Now we're safe in Australia. But the only reaction we notice is wanting to make up somehow, anyhow, for those who didn't get away.

DIVE BOMBERS OVER ITALY

Americans eagerly followed the war news on radio and in the press. Often they learned about the land campaigns and air and sea battles by reading the newspaper stories written by foreign correspondents. These American reporters covered every phase of World War II on every one of the many battle fronts. Many of these brave reporters went with the American units into battle. They shared the soldiers' daily hardships and dangers, and many of them lost their lives in battle.

Ernie Pyle, one of the most outstanding foreign war correspondents, spent many months at the battle fronts with American troops. His name and his stories were well known to most Americans by the time he died during the fighting on the Pacific island of Ie Shima in April 1945. In this selection, he writes about the war in Europe, describing American dive bombers and their crews fighting in Italy during 1943.

How did the dive-bomber groups support the army infantry? What, according to Pyle, are the most striking features of dive bombing?

Adapted from Brave Men *by Ernie Pyle. Copyright 1943, 1944 by Scripps-Howard Newspaper Alliance. Copyright 1944 by Ernie Pyle. Copyright © 1971, 1972 by Holt, Rinehart and Winston. Reprinted by permission of Holt, Rinehart and Winston, Publishers.*

I spent some time with a dive-bomber squadron of the 12th Air Support Command. There were about 50 officers and 250 enlisted men in each squadron. They all lived in a big apartment house built by the Italian government for war workers and their families. It was out in the country at the edge of a small town.

In the dive-bomber groups in Italy, pilots and mechanics believed that the dive bomber was the most wonderful machine produced in this war. Certainly, those dive-bomber boys were a spectacular part of our air force.

Their function was to work in extremely close support of our infantry. For instance, suppose there was a German gun position just over a hill which was holding us up because our troops couldn't get at it with their guns. They called on the dive bombers and gave them the location. Within an hour, and sometimes much quicker, bombers would come screaming out of the sky right on top of that gun and blow it up.

They could do the same thing to bunched enemy troops, bridges, tank columns, convoys, or ammunition dumps. Because of their great accuracy they could bomb much closer to our own troops than other kinds of planes would dare. Most of the time they worked less than a thousand yards [914 meters] ahead of our front lines—and sometimes even closer than that.

The group I was with had been in combat six months. During that time they had flown 10,000 missions, fired more than 1 million rounds of 50-caliber ammunition, and dropped 3 million pounds [1.4 million kilograms] of bombs. That's more than the entire Eighth Air Force in England dropped in its first year of operation.

Those boys dived about 8,000 feet [2,440 meters] before dropping their bombs. Without brakes their speed in such a dive would ordinarily build up to around 700 miles [1,125 kilometers] an hour, but the brakes held them down to about 390 miles [625 kilometers].

The dive bombers approached their target in formation. When the leader made sure he had spotted the target he wiggled his wings, raised his diving brakes, rolled on his back, nosed over, and down he went. The next man behind followed almost instantly, and then the next, and the next—not more than 150 feet [45 meters] apart. There was no danger of their running into each other, for the brakes held them all at the same speed.

At about 4,000 feet [1,220 meters] the pilot released his bombs. Then he started his pull-out. The strain was terrific, and all the pilots would "black out" a little bit. It was not a complete blackout, and lasted only four or five seconds. It was more a heaviness in the head and a darkness before the eyes, the pilots said.

If you ever heard a dive bombing by our planes you'd never forget it. Even in normal flight those planes made a sort of screaming noise. In a dive, the wail could be heard for miles. From the ground it sounded as though they were coming directly down on us. It was a horrifying thing.

For several months the posting period back to America [the number of missions a pilot had to fly before being sent home on leave] was set at a certain number of missions. Then it was suddenly increased by more than 20. When the order came, there were pilots who were within one mission of going home. So they had to stay and fly a few more months. Some of them never lived to finish the new allotment.

There is an odd psychological factor in the system of being sent home after a certain number of missions. When pilots got to within three or four missions of the finish, they became so nervous they almost jumped out of their skins. A good many were killed on their last mission. The squadron leaders wished there were some way they could surprise a man and send him home with six or eight missions still to go, thus sparing him the agony of those last few trips.

Nowhere in our fighting forces was cooperation closer or friendship greater than between Americans and British in the air. I never heard an American pilot make a critical remark about a British flier. Our pilots said the British were cooler under fire than we were. The British attitude and manner of speech amused them, but they were never scornful.

They liked to listen in on their radios as the British pilots talked to each other. For example, one day they heard one pilot call to another, "I say, old chap, there is a Jerry [the English nickname for Germans during the war] on your tail."

To which the pilot in danger answered, "Quite so, quite so, thanks very much, old man."

And another time, one of our dive bombers got shot up over the target. His engine was smoking and he was losing altitude. He made for the coast all alone, an easy target for any German fighter that might come along. He was just barely staying in the air, and he was a sad and lonely boy indeed. Then suddenly he heard over his earphones a distinctly British voice saying, "Cheer up, chicken we have you."

He looked around and two Spitfires [British fighter planes], one on either side, were leading him back to his home field.

WOMEN AND WAR

Although there were great changes in America during World War II, for most Americans the wartime years did not bring the severe hardships and widespread destruction endured by the peoples of Europe. Americans experienced rationing and shortages of food and other supplies, but they did not have to face enemy bombs or advancing armies.

One of the greatest changes in the United States was the profound effect the war had on the lives of American women. With millions of men in the armed forces, women took over many of the jobs in the nation's factories, farms, and businesses. Many women also now had to take care of their homes and their families alone. In this selection, written shortly after World War II, anthropologist Margaret Mead tells of some of these changes in women's lives.

According to Margaret Mead, what worries did American servicemen have about women on the home front? What did wartime jobs mean for women? What did the author think women's roles would be in the future? Was she correct? Explain.

Adapted from "The Women in the War" by Margaret Mead in While You Were Gone, *edited by Jack Goodman. Copyright © 1946 by Simon and Schuster, Inc., copyright renewed © 1973 by Simon and Schuster, Inc. Reprinted by permission of Simon and Schuster, a Division of Gulf and Western Corp.*

In wartime, men and women get out of step and begin to wonder about each other. "What will he be like after all those years in the army?" "What will she be like after all those years alone at home?" "I do hope he won't have changed too much." "I hope she will look the same."

All this is natural enough. Boys and girls grow up together in the same world, seeing a lot of each other, each knowing what the other is thinking. Husbands are used to coming home at night and telling their wives what they think of the news in the paper, and having their wives tell them they are exactly right—or exactly wrong. Either way, they know what's going on. Dramatic news, quintuplets and quads, double murders and triple suicides, all fall into place in peacetime. They are events that spice the usual events of life, in which most babies are born one at a time and husbands and wives may sometimes feel like murdering each other but hardly ever do. But in wartime, boys and girls, men and women, separated in time and in space, aren't in step any more, and both begin to wonder what the other one will be like . . . after the war.

The man overseas reads his paper or his magazines filled with news that women are doing new and therefore, by definition, "unwomanly" jobs. (A womanly job is just a job that everybody is used to seeing women do.) He reads about the mannish clothes women are wearing, the welding outfits they are wielding, and he worries. What's happening to women anyway? What will be the use of winning the war if when you go back home all the girls' heads are filled with a lot of strange and unwelcome nonsense?

The newspapers are full of wild stories: bobby soxers [a term for teenagers in the 1940's, since many of them wore heavy white socks called "bobby socks"] wandering about Times Square or storming a performance by Frank Sinatra; the riotous living of war workers. If the man overseas were at home, all this would make sense. He'd have a chance to see that being a woman worker means long hard hours doing unfamiliar work, cramped and difficult living conditions, hours of standing in line waiting for food. He'd know that for every straying bobby soxer there are a hundred youngsters who are working in factories or doing their absent brothers' work on the farm.

Besides the bobby soxers and the quadruplets in the newspapers, there has been continuous writing on the theme: "Will women be willing to return to the home?" This worrying question is often inspired by those in whose interest it will be to discharge women workers as soon as the war is over.

Statistics on how many women are working and plan to work appear in headlines which add, "Eight out of every ten women asked say they will work after the war." Most of those women who say they will go on working are women who would have been working anyway. The number of American women who work has been rising from 2.5 million in 1880 to over 5 million in 1920 and to 11 million in 1940. In 1950—if you ask for official estimates—you'll find that about 16 million women will be working in the United States. That's the kind of society we have, one in which many men aren't paid enough to support their wives, one in which women without husbands are expected to support themselves, one in which very few brothers are willing to support their unmarried sisters. In back of the headlines and the statistics and the threatening questions in the newspapers there lies the simple fact that more women in the United States have to work each year. And that more women than ever before will be working at some time in their lives.

This needn't worry the returning men very deeply. It was part of the America they left, and it's part of the America they are coming back to. The war has speeded things up a little, that's all. After the war, just as it would have been if there had been no war, most girls will plan to work between school and marriage. Many will plan to work until the first baby. Some will go back to work when their children are grown. And an increasing number will work because they have no husbands and no other means of support.

However, some striking things have happened during the war which are due to the war. During the war, over 3 million women have gone to work who would *not* have worked if there had not been a war. A million girls between 14 and 18 who would ordinarily have been in school have been working part or full time. A million young married women, with and without children, have gone to work. Many of them are wives of men in the armed forces. The remainder of the 3 million women include many women who have worked before and have gone back to work. Some are mothers who cannot stand waiting for the mail to bring news of their sons. Some are mothers who already know that their sons will never return.

There are several ways of looking at these things which have been happening to women. Some people find it more interesting that women have done jobs which no one thought they could do — become welders and machine setters, railroad conductors, and taxi drivers. Most of these are strictly wartime shifts and will become men's jobs again after the war.

To some, the fact that we have women in the armed forces in this war is the most striking thing that has happened. There are only a little over a quarter of a million women in the services. They have joined up in the face of a great deal of disapproval from brothers and boy friends and fathers. They have been given, for the most part, dull and inglorious jobs to do.

What do these figures mean? What will it mean to men that women who wouldn't otherwise have worked now have worked? That their wives have been working while they were gone? That their mothers and their mothers-in-law have worked?

It means, for one thing, that women, as a group, are better informed than they were before. They understand what a time clock is and what a checkoff is. Farm women have learned a great deal more about the drudgery and techniques of farm life. Women in homes which used to employ servants will know a great deal more about housework. Women who have left housework for the factory will come back with some new ideas of what it means to work definite hours. Millions of women will understand more of what their husbands are talking about, when their husbands talk sense, and will have a sounder idea of when they are talking nonsense. A great many more women will

understand more about money, how hard it is to make, as well as how hard or how easy it is to spend. Here, perhaps, is one of the places where the experience of women in wartime America will be a useful supplement to the men's. While the men have had four or five years less of dealing with money, the women have had that much more.

The second important experience women have had, while the men were away, is moving about. Small-town girls have gone to cities, city girls to little country towns, factory and office girls to pick beets and milk cows. Northern girls have gone south, and eastern girls have gone west. Some of this moving-about experience will match the men's. Men have lived abroad, but mostly in camps. Women have not had such strange ways of life, but they have actually had to cope with things more — buy and prepare food and convert trailers into homes.

And most of all women have waited. Many of them — those who have worked and traveled — have waited by doing something. Others have just waited. In their minds has been the echo of his "I want to find you just the same." Many women have sensibly interpreted this to mean that he wants her to be as good a 1945 model as she was a 1940 model, as smart a 23-year-old as she was an 18-year-old.

But others, less realistic, have taken boy friends and husbands at their word and tried not to change at all. They have tried to keep their minds, if not their hats, just as they were when their men left. Many of these girls, instead of moving out into the wartime world, have gone home to Mother. They have slipped back into dependent, little-girl positions, stayed 18 years old or even slipped back a little. Getting to know a wife who has tried to stay the same is really going to be more difficult than getting acquainted with a wife who has driven a truck or worn a uniform.

When the returning man looks his wife or sweetheart in the eye, between them will stand his years of danger and hardship which she cannot share or even properly imagine, her flat, empty years which she could not value because he was away. In peacetime, men and women count upon living side by side, watching children grow and gardens flower and houses go up and bank accounts increase and chins get double or beards get stubbier and life flow more quietly — together. All of our patterns for the relations between men and women were based on this simple expectation.

This generation will have to make new patterns.

Last of all, the man who left the country in 1941–42 will come back to a new generation of girls. These girls will be, inevitably, a new kind of girl, girls brought up on the war years, on a different sort of romance. They don't expect as much of boys as their older sisters did who grew up when dates were commoner. They will have practically no memory of the depression years. War has stood at the beginning of their young girlhood; war did not crash rudely into the middle of it, finding them unprepared. They will be standing on tiptoe waiting for the postwar world.

LIFE IN A RELOCATION CAMP

After the Japanese attack on Pearl Harbor, many American government officials believed that Japanese Americans were a danger to the nation's security. As a result, about 112,000 Japanese Americans were placed in detention or relocation camps. Most of these Japanese Americans were not allowed to leave the relocation camps until January of 1945. Despite the federal government's internment program, over 17,000 Japanese Americans served in the American armed forces, many winning military awards for bravery.

Monica Sone, a Nisei, or Japanese American born in the United States, wrote the following account of life in a relocation camp. She was a college student in Seattle, Washington, when the war broke out and she and her family were sent to a relocation camp in Idaho.

Today, most Americans view the wartime treatment of Japanese Americans as unfair. But during World War II most Americans accepted it as necessary.

Do you think it was fair to segregate Nisei soldiers? If you had been a Japanese American during the war, how do you think you would have felt about being placed in a relocation camp? Would you have volunteered to serve in the armed forces? Explain.

Adapted from Nisei Daughter *by Monica Sone. Copyright 1953, © 1981 by Monica Sone. Reprinted by permission of Little, Brown and Co. in association with the Atlantic Monthly Press.*

Camp Minidoka was located in the south-central part of Idaho, north of the Snake River. It was a semidesert region. When we arrived I could see nothing but flat prairies, clumps of greasewood shrubs, and jack rabbits. And of course the hundreds and hundreds of barracks, to house 10,000 of us.

Our home was one room in a large army-type barracks, measuring about 20 by 25 feet [6 by 7.5 meters]. The only furnishings were an iron pot-belly stove and cots.

On our first day in camp, we were given a rousing welcome by a dust storm. We felt as if we were standing in a gigantic sand-mixing machine as the gale lifted the loose earth up into the sky, hiding everything. Sand filled our mouths and nostrils and stung our faces and hands like a thousand darting needles.

Just as suddenly as the storm had broken out, it died away. We walked out of the mess hall under a pure blue sky, startling in its peacefulness. In the deepening blue shadows, people hurried here and there, preparing for their first night in camp. The Issei [Japanese-Americans born in Japan] men stomped along in their wooden *getas* (high sandals). The Issei women in cool cotton print *yukatas* (Japanese house kimonos) slipped along noiselessly. They bowed to each other, murmuring "Oyasumi nasai. Rest well." These familiar words in the alien darkness of the prairie were welcome sounds. I suddenly saw that these people were living through difficult circumstances with simple dignity and patience, and I felt ashamed of my own strong emotions. That night we let ourselves sink deep into the yawning silence of the prairie, which was shattered only by the barking of the coyotes.

Idaho summer sizzled on the average of 110 degrees [43 degrees Celsius]. For the first few weeks I lay on my cot from morning till night, not daring to do more than go to the mess hall three times a day.

When September came we slowly emerged from our stupor. The sun no longer stabbed the backs of our necks. Now when I awoke in the mornings, the air felt cool and crisp.

The momentum of the change carried me along into a job at the camp hospital as ward secretary. Henry [her brother] had already been working at the hospital for weeks. Sumi [her sister] and her young friends signed up as nurse's aides. Father finally settled on becoming a member of the internal security staff—a policeman, complete with an olive-drab uniform. Mother, who was not well, stayed home to mop the floor, wash the family laundry, iron and mend our clothes, and attend the English language class, choir practice, prayer meetings, and a Japanese doll-making class.

By fall, Camp Minidoka has bloomed into a full-grown town. Children went to school in the barracks, taught by professional teachers among the evacuees and people hired from the outside. Except for the members of the administration staff, the evacuees themselves supplied the entire labor force in the camp. All church activities were in full session.

During our spare hours, we confiscated scrap lumber, piece by piece, from a lumber pile. Tables and chairs gradually made their appearance in our tiny apartment. Rows of shelves lined the bare walls. We bought gallons of shellac, and white paint, yards of white organdy for curtains, and blue damask for the cots and clothes closet. We had a living room, powder room, three bedrooms, a study, storage room, and a kitchen all in one. It had everything except the kitchen sink and privacy.

Winter in Minidoka was as intense an experience as summer had been. We gave a strong cheer for the government when we were told that they would provide winter clothing for those who needed them. Mother was the first to go after her clothing. When she came home with the bundle, we all gathered around her excitedly to see what she had. She held up a pair of longjohns [men's underwear], olive-drab trousers, and a navy pea coat [jacket].

"They're good quality woolens," she said calmly, "and they'll certainly keep me warm. Only thing, it's too bad we aren't all males."

Sumi and I protested hysterically that we were all going to look like members of the internal security staff, since these clothes were exactly what Father and his friends wore on patrol duty. It was only after a man living in our block became lost one night in a snowstorm and died from exposure that we finally gave in. We ran to the clothing office. The man gave us what was left—size 40 longjohns, sleeveless, collarless vests which hung down to our knees, and wonderful thick, bear-sized pea coats. That taught us a lesson that a man, or at any rate, a woman, cannot live on pride alone.

We had lived in camps through four seasons, and each season had served as a challenge to us. In the meantime we had drifted farther and farther away from the American scene. We had been set apart, and we had become adjusted to our existence. The great struggle in which the world was engaged seemed far away.

Then one day a group of army personnel marched into our camp on a special mission.

They made a startling announcement. "The United States War Department has decided to form a special combat unit for the Nisei. We have come to recruit volunteers."

We gasped and we tried to speak. Dunks Oshima, who had brought the news to us, eyed us fiercely as he cried, "What do they take us for? Saps? First, they change my army status to 4-C because of my ancestry, and run me out of town. Now they want me to volunteer for a suicide squad so I could get killed for democracy. That's going some for sheer nerve!"

That was exactly the way most of us felt, but the recruiting officers were well prepared to cope with our emotional explosion. They called meetings and we flocked to them with an injured look.

An officer spoke to us. "You're probably wondering why we are here, recruiting for volunteers from your group. I think that my explanation is best expressed in the statement recently issued by our President, regarding a citizen's right and privilege to serve the country. I want to read it to you:

"No loyal citizens of the United States should be denied the democratic right to exercise the responsibilities of their citizenship, regardless of their ancestry. The principle on which this country was founded and by which it has always been governed is that Americanism is a matter of the mind and the heart. Americanism is not, and never was, a matter of race or ancestry. All loyal American citizens should be given the opportunity to serve this country wherever their skills will make the greatest contribution, whether it be in our armed forces, war production, agriculture, government service, or other work essential to the war effort.'"

It all sounded very well. It was the sort of declaration which rang true and clear in our hearts. But there were questions in our minds which needed answering. The speaker threw the meeting open for discussion. We said we didn't want a separate Nisei combat unit because it looked too much like segregation. We wanted to serve in the same way as other citizens, in a mixed group with the other Americans.

The man answered: "But if the Nisei men were to be scattered throughout the army, you'd lose your significance as Nisei. Maybe you want it that way, because in the past you suffered with your Japanese faces. Well, why not accept your Japanese face? Why be ashamed of it? Why not take advantage of it for a change? There are powerful organizations now campaigning on the [West] Coast to deport you all to Japan, citizens and residents alike. But there're also men and women who believe in you, who feel you should be given the chance to stand up and express yourselves. They thought that a Nisei combat unit would be just the thing. Whatever you accomplish, whatever you achieve, will be yours and yours alone."

We saw that the speaker was sincere and believed earnestly in this cause. Then we asked him another burning question. "Why had the government ever put us here in the first place? Why? Why? Why?"

The man looked at our wounded faces and said: "I can't answer that question. I can only repeat what you already know, that the government thought evacuation was necessary. The evacuation took place, and right or wrong, it's past. Now we're interested in your future. The War Department is offering you a chance to volunteer and to distinguish yourselves as Japanese-American citizens in the service of your country. Believe me, this combat unit is not segregation in the sense you think it is."

The tension in the mess hall eased, and questions and answers came more naturally. After the meeting we returned to our barracks to continue the debate. Dunks came with us.

"What's a fellow to do?" Dunks said wryly. "They've got us over a barrel. If we don't do our bit, you can bet your boots there won't be much of a future for us here. Those on the Coast who want to deport us will see to that."

I put in, "I'll bet, though, that some of those characters will be totally against a Nisei combat team."

Henry snorted, "Those scrooges will be against anything which might make us look good."

Dunks said, "It's the general public I'm thinking about. They're the ones who count. They want proof of our loyalty. Okay, I'm giving it to them, and maybe I'll die for it if I'm unlucky. But if after the war's over and our two cents don't cut any ice with the American public, well, to blazes with them!"

The next day Henry announced, "Tomorrow I'm going down to volunteer." No one said a word. Father stared down at his veined hands. Mother's face turned into a white mask.

"Please don't feel so bad, Mama."

Mother smiled thinly. "I don't feel bad, Henry. In fact, I don't feel anything just now."

Father spoke to her tenderly, "Mama, if Henry had been born in Japan, he would have been taken into the army and gone off to war long ago."

"That's right. And I guess it's about time we all stopped thinking about the past. I think we should go along with our sons from now. It's the least we can do."

Father said, gratefully, "That's what I wanted to hear. At least we're together on this matter. Imagine what Dunks must be going through."

Mrs. Oshima had refused to speak to her son ever since he had decided to volunteer. "Is this what we deserve from our children," she said, "after years and years of work and hardship for their sake? Ah, we've brought up nothing but fools! They can be insulted, their parents insulted, and still they volunteer."

Early the next morning, Dunks, and George and Paul, sons of Mr. Sawada, the clothing salesman, came into our apartment on their way to the camp hospital for their physical.

"Let's go, Hank, before the crowd gets there."

They left with a great clatter and loud shouting. Father, Mother, Sumi, and I sank to our cots feeling as if we had come out of a turbulent storm which had been raging steadily in our minds since Pearl Harbor. The birth of the Nisei combat team was the climax to our evacuee life, and the turning point. It was the road back to our rightful places.

BRAVERY AT THE BULGE

During World War II the United States armed forces continued their traditional policy of separate units for black Americans. Moreover, a large number of black Americans were put in service units — working in supply depots, driving trucks, doing repair and maintenance jobs. But some black units were assigned to combat. And for a brief period, late in the war, the barriers of racial segregation were broken down.

When the Germans broke through the Allied lines in December 1944, in their counterattack at the Battle of the Bulge, the Allies desperately needed fighting units. As a result, black units and white units fought together to stop the German advance. In this selection Walter White, who was secretary of the NAACP, tells of this history-making event of black and white Americans fighting together.

Why did army officers ask black soldiers to volunteer? Why did black Americans respond as they did? What was the attitude of white officers and soldiers who fought with black soldiers?

Adapted from A Man Called White *by Walter White. Copyright 1948 by Walter White, copyright © renewed 1976 by H. Lee Lurie. Reprinted by permission of Viking Penguin, Inc.*

One of the most dramatic examples of the abandonment of interracial antagonisms in combat by troops themselves—and a tragic reversal by the army high command—occurred during and after the Battle of the Bulge.

The Germans' sudden, effective breakthrough threatened disaster. The tide of war might have been changed at that point. At the very least, the war would have been longer if this daring maneuver had succeeded, even though more men and war materials would probably have brought Allied victory. Many Americans now alive would have died in the meantime.

Every available man was thrown into the fight to stop the German advance. But even then there were not enough. Desperate appeals were sent to the United States to rush more combat troops as quickly as possible. Many were sent by plane, but even these were not enough. It was at this point, during some of the fiercest fighting, that General John C. H. Lee issued an appeal to colored Service of Supply troops to volunteer for combat.

"It is planned to assign you without regard to color or race to units where assistance is most needed," General Lee promised. He made no effort to minimize the desperate nature of the fighting nor the great number of casualties caused by the German breakthrough. He pointed out that all noncommissioned officers would have to give up their ratings to qualify for service as combat troops.

Great numbers of volunteers answered General Lee's appeal. In some units 80 percent of the soldiers offered their services. In one engineer unit, 171 out of 186 men volunteered. One private in an ordnance company declared: "We've been giving a lot of sweat. Now I think we'll mix some blood with it!"

Negroes were delighted at this first opportunity to function as "real" soldiers. The response was so great that the army had to set up a quota to prevent complete disorganization of its service units.

Generals George Patton, Omar Bradley, and Courtney Hodges gave their approval to the use of Negro soldiers in completely unsegregated combat units. General Eisenhower was enthusiastic. But Eisenhower's chief of staff, W. Bedell Smith, insisted that the plan be submitted to General George C. Marshall, army chief of staff.

Washington was alarmed at the idea of an unsegregated, genuinely democratic army. It ordered the plan abandoned. But the need for combat troops was so critical that the high command in Washington was forced to agree to a compromise—the use of all-Negro platoons in white regiments, instead of a mixture of whites and Negroes throughout regiments. Although Negro soldiers felt that they had been let down, they were still enthusiastic. The Negro platoons were distributed among eleven combat divisions of the First and Seventh Armies. They fought in the crucial stages of the Battle of the Bulge and through the later Allied drive across Germany.

Several of the Negro volunteers won the Distinguished Service Cross or Silver Star. Others were cited for bravery beyond the call of duty.

The army took a poll among the white officers and soldiers who had fought with Negro troops. The results are to me a striking example of the fact that race prejudice is not as stubborn as some people imagine. The army poll showed that after having served in the same unit with black combat soldiers, 77 percent of the officers favored integration, as contrasted with 33 percent before the experience. The figures among enlisted men were 77 percent and 35 percent, after and before serving with Negroes.

A white South Carolina sergeant was quoted by the army as saying, "When I heard about it, I said I wouldn't wear the same shoulder patch they did. After that first day, when we saw how they fought, I changed my mind. They are just like any of the other men to us."

Another sergeant from Alabama, after telling how bitterly he had opposed serving with Negroes at first, confessed a total change of attitude. "I used to think they would be cowards in combat, but I saw them work."

Some 84 percent of white company officers and 81 percent of white platoon sergeants declared that Negro troops had fought superbly, and 17 percent of officers and 9 percent of enlisted men even went so far as to say that Negroes fought better than white troops.

General Patton highly praised the black volunteers. General Eisenhower declared: "All my commanders reported that these volunteers did excellent work." General Charles Lanham of the 104th Division, presenting combat decorations to eleven Negroes, went even further to declare: "I have never seen any soldiers who have performed better in combat than you have."

But Eisenhower, to the dismay of many of us who had faith in him, testified before the Senate armed services committee in 1948 that he believed racial segregation in the army should continue at the platoon level. And in April 1948 the Secretary of War bluntly told a distinguished group of 15 Negro leaders that the army would continue segregation.

DROPPING THE ATOMIC BOMB

When President Roosevelt died in 1945, Vice-President Harry Truman became President. The new President now faced the tremendous task of ending the war and planning for the peace.

After the war in Europe ended, Truman and the other Allied leaders met at Potsdam, Germany, in July 1945. At that meeting they agreed to demand that Japan surrender unconditionally. Japan refused. President Truman, who had been in office less than four months, now had to make the awesome decision of whether to drop an atomic bomb on Japan. Fearing that an attack on the Japanese mainland by American warships and planes would cost as many as a million American lives, Truman decided to approve the use of the atomic bomb. In this selection, taken from President Truman's memoirs, the President explains his decision to use the atomic bomb at Hiroshima.

How was it decided where and when to drop the first bomb? What was President Truman's feeling about his decision to drop the bomb? What do you think of Truman's decision?

Adapted from Memoirs, Vol. I, Year of Decisions *by Harry S. Truman. Published by Doubleday & Co., Inc., 1955. Reprinted by permission of Harry S. Truman Estate.*

The idea of the atomic bomb had been suggested to President Roosevelt by the famous and brilliant Dr. Albert Einstein. Its development turned out to be a vast undertaking. It was the achievement of the combined efforts of science, industry, labor, and the military, and it had no parallel in history. The people in charge and their staffs worked under great pressure. The whole enormous task required the services of more than 100,000 people and immense quantities of material. It required over two and a half years and the spending of $2.5 billion. Only a few of the thousands of people who worked in these plants knew what they were producing. So strict was the secrecy that even some the highest-ranking officials in Washington did not have the slightest idea of what was going on. I did not.

Before 1939 it had been generally agreed among scientists that in theory it was possible to release energy from the atom. In 1940 we had begun to share with Great Britain all scientific knowledge useful to war, although Britain was at war at that time and we were not. Following this—in 1942—we learned that the Germans were at work on a method to harness atomic energy for use as a weapon of war.

It was under the general policy of sharing knowledge between our nation and Great Britain that research on the atomic bomb started in such feverish secrecy. American and British scientists joined in the race against the Germans. Working together with the British, we thus made it possible to achieve a great scientific triumph in the field of atomic energy. Nevertheless, basic and historic as this event was, it had to be considered at the time as relatively unimportant to the far-flung war we were fighting in the Pacific at a terrible cost in American lives.

We could hope for a miracle, but the daily tragedy of a bitter war was always with us. We worked to construct a weapon of such overpowering force that the enemy could be forced to give in swiftly once we could use it. This was the primary aim of our secret and vast effort. But we also had to carry out the enormous effort of our basic and traditional military plans.

My own knowledge of these developments had come only after I became President, when Secretary of War Henry Stimson had given me the full story. He had told me at the time that the project was nearing completion and that a bomb could be expected within another four months. It was at his suggestion, too, that I had then set up a committee of top people and had asked them to study with great care the possibilities the new weapon might have for us.

It was their recommendation that the bomb be used against the enemy as soon as it could be done. They recommended further that it should be used without warning and against a target that would clearly show its devastating strength. I had realized, of course, that an atomic bomb explosion would cause damage and casualties beyond imagination. On the other hand, the scientific advisers of the committee reported, "We can propose no technical demonstration likely to bring an end to the war; we see no acceptable alternative to direct military use." It was their conclusion that no technical demonstration they might propose, such as dropping the bomb on a deserted island, would be likely to bring the war to an end. It had to be used against an enemy target.

The final decision of where and when to use the atomic bomb was up to me. Let there be no mistake about it. I regarded the bomb as a military weapon and never had any doubt that it should be used. My top military advisers recommended its use. When I talked to Churchill, he told me that he favored the use of the atomic bomb if it might help end the war.

In deciding to use this bomb, I wanted to make sure that it would be used as a weapon of war in the manner set down by the laws of war. That meant that I wanted it dropped on a military target. I had told Stimson that the bomb should be dropped as nearly as possible upon a war production center of prime military importance.

Stimson's staff had prepared a list of cities in Japan that might serve as targets. Kyoto, though favored as a center of military activity, was eliminated when Secretary Stimson pointed out that it was a cultural and religious shrine of the Japanese.

Four cities were finally recommended as targets: Hiroshima, Kokura, Niigata, and Nagasaki. They were listed in that order as targets for the first attack. The order of selection was in accordance with the military importance of these cities. But allowance would be given for weather conditions at the time of the bombing. Before the selected targets were approved as proper for military purposes, I personally went over them in detail with Secretary Stimson, General Marshall, and General Arnold, and we discussed the matter of timing and the final choice of the first target.

General Spaatz, who commanded the Strategic Air Forces, which would drop the bomb, was given some independence as to when and on which of the four targets the bomb would be dropped. That was necessary because of weather and other operational considerations. In order to get preparations under way, the War Department instructed General Spaatz that the first bomb would be dropped as soon after August 3 as weather would permit.

A specialized B-29 unit had been selected for the task. Seven modified B-29's, with pilots and crews, were ready and waiting for orders. Meanwhile ships and planes were rushing the materials for the bomb and specialists to assemble them to the Pacific island of Tinian in the Marianas.

On July 28 Radio Tokyo announced that the Japanese government would continue to fight. There was no choice now. The bomb was scheduled to be dropped after August 3 unless Japan surrendered before that day.

On August 6, the fourth day of my journey home from Potsdam, came the historic news that shook the world. I was eating lunch with members of the *Augusta's* crew when I was handed the following message:

TO THE PRESIDENT
FROM THE SECRETARY OF WAR

Big bomb dropped on Hiroshima August 5 at 7:15 P.M. Washington time. First reports indicate complete success which was even more conspicuous than earlier test.

I was greatly moved. I said to the group of sailors around me, "This is the greatest thing in history. It's time for us to get home."

A few minutes later a second message was handed to me. It read as follows:

Following information regarding Manhattan [the development of the bomb was called the Manhattan Project] received. "Hiroshima bombed visually. There was no fighter opposition and no flak. Parsons reports 15 minutes after drop as follows: 'Results clear cut successful in all respects. Visible effects greater than in any test. Conditions normal in airplane following delivery.'"

When I had read this I signaled to the crew in the mess hall that I wished to say something. I then told them of the dropping of a powerful new bomb which used an explosive twenty thousand times as powerful as a ton of TNT. I went to the wardroom, where I told the officers, who were at lunch, what had happened. I could not hide my expectation that the Pacific war might now be brought to a speedy end.

Unit Seven

Reshaping the Postwar World

1945-1960

CHAPTER 19
ASSUMING THE RESPONSIBILITIES OF WORLD LEADERSHIP

BEGINNINGS OF THE COLD WAR

Many Americans hoped that the Western powers and the Soviet Union would continue their wartime cooperation after World War II. But by 1946 the Soviet Union and the United States were sharply divided over such issues as the postwar boundaries of Eastern Europe, disarmament, and the international control of atomic energy. The so-called "Cold War" between the Western powers and the Soviet Union had now begun. It was clear that the Soviet Union was determined to maintain its influence in Eastern Europe and expand it into other areas of the world. It was equally clear that the United States was determined to stop the further expansion of Communism by the Soviet Union.

Exactly how the Cold War began and whose fault it was is a subject of continuing controversy among many historians. In the following selection, historian John Lewis Gaddis gives his analysis of how the Cold War began.

How does Gaddis feel one should approach the study of the Cold War? Which nation does he think had the primary responsibility for the Cold War? Why? Does Gaddis feel that the Cold War was inevitable? Do you think it was?

Adapted from The United States and the Origins of the Cold War 1941–47 *by John Lewis Gaddis (New York: Columbia University Press, 1972), pp. 353-361. Reprinted by permission of the publisher and Mr. John Lewis Gaddis.*

American leaders did not want a Cold War, but they wanted insecurity even less. By early 1946 President Truman and his advisers had reluctantly concluded that recent actions of the Soviet Union endangered the security of the United States. In order to understand how the leaders who made American foreign policy came to this conclusion, it is necessary to view the situation as they saw it, not as it appears today in the light of historical hindsight.

World War II had produced a revolution in United States foreign policy. Before that conflict, most Americans believed that their country could best protect itself by staying out of political entanglements overseas. The events of 1939–40 persuaded leaders of the Roosevelt administration that they had been wrong. The bombing of Pearl Harbor convinced others in the United States. From then on, American policy-makers would seek security through involvement, not isolation. They believed that to prevent new wars the whole system of relations between nations would have to be changed. They felt that only the United States had the power and influence to carry out this task. As a result, United States officials set to work, even before entering into the war, to plan a peace settlement which would accomplish such a change in relations between nations.

Lessons of the past greatly influenced how American leaders saw the future. Determined to avoid mistakes which, in their view, had caused World War II, American planners sought to disarm defeated enemies, give peoples of the world the right to shape their own future, revive world trade, and replace the League of Nations with a new and more effective organization. But without victory over the Axis, the United States would never be able to carry out its plan for peace. Given the realities of the military situation, victory depended upon cooperation with the Soviet Union, an ally whose commitment to American postwar ideals was, at best, questionable.

The leaders of the Soviet Union also looked to the past in planning for the future. But their very different experiences led them to conclusions that did not always agree with those of their American allies. For Stalin, the key to peace was simple: keep Russia strong and keep Germany weak. He showed little interest in Washington's plans for collective security [a policy designed to keep world peace by having nations join together to guarantee the security or safety of all nations], the reduction of tariff barriers, and reform of the world money system. Self-determination for the people in Eastern Europe, however, he would not allow. This region was vital to Soviet security, but the people who lived there were bitterly anti-Russian. Nor could Stalin agree with Allied efforts, also growing out of lessons of the past, to limit reparations [payments for war damages] paid by Germany. These two conflicts — Eastern Europe and Germany — became major areas of disagreement in the emerging Cold War.

Moscow's position would not have seemed so alarming to American officials, however, if it were not for the Soviet Union's continued belief in an ideology favoring the overthrow of capitalism throughout the world. Hopes that the United States might cooperate successfully with the Soviet Union after the war had been based on the belief, encouraged by Stalin himself, that the Soviets had given up their former goal of spreading communism. Soviet expansion into Eastern Europe in 1944 and 1945 caused Western observers to fear that they had been misled. Just at the moment of victory over the Axis, the old fear of world revolution reappeared.

It seems likely that American foreign policymakers mistook Stalin's determination to ensure Russian security through spheres of influence for a new effort to spread communism outside the borders of the Soviet Union. The Russians did not immediately set up Communist governments in all the countries they occupied after the war. And Stalin showed very little interest in promoting the fortunes of Communist parties in areas beyond his control. Historians now generally agree on the limited nature of Stalin's objectives. But the Soviet leader failed to make the limited nature of his objectives clear. Having just defeated one dictator, Americans could not regard the emergence of another one without the strongest feelings of alarm and anger.

Nor did they see any reason to give in to what Stalin seemed to be doing. The United States had come out of the war with complete control over the world's most powerful weapon, the atomic bomb. It also had a near-monopoly over the productive facilities which could make possible quick reestablishment of war-shattered economies. Convinced that technology had given them the means to shape the postwar world to their liking, American officials assumed that these instruments would leave the Russians no choice but to go along with American peace plans.

Frustrated in their efforts to work out an acceptable settlement with the Soviet Union, under strong pressure from Congress and the public to make no further compromises, American leaders started on a new Russian policy during the first months of 1946. From now on, expansionist moves by the Soviet Union would be resisted, even at the risk of war. Negotiations would continue, but future concessions would have to come from Moscow. Meanwhile, the United States would begin rebuilding its military forces, now badly decreased by demobilization. It would also begin an ambitious program of economic assistance to nations threatened by communism.

It is easy for historians, writing twenty-five

years later, to suggest ways in which the United States might have avoided, or at least lessened, the dangers of a postwar confrontation with the Soviet Union. President Roosevelt could have eased Russia's military burden by launching a second front in Europe in 1942 or 1943. He could have removed Eastern Europe from the provisions of the Atlantic Charter, thereby recognizing the Soviet sphere of influence in that part of the world. American officials could have helped in the giant task of repairing Russian war damage by granting a generous reconstruction loan, and by allowing extensive reparations from Germany. Finally, the United States could have attempted to lessen Soviet distrust by voluntarily giving up its monopoly over the atomic bomb.

But these were not workable alternatives at the time. An early second front would have greatly increased American casualties and might have weakened support for the war effort. Recognition of the Soviet position in Eastern Europe would have caused opposition in the Senate to American membership in the United Nations, and might have endangered Roosevelt's reelection. Economic concessions to the Russians, in the form of either a reconstruction loan or a more flexible attitude on reparations, would have created a storm of protest from a Congress still largely isolationist in its approach to foreign aid. A decision to give up the atomic bomb would have so alienated the American people and their representatives on Capitol Hill as to weaken the very functioning of the government.

Historians have debated at length the question of who caused the Cold War, but without shedding much light on the subject. Too often they view that event only as a series of actions by one side and reactions by the other. In fact, policy-makers in both the United States and the Soviet Union were constantly weighing each other's intentions, as they understood them, and modifying their own courses of action accordingly. In addition, officials in Washington and Moscow brought to the task of policy making a variety of fixed ideas, shaped by personality, ideology, political pressures, even ignorance and irrationality, all of which influenced their behavior. Once this complex interaction of stimulus and response is taken into account, it becomes clear that neither side can take complete responsibility for the Cold War.

But neither should the conflict be seen as predetermined if for no other reason than the impossibility of "proving" inevitability in history. The power vacuum in central Europe caused by Germany's collapse made a Russian-American confrontation likely. It did not make it inevitable. People as well as circumstances make foreign policy, and through such drastic methods as war, appeasement, or resignation, policy-makers can always change the difficult situations in which they find themselves. One may legitimately ask why they do not choose to go this far, but to view their actions as predetermined by blind, impersonal "forces" is to deny the complexity and particularity of human behavior, not to mention the ever-present possibility of accident. The Cold War is too complicated an event to be discussed in terms of either national guilt or inevitability.

If one must assign responsibility for the Cold War, the most meaningful way is to ask which side had the greater opportunity to adapt itself, at least in part, to the other's position, given the range of alternatives as they appeared at the time. Revisionists [those historians who hold America more responsible than the Soviet Union for causing the Cold War] have argued that American policy-makers had greater freedom of action. But this view ignores the restrictions enforced by domestic politics. Little is known even today about how Stalin determined his choices, but it does seem safe to say that the very nature of the Soviet system gave him a larger selection of alternatives than were open to leaders of the United States. The Russian dictator was free from pressures of Congress, public opinion, or the press. Even ideology did not restrict him: Stalin was the master of Communist doctrine, not a prisoner of it, and could modify or suspend Marxism-Leninism whenever it suited him. This is not to say that Stalin wanted a Cold War—he had every reason to avoid one. But his absolute powers did give him more chances to overcome the internal restraints on his policy than were available to democratic leaders in the West.

The Cold War grew out of a complicated interaction of external and internal developments inside both the United States and the Soviet Union. The external situation—circumstances beyond the control of either power—left Americans and Russians facing one another across a helpless Europe at the end of

World War II. Internal influences in the Soviet Union—the search for security, the role of ideology, massive postwar reconstruction needs, the personality of Stalin—together with those in the United States—the ideal of self-determination, fear of communism, the illusion of unlimited power fostered by American economic strength and the atomic bomb—made the resulting confrontation a hostile one. Leaders of both superpowers sought peace, but in doing so gave in to considerations which, while they did not cause war, made a resolution of differences impossible.

ORGANIZING THE UNITED NATIONS

Eleanor Roosevelt was one of the most active First Ladies in the nation's history. She took a special interest in New Deal programs to help young Americans and in efforts to improve the lives of minority groups. And she continued to play an important role in American political life after President Roosevelt's death.

One of Eleanor Roosevelt's greatest contributions was her work with the United Nations. In late 1945 she was appointed by President Truman as a member of the United States delegation to the organizing meeting of the UN General Assembly. At this meeting, held in London in 1946, she served on the committee formed to deal with humanitarian, educational, and cultural matters. In the following account, from her autobiography, she tells about her work as a delegate.

How did Eleanor Roosevelt feel about serving as a member of the United States delegation? About the committee on which she served? Why was the issue of refugees important?

Adapted from On My Own by Eleanor Roosevelt. Copyright © 1958 by Anna Eleanor Roosevelt; 1957 by The Curtis Publishing Co. Reprinted by permission of William Morris Agency, Inc. on behalf of Eleanor Roosevelt.

In December of 1945 I received a message from President Truman. He reminded me that the first organizing meeting of the United Nations General Assembly would be held in London, starting in January 1946. He asked me if I would serve as a member of the United States delegation.

"Oh, no! It would be impossible," was my first reaction. "How could I be a delegate to help organize the United Nations when I have no background or experience in international meetings?"

My secretary, however, urged me not to refuse without giving the idea careful thought. I knew in a general way what had been done about organizing the United Nations. After the San Francisco meeting in 1945, when the Charter was written, it has been accepted by the various nations, including our own. I knew, too, that we had a group of people headed by Adlai Stevenson working with representatives of other member nations in London to prepare for the formal organizing meeting. Then, as I thought about the President's offer, I knew that I believed the United Nations to be the one hope for a peaceful world. I knew that my husband had placed great importance on the establishment of this world organization. So I felt a great sense of responsibility. Finally I decided to accept.

Members of the delegation sailed on the *Queen Elizabeth* in January 1946. The dock was crowded with reporters and news photographers who surrounded the Senators and the members of the House of Representatives on the delegation. I was feeling rather lost and quite uncertain about what lay ahead. But as it turned out there was plenty to do even for a confused beginner in such affairs. The first thing I noticed in my stateroom was a pile of blue sheets of paper on the table. These blue sheets turned out to be documents—most of them marked "secret"—that apparently related to the work of delegates. I had no idea where they had come from but assumed they were meant for me, so I looked through them. They obviously contained background information on the work to be taken up by the General Assembly as well as statements of our government's position on various problems.

So, I thought, somebody is putting me to work without delay. I say down and began reading—or trying to read. It was dull and very hard work. I had great difficulty in staying awake, but I knew my duty when I saw it and read them all. By the time I finished I supposed that the Department of State had no more secrets from me. But I would have found it hard to reveal anything because I was seldom really sure of the exact meaning of what was on the blue sheets. At the time, I feared this was because I couldn't understand plain English when it concerned State Department matters. Later I changed my mind on this, because others seemed to have the same difficulty.

People on the *Queen Elizabeth* were very kind to me. Nevertheless I felt much alone at first. One day, as I was walking down the passageway to my room, I met Senator Arthur H. Vandenberg.

"Mrs. Roosevelt," he said in his rather deep voice, "we would like to know if you would serve on Committee 3."

I had two immediate and rather contradictory reactions to the question. First, I wondered who "we" might be. Was a Republican Senator deciding who would serve where? And why, since I was a delegate, had I not been consulted about about committee assignments? But my next reaction crowded these thoughts out of mind. I suddenly realized that I had no idea what Committee 3 might be. So I kept my thoughts to myself and humbly agreed to serve where I was made to serve.

"But," I added quickly, "will you or someone kindly see that I get as much information as possible on Committee 3?"

The Senator promised and I went on to my room. The truth was that at that time I did not know whom to ask for information or guidance. As I learned more about my work, I realized why I had been put on Committee 3, which dealt with humanitarian, educational, and cultural questions. There were many committees dealing with the budgetary, legal, political, and other questions. I could just see the members of our delegation puzzling over the list and saying:

"Oh, no! We can't put Mrs. Roosevelt on the political committee. What could she do on the budget committee? Does she know anything about legal questions? Ah, here's the safe spot for her—Committee 3. She can't do much harm there!"

Oddly enough, I felt very much the same way about it. On the ship coming over, however, State Department officials held briefings [information meetings] for the delegates. We listened to experts on various subjects explain the problems that would be brought up, give the background on them, and then state the general position of the United States. I attended all these sessions. Discovering that there also were briefings for newspaper people aboard the ship, I went to all their meetings, too. As a result of these briefings and various discussions, I began to realize that Committee

3 might be much more important than had been expected. And, in time, this proved to be true.

At the early sessions in London, which were largely concerned with organization, I got the strong impression that many of the old-timers in the field of diplomacy were very doubtful about the new world organization. They had seen so many failures, they had been through the collapse of the League of Nations, and they seemed to doubt that we would achieve much. The newcomers, the younger people in most cases, were the ones who showed the most enthusiasm and determination.

I might point out here that during the entire London session of the Assembly, I was very uneasy. I knew that as the only woman on the delegation I was not very welcome. Moreover, if I failed to be a useful member, it would not be considered only that I as an individual had failed, but that all women had failed. There would be little chance for others to serve in the near future.

As a normal thing, the important—and I might say, the hard—work of any organization such as the United Nations is not done in the big, public meetings of the General Assembly, but in the small and almost continuous meetings of the various committees. It was while working on Committee 3 that I really began to understand the inner workings of the United Nations. It was ironical perhaps that one of the subjects that created the greatest political heat of the London sessions came up in this "unimportant" committee to which I had been assigned.

The issue arose from the fact that there were many war refugees in Germany when the armistice was signed—Ukrainians, Poles, Czechoslovaks, Latvians, Lithuanians, Estonians and others. A great number of them were still living there in temporary camps because they did not want to return to live under the Communist rule of their own countries. There also were the Jewish survivors of the German death camps.

This situation flared up in Committee 3. It was raised originally by the Yugoslav representative, Leo Mates. The Yugoslav—and, of course, the Soviet Union—position that Mates put forward was that any war refugees who did not wish to return to their countries were traitors to their countries. He argued that the refugees in Germany should be forced to return home and to accept whatever punishment might be given to them. This position was strongly supported by the Soviet representative.

The position of the Western countries, including the United States, was that large numbers of the refugees were not traitors. We felt that they must be guaranteed the right to choose whether they would return to their homes. Since the London sessions were largely technical rather than political debates and since Committee 3 was the scene of one of the early clashes between the Soviet Union and the West, the newspapers carried much of the controversy.

I felt very strongly on the subject, as did others. We spent many hours trying to write some kind of resolution on which all could agree. We never did. Our chairman had to present a majority report to the General Assembly which was immediately challenged by the USSR. In the Assembly the minority position was handled, not by the Soviet representative on Committee 3, but by the head of the Soviet Union's delegation, Andrei Vishinsky. Vishinsky was one of the Russians' great legal minds, a skilled debater, a man with ability to use the weapons of wit and ridicule. It was clear that in view of the importance of the issue someone would have to speak for the United States. The question of who this was to be made our delegation extremely anxious. There was a hurried consultation among the male members. When they broke up, John Foster Dulles approached me rather uncertainly.

"Mrs. Roosevelt," he began, rather lamely, "the United States must speak in the debate. Since you are the one who has carried on for us in this controversy in the committee, do you think you could say a few words to the Assembly? I'm afraid nobody else is really familiar with the subject."

"Why, Mr. Dulles," I answered as meekly as I could manage, "in that case I will do my best."

Actually, I was badly frightened. I trembled at the thought of speaking against the famous Mr. Vishinsky. But when the time came I walked, tense and excited, to the platform and did my best. The hour was late and we knew the Russians would delay a vote as long as possible on the theory that some of our allies would get tired and leave. I knew we must, if possible, hold the South American delegates until the vote was taken because their votes might be decisive. So I talked about Simon Bolivar and his stand for the freedom of the people of Latin America. I talked and watched the delegates. To my joy the South American representatives stayed with us to the end and, when the vote came, we won. This vote meant that the Western nations would have to worry about the ultimate fate of the refugees for a long, long time, but the principle of the right of an individual to make his or her own decisions was a victory well worth while.

The final night the vote on Committee 3's report was taken so late that I did not get back to the hotel till about one o'clock. I was very tired. As I walked wearily up the stairs, I heard two voices behind me. Turning around, I saw Senator Vandenberg and Mr. Dulles. They obviously had something to say to me, but for the life of me I can't remember which one of them said it. Whichever it was, he seemed to be speaking for both.

"Mrs. Roosevelt," he said, "we must tell you that we did all we could to keep you off the United States delegation. We begged the President not to nominate you. But now that you are leaving we feel we must admit that we have worked with you gladly and found you good to work with. And we will be happy to do so again."

I don't think anything could have made the weariness disappear as did those words. I shall always be grateful for the encouragement they gave me.

REPORTING ON THE CONFLICT IN KOREA

In June 1950, Communist-ruled North Korea began an invasion of South Korea. The United States immediately pledged aid to South Korea, and, with the support the United Nations, helped to organize an army to defend South Korea. American military forces formed the largest part of this United Nations army, but Canada, Australia, New Zealand, and other nations also provided troops.

During the Korean War many news reporters, or correspondents, went along with American troops to report on the war in Asia. One of the most famous of these war correspondents was Marguerite Higgins, who wrote for the New York *Herald Tribune*. In this selection from her book about the war in Korea, she describes an unexpected enemy attack on American headquarters (located in a schoolhouse) in July 1950.

What were Marguerite Higgins' reactions to the attack? Do you think correspondents should be allowed in the front lines with fighting troops? Why? What effect might this have on news reports about the war?

Excerpts from War in Korea *by Marguerite Higgins. Copyright 1951 by Marguerite Higgins, copyright 1951 by Time Inc. Reprinted by permission of Doubleday & Co., Inc.*

Half a dozen officers, myself, and Harold Martin [of the *Saturday Evening Post* magazine], were finishing breakfast in the schoolhouse at seven in the morning when suddenly bullets exploded from all directions. They crackled through the windows, splintered through the thin walls. A machine-gun burst slammed the coffeepot off the table. A grenade exploded on the wooden frame on which I had been sleeping, and another grenade sent fragments flying off the roof.

"Where is the little beauty who threw that?" asked Captain William Hawkes, an intelligence officer, as he grabbed at his bleeding right hand, torn by a grenade splinter.

We tried to race down the hall, but we had to hit the floor fast and stay there. We were all bewildered and caught totally by surprise. It was impossible to judge what to do. Bullets were spattering at us from the hill rising directly behind us and from the courtyard on the other side.

Thoughts tumbled jerkily through my mind —"This can't be enemy fire . . . we're miles behind the front lines . . . that grenade must have been thrown from 15 or 20 yards [between 13 and 18 meters] . . . how could they possibly get that close? . . . if they are that close, they are right behind the schoolhouse . . . they can be through those windows and on top of us in a matter of seconds . . . nobody in here even has a carbine [rifle] . . . well, it would be too late anyway . . . why did I ever get myself into this? . . . I don't understand the [weapons] fire coming from the courtyard . . . what has happened to our defense? . . . could it possibly be that some trigger-happy GI started all this? . . ."

There was soon no doubt, however, that it was enemy fire. We were surrounded. During the night the Reds [Communists] had sneaked past our front lines, avoiding the main roads and traveling over mountain trails. In camouflaged uniforms, they crept onto the hillside behind the schoolhouse. Others, circling around, set up machine guns in a rice paddy on the other side of the schoolyard. This accounted for the vicious cross fire.

They had managed to get by our defenses for several reasons. The GIs were completely exhausted from a long patrol into enemy territory. Some of the guards fell asleep. And at least one column of the enemy was mistaken, by those officers awake and on duty, for South Korean police.

We had been warned the night before that South Koreans were helping us guard our exposed right flank. This was only one of the hundreds of cases in which confusion in identifying the enemy lost us lives. It is, of course, part of the difficulty of being involved in a civil war.

I learned all of this, of course, much later. On the schoolhouse floor, with our noses scraping the dust, the only thought was how to get out of the bullet-riddled building without getting killed in the process. The bullets cutting through the cardboard-thin walls ripped the floor boards around us, and we all kept wondering why one of us didn't get hit.

I mumbled to Harold that it looked as if we would have a very close blow-by-blow account of battle to give to the American public. But he didn't hear me because one of the officers suddenly said, "I'm getting out of here," and dove out the window into the courtyard in the direction away from the hill. We all leaped after him and found a stone wall which at least protected us from the rain of fire from the high ground.

In the courtyard we found an uproar of officers and noncoms attempting to dodge the incoming fire and at the same time trying to find their men and produce some order out of the chaos. Some of the soldiers in the courtyard, in their confusion, were firing, without aiming, dangerously close to the GIs racing in retreat down the hill.

Colonel Michaelis, his executive officer, Colonel Farthing, and company commanders were booting reluctant GIs out from under jeeps and trucks and telling them to get to their units up the hill.

A lot of yelling was coming from the opposite corner of the courtyard. I turned my head around in time to see an officer taking careful aim at one of our own machine gunners. He winged him. It was a good shot, and an unfortunate necessity. The machine gunner had gone crazy in the terror of the surprise attack and had started firing on our own vehicles and troops with the machine gun.

An officer came up with the gloomy information that several hundred Koreans had landed on the coast a thousand yards [914 meters] to the north.

I started to say something to Martin as he kneeled methodically recording the battle in his notebook. My teeth were chattering uncontrollably, I discovered, and in shame I broke off after the first disgraceful squeak of words.

Then suddenly, for the first time in the war, I experienced the cold, awful certainty that there was no escape. My reactions were commonplace. As with most people who suddenly accept death as inevitable and about to happen, I was simply filled with surprise that this was finally going to happen to me. Then as the conviction grew, I became hard inside and fairly calm. I stopped worrying. Physically the result was that my teeth stopped chattering and my hands stopped shaking. This was a relief, as I would have been extremely embarrassed had anyone caught me in that state.

Fortunately, by the time Michaelis came around the corner and asked, "How are you doing, kid?" I was able to answer in a respectably self-contained tone of voice, "Just fine, sir."

A few minutes later Michaelis, ignoring the bullets, moved suddenly into the middle of the courtyard. He yelled for a cease-fire.

"Let's get organized and find out what we're shooting at," he shouted.

Gradually the scramble in the courtyard turned into a pattern of resistance. Two heavy machine-gun squads crept up to the hill under cover of protecting rifle fire and fixed aim on the enemy trying to swarm down. Platoons and then companies followed. Light mortars were dragged up. The huge artillery guns lowered and fired point-blank at targets only a few hundred yards away.

Finally a reconnaissance officer came up and reported that the soldiers landing on the coasts were not a new enemy force to overwhelm us but South Korean allies. On the hill, soldiers were silencing some of the enemy fire. It was now 7:45. It did not seem possible that so much could have happened since the enemy had struck.

As the intensity of fire let up slightly, soldiers started bringing in the wounded from the hills, carrying them on their backs. I walked over to the aid station. Because of the sudden rush of casualties, everyone was frantically busy.

One medic was running short of plasma but did not dare leave his patients long enough to try to round up some more. I offered to administer the remaining plasma and passed about an hour there, helping out as best I could.

My most vivid memory of the hour is Captain Logan Weston limping into the station with a wound in his leg. He was patched up and promptly turned around and headed for the hills again. Half an hour later he was back with bullets in his shoulder and chest. Sitting on the floor smoking a cigarette, the captain calmly said, "I guess I'd better get a shot of morphine now. These last two are beginning to hurt."

It was at the aid station that I realized we were going to win after all. Injured after injured came in with reports that the North Koreans were "being murdered" and that they were falling back. There was a brief lull in the fighting. Then the enemy, strengthened with fresh reinforcements, struck again. But Michaelis was ready for them this time. At 1:30 in the afternoon, when the last attacking force had been driven back, more than 600 dead North Koreans were counted in the hills behind the schoolhouse. We really had been lucky.

After the schoolhouse battle I usually took a carbine along in our jeep. I'm a lousy shot, but I know I duck when bullets start flying my way. I reasoned that the enemy had the same reaction and that my bullets, however wild, might at least scare him into keeping his head down or might throw his aim off.

Most correspondents carried weapons of some kind. The enemy did not care if they shot unarmed civilians. And the fighting line changed so often that no place near the front lines was safe from sudden enemy attack.

In those days the main difference between a news reporter and a soldier in Korea was that the soldier in combat had to get out of his hole and go after the enemy, whereas the correspondent had the privilege of keeping his head down. It was commonplace for correspondents to be at the company and platoon level, and many of us frequently went on patrol. We felt it was the only honest way of covering the war. The large number of correspondents killed or captured in Korea is testimony of the dangers to which many willingly subjected themselves.

CHAPTER 20
RETURNING TO PEACE AND PROSPERITY

TRUMAN CURBS THE RAILROADS

With the end of World War II in 1945, the United States began to make the change from a wartime to a peacetime economy—a change known as reconversion. A smooth transition was one of the major goals of Harry S. Truman, who became President when Roosevelt died in the spring of the year. As this account indicates, President Truman's task was not an easy one.

Why was the union threatening to strike? How did Truman propose to settle the railroad strike? What happened to his proposal?

Adapted with permission of Macmillan Publishing Co., Inc. from The Truman Presidency *by Cabell Phillips. Copyright © 1966 by Cabell Phillips.*

The labor-management pot came to a boil late in 1945. The dire forecasts of massive unemployment had not materialized. But wave upon wave of strikes shut down one major segment of industry after another. Workers battled management for peacetime wages to match their wartime earnings and for pensions, welfare funds, union security, and other fringe benefits.

As the new year of 1946 opened, 900,000 workers, led by Walter Reuther's auto workers, were already on strike. Within weeks they were followed by 700,000 steel workers, 263,000 packinghouse workers, 200,000 electrical workers, 50,000 communications workers. Never before had the nation been faced with such a workers' revolt. The year was to register a total of 116,000,000 man-days of work lost due to strikes, which was three times higher than it ever had been before (and twice as high as in any year since then). In February, an even more menacing prospect darkened the picture—a general strike on the nation's railroads.

Months of fruitless negotiation between the twenty powerful rail brotherhoods and railroad management reached a final dead end on April 18. An arbitration board had proposed to settle the unions' demand for a $2.20-a-day wage increase at $1.28 and to put off a decision on work rules for a year. The carriers accepted and the unions rejected the proposal. Eighteen of the brotherhoods agreed to further negotia-

tion, but the Brotherhood of Locomotive Engineers, headed by Alvaney Johnston, and the Brotherhood of Railroad Trainmen, whose president was A. F. Whitney, said they were through with negotiation. They called a strike of their members in thirty days—for May 18.

Both Johnston and Whitney, paunchy, shrewd old veterans of the labor wars going back to the turn of the century, were old political friends of the President. They had given him a boost in his 1940 campaign for reelection to the Senate and were among his strongest backers for the Vice Presidential nomination. Until April 18, their defiance of Truman's arm's-length effort to settle their differences with the carriers had been conducted in good spirits. Now their attitude was to stiffen in cold hostility.

With the collapse of bargaining negotiations in April, President Truman took the rail dispute into his own hands and put John R. Steelman to work on the problem as his personal representative. Weeks of consultation and wheedling followed, but to no avail. On Wednesday, May 15, three days before the strike deadline, the President summoned the management representatives and the leaders of the twenty brotherhoods to his office. He talked to them and found that leaders of eighteen of the unions were willing to settle on the basis of the $1.28 arbitration award. But not Whitney and Johnston. Between them, they could bring every wheel on the railroads to a stop, and that was what they proposed to do. Peering coldly through his thick glasses at his two old friends, the President said:

"If you think I'm going to sit here and let you tie up this whole country, you're crazy."

"We've got to go through with it, Mr. President," Whitney said. "Our men are demanding it."

Truman got up from his desk, ending the conference. "All right, I'm going to give you the gun. You've got just 48 hours—until Thursday at this time—to reach a settlement. If you don't, I'm going to take over the railroads in the name of the government."

By now, an angry uproar from Congress and the press was arising from all across the country. The threat of paralysis in the transportation system seemed intolerable.

When the Thursday deadline came without a break in the deadlock, Truman called the railroad leaders again to his office to watch—and to be on public view to the news photographers—as he signed an executive order carrying out his threat of seizure of the railroads. Whitney and Johnston grudgingly agreed to postpone their strike for five days, but not an instant longer. That made the new and final deadline 4 o'clock on the afternoon of Saturday, May 25. On Thursday, Steelman called the leaders in for another all-day session at the White House. When it was over, Whitney and Johnston continued to hold out. That night they wrote the President a curt letter saying: "We have told you many times that the present agitation among the men is extremely serious and their demands cannot be abandoned. Therefore your offer is unacceptable."

When Harry Truman's mad is up, his eyes glint coldly behind his spectacles and his mouth is a thin, hard line pulled down at the corners. This was the image as he stalked into a specially called meeting of his Cabinet that Friday morning. In the manner of Lincoln and the Emancipation Proclamation, he had summoned them not to ask their views but to tell them what he was going to do. He was going to Congress in person the next day and demand the stiffest labor law in history—one that would give him authority to draft strikers into the armed services without respect to age or dependency when their strike threatened to bring on a national emergency. When the Attorney General raised a question about the constitutionality of such a move, the President brushed him aside. "We'll draft 'em first and think about the law later," he said.

Next, he turned to Charley Ross, his press secretary, and told him to arrange a coast-to-coast radio hookup for him that night so that he could explain to the people what he was about to do.

"Here's what I'm going to say," he snapped. "Get it typed up. I'm going to take the hide right off those so-and-so's."

Ross's blood pressure rocketed as he read what possibly will stand for all time as the angriest public message ever written in a President's own hand. It accused the labor leaders of having tried to sabotage the war effort while America's young men faced death on the battlefield. Now they were sabotaging the peace

by "holding a gun to the head of the government." He called on the ex-soldiers who had been his comrades in arms to help "eliminate the Whitneys and the Johnstons," and to "hang a few traitors and make our country safe for democracy."

It is hard to guess what might have happened if this blast had reached the public. Happily, Charley Ross was the kind of old friend who could go to the President and say, "Look, Harry, this just won't do." Which is basically what he did, and with the help of Clark Clifford a greatly toned-down version of the speech was hammered out before the President went on the air at 10 o'clock that night.

Even so, that speech was one of the sharpest attacks on a group of individuals by a President that has ever been uttered. In it Mr. Truman said:

My fellow countrymen—I come before the American people tonight at a time of great crisis.

The crisis of Pearl Harbor was the result of action by a foreign enemy. The crisis tonight is caused by a group of men within our own country who place their private interests above the welfare of the Nation. . . .

I assume that these two men [Johnston and Whitney] know the havoc which their decision has caused, and the even more extreme suffering which will result in the future. . . . This is no contest between labor and management. This is a contest between a small group of men and their government. . . .

If sufficient workers to operate the trains have not returned by 4 P.M. tomorrow, as head of your government I have no alternative but to operate the trains by using every means within my power. . . .

Saturday—the next day—was as packed with drama as a Hollywood cliffhanger. Steelman was locked in a room at the Statler Hotel with Whitney and Johnston in a last-ditch effort to make them relent. Clifford and Sam Rosenman, in the Cabinet room at the White House, were battling against both time and uncertainty trying to draft the President's speech to Congress. Would, or would not, the strike be settled by the time the President got to the Capitol? Steelman telephoned Clifford that an agreement might be signed any minute, but he couldn't be certain.

"That was going to put us in a fix if it were

settled at the last minute, and we had this speech," Clifford recalled. So he and Rosenman wrote out a couple of alternative pages that might be substituted at the last minute. The President had already left for the Capitol with the original text when they finished. Hatless, Clifford set out in pursuit, only to find on arrival at the office of Speaker Sam Rayburn that the President had already entered the House Chamber and was about to begin his speech.

Five minutes later, Clifford got a call through to Steelman at the Statler, who told him breathlessly: "It's signed!"

Clifford scribbled a note on a scrap of paper: "Mr. President, agreement signed, strike over," and gave it to the Secretary of the Senate who scurried across the corridor and into the House Chamber and thrust the note on top of the text from which the President had already begun to read. Truman halted in midsentence and then looked up with a grin:

"Gentlemen, the strike has been settled," he said. There was an outbreak of applause and shouts from the packed Chamber.

THE MIDDLE OF THE ROAD

The election of Dwight D. Eisenhower to the presidency in 1952 brought a Republican to the White House for the first time in twenty years. This victory did not mean, however, that all the programs of the previous Democratic administrations were to be discarded. Instead, Eisenhower and his advisers followed a middle-of-the-road approach, maintaining many New Deal policies but modifying others. They called their philosophy Modern, or New, Republicanism.

The meaning of New Republicanism is outlined here by Arthur Larson, who served as Eisenhower's Undersecretary of Labor. He places New Republicanism midway between two outlooks of the past: the probusiness approach of 1896 (when Republican William McKinley was elected President) and the prolabor approach of 1936 (when Democrat Franklin D. Roosevelt won a second, overwhelming victory).

How does Larson characterize New Republicanism? What reasons does Larson give for the emergence of the "American Consensus"? Why, as he sees it, is the Democratic Party unable to be the party of the center?

Adapted from pp. 10, 12–19 in A Republican Looks at His Party *by Arthur Larson. Copyright © 1956 by Arthur Larson. Reprinted by permission of Harper & Row, Publishers, Inc.*

In the nineteenth century, there was not enough government regulation and not enough labor strength and freedom. Result: unruly business expansion at the expense of the rights of people. In the nineteen-thirties there was too much government regulation and not enough business incentive and freedom. Result: deadened business activity and a long depression, accompanied by much humanitarian concern for the victims of the depression.

Now we have as much government activity as is necessary, but not enough to stifle the normal motivations of private enterprise. And we have a higher degree of government concern for the needs of people than ever before in our history. At the same time, the government is pursuing a policy of restoring responsibility to individuals and private groups. This balance, together with the restoration of a better balance between federal and state governments, is allowing all these elements in our society to make their maximum contribution to the common good.

By bringing together these best forces in American life, President Eisenhower and his associates have, for the first time in our history, discovered and established the Authentic American Center in politics. This is not a Center in the European sense of an uneasy mid-point between large and powerful left-wing and right-wing elements of varying degrees of radicalism. It is a Center in the American sense of a common meeting-ground of the great majority of our people on our own issues. [It is set] against a backdrop of our own history, our own current setting and our own responsibilities for the future.

What are the reasons for this recent emergence of the American Consensus? There are at least five.

First should be noted the common social and historical background which makes this high degree of agreement possible. We have not entered this period trailing centuries of class consciousness and class warfare. We did not, as a nation, start from a beginning-point in which people were divided into aristocrats and serfs, or into rich capitalists and propertyless laborers. Of course, during Revolutionary times there were some "aristocrats" of a sort, but they did their best to play down that fact. And there were struggling laborers, but they in turn never thought of themselves as a fixed "lower class." Above all, the great majority of people, whether farmers, pioneers, or workers, largely identified themselves in the one great enterprise of making their fortunes in a young and expanding country.

Reenforcing this common social origin was an ideological position. The American Revolution was part of a period of brilliant thought on political philosophy. The nation's leaders, in the *Federalist Papers,* the Constitution, and the Declaration of Independence, laid down a solid platform upon which all later American thought could build.

A third reason for the appearance of the Consensus is the gradual moving-together of the interests which have provided our principal conflicts. Responsible labor and business leaders are proclaiming the doctrine that labor and management have far-reaching interests in common. The business community has come to accept a wide range of governmental measures, formerly opposed as "interference," as highly helpful to business. The antagonism between farmers and "Eastern bankers," which loomed so large some years ago, seems to have dissolved. [This may be due to] the increase of ownership by farmers of their own farms, and with agreement on the need for special measures to protect farm income.

These are factors of a long-term or gradual kind which have made the Consensus possible. But why has it appeared just now?

For this there are two main reasons.

One is that there is arisen in the world an ideology—that of the Communists—which actively challenges and menaces almost everything we stand for. Principles that we have always taken for granted as the air we breathe are now denounced and denied over a large part of the world. We may even have allowed ourselves at times to think of these principles as trite—suitable perhaps for a fourth-grade civics course, but not the sort of thing you would make the subject of serious discussion among adults.

Now we suddenly find these familiar ideas to be our rallying-point in a grim struggle for the highest stakes in history. A common danger has forced us all to think about what we really think. In doing so, we are finding that we think more like each other than we ever realized, because the essential alikeness of our thoughts shines out against the looming black cloud of a system of thought we hate.

The second reason why the American Consensus has now so clearly emerged, is that the Eisenhower Administration has defined it, given voice to it and put it into practice.

This point is of crucial importance. If one were to go no further than to show that a wide area of agreement on fundamentals had been achieved, this would no doubt provide an interesting contribution to the history of political science. But it would have no practical impact on current political events. Under our two-party system, the decisive issue becomes: under which party banner does this American Center rally to carry forward these agreed principles?

The answer here given is: the New Republicanism as exemplified by the Eisenhower Administration.

The primary reason is that it is the Eisenhower Administration that "invented" the successful formula, the genius of which lies in bringing together all that is best in American life, whatever its origin.

Historians may someday very well conclude that the Democratic Party was the party adapted to radical reform and free-wheeling experimentation at a time when things were badly out of joint [during the Great Depression]. They may find that the Republican Party was the party designed to carry a more mature America forward on a course of steady progress and expansion, backed by the broad support of the American Consensus.

Given the continued existence of the two-party system, then, the Center will have to express itself in much the way it did in electing President Eisenhower in 1952. That is, [it will have to add] to the vote of one party both the independent vote and a considerable portion of the vote of the other party.

To summarize: in politics—as in chess—the man who holds the center holds a position of almost unbeatable strength.

McCARTHY'S ANTICOMMUNIST CRUSADE

In the years immediately after World War II, communism was expanding aggressively in Europe and Asia. Was the same thing happening in the United States? Many Americans were afraid of Communist subversion, and their fears were stimulated by Senator Joseph McCarthy of Wisconsin. He accused the government itself of employing "known Communists."
Political reporter Richard Rovere here sum-

marizes McCarthy's career as a crusader against communism. He calls the Senator a demagogue, meaning a political leader who appeals to people's prejudices and hatreds.

What were two meanings of the term "McCarthyism"? What effect does Rovere indicate McCarthy had on politics in America? What reality did the Senator ignore? Why, according to Rovere, was this dangerous?

Adapted from Senator Joe McCarthy © *1959 by Richard Rovere. Reprinted by permission of Harcourt Brace Jovanovich, Inc.*

At the start of 1950, Senator Joseph McCarthy was unknown to the general public outside Wisconsin. Then, on February 9, 1950, he made a speech in Wheeling, West Virginia. In it he said that the Department of State was full of Communists and that he and the Secretary of State knew their names. Later there was some dispute (there was always dispute whenever he said anything) as to whether he had stated that there were 205, 81, 57, or "a lot" of Communists. But the number was of slight importance. The fact was, he insisted, that Communists "known to the Secretary of State" were "still working and making policy."

A Senate committee was immediately appointed to look into his startling claims. It was the first of five investigations, held by four different committees. They were concerned exclusively with the problem of whether Senator McCarthy was telling the truth about others or others were telling the truth about Senator McCarthy. In the spring of 1950, when Communist power in the Far East was being mobilized for the war in Korea, political life in the United States seemed largely a matter of determining whether American diplomacy was in the hands of traitors.

Barely a month after Wheeling, "McCarthyism" was coined by Herbert Block, the cartoonist who signs himself "Herblock." The word was an oath at first—a synonym for the hatefulness of mudslinging. Later it became, for some, an affirmation, nothing more or less than a militant patriotism.

McCarthyism managed, for a time, to make politics in America seem almost entirely a matter of idiotic chatter about "loyalty risks" and "security risks." A visitor from another civilization would have been forced to conclude that in the United States the measure of political virtue was the number of unworthy civil servants a government managed to dismiss.

The parties seldom argued over the number of gifted people brought into the government. The test was how many rotten apples each had been able to find. "We're kicking the Communists and fellow travelers and security risks out of the Government . . . by the thousands," the Vice-President of the United States said. It happened to be a fact that not one certifiable Communist had been disclosed as working for the government—though quite possibly there were a few. But this was not the worst of it. The worst was that McCarthyism had led us to think that the health of the nation was war against clerks of doubtful patriotism.

McCarthyism was, among other things, a flight from reality. It elevated the ridiculous and ridiculed the important. It outraged common sense and held common sense to be outrageous. It made sages of screwballs and accused wise men of being fools. It diverted attention from the moment and fixed it on the past, which it distorted almost beyond recognition.

The reality it fled, while madly professing to be the only doctrine that faced it, was a terrible one. Only a Communist or an idiot could have denied that the Communist threat to the United States was real and great. The whole Western world was endangered, in those days as in these, by the thrust of Soviet power. Just before McCarthy erupted, it had been increased by the emergence of China as an ally of the Soviet Union and by the Russian mastery of nuclear weapons.

In the early part of the decade, the threat seemed more directly a military one than it does today. Within a few months of McCarthy's first appearance as a national figure, it was established by shellfire and tramping armies in Korea that communism was willing to risk military aggression and war. Communist power in the world was the central reality for the United States in early 1950. The problem we faced was to form and lead an alliance capable of resisting the Soviet thrust and to find strategies of resistance that would not lead to general war and universal destruction.

McCarthyism ignored this reality. "There is only one real issue for the farmer, the laborer, and the businessman—the issue of communism in government," McCarthy said in a campaign speech in 1952. He even insisted that the struggle against world communism was a diversion from the struggle against the domestic conspiracy. Speaking, in 1951, of our intervention in Korea, he said, "So the administration which would not fight communism at home undertook to prove to the American people that it was willing to fight communism abroad."

This sort of talk would have been nonsense at any time. In 1951 and 1952, it was stupid. In the 1930's and early 1940's there had been a strong Communist movement in this country, and Communists within the government. It was unquestionably the government's business to combat the movement. By 1950, this had been fairly effectively done—if, in fact, it had not been overdone. The FBI had just about abandoned its concern with bank robbers to turn its full force on communism. The Communist Party, moreover, was in an advanced state of disintegration—partly because of a spreading disillusionment among its members, partly because the government was locking up its leaders. If the conspiracy was still in any way effective, its effectiveness eluded McCarthy. He could find nothing more exciting than an army dentist [who might be a Communist], a novel by a Communist on a library shelf, and an ex-Communist here and there in some minor agency. He did no better than that.

Here and there, no doubt, there were (and probably still are) Communist agents in the government. Communism is, after all, an international conspiracy. It would be astonishing if a government employing two or three million people harbored no Communists at all. But the damage that agents can do is limited in any case. In our particular case steps had been taken long before McCarthy came along to uncover as many agents as possible and further to limit the damage any remaining ones could do.

Even if McCarthy had done far better, McCarthyism would still have been trading in dangerous illusions. It was insisting that communism was a danger, not to the United States, but in the United States. In truth it was just the other way about. It was focusing attention on the spy rather than on the power for whom the spy spies. It concentrated on the Communist or ex-Communist dentist in the United States Army rather than on the Red [Soviet] Army, combat-ready and nuclear-armed. We were supposed to dread not Stalin and Khrushchev with their armies and their satellites, not the gathering economic strength of communism, not the appeal of its propaganda in those parts of the world where bread is still scarce—we were to dread the dentist and his promotion to major.

CHAPTER 21
ENTERING AN ERA OF RAPID GROWTH AND CHANGE

A CRITICAL LOOK AT TELEVISION

Television was shown to the public at the New York World's Fair of 1939-40, but the new medium was little more than a curiosity until after World War II. Even in 1947 there were only 10,000 sets and very few hours of programs. Then the industry boomed. By 1957 there were 40 million sets in use, and over 450 television stations.

At first the very existence of television seemed so extraordinary that audiences were content to sit for hours watching dancing cigarette packages and old movies. By the end of the 1950's, however, some people were taking a closer look. One man who didn't like what he saw was Newton Minow, who became chairman of the Federal Communications Commission in 1961. In an address to the National Association of Broadcasters, he broke precedent by criticizing the industry. His speech is remembered for his description of television as "a vast wasteland."

What does Minow dislike about television?

How does he think ratings should be used? What recommendations does he make?

Adapted from Newton N. Minow, Equal Time: The Private Broadcaster and the Public Interest, edited by Lawrence Laurent. Copyright © 1964 by Newton N. Minow (New York: Atheneum, 1964). Reprinted with the permission of Atheneum Publishers.

In today's world . . . the old complacent, unbalanced fare of action-adventure and situation comedies is simply not good enough.

Your industry possesses the most powerful voice in America. It has an inescapable duty to make that voice ring with intelligence and with leadership. In a few years this exciting industry has grown from a novelty to an instrument of overwhelming impact on the American people. It should be making ready for the kind of leadership that newspapers and magazines assumed years ago, to make our people aware of their world.

Ours has been called the jet age, the atomic age, the space age. It is also, I submit, the television age. And just as history will decide whether the leaders of today's world employed the atom to destroy the world or rebuild it for mankind's benefit, so will history decide whether today's broadcasters employed their powerful voice to enrich the people or debase them.

Like everybody, I wear more than one hat. I am the Chairman of the FCC. I am also a television viewer and the husband and father of other television viewers. I have seen a great many television programs that seemed to me eminently worthwhile. When television is good, nothing—not the theater, not the magazines or newspapers—nothing is better.

But when television is bad, nothing is worse. I invite you to sit down in front of your television set when your station goes on the air and stay there without a book, magazine, newspaper, profit-and-loss sheet or rating book to distract you—and keep your eyes glued to that set until the station signs off. I can assure you that you will observe a vast wasteland.

You will see a procession of game shows, violence, audience participation shows, formula comedies about totally unbelievable families, blood and thunder, mayhem, violence, sadism, murder, Western badmen, Western good men, private eyes, gangsters, more violence and cartoons. And, endlessly, commercials—many screaming, cajoling and offending. And most of all, boredom. True, you will see a few things you will enjoy. But they will be very, very few. And if you think I exaggerate, try it.

Is there one person in this room who claims that broadcasting can't do better?

Well, a glance at next season's proposed programming can give us little heart. Of seventy-three and a half hours of prime evening time, the networks have tentatively scheduled fifty-nine hours to categories of "action-adventure," situation comedy, variety, quiz and movies.

Is there one network president in this room who claims he can't do better?

Why is so much of television so bad? I have heard many answers: demands of your advertisers; competition for ever higher ratings; the need always to attract a mass audience; the high cost of television programs; the insatiable appetite for programming material—these are some of them. Unquestionably these are tough problems not susceptible to easy answers.

But I am not convinced that you have tried hard enough to solve them.

I do not accept the idea that the present overall programming is aimed accurately at the public taste. The ratings tell us only that some people have their television sets turned on, and of that number, so many are tuned to one channel and so many to another. They don't tell us what the public might watch if they were offered half a dozen additional choices. A rating, at best, is an indication of how many people saw what you gave them. Unfortunately, it does not reveal the depth of the penetration, or the intensity of reaction. And it never reveals what the acceptance would have been if what you gave them had been better—if all the forces of art and creativity and daring and imagination had been unleashed. I believe in the people's good sense and good taste, and I am not convinced that the people's taste is as low as some of you assume.

My concern with the rating services is not with their accuracy. Perhaps they are accurate. I really don't know. What, then, is wrong with the ratings? It's not been their accuracy—it's been their use.

Certainly I hope you will agree that ratings should have little influence where children are concerned. The best estimates indicate that during the hours of 5 to 6 P.M., 60 per cent of your audience is composed of children under twelve. And most young children today, believe it or not, spend as much time watching television as they do in the schoolroom. I repeat—let that sink in—most young children today spend as much time watching television as they do in the schoolroom. It used to be said that there were three great influences on a child: home, school and church. Today there is a fourth great influence, and you ladies and gentlemen control it.

If parents, teachers, and ministers conducted their responsibilities by following the ratings, children would have a steady diet of ice cream, school holidays and no Sunday School. What about your responsibilities? Is there no room on television to teach, to inform, to uplift, to stretch, to enlarge the capacities of our children? Is there no room for programs deepening their understanding of children in other lands? Is there no room for a children's news show explaining something about the world to them at their level of understanding? Is there no room for reading the great literature of the past, teaching them the great traditions of freedom? There are some fine children's shows, but they are drowned out in the massive doses of cartoons, violence and more violence. Must these be your trademarks? Search your consciences and see if you cannot offer more to your young beneficiaries, whose future you guide so many hours each and every day.

What about adult programming and ratings? You know, newspaper publishers take popularity ratings too. The answers are pretty clear; it is almost always the comics, followed by the advice-to-the-lovelorn columns. But, ladies and gentlemen, the news is still on the front page of all newspapers, the editorials are not replaced by more comics, the newspapers have not become one long collection of advice to the lovelorn. Yet newspapers do not need a license from the government to be in business —they do not use public property. But in television—where your responsibilities as public trustees are so plain—the moment that the ratings indicate that Westerns are popular, there are new imitations of Westerns on the air faster than television can switch us from Hollywood to New York. Broadcasting cannot continue to live by the numbers. Ratings ought to be the slave of the broadcaster, not his master. And you and I both know that the rating services themselves would agree.

Let me make clear that what I am talking about is balance. I believe that the public interest is made up of many interests. There are many people in this great country, and you must serve all of us. You will get no argument from me if you say that, given a choice between a Western and a symphony, more people will watch the Western. I like Westerns and private eyes too—but a steady diet for the whole country is obviously not in the public interest. We all know that people would more often prefer to be entertained than stimulated or informed. But your obligations are not satisfied if you look only to popularity as a test of what to broadcast. You are not only in show business; you are free to communicate ideas as well as relaxation. You must provide a wider range of choices, more diversity, more alternatives. It is not enough to cater to the nation's whims—you must also serve the nation's needs.

And I would add this—that if some of you persist in a relentless search for the highest rating and the lowest common denominator, you may very well lose your audience. Because the people are wise, wiser than some of the broadcasters—and politicians—think.

THE OTHER AMERICA

The United States in the 1950's experienced greater prosperity than ever before. By 1956, for example, the average family had one and a half times the purchasing power it had had in 1929. Times were good for the majority of the American people. Things were very different, though, for a large minority. These were the people Michael Harrington calls "the other America"—the poor.

For what reasons are the poor invisible? How does Harrington think the problem of poverty is to be solved?

Excerpted and adapted with permission of Macmillan Publishing Co., from The Other America *by Michael Harrington,* © *Michael Harrington 1962.*

There is a familiar America. It is celebrated in speeches and advertised on television and in the magazines. It has the highest mass standard of living the world has ever known.

In the 1950's this America worried about itself, yet even its anxieties were products of abundance. There was worry about Madison Avenue and [the role of advertising]. There was discussion of the emotional suffering taking place in the suburbs. In all this, there was an assumption that the basic grinding economic problems had been solved in the United States. In this theory the nation's problems were no longer a matter of basic human needs, of food, shelter, and clothing. Now they were seen as a question of learning to live decently amid luxury.

While this discussion was carried on, there existed another America. In it dwelt somewhere between 40,000,000 and 50,000,000 citizens of this land. They were poor. They still are.

To be sure, the other America is not poor in the same sense as those poor nations where millions cling to hunger as a defense against starvation. This country has escaped such extremes. That does not change the fact that tens of millions of Americans are, at this very moment, maimed in body and spirit, existing at levels beneath those necessary for human decency. If these people are not starving, they are hungry, and sometimes fat with hunger, for that is what cheap foods do. They are without adequate housing and education and medical care.

The millions who are poor in the United States tend to become increasingly invisible. Here is a great mass of people, yet it takes an effort of the intellect and will even to see them.

The other America, the America of poverty, is hidden today in a way that it never was before. Its millions are socially invisible to the rest of us. One must begin a description of the other America by understanding why we do not see it.

Poverty is often off the beaten track. It always has been. The ordinary tourist never left the main highway, and today he rides interstate turnpikes. He does not go into the valleys of Pennsylvania. He does not see the company houses in rows, the rutted roads (the poor always have bad roads whether they live in the city, in towns, or on farms), where everything is black and dirty. And even if he were to pass through such a place by accident, the tourist would not meet the unemployed men in the bar or the women coming home from a sweatshop.

Then, too, beauty and myths are perennial masks of poverty. The traveler comes to the Appalachians in the lovely season. He sees the hills, the streams, the foliage—but not the poor. Or perhaps he looks at a run-down mountain house and decides that "those people" are truly fortunate to be living the way they are and that they are lucky to be exempt from the strains and tensions of the middle class. The only problem is that "those people" are undereducated underprivileged, lack medical care, and are in the process of being forced from the land into a life in the cities, where they are misfits.

These are normal and obvious causes of the invisibility of the poor. They operated a generation ago; they will be functioning a generation hence. It is more important to understand that the very development of American society is creating a new kind of blindness about poverty. The poor are increasingly slipping out of the very experience and consciousness of the nation.

If the middle class never did like ugliness and poverty, it was at least aware of them. "Across the tracks"; was not a very long way to go. Occasionally, almost everyone passed through the Negro ghetto or the blocks of tenements, if only to get downtown to work or to entertainment.

Now the American city has been transformed. The poor still inhabit the miserable housing in the central area, but they are increasingly isolated from contact with, or sight of, anybody else. The failures, the unskilled, the disabled, the aged, and the minorities are right there, across the tracks, where they have always been. But hardly anyone else is.

In short, the very development of the American city has removed poverty from the living, emotional experience of millions upon millions of middle-class Americans. Living out in the suburbs, it is easy to assume that ours is, indeed an affluent society.

This new segregation of poverty is compounded by a well-meaning ignorance. A good many concerned and sympathetic Americans are aware that there is much discussion of urban renewal. Suddenly, driving through the city, they notice that a familiar slum has been torn down and that there are towering, modern buildings where once there had been tenements or hovels. There is a warm feeling of satisfaction, of pride in the way things are working out: the poor, it is obvious, are being taken care of.

The irony in this is that the truth is nearly the exact opposite to the impression. The total impact of the various housing programs in postwar America has been to squeeze more and more people into existing slums.

Clothes make the poor invisible too: America has the best-dressed poverty the world has ever known. For a variety of reasons, the benefits of mass production have been spread much more evenly in this area than in many others. It is much easier in the United States to be decently dressed than it is to be decently housed, fed or doctored. Even people with terribly depressed incomes can look prosperous.

Then, many of the poor are the wrong age to be seen. A good number of them (over 8,000,000) are sixty-five years of age or better; an even larger number are under eighteen. The aged members of the other America are often sick, and they cannot move. Another group of them live out their lives in loneliness and frustration. They sit in rented rooms, or else they stay close to a house in a neighborhood that has completely changed from the old days. Indeed. one of the worst aspects of poverty among the aged is that these people are out of sight and out of mind, and alone.

The young are somewhat more visible, yet they too stay close to their neighborhoods. Sometimes they advertise their poverty through a newspaper story about a gang killing. But generally they do not disturb the quiet streets of the middle class.

And finally, the poor are politically invisible. It is one of the cruelest ironies of social life in advanced countries that the dispossessed at the bottom of society are unable to speak for themselves. The people of the other America do not, by far and large, belong to unions, to fraternal organizations, or to political parties. They are without lobbies of their own; they put forward no legislative program. They have no face; they have no voice.

Thus, there is not even a cynical political motive for caring about the poor, as in the old days. Because the slums are no longer centers of powerful political organizations, the politicians need not really care about their inhabitants. The slums are no longer visible to the middle class, so much of the idealistic urge to fight for those who need help is gone. Only the social agencies have a really direct involvement with the other America, and they are without any great political power. . . .

Only the larger society, with its help and resources, can really make it possible for these people to help themselves. Yet those who could make the difference too often refuse to act because of their ignorance and smugness. They view the effects of poverty—above all, the warping of the will and spirit that is a consequence of being poor—as choices. Understanding is an important step in breaking down this prejudice.

The United States contains an affluent society within its borders. Millions and tens of millions enjoy the highest standard of life the world has ever known.

But when all is said and done, after one reads the facts, either there are anger and shame, or there are not. And, as usual, the fate of the poor hangs upon the decision of the better-off. If this anger and shame are not forthcoming, someone can write a book about the other America a generation from now and it will be the same, or worse.

DESEGREGATION: ON THE FRONT LINES

A landmark in the history of American civil rights was the 1954 Supreme Court decision, *Brown v. Board of Education of Topeka.* The judges ruled that segregating black students from white students in public education was unconstitutional. They urged that schools should be desegregated "with all deliberate speed."

Desegregation went smoothly in some communities, but elsewhere it was accompanied by protests and violence. One such place was Little Rock, Arkansas. When nine black students attempted to enter Central High School in the fall of 1957, Governor Orval Faubus brought in troops to keep them out, and screaming mobs kept the town in an uproar. The students were able to go to school only when President Eisenhower federalized the National Guard—that is, brought it under federal control—and sent in paratroopers.

The story of the students' first day in school—September 25, 1957—is told here by Daisy Bates, then president of the Arkansas chapter of the National Association for the Advancement of Colored People. Although the students did enter the school, the struggle was far from over. The next year Little Rock's schools were closed down entirely. It was a long time before desegregation was an accomplished fact in the city.

What was Daisy Bates' reaction to the President's action? How does she describe the students before and after their first day?

In midafternoon [of September 24] the city was electrified by the news that President Eisenhower had federalized all ten thousand men of the Arkansas National Guard units. . . . The Secretary of Defense ordered 1,000 paratroopers to Little Rock from Fort Campbell, Kentucky. The soldiers were part of the 101st Airborne "Screaming Eagle" Division of the 327th Infantry Regiment.

When the Negro and white paratroopers arrived at Camp Robinson, an Army base in the suburb of North Little Rock, there was a general exodus of newsmen from our house. One reporter called back to me, "Come on, Mrs. Bates, aren't you going to see the troops enter the city?"

"No," I replied, "but thank God they're here."

After the newsmen were gone, I walked out onto the lawn. I heard the deep drone of big planes, and it sounded like music to my ears. I walked around the yard. I saw other women standing in their yards, looking upward, listening. I heard the subdued laughter of children and realized how long it had been since I'd heard that sound. Kept within doors in recent days, they now spilled out onto yards and driveways. From an open kitchen doorway Mrs. Anderson was heard singing, "Nobody knows the trouble I've seen . . ." A fear-paralyzed city had begun to stir again.

Around 6 P.M., the long line of trucks, jeeps,

and staff cars entered the heart of the city to the wailing sound of sirens and the dramatic flashing of lights from the police cars escorting the caravan to Central High School. The "Battle of Little Rock" was on.

*　　*　　*　　*

I knew the parents [of the schoolchildren were] waiting to hear from me, [to find out if] the children would be going back to Central tomorrow. I delayed calling them. I was awaiting a call from Superintendent [of Schools Virgil T.] Blossom. Finally, about 10 P.M., I called the parents to tell them I had not heard from Mr. Blossom. I assumed that the mob would be at the school the next morning and therefore decided that the children could not be sent to Central the next day, troops or not.

Shortly after midnight Mr. Blossom telephoned. "Mrs. Bates, I understand you instructed the children that they were not to go to Central in the morning."

"That is correct."

"But General Walker said that he is here to put the children in school. So you must have them at your house by eight thirty in the morning." Major General Edwin A. Walker, chief of the Arkansas Military District, had been put in command of the 101st Airborne Division and newly federalized Arkansas militia.

"I can't," I said. "I can't reach them. We have an agreement that if I want them, I will call *before* midnight. In order to get some sleep and avoid the harassing calls, they take their phones off the hook after midnight." How I wish I had done the same, I thought wearily, as I listened to the Superintendent's urgent tones. "I suppose I could go to each home, but I can't go alone," I said.

"I'll call Hawkins and Christophe and ask them to accompany you," Mr. Blossom said. "You may expect them shortly." Edwin Hawkins was Principal of Dunbar Junior High School and L. M. Christophe was Principal of Horace Mann High School, both Negro schools.

At about 1 A.M. the three of us set out. Our first stop was some eight blocks away, the home of fifteen-year-old Gloria Ray. We knocked for what seemed ten minutes before we got an answer. The door opened about three inches exposing the muzzle of a shotgun. Behind it stood Gloria's father.

"What do you want now?" was his none-too-cordial greeting, as he looked straight at me.

He forgot—I hope that was the reason—to remove his finger from the trigger or at least to lower the gun.

My eyes were fixed on the muzzle, and I could sense that Hawkins and Christophe, standing behind me, were riveted in attention. In my most pleasant, friendliest voice, and trying to look at him instead of the gun, I said that the children were to be at my house by eight thirty the next morning, and that those were the instructions of Superintendent Blossom.

"I don't care if the President of the United States gave you those instructions!" he said irritably. "I won't let Gloria go. She's faced two mobs and that's enough."

Both Mr. Christophe and Mr. Hawkins assured him that with the Federal troops there, the children would be safe. We all, of course, added that the decision was up to him. At this point I asked if he wouldn't mind lowering his gun. He did. I told him if he changed his mind to bring Gloria to my house in the morning. Somewhat shakily we made our way to the car.

"Good Lord," sighed Mr. Christophe, "are we going to have to go through this with all nine sets of parents?"

The children's homes were widely scattered over Little Rock, and so our tour took better than three hours. Our encounter with Mr. Ray impressed on our minds the need to identify ourselves immediately upon entering the grounds of each home. But the cautious parents still greeted us with gun in hand although they were a little more calm than Mr. Ray, and accepted the change in plans without objection.

At eight twenty-five the next morning, all the children except Gloria had arrived. My phone rang. "What time are we to be there, Mrs. Bates?" It was Gloria.

"They're all here now."

"Wait for me!" she said. "I'll be right over!"

In less than ten minutes, Mr. Ray, shy and smiling, led Gloria into the house. He looked down at his daughter with pride. "Here, Daisy, she's yours. She's determined to go. Take her. You seem to have more influence over her than I have, anyhow."

No sooner had Gloria joined the group than I was called to the telephone. A school official wanted to know whether the children were there. "All nine," I answered. I was told that a convoy for them was on its way.

*　　*　　*　　*

Soon, jeeps were rolling down Twenty-eighth Street. Two passed our house and parked at the end of the block, while two remained at the other end of the block. Paratroopers quickly jumped out and stood across the width of the street at each end of the block —those at the western end standing at attention facing west, and those at the eastern end facing east.

An Army station wagon stopped in front of our house. While photographers, perched on the tops of cars and rooftops, went into action, the paratrooper in charge of the detail leaped out of the station wagon and started up our driveway. As he approached, I heard Minnijean say gleefully, "Oh, look at them, they're so—so soldierly! It gives you goose pimples to look at them!" And then she added solemnly, "For the first time in my life, I feel like an American citizen."

The officer was at the door, and as I opened it, he saluted and said, his voice ringing through the sudden quiet of the living-room where a number of friends and parents of the nine had gathered to witness this moment in history: "Mrs. Bates, we're ready for the children. We will return them to your home at three thirty o'clock."

I watched them follow him down the sidewalk. Another paratrooper held open the door of the station wagon, and they got in. Turning back into the room, my eyes none too dry, I saw the parents with tears of happiness in their eyes as they watched the group drive off.

*   *   *   *

Tense and dramatic events were taking place in and around the school while the Negro pupils were being transported by the troops from my home to Central High.

A block from the school, a small group of hardcore segregationists ignored Mayor James Meyers' orders to disperse peacefully and return to their homes. The major [in charge of the troops] repeated the command when the surly, angry crowd refused to disperse. He was forced to radio for additional help. About thirty soldiers answered the emergency call "on the double," wearing steel helmets, carrying bayonet-fixed rifles, their gas masks in readiness, and "walkie-talkies" slung over their shoulders.

The soldiers lowered their rifles and moved slowly and deliberately into the crowd. The mob quickly gave way, shouting insults at the troops in the process. In a matter of minutes the streets, which for days had been littered with hate-filled mobs, cigarette butts, half-eaten sandwiches, and used flash bulbs, were strangely quiet.

At 9:22 A.M. the nine Negro pupils marched solemnly through the doors of Central High School, surrounded by twenty-two soldiers. An Army helicopter circled overhead. Around the massive brick schoolhouse 350 paratroopers stood grimly at attention. Scores of reporters, photographers, and TV cameramen made a mad dash for telephones, typewriters, and TV studios. Within minutes a world that had been holding its breath learned that the nine pupils, protected by the might of the United States military, had finally entered the "never-never land."

When classes ended that afternoon, the troops escorted the pupils to my home. Here we held the first of many conferences that were to take place during the hectic months ahead.

I looked into the face of each child, from the frail ninety-pound Thelma Mothershed with a cardiac condition, to the well-built, sturdy Ernest Green, oldest of them all. They sat around the room, subdued and reflective—and understandably so. Too much had happened to them in these frenzied weeks to be otherwise.

I asked if they had a rough day. Not especially, they said. Some of the white pupils were friendly and had even invited them to lunch. Some were indifferent, and only a few showed open hostility.

Minnijean Brown reported that she had been invited by her classmates to join the glee club.

"Then why the long faces?" I wanted to know.

"Well," Ernest spoke up, "you don't expect us to be jumping for joy, do you?"

Someone said, "But Ernest, we *are* in Central, and that shouldn't make us feel sad exactly."

"Sure we're in Central," Ernest shot back, somewhat impatiently. "But how did we get in? We got in, finally, because we were protected by paratroops. Some victory!" he said sarcastically.

"Are you sorry," someone asked him, "that the President sent the troops?"

"No," said Ernest. "I'm only sorry it had to be that way."

Unit Eight

Into a New Era

(1960's-1980's)

CHAPTER 22
DEVELOPMENTS ON THE DOMESTIC FRONT

AN APPRAISAL OF KENNEDY

Young, handsome, and well-educated, President Kennedy inspired many Americans to take an active interest in government and politics. His energy and idealism also made many Americans believe that the increasingly serious problems facing the nation in the 1960's could and would be solved. Thus President Kennedy's tragic death in 1963 seemed, for a time, to mark an end to many of America's hopes and dreams.

Theodore Sorensen, one of the President's advisers, tried to analyze the special appeal that Kennedy had for so many Americans. Part of the President's popularity was based on Kennedy's "style," or way of doing things. In his book about Kennedy, from which the following selection is taken, Sorensen wrote: "The Kennedy style was special—the grace, the wit, the elegance. . . . But what mattered most to him, and what in my opinion will matter most to history, was the substance—the strength of his ideas and ideals, his courage and judgment."

What events of Kennedy's Presidency does Sorensen stress? In what ways was Kennedy different from other Presidents, according to Sorensen?

Adapted from pp. 756-758 in Kennedy *by Theodore C. Sorensen. Copyright © 1965 by Theodore C. Sorensen. By permission of Harper & Row. Publishers, Inc.*

How will history judge him? It is too early to say. I am too close to say. But history will surely record that his achievements were beyond his years. In an eloquent letter to President Kennedy on nuclear testing, Prime Minister Harold Macmillan of Britain once wrote: "It is not the things one did in one's life that one regrets, but rather the opportunities missed." It can be said of John Kennedy that he missed very few opportunities.

In less than three years he presided over a new era in American race relations, a new era in American-Soviet relations, a new era in our Latin-American relations, a new era in fiscal and economic policy, and a new era in space exploration. His Presidency helped start the longest and strongest period of economic expansion in our peacetime history. It helped start the largest and swiftest build-up of our defensive strength in peacetime history. And it brought new and enlarged roles for the federal government in higher education, mental illness, civil rights, and the conservation of human and natural resources.

Some moves were dramatic, such as the Cuban missile crisis, the Test Ban Treaty, the Peace Corps, and the Alliance for Progress. Some were small day-by-day efforts on Berlin or Southeast Asia, where no real progress could be claimed. Some were simply holding our own. No nation slipped into the Communist orbit, no nuclear war raised havoc on our planet, no new recession set back our economy. But generally Kennedy was not content to hold his own. His efforts were devoted to turning the country around, starting it in new directions, getting it moving again. "He believed," said his wife, "that one man can make a difference and that every man should try." He left the nation a whole new set of basic propositions – on freedom now instead of someday for the black American – on winding down instead of "winning" the Cold War – on the unthinkability instead of the inevitability of nuclear war – on cutting taxes in times of deficit – on battling poverty in times of prosperity.

For the most part, on November 22, these problems had not been solved and these projects had not been completed. Even most of those completed will impress historians a generation from now only if this generation makes the most of them.

But I suspect that history will remember John Kennedy for what he started as well as for what he completed. The forces he released in this world will be felt for generations to come. The standards he set, the goals he outlined and the talented people he attracted to politics and public service will influence his country's course for at least ten years.

People will remember not only what he did but what he stood for. This, too, may help the historians assess his Presidency. He stood for excellence in an era of indifference – for hope in an era of doubt – for placing public service ahead of private interests – for understanding between East and West, black and white, labor and management. He had confidence in people and gave them confidence in the future.

It will not be easy for historians to compare John Kennedy with those who came before him and after him. He was unique in his effect on the office. He was the first to be elected at so young an age, the first of the Catholic faith, the first to reach for the moon and beyond, the first to announce that all racial segregation and discrimination must be abolished as a matter of right, the first to meet our enemies in a potentially nuclear confrontation, and the first to take a solid step toward nuclear arms control. And he was the first to die at so young an age.

All his life he was a winner until November 1963. In battle he became a hero. In literature he won a Pulitzer Prize. In politics he reached the Presidency. His inaugural address, his wife, his children, his policies, his conduct of crises, all reflected his pursuit of excellence.

History and the future must decide. Usually they reserve greatness for those who win great wars, not those who prevent them. But in my unobjective view I think it will be difficult to measure John Kennedy by any ordinary historical yardstick. For he was an extraordinary man, an extraordinary politician, and an extraordinary President. It is my belief that no scale of good and bad Presidents can rate John Fitzgerald Kennedy. A mind so free of fear and myth and prejudice, so opposed to clichés, so unwilling to fool or be fooled, to accept or reflect mediocrity, is rare in our world – and even rarer in American politics. Without lessening any of the great men who have held the Presidency in this century, I do not see how John Kennedy could be ranked below any one of them.

His untimely and violent death will affect the judgment of historians. The danger is that it will turn his greatness into legend. Even though he was himself almost a legendary figure in life, Kennedy was a constant critic of the myth. It would be an ironic twist of fate if his martyrdom should now make a myth of the mortal man.

In my view, the man was greater than the legend. His life, not his death, created his greatness. In November 1963, some saw it for the first time. Others realized that they had too casually accepted it. Others mourned that they had not admitted it to themselves before.

JOHNSON URGES EQUAL RIGHTS FOR ALL

When Lyndon Johnson became President after President Kennedy's assassination, he promised the nation he would continue President Kennedy's programs. Almost immediately he called on Congress to pass the civil rights bill that Kennedy had proposed. After a bitter struggle in the Senate, the Civil Rights Act of 1964 was passed into law in July of 1964. Now, for the first time, all black Americans were guaranteed the right to register to vote.

However, some voter registration drives in the South led to violence. In Selma, Alabama, a Unitarian minister was killed in March 1965 after he had taken part in a protest march. A week later, on

March 15, Johnson spoke before Congress, proposing a second civil rights bill. The following selection is taken from that speech—a moving statement of Johnson's belief in American democracy.

What does Johnson believe is the most basic right of all Americans? How does Johnson sum up his goals as President? Do you think that he achieved them? Explain.

Adapted from Lyndon B. Johnson, "The Right to Vote," in Vital Speeches of the Day. *April 1 1965.*

I speak tonight for the dignity of all human beings and the destiny of democracy. I urge every member of both parties, Americans of all religions and of all colors, from every section of this country, to join me in that cause.

At times, history and fate meet at a single time in a single place to shape a turning point in people's unending search for freedom.

So it was at Lexington and Concord. So it was a hundred years ago at Appomattox. So it was last week in Selma, Alabama.

There, long-suffering men and women peacefully protested the denial of their rights as Americans. Many were brutally assaulted. One good man—a man of God—was killed.

There is no cause for pride in what has happened in Selma. There is no cause for self-satisfaction in the long denial of equal rights of millions of Americans. But there is cause for hope and for faith in our democracy in what is happening here tonight.

For the cries of pain and the hymns and protests of oppressed people have brought together all the majesty of this great government—the government of the greatest nation on earth.

Our mission is at once the oldest and the most basic of this country—to right wrong, to do justice, to serve people.

In our time we have come to live with the moments of great crisis. Our lives have been marked with debate about great issues, issues of war and peace, issues of prosperity and depression.

But rarely in any time does an issue show the secret heart of America itself. Rarely do we meet a challenge, not to our growth or abundance, our welfare or security, but rather to the values, purposes, and meaning of our beloved nation.

The issue of equal rights for American Negroes is such an issue.

There is no Negro problem. There is no southern problem. There is no northern problem. There is only an American problem.

And we meet here tonight as Americans—not as Democrats or Republicans—to solve that problem.

This was the first nation in the history of the world to be founded with a purpose. The great statements of that purpose still sound in every American heart, North and South: "All men are created equal." "Government by consent of the governed." "Give me liberty or give me death."

Those are not just clever words. Those are not just empty theories. In their name Americans have fought and died for two hundred years.

Those words are promised to all citizens so they can share in the dignity of all human beings. This dignity cannot be found in people's possessions. It cannot be found in their power or in their position. It really rests on their right to be treated as a person equal in opportunity to all others.

It says that they shall share in freedom. They shall choose their leaders, educate their children, and provide for their family according to their ability and their merits as human beings.

To apply any other test, to deny people their hopes because of their color, race, religion, or place of birth is not only to do injustice. It is to deny America and to dishonor the dead who gave their lives for American freedom.

Our forebears believed that if this noble view of the rights of people was to flourish it must be rooted in democracy. The most basic right of all was the right to choose your own leaders.

The history of this country in large part is the history of the expansion of that right to all of our people. Many of the issues of civil rights are very complex and most difficult. But about this there can and should be no argument. Every American citizen must have an equal right to vote.

There is no reason which can excuse the denial of that right. There is no duty which weighs more heavily on us than the duty we have to insure that right. Yet the harsh fact is that in many places in this country men and women are kept from voting simply because they are Negroes.

This bill will establish a simple, uniform standard for voting. It will provide for citizens to be registered by officials of the United States government, if state officials refuse to register them.

It will eliminate tiresome, unnecessary lawsuits which delay the right to vote.

Finally, this legislation will insure that properly registered individuals are not prohibited from voting.

There is no constitutional issue here. The command of the Constitution is plain. There is no moral issue. It is wrong—deadly wrong—to deny any of your fellow Americans the right to vote in this country.

There is no issue of state's rights or national rights. There is only the struggle for human rights.

On this issue, there must be no delay, no hesitation, no compromise with our purpose.

We cannot, we must not, refuse to protect the right of every American to vote in every election that he or she may desire to participate in.

But even if we pass this bill the battle will not be over.

What happened in Selma is part of a far larger movement which reaches into every section and state of America. It is the effort of American Negroes to secure for themselves the full blessings of American life.

Their cause must be our cause too. Because it's not just Negroes, but really it's all of us, who must overcome the crippling legacy of bigotry and injustice.

And we shall overcome.

As a man whose roots go deeply into southern soil, I know how agonizing racial feelings are. I know how difficult it is to change the attitudes and the structure of our society. But a century has passed—more than a hundred years—since the Negroes were freed.

And they are not fully free tonight.

Negroes are not the only victims. How many white children have gone without an education? How many white families have lived in poverty? How many white lives have been scarred by fear, because we wasted energy to maintain the barriers of hatred and terror?

And so I say to all of you here and to all in the nation tonight that those who appeal to you to hold on to the past do so at the cost of denying you your future. This great, rich, restless country can offer opportunity and education and hope to all—all, black and white, all, North and South, sharecropper and city dweller.

These are the enemies: Poverty, ignorance, disease. They are our enemies, not our fellow humans, not our neighbors. And these enemies too—poverty, disease, and ignorance—we shall overcome.

There is really no part of America where the promise of equality has been fully kept. In Buffalo as well as in Birmingham, in Philadelphia as well as in Selma, Americans are struggling for their freedom. This is one nation. What happens in Selma and Cincinnati is a matter of concern to every American.

At the real heart of the battle for equality is a deep-seated belief in the democratic process. Equality does not depend on the force of arms or on tear gas. It depends upon the force of moral right, on respect for law and order.

The bill I am presenting to you will be known as a civil rights bill.

But in a larger sense, most of the program I am recommending is a civil rights program. Its object is to open the city of hope to all people of all races. All Americans must have the right to vote. And we are going to give them that right.

All Americans must have the privileges of citizenship, regardless of race. And they are going to have those privileges.

I would like to remind you that to exercise these privileges takes much more than just legal right. It requires a trained mind and a healthy body. It requires a decent home and the chance to find a job and the opportunity to escape from poverty.

Of course people cannot contribute to the nation if they are never taught to read or write; if their bodies are stunted from hunger; if their sickness goes uncared for; if their life is spent in hopeless poverty, just drawing a welfare check.

So we want to open the gates to opportunity. But we're also going to give all our people, black and white, the help that they need to walk through those gates.

My first job after college was as a teacher in Cotulla, Texas, in a small Mexican-American school. Few of my students could speak English and I couldn't speak much Spanish.

My students were poor and they often came to class without breakfast. They knew, even in their youth, the pain of prejudice. They never seemed to know why people disliked them, but they knew it was so, because I saw it in their eyes.

I often walked home late in the afternoon, after classes were finished, wishing there was more that I could do. But all I knew was to teach them the little that I knew, hoping that it might help them against the hardships that lay ahead.

Somehow you never forget what poverty and hatred can do when you see its scars on the hopeful face of a young child.

I never thought then, in 1928, that I would be standing here in 1965. It never occurred to me that I might have the chance to help the sons and daughters of those students, and to help people like them all over this country.

But now I do have that chance. And I'll let you in on a secret—I mean to use it.

And I hope that you will use it with me. This is the richest, most powerful country which ever occupied this globe. The might of past empires is little compared to ours. But I do not want to be the President who built empires, or sought grandeur, or extended authority. I want to be the President who educated young children to the wonders of their world.

I want to be the President who helped to feed the hungry and to prepare them to be tax-payers instead of tax eaters.

I want to be the President who helped the poor to find their own way and who protected the right of every citizen to vote in every election.

I want to be the President who helped to end hatred among people and who promoted love among the people of all races, all regions, and all parties.

THE MOON LANDING

One of the proudest American achievements of the 1960's was the successful flight of Apollo 11, which carried the first astronauts to the moon. The project had been started under President Kennedy in 1961. Several Apollo flights had taken place during the Presidency of Lyndon Johnson. And it was President Nixon who called the astronauts after the flight of Apollo 11 to congratulate them on their accomplishment. "For one priceless moment," he said, "all the people on earth are truly one."

Apollo 11 was launched from Cape Canaveral, Florida, on July 15, 1969. On board were Neil Armstrong, Edwin Aldrin, and Michael Collins. On July 20, Armstrong and Aldrin, in a detachable lunar module, landed on the surface of the moon. In the following selection, Armstrong discusses the flight and landing.

Why does Armstrong think the moon landing is important? What features of the moon impressed him most?

Adapted from "The Moon Had Been Awaiting Us a Long Time" by Neil Armstrong in Life. *August 22, 1969. Copyright © 1969 by Time Inc. Used by permission of the publisher.*

Our goal, when we were assigned to this flight last January, seemed almost impossible. There were a lot of unknowns, unproved ideas, unproved equipment. The lunar module had never flown. There were many things about the lunar surface we did not know. It remained to be seen whether it was possible for the ground to communicate simultaneously with two vehicles up there. I honestly suspected, at the time, that it was unlikely that Apollo 11 would make the first lunar landing flight. There was just too much to learn—too many chances for problems.

Then came the flights of Apollo 9 and 10, which were so magnificently successful. It began to seem that we really would get a chance at a landing. From that point on, preparations became relentless.

We were not concerned with safety, specifically, in these preparations. We were concerned with mission success, with the accomplishment of what we set out to do. I felt a successful lunar landing might inspire people around the world to believe that impossible goals really are possible, that there really is hope for solutions to humanity's problems.

We were very conscious of the symbolism of our exploration, and we wanted the small things which go along with a flight to reflect our very serious approach to the business of flying the lunar mission.

The patch we designed was meant to symbolize the peaceful American attempt at a lunar landing. We wanted the names we chose for communication to have both dignity and symbolism. The name Eagle [for the lunar module] was intended to reflect a degree of national pride in the enterprise. The name Columbia [for the space capsule] is also a national symbol. It reflected, too, the aura of adventure, exploration, and seriousness with which Columbus took on his assignment.

The day of the lunar landing was a long one and there was a lot to do every minute. We got up at 5:30 that morning and touched down about 3:20 P.M. Houston time. Our ignition for powered descent was smooth and right on time. But at about 30,000 feet [9,144 meters] we began to have computer problems. They seem to have come from overloading the computer. Mission Control analyzed the problem and the cause, and advised us promptly that we could safely override the alarms and continue our descent.

From about 30,000 feet [9,144 meters] down to 5,000 feet [1,524 meters] we were totally absorbed in analyzing and dealing with this problem, and checking our instruments. Our attention was thus taken away from the windows and from identification of landmarks outside. The first chance we had to spend some time looking out was from below 3,000 feet [914.4 meters]. It was difficult at that height to see very far ahead. The only landmark we could see was a very large, very impressive crater.

At first we considered landing just short of it. That location seemed clearly to be where our automatic guidance system was taking us. By the time we were down around 1,000 feet [305 meters], however, it was quite obvious that Eagle was attempting to land in a most undesirable area. I had an excellent view of the crater and the boulder field out of the left window. There were boulders as big as Volkswagens all around.

The rocks seemed to be coming up at us awfully fast. We reduced our descent rate from 10 to 3 feet [3 to .9 meters] per second. It would have been interesting to land in that boulder field from a scientific point of view. I was tempted, but my better judgment took over. We pitched forward to a level altitude, and scanned the surface to the west for a better touchdown area. The one we chose was only a couple of hundred feet square, about the size of a big house lot. It was ringed on one side by some fairly good-sized craters and on the other with a field of small rocks, but it still looked as if we could live with it. I put Eagle down there.

I am told that my heartbeat increased noticeably during the lunar descent, but I would really be disturbed with myself if it hadn't. During the final seconds of descent, our engine kicked up a substantial amount of lunar dust which blew out almost parallel to the surface, at very high speeds. Normally on earth if you kick up dust it hangs in the air and settles back to the ground very slowly. But since there is no atmosphere on the moon, dust sails away in a flat, low path, leaving a clear space behind it. The dust we kicked up probably still hadn't settled on the lunar surface by the time we landed, but it was a long way away from us and going fast. It was possible to see through it—I could make out rocks and craters—but its movement was distracting. It made it difficult to pick out the speeds for a smooth touchdown.

It was much like landing in a very fast-moving ground fog.

Buzz [Aldrin] and I had about 12 minutes of very post-touchdown [after landing] work, and then we could relax enough to have a sense of relief, of elation.

It took us somewhat longer to come out from Eagle than we had anticipated. It wasn't until after landing that I made up my mind what to say: "That's one small step for a man, one giant leap for mankind." Beyond those words I don't recall any particular emotion or feeling other than a little caution, a desire to be sure it was safe to put my weight on that surface outside Eagle.

From inside Eagle the sky was black, but it looked like daylight out on the surface and the surface looked tan. There is a very peculiar lighting effect on the lunar surface which seems to make the colors change. I don't understand this completely. If you look down along your own shadow, or into the sun, the moon is tan. If you look straight down at the surface, particularly in the shadows, it looks very, very dark. When you pick up material in your hands it is also dark, gray or black. The material is of a generally fine texture, almost like flour, but some coarser particles are like sand. Then there are, of course, scattered rocks and rock chips of all sizes. My only real problem on the surface was that there were so many places that I would like to have investigated.

All the things we left on the moon are pretty well known by now. We were particularly pleased to leave the patch of Apollo 1 in memory of our friends and fellow astronauts Gus Grissom, Ed White, and Roger Chaffee [three astronauts who lost their lives during an on-ground training accident in 1967] and the medals in memory of Gagarin and Komarov [two Soviet astronauts]. I believe that the Russians share our own dreams and hopes for a better world.

Looking back, touchdown was for me the most striking achievement in the flight. Lift-off was the next most striking. I thought quite a bit about that single ascent engine and how much depended upon it. When the moment came it was perfection. It gave us not only a very pleasant ride but also a beautiful, final view of our moon base as we lifted up and away from it.

My overwhelming impression of the moon as I walked on it and photographed it was that I was taking pictures of a steady-state process, a process in which some rocks are being worn down continually on the surface and other new ones are being thrown out on top by new events occurring either near or far away. In other words, no matter when humans first reached this spot—a thousand years ago or 100,000 years ago or even a million years from now—it would look generally the same. The only difference would be that at each period in time one would see slightly different rocks, slightly different surfaces, all influenced by the same processes. From what I saw I believe that most of the processes are external (that is, things like meteorite impact). But some materials indicate that there may have been internal processes on the moon at some time.

The most dramatic memories I have now are the sights themselves, those magnificent visual images. They go far beyond any other visual experiences I've had in my life. Of all the spectacular views we had, the most impressive to me was on the way toward the moon, when we flew through its shadow. We were still thousands of miles away but close enough so that the moon almost filled our circular window. It was eclipsing the sun, from our position, and the corona [the outermost part of the atmosphere] of the sun was visible around the moon. It was magnificent, but the moon itself was even more so. We were in its shadow so there was no part of it lit by the sun. It was lit only by the earth, by earthshine. This made the moon appear blue-gray. The entire scene looked three-dimensional.

I was really aware, visually aware, that the moon was in fact a sphere, not a disk. It seemed almost as if it were showing us its roundness, its similarity in shape to our earth, in a sort of welcome. I was sure then that it would be a hospitable host. It had been awaiting its first visitors for a long time.

THE MEANING OF WATERGATE

In June of 1972, five men were arrested as they attempted to break into Democratic National Committee headquarters at the Watergate building in Washington, D.C. It was soon discovered that they were working for the campaign committee to reelect President Nixon. Although President Nixon declared that he knew nothing about the burglary, news reporters discovered evidence that pointed to a White House cover-up of the burglary as well as other possible criminal activities.

The Watergate scandal soon became a national crisis, as more and more Americans came to believe that the President was covering up a crime and lying about his activities. After many months of Congressional investigations into the Watergate scandals, President Richard M. Nixon resigned from office in August 1974.

In this selection, Theodore White, the author of several best-selling books on recent Presidential election campaigns, expresses his opinion about how and why Watergate happened.

According to White, why are myths especially important to American society? How did President Nixon's administration shatter Americans' faith in the Presidency? What effect do you think the Watergate crisis had on American politics and society?

Adapted from Breach of Faith *by Theodore H. White. Copyright © 1975 by Theodore H. White. (New York: Atheneum/Reader's Digest Press, 1975). Reprinted with permission.*

The true crime of Richard Nixon was simple. He destroyed the myth that binds America together. For this he was driven from power.

The myth he broke was critical—that somewhere in American life there is at least one person who stands for law, the President. That faith overcomes all distrust all evidence or suspicion of wrongdoing by lesser leaders, all corruptions. That faith holds that all people are equal before the law and protected by it. It holds that no matter how the faith may be betrayed elsewhere, at one particular point—the Presidency—justice will be done. It was that faith that Richard Nixon broke.

All civilizations rest on myths. But in America myths have exceptional meaning. A myth is a way of giving meaning to the raw and contradictory evidence of life. It lets people make patterns in their own lives, within the larger patterns.

There is, however, an absolutely vital political difference between the mythology of other nations and the mythology of America. Other nations may fall or last. They may change their governing myths. But French people will always remain French people, Russians will be Russians, Germans remain Germans, and English people—English people. But America is different. It is the only peaceful civilization in the world made up of many races. Its people come from such diverse heritages of religion, language, habit, and color that if America did not exist it would be impossible to imagine that such a grouping could ever behave like a nation. It would be impossible unless its people were bound together by a common faith.

Politics in America is the binding faith. That begins with the founding faith of the Declaration of Independence: "We hold these truths to be self-evident: that all men are created equal, that they are endowed by their Creator with certain unalienable rights, that among these are life, liberty, and the pursuit of happiness."

Of all the political myths out of which the Republic was born, none was more hopeful than the myth of the Presidency — that the people, in their shared wisdom, would be able to choose the best person to lead them. From this came a related myth — that the Presidency, the supreme office, would make noble any person who held its responsibility. The office and its duties would, by their very weight, make an individual a superior person, wise enough to resist the clash of all selfish interests.

Richard Nixon behaved otherwise. His lawlessness exploded the myths. He left a nation approaching the 200th anniversary of its glorious independence with a President and a Vice-President neither of whom had been chosen by the people. The faith was shattered. Being shattered, it was to leave American politics more confused than ever since the Civil War.

What Richard Nixon left us is best understood as a set of questions — questions about ourselves and what we seek from government.

The simplest set of questions can be asked and answered in the formula of popular detective stories: Who did it?

Like any popular detective story, this is a story of bungling criminals. It begins with the circumstance, very difficult for Richard Nixon's enemies to accept, that most of the top people involved were strong patriots, convinced that what they were doing was best for their country. Men like Ehrlichman and Haldeman [Nixon's two most important aides] were true believers in the purpose of America as they saw it. They sought nothing for themselves. Beneath came all the others, people of little patriotism and no principle.

They entered into government, all of them, with no greater knowledge of how power worked than the intrigues of political campaigning. They could not understand the essential balance there must always be in the nation's affairs between distrust and suspicion on the one hand and faith and trust on the other.

A naive politician gets nowhere. A successful politician must be something of a hypocrite, promising all to all, knowing that, if elected, he or she must inevitably sacrifice the interests of some for others. But people in government must know when to choose trust and faith over political need. The people must trust their words at whatever cost — or they cannot govern. In the Presidency, above all, it is essential to recognize the moment for truth.

From mid-April of 1973 to his end in 1974, the President lied, lied again, and continued to lie. His lying not only added to the anger of those who were on his trail. It slowly destroyed the faith of Americans in that President's honor. He knew what he was doing, for he consciously relied on the mystique of the Presidency to carry him through what lay ahead.

If Nixon had committed a historic crime — treason, or accepting graft, or knowingly twisting American national policy for personal or partisan ends — the detective story would be enough. Its answer to the question is that the criminals were caught because they were bunglers.

But the initial crime [the Watergate break-in] was commonplace. Nixon might have erased it easily by acting as Presidents must act against lawbreakers. Instead he made it a disaster by trying to cover it up. So another set of questions arose — not how the criminals were caught, but why Nixon did what he was caught doing.

"Why?" is a political question and one that will hang over American politics for years to come. Nixon was not a stupid man. What did he think he was defending beyond his own skin and reputation?

To trace the answers to the question of "Why?" one must accept the political reality that Richard Nixon and his aides were, for the first time in American politics since 1860, carrying on an ideological war [a struggle between differing sets of ideas]. Because they felt their purpose was high and necessary and the purpose of their enemies dangerous or immoral, he and his aides believed that the laws did not bind them — or that the laws could legitimately be bent.

Again one must go back to a set of American myths to explain the intensity of the ideological war that began in the 1960's.

Wrapped around the original political myths of America — of liberty, of equality, of a government-of-laws-not-people — had been a culture, long since destroyed, with a set of social myths now twisted by time into the rigid political principles of today.

The old social myths rested on the belief that free citizens were able to control their own futures by their own efforts. In the original American community of farmers 200 years ago, it was considered a matter of thrift and constant work and planning whether a person made it or did not. But in corporate America, since the beginning of the 1900's, fewer and fewer people have been able to control their own future by their own efforts. Now, in present-day America, everyone was locked up—in corporations, in unions, in organizations, in schools, in draft boards, in the tax net—and group pressure was the thing. Nixon and his men believed in the old social myths and the old culture. His opponents believed in mobilizing group pressure to force the federal government to do their will or to protect their future.

The old myths glorified self-government. The states and the federal government originally agreed that each had separate responsibilities. But in practice, by the 1960's the heart of the problem lay in the cities and suburbs.

But the most deceptive inherited social myth was that of American power. That myth was recent. It rested on the brief dominance of American arms as they spread triumphant over the entire globe in 1945. What had happened, however, by the 1960's, was that the myth of American power had been weakened by the revolutions of the postwar world. Americans were faced with a new reality—they were engaged in the first major war that they would not win. By the time Nixon came to power, that realization had split the country at every level. Resentment at the waste and killing in Vietnam had spilled out into the streets in sputtering violence and frightening bloodshed.

Nixon had to be sure, recognized the weakening of American power abroad. As soon as he took office in 1969, he had begun to end the war in Vietnam. But he clung to the old doctrine that the President alone could make the decisions and arrange the timing for a withdrawal from Asia that would bring peace with honor. Those who opposed him, whether in the streets or in the news system, he would treat with moral fierceness.

The political detective story of Nixon's crime begins there—with his belief that he, as President, was the only caretaker of America's power. The Nixon aides saw themselves as waging war in Vietnam to make peace. They had no doubt that national security required them to carry on that war by all means possible until peace with honor had been won. If the end was good then the means, however brutal, must also be good. And from this idea of the President's authority came most of the early illegalities, the buggings, the wire-taps, the surveillances, the minor crimes. Until finally the President's aides saw no distinction between ends and means. They were making war not just in Vietnam but all across the home front, too. All the disputes over home issues, as well as foreign issues, became part of the ideological war.

But the political story does not quite answer the "Why?" or explain the particular fierceness of behavior of the men at the White House.

To explain the spite and hatred of their struggle, one must add one more condition—the change of culture that was taking place all over America in the 1960's. The Nixon aides were people of the embattled old culture. As such, they believed the new culture was not only undermining the authority of their President to make war-and-peace, but striking into their homes, families, and schools, too. It was undermining the values with which they had grown up and still held dear.

This conflict of the two cultures far surpassed in emotion the traditional American political struggle between "conservatives" and "liberals." The two cultures clashed in every form of expression—in language, in costume, in slogans. They clashed over important matters—civil rights, "law-and-order," safety in the streets, drug abuse, the dignity of women. The line of clash between the two cultures ran through families as well as communities. Fathers against sons, mothers against daughters, students against teachers, arguing over such matters as dress and manners and morals, and sex and drugs and rioting. This clash of culture and personal values was taking place at the same time as the political clash over the hard issues. And the two added to each other.

One must see all three wars—the war abroad, the ideological war, the cultural war—as crossing each other in the agony of an unstable personality in order to answer the personal "Why?" of Richard Nixon's collapse. The answer can come only by imagining that here was a man who could not, in his waking moments, accept the man he recognized in his

657

own nightmares—the outsider, the loner, the loser.

Throughout his career, except for a few brief years in 1971 and 1972, that had been his inner roles—the outsider, the loser. "They" were against him, always. His authority as President was being challenged by the news system, the rioters, the Congress, the intellectuals. The culture, the manners, the beliefs of his lonely life of striving were being wiped out by the fashions of the new culture. Losers play dirty. He, too, would change the rules. His ruthlessness, vengefulness, nastiness were the characteristics of a man who has seen himself as underdog for so long that he cannot distinguish between real and fancied enemies, a man who does not really care whom he hurts when pressed, who cannot accept or understand when or what he has won.

Always, in the crisis, he reacted as the cornered loser. He could not shake that characteristic. In 1972 he had won so largely that he could misread his victory. It was a victory for his ideas and politics. But he saw it as personal, as a loner. It was not simply an election he had won. He had conquered a land. Its citizens were the occupied. And he could use the law as he wished, however much a hostile Congress, the news system, or intellectuals protested.

A NEW DIRECTION UNDER REAGAN

When Ronald Reagan became President in 1981, the United States was facing serious problems abroad. American citizens were being held hostage in Iran. The Soviet Union was moving troops into Afghanistan, increasing international tensions.

As serious as these problems were, the crises the nation faced at home were even more severe. Inflation rates were soaring. Economic productivity was declining. Some citizens were losing confidence in the government's ability to deal with these problems.

In his Inaugural Address, President Reagan tried to reassure Americans that they could handle any present and future challenges. One way of getting the nation moving again, he declared, was to limit the growth of federal government.

According to Reagan, what was the "problem" the nation faced? What did Reagan propose to do to deal with the crisis? What did he say that government should do?

From Ronald Reagan, "Inaugural Address," in The New York Times, Jan. 21, 1981.

In this present crisis, government is not the solution to our problem; government is the problem.

From time to time we've been tempted to believe that society has become too complex to be managed by self-rule, that government by an elite group is superior to government for, by and of the people.

But if no one among us is capable of governing himself, then who among us has the capacity to govern someone else?

All of us together—in and out of government—must bear the burden. The solutions we seek must be equitable with no one group singled out to pay a higher price.

We hear much of special interest groups. Well, our concern must be for a special interest group that has been too long neglected.

It knows no sectional boundaries, or ethnic and racial divisions and it crosses political party lines. It is made up of men and women who raise our food, patrol our streets, man our mines and factories, teach our children, keep our homes and heal us when we're sick.

Professionals, industrialists, shopkeepers, clerks, cabbies and truck drivers. They are, in short, "We, the people." This breed called Americans.

Well, this Administration's objective will be a healthy, vigorous, growing economy that provides equal opportunities for all Americans with no barriers born of bigotry or discrimination.

Putting America back to work means putting all Americans back to work. Ending inflation means freeing all Americans from the terror of runaway living costs.

All must share in the productive work of this "new beginning," and all must share in the bounty of a revived economy.

With the idealism and fair play which are the core of our system and our strength, we can have a strong, prosperous America at peace with itself and the world.

So as we begin, let us take inventory.

We are a nation that has a government—not the other way around. And this makes us special among the nations of the earth.

Our government has no power except that granted it by the people. It is time to check and reverse the growth of government which shows signs of having grown beyond the consent of the governed.

It is my intention to curb the size and influence of the Federal establishment and to demand recognition of the distinction between the powers granted to the Federal Government and those reserved to the states or to the people.

All of us—all of us need to be reminded that the Federal Government did not create the states; the states created the Federal Government.

Now, so there will be no misunderstanding, it's not my intention to do away with government.

It is rather to make it work—work with us, not over us; to stand by our side, not ride on our back. Government can and must provide opportunity, not smother it; foster productivity, not stifle it.

If we look for the answer as to why for so many years we achieved so much, prospered as no other people on earth, it was because here in this land we unleashed the energy and individual genius of man to a greater extent than has ever been done before.

Freedom and dignity of the individual have been more available and assured here than in any other place on earth. The price of this freedom at times has been high, but we have never been unwilling to pay that price.

It is no coincidence that our present troubles are parallel and are proportionate to the intervention and intrusion in our lives that result from unnecessary and excessive growth of government.

It is time for us to realize that we are too great a nation to limit ourselves to small dreams. We're not, as some would have us believe, doomed to an inevitable decline. I do not believe in a fate that will fall on us no matter what we do. I do believe in a fate that will fall on us if we do nothing.

So, with all the creative energy at our command let us begin an era of national renewal. Let us renew our determination, our courage and our strength. And let us renew our faith and our hope. We have every right to dream heroic dreams.

CHAPTER 23
REEXAMINING THE NATION'S ROLE IN WORLD AFFAIRS

THE MISSILE CRISIS IN CUBA

In October of 1962, President Kennedy learned from American intelligence reports that the Soviet Union was building powerful missile bases in Cuba. These bases posed so great a danger to the United States' security that Kennedy and his advisers decided they must act immediately. They communicated with the leaders of the Soviet government and demanded that the Soviet Union dismantle and remove these missile sites. For the next few days, war seemed possible as both nations considered what action they should take.

Several years later Robert Kennedy, the President's brother, who also was one of his key advisers as well as his Attorney General, wrote a detailed account of the Cuban missile crisis. His book, called *Thirteen Days,* gives a day-by-day record of the events from October 16 through 28, 1962. In this selection, Robert Kennedy describes what happened on October 27 and 28—the most crucial and dangerous days of the missile crisis.

What troubled President Kennedy most on the evening described here? How would you describe Robert Kennedy's meeting with the Soviet ambassador? How was the Cuban missile crisis settled?

Adapted from Thirteen Days, A Memoir of the Cuban Missile Crisis, *by Robert F. Kennedy. Copyright © 1971, 1969, by W. W. Norton & Co., Inc. Copyright © 1968 by McCall Corporation. Reprinted by permission of W. W. Norton & Co., Inc.*

[*Saturday, October 27*]
The President ordered the Ex Comm [the Executive Committee for National Security, which included Secretary of State Dean Rusk, several other members of the Cabinet, and military officials] to meet again at 9:00 P.M. in the White House. While the letter was being typed and prepared to be sent, he and I sat in his office. [This was the letter President Kennedy sent to Khrushchev on October 27, requesting that the missiles in Cuba be dismantled. In return, the United States would end its naval "quarantine."] He talked about Major Anderson and

how it is always the brave and the best who die. [Anderson, a U-2 pilot, had been killed the day before by missile fire while on a reconnaissance mission over Cuba.] He talked about the mistakes that lead to war. War is rarely planned. The Russians don't wish to fight any more than we do. They do not want to go to war with us nor we with them. And yet if events continue as they have in the last several days, that struggle — which no one wishes, which will accomplish nothing — will engulf and destroy humanity.

He wanted to make sure that he had done everything in his power, everything possible, to prevent such a catastrophe. Every opportunity was to be given to the Russians to find a peaceful settlement which would not decrease their national security or be a public humiliation. It was not only for Americans that he was concerned, or primarily the older generation of any land. The thought that disturbed him the most, and that made the prospect of war much more fearful than it would otherwise have been, was the possibility of the death of the children of this country and all the world — the young people who had no role, who had no say, who knew nothing even of the confrontation, but whose lives would be ended like everyone else's. They would never have a chance to make a decision, to vote in an election, to run for office, to lead a revolution, to determine their own futures.

It was this that troubled him most, that gave him such pain. And it was then that he and Secretary Rusk decided that I should visit with [Soviet] Ambassador Dobrynin and personally make known the President's great concern.

I telephoned Ambassador Dobrynin about 7:15 P.M. and asked him to come to the Department of Justice. We met in my office at 7:45. I told him first that we knew that work was continuing on the missile bases in Cuba and that in the last few days it had been speeded up. I said that in the last few hours we had learned that our reconnaissance planes flying over Cuba had been fired upon and that one of our U-2's had been shot down and the pilot killed. That for us was a most serious turn of events.

President Kennedy did not want a military conflict. He had done everything possible to avoid a military engagement with Cuba and with the Soviet Union, but now they had forced our hand. Because of the deception of the Soviet Union, our photographic reconnaissance planes would have to continue to fly over Cuba. If the Cubans or Soviets shot at these planes, then we would have to shoot back. This would inevitably lead to further incidents and to escalation of the conflict.

He said the Cubans resented the fact that we were violating Cuban air space. I replied that if we had not violated Cuban air space, we would still be believing what Khrushchev had said — that there would be no missiles placed in Cuba. In any case, I said, this matter was far more serious than the air space of Cuba — it involved the peoples of both of our countries and, in fact, people all over the globe.

The Soviet Union had secretly established missile bases in Cuba while at the same time claiming privately and publicly that this would never be done. We had to have a commitment by tomorrow that those bases would be removed. I was not giving them an ultimatum but a statement of fact. He should understand that if they did not remove those bases, we would remove them. President Kennedy had great respect for the ambassador's country and the courage of its people. Perhaps his country might feel it necessary to take action. But before that was over, there would be not only dead Americans but dead Russians as well.

He asked me what offer the United States was making, and I told him of the letter that President Kennedy had just sent to Khrushchev. He raised the question of our removing our missiles from Turkey. I said that there could be no arrangement made under this kind of threat or pressure. In the last analysis this was a decision that would have to be made by NATO. However, I said President Kennedy had been anxious to remove those missiles from Turkey (and Italy) for a long period of time. He had ordered their removal some time ago. It was our judgment that, within a short time after this crisis was over, those missiles would be gone.

I said President Kennedy wished to have peaceful relations between our two countries. Time was running out. We had only a few more hours — we needed an answer immediately from the Soviet Union. I said we must have it the next day.

I returned to the White House. The President was not optimistic, nor was I. He ordered twenty-four troop-carrier squadrons of the Air Force Reserve to active duty. They would be necessary for an invasion. He had not given up hope, but what hope there was now rested with

660

Khrushchev's changing his course within the next few hours. It was a hope, not an expectation. The expectation was a military confrontation by Tuesday and possibly tomorrow.

[*Sunday, October 28*]

I had promised my daughters for a long time that I would take them to the horse show. Early Sunday morning I went to the Washington Armory to watch the horses jump. In any case, there was nothing I could do but wait. Around 10:00, I received a call at the horse show. It was Secretary Rusk. He said he had just received word from the Russians that they had agreed to withdraw the missiles from Cuba.

I went immediately to the White House, and there I received a call from Ambassador Dobrynin, saying he would like to visit with me. I met him in my office at 11:00 A.M.

He told me that the message was coming through that Khrushchev had agreed to dismantle and withdraw the missiles under adequate supervision and inspection; that everything was going to work out satisfactorily; and that Mr. Khrushchev wanted to send his best wishes to the President and to me.

It was quite a different meeting from the night before. I went back to the White House and talked to the President for a long time. While I was there, he placed telephone calls to former Presidents Truman and Eisenhower. As I was leaving, he said, making reference to Abraham Lincoln, "This is the night I should go to the theater." I said, "If you go, I want to go with you." As I closed the door, he was seated at the desk writing a letter to Mrs. Anderson [wife of the U-2 pilot killed on a flight over Cuba a few days earlier].

THE WAR IN VIETNAM

American involvement in the Vietnam War began in 1962 when President Kennedy sent 8,000 military "advisers" to help train the South Vietnamese army. Then, in 1964, President Johnson began to send American combat troops. And in 1965, the United States began the bombing of North Vietnam.

Almost from the beginning, American opinion on the Vietnam War was divided. Some American leaders, known as "hawks," supported the war because they felt the United States had promised to protect South Vietnam and that America's honor and world leadership role were at stake. Other leaders, called "doves," opposed the war, believing that the United States could not create a stable, democratic government in South Vietnam nor instill within the South Vietnamese people the will to fight. As the war continued and more American troops were sent to Vietnam, this debate over the role of the United States in Vietnam continued and grew more bitter.

In the following selection, President Johnson offers a defense of the war. In response, Senator William Fulbright suggests that American involvement in Vietnam is a mistake.

Why, according to President Johnson, is the United States fighting in South Vietnam? Why does Senator Fulbright believe that American involvement in South Vietnam is a mistake? Which viewpoint do you favor? Explain.

President Johnson's speech adapted from "Peace Without Conquest," an address by Lyndon B. Johnson at Johns Hopkins University, April 7, 1965, in Public Papers of the Presidents of the United States: *Vol. I. Washington, D.C.: Government Printing Office, 1966.*

Senator Fulbright's statement adapted from The Arrogance of Power *by J. William Fulbright. Copyright © 1966 by J. William Fulbright. Reprinted by permission of Random House, Inc.*

[PRESIDENT JOHNSON]

Tonight Americans and Asians are dying for a world where each people may choose its own path to change.

Why must we take this painful road?

Why must this nation endanger its ease, and its interest, and its power for the sake of a people so far away?

We fight because we must fight if we are to live in a world where every country can shape its own destiny. And only in such a world will our own freedom be finally secure.

The first reality is that North Vietnam has attacked the independent nation of South Vietnam. Its object is total conquest.

Of course, some of the people of South Vietnam are participating in an attack on their own government. But trained men and supplies, orders, and arms, flow in a constant stream from north to south.

This support is the heartbeat of the war.

Over this war—and all Asia—is another reality: Communist China. The rulers in Hanoi are urged on by Peking. This is a government which has destroyed freedom in Tibet, which has attacked India, and has been condemned by the Union Nations for aggression in Korea.

661

It is a nation which is helping the forces of violence in almost every continent. The contest in Vietnam is part of a wider pattern of aggressive purposes.

Why are we in South Vietnam?

We are there because we have a promise to keep. Since 1954 every American President has offered support to the people of South Vietnam. We have helped to build, and we have helped to defend. Thus over many years we have made a national pledge to help South Vietnam defend its independence.

And I intend to keep that promise.

To dishonor that pledge, to abandon this small and brave nation to its enemies, and to the terror that must follow, would be an unforgivable wrong.

We are also there to strengthen world order. Around the globe, from Berlin to Thailand, are people whose well-being rests, in part, on the belief that they can count on us if they are attacked. To leave Vietnam to its fate would shake the confidence of all these people in the value of an American commitment and in the value of America's word. The result would be increased unrest and instability, and even wider war.

We are also there because there are great stakes in the balance. Let no one think for a moment that retreat from Vietnam would bring an end to conflict. The battle would be started again in one country and then another. The central lesson of our time is that the appetite of aggression is never satisfied. To withdraw from one battlefield means only to prepare for the next.

Our objective is the independence of South Vietnam, and its freedom from attack. We want nothing for ourselves—only that the people of South Vietnam be allowed to guide their own country in their own way.

We will do everything necessary to reach that objective. And we will do only what is absolutely necessary.

We hope that peace will come swiftly. But that is in the hands of others besides ourselves. And we must be prepared for a long continued conflict. It will require patience as well as bravery, the will to endure as well as the will to resist.

I wish it were possible to convince others with words of what we now find it necessary to say with guns and planes: Armed hostility is useless. Our resources are equal to any challenge. Because we fight for values and we fight for principles, rather than territory or colonies, our patience and determination are unending.

Once this is clear, then it should also be clear that the only path for reasonable people is the path of peaceful settlement.

Such peace demands an independent South Vietnam—securely guaranteed and able to shape its own relationships to all others—free from outside interference—tied to no alliance—a military base for no other country.

These are the essentials of any final settlement.

[SENATOR FULBRIGHT]

We are now in a war to "defend freedom" in South Vietnam. The official war aims of the United States government, as I understand them, are to defeat what is regarded as North Vietnamese aggression, to demonstrate the uselessness of what the Communists call "wars of national liberation," and to create conditions under which the South Vietnamese people will be able freely to determine their own future.

I have not the slightest doubt of the sincerity of the President and the Vice-President and the Secretaries of State and Defense in putting forward these aims. What I do doubt, and doubt very much, is the ability of the United States to achieve these aims by the means being used. I do not question the power of our weapons and the efficiency of our military plans; they are certainly impressive. What I do question is the ability of the United States or any other Western nation to go into a small, alien, undeveloped Asian nation and create stability where there is chaos, the will to fight where there is defeatism, democracy where there is no tradition of it, and honest government where corruption is almost a way of life.

Sincere though it is, the American effort to build the foundations of freedom in South Vietnam is having an effect quite different from the one intended.

One wonders how much the American commitment to Vietnamese freedom is also a commitment to American pride—the two seem to have become part of the same package. When we talk about the freedom of South Vietnam, we may be thinking about how disagreeable it would be to accept a solution short of victory. We may be thinking about how our pride would be injured if we settled for less than we set out to achieve. We may be thinking about our reputation as a great power, fearing that a compromise settlement would shame us before

662

the world, marking us as a second-rate people with failing courage and determination.

Such fears are senseless. They are unworthy of the richest, most powerful, most productive, and best educated people in the world.

The cause of our difficulties in Southeast Asia is not a lack of power but too much of the wrong kind of power. We are trying to remake Vietnamese society, a task which certainly cannot be accomplished by force and which probably cannot be accomplished by any means available to outsiders. The objective may be desirable, but it is not practical.

With the best intentions in the world the United States has involved itself in the affairs of developing nations in Asia and Latin America, practicing what has been called a kind of "welfare imperialism." Our honest purpose is the advancement of development and democracy. To achieve this purpose, it has been thought necessary to destroy ancient and unproductive ways of life. In this latter goal we have been successful, perhaps more successful than we know. Bringing skills and knowledge, money and resources in amounts unknown in traditional societies, the Americans have overcome native groups and interests and become the dominant force in a number of countries. Far from being bumbling, wasteful, and incompetent, as critics have charged, American government officials, technicians, and economists have been very successful in breaking down the barriers to change in ancient but fragile cultures.

Here, however, our success ends. Traditional rulers, institutions, and ways of life have crumbled under the fatal impact of American wealth and power. But they have not been replaced by new institutions and new ways of life, nor has their breakdown brought about an era of democracy and development. It has rather brought an era of disorder and demoralization because, while destroying old ways of doing things, we have also destroyed the self-confidence and self-reliance which a society needs to build its own institutions. We have reduced those peoples we intended to help to a condition of dependency. We have done this for the most part without meaning to. With every good intention we have intruded on fragile societies. Although we have been successful in uprooting traditional ways of life, we have been unsuccessful in planting the democracy and advancing the development which are the honest aims of our "welfare imperialism."

A RUSSIAN WRITER WARNS AGAINST DÉTENTE

One of the major achievements of American foreign policy under President Nixon was the improvement in United States relations with both Communist China and the Soviet Union. This important effort to end the Cold War and relax world tensions became known as the policy of détente. While détente with both China and the Soviet Union seemed to be widely supported, some important voices spoke out against détente with the Soviet Union. One of them was Aleksandr Solzhenitsyn, a famous Soviet writer.

Solzhenitsyn had spent many years in Russian labor and detention camps for writings that were critical of Stalin and later Soviet leaders. Finally, in 1974, he was compelled to leave the Soviet Union to live in exile in Switzerland. The following selection is from a speech he made on a visit to the United States in 1975.

What does Solzhenitsyn describe as "a true détente"? According to Solzhenitsyn, what are the weaknesses of the policy of détente being followed by the United States? What role does he think the United States should play in the liberation movement in Communist countries? What do you think?

Adapted from "America, We Beg You to Interfere" by Aleksandr I. Solzhenitsyn, in the AFL-CIO American Federationist, *July 1975. Reprinted by permission of the American Federation of Labor and Congress of Industrial Organizations.*

The Soviet system is so closed that it is almost impossible for you to understand. Everything is done the way the [Communist] Party demands. That's our system. Judge it for yourself.

It's a system where for 40 years there haven't been genuine elections. It's a system which has no legislative bodies. It's a system without a free press or independent judges. The people have no influence either on foreign policy or on internal policy. Any thinking which is different from what the government thinks is crushed.

It's a system where leaders who have murdered millions have never been tried in the courts but instead retire with huge pensions and live in the greatest comfort. It's a system where the constitution has never been carried out for a single day. All the decisions are made in secrecy, by a small group responsible to no one, and then are released on us like a bolt of lightning.

And what are the signatures of members of such a group worth? How could anyone trust their signatures to documents of détente? Your specialists will tell you that in recent years the Soviet Union has succeeded in creating wonderful chemical weapons and missiles, even better than those used by the United States.

So what are we to conclude from that? Is détente needed or not? Not only is it needed, it's as necessary as air. It's the only way of saving the earth. Instead of a world war, we must have détente—but a true détente.

I would say that there are very few, really only three, main characteristics of such a true détente.

In the first place, there would be disarmament—not only disarmament in terms of war but also in terms of violence. We must stop using the sort of arms [weapons] which are used to destroy one's neighbors, and also the sort of arms which are used to oppress one's fellow citizens. It is not détente if we here with you today can spend our time agreeably while over there people are suffering and dying.

The second sign of détente, I would say, is the following: that it be not one based on smiles, not on verbal concessions, but only on a firm foundation. There must be a guarantee that it will not be broken overnight. This means that the other party to the agreement must have its actions subject to public opinion, to the press, and to a freely elected parliament. Until such control exists there is absolutely no guarantee.

There is a third simple condition. What sort of détente is it when the Soviet Union uses the kind of inhumane propaganda which is proudly called "ideological warfare"? Let us not have that. If we're going to be friends, let's be friends. If we're going to have détente, then let's have détente and put an end to ideological warfare.

The Soviet Union and the Communist countries can conduct negotiations. They know how to do this. For a long time they don't make any concessions and then they give in a little bit. Then everyone says triumphantly, "Look, they've made a concession. It's time to sign."

But we, from our lives there, have learned that violence can only be withstood by firmness.

You have to understand the nature of communism. The very ideology of communism, all of Lenin's teachings, holds that people who don't take what's lying in front of them are

fools. If you can take it, take it. If you can attack, attack. But if there's a wall, then go back. The Communist leaders respect only firmness. They laugh at persons who continually give in to them. Your people are now saying, "Power without any attempt at conciliation will lead to a world conflict." But I would say that power with continual surrender is no power at all.

From our experience I can tell you that only firmness will make it possible to withstand the assaults of Communist totalitarianism. We see many historic examples. Let me give you some of them. Look at tiny Finland in 1939, which by its own forces withstood Russian attack. You, in 1948, defended Berlin only by your firmness of spirit, and there was no world conflict. In Korea in 1950 you stood up against the Communists, only by your firmness, and there was no world conflict. In 1962 you forced the rockets to be removed from Cuba. Again it was only firmness, and there was no world conflict.

We, the dissidents of the USSR [those who openly disagree with Russian policy within the Soviet Union], don't have any tanks, we don't have any weapons, we have no organization. We don't have anything. Our hands are empty. We have only our hearts and what we have lived through during the past 50 years under the system. And when we have found the firmness within ourselves to stand up for our rights, we have done so. It's only by firmness of spirit that we have withstood. And if I am standing here before you, it's not because of the kindness or the good will of communism, not thanks to détente, but thanks to my own firmness and your firm support. They knew that I would not give in one inch, not one hair. And when they couldn't do more, they themselves fell back.

This is not an easy lesson. In our conditions this was taught to me by the difficulties of my own life. And if you yourselves—any one of you—were in the same difficult situation, you would have learned the same thing.

Today there are two major processes occurring in the world. One is a process of short-sighted concessions. It is a process of giving up, and giving up, and giving up, and hoping that perhaps at some point the wolf will have eaten enough.

The second process is one which I consider the key to everything and which, I will say now, will bring a new future to those under communism. For 20 years in the Soviet Union (and a shorter time in other Communist countries) there has been occurring a liberation of the human spirit. New generations are growing up which are steadfast in their struggle with evil. They are not willing to accept unprincipled compromises. They prefer to lose everything — salary, conditions of existence, life itself — rather than sacrifice conscience or make deals with evil.

This process has now gone so far that in the Soviet Union today, Marxism [the Communist teachings of Karl Marx] has become simply an object of contempt. No serious person in our country today, not even university and high school students, can talk about Marxism without laughing. But this whole process of our liberation, which obviously will involve social changes, is slower than the first one — the process of concessions. Over there, when we see these concessions, we are frightened. Why so quickly? Why give up several countries a year?

You are the allies of our liberation movement in the Communist countries. And I call upon you. Let us think together and try to see how we can adjust the relationship between these two processes. Whenever you help the persons persecuted in the Soviet Union, you're defending not only them but yourselves as well. You're defending your own future. So let us try and see how far we can go to stop this senseless and immoral process of making endless concessions to the aggressor.

On our crowded planet there are no longer any internal affairs. The Communist leaders say, "Don't interfere in our internal affairs. Let us strangle our citizens in peace and quiet." But I tell you: Interfere more and more. Interfere as much as you can. We beg you to come and interfere.

America — in me and among my friends and among people who think the way I do over there, among all ordinary Soviet citizens — brings forth a mixture of admiration and compassion. You're a country of the future; a young country; a country of still unused possibilities; a country of tremendous geographical distances; a country of tremendous spirit; a country of generosity. But these qualities — strength and generosity — usually make a person and even a whole country trusting. This already has done you a disservice several times.

I would like to call upon America to be more careful with its trust and prevent those people who are falsely using the struggle for peace and social justice to lead you down a false road. They are trying to weaken you. They are trying to disarm your strong and magnificent country in the face of this fearful threat — one which has never been seen before in the history of the world. Do not let yourselves be taken in the wrong direction. Let us try to slow down the process of concessions and help the process of liberation!

KISSINGER DEFENDS DÉTENTE

During the administrations of Richard Nixon and Gerald Ford, from 1969 to 1977, the United States improved its relations with the Communist nations of China and the Soviet Union through détente. A major figure behind this policy was Henry Kissinger, who served as Secretary of State under both Nixon and Ford. Kissinger helped negotiate the treaty ending United States military involvement in Vietnam. He also helped arrange President Nixon's historic visits to China and the Soviet Union in 1972. The following selection is from a 1975 speech that Kissinger made to explain détente.

Why is a peaceful relationship between the United States and the Soviet Union so necessary to the rest of the world? What does Kissinger say to the critics of détente? Do you think his arguments are effective? Explain.

Adapted from Henry Kissinger "The Moral Foundations of Foreign Policy," speech delivered at Minneapolis on July 15, 1975. Department of State Bulletin *No. 1884, August 4, 1975.*

Our relationship with the Communist powers has raised difficult questions for Americans ever since the Bolshevik Revolution. [The Russian Revolution took place in 1917–18.] It was understood very early that the Communist system and ideology were in conflict with our own principles. Sixteen years passed before President Franklin Roosevelt extended diplomatic recognition to the Soviet government. He did so in the belief, as he put it, that "through the resumption of normal relations the prospects of peace over all the world are greatly strengthened."

Today again courageous voices remind us of the nature of the Soviet system and of our duty to defend freedom. About this there is no disagreement.

There is, however, a clear conflict between two principles which is at the heart of the problem. Since the beginning of the nuclear age, the world's fears of catastrophe and its hopes for a better future have both depended on the relationship between the two superpowers. In an era of strategic nuclear balance —when both sides have the capacity to destroy civilized life—there is no alternative to coexistence.

In such conditions the necessity of peace is itself a moral principle. As President Kennedy pointed out: "In the final analysis our most basic common link is that we all inhabit this small planet. We all breathe the same air. We all cherish our children's future. And we are all mortal."

It is said, correctly, that the Soviet idea of "peaceful coexistence" is not the same as ours, that Soviet policies aim at the furthering of Soviet objectives. The problem of peace takes on a profound moral and practical difficulty in a world of nuclear weapons capable of destroying humankind; in a century which has seen the use of brutal force; in an age of ideology which turns the domestic policies of nations into issues of international conflict. But the issue, surely, is not whether peace and stability serve Soviet purposes, but whether they also serve our own. Constructive actions in Soviet policy are desirable whatever the Soviet motives.

This government has stated clearly and constantly the principles which we believe must guide relations between the Soviet Union and the United States and international conduct, principles that are consistent with both our values and our interests:

—We will maintain a strong and flexible military position to preserve our security. We will as a matter of principle and national interest oppose attempts by any country to achieve global or regional predominance.

—We will judge the state of U.S.–Soviet relations according to whether concrete problems are successfully resolved.

—All negotiations will be a two-way street, based on mutual benefit and observance of agreements.

—We will insist, as we always have, that progress in U.S.–Soviet economic relations must reflect progress toward stable political relationships.

—We will never abandon our ideals or our friends. We will not negotiate over the heads of, or against the interests of, other nations.

—We will respond firmly to attempts to achieve advantage by one side.

Beyond the necessities of coexistence there is the hope of a more positive relationship. The American people will never be satisfied with simply reducing tension and easing the danger of nuclear disaster. Over the longer term, we hope that firmness in the face of pressure and the creation of motives for cooperative action may bring about a more lasting pattern of stability and responsible conduct.

Today's joint manned mission in space—an area in which 15 years ago we saw ourselves in rivalry—is symbolic of the distance we have traveled. [He is referring to the Apollo-Soyuz space flight in 1975, in which an American and a Russian spacecraft met and docked in space.] Practical progress has been made on many problems. Berlin is no longer a source of conflict between East and West. Crises have been avoided. The frequency of U.S.–Soviet consultation is unprecedented. The cooperation in many fields is in dramatic contrast to the state of affairs ten, even five, years ago. The agreements already achieved to limit strategic armament programs are unparalleled in the history of diplomacy.

Our immediate attention is on the international actions of the Soviet Union not because it is our only moral concern, but because it is the sphere of action that we can most directly and confidently affect. As a result of improved foreign policy relationships, we have successfully used our influence to promote human rights. But we have done so quietly, keeping in mind the delicacy of the problem and stressing results rather than public confrontation.

Therefore critics of détente must answer: What is the alternative that they propose? What precise policies do they want us to change? Are they prepared for a prolonged situation of dramatically increased international danger? Do they wish to return to the constant crises and high arms budgets of the Cold War? Does détente encourage repression? Or is it détente that has brought about the demands for openness that we are now witnessing? Can we ask our people to support confrontation unless they know that every reasonable alternative has been explored?

In our relations with the Soviet Union, the United States will maintain its strength, defend its interests, and support its friends with determination and without illusion. We will speak up for our beliefs with vigor and without self-deception. We consider détente a means to regulate a competitive relationship—not a substitute for our own efforts in building the strength of the free world. We will continue on this course because it offers hope to our children of a more secure and a more just world.

The considerations raise a more general question: To what extent are we able to affect the internal policies of other governments and to what extent is it desirable?

There are some 150 nations in the world. Barely 20 of them are democracies in any real sense. The rest are nations whose ideology or political practices are inconsistent with our own. Yet we have political relations and often alliances with some of these countries in Asia, Latin America, Africa, and Europe.

We do not and will not overlook repressive practices. We have used, and we will use, our influence against repressive practices. Our traditions and our interests demand it.

But truth also forces a recognition of our limits. The question is whether we promote human rights more effectively by counsel and friendly relations where this serves our interest or by propaganda and discriminatory legislation. And we must also assess how foreign governments act in relation to their history and to the threats they face. We must have some understanding for the problems of countries adjoining powerful, hostile, and totalitarian regimes.

Our alliances and political relationships serve mutual ends. They contribute to regional and world security and thus support the broader welfare. They are not favors to other governments, but reflect a recognition of mutual interests. They should be withdrawn only when our interests change and not as a punishment for some act with which we do not agree.

In many countries, whatever the internal structure, the populations are unified in seeking our protection against outside aggression. In many countries our foreign policy relationships have proved to be no obstacle to the forces of change. And in many countries, especially in Asia, it is the process of American withdrawal that has weakened the sense of security and created a need for greater internal discipline — and at the same time decreased our ability to influence domestic practices.

The attempt to deal with those practices by restrictive American legislation raises a serious problem. This is not because of the moral view it expresses — which we share — but because of the mistaken impression it creates that our security ties are acts of charity. And beyond that, such acts are almost inevitably doomed to fail because they are too public, too inflexible, and too much a stimulus to nationalistic resentment.

There are no simple answers. Painful experience should have taught us that we ought not exaggerate our ability to foresee, let alone to shape, social and political change in other societies. Therefore let me state the principles that will guide our action:

— Human rights are a legitimate international concern and have been so defined in international agreements for more than a generation.

— The United States will speak up for human rights in appropriate international forums and in exchanges with other governments.

— We will be mindful of the limits of our reach. We will be conscious of the difference between public attitudes that satisfy our self-esteem and policies that bring positive results.

— We will not lose sight of either the requirements of global security or what we stand for as a nation.

CHAPTER 24
REACHING FOR GREATER FREEDOM AND JUSTICE

AN APPEAL BY MARTIN LUTHER KING, JR.

One of the greatest of modern American black leaders was Martin Luther King, Jr., a minister and crusader for civil rights. King first became well known during a bus boycott in Montgomery, Alabama, in 1955–56. After several months, black residents succeeded in desegregating local transportation. In the years that followed, King became a powerful leader of the nonviolent protest movement. He and his followers used sit-ins, boycotts, and marches to call attention to inequality and illegality in the treatment of black Americans.

Adapted from "I Have a Dream," an address by Martin Luther King. Jr. Copyright © 1963 by Martin Luther King Jr. Adapted and reprinted by permission of Joan Daves Literary Agency.

One hundred years ago a great American, in whose symbolic shadow we stand [the demonstration was held at the Lincoln Memorial], signed the Emancipation Proclamation. This momentous decree came as a great beacon light of hope to millions of Negro slaves who had been seared in the flames of withering injustice. It came as a joyous daybreak to end the long night of captivity.

But one hundred years later we must face the tragic fact that the Negro is still not free. One hundred years later the life of the Negro is still sadly crippled by the chains of segregation and discrimination. One hundred years later the Negro lives on a lonely island of poverty in the midst of a vast ocean of material prosperity. One hundred years later Negroes still find themselves exiles in their own land. So we have come here today to dramatize an appalling condition.

In a sense we have come to our nation's capital to cash a check. When the builders of our republic wrote the magnificent words of the Constitution and the Declaration of Independence, they were signing a promissory note which every American was to inherit. This note was a promise that all people would be guaranteed the unalienable rights of life, liberty, and the pursuit of happiness.

It is obvious today that America has defaulted on this promissory note insofar as its black citizens are concerned. Instead of honoring this sacred obligation, America has given the Negro people a bad check—a check which has come back marked "insufficient funds." But we refuse to believe that the bank of justice is bankrupt. We refuse to believe that there are insufficient funds in the great vaults of opportunity of this nation. So we have come to cash this check—a check that will give us upon demand the riches of freedom and the security of justice. We have also come to this hallowed spot to remind America of the fierce urgency of *now*. This is no time to engage in the luxury of cooling off or gradualism [the idea of proceeding slowly in carrying out change]. *Now* is the time to make real the promises of democracy. *Now* is the time to rise from the dark and desolate valley of segregation to the sunlit path of racial justice. *Now* is the time to open the doors of opportunity to all of God's children. *Now* is the time to lift our nation from the quicksands of racial injustice to the solid rock of brotherhood.

It would be fatal for the nation to overlook the urgency of the moment and to underestimate the determination of the Negro. This sweltering summer of the Negro's legitimate discontent will not pass until there is an invigorating autumn of freedom and equality. The year 1963 is not an end, but a beginning. Those who hope that the Negro needed to blow off steam and will now be content will have a rude awakening if the nation returns to business as usual. There will be neither rest nor tranquility in America until the Negro is granted citizenship rights. The whirlwinds of revolt will continue to shake the foundations of our nation until the bright day of justice emerges.

But there is something that I must say to my people who stand on the warm threshold which leads into the palace of justice. In the process of gaining our rightful place we must not be guilty of wrongful deeds. Let us not seek to satisfy our thirst for freedom by drinking from the cup of bitterness and hatred. We must forever conduct our struggle with dignity and discipline. We must not allow our creative protest to turn into physical violence. Again and again we must rise to the majestic heights of meeting physical force with soul force. The marvelous new militancy which has taken over the Negro community must not lead us to a distrust of all white people. Many of our white brothers, as shown by their presence here today, have come to realize that their destiny is tied up with our destiny. Their freedom is bound to our freedom. We cannot walk alone.

And as we walk, we must make the pledge that we shall march ahead. We cannot turn back. There are those who are asking us, "When will you be satisfied?" We can never be satisfied as long as the Negro is the victim of the unspeakable horrors of police brutality. We can never be satisfied as long as we cannot gain lodging in the motels of the highways and the hotels of the cities. We cannot be satisifed as long as the Negro's basic mobility is from a smaller ghetto to a larger one. We can never be satisfied as long as a Negro in Mississippi cannot vote, and a Negro in New York believes he has nothing for which to vote. No, no, we are not satisfied, and we will not be satisfied until justice rolls down like water and righteousness like a mighty stream.

I know that some of you have come here out of great trouble. Some of you have come fresh from narrow jail cells. Some of you have come from areas where your search for freedom left you battered by the storms of persecution and staggered by the winds of police brutality. You have been the veterans of creative suffering. Continue to work with the faith that unearned suffering is redeeming.

Go back to Mississippi, go back to Alabama, go back to South Carolina, go back to Georgia, go back to Louisiana, go back to the slums and ghettos of our modern cities, knowing that somehow this situation can and will be changed. Let us not wallow in the valley of despair.

I say to you today, my friends, that in spite of the difficulties and frustrations of the moment I still have a dream. It is a dream deeply rooted in the American dream.

I have a dream that one day this nation will rise up and live out the true meaning of its creed: "We hold these truths to be self-evident: that all men are created equal."

I have a dream that one day on the red hills of Georgia the sons of former slaves and the sons of former slaveowners will be able to sit down together at the table of brotherhood. •

I have a dream that one day even the state of Mississippi will be transformed into an oasis of freedom and justice.

I have a dream that my four little children will one day live in a nation where they will not be judged by the color of their skin but by the content of their character.

I have a dream today.

I have a dream that one day the state of Alabama will be changed into a situation where little black boys and black girls will be able to join hands with little white boys and white girls and walk together as sisters and brothers.

I have a dream today.

This is our hope. This is the faith with which I return to the South. With this faith we will be able to cut out of the mountain of despair a stone of hope. With this faith we will be able to change the jangling discords of our nation into a beautiful symphony of brotherhood. With this faith we will be able to work together, to pray together, to struggle together, to go to jail together, to stand up for freedom together, knowing that we will be free one day.

This will be the day when all of God's children will be able to sing with new meaning "My country 'tis of thee, sweet land of liberty, of thee I sing. Land where my fathers died, land of the pilgrim's pride, from every mountainside, let freedom ring."

And if America is to be a great nation this must become true. So let freedom ring from the hilltops of New Hampshire. Let freedom ring from the mountains of New York. Let freedom ring from the Alleghenies of Pennsylvania!

Let freedom ring from the snow-capped Rockies of Colorado!

Let freedom ring from the peaks of California!

But not only that; let freedom ring from Stone Mountain of Georgia!

Let freedom ring from Lookout Mountain of Tennessee!

Let freedrom ring from every hill and molehill of Mississippi. From every mountainside, let freedom ring.

When we let freedom ring, when we let it ring from every village and every hamlet, from every state and every city, we will be able to speed up that day when all of God's children, black people and white people, Jews, Protestants, and Catholics, will be able to join hands and sing in the words of the old Negro spiritual, "Free at last! free at last, thank God almighty, we are free at last!"

HOW MUCH PROGRESS FOR BLACKS?

The historic decision in *Brown v. Board of Education of Topeka*—calling for desegregation in public education—was handed down by the Supreme Court in 1954. Twenty-four years later a group of scholars met in Mississippi to debate the question, "Have we overcome?" The words came from the unofficial anthem of the civil rights movement, "We Shall Overcome." Here black writer Lerone Bennett, Jr., offers an answer and an explanation.

Adapted from "Have We Overcome?" by Lerone Bennett, Jr., in Have We Overcome? Race Relations Since Brown. Reprinted by permission of the University Press of Mississippi.

The question is have we overcome?

And my question is how are we to understand that dangerous word *we*?

And what does it mean *to overcome*?

Well, in the context of the song and the struggle, *we* means black people and white people who are committed to and involved in the struggle for equality and racial justice. And *to overcome,* again in the context of the song and the struggle, means the act of destroying all racial barriers and creating a new land of freedom and equality for all men, all women, and all children.

"Oh, deep in my heart I do believe we shall overcome." We shall overpass, triumph over mean sheriffs, robed riders, assassins of the spirit, segregation, discrimination, hunger, poverty, and humiliation.

Have we done it? No, a thousand times no.

We were there, some of us, and we sang the song, some of us, and saw the blood, some of us. And we know – deep in our hearts – that what the singers and dreamers and victims hoped for . . . what they struggled and died for . . . has not happened yet. Because of the passion and the pain of the singers and victims and dreamers, we have, in the past twenty-four years, crossed many barriers . . . but we are nowhere near the end of our journey, and we have miles to go before we sleep.

And so, it is necessary to say here, in the name of the dreamers and victims, that we have not yet started the process of grappling with the depth and the height of the dream. As a matter of fact, we haven't even defined what we must do in order to overcome.

To cite only one point, the admission of a handful of gifted black students and athletes to a white university controlled by whites is not – repeat – *not* integration. It is at best desegregation and a prelude to that great American dream which was written down on pieces of paper, which was promised, and which has never existed anywhere in America, except in the hearts of a handful of men and women. By any reasonable standard, then, we have failed to meet the goal.

How remote, how unimaginably distant and remote that May day [of the *Brown* decision] seems today. The events of the intervening years – Montgomery, the sit-ins, the freedom rides, the marches, and urban rebellions – came so suddenly, so dramatically. Our sense of time has been distorted and incidents and personalities of only a few days ago have been pushed into the distant past.

The internal and external changes flowing from this event have been profound and dramatic. So have the costs. Martin Luther King, Jr., is dead; Malcolm X is dead. Whitney Young, Medgar Evers, Fred Hampton [other figures associated with the civil rights movement] are all dead. And the movement they led and symbolized has ended.

It is true, and important, that blacks are going places today they couldn't go twenty-four years ago. *Everything, in fact, has changed in Mississippi and America, and yet, paradoxically, nothing has changed.*

Despite the court orders and civil rights laws, blacks are still the last hired and the first fired. They are still systematically exploited as consumers and citizens. To come right out with it, the full privileges and immunities of the U.S. Constitution do not apply to blacks tonight, in Mississippi or in Massachusetts, and they never have. You want to know how bad things are? Listen to the facts cited by Robert B. Hill of the National Urban League in a recent booklet, entitled *The Illusion of Black Progress.*

Contrary to popular belief, the economic gap between blacks and whites is widening. Between 1975 and 1976, the black to white family income ratio fell sharply from 62 to 59 percent.

Not only is black unemployment at its highest level today, but the jobless gap between blacks and whites is the widest it has ever been. . . . The proportion of middle-income black families has not significantly increased. The proportion of upper-income black families has steadily declined. White high school dropouts have lower unemployment rates (22.3%) than black youth with college education (27.2%).

These figures are terrible, and the reality is worse. How did this happen? How is it possible for black America to be in so much trouble after all the demonstrations, and marches, and court orders? What is the meaning of this terrible indictment?

The short answer to these questions is that we stopped marching too soon. The long . . . and scholarly . . . answer is embedded in the history of our journey.

It is possible, indeed likely, that the post-*Brown* struggle, despite its limitations, was a necessary stage in the social maturing of black people. And there can be little doubt that it created black America's finest hours and one of the finest hours in the history of the republic.

Because of that struggle, we have made significant gains on the political front and in the middle sectors. The movement changed, destroyed, wiped out the visible and dramatic signs of racism, but it did not and perhaps could not at that time deal with the subtle forms of institutional racism. Nor did it change or even make a dent in the economic inequities of a society that can make work for black men inside prisons after they commit crimes but cannot find work for black men outside prisons before they commit crimes.

And so, as a result of the failure of the movement to make a total breakthrough on the racial front, we find ourselves in the post-revolutionary phase of a revolution that never happened.

Does this mean that the movement was a failure? By no means. As a result of that struggle, one-third of this nation—the South—was changed, perhaps forever, and the rest of the nation made its first tentative steps toward democracy. Beyond all that, the movement created the foundations for future change.

The leaders [of the civil rights movement] didn't start the Montgomery boycott: the people started it. And when the energy of the people ran out, when they had tried everything, or almost everything, the people withdrew to retool and rethink. And what we've got to understand tonight is that this temporary withdrawal was and is natural under the circumstances. The law of history is that people cannot live forever on the heights. The law of history is that a people advance and retreat, advance and retreat, advance and retreat, until they reach a collective decision to go for broke. And this entitles us to say, I think, that if the sun continues to shine and the wind continues to blow, the movement of the sixties will reemerge in America on a higher level of development.

The sixties taught us four great lessons. First, the struggle to overcome is not a hundred-yard dash but a long-distance run. We must prepare, therefore, for the long haul. We must prepare for a struggle of five, ten, fifteen, or even fifty years.

The second lesson, growing out of the first, is that people change only when they have to change, and that it is the task of the oppressed to do whatever is required to force change.

The third is that we cannot overcome and the gains of the post-*Brown* years cannot be preserved without a total struggle for fundamental change. There have to be real changes in the tax structure and the relations between the private and public sectors, a redefinition of values, and a redistribution of income.

Finally, and most importantly, the white South and white North are going to have to deal with themselves. The great lesson of the sixties, a lesson heeded almost nowhere, is that there is no Negro problem in Mississippi and in America. The problem of race in Mississippi, and in America, is a white problem, and we shall not overcome until we confront that problem.

FOUR MINORITY VOICES

The United States was settled and built by people of many different racial and national backgrounds. In many cases the newcomers or their descendants discarded their cultural differences and became "Americanized." Indeed, for a long time the ideal America was a "melting pot." In it all the various peoples would blend, losing their individuality and ethnic identity. Instead of being Poles or Filipinos or Haitians, they would become, simple, Americans.

In recent years, however, the trend has been to emphasize ethnic consciousness—the feeling of belonging to a special group. Members of many minority groups have felt a new awareness of their cultures. This selection presents the views of four minority group members: a Mexican American, a Puerto Rican, a Chinese American, and an American Indian.

What does being Mexican American mean to Foresto Garcia? What are Ricky's feelings about his Puerto Rican identity? How does Clarence Chen describe his experiences as a Chinese American? How would you summarize Betty's attitude toward being an American Indian? Can you find any experiences or attitudes that these young people share in common?

[FORRESTO GARCIA]

I am Forresto Garcia and sixteen years old. I have five brothers and four sisters. I know how it is to work in the fields but I have been lucky and graduated from my grade school. I like to help poor people and I want to be somebody that helps poor people.

We have just come from Texas to California in our car with a trailer attached to it, and we put all our belongings in the trailer. When we arrived here we looked for a rancher, and he said, "Do you want to work picking cotton?" And we said, "Yes, we want to work," and he said, "Well, I'll give you a house if you work for me for the cotton season," and he gives us a house and that's the way we live. And when the cotton is finished we move to another town and look for another crop. When there is no house we set up our trailer near the rest of the families, but mostly we live outside the trailer. But when we are naughty my father quietly tells us to go into the trailer. You obey right away just by hearing the way he speaks. He has a twig from the prune true and when he hits you with it you know it. Just once or twice.

We get up at five in the morning so we can start work at six. My sisters get up earlier because they have to make breakfast for my dad and my brothers and then make food for the fields. We make an early start so we could earn enough money for the day. We work until about four in the afternoon.

I am trying to get a steady job to help my family so they can have more money. In Texas I have seen many American-Mexicans without shoes, with their feet all dirty, and their faces and hands dirty, and no water to take a bath.

I sometimes just stay home doing nothing but thinking about my family. On Sunday when there is no work we go to the picnic grounds and cook on an open fire and when it gets very hot we swim in the stream that runs by our house.

It makes me feel bad to see poor people. My brother, he works for the union and he talks a lot about the union and what the union is doing and I like it. When I meet some guys working in the field I say, "How would you like to join the union?" and they say, "No, I'm O.K. and I don't like to help poor people," I get mad at them.

Now when my older brothers and my father picket against picking grapes I help them. I like to see them win what they are fighting for. Some employers are better than others, but some take advantage of the workers. They are rich and my people are so poor.

[RICKY]

My name is Ricky and I'm Puerto Rican. The best thing about being Puerto Rican is just being Puerto Rican. That's where it's at. I believe Puerto Rican people are the best. They treat me very good—very good. Like they aren't cheap with their stuff. Like you're at a party and it's late. And they say right away, "We got an extra bed. Sleep here." And they feed you and they do everything for you. And they don't have that much. But they've always given to everyone, and they'll give you what they got because they're generous.

Where I live now it looks like a ghetto. But it used to be real pretty. When I was young there were no addicts there and nobody was uptight about drugs. Now everybody is, because there's a lot of junkies [drug users] hanging around all over the neighborhood. Puerto Ricans. Blacks. Dominicans. All the races mix. It doesn't matter.

There's a lot of violence where I live. I watch not because I'm interested, but because you have no choice. After all, if I'm there, what am I going to do—just look the other way? But I like to see people who deserve to get hurt get theirs, you know? The guys that hurt other people. Like the junkies—most people who get hurt in these fights are junkies, because they're the ones who go around hurting people and the others get even. They mug people, kill people, and rob houses, and the people around my way they don't have that much. Maybe they save a year for a television set, and they enjoy watching it. And then here comes somebody, some junkie after money, and he robs these people and takes all they've got and leaves them with nothing.

I know a whole lot of junkies, but they're not my friends—I don't hang out with them. I don't know how people become junkies in the first place. Maybe they're influenced by their friends or they pick it up in school—but something happens to them.

I never smoked marijuana 'cause I don't need it. I don't need anything. Maybe other people need to feel nice. Maybe it makes them feel like a big man. It's the same with violence, guns, and killings, I guess.

I feel nice when I shoot pool. I'm pretty good, too. I make money from it, in fact. I can make thirty or forty dollars on a weekend. I just go up to a guy and say, "Hey, do you want to shoot pool?" I lose a lot of times, but I've won more money than I lost. And I also like to play poker.

Another thing I've always liked to do is turn on the fire hydrant. It's fun getting wet and running around getting other people wet. One time when I was little I was playing with the fire hydrant and I was covering myself with a box so I didn't see a car coming. And I guess the car didn't see me either and the driver didn't pay any attention to the water and I got hit. That happened twice more. The person that hit me the third time was my lawyer. He was going to my house to talk to my parents about the first two cases and then he hit me. I tried to sue but I don't know what happened. I wasn't badly hurt.

I'd still like to play with the fire hydrant, but the cops picked me up for opening one last summer. The only other time I got into trouble with the police was once when they asked me my name. I gave them a phony name and a phony address. I told them I didn't have a phone number, and they believed me.

When a cop gets shot, I say that's bad. Like, they have to take care of people and they're just people, too. They weren't born cops, they just got in it. In fact, I like Puerto Rican cops. They're together people. Puerto Ricans are proud and that's good. Maybe that's why we fight a lot. We are proud people and we don't take anything off of people. We don't ask nobody for nothing. I wouldn't even borrow money from my friends. That's how proud I am.

[CLARENCE CHEN]
For most of my life I have taken for granted the fact that I am racially different from most of the people I have met and known—they are mostly Caucasian and I am not. When it occurred to me to think about who I was I would think of myself first as a boy, a student, a son, and then, somewhere near the end of the list, as a Chinese.

After all, I was like all of my American friends; we spoke the same slang, played the same games, listened to the same music, wore the same type of clothes. When we were boys, we lived and would have died for the same local baseball team—the White Sox. We played cowboys and Indians. As an adolescent, I had the same financial, emotional, and social crises everyone else did. For all practical purposes, I grew up as a typical American boy who happened to be Chinese.

Throughout my years of growing up, I encountered relatively little outward racial prejudice directed against me. The general lack of racial prejudice directed against me was at least partially due to the absence of any other Chinese people. My family were the first Chinese (and nonwhite) to move into that neighborhood on the South Side of Chicago. My brother and I were the first Chinese students at our elementary and high schools.

But while I am an American for all practical purposes, there have been times when I was acutely and uncomfortably aware that I was also different. Though my mannerisms, speech, and dress were American, my physical appearance was quite obviously Oriental. When I was about five, I believed that my Oriental features made me ugly even though I cannot recall having been told that by anyone.

In school, whenever a topic related to China was brought up in a social studies class, I would notice the other kids looking in my direction—expecting me to be knowledgeable on the subject. Since I knew practically nothing of Chinese history, culture, or language, I generally passed such moments by slumping into my seat and becoming suddenly interested in my books.

Unfortunately, some of my meetings with other Chinese have been similarly embarrassing. Whenever I have met Chinese people who have been brought up in the Chinese culture, I have been met with two sets of responses. Either I am Chinese and able to speak and act Chinese, or I am not Chinese at all but completely American or perhaps Japanese. In the former case, the other person is usually disappointed and embarrassed to learn I cannot speak Chinese. In the latter case, the other person is usually surprised and amused to find I am racially 100 percent Chinese, that my family came to this country just one generation ago, and that I actually know a few phrases in Chinese such as "Thank you" and "See you again."

Several years ago I made a trip to Taiwan. My uncles and aunts, while warmly receiving me as a member of the family, could not help but see me as more American than Chinese. They affectionately called me *wai gwo ren* — a term meaning "foreigner" but also suggesting "Westerner" or "white man." I felt I was viewed as somewhat stupid because of my inability to speak Chinese. There must have been something about my appearance and manner — perhaps my American-style clothes and hair length or my un-Chinese assertiveness — which branded me as an alien; for storekeepers, cab drivers, and waiters quickly knew I was an outsider even before I spoke.

I do not mean to suggest that I have never gotten along with other Chinese. Yes, some of my best friends are Chinese. But they have come from white-collar, middle-class families like mine who have been pretty much assimilated into the mainstream of American culture.

While it may sound as if I have never been genuinely comfortable in the company of either Americans or Chinese, the reality has not been that difficult. Most of the time when I am with other non-Chinese people, the matter of our racial differences never crosses our minds.

While I have occasionally felt uncomfortable being Chinese in a mainly Caucasian country, I am fortunate in belonging to a group of Chinese-Americans in which I can feel very much at home. This group, consisting of eight families scattered around the Chicago area, began as an informal association of Chinese student couples who found themselves stranded in the United States after the Communists came to power in China. The members meet socially once a month at one another's homes.

The people of my generation in this group will, no matter how Americanized they seem to become, always have a unique aspect in their backgrounds — their parents grew up and were brought up in the Chinese culture. Thus, despite our American characteristics, we (the American-born Chinese) have been influenced in certain ways by the traditional culture. All of us have high achievement motivations and have all won superior academic credentials.

(Scholarship was, for thousands of years in China, the most honored and respected path to higher status and public recognition.) Furthermore, academic and nonacademic achievements have been felt in our group to reflect shamefully or proudly on the individual and also on the individual's family. It is quite common in our eight-family gatherings to hear one parent praising another parent for his or her offspring's accomplishment. This is a reflection of a traditional Chinese concept: a person's reputation, whether honorable or dishonorable, directly affects the family's reputation. "Good" children in China were those who brought honor to the family name.

Last summer I went to a "Chinese Family Camp" to serve as a counselor. About thirty yards [27 meters] off the shore of Lake Wawasee, Indiana, was an anchored raft that could be used by anyone who swam out to it. One afternoon I was resting on it when I suddenly realized that the five or six of us on the raft were all Chinese-American. In that moment, a deep, warm feeling swept through me. I was just where I belonged — a temporary island on which disguises dissolved and I could be what I am — not really American, not really Chinese, but really Chinese-American.

[BETTY]

I'm like my brother. He says we're *both* going to be different Hopis than our parents were. We would like to leave the reservation. We wouldn't mind seeing how Indians live in cities. A lot of Hopis say you stop being a Hopi when you go into a city and live in big buildings and forget about our land, and our hills, and the sky over us. Maybe. I don't know. The Indian can't just sit and think of his past. My mother says it's a pity; our people were happy here for so long. Now, a lot of us want to leave. But she admits that we are living better than we used to live. And she says we can still be Hopis, even if we get the white man's knowledge, and spend some of our lives living in his land, not ours.

We're not going to have cities here. We're not going to let the white man come and tear our land up, like he's done elsewhere. But we have to live so that our children don't get sick and die, when they could live if there was a doctor and a hospital near. And we have to live in houses where the children don't freeze in the winter. Our mother said her old mother and old aunt didn't like the house we lived in at first.

They said it was a white man's house. They didn't like the electricity when it was first brought in. But now they do. They wouldn't know how to get by without it. That's why I tell my brother: it's all right to be a white man, and you can still be a Hopi.

My aunt is very fond of me. She asks me a lot of the time what I will do when I grow older. Will I stay in school? Have I thought of someone I'd like to marry? Questions like that. I have always confided in her. I told her once that I wouldn't mind going away for a while and living among white people. She wasn't as upset as my mother would be. But I don't think she really believes I'm going to go — and I'm not sure either.

She said it was all right to want to know about the white man and his cities. She said it's because of school; we learn so much. When she was young, she didn't go to school. She is right about schools. They show us pictures and movies and we read books. I read a book about France. I would like to go to Paris. I read another book about England. I would like to go to London. I would also like to see California. I would *not* like to visit Washington, D.C. That is where the BIA [Bureau of Indian Affairs] has its office.

My old aunt always asks me the same question at the end of a talk: would you come back if you traveled far away? I say yes, and she is happy. But I'm not sure. What would happen if I traveled far and liked living where I was? Would I come back then? I don't know. The white people live a different life than we do. And my father is right, they kill each other in automobile crashes when they travel, and they are always starting a war or trying to end one. And our people have lost so much to them. Our men still fight in their wars, and a long time ago, they were making war against us, and we lost a lot of people then. But the Hopis never fought the whites the way the Navajos and the Apaches did. The teachers told us that in school, and my father said they are right because we have not been fighters. My father tells us that to fight is to admit that you are weak and without control over yourself — wilder than any animal.

But the white people aren't just fighting all the time. They can be friends of the Indians; some white people are volunteers. They try to help people — and they even work for the same federal government that sends us the BIA people. My father admits that even a few of the BIA people are getting better. I think in the future Hopis and white people will become friendlier, and the Hopi people will travel more.

THE UNENDING DREAM

With all its problems, the United States in the 1980's still has a worldwide image as a land of opportunity. Every year thousands of foreigners immigrate in hopes of finding a better life. Thousands more come illegally with the same hope. In the interview that follows, Leonel Castillo, former head of the United States Immigration and Naturalization Service, talks about the American Dream. Himself the grandson of a Mexican immigrant, he is especially concerned with Mexican, and other, illegal (or undocumented) aliens.

How does Castillo describe the typical undocumented newcomer? What are Castillo's feelings about illegal aliens? What does the American Dream mean to you?

Adapted from American Dreams: Lost and Found *by Studs Terkel. Copyright © 1980 by Studs Terkel. Reprinted by permission of Pantheon Books, a Division of Random House.*

New immigrants are trying all over again to integrate themselves into the system. They have the same hunger. On any given day, there are about three million throughout the world who are applying to come to the United States and share the American Dream. . . .

The Vietnamese boat people [who fled Southeast Asia after the Communist takeover in 1975] express it as well as anyone. They don't know if they're gonna land, if the boat's gonna sink. They don't know what's gonna happen to 'em, but they've a hunch they might make it to the U.S. as the "freedom place."

There is the plain hard fact of hunger. In order to eat, a person will endure tremendous hardship. Mexican people who come here usually are not the poorest. Someone who's too poor can't afford the trip. . . .

Sometimes the whole family saves up and gives the bright young man or the bright young woman the family savings. It even goes into debt for a year or two. They pin all their hopes on this one kid, put him on a bus, let him go a thousand miles [1600 kilometers]. He doesn't speak a word of English. He's only seventeen, eighteen years old, but he's gonna save that family. A lot rides on that kid who's a busboy in some hotel.

We've had some as young as eleven who have come a thousand miles [1600 kilometers]. You have this young kid, all his family savings, everything is on him. There are a lot of songs and stories about mother and child, the son leaving who may never return. We end up deporting him [sending him back home]. It's heartrending.

He's the bright kid in the family. The slow one might not make it, might get killed. The one who's sickly can't make the trip. He couldn't walk through the desert. He's not gonna be too old, too young, too destitute, or too slow. He's the brightest and the best.

He's gonna be the first hook, the first pioneer coming into an alien society, the United States. . . . He works as a busboy all night long. They pay him minimum or less, and work him hard. He'll never complain. He might even thank his boss. He'll say as little as possible because he doesn't want anyone to know what his status is. He will often live in his apartment, except for the time he goes to work or to church or to a dance. He will stay in and watch TV. If he makes a hundred a week, he will manage to send back twenty-five. All over the country, if you go to a Western Union office on the weekend, you'll find a lot of people there sending money orders to Mexico.

After the kid learns a bit, because he's healthy and young and energetic, he'll probably get another job as a busboy. He'll work at another place as soon as the shift is over. He'll try to work his way up to be a waiter. He'll work incredible hours. He doesn't care about union scale, he doesn't care about conditions, about humiliations. He accepts all this as his fate.

He's burning underneath with this energy and ambition. He outworks the U.S. busboys and eventually becomes the waiter. Where he can maneuver, he tries to become the owner and gives a lot of competition to the locals. Restaurant owners tell me, if they have a choice, they'll always hire foreign nationals first. They're so eager and grateful. There's a little greed here, too. They pay 'em so little. . . .

At least a quarter of a million apprehensions were made last year. If we apprehend them at the border, we turn 'em around and ask them to depart voluntarily. They turn around and go back to Mexico. A few hours later, they try again. In El Paso, we deported one fellow six times in one day. There's a restaurant in Hollywood run by a fellow we deported thirty-seven times. We've deported some people more than a hundred times. They always want to come back. There's a job and there's desperation. . . .

Half the people here without papers are not Mexicans. They're from all over the world. They came legally, with papers, as tourists ten years ago. . . . All too often, the public gets the impression that all immigrants are on welfare. It's the exact opposite. Very few go on welfare. We get people coming in from Haiti, the poorest country in the western hemisphere. They come over by boat and land in Florida.

We make three thousand apprehensions at the border every weekend. It's just a little 14-mile [22-kilometer] stretch. Our border patrol knows this little fellow comin' across is hungry. He just wants to work. They know he's no security threat. They say: "It's my job." Many of them come to have a great deal of respect for the people they're deporting. What do you think of a person you deport three, four times, who just keeps coming back? You would never want to get in the same ring with that person.

I'm torn. I saw it in the Peace Corps, when I was in the Philippines. A mother offered you her infant. You're just a twenty-one-year-old kid and she says: "Take my child, take him with you to the States." When you see this multiplied by thousands, it tears you up. . . .

The only thing that helps me is remembering the history of this country. We've always managed . . . to rejuvenate ourselves, to bring in new people. Every new group comes in believing more firmly in the American Dream than the one that came a few years before. Every new group is scared of being in the welfare line or in the unemployment office. They go to night school, they learn about America. We'd be lost without them.

The old dream is still dreamt. The old neighborhood Ma-Pa stores [small stores owned and run by a husband and wife] are still around. They are not Italian or Jewish or Eastern European any more. Ma and Pa are now Korean, Vietnamese, Iraqi, Jordanian, Latin American. They live in the store. They work seven days a week. Their kids are doing well in school. They're making it. Sound familiar?

Near our office in Los Angeles is a little cafe with a sign: KOSHER BURRITOS. A *burrito* is a Mexican tortilla with meat inside. Most of the customers are black. The owner is Korean. The banker, I imagine, is WASP. This is what's happening in the United States today. It is not a melting pot, but in one way or another, there is a blending of cultures.

I see all kinds of new immigrants starting out all over again, trying to work their way into the system. They're going through new battles, yet they're old battles. They want to share in the American Dream. The stream never ends.

WOMEN'S DISSATISFACTION

In the 1950's most American women were full-time wives and mothers; only about 30 percent worked outside the home. There were very few women in politics, in the professions, or in executive positions in business and industry. Society praised the role of the housewife—but not all of those who held the job were satisfied with it.

One woman who felt that there must be more to life was a suburban mother of three, named Betty Friedan. She investigated how other women felt about themselves and reported her findings in a best-selling book, *The Feminine Mystique.* Its major point was that millions of American women were becoming aware that the world of home and family did not offer them fulfillment.

In 1964 Friedan helped found the National Organization for Women. It revived the feminist movement and led a renewed struggle for equal rights for women in employment, education, and other areas of American society.

According to the author, what is the "feminine mystique"? What is "the problem that has no name"? Does Friedan agree with the solutions explaining the problem? Why or why not?

Adapted from The Feminine Mystique *by Betty Friedan. Copyright © 1961, 1974 by Betty Friedan. Reprinted by permission of W. W. Norton & Co., Inc.*

The problem lay buried, unspoken, for many years in the minds of American women. It was a strange stirring, a sense of dissatisfaction, a yearning that women suffered in the 1950's in the United States. Each suburban wife struggled with it alone. As she made the beds, shopped for groceries, matched slipcover material, ate peanut butter sandwiches with her children, drove around Cub Scouts and Brownies, she was afraid to ask herself the silent question—"Is this all?"

For over fifteen years there was no word of this yearning in the millions of words written about women and for women by experts telling them that their role was to seek fulfillment as wives and mothers. Over and over women heard that they could desire no greater destiny than to glory in their own femininity. Experts told them how to catch a man and keep him, how to handle children; how to buy a dishwasher, bake bread, cook gourmet snails; how to dress, look, and act more feminine and make marriage more exciting. They were taught to pity the neurotic, unfeminine, unhappy women who wanted to be poets or physicists or presidents. They learned that truly feminine women do not want careers, higher education, political rights—the independence and the opportunities that the old-fashioned feminists fought for. A thousand expert voices praised women's new maturity. All they had to do was devote their lives from earliest girlhood to finding a husband and having children.

By the end of the 1950's the average marriage age of women in America had dropped to 20, and was still dropping, into the teens. Fourteen million girls were engaged by 17. The proportion of women attending college in comparison with men dropped from 47 percent in 1920 to 35 percent in 1958. A hundred years earlier, women had fought for higher education; now girls went to college to get a husband. By the mid-1950's, 60 percent dropped out of college to marry, or because they were afraid too much education would hurt their chances for marriage.

By the end of the 1950's the United States birthrate was overtaking India's. Statisticians were especially astounded at the fantastic increase in the number of babies born to college-educated women. Where once they had two children, now they had four, five, six.

Girls were growing up in America without ever having jobs outside the home. Fewer and fewer women were entering professional work. The shortages in the nursing, social work, and teaching professions caused crises in almost every American city. Concerned over the Soviet Union's lead in the space race, scientists noted that America's greatest source of unused brainpower was women. But girls would not study physics: it was "unfeminine."

The suburban housewife—she was the dream image of young American women. She was the envy, it was said, of women all over the world. The American housewife was freed by science and labor-saving appliances from the drudgery, the dangers of childbirth, and the illnesses of her grandmother. She was healthy, beautiful, educated, concerned only about her husband, her children, her home. She had found true feminine fulfillment. As a housewife and mother, she was respected as a full and equal partner to man in his world. She was free to choose automobiles, clothes, appliances, supermarkets. She had everything that women had ever dreamed of.

In the fifteen years after World War II, this mystique of feminine fulfillment became the cherished center of American culture. Millions of women lived their lives in the image of the American suburban housewife, kissing their husbands goodbye in front of the picture window, leaving their stationwagonsful of children at school, and smiling as they ran the new electric waxer over the spotless kitchen floor. They gave no thought to the unfeminine problems of the world outside the home; they wanted the men to make the major decisions. They gloried in their role as women, and wrote proudly on the census blank: "Occupation: housewife."

For over fifteen years, the words written for women, and the words women used when they talked to each other, were about problems with their children, or how to keep their husbands happy, or improve their children's school, or cook chicken or make slipcovers. Nobody argued whether women were inferior or superior to men; they were simply different. Words like "emancipation" and "career" sounded strange and embarrassing; no one had used them for years.

If a woman had a problem in the 1950's and 1960's, she knew that something must be wrong with her marriage, or with herself. Other women were satisfied with their lives, she thought. What kind of woman was she if she did not feel this mysterious fulfillment waxing the kitchen floor? She was so ashamed to admit her dissatisfaction that she never knew how many other women shared it. If she tried to tell her husband, he didn't understand what she was talking about.

But on an April morning in 1959, I heard a mother of four, having coffee with four other mothers, say in a tone of quiet desperation, "the problem." And the others knew, without words, that she was not talking about a problem with her husband, or her children, or her home. Suddenly they realized they all shared the same problem, the problem that has no name. They began, hesitantly, to talk about it. Later, after they had picked up their children at nursery school and taken them home to nap,

two of the women cried, in sheer relief, just to know they were not alone.

Gradually I came to realize that the problem that has no name was shared by countless women in America. Sometimes I sensed the problem, not as a reporter, but as a suburban housewife, for during this time I was also bringing up my own three children.

Just what was this problem that has no name? What were the words women used when they tried to express it? Sometimes a woman would say, "I feel empty somehow—incomplete." Or she would say, "I feel as if I don't exist." Sometimes she got rid of the feeling with a tranquilizer. Sometimes she thought the problem was with her husband, or her children, or that what she really needed was to redecorate her house, or move to a better neighborhood, or have another baby. Sometimes she went to a doctor with symptoms she could hardly describe: "A tired feeling—I get so angry with the children it scares me—I feel like crying without any reason."

In 1960 the problem that has no name burst through the image of the happy American housewife. In the television commercials the pretty housewives still smiled over their foaming dishpans. But the actual unhappiness of the American housewife was suddenly being reported, although almost everybody who talked about it found some easy reason to explain it away.

The problem was explained away by telling the housewife she didn t realize how lucky she was. What if she wasn't happy—did she think men were happy in this world? Did she really, secretly, still want to be a man? Didn t she know yet how lucky she was to be a woman?

The problem was also explained away by saying that there are no solutions. This is what being a woman means. What is wrong with American women that they can't accept their role gracefully?

By 1962 the plight of the trapped American housewife had become a national game. Whole issues of magazines, newspaper columns, books, educational conferences, and television panels were devoted to the problem.

Even so, most men, and some women, still did not know that this problem was real. But those who had faced it honestly knew that all the easy remedies did not work. They got all kinds of advice on how to adjust to their role as housewives. No other road to fulfillment was offered to American women in the 1950's. Most adjusted to their role and suffered or ignored the problem that has no name.

*   *   *   *

It is no longer possible to ignore, to explain away, the desperation of so many American women. This is not what being a woman means, no matter what the experts say. Perhaps the reason has not been found because the right questions have not been asked, or pressed far enough. The women who suffer from this problem have a hunger that food cannot fill. It may not even be felt by women with desperate problems of hunger poverty, or illness. And women who think it will be solved by more money, a bigger house, a second car, moving to a better suburb, often discover it gets worse.

It is no longer possible today to blame the problem on loss of femininity, or to say that education and independence and equality with men have made American women unfeminine. I have heard so many women try to deny this dissatisfied voice within themselves because it does not fit the pretty picture of femininity the experts have given them.

If I am right, the problem that has no name stirring in the minds of so many American women today is not a matter of loss of femininity or too much education or the demands of taking care of a house and family. It is far more important than anyone recognizes. It is the key to these other new and old problems which have been torturing women and their husbands and children for years. It may well be the key to our future as a nation and a culture. We can no longer ignore that voice within women that says: "I want something more than my husband and my children and my home."

THE GAINS OF FEMINISM

When Linda Gray Sexton graduated from college in the mid-1970's, she and her classmates felt that all options were open to them: career, marriage, and motherhood. Sexton's mother had given her a copy of *The Feminine Mystique* when she was a girl, and she had found Betty Friedan "a friendly girder of support" as she contemplated living in the "two worlds" of career woman and wife-mother.

But reality seemed more complex. Some of Sexton's friends were poorly prepared for vocations. Others, trying to exercise all their options, teetered constantly on the edge of exhaustion. What was wrong? Like Friedan before her, Sexton (about the right age to be Friedan's daughter) embarked on a series of interviews. Here she summarizes her findings.

What, according to Sexton, is the "feminist mystique"? Why has the women's movement failed to solve all of women's problems? What has it achieved?

From pages 253-55 in Between Two Worlds *by Linda Gray Sexton. Copyright © 1979 by Linda Gray Sexton. Adapted by permission of William Morrow & Company.*

The femin*ine* mystique preached that women didn't need a variety of choices because biology determined that they would be wives and mothers. The femin*ist* mystique said that women didn't need a variety of choices because choice in itself was unnecessary, limiting, and defeatist. In the long run, then, there was only one difference between the two. One gave birth to boredom—for those not suited to housewifery. The other led to exhaustion—for those not geared to "Superwomanhood." From the women I interviewed, one message stood out clearly: blind acceptance of the femin*ist* mystique is as much an unthinking observance of a new tradition as blind acceptance of the femin*ine* mystique was an unthinking observance of the old. Once again, a problem has arisen because a system of values has been applied to an entire population.

A few months ago, in the midst of my writing, an acquaintance told me a story that seemed to sum up some of the problems faced by our generation. She had recently become a mother, while simultaneously teaching full time at a nearby university. Using a day-care center—which she had applied to months in advance—she clockworked her schedule down to the minute. Racing between home, the university, and the center, she managed to keep it all together. Both she and her husband worked four days a week as a compromise. But now, even looking back on that time makes her feel exhausted. She realizes that her attempt not to shortchange the needs of her baby, her husband, or her career resulted in shortchanging the most important needs of all—her own. She had proved she could do it, but at what cost to herself?

The oversimplified teachings of women's liberation have been no cure-all. The movement promised that if women worked they would be happy and fulfilled. But as more and more of us have ventured out into the business world, universal happiness has not descended. Universal confusion has, however. Women are finally beginning to wake up to a basic truth, a truth men have taken for granted and accepted for generations: work is *work*—not play. Work is not always fulfillment. It is 90 percent drudgery and 10 percent illumination—like motherhood. Its satisfactions are not sufficient for everyone.

The Women's Movement has made great strides in winning the equal rights women deserve as a group. But it has failed as a miracle drug—it has not cured the unhappiness of all individual American women. Before we are women, after all, we are people. Many of our discontents can only be solved by us alone, for ourselves alone. Even when a woman adopts feminist teachings wholeheartedly and makes no choice between parenthood and career, even when her husband rearranges his own career, there is still a price to be paid. And, ultimately, it is the woman herself who bears the cost.

With nearly all doors open to us, with increasing legislation in our favor, with more and more of us flowing into the job market at one time or another, are we more content, more fulfilled than our mothers were? I think not. I think it would be accurate to say we are overwhelmingly confused about who we are—just as confused as our mothers were, if not more so. We are trapped between one mystique and the other, and the way to freedom is not at all clear. Even worse, we are often ashamed to voice our feelings of conflict because we live in a time when women are supposed to be free of conflict.

We are the products of two vastly different worlds, forged in the fire of dissent and strife. While it is difficult to generalize about fifteen women so very different as those presented [in the book Sexton has written], one feeling common to them all is frighteningly clear. Wherever they come from, whatever they do, whoever they are, they all feel an increasing need to choose between the two worlds, to simplify their lives, to stop straddling the fence. I see a new and painful light dawning in their eyes, a new acknowledgment of the need to choose. Some realize it with horror, as it increases the immediate pressure. Others realize it with heartfelt relief because facing it releases some of the tension.

Each and every one of us finds the idea of making choices frightening: to make a choice is to take a risk. Studies show that women don't like risk—they see it as a possibility only for loss, while men tend to see it as an equally balanced chance for loss *or gain.* Now, for the first time in history, an entire generation of women is being asked—as men have been for years—to choose their destiny, to take risks. Now, even if a woman elects traditional family-oriented life, it is a *choice,* a gamble—not a passive assumption of the inevitable.

Contrary to what the Women's Movement says, it matters little which kind of choice we make, so long as we take the risk of making that choice for ourselves. The opportunity to choose is that which, in the long run, feminism has really given us. This is what we have gained—and it is both a blessing and a curse, both liberating and painful, but never, as we were taught, easy or natural.

CHAPTER 25
INTO THE FUTURE

IMPROVING THE QUALITY OF LIFE

As the United States entered the last decades of the 1900's, Americans were deeply concerned about the nation's economy. They were increasingly concerned, too, about the quality of life. There was a feeling that material progress alone was not enough to satisfy society's needs. Here one observer, Angus Campbell, discusses what he calls "the public sense of well-being."

In the thirty years after World War II, what happened to economic life in America? What trends caused dissatisfaction? What "nonmaterial needs" did people want to satisfy? According to Campbell, why has government not dealt with these needs?

In his State of the Union Message in 1970, Richard M. Nixon observed: "In the next 10 years we will increase our wealth by 50 percent. The profound question is, Does this mean that we will be 50 percent richer in any real sense, 50 percent better off, 50 percent happier?" Now, 10 years later, it is clear that he overestimated the nation's economic growth. But his "profound question" still remains: Does increasing affluence mean a greater sense of public well-being?

For the last 100 years, we have had a strong faith in the power of economic prosperity to bring about the good life. It would be hard to argue that over that century of increasing affluence, the life of the average American has not been improved. Small wonder that the Gross National Product [the yearly total value of all the goods and services produced by the nation] and other economic indicators have, as a government publication put it, "become so much a part of our thinking that we tend to equate a rising national income with national well-being."

Sometime during the 30 years following World War II, however, something went wrong with this simple tie between economic welfare and the public sense of well-being. Americans experienced one of the most dazzling rises in economic affluence in the nation's history. Average family income went up by about two-thirds between 1945 and 1973, a remarkable national achievement. But, as we increased the ability of our people to purchase the material things of life, we also experienced a great increase in divorce, illegitimacy, juvenile delinquency, and suicide. In addition, there was a growing fear of criminal assault, the development of a widespread drug culture, a spreading distrust of government, and a general dissatisfaction with the state of the nation. National surveys demonstrate that as economic welfare increased during the postwar period, psychological well-being declined, especially among the young, the affluent, and the well-educated.

Many factors contributed to this turn of events. One appears to be the nature of affluence itself. Public aspirations and values can no longer be as readily satisfied by simple increases in economic affluence as they may have been earlier in our history. There appear to be a growing number of people for whom economic circumstances are no longer what determines their sense of well-being. Economic man is being replaced by psychological man. These are people for whom "higher needs" have become important. This conclusion is supported by studies in [Europe], Canada and this country that find income to be losing its relationship to the way people describe the psychological quality of their lives.

This decline in the significance of income occurs primarily among the more advantaged parts of the population. It does not mean that people have lost interest in having the material things and other benefits that income makes possible.

What appears to have happened is that an increasing number of people have achieved a degree of economic security. This has liberated them from an overwhelming concern with income. Thus there is an increase in the importance of nonmaterial needs—the need for a sensitive and responsive marital relationship, for challenging and significant work, for the respect and approval of friends, for identification with community, and for a stimulating and fulfilling life.

Senator Daniel Patrick Moynihan [of New York] once observed that governments seldom do anything about a problem until they have learned to count it. Governments have well-established ways of responding to public needs for a minimum income, adequate housing, and medical care. But they have a more difficult time with such feelings as boredom, job dissatisfaction, fear of crime, loneliness, resentment of discrimination, loss of confidence in authority, and other conditions that diminish the quality of people's lives. They do not have a clear sense of how widespread these problems are or a sure feeling of how to deal with them.

At present, inflation and unemployment are creating economic stress for many Americans. Our governmental officials are understandably obsessed with their problems. Eventually, however, the national agenda will have to give greater prominence to the psychological needs of the population than it has in the past.

We must recognize that people may be deprived psychologically as well as economically. As economic needs are met, psychological needs assume priority.

A government that aspires to raise the national quality of life must concern itself with both.

A TROUBLED ECONOMY

Beginning in the early 1970's, inflation became a serious problem in the United States. Americans were deeply concerned about its impact on their ment and a decline in productivity. They asked what could be done to help the troubled economy.

The two selections that follow discuss the nation's economic difficulties. In the first, Lester Thurow, an economist at the Massachusetts Institute of Technology, explains why he thinks the economy is in trouble. In the second, President Reagon puts forward his program for recovery.

What is a "zero-sum game," according to Thurow? Why does he feel the nation's economy is unable to handle such a situation? According to Reagan, what should the government's taxing power be used for? What should it *not* be used for? Do you find areas where Thurow and Reagan agree? Where they disagree?

From The Zero-Sum Society: Distribution and the Possibilities for Economic Change *by Lester C. Thurow. Copyright ©* *1980 by Basic Books, Inc. By permission of Basic Books, Inc., Publishers, New York.*

Condensed from Ronald Reagan "State of the Union Message on Economic Recovery," in The New York Times, *Feb. 19, 1981.*

[THUROW]

[By the late 1970's] seemingly unsolvable problems were emerging everywhere—inflation, unemployment, slow growth, environmental decay, conflicting group demands, and complex, cumbersome regulations. Were the problems unsolvable or were our leaders incompetent? Had Americans lost the work ethic? Had we stopped inventing new processes and products? Should we invest more and consume less? Do we need to junk our social welfare, health, safety, and environmental protection systems in order to compete? Why were others doing better?

The hard-core conservative solution [to our economic problems] is to "liberate free enterprise," reduce social expenditures, restructure taxes to encourage saving and investment (shift the tax burden from those who save, the rich, to those who consume, the poor), and eliminate government rules and regulations that do not help business. Only by returning to the virtues of hard work and free enterprise can the economy be saved.

In thinking about this solution, it is well to remember that none of our competitors became successful by following this route. Government absorbs slightly over 30 percent of the GNP [Gross National Product] in the United States, but over 50 percent of the GNP in West Germany. Fifteen other countries collect a larger fraction of their GNP in taxes.

Ours is not the economy with the most rules and regulations. On the contrary, it is the one with the fewest rules and regulations. As many American firms have discovered to their horror, it simply isn't possible to fire workers abroad as it is here. It is a dubious achievement, but nowhere in the world is it easier to lay off workers.

Nor have our competitors unleashed work effort and savings by increasing income differentials [that is, allowing bigger gaps between rich and poor]. Indeed, they have done exactly the opposite. If you look at the earnings gap between the top and bottom 10 percent of the population, the West Germans work hard with 36 percent less inequality than we, and the Japanese work even harder with 50 percent less inequality. If income differentials encourage individual initiative, we should be full of initiative, since among industrialized countries, only the French surpass us in terms of inequality.

Moreover, our own history shows that our economic performance since the New Deal and the onset of governmental "interference" has been better than it was prior to the New Deal. As both our experience and foreign experience demonstrate, there is no conflict between social spending or government intervention and economic success. As we, and others, have shown, social reforms can be productive, as well as just, if done in the right way. If done in the wrong way, they can, of course, be both disastrous and unjust. There may also be some merit in "liberating free enterprise" if it is done in the right way. There are certainly unnecessary rules and regulations that are now strangling our economy. The trick is not rules versus no rules, but finding the right rules.

The American problem is not returning to some golden age of economic growth (there was no such golden age) but in recognizing that we have an economic structure that has never in its entire history performed as well as Japan and West Germany have performed since World War II. We are now the ones who must copy and adapt the policies and innovations that have been successful elsewhere. To retreat into our mythical past is to guarantee that our days of economic glory are over.

But our problems are not limited to slow growth. Throughout our society there are painful, persistent problems that are not being solved. Energy, inflation, unemployment, environmental decay, ever-spreading waves of regulations, sharp income gaps between minorities and majorities—the list is almost endless. Because of our inability to solve these problems, the lament is often heard that the U.S. economy and political system have lost their ability to get things done.

The problem is real, but it has not been properly diagnosed. One cannot lose an ability that one never had. What is perceived as a lost ability to act is in fact (1) a shift from international cold war problems to domestic problems. It is also (2) an inability to impose large economic losses explicitly [that is, openly and frankly].

As domestic problems rise in importance relative to international problems, action becomes increasingly difficult. International conflicts can be, and to some extent are, portrayed as situations where everyone is fairly sharing sacrifices to hold the foreign enemy in check. Since every member of society is facing a common threat, an overwhelming consensus can be achieved. Domestic problems are much more difficult. When policies are adopted to solve domestic problems, there are American winners and American losers. Some incomes go up as a result of the solution, but others go down. Individuals do not sacrifice equally. Some gain; some lose. A program to raise the occupational position of women and minorities automatically lowers the occupational position of white men. Every black or female appointed to a President's cabinet is one less white male who can be appointed.

Secondly, the solutions to our problems have a common characteristic. Each requires that some large group—sometimes a minority and sometimes the majority—be willing to tolerate a large reduction in their real standard of living. When the economic pluses and minuses are added up, the pluses usually exceed the minuses. But there are large economic losses. These have to be allocated to someone, and no group wants to be the group that must suffer economic losses for the general good.

This is the heart of our fundamental problem. Our political and economic structure simply isn't able to cope with an economy that has a substantial zero-sum element. A zero-sum game is any game where the losses exactly equal the winnings. All sporting events are zero-sum games. For every winner there is a loser. Winners can only exist if losers exist. What the winning gambler wins, the losing gambler must lose.

When there are large losses to be allocated, any economic decision has a large zero-sum element. The economic gains may exceed the economic losses, but the losses are so large as to [cancel out much of the gain]. What is more important, the gains and losses are not allocated to the same individuals or groups. On average, society may be better off, but this average hides a large number of people who are much better off and large numbers of people who are much worse off.

The problem with zero-sum games is that the essence of problem solving is loss allocation [deciding who will suffer losses]. But this is precisely what our political process is least capable of doing. When there are economic gains to be allocated, our political process can allocate them. When there are large economic losses to be allocated, our political process is paralyzed. And with political paralysis comes economic paralysis.

Lacking a consensus on whose income ought to go down, or even the recognition that this is at the heart of the problem, we are paralyzed. We dislike the current situation, we wish to do something about our problems, but we endure them because we have not learned to play an economic game with a substantial zero-sum element.

*   *   *   *

[REAGAN]

I'm here tonight to ask that we share in restoring the promise that is offered to every citizen by this, the last, best hope of man on earth.

All of us are aware of the punishing inflation which has, for the first time in 60 years, held to double-digit figures for two years in a row [that is, figures over 9 percent]. Interest rates have reached absurd levels of more than 20 percent and over 15 percent for those who would borrow to buy a home. All across this land one can see newly built homes standing vacant, unsold because of mortgage interest rates.

Almost eight million Americans are out of

work. These are people who want to be productive. But as the months go by, despair dominates their lives. The threats of layoff and unemployment hang over other millions, and all who work are frustrated by their inability to keep up with inflation.

One worker in a Midwest city put it to me this way. He said: "I'm bringing home more dollars than I ever believed I could possibly earn but I seem to be getting worse off." And he is. Not only have hourly earnings of the American worker, after adjusting for inflation, declined 5 percent over the past five years, but in these five years, Federal personal taxes for the average family have increased 67 percent.

We can no longer procrastinate and hope that things will get better. They will not. Unless we act forcefully, and now, the economy will get worse.

Can we who man the ship of state deny it is somewhat out of control? Our national debt is approaching $1 trillion. The interest on the public debt this year will be over $90 billion.

Adding to our troubles is a mass of regulations imposed on the shopkeeper, the farmer, the craftsman, professionals and major industry that is estimated to add $100 billion to the price of the things we buy. And it reduces our ability to produce. The rate of increase in American productivity, once one of the highest in the world, is among the lowest of all major industrial nations. Indeed, it has actually declined in the last three years.

Now I've painted a pretty grim picture, but I think I've painted it accurately. It is within our power to change this picture and we can act with hope. There's nothing wrong with our internal strengths. There has been no breakdown in the human, technological and natural resources upon which the economy is built.

Based on this confidence in a system which has never failed us—but which we have failed through a lack of confidence, and sometimes through a belief that we could fine-tune the economy and get a tune to our liking—I am proposing a comprehensive four-point program.

This plan is aimed at reducing the growth in Government spending and taxing, reforming and eliminating regulations which are unnecessary and unproductive, or counterproductive, and encouraging a policy aimed at maintaining the value of the currency.

If enacted in full, this program can help America create 13 million new jobs, nearly three million more than we would without these measures. It will also help us to gain control of inflation.

It's important to note that we're only reducing the rate of increase in taxing and spending. We are not attempting to cut either spending or taxing levels below that which we presently have. This plan will get our economy moving again and thus create the jobs that our people must have.

[Reagan next discusses some details of his four main proposals: (1) reducing federal spending by tightening or eliminating various aid programs; (2) across-the-board tax cuts for individuals and businesses; (3) reducing the number of federal regulations; and (4) slowing the growth of the money supply.]

This, then, is our proposal. "America's New Beginning: A Program for Economic Recovery." I don't want it to be simply the plan of my Administration—I'm here tonight to ask you to join me in making it our plan. Together, we can embark on this road—not to make things easy, but to make things better.

Our social political and cultural, as well as our economic institutions, can no longer absorb the repeated shocks that have been dealt them over the past decades.

Can we do the job? The answer is yes. But we must begin now.

We are in control here. There's nothing wrong with America that together we can't fix.

I'm sure there will be some who will raise the familiar old cry, "Don't touch my program—cut somewhere else."

I hope I've made it plain that our approach has been even-handed; that only the programs for the truly deserving needy remain untouched.

The question is, are we simply going to go down the same path we've gone down before—carving out one special program here, another special program there? I don't think that's what they want. They are ready to return to the source of our strength.

The substance and prosperity of our nation is built by wages brought home from the factories and the mills, the farms and the shops.

They are the services provided in 10.000 corners of America; the interest on the thrift of our people and the returns for their risk-taking. The production of America is the possession of those who build, serve, create and produce.

For too long now, we've removed from our

people the decisions on how to dispose of what they created. We've strayed from first principles. We must alter our course.

The taxing power of Government must be used to provide revenues for legitimate Government purposes. It must not be used to regulate the economy or bring about social change. We've tried that and surely we must be able to see it doesn't work.

Spending by Government must be limited to those functions which are the proper province of Government. We can no longer afford things simply because we think of them.

I would direct a question to those who have indicated already an unwillingness to accept such a plan: Have they an alternative which offers a greater chance of balancing the budget, reducing and eliminating inflation, stimulating the creation of jobs and reducing the tax burden? And, if they haven't, are they suggesting we can continue on the present course without coming to a day of reckoning?

If we don't do this, inflation and the growing tax burden will put an end to everything we believe in and our dreams for the future. We don't have an option of living with inflation and its attendant tragedy, millions of productive people willing and able to work but unable to find a buyer for their work in the job market.

We have an alternative and that is a program for economic recovery.

True, it will take time for the favorable effects of our proposal to be felt. So we must begin now.

The people are watching and waiting. They don't demand miracles. They do expect us to act. Let us act together.

THE ENERGY CRISIS

One of the foundations of American prosperity was cheap energy. At home, coal and oil were abundant. Additional supplies from foreign sources seemed assured. Suddenly, in 1973, the situation changed. At this time Israel was successfully pushing back Egypt and Syria after attacks by these two Arab nations. In response the largely Arab membership of the Organization of Petroleum Exporting Countries (OPEC) cut back oil production and began an embargo of the United States and several other nations friendly to Israel. Although the boycott ended in a few months, the price of oil had soared and continued to rise in following years.

Most Americans agreed that they faced an energy crisis. They disagreed, though, about its nature and how best to cope with it. One set of solutions was offered in a report of the Energy Project of the Harvard Business School. The selection that follows is from the report's introductory chapter.

As the editors see it, what is the "key contradiction" of the energy crisis? What future do they see for the four conventional sources of domestic energy? What unconventional source do they regard most highly?

From Energy Future: Report of the Energy Project at the Harvard Business School *edited by Robert Stobaugh and Daniel Yergin. Copyright © 1979 by Robert Stobaugh and Daniel Yergin, Reprinted by permission of Random House, Inc.*

In 1970, some 111 years after the birth of the American oil industry, domestic production peaked and began to decline. But the demand for oil continued to surge. That demand could be met only by more and more oil from the Middle East. This meant increasing dependence — and increasing vulnerability. The idea that there was something threatening in the growing dependence was an idea better ignored. Even if one recognized a potential problem, what to do about it was hardly clear. . . .

The first oil shock, in late 1973 and early 1974, definitely marked the end of the era of secure and cheap oil. Arab oil producers embargoed the United States and reduced overall output and shipments to other nations. For the first time, these producers stopped negotiating a price with the oil companies. Instead they set the price on a take-it-or-leave-it basis. The oil buyers had no choice, and they took it, paying the higher price — eight times higher by the end of 1974 than five years earlier. And so the petroleum exporting countries defined a new era for the rest of the world — one of insecure supplies of expensive oil.

Yet today, as we enter the 1980's, even after the second oil shock that accompanied the fall of the Shah of Iran, the cause and consequences of the new era of oil have yet to be taken seriously in the United States. They key contradiction is this: While the declared aim of American policy is to reduce the use of imported oil, the United States is in fact becoming more and more dependent upon it. Between 1973 and early 1979, U.S. oil imports almost doubled, and had begun to provide half of the nation's oil. By current trends the United States will be even more dependent on imported oil in the 1980's.

Does this matter?

We think it does. . . . Imported oil poses too many risks to be calmly accepted. . . . The United States should make a much greater attempt to stop the growth of its oil imports.

But can the United States do this? There are four conventional sources of domestic energy: oil, natural gas, coal, and nuclear power. But all four are likely to deliver less energy than their advocates would lead one to believe.

In the debate about oil, three main domestic oil "solutions" have been put forward as alternatives to imported petroleum. They are to break up the industry, to decontrol oil prices (and lease more land), and to use unconventional technology. The first two are important and controversial political questions because they affect the distribution of income and power in America. But the "solutions" have little to do with increasing production. Whether the industry is or is not broken up, whether prices are or are not deregulated, the physical production of oil from conventional sources will continue to decline. At best, . . . unconventional means can help to keep domestic supplies flowing at current levels. To be sure, outside the United States new oil fields in Mexico and China are important and will add to world supplies. But they are unlikely to make a substantial change in the world oil balance.

Natural gas accounts for over a quarter of America's energy needs. It has also been caught in a great domestic debate. Should it continue to be deregulated, with price based on value? As in the case of oil, the debate is about money and who gets it. But . . . the best that one can expect is that a deregulated price will enable natural gas production to remain at current levels.

A major goal of President Carter's National Energy Plan has been the substitution of domestically produced coal for imported oil. Given America's great coal reserves, this appears possible on paper, but in practice it probably is not. For coal to do what the Carter Administration wants it to do, a traditionally backward industry must be suddenly transformed into a modern, technologically advanced one. Potential users are reluctant to commit themselves to coal, especially because of the uncertainty about meeting environmental requirements. Coal's contribution, . . . therefore, is likely to prove more limited than the Administration plans. However, its importance is still likely to grow, particularly for utilities.

Nuclear power is the other conventional alternative in which high hopes are placed. Yet, the further development of nuclear power is hindered by controversy. . . . It is too soon to judge the long-term consequences for the nuclear power industry of the nuclear accident at Harrisburg [the 1979 accident at Three Mile Island]. It seems safe to say that it hardly improves the industry's prospects. Even without a Harrisburg, however, the problem of what to do with nuclear waste is so confused, and so far from being settled, that it could result in a decline in the energy produced by nuclear power in the next decade. Moreover, one should remember how limited the potential of atomic power is under the best circumstances. If nuclear power capacity *doubled* in ten years, it would still be providing less than 7 percent of America's total energy.

In short, there is little reason to expect conventional alternatives to make a sizable contribution to reducing our dependence on imported oil. These energy sources . . . as a group can increase their contribution to cover, at most, one third to one half of the nation's additional energy needs over the next decade.

On the other hand, the unconventional alternatives, which tend to be played down, can make a much greater contribution than is normally assumed. The unconventional . . . alternatives should be given a fair chance. To date, they have not received anything like that. According to one estimate, conventional energy sources have received more than $120 billion in incentives and subsidies. At the same time, the unconventional sources have received virtually nothing by comparison. . . .

Among the unconventional sources of energy, conservation offers the most immediate opportunity. It should be regarded as a largely untapped source of energy. Indeed, conservation — not coal or nuclear energy — is the major alternative to imported oil. It could perhaps "supply" up to 40 percent of America's current energy usage, although we do not predict that it will. Moreover, the evidence suggests that . . . a conservation strategy could actually spur economic growth. Conservation does not require technological breakthroughs. But it has been difficult to tap, because a consistent set of signals — price, incentives, and regulations — is not in place. Moreover, . . . decisions to conserve, unlike decisions to produce energy, have to be made by millions and millions of often poorly informed people.

The range of energy possibilities grouped under the heading "solar" could meet one fifth of U.S. energy needs within two decades. Like conservation, solar energy faces a problem of decentralized decision-making. Moreover, the most promising short-term solar energy applications use existing, relatively simple technologies. These are receiving less support than the more uncertain more distant high-technology solar applications. Low-technology solar energy can make a significant contribution. But like conservation, it needs a more consistent framework of price, incentive, and regulation.

Some people may charge that the authors are romantics opposed to economic growth, or that we advocate basic changes in the way the society is organized. We are not and we do not. . . . Genuine alternatives for energy do exist and we want to contribute to the clarification of the choices. We also believe that it is unwise to ask conventional sources to do more than they really can and by so doing to block the move to a more balanced energy system. . . .

No easy remedy will solve the energy crisis. Solutions, however, will emerge from a recognition and comparison of benefits and risks, possibilities and obstacles, across a wide range. Political choices are therefore involved, which is why the energy crisis is a crisis of our political system.

CONCERN FOR THE ENVIRONMENT

For a long time Americans exploited the rich resources of their land with little thought of the future. They stripped trees and minerals from the earth, poured wastes into the water, and filled the air with smoke and chemicals. Not until the mid-1900's did they begin to see what was happening to their environment.

A major factor in their new awareness was the warning voice of Rachel Carson. A zoologist, she was particularly concerned about the effects of such insecticides and pesticides as DDT. In 1962 she published a book called *Silent Spring,* which was widely read and enormously influential. Carson's title referred to some future spring season when migratory birds—their numbers greatly reduced by pollution—would fail to arrive. It was a frightening picture of a world slowly dying. In this selection Carson warns that human beings have acquired "significant power to change the nature of their world."

Why are chemicals potentially so dangerous? What is the "endless spiral" that results? What does the author propose?

The history of life on earth has been a history of interaction between living things and their surroundings. To a large extent the physical form and the habits of the earth's plant life and its animal life have been molded by the environment. Considering the whole span of earthly time, the opposite effect, in which life actually modifies or changes its surroundings, has been relatively slight. Only within the moment of time represented by the present century has one species—human beings—acquired significant power to change the nature of their world.

During the past twenty-five years this power has not only increased to one of disturbing magnitude but it has changed in character. The most alarming of all human assaults upon the environment is the contamination of air, earth, and water with dangerous and even deadly materials. . . . The chain of evil that pollution begins, not only in the world that must support life but in living tissues, is for the most part irreversible.

In this now universal contamination of the environment, chemicals are the evil and little recognized partners of radiation in changing the very nature of the world—the very nature of its life. Strontium 90 released through nuclear explosions into the air, comes to earth in rain or drifts down as fallout. It lodges in soil, enters into the grass or corn or wheat grown there, and in time ends up in the bones of a human being, there to remain until death. Similarly, chemicals sprayed on croplands or forests or gardens lie long in soil. They enter into living organisms, passing from one to another in a chain of poisoning and death. Or they pass mysteriously by underground streams until they emerge and . . . combine into new forms that kill plants, sicken cattle, and work unknown harm on those who drink from once pure wells. . . .

It took hundreds of millions of years to produce the life that now inhabits the earth. During that time developing and evolving life reached a state of adjustment and balance with its surroundings. The environment, shaping and directing the life it supported, contained elements that were hostile as well as supporting. Certain rocks gave out dangerous radiation. Even within the light of the sun, from which all life draws its energy, there were short-wave radiations with power to injure. Given time — time not in years but in thousands of years — life adjusts, and a balance has been reached. For time is the essential ingredient. But in the modern world there is no time.

The rapidity of change and the speed with which new situations are created follow the rapid pace of humans rather than the deliberate pace of nature. Radiation is no longer just the background radiation of rocks, the bombardment of cosmic rays, the ultraviolet of the sun, that have existed since before there was any life on earth. Radiation is now the unnatural creation of people's tampering with the atom. The chemicals to which life is asked to make its adjustment are no longer . . . just the minerals washed out of the rocks and carried in rivers to the sea. They are the synthetic creations of people's inventive minds, made in their laboratories, and having no counterparts in nature.

To adjust to these chemicals would require time on the scale that is nature's. It would require not just the years of a person's life but the life of generations. And even this, if possible, would be hopeless, for the new chemicals come from our laboratories in an endless stream. Every year almost 500 chemicals find their way into actual use in the United States alone. The figure is staggering, and all its meanings are not easily grasped — 500 new chemicals to which the bodies of people and animals are required somehow to adapt each year, chemicals totally outside the limits of biologic experience.

Among them are many that are used in people's war against nature. Since the mid-1940's over 200 basic chemicals have been created for use in killing insects, weeds, rodents, and other organisms described as "pests." They are sold under several thousand different brand names.

These sprays, dusts, and aerosols are now applied almost universally to farms, gardens, forests, and homes — nonselective chemicals that have the power to kill every insect, the "good" and the "bad," to still the song of birds and the leaping of fish in the streams, to coat the leaves with a deadly film, and to linger on in the soil — all this though the intended target may be only a few weeds or insects. Can anyone believe it is possible to lay down such a barrage of poisons on the surface of the earth without making it unfit for all life? . . .

The whole process of spraying seems caught up in an endless spiral. Since DDT was released for civilian use, a process of escalation has been going on in which ever more poisonous materials must be found. This has happened because insects . . . have evolved super races immune to the particular insecticide used. Hence a deadlier one has always to be developed — and then a deadlier one than that. . . . Thus the chemical war is never won, and all life is caught in its violent crossfire. . . .

It is not my belief that chemical insecticides must never be used. I do say that we have put poisonous and biologically powerful chemicals into the hands of persons largely or wholly ignorant of their potentials for harm. We have subjected enormous numbers of people to contact with these poisons, without their consent and often without their knowledge. If the Bill of Rights contains no guarantee that a citizen shall be secure against deadly poisons distributed either by private individuals or by public officials, it is surely only because those who wrote it, despite their wisdom and foresight, could conceive of no such problem.

I say, furthermore, that we have allowed these chemicals to be used with little or no advance investigation of their effect on soil, water, wildlife, and people themselves. Future generations are unlikely to overlook our lack of wise concern for the integrity of the natural world that supports all life.

There is still very limited awareness of the nature of the threat. This is an era of specialists, each of whom sees his or her own problem and is unaware of or intolerant of the larger frame into which it fits. It is also an era dominated by industry, in which the right to make a dollar at whatever cost is seldom challenged. When the public protests, confronted with some obvious evidence of damaging results of pesticide applications, it is fed little tranquilizing pills of half truth. We urgently need an end to these false assurances, to the sugar coating of unacceptable facts. It is the public that is being asked to assume the risks that the insect controllers calculate. The public must decide whether it wishes to continue on the present road, and it can do so only when in full possession of the facts.

Historical
Atlas

of the
United States

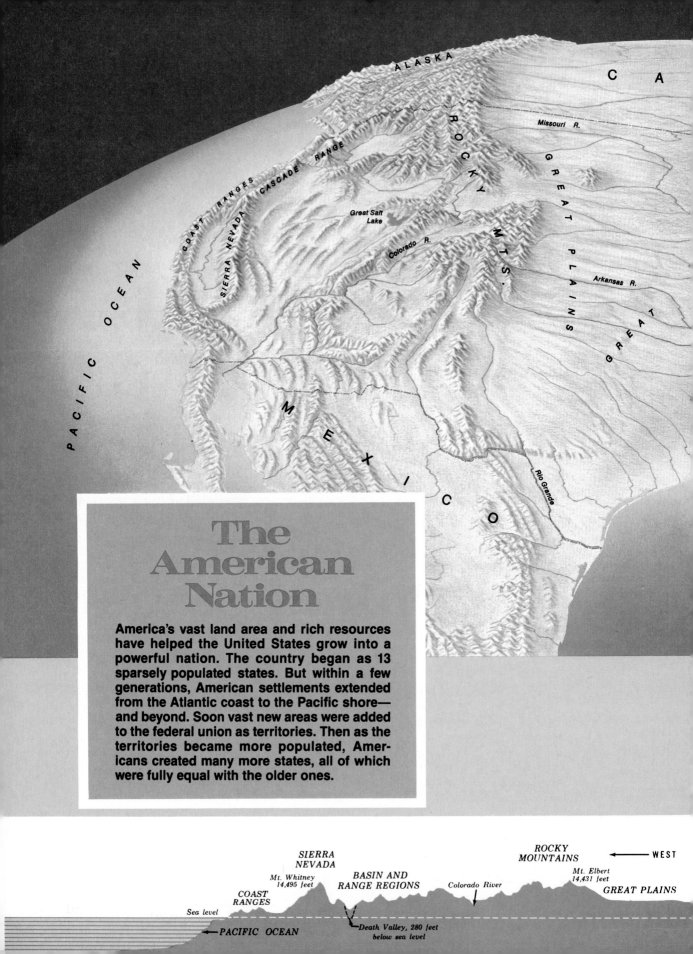

The American Nation

America's vast land area and rich resources
have helped the United States grow into a
powerful nation. The country began as 13
sparsely populated states. But within a few
generations, American settlements extended
from the Atlantic coast to the Pacific shore—
and beyond. Soon vast new areas were added
to the federal union as territories. Then as the
territories became more populated, Americans created many more states, all of which
were fully equal with the older ones.

ALASKA

CA

Missouri R.

COAST RANGES

CASCADE RANGE

SIERRA NEVADA

Great Salt
Lake

Colorado R.

ROCKY

MTS.

GREAT PLAINS

Arkansas R.

GREAT

PACIFIC OCEAN

MEXICO

Rio Grande

COAST
RANGES

Sea level

PACIFIC OCEAN

SIERRA
NEVADA

Mt. Whitney
14,495 feet

BASIN AND
RANGE REGIONS

Death Valley, 280 feet
below sea level

Colorado River

ROCKY
MOUNTAINS

Mt. Elbert
14,431 feet

GREAT PLAINS

WEST

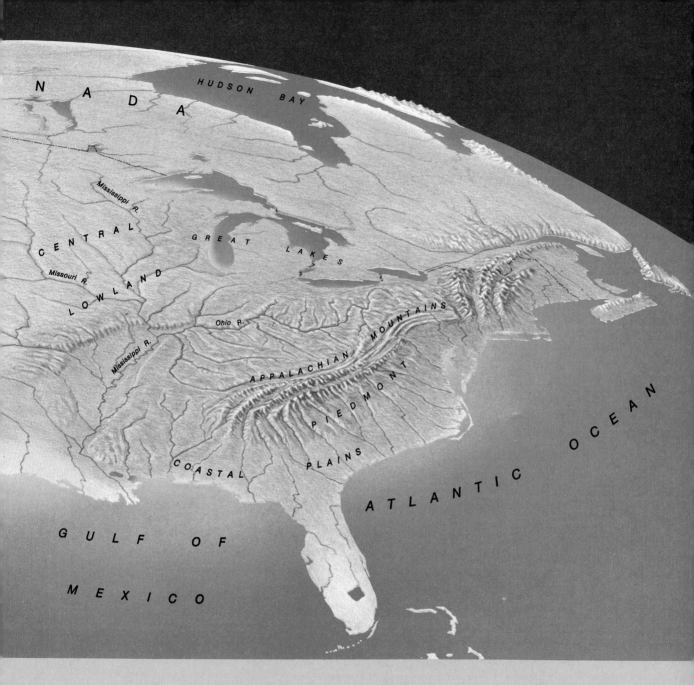

Above is a revealing view of the United States from far above the earth's surface—a view of the country's varied natural features as an astronaut might see them if there were no clouds to hinder observation. The elevation profile below has never been seen by astronauts or anyone else, for this drawing depicts how the country would look if a deep trench were cut from one end of the United States to the other. It reveals a side view of the natural features of the land. See if you can locate the same mountain ranges, plains, and river valleys depicted on both the map and the elevation profile.

EAST ⟶

CENTRAL   LOWLAND

APPALACHIAN
HIGHLANDS

Mt. Mitchell
6,684 feet

PRAIRIES OZARK MTS. ⌐Mississippi River   COASTAL
PLAIN

Sea level

ATLANTIC OCEAN ⟶

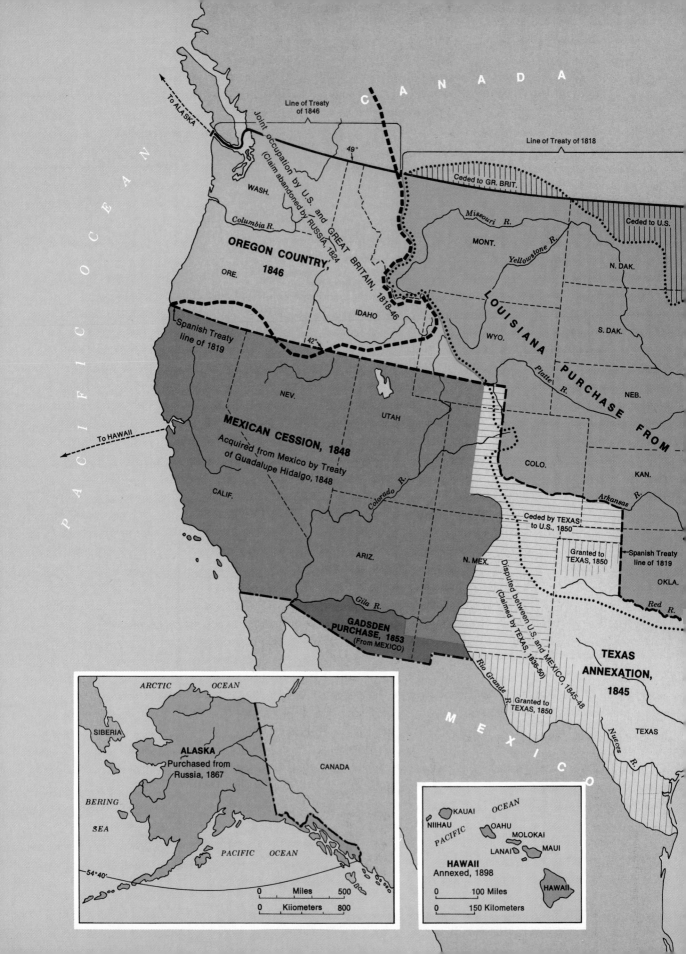

CANADA

Line of Treaty
of 1846

Line of Treaty of 1818

To ALASKA

Joint occupation by U.S. and GREAT BRITAIN, 1818-46
(Claim abandoned by RUSSIA, 1824)

49°

Ceded to GR. BRIT.

Ceded to U.S.

WASH.

Columbia R.

Missouri R.

MONT.

Yellowstone R.

N. DAK.

OREGON COUNTRY,
1846

ORE.

IDAHO

LOUISIANA

S. DAK.

WYO.

Platte R.

Spanish Treaty
line of 1819

42°

NEB.

PURCHASE FROM

NEV.

UTAH

MEXICAN CESSION, 1848

Acquired from Mexico by Treaty
of Guadalupe Hidalgo, 1848

COLO.

Ceded by TEXAS
to U.S., 1850

KAN.

To HAWAII

CALIF.

Colorado R.

ARIZ.

N. MEX.

Disputed between U.S. and MEXICO, 1845-48
(Claimed by TEXAS, 1836-50)

Granted to
TEXAS, 1850

Spanish Treaty
line of 1819

OKLA.

Arkansas R.

Red R.

Gila R.

GADSDEN
PURCHASE, 1853
(From MEXICO)

Rio Grande R.

Granted to
TEXAS, 1850

TEXAS
ANNEXATION,
1845

MEXICO

Nueces R.

TEXAS

PACIFIC OCEAN

Alaska inset:

ARCTIC OCEAN

SIBERIA

ALASKA
Purchased from
Russia, 1867

CANADA

BERING SEA

PACIFIC OCEAN

54°40'

0   Miles   500

0   Kilometers   800

Hawaii inset:

KAUAI

NIIHAU

OCEAN

OAHU

MOLOKAI

PACIFIC

LANAI   MAUI

HAWAII
Annexed, 1898

HAWAII

0   100 Miles

0   150 Kilometers

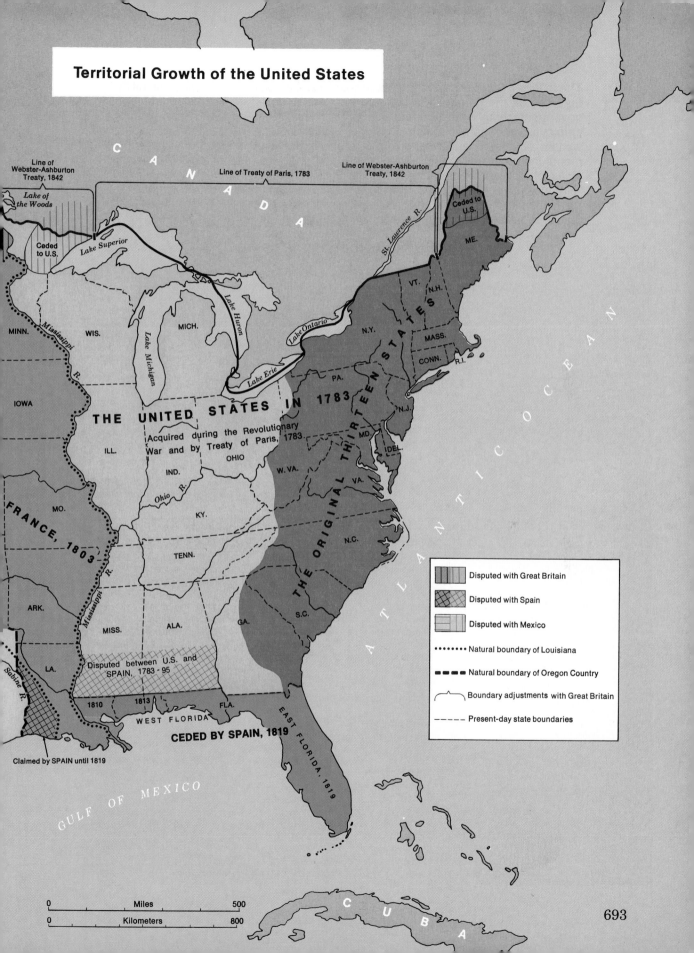

Territorial Growth of the United States

CANADA

Line of Webster-Ashburton Treaty, 1842

Line of Treaty of Paris, 1783

Line of Webster-Ashburton Treaty, 1842

Lake of the Woods

Ceded to U.S.

Ceded to U.S.

Lake Superior

St. Lawrence R.

ME.

MINN.

Mississippi R.

WIS.

Lake Michigan

MICH.

Lake Huron

Lake Ontario

VT.

N.H.

N.Y.

MASS.

CONN.

R.I.

Lake Erie

PA.

IOWA

ILL.

THE UNITED STATES IN 1783

Acquired during the Revolutionary War and by Treaty of Paris, 1783

IND.

OHIO

Ohio R.

W. VA.

N.J.

MD.

DEL.

VA.

THE ORIGINAL THIRTEEN STATES

FRANCE, 1803

MO.

KY.

Mississippi R.

TENN.

N.C.

ARK.

MISS.

ALA.

GA.

S.C.

Sabine R.

LA.

Disputed between U.S. and SPAIN, 1783 - 95

1810

1813

FLA.

WEST FLORIDA

EAST FLORIDA · 1819

CEDED BY SPAIN, 1819

Claimed by SPAIN until 1819

ATLANTIC OCEAN

GULF OF MEXICO

CUBA

Legend:

- Disputed with Great Britain
- Disputed with Spain
- Disputed with Mexico
- •••••• Natural boundary of Louisiana
- – – – Natural boundary of Oregon Country
- ⌣ Boundary adjustments with Great Britain
- – – – Present-day state boundaries

| 0 | Miles | 500 |
| 0 | Kilometers | 800 |

The federal government and the many state and local governments were small at first. But as the country's population and needs grew, so did the number of government employees. Federal, state, and local governments needed more employees and more money to meet their responsibilities in areas such as public welfare, education, and defense. To pay for the increased expenditures, governments increased taxes and added some new ones, such as income taxes and taxes for the social security fund. In recent years there have been many demands to reduce government taxes. There also have been demands for limiting government spending in many areas. You can become more informed about the issues raised in these demands by studying the graphs on the accompanying pages.

The Growth of the Federal Union

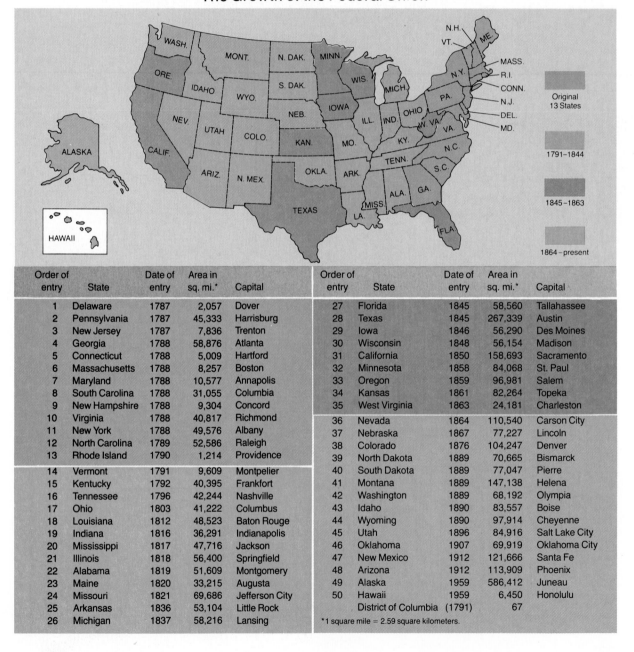

Original 13 States

1791–1844

1845–1863

1864–present

Order of entry	State	Date of entry	Area in sq. mi.*	Capital	Order of entry	State	Date of entry	Area in sq. mi.*	Capital
1	Delaware	1787	2,057	Dover	27	Florida	1845	58,560	Tallahassee
2	Pennsylvania	1787	45,333	Harrisburg	28	Texas	1845	267,339	Austin
3	New Jersey	1787	7,836	Trenton	29	Iowa	1846	56,290	Des Moines
4	Georgia	1788	58,876	Atlanta	30	Wisconsin	1848	56,154	Madison
5	Connecticut	1788	5,009	Hartford	31	California	1850	158,693	Sacramento
6	Massachusetts	1788	8,257	Boston	32	Minnesota	1858	84,068	St. Paul
7	Maryland	1788	10,577	Annapolis	33	Oregon	1859	96,981	Salem
8	South Carolina	1788	31,055	Columbia	34	Kansas	1861	82,264	Topeka
9	New Hampshire	1788	9,304	Concord	35	West Virginia	1863	24,181	Charleston
10	Virginia	1788	40,817	Richmond	36	Nevada	1864	110,540	Carson City
11	New York	1788	49,576	Albany	37	Nebraska	1867	77,227	Lincoln
12	North Carolina	1789	52,586	Raleigh	38	Colorado	1876	104,247	Denver
13	Rhode Island	1790	1,214	Providence	39	North Dakota	1889	70,665	Bismarck
14	Vermont	1791	9,609	Montpelier	40	South Dakota	1889	77,047	Pierre
15	Kentucky	1792	40,395	Frankfort	41	Montana	1889	147,138	Helena
16	Tennessee	1796	42,244	Nashville	42	Washington	1889	68,192	Olympia
17	Ohio	1803	41,222	Columbus	43	Idaho	1890	83,557	Boise
18	Louisiana	1812	48,523	Baton Rouge	44	Wyoming	1890	97,914	Cheyenne
19	Indiana	1816	36,291	Indianapolis	45	Utah	1896	84,916	Salt Lake City
20	Mississippi	1817	47,716	Jackson	46	Oklahoma	1907	69,919	Oklahoma City
21	Illinois	1818	56,400	Springfield	47	New Mexico	1912	121,666	Santa Fe
22	Alabama	1819	51,609	Montgomery	48	Arizona	1912	113,909	Phoenix
23	Maine	1820	33,215	Augusta	49	Alaska	1959	586,412	Juneau
24	Missouri	1821	69,686	Jefferson City	50	Hawaii	1959	6,450	Honolulu
25	Arkansas	1836	53,104	Little Rock		District of Columbia	(1791)	67	
26	Michigan	1837	58,216	Lansing		*1 square mile = 2.59 square kilometers.			

Federal Receipts

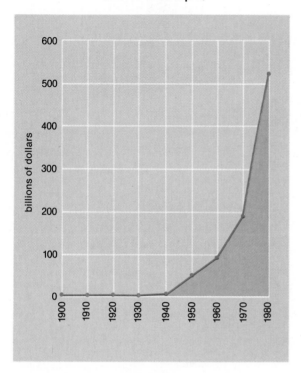

Federal Outlays

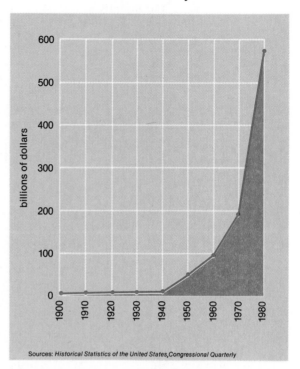

Sources: *Historical Statistics of the United States, Congressional Quarterly*

Distribution of Outlays

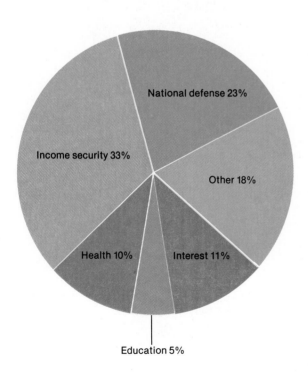

National defense 23%

Income security 33%

Other 18%

Health 10%

Interest 11%

Education 5%

Source: *The United States Budget in Brief,* 1980 data

Number of Government Employees

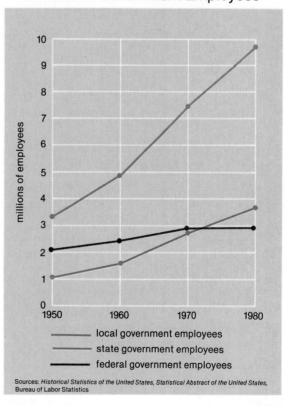

local government employees
state government employees
federal government employees

Sources: *Historical Statistics of the United States, Statistical Abstract of the United States,*
Bureau of Labor Statistics

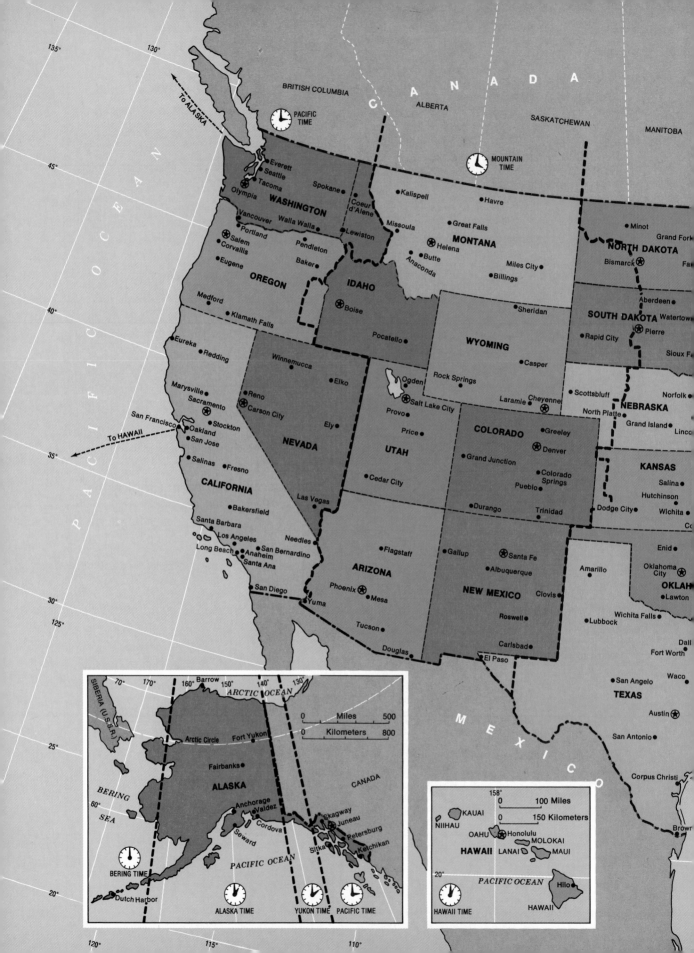

States and Cities of the United States

CENTRAL TIME

EASTERN TIME

ONTARIO

QUEBEC

NEW BRUNSWICK

NOVA SCOTIA

C A N A D A

Lake Superior

Hibbing
Duluth
Superior
Sault Ste. Marie

NESOTA

St. Paul
Minneapolis
Rochester

WISCONSIN
Eau Claire
Green Bay
Oshkosh

M I C H I G A N

Lake Huron

Lake Michigan

Grand Rapids
Flint
Lansing
Detroit
Kalamazoo

MAINE
Caribou
Augusta
Lewiston
Bangor
Portland

Burlington
Montpelier
VT.
N.H.
Concord
Manchester

NEW YORK

Syracuse
Utica
Schenectady
Troy
Albany

MASS.
Boston
Worcester

Hartford
CONN.
Providence
R.I.

Buffalo
Rochester

Lake Ontario

Lake Erie
Erie
Cleveland
Warren
Youngstown

Binghamton
Scranton

PENNSYLVANIA

Newark
New York
Trenton
Philadelphia
Camden
N.J.

Mason City
Madison
Racine
Rockford
Chicago
Milwaukee

IOWA
Dubuque

Cedar Rapids
Davenport
Rock Island

Des Moines

Peoria

ILLINOIS
Springfield

Gary
South Bend
Fort Wayne

Toledo
Akron
Canton

OHIO
Dayton
Columbus

Indianapolis

INDIANA

Cincinnati

Covington
Frankfort
Lexington
Louisville

Evansville
Owensboro

KENTUCKY

Pittsburgh
Wheeling

Harrisburg
York
Baltimore

Washington
Annapolis
MD.

DE.
Dover

W. VA.
Charleston
Huntington

VIRGINIA
Richmond

St. Joseph
Kansas City
eka
Jefferson City
St. Louis
East St. Louis

MISSOURI
Springfield
Cape Girardeau

Hannibal

Cairo
Paducah

Middlesboro

Nashville
Jackson
Jonesboro

TENNESSEE
Chattanooga

Memphis

Roanoke
Norfolk

Greensboro
Raleigh
Oak Ridge
Knoxville
Asheville
Charlotte

NORTH CAROLINA

Wilmington

Greenville
Columbia

SOUTH CAROLINA

Fort Smith
Hot Springs
Little Rock
Pine Bluff

ARKANSAS
El Dorado

MISSISSIPPI
Columbus

Huntsville
Birmingham

ALABAMA
Columbus
Montgomery

GEORGIA
Atlanta
Macon

Savannah

Charleston

Shreveport
Natchez

LOUISIANA
Alexandria

Jackson
Meridian

Albany
Valdosta

Baton Rouge
Lake Charles
New Orleans

Mobile
Biloxi
Pensacola
Tallahassee
Jacksonville
Gainesville

ont
ston
Galveston

GULF OF MEXICO

FLORIDA
Orlando
Tampa
St. Petersburg
Ft. Myers

West Palm Beach
Boca Raton
Ft. Lauderdale
Miami

Key West

CUBA

ATLANTIC OCEAN

West longitude
North latitude

★ State Capital

United States standard time zones are indicated by clocks (When it is 12:00 noon in Western Alaska, it is 6:00 p.m. along the eastern coast of the United States.)

- - - Boundaries of time zones

0   Miles   500
0   Kilometers   800

60°
45°
40°
65°
35°
30°
25°
20°

90°   85°   80°   75°   70°

697

The American People

The people who settled America came from many lands. Indeed, all Americans were immigrants or the descendants of immigrants. The American Indians, the first Americans, for example, originally were hunting peoples who came to North America from Asia. Today the United States has a diverse population, composed of people with many national and racial backgrounds, religious beliefs, and regional loyalties. The following graphs and charts tell much about these Americans. One graph portrays which decades experienced the largest immigration to this country. Another graph shows which countries were the former homes of large numbers of Americans. The following pages also provide information on how quickly the population of the country grew over the years and how specific regions, states, and cities have participated in this growth. In addition, this section of the Atlas highlights certain trends that concern all Americans. There are graphs which show a rise in average life expectancy, a growth in family income, and an increase in educational enrollment. Graphs and charts, such as these shown here, are valuable reference tools for the study of the history of the United States. They support many of the former themes stated in the text and provide a richer understanding of the American experience.

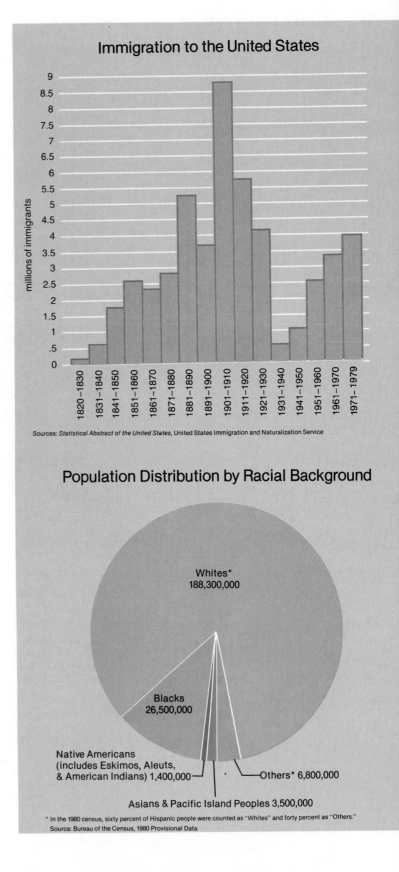

Immigration to the United States

millions of immigrants

Sources: *Statistical Abstract of the United States,* United States Immigration and Naturalization Service

Population Distribution by Racial Background

Whites*
188,300,000

Blacks
26,500,000

Native Americans
(includes Eskimos, Aleuts,
& American Indians) 1,400,000

Others* 6,800,000

Asians & Pacific Island Peoples 3,500,000

* In the 1980 census, sixty percent of Hispanic people were counted as "Whites" and forty percent as "Others."
Source: Bureau of the Census, 1980 Provisional Data

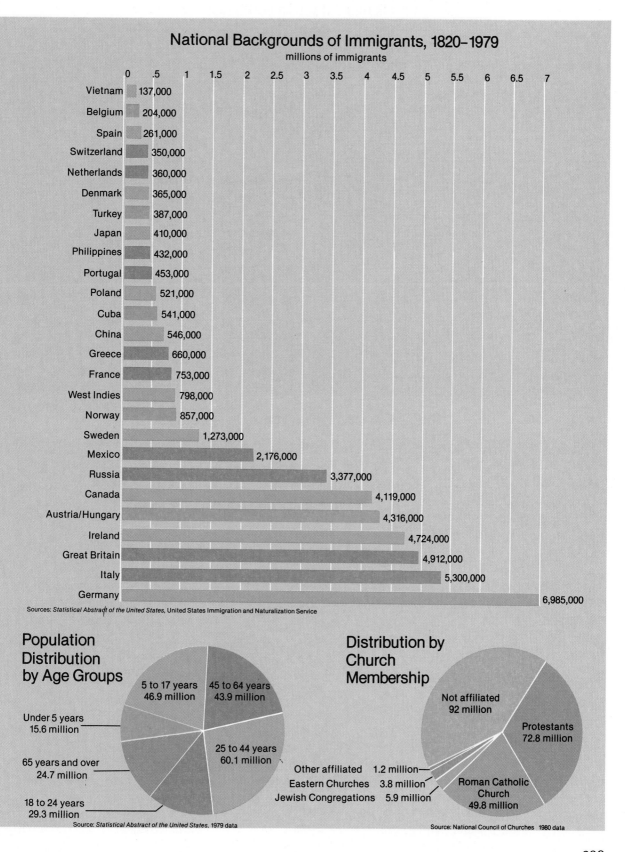

National Backgrounds of Immigrants, 1820–1979

millions of immigrants

Country	Immigrants
Vietnam	137,000
Belgium	204,000
Spain	261,000
Switzerland	350,000
Netherlands	360,000
Denmark	365,000
Turkey	387,000
Japan	410,000
Philippines	432,000
Portugal	453,000
Poland	521,000
Cuba	541,000
China	546,000
Greece	660,000
France	753,000
West Indies	798,000
Norway	857,000
Sweden	1,273,000
Mexico	2,176,000
Russia	3,377,000
Canada	4,119,000
Austria/Hungary	4,316,000
Ireland	4,724,000
Great Britain	4,912,000
Italy	5,300,000
Germany	6,985,000

Sources: *Statistical Abstract of the United States,* United States Immigration and Naturalization Service

Population Distribution by Age Groups

- 5 to 17 years 46.9 million
- 45 to 64 years 43.9 million
- Under 5 years 15.6 million
- 25 to 44 years 60.1 million
- 65 years and over 24.7 million
- 18 to 24 years 29.3 million

Source: *Statistical Abstract of the United States,* 1979 data

Distribution by Church Membership

- Not affiliated 92 million
- Protestants 72.8 million
- Other affiliated 1.2 million
- Eastern Churches 3.8 million
- Jewish Congregations 5.9 million
- Roman Catholic Church 49.8 million

Source: National Council of Churches 1980 data

699

Settlement of the United States

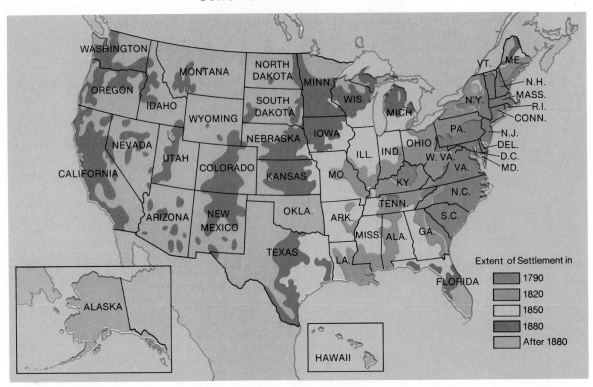

Extent of Settlement in

1790
1820
1850
1880
After 1880

Population Distribution in the United States

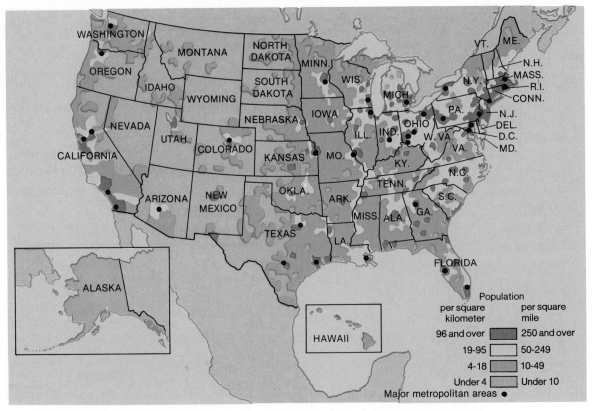

Population
per square kilometer | per square mile
96 and over | 250 and over
19-95 | 50-249
4-18 | 10-49
Under 4 | Under 10
Major metropolitan areas ●

Population Growth of States and Their Largest Cities

	State	Population at first census after entry	State population 1980 (prel.)	Represen-tatives in Congress	Largest city in 1980	City population in 1890	City population in 1930	City population 1980 (prel.)
1	Delaware	59,000	548,000	1	Wilmington	61,431	106,597	70,366
2	Pennsylvania	434,000	11,828,095	23	Philadelphia	1,046,964	1,950,961	1,680,235
3	New Jersey	184,000	7,342,164	14	Newark	181,830	442,337	329,498
4	Georgia	83,000	5,404,384	10	Atlanta	65,533	270,366	422,293
5	Connecticut	238,000	3,096,454	6	Bridgeport	48,866	146,716	142,459
6	Massachusetts	379,000	5,728,288	11	Boston	448,477	781,188	562,582
7	Maryland	320,000	4,198,113	8	Baltimore	434,439	804,874	784,554
8	South Carolina	249,000	3,069,825	6	Columbia	15,353	51,581	97,104
9	New Hampshire	142,000	919,114	2	Manchester	44,126	76,834	90,757
10	Virginia	692,000	5,323,412	10	Norfolk	34,871	129,710	262,803
11	New York	340,000	17,507,541	34	New York	2,507,414	6,930,446	7,015,608
12	North Carolina	394,000	5,847,788	11	Charlotte	11,557	82,675	310,799
13	Rhode Island	69,000	945,835	2	Providence	132,146	252,981	156,519
14	Vermont	154,000	511,299	1	Burlington	14,500	24,789	37,727
15	Kentucky	221,000	3,642,795	7	Louisville	161,129	307,745	298,161
16	Tennessee	106,000	4,545,590	9	Memphis	64,495	253,143	644,838
17	Ohio	231,000	10,772,432	21	Cleveland	261,353	900,429	572,532
18	Louisiana	153,000	4,199,542	8	New Orleans	242,039	458,762	556,913
19	Indiana	147,000	5,461,103	10	Indianapolis	105,436	364,161	695,040
20	Mississippi	75,000	2,511,491	5	Jackson	5,920	48,282	200,338
21	Illinois	55,000	11,355,062	22	Chicago	1,099,850	3,376,438	2,969,570
22	Alabama	128,000	3,870,251	7	Birmingham	26,178	259,678	282,068
23	Maine	298,000	1,123,670	2	Portland	36,425	70,810	61,575
24	Missouri	140,000	4,906,480	9	St. Louis	451,770	821,960	448,640
25	Arkansas	98,000	2,284,037	4	Little Rock	25,874	81,679	153,831
26	Michigan	212,000	9,238,634	18	Detroit	205,876	1,568,662	1,192,222
27	Florida	87,000	9,579,963	19	Jacksonville	17,201	129,549	541,269
28	Texas	213,000	14,173,876	27	Houston	27,557	292,352	1,554,992
29	Iowa	192,000	2,909,463	6	Des Moines	50,093	142,559	190,910
30	Wisconsin	305,000	4,693,941	9	Milwaukee	204,468	578,249	632,989
31	California	93,000	23,545,061	45	Los Angeles	50,395	1,238,048	2,950,010
32	Minnesota	172,000	4,069,356	8	Minneapolis	164,738	464,356	370,091
33	Oregon	52,000	2,618,126	5	Portland	46,385	301,815	364,891
34	Kansas	364,000	2,356,032	5	Wichita	23,853	111,110	279,352
35	West Virginia	442,000	1,930,787	4	Huntington	10,108	75,572	63,626
36	Nevada	42,000	800,312	2	Las Vegas	0	5,165	162,960
37	Nebraska	123,000	1,564,901	3	Omaha	148,514	214,006	312,929
38	Colorado	194,000	2,882,061	6	Denver	106,713	287,861	489,318
39	North Dakota	191,000	652,437	1	Fargo	5,664	28,619	61,281
40	South Dakota	349,000	688,217	1	Sioux Falls	7,205	33,362	81,071
41	Montana	143,000	783,698	2	Billings	836	16,380	68,361
42	Washington	357,000	4,114,738	8	Seattle	42,837	365,583	491,897
43	Idaho	89,000	943,629	2	Boise	2,311	21,544	102,125
44	Wyoming	63,000	468,954	1	Cheyenne	11,690	17,361	47,207
45	Utah	277,000	1,459,010	3	Salt Lake City	44,843	140,267	162,985
46	Oklahoma	1,657,000	3,001,252	6	Oklahoma City	4,151	185,389	401,002
47	New Mexico	360,000	1,295,474	3	Albuquerque	3,785	26,570	382,837
48	Arizona	334,000	2,719,225	5	Phoenix	3,152	48,118	781,443
49	Alaska	229,000	400,142	1	Anchorage	0	2,500	173,992
50	Hawaii	642,000	964,680	2	Honolulu	22,907	138,445	365,114
	District of Columbia	8,000 (1800)	635,233	—	Washington, D.C.	188,932	486,869	635,223

Growth of Population in the United States

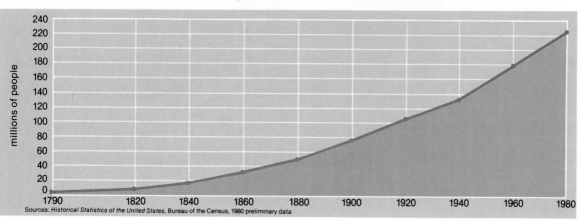

millions of people

(y-axis: 0, 20, 40, 60, 80, 100, 120, 140, 160, 180, 200, 220, 240)
(x-axis: 1790, 1820, 1840, 1860, 1880, 1900, 1920, 1940, 1960, 1980)

Sources: *Historical Statistics of the United States*, Bureau of the Census, 1980 preliminary data

701

Population Shifts Among the States

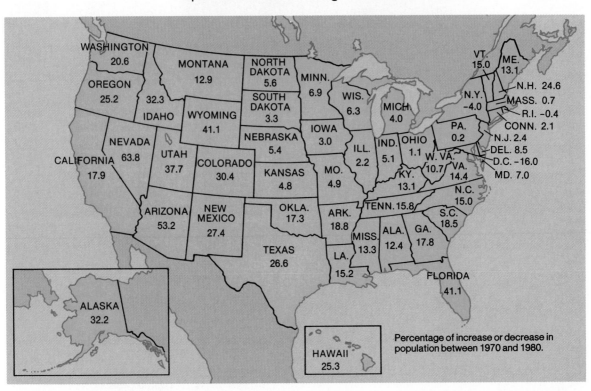

Percentage of increase or decrease in population between 1970 and 1980.

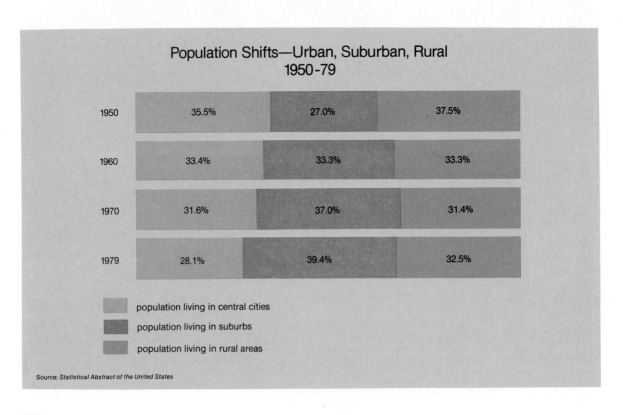

Population Shifts—Urban, Suburban, Rural 1950-79

Year	Central cities	Suburbs	Rural areas
1950	35.5%	27.0%	37.5%
1960	33.4%	33.3%	33.3%
1970	31.6%	37.0%	31.4%
1979	28.1%	39.4%	32.5%

- population living in central cities
- population living in suburbs
- population living in rural areas

Source: *Statistical Abstract of the United States*

Growth of Family Income

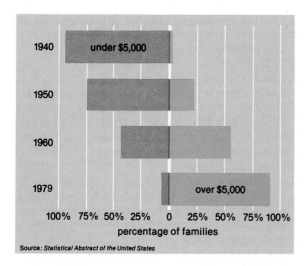

Source: *Statistical Abstract of the United States*

Average Life Expectancy

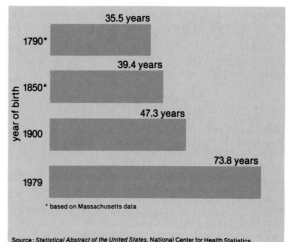

* based on Massachusetts data

Source: *Statistical Abstract of the United States*, National Center for Health Statistics

High School/College Enrollment

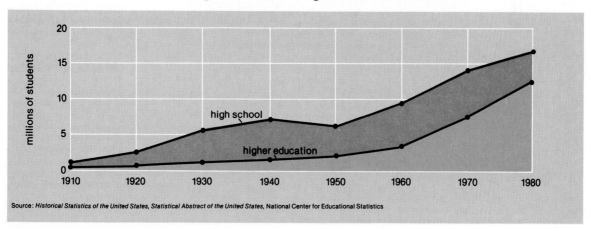

Source: *Historical Statistics of the United States, Statistical Abstract of the United States*, National Center for Educational Statistics

Birth and Death Rates

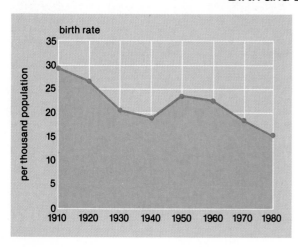

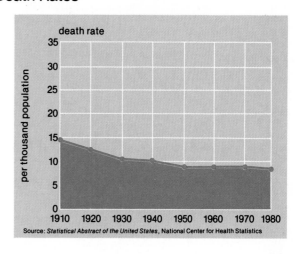

Source: *Statistical Abstract of the United States*, National Center for Health Statistics

The American Economy

Gross National Product

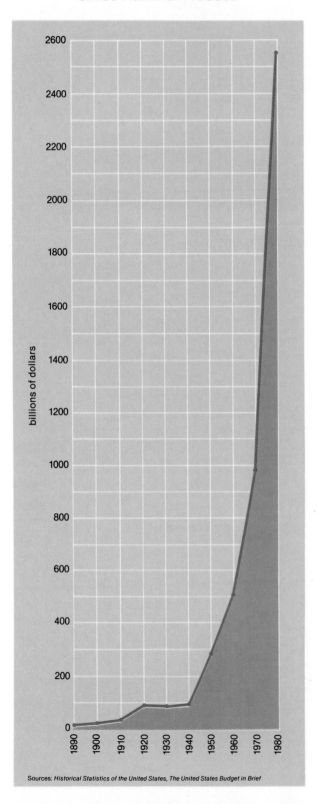

billions of dollars

2600 / 2400 / 2200 / 2000 / 1800 / 1600 / 1400 / 1200 / 1000 / 800 / 600 / 400 / 200 / 0

1890 / 1900 / 1910 / 1920 / 1930 / 1940 / 1950 / 1960 / 1970 / 1980

Sources: *Historical Statistics of the United States, The United States Budget in Brief*

The United States, with its rich resources, advanced technology, and hardworking population, has experienced remarkable economic growth. There are many ways of measuring this growth. One is the Gross National Product (GNP), or the total value of all goods and services produced in the nation. This key measure of economic growth soared from $13.1 billion in 1890 to $2.6 trillion in 1980. Workers' productivity is another indicator of economic progress. For example, each farm worker produced nearly ten times as much food in 1979 as in 1900. The kind of work Americans perform also has changed, with a notable increase in service occupations and government jobs. And the nation's economic growth has reflected advances in American know-how. From the years of hand tools to today's computer-operated machinery, each era has seen major improvements which helped raise Americans' standards of living and improve America's position in trading with other countries of the world.

Major Advances

	1607–1783
POWER	Human muscles Animal muscles Wind and water power
MANUFACTURING MATERIALS	Copper, bronze, iron Wood Clay Plant and animal fibers
FACTORY METHODS	Hand forges and tools Hand-powered equipment
AGRICULTURE	Wooden plows Spades and hoes Axes and other hand tools
TRANSPORTATION	Horses Animal-drawn vehicles Sailing vessels
COMMUNICATION	Hand-operated printing presses Newspapers
MERCHANDISING AND BUSINESS ORGANIZATION	Small shops Peddlers

Average Workweek

Year	hours
1850	(bar to ~66)
1900	(bar to ~57)
1950	(bar to ~40)
1980	(bar to ~36)

0 10 20 30 40 50 60 70
hours

Sources: *Statistical Abstract of the United States*, Bureau of Labor Statistics

Output in Manufacturing, 1950–1980

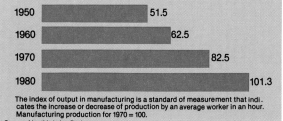

Year	Index
1950	51.5
1960	62.5
1970	82.5
1980	101.3

The index of output in manufacturing is a standard of measurement that indicates the increase or decrease of production by an average worker in an hour.
Manufacturing production for 1970 = 100.

Source: *Monthly Labor Review*

Changes in Workers' Occupations

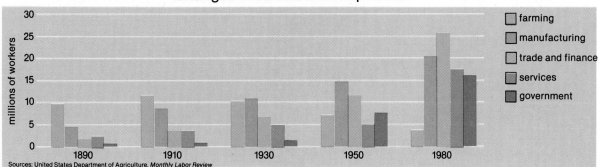

millions of workers

Legend:
- farming
- manufacturing
- trade and finance
- services
- government

Years: 1890, 1910, 1930, 1950, 1980

Sources: United States Department of Agriculture, *Monthly Labor Review*

in American Business and Industry

1783–1850	1850–1900	1900–1920	1920–Present
Steam power	Electric power Internal combustion engines		Atomic energy Solar energy Geothermal energy
Large-scale production of iron	Large-scale production of steel Development of combustion fuels: coal, oil, gas Development of light metals and alloys	Large-scale production of light metals and alloys Development of plastics and synthetics	Large-scale production of plastics and synthetics
Machinery powered by water and steam Interchangeable parts	Mass production, with centralized assembly of interchangeable parts	Conveyor-belt assembly line	Automation Computer-operated machinery
Iron and steel plows Cotton gin Mowing, threshing, and haying machines	McCormick reaper Barbed-wire fencing	Scientific agriculture	Large-scale mechanized agriculture Corporation farms
Canals Clipper ships Development of railroads and steamships	Large-scale steamship and railroad lines City trolleys, elevated trains	Automobiles, trucks, and buses Development of propeller-driven aircraft Subways	Space exploration Monorail trains Supersonic planes
Mechanized printing presses Telegraph Mass-circulation books and magazines	Transatlantic cable Telephones Phonographs Typewriters Cameras	Motion pictures Radios	Television Transistors Magnetic tape Lasers Satellite transmissions
Individual-and family-owned factories and mills General stores	Department stores Chain stores Mail-order houses Growth of corporations Trusts	National advertising Holding companies	Supermarkets Shopping centers Conglomerate corporations Multinational corporations

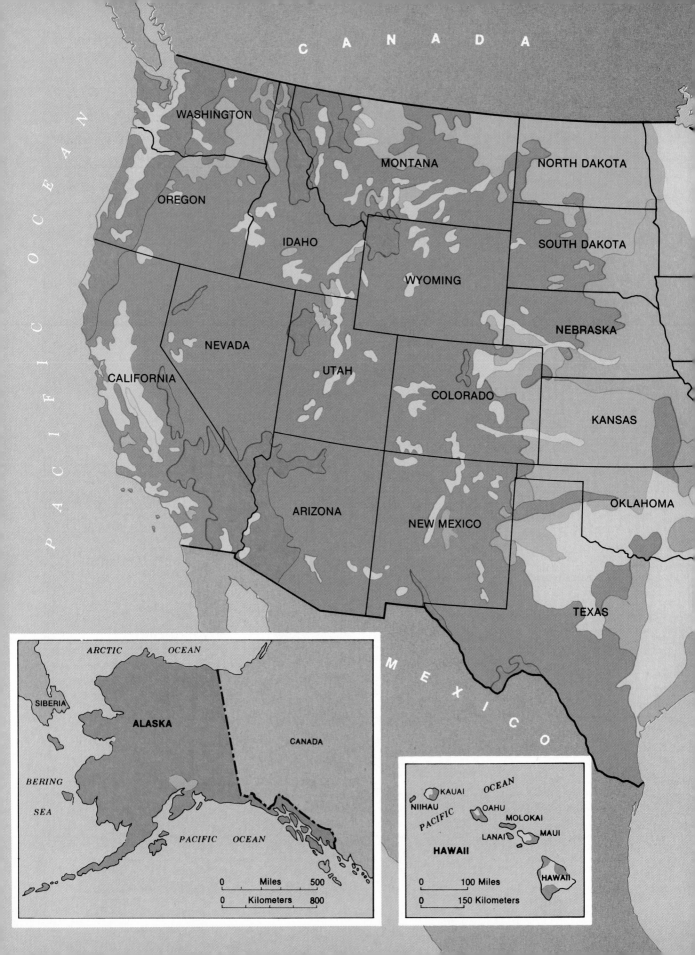

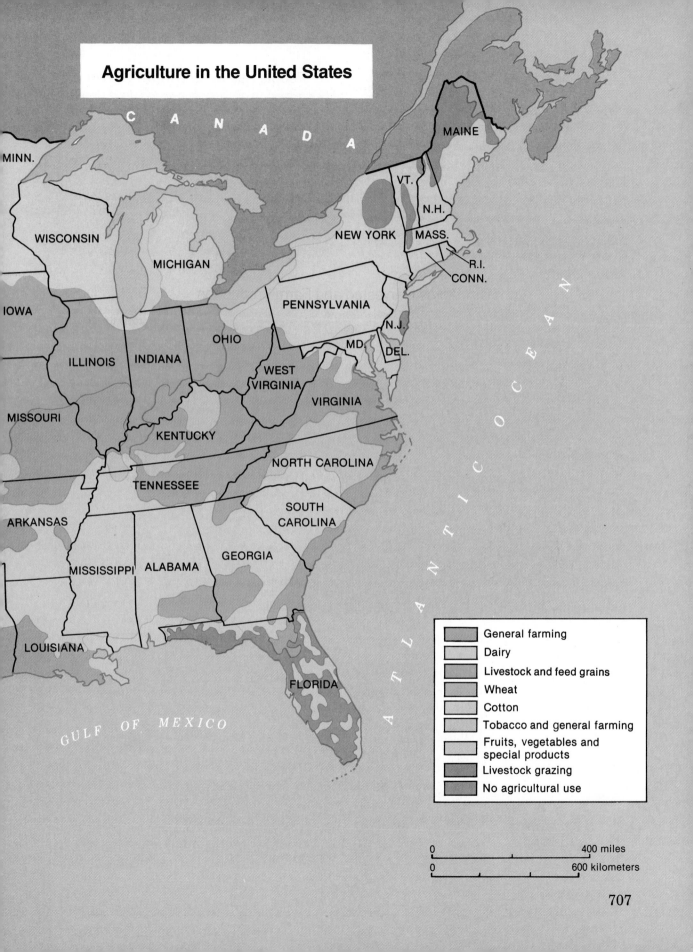

Agriculture in the United States

General farming

Dairy

Livestock and feed grains

Wheat

Cotton

Tobacco and general farming

Fruits, vegetables and special products

Livestock grazing

No agricultural use

CANADA

MINN.

WISCONSIN

MICHIGAN

MAINE

VT.

N.H.

NEW YORK

MASS.

R.I.

CONN.

IOWA

ILLINOIS

INDIANA

OHIO

PENNSYLVANIA

N.J.

MD.

DEL.

WEST VIRGINIA

VIRGINIA

MISSOURI

KENTUCKY

NORTH CAROLINA

ARKANSAS

TENNESSEE

SOUTH CAROLINA

MISSISSIPPI

ALABAMA

GEORGIA

LOUISIANA

FLORIDA

GULF OF MEXICO

ATLANTIC OCEAN

0   400 miles

0   600 kilometers

707

Average Size of Farms

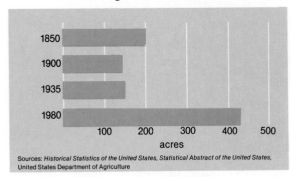

Year	acres
1850	200
1900	140
1935	150
1980	420

acres — 100, 200, 300, 400, 500

Sources: *Historical Statistics of the United States, Statistical Abstract of the United States,* United States Department of Agriculture

People Fed by One Farm Worker

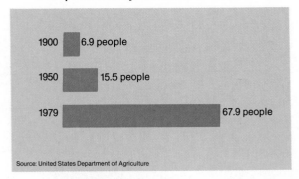

Year	people
1900	6.9 people
1950	15.5 people
1979	67.9 people

Source: United States Department of Agriculture

Farm Acres Harvested and Farm Production

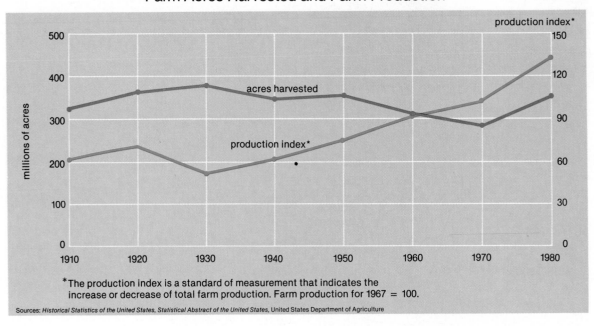

acres harvested

production index*

millions of acres: 0, 100, 200, 300, 400, 500

production index*: 0, 30, 60, 90, 120, 150

1910, 1920, 1930, 1940, 1950, 1960, 1970, 1980

*The production index is a standard of measurement that indicates the increase or decrease of total farm production. Farm production for 1967 = 100.

Sources: *Historical Statistics of the United States, Statistical Abstract of the United States,* United States Department of Agriculture

America's Exports

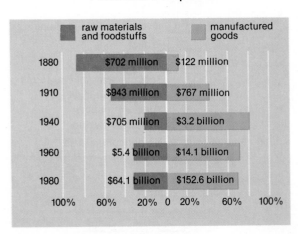

raw materials and foodstuffs / manufactured goods

Year	raw materials and foodstuffs	manufactured goods
1880	$702 million	$122 million
1910	$943 million	$767 million
1940	$705 million	$3.2 billion
1960	$5.4 billion	$14.1 billion
1980	$64.1 billion	$152.6 billion

100% 60% 20% 0 20% 60% 100%

America's Imports

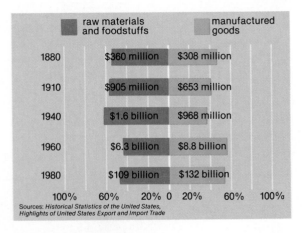

raw materials and foodstuffs / manufactured goods

Year	raw materials and foodstuffs	manufactured goods
1880	$360 million	$308 million
1910	$905 million	$653 million
1940	$1.6 billion	$968 million
1960	$6.3 billion	$8.8 billion
1980	$109 billion	$132 billion

100% 60% 20% 0 20% 60% 100%

Sources: *Historical Statistics of the United States, Highlights of United States Export and Import Trade*

The Rise and Fall of U.S. Tariffs

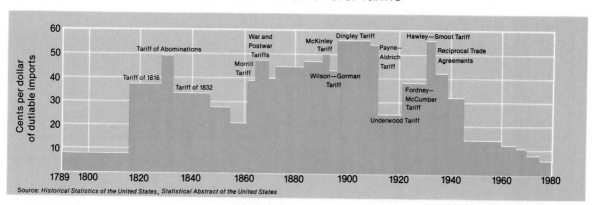

Cents per dollar of dutiable imports

- Tariff of 1816
- Tariff of Abominations
- Tariff of 1832
- Morrill Tariff
- War and Postwar Tariffs
- McKinley Tariff
- Wilson—Gorman Tariff
- Dingley Tariff
- Payne—Aldrich Tariff
- Underwood Tariff
- Fordney—McCumber Tariff
- Hawley—Smoot Tariff
- Reciprocal Trade Agreements

Source: Historical Statistics of the United States, Statistical Abstract of the United States

America's World Trade

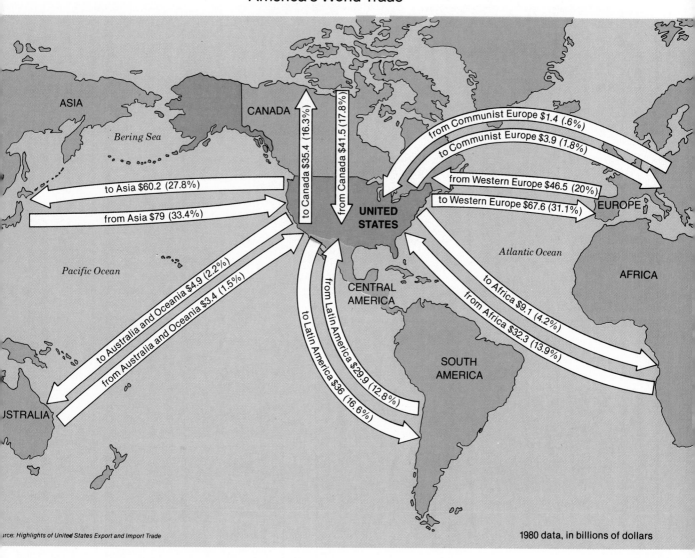

to Canada $35.4 (16.3%)

from Canada $41.5 (17.8%)

to Asia $60.2 (27.8%)

from Asia $79 (33.4%)

from Communist Europe $1.4 (.6%)

to Communist Europe $3.9 (1.8%)

from Western Europe $46.5 (20%)

to Western Europe $67.6 (31.1%)

to Australia and Oceania $4.9 (2.2%)

from Australia and Oceania $3.4 (1.5%)

from Latin America $29.9 (12.8%)

to Latin America $36 (16.6%)

to Africa $9.1 (4.2%)

from Africa $32.3 (13.9%)

UNITED STATES

CANADA

ASIA

Bering Sea

Pacific Ocean

CENTRAL AMERICA

SOUTH AMERICA

EUROPE

AFRICA

Atlantic Ocean

AUSTRALIA

Source: Highlights of United States Export and Import Trade

1980 data, in billions of dollars

709

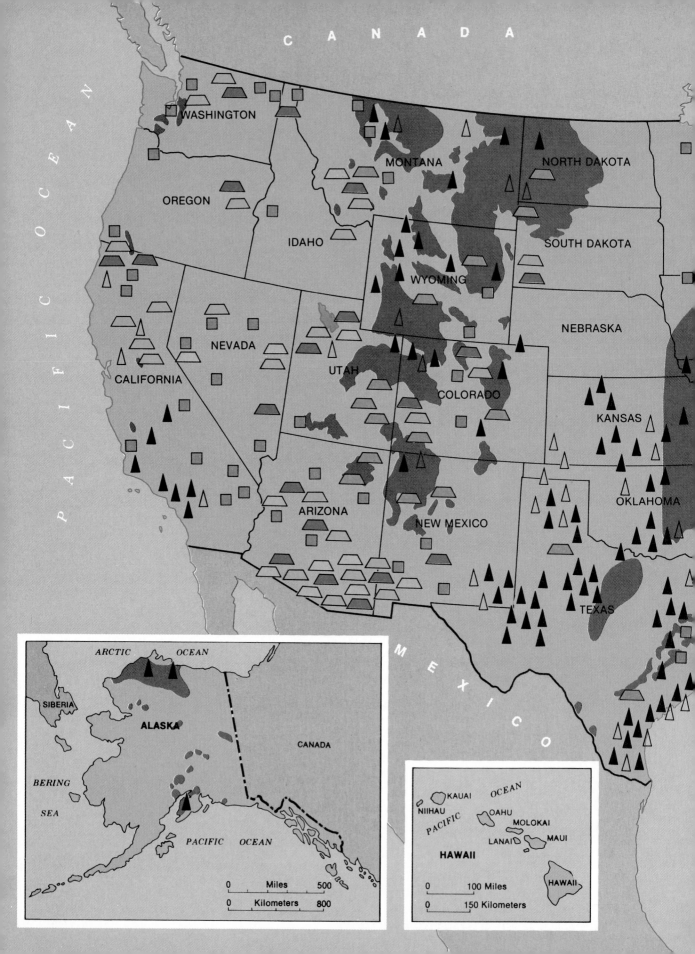

CANADA

PACIFIC OCEAN

WASHINGTON

OREGON

IDAHO

MONTANA

NORTH DAKOTA

SOUTH DAKOTA

WYOMING

NEVADA

UTAH

COLORADO

NEBRASKA

CALIFORNIA

ARIZONA

NEW MEXICO

KANSAS

OKLAHOMA

TEXAS

MEXICO

ARCTIC OCEAN

SIBERIA

ALASKA

CANADA

BERING SEA

PACIFIC OCEAN

| 0 | Miles | 500 |
| 0 | Kilometers | 800 |

KAUAI

OCEAN

NIIHAU

PACIFIC

OAHU

MOLOKAI

LANAI

MAUI

HAWAII

HAWAII

| 0 | 100 Miles |
| 0 | 150 Kilometers |

Mineral Resources in the United States

CANADA

MAINE

MINN.

VT.

N.H.

WISCONSIN

NEW YORK

MASS

MICHIGAN

R.I.
CONN.

IOWA

PENNSYLVANIA

N.J.

OHIO

MD.

INDIANA

DEL.

ILLINOIS

WEST
VIRGINIA

MISSOURI

VIRGINIA

KENTUCKY

NORTH CAROLINA

TENNESSEE

SOUTH
CAROLINA

ARKANSAS

GEORGIA

MISSISSIPPI

ALABAMA

LOUISIANA

FLORIDA

GULF OF MEXICO

ATLANTIC OCEAN

	Coal
	Petroleum
	Natural gas
	Silver
	Gold
	Copper
	Iron Ore
	Uranium

0   400 miles

0   600 kilometers

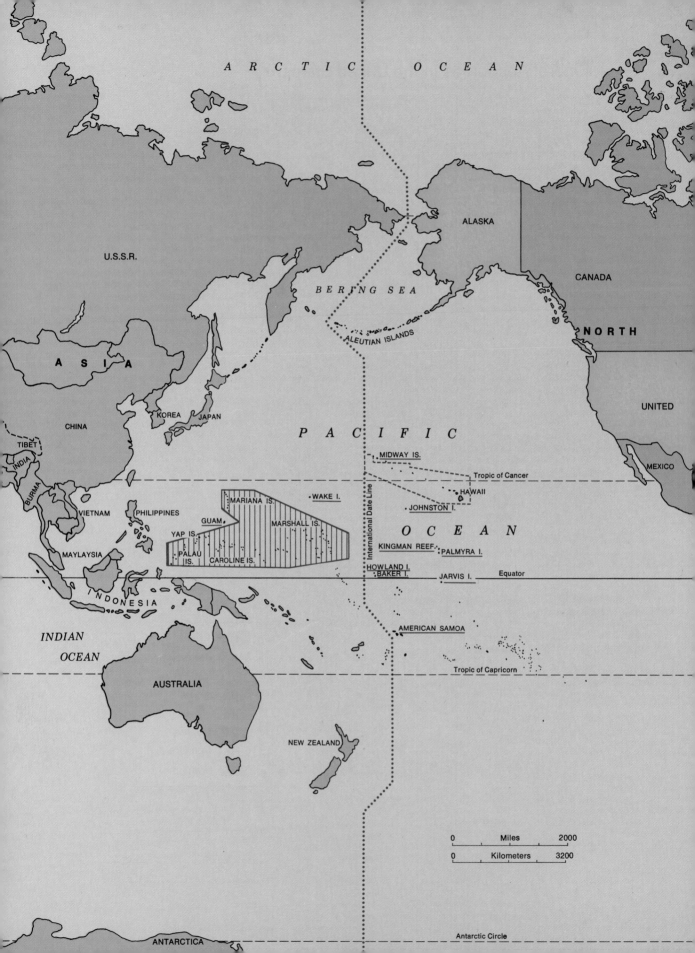

ARCTIC OCEAN

CANADA

ALASKA

BERING SEA

NORTH

U.S.S.R.

ALEUTIAN ISLANDS

UNITED

ASIA

KOREA JAPAN

PACIFIC

MEXICO

CHINA

MIDWAY IS.

TIBET

Tropic of Cancer

INDIA

WAKE I.

MARIANA IS.

HAWAII

BURMA

VIETNAM PHILIPPINES

JOHNSTON I.

GUAM

MARSHALL IS.

OCEAN

YAP IS.

MAYLAYSIA

PALAU
IS. CAROLINE IS.

KINGMAN REEF PALMYRA I.

HOWLAND I.

INDONESIA

BAKER I. JARVIS I. Equator

AMERICAN SAMOA

INDIAN

OCEAN

International Date Line

Tropic of Capricorn

AUSTRALIA

NEW ZEALAND

0	Miles	2000
0	Kilometers	3200

ANTARCTICA Antarctic Circle

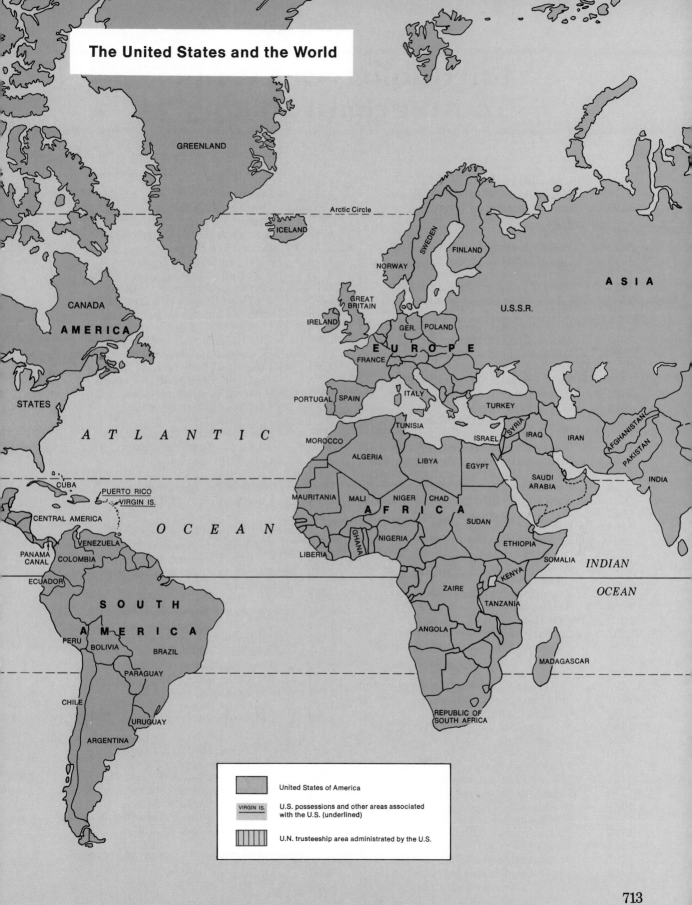

The United States and the World

GREENLAND

Arctic Circle

ICELAND

NORWAY

SWEDEN

FINLAND

ASIA

CANADA

AMERICA

GREAT BRITAIN

IRELAND

GER.

POLAND

U.S.S.R.

E U R O P E

FRANCE

STATES

PORTUGAL

SPAIN

ITALY

TURKEY

A T L A N T I C

MOROCCO

TUNISIA

ISRAEL

SYRIA

IRAQ

IRAN

AFGHANISTAN

PAKISTAN

ALGERIA

LIBYA

EGYPT

SAUDI ARABIA

INDIA

CUBA

PUERTO RICO

VIRGIN IS.

O C E A N

MAURITANIA

MALI

NIGER

CHAD

A F R I C A

SUDAN

CENTRAL AMERICA

VENEZUELA

PANAMA CANAL

COLOMBIA

LIBERIA

GHANA

NIGERIA

ETHIOPIA

SOMALIA

INDIAN

ECUADOR

ZAIRE

KENYA

OCEAN

S O U T H

A M E R I C A

PERU

BOLIVIA

BRAZIL

TANZANIA

ANGOLA

MADAGASCAR

PARAGUAY

CHILE

URUGUAY

REPUBLIC OF SOUTH AFRICA

ARGENTINA

United States of America

VIRGIN IS.

U.S. possessions and other areas associated with the U.S. (underlined)

U.N. trusteeship area administered by the U.S.

Chronology of Events in American History

1096	Crusades to Holy Land start.
1271–95	Marco Polo's travels in Far East.
1492	Columbus reaches America.
1497–98	John Cabot's explorations.
1498	Vasco da Gama reaches India.
1513	Balboa reaches Pacific Ocean.
1519	Cortés lands in Mexico.
1519–22	Magellan's ships circle earth.
1531–35	Pizarro conquers Incas.
1534	Cartier makes first voyage.
1539–42	De Soto explores Southeast.
1588	English defeat Spanish Armada.
1607	Jamestown is founded.
1609	Hudson explores Hudson River.
1619	First women arrive at Jamestown.
1619	First Africans arrive in Virginia.
1620	Pilgrims reach Cape Cod.
1620	Mayflower Compact.
1624	Virginia becomes royal colony.
1630	Massachusetts Bay Colony founded.
1632	Maryland is chartered.
1636	Roger Williams founds Providence.
1636	Harvard University founded.
1639	Fundamental Orders of Connecticut.
1643	New England Confederation formed.
1647	Massachusetts passes school law.
1649	Maryland Toleration Act.
1651–63	Principal Navigation Acts.
1663	Carolina is chartered.
1664	New Netherland becomes New Jersey and New York.
1673	Exploration by Marquette, Joliet.
1675–76	Bacon's Rebellion.
1679	New Hampshire is chartered.
1681	Pennsylvania is chartered.
1681–82	Exploration by La Salle.
1682	Delaware granted to Penn.
1686	Dominion of New England created.
1693	College of William and Mary founded.
1701	Yale University founded.
1732	Georgia is chartered.
1733	Molasses Act.
1735	Zenger trial.
1750	Iron Act.
1754	French and Indian War starts.
1754	Albany Plan of Union proposed.
1754	Columbia University founded.
1755	Braddock defeated disastrously.
1756	Pitt heads British government.
1759	British capture Quebec.
1763	Treaty of Paris.
1763	Proclamation of 1763.
1764	Sugar Act, Currency Act.

1765	Stamp Act.
1766	Stamp Act repealed.
1767	Townshend Acts.
1770	Boston Massacre.
1772	Committees of Correspondence.
1773	Boston Tea Party.
1774	First Continental Congress.
1775	Fighting at Lexington, Concord.
1775	Second Continental Congress.
1775	Battle of Breed's (Bunker) Hill.
1776	Paine's *Common Sense* appears.
1776	Declaration of Independence.
1776	American victory at Trenton.
1777–78	Howe occupies Philadelphia.
1777	Burgoyne surrenders at Saratoga.
1778	Treaty of alliance with France.
1781	Cornwallis surrenders.
1781	Articles of Confederation go into effect.
1783	Treaty of Paris: United States independence recognized.
1785	Land Ordinance.
1786–87	Shays' Rebellion.
1787	Northwest Ordinance.
1787	Constitution is drafted.

George Washington in Office 1789–1797

1789	Congress creates Departments of State, Treasury, and War.
1789	United States courts are organized.
1790	Assumption Bill is passed.
1791	Bill of Rights is ratified.
1791	Vermont enters Union.
1791	Bank of United States chartered.
1791	Lancaster Turnpike is begun.
1792	Kentucky enters Union.
1793	Proclamation of Neutrality.
1794	"Whiskey Rebellion" is put down.
1794	Jay Treaty.
1795	Pinckney Treaty.
1796	Tennessee enters Union.

John Adams in Office: 1797–1801

1797	XYZ Affair angers Americans.
1798	Navy Department is created.
1798	Eleventh Amendment ratified.
1798	Alien and Sedition Acts.
1798–99	Kentucky and Virginia Resolutions.
1801	Marshall becomes Chief Justice.

Thomas Jefferson in Office: 1801–1809

1803	Ohio enters Union.

1803	*Marbury v. Madison.*
1803	Louisiana Purchase adds vast territory to United States.
1804	Twelfth Amendment ratified.
1804–06	Lewis and Clark expedition.
1805	War with Barbary pirates ends.
1807	Embargo Act.
1809	Non-Intercourse Act.

James Madison in Office: 1809–1817

1811	Indian fight at Tippecanoe.
1811	National Road is begun.
1812	Louisiana enters Union.
1812–14	War of 1812 is fought between United States and Great Britain.
1814	Treaty of Ghent restores peace.
1815	Battle of New Orleans.
1816	Second Bank of United States chartered.
1816	Indiana enters Union.

James Monroe in Office: 1817–1825

1817–25	"Era of Good Feelings."
1817	Mississippi enters Union.
1818	Rush-Bagot Agreement approved.
1818	Illinois enters Union.
1818	Treaty settles Canadian boundary.
1819	*McCulloch v. Maryland.*
1819	*Dartmouth College v. Woodward.*
1819	Alabama enters Union.
1819	Treaty gives Florida to U.S.
1820	Missouri Compromise.
1820	Maine enters Union.
1821	Missouri enters Union.
1821	First public high school opens.
1823	Monroe Doctrine proclaimed.
1824	*Gibbons v. Ogden.*

John Quincy Adams in Office: 1825–1829

1825	Erie Canal opens.
1828	"Tariff of Abominations."
1828	Work begins on Baltimore and Ohio Railroad.

Andrew Jackson in Office: 1829–1837

1830	Webster-Hayne debate.
1831	Slave uprising in Virginia.
1831	First issue of the *Liberator.*
1832	Tariff of 1832.
1832	Ordinance of Nullification.
1832	Jackson vetoes renewal of charter for Bank of United States.
1833	Compromise tariff act.
1836	Texas declares its independence.
1836	Arkansas enters Union.
1837	Michigan enters Union.

Martin Van Buren in Office: 1837–1841

1837	Business panic; depression begins.
1837	Horace Mann starts school reform.
1838	Oberlin admits women.
1841	Jacksonian era ends.

William Henry Harrison in Office: March 4–April 4, 1841

| 1841 | Harrison dies. |

John Tyler in Office: 1841–1845

1842	Massachusetts recognizes legal right of labor unions to exist.
1842	Webster-Ashburton Treaty.
1845	Florida enters Union.

James K. Polk in Office: 1845–1849

1845	Texas enters Union.
1846	Treaty settles Oregon boundary.
1846	Iowa enters Union.
1846	Congress declares war on Mexico.
1846	Wilmot Proviso is presented.
1847	Mormons settle at Great Salt Lake.
1848	Treaty ends Mexican War; gives U.S. Mexican Cession.
1848	Women's rights convention at Seneca Falls.
1848	Wisconsin enters Union.

Zachary Taylor in Office: 1849–1850

| 1849 | Gold rush to California. |
| 1850 | Taylor dies. |

Millard Fillmore in Office: 1850–1853

1850	Compromise of 1850.
1850	California admitted to Union.
1852	*Uncle Tom's Cabin* is published.

Franklin Pierce in Office: 1853–1857

1853	Gadsden Purchase approved.
1853	Perry arrives in Japan.
1854	Kansas-Nebraska Act.
1854	Republican Party is formed.
1856	Violence breaks out in Kansas.

James Buchanan in Office: 1857–1861

1857	Dred Scott decision.
1858	Lincoln-Douglas debates.
1858	Minnesota enters Union.
1859	John Brown raids Harpers Ferry.
1859	Oregon enters Union.
1860	South Carolina secedes.
1861	Kansas enters Union.
1861	Confederacy is formed.
1861	Morrill Tariff Act.

Abraham Lincoln in Office: 1861–1865

1861	South fires on Fort Sumter; Civil War (1861–65) begins.
1861	First Battle of Bull Run.
1862	Battle of *Monitor* and *Merrimac.*
1862	Second Battle of Bull Run.
1862	Battle of Antietam.
1862	Emancipation Proclamation.
1862	Union forces reach Vicksburg.
1862	Homestead Act.
1862	Morrill Act for agricultural and industrial education.

1862	Department of Agriculture formed.
1863	Battle of Gettysburg.
1863	Grant takes Vicksburg.
1863	West Virginia enters Union.
1864	Sherman takes Atlanta, Savannah.
1864	Nevada enters Union.
1865	Freedmen's Bureau is created.
1865	Lee surrenders to Grant.
1865	Lincoln is assassinated.

Andrew Johnson in Office: 1865–1869

1865	Johnson recognizes four reconstructed state governments.
1865	Thirteenth Amendment ratified.
1865–86	Conflict between settlers and Indians on the plains.
1866	National Labor Union is formed.
1867	Nebraska enters Union.
1867	U.S. buys Alaska.
1867	Congressional plan of reconstruction is set up.
1867	Grange is organized.
1868	Fourteenth Amendment ratified.
1868	House impeaches Johnson.
1868	Senate acquits Johnson.

Ulysses S. Grant in Office: 1869–1877

1869	First transcontinental railroad completed.
1869	Knights of Labor founded.
1870	Fifteenth Amendment ratified.
1870–71	Force Acts.
1872	Amnesty Act.
1872	Crédit Mobilier scandal.
1873	Nationwide economic depression.
1875	Resumption Act.
1876	Colorado enters Union.
1876	Centennial Exhibition.
1876	Presidential election disputed.
1876–77	"Granger cases" decided.

Rutherford B. Hayes in Office: 1877–1881

1877	Troops withdrawn from South.
1877	Series of railroad strikes.
1878	Bland-Allison Act.
1880–90	New Immigration from eastern and southern Europe.

James A. Garfield in Office:
March 4–September 19, 1881

1881	Garfield is assassinated.

Chester A. Arthur in Office: 1881–1885

1882	Chinese Exclusion Act.
1882	Standard Oil Trust organized.
1883	Civil Service Commission set up.

Grover Cleveland in Office: 1885–1889

1886	Presidential Succession Act.
1886	A. F. of L. is organized.
1886	Haymarket Riot.

1887	Interstate Commerce Act.
1887	Hatch Act.
1887	Dawes Act tries to "Americanize" Indians.

Benjamin Harrison in Office: 1889–1893

1889	Washington, Montana, North Dakota, South Dakota enter Union.
1890	Wyoming, Idaho enter Union.
1890	McKinley Tariff.
1890	Sherman Antitrust Act.
1890	Sherman Silver Purchase Act.
1891	Populist Party is organized.
1892	Homestead steel strike.

Grover Cleveland in Office: 1893–1897

1893	Silver Purchase Act is repealed.
1893	World's Fair held in Chicago.
1894	Wilson-Gorman Tariff.
1894	Pullman strike.
1895	Cubans revolt against Spain.
1896	Bryan is free silver candidate.
1896	Utah enters Union.
1896	Gold discovered in Klondike.

William McKinley in Office: 1897–1901

1897	Dingley Tariff.
1898	Spanish-American War.
1898	Treaty of Paris gives U.S. Puerto Rico, Guam, Philippines.
1898	U.S. annexes Hawaiian Islands.
1899	First Hague Conference.
1899–1900	Open Door policy proclaimed.
1900	Boxer Rebellion.
1901	Platt Amendment.
1901	McKinley is assassinated.

Theodore Roosevelt in Office: 1901–1909

1901	Hay-Pauncefote Treaty.
1901–02	Pan-American Conference.
1902	Newlands Reclamation Act.
1902	Drago Doctrine is announced.
1902	American forces withdrawn from Cuba.
1903	Department of Commerce and Labor is created.
1903	Elkins Act.
1903	Wisconsin adopts direct primary.
1903	Canal Zone is acquired by U.S.
1904	Northern Securities Company ruling.
1904	Roosevelt Corollary to Monroe Doctrine.
1905	Treaty of Portsmouth.
1906	Pure Food and Drug Act.
1906	Meat Inspection Act.
1906	Burke Act modifies Dawes Act.
1906	Pan-American Conference.
1907	Oklahoma enters Union.
1907	"Gentlemen's Agreement" with Japan.
1907	Second Hague Conference.
1908	White House Conservation Conference.

1908	Danbury Hatters ruling.

William H. Taft in Office: 1909–1913

1909	Payne-Aldrich Tariff.
1910	Mann-Elkins Act.
1910	Pan-American Conference.
1911	Transcontinental plane flight.
1912	New Mexico, Arizona enter Union.
1912	Progressive Party is formed.
1912	First state minimum-wage law.
1913	Sixteenth Amendment ratified.

Woodrow Wilson in Office: 1913–1921

1913	Seventeenth Amendment ratified.
1913	Underwood Tariff.
1913	Federal Reserve Act.
1914	World War I starts.
1914	Panama Canal opened to shipping.
1914	FTC is created.
1914	Clayton Antitrust Act.
1916	Jones Act.
1917	Russian Revolution.
1917	U.S. enters World War I.
1917	Smith-Hughes Act.
1917	U.S. buys Virgin Islands.
1918	World War I ends.
1918	Wilson presents Fourteen Points.
1919	Eighteenth Amendment ratified.
1919	"Palmer raids."
1919	Treaty of Versailles (with provision for League of Nations).
1920	Nineteenth Amendment ratified.

Warren G. Harding in Office: 1921–1923

1921	Bureau of the Budget created.
1921	Veterans' Bureau created.
1921–22	Washington Naval Conference.
1921–29	Laws restricting immigration passed.
1922	Mussolini seizes power in Italy.
1922	Fordney-McCumber Tariff.
1923	Harding dies suddenly.

Calvin Coolidge in Office: 1923–1929

1923	Pan-American Conference.
1924	Teapot Dome scandal.
1924	Veterans' bonus bill passed.
1924	All Indians given citizenship.
1927	McNary-Haugen Bill vetoed.
1928	Kellogg-Briand Pact.
1928	Pan-American Conference.

Herbert Hoover in Office: 1929–1933

1929	Stock market crash; start of Great Depression.
1930	Public-works programs started.
1930	Hawley-Smoot Tariff.
1931	Japan invades Manchuria.
1932	RFC is created.
1932	Stimson Doctrine is announced.
1932–33	Federal Reserve powers increased.
1933	Hitler comes to power in Germany.
1933	Twentieth Amendment ratified.

Franklin D. Roosevelt in Office: 1933–1945

1933	CCC is created.
1933	Agricultural Adjustment Act.
1933	Roosevelt declares bank holiday.
1933	NIRA goes into effect.
1933	TVA is created.
1933	U.S. recognizes Soviet Union.
1933	Good Neighbor policy announced.
1933	Twenty-first Amendment ratified.
1934	Roosevelt "devalues" dollar.
1934	SEC is created.
1934	Indian Reorganization Act (Wheeler-Howard Act).
1934	Trade Agreements Act.
1934	Platt Amendment canceled.
1935	WPA is created.
1935	NIRA declared unconstitutional.
1935	National Labor Relations Act.
1935	Social Security Act.
1935–37	Neutrality Acts.
1936	AAA ruled unconstitutional.
1936	Pan-American Conference.
1937	Plan to reorganize Supreme Court.
1937–38	Business slump.
1938	CIO separates from A. F. of L.
1938	Fair Labor Standards Act.
1938	Food, Drug, and Cosmetic Act.
1938	Declaration of Lima.
1939	Germany invades Poland; World War II begins.
1939	Neutrality Act of 1937 amended.
1940	France signs armistice.
1941	"Four Freedoms" speech.
1941	Lend-Lease Act.
1941	Hitler attacks U.S.S.R.
1941	Atlantic Charter states war aims.
1941	Japanese attack Pearl Harbor; U.S. enters World War II.
1942	Corregidor surrenders to Japanese.
1942	Marines invade Guadalcanal.
1942	Allied invasion of North Africa.
1942	OPA is established.
1943	Allied invasion of Italy.
1943	Cairo and Teheran Conferences.
1944	Allies invade Western Europe.
1944	France is liberated.
1945	Yalta Conference.
1945	Roosevelt dies suddenly.

Harry S. Truman in Office: 1945–1953

1945	San Francisco Conference.
1945	War ends in Europe.
1945	Atomic bombs destroy Hiroshima and Nagasaki.
1945	Truman signs UN Charter.
1945	World War II ends.
1946	Philippines become independent.
1946	Wage and price controls ended.
1947	Truman Doctrine is announced.
1947	Marshall Plan is proposed.
1947	Taft-Hartley Act.

1947	Presidential Succession Act.
1948–49	Berlin airlift.
1949	Point Four program is announced.
1949	NATO is formed.
1949	Communists control China.
1950	Internal Security Act.
1950	Korean War starts.
1951	Twenty-second Amendment ratified.
1952	U.S. tests hydrogen bomb.

Dwight D. Eisenhower in Office: 1953–1961

1953	Department of Health, Education, and Welfare created.
1953	States get title to offshore oil.
1953	Korean armistice signed.
1954	Supreme Court rules segregated public schools unconstitutional.
1954	West Germany is admitted to NATO.
1954	Both U.S. and U.S.S.R. have H-bombs.
1955	Summit conference.
1956	Suez crisis.
1957	Civil Rights Commission created.
1957	*Sputnik* in orbit.
1958	First U.S. satellite in orbit.
1958	Congress admits Alaska to the Union.
1958–59	Berlin crisis.
1959	St. Lawrence Seaway is opened.
1959	Congress admits Hawaii to the Union.
1960	Summit Conference called off.

John F. Kennedy in Office: 1961–1963

1961	Peace Corps created.
1961	Alliance for Progress started.
1961	First Soviet cosmonaut orbits earth.
1961	Invasion of Cuba fails.
1961	Berlin wall built.
1962	First American astronaut orbits earth.
1962	U.S. troops sent to South Vietnam.
1962	Trade Expansion Act.
1962	Cuban missile crisis.
1963	Nuclear test-ban treaty.
1963	Kennedy is assassinated.

Lyndon B. Johnson in Office: 1963–1969

1964	Economic Opportunity Act.
1964	Civil Rights Act.
1964	Twenty-fourth Amendment ratified.
1965	Voting Rights Act.
1965	Medicare established.
1965	Escalation in South Vietnam.
1965	Department of Housing and Urban Development created.
1966	National Organization for Women (NOW) is founded.
1966	Department of Transportation created.
1967	Racial disturbances occur in several large cities.
1967	Twenty-fifth Amendment ratified.

1968	Martin Luther King, Jr., is assassinated.
1968	Vietnam peace talks begin in Paris.

Richard M. Nixon in Office: 1969–1974

1969	American troop withdrawals from Vietnam begin.
1969	American astronauts land on the moon.
1971	President Nixon visits Communist China and the Soviet Union.
1972	Twenty-seventh Amendment passed by Congress and sent to states for ratification.
1973	Vice-President Agnew resigns.
1973	Vietnam cease-fire.
1974	President Nixon resigns; Gerald Ford becomes President.

Gerald Ford in Office: 1974–1977

1975	Vietnam falls to Communists.
1975	Joint U.S.-Soviet space mission.
1976	The nation celebrates its Bicentennial.
1976	U.S. Viking spacecraft land on Mars.

Jimmy Carter in Office: 1977–1981

1977	Carter announces plan to pardon Vietnam draft evaders.
1977	Department of Energy created.
1978	Panama Canal treaties approved.
1978	Carter proposes voluntary wage and price guidelines.
1978	Carter meets with Begin of Israel and Sadat of Egypt at Camp David for peace talks.
1979	Revolution in Iran; American hostages seized in November.
1979	Accident at Three Mile Island nuclear plant.
1979	Gasoline shortages in U.S.
1979	Soviet Union invades Afghanistan.
1980	"Carter Doctrine" announced.
1980	U.S. cuts off grain shipments to Soviet Union and boycotts Olympics to protest Afghanistan invasion.
1980	U.S. mission to free hostages in Iran fails.
1980	"Freedom flotilla" from Cuba to U.S.

Ronald Reagan in Office: 1981–

1981	Iran releases U.S. hostages.
1981	Reagan survives assassination attempt.
1981	Flight of U.S. space shuttle *Columbia*.
1981	Sandra Day O'Connor becomes first woman appointed to Supreme Court.

Living American Documents

The Declaration of Independence

and

The Constitution of the United States

The Declaration of Independence is one of the noblest documents in human history. It proclaims in memorable language the universal desire for freedom. Thomas Jefferson, who was chiefly responsible for writing the Declaration, said that he had intended it "to be an expression of the American mind." However, it is also an expression of the ideals of all who seek those fundamental human rights which go with human dignity. It is probably the best summary of the watchwords of democracy in political literature.

Adopted by the Continental Congress in 1776, the Declaration marked a complete break between the colonies and the mother country. It represented a formal declaration of war and a new conception of government.

The Constitution of the United States represents the classic solution to one of the great political problems: How can a group of small states combine into a strong union without losing their individuality and surrendering their control over local affairs? The fifty-five delegates who met at Philadelphia during the hot summer days of 1787 answered this question with a document that called for a federal system of government, a separation of powers with checks and balances, and a procedure for orderly change to meet future needs. Adopted on September 17, 1787, it was ratified in June 1788. Since that time the Constitution has served as a model for many newly formed nations.

A serious objection to the new Constitution, however, was its lack of a "bill of rights." Determined to safeguard their hard-won rights, many Americans accepted the new government on the condition that provision be made for the protection of their fundamental liberties. On December 15, 1791, the first ten amendments to the Constitution were ratified. Gradually, over the years, more amendments were added as political, economic, and social problems called for solution.

The Declaration of Independence

PREAMBLE

When, in the course of human events, it becomes necessary for one people to dissolve the political bands which have connected them with another, and to assume, among the powers of the earth, the separate and equal station to which the laws of nature and of nature's God entitle them, a decent respect to the opinions of mankind requires that they should declare the causes which impel them to the separation.

A NEW THEORY OF GOVERNMENT

We hold these truths to be self-evident: that all men are created equal, that they are endowed by their Creator with certain unalienable rights, that among these are life, liberty, and the pursuit of happiness.

That, to secure these rights, governments are instituted among men, deriving their just powers from the consent of the governed;

That whenever any form of government becomes destructive of these ends, it is the right of the people to alter or to abolish it, and to institute new government, laying its foundation on such principles, and organizing its powers in such form, as to them shall seem most likely to effect their safety and happiness. Prudence, indeed, will dictate that governments long established should not be changed for light and transient causes; and accordingly all experience hath shown that mankind are more disposed to suffer while evils are sufferable, than to right themselves by abolishing the forms to which they are accustomed. But when a long train of abuses and usurpations, pursuing invariably the same object, evinces a design to reduce them under absolute despotism, it is their right, it is their duty, to throw off such government, and to provide new guards for their future security.

REASONS FOR SEPARATION

Such has been the patient sufferance of these colonies; and such is now the necessity which constrains them to alter their former systems of government. The history of the present king of Great Britain is a history of repeated injuries and usurpations, all having in direct object the establishment of an absolute tyranny over these states. To prove this, let facts be submitted to a candid world.

He has refused his assent to laws the most wholesome and necessary for the public good.

He has forbidden his governors to pass laws of immediate and pressing importance unless suspended in their operation till his assent should be obtained; and when so suspended, he has utterly neglected to attend to them.

He has refused to pass other laws for the accommodation of large districts of people, unless those people would relinquish the right of representation in the legislature, a right inestimable to them, and formidable to tyrants only.

He has called together legislative bodies at places unusual, uncomfortable, and distant from the depository of their public records, for the sole purpose of fatiguing them into compliance with his measures.

He has dissolved representative houses repeatedly, for opposing, with manly firmness, his invasions on the rights of the people.

He has refused, for a long time after such dissolutions, to cause others to be elected; whereby the legislative powers, incapable of annihilation, have returned to the people at large for their exercise; the state remaining, in the mean time, exposed to all the dangers of invasion from without and convulsions within.

He has endeavored to prevent the population of these states; for that purpose obstructing the laws of naturalization of foreigners, refusing to pass others to encourage their migration hither, and raising the conditions of new appropriations of lands.

He has obstructed the administration of justice, by refusing his assent to laws for establishing judiciary powers.

He has made judges dependent on his will alone for the tenure of their offices, and the amount and payment of their salaries.

He has erected a multitude of new offices, and sent hither swarms of officers to harass our people and eat out their substance.

He has kept among us, in times of peace, standing armies, without the consent of our legislature.

He has affected to render the military independent of, and superior to, the civil power.

He has combined with others to subject us to a jurisdiction foreign to our constitution and unacknowledged by our laws, giving his assent to their acts of pretended legislation:

For quartering large bodies of armed troops among us;

For protecting them, by a mock trial, from punishment for any murders which they should commit on the inhabitants of these states;

For cutting off our trade with all parts of the world;

For imposing taxes on us without our consent;

For depriving us, in many cases, of the benefits of trial by jury;

For transporting us beyond seas, to be tried for pretended offenses;

For abolishing the free system of English laws in a neighboring province, establishing therein an arbitrary government, and enlarging its boundaries, so as to render it at once an example and fit instrument for introducing the same absolute rule into these colonies;

For taking away our charters, abolishing our most valuable laws, and altering, fundamentally, the forms of our governments;

For suspending our own legislature, and declaring themselves invested with power to legislate for us in all cases whatsoever.

He has abdicated government here, by declaring us out of his protection and waging war against us.

He has plundered our seas, ravaged our coasts, burned our towns, and destroyed the lives of our people.

He is at this time transporting large armies of foreign mercenaries to complete the works of death, desolation, and tyranny already begun with circumstances of cruelty and perfidy scarcely paralleled in the most barbarous ages, and totally unworthy the head of a civilized nation.

He has constrained our fellow-citizens, taken captive on the high seas, to bear arms against their country, to become the executioners of their friends and brethren, or to fall themselves by their hands.

He has excited domestic insurrections among us, and has endeavored to bring on the inhabitants of our frontiers the merciless Indian savages, whose known rule of warfare is an undistinguished destruction of all ages, sexes, and conditions.

In every stage of these oppressions we have petitioned for redress in the most humble terms; our repeated petitions have been answered only by repeated injury. A prince whose character is thus marked by every act which may define a tyrant is unfit to be the ruler of a free people.

Nor have we been wanting in attention to our British brethren. We have warned them, from time to time, of attempts by their legislature to extend an unwarrantable jurisdiction over us. We have reminded them of the circumstances of our emigration and settlement here. We have appealed to their native justice and magnanimity; and we have conjured them, by the ties of our common kindred, to disavow these usurpations, which would inevitably interrupt our connections and correspondence. They, too, have been deaf to the voice of justice and of consanguinity. We must, therefore, acquiesce in the necessity which denounces our separation, and hold them, as we hold the rest of mankind, enemies in war, in peace, friends.

A FORMAL DECLARATION OF WAR

We, therefore, the representatives of the United States of America, in General Congress assembled, appealing to the Supreme Judge of the world for the rectitude of our intentions, do, in the name and by authority of the good people of these colonies, solemnly publish and declare, that these united colonies are, and of right ought to be, free and independent states; that they are absolved from all allegiance to the British crown, and that all political connection between them and the state of Great Britain is, and ought to be, totally dissolved; and that, as free and independent states, they have full power to levy war, conclude peace, contract alliances, establish commerce, and to do all other acts and things which independent states may of right do. And, for the support of this declaration, with a firm reliance on the protection of Divine Providence, we mutually pledge to each other our lives, our fortunes, and our sacred honor.

Constitution
of the United States

¶ In addition to stating the purposes of the Constitution, the Preamble makes it clear that the government is established by consent of the governed. "We the people, . . . ordain and establish" the government. We, the people, have supreme power in establishing the government of the United States of America.

¶ By separating the functions of government among branches concerned with lawmaking (Article 1), law executing (Article 2), and law interpreting (Article 3), the framers of the Constitution were applying the principle of separation of powers and developing a system of checks and balances as a defense against tyranny.

¶ Practice has modified the provision that all lawmaking powers granted in the Constitution are vested in Congress. For example, such administrative agencies as the Interstate Commerce Commission can issue regulations that in some ways have the force of laws.

¶ *Clause 1.* The members of the House of Representatives are elected every two years by the "electors" (voters) of the states. Except for the provisions of Amendments 15, 19, 24, and 26, the individual states decide who may or may not vote.

¶ *Clause 2.* This clause specifies that a member of the House of Representatives must be (1) at least 25 years of age, (2) a United States citizen for at least 7 years, and (3) a resident of the state in which elected. (Custom has added the requirement of residence in the Congressional district from which a Representative is elected.) Each state is divided into Congressional districts for the purpose of electing Representatives; each district elects one. ¶ TERM OF OFFICE: 2 years.

PREAMBLE

We the people of the United States, in order to form a more perfect Union, establish justice, insure domestic tranquillity, provide for the common defense, promote the general welfare, and secure the blessings of liberty to ourselves and our posterity, do ordain and establish this CONSTITUTION for the United States of America.

ARTICLE 1.
LEGISLATIVE DEPARTMENT

SECTION 1. CONGRESS

All legislative powers herein granted shall be vested in a Congress of the United States, which shall consist of a Senate and House of Representatives.

SECTION 2. HOUSE OF REPRESENTATIVES

1. Election and term of members. The House of Representatives shall be composed of members chosen every second year by the people of the several states, and the electors in each state shall have the qualifications requisite for electors of the most numerous branch of the state legislature.

2. Qualifications. No person shall be a Representative who shall not have attained to the age of twenty-five years, and been seven years a citizen of the United States, and who shall not, when elected, be an inhabitant of that state in which he shall be chosen.

722

THE THREE BRANCHES OF THE FEDERAL GOVERNMENT

LEGISLATIVE BRANCH

HOUSE OF REPRESENTATIVES
Each state is represented in the House of Representatives based on population.

SENATE
Each state is represented in the Senate equally by two Senators.

Standing Committees of the House

Agriculture
Appropriations
Armed Services
Banking, Finance, and Urban Affairs
Budget
District of Columbia
Education and Labor
Foreign Affairs
Government Operations
House Administration
Interior and Insular Affairs
Interstate and Foreign Commerce
Judiciary
Merchant Marine and Fisheries
Post Office and Civil Service
Public Works and Transportation
Rules
Science and Technology
Small Business
Standards of Official Conduct
Veterans' Affairs
Ways and Means

Standing Committees of the Senate

Agriculture, Nutrition, and Forestry
Appropriations
Armed Services
Banking, Housing, and Urban Affairs
Budget
Commerce, Science, and Transportation
Energy and Natural Resources
Environment and Public Works
Finance
Foreign Relations
Governmental Affairs
Judiciary
Labor and Human Resources
Rules and Administration
Veterans' Affairs

EXECUTIVE BRANCH

Executive Departments

Department of State
Department of the Treasury
Department of Defense
Department of Justice
Department of the Interior
Department of Agriculture
Department of Commerce
Department of Labor
Department of Health and Human Services
Department of Education
Department of Housing and Urban Development
Department of Transportation
Department of Energy

The Executive Office

The White House
Office of Management and Budget
Council of Economic Advisers
Council on Environmental Quality
Domestic Policy Staff
National Security Council
Central Intelligence Agency
Office of Administration
Office of Science and Technology Policy
Office of the Special Representative for Trade

Independent Federal Agencies (Partial Listing)

ACTION
American Red Cross
Board of Governors of the Federal Reserve System
Environmental Protection Agency
Equal Employment Opportunity Commission
Farm Credit Administration
Federal Communications Commission

Federal Deposit Insurance Corporation
Federal Election Commission
Federal Mediation and Conciliation Service
Federal Trade Commission
General Services Administration
Interstate Commerce Commission

National Academy of Sciences
National Aeronautics and Space Administration
National Foundation on the Arts and Humanities
National Labor Relations Board
National Science Foundation
National Transportation Safety Board

Nuclear Regulatory Commission
Securities and Exchange Commission
Small Business Administration
Smithsonian Institution
Tennessee Valley Authority
United States Postal Service
Veterans Administration

JUDICIAL BRANCH

SUPREME COURT

Courts of Appeals

District Courts

Courts of the District of Columbia

Special Courts

Court of Claims
Court of Customs and Patent Appeals
Customs Court
Tax Court
Court of Military Appeals
Territorial Courts

¶ *Clause 3.* The bracketed portion of this clause beginning on line 5 forms what came to be called the "three-fifths compromise." Amendment 13 and Section 2 of Amendment 14 overruled this provision in the case of black Americans but not for Indians. However, since 1940 Indians have been included in the population census. ¶ Originally each state was entitled to one Representative for every 30,000 people. Later, membership was limited by law to a total of 435. ¶ A population census of the United States is taken every ten years to determine the number of Representatives to which each state is entitled. Regardless of its population, however, each state is entitled to at least one Representative in Congress.

¶ *Clause 4.* The "executive authority" refers to the governor of the state; a "writ of election" is an order for a special election to fill the vacant seat.

¶ *Clause 5.* In actual practice it is the majority party—the political party having the largest number of members in the House—that chooses the Speaker of the House and other House officials (clerk, doorkeeper, sergeant-at-arms, postmaster, and chaplain). The Speaker is the only official chosen from among the members of the House. ¶ The House, by a majority vote, can impeach (accuse) an Executive Department officer or a federal judge. The trial of the impeached official takes place in the Senate. (See Section 3, Clause 6.)

¶ *Clause 1.* Under the provisions of Amendment 17, the 100 Senators are now elected directly by the voters of the states in the same manner as the Representatives. The method of electing Senators provided here, by which the state legislatures chose Senators, came to be considered undemocratic and was therefore changed.

¶ *Clause 2.* One third of the Senate comes up for election every two years. This procedure was established in the first Senate, whose Senators were divided into three groups. One group was to serve for two years, the second for four years, and the third for six years. As a result, the terms of Senators today overlap, making the Senate a "continuing" body, in which two thirds of the members are "carried over" through every election. In contrast, the total membership of the House of Representatives is elected every two years. ¶ Under Amendment 17, if a Senator resigns or dies, the state governor can call a special election to fill the vacancy. The state legislature, however, may empower the governor to name a temporary Senator.

724

3. Apportionment of Representatives and direct taxes. Representatives [and direct taxes] shall be apportioned among the several states which may be included within this Union, according to their respective numbers [which shall be determined by adding to the whole number of free persons, including those bound to service for a term of years, and excluding Indians not taxed, three fifths of all other persons]. The actual enumeration shall be made within three years after the first meeting of the Congress of the United States, and within every subsequent term of ten years, in such manner as they shall by law direct. The number of Representatives shall not exceed 1 for every 30,000, but each state shall have at least 1 Representative; [and until such enumeration shall be made, the state of New Hampshire shall be entitled to choose 3; Massachusetts, 8; Rhode Island and Providence Plantations, 1; Connecticut, 5; New York, 6; New Jersey, 4; Pennsylvania, 8; Delaware, 1; Maryland, 6; Virginia, 10; North Carolina, 5; South Carolina, 5; and Georgia, 3.]

4. Filling vacancies. When vacancies happen in the representation from any state, the executive authority thereof shall issue writs of election to fill such vacancies.

5. Officers; impeachment. The House of Representatives shall choose their Speaker and other officers; and shall have the sole power of impeachment.

SECTION 3. SENATE

1. Number of members and terms of office. The Senate of the United States shall be composed of two Senators from each state [chosen by the legislature thereof], for six years, and each Senator shall have one vote.

2. Classification; filling vacancies. [Immediately after they shall be assembled in consequence of the first election, they shall be divided as equally as may be into three classes. The seats of the Senators of the first class shall be vacated at the expiration of the second year, of the second class at the expiration of the fourth year, and of the third class at the expiration of the sixth year, so that one third may be chosen every second year; and if vacancies happen by resignation, or otherwise, during the recess of the legislature of any state, the executive thereof may make temporary appointments until the next meeting of the legislature, which shall then fill such vacancies.]

3. Qualifications. No person shall be a Senator who shall not have attained to the age of thirty years, and been nine years a citizen of the United States, and who shall not, when elected, be an inhabitant of that state for which he shall be chosen.

¶ *Clause 3.* This clause specifies that a Senator must be (1) at least 30 years of age, (2) a United States citizen for at least 9 years, and (3) a resident of the state in which elected. ¶ TERM OF OFFICE: 6 years.

4. President of the Senate. The Vice-President of the United States shall be president of the Senate, but shall have no vote, unless they be equally divided.

Clause 4. To serve as president of the Senate and vote only in case of a tie is the sole duty the Constitution assigns to the Vice-President. In recent years the Vice-President has assumed additional duties at the President's request, such as attending cabinet meetings, traveling abroad on good-will tours, and carrying out such ceremonial duties as entertaining leading officials from abroad and representing the government at important events.

5. Other officers. The Senate shall choose their other officers, and also a president *pro tempore,* in the absence of the Vice-President, or when he shall exercise the office of the President of the United States.

¶ *Clause 5.* "Other officers" include a secretary, chaplain, and sergeant-at-arms. These officers are not members of the Senate. *Pro tempore* is a Latin expression meaning "for the time being," or "temporarily." Thus, the president *pro tempore* acts as a temporary president of the Senate.

6. Trial of impeachments. The Senate shall have the sole power to try all impeachments. When sitting for that purpose, they shall be on oath or affirmation. When the President of the United States is tried, the Chief Justice shall preside; and no person shall be convicted without the concurrence of two thirds of the members present.

¶ *Clause 6.* Only the President, Vice-President, cabinet officials, and federal judges are subject to impeachment and removal from office. Members of the House and Senate cannot be impeached, but they can be censured and even removed from office by the members of their respective houses. ¶ Officials may be impeached only for committing "treason, bribery, or other high crimes and misdemeanors" (see Article 2, Section 4). The Chief Justice of the Supreme Court presides at the impeachment trial of a President. The Vice-President presides over all other impeachment trials. The Senate can find an impeached official guilty only if two thirds of the Senators present agree on the verdict. The only President ever impeached was Andrew Johnson, in 1867; he was saved from conviction by one vote. In 1974 Richard M. Nixon resigned as President after the Judiciary Committee of the House of Representatives recommended to the House that he be impeached.

7. Penalty for conviction. Judgment in cases of impeachment shall not extend further than to removal from office, and disqualification to hold and enjoy any office of honor, trust, or profit under the United States; but the party convicted shall nevertheless be liable and subject to indictment, trial, judgment, and punishment, according to law.

¶ *Clause 7.* The punishment for conviction in impeachment cases can consist only of removal from office and disqualification from holding any other federal office. However, the convicted person may also be tried in a regular court of law for this same offense. Although not impeached, President Nixon was granted a Presidential pardon, which spared him a possible criminal court trial.

¶ *Clause 1.* Under this provision Congress has passed a law stating that, unless the constitution of a state provides otherwise, Congressional elections must be held on the Tuesday following the first Monday in November of even-numbered years. (Until 1960 Maine held elections in September.) Congress has also ruled that Representatives must be elected by districts, rather than by the state as a whole, and that secret ballots (or voting machines, where required by state law) must be used.

¶ *Clause 2.* Under Amendment 20 Congress now meets on January 3, unless it sets another day by law.

¶ *Clause 1.* Until 1969 Congress used this clause to disqualify elected candidates and prevent them from taking office on the grounds of public policy. On one occasion the House refused to admit to membership an elected candidate who had violated the criminal laws. On another occasion the Senate refused to seat a victorious candidate whose election campaign had been characterized by "fraud and corruption." When the House refused to seat Adam Clayton Powell in 1967 on grounds of "gross misconduct," he sued. Two years later, the Supreme Court ruled that Congress had to seat all Senators and Representatives who met the requirements of Article 1, Section 2, Clause 2. ¶ A *quorum* is the minimum number of persons required to be present to transact business; a majority of the House or Senate constitutes a quorum. In practice, business is often transacted with less than a quorum present, and may go on as long as no member objects to the lack of a quorum.

¶ *Clause 2.* Each house has extensive rules of procedure. Each house can censure, punish, or expel a member. Expulsion requires a two-thirds vote.

¶ *Clause 3.* Each house is required to keep a journal of its activities. These journals, called the *House Journal* and the *Senate Journal*, are published at the end of each session of Congress. A third journal, called the *Congressional Record*, is published every day that Congress is in session, and furnishes a daily account of what Representatives and Senators do and say. ¶ If one fifth of those present insist on a roll call of the members' votes, each member's vote must be recorded in the proper house journal.

¶ *Clause 4.* Both houses must remain in session for the same period of time and in the same place.

SECTION 4. ELECTIONS AND MEETINGS

1. Holding elections. The times, places, and manner of holding elections for Senators and Representatives shall be prescribed in each state by the legislature thereof; but the Congress may at any time by law make or alter such regulations, except as to the places of choosing Senators.

2. Meetings. The Congress shall assemble at least once in every year, [and such meeting shall be on the first Monday in December,] unless they shall by law appoint a different day.

SECTION 5. RULES OF PROCEDURE

1. Organization. Each house shall be the judge of the elections, returns, and qualifications of its own members, and a majority of each shall constitute a quorum to do business; but a smaller number may adjourn from day to day, and may be authorized to compel the attendance of absent members, in such manner, and under such penalties, as each house may provide.

2. Proceedings. Each house may determine the rules of its proceedings, punish its members for disorderly behavior, and with the concurrence of two thirds, expel a member.

3. Journal. Each house shall keep a journal of its proceedings, and from time to time publish the same, excepting such parts as may in their judgment require secrecy; and the yeas and nays of the members of either house on any question shall, at the desire of one fifth of those present, be entered on the journal.

4. Adjournment. Neither house, during the session of Congress, shall, without the consent of the other, adjourn for more than three days, nor to any other place than that in which the two houses shall be sitting.

SECTION 6. PRIVILEGES AND RESTRICTIONS

1. Pay and privileges. The Senators and Representatives shall receive a compensation for their services, to be ascertained by law and paid out of the Treasury of the United States. They shall in all cases, except treason, felony, and breach of the peace, be privileged from arrest during their attendance at the session of their respective houses, and in going to and returning from the same; and for any speech or debate in either house, they shall not be questioned in any other place.

¶ *Clause 1.* In 1981 the salary of a member of Congress was $60,662.50 a year. ¶ The provision concerning privilege from arrest establishes the principle of "Congressional immunity." According to this principle, members cannot be arrested or brought into court for what they say in speeches and debates in Congress. The aim of this provision is to enable members of Congress to speak freely. They are subject to arrest, however, if they commit a crime, and, under the laws governing slander and libel, are liable for any false or defamatory statements they may make outside Congress.

2. Restrictions. No Senator or Representative shall, during the time for which he was elected, be appointed to any civil office under the authority of the United States, which shall have been created, or the emoluments whereof shall have been increased, during such time; and no person holding any office under the United States shall be a member of either house during his continuance in office.

¶ *Clause 2.* This clause emphasizes the separation of powers in the federal government. Legislators cannot, while they are members of Congress, hold positions also in the executive or judicial departments. Nor can legislators resign and then accept positions that were created during their term of office. Thus members of Congress cannot set up jobs for themselves in the executive or judicial branches of the government. Furthermore, if a member resigns and is appointed to an existing executive or judicial position, he or she cannot profit from any increase in pay in this position that was voted during the member's term in Congress.

SECTION 7. METHOD OF PASSING LAWS

1. Revenue bills. All bills for raising revenue shall originate in the House of Representatives; but the Senate may propose or concur with amendments as on other bills.

¶ *Clause 1.* All revenue, or money-raising, bills must be introduced in the House of Representatives. This provision grew out of a demand that the popularly elected branch of the legislature should have the "power of the purse." (Until Amendment 17 was ratified, the House was the only popularly elected branch.) It was also felt that the voters had more control over Representatives, who are elected for two-year terms, than over Senators, who are elected for six-year terms. Thus Representatives would be more careful than Senators in considering revenue bills. Since the Senate has the power to amend any bill, however, it can amend a revenue bill in such a way as actually to introduce a revenue bill of its own.

2. How a bill becomes a law. Every bill which shall have passed the House of Representatives and the Senate shall, before it become a law, be presented to the President of the United States; if he approve, he shall sign it, but if not, he shall return it, with his objections, to that house in which it shall have originated, who shall enter the objections at large on their journal, and proceed to reconsider it. If after such reconsideration two-thirds of that house shall agree to pass the bill, it shall be sent, together with the objections, to the other house, by which it shall likewise be reconsidered, and, if approved by two-thirds of that house, it shall become a law. But in all such cases the votes of

¶ *Clause 2.* When both houses of Congress pass a law, it is then sent to the President. ¶ If the President does not approve of a bill, one of several things may occur. The President may (1) veto, or refuse to sign, the bill; (2) permit the bill to become a law without signing it by holding it for ten days (not counting Sundays) while Congress is in session; (3) hold the bill near the end of a session in the hope that Congress will adjourn within ten days. In that case, the bill fails to become a law, just as though the President had formally vetoed it. This type of veto is called a "pocket veto." ¶ A bill vetoed by the President can become a law, however, if two thirds or more of both houses vote for the bill a second time. When this happens, Congress is said to have "overridden the Presidential veto."

HOW A BILL BECOMES A LAW

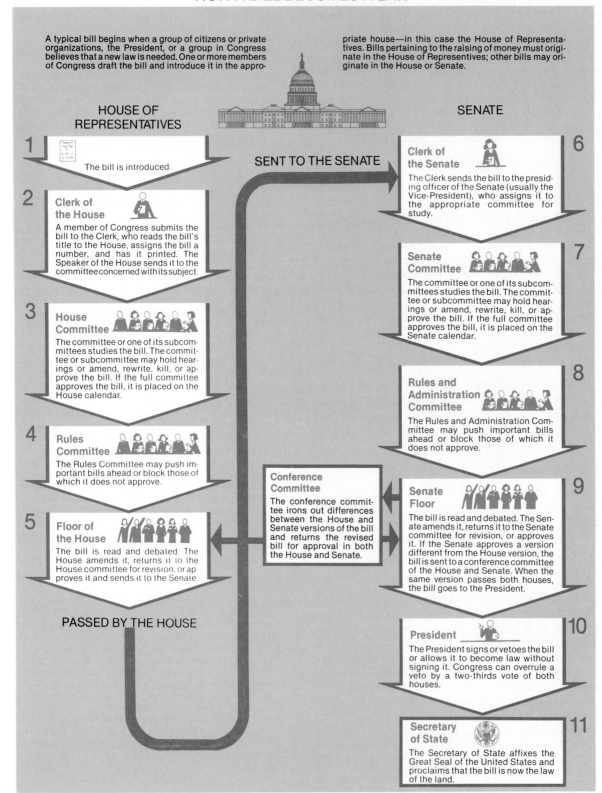

A typical bill begins when a group of citizens or private organizations, the President, or a group in Congress believes that a new law is needed. One or more members of Congress draft the bill and introduce it in the appro-priate house—in this case the House of Representatives. Bills pertaining to the raising of money must originate in the House of Representives; other bills may originate in the House or Senate.

HOUSE OF REPRESENTATIVES

SENATE

SENT TO THE SENATE

1 The bill is introduced.

2 Clerk of the House
A member of Congress submits the bill to the Clerk, who reads the bill's title to the House, assigns the bill a number, and has it printed. The Speaker of the House sends it to the committee concerned with its subject.

3 House Committee
The committee or one of its subcommittees studies the bill. The committee or subcommittee may hold hearings or amend, rewrite, kill, or approve the bill. If the full committee approves the bill, it is placed on the House calendar.

4 Rules Committee
The Rules Committee may push important bills ahead or block those of which it does not approve.

5 Floor of the House
The bill is read and debated. The House amends it, returns it to the House committee for revision, or approves it and sends it to the Senate.

PASSED BY THE HOUSE

6 Clerk of the Senate
The Clerk sends the bill to the presiding officer of the Senate (usually the Vice-President), who assigns it to the appropriate committee for study.

7 Senate Committee
The committee or one of its subcommittees studies the bill. The committee or subcommittee may hold hearings or amend, rewrite, kill, or approve the bill. If the full committee approves the bill, it is placed on the Senate calendar.

8 Rules and Administration Committee
The Rules and Administration Committee may push important bills ahead or block those of which it does not approve.

Conference Committee
The conference committee irons out differences between the House and Senate versions of the bill and returns the revised bill for approval in both the House and Senate.

9 Senate Floor
The bill is read and debated. The Senate amends it, returns it to the Senate committee for revision, or approves it. If the Senate approves a version different from the House version, the bill is sent to a conference committee of the House and Senate. When the same version passes both houses, the bill goes to the President.

10 President
The President signs or vetoes the bill or allows it to become law without signing it. Congress can overrule a veto by a two-thirds vote of both houses.

11 Secretary of State
The Secretary of State affixes the Great Seal of the United States and proclaims that the bill is now the law of the land.

728

both houses shall be determined by yeas and nays, and the names of the persons voting for and against the bill shall be entered on the journal of each house respectively. If any bill shall not be returned by the President within ten days (Sundays excepted) after it shall have been presented to him, the same bill shall be a law, in like manner as if he had signed it, unless the Congress by their adjournment prevent its return, in which case it shall not be a law.

3. Presidential approval or veto. Every order, resolution, or vote to which the concurrence of the Senate and House of Representatives may be necessary (except on a question of adjournment) shall be presented to the President of the United States; and before the same shall take effect, shall be approved by him, or being disapproved by him, shall be repassed by two thirds of the Senate and House of Representatives, according to the rules and limitations prescribed in the case of a bill.

SECTION 8. POWERS DELEGATED TO CONGRESS

The Congress shall have power

1. To lay and collect taxes, duties, imposts, and excises, to pay the debts and provide for the common defense and general welfare of the United States; but all duties, imposts, and excises shall be uniform throughout the United States;

2. To borrow money on the credit of the United States;

3. To regulate commerce with foreign nations, and among the several states, [and with the Indian tribes];

¶ *Clause 3.* A *joint resolution* results from declarations passed by both houses of Congress on the same subject. It becomes a law in the same manner as a bill. A Congressional declaration of war takes the form of a joint resolution. A *concurrent resolution* represents only an expression of opinion on the part of either house of Congress. It does not have the force of law and, therefore, does not require Presidential approval. The process of amending the Constitution may start this way. A vote censuring a Representative or Senator, or an expression of sympathy, takes the form of a concurrent resolution.

¶ Section 8 places important powers in the hands of Congress, indicating that the framers of the Constitution were aware of the weaknesses of the Congress under the Articles of Confederation. This section lists 18 powers granted to Congress—the *delegated* or *enumerated powers*. The first 17 are expressed powers because they clearly designate specific areas in which Congress may exercise its authority. The eighteenth power is contained in the famous elastic clause, from which has come the doctrine of implied powers. The elastic clause permits the stretching of the other 17 powers.

¶ *Clause 1.* This clause gives Congress the power to levy and collect taxes, duties, or tariffs (taxes on imported goods collected at customhouses), and excises (taxes on goods produced, sold, or consumed within the country). The term "imposts" includes duties and excise taxes. Notice that these taxes must be uniform throughout the United States. According to this clause, the power to tax may be used only (1) to pay the government's debts and (2) to provide for the common defense and general welfare. The Social Security tax on payrolls is a present-day use of the power to tax.

¶ *Clause 2.* The power granted in Clause 2 enables the government to borrow money by issuing bonds for sale, on which the government pays interest. This clause, extended by Clause 18, has also given Congress the power to establish national banks and the Federal Reserve System.

¶ *Clause 3.* Congress is given direct control over interstate and foreign commerce. This provision has been extended, by the use of Clause 18, to give Congress control over transportation, communication, and navigation. In order to exercise this broad power, Congress has set up administrative agencies, such as the Interstate Commerce Commission and the Federal Communications Commission.

729

¶ *Clause 4.* This clause provides the power to regulate the methods by which aliens become citizens of the United States and to form rules regarding bankruptcy.

¶ *Clause 5.* Congress is permitted to coin money, to determine the gold and silver content of money, and to order the printing of paper money. It also permits Congress to set up uniform standards for measuring weights and distances.

¶ *Clause 6.* Under this clause Congress authorizes the Treasury Department to investigate counterfeiting of money or of government bonds.

¶ *Clause 7.* In 1970 Congress transferred authority over the postal system to the executive branch in the Postal Reorganization Act. The Post Office Department was replaced by an independent agency, the United States Postal Service.

¶ *Clause 8.* This clause shows that the framers of the Constitution were eager to promote the progress of science and the arts. Under this power Congress has passed laws providing that inventors be granted *patents* (exclusive rights to manufacture and sell their inventions for 17 years) and that authors and composers be granted *copyrights* (exclusive rights to control the publication or performance of their works for their lifetimes plus 50 years).

¶ *Clause 9.* Congress is granted the power to establish the federal district courts, the Courts of Appeals, and special courts.

¶ *Clause 10.* Congress protects and controls citizens and ships of the United States when they are out of the country. It may also punish counterfeiting in the United States of bonds and notes of a foreign government.

¶ *Clause 11.* Congress is given the power to declare war. Although Congress alone has this power, several Presidents have taken military action without prior consent of Congress. In 1846 President Polk sent troops into an area claimed by both the United States and Mexico. In 1950 President Truman ordered American troops into Korea. And in the mid-1960's, through executive order, American troops became involved in the conflict in South Vietnam without a formal declaration of war. The War Powers Act of 1973 requires the President to report to Congress within 48 hours any new commitment of American troops to a foreign war. Unless Congress declares war, the President must end hostilities within 60 days and withdraw the troops within 90 days. Congress can require earlier withdrawal by passing a joint resolution, which the President cannot veto. ¶ Letters of marque and reprisal were licenses issued by the government to privateers (armed ships, privately owned), allowing them to attack enemy ships during wartime. In the War of 1812, the government of the United States issued many of these licenses to American privateers, who did extensive damage to British trade. Today, the issuing of such licenses is outlawed by international agreement.

4. To establish a uniform rule of naturalization, and uniform laws on the subject of bankruptcies throughout the United States;

5. To coin money, regulate the value thereof, and of foreign coin, and fix the standard of weights and measures;

6. To provide for the punishment of counterfeiting the securities and current coin of the United States;

7. To establish post offices and post roads;

8. To promote the progress of science and useful arts by securing for limited times to authors and inventors the exclusive right to their respective writings and discoveries;

9. To constitute tribunals inferior to the Supreme Court;

10. To define and punish piracies and felonies committed on the high seas and offenses against the law of nations;

11. To declare war, [grant letters of marque and reprisal,] and make rules concerning captures on land and water;

730

12. To raise and support armies, but no appropriation of money to that use shall be for a longer term than two years;

13. To provide and maintain a navy;

14. To make rules for the government and regulation of the land and naval forces;

15. To provide for calling forth the militia to execute the laws of the Union, suppress insurrections, and repel invasions;

16. To provide for organizing, arming, and disciplining the militia, and for governing such part of them as may be employed in the service of the United States, reserving to the states, respectively, the appointment of the officers, and the authority of training the militia according to the discipline prescribed by Congress;

17. To exercise exclusive legislation in all cases whatsoever, over such district (not exceeding ten miles square) as may, by cession of particular states, and the acceptance of Congress, become the seat of government of the United States, and to exercise like authority over all places purchased by the consent of the legislature of the state in which the same shall be, for the erection of forts, magazines, arsenals, dock-yards, and other needful buildings;—and

18. To make all laws which shall be necessary and proper for carrying into execution the foregoing powers, and all other powers vested by this Constitution in the government of the United States, or in any department or officer thereof.

SECTION 9. POWERS DENIED TO THE FEDERAL GOVERNMENT

1. [The migration or importation of such persons as any of the states now existing shall think proper to admit shall not be prohibited by the Congress prior to the year 1808; but a tax or duty may be imposed on such importation, not exceeding $10 for each person.]

¶ *Clause 12.* The two-year limit in Clause 12 on money appropriations for the army was included to keep the major military power under strict civilian control.

¶ *Clause 13.* Notice that appropriations for the navy were not limited. An air force, of course, was not dreamed of when the Constitution was written.

¶ *Clause 14.* Under the power granted in this clause, Congress has established rules and regulations governing military discipline and the procedure of courts-martial.

¶ *Clause 15.* The term "militia" now refers to the National Guard units of the states. These units may now be called up by the President to keep law and order. They can become part of the United States Army in emergencies.

¶ *Clause 16.* Congress is authorized to help states support their militia.

¶ *Clause 17.* This clause enables Congress to exercise exclusive control over the government of the District of Columbia. In 1973 Congress relinquished some of this control by allowing the District to choose local officials. By this clause Congress also controls all installations owned and operated by the federal government in the various states.

¶ *Clause 18.* "Necessary and proper" are the key words in the so-called *elastic clause.* Only by combining the power granted in this clause with one of the other 17 powers can Congress use the implied powers granted to it in the Constitution. Laws based on this clause are, of course, subject to review by the judicial branch.

¶ Section 9 limits the powers of Congress.

¶ *Clause 1.* "Such persons" refers to slaves. This provision grew out of the commerce compromise at the Constitutional Convention held in Philadelphia in 1787. It was agreed that Congress would not prohibit the importation of slaves prior to 1808, and that it would not impose an import tax of more than $10 per slave. The importation of slaves into the United States became illegal in 1808.

¶ *Clause 2*. The guarantee of the *writ of habeas corpus* (meaning "you may have the body, or person") has been called the most important single safeguard of personal liberty under Anglo-American law. It protects a person against being held in jail on insufficient evidence or no evidence at all. The lawyer of a person arrested can obtain a writ, or court order, that requires the arrested person to be brought before a judge who must determine whether there are sufficient grounds to hold the person in jail. If there are no such grounds, the person must be freed.

¶ *Clause 3*. A "bill of attainder" is a legislative measure that condemns and punishes a person without a jury trial. Such measures were used in England, where Parliament could, by law, declare persons guilty of treason and punish them by death and confiscation of property. Under the Constitution Congress cannot by law single out certain persons and inflict punishment on them. The power to punish belongs to the judiciary. ¶ An *ex post facto law* is a law that punishes a person for doing something that was legal before the law was passed, or that increases the penalty for earlier actions. Because of this clause, the Lindbergh kidnaping law of 1932, for example, could not be applied to persons who committed the crime of kidnaping before that year.

¶ *Clause 4*. A capitation tax is a direct tax imposed on each person, such as the poll tax on persons voting. This provision was inserted to prevent Congress from taxing slaves per poll, or per person, for the purpose of abolishing slavery. Amendment 16 overrules this clause. Amendment 24 outlaws federal poll taxes.

¶ *Clause 5*. This clause also resulted from the commerce compromise. The southern states wanted to make sure that Congress could not use its taxing power to impose taxes on southern exports, such as cotton and tobacco.

¶ *Clause 6*. This clause declares that the United States is an open market in which all states have equal trading and commercial opportunities.

¶ *Clause 7*. This clause concerns the all-important power of the purse. Since Congress controls expenditures, it can limit the powers of the President by limiting the amount of money the Chief Executive may spend to run the government. This clause is perhaps the single most important curb on Presidential power in the Constitution. Furthermore, the requirement to account for money spent and received helps to protect against misuse of funds.

¶ *Clause 8*. This clause prohibits the establishment of a nobility. It also discourages bribery of American officials by foreign governments.

2. The privilege of the writ of *habeas corpus* shall not be suspended, unless when in cases of rebellion or invasion the public safety may require it.

3. No bill of attainder or *ex post facto* law shall be passed.

4. [No capitation or other direct tax shall be laid, unless in proportion to the census herein before directed to be taken.]

5. No tax or duty shall be laid on articles exported from any state.

6. No preference shall be given any regulation of commerce or revenue to the ports of one state over those of another; nor shall vessels bound to, or from, one state, be obliged to enter, clear, or pay duties in another.

7. No money shall be drawn from the Treasury, but in consequence of appropriations made by law; and a regular statement and account of the receipts and expenditures of all public money shall be published from time to time.

8. No title of nobility shall be granted by the United States; and no person holding any office of profit or trust under them, shall, without the consent of the Congress, accept of any present, emolument, office, or title, of any kind whatever, from any king, prince, or foreign state.

SECTION 10.
POWERS DENIED TO THE STATES

1. No state shall enter into any treaty, alliance, or confederation; grant letters of marque and reprisal; coin money; emit bills of credit; make anything but gold and silver coin a tender in payment of debts; pass any bill of attainder, *ex post facto* law, or law impairing the obligation of contracts, or grant any title of nobility.

2. No state shall, without the consent of the Congress, lay any imposts or duties on imports or exports, except what may be absolutely necessary for executing its inspection laws; and the net produce of all duties and imposts, laid by any state on imports or exports, shall be for the use of the Treasury of the United States; and all such laws shall be subject to the revision and control of the Congress.

3. No state shall, without the consent of Congress, lay any duty of tonnage, keep troops, or ships of war in time of peace, enter into any agreement or compact with another state, or with a foreign power, or engage in war, unless actually invaded, or in such imminent danger as will not admit of delay.

ARTICLE 2.
EXECUTIVE DEPARTMENT

SECTION 1. PRESIDENT AND VICE-PRESIDENT

1. Term of office. The executive power shall be vested in a President of the United States of America. He shall hold his office during the term of four years, and together with the Vice-President, chosen for the same term, be elected as follows:

¶ According to Section 10, states cannot (1) make treaties, (2) coin money, (3) pass either bills of attainder or *ex post facto* laws, (4) impair obligations of contract, (5) grant titles of nobility, (6) tax imports or exports without the consent of Congress, (7) keep troops or warships in time of peace, (8) deal with another state or foreign power without the consent of Congress, and (9) engage in war unless invaded.

¶ *Clause 1.* Because Shays' Rebellion was still fresh in the minds of the delegates to the Constitutional Convention, and since several of the states at that time were being urged to pass legislation relieving debtors from the payment of their debts, the delegates decided to protect creditors once and for all by denying states the right to pass laws that would impair obligations of contract. During the Great Depression, which began in 1929, and the New Deal period (1933–45), the Supreme Court upheld state laws relieving debtors or mortgagees from paying their debts on the due dates, but payments were simply postponed, not canceled.

¶ *Clause 2.* The powers forbidden to the states in this clause are to vote for taxes on goods sent in or out of a state, unless Congress agrees.

¶ *Clause 3.* This clause forbids the states to keep troops or warships in peacetime or to deal with another state or a foreign nation, unless Congress agrees.

¶ *Clause 1.* This provision gives the executive power to the President. The President may use all of the means available to carry out the laws or refrain from using some of these means. Of course, the power and prestige of the Presidency depend to some extent on the personality of the person who holds the office.

733

THE FEDERAL SYSTEM

DIVISION OF POWERS

FEDERAL GOVERNMENT

Enumerated powers delegated to the Congress:

- to regulate interstate and foreign commerce
- to establish laws governing citizenship
- to coin money
- to control the postal system
- to regulate patents and copyrights
- to establish federal courts lower than the Supreme Court
- to declare war
- to establish and support the armed forces
- to pass all laws necessary and proper for carrying out the preceding powers

FEDERAL AND STATE GOVERNMENTS

Concurrent powers shared by the federal and state governments:

- to tax
- to borrow money
- to establish penal laws
- to charter banks
- to take property for public purposes by eminent domain

STATE GOVERNMENTS

Reserved powers retained by the state governments:

- to regulate suffrage for state elections
- to maintain a system of public education
- to establish marriage and divorce laws
- to establish laws governing corporations
- to establish traffic laws
- to regulate intrastate commerce
- Amendment 10 of the Constitution reserves to the state governments all powers not delegated to the federal government or prohibited by the Constitution.

PROHIBITED POWERS

Powers denied the federal government:

- to suspend the writ of *habeas corpus* except in cases of rebellion or invasion
- to levy taxes on exports
- to give preferential treatment in commerce or revenue to the ports of any state
- to draw money from the Treasury except by appropriation under a specific law
- to permit persons holding federal office to accept gifts from a foreign country without consent of Congress

Powers denied the federal and state governments:

- to pass bills of attainder
- to pass *ex post facto* laws
- to grant titles of nobility

Powers denied the state governments:

- to enter into treaties with other nations or with other states without the consent of Congress
- to coin money
- to impair obligations of contract
- to place a tax on imports or exports except to carry out their inspection laws
- to keep troops or ships in time of peace without consent of Congress

2. Electoral system. Each state shall appoint, in such manner as the legislature thereof may direct, a number of electors, equal to the whole number of Senators and Representatives to which the state may be entitled in the Congress; but no Senator or Representative, or person holding an office of trust or profit under the United States, shall be appointed an elector.

3. Former method of using the electoral system. [The electors shall meet in their respective states, and vote by ballot for two persons, of whom one at least shall not be an inhabitant of the same state with themselves. And they shall make a list of all the persons voted for, and of the number of votes for each; which list they shall sign and certify, and transmit sealed to the seat of the government of the United States, directed to the president of the Senate. The president of the Senate shall, in the presence of the Senate and House of Representatives, open all the certificates, and the votes shall then be counted. The person having the greatest number of votes shall be the President, if such number be a majority of the whole number of electors appointed; and if there be more than one who have such majority, and have an equal number of votes, then the House of Representatives shall immediately choose by ballot one of them for President; and if no person have a majority, then from the five highest on the list the said House shall in like manner choose the President. But in choosing the President the votes shall be taken by states, the representation from each state having one vote. A quorum for this purpose shall consist of a member or members from two thirds of the states, and a majority of all the states shall be necessary to a choice. In every case, after the choice of the President, the person having the greatest number of votes of the electors shall be the Vice-President. But if there should remain two or more who have equal votes, the Senate shall choose from them by ballot the Vice-President.]

4. Time of elections. The Congress may determine the time of choosing the electors, and the day on which they shall give their votes; which day shall be the same throughout the United States.

¶ *Clauses 2, 3.* These clauses established the electoral system, but very little that the framers decided about electing a President has survived in the form they intended. The delegates to the Constitutional Convention, still fearful of popular rule, decided that the President and Vice-President ought to be elected by a small group of persons called "electors" chosen according to a method determined by each state legislature. Until Andrew Jackson's Presidency, electors were chosen by state legislatures. Since then the people have voted directly for the electors. Some changes in the method of electing a President have been made by formal amendment, as in Amendment 12; other changes have resulted from political practice.

¶ *Clause 4.* Today Presidential elections are held on the Tuesday after the first Monday in November. Electoral votes are cast on the Monday after the second Wednesday in December.

¶ *Clause 5*. This clause specifies that the President must be (1) a native-born citizen of the United States, (2) at least 35 years of age, and (3) a resident of the United States for at least 14 years. ¶ TERM OF OFFICE: 4 years.

¶ *Clause 6*. If a President dies or is removed from office, the Vice-President succeeds to the office. John Tyler, in 1841, was the first Vice-President to succeed to the Presidency. By assuming the office of President, not simply serving as an acting President, Tyler established a precedent that has since been followed. ¶ Under the Presidential Succession Act of 1947, if both the President and the Vice-President die or are removed from office, the order of succession is as follows: (1) Speaker of the House, (2) President *pro tempore* of the Senate, and (3) the cabinet members in the order in which their offices were created. ¶ Amendment 25, adopted in 1967, clarifies the procedure to be followed in case the President or Vice-President is unable to serve or resigns.

¶ *Clause 7*. In 1981 the President's salary was $200,000 a year, plus a $50,000 expense account and a nontaxable fund for travel and official entertainment limited to $112,000. The Vice-President's salary was $79,125 a year plus a $10,000 expense allowance.

¶ *Clause 8*. The President assumes office officially only after taking the oath of office, which is administered by the Chief Justice of the United States.

¶ *Clause 1*. The important point in this provision is that it places the armed forces under civilian control. The President is a civilian but is superior in military power to any military officer. ¶ The words "principal officer in each of the executive departments" are the basis for the creation of the President's cabinet. Each cabinet member is the head of one of the executive departments. The President chooses the cabinet members, with the consent of the Senate, and can remove any cabinet official without asking Senate approval.

¶ *Clause 2*. The President makes treaties with the advice and consent of two thirds of the Senate. A treaty ratified by the Senate becomes the supreme law of the land. The Pres-

5. Qualifications for President. No person except a natural-born citizen [or a citizen of the United States, at the time of the adoption of this Constitution], shall be eligible to the office of the President; neither shall any person be eligible to that office who shall not have attained to the age of thirty-five years, and been fourteen years a resident within the United States.

6. Filling vacancies. In case of the removal of the President from office, or of his death, resignation, or inability to discharge the powers and duties of the said office, the same shall devolve on the Vice-President, and the Congress may by law provide for the case of removal, death, resignation, or inability, both of the President and Vice-President, declaring what officer shall then act as President, and such officer shall act accordingly, until the disability be removed, or a President shall be elected.

7. Salary. The President shall, at stated times, receive for his services, a compensation, which shall neither be increased nor diminished during the period for which he shall have been elected, and he shall not receive within that period any other emolument from the United States, or any of them.

8. Oath of office. Before he enter on the execution of his office, he shall take the following oath or affirmation:—"I do solemnly swear (or affirm) that I will faithfully execute the office of President of the United States, and will to the best of my ability, preserve, protect, and defend the Constitution of the United States."

SECTION 2. POWERS OF THE PRESIDENT

1. Military powers. The President shall be Commander in Chief of the Army and Navy of the United States, and of the militia of the several states, when called into the actual service of the United States; he may require the option, in writing, of the principal officer in each of the executive departments, upon any subject relating to the duties of their respective offices, and he shall have power to grant reprieves and pardons for offenses against the United States, except in cases of impeachment.

2. Treaties and appointments. He shall have power, by and with the advice and consent of the Senate, to make treaties, provided two thirds of the

736

Senators present concur; and he shall nominate, and by and with the advice and consent of the Senate, shall appoint ambassadors, other public ministers and consuls, judges of the Supreme Court, and all other officers of the United States, whose appointments are not herein otherwise provided for, and which shall be established by law; but the Congress may by law vest the appointment of such inferior officers, as they think proper, in the President alone, in the courts of law, or in the heads of departments.

3. Filling vacancies. The President shall have power to fill up all vacancies that may happen during the recess of the Senate, by granting commissions which shall expire at the end of their next session.

ident can also enter into executive agreements with foreign governments that have the same force as treaties but do not require Senate approval. ¶ With the consent of the Senate, the President can appoint ambassadors, public ministers, consuls, and other diplomatic officials, as well as federal judges, military officers, and members of administrative agencies. "Inferior officers" are those subordinate to the cabinet members or to federal judges. ¶ At the present time, a majority of federal government positions are filled by men and women who have passed examinations given by the United States Civil Service Commission.

¶ *Clause 3.* If a vacancy in an important position occurs when Congress is not in session, the President has the power to fill such a vacancy with an interim appointment. When Congress meets again, this appointment or a new appointment must be submitted to the Senate so that it may be approved.

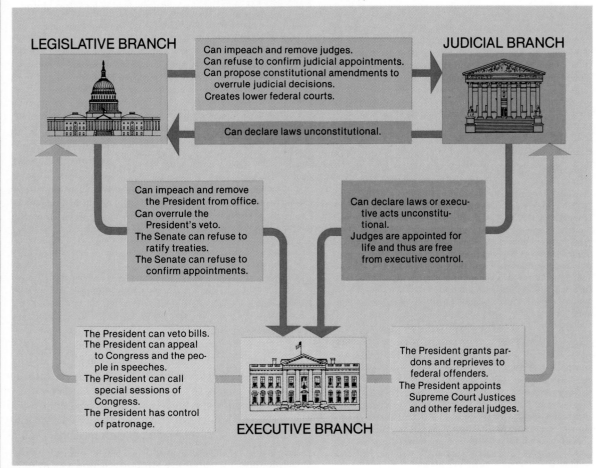

SEPARATION OF FEDERAL POWERS: Examples of Checks and Balances

LEGISLATIVE BRANCH

JUDICIAL BRANCH

Can impeach and remove judges.
Can refuse to confirm judicial appointments.
Can propose constitutional amendments to overrule judicial decisions.
Creates lower federal courts.

Can declare laws unconstitutional.

Can impeach and remove the President from office.
Can overrule the President's veto.
The Senate can refuse to ratify treaties.
The Senate can refuse to confirm appointments.

Can declare laws or executive acts unconstitutional.
Judges are appointed for life and thus are free from executive control.

The President can veto bills.
The President can appeal to Congress and the people in speeches.
The President can call special sessions of Congress.
The President has control of patronage.

The President grants pardons and reprieves to federal offenders.
The President appoints Supreme Court Justices and other federal judges.

EXECUTIVE BRANCH

¶ The President's duties include the following: (1) *Legislative duties:* delivering annual and special messages to Congress; calling special sessions of Congress; approving or vetoing bills (see Article 1, Section 7). (2) *Diplomatic duties:* receiving (or refusing to receive) ambassadors or ministers of foreign countries to indicate that the United States recognizes (or refuses to recognize) the government of these countries. The President can also send home the ambassador of a foreign country as a sign that the United States is breaking off diplomatic relations with that country. (3) *Executive duties:* executing all the laws. In actual fact the administration and enforcement of the laws are in the hands of the various government departments, commissions, and administrative agencies; but the President is responsible for seeing that they are carried out. (4) *Military duties:* commissioning of United States armed forces officers.

¶ (See annotation of Article 1, Section 3, Clauses 6–7.)

¶ By authorizing the establishment of a system of federal courts, Article 3 creates the judicial power — the power to hear and decide cases. Under the judicial powers granted by the Constitution or developed through Supreme Court decisions, the courts have declared unconstitutional certain laws of Congress, acts of the President, laws of the state legislatures, and decisions of the state courts.

¶ Only the Supreme Court is established by the Constitution itself, but the Constitution gives Congress the authority to establish the lower courts that exist today. Since the Constitution does not state the number of justices to be appointed to the Supreme Court, Congress decides the number by law. Today the Supreme Court has nine justices. ¶ Congress has created two types of lower courts. One type includes federal district courts and Courts of Appeals, which review cases sent up by the district courts. District courts and Courts of Appeals are called "constitutional courts" because they are general courts deriving their power directly from the Constitution. The second type of court deals with cases of a specialized nature. The Court of Claims, the Tax Court, and the Court of Customs and Patent Appeals are included in this second group. ¶ The framers of the Constitution wanted to make sure that federal judges would be independent of political influence. Accordingly federal judges are appointed for life, subject to good behavior, and their pay cannot be reduced by law during their term of office.

¶ *Clause 1.* Here the words "law" and "equity" have special meanings. "Law" means the common law — the laws that originated in England and that have been based on centuries of judicial decisions. "Equity" refers to principles of justice also developed in England to remedy wrongs in situations in which the common law was inadequate. Today, in the United States, law and equity are applied by the same judges in the same courts. ¶ The power of the federal courts extends to two types of cases: (1) those involv-

SECTION 3. DUTIES OF THE PRESIDENT

He shall from time to time give to the Congress information of the state of the Union, and recommend to their consideration such measures as he shall judge necessary and expedient; he may, on extraordinary occasions, convene both houses, or either of them, and in case of disagreement between them, with respect to the time of adjournment, he may adjourn them to such time as he shall think proper; he shall receive ambassadors and other public ministers; he shall take care that the laws be faithfully executed, and shall commission all the officers of the United States.

SECTION 4. IMPEACHMENT

The President, Vice-President, and all civil officers of the United States, shall be removed from office on impeachment for, and conviction of, treason, bribery, or other high crimes and misdemeanors.

ARTICLE 3.
JUDICIAL DEPARTMENT

SECTION 1. FEDERAL COURTS

The judicial power of the United States shall be vested in one Supreme Court, and in such inferior courts as the Congress may from time to time ordain and establish. The judges, both of the Supreme and inferior courts, shall hold their offices during good behavior, and shall, at stated times, receive for their services a compensation, which shall not be diminished during their continuance in office.

SECTION 2. JURISDICTION OF FEDERAL COURTS

1. General jurisdiction. The judicial power shall extend to all cases, in law and equity, arising under this Constitution, the laws of the United States, and treaties made or which shall be made, under their authority; to all cases affecting ambassadors, other public ministers and consuls; to all cases of admiralty and maritime jurisdiction; to controversies to which the United States shall be a party; to controversies between two or more states; [between a state and citizens of another state;] between citizens of different states; between citizens of the same state claiming lands under grants of different states, and between a state or the citizens thereof, and foreign states, citizens, or subjects.

2. Supreme Court. In all cases affecting ambassadors, other public ministers and consuls, and those in which a state shall be a party, the Supreme Court shall have original jurisdiction. In all the other cases before mentioned, the Supreme Court shall have appellate jurisdiction, both as to law and fact, with such exceptions, and under such regulations as the Congress shall make.

3. Conduct of trials. The trial of all crimes, except in cases of impeachment, shall be by jury; and such trial shall be held in the state where the said crimes shall have been committed; but when not committed within any state, the trial shall be at such place or places as the Congress may by law have directed.

SECTION 3. TREASON

1. Definition. Treason against the United States shall consist only in levying war against them, or in adhering to their enemies, giving them aid and comfort. No person shall be convicted of treason unless on the testimony of two witnesses to the same overt act, or on confession in open court.

2. Punishment. The Congress shall have power to declare the punishment of treason, but no attainder of treason shall work corruption of blood or forfeiture except during the life of the person attainted.

ARTICLE 4.
RELATIONS AMONG THE STATES

SECTION 1. OFFICIAL ACTS

Full faith and credit shall be given in each state to the public acts, records, and judicial proceedings of every other state. And the Congress may by general laws prescribe the manner in which such acts, records, and proceedings shall be proved, and the effect thereof.

ing the interpretation of the Constitution, federal laws, treaties, and laws relating to ships on the high seas and navigable waters; and (2) those involving the United States government itself, foreign diplomatic officials, two or more state governments, citizens of different states when the sum involved is more than $10,000, and a state or its citizens versus foreign countries or citizens of foreign countries.

¶ *Clause 2.* "Original jurisdiction" means the right to try a case before any other court may hear it. "Appellate jurisdiction" means the right of a court to try cases appealed from lower courts. Most of the cases tried by the Supreme Court are cases appealed from lower federal and state courts. Cases involving foreign diplomats and any state of the United States may be started directly in the Supreme Court.

¶ *Clause 3.* Every person accused of a federal crime is guaranteed a jury trial near the scene of the crime. But accused persons may give up this privilege, if they wish. ¶ Amendments 5, 6, and 7 expand the provisions of this clause.

¶ *Clause 1.* Treason is the only crime specifically defined in the Constitution. To be found guilty of treason, a person must be shown to have helped wage war against the United States, or to have given aid and comfort to its enemies. A person cannot be convicted without the testimony of two witnesses to the same act unless the person confesses in open court.

¶ *Clause 2.* The punishment for treason, as determined by Congress, is death or a fine of $10,000 and imprisonment for not less than five years. This clause further states that the punishment for treason cannot be extended to the children of a traitor. They cannot be deprived of their rights and their property — as had been done in England.

¶ The purpose of this provision is to make sure that the official records of one state are respected in all the other states. Official records of this kind include birth certificates, marriage licenses, death certificates, corporation charters, wills, and court decisions. This provision also protects a citizen's right to collect money that has been awarded by a court decision in one state, even if the person who owes the money moves to another state.

¶ *Clause 1.* The terms "privileges" and "immunities" simply mean the rights of citizens. Thus a state cannot discriminate against citizens of other states in favor of its own citizens, except in certain very special areas—such as voting, for example. A state can impose residence requirements for voting, so that citizens of another state must reside in the state for a specified period before they can vote as citizens of their new state.

¶ *Clause 2.* This provision prevents a prisoner or a person charged with a crime from escaping justice by fleeing across a state line. It provides that a criminal be returned by the state where captured to the state where the crime was committed—a process known as extradition. A governor of a state cannot be forced to extradite, or return, a prisoner, however, if the governor feels that such action will result in injustice to the accused person.

¶ *Clause 3.* Since the ratification of Amendment 13 in 1865 brought an end to slavery in this country, the clause is now of historical interest only.

¶ *Clause 1.* The Northwest Ordinance of 1787 provided that new states be admitted to the Union on completely equal footing with the original thirteen states. Although the Constitution declares here that new states may not be created within the territory of any other state without its consent, an exception did occur in 1863, when West Virginia was formed from the western part of the state of Virginia. This exception occurred during the Civil War, and West Virginia received permission from the loyal, rather than the secessionist, government of Virginia.

¶ *Clause 2.* Under this provision Congress has the power to control all property belonging to the federal government. It can set up governments for territories and colonies of the United States. It can grant independence to a colony, as it did to the Philippines in 1946. It can set aside land for national parks and build dams for flood control.

¶ If public property is being destroyed and public safety endangered in a state, the President may decide to send troops into that state without having been requested to do so by local authorities. The President may even proclaim martial law in a state. This section also guarantees that states can govern only by consent of the governed.

SECTION 2. PRIVILEGES OF CITIZENS

1. Privileges. The citizens of each state shall be entitled to all privileges and immunities of citizens in the several states.

2. Extradition. A person charged in any state with treason, felony, or other crime, who shall flee from justice, and be found in another state, shall on demand of the executive authority of the state from which he fled, be delivered up, to be removed to the state having jurisdiction of the crime.

3. Fugitive slaves. [No person held in service or labor in one state, under the laws thereof, escaping into another, shall in consequence of any law or regulation therein, be discharged from such service or labor, but shall be delivered up on claim of the party to whom such service or labor may be due.]

SECTION 3. NEW STATES AND TERRITORIES

1. Admission of new states. New states may be admitted by the Congress into this Union; but no new state shall be formed or erected within the jurisdiction of any other state; nor any state be formed by the junction of two or more states, or parts of states, without the consent of the legislatures of the states concerned as well as of the Congress.

2. Powers of Congress over territories and other property. The Congress shall have power to dispose of and make all needful rules and regulations respecting the territory or other property belonging to the United States; and nothing in this Constitution shall be so construed as to prejudice any claims of the United States, or of any particular state.

SECTION 4. GUARANTEES TO THE STATES

The United States shall guarantee to every state in this Union a republican form of government, and shall protect each of them against invasion; and on application of the legislature, or of the executive (when the legislature cannot be convened) against domestic violence.

HOW THE CONSTITUTION MAY BE AMENDED

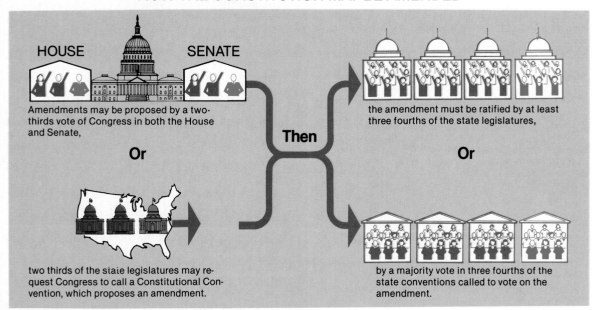

HOUSE   SENATE

Amendments may be proposed by a two-thirds vote of Congress in both the House and Senate,

Or

two thirds of the state legislatures may request Congress to call a Constitutional Convention, which proposes an amendment.

Then

the amendment must be ratified by at least three fourths of the state legislatures,

Or

by a majority vote in three fourths of the state conventions called to vote on the amendment.

ARTICLE 5.
METHODS OF AMENDMENT

The Congress, whenever two thirds of both houses shall deem it necessary, shall propose amendments to this Constitution, or, on the application of the legislatures of two thirds of the several states, shall call a convention for proposing amendments, which, in either case, shall be valid to all intents and purposes, as part of this Constitution, when ratified by the legislatures of three fourths of the several states, or by conventions in three fourths thereof, as the one or the other mode of ratification may be proposed by the Congress; provided that [no amendments which may be made prior to the year 1808 shall in any manner affect the first and fourth clauses in the Ninth Section of the First Article; and that] no state, without its consent, shall be deprived of its equal suffrage in the Senate.

¶ One of the most important features of the Constitution is that it can be amended, or changed. This adaptability is one of the four main principles of the Constitution. ¶ An amendment must first be *proposed* and then *ratified*. There are four methods of amending the Constitution. So far, all amendments have been proposed by Congress and ratified by state legislatures except Amendment 21, which was ratified by the convention method. ¶ The fact that only 26 amendments have been adopted since 1789 — and only 16 since 1791 — indicates that it is not easy to change the Constitution, and that changing it is a serious matter, requiring much thought and discussion in Congress, in the state legislatures, and among the people. ¶ Notice that there are two areas in which the Constitution cannot be amended under any circumstances. The first exception is obsolete because it is a reference to the period that preceded 1808. The second exception is still very important because it guarantees that every state shall have equal representation in the Senate.

ARTICLE 6.
GENERAL PROVISIONS

1. Public debts. All debts contracted and engagements entered into, before the adoption of this Constitution, shall be as valid against the United States under this Constitution, as under the Confederation.

¶ *Clause 1.* This provision was important because it announced to all that the new government would assume and pay back all debts of the government under the Articles of Confederation. It was one of several actions favored by Alexander Hamilton and undertaken by Congress in order to establish the credit of the new government.

¶ *Clause 2.* This is the famous "supremacy clause" of the Constitution. It declares that the "supreme law of the land" is (1) the Constitution, (2) the laws of the United States passed under this Constitution, and (3) the treaties made under the authority of the United States. ¶ According to the supremacy clause, the power of the national government is superior to the power of the state governments, provided that its actions are in accordance with the Constitution. The Supreme Court determines whether the actions of the President and Congress are constitutional.

¶ *Clause 3.* No religious qualification shall ever be required as a condition for holding public office. This provision results from the fact that in the United States there is separation of church and state. This means that a person's religion is supposed to remain a private matter, with no bearing on consideration for public office.

¶ The Constitutional Convention was summoned by the Congress of the Confederation to amend the Articles of Confederation. Under the Articles amendments had to be approved by all thirteen states. Instead of amending the Articles, however, the delegates to the Constitutional Convention drafted an entirely new plan of government. Realizing that it would be difficult to get the approval of all the states—Rhode Island, for example, had not even sent delegates to Philadelphia—the framers provided that the Constitution would go into effect after ratification by only nine states, not thirteen. As a result opponents of the Constitution said it had been adopted by revolutionary means.

2. The supreme law. This Constitution, and the laws of the United States which shall be made in pursuance thereof, and all treaties made, or which shall be made, under the authority of the United States, shall be the supreme law of the land; and the judges in every state shall be bound thereby, anything in the constitution or laws of any state to the contrary notwithstanding.

3. Oaths of office. The Senators and Representatives before mentioned, and the members of the several state legislatures, and all executive and judicial officers, both of the United States and of the several states, shall be bound by oath or affirmation, to support this Constitution; but no religious test shall ever be required as a qualification to any office or public trust under the United States.

ARTICLE 7. RATIFICATION

The ratification of the convention of nine states shall be sufficient for the establishment of the Constitution between the states so ratifying the same.

DONE in Convention by the unanimous consent of the States present the seventeenth day of September in the year of our Lord one thousand seven hundred and eighty-seven and of the independence of the United States of America the twelfth. In witness whereof we have hereunto subscribed our names.

G Washington —*President and deputy from Virginia*

NEW HAMPSHIRE

John Langdon
Nicholas Gilman

MASSACHUSETTS

Nathaniel Gorman
Rufus King

CONNECTICUT

William Samuel Johnson
Roger Sherman

NEW YORK

Alexander Hamilton

NEW JERSEY

William Livingston
David Brearley
William Paterson
Jonathan Dayton

PENNSYLVANIA

Benjamin Franklin
Thomas Mifflin
Robert Morris
George Clymer
Thomas FitzSimons
Jared Ingersoll
James Wilson
Gouverneur Morris

DELAWARE

George Read
Gunning Bedford
John Dickinson
Richard Bassett
Jacob Broom

MARYLAND

James McHenry
Daniel of St. Thomas Jenifer
Daniel Carroll

VIRGINIA

John Blair
James Madison

NORTH CAROLINA

William Blount
Richard Dobbs Spaight
Hugh Williamson

SOUTH CAROLINA

John Rutledge
Charles Cotesworth Pinckney
Charles Pinckney
Pierce Butler

GEORGIA

William Few
Abraham Baldwin

Amendments to the Constitution

(The first ten amendments to the Constitution are called the Bill of Rights. The Bill of Rights limits the powers of the federal government but not the powers of the states. The Supreme Court has ruled, however, that the "due process" clause of Amendment 14 protects individuals against denial by the states of certain rights included in the Bill of Rights. For example, the Supreme Court has decided that neither the federal government nor the states can deprive any individual of freedom of religion, speech, press, petition, assembly, or of several other rights that pertain to the fair treatment of an accused person.)

AMENDMENT 1.
FREEDOM OF RELIGION, SPEECH, PRESS, ASSEMBLY, AND PETITION (1791)

Congress shall make no law respecting an establishment of religion, or prohibiting the free exercise thereof; or abridging the freedom of speech, or of the press; or the right of the people peaceably to assemble, and to petition the government for a redress of grievances.

¶ Amendment 1 protects five great civil liberties: (1) Freedom of religion means that Congress cannot interfere with the right to worship as one sees fit. The Supreme Court, however, has ruled that Congress can require "conscientious objectors" to bear arms during wartime. Congress has, however, made special provisions to permit conscientious objectors to participate in war work without bearing arms. In interpreting the phrase "establishment of religion," the Supreme Court has decided that this phrase erects a wall of separation between church and state. The Supreme Court has prohibited state and local school authorities from requiring prayers or devotional reading of the Bible in public schools. (2) Freedom of speech means the right to speak out privately and publicly. However, this right does not permit anyone to slander people (make false and malicious remarks about them). Furthermore, the Supreme Court has declared that freedom of speech can be limited by the federal government if there is a "clear and present" danger that what is said may injure the general welfare. (3) Freedom of the press gives newspapers, television, and magazines the right to express ideas and opinions provided they do not libel people (publish false and malicious remarks about them) or incite the violent overthrow of the government. Also, the use of the United States mails may be denied to those publications that spread obscenity and fraudulent ideas. (4) Freedom to assemble is the right to attend meetings and join clubs. (5) The right to petition for redress of grievances means the opportunity to express complaints to any official of the federal government.

AMENDMENT 2.
RIGHT TO KEEP ARMS (1791)

A well-regulated militia, being necessary to the security of a free state, the right of the people to keep and bear arms shall not be infringed.

¶ The purpose of this amendment was to prevent Congress from denying states the right to have a militia (or National Guard) of armed citizens. It also protected Americans' right to keep weapons in order to resist a tyrannical government. In the public interest, however, Congress and many states have regulated the ownership and use of weapons by citizens through gun control legislation.

AMENDMENT 3.
QUARTERING OF TROOPS (1791)

No soldier shall, in time of peace, be quartered in any house, without the consent of the owner; nor in time of war, but in a manner to be prescribed by law.

¶ Amendments 3 and 4 guarantee all citizens the right to privacy and security in their own homes. ¶ Amendment 3 was designed to prevent the national government from requiring citizens to house and feed military personnel in their homes. The quartering of troops in the colonists' homes by the British government had been a source of friction between the American colonists and the British before the American Revolution.

743

¶ With the hated writs of assistance still fresh in their minds, the supporters of this amendment aimed to limit issuance of search warrants to the following conditions: (1) The warrant must be issued by a judge. (2) There must be a good reason for its use. (3) The officer who asks for a search warrant must take an oath affirming reasons for demanding the warrant. (4) The warrant must describe the place to be searched and the persons or things to be seized. ¶ The Supreme Court has decided that evidence illegally seized cannot be used in either federal or state courts. Under this amendment the federal government prohibits wiretapping unless a court permit is obtained showing a reasonable certainty that one of a certain list of crimes is being committed. ¶ In 1967 the Supreme Court held that eavesdropping and bugging by electronic means are permissible but only within certain limits; for example, police may use electronic eavesdropping devices if they secure a warrant in advance by showing probable cause. ¶ In 1968 the Supreme Court forbade the use of criminal evidence obtained by police listening in on a party line, but evidence derived from wiretapping is permitted in federal courts in some crimes.

¶ This amendment lists the rights of an accused person: (1) A person accused of a capital crime or any other serious crime must first be accused by a grand jury (a jury of 12 to 23 persons) before being brought to trial. An indictment or presentment by a grand jury is merely a formal accusation. (2) A person cannot be tried twice for the same crime. (3) A person cannot be required to give incriminating testimony in a courtroom or before a grand jury or Congressional committee. However, under the Immunity Act of 1954, a witness can be required to testify in certain cases if the evidence he or she may provide cannot be used in any trial of that person. (4) A person cannot be deprived of life, liberty, or property without due process of law—or according to the law of the land. (5) Congress cannot take private property for public use without paying a fair price for it. This provision, an important protection of property rights, establishes the principle of eminent domain. ¶ Members of the armed forces are tried by military courts and commissions and are not subject to the provision calling for indictment by a grand jury.

¶ This amendment continues the rights of an accused person. Notice that all witnesses against an accused person must appear on the witness stand, and that the government must help the accused to produce favorable witnesses. If an accused person cannot afford to hire a lawyer, the judge will assign one, and the government will pay the lawyer's fee. These provisions under Amendment 6 apply to federal courts. However, under the "due process" clause of Amendment 14, the Supreme Court has decided that state courts must also assign a lawyer to defend an accused person who cannot afford one.

AMENDMENT 4.
SEARCH AND SEIZURE; WARRANTS (1791)

The right of the people to be secure in their persons, houses, papers, and effects, against unreasonable searches and seizures, shall not be violated; and no warrants shall issue but upon probable cause, supported by oath or affirmation, and particularly describing the place to be searched, and the person or things to be seized.

AMENDMENT 5.
RIGHTS OF ACCUSED PERSONS (1791)

No person shall be held to answer for a capital, or otherwise infamous, crime, unless on a presentment or indictment of a grand jury, except in cases arising in the land or naval forces, or in the militia, when in actual service in time of war or public danger; nor shall any person be subject for the same offense to be twice put in jeopardy of life and limb; nor shall be compelled, in any criminal case, to be a witness against himself; nor be deprived of life, liberty, or property, without due process of law; nor shall private property be taken for public use, without just compensation.

AMENDMENT 6.
RIGHT TO SPEEDY TRIAL (1791)

In all criminal prosecutions, the accused shall enjoy the right to a speedy and public trial, by an impartial jury of the state and district wherein the crime shall have been committed, which district shall have been previously ascertained by law, and to be informed of the nature and cause of the accusation; to be confronted with the witnesses against him; to have compulsory process for obtaining witnesses in his favor, and to have the assistance of counsel for his defense.

AMENDMENT 7.
JURY TRIAL IN CIVIL CASES
(1791)

In suits at common law, where the value in controversy shall exceed $20, the right of trial by jury shall be preserved, and no fact tried by a jury shall be otherwise re-examined in any court of the United States than according to the rules of the common law.

¶ This amendment provides for a jury trial in federal civil cases (trials where one person sues another) in which more than $20 is involved. By custom, however, civil cases are not tried before federal courts unless they involve much larger sums of money.

AMENDMENT 8.
BAILS, FINES, PUNISHMENTS
(1791)

Excessive bail shall not be required, nor excessive fines imposed, nor cruel and unusual punishments inflicted.

¶ Persons accused of a crime and awaiting trial may be permitted to leave jail if they or someone else posts bail — a sum of money serving as a guarantee that the accused will appear for trial. The courts determine the amount of bail asked for. Cruel and unusual punishments, such as torture and beheading, are prohibited. ¶ In a series of rulings, the Supreme Court declared invalid convictions of accused persons based on confessions secured by torture or other "third degree" methods.

AMENDMENT 9.
POWERS RESERVED
TO THE PEOPLE (1791)

The enumeration in the Constitution, of certain rights, shall not be construed to deny or disparage others retained by the people.

¶ The Constitution does not describe specifically all the rights to be retained by the people. This amendment was added in order to guarantee that those fundamental rights not enumerated must be respected by the national government at all times.

AMENDMENT 10.
POWERS RESERVED
TO THE STATES (1791)

The powers not delegated to the United States by the Constitution, nor prohibited by it to the states, are reserved to the states respectively, or to the people.

¶ This is known as the reserved power amendment. Powers delegated to the national government are listed in Article 1, Section 8. Powers prohibited to the states are found in Article 1, Section 10. Amendment 10 makes it clear that all other powers — the so-called reserved powers — are left to the states or to the people.

AMENDMENT 11.
SUITS AGAINST STATES (1798)

The judicial power of the United States shall not be construed to extend to any suit in law or equity, commenced or prosecuted against one of the United States, by citizens of another state, or by citizens or subjects of any foreign state.

¶ This is the first amendment to the Constitution that was designed to overrule a Supreme Court decision. In the case of *Chisholm v. Georgia* (1793), the Supreme Court ruled that two citizens of South Carolina could sue Georgia in a federal court for property that Georgia had confiscated. The states objected, arguing that since the states were sovereign, it was undignified to permit a state to be sued by a citizen of another state in a federal court. As a result of this amendment, a citizen of the United States or of a foreign nation who wishes to bring suit against any state is required to introduce the case in the courts of the state that is being sued.

745

¶ This amendment alters Article 2, Section 1, Clause 3. Before this amendment the electors voted for two persons, without designating which was to be President and which Vice-President. As a result in 1796 the people elected a Federalist President (John Adams) and a Republican Vice-President (Jefferson). In 1800 the electors of the victorious Republican Party each cast one vote for Jefferson, whom they wanted to be President, and one vote for Burr, whom they wanted to be Vice-President. The result, of course, was a tie. Amendment 12, which instructs electors to cast separate ballots for President and Vice-President, prevents such situations. (See also Amendment 23, which makes provision for choosing electors of President and Vice-President by the District of Columbia.)

AMENDMENT 12.
ELECTION OF PRESIDENT
AND VICE-PRESIDENT (1804)

The electors shall meet in their respective states, and vote by ballot for President and Vice-President, one of whom, at least, shall not be an inhabitant of the same state with themselves; they shall name in their ballots the person voted for as President, and in distinct ballots the person voted for as Vice-President, and they shall make distinct lists of all persons voted for as President, and of all persons voted for as Vice-President, and of the number of votes for each, which lists they shall sign and certify, and transmit, sealed, to the seat of government of the United States, directed to the President of the Senate; the President of the Senate shall, in the presence of the Senate and House of Representatives, open all the certificates and the votes shall then be counted; the person having the greatest number of votes for President shall be the President, if such number be a majority of the whole number of electors appointed; and if no person have such majority, then from the persons having the highest numbers not exceeding three on the list of those voted for as President, the House of Representatives shall choose immediately, by ballot, the President. But in choosing the President, the votes shall be taken by states, the representation from each state having one vote; a quorum for this purpose shall consist of a member or members from two thirds of the states, and a majority of all the states shall be necessary to a choice. [And if the House of Representatives shall not choose a President whenever the right of choice shall devolve upon them, before the fourth day of March next following, then the Vice-President shall act as President, as in the case of the death or other constitutional disability of the President.] The person having the greatest number of votes as Vice-President, shall be the Vice-President, if such number be a majority of the whole number of electors appointed, and if no person have a majority, then, from the two highest numbers on the list, the Senate shall choose the Vice-President; a quorum for the purpose shall consist of two thirds of the whole number of Senators, and a majority of the whole number shall be necessary to a choice. But no person constitutionally ineligible to the office of President shall be eligible to that of Vice-President of the United States.

HOW A PRESIDENT IS ELECTED

TIME SEQUENCE			
WINTER AND SPRING OF ELECTION YEAR	STATE PRIMARIES 	STATE CAUCUSES 	STATE PARTY LEADERS 

In some states political parties hold primaries and caucuses to choose delegates to their national conventions. In other states party leaders choose these delegates.

SUMMER OF ELECTION YEAR

REPUBLICAN NATIONAL CONVENTION

The delegates to the Republican National Convention nominate candidates for President and Vice-President and adopt a platform on which they run.

DEMOCRATIC NATIONAL CONVENTION

The delegates to the Democratic National Convention nominate candidates for President and Vice-President and adopt a platform on which they run.

BEFORE ELECTION

STATE REPUBLICAN HEADQUARTERS

The Republican Party in each state chooses electors who promise to vote for the party's candidates for President and Vice-President. The number of electors chosen is equal to the number of the state's Senators and Representatives.

STATE DEMOCRATIC HEADQUARTERS

The Democratic Party in each state chooses electors who promise to vote for the party's candidates for President and Vice-President. The number of electors chosen is equal to the number of the state's Senators and Representatives.

ELECTION DAY (NOVEMBER)

In voting for a Presidential nominee, the voters actually vote for the electors of the nominee's party. This is the popular vote.

DECEMBER

IF PARTY WINS...   IF PARTY WINS...

In each state the electors of the party with the greatest popular vote assemble at the state capital. There they vote separately for Presidential and Vice-Presidential candidates, usually those of their own party. This is the electoral vote. Certified copies of the vote are sent to the President of the United States Senate.

JANUARY

The President of the Senate counts the electoral votes in the presence of both houses of Congress.

To be elected, a candidate must receive a majority of the electoral vote.

¶ Amendments 13, 14, and 15 resulted from the Civil War. Amendment 13 freed the slaves, Amendment 14 made blacks citizens, and Amendment 15 forbade the states to deny black Americans the right to vote. ¶ Amendment 13 forbids slavery, and under Section 2, Congress has the power to enforce this order.

¶ This section contains a number of important provisions. By the definition of citizenship given here, black Americans were granted citizenship. The second sentence, forbidding states to abridge the privileges and immunities — the rights — of citizens, meant that the states could not interfere with the right of black Americans and other citizens to live a peaceful, useful life or to travel. ¶ This amendment, like Amendment 5, contains a "due process of law" clause. Amendment 5 denies to Congress and Amendment 14 denies to the states the power to deprive any person of life, liberty, or property without due process of law. This amendment, originally intended to protect black citizenship, has been broadly interpreted by the courts as a protection for corporations. Corporations, under this interpretation, are considered as persons. Their property cannot be taken away except by fair, legal methods. Thus, for example, the Interstate Commerce Commission can fix railroad rates only after giving railroad corporations an opportunity to present their side of the case. ¶ The "due process" clause also protects individuals from unfair actions by their state governments. It protects their rights of freedom of religion, speech, press, petition, and peaceful assembly and the rights of persons accused of crimes against state abuses. It prevents a state, in the exercise of its police power (the power to protect its people), from depriving anyone of civil liberties, except during a national emergency. ¶ The last provision of Section 1 prevents a state from denying equal protection of the laws. In 1954, in the case of *Brown v. Board of Education of Topeka,* the Supreme Court interpreted this provision to mean that segregation in public schools is unconstitutional. Also, in *Baker v. Carr* (1962) the Supreme Court ruled that unfair apportionment of representation in state legislatures violates the "equal protection" clause of this amendment.

¶ This section was never implemented, but later civil rights laws and Amendment 24 guaranteed the vote to black Americans. Amendment 19 gave women the right to vote. The Dawes Act and the 1924 citizenship law enfranchised Indians. And Amendment 26 changed the voting age from 21 to 18. This section dealing with apportionment of Representatives is sometimes called the "dead letter clause" of Amendment 14 since its provisions were never carried out.

AMENDMENT 13.
SLAVERY ABOLISHED (1865)

SECTION 1. Neither slavery nor involuntary servitude, except as a punishment for crime whereof the party shall have been duly convicted, shall exist within the United States, or any place subject to their jurisdiction.

SECTION 2. Congress shall have power to enforce this article by appropriate legislation.

AMENDMENT 14.
RIGHTS OF CITIZENS (1868)

SECTION 1. Citizenship defined. All persons born or naturalized in the United States and subject to the jurisdiction thereof, are citizens of the United States and of the state wherein they reside. No state shall make or enforce any law which shall abridge the privileges or immunities of citizens of the United States; nor shall any state deprive any person of life, liberty, or property, without due process of law; nor deny to any person within its jurisdiction the equal protection of the laws.

SECTION 2. Apportionment of Representatives. Representatives shall be apportioned among the several states according to their respective numbers, counting the whole number of persons in each state [excluding Indians not taxed]. But when the right to vote at any election for the choice of electors for President and Vice-President of the United States, Representatives in Congress, the executive and judicial officers of a state, or the members of the legislature thereof, is denied to any of the [male] inhabitants of such state, [being twenty-one years of age] and citizens of the United States, or in any way abridged, except for participation in rebellion, or other crime, the basis of representation therein shall be reduced in the proportion which the number of such [male] citizens shall bear to the whole number of male citizens [twenty-one years of age] in such state.

SECTION 3. Disability for engaging in insurrection. No person shall be a Senator or Representative in Congress, or elector of President and Vice-President, or hold any office, civil or military, under the United States, or under any state, who, having previously taken an oath, as a member of Congress, or as an officer of the United States, or as a member of any state legislature, or as an executive or judicial officer of any state, to support the Constitution of the United States, shall have engaged in insurrection or rebellion against the same, or given aid or comfort to the enemies thereof. But Congress may, by vote of two thirds of each house, remove such disability.

¶ This section aimed to punish the leaders of the Confederacy for having broken their oath to support the Constitution of the United States. All officials who had taken this oath and who later joined the Confederacy in the Civil War were disqualified from holding federal or state offices. Although many southern leaders were excluded under this section from holding office after the war, by 1872 most of them were permitted to return to political life. In 1898 all of the others were pardoned.

SECTION 4. Public debt. The validity of the public debt of the United States, authorized by law, including debts incurred for payment of pensions and bounties for services in suppressing insurrection or rebellion, shall not be questioned. But neither the United States nor any state shall assume or pay any debt or obligation incurred in aid of insurrection or rebellion against the United States [or any claim for the loss or emancipation of any slave]; but all such debts, obligations, and claims shall be held illegal and void.

¶ This section makes three important points: (1) The public debt of the United States incurred in fighting the Civil War was valid and could never be questioned by southerners. (2) The Confederate debt was void. It was illegal for the federal government or the states to pay any money on Confederate debts. This provision was meant to serve as a harsh lesson to all who had invested money in Confederate bonds. (3) No payment was to be made for the loss of former slaves.

SECTION 5. Enforcement. The Congress shall have power to enforce, by appropriate legislation, the provisions of this article.

AMENDMENT 15.
RIGHT OF SUFFRAGE (1870)

¶ The purpose of this amendment was to extend the *franchise,* or the right to vote, to blacks. Thus, according to this amendment, any person who can meet all of the qualifications for suffrage in a particular state cannot be deprived of the right to vote simply because of race or color.

SECTION 1. The right of citizens of the United States to vote shall not be denied or abridged by the United States or any state on account of race, color, or previous condition of servitude.

SECTION 2. The Congress shall have power to enforce this article by appropriate legislation.

¶ In 1894 Congress passed an income tax law. The following year the Supreme Court declared this tax law unconstitutional. The Court stated that the income tax was a direct tax and, therefore, according to the Constitution (Article 1, Section 2, Clause 3; Article 1, Section 9, Clause 4) should have been apportioned among the states according to their population. This decision was unpopular because it prevented the government from taxing people on the basis of their incomes in order to pay for government expenses, which were already large and growing larger. Amendment 16 overruled the Supreme Court decision and gave Congress the power to tax incomes from any source and without apportionment among the states according to population. Today income taxes are the federal government's major source of income.

¶ Before the passage of this amendment, Senators were chosen by the state legislatures (see Article 1, Section 3, Clause 1). There was a great deal of dissatisfaction with this method because it gave the voters little control over the Senate. Amendment 17 provides for the direct election of Senators by the voters of each state, thus making Senators more responsive to the will of the voters who put them in office.

¶ This amendment outlawed the making, sale, or transportation of alcoholic beverages in the United States except for special purposes. This amendment was later repealed by Amendment 21.

AMENDMENT 16.
INCOME TAX (1913)

The Congress shall have power to lay and collect taxes on incomes, from whatever source derived, without apportionment among the several states, and without regard to any census or enumeration.

AMENDMENT 17.
ELECTION OF SENATORS (1913)

SECTION 1. Method of election. The Senate of the United States shall be composed of two Senators from each state, elected by the people thereof, for six years; and each Senator shall have one vote. The electors in each state shall have the qualifications requisite for electors of the most numerous branch of the state legislatures.

SECTION 2. Filling vacancies. When vacancies happen in the representation of any state in the Senate, the executive authority of such state shall issue writs of election to fill such vacancies: *Provided* that the legislature of any state may empower the executive thereof to make temporary appointments until the people fill the vacancies by election as the legislature may direct.

[**SECTION 3. Not retroactive.** This amendment shall not be so construed as to affect the election or term of any Senator chosen before it becomes valid as part of the Constitution.]

AMENDMENT 18.
NATIONAL PROHIBITION (1919)

[**SECTION 1.** After one year from the ratification of this article the manufacture, sale, or transportation of intoxicating liquors within, the importation thereof into, or the exportation thereof from, the United States and all territory subject to the jurisdiction thereof for beverage purposes is hereby prohibited.

SECTION 2. The Congress and the several states shall have concurrent power to enforce this article by appropriate legislation.

SECTION 3. This article shall be inoperative unless it shall have been ratified as an amendment to the Constitution by the legislatures of the several states, as provided in the Constitution, within seven years from the date of the submission hereof to the states by the Congress.]

AMENDMENT 19.
WOMAN SUFFRAGE (1920)

SECTION 1. The right of citizens of the United States to vote shall not be denied or abridged by the United States or by any state on account of sex.

SECTION 2. Congress shall have power to enforce this article by appropriate legislation.

¶ This amendment, extending the right to vote to all qualified women, marked the greatest single step in extending the suffrage in the United States. Women's struggle to win this basic right began many years before Amendment 19 was finally ratified.

AMENDMENT 20.
"LAME DUCK" AMENDMENT (1933)

SECTION 1. Beginning of terms. The terms of the President and Vice-President shall end at noon on the 20th day of January, and the terms of Senators and Representatives at noon on the 3rd day of January, of the years in which such terms would have ended if this article had not been ratified; and the terms of their successors shall then begin.

SECTION 2. Beginning of Congressional sessions. The Congress shall assemble at least once in every year, and such meeting shall begin at noon on the 3d day of January, unless they shall by law appoint a different day.

SECTION 3. Presidential succession. If at the time fixed for the beginning of the term of the President, the President-elect shall have died, the Vice-President-elect shall become President. If a President shall not have been chosen before the time fixed for the beginning of his term, or if the President-elect shall have failed to qualify, then the Vice-President-elect shall act as President until a President shall have qualified; and the Congress may by law provide for the case wherein neither a President-elect nor a Vice-President-elect shall have qualified, declaring who shall then act as President, or the manner in which one who is to act shall be selected, and such person shall act accordingly until a President or Vice-President shall have qualified.

¶ When the Constitution was written, transportation and communication were so slow that a new President and new members of Congress elected in November could not reach the capital to take office until March 4. However, since sessions of Congress began in December, a session including newly elected members could not be held until 13 months after their election. Thus, even if a member running for reelection were defeated in November, he or she would serve in the session of Congress that began the month after this election and continue to serve several more months. Since defeated candidates had been rejected by the voters, they were called "lame ducks," suggesting that their political wings had been clipped. One purpose of Amendment 20 was to limit the term and power of lame duck members.

SECTION 4. Filling Presidential vacancy. The Congress may by law provide for the case of the death of any of the persons from whom the House of Representatives may choose a President whenever the right of choice shall have devolved upon them, and for the case of the death of any of the persons from whom the Senate may choose a Vice-President whenever the right of choice shall have devolved upon them.

[**SECTION 5. Effective date.** Sections 1 and 2 shall take effect on the 15th day of October following the ratification of this article.

SECTION 6. Time limit for ratification. This article shall be inoperative unless it shall have been ratified as an amendment to the Constitution by the legislatures of three fourths of the several states within seven years from the date of its submission.]

AMENDMENT 21.
REPEAL OF PROHIBITION (1933)

SECTION 1. The eighteenth article of amendment to the Constitution of the United States is hereby repealed.

SECTION 2. The transportation or importation into any state, territory, or possession of the United States for delivery or use therein of intoxicating liquors, in violation of the laws thereof, is hereby prohibited.

[**SECTION 3.** This article shall be inoperative unless it shall have been ratified as an amendment to the Constitution by conventions in the several states, as provided in the Constitution, within seven years from the date of the submission hereof to the states by the Congress.]

AMENDMENT 22.
TWO-TERM LIMIT FOR PRESIDENTS (1951)

SECTION 1. No person shall be elected to the office of the President more than twice, and no person who has held the office of President, or acted as President, for more than two years of a term to which some other person was elected President shall be elected to the office of the President more than once. [But this Article shall not apply to any

¶ This amendment, which repealed Amendment 18, was the only amendment ratified by special state conventions instead of state legislatures. Congress felt that a popular referendum (vote) would give the people a better chance to voice their opinions on prohibition. As in Amendments 18 and 20, Congress included a provision that the amendment, to become law, have a seven-year limit for ratification by the states.

¶ The original Constitution placed no limit on the number of terms a President could be elected to office. Washington and Jefferson, however, set a two-term precedent. In 1940 this tradition was broken when Franklin D. Roosevelt was elected for a third term, and in 1944, when he won a fourth term. The purpose of this amendment was to write the two-term precedent into law. The bracket portion was included so that the amendment would not apply to President Truman, who was in office at the time the amendment was ratified. Note that anyone who succeeds to the Presidency and completes less than two years of another person's term may be elected for two more terms.

752

person holding the office of President when this Article was proposed by the Congress, and shall not prevent any person who may be holding the office of President, or acting as President, during the term within which this Article becomes operative from holding the office of President or acting as President during the remainder of such term.]

[**SECTION 2.** This Article shall be inoperative unless it shall have been ratified as an amendment to the Constitution by the legislatures of three fourths of the several states within seven years from the date of its submission to the states by the Congress.]

AMENDMENT 23.
PRESIDENTIAL ELECTORS FOR DISTRICT OF COLUMBIA (1961)

SECTION 1. The District constituting the seat of Government of the United States shall appoint in such manner as the Congress may direct:

A number of electors of President and Vice-President equal to the whole number of Senators and Representatives in Congress to which the District would be entitled if it were a State, but in no event more than the least populous State; they shall be in addition to those appointed by the States, but they shall be considered, for the purposes of the election of President and Vice-President, to be electors appointed by a State; and they shall meet in the District and perform such duties as provided by the twelfth article of amendment.

SECTION 2. The Congress shall have power to enforce this article by appropriate legislation.

AMENDMENT 24.
POLL TAX BANNED IN NATIONAL ELECTIONS (1964)

SECTION 1. The right of citizens of the United States to vote in any primary or other election for President or Vice-President, for electors of President or Vice-President, or for Senator or Representative in Congress, shall not be denied or abridged by the United States or any state by reason of failure to pay any poll tax or other tax.

SECTION 2. The Congress shall have the power to enforce this article by appropriate legislation.

¶ Amendment 23 enabled residents of the District of Columbia to vote for President and Vice-President. In effect, it gave the capital city three members in the Electoral College, the same number elected by each of the six least populous states.

¶ This amendment forbade the collection of poll taxes—taxes persons had to pay before they were able to vote—as a requirement for voting in federal elections. (In 1964 five southern states still had poll taxes.) In 1966 the Supreme Court ruled that poll taxes were illegal as a requirement for voting in state and local elections as well.

753

¶ This amendment was intended to clarify Article 2, Section 1, Clause 6, particularly in the case of the temporary disability of a President. The problem of disability in office existed during the last part of President Wilson's term and occurred again when President Eisenhower was disabled by a heart attack. This amendment provided two ways (see sections 3 and 4) the Vice-President could assume the duties of the office of the President, as well as a procedure by which the President could again perform the duties of office when the disability ended.

¶ However, the first use of this amendment did not involve Presidential disability. It involved a Presidential resignation. In 1974 Richard M. Nixon became the first President in American history to resign from office. And Vice-President Gerald R. Ford, who succeeded as President, became the first person to become President without being first elected to that office or to the Vice-Presidency. ¶ This unique situation occurred in the following way. In 1973 Vice-President Spiro T. Agnew had resigned, and President Nixon had filled the vacancy according to the provisions of Section 2 of this amendment. Gerald R. Ford, a member of the House of Representatives, had been named Vice-President with the approval of Congress. Therefore when Nixon resigned as President during the Watergate scandal, Ford took over the Presidency. A vacancy then existed in the Vice-Presidency (see Section 2). President Ford named Nelson A. Rockefeller as Vice-President, and this nomination was also approved by a majority vote of both houses of Congress.

AMENDMENT 25. PRESIDENTAL DISABILITY AND SUCCESSION (1967)

1. In case of the removal of the President from office or his death or resignation, the Vice-President shall become President.

2. Whenever there is a vacancy in the office of the Vice-President, the President shall nominate a Vice-President who shall take the office upon confirmation by a majority vote of both houses of Congress.

3. Whenever the President transmits to the President *pro tempore* of the Senate and the Speaker of the House of Representatives his written declaration that he is unable to discharge the powers and duties of his office, and until he transmits to them a written declaration to the contrary, such powers and duties shall be discharged by the Vice-President as Acting President.

4. Whenever the Vice-President and a majority of either the principal officers of the executive departments or of such other body as Congress may by law provide, transmit to the President *pro tempore* of the Senate and the Speaker of the House of Representatives their written declaration that the President is unable to discharge the powers and duties of his office, the Vice-President shall immediately assume the powers and duties of the office as Acting President.

Thereafter, when the President transmits to the President *pro tempore* of the Senate and the Speaker of the House of Representatives his written declaration that no inability exists, he shall resume the powers and duties of his office unless the Vice-President and a majority of either the principal officers of the executive department or of such other body as Congress may by law provide, transmit within four days to the President *pro tempore* of the Senate and the Speaker of the House of Representatives their written declaration that the President is unable to discharge the powers and duties of his office. Thereupon Congress shall decide the issue, assembling within 48 hours for that purpose if not in session. If the Congress, within 21 days after receipt of the latter written declaration, or, if Congress is not in session, within 21 days after Congress is required to assemble, determines by two-thirds vote of both houses that the President is unable to discharge the powers and duties of his office, the Vice-President shall continue to discharge the same as Acting President; otherwise, the President shall assume the powers and duties of his office.

AMENDMENT 26.
VOTING AGE LOWERED TO 18 (1971)

SECTION 1. The right of citizens of the United States, who are 18 years of age or older, to vote shall not be denied or abridged by the United States or any State on account of age.

SECTION 2. The Congress shall have the power to enforce this article by appropriate legislation.

PROPOSED AMENDMENT.
THE WOMEN'S RIGHTS AMENDMENT

SECTION 1. Equality of rights under the law shall not be denied or abridged by the United States or by any State on account of sex.

SECTION 2. Congress shall have the power to enforce, by appropriate legislation, the provisions of this article.

PROPOSED AMENDMENT.
REPRESENTATION FOR THE DISTRICT OF COLUMBIA

1. For purposes of representation in the Congress, election of the President and Vice-President, and article 5 of this Constitution, the District constituting the seat of government of the United States shall be treated as though it were a State.

2. The exercise of the rights and powers conferred under this article shall be by the people of the District constituting the seat of government, and as shall be provided by the Congress.

3. The twenty-third article of amendment to the Constitution of the United States is hereby repealed.

¶ Congress, in the Voting Rights Act of 1970, had lowered the minimum voting age from 21 to 18, but the Supreme Court ruled that this law applied only to federal elections. Amendment 26 specified that 18 was the legal voting age in state, local, and federal elections.

¶ This amendment, submitted to the states for ratification in 1972, would prohibit discrimination based on a person's sex.

¶ This amendment, proposed in 1978, would give the District of Columbia two Senators and one or two Representatives. The number of Presidential electors—three, at present—would be changed to the total number of Senators and Representatives. The District would also acquire the power of a state in amending the Constitution.

Index

Italicized page numbers preceded by *m* or *p* refer to a *map* (*m*) or picture or feature (*p*) on the page. Italicized page numbers preceded by *c* refer to a chart or graph on the page. **Boldface** page numbers are pages on which a definition or explanation is given.

Bay of Pigs, Cuba, 428
Begin, Menachem, 441, *p441*
Belgium: in World War I, *m220,* 222–23, *m223,* 231, *m231,* 232; post-World War I, *m234,* 235; in World War II, 323, *m332, m342*
Belknap, William W., 59
Bell, Alexander Graham, *p63,* 93
Bellamy, Edward, 148
Belleau Wood, France, 231, *m231*
Bell Telephone Company, 389
Benson, Ezra Taft, 376
Benton, Thomas Hart, *p280*
Berger, Victor, 117
Berlin, Germany: airlift to, 357; crisis in (1958), 365; wall built in, 430; in World War II, *m332,* 341, 342, *m342*
Berryman, Clifford, *p165*
Bessemer, Henry, 95
Bessemer converter, *p107*
Bethlehem Steel Corporation, 191
Bethune, Mary McLeod, 293
Bicentennial, *p427*
Bill of Rights: in U.S. Constitution, 743–45
Bimetallism, 133–34. *See also* Gold; Silver
Birdseye, Clarence, 281
Birmingham, Alabama, 52
Birth and death rates, *c703*
Black Americans: civil rights movement of, 399–400, 449–52; in post-Civil War period, 49–55, *p53;* as cowboys, 77; in Farmers' Alliances, 131; Fifteenth Amendment and, 45; Harlem Renaissance of, 295–96; in Indian wars, 72; labor unions and, 114, 267; literature of, in late 1800's, 149; muckrakers and, 159; poll tax and, 407; Populist Party and, 132–33; during Reconstruction, 36, 39–43, *p39,* 46–47, *p46, p48,* 49; F. D. Roosevelt and, 265, 269; T. Roosevelt and, 162; in rural society, in late 1800's, 123; in Spanish-American War, 194; Wilson and, 174; women, in late 1800's, 144; in World War I, 226–27; in World War II, 336, 338; in 1920's and Great Depression, 284, 291–93. See also Slaves and slavery
Black Hills (South Dakota and Wyoming), 73, 85
Black lists, 114
Blackmun, Harry, 413
Black Muslims, 450–51
Black Panther Party, 451
Blackwell, Henry, 144
Blaine, James G., 62–64
Bland, Richard P., 130
Bland-Allison Act, 130
Blue Lake, New Mexico, 457, *p457*
Bok, Edward, 148

Bolsheviks. *See* Russian Revolution
Bond, Julian, 451
"Bonus Army," 290
Booth, John Wilkes, 37, *p37*
Borneo, 329, *m344*
Bougainville, Solomon Islands, *p330*
Boulder Dam, 251
Boxer Rebellion, 199–200
Boycotts, 378, 400, 449, 453
Bracero program, 338, 398
Brazil, 215
Brest-Litovsk, Treaty of (1918), 229, 232
Brezhnev, Leonid, 437–38
Briand, Aristide, 309
Bristow, Benjamin H., 59
Britain. *See* Great Britain
Britain, Battle of, 323–24
British Guiana, *m205,* 210
British West Indies. *See* West Indies
Brooke, Edward W., 451
Brown, A. W., 178
Brown, Dee, 456
Brown, William Wells, 149
Brown v. Board of Education of Topeka (1954), 399
Browne, Carl, *p116*
Bruce, Blanche K., 47
Bryan, William Jennings: in election of 1896, 135, 157; in election of 1900, 161; in election of 1908, 168–69; as Secretary of State, 219, 225
Brzezinski, Zbigniew, 440, 442
Bucharest, Treaty of, 232
Budapest, Hungary, 363, 364
Budget, Bureau of, 244–45
Budget and Accounting Act (1921), 244
Buenos Aires Conference (1936), 319
Buffalo, 70–72
Bulgaria, *m220,* 232, *m234*
Bulge, Battle of the, 341, *m342*
Bull Moose Party. *See* Progressive Parties
Bunau-Varilla, Philippe, 208
Bunche, Ralph, 293, 358, *p359*
Bureau of Indian Affairs, 71, 75, 398, 456, 457
Burger, Warren E., 413
Burke Act (1906), 76
Burke-Wadsworth Act, 325
Burlingame Treaty (1868), 109, 110
Burma, 329, *m344*
Bush, George, 423, *p424*
Business: advances in, *c704–05;* automation of, 389–90; efficiency in, in 1920's, 281, 283; inflation and, 468–69; New Deal and, 261, 262, 266–270; T. Roosevelt and, 163–64; World War I profits by, 315; in late 1800's, 94–103; in 1950's, 376–77. *See also* Capitalism and capitalists; Corporations; Industry; Trade and commerce; *specific industries*
Business cycles, 107–08, 250

Butte, Montana, *p106*
Byrd, Richard E., 288
Byrne, Jane N., 459

Cable, George Washington, 149
Cabrini, Francis Xavier, 143
California: Chinese immigrants in, 109; gold rush to, 84; population of, 446
Cambodia, 362, 430, *m431,* 436, 438; U.S. invasion of, 413, 435
Camp David Agreements (1979), 441, *m441*
Canada: Monroe Doctrine and, 319
Canal, Panama, 206–09, *p208,* 306
Cannon, Joseph, 170
Cantigny, France, 231, *m231*
Capitalism and capitalists: business organization of, 96–98; cold war and, 355; finance, 103; industrial, 103. *See also* Business; Industry
Capone, Al, 287
Caporetto, Italy, 220, 229
Capra, Frank, 297
Cárdenas, Lázaro, 313
Caribbean Sea, *m205;* policy in (1898–1914), 204–15; policy in (1920's), 305–06
Carmichael, Stokely, 451
Carnegie, Andrew, 101–03, *p101,* 143
Carnegie Steel Company, 102
Carpetbaggers, 45–46
Carranza, Venustiano, 214, 215
Carroll, James, *p207*
Carson, Rachel, 476
Carter, Jimmy, *p421, p424;* blacks appointed by, 452; economy and, 420–21, 468; energy policy of, 422–23, 474; foreign policy of, 439–43, *p441;* as President, 455, 475
Carter Doctrine, 442
Cartwright, Alexander, *p152*
Cassatt, Mary, 150
Castro, Fidel, 428, 429, 455
Cather, Willa, 295
Catlin, George, *p70*
Catt, Carrie Chapman, 144
Cattle industry, 76–80, *p77, m78, p79,* 83
Celebes, 329, *m344*
Centennial Exhibition (Philadelphia; 1876), 92
Central America. *See* Latin America; *specific countries*
Central Intelligence Agency (CIA), 370, 417, 428, 437
Central Pacific Railroad, 58, 71, *m78*
Central Powers (World War I), 220, *m220,* 222, 223, 229, 232
Cervera, Pascual, 193, 194
Chamberlain, Neville, 318, 323

Chaplin, Charlie, 297
Chase, Salmon P., 44
Château-Thierry, France, 231, *m231*
Chautauqua movement, 151
Chavez, Cesar, 453
Cherokees (Indians), 83, 84
Chestnutt, Charles W., 149
Cheyennes (Indians), 73, 84
Chiang Kai-shek, 346, 358, 360
Chicago, Ill., *p91;* Columbian Exposition in, 149–50; Democratic Convention (1968) in, 411, 412, *p412;* Haymarket Affair in, 112
Chicano movement, 454
Chickasaws (Indians), 83
Child labor, 182, 269
Chile, 215, 437
China, *m431;* Boxer Rebellion in, 199–200, *p199;* early relations with, 198–99; foreign policy of (1960's), 430; imperialism in, 189; Indochina and, 362; invaded by Japan, 309, 315; in Korean War, 360, *m360;* Nixon's policy toward, 437, *p437;* in Sino-Japanese War, 201; split between Soviet Union and, 427; United Nations and, 353, 354; in World War II, 317, 325, *m344,* 347; Yalta Conference and, 346
Chinese Exclusion Act (1882), 110, 111
Chinese immigrants, 71, 109–10
Choctaws (Indians), 83
Chopin, Kate, 149
Christian Science, 143
Churchill, Winston, 353; in World War II, 323–25, *p324,* 331, 334, 338, 342; at Yalta, 346, 347
Cisneros, Joseph, 453
Cities: corruption in, 59–60; growth in late 1800's, 142–45; growth in 1920's of, 283; Hispanics in, 454, 455; migration from farms to, 108, 141; progressive reforms in, 161; riots in, 450–02; skyscrapers of, 150, *p150;* transportation and communications for, in late 1800's, 91–93; urban renewal programs for, 393–94; in early 1900's, 181; in 1970's and 1980's, 447–48
Civilian Conservation Corps, 258, 271, 293
Civil liberties: McCarthy and, 440; "Red scare" and, 243
Civil rights: election of 1948 and, 371; as issue in 1968, 411–12; movement for, 399–400, 449–52, 458; in 1920's, 293
Civil Rights Acts: of 1866, 42; of 1875, 53–54; of 1957, 400, 448; of 1964, 409, 449, 458; of 1968, 451

757

of, 170. *See also* Congress, U.S.

Housing: discrimination barred in, 451; New Deal programs for, 260, 270; of pioneers, *p81,* 82; in suburbs, 394–95, *p394;* urban renewal programs and, 393; post-World War II, 370

Housing Act (1961), 406
Howard, Oliver Otis, 40, 75
Howard University, 40
Howard-Wheeler Act (Indian Reorganization Act; 1934), 294, 397
Howe, Julia Ward, 144
Howells, William Dean, 148
Huerta, Victoriano, 214, 215
Hughes, Charles Evans, 158, 174, 245, 308
Hughes, Langston, 296
Hull, Cordell, 314, 317, 324
Hull House, 144, *p144,* 145
Human rights, 437, 440
Humphrey, Hubert H., 371; in election of 1964, 409; in election of 1968, 411–13
Humphrey-Hawkins Act (1978), 421
Hungary, *m234;* revolution (1956) in, 363–64, *p363;* in World War II, *m332,* 341, *m342;* post-World War II, 355
Hunt, Richard Morris, 149
Hydroelectricity, 473
Hydrogen bomb. *See* Nuclear weapons

Ice box, *p282*
Iceland, *m320,* 325
Idaho, 84, 131, 160
Immigration and immigrants, 445, *c698;* in Great Depression, 289; labor unions and, 113; from Mexico, 215, 294, 398, 453–54; national backgrounds, *c683;* restrictions on, in 1920's, 303–04; settlement of Great Plains by, 80–81, 123; in late 1800's, 108–10; 1890–1939, *c304;* 1940–1979, *c446;* in 1950's, 393; in 1960's and 1970's, 448
Immigration and Nationality Act (1965), 448
Impeachment: Constitution on, 725, 738; of A. Johnson, *p42, 43*–44; Nixon and, 417
Imperialism, 189–90; as cause of World War I, 221; by Japan, 201; as U.S. policy, 196–98
Imports, *c708*
Inchon, Korea, 359, *m360*
Income, family: growth of, *c703;* median, *c399*
Income taxes: Constitution on, 169, 750; Supreme Court on, 67; under Wilson, 172; during World War II, 336, 337
India, 430, 437
Indianapolis, Indiana, *p142*

Indian Reorganization Act (Howard-Wheeler Act; 1934), 294, 397
Indians (Native Americans): attempt to "Americanize," 74–76, *p75;* gold discovered on land of, 85; of Great Plains, 69–72, *p70,* 83, 84; termination policy toward, 397–98; in wars with U.S., 72–74; in World War II, 336; in 1920's and Great Depression, 293–94; in 1960's and 1970's, 456–57
Indochina: under France, 362; in World War II, 325, *m344. See also* Vietnam War
Industrialization, *p137–40*
Industrial Revolution: energy for, 470; imperialism and, 189; in late 1800's, *p97*
Industrial Workers of the World (IWW), 184
Industry: advances in, *c704–05;* business organization of, 96–100; of post-Civil War South, 51–52; education influenced by, 146; growth of cities and, 142–45; labor for, in late 1800's, 106–08; leaders of, 100–03; output in, *c705;* pollution and wastes of, 475; settlement of Great Plains and, 83; southern workers employed in, *c51;* unions and, in late 1900's, 114–17; during World War I, 227; during World War II, 334–36; in late 1800's, 94–96; in early 1900's, 178–80; in 1920's, 281–82; in 1950's, 389–92; in 1960's and 1970's, 468–70. *See also* Business; *specific industries*
Inflation, 271, 466–69; consumer prices, 468; post-World War II, 370; in 1960's, 414; in 1970's, 419, 421. *See also* Economy
Initiative (election), 159
Inness, George, 150
Insular Cases, 204–05
Interlocking directorates, 100
Internal combustion engine, *p286*
Internal Security Act (1950), 372
International Atomic Energy Commission, 355
International Bank for Reconstruction and Development, 354
International Brigade, 317
International Court of Justice, 354
International Geophysical Year, 389
International Ladies Garment Workers Union (ILGWU), 113
International Monetary Fund (IMF), 355

International News Service, 297
International Union of American Republics (Pan-American Union), 219
Interstate Commerce Act (1887), 65, 128–29, 165, 168, 169
Interstate Commerce Commission (ICC), 129, 165, 261
Iowa (Indians), 84
Iran, 358, *m438,* 443; revolution in, 422, 441–42, 470–71
Iraq, 365, *m438,* 442
Irish immigrants, 71
Iron industry, 94–95
Isolationism, 314–20
Israel: establishment of, 358; OPEC and, 414; Suez crisis (1956) and, 364; in wars with Arabs, 438–39, *m438,* 441
Italy: under Mussolini, 314–17; in World War I, *m220,* 221, 223, 229, 232, 234; post-World War I, *m234,* 235; in World War II, 318, 320, 323, 325, 328, 331, *m332,* 339–40, *m342;* post-World War II, 355
Iwo Jima, 344, 347, *m347*

Jackson, Helen Hunt, 75, 149
Jackson, Henry, 439
James, Henry, 148
James, William, 285
Japan: atomic bombing of, 348, *p348,* 388; immigration restrictions on, 304; Manchuria invaded by, 309; Perry in, *p200;* in Russo-Japanese War, 201, 219; in Sino-Japanese War, 199; trade with, 421, 427; at Washington Conference (1921–22), 308; in World War I, 234; pre-World War II, 314–17; in World War II, *m321,* 325–26, *p326,* 328–31, 343–47, *m344–45;* post-World War II, 358
Japanese Americans, *p337,* 338
Java Sea, Battle of, 329, *m344*
Jazz, 288, 295–96, 298
Jewett, Sarah Orne, 149
Jews: in Germany, *p322,* 342; in Israel, 358; in Soviet Union, 439
Jim Crow laws, 54
Joffre, Joseph, 222, 223
Johnson, Andrew: impeachment of, *p42, 43*–44; as President, 37; reconstruction program of, 38, 41–43, 48
Johnson, Edward A., *p162*
Johnson, Henry, 226–27
Johnson, Hiram, 158
Johnson, Lyndon B., 389,

p410; in election of 1960, 405; foreign policy of, 427–30; as President, 408–11, 451, 456, 467; Vietnam War and, 412, 432–35, *p432*
Johnson Debt Default Act (1934), 314
Jones, James, 396
Jones Acts (1916, 1917), 197, 205, 312
Jordan, 365, 438, *m438*
Joseph (Nez Percé chief), 69, 73
J. Pierpont Morgan and Company, 172
Juárez, Benito, 209, 210
Judicial branch: in Constitution, 738–39; labor unions and, 116–17. *See also* Courts; Supreme Court

Kanagawa, Treaty of (1854), *p200,* 201
Kansas Pacific Railroad, 77
Keaton, Buster, 297
Kefauver, Estes, 378
Kelley, Florence, 158
Kelley, Oliver Hudson, 127
Kellogg, Frank B., 309
Kellogg-Briand Pact (Pact of Paris; 1928), 309
Kelly, William, 95
Kennedy, Edward M., 421, 423
Kennedy, John F., *p405,* 464; assassination of, 407–08; in election of 1960, 405; foreign policy of, 427–32; moon landing and, 413, *p414;* as President, 406–07
Kennedy, Robert F., 410–11
Kent State University, 413
Keppler, Joseph J., *p164*
Kerner Commission (National Advisory Commission on Civil Disorders), 451–52
Kerosene, 94
Khomeini, Ayatollah Ruhollah, 442
Khrushchev, Nikita, 363, 365–66, 428–30
Kickapoo (Indians), 84
King, Grace, 149
King, Mackenzie, 325
King, Martin Luther, Jr., 400, 449, *p450,* 451; assassination of, 411, 452
Kissinger, Henry, 436–40
Klamaths (Indians), 398
Knights of Labor, 111–12, 114
Knights of the White Camellia, 47
Knox, Frank, 194
Korea: division of and war in, 358–60, *m360, p361;* under Japan, 199, 201; Yalta Conference and, 346–47
Kreps, Juanita, 459
Ku Klux Klan, 47, 48, 291
Kwajalein, Marshall Islands, 343

360; Nixon's policy toward, 437–38; Reagan's policy toward, 443; recognized by U.S., 312; space program of, 407, 462; Spanish Civil War and, 317; split between China and, 427; under Stalin, 314; in United Nations, 353, 354; in World War II, 319–20, *m320-21,* 325, 330, *m332-33,* 334, 339–42, *m342, m344,* 346–48. *See also* Russia; Russian Revolution

Soyer, Raphael, *p289*

Space programs, 391, *p391;* J. F. Kennedy and, 407; moon landings and, 388, 412, *p414;* shuttle, 462, *p463; Sputnik* and, 365; treaty on, 389

Spain: Civil War in, 314–17, *m318;* Treaty of Paris (1898) and, 203; war with, 191–94, *m193, m194, p195*

Spanish-American War, 193–94, *m193, m194;* events leading up to, 191–93; Rough Riders in, 162, *p195;* Treaty of Paris (1898) ending, 203

Spanish Civil War, 314–17, *m318*

Spanish language, *p79*

Spanish-speaking Americans, 398–99, 448, 453–55. *See also* Mexican Americans; Puerto Ricans

Sparkman, John, 373

Spoils system, 60

Sports: 275–78; in late 1800's, 151–52; in 1920's, 288

Sputnik, 365, 396, 462

"Square Deal," 156, 161–66

Stagflation, 468

Stalin, Josef, 314, 346, 347, 353, 363

Stalingrad, Battle of, 330, *m333,* 334

"Stalwarts," 62, 63

Standard Oil Company, 103

Stanford, Leland, 142

Stanton, Edwin M., 37, 44

Stanton, Elizabeth Cady, 144

States: Constitution on, 733, 739–40, 745; "one person, one vote" in, 407; railroads regulated by, 128; reconstruction governments of, 38, 40–41, 46–48; "Red scare" in, 243; social legislation of, **182–83;** vote given to women by, 144, 160, 177

States' Rights Party, 371

Staunton, Virginia, 161

Steel industry, 94–95, *p111;* Bessemer converter and, *p107;* Carnegie and, 102–03; production of raw steel, *c98;* strikes in, 242, 379

Steffens, Lincoln, 158, 159

Steinbeck, John, 295

Steiner, Saul, 456

Stephens, Uriah S., 111, 112

Stevens, Thaddeus, 36, 41, 42, *p42,* 48

Stevenson, Adlai E., 373, 378, *p378*

Stilwell Road, *m344,* 347

Stimson, Henry L., 309

Stobaugh, Robert, 474

Stocks and stock market, 97–98; crash of 1929 on, 249, *p249;* New Deal and, 262; panic of 1893 and, 67, *p67;* prices, *c250*

Stokes, Carl B., 451

Stone, Lucy, 144

Stoves, in late 1800's, *p143*

Strategic Arms Limitation Talks (SALT), 438

Strikes: attempts to break, 115–17; Clayton Act and, 173; by Industrial Workers of the World, 184; by Knights of Labor, 111–12; NLRB and, 261; during New Deal, 268–69; in steel industry, 379; post-World War I, 241–42; during World War II, 337; post-World War II, 370

Strong, Josiah, 190

Submarines: nuclear, *p366;* in World War I, 223–26, 229; in World War II, 325, 331, 340

Submerged Lands Act (1953), 376

Suburbs, 394–95, *p394,* 447–48

Sudetenland, 317, *m318*

Suez Canal, 331, *m333,* 339, 364

Suffrage: Constitution on, 407, 415, 464, 748–49, 751, 753; for women, 144, 160, *p160,* 285. *See also* Voting

Sugar, 191

Sugar trust, 66

Sullivan, Louis H., 149–50, 297

Sumner, Charles, 41, 48

Supreme Court: on abortion, 458–59; on civil rights cases, 399, 400, 449, 450; Constitution on, 739; on Granger cases, 128; on income taxes, 67; on Insular Cases, 204–05; on labor legislation, 183, 242; on New Deal legislation, 259, 261, 265, 266, 269; on new life forms, 462; Nixon's appointments to, 413; on "one person, one vote," 407; on "separate but equal," 54; on Sherman Antitrust Act, 99–100, 117, 163–64; on Watergate tapes, 417; woman appointed to, 459. *See also* Judicial branch

Sussex (ship), 224–25

Syria, 364, 438, *m438*

Taft, Robert A., 373

Taft, William Howard, 156;

in election of 1908, 168–69; in election of 1912, 171; foreign policy of, 219, 306; in Philippines, 196; as President, 169–70

Taft-Hartley Act (Labor-Management Relations Act; 1947), 370–72, 379

Taiwan (Formosa), 199, 358, 437

Tammany Hall, 59–60, *p61,* 247

Taos Pueblo (New Mexico), 457, *p457*

Tarawa, 343, *m343*

Tarbell, Ida M., 158

Tariffs: agricultural prices and, 124; Great Depression and, 250; rise and fall of, *c709;* of 1890 (McKinley), 65, 66, *p124,* 131, 191; of 1894 (Wilson-Gorman), 66, 191; of 1897 (Dingley), 157; of 1909 (Payne-Aldrich), 169; of 1913 (Underwood), 172, 174; of 1921 (Emergency), 244; of 1922 (Fordney-McCumber), 245, 304; of 1930 (Hawley-Smoot), 304; of 1934 (Tydings-McDuffie; Trade Agreements Act), 312–14; of 1962 (Trade Expansion Act), 406–07. *See also* Trade and commerce

Taxation: Carter's program on, 421; Constitution on, 169, 729, 750; excise, 410; of income, 67; during New Deal, 272; Reagan's program on, 424, 470; receipts from, *c695;* Revenue Act (1964) and, 408; for Social Security, 262; under Wilson, 172; during World War I, 227; during World War II, 335–37

Taylor, Frederick W., 179

Taylor, Nevada, *p85*

Teamsters, International Brotherhood of, 378

Teapot Dome scandal, 245–46

Technology, 388–92, 462–63

Teheran, Iran, 442

Telegraph, 92–93

Telephone, 93, 389

Television, 395, *p396*

Teller Resolution (1898), 193

Temperance movements, 149, *p158*

Tenant farmers, 49, 121, 248, 269

Tennessee: Jim Crow laws in, 54; readmission of, 43

Tennessee Valley Authority (TVA), 263–64, *m263, p264,* 269, 376–77

Tenure of Office Act (1867), 43–44

Terrell, Mary Church, 144

Territories: *m692-93;* Constitution on, 740; government in, 85–86

Tet offensive, 434

Texas: cattle industry in, 77, *m78*

Textile industry: in post-Civil War South, 51

Thailand, 329, *m344, m431*

Theater: in late 1800's, 151

Thieu, Nguyen Van, 433

Third World, 427

Thorndike, Edward L., 285

Thorpe, Jim, 288

Three Mile Island nuclear power plant, *p471,* 472

Thurmond, J. Strom, 371, 372

Tibet, 430

Tidal energy, 473

Tientsin, China, 199, 200

Tilden, Samuel J., 61–62

Tillman, "Pitchfork Ben," 131

Time, 296

Tobacco: sharecropping of, 50

Towne, Laura, 39

Trade Agreements Act (1934), 313–14

Trade and commerce: *m709;* with China, 198, 199; Constitution on, 729; exports and imports, *c708-09;* Interstate Commerce Act and, 65, 128–29; with Japan, *p200,* 201; under F. D. Roosevelt, 313–14; T. Roosevelt and, 165; with Soviet Union, 439, 443; Wilson and, 173; in 1960's and 1970's, 406–07, 427–28; world trade, *m709. See also* Tariffs

Trade Expansion Act (1962), 406–07, 427–28

Transportation: Interstate Commerce Act and, 129; New Deal programs for, 260–61; in late 1800's, 91–93; in early 1900's, 177–78; in 1920's, 281–83, 285–86; in 1950's, 392–93. *See also* Automobiles and automobile industry; Railroads; Roads and highways

Treaties: on Antarctica and outer space, 389; Constitution on, 736–37; World War I and, 219, 221, 232–34. *See also specific treaties*

Treblinka, Poland, *p322*

Triangle fire, 107

Triple Alliance, 221

Triple Entente, 221

Truk, 343, *m344*

Truman, Harry S., *p371,* 373; atomic bomb used by, 348; foreign policy of, 312, 354, 356–60, 362; as President, 342, 368–72, 382, 399; as Vice-President, 341

Truman Doctrine, 356

Trusts, 66, 99–100, *p164;* T. Roosevelt and, 163–65, *p165. See also* Antitrust Acts

Turkey: in World War I, *m220,* 221, 223, 232, *m234;* post-World War II, 356

Tuskegee Institute, *p54,* 55

Acknowledgments

Cover illustration by Sisee Brimberg/Woodfin Camp, Inc. and Bettmann Archive. Title page by Sisee Brimberg. Drawings by Samuel H. Bryant and Manny Haller. Illustration of American bald eagle with banner and shield on *Changing Ways of American Life* chapters by Raul Mina Mora. Maps by Harold K. Faye and Paul Pugliese; charts by Ed Malsberg and Graphic Arts International.

UNIT ONE: p. 33, Bettmann Archive; 35, Library of Congress; 37, Brown University Library; 39, Courtesy, HBJ Library; 43, both, Bettmann Archive; 44, Smithsonian Institution; 46, Library of Congress; 48, Chicago Historical Society; 50, Bettmann Archive; 52, *Harper's Weekly,* March 16, 1867; 54, Library of Congress; 59, Brown Brothers; 61, Brown Brothers; 63, New York Public Library, Frank Leslie's *Illustrated Newspaper,* August 20, 1881; 65, Bettmann Archive; 67, New York Public Library, *Harper's Weekly,* August 12, 1893; 70, National Museum of American Art, Smithsonian Institution; 72, West Point Museum collection, U.S. Military Academy; 74, Bettmann Archive; 75, Nevada State Historical Society; 77, U.S. Department of Agriculture; 79, The Thomas Gilcrease Institute of American History and Art; 79, Nebraska State Historical Society; 85, Nevada State Historical Society; 86, Courtesy of Gene Autry.

UNIT TWO: p. 69, Chicago Historical Society; 71, Bettmann Archive; 73, Bettmann Archive, 75, New York Public Library, *Century Magazine,* Vol. XXVI-31; 77, Bettmann Archive; 101, both, Bettmann Archive; 102, Bettmann Archive; 106, Bettmann Archive; 109, Thomas Gilcrease Institute of American History and Art, Tulsa, Oklahoma; 111, Permission of The Fine Arts Museums of San Francisco; 115, Granger Collection; 116, Bettmann Archive; 120, Metropolitan Museum of Art, Gift of Christian A. Zabrisiae; 122, New York State Historical Association; 124, Granger Collection; 128, Bettmann Archive; 130, Granger Collection; 133, Granger Collection; 134, Chicago Historical Society; 137, t, Bettmann Archive, b, Metropolitan Museum of Art, Gift of Lyman G. Bloomingdale, 1901; 138, t, Chicago Historical Society, bl, Barfoot, The Progress of Cotton: #6 Spinning, Yale University Art Gallery, Mabel Brady Garvan Collection, br, Bettmann Archive; 139, t, Courtesy HBJ Library, San Francisco, c, Bettmann Archive, b, Department of the Interior; 140, t. J. Alex Langley/DPI, c, © Steve Thompson/Uniphoto, b, © George Hall, Woodfin Camp & Associates; 142, Indianapolis Museum of Art, Gift of A Couple of Old Hoosiers; 144, Culver Pictures; 146, Brown Brothers; 148, Bettmann Archive; 150, Museum of the City of New York; 152, Bettmann Archive.

UNIT THREE: p. 155, Kennedy Galleries; 157, Kennedy Galleries; 158, Historical Picture Service; 160, Bettmann Archive; 162, both, Association for the Study of Afro-American Life and History, Inc., Washington, D.C.; 164, Library of Congress; 165, Library of Congress; 167, National Museum of American Art, Smithsonian Institution, Gift of Mrs. Sarah Harrison; 168, Harvard College Library; 170, Historical Picture Service; 173, Bettmann Archive; 177, Museum of the City of New York; 179, Historical Picture Service; 180, Library of Congress; 183, Library of Congress.

UNIT FOUR: p. 187, l, Collection of George J. Goodstadt, c, West Point Museum collection, U.S. Military Academy, r, Granger; 190, Library of Congress; 195, Chicago Historical Society; 196, Culver Pictures; 197, Culver Pictures; 199, Brown Brothers; 200, Courtesy, Franklin D. Roosevelt Library; 204, Culver Pictures; 207, Granger Collection; 208, Courtesy, HBJ Library; 211, New York Public Library, *New York Herald,* December 16, 1902; 212, Brown Brothers; 214, M. Farbman, © TIME, Inc., 1960; 218, Photoworld/FPG; 222, Bettmann Archive; 224, Brown Brothers; 227, Granger Collection; 228, Collection of George J. Goodstadt; 230, Bettmann Archive; 235, Imperial War Museum.

UNIT FIVE: p. 239, Department of the Interior; 242, Courtesy Whitney Museum of American Art; 244, Bettmann Archive; 245, Brown Brothers; 246, The New York Historical Society; 249, Brown Brothers; 252, Courtesy, Franklin D. Roosevelt Library; 255, Brown Brothers; 257, Photoworld/FPG; 259, Bettmann Archive; 265, Photo: E. Irving Blomstrann, New Britain Museum of American Art; 266, Library of Congress; 268, UPI; 272, Brown Brothers; 273, Wide World; 275, all, Bettmann Archive; 276, *Harper's Weekly,* October 13, 1883, lc, The Brooklyn Museum, rc, b, Bettmann Archive; 277, t, Bettmann Archive, c, Museum of the City of New York, Byron Collection, b, Richard Pilling/Focus on Sports; 278, t, Russell-Kelly/Focus on Sports, b, Focus on Sports; 280, Memorial Art Gallery of the University of Rochester; 287, Bettmann Archive; 289, Private Collection; 292, Courtesy, The Phillips Collection; 296, Courtesy, Whitney Museum of American Art; 298, Bettmann Archive.

UNIT SIX: p. 301, Charles Phelps Cushing/H. Armstrong Roberts; 303, Granger Collection; 306, Photoworld/FPG; 308, Bettmann Archive; 313, © Edward B. Marks Music Corporation. Used by permission; 315, Historical Picture Service; 316, Culver Pictures; 322, Bettmann Archive; 323, Wide World; 324, Bettmann Archive; 326, Brown Brothers; 330, Courtesy U.S. Navy; 331, UPI; 335, UPI; 337, Brown Brothers; 339, Bettmann Archive; 341, Courtesy, Franklin D. Roosevelt Library; 347, Charles Phelps Cushing/H. Armstrong Roberts; 348, Brown Brothers.

UNIT SEVEN: p. 351, Grant Heilman; 353, United Nations; 356, UPI; 359, UPI; 361, UPI; 362, French Embassy, Press and Information Division; 363, Wide World; 366, UPI; 369, UPI; 371, UPI; 373, Wayne Miller/Magnum; 374, Bettmann Archive; 375, Pictorial Parade; 376, Wide World; 378, UPI; 379, Erich Hartmann/Magnum; 380, Steve McCutcheon; 381, Wide World; 383, t, Bettmann Archive, b, © James Foote/Photo Researchers; 384, t, Museum of the American Indian, cl, Historical Picture Service, bl, br, Bettmann Archive; 385, all, Bettmann Archive; 386, t, © Margot Granitsas/Photo Researchers, bl, © Larry Mulvehill/Photo Researchers, br, Radio Shack, A Division of Tandy Corporation; 388, Atomic Energy Commission/UPI; 389, Historical Picture Service; 391, UPI; 392, © 1980 George Hall/Woodfin Camp & Associates; 394, Photo Trends; 396, Merrim/Monkmeyer Press Photo; 398, Katrina Thomas/Photo Researchers; 400, UPI.

UNIT EIGHT: p. 403, NASA; 405, UPI; 409, Sybil Shackman/Monkmeyer Press Photo; 410, Shanks in *The Buffalo Evening News;* 412, Fred Ward/Black Star; 413, Liederman, *L.I. Press,* N.Y.; 414, NASA; 418, Wally McNamee/Woodfin Camp & Associates; 419, Tiziou/Sygma; 421, M. Naythons/Gamma-Liaison; 422, Andy Leven/Black Star; 424, Rick Friedman/Black Star; 427, Reprinted by permission of the Chicago Tribune-New York News Syndicate, Inc.; 429, Pictorial Parade; 432, Fred Ward/Black Star; 437, Tashi/Black Star; 441, Owen/Black Star; 443, Shelly Katz/Black Star; 447, Wide World; 448, Owen Franken/Sygma; 450, Bob Adel/Magnum; 453, Herman J. Kokojan/Black Star; 455, UPI; 457, © 1970 Dan Budnik/Woodfin Camp & Associates; 459, White House Photo/Black Star; 463, NASA; 467, UPI; 469, Dick Durrance II/Woodfin Camp & Associates; 471, Skoogsfors/Gamma-Liaison; 474, J. H. Pickerell/Black Star; 475, Tom McHugh/Photo Researchers; 477, UPI; 478, Steve McCutcheon.

E 6
F 7
G 8
H 9
I 0
J 1